LEADING CASES IN CIVIL PROCEDURE

Second Edition

■ ■ ■

By

Linda S. Mullenix

Morris and Rita Atlas Chair in Advocacy
University of Texas School of Law

AMERICAN CASEBOOK SERIES®

WEST®

A Thomson Reuters business

Mat #41122612

American Casebook Series is a trademark registered in the U.S. Patent and Trademark Office.

© 2010 Thomson Reuters
© 2012 Thomson Reuters

    610 Opperman Drive
    St. Paul, MN 55123
    1–800–313–9378

Printed in the United States of America

ISBN: 978–0–314–27454–0

PREFACE TO THE SECOND EDITION

This second edition of LEADING CASES IN CIVIL PROCEDURE was prompted by two sets of statutory and rule revisions that have occurred since publication of the first edition. This new text contains the amendments and revisions to the Federal Rules of Civil Procedure that went into effect on December 1, 2010, including language revisions as a consequence of the Advisory Committee on Civil Rules style project, as well as rule changes relating to the timing of motions and other papers in federal court. In addition, the revised second edition text includes all amendments and revisions to the jurisdiction, venue, and removal statutes in the Federal Courts Jurisdiction and Venue Clarification Act of 2011, which the President signed into law on December 7, 2011 and which took effect on January 6, 2012. The second edition text is entirely up-to-date on new jurisdiction, venue, and removal provisions. Finally, this second edition includes a few new Supreme Court decisions, including *J. McIntyre v. Nicastro* (on personal jurisdiction); *Mims v. Arrow Financial Services* (relating to federal subject matter jurisdiction), and *Krupski v. Costa Crociere* (on Rule 15 amendments to pleadings).

The PREFACE to the first edition has been retained because it sets forth the underlying philosophy and design of the text. The text is based on a 14–week one-semester curriculum, with 14 chapters that provide simple guidance for working through the course. Each week assembles the core cases, statutes, and rules that students and professors reasonably may study in four hours of class time. The text also offers substitute materials for alternative weeks. Hence, this compact book focuses on a select core canon of the leading cases in civil procedure, including concurring and dissenting opinions omitted in many other casebooks.

In keeping with this compact approach, this second edition has reduced or eliminated some materials from the first edition. For all new material added, some pre-existing material has been removed. Thanks to comments from various readers, the text has been cleaned up to correct minor typographical glitches. Special thanks to Professor Suja Thomas, whose very careful reading and use of the first edition has contributed greatly to this revised second edition.

LINDA S. MULLENIX

March 7, 2012

PREFACE TO THE FIRST EDITION

This basic text is intended to fill a gap in the very crowded field of first-year civil procedure casebooks. The book has been designed to serve three purposes: (1) to identify the leading cases in civil procedure that every law student needs to know as an educated attorney in his or her professional life, (2) to reduce or eliminate the amount of detailed nuance relating to civil procedure contained in most civil procedure courses, and (3) to provide a one volume book that includes cases, constitutional provisions, statutes, and rules, suitable for a one-semester, fourteen-week course. As many law schools now have eliminated the traditional year-long course in civil procedure, the need for at least one text tailored to the one-semester civil procedure course is apparent.

This book's design is based on the author's thirty years experience in teaching civil procedure. First, the book assembles a core "canon" of decisional law in civil procedure, accompanied by the constitutional provisions, statutes, and rules involved in those cases. The author believes that there is such a canon and that most procedure teachers, if pressed, would agree on certain canonical cases. In assembling these leading cases in civil procedure, then, the selection has been guided by several questions: "What are the essential decisions in civil procedure that every educated attorney needs to know, and would be familiar with?" "What are the essential topics or problems in civil procedure that every educated attorney needs some passing familiarity?" "What procedural problems may be treated in other courses, or are better suited for an advanced procedure course?" The text covers topics, then, essential to a fundamental knowledge of civil procedure.

The second goal of this book is to drastically reduce or eliminate the huge amount of in-depth coverage, source materials, and procedural nuance that characterize current civil procedure textbooks. This book is completely shorn of the bells and whistles that characterize many of our current casebooks. As our course credit hours have shrunk, our casebooks have grown fatter and more detailed. This text instead focuses on a core canon and therefore reduces topic coverage as well as collateral materials. Our students need to gain a basic grasp of the procedural process in fourteen weeks; we are not training them to become procedural scholars. Entire topics in civil procedure that currently are covered in other casebooks have been eliminated from this book. Hence, this book does not cover topics such as service of process, interpleader, historical materials on common law pleading, discovery mechanisms, interlocutory appeal, default judgments, voluntary and involuntary dismissal, execution of judgments, and trial. In addition, coverage of those topics selected for inclusion also has been drastically reduced, focusing on a few core decisions that illustrate the problems and issues related to that topic. The book is assembled in the belief that our first year students do not need to be *Erie* scholars, but do need to be familiar with basic *Erie* doctrine. In addition, cases have been edited to eliminate most internal citation. Finally, this book eliminates the notes, comments, and questions that typically accompany decisions in existing casebooks.

The book has been assembled based on the structure of a fourteen-week, four-hour course. Rather than assembled in chapters, the book is designed based on a fourteen-week curriculum. Hopefully, this structure provides easy and simple guidance for students and the professor to work through the one-semester course. Each week addresses a topic in civil procedure and assembles the core cases, statutes, or rules that reasonably may be studied by students and taught by the professor in four hours of class time. The topic selection reflects the author's evaluation of core coverage. Although the number of cases has been reduced, the presentation of cases departs from many current casebooks. Thus, in most instances decisions are reported fully, and concurring and dissenting opinions also are set out at length. This presentation supplies students with a fuller appreciation of underlying facts, procedural developments, doctrinal analysis, and competing judicial views. The materials for each week aim to cover approximately forty pages of assigned reading, focusing on four leading cases and related statutory material that illustrate the core concepts an educated lawyer needs to appreciate.

In recognition that other professors might have selected other topics for coverage, the second portion of the book sets forth materials for alternative weeks that may be substituted for coverage other than the topics in the main text. The alternative materials replicate the basic concept that topic coverage should be streamlined and self-contained within a reasonable teaching unit.

The third goal of this book is to provide students with a readily accessible one-volume, affordable paperback text in civil procedure that combines decisional law along with relevant constitutional provisions, statutes, and rules. Our first year students are compelled to purchase both a text and a statutory supplement for use in civil procedure, but the first year course implicates only selected constitutional provisions, statutes, and rules. While there is an argument for compelling students to purchase an entire statutory supplement, there are countervailing arguments for relieving students of this requirement in their first year of law school. Moreover, some procedure professors eschew teaching the rules portion of the course, altogether. This text, then, integrates relevant constitutional, statutory, and rule provisions along with the cases in which those sources are implicated by the decision.

This text attempts to replicate the concept of the introductory "survey course" in the undergraduate curriculum. The text is intended to accomplish breadth of coverage, rather than depth. It does not attempt to present any theories or themes of the procedural process. The text does, however, enable the procedure professor to enhance students' understanding of the procedural process through the professor's in-depth knowledge of the core canon, authoritative bases for the decisional law, contested or unresolved issues, and academic controversies surrounding the materials.

LINDA S. MULLENIX
MORRIS & RITA ATLAS CHAIR
IN ADVOCACY
UNIVERSITY OF TEXAS SCHOOL OF LAW

November 2009

TABLE OF CONTENTS

Page

PREFACE TO THE SECOND EDITION ---- iii
PREFACE TO THE FIRST EDITION ---- v
TABLE OF CASES ---- xv

PART ONE. LEADING CASES IN CIVIL PROCEDURE

Sec.

I. Choosing the Forum (Personal Jurisdiction) ---- 1
    A. The Professional Responsibility of the Lawyer ---- 1
        American Bar Association Model Rules of Professional Conduct ---- 1
    B. Traditional Bases: Territorial Jurisdiction ---- 5
        Constitutional Provisions ---- 5
        U.S. Const. Article IV § 1 ---- 5
        U.S. Const. Amend. XIV § 1 ---- 5
        Federal Rule of Civil Procedure 55 ---- 5
        28 U.S.C. § 1738 ---- 6
        Pennoyer v. Neff ---- 6
    C. Implied Consent ---- 14
        Hess v. Pawloski ---- 14
    D. Due Process Minimum Contacts ---- 17
        U.S. Const. Amend. I: Freedom of Religion, Speech and Press; Peaceful
          Assemblage; Petition of Grievances ---- 17
        U.S. Const. Amend. X: Reserved Powers to States ---- 17
        Federal Rule of Civil Procedure 12 ---- 17
        International Shoe Co. v. State of Washington ---- 18

II. Choosing the Forum (Personal Jurisdiction) ---- 26
    A. Minimum Contacts at the Extreme ---- 26
        McGee v. International Life Insurance Company ---- 26
    B. Minimum Contacts Retrenched ---- 28
        Hanson v. Denckla ---- 28
    C. Long Arm Statutes and the Stream of Commerce ---- 40
        Illinois Long Arm Statute: Ill. Comp. Statutes § 2–209 ---- 40
        California Long Arm Statute: Cal. Code Civ. Pro. § 410.10 ---- 42
        Gray v. American Radiator & Standard Sanitary Corporation ---- 42
        Kulko v. Superior Court of California ---- 48
    D. Property Revisited ---- 56
        Shaffer v. Heitner ---- 56

III. Choosing the Forum (Personal Jurisdiction) ---- 74
    A. Affiliating Circumstances ---- 74
        World-Wide Volkswagen Corporation v. Woodson ---- 74
    B. General and Specific Jurisdiction ---- 90
        Helicopteros Nacionales de Colombia, S.A. v. Hall ---- 90
    C. First Amendment Considerations ---- 100
        Keeton v. Hustler Magazine ---- 100
        Calder v. Jones ---- 105

Page

Sec.

D. Jurisdiction Based on Contract Revisited ---------------- 108
    Federal Rule of Civil Procedure 4 [Selected Provisions] ---------------- 108
    Burger King Corporation v. Rudzewicz ---------------- 109

IV. Choosing the Forum (Personal Jurisdiction) ---------------- 124
  A. Stream of Commerce Revisited ---------------- 124
    Asahi Metal Industry Co., Ltd. v. Superior Court of California ---------------- 124
  B. Stream of Commerce: Muddy Waters ---------------- 134
    J. Mcintyre Machinery, Ltd. v. Nicastro ---------------- 134
  C. Tag Jurisdiction ---------------- 152
    Burnham v. Superior Court of California ---------------- 152
  D. Consent Revisited ---------------- 168
    M/S Bremen v. Zapata Off-Shore Company ---------------- 168
    Carnival Cruise Lines, Inc. v. Shute ---------------- 179

V. Choosing the Forum (Subject Matter Jurisdiction) ---------------- 189
  A. Diversity Jurisdiction and Special Diversity Problems ---------------- 189
    28 U.S.C. § 1332 ---------------- 189
    Federal Rule of Civil Procedure 12 ---------------- 190
    Federal Rule of Civil Procedure 17. Plaintiff and Defendant; Capacity;
      Public Officers ---------------- 190
    Mas v. Perry ---------------- 191
    28 U.S.C. § 1441. Removal of Civil Actions ---------------- 195
    The Hertz Corporation v. Friend ---------------- 195
  B. Special Problems in Diversity Jurisdiction: Collusive Joinder ---------------- 204
    28 U.S.C. § 1359. Parties Collusively Joined or Made ---------------- 204
    Kramer v. Caribbean Mills, Inc. ---------------- 204
    Rose v. Giamatti ---------------- 208
  C. Federal Question Jurisdiction—"Arising Under" Jurisdiction ---------------- 219
    Art. III, Section 2, Clause 1. Jurisdiction of Courts ---------------- 219
    28 U.S.C. § 1331. Federal Question ---------------- 220
    28 U.S.C. § 1338. Patents, Plant Variety Protection, Copyrights, Mask
      Works, Designs, Trademarks, and Unfair Competition ---------------- 220
    American National Red Cross v. S.G. and A.E. ---------------- 220
    T. B. Harms Company v. Eliscu ---------------- 234
  D. Federal Question Jurisdiction—The Well-Pleaded Complaint
    Rule ---------------- 238
    Louisville & Nashville Railroad Company v. Mottley ---------------- 238

VI. Choosing the Forum—Subject Matter Jurisdiction ---------------- 241
  A. Federal Question Jurisdiction—Express and Implied Actions ---------------- 241
    Merrell Dow Pharmaceuticals Inc. v. Thompson ---------------- 241
  B. Statutory Bases ---------------- 253
    Grable & Sons Metal Products, Inc. v. Darue Engineering ---------------- 253
    Mims v. Arrow Financial Services, LLC. ---------------- 259
  C. Supplemental Jurisdiction—Common Law Principles ---------------- 267
    Pendent Claim and Pendent Party Jurisdiction ---------------- 267
    Federal Rule of Civil Procedure 2. One Form of Action ---------------- 267
    Federal Rule of Civil Procedure 42. Consolidation; Separate Trials ---------------- 267
    United Mine Workers of America v. Gibbs ---------------- 267
    Finley v. United States ---------------- 272
  D. Supplemental Jurisdiction—Common Law Principles ---------------- 283
    Ancillary Jurisdiction ---------------- 283

Page

Sec.

VI. Choosing the Forum—Subject Matter Jurisdiction—Continued
Federal Rule of Civil Procedure 14. Third–Party Practice 283
Owen Equipment and Erection Company v. Kroger 284

VII. Choosing the Forum— Supplemental Jurisdiction, Removal, Venue 294
A. The Supplemental Jurisdiction Statute 294
28 U.S.C. § 1367. Supplemental Jurisdiction 294
Exxon Mobil Corporation v. Allapattah Services, Inc. 295
B. Removal Jurisdiction 316
28 U.S.C. § 1441. Removal of civil actions 316
28 U.S.C. § 1442. Federal officers or agencies sued or prosecuted 318
28 U.S.C. § 1443. Civil rights cases 319
28 U.S.C. § 1445. Nonremovable actions 320
28 U.S.C. § 1446. Procedure for removal of civil actions 320
28 U.S.C. § 1447. Procedure after removal generally 322
28 U.S.C. § 1448. Process after removal 323
Carlsbad Technology, Inc. v. HIF Bio, Inc. 323
C. Venue and Transfer of Venue 328
28 U.S.C. § 1391. Venue generally 328
28 U.S.C. § 1404. Change of venue 330
28 U.S.C. § 1406. Cure or waiver of defects 330
28 U.S.C. § 1407. Multidistrict litigation 331
Bates v. C & S Adjusters, Inc. 333
Hoffman v. Blaski 336
D. Forum Non Conveniens 339
Piper Aircraft Company v. Reyno 339

VIII. Modern Pleading 352
A. Selections From the Field Code (N.Y. Laws 1848) 352
B. Notice Pleading 353
Federal Rule of Civil Procedure 1. Scope and Purpose 353
Federal Rule of Civil Procedure 2. One Form of Action 353
Federal Rule of Civil Procedure 7. Pleadings Allowed; Form of Motions
and Other Papers 353
Federal Rule of Civil Procedure 7.1. Disclosure Statement 354
Federal Rule of Civil Procedure 8. General Rules of Pleading 354
Dioguardi v. Durning 354
Conley v. Gibson 358
C. The Limits of Notice Pleading 361
Federal Rule of Civil Procedure 12(b)(6) 361
Bell Atlantic Corporation v. Twombly 361
Ashcroft v. Iqbal 376
D. Fact Pleading Revitalized 391
Federal Rule of Civil Procedure 9. Pleading Special Matters 391
Tellabs, Inc. v. Makor Issues & Rights, Ltd. 392

IX. Week Nine: Modern Pleading 404
A. Responding to the Complaint 404
Federal Rule of Civil Procedure 12 404
Federal Rule of Civil Procedure 8(d) 404
PAE Government Services, Inc. v. MPRI, Inc. 404
Garcia v. Hilton Hotels International, Inc. 410
Rubert–Torres v. Hospital San Pablo, Inc. 415

Page

Sec.
IX. Week Nine: Modern Pleading—Continued
B. The Answer; Denials and Affirmative Defenses ---------------------- 418
Federal Rule of Civil Procedure 8(b)–(c) ----------------------------- 418
Zielinski v. Philadelphia Piers, Inc. ------------------------------ 419
C. Amendments to Pleadings-- 424
Federal Rule of Civil Procedure 15. Amended and Supplemental Plead-
ings --- 424
Krupski v. Costa Crociere S. p. A. --------------------------------- 426
D. Truthful Pleadings and Sanctions --------------------------------- 435
Federal Rule of Civil Procedure 11. Signing Pleadings, Motions, and
Other Papers; Representations to the Court; Sanctions--------------- 435
28 U.S.C. § 1927. Counsel's Liability for Excessive Costs------------ 437
Roth v. Green -- 437

X. Week Ten: Joinder of Parties and Claims ------------------------- 449
A. Counterclaims -- 449
Federal Rule of Civil Procedure 13. Counterclaim and Crossclaim---------- 449
Federal Rule of Civil Procedure 14. Third–Party Practice ------------ 450
Jones v. Ford Motor Credit Company -------------------------------- 451
B. Cross–Claims --- 460
Federal Rule of Civil Procedure 13(g), (h), (i) --------------------- 460
Federal Rule of Civil Procedure 18. Joinder of Claims --------------- 460
Federal Rule of Civil Procedure 20. Permissive Joinder of Parties---------- 460
Federal Rule of Civil Procedure 42. Consolidation; Separate Trials-------- 461
*Lasa Per L'Industria Del Marmo Societa Per Azioni of Lasa, Italy v.
Alexander* -- 461
C. Persons Needed for a Just Adjudication --------------------------- 471
Review Federal Rule of Civil Procedure 12(b)(7) --------------------- 471
Federal Rule of Civil Procedure 19.   Required Joinder of Parties --------- 471
The Bank of California v. The Superior Court of San Francisco ----------- 472
Provident Tradesmens Bank & Trust Co. v. Patterson ---------------- 477
D. Intervention--- 484
Federal Rule of Civil Procedure 24.   Intervention ------------------ 484
Grutter v. Bollinger -- 485

XI. Week Eleven: Discovery --- 492
A. Scope and Constitutionality of Discovery------------------------- 492
Federal Rule of Civil Procedure 26.   Duty to Disclose; General Provi-
sions Governing Discovery --- 492
Federal Rule of Civil Procedure 35.   Physical and Mental Examinations 499
Schlagenhauf v. Holder-- 500
B. Protective Orders --- 510
Federal Rule of Civil Procedure 26(c)------------------------------- 510
Federal Rule of Civil Procedure 37.   Failure to Make Disclosures or to
Cooperate in Discovery; Sanctions ---------------------------------- 511
Seattle Times Company v. Rhinehart ------------------------------- 515
C. Work Product Immunity-- 524
Federal Rule of Civil Procedure 26(b)(3)--------------------------- 524
Federal Rule of Civil Procedure 30.   Depositions by Oral Examination -- 525
Federal Rule of Civil Procedure 33.   Interrogatories to Parties ----------- 530
Federal Rule of Civil Procedure 34.   Producing Documents, Electroni-
cally Stored Information, and Tangible Things, or Entering onto
Land, for Inspection and Other Purposes ---------------------------- 531
Hickman v. Taylor -- 532
D. Attorney–Client Privilege-- 544
Upjohn Company v. United States ---------------------------------- 544

Page

Sec.

XII. Summary Judgment, Trial Motions, and Post–Trial Motions 555
  A. Evidentiary Burdens and Credibility Issues 555
      Federal Rule of Civil Procedure 56. Summary Judgment 555
      Lundeen v. Cordner 556
      Cross v. United States 565
  B. Modern Summary Judgment Standards 569
      Celotex Corporation v. Catrett 569
      Scott v. Harris 579
  C. Judgment as a Matter of Law (Directed Verdict) 589
      Federal Rule of Civil Procedure 50. Judgment as a Matter of Law in a
        Jury Trial; Related Motion for a New Trial; Conditional Ruling 589
      Galloway v. United States 590
  D. Judgment as a Matter of Law (Post–Trial Motions) 609
      Neely v. Martin K. Eby Construction Co., Inc. 609

XIII. Choice of Applicable Law (Erie Doctrine) 620
  A. Historical Basis: The Rules of Decision Act 620
      28 U.S.C. § 1652.   State Laws as Rules of Decision 620
      Erie R. Co. v. Tompkins 620
      Klaxon Co. v. Stentor Electric Mfg. Co., Inc. 631
  B. The Outcome Determination Test 633
      Guaranty Trust Co. of New York v. York 633
  C. Constitutional Concerns: The Byrd Balancing Test 643
      Byrd v. Blue Ridge Rural Electric Cooperative, Inc. 643
  D. The Rules Enabling Act 651
      28 U.S.C. § 2071. Rule–Making Power Generally 651
      28 U.S.C. § 2072. Rules of Procedure and Evidence; Power to Prescribe 651
      Federal Rule of Civil Procedure 83.   Rules by District Courts; Judge's
        Directives 652
      Hanna v. Plumer 652

XIV. Representational Class Action Litigation 662
  A. Due Process Considerations 662
      Hansberry v. Lee 662
  B. Class Certification 666
      Federal Rule of Civil Procedure 23.   Class Actions 666
      In the Matter of Rhone–Poulenc Rorer Inc. 671
  C. Jurisdiction and Choice of Law Issues 681
      28 U.S.C. § 1332(d). Class Actions; Diversity of Citizenship; Amount in
        Controversy 681
      28 U.S.C. § 1453.   Removal of Class Actions 685
      Phillips Petroleum Company v. Shutts 686
  D. Settlement Classes 704
      Amchem Products, Inc. v. Windsor 704

PART TWO. ALTERNATIVE WEEKS

I. Procedural Due Process 726
  A. Reasonable Notice 726
      U.S. Const. Amend. V. 726
      U.S. Const. Amend. XIV. 726
      Mullane v. Central Hanover Bank & Trust Co. 726
  B. Service of Process 734
      Federal Rule of Civil Procedure 4. Summons 734
      National Equipment Rental, Ltd. v. Szukhent 739

Page

Sec.

I. Procedural Due Process—Continued

    C. Opportunity to be Heard: Prior Hearing 750

        Fuentes v. Shevin 750

    D. Attachment Statutes 763

        Connecticut v. Doehr 763

II. Right to Trial by Jury 776

    A. Historical Bases and Modern Approach 776

        U.S. Const. Amend. VII. Civil Trials 776

        Federal Rule of Civil Procedure 38. Right to a Jury Trial; Demand 776

        Federal Rule of Civil Procedure 39. Trial by Jury or by the Court 776

        Federal Rule of Civil Procedure 57. Declaratory Judgment 777

        28 U.S.C. § 2201. Creation of Remedy 777

        28 U.S.C. § 2202. Further Relief 777

        Beacon Theatres, Inc. v. Westover 777

    B. Characterizing the Issue 786

        Dairy Queen, Inc. v. Wood 786

        Ross v. Bernhard 791

    C. Administrative Forum 800

        Atlas Roofing Co., Inc. v. Occupational Safety and Health Review Comm. 800

    D. Statutory Civil Penalty Actions 807

        Tull v. United States 807

III. Interlocutory Appeal 816

    A. The Final Judgment Rule 816

        Federal Rule of Civil Procedure 54. Judgment; Costs 816

        28 U.S.C. § 1291. Final Decisions of District Courts 817

        28 U.S.C. § 1292. Interlocutory Decisions 817

        Liberty Mutual Insurance Company v. Wetzel 818

        Curtiss–Wright Corp. v. General Electric Co. 821

    B. Collateral Order Doctrine 827

        Cohen v. Beneficial Industrial Loan Corp. 827

        Mohawk Industries, Inc. v. Carpenter 829

    C. Certified Orders 838

        Yamaha Motor Corp., U.S.A. v. Calhoun 838

        United States v. Philip Morris USA Inc. 840

    D. The Writ of Mandamus 851

        Federal Rule of Civil Procedure 53. Masters 851

        28 U.S.C. § 1651. Writs 854

        La Buy v. Howes Leather Company 854

IV. Res Judicata and Preclusion Doctrine 862

    A. Res Judicata and the Finality of Judgments 862

        Cromwell v. County of Sac 862

        Russell v. Place 873

    B. Collateral Estoppel: Identity of Issues 875

        Commissioner of Internal Revenue v. Sunnen 875

    C. Mutuality of Estoppel 881

        Parklane Hosiery Company, Inc. v. Shore 881

    D. Federalism Issues 896

        Review U.S. Const. Article IV § 1; 28 U.S.C. § 1738; Fed. R. Civ. P. 8(c)(1) 896

        Durfee v. Duke 896

Page

Sec.

IV. Res Judicata and Preclusion Doctrine—Continued
    Federal Rule of Civil Procedure 41. Dismissal of Actions......................... 900
    Semtek Int'l Corp. v. Lockheed Martin Corp. 901

TABLE OF CASES

References are to pages. Cases cited in principal cases and within other quoted materials are not included.

Amchem Products, Inc. v. Windsor, 521 U.S. 591, 117 S.Ct. 2231, 138 L.Ed.2d 689 (1997), **704**

American National Red Cross v. S.G. and A.E., 505 U.S. 247, 112 S.Ct. 2465, 120 L.Ed.2d 201 (1992), **220**

Asahi Metal Industry Co., Ltd. v. Superior Court of California, 480 U.S. 102, 107 S.Ct. 1026, 94 L.Ed.2d 92 (1987), **124**

Ashcroft v. Iqbal, 556 U.S. 662, 129 S.Ct. 1937, 173 L.Ed.2d 868 (2009), **376**

Atlas Roofing Co., Inc. v. Occupational Safety and Health Review Com'n, 430 U.S. 442, 97 S.Ct. 1261, 51 L.Ed.2d 464 (1977), **800**

Bank of California Nat. Ass'n v. Superior Court of San Francisco, 16 Cal.2d 516, 106 P.2d 879 (Cal.1940), **472**

Bates v. C & S Adjusters, Inc., 980 F.2d 865 (2nd Cir.1992), **333**

Beacon Theatres, Inc. v. Westover, 359 U.S. 500, 79 S.Ct. 948, 3 L.Ed.2d 988 (1959), **777**

Bell Atlantic Corp. v. Twombly, 550 U.S. 544, 127 S.Ct. 1955, 167 L.Ed.2d 929 (2007), **361**

Burger King Corp. v. Rudzewicz, 471 U.S. 462, 105 S.Ct. 2174, 85 L.Ed.2d 528 (1985), **109**

Burnham v. Superior Court of California, County of Marin, 495 U.S. 604, 110 S.Ct. 2105, 109 L.Ed.2d 631 (1990), **152**

Byrd v. Blue Ridge Rural Elec. Co-op., Inc., 356 U.S. 525, 78 S.Ct. 893, 2 L.Ed.2d 953 (1958), **643**

Calder v. Jones, 465 U.S. 783, 104 S.Ct. 1482, 79 L.Ed.2d 804 (1984), **105**

Carlsbad Technology, Inc. v. HIF Bio, Inc., 556 U.S. 635, 129 S.Ct. 1862, 173 L.Ed.2d 843 (2009), **323**

Carnival Cruise Lines, Inc. v. Shute, 499 U.S. 585, 111 S.Ct. 1522, 113 L.Ed.2d 622 (1991), **179**

Celotex Corp. v. Catrett, 477 U.S. 317, 106 S.Ct. 2548, 91 L.Ed.2d 265 (1986), **569**

Cohen v. Beneficial Indus. Loan Corp., 337 U.S. 541, 69 S.Ct. 1221, 93 L.Ed. 1528 (1949), **827**

Conley v. Gibson, 355 U.S. 41, 78 S.Ct. 99, 2 L.Ed.2d 80 (1957), **358**

Connecticut v. Doehr, 501 U.S. 1, 111 S.Ct. 2105, 115 L.Ed.2d 1 (1991), **763**

Cromwell v. County of Sac, 94 U.S. 351, 4 Otto 351, 24 L.Ed. 195 (1876), **862**

Cross v. United States, 336 F.2d 431 (2nd Cir.1964), **565**

Curtiss–Wright Corp. v. General Elec. Co., 446 U.S. 1, 100 S.Ct. 1460, 64 L.Ed.2d 1 (1980), **821**

Dairy Queen, Inc. v. Wood, 369 U.S. 469, 82 S.Ct. 894, 8 L.Ed.2d 44 (1962), **786**

Dioguardi v. Durning, 139 F.2d 774 (2nd Cir.1944), **354**

Durfee v. Duke, 375 U.S. 106, 84 S.Ct. 242, 11 L.Ed.2d 186 (1963), **896**

Erie R. Co. v. Tompkins, 304 U.S. 64, 58 S.Ct. 817, 82 L.Ed. 1188 (1938), **620**

Exxon Mobil Corp. v. Allapattah Services, Inc., 545 U.S. 546, 125 S.Ct. 2611, 162 L.Ed.2d 502 (2005), **295**

Finley v. United States, 490 U.S. 545, 109 S.Ct. 2003, 104 L.Ed.2d 593 (1989), **272**

Fuentes v. Shevin, 407 U.S. 67, 92 S.Ct. 1983, 32 L.Ed.2d 556 (1972), **750**

Galloway v. United States, 319 U.S. 372, 63 S.Ct. 1077, 87 L.Ed. 1458 (1943), **590**

Garcia v. Hilton Hotels Intern., 97 F.Supp. 5 (D.Puerto Rico 1951), **410**

Grable & Sons Metal Products, Inc. v. Darue Engineering & Mfg., 545 U.S. 308, 2006-14 I.R.B. 697, 125 S.Ct. 2363, 162 L.Ed.2d 257 (2005), **253**

Gray v. American Radiator & Standard Sanitary Corp., 22 Ill.2d 432, 176 N.E.2d 761 (Ill.1961), **42**

Grutter v. Bollinger, 188 F.3d 394 (6th Cir. 1999), **485**

Guaranty Trust Co. of N.Y. v. York, 326 U.S. 99, 65 S.Ct. 1464, 89 L.Ed. 2079 (1945), **633**

Hanna v. Plumer, 380 U.S. 460, 85 S.Ct. 1136, 14 L.Ed.2d 8 (1965), **652**

Hansberry v. Lee, 311 U.S. 32, 61 S.Ct. 115, 85 L.Ed. 22 (1940), **662**

Hanson v. Denckla, 357 U.S. 235, 78 S.Ct. 1228, 2 L.Ed.2d 1283 (1958), **28**

Helicopteros Nacionales de Colombia, S.A. v. Hall, 466 U.S. 408, 104 S.Ct. 1868, 80 L.Ed.2d 404 (1984), **90**

Hertz Corp. v. Friend, ___ U.S. ___, 130 S.Ct. 1181, 175 L.Ed.2d 1029 (2010), **195**

Hess v. Pawloski, 274 U.S. 352, 47 S.Ct. 632, 71 L.Ed. 1091 (1927), **14**

Hickman v. Taylor, 329 U.S. 495, 67 S.Ct. 385, 91 L.Ed. 451 (1947), **532**

Hoffman v. Blaski, 363 U.S. 335, 80 S.Ct. 1084, 4 L.Ed.2d 1254 (1960), **336**

International Shoe Co. v. State of Washington, 326 U.S. 310, 66 S.Ct. 154, 90 L.Ed. 95 (1945), **18**

J. McIntyre Machinery, Ltd. v. Nicastro, ___ U.S. ___, 131 S.Ct. 2780, 180 L.Ed.2d 765 (2011), **134**

Jones v. Ford Motor Credit Co., 358 F.3d 205 (2nd Cir.2004), **451**

Keeton v. Hustler Magazine, Inc., 465 U.S. 770, 104 S.Ct. 1473, 79 L.Ed.2d 790 (1984), **100**

Klaxon Co. v. Stentor Electric Mfg. Co., 313 U.S. 487, 61 S.Ct. 1020, 85 L.Ed. 1477 (1941), **631**

Kramer v. Caribbean Mills, Inc., 394 U.S. 823, 89 S.Ct. 1487, 23 L.Ed.2d 9 (1969), **204**

Krupski v. Costa Crociere S. p. A., ___ U.S. ___, 130 S.Ct. 2485, 177 L.Ed.2d 48 (2010), **426**

Kulko v. Superior Court of California In and For City and County of San Francisco, 436 U.S. 84, 98 S.Ct. 1690, 56 L.Ed.2d 132 (1978), **48**

La Buy v. Howes Leather Company, 352 U.S. 249, 77 S.Ct. 309, 1 L.Ed.2d 290 (1957), **854**

LASA Per L'Industria Del Marmo Societa Per Azioni of Lasa, Italy v. Alexander, 414 F.2d 143 (6th Cir.1969), **461**

Liberty Mut. Ins. Co. v. Wetzel, 424 U.S. 737, 96 S.Ct. 1202, 47 L.Ed.2d 435 (1976), **818**

Louisville & Nashville R. Co. v. Mottley, 211 U.S. 149, 29 S.Ct. 42, 53 L.Ed. 126 (1908), **238**

Lundeen v. Cordner, 354 F.2d 401 (8th Cir. 1966), **556**

Mas v. Perry, 489 F.2d 1396 (5th Cir.1974), **191**

Matter of (see name of party)

McGee v. International Life Ins. Co., 355 U.S. 220, 78 S.Ct. 199, 2 L.Ed.2d 223 (1957), **26**

Merrell Dow Pharmaceuticals Inc. v. Thompson, 478 U.S. 804, 106 S.Ct. 3229, 92 L.Ed.2d 650 (1986), **241**

Mims v. Arrow Financial Services, LLC, ___ U.S. ___, 132 S.Ct. 740, 181 L.Ed.2d 881 (2012), **259**

Mohawk Industries, Inc. v. Carpenter, ___ U.S. ___, 130 S.Ct. 599, 175 L.Ed.2d 458 (2009), **829**

M/S Bremen v. Zapata Off–Shore Co., 407 U.S. 1, 92 S.Ct. 1907, 32 L.Ed.2d 513 (1972), **168**

Mullane v. Central Hanover Bank & Trust Co., 339 U.S. 306, 70 S.Ct. 652, 94 L.Ed. 865 (1950), **726**

National Equipment Rental, Limited v. Szukhent, 375 U.S. 311, 84 S.Ct. 411, 11 L.Ed.2d 354 (1964), **739**

Neely v. Martin K. Eby Const. Co., 386 U.S. 317, 87 S.Ct. 1072, 18 L.Ed.2d 75 (1967), **609**

Owen Equipment & Erection Co. v. Kroger, 437 U.S. 365, 98 S.Ct. 2396, 57 L.Ed.2d 274 (1978), **284**

PAE Government Services, Inc. v. MPRI, Inc., 514 F.3d 856 (9th Cir.2007), **404**

Parklane Hosiery Co., Inc. v. Shore, 439 U.S. 322, 99 S.Ct. 645, 58 L.Ed.2d 552 (1979), **881**

Pennoyer v. Neff, 95 U.S. 714, 5 Otto 714, 24 L.Ed. 565 (1877), **6**

Philip Morris USA, Inc., United States v., 396 F.3d 1190, 364 U.S.App.D.C. 454 (D.C.Cir.2005), **840**

Phillips Petroleum Co. v. Shutts, 472 U.S. 797, 105 S.Ct. 2965, 86 L.Ed.2d 628 (1985), **686**

Piper Aircraft Co. v. Reyno, 454 U.S. 235, 102 S.Ct. 252, 70 L.Ed.2d 419 (1981), **339**

Provident Tradesmens Bank & Trust Co. v. Patterson, 390 U.S. 102, 88 S.Ct. 733, 19 L.Ed.2d 936 (1968), **477**

Rhone–Poulenc Rorer, Inc., Matter of, 51 F.3d 1293 (7th Cir.1995), **671**

Rose v. Giamatti, 721 F.Supp. 906 (S.D.Ohio 1989), **208**

Ross v. Bernhard, 396 U.S. 531, 90 S.Ct. 733, 24 L.Ed.2d 729 (1970), **791**

Roth v. Green, 466 F.3d 1179 (10th Cir. 2006), **437**

Rubert–Torres v. Hospital San Pablo, Inc., 205 F.3d 472 (1st Cir.2000), **415**

Russell v. Place, 94 U.S. 606, 4 Otto 606, 24 L.Ed. 214 (1876), **873**

Schlagenhauf v. Holder, 379 U.S. 104, 85 S.Ct. 234, 13 L.Ed.2d 152 (1964), **500**

Scott v. Harris, 550 U.S. 372, 127 S.Ct. 1769, 167 L.Ed.2d 686 (2007), **579**

Seattle Times Co. v. Rhinehart, 467 U.S. 20, 104 S.Ct. 2199, 81 L.Ed.2d 17 (1984), **515**

Semtek Intern. Inc. v. Lockheed Martin Corp., 531 U.S. 497, 121 S.Ct. 1021, 149 L.Ed.2d 32 (2001), **901**

Shaffer v. Heitner, 433 U.S. 186, 97 S.Ct. 2569, 53 L.Ed.2d 683 (1977), **56**

Sunnen, Commissioner v., 333 U.S. 591, 68 S.Ct. 715, 92 L.Ed. 898 (1948), **875**

T. B. Harms Co. v. Eliscu, 339 F.2d 823 (2nd Cir.1964), **234**

Tellabs, Inc. v. Makor Issues & Rights, Ltd., 551 U.S. 308, 127 S.Ct. 2499, 168 L.Ed.2d 179 (2007), **392**

Tull v. United States, 481 U.S. 412, 107 S.Ct. 1831, 95 L.Ed.2d 365 (1987), **807**

United Mine Workers of America v. Gibbs, 383 U.S. 715, 86 S.Ct. 1130, 16 L.Ed.2d 218 (1966), **267**

United States v. _____ (see opposing party)

Upjohn Co. v. United States, 449 U.S. 383, 101 S.Ct. 677, 66 L.Ed.2d 584 (1981), **544**

World–Wide Volkswagen Corp. v. Woodson, 444 U.S. 286, 100 S.Ct. 559, 62 L.Ed.2d 490 (1980), **74**

Yamaha Motor Corp., U.S.A. v. Calhoun, 516 U.S. 199, 116 S.Ct. 619, 133 L.Ed.2d 578 (1996), **838**

Zielinski v. Philadelphia Piers, Inc., 139 F.Supp. 408 (E.D.Pa.1956), **419**

LEADING CASES IN CIVIL PROCEDURE

PART ONE

LEADING CASES IN CIVIL PROCEDURE

■ ■ ■

I. CHOOSING THE FORUM (PERSONAL JURISDICTION)

A. THE PROFESSIONAL RESPONSIBILITY OF THE LAWYER

AMERICAN BAR ASSOCIATION
MODEL RULES OF PROFESSIONAL CONDUCT

PREAMBLE: A LAWYER'S RESPONSIBILITIES

[1]   A lawyer, as a member of the legal profession, is a representative of clients, an officer of the legal system and a public citizen having special responsibility for the quality of justice.

[2]   As a representative of clients, a lawyer performs various functions. As advisor, a lawyer provides a client with an informed understanding of the client's legal rights and obligations and explains their practical implications. As advocate, a lawyer zealously asserts the client's position under the rules of the adversary system. As negotiator, a lawyer seeks a result advantageous to the client but consistent with requirements of honest dealings with others. As an evaluator, a lawyer acts by examining a client's legal affairs and reporting about them to the client or to others.

[3]   In addition to these representational functions, a lawyer may serve as a third-party neutral, a nonrepresentational role helping the parties to resolve a dispute or other matter. Some of these Rules apply directly to lawyers who are or have served as third-party neutrals. See, e.g., Rules 1.12 and 2.4. In addition, there are Rules that apply to lawyers who are not active in the practice of law or to practicing lawyers even when they are acting in a nonprofessional capacity. For example, a lawyer who commits fraud in the conduct of a business is subject to discipline for engaging in conduct involving dishonesty, fraud, deceit or misrepresentation. See Rule 8.4.

[4]   In all professional functions a lawyer should be competent, prompt and diligent. A lawyer should maintain communication with a

1

client concerning the representation. A lawyer should keep in confidence information relating to representation of a client except so far as disclosure is required or permitted by the Rules of Professional Conduct or other law.

[5] A lawyer's conduct should conform to the requirements of the law, both in professional service to clients and in the lawyer's business and personal affairs. A lawyer should use the law's procedures only for legitimate purposes and not to harass or intimidate others. A lawyer should demonstrate respect for the legal system and for those who serve it, including judges, other lawyers and public officials. While it is a lawyer's duty, when necessary, to challenge the rectitude of official action, it is also a lawyer's duty to uphold legal process.

[6] As a public citizen, a lawyer should seek improvement of the law, access to the legal system, the administration of justice and the quality of service rendered by the legal profession. As a member of a learned profession, a lawyer should cultivate knowledge of the law beyond its use for clients, employ that knowledge in reform of the law and work to strengthen legal education. In addition, a lawyer should further the public's understanding of and confidence in the rule of law and the justice system because legal institutions in a constitutional democracy depend on popular participation and support to maintain their authority. A lawyer should be mindful of deficiencies in the administration of justice and of the fact that the poor, and sometimes persons who are not poor, cannot afford adequate legal assistance. Therefore, all lawyers should devote professional time and resources and use civic influence to ensure equal access to our system of justice for all those who because of economic or social barriers cannot afford or secure adequate legal counsel. A lawyer should aid the legal profession in pursuing these objectives and should help the bar regulate itself in the public interest.

[7] Many of a lawyer's professional responsibilities are prescribed in the Rules of Professional Conduct, as well as substantive and procedural law. However, a lawyer is also guided by personal conscience and the approbation of professional peers. A lawyer should strive to attain the highest level of skill, to improve the law and the legal profession and to exemplify the legal profession's ideals of public service.

[8] A lawyer's responsibilities as a representative of clients, an officer of the legal system and a public citizen are usually harmonious. Thus, when an opposing party is well represented, a lawyer can be a zealous advocate on behalf of a client and at the same time assume that justice is being done. So also, a lawyer can be sure that preserving client confidences ordinarily serves the public interest because people are more likely to seek legal advice, and thereby heed their legal obligations, when they know their communications will be private.

[9] In the nature of law practice, however, conflicting responsibilities are encountered. Virtually all difficult ethical problems arise from conflict between a lawyer's responsibilities to clients, to the legal system and to

the lawyer's own interest in remaining an ethical person while earning a satisfactory living. The Rules of Professional Conduct often prescribe terms for resolving such conflicts. Within the framework of these Rules, however, many difficult issues of professional discretion can arise. Such issues must be resolved through the exercise of sensitive professional and moral judgment guided by the basic principles underlying the Rules. These principles include the lawyer's obligation zealously to protect and pursue a client's legitimate interests, within the bounds of the law, while maintaining a professional, courteous and civil attitude toward all persons involved in the legal system.

[10] The legal profession is largely self-governing. Although other professions also have been granted powers of self-government, the legal profession is unique in this respect because of the close relationship between the profession and the processes of government and law enforcement. This connection is manifested in the fact that ultimate authority over the legal profession is vested largely in the courts.

[11] To the extent that lawyers meet the obligations of their professional calling, the occasion for government regulation is obviated. Self-regulation also helps maintain the legal profession's independence from government domination. An independent legal profession is an important force in preserving government under law, for abuse of legal authority is more readily challenged by a profession whose members are not dependent on government for the right to practice.

[12] The legal profession's relative autonomy carries with it special responsibilities of self-government. The profession has a responsibility to assure that its regulations are conceived in the public interest and not in furtherance of parochial or self-interested concerns of the bar. Every lawyer is responsible for observance of the Rules of Professional Conduct. A lawyer should also aid in securing their observance by other lawyers. Neglect of these responsibilities compromises the independence of the profession and the public interest which it serves.

[13] Lawyers play a vital role in the preservation of society. The fulfillment of this role requires an understanding by lawyers of their relationship to our legal system. The Rules of Professional Conduct, when properly applied, serve to define that relationship.

SCOPE

[14] The Rules of Professional Conduct are rules of reason. They should be interpreted with reference to the purposes of legal representation and of the law itself. Some of the Rules are imperatives, cast in the terms "shall" or "shall not." These define proper conduct for purposes of professional discipline. Others, generally cast in the term "may," are permissive and define areas under the Rules in which the lawyer has discretion to exercise professional judgment. No disciplinary action should be taken when the lawyer chooses not to act or acts within the bounds of such discretion. Other Rules define the nature of relationships between

the lawyer and others. The Rules are thus partly obligatory and disciplinary and partly constitutive and descriptive in that they define a lawyer's professional role. Many of the Comments use the term "should." Comments do not add obligations to the Rules but provide guidance for practicing in compliance with the Rules.

[15] The Rules presuppose a larger legal context shaping the lawyer's role. That context includes court rules and statutes relating to matters of licensure, laws defining specific obligations of lawyers and substantive and procedural law in general. The Comments are sometimes used to alert lawyers to their responsibilities under such other law.

[16] Compliance with the Rules, as with all law in an open society, depends primarily upon understanding and voluntary compliance, secondarily upon reinforcement by peer and public opinion and finally, when necessary, upon enforcement through disciplinary proceedings. The Rules do not, however, exhaust the moral and ethical considerations that should inform a lawyer, for no worthwhile human activity can be completely defined by legal rules. The Rules simply provide a framework for the ethical practice of law.

[17] Furthermore, for purposes of determining the lawyer's authority and responsibility, principles of substantive law external to these Rules determine whether a client-lawyer relationship exists. Most of the duties flowing from the client-lawyer relationship attach only after the client has requested the lawyer to render legal services and the lawyer has agreed to do so. But there are some duties, such as that of confidentiality under Rule 1.6, that attach when the lawyer agrees to consider whether a client-lawyer relationship shall be established. *See* Rule 1.18. Whether a client-lawyer relationship exists for any specific purpose can depend on the circumstances and may be a question of fact.

[18] Under various legal provisions, including constitutional, statutory and common law, the responsibilities of government lawyers may include authority concerning legal matters that ordinarily reposes in the client in private client-lawyer relationships. For example, a lawyer for a government agency may have authority on behalf of the government to decide upon settlement or whether to appeal from an adverse judgment. Such authority in various respects is generally vested in the attorney general and the state's attorney in state government, and their federal counterparts, and the same may be true of other government law officers. Also, lawyers under the supervision of these officers may be authorized to represent several government agencies in intra-governmental legal controversies in circumstances where a private lawyer could not represent multiple private clients. These Rules do not abrogate any such authority.

[19] Failure to comply with an obligation or prohibition imposed by a Rule is a basis for invoking the disciplinary process. The Rules presuppose that disciplinary assessment of a lawyer's conduct will be made on the basis of the facts and circumstances as they existed at the time of the conduct in question and in recognition of the fact that a lawyer often has

to act upon uncertain or incomplete evidence of the situation. Moreover, the Rules presuppose that whether or not discipline should be imposed for a violation, and the severity of a sanction, depend on all the circumstances, such as the willfulness and seriousness of the violation, extenuating factors and whether there have been previous violations.

[20]   Violation of a Rule should not itself give rise to a cause of action against a lawyer nor should it create any presumption in such a case that a legal duty has been breached. In addition, violation of a Rule does not necessarily warrant any other non-disciplinary remedy, such as disqualification of a lawyer in pending litigation. The Rules are designed to provide guidance to lawyers and to provide a structure for regulating conduct through disciplinary agencies. They are not designed to be a basis for civil liability. Furthermore, the purpose of the Rules can be subverted when they are invoked by opposing parties as procedural weapons. The fact that a Rule is a just basis for a lawyer's self-assessment, or for sanctioning a lawyer under the administration of a disciplinary authority, does not imply that an antagonist in a collateral proceeding or transaction has standing to seek enforcement of the Rule. Nevertheless, since the Rules do establish standards of conduct by lawyers, a lawyer's violation of a Rule may be evidence of breach of the applicable standard of conduct.

* * *

B.   TRADITIONAL BASES: TERRITORIAL JURISDICTION

CONSTITUTIONAL PROVISIONS

U.S. CONST. ARTICLE IV § 1

Section 1. Full Faith and Credit shall be given in each State to the public Acts, Records, and judicial Proceedings of every other State. And the Congress may by general Laws prescribe the Manner in which such Acts, Records and Proceedings shall be proved, and the Effect thereof.

U.S. CONST. AMEND. XIV § 1

Section 1. All persons born or naturalized in the United States, and subject to the jurisdiction thereof, are citizens of the United States and of the State wherein they reside. No State shall make or enforce any law which shall abridge the privileges or immunities of citizens of the United States; nor shall any State deprive any person of life, liberty, or property, without due process of law; nor deny to any person within its jurisdiction the equal protection of the laws.

* * *

FEDERAL RULE OF CIVIL PROCEDURE 55

(a) **Entering a Default**. When a party against whom a judgment for affirmative relief is sought has failed to plead or otherwise defend, and that failure is shown by affidavit or otherwise, the clerk must enter the party's default.

* * *

28 U.S.C. § 1738

The records and judicial proceedings of any court of any ... State, Territory or Possession ... shall have the same full faith and credit in every court within the United States and its Territories and Possessions as they have by law or usage in the courts of such State, Territory or Possession from which they are taken.

* * *

PENNOYER v. NEFF

95 U.S. 714 (1877)

MR. JUSTICE FIELD delivered the opinion of the court.

This is an action to recover the possession of a tract of land, of the alleged value of $15,000, situated in the State of Oregon. The plaintiff asserts title to the premises by a patent of the United States issued to him in 1866, under the act of Congress of Sept. 27, 1850, usually known as the Donation Law of Oregon. The defendant claims to have acquired the premises under a sheriff's deed, made upon a sale of the property on execution issued upon a judgment recovered against the plaintiff in one of the circuit courts of the State. The case turns upon the validity of this judgment.

It appears from the record that the judgment was rendered in February, 1866, in favor of J. H. Mitchell, for less than $300, including costs, in an action brought by him upon a demand for services as an attorney; that, at the time the action was commenced and the judgment rendered, the defendant therein, the plaintiff here, was a non-resident of the State that he was not personally served with process, and did not appear therein; and that the judgment was entered upon his default in not answering the complaint, upon a constructive service of summons by publication.

The Code of Oregon provides for such service when an action is brought against a non-resident and absent defendant, who has property within the State. It also provides, where the action is for the recovery of money or damages, for the attachment of the property of the non-resident. And it also declares that no natural person is subject to the jurisdiction of a court of the State, "unless he appear in the court, or be found within the State, or be a resident thereof, or have property therein; and, in the last case, only to the extent of such property at the time the jurisdiction attached." Construing this latter provision to mean, that, in an action for money or damages where a defendant does not appear in the court, and is not found within the State, and is not a resident thereof, but has property therein, the jurisdiction of the court extends only over such property, the declaration expresses a principle of general, if not universal, law. The authority of every tribunal is necessarily restricted by the territorial limits of the State in which it is established. Any attempt to exercise authority beyond those limits would be deemed in every other forum, as has been said by this court, in illegitimate assumption of power, and be resisted as mere abuse. In the case against the plaintiff, the property here in controversy sold under the judgment rendered was not attached, nor in any way brought under the jurisdiction of the court. Its first connection with the case was caused by a levy of the execution. It was not, therefore, disposed of pursuant to any adjudication, but only in enforcement of a personal judgment, having no relation to the property, rendered against a non-resident without service of process upon him in the action, or his appearance therein. The court below did not consider that an attachment of the property was essential to its jurisdiction or to the validity of the sale, but held that the judgment was invalid from defects in the affidavit upon which the order of publication was obtained, and in the affidavit by which the publication was proved.

There is some difference of opinion among the members of this court as to the rulings upon these alleged defects. * * * If, therefore, we were confined to the rulings of the court below upon the defects in the affidavits mentioned, we should be unable to uphold its decision. But it was also contended in that court, and is insisted upon here, that the judgment in the State court against the plaintiff was void for want of personal service of process on him, or of his appearance in the action in which it was rendered and that the premises in controversy could not be subjected to the payment of the demand of a resident creditor except by a proceeding *in rem;* that is, by a direct proceeding against the property for that purpose. If these positions are sound, the ruling of the Circuit Court as to the invalidity of that judgment must be sustained, notwithstanding our dissent from the reasons upon which it was made. And that they are sound would seem to follow from two well-established principles of public law respecting the jurisdiction of an independent State over persons and property. The several States of the Union are not, it is true, in every respect independent, many of the right and powers which originally belonged to them being now vested in the government created by the Constitution. But, except as restrained and limited by that instrument, they possess and exercise the authority of independent States, and the principles of public law to which we have referred are applicable to them. One of these principles is, that every State possesses exclusive jurisdiction and sovereignty over persons and property within its territory. As a consequence, every State has the power to determine for itself the civil *status* and capacities of its inhabitants; to prescribe the subjects upon which they may contract, the forms and solemnities with which their contracts shall be executed, the rights and obligations arising from them, and the mode in which their validity shall be determined and their obligations enforced; and also the regulate the manner and conditions upon which property situated within such territory, both personal and real, may be acquired, enjoyed, and transferred. The other principle of public law referred to follows from the one mentioned; that is, that no State can exercise direct jurisdiction and authority over persons or property without its territory. The several States are of equal dignity and authority, and the independence of one implies the exclusion of power from all others. And so it is laid down by jurists, as an elementary principle, that the laws of one State have no operation outside of its territory, except so far as is allowed by comity; and that no tribunal established by it can extend its process beyond that territory so as to subject either persons or property to its decisions. "Any exertion of authority of this sort beyond this limit," says Story, "is a mere nullity, and incapable of binding such persons or property in any other tribunals."

But as contracts made in one State may be enforceable only in another State, and property may be held by non-residents, the exercise of the jurisdiction which every State is admitted to possess over persons and property within its own territory will often affect persons and property without it. To any influence exerted in this way by a State affecting persons resident or property situated elsewhere, no objection can be justly taken; whilst any direct exertion of authority upon them, in an attempt to give ex-territorial operation to its laws, or to enforce an ex-territorial jurisdiction by its tribunals, would be deemed an encroachment upon the independence of the State in which the persons are domiciled or the property is situated, and be resisted as usurpation.

Thus the State, through its tribunals, may compel persons domiciled within its limits to execute, in pursuance of their contracts respecting property elsewhere situated, instruments in such form and with such solemnities as to transfer the title, so far as such formalities can be complied with; and the exercise of this jurisdiction in no manner interferes with the supreme control over the property by the State within which it is situated.

So the State, through its tribunals, may subject property situated within its limits owned by non-residents to the payment of the demand of its own citizens against them; and the exercise of this jurisdiction in no respect infringes upon the sovereignty of the State where the owners are domiciled. Every State owes protection to its own citizens; and, when non-residents deal with them, it is a legitimate and just exercise of authority to hold and appropriate any property owned by such non-residents to satisfy the claims of its citizens. It is in virtue of the State's jurisdiction over the property of the non-resident situated within its limits that its tribunals can inquire into that non-resident's obligations to its own citizens, and the inquiry can then be carried only to the extent necessary to control the disposition of the property. If the non-resident have no property in the State, there is nothing upon which the tribunals can adjudicate.

These views are not new. They have been frequently expressed, with more or less distinctness, in opinions of eminent judges, and have been carried into adjudications in numerous cases. Thus, . . . Mr. Justice Story said:

> Where a party is within a territory, he may justly be subjected to its process, and bound personally by the judgment pronounced on such process against him. Where he is not within such territory, and is not personally subject to its laws, if, on account of his supposed or actual property being within the territory, process by the local laws may, by attachment, go to compel his appearance, and for his default to appear judgment may be pronounced against him, such a judgment must, upon general principles, be deemed only to bind him to the extent of such property, and cannot have the effect of a conclusive judgment *in personam*, for the plain reason, that, except so far as the property is concerned, it is a judgment *coram non judice*.

And, where the title of the plaintiff in ejectment was acquired on a sheriff's sale, under a money decree rendered upon publication of notice against non-residents, in a suit brought to enforce a contract relating to land, Mr. Justice McLean said:

> Jurisdiction is acquired in one of two modes: first, as against the person of the defendant by the service of process; or, secondly, by a procedure against the property of the defendant within the jurisdiction of the court. In the latter case, the defendant is not personally bound by the judgment beyond the property in question. And it is immaterial whether the proceeding against the property be by an attachment or bill in chancery. It must be substantially a proceeding *in rem*.

* * * It is the only doctrine consistent with proper protection to citizens of other States. If, without personal service, judgments *in personam*, obtained *ex parte* against non-residents and absent parties, upon mere publication of process, which, in the great majority of cases, would never be seen by the parties interested, could be upheld and enforced, they would be the constant instruments of fraud and oppression. Judgments for all sorts of claims upon contracts and for torts, real or pretended, would be thus obtained, under which property would be seized, when the evidence of the transactions upon which they were founded, if they ever had any existence, had perished.

Substituted service by publication, or in any other authorized form, may be sufficient to inform parties of the object of proceedings taken where property is once brought under the control of the court by seizure or some equivalent act. The law assumes that property is always in the possession of its owner, in person or by agent; and it proceeds upon the theory that its seizure will inform him, not only that it is taken into the custody of the court, but that he must look to any proceedings authorized by law upon such seizure for its condemnation and sale. Such service may also be sufficient in cases where the object of the action is to reach and dispose of property in the State, or of some interest therein, by enforcing a contract or a lien respecting the same, or to partition it among different owners, or, when the public is a party, to condemn and appropriate it for a public purpose. In other words, such service may answer in all actions which are substantially proceedings *in rem*. But where the entire object of the action is to determine the personal rights and obligations of the defendants, that is, where the suit is merely *in personam*, constructive service in this form upon a non-resident is ineffectual for any purpose. Process from the tribunals of one State cannot run into another State, and summon parties there domiciled to leave its territory and respond to proceedings against them. Publication of process or notice within the State where the tribunal sits cannot create any greater obligation upon the non-resident to appear. Process sent to him out of the State, and process published within it, are equally unavailing in proceedings to establish his personal liability.

The want of authority of the tribunals of a State to adjudicate upon the obligations of non-residents, where they have no property within its limits, is not denied by the court below: but the position is assumed, that, where they have property within the State, it is immaterial whether the property is in the first instance brought under the control of the court by attachment or some other equivalent act, and afterwards applied by its judgment to the satisfaction of demands against its owner; or such demands be first established in a personal action, and the property of the non-resident be afterwards seized and sold on execution. But the answer to this position has already been given in the statement, that the jurisdiction of the court to inquire into and determine his obligations at all is only incidental to its jurisdiction over the property. Its jurisdiction in that respect cannot be made to depend upon facts to be ascertained after it has tried the cause and rendered the judgment. If the judgment be previously void, it will not become valid by the subsequent discovery of property of the defendant, or by his subsequent acquisition of it. The judgment, if void when rendered, will always remain void: it cannot occupy the doubtful position of being valid if property be found, and void if there be none. Even if the position assumed were confined to cases where the non-resident defendant possessed property in the State at the commencement of the action, it would still make the validity of the proceedings and judgment depend upon the question whether, before the levy of the execution, the defendant had or had not disposed of the property. If before the levy the property should be sold, then, according to this position, the judgment would not be binding. This doctrine would introduce a new element of uncertainty in judicial proceedings. The contrary is the law: the validity of every judgment depends upon the jurisdiction of the court before it is rendered, not upon what may occur subsequently. [Where a] plaintiff claimed title to land sold under judgments recovered in suits brought in a territorial court of Iowa, upon publication of notice under a law of the territory, without service of process; and the court said:

> These suits were not a proceeding *in rem* against the land, but were *in personam* against the owners of it. Whether they all resided within the territory or not does not appear, nor is it a matter of any

importance. No person is required to answer in a suit on whom process has not been served, or whose property has not been attached. In this case, there was no personal notice, nor an attachment or other proceeding against the land, until after the judgments. The judgments, therefore, are nullities, and did not authorize the executions on which the land was sold.

The force and effect of judgments rendered against non-residents without personal service of process upon them, or their voluntary appearance, have been the subject of frequent consideration in the courts of the United States and of the several States, as attempts have been made to enforce such judgments in States other than those in which they were rendered, under the provision of the Constitution requiring that "full faith and credit shall be given in each State to the public acts, records, and judicial proceedings of every other State;" and the act of Congress providing for the mode of authenticating such acts, records, and proceedings, and declaring that, when thus authenticated, "they shall have such faith and credit given to them in every court within the United States as they have by law or usage in the courts of the State from which they are or shall or taken." In the earlier cases, it was supposed that the act gave to all judgments the same effect in other States which they had by law in the State where rendered. But this view was afterwards qualified so as to make the act applicable only when the court rendering the judgment had jurisdiction of the parties and of the subject-matter, and not to preclude an inquiry into the jurisdiction of the court in which the judgment was rendered, or the right of the State itself to exercise authority over the person or the subject-matter. In [another case] this view is stated with great clearness. That was an action in the Circuit Court of the United States for Louisiana, brought upon a judgment rendered in New York under a State statute, against two joint debtors, only one of whom had been served with process, the other being a non-resident of the State. The Circuit Court held the judgment conclusive and binding upon the non-resident not served with process; but this court reversed its decision, observing, that it was a familiar rule that countries foreign to our own disregarded a judgment merely against the person, where the defendant had not been served with process nor had a day in court; that national comity was never thus extended; that the proceeding was deemed an illegitimate assumption of power, and resisted as mere abuse; that no faith and credit or force and effect had been given to such judgments by any State of the Union, so far as known; and that the State courts had uniformly, and in many instances, held them to be void. "The international law," said the court, "as it existed among the States in 1790, was that a judgment rendered in one State, assuming to bind the person of a citizen of another, was void within the foreign State, when the defendant had not been served with process or voluntarily made defence; because neither the legislative jurisdiction nor that of courts of justice had binding force." And the court held that the act of Congress did not intend to declare a new rule, or to embrace judicial records of this description. As was stated in a subsequent case, the doctrine of this court is, that the act "was not designed to displace that principle of natural justice which requires a person to have notice of a suit before he can be conclusively bound by its result, nor those rules of public law which protect persons and property within one State from the exercise of jurisdiction over them by another."

* * * In several [ ] cases, the decision has been accompanied with the observation that a personal judgment thus recovered has no binding force without the State in which it is rendered, implying that in such State it may be valid and binding. But if the court has no jurisdiction over the person of the defendant by reason of his non-residence, and, consequently, no authority to pass upon his personal rights and obligations; if the whole proceeding, without service upon him or his appearance, is *coram non judice* and void; if to hold a defendant bound by such a judgment is contrary to the first principles of justice—it is difficult to see how the judgment can legitimately have any force within the State. The language used can be justified only on the ground that there was no mode of directly reviewing such judgment or impeaching its validity within the State where rendered; and that, therefore, it could be called in question only when its enforcement was elsewhere attempted. In later cases, this language is repeated with less frequency than formerly, it beginning to be considered, as it always ought to have been, that a judgment which can be treated in any State of this Union as contrary to the first principles of justice, and as an absolute nullity, because rendered without any jurisdiction of the tribunal over the party, is not entitled to any respect in the State where rendered.

Be that as it may, the courts of the United States are not required to give effect to judgments of this character when any right is claimed under them. Whilst they are not foreign tribunals in their relations to the State courts, they are tribunals of a different sovereignty, exercising a distinct and independent jurisdiction, and are bound to give to the judgments of the State courts only the same faith and credit which the courts of another State are bound to give to them.

Since the adoption of the Fourteenth Amendment to the Federal Constitution, the validity of such judgments may be directly questioned, and their enforcement in the State resisted, on the ground that proceedings in a court of justice to deter mine the personal rights and obligations of parties over whom that court has no jurisdiction do not constitute due process of law. Whatever difficulty may be experienced in giving to those terms a definition which will embrace every permissible exertion of power affecting private rights, and exclude such as is forbidden, there can be no doubt of their meaning when applied to judicial proceedings. They then mean a course of legal proceedings according to those rules and principles which have been established in our systems of jurisprudence for the protection and enforcement of private rights. To give such proceedings any validity, there must be a tribunal competent by its constitution—that is, by the law of its creation—to pass upon the subject-matter of the suit; and, if that involves merely a determination of the personal liability of the defendant, he must be brought within its jurisdiction by service of process within the State, or his voluntary appearance.

Except in cases affecting the personal *status* of the plaintiff, and cases in which that mode of service may be considered to have been assented to in advance, as hereinafter mentioned, the substituted service of process by publication, allowed by the law of Oregon and by similar laws in other States, where actions are brought against non-residents, is effectual only where, in connection with process against the person for commencing the action, property in the State is brought under the control of the court, and subjected to its disposition by process adapted to that purpose, or where the judgment is sought as a means of reaching such property or affecting some interest therein; in other words, where the action is in the nature of a proceeding *in rem*. As stated by Cooley in his Treatise on Constitutional Limitations, 405, for any other purpose than to subject the property of a non-resident to valid claims against him in the State, "due process of law would require appearance or personal service before the defendant could be personally bound by any judgment rendered."

It is true that, in a strict sense, a proceeding *in rem* is one taken directly against property, and has for its object the disposition of the property, without reference to the title of individual claimants; but, in a larger and more general sense, the terms are applied to actions between parties, where the direct object is to reach and dispose of property owned by them, or of some interest therein. Such are cases commenced by attachment against the property of debtors, or instituted to partition real estate, foreclose a mortgage, or enforce a lien. So far as they affect property in the State, they are substantially proceedings *in rem* in the broader sense which we have mentioned.

It is hardly necessary to observe, that in all we have said we have had reference to proceedings in courts of first instance, and to their jurisdiction, and not to proceedings in an appellate tribunal to review the action of such courts. The latter may be taken upon such notice, personal or constructive, as the State creating the tribunal may provide. They are considered as rather a continuation of the original litigation than the commencement of a new action.

It follows from the views expressed that the personal judgment recovered in the State court of Oregon against the plaintiff herein, then a non-resident of the State, was without any validity, and did not authorize a sale of the property in controversy.

To prevent any misapplication of the views expressed in this opinion, it is proper to observe that we do not mean to assert, by any thing we have said, that a State may not authorize proceedings to determine the *status* of one of its citizens towards a non-resident, which would be binding within the State, though made without service of process or personal notice to the non-resident. The jurisdiction which every State possesses to determine the civil *status* and capacities of all its inhabitants involves authority to prescribe the conditions on which proceedings affecting them may be commenced and carried on within its territory. The State, for example, has absolute right to prescribe the conditions upon which the marriage relation between its own citizens shall be created, and the causes for which it may be dissolved. One of the parties guilty of acts for which, by the law of the State, a dissolution may be granted, may have removed to a State where no dissolution is permitted. The complaining party would, therefore, fail if a divorce were sought in the State of the defendant; and if application could not be made to the tribunals of the complainant's domicile in such case, and proceedings be there instituted without personal service of process or personal notice to the offending party, the injured citizen would be without redress.

Neither do we mean to assert that a State may not require a non-resident entering into a partnership or association within its limits, or making contracts enforceable there, to appoint an agent or representative in the State to receive service of process and notice in legal proceedings instituted with respect to such partnership, association, or contracts, or to designate a place where such service may be made and notice given, and provide, upon their failure, to make such appointment or to designate such place that service may be made upon a public officer designated for that purpose, or in some other prescribed way, and that judgments rendered upon such service may not be binding upon the non-residents both within and without the State.... Nor do we doubt that a State, on creating corporations or other institutions for pecuniary or charitable purposes, may provide a mode in which their conduct may be investigated, their obligations enforced, or their charters revoked, which shall require other than personal service upon their officers or members. Parties becoming members of such corporations or institutions would hold their interest subject to the conditions prescribed by law.

In the present case, there is no feature of this kind, and, consequently, no consideration of what would be the effect of such legislation in enforcing the contract of a non-resident can arise. The question here respects only the validity of a money judgment rendered in one State, in an action upon a simple contract against the resident of another, without service of process upon him, or his appearance therein.

Judgment affirmed.

* * *

C. IMPLIED CONSENT

HESS v. PAWLOSKI

274 U.S. 352 (1927)

MR. JUSTICE BUTLER delivered the opinion of the Court.

This action was brought by defendant in error to recover damages for personal injuries. The declaration alleged that plaintiff in error negligently and wantonly drove a motor vehicle on a public highway in Massachusetts, and that by reason thereof the vehicle struck and injured defendant in error. Plaintiff in error is a resident of Pennsylvania. No personal service was made on him, and no property belonging to him was attached. The service of process was made in compliance with chapter 90, General Laws of Massachusetts, as amended by Stat. 1923, c. 431, § 2, the material parts of which follow:

> The acceptance by a nonresident of the rights and privileges conferred by section three or four, as evidence by his operating a motor vehicle thereunder, or the operation by a nonresident of a motor vehicle on a public way in the commonwealth other than under said sections, shall be deemed equivalent to an appointment by such nonresident of the registrar or his successor in office, to be his true and lawful attorney upon whom may be served all lawful processes in any action or proceeding against him, growing out of any accident or collision in which said nonresident may be involved while operating a motor vehicle on such a way, and said acceptance or operation shall be a signification of his agreement that any such process against him which is so served shall be of the same legal force and validity as if served on him personally. Service of such process shall be made by leaving a copy of the process with a fee of two dollars in the hands of the registrar, or in his office, and such service shall be sufficient service upon the said nonresident: Provided, that notice of such service and a copy of the process are forthwith sent by registered mail by the plaintiff to the defendant, and the defendant's return receipt and the plaintiff's affidavit of compliance herewith are appended to the writ and entered with the declaration. The court in which the action is pending may order such continuances as may be necessary to afford the defendant reasonable opportunity to defend the action.

Plaintiff in error appeared specially for the purpose of contesting jurisdiction, and filed an answer in abatement and moved to dismiss on the ground that the service of process, if sustained, would deprive him of his property without due process of law, in violation of the Fourteenth Amendment. The court overruled the answer in abatement and denied the motion. The Supreme Judicial Court held the statute to be a valid exercise of the police power, and affirmed the order. At the trial the contention was renewed and again denied. Plaintiff in error excepted. The jury returned a verdict for defendant in error. The exceptions were overruled by the Supreme Judicial Court. Thereupon the superior court entered judgment. The writ of error was allowed by the Chief Justice of that court.

The question is whether the Massachusetts enactment contravenes the due process clause of the Fourteenth Amendment.

The process of a court of one state cannot run into another and summon a party there domiciled to respond to proceedings against him. Notice sent outside the state to a nonresident is unavailing to give jurisdiction in an action against him personally for money recovery. *Pennoyer v. Neff.* There must be actual service within the state of notice upon him or upon some one authorized to accept service for him. A personal judgment rendered against a nonresident, who has neither been served with process nor appeared in the suit, is without validity. The mere transaction of business in a state by nonresident natural persons does not imply consent to be bound by the process of its courts. The power of a state to exclude foreign corporations, although not absolute, but qualified, is the ground on which such an implication is supported as to them. But a state may not withhold from nonresident individuals the right of doing business therein. The privileges and immunities clause of the Constitution safeguards to the citizens of one state the right "to pass through, or to reside in any other state for purposes of trade, agriculture, professional pursuits, or otherwise." And it prohibits state legislation discriminating against citizens of other states.

Motor vehicles are dangerous machines, and, even when skillfully and carefully operated, their use is attended by serious dangers to persons and property. In the public interest the state may make and enforce regulations reasonable calculated to promote care on the part of all, residents and nonresidents alike, who use its highways. The measure in question operates to require a nonresident to answer for his conduct in the state where arise causes of action alleged against him, as well as to provide for a claimant a convenient method by which he may sue to enforce his rights. Under the statute the implied consent is limited to proceedings growing out of accidents or collisions on a highway in which the nonresident may be involved. It is required that he shall actually receive and receipt for notice of the service and a copy of the process. And it contemplates such continuances as may be found necessary to give reasonable time and opportunity for defense. It makes no hostile discrimination against nonresidents, but tends to put them on the same footing as residents. Literal and precise equality in respect of this matter is not attainable; it is not required. The state's power to regulate the use of its highways extends to their use by nonresidents as well as by residents. And, in advance of the operation of a motor vehicle on its highway by a nonresident, the state may require him to appoint one of its officials as his agent on whom process may be served in proceedings growing out of such use. That case recognized power of the state to exclude a nonresident until the formal appointment is made. And, having the power so to exclude, the state may declare that the use of the highway by the nonresident is the equivalent of the appointment of the registrar as agent on whom process may be served. The difference between the formal and implied appointment is not substantial, so far as concerns the application of the due process clause of the Fourteenth Amendment.

Judgment affirmed.

* * *

D. DUE PROCESS MINIMUM CONTACTS

U.S. CONST. AMEND. I: FREEDOM OF RELIGION, SPEECH AND PRESS; PEACEFUL ASSEMBLAGE; PETITION OF GRIEVANCES

Congress shall make no law respecting an establishment of religion, or prohibiting the free exercise thereof; or abridging the freedom of speech, or of the press; or the right of the people peaceably to assemble, and to petition the Government for a redress of grievances.

* * *

U.S. CONST. AMEND. X: RESERVED POWERS TO STATES

The powers not delegated to the United States by the Constitution, nor prohibited by it to the States, are reserved to the States respectively, or to the people.

* * *

FEDERAL RULE OF CIVIL PROCEDURE 12

RULE 12. DEFENSES AND OBJECTIONS: WHEN AND HOW PRESENTED

* * *

(a) Time to Serve a Responsive Pleading.

    (1) *In General.* Unless another time is specified by this rule or a federal statute, the time for serving a responsive pleading is as follows:

        (A) A defendant must serve an answer:

            (i) within 21 days after being served with the summons and complaint; or

            (ii) if it has timely waived service under Rule 4(d), within 60 days after the request for a waiver was sent, or within 90 days after it was sent to the defendant outside any judicial district of the United States.

        (B) A party must serve an answer to a counterclaim or cross-claim within 21 days after being served with the pleading that states the counterclaim or cross-claim.

        (C) A party must serve a reply to an answer within 21 days after being served with an order to reply, unless the order specifies a different time.

* * *

    (4) *Effect of a Motion.* Unless the court sets a different time, serving a motion under this rule alters these periods as follows:

    (A) if the court denies the motion or postpones its disposition until trial, the responsive pleading must be served within 14 days after notice of the court's action; or

    (B) if the court grants a motion for a more definite statement, the responsive pleading must be served within 14 days after the more definite statement is served.

(b) How to Present Defenses. Every defense to a claim for relief in any pleading must be asserted in the responsive pleading if one is required. But a party may assert the following defenses by motion:

    (1) lack of subject-matter jurisdiction;

    (2) lack of personal jurisdiction;

    (3) improper venue;

    (4) insufficient process;

    (5) insufficient service of process;

    (6) failure to state a claim upon which relief can be granted; and

    (7) failure to join a party under Rule 19.

A motion asserting any of these defenses must be made before pleading if a responsive pleading is allowed. If a pleading sets out a claim for relief that does not require a responsive pleading, an opposing party may assert at trial any defense to that claim. No defense or objection is waived by joining it with one or more other defenses or objections in a responsive pleading or in a motion.

* * *

INTERNATIONAL SHOE CO. v. STATE OF WASHINGTON

326 U.S. 310 (1945)

MR. CHIEF JUSTICE STONE delivered the opinion of the Court.

The questions for decision are (1) whether, within the limitations of the due process clause of the Fourteenth Amendment, appellant, a Delaware corporation, has by its activities in the State of Washington rendered itself amenable to proceedings in the courts of that state to recover unpaid contributions to the state unemployment compensation fund exacted by state statutes, Washington Unemployment Compensation Act, Washington Revised Statutes, and (2) whether the state can exact those contributions consistently with the due process clause of the Fourteenth Amendment.

The statutes in question set up a comprehensive scheme of unemployment compensation, the costs of which are defrayed by contributions required to be made by employers to a state unemployment compensation fund. The contributions are a specified percentage of the wages payable annually by each employer for his employees' services in the state. The assessment and collection of the contributions and the fund are administered by respondents. Section 14(c) of the Act authorizes respondent Commissioner to issue an order and notice of assessment of delinquent contributions upon prescribed personal service of the notice upon the employer if found within the state, or, if not so found, by mailing the notice to the employer by registered mail at his last known address. That section also authorizes the Commissioner to collect the assessment by distraint if it is not paid within ten days after service of the notice. * * *

In this case notice of assessment for the years in question was personally served upon a sales solicitor employed by appellant in the State of Washington, and a copy of the notice was mailed by registered mail to appellant at its address in St. Louis, Missouri. Appellant appeared specially before the office of unemployment and moved to set aside the order and notice of assessment on the ground that the service upon appellant's salesman was not proper service upon appellant; that appellant was not a corporation of the State of Washington and was not doing business within the state; that it had no agent within the state upon whom service could be made; and that appellant is not an employer and does not furnish employment within the meaning of the statute.

The motion was heard on evidence and a stipulation of facts by the appeal tribunal which denied the motion and ruled that respondent Commissioner was entitled to recover the unpaid contributions. That action was affirmed by the Commissioner; both the Superior Court and the Supreme Court affirmed. Appellant in each of these courts assailed the statute as applied, as a violation of the due process clause of the Fourteenth Amendment, and as imposing a constitutionally prohibited burden on interstate commerce. The cause comes here on appeal, appellant assigning as error that the challenged statutes as applied infringe the due process clause of the Fourteenth Amendment and the commerce clause.

The facts as found by the appeal tribunal and accepted by the state Superior Court and Supreme Court, are not in dispute. Appellant is a Delaware corporation, having its principal place of business in St. Louis, Missouri, and is engaged in the manufacture and sale of shoes and other footwear. It maintains places of business in several states, other than Washington, at which its manufacturing is carried on and from which its merchandise is distributed interstate through several sales units or branches located outside the State of Washington.

Appellant has no office in Washington and makes no contracts either for sale or purchase of merchandise there. It maintains no stock of merchandise in that state and makes there no deliveries of goods in intrastate commerce. During the years from 1937 to 1940, now in question, appellant employed eleven to thirteen salesmen under direct supervision and control of sales managers located in St. Louis. These salesmen resided in Washington; their principal activities were confined to that state; and they were compensated by commissions based upon the amount of their sales. The commissions for each year totaled more than $31,000.

Appellant supplies its salesmen with a line of samples, each consisting of one shoe of a pair, which they display to prospective purchasers. On occasion they rent permanent sample rooms, for exhibiting samples, in business buildings, or rent rooms in hotels or business buildings temporarily for that purpose. The cost of such rentals is reimbursed by appellant.

The authority of the salesmen is limited to exhibiting their samples and soliciting orders from prospective buyers, at prices and on terms fixed by appellant. The salesmen transmit the orders to appellant's office in St. Louis for acceptance or rejection, and when accepted the merchandise for filling the orders is shipped f.o.b. from points outside Washington to the purchasers within the state. All the merchandise shipped into Washington is invoiced at the place of shipment from which collections are made. No salesman has authority to enter into contracts or to make collections.

The Supreme Court of Washington was of opinion that the regular and systematic solicitation of orders in the state by appellant's salesmen, resulting in a continuous flow of appellant's product into the state, was sufficient to constitute doing business in the state so as to make appellant amenable to suit in its courts. But it was also of opinion that there were sufficient additional activities shown to bring the case within the rule frequently stated, that solicitation within a state by the agents of a foreign corporation plus some additional activities there are sufficient to render the corporation amenable to suit brought in the courts of the state to enforce an obligation arising out of its activities there. The court found such additional activities in the salesmen's display of samples sometimes in permanent display rooms, and the salesmen's residence within the state, continued over a period of years, all resulting in a substantial volume of merchandise regularly shipped by appellant to purchasers within the state. The court also held that the statute as applied did not invade the constitutional power of Congress to regulate interstate commerce and did not impose a prohibited burden on such commerce.

Appellant's argument, renewed here, that the statute imposes an unconstitutional burden on interstate commerce need not detain us. For 53 Stat. 1391, 26 U.S.C. § 1606(a), 26 U.S.C.A. Int. Rev. Code, § 1606(a), provides that "No person required under a State law to make payments to an unemployment fund shall be relieved from compliance therewith on the ground that he is engaged in interstate or foreign commerce, or that the State law does not distinguish between employees engaged in interstate or foreign commerce and those engaged in intrastate commerce." It is no longer debatable that Congress, in the exercise of the commerce power, may authorize the states, in specified ways, to regulate interstate commerce or impose burdens upon it.

Appellant also insists that its activities within the state were not sufficient to manifest its "presence" there and that in its absence the state courts were without jurisdiction, that consequently it was a denial of due process for the state to subject appellant to suit. It refers to those cases in which it was said that the mere solicitation of orders for the purchase of goods within a state, to be accepted without the state and filled by shipment of the purchased goods interstate, does not render the corporation seller amenable to suit within the state. And appellant further argues that since it was not present within the state, it is a denial of due process to subject it to taxation or other money exaction. It thus denies the power of the state to lay the tax or to subject appellant to a suit for its collection.

Historically the jurisdiction of courts to render judgment *in personam* is grounded on their de facto power over the defendant's person. Hence his presence within the territorial jurisdiction of court was prerequisite to its rendition of a judgment personally binding him. *Pennoyer v. Neff.* But now that the *capias ad respondendum* has given way to personal service of summons or other form of notice, due process requires only that in order to subject a defendant to a judgment *in personam*, if he be not present within the territory of the forum, he have certain minimum contacts with it such that the maintenance of the suit does not offend "traditional notions of fair play and substantial justice."

Since the corporate personality is a fiction, although a fiction intended to be acted upon as though it were a fact, it is clear that unlike an individual its "presence" without, as well as within, the state of its origin can be manifested only by activities carried on in its behalf by those who are authorized to act for it. To say that the corporation is so far "present" there as to satisfy due process requirements, for purposes of taxation or the maintenance of suits against it in the courts of the state, is to beg the question to be decided. For the terms "present" or "presence" are used merely to symbolize those activities of the corporation's agent within the state which courts will deem to be sufficient to satisfy the demands of due process. Those demands may be met by such contacts of the corporation with the state of the forum as make it reasonable, in the context of our federal system of government, to require the corporation to defend the particular suit which is brought there. An "estimate of the inconveniences" which would result to the corporation from a trial away from its "home" or principal place of business is relevant in this connection.

"Presence" in the state in this sense has never been doubted when the activities of the corporation there have not only been continuous and systematic, but also give rise to the liabilities sued on, even though no consent to be sued or authorization to an agent to accept service of process has been given. Conversely it has been generally recognized that the casual presence of the corporate agent or even his conduct of single or isolated items of activities in a state in the corporation's behalf are not enough to subject it to suit on causes of action unconnected with the activities there. To require the corporation in such circumstances to defend the suit away from its home or other jurisdiction where it carries on more substantial activities has been thought to lay too great and unreasonable a burden on the corporation to comport with due process.

While it has been held in cases on which appellant relies that continuous activity of some sorts within a state is not enough to support the demand that the corporation be amenable to suits unrelated to that activity, there have been instances in which the continuous corporate operations within a state were thought so substantial and of such a nature as to justify suit against it on causes of action arising from dealings entirely distinct from those activities.

Finally, although the commission of some single or occasional acts of the corporate agent in a state sufficient to impose an obligation or liability on the corporation has not been thought to confer upon the state authority to enforce it, other such acts, because of their nature and quality and the circumstances of their commission, may be deemed sufficient to render the corporation liable to suit. True, some of the decisions holding the corporation amenable to suit have been supported by resort to the legal fiction that it has given its consent to service and suit, consent being implied from its presence in the state through the acts of its authorized agents. But more realistically it may be said that those authorized acts were of such a nature as to justify the fiction.

It is evident that the criteria by which we mark the boundary line between those activities which justify the subjection of a corporation to suit, and those which do not, cannot be simply mechanical or quantitative. The test is not merely, as has sometimes been suggested, whether the activity, which the corporation has seen fit to procure through its agents in another state, is a little more or a little less. Whether due process is satisfied must depend rather upon the quality and nature of the activity in relation to the fair and orderly administration of the laws which it was the purpose of the due process clause to insure. That clause does not contemplate that a state may make binding a judgment *in personam* against an individual or corporate defendant with which the state has no contacts, ties, or relations. *Cf. Pennoyer v. Neff.*

But to the extent that a corporation exercises the privilege of conducting activities within a state, it enjoys the benefits and protection of the laws of that state. The exercise of that privilege may give rise to obligations; and, so far as those obligations arise out of or are connected with the activities within the state, a procedure which requires the corporation to respond to a suit brought to enforce them can, in most instances, hardly be said to be undue.

Applying these standards, the activities carried on in behalf of appellant in the State of Washington were neither irregular nor casual. They were systematic and continuous throughout the years in question. They resulted in a large volume of interstate business, in the course of which appellant received the benefits and protection of the laws of the state, including the right to resort to the courts for the enforcement of its rights. The obligation which is here sued upon arose out of those very activities. It is evident that these operations establish sufficient contacts or ties with the state of the forum to make it reasonable and just according to our traditional conception of fair play and substantial justice to permit the state to enforce the obligations which appellant has incurred there. Hence we cannot say that the maintenance of the present suit in the State of Washington involves an unreasonable or undue procedure.

We are likewise unable to conclude that the service of the process within the state upon an agent whose activities establish appellant's "presence" there was not sufficient notice of the suit, or that the suit was so unrelated to those activities as to make the agent an inappropriate vehicle for communicating the notice. It is enough that appellant has established such contacts with the state that the particular form of substituted service adopted there gives reasonable assurance that the notice will be actual. Nor can we say that the mailing of the notice of suit to appellant by registered mail at its home office was not reasonably calculated to apprise appellant of the suit.

* * * Appellant having rendered itself amenable to suit upon obligations arising out of the activities of its salesmen in Washington, the state may maintain the present suit *in personam* to collect the tax laid upon the exercise of the privilege of employing appellant's salesmen within the state. For Washington has made one of those activities, which taken together establish appellant's "presence" there for purposes of suit, the taxable event by which the state brings appellant within the reach of its taxing power. The state thus has constitutional power to lay the tax and to subject appellant to a suit to recover it. The activities which establish its "presence" subject it alike to taxation by the state and to suit to recover the tax.

Affirmed.

MR. JUSTICE JACKSON took no part in the consideration or decision of this case. MR. JUSTICE BLACK delivered the following opinion.

Congress, pursuant to its constitutional power to regulate commerce, has expressly provided that a State shall not be prohibited from levying the kind of unemployment compensation tax here challenged. We have twice decided that this Congressional consent is an adequate answer to a claim that imposition of the tax violates the Commerce Clause. Two determinations by this Court of an issue so palpably without merit are sufficient. Consequently that part of this appeal which again seeks to raise the question seems so patently frivolous as to make the case a fit candidate for dismissal. Nor is the further ground advanced on this appeal, that the State of Washington has denied appellant due process of law, any less devoid of substance. It is my view, therefore, that we should dismiss the appeal as unsubstantial, and decline the invitation to formulate broad rules as to the meaning of due process, which here would amount to deciding a constitutional question "in advance of the necessity for its decision."

Certainly appellant cannot in the light of our past decisions meritoriously claim that notice by registered mail and by personal service on its sales solicitors in Washington did not meet the requirements of procedural due process. And the due process clause is not brought in issue any more by appellant's further conceptualistic contention that Washington could not levy a tax or bring suit against the corporation because it did not honor that State with its mystical "presence." For it is unthinkable that the vague due process clause was ever intended to prohibit a State from regulating or taxing a business carried on within its boundaries simply because this is done by agents of a corporation organized and having its headquarters elsewhere. To read this into the due process clause would in fact result in depriving a State's citizens of due process by taking from the State the power to protect them in their business dealings within its boundaries with representatives of a foreign corporation. Nothing could be more irrational or more designed to defeat the function of our federative system of government. Certainly a State, at the very least, has power to tax and sue those dealing with its citizens within its boundaries, as we have held before. Were the Court to follow this principle, it would provide a workable standard for cases where, as here, no other questions are involved. The Court has not chosen to do so, but instead has engaged in an unnecessary discussion in the course of which it has announced vague Constitutional criteria applied for the first time to the issue before us. It has thus introduced uncertain elements confusing the simple pattern and tending to curtail the exercise of State powers to an extent not justified by the Constitution.

The criteria adopted insofar as they can be identified read as follows: Due process does permit State courts to "enforce the obligations which appellant has incurred" if it be found "reasonable and just according to our traditional conception of fair play and substantial justice." And this in turn means that we will "permit" the State to act if upon "an 'estimate of the inconveniences' which would result to the corporation from a trial away from its 'home' or principal place of business", we conclude that it is "reasonable" to subject it to suit in a State where it is doing business.

It is true that this Court did use the terms "fair play" and "substantial justice" in explaining the philosophy underlying the holding that it could not be "due process of law" to render a personal judgment against a defendant without notice to and an opportunity to be heard by him. * * * Mr. Justice Holmes speaking for the Court warned against judicial curtailment of this opportunity to be heard and referred to such a curtailment as a denial of "fair play", which even the common law would have deemed "contrary to natural justice." And previous cases had indicated that the ancient rule against judgments without notice had stemmed from "natural justice" concepts. These cases, while giving additional reasons why notice under particular circumstances is inadequate, did not mean thereby that all legislative enactments which this Court might deem to be contrary to natural justice ought to be held invalid under the due process clause. None of the cases purport to support or could support a holding that a State can tax and sue corporations only if its action comports with this Court's notions of "natural justice." I should have thought the Tenth Amendment settled that.

I believe that the Federal Constitution leaves to each State, without any "ifs" or "buts", a power to tax and to open the doors of its courts for its citizens to sue corporations whose agents do business in those States.

Believing that the Constitution gave the States that power, I think it a judicial deprivation to condition its exercise upon this Court's notion of "fairplay", however appealing that term may be. Nor can I stretch the meaning of due process so far as to authorize this Court to deprive a State of the right to afford judicial protection to its citizens on the ground that it would be more "convenient" for the corporation to be sued somewhere else.

There is a strong emotional appeal in the words "fair play", "justice", and "reasonableness." But they were not chosen by those who wrote the original Constitution or the Fourteenth Amendment as a measuring rod for this Court to use in invalidating State or Federal laws passed by elected legislative representatives. No one, not even those who most feared a democratic government, ever formally proposed that courts should be given power to invalidate legislation under any such elastic standards. Express prohibitions against certain types of legislation are found in the Constitution, and under the long settled practice, courts invalidate laws found to conflict with them. This requires interpretation, and interpretation, it is true, may result in extension of the Constitution's purpose. But that is no reason for reading the due process clause so as to restrict a State's power to tax and sue those whose activities affect persons and businesses within the State, provided proper service can be had. Superimposing the natural justice concept on the Constitution's specific prohibitions could operate as a drastic abridgment of democratic safeguards they embody, such as freedom of speech, press and religion, and the right to counsel.[2] This has already happened. For application of this natural law concept, whether under the terms "reasonableness", "justice", or "fair play", makes judges the supreme arbiters of the country's laws and practices. This result, I believe, alters the form of government our Constitution provides. I cannot agree.

True, the State's power is here upheld. But the rule announced means that tomorrow's judgment may strike down a State or Federal enactment on the ground that it does not conform to this Court's idea of natural justice. I therefore find myself moved by the same fears that caused Mr. Justice Holmes to say in 1930:

> I have not yet adequately expressed the more than anxiety that I feel at the ever increasing scope given to the Fourteenth Amendment in cutting down what I believe to be the constitutional rights of the States. As the decisions now stand, I see hardly any limit but the sky to the invalidating of those rights if they happen to strike a majority of this Court as for any reason undesirable.

* * *

---

2. These First Amendment liberties—freedom of speech, press and religion—provide a graphic illustration of the potential restrictive capacity of a rule under which they are protected at a particular time only because the Court, as then constituted believes them to be a requirement of fundamental justice. Consequently, under the same rule, another Court, with a different belief as to fundamental justice, could at least as against State action, completely or partially withdraw Constitutional protection from these basic freedoms, just as though the First Amendment had never been written.

II. CHOOSING THE FORUM (PERSONAL JURISDICTION)

A. MINIMUM CONTACTS AT THE EXTREME

McGEE v. INTERNATIONAL LIFE INSURANCE COMPANY

355 U.S. 220 (1957)

Opinion of the Court by MR. JUSTICE BLACK, announced by MR. JUSTICE DOUGLAS.

Petitioner, Lulu B. McGee, recovered a judgment in a California state court against respondent, International Life Insurance Company, on a contract of insurance. Respondent was not served with process in California but by registered mail at its principal place of business in Texas. The California court based its jurisdiction on a state statute which subjects foreign corporations to suit in California on insurance contracts with residents of that State even though such corporations cannot be served with process within its borders.

Unable to collect the judgment in California petitioner went to Texas where she filed suit on the judgment in a Texas court. But the Texas courts refused to enforce her judgment holding it was void under the Fourteenth Amendment because service of process outside California could not give the courts of that State jurisdiction over respondent. Since the case raised important questions, not only to California but to other States which have similar laws, we granted certiorari. It is not controverted that if the California court properly exercised jurisdiction over respondent the Texas courts erred in refusing to give its judgment full faith and credit.

The material facts are relatively simple. In 1944, Lowell Franklin, a resident of California, purchased a life insurance policy from the Empire Mutual Insurance Company, an Arizona corporation. In 1948 the respondent agreed with Empire Mutual to assume its insurance obligations. Respondent then mailed a reinsurance certificate to Franklin in California offering to insure him in accordance with the terms of the policy he held with Empire Mutual. He accepted this offer and from that time until his death in 1950 paid premiums by mail from his California home to respondent's Texas office. Petitioner Franklin's mother, was the beneficiary under the policy. She sent proofs of his death to the respondent but it refused to pay claiming that he had committed suicide. It appears that neither Empire Mutual nor respondent has ever had any office or agent in California. And so far as the record before us shows, respondent has never solicited or done any insurance business in California apart from the policy involved here.

Since *Pennoyer v. Neff*, this Court has held that the Due Process Clause of the Fourteenth Amendment places some limit on the power of state courts to enter binding judgments against persons not served with process within their boundaries. But just where this line of limitation falls has been the subject of prolific controversy, particularly with respect to foreign corporations. In a continuing process of evolution this Court accepted and then abandoned "consent," "doing business," and "presence" as the standard for measuring the extent of state judicial power over such corporations. More recently in *International Shoe Co. v. State of Washington*, the Court decided that "due process requires only that in order to subject a defendant to a judgment *in personam*, if he be not present within the territory of the forum, he have certain minimum contacts with it such that the maintenance of the suit does not offend 'traditional notions of fair play and substantial justice.' "

Looking back over this long history of litigation a trend is clearly discernible toward expanding the permissible scope of state jurisdiction over foreign corporations and other nonresidents. In part this is attributable to the fundamental transformation of our national economy over the years. Today many commercial transactions touch two or more States and may involve parties separated by the full continent. With this increasing nationalization of commerce has come a great increase in the amount of business conducted by mail across state lines. At the same time modern transportation and communication have made it much less burdensome for a party sued to defend himself in a State where he engages in economic activity.

Turning to this case we think it apparent that the Due Process Clause did not preclude the California court from entering a judgment binding on respondent. It is sufficient for purposes of due process that the suit was based on a contract which had substantial connection with that State. *Cf. Hess v. Pawloski*; *Pennoyer v. Neff*. The contract was delivered in California, the premiums were mailed from there and the insured was a resident of that State when he died. It cannot be denied that California has a manifest interest in providing effective means of redress for its residents when their insurers refuse to pay claims. These residents would be at a severe disadvantage if they were forced to follow the insurance company to a distant State in order to hold it legally accountable. When claims were small or moderate individual claimants frequently could not afford the cost of bringing an action in a foreign forum—thus in effect making the company judgment proof. Often the crucial witnesses—as here on the company's defense of suicide—will be found in the insured's locality. Of course there may be inconvenience to the insurer if it is held amenable to suit in California where it had this contract but certainly nothing which amounts to a denial of due process. There is no contention that respondent did not have adequate notice of the suit or sufficient time to prepare its defenses and appear.

The California statute became law in 1949, after respondent had entered into the agreement with Franklin to assume Empire Mutual's obligation to him. Respondent contends that application of the statute to this existing contract improperly impairs the obligation of the contract. We believe that contention is devoid of merit. The statute was remedial, in the purest sense of that term, and neither enlarged nor impaired respondent's substantive rights or obligations under the contract. It did nothing more than to provide petitioner with a California forum to enforce whatever substantive rights she might have against respondent. At the same time respondent was given a reasonable time to appear and defend on the merits after being notified of the suit. Under such circumstances it had no vested right not to be sued in California.

The judgment is reversed and the cause is remanded to the Court of Civil Appeals of the State of Texas, First Supreme Judicial District, for further proceedings not inconsistent with this opinion.

It is so ordered.

Judgment reversed and cause remanded with directions.

The CHIEF JUSTICE took no part in the consideration or decision of this case.

* * *

B. MINIMUM CONTACTS RETRENCHED

HANSON v. DENCKLA

357 U.S. 235 (1958)

MR. CHIEF JUSTICE WARREN delivered the opinion of the Court.

This controversy concerns the right to $400,000, part of the corpus of a trust established in Delaware by a settlor who later became domiciled in Florida. One group of claimants, "legatees," urge that this property passed under the residuary clause of the settlor's will, which was admitted to probate in Florida. The Florida courts have sustained this position. Other claimants, "appointees" and "beneficiaries," contend that the property passed pursuant to the settlor's exercise of the *inter vivos* power of appointment created in the deed of trust. The Delaware courts adopted this position and refused to accord full faith and credit to the Florida determination because the Florida court had not acquired jurisdiction over an indispensable party, the Delaware trustee.

The trust whose validity is contested here was created in 1935. Dora Browning Donner, then a domiciliary of Pennsylvania, executed a trust instrument in Delaware naming the Wilmington Trust Co., of Wilmington, Delaware, as trustee. The corpus was composed of securities. Mrs. Donner reserved the income for life, and stated that the remainder should be paid to such persons or upon such trusts as she should appoint by *inter vivos* or testamentary instrument. The trust agreement provided that Mrs. Donner could change the trustee, and that she could amend, alter or revoke the agreement at any time. A measure of control over trust administration was assured by the provision that only with the consent of a trust 'advisor' appointed by the settlor could the trustee (1) sell trust assets, (2) make investments, and (3) participate in any plan, proceeding, reorganization or merger involving securities held in the trust. A few days after the trust was established Mrs. Donner exercised her power of appointment. That appointment was replaced by another in 1939. Thereafter she left Pennsylvania, and in 1944 became domiciled in Florida, where she remained until her death in 1952. Mrs. Donner's will was executed Dec. 3, 1949. On that same day she executed the inter vivos power of appointment whose terms are at issue here. After making modest appointments in favor of a hospital and certain family retainers (the "appointees"), she appointed the sum of $200,000 to each of two trusts previously established with another Delaware trustee, the Delaware Trust Co. The balance of the trust corpus, over $1,000,000 at the date of her death, was appointed to her executrix. That amount passed under the residuary clause of her will and is not at issue here.

The two trusts with the Delaware Trust Co. were created in 1948 by Mrs. Donner's daughter, Elizabeth Donner Hanson, for the benefit of Elizabeth's children, Donner Hanson and Joseph Donner Winsor. In identical terms they provide that the income not required for the beneficiary's support should be accumulated to age 25, when the beneficiary should be paid 1/4 of the corpus and receive the income from the balance for life. Upon the death of the beneficiary the remainder was to go to such of the beneficiary's issue or Elizabeth Donner Hanson's issue as the beneficiary should appoint by *inter vivos* or testamentary instrument; in default of appointment to the beneficiary's issue alive at the time of his death, and if none to the issue of Elizabeth Donner Hanson.

Mrs. Donner died Nov. 20, 1952. Her will, which was admitted to probate in Florida, named Elizabeth Donner Hanson as executrix. She was instructed to pay all debts and taxes, including any which might be payable by reason of the property appointed under the power of appointment in the trust agreement with the Wilmington Trust Co. After disposing of personal and household effects, Mrs. Donner's will directed that the balance of her property (the $1,000,000 appointed from the Delaware trust) be paid in equal parts to two trusts for the benefit of her daughters Katherine N. R. Denckla and Dorothy B. R. Stewart.

This controversy grows out of the residuary clause that created the last-mentioned trusts. It begins:

> All the rest, residue and remainder of my estate, real, personal and mixed, whatsoever and wheresoever the same may be at the time of my death, including any and all property, rights and interest over which I may have power of appointment which prior to my death has not been effectively exercised by me or has been exercised by me in favor of my Executrix, I direct my Executrix to deal with as follows * * *.

Residuary legatees Denckla and Stewart, already the recipients of over $500,000 each, urge that the power of appointment over the $400,000 appointed to sister Elizabeth's children was not "effectively exercised" and that the property should accordingly pass to them. Fourteen months after Mrs. Donner's death these parties petitioned a Florida chancery court for a declaratory judgment "concerning what property passes under the residuary clause" of the will. Personal service was had upon the following defendants: (1) executrix Elizabeth Donner Hanson, (2) beneficiaries Donner Hanson and Joseph Donner Winsor, and (3) potential beneficiary William Donner Roosevelt, also one of Elizabeth's children. Curtin Winsor, Jr., another of Elizabeth's children and also a potential beneficiary of the Delaware trusts, was not named as a party and was not served. About a dozen other defendants were nonresidents and could not be personally served. These included the Wilmington Trust Co. ("trustee"), the Delaware Trust Co. (to whom the $400,000 had been paid shortly after Mrs. Donner's death), certain individuals who were potential successors in interest to complainants Denckla and Stewart, and most of the named appointees in Mrs. Donner's 1949 appointment. A copy of the pleadings and a "Notice to Appear and Defend" were sent to each of these defendants by ordinary mail, and notice was published locally as required by the Florida statutes dealing with constructive service. With the exception of two individuals whose interests coincided with complainants Denckla and Stewart, none of the nonresident defendants made any appearance.

The appearing defendants (Elizabeth Donner Hanson and her children) moved to dismiss the suit because the exercise of jurisdiction over indispensable parties, the Delaware trustees, would offend Section 1 of the Fourteenth Amendment. The Chancellor ruled that he lacked jurisdiction over these nonresident defendants because no personal service was had and because the trust corpus was outside the territorial jurisdiction of the court. The cause was dismissed as to them. As far as parties before the court were concerned, however, he ruled that the power of appointment was testamentary and void under the applicable Florida law. In a decree dated Jan. 14, 1955, he ruled that the $400,000 passed under the residuary clause of the will.

After the Florida litigation began, but before entry of the decree, the executrix instituted a declaratory judgment action in Delaware to determine who was entitled to participate in the trust assets held in that State. Except for the addition of beneficiary Winsor and several appointees, the parties were substantially the same as in the Florida litigation. Nonresident defendants were notified by registered mail. All of the trust companies, beneficiaries, and legatees except Katherine N. R. Denckla, appeared and participated in the litigation. After the Florida court enjoined executrix Hanson from further participation, her children pursued their own interests. When the Florida decree was entered the legatees unsuccessfully urged it as res judicata of the Delaware dispute. In a decree dated Jan. 13, 1956, the Delaware Chancellor ruled that the trust and power of appointment were valid under the applicable Delaware law, and that the trust corpus had properly been paid to the Delaware Trust Co. and the other appointees.

Alleging that she would be bound by the Delaware decree, the executrix moved the Florida Supreme Court to remand with instructions to dismiss the Florida suit then pending on appeal. No full faith and credit question was raised. The motion was denied. The Florida Supreme Court affirmed its Chancellor's conclusion that Florida law applied to determine the validity of the trust and power of appointment. Under that law the trust was invalid because the settlor had reserved too much power over the trustee and trust corpus, and the power of appointment was not independently effective to pass the property because it was a testamentary act not accompanied by the requisite formalities. The Chancellor's conclusion that there was no jurisdiction over the trust companies and other absent defendants was reversed. The court ruled that jurisdiction to construe the will carried with it "substantive" jurisdiction "over the persons of the absent defendants" even though the trust assets were not "physically in this state." Whether this meant jurisdiction over the person of the defendants or jurisdiction over the trust assets is open to doubt. In a motion for rehearing the beneficiaries and appointees urged for the first time that Florida should have given full faith and credit to the decision of the Delaware Chancellor. The motion was denied without opinion, Nov. 28, 1956.

The full faith and credit question was first raised in the Delaware litigation by an unsuccessful motion for new trial filed with the Chancellor Jan. 20, 1956. After the Florida Supreme Court decision the matter was renewed by a motion to remand filed with the Delaware Supreme Court. In a decision of Jan. 14, 1957, that court denied the motion and affirmed its Chancellor in all respects. The Florida decree was held not binding for purposes of full faith and credit because the Florida court had no personal jurisdiction over the trust companies and no jurisdiction over the trust res.

The issues for our decision are, first, whether Florida erred in holding that it had jurisdiction over the nonresident defendants, and second, whether Delaware erred in refusing full faith and credit to the Florida decree. We need not determine whether Florida was bound to give full faith and credit to the decree of the Delaware Chancellor since the question was not seasonably presented to the Florida court.

The Florida Appeal. * * * Treating the papers whereon appeal was taken as a petition for certiorari, certiorari is granted.

Appellants charge that this judgment is offensive to the Due Process Clause of the Fourteenth Amendment because the Florida court was without jurisdiction. There is no suggestion that the court failed to employ a means of notice reasonably calculated to inform nonresident defendants of the pending proceedings, or denied them an opportunity to be heard in defense of their interests. The alleged defect is the absence of those "affiliating circumstances" without which the courts of a state may not enter a judgment imposing obligations on persons (jurisdiction in *personam*) or affecting interests in property (jurisdiction *in rem* or *quasi in rem*).[12] While the *in rem* and *in personam* classifications do not exhaust all the situations that give rise to jurisdiction, they are adequate to describe the affiliating circumstances suggested here, and accordingly serve as a useful means of approach to this case.

In rem jurisdiction. Founded on physical power, the *in rem* jurisdiction of a state court is limited by the extent of its power and by the coordinate authority of sister States. The basis of the jurisdiction is the presence of the subject property within the territorial jurisdiction of the forum State. Tangible property poses no problem for the application of this rule, but the situs of intangibles is often a matter of controversy.[15] In considering restrictions on the power to tax, this Court has concluded that "jurisdiction" over intangible property is not limited to a single State. Whether the type of "jurisdiction" with which this opinion deals may be exercised by more than one State we need not decide. The parties seem to assume that the trust assets that form the subject matter of this action were located in Delaware and not in Florida. We can see nothing in the record contrary to that assumption, or sufficient to establish a situs in Florida.[17]

The Florida court held that the presence of the subject property was not essential to its jurisdiction. Authority over the probate and construction of its domiciliary's will, under which the assets might pass, was thought sufficient to confer the requisite jurisdiction. But jurisdiction cannot be predicated upon the contingent role of this Florida will. Whatever the efficacy of a so-called *"in rem"* jurisdiction over assets admittedly passing under a local will, a State acquires no *in rem* jurisdiction to adjudicate the validity of *inter vivos* dispositions simply because its decision might augment an estate passing under a will probated in its courts. If such a basis of jurisdiction were sustained, probate courts would enjoy nationwide service of process to adjudicate interests in property with which neither the State nor the decedent could claim any affiliation. The settlor-decedent's Florida domicile is equally unavailing as a basis for

---

12. A judgment *in personam* imposes a personal liability or obligation on one person in favor of another. A judgment *in rem* affects the interests of all persons in designated property. A judgment *quasi in rem* affects the interests of particular persons in designated property. The latter is of two types. In one the plaintiff is seeking to secure a pre-existing claim in the subject property and to extinguish or establish the nonexistence of similar interests of particular persons. In the other the plaintiff seeks to apply what he concedes to be the property of the defendant to the satisfaction of a claim against him. For convenience of terminology this opinion will use "in rem" in lieu of "in rem and quasi in rem."

15. This case does not concern the situs of a beneficial interest in trust property. These appellees were contesting the validity of the trust. Their concern was with the legal interest of the trustee or, if the trust was invalid, the settlor. Therefore, the relevant factor here is the situs of the stocks, bonds, and notes that make up the corpus of the trust. Properly speaking such assets are intangibles that have no "physical" location. But their embodiment in documents treated for most purposes as the assets themselves makes them partake of the nature of tangibles.

17. The documents evidencing ownership of the trust property were held in Delaware, by a Delaware trustee who was the obligee of the credit instruments and the record owner of the stock. The location of the obligors and the domicile of the corporations do not appear. The trust instrument was executed in Delaware by a settlor then domiciled in Pennsylvania. Without expressing any opinion on the significance of these or other factors unnamed, we note that none relates to Florida.

jurisdiction over the trust assets. For the purpose of jurisdiction *in rem* the maxim that personalty has its situs at the domicile of its owner is a fiction of limited utility. The maxim is no less suspect when the domicile is that of a decedent. In analogous cases, this Court has rejected the suggestion that the probate decree of the State where decedent was domiciled has an *in rem* effect on personalty outside the forum State that could render it conclusive on the interests f nonresidents over whom there was no personal jurisdiction. The fact that the owner is or was domiciled within the forum State is not a sufficient affiliation with the property upon which to base jurisdiction *in rem*. Having concluded that Florida had no *in rem* jurisdiction, we proceed to consider whether a judgment purporting to rest on that basis is invalid in Florida and must therefore be reversed.

Prior to the Fourteenth Amendment an exercise of jurisdiction over persons or property outside the forum State was thought to be an absolute nullity, but the matter remained a question of state law over which this Court exercised no authority. With the adoption of that Amendment, any judgment purporting to bind the person of a defendant over whom the court had not acquired *in personam* jurisdiction was void within the State as well as without. *Pennoyer v. Neff*. Nearly a century has passed without this Court being called upon to apply that principle to an *in rem* judgment dealing with property outside the forum State. The invalidity of such a judgment within the forum State seems to have been assumed-and with good reason. Since a State is forbidden to enter a judgment attempting to bind a person over whom it has no jurisdiction, it has even less right to enter a judgment purporting to extinguish the interest of such a person in property over which the court has no jurisdiction.[23] Therefore, so far as it purports to rest upon jurisdiction over the trust assets, the judgment of the Florida court cannot be sustained.

In personam jurisdiction. Appellees' stronger argument is for *in personam* jurisdiction over the Delaware trustee. They urge that the circumstances of this case amount to sufficient affiliation with the State of Florida to empower its courts to exercise personal jurisdiction over this nonresident defendant. Principal reliance is placed upon *McGee v. International Life Ins. Co.* In *McGee* the Court noted the trend of expanding personal jurisdiction over nonresidents. As technological progress has increased the flow of commerce between States, the need for jurisdiction over nonresidents has undergone a similar increase. At the same time, progress in communications and transportation has made the defense of a suit in a foreign tribunal less burdensome. In response to these changes, the requirements for personal jurisdiction over nonresidents have evolved from the rigid rule of *Pennoyer v. Neff*, to the flexible standard of *International Shoe Co. v. State of Washington*. But it is a mistake to

---

23. This holding was forecast in *Pennoyer v. Neff*. When considering the effect of the Fourteenth Amendment, this Court declared that in actions against nonresidents substituted service was permissible only where "property in the State is brought under the control of the court, and subjected to its disposition by process adapted to that purpose * * *."

assume that this trend heralds the eventual demise of all restrictions on the personal jurisdiction of state courts. Those restrictions are more than a guarantee of immunity from inconvenient or distant litigation. They are a consequence of territorial limitations on the power of the respective States. However minimal the burden of defending in a foreign tribunal, a defendant may not be called upon to do so unless he has had the "minimal contacts" with that State that are a prerequisite to its exercise of power over him. *See International Shoe Co. v. State of Washington.*

We fail to find such contacts in the circumstances of this case. The defendant trust company has no office in Florida, and transacts no business there. None of the trust assets has ever been held or administered in Florida, and the record discloses no solicitation of business in that State either in person or by mail. *Cf. International Shoe Co. v. State of Washington; McGee v. International Life Ins. Co.*

The cause of action in this case is not one that arises out of an act done or transaction consummated in the forum State. In that respect, it differs from *McGee v. International Life Ins. Co.*, and the cases there cited. In *McGee*, the nonresident defendant solicited a reinsurance agreement with a resident of California. The offer was accepted in that State, and the insurance premiums were mailed from there until the insured's death. Noting the interest California has in providing effective redress for its residents when nonresident insurers refuse to pay claims on insurance they have solicited in that State, the Court upheld jurisdiction because the suit "was based on a contract which had substantial connection with that State." In contrast, this action involves the validity of an agreement that was entered without any connection with the forum State. The agreement was executed in Delaware by a trust company incorporated in that State and a settlor domiciled in Pennsylvania. The first relationship Florida had to the agreement was years later when the settlor became domiciled there, and the trustee remitted the trust income to her in that State. From Florida Mrs. Donner carried on several bits of trust administration that may be compared to the mailing of premiums in *McGee*.[24] But the record discloses no instance in which the trustee performed any acts in Florida that bear the same relationship to the agreement as the solicitation in *McGee*. Consequently, this suit cannot be said to be one to enforce an obligation that arose from a privilege the defendant exercised in Florida. *Cf. International Shoe Co. v. State of Washington.* This case is also different from *McGee* in that there the State had enacted special legislation to exercise what McGee called its "manifest interest" in providing effective redress for citizens who had been injured by nonresidents engaged in an activity that the State treats as exceptional and subjects to special regulation.

---

24. By a letter dated Feb. 5, 1946, Mrs. Donner changed the compensation to be paid the trust advisor. April 2, 1947, she revoked the trust as to $75,000, returning that amount to the trustee December 22, 1947. To these acts may be added the execution of the two powers of appointment mentioned earlier.

The execution in Florida of the powers of appointment under which the beneficiaries and appointees claim does not give Florida a substantial connection with the contract on which this suit is based. It is the validity of the trust agreement, not the appointment, that is at issue here. For the purpose of applying its rule that the validity of a trust is determined by the law of the State of its creation, Florida ruled that the appointment amounted to a "republication" of the original trust instrument in Florida. For choice-of-law purposes such a ruling may be justified, but we think it an insubstantial connection with the trust agreement for purposes of determining the question of personal jurisdiction over a nonresident defendant. The unilateral activity of those who claim some relationship with a nonresident defendant cannot satisfy the requirement of contact with the forum State. The application of that rule will vary with the quality and nature of the defendant's activity, but it is essential in each case that there be some act by which the defendant purposefully avails itself of the privilege of conducting activities within the forum State, thus invoking the benefits and protections of its laws. *International Shoe Co. v. State of Washington.* The settlor's execution in Florida of her power of appointment cannot remedy the absence of such an act in this case.

It is urged that because the settlor and most of the appointees and beneficiaries were domiciled in Florida the courts of that State should be able to exercise personal jurisdiction over the nonresident trustees. This is a non-sequitur. With personal jurisdiction over the executor, legatees, and appointees, there is nothing in federal law to prevent Florida from adjudicating concerning the respective rights and liabilities of those parties. But Florida has not chosen to do so. As we understand its law, the trustee is an indispensable party over whom the court must acquire jurisdiction before it is empowered to enter judgment in a proceeding affecting the validity of a trust. It does not acquire that jurisdiction by being the "center of gravity" of the controversy, or the most convenient location for litigation. The issue is personal jurisdiction, not choice of law. It is resolved in this case by considering the acts of the trustee. As we have indicated, they are insufficient to sustain the jurisdiction.

Because it sustained jurisdiction over the nonresident trustees, the Florida Supreme Court found it unnecessary to determine whether Florida law made those defendants indispensable parties in the circumstances of this case. Our conclusion that Florida was without jurisdiction over the Delaware trustee, or over the trust corpus held in that State, requires that we make that determination in the first instance. As we have noted earlier, the Florida Supreme Court has repeatedly held that a trustee is an indispensable party without whom a Florida court has no power to adjudicate controversies affecting the validity of a trust. For that reason the Florida judgment must be reversed not only as to the nonresident trustees but also as to appellants, over whom the Florida court admittedly had jurisdiction.

The Delaware Certiorari. The same reasons that compel reversal of the Florida judgment require affirmance of the Delaware one. Delaware is under no obligation to give full faith and credit to a Florida judgment invalid in Florida because offensive to the Due Process Clause of the Fourteenth Amendment. Even before passage of the Fourteenth Amendment this Court sustained state courts in refusing full faith and credit to judgments entered by courts that were without jurisdiction over nonresident defendants. Since Delaware was entitled to conclude that Florida law made the trust company an indispensable party, it was under no obligation to give the Florida judgment any faith and credit—even against parties over whom Florida's jurisdiction was unquestioned.

It is suggested that this disposition is improper—that the Delaware case should be held while the Florida cause is remanded to give that court an opportunity to determine whether the trustee is an indispensable party in the circumstances of this case. * * * The rule of primacy to the first final judgment is a necessary incident to the requirement of full faith and credit. Our only function is to determine whether judgments are consistent with the Federal Constitution. In determining the correctness of Delaware's judgment we look to what Delaware was entitled to conclude from the Florida authorities at the time the Delaware court's judgment was entered. To withhold affirmance of a correct Delaware judgment until Florida has had time to rule on another question would be participating in the litigation instead of adjudicating its outcome.

The judgment of the Delaware Supreme Court is affirmed, and the judgment of the Florida Supreme Court is reversed and the cause is remanded for proceedings not inconsistent with this opinion.

It is so ordered.

MR. JUSTICE BLACK, whom MR. JUSTICE BURTON and MR. JUSTICE BRENNAN join, dissenting.

I believe the courts of Florida had power to adjudicate the effectiveness of the appointment made in Florida by Mrs. Donner with respect to all those who were notified of the proceedings and given an opportunity to be heard without violating the Due Process Clause of the Fourteenth Amendment. If this is correct, it follows that the Delaware courts erred in refusing to give the prior Florida judgment full faith and credit.

Mrs. Donner was domiciled in Florida from 1944 until her death in 1952. The controversial appointment was made there in 1949. It provided that certain persons were to receive a share of the property held by the Delaware "trustee" under the so-called trust agreement upon her death. Until she died Mrs. Donner received the entire income from this property, and at all times possessed absolute power to revoke or alter the appointment and to dispose of the property as she pleased. As a practical matter she also retained control over the management of the property, the "trustee" in Delaware being little more than a custodian. A number of the beneficiaries of the appointment, including those who were to receive more than 95% of the assets involved, were residents of Florida at the time the appointment was made as well as when the present suit was filed. The appointed property consisted of intangibles which had no real situs in any particular State although Mrs. Donner paid taxes on the property in Florida.

The same day the 1949 appointment was made Mrs. Donner executed a will, which after her death was duly probated in a Florida court. The will contained a residuary clause providing for the distribution of all of her property not previously bequeathed, including "any and all property, rights and interest over which I may have power of appointment which prior to my death has not been effectively exercised by me * * *." Thus if the 1949 appointment was ineffective the property involved came back into Mrs. Donner's estate to be distributed under the residuary clause of her will. As might be anticipated the present litigation arose when legatees brought an action in the Florida courts seeking a determination whether the appointment was valid. The beneficiaries of the appointment, some of whom live outside Florida, and the Delaware trustee were defendants. They had timely notice of the suit and an adequate opportunity to obtain counsel and appear.

In light of the foregoing circumstances it seems quite clear to me that there is nothing in the Due Process Clause which denies Florida the right to determine whether Mrs. Donner's appointment was valid as against its statute of wills. This disposition, which was designed to take effect after her death, had very close and substantial connections with that State. Not only was the appointment made in Florida by a domiciliary of Florida, but the primary beneficiaries also lived in that State. In my view it could hardly be denied that Florida had sufficient interest so that a court with jurisdiction might properly apply Florida law, if it chose, to determine whether the appointment was effectual. True, the question whether the law of a State can be applied to a transaction is different from the question whether the courts of that State have jurisdiction to enter a judgment, but the two are often closely related and to a substantial degree depend upon similar considerations. It seems to me that where a transaction has as much relationship to a State as Mrs. Donner's appointment had to Florida its courts ought to have power to adjudicate controversies arising out of that transaction, unless litigation there would impose such a heavy and disproportionate burden on a nonresident defendant that it would offend what this Court has referred to as "traditional notions of fair play and substantial justice." *International Shoe Co. v. State of Washington.* So far as the nonresident defendants here are concerned I can see nothing which approaches that degree of unfairness. Florida, the home of the principal contenders for Mrs. Donner's largess, was a reasonably convenient forum for all.[3] Certainly there is nothing fundamentally unfair in subjecting the corporate trustee to the jurisdiction of the Florida courts. It chose to maintain business relations with Mrs. Donner in that State for eight years, regularly communicating with her with respect to the business of the trust including the very appointment in question.

---

3. The suggestion is made that Delaware was a more suitable forum, but the plain fact is that none of the beneficiaries or legatees has ever resided in that State.

Florida's interest in the validity of Mrs. Donner's appointment is made more emphatic by the fact that her will is being administered in that State. It has traditionally been the rule that the State where a person is domiciled at the time of his death is the proper place to determine the validity of his will, to construe its provisions and to marshal and distribute his personal property. Here Florida was seriously concerned with winding up Mrs. Donner's estate and with finally determining what property was to be distributed under her will. In fact this suit was brought for that very purpose.

The Court's decision that Florida did not have jurisdiction over the trustee (and inferentially the nonresident beneficiaries) stems from principles stated the better part of a century ago in *Pennoyer v. Neff*. That landmark case was decided in 1878, at a time when business affairs were predominantly local in nature and travel between States was difficult, costly and sometimes even dangerous. There the Court laid down the broad principle that a State could not subject nonresidents to the jurisdiction of its courts unless they were served with process within its boundaries or voluntarily appeared, except to the extent they had property in the State. But as the years have passed the constantly increasing ease and rapidity of communication and the tremendous growth of interstate business activity have led to a steady and inevitable relaxation of the strict limits on state jurisdiction announced in that case. In the course of this evolution the old jurisdictional landmarks have been left far behind so that in many instances States may now properly exercise jurisdiction over nonresidents not amenable to service within their borders. Yet further relaxation seems certain. Of course we have not reached the point where state boundaries are without significance, and I do not mean to suggest such a view here. There is no need to do so. For we are dealing with litigation arising from a transaction that had an abundance of close and substantial connections with the State of Florida.

Perhaps the decision most nearly in point is *Mullane v. Central Hanover Bank & Trust Co.* In that case the Court held that a State could enter a personal judgment in favor of a trustee against nonresident beneficiaries of a trust even though they were not served with process in that State. So far as appeared, their only connection with the State was the fact that the trust was being administered there. In upholding the State's jurisdiction the Court emphasized its great interest in trusts administered within its boundaries and governed by its laws. Also implicit in the result was a desire to avoid the necessity for multiple litigation with its accompanying waste and possibility of inconsistent results. It seems to me that the same kind of considerations are present here supporting Florida's jurisdiction over the nonresident defendants.

Even if it be assumed that the Court is right in its jurisdictional holding, I think its disposition of the two cases is unjustified. It reverses the judgment of the Florida Supreme Court on the ground that the trustee may be, but need not be, an indispensable party to the Florida litigation under Florida law. At the same time it affirms the subsequent Delaware judgment. Although in form the Florida case is remanded for further proceedings not inconsistent with the Court's opinion, the effect is that the Florida courts will be obliged to give full faith and credit to the Delaware judgment. This means the Florida courts will never have an opportunity to determine whether the trustee is an indispensable party. The Florida judgment is thus completely wiped out even as to those parties who make their homes in that State, and even though the Court acknowledges there is nothing in the Constitution which precludes Florida from entering a binding judgment for or against them. It may be argued that the Delaware judgment is the first to become final and therefore is entitled to prevail. But it only comes first because the Court makes it so. In my judgment the proper thing to do would be to hold the Delaware case until the Florida courts had an opportunity to decide whether the trustee is an indispensable party. Under the circumstances of this case I think it is quite probable that they would say he is not. I can see no reason why this Court should deprive Florida plaintiffs of their judgment against Florida defendants on the basis of speculation about Florida law which might well turn out to be unwarranted.

MR. JUSTICE DOUGLAS, dissenting.

The testatrix died domiciled in Florida. Her will, made after she had acquired a domicile in Florida, was probated there. Prior to the time she established a domicile in Florida she executed a trust instrument in Delaware. By its terms she was to receive the income during her life. On her death the principal and undistributed income were to go as provided in any power of appointment or, failing that, in her last will and testament.

After she had become domiciled in Florida she executed a power of appointment; and she also provided in her will that if the power of appointment had not been effectively exercised, the property under the trust, consisting of intangibles, should pass to certain designated trusts.

The Florida court held that the power of appointment was testamentary in character and not being a valid testamentary disposition for lack of the requisite witnesses, failed as a will under Florida law. Therefore the property passed under the will.

Distribution of the assets of the estate could not be made without determining the validity of the power of appointment. The power of appointment, being integrated with the will, was as much subject to construction and interpretation by the Florida court as the will itself. Of course one not a party or privy to the Florida proceedings is not bound by it and can separately litigate the right to assets in other States. But we have no such situation here. The trustee of the trust was in privity with the deceased. She was the settlor; and under the trust, the trustee was to do her bidding. That is to say, the trustee, though managing the res during the life of the settlor, was on her death to transfer the property to such persons as the settlor designated by her power of appointment or by her last will and testament, or, failing that, to designated classes of persons. So far as the present controversy is concerned the trustee was purely and simply a stakeholder or an agent holding assets of the settlor to dispose of as she designated. It had a community of interest with the deceased. I see no reason therefore why Florida could not say that the deceased and her executrix may stand in judgment for the trustee so far as the disposition of the property under the power of appointment and the will is concerned. The question in cases of this kind is whether the procedure is fair and just, considering the interests of the parties. Florida has such a plain and compelling relation to these out-of-state intangibles, and the nexus between the settlor and trustee is so close, as to give Florida the right to make the controlling determination even without personal service over the trustee and those who claim under it. We must remember this is not a suit to impose liability on the Delaware trustee or on any other absent person. It is merely a suit to determine interests in those intangibles. Under closely analogous facts the California Supreme Court held that California had jurisdiction over an absent trustee. I would hold the same here. The decedent was domiciled in Florida; most of the legatees are there; and the absent trustee through whom the others claim was an agency so close to the decedent as to be held to be privy with her—in other words so identified in interest with her as to represent the same legal right.

* * *

C. LONG ARM STATUTES AND THE STREAM OF COMMERCE

ILLINOIS LONG ARM STATUTE: ILL. COMP. STATUTES § 2–209

§ 2–209. ACT SUBMITTING TO JURISDICTION.

(a) Any person, whether or not a citizen or resident of this State, who in person or through an agent does any of the acts hereinafter enumerated, thereby submits such person, and, if an individual, his or her personal representative, to the jurisdiction of the courts of this State as to any cause of action arising from the doing of any of such acts:

(1) The transaction of any business within this State;

(2) The commission of a tortious act within this State;

(3) The ownership, use, or possession of any real estate situated in this State;

(4) Contracting to insure any person, property or risk located within this State at the time of contracting;

(5) With respect to actions of dissolution of marriage, declaration of invalidity of marriage and legal separation, the maintenance in this State of a matrimonial domicile at the time this cause of action arose or the commission in this State of any act giving rise to the cause of action;

(6) With respect to actions brought under the Illinois Parentage Act of 1984, as now or hereafter amended, the performance of an act of sexual intercourse within this State during the possible period of conception;

(7) The making or performance of any contract or promise substantially connected with this State;

(8) The performance of sexual intercourse within this State which is claimed to have resulted in the conception of a child who resides in this State;

(9) The failure to support a child, spouse or former spouse who has continued to reside in this State since the person either formerly resided with them in this State or directed them to reside in this State;

(10) The acquisition of ownership, possession or control of any asset or thing of value present within this State when ownership, possession or control was acquired;

(11) The breach of any fiduciary duty within this State;

(12) The performance of duties as a director or officer of a corporation organized under the laws of this State or having its principal place of business within this State;

(13) The ownership of an interest in any trust administered within this State; or

(14) The exercise of powers granted under the authority of this State as a fiduciary.

(b) A court may exercise jurisdiction in any action arising within or without this State against any person who:

(1) Is a natural person present within this State when served;

(2) Is a natural person domiciled or resident within this State when the cause of action arose, the action was commenced, or process was served;

(3) Is a corporation organized under the laws of this State; or

(4) Is a natural person or corporation doing business within this State.

(b–5) Foreign defamation judgment. The courts of this State shall have personal jurisdiction over any person who obtains a judgment in a defamation proceeding outside the United States against any person who is a resident of Illinois or, if not a natural person, has its principal place of business in Illinois, for the purposes of rendering declaratory relief with respect to that resident's liability for the judgment, or for the purpose of determining whether said judgment should be deemed nonrecognizable pursuant to this Code, to the fullest extent permitted by the United States Constitution, provided:

(1) the publication at issue was published in Illinois, and

(2) that resident (i) has assets in Illinois which might be used to satisfy the foreign defamation judgment, or (ii) may have to take actions in Illinois to comply with the foreign defamation judgment.

The provisions of this subsection (b–5) shall apply to persons who obtained judgments in defamation proceedings outside the United States prior to, on, or after the effective date of this amendatory Act of the 95th General Assembly.

(c) A court may also exercise jurisdiction on any other basis now or hereafter permitted by the Illinois Constitution and the Constitution of the United States.

* * *

(f) Only causes of action arising from acts enumerated herein may be asserted against a defendant in an action in which jurisdiction over him or her is based upon subsection (a).

(g) Nothing herein contained limits or affects the right to serve any process in any other manner now or hereafter provided by law.

* * *

CALIFORNIA LONG ARM STATUTE: CAL. CODE CIV. PRO. § 410.10

A court of this state may exercise jurisdiction on any basis not inconsistent with the Constitution of this state or of the United States.

* * *

GRAY v. AMERICAN RADIATOR & STANDARD SANITARY CORPORATION

22 Ill.2d 432, 176 N.E.2d 761 (1961)

KLINGBIEL, JUSTICE.

Phyllis Gray appeals from a judgment of the circuit court of Cook County dismissing her action for damages. The issues are concerned with the construction and validity of our statute providing for substituted service of process on nonresidents. Since a constitutional question is involved, the appeal is direct to this court.

The suit was brought against the Titan Valve Manufacturing Company and others, on the ground that a certain water heater had exploded and injured the plaintiff. The complaint charges, inter alia, that the Titan company, a foreign corporation, had negligently constructed the safety valve; and that the injuries were suffered as a proximate result thereof. Summons issued and was duly served on Titan's registered agent in Cleveland, Ohio. The corporation appeared specially, filing a motion to quash on the ground that it had not committed a tortious act in Illinois. Its affidavit stated that it does no business here; that it has no agent physically present in Illinois; and that it sells the completed valves to defendant, American Radiator & Standard Sanitary Corporation, outside Illinois. The American Radiator & Standard Sanitary Corporation (also made a defendant) filed an answer in which it set up a cross claim against Titan, alleging that Titan made certain warranties to American Radiator, and that if the latter is held liable to the plaintiff it should be indemnified and held harmless by Titan. The court granted Titan's motion, dismissing both the complaint and the cross claim.

Section 16 of the Civil Practice Act provides that summons may be personally served upon any party outside the State; and that as to nonresidents who have submitted to the jurisdiction of our courts, such service has the force and effect of personal service within Illinois. Under section 17(1)(b) a nonresident who, either in person or through an agent, commits a tortious act within this State submits to jurisdiction. The questions in this case are (1) whether a tortious act was committed here, within the meaning of the statute, despite the fact that the Titan corporation had no agent in Illinois; and (2) whether the statute, if so construed, violates due process of law.

The first aspect to which we must direct our attention is one of statutory construction. Under section 17(1)(b) jurisdiction is predicated on the committing of a tortious act in this State. It is not disputed, for the purpose of this appeal, that a tortious act was committed. The issue depends on whether it was committed in Illinois, so as to warrant the assertion of personal jurisdiction by service of summons in Ohio.

The wrong in the case at bar did not originate in the conduct of a servant physically present here, but arose instead from acts performed at the place of manufacture. Only the consequences occurred in Illinois. It is well established, however, that in law the place of a wrong is where the last event takes place which is necessary to render the actor liable. Restatement, *Conflict of Laws* § 377. A second indication that the place of injury is the determining factor is found in rules governing the time within which an action must be brought. In applying statutes of limitation our court has computed the period from the time when the injury is done. We think it is clear that the alleged negligence in manufacturing the valve cannot be separated from the resulting injury; and that for present purposes, like those of liability and limitations, the tort was committed in Illinois.

Titan seeks to avoid this result by arguing that instead of using the word "tort," the legislature employed the term "tortious act"; and that the latter refers only to the act or conduct, separate and apart from any consequences thereof. We cannot accept the argument. To be tortious an act must cause injury. The concept of injury is an inseparable part of the phrase. In determining legislative intention courts will read words in their ordinary and popularly understood sense. We think the intent should be determined less from technicalities of definition than from considerations of general purpose and effect. To adopt the criteria urged by defendant would tend to promote litigation over extraneous issues concerning the elements of a tort and the territorial incidence of each, whereas the test should be concerned more with those substantial elements of convenience and justice presumably contemplated by the legislature. As we observed in *Nelson v. Miller*, the statute contemplates the exertion of jurisdiction over nonresident defendants to the extent permitted by the due-process clause.

The Titan company contends that if the statute is applied so as to confer jurisdiction in this case it violates the requirement of due process of law. The precise constitutional question thus presented has not heretofore been considered by this court. In the Nelson case the validity of the statute was upheld in an action against a nonresident whose employee, while physically present in Illinois, allegedly caused the injury. The *ratio decidendi* was that Illinois has an interest in providing relief for injuries caused by persons having "substantial contacts within the State." A standard of fairness or reasonableness was announced, within the limitation that defendant be given a realistic opportunity to appear and be heard. The case at bar concerns the extent to which due process permits substituted service where defendant had no agent or employee in the State of the forum.

Under modern doctrine the power of a State court to enter a binding judgment against one not served with process within the State depends upon two questions: first, whether he has certain minimum contacts with the State (*see International Shoe Co. v. State of Washington*), and second, whether there has been a reasonable method of notification. *See International Shoe Co. v. State of Washington*. In the case at bar there is no contention that section 16 provides for inadequate notice or that its provisions were not followed. Defendant's argument on constitutionality is confined to the proposition that applying section 17(1)(b), where the injury is defendant's only contact with the State, would exceed the limits of due process.

A proper determination of the question presented requires analysis of those cases which have dealt with the quantum of contact sufficient to warrant jurisdiction. Since the decision in *Pennoyer v. Neff*, the power of a State to exert jurisdiction over nonresidents has been greatly expanded, particularly with respect to foreign corporations. *International Shoe Co. v. State of Washington*, was a proceeding to collect unpaid contributions to the unemployment compensation fund of the State of Washington. A statute purported to authorize such proceedings, where the employer was not found within the State, by sending notice by registered mail to its last known address. The defendant foreign corporation, a manufacturer of shoes, employed certain salesmen who resided in Washington and who solicited orders there. In holding that maintenance of the suit did not violate due process the court pointed out that the activities of the corporation in Washington were not only continuous and systematic but also gave rise to the liability sued on. It was observed that such operations, which resulted in a large volume of business, established "sufficient contacts or ties with the state of the forum to make it reasonable and just according to our traditional conception of fair play and substantial justice to permit the state to enforce the obligations which appellant has incurred there."

Where the business done by a foreign corporation in the State of the forum is of a sufficiently substantial nature, it has been held permissible for the State to entertain a suit against it even though the cause of action arose from activities entirely distinct from its conduct within the State. *Perkins v. Benguet Consolidated Mining Co.* But where such business or other activity is not substantial, the particular act or transaction having no connection with the State of the forum, the requirement of "contact" is not satisfied. *Hanson v. Denckla.*

In the case at bar the defendant's only contact with this State is found in the fact that a product manufactured in Ohio was incorporated in Pennsylvania, into a hot water heater which in the course of commerce was sold to an Illinois consumer. The record fails to disclose whether defendant has done any other business in Illinois, either directly or indirectly; and it is argued, in reliance on the International Shoe test, that since a course of business here has not been shown there are no "minimum contacts" sufficient to support jurisdiction. We do not think, however, that doing a given volume of business is the only way in which a nonresident can form the required connection with this State. Since the *International Shoe* case was decided the requirements for jurisdiction have been further relaxed, so that at the present time it is sufficient if the act or transaction itself has a substantial connection with the State of the forum.

In *McGee v. International Life Insurance Co.*, suit was brought in California against a foreign insurance company on a policy issued to a resident of California. The defendant was not served with process in that State but was notified by registered mail at its place of business in Texas, pursuant to a statute permitting such service in suits on insurance contracts. The contract in question was delivered in California, the premiums were mailed from there and the insured was a resident of that State when he died, but defendant had no office or agent in California nor did it solicit any business there apart from the policy sued on. After referring briefly to the *International Shoe* case the court held that *"it is sufficient for purposes of due process that the suit was based on a contract which had substantial connection"* with California.

In *Smyth v. Twin State Improvement Corp.*, a Vermont resident engaged a foreign corporation to re-roof his house. While doing the work the corporation negligently damaged the building, and an action was brought for damages. Service of process was made on the Secretary of State and a copy was forwarded to defendant by registered mail at its principal place of business in Massachusetts. A Vermont statute provided for such substituted service on foreign corporations committing a tort in Vermont against a resident of Vermont. In holding that the statute affords due process of law, the court discussed the principal authorities on the question and concluded, inter alia, that "continuous activity within the state is not necessary as a prerequisite to jurisdiction."

In *Nelson v. Miller*, the commission of a single tort within this State was held sufficient to sustain jurisdiction under the present statute. The defendant in that case, a resident of Wisconsin, was engaged in the business of selling appliances. It was alleged that in the process of delivering a stove in Illinois, an employee of the defendant negligently caused injury to the plaintiff. In holding that the defendant was not denied due process by being required to defend in Illinois, this court observed: "The defendant sent his employee into Illinois in the advancement of his own interests. While he was here, the employee and the defendant enjoyed the benefit and protection of the laws of Illinois, including the right to resort to our courts. In the course of his stay here the employee performed acts that gave rise to an injury. The law of Illinois will govern the substantive rights and duties stemming from the incident. Witnesses, other than the defendant's employee, are likely to be found here, and not in Wisconsin. In such circumstances, it is not unreasonable to require the defendant to make his defense here."

Whether the type of activity conducted within the State is adequate to satisfy the requirement depends upon the facts in the particular case. *Perkins v. Benguet Consolidated Mining Co*. The question cannot be answered by applying a mechanical formula or rule of thumb but by ascertaining what is fair and reasonable in the circumstances. In the application of this flexible test the relevant inquiry is whether defendant engaged in some act or conduct by which he may be said to have invoked the benefits and protections of the law of the forum. *See Hanson v. Denckla*; *International Shoe Co. v. State of Washington*. The relevant decisions since *Pennoyer v. Neff* show a development of the concept of personal jurisdiction from one which requires service of process within the State to one which is satisfied either if the act or transaction sued on occurs there or if defendant has engaged in a sufficiently substantial course of activity in the State, provided always that reasonable notice and opportunity to be heard are afforded. As the Vermont court recognized the Smyth case, the trend in defining due process of law is away from the emphasis on territorial limitations and toward emphasis on providing adequate notice and opportunity to be heard: from the court with immediate power over the defendant, toward the court in which both parties can most conveniently settle their dispute.

In the *McGee* case the court commented on the trend toward expanding State jurisdiction over nonresidents, observing that: "In part this is attributable to the fundamental transformation of our national economy over the years. Today many commercial transactions touch two or more States and may involve parties separated by the full continent. With this increasing nationalization of commerce has come a great increase in the amount of business conducted by mail across state lines. At the same time modern transportation and communication have made it much less burdensome for a party sued to defend himself in a State where he engages in economic activity."

It is true that courts cannot "assume that this trend heralds the eventual demise of all restrictions on the personal jurisdiction of state courts." *Hanson v. Denckla*. An orderly and fair administration of the law throughout the nation requires protection against being compelled to answer claims brought in distant States with which the defendant has little or no association and in which he would be faced with an undue burden or disadvantage in making his defense. It must be remembered that lawsuits can be brought on frivolous demands or groundless claims as well as on legitimate ones, and that procedural rules must be designed and appraised in the light of what is fair and just to both sides in the dispute. Interpretations of basic rights which consider only those of a claimant are not consonant with the fundamental requisites of due process.

In the case at bar defendant does not claim that the present use of its product in Illinois is an isolated instance. While the record does not disclose the volume of Titan's business or the territory in which appliances incorporating its valves are marketed, it is a reasonable inference that its commercial transactions, like those of other manufacturers, result in substantial use and consumption in this State. To the extent that its business may be directly affected by transactions occurring here it enjoys benefits from the laws of this State, and it has undoubtedly benefited, to a degree, from the protection which our law has given to the marketing of hot water heaters containing its valves. Where the alleged liability arises, as in this case, from the manufacture of products presumably sold in contemplation of use here, it should not matter that the purchase was made from an independent middleman or that someone other than the defendant shipped the product into this State.

With the increasing specialization of commercial activity and the growing interdependence of business enterprises it is seldom that a manufacturer deals directly with consumers in other States. The fact that the benefit he derives from its laws is an indirect one, however, does not make it any the less essential to the conduct of his business; and it is not unreasonable, where a cause of action arises from alleged defects in his product, to say that the use of such products in the ordinary course of commerce is sufficient contact with this State to justify a requirement that he defend here.

As a general proposition, if a corporation elects to sell its products for ultimate use in another State, it is not unjust to hold it answerable there for any damage caused by defects in those products. Advanced means of distribution and other commercial activity have made possible these modern methods of doing business, and have largely effaced the economic significance of State lines. By the same token, today's facilities for transportation and communication have removed much of the difficulty and inconvenience formerly encountered in defending lawsuits brought in other States.

Unless they are applied in recognition of the changes brought about by technological and economic progress, jurisdictional concepts which may have been reasonable enough in a simpler economy lose their relation to reality, and injustice rather than justice is promoted. Our unchanging principles of justice, whether procedural or substantive in nature, should be scrupulously observed by the courts. But the rules of law which grow and develop within those principles must do so in the light of the facts of economic life as it is lived today. Otherwise the need for adaptation may become so great that basic rights are sacrificed in the name of reform, and the principles themselves become impaired.

The principles of due process relevant to the issue in this case support jurisdiction in the court where both parties can most conveniently settle their dispute. The facts show that the plaintiff, an Illinois resident, was injured in Illinois. The law of Illinois will govern the substantive questions, and witnesses on the issues of injury, damages and other elements relating to the occurrence are most likely to be found here. Under such circumstances the courts of the place of injury usually provide the most convenient forum for trial. * * *

We are aware of decisions, cited by defendant, wherein the opposite result was reached on somewhat similar factual situations. Little purpose can be served, however, by discussing such cases in detail, since the existence of sufficient "contact" depends upon the particular facts in each case. In any event we think the better rule supports jurisdiction in cases of the present kind. We conclude accordingly that defendant's association with this State is sufficient to support the exercise of jurisdiction.

We construe section 17(1)(b) as providing for jurisdiction under the circumstances shown in this case, and we hold that as so construed the statute does not violate due process of law.

The trial court erred in quashing service of summons and in dismissing the complaint and cross claim. The judgment is reversed and the cause is remanded to the circuit court of Cook County, with directions to deny the motion to quash.

Reversed and remanded, with directions.

* * *

KULKO v. SUPERIOR COURT OF CALIFORNIA

436 U.S. 84 (1978)

MR. JUSTICE MARSHALL delivered the opinion of the Court.

The issue before us is whether, in this action for child support, the California state courts may exercise *in personam* jurisdiction over a nonresident, non-domiciliary parent of minor children domiciled within the State. For reasons set forth below, we hold that the exercise of such jurisdiction would violate the Due Process Clause of the Fourteenth Amendment.

I

Appellant Ezra Kulko married appellee Sharon Kulko Horn in 1959, during appellant's three-day stopover in California en route from a military base in Texas to a tour of duty in Korea. At the time of this marriage, both parties were domiciled in and residents of New York State. Immediately following the marriage, Sharon Kulko returned to New York, as did appellant after his tour of duty. Their first child, Darwin, was born to the Kulkos in New York in 1961, and a year later their second child, Ilsa, was born, also in New York. The Kulkos and their two children resided together as a family in New York City continuously until March 1972, when the Kulkos separated.

Following the separation, Sharon Kulko moved to San Francisco. A written separation agreement was drawn up in New York; in September 1972, Sharon Kulko flew to New York City in order to sign this agreement. The agreement provided, *inter alia,* that the children would remain with their father during the school year but would spend their Christmas, Easter, and summer vacations with their mother. While Sharon Kulko waived any claim for her own support or maintenance, Ezra Kulko agreed to pay his wife $3,000 per year in child support for the periods when the children were in her care, custody, and control. Immediately after execution of the separation agreement, Sharon Kulko flew to Haiti and procured a divorce there; the divorce decree incorporated the terms of the agreement. She then returned to California, where she remarried and took the name Horn.

The children resided with appellant during the school year and with their mother on vacations, as provided by the separation agreement, until December 1973. At this time, just before Ilsa was to leave New York to spend Christmas vacation with her mother, she told her father that she wanted to remain in California after her vacation. Appellant bought his daughter a one-way plane ticket, and Ilsa left, taking her clothing with her. Ilsa then commenced living in California with her mother during the school year and spending vacations with her father. In January 1976, appellant's other child, Darwin, called his mother from New York and advised her that he wanted to live with her in California. Unbeknownst to appellant, appellee Horn sent a plane ticket to her son, which he used to fly to California where he took up residence with his mother and sister.

Less than one month after Darwin's arrival in California, appellee Horn commenced this action against appellant in the California Superior Court. She sought to establish the Haitian divorce decree as a California judgment; to modify the judgment so as to award her full custody of the children; and to increase appellant's child-support obligations. Appellant appeared specially and moved to quash service of the summons on the ground that he was not a resident of California and lacked sufficient "minimum contacts" with the State under *International Shoe Co. v. Washington* to warrant the State's assertion of personal jurisdiction over him.

The trial court summarily denied the motion to quash, and appellant sought review in the California Court of Appeal by petition for a writ of mandate. Appellant did not contest the court's jurisdiction for purposes of the custody determination, but, with respect to the claim for increased support, he renewed his argument that the California courts lacked personal jurisdiction over him. The appellate court affirmed the denial of appellant's motion to quash, reasoning that, by consenting to his children's living in California, appellant had "caused an effect in th[e] state" warranting the exercise of jurisdiction over him.

The California Supreme Court granted appellant's petition for review, and in a 4–2 decision sustained the rulings of the lower state courts. It noted first that the California Code of Civil Procedure demonstrated an intent that the courts of California utilize all bases of *in personam* jurisdiction "not inconsistent with the Constitution."[3] Agreeing with the court below, the Supreme Court stated that, where a nonresident defendant has caused an effect in the State by an act or omission outside the State, personal jurisdiction over the defendant in causes arising from that effect may be exercised whenever "reasonable." It went on to hold that such an exercise was "reasonable" in this case because appellant had "purposely availed himself of the benefits and protections of the laws of California" by sending Ilsa to live with her mother in California. While noting that appellant had not, "with respect to his other child, Darwin, caused an effect in [California]"—since it was appellee Horn who had arranged for Darwin to fly to California in January 1976—the court concluded that it was "fair and reasonable for defendant to be subject to personal jurisdiction for the support of both children, where he has committed acts with respect to one child which confers *[sic]* personal jurisdiction and has consented to the permanent residence of the other child in California."

In the view of the two dissenting justices, permitting a minor child to move to California could not be regarded as a purposeful act by which appellant had invoked the benefits and protection of state law. Since appellant had been in the State of California on only two brief occasions many years before on military stopovers, and lacked any other contact with the State, the dissenting opinion argued that appellant could not reasonably be subjected to the *in personam* jurisdiction of the California state courts.

On Ezra Kulko's appeal to this Court, probable jurisdiction was postponed. We have concluded that jurisdiction by appeal does not lie, but, treating the papers as a petition for a writ of certiorari, we hereby grant the petition and reverse the judgment below.

II

The Due Process Clause of the Fourteenth Amendment operates as a limitation on the jurisdiction of state courts to enter judgments affecting

---

3.   Section 410.10, Cal. Civ. Proc. Code Ann., provides:

A court of this state may exercise jurisdiction on any basis not inconsistent with the Constitution of this state or of the United States.

rights or interests of nonresident defendants. See *Shaffer v. Heitner*. It has long been the rule that a valid judgment imposing a personal obligation or duty in favor of the plaintiff may be entered only by a court having jurisdiction over the person of the defendant. *Pennoyer v. Neff*; *International Shoe Co. v. Washington*. The existence of personal jurisdiction, in turn, depends upon the presence of reasonable notice to the defendant that an action has been brought. *Mullane v. Central Hanover Trust Co.*, and a sufficient connection between the defendant and the forum State to make it fair to require defense of the action in the forum. *Milliken v. Meyer*. In this case, appellant does not dispute the adequacy of the notice that he received, but contends that his connection with the State of California is too attenuated, under the standards implicit in the Due Process Clause of the Constitution, to justify imposing upon him the burden and inconvenience of defense in California.

The parties are in agreement that the constitutional standard for determining whether the State may enter a binding judgment against appellant here is that set forth in this Court's opinion in *International Shoe Co. v. Washington:* that a defendant "have certain minimum contacts with [the forum State] such that the maintenance of the suit does not offend 'traditional notions of fair play and substantial.'" While the interests of the forum State and of the plaintiff in proceeding with the cause in the plaintiff's forum of choice are, of course, to be considered, *see McGee v. International Life Insurance Co.*, an essential criterion in all cases is whether the "quality and nature" of the defendant's activity is such that it is "reasonable" and "fair" to require him to conduct his defense in that State. *International Shoe Co. v. Washington*.

Like any standard that requires a determination of "reasonableness," the "minimum contacts" test of *International Shoe* is not susceptible of mechanical application; rather, the facts of each case must be weighed to determine whether the requisite "affiliating circumstances" are present. *Hanson v. Denckla*. We recognize that this determination is one in which few answers will be written "in black and white. The greys are dominant and even among them the shades are innumerable." But we believe that the California Supreme Court's application of the minimum-contacts test in this case represents an unwarranted extension of *International Shoe* and would, if sustained, sanction a result that is neither fair, just, nor reasonable.

A

In reaching its result, the California Supreme Court did not rely on appellant's glancing presence in the State some 13 years before the events that led to this controversy, nor could it have. Appellant has been in California on only two occasions, once in 1959 for a three-day military stopover on his way to Korea, and again in 1960 for a 24-hour stopover on his return from Korean service. To hold such temporary visits to a State a basis for the assertion of *in personam* jurisdiction over unrelated actions arising in the future would make a mockery of the limitations on state jurisdiction imposed by the Fourteenth Amendment. Nor did the California court rely on the fact that appellant was actually married in California on one of his two brief visits. We agree that where two New York domiciliaries, for reasons of convenience, marry in the State of California and thereafter spend their entire married life in New York, the fact of their California marriage by itself cannot support a California court's exercise of jurisdiction over a spouse who remains a New York resident in an action relating to child support.

Finally, in holding that personal jurisdiction existed, the court below carefully disclaimed reliance on the fact that appellant had agreed at the time of separation to allow his children to live with their mother three months a year and that he had sent them to California each year pursuant to this agreement. As was noted below, to find personal jurisdiction in a State on this basis, merely because the mother was residing there, would discourage parents from entering into reasonable visitation agreements. Moreover, it could arbitrarily subject one parent to suit in any State of the Union where the other parent chose to spend time while having custody of their offspring pursuant to a separation agreement. As we have emphasized:

> The unilateral activity of those who claim some relationship with a nonresident defendant cannot satisfy the requirement of contact with the forum State.... [I]t is essential in each case that there be some act by which the defendant purposefully avails [him]self of the privilege of conducting activities within the forum State.... *Hanson v. Denckla.*

The "purposeful act" that the California Supreme Court believed did warrant the exercise of personal jurisdiction over appellant in California was his "actively and fully consent[ing] to Ilsa living in California for the school year ... and ... sen[ding] her to California for that purpose." We cannot accept the proposition that appellant's acquiescence in Ilsa's desire to live with her mother conferred jurisdiction over appellant in the California courts in this action. A father who agrees, in the interests of family harmony and his children's preferences, to allow them to spend more time in California than was required under a separation agreement can hardly be said to have "purposefully availed himself" of the "benefits and protections" of California's laws. *See Shaffer v. Heitner.*[7]

Nor can we agree with the assertion of the court below that the exercise of *in personam* jurisdiction here was warranted by the financial benefit appellant derived from his daughter's presence in California for nine months of the year. This argument rests on the premise that, while appellant's liability for support payments remained unchanged, his yearly expenses for supporting the child in New York decreased. But this

---

7. The court below stated that the presence in California of appellant's daughter gave appellant the benefit of California's "police and fire protection, its school system, its hospital services, its recreational facilities, its libraries and museums...." But, in the circumstances presented here, these services provided by the State were essentially benefits to the child, not the father, and in any event were not benefits that appellant purposefully sought for himself.

circumstance, even if true, does not support California's assertion of jurisdiction here. Any diminution in appellant's household costs resulted, not from the child's presence in California, but rather from her absence from appellant's home. Moreover, an action by appellee Horn to increase support payments could now be brought, and could have been brought when Ilsa first moved to California, in the State of New York; a New York court would clearly have personal jurisdiction over appellant and, if a judgment were entered by a New York court increasing appellant's child-support obligations, it could properly be enforced against him in both New York and California.[9] Any ultimate financial advantage to appellant thus results not from the child's presence in California, but from appellee's failure earlier to seek an increase in payments under the separation agreement. The argument below to the contrary, in our view, confuses the question of appellant's liability with that of the proper forum in which to determine that liability.

In light of our conclusion that appellant did not purposefully derive benefit from any activities relating to the State of California, it is apparent that the California Supreme Court's reliance on appellant's having caused an "effect" in California was misplaced. This "effects" test is derived from the American Law Institute's *Restatement (Second) of Conflict of Laws* § 37, which provides:

> "A state has power to exercise judicial jurisdiction over an individual who causes effects in the state by an act done elsewhere with respect to any cause of action arising from these effects unless the nature of the effects and of the individual's relationship to the state make the exercise of such jurisdiction unreasonable."

While this provision is not binding on this Court, it does not in any event support the decision below. As is apparent from the examples accompanying § 37 in the Restatement, this section was intended to reach wrongful activity outside of the State causing injury within the State, *see*, *e. g.*, Comment *a*, p. 157 (shooting bullet from one State into another), or commercial activity affecting state residents. Even in such situations, moreover, the Restatement recognizes that there might be circumstances that would render "unreasonable" the assertion of jurisdiction over the nonresident defendant.

The circumstances in this case clearly render "unreasonable" California's assertion of personal jurisdiction. There is no claim that appellant has visited physical injury on either property or persons within the State of California. *Cf. Hess v. Pawloski.* The cause of action herein asserted arises, not from the defendant's commercial transactions in interstate commerce, but rather from his personal, domestic relations. It thus cannot be said that appellant has sought a commercial benefit from solicitation of business from a resident of California that could reasonably render him

---

9. A final judgment entered by a New York court having jurisdiction over the defendant's person and over the subject matter of the lawsuit would be entitled to full faith and credit in any State.

liable to suit in state court; appellant's activities cannot fairly be analogized to an insurer's sending an insurance contract and premium notices into the State to an insured resident of the State. *Cf. McGee v. International Life Insurance Co.* Furthermore, the controversy between the parties arises from a separation that occurred in the State of New York; appellee Horn seeks modification of a contract that was negotiated in New York and that she flew to New York to sign. As in *Hanson v. Denckla,* the instant action involves an agreement that was entered into with virtually no connection with the forum State.

Finally, basic considerations of fairness point decisively in favor of appellant's State of domicile as the proper forum for adjudication of this case, whatever the merits of appellee's underlying claim. It is appellant who has remained in the State of the marital domicile, whereas it is appellee who has moved across the continent. Appellant has at all times resided in New York State, and, until the separation and appellee's move to California, his entire family resided there as well. As noted above, appellant did no more than acquiesce in the stated preference of one of his children to live with her mother in California. This single act is surely not one that a reasonable parent would expect to result in the substantial financial burden and personal strain of litigating a child-support suit in a forum 3,000 miles away, and we therefore see no basis on which it can be said that appellant could reasonably have anticipated being "haled before a [California] court," *Shaffer v. Heitner.* To make jurisdiction in a case such as this turn on whether appellant bought his daughter her ticket or instead unsuccessfully sought to prevent her departure would impose an unreasonable burden on family relations, and one wholly unjustified by the "quality and nature" of appellant's activities in or relating to the State of California. *International Shoe Co. v. Washington.*

III

In seeking to justify the burden that would be imposed on appellant were the exercise of *in personam* jurisdiction in California sustained, appellee argues that California has substantial interests in protecting the welfare of its minor residents and in promoting to the fullest extent possible a healthy and supportive family environment in which the children of the State are to be raised. These interests are unquestionably important. But while the presence of the children and one parent in California arguably might favor application of California law in a lawsuit in New York, the fact that California may be the " 'center of gravity' " for choice-of-law purposes does not mean that California has personal jurisdiction over the defendant. *Hanson v. Denckla.* And California has not attempted to assert any particularized interest in trying such cases in its courts by, *e. g.,* enacting a special jurisdictional statute. *Cf. McGee v. International Life Ins. Co.*

California's legitimate interest in ensuring the support of children resident in California without unduly disrupting the children's lives, moreover, is already being served by the State's participation in the

Revised Uniform Reciprocal Enforcement of Support Act of 1968. This statute provides a mechanism for communication between court systems in different States, in order to facilitate the procurement and enforcement of child-support decrees where the dependent children reside in a State that cannot obtain personal jurisdiction over the defendant. California's version of the Act essentially permits a California resident claiming support from a nonresident to file a petition in California and have its merits adjudicated in the State of the alleged obligor's residence, without either party's having to leave his or her own State. New York State is a signatory to a similar Act. Thus, not only may plaintiff-appellee here vindicate her claimed right to additional child support from her former husband in a New York court, but also the Uniform Acts will facilitate both her prosecution of a claim for additional support and collection of any support payments found to be owed by appellant.[15]

It cannot be disputed that California has substantial interests in protecting resident children and in facilitating child-support actions on behalf of those children. But these interests simply do not make California a "fair forum" in which to require appellant, who derives no personal or commercial benefit from his child's presence in California and who lacks any other relevant contact with the State, either to defend a child-support suit or to suffer liability by default.

IV

We therefore believe that the state courts in the instant case failed to heed our admonition that "the flexible standard of *International Shoe*" does not "heral[d] the eventual demise of all restrictions on the personal jurisdiction of state courts." *Hanson v. Denckla*. In *McGee v. International Life Ins. Co.*, we commented on the extension of *in personam* jurisdiction under evolving standards of due process, explaining that this trend was in large part "attributable to the . . . increasing nationalization of commerce . . . [accompanied by] modern transportation and communication [that] have made it much less burdensome for a party sued to defend himself in a State where he engages in economic activity." But the mere act of sending a child to California to live with her mother is not a commercial act and connotes no intent to obtain or expectancy of receiving a corresponding benefit in the State that would make fair the assertion of that State's judicial jurisdiction.

Accordingly, we conclude that the appellant's motion to quash service, on the ground of lack of personal jurisdiction, was erroneously denied by the California courts. The judgment of the California Supreme Court is, therefore,

Reversed.

---

15. Thus, it cannot here be concluded, as it was in *McGee v. International Life Insurance Co.*, with respect to actions on insurance contracts, that resident plaintiffs would be at a "severe disadvantage" if *in personam* jurisdiction over out-of-state defendants were sometimes unavailable.

MR. JUSTICE BRENNAN, with whom MR. JUSTICE WHITE and MR. JUSTICE POWELL join, dissenting.

The Court properly treats this case as presenting a single narrow question. That question is whether the California Supreme Court correctly "weighed" "the facts" of this particular case in applying the settled "constitutional standard," that before state courts may exercise *in personam* jurisdiction over a nonresident, non-domiciliary parent of minor children domiciled in the State, it must appear that the nonresident has "certain minimum contacts [with the forum State] such that the maintenance of the suit does not offend 'traditional notions of fair play and substantial justice.'" *International Shoe Co. v. Washington.* The Court recognizes that "this determination is one in which few answers will be written 'in black and white.'" I cannot say that the Court's determination against state-court *in personam* jurisdiction is implausible, but, though the issue is close, my independent weighing of the facts leads me to conclude, in agreement with the analysis and determination of the California Supreme Court, that appellant's connection with the State of California was not too attenuated, under the standards of reasonableness and fairness implicit in the Due Process Clause, to require him to conduct his defense in the California courts. I therefore dissent.

* * *

D. PROPERTY REVISITED

SHAFFER v. HEITNER

433 U.S. 186 (1977)

MR. JUSTICE MARSHALL delivered the opinion of the Court.

The controversy in this case concerns the constitutionality of a Delaware statute that allows a court of that State to take jurisdiction of a lawsuit by sequestering any property of the defendant that happens to be located in Delaware. Appellants contend that the sequestration statute as applied in this case violates the Due Process Clause of the Fourteenth Amendment both because it permits the state courts to exercise jurisdiction despite the absence of sufficient contacts among the defendants, the litigation, and the State of Delaware and because it authorizes the deprivation of defendants' property without providing adequate procedural safeguards. We find it necessary to consider only the first of these contentions.

I

Appellee Heitner, a nonresident of Delaware, is the owner of one share of stock in the Greyhound Corp., a business incorporated under the laws of Delaware with its principal place of business in Phoenix, Ariz. On May 22, 1974, he filed a shareholder's derivative suit in the Court of Chancery for New Castle County, Del., in which he named as defendants

Greyhound, its wholly owned subsidiary Greyhound Lines, Inc.,[1] and 28 present or former officers or directors of one or both of the corporations. In essence, Heitner alleged that the individual defendants had violated their duties to Greyhound by causing it and its subsidiary to engage in actions that resulted in the corporations being held liable for substantial damages in a private antitrust suit and a large fine in a criminal contempt action. The activities which led to these penalties took place in Oregon.

Simultaneously with his complaint, Heitner filed a motion for an order of sequestration of the Delaware property of the individual defendants pursuant to Del. Code Ann., Tit. 10, § 366 (1975). This motion was accompanied by a supporting affidavit of counsel which stated that the individual defendants were nonresidents of Delaware. The affidavit identified the property to be sequestered as

> "common stock, 3% Second Cumulative Preferred Stock and stock unit credits of the Defendant Greyhound Corporation, a Delaware corporation, as well as all options and all warrants to purchase said stock issued to said individual Defendants and all contractural (sic) obligations, all rights, debts or credits due or accrued to or for the benefit of any of the said Defendants under any type of written agreement, contract or other legal instrument of any kind whatever between any of the individual Defendants and said corporation."

The requested sequestration order was signed the day the motion was filed. Pursuant to that order, the sequestrator "seized" approximately 82,000 shares of Greyhound common stock belonging to 19 of the defendants, and options belonging to another 2 defendants. These seizures were accomplished by placing "stop transfer" orders or their equivalents on the books of the Greyhound Corp. So far as the record shows, none of the certificates representing the seized property was physically present in Delaware. The stock was considered to be in Delaware, and so subject to seizure, by virtue of Del. Code Ann., Tit. 8, § 169, which makes Delaware the situs of ownership of all stock in Delaware corporations.

All 28 defendants were notified of the initiation of the suit by certified mail directed to their last known addresses and by publication in a New Castle County newspaper. The 21 defendants whose property was seized (hereafter referred to as appellants) responded by entering a special appearance for the purpose of moving to quash service of process and to vacate the sequestration order. They contended that the ex parte sequestration procedure did not accord them due process of law and that the property seized was not capable of attachment in Delaware. In addition, appellants asserted that under the rule of *International Shoe Co. v. Washington*, they did not have sufficient contacts with Delaware to sustain the jurisdiction of that State's courts.

The Court of Chancery rejected these arguments in a letter opinion which emphasized the purpose of the Delaware sequestration procedure:

---

1. Greyhound Lines, Inc. is incorporated in California and has its principal place of business in Phoenix, Ariz.

The primary purpose of "sequestration" is not to secure possession of property pending a trial between resident debtors and creditors on the issue of who has the right to retain it. On the contrary, as here employed, "sequestration" is a process used to compel the personal appearance of a nonresident defendant to answer and defend a suit brought against him in a court of equity. It is accomplished by the appointment of a sequestrator by this Court to seize and hold property of the nonresident located in this State subject to further Court order. If the defendant enters a general appearance, the sequestered property is routinely released, unless the plaintiff makes special application to continue its seizure, in which event the plaintiff has the burden of proof and persuasion.

This limitation on the purpose and length of time for which sequestered property is held, the court concluded, rendered inapplicable the due process requirements. ... The court also found no state-law or federal constitutional barrier to the sequestrator's reliance on Del. Code Ann., Tit. 8, § 169. Finally, the court held that the statutory Delaware situs of the stock provided a sufficient basis for the exercise of *quasi in rem* jurisdiction by a Delaware court.

On appeal, the Delaware Supreme Court affirmed the judgment of the Court of Chancery. Most of the Supreme Court's opinion was devoted to rejecting appellants' contention that the sequestration procedure is inconsistent with the due process analysis. The court based its rejection of that argument in part on its agreement with the Court of Chancery that the purpose of the sequestration procedure is to compel the appearance of the defendant. The court also relied on what it considered the ancient origins of the sequestration procedure and approval of that procedure in the opinions of this Court,[10] Delaware's interest in asserting jurisdiction to adjudicate claims of mismanagement of a Delaware corporation, and the safeguards for defendants that it found in the Delaware statute.

Appellants' claim that the Delaware courts did not have jurisdiction to adjudicate this action received much more cursory treatment. The court's analysis of the jurisdictional issue is contained in two paragraphs:

> There are significant constitutional questions at issue here but we say at once that we do not deem the rule of *International Shoe* to be one of them.... The reason of course, is that jurisdiction ... remains ... *quasi in rem* founded on the presence of capital stock here, not on prior contact by defendants with this forum. Under [Delaware statutes] the "situs of the ownership of the capital stock of all corporations existing under the laws of this State ... (is) in this State," and that provides the initial basis for jurisdiction. Delaware may constitutionally establish situs of such shares here ... it has done so and the presence thereof provides the foundation for [jurisdiction] in this case.

---

10. Sequestration is the equity counterpart of the process of foreign attachment in suits at law. Delaware's sequestration statute was modeled after its attachment statute.

We hold that seizure of the Greyhound shares is not invalid because plaintiff has failed to meet the prior contacts tests of *International Shoe*.

We noted probable jurisdiction. We reverse.

II

The Delaware courts rejected appellants' jurisdictional challenge by noting that this suit was brought as a *quasi in rem* proceeding. Since *quasi in rem* jurisdiction is traditionally based on attachment or seizure of property present in the jurisdiction, not on contacts between the defendant and the State, the courts considered appellants' claimed lack of contacts with Delaware to be unimportant. This categorical analysis assumes the continued soundness of the conceptual structure founded on the century-old case of *Pennoyer v. Neff*.

Pennoyer was an ejectment action brought in federal court under the diversity jurisdiction. Pennoyer, the defendant in that action, held the land under a deed purchased in a sheriff's sale conducted to realize on a judgment for attorney's fees obtained against Neff in a previous action by one Mitchell. At the time of Mitchell's suit in an Oregon State court, Neff was a nonresident of Oregon. An Oregon statute allowed service by publication on nonresident who had property in the State, and Mitchell had used that procedure to bring Neff before the court. The United States Circuit Court for the District of Oregon, in which Neff brought his ejectment action, refused to recognize the validity of the judgment against Neff in Mitchell's suit, and accordingly awarded the land to Neff. This Court affirmed.

Mr. Justice Field's opinion for the Court focused on the territorial limits of the States' judicial powers. Although recognizing that the States are not truly independent sovereigns, Mr. Justice Field found that their jurisdiction was defined by the "principles of public law" that regulate the relationships among independent nations. The first of those principles was "that every State possesses exclusive jurisdiction and sovereignty over persons and property within its territory." The second was "that no State can exercise direct jurisdiction and authority over persons or property without its territory." Thus, "in virtue of the State's jurisdiction over the property of the non-resident situated within its limits," the state courts "can inquire into that non-resident's obligations to its own citizens . . . to the extent necessary to control the disposition of the property." The Court recognized that if the conclusions of that inquiry were adverse to the non-resident property owner, his interest in the property would be affected. Similarly, if the defendant consented to the jurisdiction of the state courts or was personally served within the State, a judgment could affect his interest in property outside the State. But any attempt "directly" to assert extraterritorial jurisdiction over persons or property would offend sister States and exceed the inherent limits of the State's power. A judgment resulting from such an attempt, Mr. Justice Field concluded, was not only unenforceable in other States, but was also void in the rendering State because it had been obtained in violation of the Due Process Clause of the Fourteenth Amendment.

This analysis led to the conclusion that Mitchell's judgment against Neff could not be validly based on the State's power over persons within its borders, because Neff had not been personally served in Oregon, nor had he consensually appeared before the Oregon court. The Court reasoned that even if Neff had received personal notice of the action, service of process outside the State would have been ineffectual since the State's power was limited by its territorial boundaries. Moreover, the Court held, the action could not be sustained on the basis of the State's power over property within its borders because that property had not been brought before the court by attachment or any other procedure prior to judgment. Since the judgment which authorized the sheriff's sale was therefore invalid, the sale transferred no title. Neff regained his land.

From our perspective, the importance of *Pennoyer* is not its result, but the fact that its principles and corollaries derived from them became the basic elements of the constitutional doctrine governing state-court jurisdiction. As we have noted, under *Pennoyer* state authority to adjudicate was based on the jurisdiction's power over either persons or property. This fundamental concept is embodied in the very vocabulary which we use to describe judgments. If a court's jurisdiction is based on its authority over the defendant's person, the action and judgment are denominated "*in personam*" and can impose a personal obligation on the defendant in favor of the plaintiff. If jurisdiction is based on the court's power over property within its territory, the action is called "*in rem*" or "*quasi in rem*." The effect of a judgment in such a case is limited to the property that supports jurisdiction and does not impose a personal liability on the property owner, since he is not before the court.[17] In *Pennoyer's* terms, the owner is affected only "indirectly" by an *in rem* judgment adverse to his interest in the property subject to the court's disposition.

By concluding that "(t)he authority of every tribunal is necessarily restricted by the territorial limits of the State in which it is established," *Pennoyer* sharply limited the availability of *in personam* jurisdiction over defendants not resident in the forum State. If a nonresident defendant could not be found in a State, he could not be sued there. On the other hand, since the State in which property was located was considered to have exclusive sovereignty over that property, *in rem* actions could proceed regardless of the owner's location. Indeed, since a State's process could not reach beyond its borders, this Court held after *Pennoyer* that

---

17. "A judgment *in rem* affects the interests of all persons in designated property. A judgment *quasi in rem* affects the interests of particular persons in designated property. The latter is of two types. In one the plaintiff is seeking to secure a pre-existing claim in the subject property and to extinguish or establish the nonexistence of similar interests of particular persons. In the other the plaintiff seeks to apply what he concedes to be the property of the defendant to the satisfaction of a claim against him. *Restatement, Judgments*, 5–9." *Hanson v. Denckla*.

As did the Court in *Hanson*, we will for convenience generally use the term "*in rem*" in place of "*in rem* and *quasi in rem*."

due process did not require any effort to give a property owner personal notice that his property was involved in an *in rem* proceeding.

The *Pennoyer* rules generally favored nonresident defendants by making them harder to sue. This advantage was reduced, however, by the ability of a resident plaintiff to satisfy a claim against a nonresident defendant by bringing into court any property of the defendant located in the plaintiff's State. For example, in the well-known case of *Harris v. Balk*, 198 U.S. 215 (1905), Epstein, a resident of Maryland, had a claim against Balk, a resident of North Carolina. Harris, another North Carolina resident, owed money to Balk. When Harris happened to visit Maryland, Epstein garnished his debt to Balk. Harris did not contest the debt to Balk and paid it to Epstein's North Carolina attorney. When Balk later sued Harris in North Carolina, this Court held that the Full Faith and Credit Clause, U.S. Const., Art. IV, § 1, required that Harris' payment to Epstein be treated as a discharge of his debt to Balk. This Court reasoned that the debt Harris owed Balk was an intangible form of property belonging to Balk, and that the location of that property traveled with the debtor. By obtaining personal jurisdiction over Harris, Epstein had "arrested" his debt to Balk, and brought it into the Maryland court. Under the structure established by *Pennoyer*, Epstein was then entitled to proceed against that debt to vindicate his claim against Balk, even though Balk himself was not subject to the jurisdiction of a Maryland tribunal.

Pennoyer itself recognized that its rigid categories, even as blurred by the kind of action typified by Harris, could not accommodate some necessary litigation. Accordingly, Mr. Justice Field's opinion carefully noted that cases involving the personal status of the plaintiff, such as divorce actions, could be adjudicated in the plaintiff's home State even though the defendant could not be served within that State. Similarly, the opinion approved the practice of considering a foreign corporation doing business in a State to have consented to being sued in that State. This basis for *in personam* jurisdiction over foreign corporations was later supplemented by the doctrine that a corporation doing business in a State could be deemed "present" in the State, and so subject to service of process under the rule of *Pennoyer*.

The advent of automobiles, with the concomitant increase in the incidence of individuals causing injury in States where they were not subject to *in personam* actions under *Pennoyer*, required further moderation of the territorial limits on jurisdictional power. This modification, like the accommodation to the realities of interstate corporate activities, was accomplished by use of a legal fiction that left the conceptual structure established in *Pennoyer* theoretically unaltered. The fiction used was that the out-of-state motorist, who it was assumed could be excluded altogether from the State's highways, had by using those highways appointed a designated state official as his agent to accept process. *See Hess v. Pawloski.* Since the motorist's "agent" could be personally served within the State, the state courts could obtain *in personam* jurisdiction over the nonresident driver.

The motorists' consent theory was easy to administer since it required only a finding that the out-of-state driver had used the State's roads. By contrast, both the fictions of implied consent to service on the part of a foreign corporation and of corporate presence required a finding that the corporation was "doing business" in the forum State. Defining the criteria for making that finding and deciding whether they were met absorbed much judicial energy. *See, e.g., International Shoe Co. v. Washington.* While the essentially quantitative tests which emerged from these cases purported simply to identify circumstances under which presence or consent could be attributed to the corporation, it became clear that they were in fact attempting to ascertain "what dealings make it just to subject a foreign corporation to local suit". *In International Shoe,* we acknowledged that fact.

The question in *International Shoe* was whether the corporation was subject to the judicial and taxing jurisdiction of Washington. Mr. Chief Justice Stone's opinion for the Court began its analysis of that question by noting that the historical basis of *in personam* jurisdiction was a court's power over the defendant's person. That power, however, was no longer the central concern:

> But now that the *capias ad respondendum* has given way to personal service of summons or other form of notice, due process requires only that in order to subject a defendant to a judgment *in personam*, if he be not present within the territory of the forum, he have certain minimum contacts with it such that the maintenance of the suit does not offend "traditional notions of fair play and substantial justice."

Thus, the inquiry into the State's jurisdiction over a foreign corporation appropriately focused not on whether the corporation was "present" but on whether there have been "such contacts of the corporation with the state of the forum as make it reasonable, in the context of our federal system of government, to require the corporation to defend the particular suit which is brought there."

Mechanical or quantitative evaluations of the defendant's activities in the forum could not resolve the question of reasonableness:

> Whether due process is satisfied must depend rather upon the quality and nature of the activity in relation to the fair and orderly administration of the laws which it was the purpose of the due process clause to insure. That clause does not contemplate that a state may make binding a judgment *in personam* against an individual or corporate defendant with which the state has no contacts, ties, or relations.[19]

---

19. As the language quoted indicates, the *International Shoe* Court believed that the standard it was setting forth governed actions against natural persons as well as corporations, and we see no reason to disagree. *See also McGee v. International Life Ins. Co. (International Shoe* culmination of trend toward expanding state jurisdiction over "foreign corporations and other nonresidents"). The differences between individuals and corporations may, of course, lead to the

Thus, the relationship among the defendant, the forum, and the litigation, rather than the mutually exclusive sovereignty of the States on which the rules of *Pennoyer* rest, became the central concern of the inquiry into personal jurisdiction.[20] The immediate effect of this departure from *Pennoyer's* conceptual apparatus was to increase the ability of the state courts to obtain personal jurisdiction over nonresident defendants.

No equally dramatic change has occurred in the law governing jurisdiction *in rem*. There have, however, been intimations that the collapse of the *in personam* wing of *Pennoyer* has not left that decision unweakened as a foundation for *in rem* jurisdiction. Well-reasoned lower court opinions have questioned the proposition that the presence of property in a State gives that State jurisdiction to adjudicate rights to the property regardless of the relationship of the underlying dispute and the property owner to the forum. * * * The overwhelming majority of commentators have also rejected *Pennoyer's* premise that a proceeding "against" property is not a proceeding against the owners of that property. Accordingly, they urge that the "traditional notions of fair play and substantial justice" that govern a State's power to adjudicate *in personam* should also govern its power to adjudicate personal rights to property located in the State.

Although this Court has not addressed this argument directly, we have held that property cannot be subjected to a court's judgment unless reasonable and appropriate efforts have been made to give the property owners actual notice of the action. This conclusion recognizes, contrary to *Pennoyer*, that an adverse judgment *in rem* directly affects the property owner by divesting him of his rights in the property before the court. Moreover, in *Mullane* we hold that Fourteenth Amendment rights cannot depend on the classification of an action as *in rem* or *in personam*, since that is "a classification for which the standards are so elusive and confused generally and which, being primarily for state courts to define, may and do vary from state to state."

It is clear, therefore, that the law of state-court jurisdiction no longer stands securely on the foundation established in Pennoyer. We think that the time is ripe to consider whether the standard of fairness and substantial justice set forth in *International Shoe* should be held to govern actions *in rem* as well as *in personam*.

III

The case for applying to jurisdiction *in rem* the same test of "fair play and substantial justice" as governs assertions of jurisdiction *in personam* is simple and straightforward. It is premised on recognition that "(t)he

---

conclusion that a given set of circumstances establishes state jurisdiction over one type of defendant but not over the other.

20. Nothing in *Hanson v. Denckla*, is to the contrary. The *Hanson* Court's statement that restrictions on state jurisdiction "are a consequence of territorial limitations on the power of the respective States" simply makes the point that the States are defined by their geographical territory. After making this point, the Court in *Hanson* determined that the defendant over which personal jurisdiction was claimed had not committed any acts sufficiently connected to the State to justify jurisdiction under the *International Shoe* standard.

phrase, 'judicial jurisdiction over a thing', is a customary elliptical way of referring to jurisdiction over the interests of persons in a thing." *Restatement (Second) of Conflict of Laws* § 56, Introductory Note. This recognition leads to the conclusion that in order to justify an exercise of jurisdiction *in rem*, the basis for jurisdiction must be sufficient to justify exercising "jurisdiction over the interests of persons in a thing."[23] The standard for determining whether an exercise of jurisdiction over the interests of persons is consistent with the Due Process Clause is the minimum-contacts standard elucidated in *International Shoe*.

This argument, of course, does not ignore the fact that the presence of property in a State may bear on the existence of jurisdiction by providing contacts among the forum State, the defendant, and the litigation. For example, when claims to the property itself are the source of the underlying controversy between the plaintiff and the defendant, it would be unusual for the State where the property is located not to have jurisdiction. In such cases, the defendant's claim to property located in the State would normally indicate that he expected to benefit from the State's protection of his interest. The State's strong interests in assuring the marketability of property within its borders and in providing a procedure for peaceful resolution of disputes about the possession of that property would also support jurisdiction, as would the likelihood that important records and witnesses will be found in the State. The presence of property may also favor jurisdiction in cases such as suits for injury suffered on the land of an absentee owner, where the defendant's ownership of the property is conceded but the cause of action is otherwise related to rights and duties growing out of that ownership.

It appears, therefore, that jurisdiction over many types of actions which now are or might be brought *in rem* would not be affected by a holding that any assertion of state-court jurisdiction must satisfy the *International Shoe* standard. For the type of *quasi in rem* action typified by *Harris v. Balk* and the present case, however, accepting the proposed analysis would result in significant change. These are cases where the property which now serves as the basis for state-court jurisdiction is completely unrelated to the plaintiff's cause of action. Thus, although the presence of the defendant's property in a State might suggest the existence of other ties among the defendant, the State, and the litigation, the presence of the property alone would not support the State's jurisdiction. If those other ties did not exist, cases over which the State is now thought to have jurisdiction could not be brought in that forum.

Since acceptance of the *International Shoe* test would most affect this class of cases, we examine the arguments against adopting that standard as they relate to this category of litigation. Before doing so, however, we note that this type of case also presents the clearest illustration of the argument in favor of assessing assertions of jurisdiction by a single

---

23. It is true that the potential liability of a defendant in an *in rem* action is limited by the value of the property, but that limitation does not affect the argument. The fairness of subjecting a defendant to state-court jurisdiction does not depend on the size of the claim being litigated.

standard. For in cases such as *Harris* and this one, the only role played by the property is to provide the basis for bringing the defendant into court. Indeed, the express purpose of the Delaware sequestration procedure is to compel the defendant to enter a personal appearance. In such cases, if a direct assertion of personal jurisdiction over the defendant would violate the Constitution, it would seem that an indirect assertion of that jurisdiction should be equally impermissible.

The primary rationale for treating the presence of property as a sufficient basis for jurisdiction to adjudicate claims over which the State would not have jurisdiction if *International Shoe* applied is that a wrongdoer "should not be able to avoid payment of his obligations by the expedient of removing his assets to a place where he is not subject to an *in personam* suit." *Restatement* § 66, Comment a.

This justification, however, does not explain why jurisdiction should be recognized without regard to whether the property is present in the State because of an effort to avoid the owner's obligations. Nor does it support jurisdiction to adjudicate the underlying claim. At most, it suggests that a State in which property is located should have jurisdiction to attach that property, by use of proper procedures, as security for a judgment being sought in a forum where the litigation can be maintained consistently with *International Shoe*. Moreover, we know of nothing to justify the assumption that a debtor can avoid paying his obligations by removing his property to a State in which his creditor cannot obtain personal jurisdiction over him. The Full Faith and Credit Clause, after all, makes the valid *in personam* judgment of one State enforceable in all other States.

It might also be suggested that allowing *in rem* jurisdiction avoids the uncertainty inherent in the *International Shoe* standard and assures a plaintiff of a forum. We believe, however, that the fairness standard of *International Shoe* can be easily applied in the vast majority of cases. Moreover, when the existence of jurisdiction in a particular forum under *International Shoe* is unclear, the cost of simplifying the litigation by avoiding the jurisdictional question may be the sacrifice of "fair play and substantial justice." That cost is too high.

We are left, then, to consider the significance of the long history of jurisdiction based solely on the presence of property in a State. Although the theory that territorial power is both essential to and sufficient for jurisdiction has been undermined, we have never held that the presence of property in a State does not automatically confer jurisdiction over the owner's interest in that property. This history must be considered as supporting the proposition that jurisdiction based solely on the presence of property satisfies the demands of due process, but it is not decisive. "(T)raditional notions of fair play and substantial justice" can be as readily offended by the perpetuation of ancient forms that are no longer justified as by the adoption of new procedures that are inconsistent with the basic values of our constitutional heritage. The fiction that an assertion of jurisdiction over property is anything but an assertion of jurisdiction over the owner of the property supports an ancient form without substantial modern justification. Its continued acceptance would serve only to allow state-court jurisdiction that is fundamentally unfair to the defendant.

We therefore conclude that all assertions of state-court jurisdiction must be evaluated according to the standards set forth in *International Shoe* and its progeny.[39]

IV

The Delaware courts based their assertion of jurisdiction in this case solely on the statutory presence of appellants' property in Delaware. Yet that property is not the subject matter of this litigation, nor is the underlying cause of action related to the property. Appellants' holdings in Greyhound do not, therefore, provide contacts with Delaware sufficient to support the jurisdiction of that State's courts over appellants. If it exists, that jurisdiction must have some other foundation.

Appellee Heitner did not allege and does not now claim that appellants have ever set foot in Delaware. Nor does he identify any act related to his cause of action as having taken place in Delaware. Nevertheless, he contends that appellants' positions as directors and officers of a corporation chartered in Delaware provide sufficient "contacts, ties, or relations", *International Shoe Co. v. Washington*, with that State to give its courts jurisdiction over appellants in this stockholder's derivative action. This argument is based primarily on what Heitner asserts to be the strong interest of Delaware in supervising the management of a Delaware corporation. That interest is said to derive from the role of Delaware law in establishing the corporation and defining the obligations owed to it by its officers and directors. In order to protect this interest, appellee concludes, Delaware's courts must have jurisdiction over corporate fiduciaries such as appellants.

This argument is undercut by the failure of the Delaware Legislature to assert the state interest appellee finds so compelling. Delaware law bases jurisdiction, not on appellants' status as corporate fiduciaries, but rather on the presence of their property in the State. Although the sequestration procedure used here may be most frequently used in derivative suits against officers and directors, the authorizing statute evinces no specific concern with such actions. Sequestration can be used in any suit against a nonresident, and reaches corporate fiduciaries only if they happen to own interests in a Delaware corporation, or other property in the State. But as Heitner's failure to secure jurisdiction over seven of the defendants named in his complaint demonstrates, there is no necessary relationship between holding a position as a corporate fiduciary and

---

39. It would not be fruitful for us to re-examine the facts of cases decided on the rationales of *Pennoyer* and *Harris* to determine whether jurisdiction might have been sustained under the standard we adopt today. To the extent that prior decisions are inconsistent with this standard, they are overruled.

owning stock or other interests in the corporation. If Delaware perceived its interest in securing jurisdiction over corporate fiduciaries to be as great as Heitner suggests, we would expect it to have enacted a statute more clearly designed to protect that interest.

Moreover, even if Heitner's assessment of the importance of Delaware's interest is accepted, his argument fails to demonstrate that Delaware is a fair forum for this litigation. The interest appellee has identified may support the application of Delaware law to resolve any controversy over appellants' actions in their capacities as officers and directors. But we have rejected the argument that if a State's law can properly be applied to a dispute, its courts necessarily have jurisdiction over the parties to that dispute. "(The State) does not acquire . . . jurisdiction by being the 'center of gravity' of the controversy, or the most convenient location for litigation. The issue is personal jurisdiction, not choice of law. It is resolved in this case by considering the acts of the (appellants)." *Hanson v. Denckla.*

Appellee suggests that by accepting positions as officers or directors of a Delaware corporation, appellants performed the acts required by *Hanson v. Denckla.* He notes that Delaware law provides substantial benefits to corporate officers and directors, and that these benefits were at least in part the incentive for appellants to assume their positions. It is, he says, "only fair and just" to require appellants, in return for these benefits, to respond in the State of Delaware when they are accused of misusing their power.

But like Heitner's first argument, this line of reasoning establishes only that it is appropriate for Delaware law to govern the obligations of appellants to Greyhound and its stockholders. It does not demonstrate that appellants have "purposefully avail(ed themselves) of the privilege of conducting activities within the forum State," *Hanson v. Denckla*, in a way that would justify bringing them before a Delaware tribunal. Appellants have simply had nothing to do with the State of Delaware. Moreover, appellants had no reason to expect to be haled before a Delaware court. Delaware, unlike some States, has not enacted a statute that treats acceptance of a directorship as consent to jurisdiction in the State. And "(i)t strains reason . . . to suggest that anyone buying securities in a corporation formed in Delaware 'impliedly consents' to subject himself to Delaware's . . . jurisdiction on any cause of action." Appellants, who were not required to acquire interests in Greyhound in order to hold their positions, did not by acquiring those interests surrender their right to be brought to judgment only in States with which they had had "minimum contacts."

The Due Process Clause "does not contemplate that a state may make binding a judgment . . . against an individual or corporate defendant with which the state has no contacts, ties, or relations." *International Shoe Co. v. Washington.*

Delaware's assertion of jurisdiction over appellants in this case is inconsistent with that constitutional limitation on state power. The judgment of the Delaware Supreme Court must, therefore, be reversed.

It is so ordered.

MR. JUSTICE REHNQUIST took no part in the consideration or decision of this case. MR. JUSTICE POWELL, concurring.

I agree that the principles of *International Shoe Co. v. Washington,* should be extended to govern assertions of *in rem* as well as *in personam* jurisdiction in a state court. I also agree that neither the statutory presence of appellants' stock in Delaware nor their positions as directors and officers of a Delaware corporation can provide sufficient contacts to support the Delaware courts' assertion of jurisdiction in this case.

I would explicitly reserve judgment, however, on whether the ownership of some forms of property whose situs is indisputably and permanently located within a State may, without more, provide the contacts necessary to subject a defendant to jurisdiction within the State to the extent of the value of the property. In the case of real property, in particular, preservation of the common-law concept of *quasi in rem* jurisdiction arguably would avoid the uncertainty of the general *International Shoe* standard without significant cost to " 'traditional notions of fair play and substantial justice.' "

Subject to the foregoing reservation, I join the opinion of the Court.

MR. JUSTICE STEVENS, concurring in the judgment.

The Due Process Clause affords protection against "judgments without notice." *International Shoe Co. v. Washington.* Throughout our history the acceptable exercise of *in rem* and *quasi in rem* jurisdiction has included a procedure giving reasonable assurance that actual notice of the particular claim will be conveyed to the defendant. Thus, publication, notice by registered mail, or extraterritorial personal service has been an essential ingredient of any procedure that serves as a substitute for personal service within the jurisdiction.

The requirement of fair notice also, I believe, includes fair warning that a particular activity may subject a person to the jurisdiction of a foreign sovereign. If I visit another State, or acquire real estate or open a bank account in it, I knowingly assume some risk that the State will exercise its power over my property or my person while there. My contact with the State, though minimal, gives rise to predictable risks.

Perhaps the same consequences should flow from the purchase of stock of a corporation organized under the laws of a foreign nation, because to some limited extent one's property and affairs then become subject to the laws of the nation of domicile of the corporation. As a matter of international law, that suggestion might be acceptable because a foreign investment is sufficiently unusual to make it appropriate to require the investor to study the ramifications of his decision. But a purchase of securities in the domestic market is an entirely different matter.

One who purchases shares of stock on the open market can hardly be expected to know that he has thereby become subject to suit in a forum remote from his residence and unrelated to the transaction. As a practical matter, the Delaware sequestration statute creates an unacceptable risk of judgment without notice. Unlike the 49 other States, Delaware treats the place of incorporation as the situs of the stock, even though both the owner and the custodian of the shares are elsewhere. Moreover, Delaware denies the defendant the opportunity to defend the merits of the suit unless he subjects himself to the unlimited jurisdiction of the court. Thus, it coerces a defendant either to submit to personal jurisdiction in a forum which could not otherwise obtain such jurisdiction or to lose the securities which have been attached. If its procedure were upheld, Delaware would, in effect, impose a duty of inquiry on every purchaser of securities in the national market. For unless the purchaser ascertains both the State of incorporation of the company whose shares he is buying, and also the idiosyncrasies of its law, he may be assuming an unknown risk of litigation. I therefore agree with the Court that on the record before us no adequate basis for jurisdiction exists and that the Delaware statute is unconstitutional on its face.

How the Court's opinion may be applied in other contexts is not entirely clear to me. I agree with Mr. Justice Powell that it should not be read to invalidate *quasi in rem* jurisdiction where real estate is involved. I would also not read it as invalidating other long-accepted methods of acquiring jurisdiction over persons with adequate notice of both the particular controversy and the fact that their local activities might subject them to suit. My uncertainty as to the reach of the opinion, and my fear that it purports to decide a great deal more than is necessary to dispose of this case, persuade me merely to concur in the judgment.

MR. JUSTICE BRENNAN, concurring in part and dissenting in part.

I join Parts I–III of the Court's opinion. I fully agree that the minimum-contacts analysis developed in *International Shoe Co. v. Washington* represents a far more sensible construct for the exercise of state-court jurisdiction than the patchwork of legal and factual fictions that has been generated from the decision in *Pennoyer v. Neff*. It is precisely because the inquiry into minimum contacts is now of such overriding importance, however, that I must respectfully dissent from Part IV of the Court's opinion.

I

The primary teaching of Parts I–III of today's decision is that a State, in seeking to assert jurisdiction over a person located outside its borders, may only do so on the basis of minimum contacts among the parties, the contested transaction, and the forum State. The Delaware Supreme Court could not have made plainer, however, that its sequestration statute does not operate on this basis, but instead is strictly an embodiment of *quasi in rem* jurisdiction, a jurisdictional predicate no longer constitutionally viable.

This state-court ruling obviously comports with the understanding of the parties, for the issue of the existence of minimum contacts was never pleaded by appellee, made the subject of discovery, or ruled upon by the Delaware courts. These facts notwithstanding, the Court in Part IV reaches the minimum-contacts question and finds such contacts lacking as applied to appellants. Succinctly stated, once having properly and persuasively decided that the *quasi in rem* statute that Delaware admits to having enacted is invalid, the Court then proceeds to find that a minimum-contacts law that Delaware expressly denies having enacted also could not be constitutionally applied in this case.

In my view, a purer example of an advisory opinion is not to be found. True, appellants do not deny having received actual notice of the action in question. However, notice is but one ingredient of a proper assertion of state-court jurisdiction. The other is a statute authorizing the exercise of the State's judicial power along constitutionally permissible grounds which henceforth means minimum contacts. As of today, § 366 is not such a law.[1] Recognizing that today's decision fundamentally alters the relevant jurisdictional ground rules, I certainly would not want to rule out the possibility that Delaware's courts might decide that the legislature's overriding purpose of securing the personal appearance in state courts of defendants would best be served by reinterpreting its statute to permit state jurisdiction on the basis of constitutionally permissible contacts rather than stock ownership. Were the state courts to take this step, it would then become necessary to address the question of whether minimum contacts exist here. But in the present posture of this case, the Court's decision of this important issue is purely an abstract ruling.

My concern with the inappropriateness of the Court's action is highlighted by two other considerations. First, an inquiry into minimum contacts inevitably is highly dependent on creating a proper factual foundation detailing the contacts between the forum State and the controversy in question. Because neither the plaintiff-appellee nor the state courts viewed such an inquiry as germane in this instance, the Court today is unable to draw upon a proper factual record in reaching its conclusion; moreover, its disposition denies appellee the normal opportunity to seek discovery on the contacts issue. Second, it must be remembered that the Court's ruling is a constitutional one and necessarily will affect the reach of the jurisdictional laws of all 50 States. Ordinarily this would counsel restraint in constitutional pronouncements. Certainly it should have cautioned the Court against reaching out to decide a question that,

---

1. Indeed, the Court's decision to proceed to the minimum-contacts issue treats Delaware's sequestration statute as if it were the equivalent of Rhode Island's long-arm law, which specifically authorizes its courts to assume jurisdiction to the limit permitted by the Constitution, R.I. Gen. Laws Ann. § 9–5–33, thereby necessitating judicial consideration of the frontiers of minimum contacts in every case arising under that statute.

as here, has yet to emerge from the state courts ripened for review on the federal issue.

II

Nonetheless, because the Court rules on the minimum-contacts question, I feel impelled to express my view. While evidence derived through discovery might satisfy me that minimum contacts are lacking in a given case, I am convinced that as a general rule a state forum has jurisdiction to adjudicate a shareholder derivative action centering on the conduct and policies of the directors and officers of a corporation chartered by that State. Unlike the Court, I therefore would not foreclose Delaware from asserting jurisdiction over appellants were it persuaded to do so on the basis of minimum contacts.

It is well settled that a derivative lawsuit as presented here does not inure primarily to the benefit of the named plaintiff. Rather, the primary beneficiaries are the corporation and its owners, the shareholders. "The cause of action which such a plaintiff brings before the court is not his own but the corporation's. . . . Such a plaintiff often may represent an important public and stockholder interest in bringing faithless managers to book."

Viewed in this light, the chartering State has an unusually powerful interest in insuring the availability of a convenient forum for litigating claims involving a possible multiplicity of defendant fiduciaries and for vindicating the State's substantive policies regarding the management of its domestic corporations. I believe that our cases fairly establish that the States's valid substantive interests are important considerations in assessing whether it constitutionally may claim jurisdiction over a given cause of action.

In this instance, Delaware can point to at least three interrelated public policies that are furthered by its assertion of jurisdiction. First, the State has a substantial interest in providing restitution for its local corporations that allegedly have been victimized by fiduciary misconduct, even if the managerial decisions occurred outside the State. The importance of this general state interest in assuring restitution for its own residents previously found expression in cases that went outside the then-prevailing due process framework to authorize state-court jurisdiction over nonresident motorists who injure others within the State. *Hess v. Pawloski.* More recently, it has led States to seek and to acquire jurisdiction over nonresident tortfeasors whose purely out-of-state activities produce domestic consequences. *E.g., Gray v. American Radiator & Standard Sanitary Corp.* Second, state courts have legitimately read their jurisdiction expansively when a cause of action centers in an area in which the forum State possesses a manifest regulatory interest. *E.g., McGee v. International Life Ins. Co.* (insurance regulation). Only this Term we reiterated that the conduct of corporate fiduciaries is just such a matter in which the policies and interests of the domestic forum are ordinarily presumed to be paramount. Finally, a State like Delaware has a recognized interest in affording a convenient forum for supervising and overseeing the affairs of an entity that is purely the creation of that State's law. For example, even following our decision in *International Shoe*, New York courts were permitted to exercise complete judicial authority over nonresident beneficiaries of a trust created under state law, even though, unlike appellants here, the beneficiaries personally entered into no association whatsoever with New York. I, of course, am not suggesting that Delaware's varied interests would justify its acceptance of jurisdiction over any transaction touching upon the affairs of its domestic corporations. But a derivative action which raises allegations of abuses of the basic management of an institution whose existence is created by the State and whose powers and duties are defined by state law fundamentally implicates the public policies of that forum.

To be sure, the Court is not blind to these considerations. It notes that the State's interests "may support the application of Delaware law to resolve any controversy over appellants' actions in their capacities as officers and directors." But this, the Court argues, pertains to choice of law, not jurisdiction. I recognize that the jurisdictional and choice-of-law inquiries are not identical. *Hanson v. Denckla.* But I would not compartmentalize thinking in this area quite so rigidly as it seems to me the Court does today, for both inquiries "are often closely related and to a substantial degree depend upon similar considerations." In either case an important linchpin is the extent of contacts between the controversy, the parties, and the forum State. While constitutional limitations on the choice of law are by no means settled, important considerations certainly include the expectancies of the parties and the fairness of governing the defendants' acts and behavior by rules of conduct created by a given jurisdiction. These same factors bear upon the propriety of a State's exercising jurisdiction over a legal dispute. At the minimum, the decision that it is fair to bind a defendant by a State's laws and rules should prove to be highly relevant to the fairness of permitting that same State to accept jurisdiction for adjudicating the controversy.

Furthermore, I believe that practical considerations argue in favor of seeking to bridge the distance between the choice-of-law and jurisdictional inquiries. Even when a court would apply the law of a different forum, as a general rule it will feel less knowledgeable and comfortable in interpretation, and less interested in fostering the policies of that foreign jurisdiction, than would the courts established by the State that provides the applicable law. Obviously, such choice-of-law problems cannot entirely be avoided in a diverse legal system such as our own. Nonetheless, when a suitor seeks to lodge a suit in a State with a substantial interest in seeing its own law applied to the transaction in question, we could wisely act to minimize conflicts, confusion, and uncertainty by adopting a liberal view of jurisdiction, unless considerations of fairness or efficiency strongly point in the opposite direction.

This case is not one where, in my judgment, this preference for jurisdiction is adequately answered. Certainly nothing said by the Court persuades me that it would be unfair to subject appellants to suit in Delaware. The fact that the record does not reveal whether they "set foot" or committed "act(s) related to (the) cause of action" in Delaware, is not decisive, for jurisdiction can be based strictly on out-of-state acts having foreseeable effects in the forum State. *E.g., McGee v. International Life Ins. Co; Gray v. American Radiator & Standard Sanitary Corp.* I have little difficulty in applying this principle to nonresident fiduciaries whose alleged breaches of trust are said to have substantial damaging effect on the financial posture of a resident corporation. Further, I cannot understand how the existence of minimum contacts in a constitutional sense is at all affected by Delaware's failure statutorily to express an interest in controlling corporate fiduciaries. To me this simply demonstrates that Delaware did not elect to assert jurisdiction to the extent the Constitution would allow. Nor would I view as controlling or even especially meaningful Delaware's failure to exact from appellants their consent to be sued. Once we have rejected the jurisdictional framework created in *Pennoyer v. Neff,* I see no reason to rest jurisdiction on a fictional outgrowth of that system such as the existence of a consent statute, expressed or implied.[6]

I, therefore, would approach the minimum-contacts analysis differently than does the Court. Crucial to me is the fact that appellants voluntarily associated themselves with the State of Delaware, "invoking the benefits and protections of its laws," *Hanson v. Denckla; International Shoe Co. v. Washington,* by entering into a long-term and fragile relationship with one of its domestic corporations. They thereby elected to assume powers and to undertake responsibilities wholly derived from that State's rules and regulations, and to become eligible for those benefits that Delaware law makes available to its corporations' officials. While it is possible that countervailing issues of judicial efficiency and the like might clearly favor a different forum, they do not appear on the meager record before us; and, of course, we are concerned solely with "minimum" contacts, not the "best" contacts. I thus do not believe that it is unfair to insist that appellants make themselves available to suit in a competent forum that Delaware might create for vindication of its important public policies directly pertaining to appellants' fiduciary associations with the State.

* * *

---

6. Admittedly, when one consents to suit in a forum, his expectation is enhanced that he may be haled into that State's courts. To this extent, I agree that consent may have bearing on the fairness of accepting jurisdiction. But whatever is the degree of personal expectation that is necessary to warrant jurisdiction should not depend on the formality of establishing a consent law. Indeed, if one's expectations are to carry such weight, then appellants here might be fairly charged with the understanding that Delaware would decide to protect its substantial interests through its own courts, for they certainly realized that in the past the sequestration law has been employed primarily as a means of securing the appearance of corporate officials in the State's courts. Even in the absence of such a statute, however, the close and special association between a state corporation and its managers should apprise the latter that the State may seek to offer a convenient forum for addressing claims of fiduciary breach of trust.

III. CHOOSING THE FORUM (PERSONAL JURISDICTION)

A. AFFILIATING CIRCUMSTANCES

WORLD-WIDE VOLKSWAGEN CORPORATION v. WOODSON

444 U.S. 286 (1980)

MR. JUSTICE WHITE delivered the opinion of the Court.

The issue before us is whether, consistently with the Due Process Clause of the Fourteenth Amendment, an Oklahoma court may exercise *in personam* jurisdiction over a nonresident automobile retailer and its wholesale distributor in a products-liability action, when the defendants' only connection with Oklahoma is the fact that an automobile sold in New York to New York residents became involved in an accident in Oklahoma.

Respondents Harry and Kay Robinson purchased a new Audi automobile from petitioner Seaway Volkswagen, Inc. (Seaway), in Massena, N. Y., in 1976. The following year the Robinson family, who resided in New York, left that State for a new home in Arizona. As they passed through the State of Oklahoma, another car struck their Audi in the rear, causing a fire which severely burned Kay Robinson and her two children.

The Robinsons subsequently brought a products-liability action in the District Court for Creek County, Okla., claiming that their injuries resulted from defective design and placement of the Audi's gas tank and fuel system. They joined as defendants the automobile's manufacturer, Audi NSU Auto Union Aktiengesellschaft (Audi); its importer Volkswagen of America, Inc. (Volkswagen); its regional distributor, petitioner World–Wide Volkswagen Corp. (World–Wide); and its retail dealer, petitioner Seaway. Seaway and World–Wide entered special appearances,[3] claiming that Oklahoma's exercise of jurisdiction over them would offend the limitations on the State's jurisdiction imposed by the Due Process Clause of the Fourteenth Amendment.

The facts presented to the District Court showed that World–Wide is incorporated and has its business office in New York. It distributes vehicles, parts, and accessories, under contract with Volkswagen, to retail dealers in New York, New Jersey, and Connecticut. Seaway, one of these retail dealers, is incorporated and has its place of business in New York. Insofar as the record reveals, Seaway and World–Wide are fully independent corporations whose relations with each other and with Volkswagen and Audi are contractual only. Respondents adduced no evidence that either World–Wide or Seaway does any business in Oklahoma, ships or sells any products to or in that State, has an agent to receive process

---

3. Volkswagen also entered a special appearance in the District Court, but unlike World–Wide and Seaway did not seek review in the Supreme Court of Oklahoma and is not a petitioner here. Both Volkswagen and Audi remain as defendants in the litigation pending before the District Court in Oklahoma.

there, or purchases advertisements in any media calculated to reach Oklahoma. In fact, as respondents' counsel conceded at oral argument, there was no showing that any automobile sold by World–Wide or Seaway has ever entered Oklahoma with the single exception of the vehicle involved in the present case.

Despite the apparent paucity of contacts between petitioners and Oklahoma, the District Court rejected their constitutional claim and reaffirmed that ruling in denying petitioners' motion for reconsideration. Petitioners then sought a writ of prohibition in the Supreme Court of Oklahoma to restrain the District Judge, respondent Charles S. Woodson, from exercising *in personam* jurisdiction over them. They renewed their contention that, because they had no "minimal contacts," with the State of Oklahoma, the actions of the District Judge were in violation of their rights under the Due Process Clause.

The Supreme Court of Oklahoma denied the writ, 585 P.2d 351 (1978), holding that personal jurisdiction over petitioners was authorized by Oklahoma's "long-arm" statute.[7] Although the court noted that the proper approach was to test jurisdiction against both statutory and constitutional standards, its analysis did not distinguish these questions, probably because [Oklahoma's long-arm statute] has been interpreted as conferring jurisdiction to the limits permitted by the United States Constitution. The court's rationale was contained in the following paragraph:

> In the case before us, the product being sold and distributed by the petitioners is by its very design and purpose so mobile that petitioners can foresee its possible use in Oklahoma. This is especially true of the distributor, who has the exclusive right to distribute such automobile in New York, New Jersey and Connecticut. The evidence presented below demonstrated that goods sold and distributed by the petitioners were used in the State of Oklahoma, and under the facts we believe it reasonable to infer, given the retail value of the automobile, that the petitioners derive substantial income from automobiles which from time to time are used in the State of Oklahoma. This being the case, we hold that under the facts presented, the trial court was justified in concluding that the petitioners derive substantial revenue from goods used or consumed in this State.

We granted certiorari, to consider an important constitutional question with respect to state-court jurisdiction and to resolve a conflict between the Supreme Court of Oklahoma and the highest courts of at least four other States. We reverse.

---

7. This subsection provides:

A court may exercise personal jurisdiction over a person, who acts directly or by an agent, as to a cause of action or claim for relief arising from the person's ... causing tortious injury in this state by an act or omission outside this state if he regularly does or solicits business or engages in any other persistent course of conduct, or derives substantial revenue from goods used or consumed or services rendered, in this state....

The State Supreme Court rejected jurisdiction based on [the long-arm statute], which authorizes jurisdiction over any person "causing tortious injury in this state by an act or omission in this state." Something in addition to the infliction of tortious injury was required.

II

The Due Process Clause of the Fourteenth Amendment limits the power of a state court to render a valid personal judgment against a nonresident defendant. *Kulko v. California Superior Court*. A judgment rendered in violation of due process is void in the rendering State and is not entitled to full faith and credit elsewhere. *Pennoyer v. Neff*. Due process requires that the defendant be given adequate notice of the suit, *Mullane v. Central Hanover Trust Co.*, and be subject to the personal jurisdiction of the court, *International Shoe Co. v. Washington*. In the present case, it is not contended that notice was inadequate; the only question is whether these particular petitioners were subject to the jurisdiction of the Oklahoma courts.

As has long been settled, and as we reaffirm today, a state court may exercise personal jurisdiction over a nonresident defendant only so long as there exist "minimum contacts" between the defendant and the forum State. *International Shoe Co. v. Washington*. The concept of minimum contacts, in turn, can be seen to perform two related, but distinguishable, functions. It protects the defendant against the burdens of litigating in a distant or inconvenient forum. And it acts to ensure that the States through their courts, do not reach out beyond the limits imposed on them by their status as coequal sovereigns in a federal system.

The protection against inconvenient litigation is typically described in terms of "reasonableness" or "fairness." We have said that the defendant's contacts with the forum State must be such that maintenance of the suit "does not offend 'traditional notions of fair play and substantial justice.'" *International Shoe Co. v. Washington,* quoting *Milliken v. Meyer*. The relationship between the defendant and the forum must be such that it is "reasonable ... to require the corporation to defend the particular suit which is brought there." Implicit in this emphasis on reasonableness is the understanding that the burden on the defendant, while always a primary concern, will in an appropriate case be considered in light of other relevant factors, including the forum State's interest in adjudicating the dispute, *see McGee v. International Life Ins. Co.*; the plaintiff's interest in obtaining convenient and effective relief, *see Kulko v. California Superior Court,* at least when that interest is not adequately protected by the plaintiff's power to choose the forum, *cf. Shaffer v. Heitner*; the interstate judicial system's interest in obtaining the most efficient resolution of controversies; and the shared interest of the several States in furthering fundamental substantive social policies, *see Kulko v. California Superior Court*.

The limits imposed on state jurisdiction by the Due Process Clause, in its role as a guarantor against inconvenient litigation, have been substantially relaxed over the years. As we noted in *McGee v. International Life Ins. Co.,* this trend is largely attributable to a fundamental transformation in the American economy:

Today many commercial transactions touch two or more States and may involve parties separated by the full continent. With this increasing nationalization of commerce has come a great increase in the amount of business conducted by mail across state lines. At the same time modern transportation and communication have made it much less burdensome for a party sued to defend himself in a State where he engages in economic activity.

The historical developments noted in *McGee*, of course, have only accelerated in the generation since that case was decided.

Nevertheless, we have never accepted the proposition that state lines are irrelevant for jurisdictional purposes, nor could we, and remain faithful to the principles of interstate federalism embodied in the Constitution. The economic interdependence of the States was foreseen and desired by the Framers. In the Commerce Clause, they provided that the Nation was to be a common market, a "free trade unit" in which the States are debarred from acting as separable economic entities. But the Framers also intended that the States retain many essential attributes of sovereignty, including, in particular, the sovereign power to try causes in their courts. The sovereignty of each State, in turn, implied a limitation on the sovereignty of all of its sister States—a limitation express or implicit in both the original scheme of the Constitution and the Fourteenth Amendment.

Hence, even while abandoning the shibboleth that "[t]he authority of every tribunal is necessarily restricted by the territorial limits of the State in which it is established," *Pennoyer v. Neff*, we emphasized that the reasonableness of asserting jurisdiction over the defendant must be assessed "in the context of our federal system of government," *International Shoe Co. v. Washington*, and stressed that the Due Process Clause ensures not only fairness, but also the "orderly administration of the laws." As we noted in *Hanson v. Denckla*:

> "As technological progress has increased the flow of commerce between the States, the need for jurisdiction over nonresidents has undergone a similar increase. At the same time, progress in communications and transportation has made the defense of a suit in a foreign tribunal less burdensome. In response to these changes, the requirements for personal jurisdiction over nonresidents have evolved from the rigid rule of *Pennoyer v. Neff* to the flexible standard of *International Shoe Co. v. Washington*. But it is a mistake to assume that this trend heralds the eventual demise of all restrictions on the personal jurisdiction of state courts. Those restrictions are more than a guarantee of immunity from inconvenient or distant litigation. They are a consequence of territorial limitations on the power of the respective States."

Thus, the Due Process Clause "does not contemplate that a state may make binding a judgment *in personam* against an individual or corporate defendant with which the state has no contacts, ties, or relations."

International Shoe Co. v. Washington. Even if the defendant would suffer minimal or no inconvenience from being forced to litigate before the tribunals of another State; even if the forum State has a strong interest in applying its law to the controversy; even if the forum State is the most convenient location for litigation, the Due Process Clause, acting as an instrument of interstate federalism, may sometimes act to divest the State of its power to render a valid judgment. *Hanson v. Denckla.*

<h1 style="text-align:center">III</h1>

Applying these principles to the case at hand, we find in the record before us a total absence of those affiliating circumstances that are a necessary predicate to any exercise of state-court jurisdiction. Petitioners carry on no activity whatsoever in Oklahoma. They close no sales and perform no services there. They avail themselves of none of the privileges and benefits of Oklahoma law. They solicit no business there either through salespersons or through advertising reasonably calculated to reach the State. Nor does the record show that they regularly sell cars at wholesale or retail to Oklahoma customers or residents or that they indirectly, through others, serve or seek to serve the Oklahoma market. In short, respondents seek to base jurisdiction on one, isolated occurrence and whatever inferences can be drawn therefrom: the fortuitous circumstance that a single Audi automobile, sold in New York to New York residents, happened to suffer an accident while passing through Oklahoma.

It is argued, however, that because an automobile is mobile by its very design and purpose it was "foreseeable" that the Robinsons' Audi would cause injury in Oklahoma. Yet "foreseeability" alone has never been a sufficient benchmark for personal jurisdiction under the Due Process Clause. In *Hanson v. Denckla,* it was no doubt foreseeable that the settlor of a Delaware trust would subsequently move to Florida and seek to exercise a power of appointment there; yet we held that Florida courts could not constitutionally exercise jurisdiction over a Delaware trustee that had no other contacts with the forum State. In *Kulko v. California Superior Court*, it was surely "foreseeable" that a divorced wife would move to California from New York, the domicile of the marriage, and that a minor daughter would live with the mother. Yet we held that California could not exercise jurisdiction in a child-support action over the former husband who had remained in New York.

If foreseeability were the criterion, a local California tire retailer could be forced to defend in Pennsylvania when a blowout occurs there; a Wisconsin seller of a defective automobile jack could be haled before a distant court for damage caused in New Jersey; or a Florida soft-drink concessionaire could be summoned to Alaska to account for injuries happening there. Every seller of chattels would in effect appoint the chattel his agent for service of process. His amenability to suit would travel with the chattel. We recently abandoned the outworn rule of *Harris v. Balk,* that the interest of a creditor in a debt could be extinguished or otherwise affected by any State having transitory jurisdiction over the debtor. *Shaffer v. Heitner.* Having inferred the mechanical rule that a creditor's amenability to a *quasi in rem* action travels with his debtor, we are unwilling to endorse an analogous principle in the present case.[11]

This is not to say, of course, that foreseeability is wholly irrelevant. But the foreseeability that is critical to due process analysis is not the mere likelihood that a product will find its way into the forum State. Rather, it is that the defendant's conduct and connection with the forum State are such that he should reasonably anticipate being haled into court there. *See Kulko v. California Superior Court*; *Shaffer v. Heitner.* The Due Process Clause, by ensuring the "orderly administration of the laws," *International Shoe Co. v. Washington*, gives a degree of predictability to the legal system that allows potential defendants to structure their primary conduct with some minimum assurance as to where that conduct will and will not render them liable to suit.

When a corporation "purposefully avails itself of the privilege of conducting activities within the forum State," *Hanson v. Denckla*, it has clear notice that it is subject to suit there, and can act to alleviate the risk of burdensome litigation by procuring insurance, passing the expected costs on to customers, or, if the risks are too great, severing its connection with the State. Hence if the sale of a product of a manufacturer or distributor such as Audi or Volkswagen is not simply an isolated occurrence, but arises from the efforts of the manufacturer or distributor to serve directly or indirectly, the market for its product in other States, it is not unreasonable to subject it to suit in one of those States if its allegedly defective merchandise has there been the source of injury to its owner or to others. The forum State does not exceed its powers under the Due Process Clause if it asserts personal jurisdiction over a corporation that delivers its products into the stream of commerce with the expectation that they will be purchased by consumers in the forum State. *Cf. Gray v. American Radiator & Standard Sanitary Corp.*

But there is no such or similar basis for Oklahoma jurisdiction over World–Wide or Seaway in this case. Seaway's sales are made in Massena, N. Y. World–Wide's market, although substantially larger, is limited to dealers in New York, New Jersey, and Connecticut. There is no evidence of record that any automobiles distributed by World–Wide are sold to retail customers outside this tristate area. It is foreseeable that the purchasers of automobiles sold by World–Wide and Seaway may take them to Oklahoma. But the mere "unilateral activity of those who claim some

---

11. Respondents' counsel at oral argument sought to limit the reach of the foreseeability standard by suggesting that there is something unique about automobiles. It is true that automobiles are uniquely mobile, that they did play a crucial role in the expansion of personal jurisdiction through the fiction of implied consent, *e.g., Hess v. Pawloski*, and that some of the cases have treated the automobile as a "dangerous instrumentality." But today, under the regime of *International Shoe*, we see no difference for jurisdictional purposes between an automobile and any other chattel. The "dangerous instrumentality" concept apparently was never used to support personal jurisdiction; and to the extent it has relevance today it bears not on jurisdiction but on the possible desirability of imposing substantive principles of tort law such as strict liability.

relationship with a nonresident defendant cannot satisfy the requirement of contact with the forum State." *Hanson v. Denckla.*

In a variant on the previous argument, it is contended that jurisdiction can be supported by the fact that petitioners earn substantial revenue from goods used in Oklahoma. The Oklahoma Supreme Court so found, drawing the inference that because one automobile sold by petitioners had been used in Oklahoma, others might have been used there also. While this inference seems less than compelling on the facts of the instant case, we need not question the court's factual findings in order to reject its reasoning.

This argument seems to make the point that the purchase of automobiles in New York, from which the petitioners earn substantial revenue, would not occur *but for* the fact that the automobiles are capable of use in distant States like Oklahoma. Respondents observe that the very purpose of an automobile is to travel, and that travel of automobiles sold by petitioners is facilitated by an extensive chain of Volkswagen service centers throughout the country, including some in Oklahoma.[12] However, financial benefits accruing to the defendant from a collateral relation to the forum State will not support jurisdiction if they do not stem from a constitutionally cognizable contact with that State. *See Kulko v. California Superior Court.* In our view, whatever marginal revenues petitioners may receive by virtue of the fact that their products are capable of use in Oklahoma is far too attenuated a contact to justify that State's exercise of *in personam* jurisdiction over them.

Because we find that petitioners have no "contacts, ties, or relations" with the State of Oklahoma, *International Shoe Co. v. Washington,* the judgment of the Supreme Court of Oklahoma is

Reversed.

MR. JUSTICE MARSHALL, with whom MR. JUSTICE BLACKMUN joins, dissenting.

For over 30 years the standard by which to measure the constitutionally permissible reach of state-court jurisdiction has been well established:

> "[D]ue process requires only that in order to subject a defendant to a judgment *in personam,* if he be not present within the territory of the forum, he have certain minimum contacts with it such that the maintenance of the suit does not offend 'traditional notions of fair play and substantial justice.'" *International Shoe, Co. v. Washington,* quoting *Milliken v. Meyer.*

The corollary, that the Due Process Clause forbids the assertion of jurisdiction over a defendant "with which the state has no contacts, ties, or relations," is equally clear. The concepts of fairness and substantial justice as applied to an evaluation of "the quality and nature of the [defendant's] activity," are not readily susceptible of further definition,

---

12.   As we have noted, petitioners earn no direct revenues from these service centers.

however, and it is not surprising that the constitutional standard is easier to state than to apply.

This is a difficult case, and reasonable minds may differ as to whether respondents have alleged a sufficient "relationship among the defendant[s], the forum, and the litigation," *Shaffer v. Heitner*, to satisfy the requirements of *International Shoe*. I am concerned, however, that the majority has reached its result by taking an unnecessarily narrow view of petitioners' forum-related conduct. The majority asserts that "respondents seek to base jurisdiction on one, isolated occurrence and whatever inferences can be drawn therefrom: the fortuitous circumstance that a single Audi automobile, sold in New York to New York residents, happened to suffer an accident while passing through Oklahoma." If that were the case, I would readily agree that the minimum contacts necessary to sustain jurisdiction are not present. But the basis for the assertion of jurisdiction is not the happenstance that an individual over whom petitioner had no control made a unilateral decision to take a chattel with him to a distant State. Rather, jurisdiction is premised on the deliberate and purposeful actions of the defendants themselves in choosing to become part of a nationwide, indeed a global, network for marketing and servicing automobiles.

Petitioners are sellers of a product whose utility derives from its mobility. The unique importance of the automobile in today's society, which is discussed in Mr. Justice Blackmun's dissenting opinion, needs no further elaboration. Petitioners know that their customers buy cars not only to make short trips, but also to travel long distances. In fact, the nationwide service network with which they are affiliated was designed to facilitate and encourage such travel. Seaway would be unlikely to sell many cars if authorized service were available only in Massena, N. Y. Moreover, local dealers normally derive a substantial portion of their revenues from their service operations and thereby obtain a further economic benefit from the opportunity to service cars which were sold in other States. It is apparent that petitioners have not attempted to minimize the chance that their activities will have effects in other States; on the contrary, they have chosen to do business in a way that increases that chance, because it is to their economic advantage to do so.

To be sure, petitioners could not know in advance that this particular automobile would be driven to Oklahoma. They must have anticipated, however, that a substantial portion of the cars they sold would travel out of New York. Seaway, a local dealer in the second most populous State, and World–Wide one of only seven regional Audi distributors in the entire country, would scarcely have been surprised to learn that a car sold by them had been driven in Oklahoma on Interstate 44, a heavily traveled transcontinental highway. In the case of the distributor, in particular, the probability that some of the cars it sells will be driven in every one of the contiguous States must amount to a virtual certainty. This knowledge should alert a reasonable businessman to the likelihood that a defect in the product might manifest itself in the forum State-not because of some unpredictable, aberrant, unilateral action by a single buyer, but in the normal course of the operation of the vehicles for their intended purpose.

It is misleading for the majority to characterize the argument in favor of jurisdiction as one of " 'foreseeability' alone." As economic entities petitioners reach out from New York, knowingly causing effects in other States and receiving economic advantage both from the ability to cause such effects themselves and from the activities of dealers and distributors in other States. While they did not receive revenue from making direct sales in Oklahoma, they intentionally became part of an interstate economic network, which included dealerships in Oklahoma, for pecuniary gain. In light of this purposeful conduct I do not believe it can be said that petitioners "had no reason to expect to be haled before a[n Oklahoma] court." *Shaffer v. Heitner*; *Kulko v. California Superior Court*.

The majority apparently acknowledges that if a product is purchased in the forum State by a consumer, that State may assert jurisdiction over everyone in the chain of distribution. With this I agree. But I cannot agree that jurisdiction is necessarily lacking if the product enters the State not through the channels of distribution but in the course of its intended use by the consumer. We have recognized the role played by the automobile in the expansion of our notions of personal jurisdiction. *See Shaffer v. Heitner*; *Hess v. Pawloski*. Unlike most other chattels, which may find their way into States far from where they were purchased because their owner takes them there, the intended use of the automobile is precisely as a means of traveling from one place to another. In such a case, it is highly artificial to restrict the concept of the "stream of commerce" to the chain of distribution from the manufacturer to the ultimate consumer.

I sympathize with the majority's concern that the persons ought to be able to structure their conduct so as not to be subject to suit in distant forums. But that may not always be possible. Some activities by their very nature may foreclose the option of conducting them in such a way as to avoid subjecting oneself to jurisdiction in multiple forums. This is by no means to say that all sellers of automobiles should be subject to suit everywhere; but a distributor of automobiles to a multistate market and a local automobile dealer who makes himself part of a nationwide network of dealerships can fairly expect that the cars they sell may cause injury in distant States and that they may be called on to defend a resulting lawsuit there.

In light of the quality and nature of petitioners' activity, the majority's reliance on *Kulko v. California Superior Court, supra,* is misplaced. *Kulko* involved the assertion of state-court jurisdiction over a nonresident individual in connection with an action to modify his child custody rights and support obligations. His only contact with the forum State was that he gave his minor child permission to live there with her mother. In holding that exercise of jurisdiction violated the Due Process Clause, we emphasized that the cause of action as well as the defendant's actions in relation to the forum State arose "*not from the defendant's commercial* *transactions in interstate commerce*, but rather from his personal, domestic relations," contrasting Kulko's actions with those of the insurance company in *McGee v. International Life Ins. Co.*, which were undertaken for commercial benefit.*

Manifestly, the "quality and nature" of commercial activity is different, for purposes of the *International Shoe* test, from actions from which a defendant obtains no economic advantage. Commercial activity is more likely to cause effects in a larger sphere, and the actor derives an economic benefit from the activity that makes it fair to require him to answer for his conduct where its effects are felt. The profits may be used to pay the costs of suit, and knowing that the activity is likely to have effects in other States the defendant can readily insure against the costs of those effects, thereby sparing himself much of the inconvenience of defending in a distant forum.

Of course, the Constitution forbids the exercise of jurisdiction if the defendant had no judicially cognizable contacts with the forum. But as the majority acknowledges, if such contacts are present the jurisdictional inquiry requires a balancing of various interests and policies. I believe such contacts are to be found here and that, considering all of the interests and policies at stake, requiring petitioners to defend this action in Oklahoma is not beyond the bounds of the Constitution. Accordingly, I dissent.

MR. JUSTICE BLACKMUN, dissenting.

I confess that I am somewhat puzzled why the plaintiffs in this litigation are so insistent that the regional distributor and the retail dealer, the petitioners here, who handled the ill-fated Audi automobile involved in this litigation, be named defendants. It would appear that the manufacturer and the importer, whose subjectability to Oklahoma jurisdiction is not challenged before this Court, ought not to be judgment-proof. It may, of course, ultimately amount to a contest between insurance companies that, once begun, is not easily brought to a termination. Having made this much of an observation, I pursue it no further.

For me, a critical factor in the disposition of the litigation is the nature of the instrumentality under consideration. It has been said that we are a nation on wheels. What we are concerned with here is the automobile and its peripatetic character. One need only examine our national network of interstate highways, or make an appearance on one of them, or observe the variety of license plates present not only on those highways but in any metropolitan area, to realize that any automobile is likely to wander far from its place of licensure or from its place of distribution and retail sale. Miles per gallon on the highway (as well as in the city) and mileage per tankful are familiar allegations in manufacturers' advertisements today. To expect that any new automobile will remain in the vicinity of its retail sale—like the 1914 electric driven car by the

---

* Similarly, I believe the Court in *Hanson v. Denckla*, was influenced by the fact that trust administration has traditionally been considered a peculiarly local activity.

proverbial "little old lady"—is to blink at reality. The automobile is intended for distance as well as for transportation within a limited area.

It therefore seems to me not unreasonable—and certainly not unconstitutional and beyond the reach of the principles laid down in *International Shoe Co. v. Washington*, and its progeny—to uphold Oklahoma jurisdiction over this New York distributor and this New York dealer when the accident happened in Oklahoma. I see nothing more unfair for them than for the manufacturer and the importer. All are in the business of providing vehicles that spread out over the highways of our several States. It is not too much to anticipate at the time of distribution and at the time of retail sale that this Audi would be in Oklahoma. Moreover, in assessing "minimum contacts," foreseeable use in another State seems to me to be little different from foreseeable resale in another State. Yet the Court declares this distinction determinative.

Mr. Justice Brennan points out in his dissent that an automobile dealer derives substantial benefits from States other than its own. The same is true of the regional distributor. Oklahoma does its best to provide safe roads. Its police investigate accidents. It regulates driving within the State. It provides aid to the victim and thereby, it is hoped, lessens damages. Accident reports are prepared and made available. All this contributes to and enhances the business of those engaged professionally in the distribution and sale of automobiles. All this also may benefit defendants in the very lawsuits over which the State asserts jurisdiction.

My position need not now take me beyond the automobile and the professional who does business by way of distributing and retailing automobiles. Cases concerning other instrumentalities will be dealt with as they arise and in their own contexts.

I would affirm the judgment of the Supreme Court of Oklahoma. Because the Court reverses that judgment, it will now be about parsing every variant in the myriad of motor vehicles fact situations that present themselves. Some will justify jurisdiction and others will not. All will depend on the "contact" that the Court sees fit to perceive in the individual case.

* * *

MR. JUSTICE BRENNAN, dissenting.

The Court holds that the Due Process Clause of the Fourteenth Amendment bars the States from asserting jurisdiction over the defendants in these two cases. In each case the Court so decides because it fails to find the "minimum contacts" that have been required since *International Shoe Co.* Because I believe that the Court reads *International Shoe* and its progeny too narrowly, and because I believe that the standards enunciated by those cases may already be obsolete as constitutional boundaries, I dissent.

I

The Court's opinions focus tightly on the existence of contacts between the forum and the defendant. In so doing, they accord too little weight to the strength of the forum State's interest in the case and fail to explore whether there would be any actual inconvenience to the defendant. The essential inquiry in locating the constitutional limits on state-court jurisdiction over absent defendants is whether the particular exercise of jurisdiction offends " 'traditional notions of fair play and substantial justice.' " *International Shoe*. The clear focus in *International Shoe* was on fairness and reasonableness. *Kulko*. The Court specifically declined to establish a mechanical test based on the quantum of contacts between a State and the defendant:

> Whether due process is satisfied must depend rather upon the quality and nature of the activity *in relation to the fair and orderly administration of the laws which it was the purpose of the due process clause to insure*. That clause does not contemplate that a state may make binding a judgment *in personam* against an individual or corporate defendant with which the state has *no* contacts, ties, or relations."

The existence of contacts, so long as there were some, was merely one way of giving content to the determination of fairness and reasonableness.

Surely *International Shoe* contemplated that the significance of the contacts necessary to support jurisdiction would diminish if some other consideration helped establish that jurisdiction would be fair and reasonable. The interests of the State and other parties in proceeding with the case in a particular forum are such considerations. *McGee*, for instance, accorded great importance to a State's "manifest interest in providing effective means of redress" for its citizens. See also *Kulko*; *Shaffer*.

Another consideration is the actual burden a defendant must bear in defending the suit in the forum. *McGee*. Because lesser burdens reduce the unfairness to the defendant, jurisdiction may be justified despite less significant contacts. The burden, of course, must be of constitutional dimension. Due process limits on jurisdiction do not protect a defendant from all inconvenience of travel, *McGee,* and it would not be sensible to make the constitutional rule turn solely on the number of miles the defendant must travel to the courtroom. Instead, the constitutionally significant "burden" to be analyzed relates to the mobility of the defendant's defense. For instance, if having to travel to a foreign forum would hamper the defense because witnesses or evidence or the defendant himself were immobile, or if there were a disproportionately large number of witnesses or amount of evidence that would have to be transported at the defendant's expense, or if being away from home for the duration of the trial would work some special hardship on the defendant, then the Constitution would require special consideration for the defendant's interests.

That considerations other than contacts between the forum and the defendant are relevant necessarily means that the Constitution does not require that trial be held in the State which has the "best contacts" with the defendant. See *Shaffer* (Brennan, J., dissenting). The defendant has no constitutional entitlement to the best forum or, for that matter, to any particular forum. Under even the most restrictive view of *International Shoe*, several States could have jurisdiction over a particular cause of action. We need only determine whether the forum States in these cases satisfy the constitutional minimum.

II

... I would find that the forum State has an interest in permitting the litigation to go forward, the litigation is connected to the forum, the defendant is linked to the forum, and the burden of defending is not unreasonable. Accordingly, I would hold that it is neither unfair nor unreasonable to require these defendants to defend in the forum State.

B

In [*Volkswagen*], the interest of the forum State and its connection to the litigation is strong. The automobile accident underlying the litigation occurred in Oklahoma. The plaintiffs were hospitalized in Oklahoma when they brought suit. Essential witnesses and evidence were in Oklahoma. See *Shaffer*. The State has a legitimate interest in enforcing its laws designed to keep its highway system safe, and the trial can proceed at least as efficiently in Oklahoma as anywhere else.

The petitioners are not unconnected with the forum. Although both sell automobiles within limited sales territories, each sold the automobile which in fact was driven to Oklahoma where it was involved in an accident.[8] It may be true, as the Court suggests, that each sincerely intended to limit its commercial impact to the limited territory, and that each intended to accept the benefits and protection of the laws only of those States within the territory. But obviously these were unrealistic hopes that cannot be treated as an automatic constitutional shield.

An automobile simply is not a stationary item or one designed to be used in one place. An automobile is *intended* to be moved around. Someone in the business of selling large numbers of automobiles can hardly plead ignorance of their mobility or pretend that the automobiles stay put after they are sold. It is not merely that a dealer in automobiles foresees that they will move. The dealer actually intends that the purchasers will use the automobiles to travel to distant States where the dealer does not directly "do business." The sale of an automobile does *purposefully* inject the vehicle into the stream of interstate commerce so that it can travel to distant States. See *Kulko*; *Hanson*.

This case is similar to *Ohio v. Wyandotte Chemicals Corp.* There we indicated, in the course of denying leave to file an original-jurisdiction

---

8. On the basis of this fact the state court inferred that the petitioners derived substantial revenue from goods used in Oklahoma. The inference is not without support. Certainly, were use of goods accepted as a relevant contact, a plaintiff would not need to have an exact count of the number of petitioners' cars that are used in Oklahoma.

case, that corporations having no direct contact with Ohio could constitutionally be brought to trial in Ohio because they dumped pollutants into streams outside Ohio's limits which ultimately, through the action of the water, reach Lake Erie and affected Ohio. No corporate acts, only their consequences, occurred in Ohio. The stream of commerce is just as natural a force as a stream of water, and it was equally predictable that the cars petitioners released would reach distant States.

The Court accepts that a State may exercise jurisdiction over a distributor which "serves" that State "indirectly" by "deliver[ing] its products into the stream of commerce with the expectation that they will be purchased by consumers in the forum State." It is difficult to see why the Constitution should distinguish between a case involving goods which reach a distant State through a chain of distribution and a case involving goods which reach the same State because a consumer, using them as the dealer knew the customer would, took them there. In each case the seller purposefully injects the goods into the stream of commerce and those goods predictably are used in the forum State.[12]

Furthermore, an automobile seller derives substantial benefits from States other than its own. A large part of the value of automobiles is the extensive, nationwide network of highways. Significant portions of that network have been constructed by and are maintained by the individual States, including Oklahoma. The States, through their highway programs, contribute in a very direct and important way to the value of petitioners' businesses. Additionally, a network of other related dealerships with their service departments operates throughout the country under the protection of the laws of the various States, including Oklahoma, and enhances the value of petitioners' businesses by facilitating their customers' traveling.

Thus, the Court errs in its conclusion, that "petitioners have *no* 'contacts, ties, or relations'" with Oklahoma. There obviously are contacts, and, given Oklahoma's connection to the litigation, the contacts are sufficiently significant to make it fair and reasonable for the petitioners to submit to Oklahoma's jurisdiction.

III

It may be that affirmance of the judgments in these cases would approach the outer limits of *International Shoe's* jurisdictional principle. But that principle, with its almost exclusive focus on the rights of defendants, may be outdated. As Mr. Justice Marshall wrote in *Shaffer*: "'[T]raditional notions of fair play and substantial justice' can be as readily offended by the perpetuation of ancient forms that are no longer justified as by the adoption of new procedures.... "

International Shoe inherited its defendant focus from *Pennoyer*, and represented the last major step this Court has taken in the long process of

---

12. The manufacturer in the case cited by the Court, *Gray v. American Radiator & Standard Sanitary Corp.*, had no more control over which States its goods would reach than did the petitioners in this case.

liberalizing the doctrine of personal jurisdiction. Though its flexible approach represented a major advance, the structure of our society has changed in many significant ways since *International Shoe* was decided in 1945. Mr. Justice Black, writing for the Court in *McGee*, recognized that "a trend is clearly discernible toward expanding the permissible scope of state jurisdiction over foreign corporations and other nonresidents." He explained the trend as follows:

> In part this is attributable to the fundamental transformation of our national economy over the years. Today many commercial transactions touch two or more States and may involve parties separated by the full continent. With this increasing nationalization of commerce has come a great increase in the amount of business conducted by mail across state lines. At the same time modern transportation and communication have made it much less burdensome for a party sued to defend himself in a State where he engages in economic activity.

As the Court acknowledges, both the nationalization of commerce and the ease of transportation and communication have accelerated in the generation since 1957. The model of society on which the *International Shoe* Court based its opinion is no longer accurate. Business people, no matter how local their businesses, cannot assume that goods remain in the business' locality. Customers and goods can be anywhere else in the country usually in a matter of hours and always in a matter of a very few days.

In answering the question whether or not it is fair and reasonable to allow a particular forum to hold a trial binding on a particular defendant, the interests of the forum State and other parties loom large in today's world and surely are entitled to as much weight as are the interests of the defendant. The "orderly administration of the laws" provides a firm basis for according some protection to the interests of plaintiffs and States as well as of defendants. Certainly, I cannot see how a defendant's right to due process is violated if the defendant suffers no inconvenience.

The conclusion I draw is that constitutional concepts of fairness no longer require the extreme concern for defendants that was once necessary. Rather, as I wrote in dissent from *Shaffer*, minimum contacts must exist "among the *parties*, the contested transaction, and the forum State." The contacts between any two of these should not be determinative. "[W]hen a suitor seeks to lodge a suit in a State with a substantial interest in seeing its own law applied to the transaction in question, we could wisely act to minimize conflicts, confusion, and uncertainty by adopting a liberal view of jurisdiction, unless considerations of fairness or efficiency strongly point in the opposite direction." Mr. Justice Black, dissenting in *Hanson,* expressed similar concerns by suggesting that a State should have jurisdiction over a case growing out of a transaction significantly related to that State "unless litigation there would impose such a heavy and disproportionate burden on a nonresident defendant that it would offend what this Court has referred to as 'traditional notions of fair play and substantial justice.' '' Assuming that a State gives a nonresident defendant adequate notice and opportunity to defend, I do not think the Due Process Clause is offended merely because the defendant has to board a plane to get to the site of the trial.

The Court's opinion suggests that the defendant ought to be subject to a State's jurisdiction only if he has contacts with the State "such that he should reasonably anticipate being haled into court there."[18] There is nothing unreasonable or unfair, however, about recognizing commercial reality. Given the tremendous mobility of goods and people, and the inability of businessmen to control where goods are taken by customers (or retailers), I do not think that the defendant should be in complete control of the geographical stretch of his amenability to suit. Jurisdiction is no longer premised on the notion that nonresident defendants have somehow impliedly consented to suit. People should understand that they are held responsible for the consequences of their actions and that in our society most actions have consequences affecting many States. When an action in fact causes injury in another State, the actor should be prepared to answer for it there unless defending in that State would be unfair for some reason other than that a state boundary must be crossed.[19]

In effect the Court is allowing defendants to assert the sovereign rights of their home States. The expressed fear is that otherwise all limits on personal jurisdiction would disappear. But the argument's premise is wrong. I would not abolish limits on jurisdiction or strip state boundaries of all significance, see *Hanson*; I would still require the plaintiff to demonstrate sufficient contacts among the parties, the forum, and the litigation to make the forum a reasonable State in which to hold the trial.

I would also, however, strip the defendant of an unjustified veto power over certain very appropriate fora—a power the defendant justifiably enjoyed long ago when communication and travel over long distances were slow and unpredictable and when notions of state sovereignty were impractical and exaggerated. But I repeat that that is not today's world. If a plaintiff can show that his chosen forum State has a sufficient interest in the litigation (or sufficient contacts with the defendant), then the defendant who cannot show some real injury to a constitutionality protected interest should have no constitutional excuse not to appear.

The plaintiffs ... brought suit in a forum with which they had significant contacts and which had significant contacts with the litigation. I am not convinced that the defendants would suffer any "heavy and disproportionate burden" in defending the suits. Accordingly, I would hold

---

18. The Court suggests that this is the critical foreseeability rather than the likelihood that the product will go to the forum State. But the reasoning begs the question. A defendant cannot know if his actions will subject him to jurisdiction in another State until we have declared what the law of jurisdiction is.

19. One consideration that might create some unfairness would be if the choice of forum also imposed on the defendant an unfavorable substantive law which the defendant could justly have assumed would not apply.

that the Constitution should not shield the defendants from appearing and defending in the plaintiffs' chosen fora.

* * *

B. GENERAL AND SPECIFIC JURISDICTION

HELICOPTEROS NACIONALES de COLOMBIA, S.A. v. HALL

466 U.S. 408 (1984)

JUSTICE BLACKMUN delivered the opinion of the Court.

We granted certiorari in this case to decide whether the Supreme Court of Texas correctly ruled that the contacts of a foreign corporation with the State of Texas were sufficient to allow a Texas state court to assert jurisdiction over the corporation in a cause of action not arising out of or related to the corporation's activities within the State.

I

Petitioner Helicopteros Nacionales de Colombia, S.A. (Helicol), is a Colombian corporation with its principal place of business in the city of Bogota in that country. It is engaged in the business of providing helicopter transportation for oil and construction companies in South America. On January 26, 1976, a helicopter owned by Helicol crashed in Peru. Four United States citizens were among those who lost their lives in the accident. Respondents are the survivors and representatives of the four decedents.

At the time of the crash, respondents' decedents were employed by Consorcio, a Peruvian consortium, and were working on a pipeline in Peru. Consorcio is the alter ego of a joint venture named Williams–Sedco–Horn (WSH). The venture had its headquarters in Houston, Tex. Consorcio had been formed to enable the venturers to enter into a contract with Petro Peru, the Peruvian state-owned oil company. Consorcio was to construct a pipeline for Petro Peru running from the interior of Peru westward to the Pacific Ocean. Peruvian law forbade construction of the pipeline by any non-Peruvian entity.

Consorcio/WSH needed helicopters to move personnel, materials, and equipment into and out of the construction area. In 1974, upon request of Consorcio/WSH, the chief executive officer of Helicol, Francisco Restrepo, flew to the United States and conferred in Houston with representatives of the three joint venturers. At that meeting, there was a discussion of prices, availability, working conditions, fuel, supplies, and housing. Restrepo represented that Helicol could have the first helicopter on the job in 15 days. The Consorcio/WSH representatives decided to accept the contract proposed by Restrepo. Helicol began performing before the agreement was formally signed in Peru on November 11, 1974. The contract was written in Spanish on official government stationery and provided that the residence of all the parties would be Lima, Peru. It further stated that controversies arising out of the contract would be submitted to the jurisdiction of Peruvian courts. In addition, it provided that Consorcio/WSH would make payments to Helicol's account with the Bank of America in New York City.

Aside from the negotiation session in Houston between Restrepo and the representatives of Consorcio/WSH, Helicol had other contacts with Texas. During the years 1970–1977, it purchased helicopters (approximately 80% of its fleet), spare parts, and accessories for more than $4 million from Bell Helicopter Company in Fort Worth. In that period, Helicol sent prospective pilots to Fort Worth for training and to ferry the aircraft to South America. It also sent management and maintenance personnel to visit Bell Helicopter in Fort Worth during the same period in order to receive "plant familiarization" and for technical consultation. Helicol received into its New York City and Panama City, Fla., bank accounts over $5 million in payments from Consorcio/WSH drawn upon First City National Bank of Houston.

Beyond the foregoing, there have been no other business contacts between Helicol and the State of Texas. Helicol never has been authorized to do business in Texas and never has had an agent for the service of process within the State. It never has performed helicopter operations in Texas or sold any product that reached Texas, never solicited business in Texas, never signed any contract in Texas, never had any employee based there, and never recruited an employee in Texas. In addition, Helicol never has owned real or personal property in Texas and never has maintained an office or establishment there. Helicol has maintained no records in Texas and has no shareholders in that State. None of the respondents or their decedents were domiciled in Texas,[5] but all of the decedents were hired in Houston by Consorcio/WSH to work on the Petro Peru pipeline project.

Respondents instituted wrongful-death actions in the District Court of Harris County, Tex., against Consorcio/WSH, Bell Helicopter Company, and Helicol. Helicol filed special appearances and moved to dismiss the actions for lack of *in personam* jurisdiction over it. The motion was denied. After a consolidated jury trial, judgment was entered against Helicol on a jury verdict of $1,141,200 in favor of respondents.

The Texas Court of Civil Appeals, Houston, First District, reversed the judgment of the District Court, holding that in personam jurisdiction over Helicol was lacking. The Supreme Court of Texas, with three justices dissenting, initially affirmed the judgment of the Court of Civil Appeals. Seven months later, however, on motion for rehearing, the court withdrew

---

5. Respondents' lack of residential or other contacts with Texas of itself does not defeat otherwise proper jurisdiction. *Keeton v. Hustler Magazine, Inc.*.; *Calder v. Jones*. We mention respondents' lack of contacts merely to show that nothing in the nature of the relationship between respondents and Helicol could possibly enhance Helicol's contacts with Texas. The harm suffered by respondents did not occur in Texas. Nor is it alleged that any negligence on the part of Helicol took place in Texas.

its prior opinions and, again with three justices dissenting, reversed the judgment of the intermediate court. In ruling that the Texas courts had *in personam* jurisdiction, the Texas Supreme Court first held that the State's long-arm statute[7] reaches as far as the Due Process Clause of the Fourteenth Amendment permits. Thus, the only question remaining for the court to decide was whether it was consistent with the Due Process Clause for Texas courts to assert *in personam* jurisdiction over Helicol.

II

The Due Process Clause of the Fourteenth Amendment operates to limit the power of a State to assert *in personam* jurisdiction over a nonresident defendant. *Pennoyer v. Neff.* Due process requirements are satisfied when *in personam* jurisdiction is asserted over a nonresident corporate defendant that has "certain minimum contacts with [the forum] such that the maintenance of the suit does not offend 'traditional notions of fair play and substantial justice.' " *International Shoe Co. v. Washington*, quoting *Milliken v. Meyer.* When a controversy is related to or "arises out of" a defendant's contacts with the forum, the Court has said that a "relationship among the defendant, the forum, and the litigation" is the essential foundation of *in personam* jurisdiction. *Shaffer v. Heitner.*[8]

Even when the cause of action does not arise out of or relate to the foreign corporation's activities in the forum State,[9] due process is not offended by a State's subjecting the corporation to its *in personam* jurisdiction when there are sufficient contacts between the State and the foreign corporation. *Perkins v. Benguet Consolidated Mining Co.*, 342 U.S. 437 (1952); *see Keeton v. Hustler Magazine, Inc.* In *Perkins*, the Court addressed a situation in which state courts had asserted general jurisdiction over a defendant foreign corporation. During the Japanese occupation

---

7. The State's long-arm statute reads in relevant part:

Sec. 3. Any foreign corporation ... that engages in business in this State, irrespective of any Statute or law respecting designation or maintenance of resident agents, and does not maintain a place of regular business in this State or a designated agent upon whom service may be made upon causes of action arising out of such business done in this State, the act or acts of engaging in such business within this State shall be deemed equivalent to an appointment by such foreign corporation ... of the Secretary of State of Texas as agent upon whom service of process may be made in any action, suit or proceedings arising out of such business done in this State, wherein such corporation ... is a party or is to be made a party.

Sec. 4. For the purpose of this Act, and without including other acts that may constitute doing business, any foreign corporation ... shall be deemed doing business in this State by entering into contract by mail or otherwise with a resident of Texas to be performed in whole or in part by either party in this State, or the committing of any tort in whole or in part in this State. The act of recruiting Texas residents, directly or through an intermediary located in Texas, for employment inside or outside of Texas shall be deemed doing business in this State.

* * * It is not within our province, of course, to determine whether the Texas Supreme Court correctly interpreted the State's long-arm statute. We therefore accept that court's holding that the limits of the Texas statute are coextensive with those of the Due Process Clause.

8. It has been said that when a State exercises personal jurisdiction over a defendant in a suit arising out of or related to the defendant's contacts with the forum, the State is exercising "specific jurisdiction" over the defendant.

9. When a State exercises personal jurisdiction over a defendant in a suit not arising out of or related to the defendant's contacts with the forum, the State has been said to be exercising "general jurisdiction" over the defendant.

of the Philippine Islands, the president and general manager of a Philippine mining corporation maintained an office in Ohio from which he conducted activities on behalf of the company. He kept company files and held directors' meetings in the office, carried on correspondence relating to the business, distributed salary checks drawn on two active Ohio bank accounts, engaged an Ohio bank to act as transfer agent, and supervised policies dealing with the rehabilitation of the corporation's properties in the Philippines. In short, the foreign corporation, through its president, "ha[d] been carrying on in Ohio a continuous and systematic, but limited, part of its general business," and the exercise of general jurisdiction over the Philippine corporation by an Ohio court was "reasonable and just."

All parties to the present case concede that respondents' claims against Helicol did not "arise out of," and are not related to, Helicol's activities within Texas.[10] We thus must explore the nature of Helicol's contacts with the State of Texas to determine whether they constitute the kind of continuous and systematic general business contacts the Court found to exist in Perkins. We hold that they do not.

It is undisputed that Helicol does not have a place of business in Texas and never has been licensed to do business in the State. Basically, Helicol's contacts with Texas consisted of sending its chief executive officer to Houston for a contract-negotiation session; accepting into its New York bank account checks drawn on a Houston bank; purchasing helicopters, equipment, and training services from Bell Helicopter for substantial sums; and sending personnel to Bell's facilities in Fort Worth for training.

The one trip to Houston by Helicol's chief executive officer for the purpose of negotiating the transportation-services contract with Consorcio/WSH cannot be described or regarded as a contact of a "continuous and systematic" nature, as *Perkins* described it, *see also International Shoe Co. v. Washington*, and thus cannot support an assertion of in personam jurisdiction over Helicol by a Texas court. Similarly, Helicol's acceptance from Consorcio/WSH of checks drawn on a Texas bank is of

---

10. Because the parties have not argued any relationship between the cause of action and Helicol's contacts with the State of Texas, we, contrary to the dissent's implication, assert no "view" with respect to that issue.

The dissent suggests that we have erred in drawing no distinction between controversies that "relate to" a defendant's contacts with a forum and those that "arise out of" such contacts. This criticism is somewhat puzzling, for the dissent goes on to urge that, for purposes of determining the constitutional validity of an assertion of specific jurisdiction, there really should be no distinction between the two.

We do not address the validity or consequences of such a distinction because the issue has not been presented in this case. Respondents have made no argument that their cause of action either arose out of or is related to Helicol's contacts with the State of Texas. Absent any briefing on the issue, we decline to reach the questions (1) whether the terms "arising out of" and "related to" describe different connections between a cause of action and a defendant's contacts with a forum, and (2) what sort of tie between a cause of action and a defendant's contacts with a forum is necessary to a determination that either connection exists. Nor do we reach the question whether, if the two types of relationship differ, a forum's exercise of personal jurisdiction in a situation where the cause of action "relates to," but does not "arise out of," the defendant's contacts with the forum should be analyzed as an assertion of specific jurisdiction.

negligible significance for purposes of determining whether Helicol had sufficient contacts in Texas. There is no indication that Helicol ever requested that the checks be drawn on a Texas bank or that there was any negotiation between Helicol and Consorcio/WSH with respect to the location or identity of the bank on which checks would be drawn. Common sense and everyday experience suggest that, absent unusual circumstances, the bank on which a check is drawn is generally of little consequence to the payee and is a matter left to the discretion of the drawer. Such unilateral activity of another party or a third person is not an appropriate consideration when determining whether a defendant has sufficient contacts with a forum State to justify an assertion of jurisdiction. *See Kulko v. California Superior Court* (arbitrary to subject one parent to suit in any State where other parent chooses to spend time while having custody of child pursuant to separation agreement); *Hanson v. Denckla* ("The unilateral activity of those who claim some relationship with a nonresident defendant cannot satisfy the requirement of contact with the forum State").

The Texas Supreme Court focused on the purchases and the related training trips in finding contacts sufficient to support an assertion of jurisdiction. We do not agree with that assessment, for the Court's opinion in *Rosenberg Bros. & Co. v. Curtis Brown Co.* makes clear that purchases and related trips, standing alone, are not a sufficient basis for a State's assertion of jurisdiction.

The defendant in *Rosenberg* was a small retailer in Tulsa, Okla., who dealt in men's clothing and furnishings. It never had applied for a license to do business in New York, nor had it at any time authorized suit to be brought against it there. It never had an established place of business in New York and never regularly carried on business in that State. Its only connection with New York was that it purchased from New York wholesalers a large portion of the merchandise sold in its Tulsa store. The purchases sometimes were made by correspondence and sometimes through visits to New York by an officer of the defendant. The Court concluded: "Visits on such business, even if occurring at regular intervals, would not warrant the inference that the corporation was present within the jurisdiction of [New York]."

This Court in *International Shoe* acknowledged and did not repudiate its holding in *Rosenberg*. In accordance with *Rosenberg*, we hold that mere purchases, even if occurring at regular intervals, are not enough to warrant a State's assertion of *in personam* jurisdiction over a nonresident corporation in a cause of action not related to those purchase transactions.[12] Nor can we conclude that the fact that Helicol sent personnel into

---

12. This Court in *International Shoe* cited *Rosenberg* for the proposition that "the commission of some single or occasional acts of the corporate agent in a state sufficient to impose an obligation or liability on the corporation has not been thought to confer upon the state authority to enforce it." Arguably, therefore, *Rosenberg* also stands for the proposition that mere purchases are not a sufficient basis for either general or specific jurisdiction. Because the case before us is one in which there has been an assertion of general jurisdiction over a foreign defendant, we need not decide the continuing validity of *Rosenberg* with respect to an assertion of specific jurisdic-

Texas for training in connection with the purchase of helicopters and equipment in that State in any way enhanced the nature of Helicol's contacts with Texas. The training was a part of the package of goods and services purchased by Helicol from Bell Helicopter. The brief presence of Helicol employees in Texas for the purpose of attending the training sessions is no more a significant contact than were the trips to New York made by the buyer for the retail store in *Rosenberg*. *See also Kulko v. California Superior Court*, (basing California jurisdiction on 3–day and 1–day stopovers in that State "would make a mockery of" due process limitations on assertion of personal jurisdiction).

III

We hold that Helicol's contacts with the State of Texas were insufficient to satisfy the requirements of the Due Process Clause of the Fourteenth Amendment. Accordingly, we reverse the judgment of the Supreme Court of Texas.

It is so ordered.

JUSTICE BRENNAN, dissenting.

Decisions applying the Due Process Clause of the Fourteenth Amendment to determine whether a State may constitutionally assert *in personam* jurisdiction over a particular defendant for a particular cause of action most often turn on a weighing of facts. *See, e.g., Kulko v. California Superior Court* (Brennan, J., dissenting). To a large extent, today's decision follows the usual pattern. Based on essentially undisputed facts, the Court concludes that petitioner Helicol's contacts with the State of Texas were insufficient to allow the Texas state courts constitutionally to assert "general jurisdiction" over all claims filed against this foreign corporation. Although my independent weighing of the facts leads me to a different conclusion, the Court's holding on this issue is neither implausible nor unexpected.

What is troubling about the Court's opinion, however, are the implications that might be drawn from the way in which the Court approaches the constitutional issue it addresses. First, the Court limits its discussion to an assertion of general jurisdiction of the Texas courts because, in its view, the underlying cause of action does "not aris[e] out of or relat[e] to the corporation's activities within the State." Then, the Court relies on a 1923 decision in *Rosenberg*, without considering whether that case retains any validity after our more recent pronouncements concerning the permissible reach of a State's jurisdiction. By posing and deciding the question presented in this manner, I fear that the Court is saying more than it realizes about constitutional limitations on the potential reach of *in personam* jurisdiction. In particular, by relying on a precedent whose premises have long been discarded, and by refusing to consider any distinction between controversies that "relate to" a defendant's contacts

---

tion, i.e., where the cause of action arises out of or relates to the purchases by the defendant in the forum State.

with the forum and causes of action that "arise out of" such contacts, the Court may be placing severe limitations on the type and amount of contacts that will satisfy the constitutional minimum.

In contrast, I believe that the undisputed contacts in this case between petitioner Helicol and the State of Texas are sufficiently important, and sufficiently related to the underlying cause of action, to make it fair and reasonable for the State to assert personal jurisdiction over Helicol for the wrongful-death actions filed by the respondents. Given that Helicol has purposefully availed itself of the benefits and obligations of the forum, and given the direct relationship between the underlying cause of action and Helicol's contacts with the forum, maintenance of this suit in the Texas courts "does not offend [the] 'traditional notions of fair play and substantial justice,' " *International Shoe Co. v. Washington*, that are the touchstone of jurisdictional analysis under the Due Process Clause. I therefore dissent.

I

The Court expressly limits its decision in this case to "an assertion of general jurisdiction over a foreign defendant." Having framed the question in this way, the Court is obliged to address our prior holdings in *Perkins* and *Rosenberg*. In *Perkins*, the Court considered a State's assertion of general jurisdiction over a foreign corporation that "ha[d] been carrying on ... a continuous and systematic, but limited, part of its general business" in the forum. Under the circumstances of that case, we held that such contacts were constitutionally sufficient "to make it reasonable and just to subject the corporation to the jurisdiction" of that State. Nothing in *Perkins* suggests, however, that such "continuous and systematic" contacts are a necessary minimum before a State may constitutionally assert general jurisdiction over a foreign corporation.

The Court therefore looks for guidance to our 1923 decision in *Rosenberg*, which until today was of dubious validity given the subsequent expansion of personal jurisdiction that began with *International Shoe*, in 1945. In *Rosenberg*, the Court held that a company's purchases within a State, even when combined with related trips to the State by company officials, would not allow the courts of that State to assert general jurisdiction over all claims against the nonresident corporate defendant making those purchases.[1] Reasoning by analogy, the Court in this case concludes that Helicol's contacts with the State of Texas are no more significant than the purchases made by the defendant in Rosenberg. The

---

1. The Court leaves open the question whether the decision in *Rosenberg* was intended to address any constitutional limits on an assertion of "specific jurisdiction." If anything is clear from Justice Brandeis' opinion for the Court in *Rosenberg*, however, it is that the Court was concerned only with general jurisdiction over the corporate defendant. ("The sole question for decision is whether ... defendant was doing business within the State of New York in such manner and to such extent as to warrant the inference that it was present there"); (the corporation's contacts with the forum "would not warrant the inference that the corporation was present within the jurisdiction of the State"). The Court's resuscitation of *Rosenberg*, therefore, should have no bearing upon any forum's assertion of jurisdiction over claims that arise out of or relate to a defendant's contacts with the State.

Court makes no attempt, however, to ascertain whether the narrow view of *in personam* jurisdiction adopted by the Court in *Rosenberg* comports with "the fundamental transformation of our national economy" that has occurred since 1923. *McGee v. International Life Ins. Co. See also World–Wide Volkswagen Corp. v. Woodson* (Brennan, J., dissenting); *Hanson v. Denckla* (Black, J., dissenting). This failure, in my view, is fatal to the Court's analysis.

The vast expansion of our national economy during the past several decades has provided the primary rationale for expanding the permissible reach of a State's jurisdiction under the Due Process Clause. By broadening the type and amount of business opportunities available to participants in interstate and foreign commerce, our economy has increased the frequency with which foreign corporations actively pursue commercial transactions throughout the various States. In turn, it has become both necessary and, in my view, desirable to allow the States more leeway in bringing the activities of these nonresident corporations within the scope of their respective jurisdictions.

This is neither a unique nor a novel idea. As the Court first noted in 1957:

> "[M]any commercial transactions touch two or more States and may involve parties separated by the full continent. With this increasing nationalization of commerce has come a great increase in the amount of business conducted by mail across state lines. At the same time modern transportation and communication have made it much less burdensome for a party sued to defend himself in a State where he engages in economic activity." *McGee.*

See also World–Wide Volkswagen (reaffirming that "[t]he historical developments noted in *McGee* . . . have only accelerated in the generation since that case was decided"); *Hanson v. Denckla.*

Moreover, this "trend . . . toward expanding the permissible scope of state jurisdiction over foreign corporations and other nonresidents," *McGee*, is entirely consistent with the "traditional notions of fair play and substantial justice," *International Shoe*, that control our inquiry under the Due Process Clause. As active participants in interstate and foreign commerce take advantage of the economic benefits and opportunities offered by the various States, it is only fair and reasonable to subject them to the obligations that may be imposed by those jurisdictions. And chief among the obligations that a nonresident corporation should expect to fulfill is amenability to suit in any forum that is significantly affected by the corporation's commercial activities.

As a foreign corporation that has actively and purposefully engaged in numerous and frequent commercial transactions in the State of Texas, Helicol clearly falls within the category of nonresident defendants that may be subject to that forum's general jurisdiction. Helicol not only purchased helicopters and other equipment in the State for many years, but also sent pilots and management personnel into Texas to be trained in the use of this equipment and to consult with the seller on technical matters.[2] Moreover, negotiations for the contract under which Helicol provided transportation services to the joint venture that employed the respondents' decedents also took place in the State of Texas. Taken together, these contacts demonstrate that Helicol obtained numerous benefits from its transaction of business in Texas. In turn, it is eminently fair and reasonable to expect Helicol to face the obligations that attach to its participation in such commercial transactions. Accordingly, on the basis of continuous commercial contacts with the forum, I would conclude that the Due Process Clause allows the State of Texas to assert general jurisdiction over petitioner Helicol.

II

The Court also fails to distinguish the legal principles that controlled our prior decisions in *Perkins* and *Rosenberg*. In particular, the contacts between petitioner Helicol and the State of Texas, unlike the contacts between the defendant and the forum in each of those cases, are significantly related to the cause of action alleged in the original suit filed by the respondents. Accordingly, in my view, it is both fair and reasonable for the Texas courts to assert specific jurisdiction over Helicol in this case.

By asserting that the present case does not implicate the specific jurisdiction of the Texas courts, the Court necessarily removes its decision from the reality of the actual facts presented for our consideration. Moreover, the Court refuses to consider any distinction between contacts that are "related to" the underlying cause of action and contacts that "give rise" to the underlying cause of action. In my view, however, there is a substantial difference between these two standards for asserting specific jurisdiction. Thus, although I agree that the respondents' cause of action did not formally "arise out of" specific activities initiated by Helicol in the State of Texas, I believe that the wrongful-death claim filed by the respondents is significantly related to the undisputed contacts between Helicol and the forum. On that basis, I would conclude that the Due Process Clause allows the Texas courts to assert specific jurisdiction over this particular action.

The wrongful-death actions filed by the respondents were premised on a fatal helicopter crash that occurred in Peru. Helicol was joined as a defendant in the lawsuits because it provided transportation services,

---

2. Although the Court takes note of these contacts, it concludes that they did not "enhanc[e] the nature of Helicol's contacts with Texas [because the] training was a part of the package of goods and services purchased by Helicol." Presumably, the Court's statement simply recognizes that participation in today's interdependent markets often necessitates the use of complicated purchase contracts that provide for numerous contacts between representatives of the buyer and seller, as well as training for related personnel. Ironically, however, while relying on these modern-day realities to denigrate the significance of Helicol's contacts with the forum, the Court refuses to acknowledge that these same realities require a concomitant expansion in a forum's jurisdictional reach. As a result, when deciding that the balance in this case must be struck against jurisdiction, the Court loses sight of the ultimate inquiry: whether it is fair and reasonable to subject a nonresident corporate defendant to the jurisdiction of a State when that defendant has purposefully availed itself of the benefits and obligations of that particular forum. *Cf. Hanson v. Denckla*.

including the particular helicopter and pilot involved in the crash, to the joint venture that employed the decedents. Specifically, the respondent Hall claimed in her original complaint that "Helicol is ... legally responsible for its own negligence through its pilot employee." Viewed in light of these allegations, the contacts between Helicol and the State of Texas are directly and significantly related to the underlying claim filed by the respondents. The negotiations that took place in Texas led to the contract in which Helicol agreed to provide the precise transportation services that were being used at the time of the crash. Moreover, the helicopter involved in the crash was purchased by Helicol in Texas, and the pilot whose negligence was alleged to have caused the crash was actually trained in Texas. This is simply not a case, therefore, in which a state court has asserted jurisdiction over a nonresident defendant on the basis of wholly unrelated contacts with the forum. Rather, the contacts between Helicol and the forum are directly related to the negligence that was alleged in the respondent Hall's original complaint.[4] Because Helicol should have expected to be amenable to suit in the Texas courts for claims directly related to these contacts, it is fair and reasonable to allow the assertion of jurisdiction in this case.

Despite this substantial relationship between the contacts and the cause of action, the Court declines to consider whether the courts of Texas may assert specific jurisdiction over this suit. Apparently, this simply reflects a narrow interpretation of the question presented for review. It is nonetheless possible that the Court's opinion may be read to imply that the specific jurisdiction of the Texas courts is inapplicable because the cause of action did not formally "arise out of" the contacts between Helicol and the forum. In my view, however, such a rule would place unjustifiable limits on the bases under which Texas may assert its jurisdictional power.

Limiting the specific jurisdiction of a forum to cases in which the cause of action formally arose out of the defendant's contacts with the State would subject constitutional standards under the Due Process Clause to the vagaries of the substantive law or pleading requirements of each State. For example, the complaint filed against Helicol in this case alleged negligence based on pilot error. Even though the pilot was trained in Texas, the Court assumes that the Texas courts may not assert jurisdiction over the suit because the cause of action "did not 'arise out of,' and [is] not related to," that training. If, however, the applicable substantive law required that negligent training of the pilot was a necessary element of a cause of action for pilot error, or if the respondents had simply added an allegation of negligence in the training provided for the Helicol pilot, then presumably the Court would concede that the specific jurisdiction of the Texas courts was applicable.

---

4. The jury specifically found that "the pilot failed to keep the helicopter under proper control," that "the helicopter was flown into a treetop fog condition, whereby the vision of the pilot was impaired," that "such flying was negligence," and that "such negligence ... was a proximate cause of the crash." On the basis of these findings, Helicol was ordered to pay over $1 million in damages to the respondents.

Our interpretation of the Due Process Clause has never been so dependent upon the applicable substantive law or the State's formal pleading requirements. At least since *International Shoe Co. v. Washington*, the principal focus when determining whether a forum may constitutionally assert jurisdiction over a nonresident defendant has been on fairness and reasonableness to the defendant. To this extent, a court's specific jurisdiction should be applicable whenever the cause of action arises out of or relates to the contacts between the defendant and the forum. It is eminently fair and reasonable, in my view, to subject a defendant to suit in a forum with which it has significant contacts directly related to the underlying cause of action. Because Helicol's contacts with the State of Texas meet this standard, I would affirm the judgment of the Supreme Court of Texas.

* * *

C. FIRST AMENDMENT CONSIDERATIONS

KEETON v. HUSTLER MAGAZINE

465 U.S. 770 (1984)

JUSTICE REHNQUIST delivered the opinion of the Court.

Petitioner Kathy Keeton sued respondent Hustler Magazine, Inc., and other defendants in the United States District Court for the District of New Hampshire, alleging jurisdiction over her libel complaint by reason of diversity of citizenship. The district court dismissed her suit because it believed that the Due Process Clause of the Fourteenth Amendment to the United States Constitution forbade the application of New Hampshire's long-arm statute in order to acquire personal jurisdiction over respondent. The Court of Appeals for the First Circuit affirmed, summarizing its concerns with the statement that "the New Hampshire tail is too small to wag so large an out-of-state dog." We granted certiorari, and we now reverse.

Petitioner Keeton is a resident of New York. Her only connection with New Hampshire is the circulation there of copies of a magazine that she assists in producing. The magazine bears petitioner's name in several places crediting her with editorial and other work. Respondent Hustler Magazine, Inc., is an Ohio corporation, with its principal place of business in California. Respondent's contacts with New Hampshire consist of the sale of some 10 to 15,000 copies of *Hustler* magazine in that State each month. Petitioner claims to have been libeled in five separate issues of respondent's magazine published between September, 1975, and May, 1976.[1]

---

1. Initially, petitioner brought suit for libel and invasion of privacy in Ohio, where the magazine was published. Her libel claim, however, was dismissed as barred by the Ohio statute of limitations, and her invasion of privacy claim was dismissed as barred by the New York statute of limitations, which the Ohio court considered to be "migratory." Petitioner then filed the present action in October, 1980.

The Court of Appeals, in its opinion affirming the District Court's dismissal of petitioner's complaint, held that petitioner's lack of contacts with New Hampshire rendered the State's interest in redressing the tort of libel to petitioner too attenuated for an assertion of personal jurisdiction over respondent. The Court of Appeals observed that the "single publication rule" ordinarily applicable in multistate libel cases would require it to award petitioner "damages caused in *all* states" should she prevail in her suit, even though the bulk of petitioner's alleged injuries had been sustained outside New Hampshire. The court also stressed New Hampshire's unusually long (6–year) limitations period for libel actions. New Hampshire was the only State where petitioner's suit would not have been time-barred when it was filed. Under these circumstances, the Court of Appeals concluded that it would be "unfair" to assert jurisdiction over respondent. New Hampshire has a minimal interest in applying its unusual statute of limitations to, and awarding damages for, injuries to a nonresident occurring outside the State, particularly since petitioner suffered such a small proportion of her total claimed injury within the State.

We conclude that the Court of Appeals erred when it affirmed the dismissal of petitioner's suit for lack of personal jurisdiction. Respondent's regular circulation of magazines in the forum State is sufficient to support an assertion of jurisdiction in a libel action based on the contents of the magazine. This is so even if New Hampshire courts, and thus the District Court under *Klaxon Co. v. Stentor Co.*, would apply the so-called "single publication rule" to enable petitioner to recover in the New Hampshire action her damages from "publications" of the alleged libel throughout the United States.

The district court found that "[t]he general course of conduct in circulating magazines throughout the state was purposefully directed at New Hampshire, and inevitably affected persons in the state." Such regular monthly sales of thousands of magazines cannot by any stretch of the imagination be characterized as random, isolated, or fortuitous. It is, therefore, unquestionable that New Hampshire jurisdiction over a complaint based on those contacts would ordinarily satisfy the requirement of the Due Process Clause that a State's assertion of personal jurisdiction over a nonresident defendant be predicated on "minimum contacts" between the defendant and the State. *See World–Wide Volkswagen Corp. v. Woodson,; International Shoe Corp. v. Washington*. And, as the Court of Appeals acknowledged, New Hampshire has adopted a "long-arm" statute authorizing service of process on nonresident corporations whenever permitted by the Due Process Clause. Thus, all the requisites for personal jurisdiction over Hustler Magazine, Inc., in New Hampshire are present.

We think that the three concerns advanced by the Court of Appeals, whether considered singly or together, are not sufficiently weighty to merit a different result. The "single publication rule," New Hampshire's unusually long statute of limitations, and plaintiff's lack of contacts with the forum State do not defeat jurisdiction otherwise proper under both New Hampshire law and the Due Process Clause.

In judging minimum contacts, a court properly focuses on "the relationship among the defendant, the forum, and the litigation." *Shaffer v. Heitner*. Thus, it is certainly relevant to the jurisdictional inquiry that petitioner is *seeking* to recover damages suffered in all States in this one suit. The contacts between respondent and the forum must be judged in the light of that claim, rather than a claim only for damages sustained in New Hampshire. That is, the contacts between respondent and New Hampshire must be such that it is "fair" to compel respondent to defend a multistate lawsuit in New Hampshire seeking nationwide damages for all copies of the five issues in question, even though only a small portion of those copies were distributed in New Hampshire.

The Court of Appeals expressed the view that New Hampshire's "interest" in asserting jurisdiction over plaintiff's multistate claim was minimal. We agree that the "fairness" of haling respondent into a New Hampshire court depends to some extent on whether respondent's activities relating to New Hampshire are such as to give that State a legitimate interest in holding respondent answerable on a claim related to those activities. See *World-Wide Volkswagen Corp. v. Woodson*; *McGee v. International Life Insurance Co.* But insofar as the State's "interest" in adjudicating the dispute is a part of the Fourteenth Amendment due process equation, as a surrogate for some of the factors already mentioned, we think the interest is sufficient.

The Court of Appeals acknowledged that petitioner was suing, at least in part, for damages suffered in New Hampshire. And it is beyond dispute that New Hampshire has a significant interest in redressing injuries that actually occur within the State.

This interest extends to libel actions brought by nonresidents. False statements of fact harm both the subject of the falsehood *and* the readers of the statement. New Hampshire may rightly employ its libel laws to discourage the deception of its citizens. There is "no constitutional value in false statements of fact."

New Hampshire may also extend its concern to the injury that instate libel causes within New Hampshire to a nonresident. The tort of libel is generally held to occur wherever the offending material is circulated. The reputation of the libel victim may suffer harm even in a state in which he has hitherto been anonymous. The communication of the libel may create a negative reputation among the residents of a jurisdiction where the plaintiff's previous reputation was, however small, at least unblemished.

New Hampshire has clearly expressed its interest in protecting such persons from libel, as well as in safeguarding its populace from falsehoods. Its criminal defamation statute bears no restriction to libels of which residents are the victim. Moreover, in 1971 New Hampshire specifically deleted from its long-arm statute the requirement that a tort be committed "against a resident of New Hampshire."

New Hampshire also has a substantial interest in cooperating with other States, through the "single publication rule," to provide a forum for efficiently litigating all issues and damage claims arising out of a libel in a unitary proceeding. This rule reduces the potential serious drain of libel cases on judicial resources. It also serves to protect defendants from harassment resulting from multiple suits. In sum, the combination of New Hampshire's interest in redressing injuries that occur within the State and its interest in cooperating with other States in the application of the "single publication rule" demonstrate the propriety of requiring respondent to answer to a multistate libel action in New Hampshire.

The Court of Appeals also thought that there was an element of due process "unfairness" arising from the fact that the statutes of limitations in every jurisdiction except New Hampshire had run on the plaintiff's claim in this case. Strictly speaking, however, any potential unfairness in applying New Hampshire's statute of limitations to all aspects of this nationwide suit has nothing to do with the jurisdiction of the Court to adjudicate the claims. "The issue is personal jurisdiction, not choice of law." *Hanson v. Denckla.* The question of the applicability of New Hampshire's statute of limitations to claims for out-of-state damages presents itself in the course of litigation only after jurisdiction over respondent is established, and we do not think that such choice of law concerns should complicate or distort the jurisdictional inquiry.

The chance duration of statutes of limitations in non-forum jurisdictions has nothing to do with the contacts among respondent, New Hampshire, and this multistate libel action. Whether Ohio's limitations period is six months or six years does not alter the jurisdictional calculus in New Hampshire. Petitioner's successful search for a State with a lengthy statute of limitations is no different from the litigation strategy of countless plaintiffs who seek a forum with favorable substantive or procedural rules or sympathetic local populations. Certainly Hustler Magazine, Inc., which chose to enter the New Hampshire market, can be charged with knowledge of its laws and no doubt would have claimed the benefit of them if it had a complaint against a subscriber, distributor, or other commercial partner.

Finally, implicit in the Court of Appeals' analysis of New Hampshire's interest is an emphasis on the extremely limited contacts of the *plaintiff* with New Hampshire. But we have not to date required a plaintiff to have "minimum contacts" with the forum State before permitting that State to assert personal jurisdiction over a nonresident defendant. On the contrary, we have upheld the assertion of jurisdiction where such contacts were entirely lacking. In *Perkins v. Benguet Mining Co.,* none of the parties was a resident of the forum State; indeed, neither the plaintiff nor the subject-matter of his action had any relation to that State. Jurisdiction was based solely on the fact that the defendant corporation had been carrying on in the forum "a continuous and systematic, but limited, part of its general business." In the instant case, respondent's activities in the forum may not be so substantial as to support jurisdiction over a cause of action unrelated to those activities. But respondent is carrying on a "part of its general business" in New Hampshire, and that is sufficient to support jurisdiction when the cause of action arises out of the very activity being conducted, in part, in New Hampshire.

The plaintiff's residence is not, of course, completely irrelevant to the jurisdictional inquiry. As noted, that inquiry focuses on the relations among the defendant, the forum and the litigation. Plaintiff's residence may well play an important role in determining the propriety of entertaining a suit against the defendant in the forum. That is, plaintiff's residence in the forum may, because of defendant's relationship with the plaintiff, enhance defendant's contacts with the forum. Plaintiff's residence may be the focus of the activities of the defendant out of which the suit arises. See *Calder v. Jones; McGee v. International Life Ins. Co.* But plaintiff's residence in the forum State is not a separate requirement, and lack of residence will not defeat jurisdiction established on the basis of defendant's contacts.

It is undoubtedly true that the bulk of the harm done to petitioner occurred outside New Hampshire. But that will be true in almost every libel action brought somewhere other than the plaintiff's domicile. There is no justification for restricting libel actions to the plaintiff's home forum.[12] The victim of a libel, like the victim of any other tort, may choose to bring suit in any forum with which the defendant has "certain minimum contacts ... such that the maintenance of the suit does not offend 'traditional notions of fair play and substantial justice.'" *International Shoe Co. v. Washington.*

Where, as in this case, respondent Hustler Magazine, Inc., has continuously and deliberately exploited the New Hampshire market, it must reasonably anticipate being haled into court there in a libel action based on the contents of its magazine. *World-Wide Volkswagen Corp. v. Woodson.* And, since respondent can be charged with knowledge of the "single publication rule," it must anticipate that such a suit will seek nationwide damages. Respondent produces a national publication aimed at a nationwide audience. There is no unfairness in calling it to answer for the contents of that publication wherever a substantial number of copies are regularly sold and distributed.

The judgment of the Court of Appeals is reversed and the cause is remanded for proceedings consistent with this opinion.

It is so ordered.

JUSTICE BRENNAN, concurring in the judgment.

I agree with the Court that "[r]espondent's regular circulation of magazines in the forum State is sufficient to support an assertion of jurisdiction in a libel action based on the contents of the magazine." These

---

12. As noted in *Calder v. Jones,* we reject categorically the suggestion that invisible radiations from the First Amendment may defeat jurisdiction otherwise proper under the Due Process Clause.

contacts between the respondent and the forum State are sufficiently important and sufficiently related to the underlying cause of action to foreclose any concern that the constitutional limits of the Due Process Clause are being violated. This is so, moreover, irrespective of the state's interest in enforcing its substantive libel laws or its unique statute of limitations. Indeed, as we recently explained in *Insurance Corp. v. Compagnie des Bauxites,* these interests of the State should be relevant only to the extent that they bear upon the liberty interests of the respondent that are protected by the Fourteenth Amendment. "The restriction on state sovereign power described in *World-Wide Volkswagen Corp.* [*v. Woodson*] must be seen as ultimately a function of the individual liberty interest preserved by the Due Process Clause. That Clause is the only source of the personal jurisdiction requirement and the Clause itself makes no mention of federalism concerns."

* * *

CALDER v. JONES

465 U.S. 783 (1984)

JUSTICE REHNQUIST delivered the opinion of the Court.

Respondent Shirley Jones brought suit in California Superior Court claiming that she had been libeled in an article written and edited by petitioners in Florida. The article was published in a national magazine with a large circulation in California. Petitioners were served with process by mail in Florida and caused special appearances to be entered on their behalf, moving to quash the service of process for lack of personal jurisdiction. The superior court granted the motion on the ground that First Amendment concerns weighed against an assertion of jurisdiction otherwise proper under the Due Process Clause. The California Court of Appeal reversed, rejecting the suggestion that First Amendment considerations enter into the jurisdictional analysis. We now affirm.

Respondent lives and works in California. She and her husband brought this suit against the National Enquirer, Inc., its local distributing company, and petitioners for libel, invasion of privacy, and intentional infliction of emotional harm. The Enquirer is a Florida corporation with its principal place of business in Florida. It publishes a national weekly newspaper with a total circulation of over 5 million. About 600,000 of those copies, almost twice the level of the next highest State, are sold in California.[2] Respondent's and her husband's claims were based on an article that appeared in the Enquirer's October 9, 1979 issue. Both the Enquirer and the distributing company answered the complaint and made no objection to the jurisdiction of the California court.

---

2. A geographic analysis of the total paid circulation for the September 18, 1979 issue of the *Enquirer* showed total sales, national and international, of 5,292,200. Sales in California were 604,431. The State with the next highest total was New York, with 316,911.

Petitioner South is a reporter employed by the Enquirer. He is a resident of Florida, though he frequently travels to California on business. South wrote the first draft of the challenged article, and his byline appeared on it. He did most of his research in Florida, relying on phone calls to sources in California for the information contained in the article.[4] Shortly before publication, South called respondent's home and read to her husband a draft of the article so as to elicit his comments upon it. Aside from his frequent trips and phone calls, South has no other relevant contacts with California.

Petitioner Calder is also a Florida resident. He has been to California only twice—once, on a pleasure trip, prior to the publication of the article and once after to testify in an unrelated trial. Calder is president and editor of the Enquirer. He "oversee[s] just about every function of the Enquirer." He reviewed and approved the initial evaluation of the subject of the article and edited it in its final form. He also declined to print a retraction requested by respondent. Calder has no other relevant contacts with California.

In considering petitioners' motion to quash service of process, the superior court surmised that the actions of petitioners in Florida, causing injury to respondent in California, would ordinarily be sufficient to support an assertion of jurisdiction over them in California.[5] But the court felt that special solicitude was necessary because of the potential "chilling effect" on reporters and editors which would result from requiring them to appear in remote jurisdictions to answer for the content of articles upon which they worked. The court also noted that respondent's rights could be "fully satisfied" in her suit against the publisher without requiring petitioners to appear as parties. The superior court, therefore, granted the motion.

The California Court of Appeal reversed. The court agreed that neither petitioner's contacts with California would be sufficient for an assertion of jurisdiction on a cause of action unrelated to those contacts. *See Perkins v. Benguet Mining Co.* (permitting general jurisdiction where defendant's contacts with the forum were "continuous and systematic"). But the court concluded that a valid basis for jurisdiction existed on the theory that petitioners intended to, and did, cause tortious injury to respondent in California. The fact that the actions causing the effects in California were performed outside the State did not prevent the State from asserting jurisdiction over a cause of action arising out of those effects. The court rejected the superior court's conclusion that First

---

4. The superior court found that South made at least one trip to California in connection with the article. South hotly disputes this finding, claiming that an uncontroverted affidavit shows that he never visited California to research the article. Since we do not rely for our holding on the alleged visit, we find it unnecessary to consider the contention.

5. California's "long-arm" statute permits an assertion of jurisdiction over a nonresident defendant whenever permitted by the state and federal Constitutions. Section 410.10 of the California Code of Civil Procedure provides: "A court of this state may exercise jurisdiction on any basis not inconsistent with the Constitution of this state or of the United States."

Amendment considerations must be weighed in the scale against jurisdiction.

A timely petition for hearing was denied by the Supreme Court of California. Treating the jurisdictional statement as a petition for writ of certiorari, we hereby grant the petition.

The Due Process Clause of the Fourteenth Amendment to the United States Constitution permits personal jurisdiction over a defendant in any State with which the defendant has "certain minimum contacts ... such that the maintenance of the suit does not offend 'traditional notions of fair play and substantial justice.'" *International Shoe Co. v. Washington.* In judging minimum contacts, a court properly focuses on "the relationship among the defendant, the forum, and the litigation." *Shaffer v. Heitner.* The plaintiff's lack of "contacts" will not defeat otherwise proper jurisdiction, see *Keeton v. Hustler Magazine, Inc.*, but they may be so manifold as to permit jurisdiction when it would not exist in their absence. Here, the plaintiff is the focus of the activities of the defendants out of which the suit arises. *See McGee v. International Life Ins. Co.*

The allegedly libelous story concerned the California activities of a California resident. It impugned the professionalism of an entertainer whose television career was centered in California.[9] The article was drawn from California sources, and the brunt of the harm, in terms both of respondent's emotional distress and the injury to her professional reputation, was suffered in California. In sum, California is the focal point both of the story and of the harm suffered. Jurisdiction over petitioners is therefore proper in California based on the "effects" of their Florida conduct in California. *World-Wide Volkswagen Corp. v. Woodson.*

Petitioners argue that they are not responsible for the circulation of the article in California. A reporter and an editor, they claim, have no direct economic stake in their employer's sales in a distant State. Nor are ordinary employees able to control their employer's marketing activity. The mere fact that they can "foresee" that the article will be circulated and have an effect in California is not sufficient for an assertion of jurisdiction. *World-Wide Volkswagen Corp. v. Woodson.* They do not "in effect appoint the [article their] agent for service of process." *World-Wide Volkswagen Corp. v. Woodson.* Petitioners liken themselves to a welder employed in Florida who works on a boiler which subsequently explodes in California. Cases which hold that jurisdiction will be proper over the manufacturer, *Gray v. American Radiator & Standard Sanitary Corp.*, should not be applied to the welder who has no control over and derives no direct benefit from his employer's sales in that distant State.

Petitioners' analogy does not wash. Whatever the status of their hypothetical welder, petitioners are not charged with mere untargeted negligence. Rather, their intentional, and allegedly tortious, actions were expressly aimed at California. Petitioner South wrote and petitioner

---

9. The article alleged that respondent drank so heavily as to prevent her from fulfilling her professional obligations.

Calder edited an article that they knew would have a potentially devastating impact upon respondent. And they knew that the brunt of that injury would be felt by respondent in the State in which she lives and works and in which the *National Enquirer* has its largest circulation. Under the circumstances, petitioners must "reasonably anticipate being haled into court there" to answer for the truth of the statements made in their article. *World-Wide Volkswagen Corp. v. Woodson*; *Kulko v. Superior Court*; *Shaffer v. Heitner*. An individual injured in California need not go to Florida to seek redress from persons who, though remaining in Florida, knowingly cause the injury in California.

Petitioners are correct that their contacts with California are not to be judged according to their employer's activities there. On the other hand, their status as employees does not somehow insulate them from jurisdiction. Each defendant's contacts with the forum State must be assessed individually. ("The requirements of *International Shoe* ... must be met as to each defendant over whom a state court exercises jurisdiction"). In this case, petitioners are primary participants in an alleged wrongdoing intentionally directed at a California resident, and jurisdiction over them is proper on that basis.

We also reject the suggestion that First Amendment concerns enter into the jurisdictional analysis. The infusion of such considerations would needlessly complicate an already imprecise inquiry. Moreover, the potential chill on protected First Amendment activity stemming from libel and defamation actions is already taken into account in the constitutional limitations on the substantive law governing such suits. To reintroduce those concerns at the jurisdictional stage would be a form of double counting. We have already declined in other contexts to grant special procedural protections to defendants in libel and defamation actions in addition to the constitutional protections embodied in the substantive laws.

We hold that jurisdiction over petitioners in California is proper because of their intentional conduct in Florida calculated to cause injury to respondent in California. The judgment of the California Court of Appeal is

Affirmed.

* * *

D. JURISDICTION BASED ON CONTRACT REVISITED

FEDERAL RULE OF CIVIL PROCEDURE 4 [selected provisions]

(k) Territorial Limits of Effective Service.

    (1) *In General.* Serving a summons or filing a waiver of service establishes personal jurisdiction over a defendant:

        (A) who is subject to the jurisdiction of a court of general jurisdiction in the state where the district court is located;

(B) who is a party joined under Rule 14 or 19 and is served within a judicial district of the United States and not more than 100 miles from where the summons was issued; or

(C) when authorized by a federal statute.

(2) ***Federal Claim Outside State–Court Jurisdiction.*** For a claim that arises under federal law, serving a summons or filing a waiver of service establishes personal jurisdiction over a defendant if:

(A) the defendant is not subject to jurisdiction in any state's courts of general jurisdiction; and

(B) exercising jurisdiction is consistent with the United States Constitution and laws.

* * *

(n) Asserting Jurisdiction over Property or Assets.

(1) ***Federal Law.*** The court may assert jurisdiction over property if authorized by a federal statute. Notice to claimants of the property must be given as provided in the statute or by serving a summons under this rule.

(2) ***State Law.*** On a showing that personal jurisdiction over a defendant cannot be obtained in the district where the action is brought by reasonable efforts to serve a summons under this rule, the court may assert jurisdiction over the defendant's assets found in the district. Jurisdiction is acquired by seizing the assets under the circumstances and in the manner provided by state law in that district.

* * *

BURGER KING CORPORATION v. RUDZEWICZ

471 U.S. 462 (1985)

JUSTICE BRENNAN delivered the opinion of the Court.

The State of Florida's long-arm statute extends jurisdiction to "[a]ny person, whether or not a citizen or resident of this state," who, *inter alia,* "[b]reach[es] a contract in this state by failing to perform acts required by the contract to be performed in this state," so long as the cause of action arises from the alleged contractual breach. The United States District Court for the Southern District of Florida, sitting in diversity, relied on this provision in exercising personal jurisdiction over a Michigan resident who allegedly had breached a franchise agreement with a Florida corporation by failing to make required payments in Florida. The question presented is whether this exercise of long-arm jurisdiction offended "traditional conception[s] of fair play and substantial justice" embodied in the Due Process Clause of the Fourteenth Amendment. *International Shoe Co. v. Washington.*

I

A

Burger King Corporation is a Florida corporation whose principal offices are in Miami. It is one of the world's largest restaurant organizations, with over 3,000 outlets in the 50 States, the Commonwealth of Puerto Rico, and 8 foreign nations. Burger King conducts approximately 80% of its business through a franchise operation that the company styles the "Burger King System"—"a comprehensive restaurant format and operating system for the sale of uniform and quality food products." Burger King licenses its franchisees to use its trademarks and service marks for a period of 20 years and leases standardized restaurant facilities to them for the same term. In addition, franchisees acquire a variety of proprietary information concerning the "standards, specifications, procedures and methods for operating a Burger King Restaurant." They also receive market research and advertising assistance; ongoing training in restaurant management;[2] and accounting, cost-control, and inventory-control guidance. By permitting franchisees to tap into Burger King's established national reputation and to benefit from proven procedures for dispensing standardized fare, this system enables them to go into the restaurant business with significantly lowered barriers to entry.

In exchange for these benefits, franchisees pay Burger King an initial $40,000 franchise fee and commit themselves to payment of monthly royalties, advertising and sales promotion fees, and rent computed in part from monthly gross sales. Franchisees also agree to submit to the national organization's exacting regulation of virtually every conceivable aspect of their operations. Burger King imposes these standards and undertakes its rigid regulation out of conviction that "[u]niformity of service, appearance, and quality of product is essential to the preservation of the Burger King image and the benefits accruing therefrom to both Franchisee and Franchisor."

Burger King oversees its franchise system through a two-tiered administrative structure. The governing contracts provide that the franchise relationship is established in Miami and governed by Florida law, and call for payment of all required fees and forwarding of all relevant notices to the Miami headquarters. The Miami headquarters sets policy and works directly with its franchisees in attempting to resolve major problems. Day-to-day monitoring of franchisees, however, is conducted through a network of 10 district offices which in turn report to the Miami headquarters.

The instant litigation grows out of Burger King's termination of one of its franchisees and is aptly described by the franchisee as "a divorce proceeding among commercial partners." The appellee John Rudzewicz, a Michigan citizen and resident, is the senior partner in a Detroit accounting firm. In 1978, he was approached by Brian MacShara, the son of a business acquaintance, who suggested that they jointly apply to Burger King for a franchise in the Detroit area. MacShara proposed to serve as

---

2. Mandatory training seminars are conducted at Burger King University in Miami and at Whopper College Regional Training Centers around the country.

the manager of the restaurant if Rudzewicz would put up the investment capital; in exchange, the two would evenly share the profits. Believing that MacShara's idea offered attractive investment and tax-deferral opportunities, Rudzewicz agreed to the venture.

Rudzewicz and MacShara jointly applied for a franchise to Burger King's Birmingham, Michigan, district office in the autumn of 1978. Their application was forwarded to Burger King's Miami headquarters, which entered into a preliminary agreement with them in February 1979. During the ensuing four months it was agreed that Rudzewicz and MacShara would assume operation of an existing facility in Drayton Plains, Michigan. MacShara attended the prescribed management courses in Miami during this period, and the franchisees purchased $165,000 worth of restaurant equipment from Burger King's Davmor Industries division in Miami. Even before the final agreements were signed, however, the parties began to disagree over site-development fees, building design, computation of monthly rent, and whether the franchisees would be able to assign their liabilities to a corporation they had formed.[6] During these disputes Rudzewicz and MacShara negotiated both with the Birmingham district office and with the Miami headquarters.[7] With some misgivings, Rudzewicz and MacShara finally obtained limited concessions from the Miami headquarters, signed the final agreements, and commenced operations in June 1979. By signing the final agreements, Rudzewicz obligated himself personally to payments exceeding $1 million over the 20–year franchise relationship.

The Drayton Plains facility apparently enjoyed steady business during the summer of 1979, but patronage declined after a recession began later that year. Rudzewicz and MacShara soon fell far behind in their monthly payments to Miami. Headquarters sent notices of default, and an extended period of negotiations began among the franchisees, the Birmingham district office, and the Miami headquarters. After several Burger King officials in Miami had engaged in prolonged but ultimately unsuccessful negotiations with the franchisees by mail and by telephone,[9] headquarters

---

6. The latter two matters were the major areas of disagreement. Notwithstanding that Burger King's franchise offering advised that minimum rent would be based on a percentage of "approximated capitalized site acquisition and construction costs," Rudzewicz assumed that rent would be a function solely of renovation costs, and he thereby underestimated the minimum monthly rent by more than $2,000. The District Court found Rudzewicz' interpretation "incredible."

With respect to assignment, Rudzewicz and MacShara had formed RMBK Corp. with the intent of assigning to it all of their interest and liabilities in the franchise. Consistent with the contract documents, however, Burger King insisted that the two remain personally liable for their franchise obligations. Although the franchisees contended that Burger King officials had given them oral assurances concerning assignment, the District Court found that pursuant to the parol evidence rule any such assurances "even if they had been made and were misleading were joined and merged" into the final agreement.

7. Although Rudzewicz and MacShara dealt with the Birmingham district office on a regular basis, they communicated directly with the Miami headquarters in forming the contracts; moreover, they learned that the district office had "very little" decision-making authority and accordingly turned directly to headquarters in seeking to resolve their disputes.

9. Miami's policy was to "deal directly" with franchisees when they began to encounter financial difficulties, and to involve district office personnel only when necessary. In the instant

terminated the franchise and ordered Rudzewicz and MacShara to vacate the premises. They refused and continued to occupy and operate the facility as a Burger King restaurant.

B

Burger King commenced the instant action in the United States District Court for the Southern District of Florida in May 1981, invoking that court's diversity jurisdiction pursuant to 28 U.S.C. § 1332(a) and its original jurisdiction over federal trademark disputes pursuant to § 1338(a).[10] Burger King alleged that Rudzewicz and MacShara had breached their franchise obligations "within [the jurisdiction of] this district court" by failing to make the required payments "at plaintiff's place of business in Miami, Dade County, Florida," and also charged that they were tortiously infringing its trademarks and service marks through their continued, unauthorized operation as a Burger King restaurant. Burger King sought damages, injunctive relief, and costs and attorney's fees. Rudzewicz and MacShara entered special appearances and argued that because they were Michigan residents and because Burger King's claim did not "arise" within the Southern District of Florida, the District Court lacked personal jurisdiction over them. The District Court denied their motions after a hearing, holding that, pursuant to Florida's long-arm statute, "a non-resident Burger King franchisee is subject to the personal jurisdiction of this Court in actions arising out of its franchise agreements." Rudzewicz and MacShara then filed an answer and a counterclaim seeking damages for alleged violations by Burger King of Michigan's Franchise Investment Law.

After a 3-day bench trial, the court again concluded that it had "jurisdiction over the subject matter and the parties to this cause." Finding that Rudzewicz and MacShara had breached their franchise agreements with Burger King and had infringed Burger King's trademarks and service marks, the court entered judgment against them, jointly and severally, for $228,875 in contract damages. The court also ordered them "to immediately close Burger King Restaurant Number 775 from continued operation or to immediately give the keys and possession of said restaurant to Burger King Corporation," found that they had failed to prove any of the required elements of their counterclaim, and awarded costs and attorney's fees to Burger King.

Rudzewicz appealed to the Court of Appeals for the Eleventh Circuit. A divided panel of that Circuit reversed the judgment concluding that the District Court could not properly exercise personal jurisdiction over Rudzewicz pursuant to [the Florida long-arm statute] because "the circumstances of the Drayton Plains franchise and the negotiations which led to

---

case, for example, the Miami office handled all credit problems, ordered cost-cutting measures, negotiated for a partial refinancing of the franchisees' debts, communicated directly with the franchisees in attempting to resolve the dispute, and was responsible for all termination matters.

10. Rudzewicz and MacShara were served in Michigan with summonses and copies of the complaint pursuant to Federal Rule of Civil Procedure 4.

it left Rudzewicz bereft of reasonable notice and financially unprepared for the prospect of franchise litigation in Florida." Accordingly, the panel majority concluded that "[j]urisdiction under these circumstances would offend the fundamental fairness which is the touchstone of due process."

Burger King appealed the Eleventh Circuit's judgment to this Court * * * Treating the jurisdictional statement as a petition for a writ of certiorari, we grant the petition and now reverse.

II

A

The Due Process Clause protects an individual's liberty interest in not being subject to the binding judgments of a forum with which he has established no meaningful "contacts, ties, or relations." *International Shoe Co. v. Washington.*[13] By requiring that individuals have "fair warning that a particular activity may subject [them] to the jurisdiction of a foreign sovereign," *Shaffer v. Heitner,* the Due Process Clause "gives a degree of predictability to the legal system that allows potential defendants to structure their primary conduct with some minimum assurance as to where that conduct will and will not render them liable to suit," *World-Wide Volkswagen Corp. v. Woodson.*

Where a forum seeks to assert specific jurisdiction over an out-of-state defendant who has not consented to suit there,[14] this "fair warning" requirement is satisfied if the defendant has "purposefully directed" his activities at residents of the forum, *Keeton v. Hustler Magazine, Inc.,* and the litigation results from alleged injuries that "arise out of or relate to" those activities, *Helicopteros Nacionales de Colombia, S.A. v. Hall.*[15] Thus "[t]he forum State does not exceed its powers under the Due Process Clause if it asserts personal jurisdiction over a corporation that delivers its products into the stream of commerce with the expectation that they will be purchased by consumers in the forum State" and those products subsequently injure forum consumers. *World-Wide Volkswagen Corp. v. Woodson.* Similarly, a publisher who distributes magazines in a distant State may fairly be held accountable in that forum for damages resulting

---

13. Although this protection operates to restrict state power, it "must be seen as ultimately a function of the individual liberty interest preserved by the Due Process Clause" rather than as a function "of federalism concerns." *Insurance Corp. of Ireland v. Compagnie des Bauxites de Guinee,* 456 U.S. 694, 702–703 (1982).

14. We have noted that, because the personal jurisdiction requirement is a waivable right, there are a "variety of legal arrangements" by which a litigant may give "express or implied consent to the personal jurisdiction of the court." *Insurance Corp. of Ireland v. Compagnie des Bauxites de Guinee.* For example, particularly in the commercial context, parties frequently stipulate in advance to submit their controversies for resolution within a particular jurisdiction. *See National Equipment Rental, Ltd. v. Szukhent,* 375 U.S. 311 (1964). Where such forum-selection provisions have been obtained through "freely negotiated" agreements and are not "unreasonable and unjust," *The Bremen v. Zapata Off–Shore Co.,* their enforcement does not offend due process.

15. "Specific" jurisdiction contrasts with "general" jurisdiction, pursuant to which "a State exercises personal jurisdiction over a defendant in a suit not arising out of or related to the defendant's contacts with the forum." *Helicopteros Nacionales de Colombia, S.A. v. Hall*; *see also Perkins v. Benguet Consolidated Mining Co.*

there from an allegedly defamatory story. *Keeton v. Hustler Magazine, Inc.; see also Calder v. Jones* (suit against author and editor). And with respect to interstate contractual obligations, we have emphasized that parties who "reach out beyond one state and create continuing relationships and obligations with citizens of another state" are subject to regulation and sanctions in the other State for the consequences of their activities. See also *McGee v. International Life Insurance Co.*

We have noted several reasons why a forum legitimately may exercise personal jurisdiction over a nonresident who "purposefully directs" his activities toward forum residents. A State generally has a "manifest interest" in providing its residents with a convenient forum for redressing injuries inflicted by out-of-state actors. *See also Keeton v. Hustler Magazine, Inc.* Moreover, where individuals "purposefully derive benefit" from their interstate activities, *Kulko v. California Superior Court,* it may well be unfair to allow them to escape having to account in other States for consequences that arise proximately from such activities; the Due Process Clause may not readily be wielded as a territorial shield to avoid interstate obligations that have been voluntarily assumed. And because "modern transportation and communications have made it much less burdensome for a party sued to defend himself in a State where he engages in economic activity," it usually will not be unfair to subject him to the burdens of litigating in another forum for disputes relating to such activity. *McGee v. International Life Insurance Co.*

Notwithstanding these considerations, the constitutional touchstone remains whether the defendant purposefully established "minimum contacts" in the forum State. *International Shoe Co. v. Washington.* Although it has been argued that foreseeability of causing *injury* in another State should be sufficient to establish such contacts there when policy considerations so require,[16] the Court has consistently held that this kind of foreseeability is not a "sufficient benchmark" for exercising personal jurisdiction. *World-Wide Volkswagen Corp. v. Woodson.* Instead, "the foreseeability that is critical to due process analysis ... is that the defendant's conduct and connection with the forum State are such that he should reasonably anticipate being haled into court there." In defining when it is that a potential defendant should "reasonably anticipate" out-of-state litigation, the Court frequently has drawn from the reasoning of *Hanson v. Denckla*:

> The unilateral activity of those who claim some relationship with a nonresident defendant cannot satisfy the requirement of contact with the forum State. The application of that rule will vary with the quality and nature of the defendant's activity, but it is essential in each case that there be some act by which the defendant purposefully avails itself of the privilege of conducting activities within the forum State, thus invoking the benefits and protections of its laws.

---

16. *See, e.g., World–Wide Volkswagen Corp. v. Woodson* (Brennan, J., dissenting); *Shaffer v. Heitner* (Brennan, J., concurring in part and dissenting in part).

This "purposeful availment" requirement ensures that a defendant will not be haled into a jurisdiction solely as a result of "random," "fortuitous," or "attenuated" contacts, *Keeton v. Hustler Magazine, Inc.*; *World-Wide Volkswagen Corp. v. Woodson,* or of the "unilateral activity of another party or a third person," *Helicopteros Nacionales de Colombia, S.A. v. Hall.*[17] Jurisdiction is proper, however, where the contacts proximately result from actions by the defendant *himself* that create a "substantial connection" with the forum State. *McGee v. International Life Insurance Co.*; *see also Kulko v. California Superior Court.*[18] Thus where the defendant "deliberately" has engaged in significant activities within a State, *Keeton v. Hustler Magazine, Inc.,* or has created "continuing obligations" between himself and residents of the forum, he manifestly has availed himself of the privilege of conducting business there, and because his activities are shielded by "the benefits and protections" of the forum's laws it is presumptively not unreasonable to require him to submit to the burdens of litigation in that forum as well.

Jurisdiction in these circumstances may not be avoided merely because the defendant did not *physically* enter the forum State. Although territorial presence frequently will enhance a potential defendant's affiliation with a State and reinforce the reasonable foreseeability of suit there, it is an inescapable fact of modern commercial life that a substantial amount of business is transacted solely by mail and wire communications across state lines, thus obviating the need for physical presence within a State in which business is conducted. So long as a commercial actor's efforts are "purposefully directed" toward residents of another State, we have consistently rejected the notion that an absence of physical contacts can defeat personal jurisdiction there. *Keeton v. Hustler Magazine, Inc.*; *see also Calder v. Jones*; *McGee v. International Life Insurance Co.*

Once it has been decided that a defendant purposefully established minimum contacts within the forum State, these contacts may be considered in light of other factors to determine whether the assertion of personal jurisdiction would comport with "fair play and substantial justice." *International Shoe Co. v. Washington.* Thus courts in "appropriate

---

17. Applying this principle, the Court has held that the Due Process Clause forbids the exercise of personal jurisdiction over an out-of-state automobile distributor whose only tie to the forum resulted from a customer's decision to drive there, *World-Wide Volkswagen Corp. v. Woodson;* over a divorced husband sued for child-support payments whose only affiliation with the forum was created by his former spouse's decision to settle there, *Kulko v. California Superior Court*; and over a trustee whose only connection with the forum resulted from the settlor's decision to exercise her power of appointment there, *Hanson v. Denckla.* In such instances, the defendant has had no "clear notice that it is subject to suit" in the forum and thus no opportunity to "alleviate the risk of burdensome litigation" there. *World-Wide Volkswagen Corp. v. Woodson.*

18. So long as it creates a "substantial connection" with the forum, even a single act can support jurisdiction. *McGee v. International Life Insurance Co.* The Court has noted, however, that "some single or occasional acts" related to the forum may not be sufficient to establish jurisdiction if "their nature and quality and the circumstances of their commission" create only an "attenuated" affiliation with the forum. *International Shoe Co. v. Washington*; *World-Wide Volkswagen Corp. v. Woodson.* This distinction derives from the belief that, with respect to this category of "isolated" acts, the reasonable foreseeability of litigation in the forum is substantially diminished.

case[s]" may evaluate "the burden on the defendant," "the forum State's interest in adjudicating the dispute," "the plaintiff's interest in obtaining convenient and effective relief," "the interstate judicial system's interest in obtaining the most efficient resolution of controversies," and the "shared interest of the several States in furthering fundamental substantive social policies." *World-Wide Volkswagen Corp. v. Woodson*. These considerations sometimes serve to establish the reasonableness of jurisdiction upon a lesser showing of minimum contacts than would otherwise be required. *See, e.g., Keeton v. Hustler Magazine, Inc.*; *Calder v. Jones*; *McGee v. International Life Insurance Co.* On the other hand, where a defendant who purposefully has directed his activities at forum residents seeks to defeat jurisdiction, he must present a compelling case that the presence of some other considerations would render jurisdiction unreasonable. Most such considerations usually may be accommodated through means short of finding jurisdiction unconstitutional. For example, the potential clash of the forum's law with the "fundamental substantive social policies" of another State may be accommodated through application of the forum's choice-of-law rules. Similarly, a defendant claiming substantial inconvenience may seek a change of venue. Nevertheless, minimum requirements inherent in the concept of "fair play and substantial justice" may defeat the reasonableness of jurisdiction even if the defendant has purposefully engaged in forum activities. *World-Wide Volkswagen Corp. v. Woodson*. As we previously have noted, jurisdictional rules may not be employed in such a way as to make litigation "so gravely difficult and inconvenient" that a party unfairly is at a "severe disadvantage" in comparison to his opponent. *The Bremen v. Zapata Off–Shore C.* (*re* forum-selection provisions); *McGee v. International Life Insurance Co.*

B

(1)

Applying these principles to the case at hand, we believe there is substantial record evidence supporting the District Court's conclusion that the assertion of personal jurisdiction over Rudzewicz in Florida for the alleged breach of his franchise agreement did not offend due process. At the outset, we note a continued division among lower courts respecting whether and to what extent a contract can constitute a "contact" for purposes of due process analysis. If the question is whether an individual's contract with an out-of-state party *alone* can automatically establish sufficient minimum contacts in the other party's home forum, we believe the answer clearly is that it cannot. The Court long ago rejected the notion that personal jurisdiction might turn on "mechanical" tests, *International Shoe Co. v. Washington,* or on "conceptualistic . . . theories of the place of contracting or of performance." Instead, we have emphasized the need for a "highly realistic" approach that recognizes that a "contract" is "ordinarily but an intermediate step serving to tie up prior business negotiations with future consequences which themselves are the real object of the business transaction." It is these factors—prior negotiations and contemplated future consequences, along with the terms of the contract and the parties' actual course of dealing—that must be evaluated in determining whether the defendant purposefully established minimum contacts within the forum.

In this case, no physical ties to Florida can be attributed to Rudzewicz other than MacShara's brief training course in Miami.[22] Rudzewicz did not maintain offices in Florida and, for all that appears from the record, has never even visited there. Yet this franchise dispute grew directly out of "a contract which had a *substantial* connection with that State." *McGee v. International Life Insurance Co.* Eschewing the option of operating an independent local enterprise, Rudzewicz deliberately "reach[ed] out beyond" Michigan and negotiated with a Florida corporation for the purchase of a long-term franchise and the manifold benefits that would derive from affiliation with a nationwide organization. Upon approval, he entered into a carefully structured 20–year relationship that envisioned continuing and wide-reaching contacts with Burger King in Florida. In light of Rudzewicz' voluntary acceptance of the long-term and exacting regulation of his business from Burger King's Miami headquarters, the "quality and nature" of his relationship to the company in Florida can in no sense be viewed as "random," "fortuitous," or "attenuated." *Hanson v. Denckla*; *Keeton v. Hustler Magazine, Inc.; World–Wide Volkswagen Corp. v. Woodson.* Rudzewicz' refusal to make the contractually required payments in Miami, and his continued use of Burger King's trademarks and confidential business information after his termination, caused foreseeable injuries to the corporation in Florida. For these reasons it was, at the very least, presumptively reasonable for Rudzewicz to be called to account there for such injuries.

The Court of Appeals concluded, however, that in light of the supervision emanating from Burger King's district office in Birmingham, Rudzewicz reasonably believed that "the Michigan office was for all intents and purposes the embodiment of Burger King" and that he therefore had no "reason to anticipate a Burger King suit outside of Michigan." This reasoning overlooks substantial record evidence indicating that Rudzewicz most certainly knew that he was affiliating himself with an enterprise based primarily in Florida. The contract documents themselves emphasize that Burger King's operations are conducted and supervised from the Miami headquarters, that all relevant notices and payments must be sent there, and that the agreements were made in and enforced from Miami.

---

22. The Eleventh Circuit held that MacShara's presence in Florida was irrelevant to the question of Rudzewicz's minimum contacts with that forum, reasoning that "Rudzewicz and MacShara never formed a partnership" and "signed the agreements in their individual capacities." The two did jointly form a corporation through which they were seeking to conduct the franchise, however. They were required to decide which one of them would travel to Florida to satisfy the training requirements so that they could commence business, and Rudzewicz participated in the decision that MacShara would go there. We have previously noted that when commercial activities are "carried on in behalf of" an out-of-state party those activities may sometimes be ascribed to the party, *International Shoe Co. v. Washington*, at least where he is a "primary participan[t]" in the enterprise and has acted purposefully in directing those activities, *Calder v. Jones*. Because MacShara's matriculation at Burger King University is not pivotal to the disposition of this case, we need not resolve the permissible bounds of such attribution.

Moreover, the parties' actual course of dealing repeatedly confirmed that decisionmaking authority was vested in the Miami headquarters and that the district office served largely as an intermediate link between the headquarters and the franchisees. When problems arose over building design, site-development fees, rent computation, and the defaulted payments, Rudzewicz and MacShara learned that the Michigan office was powerless to resolve their disputes and could only channel their communications to Miami. Throughout these disputes, the Miami headquarters and the Michigan franchisees carried on a continuous course of direct communications by mail and by telephone, and it was the Miami headquarters that made the key negotiating decisions out of which the instant litigation arose.

Moreover, we believe the Court of Appeals gave insufficient weight to provisions in the various franchise documents providing that all disputes would be governed by Florida law. The franchise agreement, for example, stated:

> This Agreement shall become valid when executed and accepted by BKC at Miami, Florida; it shall be deemed made and entered into in the State of Florida and shall be governed and construed under and in accordance with the laws of the State of Florida. The choice of law designation does not require that all suits concerning this Agreement be filed in Florida.

The Court of Appeals reasoned that choice-of-law provisions are irrelevant to the question of personal jurisdiction, relying on *Hanson v. Denckla* for the proposition that "the center of gravity for choice-of-law purposes does not necessarily confer the sovereign prerogative to assert jurisdiction." This reasoning misperceives the import of the quoted proposition. The Court in *Hanson* and subsequent cases has emphasized that choice-of-law *analysis*—which focuses on all elements of a transaction, and not simply on the defendant's conduct—is distinct from minimum-contacts jurisdictional analysis—which focuses at the threshold solely on the defendant's purposeful connection to the forum. Nothing in our cases, however, suggests that a choice-of-law *provision* should be ignored in considering whether a defendant has "purposefully invoked the benefits and protections of a State's laws" for jurisdictional purposes. Although such a provision standing alone would be insufficient to confer jurisdiction, we believe that, when combined with the 20–year interdependent relationship Rudzewicz established with Burger King's Miami headquarters, it reinforced his deliberate affiliation with the forum State and the reasonable foreseeability of possible litigation there. As Judge Johnson argued in his dissent below, Rudzewicz "purposefully availed himself of the benefits and protections of Florida's laws" by entering into contracts expressly providing that those laws would govern franchise disputes.[24]

---

24. In addition, the franchise agreement's disclaimer that the "choice of law designation does not *require* that all suits concerning this Agreement be filed in Florida," reasonably should have suggested to Rudzewicz that by negative implication such suits *could* be filed there.

(2)

Nor has Rudzewicz pointed to other factors that can be said persuasively to outweigh the considerations discussed above and to establish the *unconstitutionality* of Florida's assertion of jurisdiction. We cannot conclude that Florida had no "legitimate interest in holding [Rudzewicz] answerable on a claim related to" the contacts he had established in that State. *Keeton v. Hustler Magazine, Inc.*; *see also McGee v. International Life Insurance* (noting that State frequently will have a "manifest interest in providing effective means of redress for its residents").[25] Moreover, although Rudzewicz has argued at some length that Michigan's Franchise Investment Law governs many aspects of this franchise relationship, he has not demonstrated how Michigan's acknowledged interest might possibly render jurisdiction in Florida *unconstitutional*.[26] Finally, the Court of Appeals' assertion that the Florida litigation "severely impaired [Rudzewicz'] ability to call Michigan witnesses who might be essential to his defense and counterclaim," is wholly without support in the record. And even to the extent that it is inconvenient for a party who has minimum contacts with a forum to litigate there, such considerations most frequently can be accommodated through a change of venue. Although the Court has suggested that inconvenience may at some point become so substantial as to achieve *constitutional* magnitude, *McGee v. International Life Insurance Co.*, this is not such a case.

The Court of Appeals also concluded, however, that the parties' dealings involved "a characteristic disparity of bargaining power" and "elements of surprise," and that Rudzewicz "lacked fair notice" of the potential for litigation in Florida because the contractual provisions suggesting to the contrary were merely "boilerplate declarations in a lengthy printed contract." Rudzewicz presented many of these arguments to the District Court, contending that Burger King was guilty of misrepresentation, fraud, and duress; that it gave insufficient notice in its dealings with him; and that the contract was one of adhesion. After a 3–day bench trial,

---

The lease also provided for binding arbitration in Miami of certain condemnation disputes, and Rudzewicz conceded the validity of this provision at oral argument. Although it does not govern the instant dispute, this provision also should have made it apparent to the franchisees that they were dealing directly with the Miami headquarters and that the Birmingham district office was *not* "for all intents and purposes the embodiment of Burger King."

25. Complaining that "when Burger King is the plaintiff, you won't 'have it your way' because it sues all franchisees in Miami," Rudzewicz contends that Florida's interest in providing a convenient forum is negligible given the company's size and ability to conduct litigation anywhere in the country. We disagree. Absent compelling considerations, *cf. McGee v. International Life Insurance Co.*, a defendant who has purposefully derived commercial benefit from his affiliations in a forum may not defeat jurisdiction there simply because of his adversary's greater net wealth.

26. Rudzewicz has failed to show how the District Court's exercise of jurisdiction in this case might have been at all inconsistent with Michigan's interests. To the contrary, the court found that Burger King had fully complied with Michigan law, and there is nothing in Michigan's franchise Act suggesting that Michigan would attempt to assert exclusive jurisdiction to resolve franchise disputes affecting its residents. In any event, minimum-contacts analysis presupposes that two or more States may be interested in the outcome of a dispute, and the process of resolving potentially conflicting "fundamental substantive social policies," *World-Wide Volkswagen Corp. v. Woodson,* can usually be accommodated through choice-of-law rules rather than through outright preclusion of jurisdiction in one forum.

the District Court found that Burger King had made no misrepresentations, that Rudzewicz and MacShara "were and are experienced and
sophisticated businessmen," and that "at no time" did they "ac[t] under
economic duress or disadvantage imposed by" Burger King. * * * neither
Rudzewicz nor the Court of Appeals has pointed to record evidence that
would support a "definite and firm conviction" that the District Court's
findings are mistaken. To the contrary, Rudzewicz was represented by
counsel throughout these complex transactions and, as Judge Johnson
observed in dissent below, was himself an experienced accountant "who
for five months conducted negotiations with Burger King over the terms
of the franchise and lease agreements, and who obligated himself personally to contracts requiring overtime payments that exceeded $1 million."
Rudzewicz was able to secure a modest reduction in rent and other
concessions from Miami headquarters; moreover, to the extent that Burger King's terms were inflexible, Rudzewicz presumably decided that the
advantages of affiliating with a national organization provided sufficient
commercial benefits to offset the detriments.[28]

III

Notwithstanding these considerations, the Court of Appeals apparently believed that it was necessary to reject jurisdiction in this case as a
prophylactic measure, reasoning that an affirmance of the District Court's
judgment would result in the exercise of jurisdiction over "out-of-state
consumers to collect payments due on modest personal purchases" and
would "sow the seeds of default judgments against franchisees owing
smaller debts." We share the Court of Appeals' broader concerns and
therefore reject any talismanic jurisdictional formulas; "the facts of each
case must [always] be weighed" in determining whether personal jurisdiction would comport with "fair play and substantial justice." *Kulko v.
California Superior Court.*[29] The "quality and nature" of an interstate
transaction may sometimes be so "random," "fortuitous," or "attenuated" that it cannot fairly be said that the potential defendant "should
reasonably anticipate being haled into court" in another jurisdiction.
World-Wide Volkswagen Corp. v. Woodson. We also have emphasized that
jurisdiction may not be grounded on a contract whose terms have been
obtained through "fraud, undue influence, or overweening bargaining
power" and whose application would render litigation "so gravely difficult
and inconvenient that [a party] will for all practical purposes be deprived

---

28. We do not mean to suggest that the jurisdictional outcome will always be the same in
franchise cases. Some franchises may be primarily intrastate in character or involve different
decision-making structures, such that a franchisee should not reasonably anticipate out-of-state
litigation. Moreover, commentators have argued that franchise relationships may sometimes
involve unfair business practices in their inception and operation. For these reasons, we reject
Burger King's suggestion for "a general rule, or at least a presumption, that participation in an
interstate franchise relationship" represents consent to the jurisdiction of the franchisor's
principal place of business.

29. This approach does, of course, preclude clear-cut jurisdictional rules. But any inquiry into
"fair play and substantial justice" necessarily requires determinations "in which few answers will
be written 'in black and white. The greys are dominant and even among them the shades are
innumerable.'" *Kulko v. California Superior Court.*

of his day in court." *The Bremen v. Zapata Off–Shore Co.* Just as the Due Process Clause allows flexibility in ensuring that commercial actors are not effectively "judgment proof" for the consequences of obligations they voluntarily assume in other States, *McGee v. International Life Insurance Co.,* so too does it prevent rules that would unfairly enable them to obtain default judgments against unwitting customers.

For the reasons set forth above, however, these dangers are not present in the instant case. Because Rudzewicz established a substantial and continuing relationship with Burger King's Miami headquarters, received fair notice from the contract documents and the course of dealing that he might be subject to suit in Florida, and has failed to demonstrate how jurisdiction in that forum would otherwise be fundamentally unfair, we conclude that the District Court's exercise of jurisdiction pursuant to [the Florida long-arm statute] did not offend due process. The judgment of the Court of Appeals is accordingly reversed, and the case is remanded for further proceedings consistent with this opinion.

It is so ordered.

JUSTICE POWELL took no part in the consideration or decision of this case.

JUSTICE STEVENS, with whom JUSTICE WHITE joins, dissenting.

In my opinion there is a significant element of unfairness in requiring a franchisee to defend a case of this kind in the forum chosen by the franchisor. It is undisputed that appellee maintained no place of business in Florida, that he had no employees in that State, and that he was not licensed to do business there. Appellee did not prepare his French fries, shakes, and hamburgers in Michigan, and then deliver them into the stream of commerce "with the expectation that they [would] be purchased by consumers in" Florida. To the contrary, appellee did business only in Michigan, his business, property, and payroll taxes were payable in that State, and he sold all of his products there.

Throughout the business relationship, appellee's principal contacts with appellant were with its Michigan office. Notwithstanding its disclaimer, the Court seems ultimately to rely on nothing more than standard boilerplate language contained in various documents to establish that appellee " 'purposefully availed himself of the benefits and protections of Florida's laws.' " Such superficial analysis creates a potential for unfairness not only in negotiations between franchisors and their franchisees but, more significantly, in the resolution of the disputes that inevitably arise from time to time in such relationships.

Judge Vance's opinion for the Court of Appeals for the Eleventh Circuit adequately explains why I would affirm the judgment of that court. I particularly find the following more persuasive than what this Court has written today:

> Nothing in the course of negotiations gave Rudzewicz reason to anticipate a Burger King suit outside of Michigan. The only face-to-

face or even oral contact Rudzewicz had with Burger King throughout months of protracted negotiations was with representatives of the Michigan office. Burger King had the Michigan office interview Rudzewicz and MacShara, appraise their application, discuss price terms, recommend the site which the defendants finally agreed to, and attend the final closing ceremony. There is no evidence that Rudzewicz ever negotiated with anyone in Miami or even sent mail there during negotiations. He maintained no staff in the state of Florida, and as far as the record reveals, he has never even visited the state.

The contracts contemplated the startup of a local Michigan restaurant whose profits would derive solely from food sales made to customers in Drayton Plains. The sale, which involved the use of an intangible trademark in Michigan and occupancy of a Burger King facility there, required no performance in the state of Florida. Under the contract, the local Michigan district office was responsible for providing all of the services due Rudzewicz, including advertising and management consultation. Supervision, moreover, emanated from that office alone. To Rudzewicz, the Michigan office was for all intents and purposes the embodiment of Burger King. He had reason to believe that his working relationship with Burger King began and ended in Michigan, not at the distant and anonymous Florida headquarters. . . .

Given that the office in Rudzewicz' home state conducted all of the negotiations and wholly supervised the contract, we believe that he had reason to assume that the state of the supervisory office would be the same state in which Burger King would file suit. Rudzewicz lacked fair notice that the distant corporate headquarters which insulated itself from direct dealings with him would later seek to assert jurisdiction over him in the courts of its own home state. . . .

Just as Rudzewicz lacked notice of the possibility of suit in Florida, he was financially unprepared to meet its added costs. The franchise relationship in particular is fraught with potential for financial surprise. The device of the franchise gives local retailers the access to national trademark recognition which enables them to compete with better-financed, more efficient chain stores. This national affiliation, however, does not alter the fact that the typical franchise store is a local concern serving at best a neighborhood or community. Neither the revenues of a local business nor the geographical range of its market prepares the average franchise owner for the cost of distant litigation. . . .

The particular distribution of bargaining power in the franchise relationship further impairs the franchisee's financial preparedness. In a franchise contract, "the franchisor normally occupies [the] dominant role". . . .

We discern a characteristic disparity of bargaining power in the facts of this case. There is no indication that Rudzewicz had any latitude to negotiate a reduced rent or franchise fee in exchange for the added risk of suit in Florida. He signed a standard form contract whose terms were non-negotiable and which appeared in some respects to vary from the more favorable terms agreed to in earlier discussions. In fact, the final contract required a minimum monthly rent computed on a base far in excess of that discussed in oral negotiations. Burger King resisted price concessions, only to sue Rudzewicz far from home. In doing so, it severely impaired his ability to call Michigan witnesses who might be essential to his defense and counterclaim.

In sum, we hold that the circumstances of the Drayton Plains franchise and the negotiations which led to it left Rudzewicz bereft of reasonable notice and financially unprepared for the prospect of franchise litigation in Florida. Jurisdiction under these circumstances would offend the fundamental fairness which is the touchstone of due process.

Accordingly, I respectfully dissent.

* * *

IV. CHOOSING THE FORUM (PERSONAL JURISDICTION)

A. STREAM OF COMMERCE REVISITED

ASAHI METAL INDUSTRY CO., LTD. v. SUPERIOR COURT OF CALIFORNIA

480 U.S. 102 (1987)

JUSTICE O'CONNOR announced the judgment of the Court and delivered the unanimous opinion of the Court with respect to Part I, the opinion of the Court with respect to Part II–B, in which THE CHIEF JUSTICE, JUSTICE BRENNAN, JUSTICE WHITE, JUSTICE MARSHALL, JUSTICE BLACKMUN, JUSTICE POWELL, and JUSTICE STEVENS join, and an opinion with respect to Parts II–A and III, in which THE CHIEF JUSTICE, JUSTICE POWELL, and JUSTICE SCALIA join.

This case presents the question whether the mere awareness on the part of a foreign defendant that the components it manufactured, sold, and delivered outside the United States would reach the forum State in the stream of commerce constitutes "minimum contacts" between the defendant and the forum State such that the exercise of jurisdiction "does not offend 'traditional notions of fair play and substantial justice.'" *International Shoe Co. v. Washington.*

I

On September 23, 1978, on Interstate Highway 80 in Solano County, California, Gary Zurcher lost control of his Honda motorcycle and collided with a tractor. Zurcher was severely injured, and his passenger and wife, Ruth Ann Moreno, was killed. In September 1979, Zurcher filed a product liability action in the Superior Court of the State of California in and for the County of Solano. Zurcher alleged that the 1978 accident was caused by a sudden loss of air and an explosion in the rear tire of the motorcycle, and alleged that the motorcycle tire, tube, and sealant were defective. Zurcher's complaint named, *inter alia,* Cheng Shin Rubber Industrial Co., Ltd. (Cheng Shin), the Taiwanese manufacturer of the tube. Cheng Shin in turn filed a cross-complaint seeking indemnification from its codefendants and from petitioner, Asahi Metal Industry Co., Ltd. (Asahi), the manufacturer of the tube's valve assembly. Zurcher's claims against Cheng Shin and the other defendants were eventually settled and dismissed, leaving only Cheng Shin's indemnity action against Asahi.

California's long-arm statute authorizes the exercise of jurisdiction "on any basis not inconsistent with the Constitution of this state or of the United States." Asahi moved to quash Cheng Shin's service of summons, arguing the State could not exert jurisdiction over it consistent with the Due Process Clause of the Fourteenth Amendment.

In relation to the motion, the following information was submitted by Asahi and Cheng Shin. Asahi is a Japanese corporation. It manufactures tire valve assemblies in Japan and sells the assemblies to Cheng Shin, and to several other tire manufacturers, for use as components in finished tire tubes. Asahi's sales to Cheng Shin took place in Taiwan. The shipments from Asahi to Cheng Shin were sent from Japan to Taiwan. Cheng Shin bought and incorporated into its tire tubes 150,000 Asahi valve assemblies in 1978; 500,000 in 1979; 500,000 in 1980; 100,000 in 1981; and 100,000 in 1982. Sales to Cheng Shin accounted for 1.24 percent of Asahi's income in 1981 and 0.44 percent in 1982. Cheng Shin alleged that approximately 20 percent of its sales in the United States are in California. Cheng Shin purchases valve assemblies from other suppliers as well, and sells finished tubes throughout the world.

In 1983 an attorney for Cheng Shin conducted an informal examination of the valve stems of the tire tubes sold in one cycle store in Solano County. The attorney declared that of the approximately 115 tire tubes in the store, 97 were purportedly manufactured in Japan or Taiwan, and of those 97, 21 valve stems were marked with the circled letter "A", apparently Asahi's trademark. Of the 21 Asahi valve stems, 12 were incorporated into Cheng Shin tire tubes. The store contained 41 other Cheng Shin tubes that incorporated the valve assemblies of other manufacturers. An affidavit of a manager of Cheng Shin whose duties included the purchasing of component parts stated: " 'In discussions with Asahi regarding the purchase of valve stem assemblies the fact that my Company sells tubes throughout the world and specifically the United States has been discussed. I am informed and believe that Asahi was fully aware that valve stem assemblies sold to my Company and to others would end up throughout the United States and in California.' " An affidavit of the president of Asahi, on the other hand, declared that Asahi " 'has never contemplated that its limited sales of tire valves to Cheng Shin in Taiwan would subject it to lawsuits in California.' " The record does not include any contract between Cheng Shin and Asahi.

Primarily on the basis of the above information, the Superior Court denied the motion to quash summons, stating: "Asahi obviously does business on an international scale. It is not unreasonable that they defend claims of defect in their product on an international scale."

The Court of Appeal of the State of California issued a peremptory writ of mandate commanding the Superior Court to quash service of summons. The court concluded that "it would be unreasonable to require Asahi to respond in California solely on the basis of ultimately realized foreseeability that the product into which its component was embodied would be sold all over the world including California."

The Supreme Court of the State of California reversed and discharged the writ issued by the Court of Appeal. The court observed: "Asahi has no offices, property or agents in California. It solicits no business in California and has made no direct sales [in California]." Moreover, "Asahi did not design or control the system of distribution that carried its valve assemblies into California." Nevertheless, the court found the exercise of jurisdiction over Asahi to be consistent with the Due Process Clause. It concluded that Asahi knew that some of the valve assemblies sold to Cheng Shin would be incorporated into tire tubes sold in California, and that Asahi benefited indirectly from the sale in California of products incorporating its components. The court considered Asahi's intentional act of placing its components into the stream of commerce—that is, by delivering the components to Cheng Shin in Taiwan—coupled with Asahi's awareness that some of the components would eventually find their way into California, sufficient to form the basis for state court jurisdiction under the Due Process Clause.

We granted certiorari and now reverse.

II

A

The Due Process Clause of the Fourteenth Amendment limits the power of a state court to exert personal jurisdiction over a nonresident defendant. "[T]he constitutional touchstone" of the determination whether an exercise of personal jurisdiction comports with due process "remains whether the defendant purposefully established 'minimum contacts' in the forum State." *Burger King Corp. v. Rudzewicz*, quoting *International Shoe Co. v. Washington*. Most recently we have reaffirmed the oft-quoted reasoning of *Hanson v. Denckla,* that minimum contacts must have a basis in "some act by which the defendant purposefully avails itself of the privilege of conducting activities within the forum State, thus invoking the benefits and protections of its laws." *Burger King*. "Jurisdiction is proper . . . where the contacts proximately result from actions by the defendant *himself* that create a 'substantial connection' with the forum State." *Ibid.,* quoting *McGee v. International Life Insurance Co.*

Applying the principle that minimum contacts must be based on an act of the defendant, the Court in *World-Wide Volkswagen Corp. v. Woodson,* rejected the assertion that a *consumer's* unilateral act of bringing the defendant's product into the forum State was a sufficient constitutional basis for personal jurisdiction over the defendant. It had been argued in *World-Wide Volkswagen* that because an automobile retailer and its wholesale distributor sold a product mobile by design and purpose, they could foresee being haled into court in the distant States into which their customers might drive. The Court rejected this concept of foreseeability as an insufficient basis for jurisdiction under the Due Process Clause. The Court disclaimed, however, the idea that "foreseeability is wholly irrelevant" to personal jurisdiction, concluding that "[t]he forum State does not exceed its powers under the Due Process Clause if it asserts personal jurisdiction over a corporation that delivers its products into the stream of commerce with the expectation that they will be purchased by consumers in the forum State." The Court reasoned:

> "When a corporation 'purposefully avails itself of the privilege of conducting activities within the forum State,' *Hanson v. Denckla,* it

has clear notice that it is subject to suit there, and can act to alleviate the risk of burdensome litigation by procuring insurance, passing the expected costs on to customers, or, if the risks are too great, severing its connection with the State. Hence if the sale of a product of a manufacturer or distributor ... is not simply an isolated occurrence, but arises from the efforts of the manufacturer or distributor to serve, directly or indirectly, the market for its product in other States, it is not unreasonable to subject it to suit in one of those States if its allegedly defective merchandise has there been the source of injury to its owners or to others."

In *World-Wide Volkswagen* itself, the state court sought to base jurisdiction not on any act of the defendant, but on the foreseeable unilateral actions of the consumer. Since *World-Wide Volkswagen,* lower courts have been confronted with cases in which the defendant acted by placing a product in the stream of commerce, and the stream eventually swept defendant's product into the forum State, but the defendant did nothing else to purposefully avail itself of the market in the forum State. Some courts have understood the Due Process Clause, as interpreted in *World-Wide Volkswagen,* to allow an exercise of personal jurisdiction to be based on no more than the defendant's act of placing the product in the stream of commerce. Other courts have understood the Due Process Clause and the above-quoted language in *World-Wide Volkswagen* to require the action of the defendant to be more purposefully directed at the forum State than the mere act of placing a product in the stream of commerce.

The reasoning of the Supreme Court of California in the present case illustrates the former interpretation of *World-Wide Volkswagen.* The Supreme Court of California held that, because the stream of commerce eventually brought some valves Asahi sold Cheng Shin into California, Asahi's awareness that its valves would be sold in California was sufficient to permit California to exercise jurisdiction over Asahi consistent with the requirements of the Due Process Clause. The Supreme Court of California's position was consistent with those courts that have held that mere foreseeability or awareness was a constitutionally sufficient basis for personal jurisdiction if the defendant's product made its way into the forum State while still in the stream of commerce.

Other courts, however, have understood the Due Process Clause to require something more than that the defendant was aware of its product's entry into the forum State through the stream of commerce in order for the State to exert jurisdiction over the defendant. In the present case, for example, the State Court of Appeal did not read the Due Process Clause, as interpreted by *World-Wide Volkswagen,* to allow "mere foreseeability that the product will enter the forum state [to] be enough by itself to establish jurisdiction over the distributor and retailer." In *Humble v. Toyota Motor Co.,* an injured car passenger brought suit against Arakawa Auto Body Company, a Japanese corporation that manufactured car seats for Toyota. Arakawa did no business in the United States; it had no office, affiliate, subsidiary, or agent in the United States; it manufactured its component parts outside the United States and delivered them to Toyota Motor Company in Japan. The Court of Appeals, adopting the reasoning of the District Court in that case, noted that although it "does not doubt that Arakawa could have foreseen that its product would find its way into the United States," it would be "manifestly unjust" to require Arakawa to defend itself in the United States.

We now find this latter position to be consonant with the requirements of due process. The "substantial connection," *Burger King*; *McGee;* between the defendant and the forum State necessary for a finding of minimum contacts must come about by *an action of the defendant purposefully directed toward the forum State. Burger King*; *Keeton v. Hustler Magazine, Inc.* The placement of a product into the stream of commerce, without more, is not an act of the defendant purposefully directed toward the forum State. Additional conduct of the defendant may indicate an intent or purpose to serve the market in the forum State, for example, designing the product for the market in the forum State, advertising in the forum State, establishing channels for providing regular advice to customers in the forum State, or marketing the product through a distributor who has agreed to serve as the sales agent in the forum State. But a defendant's awareness that the stream of commerce may or will sweep the product into the forum State does not convert the mere act of placing the product into the stream into an act purposefully directed toward the forum State.

Assuming, *arguendo,* that respondents have established Asahi's awareness that some of the valves sold to Cheng Shin would be incorporated into tire tubes sold in California, respondents have not demonstrated any action by Asahi to purposefully avail itself of the California market. Asahi does not do business in California. It has no office, agents, employees, or property in California. It does not advertise or otherwise solicit business in California. It did not create, control, or employ the distribution system that brought its valves to California. There is no evidence that Asahi designed its product in anticipation of sales in California. On the basis of these facts, the exertion of personal jurisdiction over Asahi by the Superior Court of California exceeds the limits of due process.

B

The strictures of the Due Process Clause forbid a state court to exercise personal jurisdiction over Asahi under circumstances that would offend " 'traditional notions of fair play and substantial justice.' " *International Shoe Co. v. Washington.*

We have previously explained that the determination of the reasonableness of the exercise of jurisdiction in each case will depend on an evaluation of several factors. A court must consider the burden on the defendant, the interests of the forum State, and the plaintiff's interest in obtaining relief. It must also weigh in its determination "the interstate judicial system's interest in obtaining the most efficient resolution of controversies; and the shared interest of the several States in furthering fundamental substantive social policies." *World-Wide Volkswagen.*

A consideration of these factors in the present case clearly reveals the unreasonableness of the assertion of jurisdiction over Asahi, even apart from the question of the placement of goods in the stream of commerce.

Certainly the burden on the defendant in this case is severe. Asahi has been commanded by the Supreme Court of California not only to traverse the distance between Asahi's headquarters in Japan and the Superior Court of California in and for the County of Solano, but also to submit its dispute with Cheng Shin to a foreign nation's judicial system. The unique burdens placed upon one who must defend oneself in a foreign legal system should have significant weight in assessing the reasonableness of stretching the long arm of personal jurisdiction over national borders.

When minimum contacts have been established, often the interests of the plaintiff and the forum in the exercise of jurisdiction will justify even the serious burdens placed on the alien defendant. In the present case, however, the interests of the plaintiff and the forum in California's assertion of jurisdiction over Asahi are slight. All that remains is a claim for indemnification asserted by Cheng Shin, a Taiwanese corporation, against Asahi. The transaction on which the indemnification claim is based took place in Taiwan; Asahi's components were shipped from Japan to Taiwan. Cheng Shin has not demonstrated that it is more convenient for it to litigate its indemnification claim against Asahi in California rather than in Taiwan or Japan.

Because the plaintiff is not a California resident, California's legitimate interests in the dispute have considerably diminished. The Supreme Court of California argued that the State had an interest in "protecting its consumers by ensuring that foreign manufacturers comply with the state's safety standards." The State Supreme Court's definition of California's interest, however, was overly broad. The dispute between Cheng Shin and Asahi is primarily about indemnification rather than safety standards. Moreover, it is not at all clear at this point that California law should govern the question whether a Japanese corporation should indemnify a Taiwanese corporation on the basis of a sale made in Taiwan and a shipment of goods from Japan to Taiwan. The possibility of being haled into a California court as a result of an accident involving Asahi's components undoubtedly creates an additional deterrent to the manufacture of unsafe components; however, similar pressures will be placed on Asahi by the purchasers of its components as long as those who use Asahi components in their final products, and sell those products in California, are subject to the application of California tort law.

World-Wide Volkswagen also admonished courts to take into consideration the interests of the "several States," in addition to the forum State, in the efficient judicial resolution of the dispute and the advancement of substantive policies. In the present case, this advice calls for a court to consider the procedural and substantive policies of other *nations* whose interests are affected by the assertion of jurisdiction by the California court. The procedural and substantive interests of other nations in a state court's assertion of jurisdiction over an alien defendant will differ from case to case. In every case, however, those interests, as well as the Federal interest in Government's foreign relations policies, will be best served by a careful inquiry into the reasonableness of the assertion of jurisdiction in the particular case, and an unwillingness to find the serious burdens on an alien defendant outweighed by minimal interests on the part of the plaintiff or the forum State. "Great care and reserve should be exercised when extending our notions of personal jurisdiction into the international field."

Considering the international context, the heavy burden on the alien defendant, and the slight interests of the plaintiff and the forum State, the exercise of personal jurisdiction by a California court over Asahi in this instance would be unreasonable and unfair.

III

Because the facts of this case do not establish minimum contacts such that the exercise of personal jurisdiction is consistent with fair play and substantial justice, the judgment of the Supreme Court of California is reversed, and the case is remanded for further proceedings not inconsistent with this opinion.

It is so ordered.

JUSTICE BRENNAN, with whom JUSTICE WHITE, JUSTICE MARSHALL, and JUSTICE BLACKMUN join, concurring in part and concurring in the judgment.

I do not agree with the interpretation in Part II–A of the stream-of-commerce theory, nor with the conclusion that Asahi did not "purposely avail itself of the California market." I do agree, however, with the Court's conclusion in Part II–B that the exercise of personal jurisdiction over Asahi in this case would not comport with "fair play and substantial justice," *International Shoe Co. v. Washington.* This is one of those rare cases in which "minimum requirements inherent in the concept of 'fair play and substantial justice' . . . defeat the reasonableness of jurisdiction even [though] the defendant has purposefully engaged in forum activities." *Burger King Corp. v. Rudzewicz.* I therefore join Parts I and II–B of the Court's opinion, and write separately to explain my disagreement with Part II–A.

Part II–A states that "a defendant's awareness that the stream of commerce may or will sweep the product into the forum State does not convert the mere act of placing the product into the stream into an act purposefully directed toward the forum State." Under this view, a plaintiff would be required to show "[a]dditional conduct" directed toward the forum before finding the exercise of jurisdiction over the defendant to be consistent with the Due Process Clause. I see no need for such a showing, however. The stream of commerce refers not to unpredictable currents or eddies, but to the regular and anticipated flow of products from manufacture to distribution to retail sale. As long as a participant in this process is aware that the final product is being marketed in the forum State, the possibility of a lawsuit there cannot come as a surprise. Nor will the litigation present a burden for which there is no corresponding benefit. A defendant who has placed goods in the stream of commerce benefits economically from the retail sale of the final product in the forum State, and indirectly benefits from the State's laws that regulate and facilitate commercial activity. These benefits accrue regardless of whether that participant directly conducts business in the forum State, or engages in additional conduct directed toward that State. Accordingly, most courts and commentators have found that jurisdiction premised on the placement of a product into the stream of commerce is consistent with the Due Process Clause, and have not required a showing of additional conduct.

The endorsement in Part II–A of what appears to be the minority view among Federal Courts of Appeals[2] represents a marked retreat from the analysis in *World-Wide Volkswagen v. Woodson.* In that case, "respondents [sought] to base jurisdiction on one, isolated occurrence and whatever inferences can be drawn therefrom: the fortuitous circumstance that a single Audi automobile, sold in New York to New York residents, happened to suffer an accident while passing through Oklahoma." The Court held that the possibility of an accident in Oklahoma, while to some extent foreseeable in light of the inherent mobility of the automobile, was not enough to establish minimum contacts between the forum State and the retailer or distributor. The Court then carefully explained:

> [T]his is not to say, of course, that foreseeability is wholly irrelevant. But the foreseeability that is critical to due process analysis is not the mere likelihood that a product will find its way into the forum State. Rather, it is that the defendant's conduct and connection with the forum State are such that he should reasonably anticipate being haled into Court there.

The Court reasoned that when a corporation may reasonably anticipate litigation in a particular forum, it cannot claim that such litigation is unjust or unfair, because it "can act to alleviate the risk of burdensome litigation by procuring insurance, passing the expected costs on to consumers, or, if the risks are too great, severing its connection with the State."

---

   2. The Court of Appeals for the Eighth Circuit appears to be the only Court of Appeals to have expressly adopted a narrow construction of the stream-of-commerce theory analogous to the one articulated in Part II–A today, although the Court of Appeals for the Eleventh Circuit has implicitly adopted it. Two other Courts of Appeals have found the theory inapplicable when only a single sale occurred in the forum State, but do not appear committed to the interpretation of the theory that the Court adopts today. Similarly, the Court of Appeals for the Third Circuit has not interpreted the theory as Justice O'Connor's opinion has but has rejected stream-of-commerce arguments for jurisdiction when the relationship between the distributor and the defendant "remains in dispute" and "evidence indicating that [defendant] could anticipate either use of its product or litigation in [the forum State] is totally lacking," and when the defendant's product was not sold in the forum State and the defendant "did not take advantage of an indirect marketing scheme."

To illustrate the point, the Court contrasted the foreseeability of litigation in a State to which a consumer fortuitously transports a defendant's product (insufficient contacts) with the foreseeability of litigation in a State where the defendant's product was regularly *sold* (sufficient contacts). The Court stated:

> "Hence if the *sale* of a product of a manufacturer or distributor such as Audi or Volkswagen is not simply an isolated occurrence, but arises from the efforts of the manufacturer or distributor to serve, *directly or indirectly,* the market for its product in other States, it is not unreasonable to subject it to suit in one of those States if its allegedly defective merchandise has there been the source of injury to its owner or to others. The forum State does not exceed its powers under the Due Process Clause if it asserts personal jurisdiction over a corporation that delivers its products into the stream of commerce *with the expectation that they will be purchased by consumers* in the forum State." (emphasis added).

The Court concluded its illustration by referring to *Gray v. American Radiator & Standard Sanitary Corp.,* a well-known stream-of-commerce case in which the Illinois Supreme Court applied the theory to assert jurisdiction over a component-parts manufacturer that sold no components directly in Illinois, but did sell them to a manufacturer who incorporated them into a final product that was sold in Illinois.

The Court in *World-Wide Volkswagen* thus took great care to distinguish "between a case involving goods which reach a distant State through a chain of distribution and a case involving goods which reach the same State because a consumer . . . took them there." (Brennan, J., dissenting).[3] The California Supreme Court took note of this distinction, and correctly concluded that our holding in *World-Wide Volkswagen* preserved the stream-of-commerce theory.

In this case, the facts found by the California Supreme Court support its finding of minimum contacts. The court found that "[a]lthough Asahi did not design or control the system of distribution that carried its valve assemblies into California, Asahi was aware of the distribution system's operation, and it knew that it would benefit economically from the sale in California of products incorporating its components."[4] Accordingly, I

---

3. In dissent, I argued that the distinction was without constitutional significance, because in my view the foreseeability that a customer would use a product in a distant State was a sufficient basis for jurisdiction. *See also* (Marshall, J., dissenting) ("I cannot agree that jurisdiction is necessarily lacking if the product enters the State not through the channels of distribution but in the course of its intended use by the consumer"); (Blackmun, J., dissenting) ("[F]oreseeable use in another State seems to me little different from foreseeable resale in another State"). But I do not read the decision in *World-Wide Volkswagen* to establish a *per se* rule against the exercise of jurisdiction where the contacts arise from a consumer's use of the product in a given State, but only a rule against jurisdiction in cases involving "one, isolated occurrence [of consumer use, amounting to] . . . the fortuitous circumstance. . . ."

4. Moreover, the Court found that "at least 18 percent of the tubes sold in a particular California motorcycle supply shop contained Asahi valve assemblies," and that Asahi had an ongoing business relationship with Cheng Shin involving average annual sales of hundreds of thousands of valve assemblies.

cannot join the determination in Part II–A that Asahi's regular and extensive sales of component parts to a manufacturer it knew was making regular sales of the final product in California is insufficient to establish minimum contacts with California.

JUSTICE STEVENS, with whom JUSTICE WHITE and JUSTICE BLACKMUN join, concurring in part and concurring in the judgment.

The judgment of the Supreme Court of California should be reversed for the reasons stated in Part II–B of the Court's opinion. While I join Parts I and II–B, I do not join Part II–A for two reasons. First, it is not necessary to the Court's decision. An examination of minimum contacts is not always necessary to determine whether a state court's assertion of personal jurisdiction is constitutional. *See Burger King Corp. v. Rudzewicz*. Part II–B establishes, after considering the factors set forth in *World-Wide Volkswagen Corp. v. Woodson*, that California's exercise of jurisdiction over Asahi in this case would be "unreasonable and unfair." This finding alone requires reversal; this case fits within the rule that "minimum requirements inherent in the concept of 'fair play and substantial justice' may defeat the reasonableness of jurisdiction even if the defendant has purposefully engaged in forum activities." *Burger King* (quoting *International Shoe Co. v. Washington*). Accordingly, I see no reason in this case for the plurality to articulate "purposeful direction" or any other test as the nexus between an act of a defendant and the forum State that is necessary to establish minimum contacts.

Second, even assuming that the test ought to be formulated here, Part II–A misapplies it to the facts of this case. The plurality seems to assume that an unwavering line can be drawn between "mere awareness" that a component will find its way into the forum State and "purposeful availment" of the forum's market. Over the course of its dealings with Cheng Shin, Asahi has arguably engaged in a higher quantum of conduct than "[t]he placement of a product into the stream of commerce, without more...." Whether or not this conduct rises to the level of purposeful availment requires a constitutional determination that is affected by the volume, the value, and the hazardous character of the components. In most circumstances I would be inclined to conclude that a regular course of dealing that results in deliveries of over 100,000 units annually over a period of several years would constitute "purposeful availment" even though the item delivered to the forum State was a standard product marketed throughout the world.

* * *

B. STREAM OF COMMERCE: MUDDY WATERS

J. McINTYRE MACHINERY, LTD. v. NICASTRO

131 S.Ct. 2780 (2011)

KENNEDY, J., announced the judgment of the Court and delivered an opinion, in which ROBERTS, C.J., and SCALIA and THOMAS, JJ., joined. BREYER, J., filed an opinion concurring in the judgment, in which ALITO, J., joined. GINSBURG, J., filed a dissenting opinion, in which SOTOMAYOR and KAGAN, JJ., joined.

JUSTICE KENNEDY announced the judgment of the Court and delivered an opinion, in which THE CHIEF JUSTICE, JUSTICE SCALIA, and JUSTICE THOMAS join.

Whether a person or entity is subject to the jurisdiction of a state court despite not having been present in the State either at the time of suit or at the time of the alleged injury, and despite not having consented to the exercise of jurisdiction, is a question that arises with great frequency in the routine course of litigation. The rules and standards for determining when a State does or does not have jurisdiction over an absent party have been unclear because of decades-old questions left open in *Asahi Metal Industry Co. v. Superior Court of Cal.*

Here, the Supreme Court of New Jersey, relying in part on *Asahi*, held that New Jersey's courts can exercise jurisdiction over a foreign manufacturer of a product so long as the manufacturer "knows or reasonably should know that its products are distributed through a nationwide distribution system that might lead to those products being sold in any of the fifty states." Applying that test, the court concluded that a British manufacturer of scrap metal machines was subject to jurisdiction in New Jersey, even though at no time had it advertised in, sent goods to, or in any relevant sense targeted the State.

That decision cannot be sustained. Although the New Jersey Supreme Court issued an extensive opinion with careful attention to this Court's cases and to its own precedent, the "stream of commerce" metaphor carried the decision far afield. Due process protects the defendant's right not to be coerced except by lawful judicial power. As a general rule, the exercise of judicial power is not lawful unless the defendant "purposefully avails itself of the privilege of conducting activities within the forum State, thus invoking the benefits and protections of its laws." There may be exceptions, say, for instance, in cases involving an intentional tort. But the general rule is applicable in this products-liability case, and the so-called "stream-of-commerce" doctrine cannot displace it.

I

This case arises from a products-liability suit filed in New Jersey state court. Robert Nicastro seriously injured his hand while using a metal-shearing machine manufactured by J. McIntyre Machinery, Ltd. (J. McIntyre). The accident occurred in New Jersey, but the machine was manufactured in England, where J. McIntyre is incorporated and operates. The question here is whether the New Jersey courts have jurisdiction over J. McIntyre, notwithstanding the fact that the company at no time either marketed goods in the State or shipped them there. Nicastro was a plaintiff in the New Jersey trial court and is the respondent here; J. McIntyre was a defendant and is now the petitioner.

At oral argument in this Court, Nicastro's counsel stressed three primary facts in defense of New Jersey's assertion of jurisdiction over J. McIntyre.

First, an independent company agreed to sell J. McIntyre's machines in the United States. J. McIntyre itself did not sell its machines to buyers in this country beyond the U.S. distributor, and there is no allegation that the distributor was under J. McIntyre's control.

Second, J. McIntyre officials attended annual conventions for the scrap recycling industry to advertise J. McIntyre's machines alongside the distributor. The conventions took place in various States, but never in New Jersey.

Third, no more than four machines, including the machine that caused the injuries that are the basis for this suit, ended up in New Jersey.

In addition to these facts emphasized by petitioner, the New Jersey Supreme Court noted that J. McIntyre held both United States and European patents on its recycling technology. It also noted that the U.S. distributor "structured [its] advertising and sales efforts in accordance with" J. McIntyre's "direction and guidance whenever possible," and that "at least some of the machines were sold on consignment to" the distributor.

In light of these facts, the New Jersey Supreme Court concluded that New Jersey courts could exercise jurisdiction over petitioner without contravention of the Due Process Clause. Jurisdiction was proper, in that court's view, because the injury occurred in New Jersey; because petitioner knew or reasonably should have known "that its products are distributed through a nationwide distribution system that might lead to those products being sold in any of the fifty states"; and because petitioner failed to "take some reasonable step to prevent the distribution of its products in this State."

Both the New Jersey Supreme Court's holding and its account of what it called "[t]he stream-of-commerce doctrine of jurisdiction" were incorrect, however. This Court's *Asahi* decision may be responsible in part for that court's error regarding the stream of commerce, and this case presents an opportunity to provide greater clarity.

II

The Due Process Clause protects an individual's right to be deprived of life, liberty, or property only by the exercise of lawful power. (The Clause "protect[s] a person against having the Government impose burdens upon him except in accordance with the valid laws of the land"). This is no less true with respect to the power of a sovereign to resolve disputes through judicial process than with respect to the power of a sovereign to prescribe rules of conduct for those within its sphere. As a general rule, neither statute nor judicial decree may bind strangers to the State. Cf. *Burnham v. Superior Court of Cal.,* invoking "the phrase *coram non judice,* 'before a person not a judge'—meaning, in effect, that the proceeding in question was not a *judicial* proceeding because lawful judicial authority was not present, and could therefore not yield a *judgment*").

A court may subject a defendant to judgment only when the defendant has sufficient contacts with the sovereign "such that the maintenance of the suit does not offend 'traditional notions of fair play and substantial justice.'" *International Shoe Co.* Free-form notions of fundamental fairness divorced from traditional practice cannot transform a judgment rendered in the absence of authority into law. As a general rule, the sovereign's exercise of power requires some act by which the defendant "purposefully avails itself of the privilege of conducting activities within the forum State, thus invoking the benefits and protections of its laws," *Hanson,* though in some cases, as with an intentional tort, the defendant might well fall within the State's authority by reason of his attempt to obstruct its laws. In products-liability cases like this one, it is the defendant's purposeful availment that makes jurisdiction consistent with "traditional notions of fair play and substantial justice."

A person may submit to a State's authority in a number of ways. There is, of course, explicit consent. Presence within a State at the time suit commences through service of process is another example. See *Burnham.* Citizenship or domicile—or, by analogy, incorporation or principal place of business for corporations—also indicates general submission to a State's powers. Each of these examples reveals circumstances, or a course of conduct, from which it is proper to infer an intention to benefit from and thus an intention to submit to the laws of the forum State. Cf. *Burger King Corp.* These examples support exercise of the general jurisdiction of the State's courts and allow the State to resolve both matters that originate within the State and those based on activities and events elsewhere. *Helicopteros Nacionales de Colombia.* By contrast, those who live or operate primarily outside a State have a due process right not to be subjected to judgment in its courts as a general matter.

There is also a more limited form of submission to a State's authority for disputes that "arise out of or are connected with the activities within the state." *International Shoe Co.* Where a defendant "purposefully avails itself of the privilege of conducting activities within the forum State, thus invoking the benefits and protections of its laws," *Hanson,* it submits to the judicial power of an otherwise foreign sovereign to the extent that power is exercised in connection with the defendant's activities touching on the State. In other words, submission through contact with and activity directed at a sovereign may justify specific jurisdiction "in a suit arising out of or related to the defendant's contacts with the forum." *Helicopteros*.

The imprecision arising from *Asahi,* for the most part, results from its statement of the relation between jurisdiction and the "stream of commerce." The stream of commerce, like other metaphors, has its deficiencies as well as its utility. It refers to the movement of goods from manufacturers through distributors to consumers, yet beyond that descriptive purpose its meaning is far from exact. This Court has stated that a defendant's placing goods into the stream of commerce "with the expectation that they will be purchased by consumers within the forum State" may indicate purposeful availment. *World–Wide Volkswagen Corp.* (finding that expectation lacking). But that statement does not amend the general rule of personal jurisdiction. It merely observes that a defendant may in an appropriate case be subject to jurisdiction without entering the forum—itself an unexceptional proposition—as where manufacturers or distributors "seek to serve" a given State's market. The principal inquiry in cases of this sort is whether the defendant's activities manifest an intention to submit to the power of a sovereign. In other words, the defendant must "purposefully avai[l] itself of the privilege of conducting activities within the forum State, thus invoking the benefits and protections of its laws." *Hanson* ("[A]ctions of the defendant may amount to a legal submission to the jurisdiction of the court"). Sometimes a defendant does so by sending its goods rather than its agents. The defendant's transmission of goods permits the exercise of jurisdiction only where the defendant can be said to have targeted the forum; as a general rule, it is not enough that the defendant might have predicted that its goods will reach the forum State.

In *Asahi,* an opinion by Justice Brennan for four Justices outlined a different approach. It discarded the central concept of sovereign authority in favor of considerations of fairness and foreseeability. As that concurrence contended, "jurisdiction premised on the placement of a product into the stream of commerce [without more] is consistent with the Due Process Clause," for "[a]s long as a participant in this process is aware that the final product is being marketed in the forum State, the possibility of a lawsuit there cannot come as a surprise." It was the premise of the concurring opinion that the defendant's ability to anticipate suit renders the assertion of jurisdiction fair. In this way, the opinion made foreseeability the touchstone of jurisdiction.

The standard set forth in Justice Brennan's concurrence was rejected in an opinion written by Justice O'Connor; but the relevant part of that opinion, too, commanded the assent of only four Justices, not a majority of the Court. That opinion stated: "The 'substantial connection' between the defendant and the forum State necessary for a finding of minimum contacts must come about by an action of the defendant purposefully directed toward the forum State. The placement of a product into the stream of commerce, without more, is not an act of the defendant purposefully directed toward the forum State."

Since *Asahi* was decided, the courts have sought to reconcile the competing opinions. But Justice Brennan's concurrence, advocating a rule based on general notions of fairness and foreseeability, is inconsistent with the premises of lawful judicial power. This Court's precedents make clear that it is the defendant's actions, not his expectations, that empower a State's courts to subject him to judgment.

The conclusion that jurisdiction is in the first instance a question of authority rather than fairness explains, for example, why the principal opinion in *Burnham* "conducted no independent inquiry into the desirability or fairness" of the rule that service of process within a State suffices to establish jurisdiction over an otherwise foreign defendant. As that opinion explained, "[t]he view developed early that each State had the power to hale before its courts any individual who could be found within its borders." Furthermore, were general fairness considerations the touchstone of jurisdiction, a lack of purposeful availment might be excused where carefully crafted judicial procedures could otherwise protect the defendant's interests, or where the plaintiff would suffer substantial hardship if forced to litigate in a foreign forum. That such considerations have not been deemed controlling is instructive. See, *e.g., World–Wide Volkswagen.*

Two principles are implicit in the foregoing. First, personal jurisdiction requires a forum-by-forum, or sovereign-by-sovereign, analysis. The question is whether a defendant has followed a course of conduct directed at the society or economy existing within the jurisdiction of a given sovereign, so that the sovereign has the power to subject the defendant to judgment concerning that conduct. Personal jurisdiction, of course, restricts "judicial power not as a matter of sovereignty, but as a matter of individual liberty," for due process protects the individual's right to be subject only to lawful power. But whether a judicial judgment is lawful depends on whether the sovereign has authority to render it.

The second principle is a corollary of the first. Because the United States is a distinct sovereign, a defendant may in principle be subject to the jurisdiction of the courts of the United States but not of any particular State. This is consistent with the premises and unique genius of our Constitution. Ours is "a legal system unprecedented in form and design, establishing two orders of government, each with its own direct relationship, its own privity, its own set of mutual rights and obligations to the people who sustain it and are governed by it." For jurisdiction, a litigant may have the requisite relationship with the United States Government but not with the government of any individual State. That would be an exceptional case, however. If the defendant is a domestic domiciliary, the courts of its home State are available and can exercise general jurisdiction. And if another State were to assert jurisdiction in an inappropriate case, it would upset the federal balance, which posits that each State has a sovereignty that is not subject to unlawful intrusion by other States. Furthermore, foreign corporations will often target or concentrate on particular States, subjecting them to specific jurisdiction in those forums.

It must be remembered, however, that although this case and *Asahi* both involve foreign manufacturers, the undesirable consequences of Justice Brennan's approach are no less significant for domestic producers. The owner of a small Florida farm might sell crops to a large nearby distributor, for example, who might then distribute them to grocers across the country. If foreseeability were the controlling criterion, the farmer could be sued in Alaska or any number of other States' courts without ever leaving town. And the issue of foreseeability may itself be contested so that significant expenses are incurred just on the preliminary issue of jurisdiction. Jurisdictional rules should avoid these costs whenever possible.

The conclusion that the authority to subject a defendant to judgment depends on purposeful availment, consistent with Justice O'Connor's opinion in *Asahi,* does not by itself resolve many difficult questions of jurisdiction that will arise in particular cases. The defendant's conduct and the economic realities of the market the defendant seeks to serve will differ across cases, and judicial exposition will, in common-law fashion, clarify the contours of that principle.

III

In this case, petitioner directed marketing and sales efforts at the United States. It may be that, assuming it were otherwise empowered to legislate on the subject, the Congress could authorize the exercise of jurisdiction in appropriate courts. That circumstance is not presented in this case, however, and it is neither necessary nor appropriate to address here any constitutional concerns that might be attendant to that exercise of power. See *Asahi.* Nor is it necessary to determine what substantive law might apply were Congress to authorize jurisdiction in a federal court in New Jersey. See *Hanson* ("The issue is personal jurisdiction, not choice of law"). A sovereign's legislative authority to regulate conduct may present considerations different from those presented by its authority to subject a defendant to judgment in its courts. Here the question concerns the authority of a New Jersey state court to exercise jurisdiction, so it is petitioner's purposeful contacts with New Jersey, not with the United States, that alone are relevant.

Respondent has not established that J. McIntyre engaged in conduct purposefully directed at New Jersey. Recall that respondent's claim of jurisdiction centers on three facts: The distributor agreed to sell J. McIntyre's machines in the United States; J. McIntyre officials attended trade shows in several States but not in New Jersey; and up to four machines ended up in New Jersey. The British manufacturer had no office in New Jersey; it neither paid taxes nor owned property there; and it neither advertised in, nor sent any employees to, the State. Indeed, after discovery the trial court found that the "defendant does not have a single contact with New Jersey short of the machine in question ending up in this state." These facts may reveal an intent to serve the U.S. market, but they do not show that J. McIntyre purposefully availed itself of the New Jersey market.

It is notable that the New Jersey Supreme Court appears to agree, for it could "not find that J. McIntyre had a presence or minimum contacts in this State—in any jurisprudential sense—that would justify a New Jersey court to exercise jurisdiction in this case." The court nonetheless held that petitioner could be sued in New Jersey based on a "stream-of-commerce theory of jurisdiction." As discussed, however, the stream-of-commerce metaphor cannot supersede either the mandate of the Due Process Clause or the limits on judicial authority that Clause ensures. The New Jersey Supreme Court also cited "significant policy reasons" to justify its holding, including the State's "strong interest in protecting its citizens from defective products." That interest is doubtless strong, but the Constitution commands restraint before discarding liberty in the name of expediency.

* * *

Due process protects petitioner's right to be subject only to lawful authority. At no time did petitioner engage in any activities in New Jersey that reveal an intent to invoke or benefit from the protection of its laws. New Jersey is without power to adjudge the rights and liabilities of J. McIntyre, and its exercise of jurisdiction would violate due process. The contrary judgment of the New Jersey Supreme Court is

Reversed.

JUSTICE BREYER, with whom JUSTICE ALITO joins, concurring in the judgment.

The Supreme Court of New Jersey adopted a broad understanding of the scope of personal jurisdiction based on its view that "[t]he increasingly fast-paced globalization of the world economy has removed national borders as barriers to trade." I do not doubt that there have been many recent changes in commerce and communication, many of which are not anticipated by our precedents. But this case does not present any of those issues. So I think it unwise to announce a rule of broad applicability without full consideration of the modern-day consequences.

In my view, the outcome of this case is determined by our precedents. Based on the facts found by the New Jersey courts, respondent Robert Nicastro failed to meet his burden to demonstrate that it was constitutionally proper to exercise jurisdiction over petitioner J. McIntyre Machinery, Ltd. (British Manufacturer), a British firm that manufactures scrap-metal machines in Great Britain and sells them through an independent distributor in the United States (American Distributor). On that basis, I agree with the plurality that the contrary judgment of the Supreme Court of New Jersey should be reversed.

I

In asserting jurisdiction over the British Manufacturer, the Supreme Court of New Jersey relied most heavily on three primary facts as providing constitutionally sufficient "contacts" with New Jersey, thereby making it fundamentally fair to hale the British Manufacturer before its courts: (1) The American Distributor on one occasion sold and shipped one machine to a New Jersey customer, namely, Mr. Nicastro's employer, Mr. Curcio; (2) the British Manufacturer permitted, indeed wanted, its independent American Distributor to sell its machines to anyone in America willing to buy them; and (3) representatives of the British Manufacturer attended trade shows in "such cities as Chicago, Las Vegas, New Orleans, Orlando, San Diego, and San Francisco." In my view, these facts do not provide contacts between the British firm and the State of New Jersey constitutionally sufficient to support New Jersey's assertion of jurisdiction in this case.

None of our precedents finds that a single isolated sale, even if accompanied by the kind of sales effort indicated here, is sufficient. Rather, this Court's previous holdings suggest the contrary. The Court has held that a single sale to a customer who takes an accident-causing product to a different State (where the accident takes place) is not a sufficient basis for asserting jurisdiction. See *World–Wide Volkswagen Corp.* And the Court, in separate opinions, has strongly suggested that a single sale of a product in a State does not constitute an adequate basis for asserting jurisdiction over an out-of-state defendant, even if that defendant places his goods in the stream of commerce, fully aware (and hoping) that such a sale will take place. See *Asahi Metal Industry Co.* (opinion of O'Connor, J.) (requiring "something more" than simply placing "a product into the stream of commerce," even if defendant is "awar[e]" that the stream "may or will sweep the product into the forum State"); (Brennan, J., concurring in part and concurring in judgment) (jurisdiction should lie where a sale in a State is part of "the regular and anticipated flow" of commerce into the State, but not where that sale is only an "edd[y]," *i.e.*, an isolated occurrence); (Stevens, J., concurring in part and concurring in judgment) (indicating that "the volume, the value, and the hazardous character" of a good may affect the jurisdictional inquiry and emphasizing Asahi's "regular course of dealing").

Here, the relevant facts found by the New Jersey Supreme Court show no "regular ... flow" or "regular course" of sales in New Jersey; and there is no "something more," such as special state-related design, advertising, advice, marketing, or anything else. Mr. Nicastro, who here bears the burden of proving jurisdiction, has shown no specific effort by the British Manufacturer to sell in New Jersey. He has introduced no list of potential New Jersey customers who might, for example, have regularly attended trade shows. And he has not otherwise shown that the British Manufacturer "purposefully avail[ed] itself of the privilege of conducting activities" within New Jersey, or that it delivered its goods in the stream of commerce "with the expectation that they will be purchased" by New Jersey users. *World–Wide Volkswagen.*

There may well have been other facts that Mr. Nicastro could have demonstrated in support of jurisdiction. And the dissent considers some of those facts. See opinion of Ginsburg, J. (describing the size and scope of New Jersey's scrap-metal business). But the plaintiff bears the burden of establishing jurisdiction, and here I would take the facts precisely as the New Jersey Supreme Court stated them.

Accordingly, on the record present here, resolving this case requires no more than adhering to our precedents.

II

I would not go further. Because the incident at issue in this case does not implicate modern concerns, and because the factual record leaves many open questions, this is an unsuitable vehicle for making broad pronouncements that refashion basic jurisdictional rules.

A

The plurality seems to state strict rules that limit jurisdiction where a defendant does not "inten[d] to submit to the power of a sovereign" and cannot "be said to have targeted the forum." But what do those standards mean when a company targets the world by selling products from its Web site? And does it matter if, instead of shipping the products directly, a company consigns the products through an intermediary (say, Amazon.com) who then receives and fulfills the orders? And what if the company markets its products through popup advertisements that it knows will be viewed in a forum? Those issues have serious commercial consequences but are totally absent in this case.

B

But though I do not agree with the plurality's seemingly strict no-jurisdiction rule, I am not persuaded by the absolute approach adopted by the New Jersey Supreme Court and urged by respondent and his *amici.* Under that view, a producer is subject to jurisdiction for a products-liability action so long as it "knows or reasonably should know that its products are distributed through a nationwide distribution system that *might* lead to those products being sold in any of the fifty states." In the context of this case, I cannot agree.

For one thing, to adopt this view would abandon the heretofore accepted inquiry of whether, focusing upon the relationship between "the defendant, the *forum,* and the litigation," it is fair, in light of the defendant's contacts *with that forum,* to subject the defendant to suit there. *Shaffer v. Heitner.* It would ordinarily rest jurisdiction instead upon no more than the occurrence of a product-based accident in the forum State. But this Court has rejected the notion that a defendant's amenability to suit "travel[s] with the chattel." *World–Wide Volkswagen.*

For another, I cannot reconcile so automatic a rule with the constitutional demand for "minimum contacts" and "purposefu[l] avail[ment]," each of which rest upon a particular notion of defendant-focused fairness. A rule like the New Jersey Supreme Court's would permit every State to assert jurisdiction in a products-liability suit against any domestic manufacturer who sells its products (made anywhere in the United States) to a national distributor, no matter how large or small the manufacturer, no matter how distant the forum, and no matter how few the number of items that end up in the particular forum at issue. What might appear fair in the case of a large manufacturer which specifically seeks, or expects, an equal-sized distributor to sell its product in a distant State might seem unfair in the case of a small manufacturer (say, an Appalachian potter) who sells his product (cups and saucers) exclusively to a large distributor, who resells a single item (a coffee mug) to a buyer from a distant State (Hawaii). I know too little about the range of these or in-between possibilities to abandon in favor of the more absolute rule what has previously been this Court's less absolute approach.

Further, the fact that the defendant is a foreign, rather than a domestic, manufacturer makes the basic fairness of an absolute rule yet more uncertain. I am again less certain than is the New Jersey Supreme Court that the nature of international commerce has changed so significantly as to require a new approach to personal jurisdiction.

It may be that a larger firm can readily "alleviate the risk of burdensome litigation by procuring insurance, passing the expected costs on to customers, or, if the risks are too great, severing its connection with the State." *World–Wide Volkswagen*. But manufacturers come in many shapes and sizes. It may be fundamentally unfair to require a small Egyptian shirt maker, a Brazilian manufacturing cooperative, or a Kenyan coffee farmer, selling its products through international distributors, to respond to products-liability tort suits in virtually every State in the United States, even those in respect to which the foreign firm has no connection at all but the sale of a single (allegedly defective) good. And a rule like the New Jersey Supreme Court suggests would require every product manufacturer, large or small, selling to American distributors to understand not only the tort law of every State, but also the wide variance in the way courts within different States apply that law.

C

At a minimum, I would not work such a change to the law in the way either the plurality or the New Jersey Supreme Court suggests without a better understanding of the relevant contemporary commercial circumstances. Insofar as such considerations are relevant to any change in present law, they might be presented in a case (unlike the present one) in which the Solicitor General participates.

This case presents no such occasion, and so I again reiterate that I would adhere strictly to our precedents and the limited facts found by the New Jersey Supreme Court. And on those grounds, I do not think we can find jurisdiction in this case. Accordingly, though I agree with the plurality as to the outcome of this case, I concur only in the judgment of that opinion and not its reasoning.

JUSTICE GINSBURG, with whom JUSTICE SOTOMAYOR and JUSTICE KAGAN join, dissenting.

A foreign industrialist seeks to develop a market in the United States for machines it manufactures. It hopes to derive substantial revenue from sales it makes to United States purchasers. Where in the United States buyers reside does not matter to this manufacturer. Its goal is simply to sell as much as it can, wherever it can. It excludes no region or State from the market it wishes to reach. But, all things considered, it prefers to avoid products liability litigation in the United States. To that end, it engages a U.S. distributor to ship its machines stateside. Has it succeeded in escaping personal jurisdiction in a State where one of its products is sold and causes injury or even death to a local user?

Under this Court's path-marking precedent in *International Shoe Co.*, and subsequent decisions, one would expect the answer to be unequivocally "No." But instead, six Justices of this Court, in divergent opinions, tell us that the manufacturer has avoided the jurisdiction of our state courts, except perhaps in States where its products are sold in sizeable quantities. Inconceivable as it may have seemed yesterday, the splintered majority today "turn[s] the clock back to the days before modern long-arm statutes when a manufacturer, to avoid being haled into court where a user is injured, need only Pilate-like wash its hands of a product by having independent distributors market it."

I

On October 11, 2001, a three-ton metal shearing machine severed four fingers on Robert Nicastro's right hand. Alleging that the machine was a dangerous product defectively made, Nicastro sought compensation from the machine's manufacturer, J. McIntyre Machinery Ltd. (McIntyre UK). Established in 1872 as a United Kingdom corporation, and headquartered in Nottingham, England, McIntyre UK "designs, develops and manufactures a complete range of equipment for metal recycling." The company's product line, as advertised on McIntyre UK's Web site, includes "metal shears, balers, cable and can recycling equipment, furnaces, casting equipment and ... the world's best aluminium dross processing and cooling system." McIntyre UK holds both United States and European patents on its technology.

The machine that injured Nicastro, a "McIntyre Model 640 Shear," sold in the United States for $24,900 in 1995, *id.*, at 43a, and features a "massive cutting capacity," According to McIntyre UK's product brochure, the machine is "use[d] throughout the [w]orld." McIntyre UK represented in the brochure that, by "incorporat[ing] off-the-shelf hydraulic parts from suppliers with international sales outlets," the 640 Shear's design guarantees serviceability "wherever [its customers] may be based."

The instruction manual advises "owner[s] and operators of a 640 Shear [to] make themselves aware of [applicable health and safety regulations]," including "the American National Standards Institute Regulations (USA) for the use of Scrap Metal Processing Equipment."

Nicastro operated the 640 Shear in the course of his employment at Curcio Scrap Metal (CSM) in Saddle Brook, New Jersey. "New Jersey has long been a hotbed of scrap-metal businesses. . . . " In 2008, New Jersey recycling facilities processed 2,013,730 tons of scrap iron, steel, aluminum, and other metals—more than any other State—outpacing Kentucky, its nearest competitor, by nearly 30 percent.

CSM's owner, Frank Curcio, "first heard of [McIntyre UK's] machine while attending an Institute of Scrap Metal Industries [(ISRI)] convention in Las Vegas in 1994 or 1995, where [McIntyre UK] was an exhibitor." ISRI "presents the world's largest scrap recycling industry trade show each year." The event attracts "owners [and] managers of scrap processing companies" and others "interested in seeing—and purchasing—new equipment." According to ISRI, more than 3,000 potential buyers of scrap processing and recycling equipment attend its annual conventions, "primarily because th[e] exposition provides them with the most comprehensive industry-related shopping experience concentrated in a single, convenient location." Exhibitors who are ISRI members pay $3,000 for 10' x 10' booth space.

McIntyre UK representatives attended every ISRI convention from 1990 through 2005. These annual expositions were held in diverse venues across the United States; in addition to Las Vegas, conventions were held 1990–2005 in New Orleans, Orlando, San Antonio, and San Francisco. McIntyre UK's president, Michael Pownall, regularly attended ISRI conventions. He attended ISRI's Las Vegas convention the year CSM's owner first learned of, and saw, the 640 Shear. McIntyre UK exhibited its products at ISRI trade shows, the company acknowledged, hoping to reach "anyone interested in the machine from anywhere in the United States."

Although McIntyre UK's U.S. sales figures are not in the record, it appears that for several years in the 1990's, earnings from sales of McIntyre UK products in the United States "ha[d] been good" in comparison to "the rest of the world." In response to interrogatories, McIntyre UK stated that its commissioning engineer had installed the company's equipment in several States—Illinois, Iowa, Kentucky, Virginia, and Washington.

From at least 1995 until 2001, McIntyre UK retained an Ohio-based company, McIntyre Machinery America, Ltd. (McIntyre America), "as its exclusive distributor for the entire United States." Though similarly named, the two companies were separate and independent entities with "no commonality of ownership or management." In invoices and other written communications, McIntyre America described itself as McIntyre UK's national distributor, "America's Link" to "Quality Metal Processing Equipment" from England.

In a November 23, 1999 letter to McIntyre America, McIntyre UK's president spoke plainly about the manufacturer's objective in authorizing the exclusive distributorship: "All we wish to do is sell our products in the [United] States—and get paid!" Notably, McIntyre America was concerned about U.S. litigation involving McIntyre UK products, in which the distributor had been named as a defendant. McIntyre UK counseled McIntyre America to respond personally to the litigation, but reassured its distributor that "the product was built and designed by McIntyre Machinery in the UK and the buck stops here—if there's something wrong with the machine." Answering jurisdictional interrogatories, McIntyre UK stated that it had been named as a defendant in lawsuits in Illinois, Kentucky, Massachusetts, and West Virginia. And in correspondence with McIntyre America, McIntyre UK noted that the manufacturer had products liability insurance coverage.

Over the years, McIntyre America distributed several McIntyre UK products to U.S. customers, including, in addition to the 640 Shear, McIntyre UK's "Niagara" and "Tardis" systems, wire strippers, and can machines. In promoting McIntyre UK's products at conventions and demonstration sites and in trade journal advertisements, McIntyre America looked to McIntyre UK for direction and guidance. To achieve McIntyre UK's objective, *i.e.,* "to sell [its] machines to customers throughout the United States," "the two companies [were acting] closely in concert with each other," McIntyre UK never instructed its distributor to avoid certain States or regions of the country; rather, as just noted, the manufacturer engaged McIntyre America to attract customers "from anywhere in the United States."

In sum, McIntyre UK's regular attendance and exhibitions at ISRI conventions was surely a purposeful step to reach customers for its products "anywhere in the United States." At least as purposeful was McIntyre UK's engagement of McIntyre America as the conduit for sales of McIntyre UK's machines to buyers "throughout the United States." Given McIntyre UK's endeavors to reach and profit from the United States market as a whole, Nicastro's suit, I would hold, has been brought in a forum entirely appropriate for the adjudication of his claim. He alleges that McIntyre UK's shear machine was defectively designed or manufactured and, as a result, caused injury to him at his workplace. The machine arrived in Nicastro's New Jersey workplace not randomly or fortuitously, but as a result of the U.S. connections and distribution system that McIntyre UK deliberately arranged.[3] On what sensible view of the allocation of adjudicatory authority could the place of Nicastro's injury within the United States be deemed off limits for his products liability

---

3. McIntyre UK resisted Nicastro's efforts to determine whether other McIntyre machines had been sold to New Jersey customers. McIntyre did allow that McIntyre America "may have resold products it purchased from [McIntyre UK] to a buyer in New Jersey," but said it kept no record of the ultimate destination of machines it shipped to its distributor. A private investigator engaged by Nicastro found at least one McIntyre UK machine, of unspecified type, in use in New Jersey. But McIntyre UK objected that the investigator's report was "unsworn and based upon hearsay."

claim against a foreign manufacturer who targeted the United States (including all the States that constitute the Nation) as the territory it sought to develop?

II

A few points on which there should be no genuine debate bear statement at the outset. First, all agree, McIntyre UK surely is not subject to general (all-purpose) jurisdiction in New Jersey courts, for that foreign-country corporation is hardly "at home" in New Jersey. The question, rather, is one of specific jurisdiction, which turns on an "affiliatio[n] between the forum and the underlying controversy."

Second, no issue of the fair and reasonable allocation of adjudicatory authority among States of the United States is present in this case. New Jersey's exercise of personal jurisdiction over a foreign manufacturer whose dangerous product caused a workplace injury in New Jersey does not tread on the domain, or diminish the sovereignty, of any sister State. Indeed, among States of the United States, the State in which the injury occurred would seem most suitable for litigation of a products liability tort claim. See *World–Wide Volkswagen Corp.* (if a manufacturer or distributor endeavors to develop a market for a product in several States, it is reasonable "to subject it to suit in one of those States if its allegedly defective [product] has there been the source of injury"); 28 U.S.C. § 1391(a)-(b) (in federal-court suits, whether resting on diversity or federal-question jurisdiction, venue is proper in the judicial district "in which a substantial part of the events or omissions giving rise to the claim occurred").

Third, the constitutional limits on a state court's adjudicatory authority derive from considerations of due process, not state sovereignty. As the Court clarified in *Insurance Corp. of Ireland v. Compagnie des Bauxites de Guinee*:

> The restriction on state sovereign power described in *World–Wide Volkswagen Corp.* . . . must be seen as ultimately a function of the individual liberty interest preserved by the Due Process Clause. That Clause is the only source of the personal jurisdiction requirement and the Clause itself makes no mention of federalism concerns. Furthermore, if the federalism concept operated as an independent restriction on the sovereign power of the court, it would not be possible to waive the personal jurisdiction requirement: Individual actions cannot change the powers of sovereignty, although the individual can subject himself to powers from which he may otherwise be protected.

See also *Shaffer v. Heitner* (recognizing that "the mutually exclusive sovereignty of the States [is not] the central concern of the inquiry into personal jurisdiction").

Finally, in *International Shoe* itself, and decisions thereafter, the Court has made plain that legal fictions, notably "presence" and "implied consent," should be discarded, for they conceal the actual bases on which jurisdiction rests. "[T]he relationship among the defendant, the forum, and the litigation" determines whether due process permits the exercise of personal jurisdiction over a defendant, *Shaffer,* and "fictions of implied consent" or "corporate presence" do not advance the proper inquiry. See also *Burnham* (plurality opinion) (*International Shoe* "cast ... aside" fictions of "consent" and "presence").

Whatever the state of academic debate over the role of consent in modern jurisdictional doctrines, the plurality's notion that consent is the animating concept draws no support from controlling decisions of this Court. Quite the contrary, the Court has explained, a forum can exercise jurisdiction when its contacts with the controversy are sufficient; invocation of a fictitious consent, the Court has repeatedly said, is unnecessary and unhelpful. See, *e.g., Burger King Corp.* (Due Process Clause permits "forum ... to assert specific jurisdiction over an out-of-state defendant who has not consented to suit there"); *McGee* ("[T]his Court [has] abandoned 'consent,' 'doing business,' and 'presence' as the standard for measuring the extent of state judicial power over [out-of-state] corporations.").[5]

<h1 style="text-align:center">III</h1>

This case is illustrative of marketing arrangements for sales in the United States common in today's commercial world.[6] A foreign-country manufacturer engages a U.S. company to promote and distribute the manufacturer's products, not in any particular State, but anywhere and everywhere in the United States the distributor can attract purchasers. The product proves defective and injures a user in the State where the user lives or works. Often, as here, the manufacturer will have liability insurance covering personal injuries caused by its products.

When industrial accidents happen, a long-arm statute in the State where the injury occurs generally permits assertion of jurisdiction, upon giving proper notice, over the foreign manufacturer. For example, the State's statute might provide, as does New York's long-arm statute, for the "exercise [of] personal jurisdiction over any non-domiciliary ... who ...

> commits a tortious act without the state causing injury to person or property within the state, ... if he ... expects or should reasonably expect the act to have consequences in the state and derives substantial revenue from interstate or international commerce.

---

5. But see plurality opinion (maintaining that a forum may be fair and reasonable, based on its links to the episode in suit, yet off limits because the defendant has not submitted to the State's authority). The plurality's notion that jurisdiction over foreign corporations depends upon the defendant's "submission," seems scarcely different from the long-discredited fiction of implied consent. It bears emphasis that a majority of this Court's members do not share the plurality's view.

6. Last year, the United States imported nearly 2 trillion dollars in foreign goods. Capital goods, such as the metal shear machine that injured Nicastro, accounted for almost 450 billion dollars in imports for 2010. New Jersey is the fourth-largest destination for manufactured commodities imported into the United States, after California, Texas, and New York.

Or, the State might simply provide, as New Jersey does, for the exercise of jurisdiction "consistent with due process of law."

The modern approach to jurisdiction over corporations and other legal entities, ushered in by *International Shoe,* gave prime place to reason and fairness. Is it not fair and reasonable, given the mode of trading of which this case is an example, to require the international seller to defend at the place its products cause injury? Do not litigational convenience and choice-of-law considerations point in that direction? On what measure of reason and fairness can it be considered undue to require McIntyre UK to defend in New Jersey as an incident of its efforts to develop a market for its industrial machines anywhere and everywhere in the United States?[12] Is not the burden on McIntyre UK to defend in New Jersey fair, *i.e.,* a reasonable cost of transacting business internationally, in comparison to the burden on Nicastro to go to Nottingham, England to gain recompense for an injury he sustained using McIntyre's product at his workplace in Saddle Brook, New Jersey?

McIntyre UK dealt with the United States as a single market. Like most foreign manufacturers, it was concerned not with the prospect of suit in State X as opposed to State Y, but rather with its subjection to suit anywhere in the United States. As a McIntyre UK officer wrote in an e-mail to McIntyre America: "American law—who needs it?!" If McIntyre UK is answerable in the United States at all, is it not "perfectly appropriate to permit the exercise of that jurisdiction . . . at the place of injury"?

In sum, McIntyre UK, by engaging McIntyre America to promote and sell its machines in the United States, "purposefully availed itself" of the United States market nationwide, not a market in a single State or a discrete collection of States. McIntyre UK thereby availed itself of the market of all States in which its products were sold by its exclusive distributor. "Th[e] 'purposeful availment' requirement," this Court has explained, simply "ensures that a defendant will not be haled into a jurisdiction solely as a result of 'random,' 'fortuitous,' or 'attenuated' contacts." *Burger King.* Adjudicatory authority is appropriately exercised where "actions by the defendant *himself* "give rise to the affiliation with the forum. How could McIntyre UK not have intended, by its actions targeting a national market, to sell products in the fourth largest destination for imports among all States of the United States and the largest scrap metal market?

Courts, both state and federal, confronting facts similar to those here, have rightly rejected the conclusion that a manufacturer selling its products across the USA may evade jurisdiction in any and all States, including the State where its defective product is distributed and causes injury.

---

12. The plurality suggests that the Due Process Clause might permit a federal district court in New Jersey, sitting in diversity and applying New Jersey law, to adjudicate McIntyre UK's liability to Nicastro. In other words, McIntyre UK might be compelled to bear the burden of traveling to New Jersey and defending itself there under New Jersey's products liability law, but would be entitled to federal adjudication of Nicastro's state-law claim. I see no basis in the Due Process Clause for such a curious limitation.

They have held, instead, that it would undermine principles of fundamental fairness to insulate the foreign manufacturer from accountability in court at the place within the United States where the manufacturer's products caused injury.

IV

A

While this Court has not considered in any prior case the now-prevalent pattern presented here—a foreign-country manufacturer enlisting a U.S. distributor to develop a market in the United States for the manufacturer's products—none of the Court's decisions tug against the judgment made by the New Jersey Supreme Court. McIntyre contends otherwise, citing *World–Wide Volkswagen,* and *Asahi Metal Industry Co.*

World–Wide Volkswagen concerned a New York car dealership that sold solely in the New York market, and a New York distributor who supplied retailers in three States only: New York, Connecticut, and New Jersey. New York residents had purchased an Audi from the New York dealer and were driving the new vehicle through Oklahoma en route to Arizona. On the road in Oklahoma, another car struck the Audi in the rear, causing a fire which severely burned the Audi's occupants. Rejecting the Oklahoma courts' assertion of jurisdiction over the New York dealer and distributor, this Court observed that the defendants had done nothing to serve the market for cars in Oklahoma. Jurisdiction, the Court held, could not be based on the *customer's* unilateral act of driving the vehicle to Oklahoma. See *Asahi* (opinion of O'Connor, J.) (*World–Wide Volkswagen* "rejected the assertion that a *consumer's* unilateral act of bringing the defendant's product into the forum State was a sufficient constitutional basis for personal jurisdiction over the defendant").

Notably, the foreign manufacturer of the Audi in *World–Wide Volkswagen* did not object to the jurisdiction of the Oklahoma courts and the U.S. importer abandoned its initially stated objection. And most relevant here, the Court's opinion indicates that an objection to jurisdiction by the manufacturer or national distributor would have been unavailing. To reiterate, the Court said in *World–Wide Volkswagen* that, when a manufacturer or distributor aims to sell its product to customers in several States, it is reasonable "to subject it to suit in [any] one of those States if its allegedly defective [product] has there been the source of injury."

Asahi arose out of a motorcycle accident in California. Plaintiff, a California resident injured in the accident, sued the Taiwanese manufacturer of the motorcycle's tire tubes, claiming that defects in its product caused the accident. The tube manufacturer cross-claimed against Asahi, the Japanese maker of the valve assembly, and Asahi contested the California courts' jurisdiction. By the time the case reached this Court, the injured plaintiff had settled his case and only the indemnity claim by the Taiwanese company against the Japanese valve-assembly manufacturer remained.

The decision was not a close call. The Court had before it a foreign plaintiff, the Taiwanese manufacturer, and a foreign defendant, the Japanese valve-assembly maker, and the indemnification dispute concerned a transaction between those parties that occurred abroad. All agreed on the bottom line: The Japanese valve-assembly manufacturer was not reasonably brought into the California courts to litigate a dispute with another foreign party over a transaction that took place outside the United States.

Given the confines of the controversy, the dueling opinions of Justice Brennan and Justice O'Connor were hardly necessary. How the Court would have "estimate[d] . . . the inconveniences," see *International Shoe,* had the injured Californian originally sued Asahi is a debatable question. Would this Court have given the same weight to the burdens on the foreign defendant had those been counterbalanced by the burdens litigating in Japan imposed on the local California plaintiff? Cf. *Calder v. Jones* (a plaintiff's contacts with the forum "may be so manifold as to permit jurisdiction when it would not exist in their absence").

In any event, Asahi, unlike McIntyre UK, did not itself seek out customers in the United States, it engaged no distributor to promote its wares here, it appeared at no tradeshows in the United States, and, of course, it had no Web site advertising its products to the world. Moreover, Asahi was a component-part manufacturer with "little control over the final destination of its products once they were delivered into the stream of commerce." It was important to the Court in *Asahi* that "those who use Asahi components in their final products, and sell those products in California, [would be] subject to the application of California tort law." To hold that *Asahi* controls this case would, to put it bluntly, be dead wrong.[15]

B

The Court's judgment also puts United States plaintiffs at a disadvantage in comparison to similarly situated complainants elsewhere in the world. Of particular note, within the European Union, in which the United Kingdom is a participant, the jurisdiction New Jersey would have exercised is not at all exceptional. The European Regulation on Jurisdiction and the Recognition and Enforcement of Judgments provides for the exercise of specific jurisdiction "in matters relating to tort . . . in the courts for the place where the harmful event occurred." The European Court of Justice has interpreted this prescription to authorize jurisdiction either where the harmful act occurred or at the place of injury.

V

The commentators who gave names to what we now call "general jurisdiction" and "specific jurisdiction" anticipated that when the latter

---

15. The plurality notes the low volume of sales in New Jersey. A $24,900 shearing machine, however, is unlikely to sell in bulk worldwide, much less in any given State. By dollar value, the price of a single machine represents a significant sale. Had a manufacturer sold in New Jersey $24,900 worth of flannel shirts, cigarette lighters, or wire-rope splices, the Court would presumably find the defendant amenable to suit in that State.

achieves its full growth, considerations of litigational convenience and the respective situations of the parties would determine when it is appropriate to subject a defendant to trial in the plaintiff's community. Litigational considerations include "the convenience of witnesses and the ease of ascertaining the governing law." As to the parties, courts would differently appraise two situations: (1) cases involving a substantially local plaintiff, like Nicastro, injured by the activity of a defendant engaged in interstate or international trade; and (2) cases in which the defendant is a natural or legal person whose economic activities and legal involvements are largely home-based, *i.e.,* entities without designs to gain substantial revenue from sales in distant markets.... Courts presented with von Mehren and Trautman's first scenario—a local plaintiff injured by the activity of a manufacturer seeking to exploit a multistate or global market—have repeatedly confirmed that jurisdiction is appropriately exercised by courts of the place where the product was sold and caused injury.

* * *

For the reasons stated, I would hold McIntyre UK answerable in New Jersey for the harm Nicastro suffered at his workplace in that State using McIntyre UK's shearing machine. While I dissent from the Court's judgment, I take heart that the plurality opinion does not speak for the Court, for that opinion would take a giant step away from the "notions of fair play and substantial justice" underlying *International Shoe*.

C. TAG JURISDICTION

BURNHAM v. SUPERIOR COURT OF CALIFORNIA
495 U.S. 604 (1990)

JUSTICE SCALIA announced the judgment of the Court and delivered an opinion in which THE CHIEF JUSTICE and JUSTICE KENNEDY join, and in which JUSTICE WHITE joins with respect to Parts I, II–A, II–B, and II–C.

The question presented is whether the Due Process Clause of the Fourteenth Amendment denies California courts jurisdiction over a nonresident, who was personally served with process while temporarily in that State, in a suit unrelated to his activities in the State.

I

Petitioner Dennis Burnham married Francie Burnham in 1976 in West Virginia. In 1977 the couple moved to New Jersey, where their two children were born. In July 1987 the Burnhams decided to separate. They agreed that Mrs. Burnham, who intended to move to California, would take custody of the children. Shortly before Mrs. Burnham departed for California that same month, she and petitioner agreed that she would file for divorce on grounds of "irreconcilable differences."

In October 1987, petitioner filed for divorce in New Jersey state court on grounds of "desertion." Petitioner did not, however, obtain an issuance of summons against his wife and did not attempt to serve her with process. Mrs. Burnham, after unsuccessfully demanding that petitioner adhere to their prior agreement to submit to an "irreconcilable differences" divorce, brought suit for divorce in California state court in early January 1988.

In late January, petitioner visited southern California on business, after which he went north to visit his children in the San Francisco Bay area, where his wife resided. He took the older child to San Francisco for the weekend. Upon returning the child to Mrs. Burnham's home on January 24, 1988, petitioner was served with a California court summons and a copy of Mrs. Burnham's divorce petition. He then returned to New Jersey.

Later that year, petitioner made a special appearance in the California Superior Court, moving to quash the service of process on the ground that the court lacked personal jurisdiction over him because his only contacts with California were a few short visits to the State for the purposes of conducting business and visiting his children. The Superior Court denied the motion, and the California Court of Appeal denied mandamus relief, rejecting petitioner's contention that the Due Process Clause prohibited California courts from asserting jurisdiction over him because he lacked "minimum contacts" with the State. The court held it to be "a valid jurisdictional predicate for *in personam* jurisdiction" that the "defendant [was] present in the forum state and personally served with process." We granted certiorari.

II

A

The proposition that the judgment of a court lacking jurisdiction is void traces back to the English Year Books, and was made settled law by Lord Coke. Traditionally that proposition was embodied in the phrase *coram non judice,* "before a person not a judge"—meaning, in effect, that the proceeding in question was not a *judicial* proceeding because lawful judicial authority was not present, and could therefore not yield a *judgment.* American courts invalidated, or denied recognition to, judgments that violated this common-law principle long before the Fourteenth Amendment was adopted. In *Pennoyer v. Neff,* we announced that the judgment of a court lacking personal jurisdiction violated the Due Process Clause of the Fourteenth Amendment as well.

To determine whether the assertion of personal jurisdiction is consistent with due process, we have long relied on the principles traditionally followed by American courts in marking out the territorial limits of each State's authority. That criterion was first announced in *Pennoyer v. Neff,* in which we stated that due process "mean[s] a course of legal proceedings according to those rules and principles which have been established in our systems of jurisprudence for the protection and enforcement of private rights," including the "well-established principles of public law respecting the jurisdiction of an independent State over persons and property." In what has become the classic expression of the criterion, we said in *International Shoe Co. v. Washington,* that a state court's assertion of personal jurisdiction satisfies the Due Process Clause if it does not violate " 'traditional notions of fair play and substantial justice.' " *See also Insurance Corp. of Ireland v. Compagnie des Bauxites de Guinee.* Since *International Shoe,* we have only been called upon to decide whether these "traditional notions" permit States to exercise jurisdiction over absent defendants in a manner that deviates from the rules of jurisdiction applied in the 19th century. We have held such deviations permissible, but only with respect to suits arising out of the absent defendant's contacts with the State.[1] *See, e.g., Helicopteros Nacionales de Colombia v. Hall.* The question we must decide today is whether due process requires a similar connection between the litigation and the defendant's contacts with the State in cases where the defendant is physically present in the State at the time process is served upon him.

B

Among the most firmly established principles of personal jurisdiction in American tradition is that the courts of a State have jurisdiction over nonresidents who are physically present in the State. The view developed early that each State had the power to hale before its courts any individual who could be found within its borders, and that once having acquired jurisdiction over such a person by properly serving him with process, the State could retain jurisdiction to enter judgment against him, no matter how fleeting his visit. That view had antecedents in English common-law practice, which sometimes allowed "transitory" actions, arising out of events outside the country, to be maintained against seemingly nonresident defendants who were present in England. Justice Story believed the principle, which he traced to Roman origins, to be firmly grounded in English tradition: "[B]y the common law[,] personal actions, being transitory, may be brought in any place, where the party defendant may be found," for "every nation may . . . rightfully exercise jurisdiction over all persons within its domains." (Story, J.) ("Where a party is within a territory, he may justly be subjected to its process, and bound personally by the judgment pronounced, on such process, against him").

Recent scholarship has suggested that English tradition was not as clear as Story thought. Accurate or not, however, judging by the evidence

---

1. We have said that "[e]ven when the cause of action does not arise out of or relate to the foreign corporation's activities in the forum State, due process is not offended by a State's subjecting the corporation to its *in personam* jurisdiction when there are sufficient contacts between the State and the foreign corporation." *Helicopteros Nacionales de Colombia v. Hall.* Our only holding supporting that statement, however, involved "regular service of summons upon [the corporation's] president while he was in [the forum State] acting in that capacity." See *Perkins v. Benguet Consolidated Mining Co.* It may be that whatever special rule exists permitting "continuous and systematic" contacts to support jurisdiction with respect to matters unrelated to activity in the forum applies *only* to corporations, which have never fitted comfortably in a jurisdictional regime based primarily upon "de facto power over the defendant's person." *International Shoe Co. v. Washington.* We express no views on these matters—and, for simplicity's sake, omit reference to this aspect of "contacts"—based jurisdiction in our discussion.

of contemporaneous or near-contemporaneous decisions, one must conclude that Story's understanding was shared by American courts at the crucial time for present purposes: 1868, when the Fourteenth Amendment was adopted. The following passage in a decision of the Supreme Court of Georgia, in an action on a debt having no apparent relation to the defendant's temporary presence in the State, is representative:

> "Can a citizen of Alabama be sued in this State, as he passes through it?

> "Undoubtedly he can. The second of the axioms of *Huberus,* as translated by *Story,* is: 'that all persons who are found within the limits of a government, whether their residence is permanent or temporary, are to be deemed subjects thereof.'

> "... [A] citizen of another State, who is merely passing through this, resides, as he passes, wherever he is. Let him be sued, therefore, wherever he may, he will be sued where he resides.

> "The plaintiff in error, although a citizen of Alabama, was passing through the County of Troup, in this State, and whilst doing so, he was sued in Troup. He was liable to be sued in this State, and in Troup County of this State."

Decisions in the courts of many States in the 19th and early 20th centuries held that personal service upon a physically present defendant sufficed to confer jurisdiction, without regard to whether the defendant was only briefly in the State or whether the cause of action was related to his activities there.[2] Although research has not revealed a case deciding the issue in every State's courts, that appears to be because the issue was so well settled that it went unlitigated. Opinions from the courts of other States announced the rule in dictum. Most States, moreover, had statutes or common-law rules that exempted from service of process individuals who were brought into the forum by force or fraud, or who were there as a party or witness in unrelated judicial proceedings. These exceptions obviously rested upon the premise that service of process conferred jurisdiction. Particularly striking is the fact that, as far as we have been able to determine, *not one* American case from the period (or, for that matter, not one American case until 1978) held, or even suggested, that in-state personal service on an individual was insufficient to confer personal jurisdiction.[3] Commentators were also seemingly unanimous on the rule.

---

    2. Justice Brennan's assertion that some of these cases involved dicta rather than holdings, is incorrect. In each case, personal service within the State was the exclusive basis for the judgment that jurisdiction existed, and no other factor was relied upon. Nor is it relevant for present purposes these holdings might instead have been rested on other available grounds.

    3. Given this striking fact, and the unanimity of both cases and commentators in supporting the in-state service rule, one can only marvel at Justice Brennan's assertion that the rule "was rather weakly implanted in American jurisprudence," and "did not receive wide currency until well after our decision in *Pennoyer v. Neff.*" I have cited pre-*Pennoyer* cases clearly supporting the rule from no less than nine States, ranging from Mississippi to Colorado to New Hampshire, and two highly respected pre-*Pennoyer* commentators. (It is, moreover, impossible to believe that the many other cases decided shortly after *Pennoyer* represented some sort of instant mutation—or, for that matter, that *Pennoyer* itself was not drawing upon clear contemporary understanding.)

This American jurisdictional practice is, moreover, not merely old; it is continuing. It remains the practice of, not only a substantial number of the States, but as far as we are aware *all* the States and the Federal Government—if one disregards (as one must for this purpose) the few opinions since 1978 that have erroneously said, on grounds similar to those that petitioner presses here, that this Court's due process decisions render the practice unconstitutional. We do not know of a single state or federal statute, or a single judicial decision resting upon state law, that has abandoned in-state service as a basis of jurisdiction. Many recent cases reaffirm it.

C

Despite this formidable body of precedent, petitioner contends, in reliance on our decisions applying the *International Shoe* standard, that in the absence of "continuous and systematic" contacts with the forum, a nonresident defendant can be subjected to judgment only as to matters that arise out of or relate to his contacts with the forum. This argument rests on a thorough misunderstanding of our cases.

The view of most courts in the 19th century was that a court simply could not exercise *in personam* jurisdiction over a nonresident who had not been personally served with process in the forum. * * * *Pennoyer v. Neff,* while renowned for its statement of the principle that the Fourteenth Amendment prohibits such an exercise of jurisdiction, in fact set that forth only as dictum and decided the case (which involved a judgment rendered more than two years before the Fourteenth Amendment's ratification) under "well-established principles of public law." Those principles,

---

Justice Brennan cites neither cases nor commentators from the relevant period to support his thesis (with exceptions I shall discuss presently), and instead relies upon modern secondary sources that do not mention, and were perhaps unaware of, many of the materials I have discussed. The cases cited by Justice Brennan, do not remotely support his point. The dictum he quotes from *Coleman's Appeal,* to the effect that "a man shall only be liable to be called on to answer for civil wrongs in the forum of his home, and the tribunal of his vicinage," was addressing the situation where no personal service in the State had been obtained. This is clear from the court's earlier statements that "there is no mode of reaching by any process issuing from a court of common law, the person of a non-resident defendant not found within the jurisdiction," and "[u]pon a summons, unless there is service within the jurisdiction, there can be no judgment for want of appearance against the defendant." *Gardner v. Thomas* and *Molony v. Dows* are irrelevant to the present discussion. *Gardner,* in which the court declined to adjudicate a tort action between two British subjects for a tort that occurred on the high seas aboard a British vessel, specifically affirmed that jurisdiction did exist, but said that its exercise "must, on principles of policy, often rest in the sound discretion of the Court." The decision is plainly based, in modern terms, upon the doctrine of *forum non conveniens. Molony* did indeed hold that in-state service could not support the adjudication of an action for physical assault by one Californian against another in California (acknowledging that this appeared to contradict an earlier New York case), but it rested that holding upon a doctrine akin to the principle that no State will enforce the penal laws of another—that is, resting upon the injury to the public peace of the other State that such an assault entails, and upon the fact that the damages awarded include penal elements. The fairness or propriety of exercising jurisdiction over the parties had nothing to do with the decision, as is evident from the court's acknowledgment that if the Californians were suing one another over a contract dispute jurisdiction would lie, no matter where the contract arose. As for Justice Brennan's citation of the 1880 commentator John Cleland Wells, it suffices to quote what is set forth on the very page cited: "It is held to be a principle of the common law that any non-resident defendant voluntarily coming within the jurisdiction may be served with process, and compelled to answer."

embodied in the Due Process Clause, required (we said) that when proceedings "involv[e] merely a determination of the personal liability of the defendant, he must be brought within [the court's] jurisdiction by service of process within the State, or his voluntary appearance." We invoked that rule in a series of subsequent cases, as either a matter of due process or a "fundamental principl[e] of jurisprudence."

Later years, however, saw the weakening of the *Pennoyer* rule. In the late 19th and early 20th centuries, changes in the technology of transportation and communication, and the tremendous growth of interstate business activity, led to an "inevitable relaxation of the strict limits on state jurisdiction" over nonresident individuals and corporations. *Hanson v. Denckla* (Black, J., dissenting). States required, for example, that nonresident corporations appoint an in-state agent upon whom process could be served as a condition of transacting business within their borders, and provided in-state "substituted service" for nonresident motorists who caused injury in the State and left before personal service could be accomplished, *Hess v. Pawloski*. We initially upheld these laws under the Due Process Clause on grounds that they complied with *Pennoyer*'s rigid requirement of either "consent," *see, e.g., Hess v. Pawloski*. As many observed, however the consent and presence were purely fictional. Our opinion in *International Shoe* cast those fictions aside and made explicit the underlying basis of these decisions: Due process does not necessarily *require* the States to adhere to the unbending territorial limits on jurisdiction set forth in *Pennoyer*. The validity of assertion of jurisdiction over a non-consenting defendant who is not present in the forum depends upon whether "the quality and nature of [his] activity" in relation to the forum, renders such jurisdiction consistent with " 'traditional notions of fair play and substantial justice.' " Subsequent cases have derived from the *International Shoe* standard the general rule that a State may dispense with in-forum personal service on nonresident defendants in suits arising out of their activities in the State. *See generally Helicopteros Nacionales de Colombia v. Hall*. As *International Shoe* suggests, the defendant's litigation-related "minimum contacts" may take the place of physical presence as the basis for jurisdiction:

> Historically the jurisdiction of courts to render judgment *in personam* is grounded on their de facto power over the defendant's person. Hence his presence within the territorial jurisdiction of a court was prerequisite to its rendition of a judgment personally binding on him. *Pennoyer v. Neff*. But now that the *capias ad respondendum* has given way to personal service of summons or other form of notice, due process requires only that in order to subject a defendant to a judgment *in personam,* if he be not present within the territory of the forum, he have certain minimum contacts with it such that the maintenance of the suit does not offend "traditional notions of fair play and substantial justice."

Nothing in *International Shoe* or the cases that have followed it, however, offers support for the very different proposition petitioner seeks to establish today: that a defendant's presence in the forum is not only unnecessary to validate novel, nontraditional assertions of jurisdiction, but is itself no longer sufficient to establish jurisdiction. That proposition is unfaithful to both elementary logic and the foundations of our due process jurisprudence. The distinction between what is needed to support novel procedures and what is needed to sustain traditional ones is fundamental, as we observed over a century ago:

> [A] process of law, which is not otherwise forbidden, must be taken to be due process of law, if it can show the sanction of settled usage both in England and in this country; but it by no means follows that nothing else can be due process of law.... [That which], in substance, has been immemorially the actual law of the land ... therefor[e] is due process of law. But to hold that such a characteristic is essential to due process of law, would be to deny every quality of the law but its age, and to render it incapable of progress or improvement. It would be to stamp upon our jurisprudence the unchangeableness attributed to the laws of the Medes and Persians.

The short of the matter is that jurisdiction based on physical presence alone constitutes due process because it is one of the continuing traditions of our legal system that define the due process standard of "traditional notions of fair play and substantial justice." That standard was developed by *analogy* to "physical presence," and it would be perverse to say it could now be turned against that touchstone of jurisdiction.

D

Petitioner's strongest argument, though we ultimately reject it, relies upon our decision in *Shaffer v. Heitner.* In that case, a Delaware court hearing a shareholder's derivative suit against a corporation's directors secured jurisdiction *quasi in rem* by sequestering the out-of-state defendants' stock in the company, the situs of which was Delaware under Delaware law. Reasoning that Delaware's sequestration procedure was simply a mechanism to compel the absent defendants to appear in a suit to determine their personal rights and obligations, we concluded that the normal rules we had developed under *International Shoe* for jurisdiction over suits against absent defendants should apply—*viz.*, Delaware could not hear the suit because the defendants' sole contact with the State (ownership of property there) was unrelated to the lawsuit.

It goes too far to say, as petitioner contends, that *Shaffer* compels the conclusion that a State lacks jurisdiction over an individual unless the litigation arises out of his activities in the State. *Shaffer,* like *International Shoe,* involved jurisdiction over an *absent defendant,* and it stands for nothing more than the proposition that when the "minimum contact" that is a substitute for physical presence consists of property ownership it must, like other minimum contacts, be related to the litigation. Petitioner wrenches out of its context our statement in *Shaffer* that "all assertions of state-court jurisdiction must be evaluated according to the standards set forth in *International Shoe* and its progeny." When read together with the two sentences that preceded it, the meaning of this statement becomes clear:

> "The fiction that an assertion of jurisdiction over property is anything but an assertion of jurisdiction over the owner of the property supports an ancient form without substantial modern justification. Its continued acceptance would serve only to allow state-court jurisdiction that is fundamentally unfair to the defendant.

> "We *therefore conclude* that all assertions of state-court jurisdiction must be evaluated according to the standards set forth in *International Shoe* and its progeny." (emphasis added).

Shaffer was saying, in other words, not that all bases for the assertion of *in personam* jurisdiction (including, presumably, in-state service) must be treated alike and subjected to the "minimum contacts" analysis of *International Shoe;* but rather that *quasi in rem* jurisdiction, that fictional "ancient form," and *in personam* jurisdiction, are really one and the same and must be treated alike—leading to the conclusion that *quasi in rem* jurisdiction, *i.e.,* that form of *in personam* jurisdiction based upon a "property ownership" contact and by definition unaccompanied by personal, in-state service, must satisfy the litigation-relatedness requirement of *International Shoe.* The logic of *Shaffer*'s holding-which places all suits against absent nonresidents on the same constitutional footing, regardless of whether a separate Latin label is attached to one particular basis of contact—does not compel the conclusion that physically present defendants must be treated identically to absent ones. As we have demonstrated at length, our tradition has treated the two classes of defendants quite differently, and it is unreasonable to read *Shaffer* as casually obliterating that distinction. *International Shoe* confined its "minimum contacts" requirement to situations in which the defendant "be not present within the territory of the forum," and nothing in *Shaffer* expands that requirement beyond that.

It is fair to say, however, that while our holding today does not contradict *Shaffer,* our basic approach to the due process question is different. We have conducted no independent inquiry into the desirability or fairness of the prevailing in-state service rule, leaving that judgment to the legislatures that are free to amend it; for our purposes, its validation is its pedigree, as the phrase *"traditional notions* of fair play and substantial justice" makes clear. *Shaffer* did conduct such an independent inquiry, asserting that " 'traditional notions of fair play and substantial justice' can be as readily offended by the perpetuation of ancient forms that are no longer justified as by the adoption of new procedures that are inconsistent with the basic values of our constitutional heritage." Perhaps that assertion can be sustained when the "perpetuation of ancient forms" is engaged in by only a very small minority of the States. Where, however, as in the present case, a jurisdictional principle is both firmly approved by tradition and still favored, it is impossible to imagine what standard we could appeal to for the judgment that it is "no longer justified." While in no way receding from or casting doubt upon the holding of *Shaffer* or any other case, we reaffirm today our time-honored approach. For new procedures, hitherto unknown, the Due Process Clause requires analysis to determine whether "traditional notions of fair play and substantial justice" have been offended. *International Shoe*. But a doctrine of personal jurisdiction that dates back to the adoption of the Fourteenth Amendment and is still generally observed unquestionably meets that standard.

III

A few words in response to Justice Brennan's opinion concurring in the judgment: It insists that we apply "contemporary notions of due process" to determine the constitutionality of California's assertion of jurisdiction. But our analysis today comports with that prescription, at least if we give it the only sense allowed by our precedents. The "contemporary notions of due process" applicable to personal jurisdiction are the enduring "*traditional* notions of fair play and substantial justice" established as the test by *International Shoe*. By its very language, that test is satisfied if a state court adheres to jurisdictional rules that are generally applied and have always been applied in the United States.

But the concurrence's proposed standard of "contemporary notions of due process" requires more: It measures state-court jurisdiction not only against traditional doctrines in this country, including current state-court practice, but also against each Justice's subjective assessment of what is fair and just. Authority for that seductive standard is not to be found in any of our personal jurisdiction cases. It is, indeed, an outright break with the test of "traditional notions of fair play and substantial justice," which would have to be reformulated "*our* notions of fair play and substantial justice."

The subjectivity, and hence inadequacy, of this approach becomes apparent when the concurrence tries to explain *why* the assertion of jurisdiction in the present case meets its standard of continuing-American-tradition-*plus*-innate-fairness. Justice Brennan lists the "benefits" Mr. Burnham derived from the State of California-the fact that, during the few days he was there, "[h]is health and safety [were] guaranteed by the State's police, fire, and emergency medical services; he [was] free to travel on the State's roads and waterways; he likely enjoy[ed] the fruits of the State's economy." Three days' worth of these benefits strike us as powerfully inadequate to establish, as an abstract matter, that it is "fair" for California to decree the ownership of all Mr. Burnham's worldly goods acquired during the 10 years of his marriage, and the custody over his children. We daresay a contractual exchange swapping those benefits for that power would not survive the "unconscionability" provision of the Uniform Commercial Code. Even less persuasive are the other "fairness" factors alluded to by Justice Brennan. It would create "an asymmetry," we are told, if Burnham were *permitted* (as he is) to appear in California courts as a plaintiff, but were not *compelled* to appear in California courts as defendant; and travel being as easy as it is nowadays, and modern procedural devices being so convenient, it is no great hardship to appear in California courts. The problem with these assertions is that they justify the exercise of jurisdiction over *everyone, whether or not* he ever comes to California. The only "fairness" elements setting Mr. Burnham apart from the rest of the world are the three days' "benefits" referred to above—and even those, do not set him apart from many other people who have enjoyed three days in the Golden State (savoring the fruits of its economy, the availability of its roads and police services) but who were fortunate enough not to be served with process while they were there and thus are not (simply by reason of that savoring) subject to the general jurisdiction of California's courts. *See, e.g., Helicopteros Nacionales de Colombia v. Hall.* In other words, even if one agreed with Justice Brennan's conception of an equitable bargain, the "benefits" we have been discussing would explain why it is "fair" to assert general jurisdiction over Burnham-returned-to-New–Jersey-after-service only at the expense of proving that it is also "fair" to assert general jurisdiction over Burnham-returned-to-New–Jersey-*without*-service-which we *know* does not conform with "contemporary notions of due process."

There is, we must acknowledge, one factor mentioned by Justice Brennan that *both* relates distinctively to the assertion of jurisdiction on the basis of personal in-state service *and* is fully persuasive—namely, the fact that a defendant voluntarily present in a particular State has a "reasonable expectatio[n]" that he is subject to suit there. By formulating it as a "reasonable expectation" Justice Brennan makes that seem like a "fairness" factor; but in reality, of course, it is just tradition masquerading as "fairness." The only reason for charging Mr. Burnham with the reasonable expectation of being subject to suit is that the States of the Union assert adjudicatory jurisdiction over the person, and have always asserted adjudicatory jurisdiction over the person, by serving him with process during his temporary physical presence in their territory. That continuing tradition, which anyone entering California should have known about, renders it "fair" for Mr. Burnham, who voluntarily entered California, to be sued there for divorce—at least "fair" in the limited sense that he has no one but himself to blame. Justice Brennan's long journey is a circular one, leaving him, at the end of the day, in complete reliance upon the very factor he sought to avoid: The existence of a continuing tradition is not enough, fairness also must be considered; fairness exists here because there is a continuing tradition.

While Justice Brennan's concurrence is unwilling to confess that the Justices of this Court can possibly be bound by a continuing American tradition that a particular procedure is fair, neither is it willing to embrace the logical consequences of that refusal—or even to be clear about what consequences (logical or otherwise) it does embrace. Justice Brennan says that "[f]or these reasons [*i.e.,* because of the reasonableness factors enumerated above], as a rule the exercise of personal jurisdiction over a defendant based on his voluntary presence in the forum will satisfy the requirements of due process." The use of the word "rule" conveys the reassuring feeling that he is establishing a principle of law one can rely upon—but of course he is not. Since Justice Brennan's only criterion of constitutionality is "fairness," the phrase "as a rule" represents nothing more than his estimation that, *usually,* all the elements of "fairness" he discusses in the present case will exist. But what if they do not? Suppose, for example, that a defendant in Mr. Burnham's situation enjoys not three days' worth of California's "benefits," but 15 minutes' worth. Or suppose we remove one of those "benefits"—"enjoy[ment of] the fruits of the State's economy"—by positing that Mr. Burnham had not come to California on business, but only to visit his children. Or suppose that Mr. Burnham were demonstrably so impecunious as to be unable to take advantage of the modern means of transportation and communication that Justice Brennan finds so relevant. Or suppose, finally, that the California courts lacked the "variety of procedural devices," that Justice Brennan says can reduce the burden upon out-of-state litigants. One may also make additional suppositions, relating not to the absence of the factors that Justice BRENNAN discusses, but to the presence of additional factors bearing upon the ultimate criterion of "fairness." What if, for example, Mr. Burnham were visiting a sick child? Or a dying child? *Cf. Kulko v. Superior Court of California* (finding the exercise of long-arm jurisdiction over an absent parent unreasonable because it would "discourage parents from entering into reasonable visitation agreements"). Since, so far as one can tell, Justice Brennan's approval of applying the in-state service rule in the present case rests on the presence of *all* the factors he lists, and on the absence of any others, every different case will present a different litigable issue. Thus, despite the fact that he manages to work the word "rule" into his formulation, Justice Brennan's approach does not establish a rule of law at all, but only a "totality of the circumstances" test, guaranteeing what traditional territorial rules of jurisdiction were designed precisely to avoid: uncertainty and litigation over the preliminary issue of the forum's competence. It may be that those evils, necessarily accompanying a freestanding "reasonableness" inquiry, must be accepted at the margins, when we evaluate *non*traditional forms of jurisdiction newly adopted by the States, see, *e.g., Asahi Metal Industry Co. v. Superior Court of California.* But that is no reason for injecting them into the core of our American practice, exposing to such a "reasonableness" inquiry the ground of jurisdiction that has hitherto been considered the very *baseline* of reasonableness, physical presence.

The difference between us and Justice Brennan has nothing to do with whether "further progress [is] to be made" in the "evolution of our legal system." It has to do with whether changes are to be adopted as progressive by the American people or decreed as progressive by the Justices of this Court. Nothing we say today prevents individual States from limiting or entirely abandoning the in-state-service basis of jurisdiction. And nothing prevents an overwhelming majority of them from doing so, with the consequence that the "traditional notions of fairness" that this Court applies may change. But the States have overwhelmingly declined to adopt such limitation or abandonment, evidently not consider-ing it to be progress.[5] The question is whether, armed with no authority other than individual Justices' perceptions of fairness that conflict with both past and current practice, this Court can compel the States to make such a change on the ground that "due process" requires it. We hold that it cannot.

Because the Due Process Clause does not prohibit the California courts from exercising jurisdiction over petitioner based on the fact of in-state service of process, the judgment is

Affirmed.

JUSTICE WHITE, concurring in part and concurring in the judgment.

I join Parts I, II–A, II–B, and II–C of Justice Scalia's opinion and concur in the judgment of affirmance. The rule allowing jurisdiction to be obtained over a nonresident by personal service in the forum State, without more, has been and is so widely accepted throughout this country that I could not possibly strike it down, either on its face or as applied in this case, on the ground that it denies due process of law guaranteed by the Fourteenth Amendment. Although the Court has the authority under the Amendment to examine even traditionally accepted procedures and declare them invalid, *e.g., Shaffer v. Heitner,* there has been no showing here or elsewhere that as a general proposition the rule is so arbitrary and lacking in common sense in so many instances that it should be held violative of due process in every case. Furthermore, until such a showing is made, which would be difficult indeed, claims in individual cases that the rule would operate unfairly as applied to the particular nonresident involved need not be entertained. At least this would be the case where presence in the forum State is intentional, which would almost always be the fact. Otherwise, there would be endless, fact-specific litigation in the trial and appellate courts, including this one. Here, personal service in California, without more, is enough, and I agree that the judgment should be affirmed.

JUSTICE BRENNAN, with whom JUSTICE MARSHALL, JUSTICE BLACKMUN, and JUSTICE O'CONNOR join, concurring in the judgment.

I agree with Justice Scalia that the Due Process Clause of the Fourteenth Amendment generally permits a state court to exercise juris-diction over a defendant if he is served with process while voluntarily present in the forum State. I do not perceive the need, however, to decide

---

5. I find quite unacceptable as a basis for this Court's decisions Justice Brennan's view that "the *raison d'être* of various constitutional doctrines designed to protect out-of-staters, such as the Art. IV Privileges and Immunities Clause and the Commerce Clause," entitles this Court to brand as "unfair," and hence unconstitutional, the refusal of all 50 States "to limit or abandon bases of jurisdiction that have become obsolete." "Due process" (which is the constitutional text at issue here) does not mean that process which shifting majorities of this Court feel to be "due"; but that process which American society—self-interested American society, which expresses its judgments in the laws of self-interested States—has traditionally considered "due." The notion that the Constitution, through some penumbra emanating from the Privileges and Immunities Clause and the Commerce Clause, establishes this Court as a Platonic check upon the society's greedy adherence to its traditions can only be described as imperious.

that a jurisdictional rule that " 'has been immemorially the actual law of the land,' " automatically comports with due process simply by virtue of its "pedigree." Although I agree that history is an important factor in establishing whether a jurisdictional rule satisfies due process requirements, I cannot agree that it is the *only* factor such that all traditional rules of jurisdiction are, *ipso facto,* forever constitutional. Unlike Justice Scalia, I would undertake an "independent inquiry into the . . . fairness of the prevailing in-state service rule." I therefore concur only in the judgment.

I

I believe that the approach adopted by Justice Scalia's opinion today—reliance solely on historical pedigree—is foreclosed by our decisions in *International Shoe Co. v. Washington* and *Shaffer v. Heitner.* In *International Shoe,* we held that a state court's assertion of personal jurisdiction does not violate the Due Process Clause if it is consistent with " 'traditional notions of fair play and substantial justice.' "[2] In *Shaffer,* we stated that "*all* assertions of state-court jurisdiction must be evaluated according to the standards set forth in *International Shoe* and its progeny." The critical insight of *Shaffer* is that all rules of jurisdiction, even ancient ones, must satisfy contemporary notions of due process. No longer were we content to limit our jurisdictional analysis to pronouncements that "[t]he foundation of jurisdiction is physical power," and that "every State possesses exclusive jurisdiction and sovereignty over persons and property within its territory." *Pennoyer v. Neff.* While acknowledging that "history must be considered as supporting the proposition that jurisdiction based solely on the presence of property satisfie[d] the demands of due process," we found that this factor could not be "decisive." We recognized that " '[t]raditional notions of fair play and substantial justice' can be as readily offended by the perpetuation of ancient forms that are no longer justified as by the adoption of new procedures that are inconsistent with the basic values of our constitutional heritage." I agree with this approach and continue to believe that "the minimum-contacts analysis developed in *International Shoe* . . . represents a far more sensible construct for the exercise of state-court jurisdiction than the patchwork of legal and factual fictions that has been generated from the decision in *Pennoyer v. Neff.*"

While our *holding* in *Shaffer* may have been limited to *quasi in rem* jurisdiction, our mode of analysis was not. Indeed, that we were willing in *Shaffer* to examine anew the appropriateness of the *quasi in rem* rule—until that time dutifully accepted by American courts for at least a century—demonstrates that we did not believe that the "pedigree" of a jurisdictional practice was dispositive in deciding whether it was consis-

---

2. Our reference in *International Shoe* to " 'traditional notions of fair play and substantial justice,' " meant simply that those concepts are indeed traditional ones, not that, as Justice Scalia's opinion suggests, their specific *content* was to be determined by tradition alone. We recognized that contemporary societal norms must play a role in our analysis (considerations of "reasonable[ness], in the context of our federal system of government").

tent with due process. We later characterized *Shaffer* as "abandon[ing] the outworn rule of *Harris v. Balk,* that the interest of a creditor in a debt could be extinguished or otherwise affected by any State having transitory jurisdiction over the debtor." *World-Wide Volkswagen Corp. v. Woodson.* If we could discard an "ancient form without substantial modern justification" in *Shaffer,* again.[3] Lower courts, commentators,[5] and the American Law Institute.

II

Tradition, though alone not dispositive, is of course *relevant* to the question whether the rule of transient jurisdiction is consistent with due process.[7] Tradition is salient not in the sense that practices of the past are automatically reasonable today; indeed, under such a standard, the legitimacy of transient jurisdiction would be called into question because the rule's historical "pedigree" is a matter of intense debate. The rule was a stranger to the common law[8] and was rather weakly implanted in American jurisprudence "at the crucial time for present purposes: 1868, when the Fourteenth Amendment was adopted." For much of the 19th century, American courts did not uniformly recognize the concept of transient jurisdiction,[9] and it appears that the transient rule did not receive wide

---

3. Even Justice Scalia's opinion concedes that *sometimes* courts may discard "traditional" rules when they no longer comport with contemporary notions of due process. For example, although, beginning with the Romans, judicial tribunals for over a millenium permitted jurisdiction to be acquired by force, by the 19th century, as Justice Scalia acknowledges, this method had largely disappeared. I do not see why Justice Scalia's opinion assumes that there is no further progress to be made and that the evolution of our legal system, and the society in which it operates, ended 100 years ago.

5. Although commentators have disagreed over whether the rule of transient jurisdiction is consistent with modern conceptions of due process, that they have engaged in such a debate at all shows that they have rejected the methodology employed by Justice Scalia's opinion today.

7. I do not propose that the "contemporary notions of due process" to be applied are no more than "each Justice's subjective assessment of what is fair and just." Rather, the inquiry is guided by our decisions beginning with *International Shoe Co. v. Washington,* and the specific factors that we have developed to ascertain whether a jurisdictional rule comports with "traditional notions of fair play and substantial justice." *See, e.g., Asahi Metal Industry Co. v. Superior Court of California* (noting "several factors," including "the burden on the defendant, the interests of the forum State, and the plaintiff's interest in obtaining relief"). This analysis may not be "mechanical or quantitative," *International Shoe,* but neither is it "freestanding," or dependent on personal whim. Our experience with this approach demonstrates that it is well within our competence to employ.

8. As Justice Scalia's opinion acknowledges, American courts in the 19th century erected the theory of transient jurisdiction largely upon Justice Story's historical interpretation of Roman and continental sources. Justice Scalia's opinion concedes that the rule's tradition "was not as clear as Story thought;" in fact, it now appears that as a historical matter Story was almost surely wrong. Undeniably, Story's views are in considerable tension with English common law—a "tradition" closer to our own and thus, I would imagine, one that in Justice Scalia's eyes is more deserving of our study than civil law practice. ("The [British] cases evidence a judicial intent to limit the rules to those instances where their application is consonant with the demands of 'fair play' and 'substantial justice' ").

It seems that Justice Story's interpretation of historical practice amounts to little more than what Justice Story himself perceived to be "fair and just." (quoting Justice Story's statement that " '[w]here a party is within a territory, he may *justly* be subjected to its process' ") (emphasis added and citation omitted). I see no reason to bind ourselves forever to that perception.

9. In *Molony v. Dows,* for example, the court dismissed an action for a tort that had occurred in California, even though the defendant was served with process while he was in the forum State

currency until well after our decision in *Pennoyer v. Neff.*[10]

Rather, I find the historical background relevant because, however murky the jurisprudential origins of transient jurisdiction, the fact that American courts have announced the rule for perhaps a century (first in dicta, more recently in holdings) provides a defendant voluntarily present in a particular State *today* "clear notice that [he] is subject to suit" in the forum. *World-Wide Volkswagen Corp. v. Woodson.* Regardless of whether Justice Story's account of the rule's genesis is mythical, our common

---

of New York. The court rejected the plaintiff's contention that it possessed "jurisdiction of all actions, local and transitory, where the defendant resides, or is personally served with process," with the comment that "an action cannot be maintained in this court, or in any court of this State, to recover a pecuniary satisfaction in damages for a willful injury to the person, inflicted in another State, where, at the time of the act, both the wrongdoer and the party injured were domiciled in that State as resident citizens." The court reasoned that it could not "undertake to redress every wrong that may have happened in any part of the world, [merely] because the parties, plaintiff or defendant, may afterwards happen to be within [the court's] jurisdiction." Similarly, the Pennsylvania Supreme Court declared it "the *most important* principle of *all* municipal law of Anglo–Saxon origin, that a man shall only be liable to be called upon to answer for civil wrongs in the forum of his home, and the tribunal of his vicinage." And in *Gardner v. Thomas,* the court was faced with the question "whether this Court will take cognizance of a tort committed on the high seas, on board of a foreign vessel, both the parties being subjects or citizens of the country to which the vessel belongs," after the ship had docked in New York and suit was commenced there. The court observed that Lord Mansfield had appeared "to doubt whether an action may be maintained in *England* for an injury in consequence of two persons fighting in *France,* [even] when both are within the jurisdiction of the Court." The court distinguished the instant case as an action "for an injury on the high seas"—a location, "of course, without the actual or exclusive territory of any nation." Nevertheless, the court found that while "our Courts may take cognizance of torts committed on the high seas, on board of a foreign vessel where both parties are foreigners, . . . it must, on principles of policy, often rest in the sound discretion of the Court to afford jurisdiction or not, according to the circumstances of the case." In the particular case before it, the court found jurisdiction lacking. * * *

It is possible to distinguish these cases narrowly on their facts, as Justice Scalia demonstrates. Thus, *Molony* could be characterized as a case about the reluctance of one State to punish assaults occurring in another, *Gardner* as a *forum non conveniens* case, and *Coleman's Appeal* as a case in which there was no in-state service of process. But such an approach would mistake the trees for the forest. The truth is that the transient rule as we now conceive it had no clear counterpart at common law. Just as today there is an interaction among rules governing jurisdiction, *forum non conveniens,* and choice of law, see, *e.g., Ferens v. John Deere Co.*; *Shaffer* (Brennan, J., concurring in part and dissenting in part); *Hanson v. Denckla* (Black, J., dissenting), at common law there was a complex interplay among pleading requirements, venue, and substantive law—an interplay which in large part substituted for a theory of "jurisdiction":

A theory of territorial jurisdiction would in any event have been premature in England before, say, 1688, or perhaps even 1832. Problems of jurisdiction were the essence of medieval English law and remained significant until the period of Victorian reform. But until after 1800 it would have been impossible, even if it had been thought appropriate, to disentangle the question of territorial limitations on jurisdiction from those arising out of charter, prerogative, personal privilege, corporate liberty, ancient custom, and the fortuities of rules of pleading, venue, and process. The intricacies of English jurisdictional law of that time resist generalization on any theory except a franchisal one; they seem certainly not reducible to territorial dimension. "The English precedents on jurisdiction were therefore of little relevance to American problems of the nineteenth century."

The salient point is that many American courts followed English precedents and restricted the place where certain actions could be brought, regardless of the defendant's presence or whether he was served there.

10. One distinguished legal historian has observed that "notwithstanding dogmatic generalizations later sanctioned by the *Restatement* [of Conflict of Laws], appellate courts hardly ever in fact held transient service sufficient as such" and that "although the transient rule has often been mouthed by the courts, it has but rarely been applied." Many of the cases cited in Justice Scalia's opinion, involve either announcement of the rule in dictum or situations where factors other than in-state service supported the exercise of jurisdiction.

understanding *now,* fortified by a century of judicial practice, is that jurisdiction is often a function of geography. The transient rule is consistent with reasonable expectations and is entitled to a strong presumption that it comports with due process. "If I visit another State, ... I knowingly assume some risk that the State will exercise its power over my property or my person while there. My contact with the State, though minimal, gives rise to predictable risks." *Shaffer* (Stevens, J., concurring in judgment); *see also Burger King Corp. v. Rudzewicz* ("Territorial presence frequently will enhance a potential defendant's affiliation with a State and reinforce the reasonable foreseeability of suit there"). Thus, proposed revisions to the Restatement (Second) of Conflict of Laws § 28 (1986), provide that "[a] state has power to exercise judicial jurisdiction over an individual who is present within its territory unless the individual's relationship to the state is so attenuated as to make the exercise of such jurisdiction unreasonable."

By visiting the forum State, a transient defendant actually "avail[s]" himself, *Burger King,,* of significant benefits provided by the State. His health and safety are guaranteed by the State's police, fire, and emergency medical services; he is free to travel on the State's roads and waterways; he likely enjoys the fruits of the State's economy as well. Moreover, the Privileges and Immunities Clause of Article IV prevents a state government from discriminating against a transient defendant by denying him the protections of its law or the right of access to its courts.[12] Subject only to the doctrine of *forum non conveniens,* an out-of-state plaintiff may use state courts in all circumstances in which those courts would be available to state citizens. Without transient jurisdiction, an asymmetry would arise: A transient would have the full benefit of the power of the forum State's courts as a plaintiff while retaining immunity from their authority as a defendant.

The potential burdens on a transient defendant are slight. " '[M]odern transportation and communications have made it much less burdensome for a party sued to defend himself' " in a State outside his place of residence. *Burger King,* quoting *McGee v. International Life Ins. Co.* That the defendant has already journeyed at least once before to the forum—as evidenced by the fact that he was served with process there—is an indication that suit in the forum likely would not be prohibitively inconvenient. Finally, any burdens that do arise can be ameliorated by a variety of procedural devices.[13] For these reasons, as a rule the exercise of

---

12. That these privileges may independently be required by the Constitution does not mean that they must be ignored for purposes of determining the fairness of the transient jurisdiction rule. For example, in the context of specific jurisdiction, we consider whether a defendant "has availed himself of the privilege of conducting business" in the forum State, *Burger King Corp. v. Rudzewicz,* or has " 'invok[ed] the benefits and protections of its laws,' " quoting *Hanson v. Denckla,* even though the State could not deny the defendant the right to do so. *See also Asahi Metal Industry Co. v. Superior Court of California* (plurality opinion); *Keeton v. Hustler Magazine, Inc.; World-Wide Volkswagen Corp. v. Woodson.*

13. For example, in the federal system, a transient defendant can avoid protracted litigation of a spurious suit through a motion to dismiss for failure to state a claim or though a motion for summary judgment. Fed. Rules Civ. Proc. 12(b)(6) and 56. He can use relatively inexpensive

personal jurisdiction over a defendant based on his voluntary presence in the forum will satisfy the requirements of due process.[14]

In this case, it is undisputed that petitioner was served with process while voluntarily and knowingly in the State of California. I therefore concur in the judgment.

Justice Stevens, concurring in the judgment.

As I explained in my separate writing, I did not join the Court's opinion in *Shaffer v. Heitner,* because I was concerned by its unnecessarily broad reach. The same concern prevents me from joining either Justice Scalia's or Justice Brennan's opinion in this case. For me, it is sufficient to note that the historical evidence and consensus identified by Justice Scalia, the considerations of fairness identified by Justice Brennan, and the common sense displayed by Justice White, all combine to demonstrate that this is, indeed, a very easy case.* Accordingly, I agree that the judgment should be affirmed.

* * *

D. CONSENT REVISITED

M/S BREMEN v. ZAPATA OFF–SHORE COMPANY
407 U.S. 1 (1972)

Mr. Chief Justice Burger delivered the opinion of the Court.

We granted certiorari to review a judgment of the United States Court of Appeals for the Fifth Circuit declining to enforce a forum-selection

---

methods of discovery, such as oral deposition by telephone (Rule 30(b)(7)), deposition upon written questions (Rule 31), interrogatories (Rule 33), and requests for admission (Rule 36), while enjoying protection from harassment (Rule 26(c)), and possibly obtaining costs and attorney's fees for some of the work involved (Rules 37(a)(4), (b)–(d)). Moreover, a change of venue may be possible. 28 U.S.C. § 1404. In state court, many of the same procedural protections are available, as is the doctrine of *forum non conveniens,* under which the suit may be dismissed.

14. Justice Scalia's opinion maintains that, viewing transient jurisdiction as a contractual bargain, the rule is "unconscionabl[e]," according to contemporary conceptions of fairness. But the opinion simultaneously insists that because of its historical "pedigree," the rule is "the very *baseline* of reasonableness." Thus is revealed Justice Scalia's belief that tradition *alone* is completely dispositive and that no showing of unfairness can ever serve to invalidate a traditional jurisdictional practice. I disagree both with this belief and with Justice Scalia's assessment of the fairness of the transient jurisdiction bargain.

I note, moreover, that the dual conclusions of Justice Scalia's opinion create a singularly unattractive result. Justice Scalia suggests that when and if a jurisdictional rule becomes substantively unfair or even "unconscionable," this Court is powerless to alter it. Instead, he is willing to rely on individual States to limit or abandon bases of jurisdiction that have become obsolete. This reliance is misplaced, for States have little incentive to limit rules such as transient jurisdiction that make it *easier* for their own citizens to sue out-of-state defendants. That States are more likely to expand their jurisdiction is illustrated by the adoption by many States of long-arm statutes extending the reach of personal jurisdiction to the limits established by the Federal Constitution. Out-of-staters do not vote in state elections or have a voice in state government. We should not assume, therefore, that States will be motivated by "notions of fairness" to curb jurisdictional rules like the one at issue here. The reasoning of Justice Scalia's opinion today is strikingly oblivious to the *raison d'être* of various constitutional doctrines designed to protect out-of-staters, such as the Art. IV Privileges and Immunities Clause and the Commerce Clause.

* Perhaps the adage about hard cases making bad law should be revised to cover easy cases.

clause governing disputes arising under an international towage contract between petitioners and respondent. The circuits have differed in their approach to such clauses. For the reasons stated hereafter, we vacate the judgment of the Court of Appeals.

In November 1967, respondent Zapata, a Houston-based American corporation, contracted with petitioner Unterweser, a German corporation, to tow Zapata's ocean-going, self-elevating drilling rig Chaparral from Louisiana to a point off Ravenna, Italy, in the Adriatic Sea, where Zapata had agreed to drill certain wells.

Zapata had solicited bids for the towage, and several companies including Unterweser had responded. Unterweser was the low bidder and Zapata requested it to submit a contract, which it did. The contract submitted by Unterweser contained the following provision, which is at issue in this case: "Any dispute arising must be treated before the London Court of Justice."

In addition the contract contained two clauses purporting to exculpate Unterweser from liability for damages to the towed barge.

After reviewing the contract and making several changes, but without any alteration in the forum-selection or exculpatory clauses, a Zapata vice president executed the contract and forwarded it to Unterweser in Germany, where Unterweser accepted the changes, and the contract became effective.

On January 5, 1968, Unterweser's deep sea tug Bremen departed Venice, Louisiana, with the Chaparral in tow bound for Italy. On January 9, while the flotilla was in international waters in the middle of the Gulf of Mexico, a severe storm arose. The sharp roll of the Chaparral in Gulf waters caused its elevator legs, which had been raised for the voyage, to break off and fall into the sea, seriously damaging the Chaparral. In this emergency situation Zapata instructed the Bremen to tow its damaged rig to Tampa, Florida, the nearest port of refuge.

On January 12, Zapata, ignoring its contract promise to litigate "any dispute arising" in the English courts, commenced a suit in admiralty in the United States District Court at Tampa, seeking $3,500,000 damages against Unterweser *in personam* and the Bremen *in rem*, alleging negligent towage and breach of contract.[3] Unterweser responded by invoking the forum clause of the towage contract, and moved to dismiss for lack of jurisdiction or on forum non conveniens grounds, or in the alternative to stay the action pending submission of the dispute to the London Court of Justice. Shortly thereafter, in February, before the District Court had ruled on its motion to stay or dismiss the United States action, Unterweser commenced an action against Zapata seeking damages for breach of the towage contract in the High Court of Justice in London, as the contract provided. Zapata appeared in that court to contest jurisdiction, but its

---

3. The Bremen was arrested by a United States marshal acting pursuant to Zapata's complaint immediately upon her arrival in Tampa. The tug was subsequently released when Unterweser furnished security in the amount of $3,500,000.

challenge was rejected, the English courts holding that the contractual forum provision conferred jurisdiction.[4]

In the meantime, Unterweser was faced with a dilemma in the pending action in the United States court at Tampa. The six-month period for filing action to limit its liability to Zapata and other potential claimants was about to expire, but the United States District Court in Tampa had not yet ruled on Unterweser's motion to dismiss or stay Zapata's action. On July 2, 1968, confronted with difficult alternatives, Unterweser filed an action to limit its liability in the District Court in Tampa. That court entered the customary injunction against proceedings outside the limitation court, and Zapata refiled its initial claim in the limitation action.

It was only at this juncture, on July 29, after the six-month period for filing the limitation action had run, that the District Court denied Unterweser's January motion to dismiss or stay Zapata's initial action. In denying the motion, that court relied on the prior decision of the *Court of Appeals in Carbon Black Export, Inc. v. The Monrosa*. In that case the Court of Appeals had held a forum-selection clause unenforceable, reiterating the traditional view of many American courts that "agreements in advance of controversy whose object is to oust the jurisdiction of the courts are contrary to public policy and will not be enforced." Apparently concluding that it was bound by the *Carbon Black* case, the District Court gave the forum-selection clause little, if any, weight. Instead, the court treated the motion to dismiss under normal forum non conveniens doctrine applicable in the absence of such a clause, citing *Gulf Oil Corp. v. Gilbert*, 330 U.S. 501 (1947). Under that doctrine "unless the balance is strongly in favor of the defendant, the plaintiff's choice of forum should rarely be disturbed." The District Court concluded: "the balance of conveniences here is not strongly in favor of (Unterweser) and (Zapata's) choice of forum should not be disturbed."

Thereafter, on January 21, 1969, the District Court denied another motion by Unterweser to stay the limitation action pending determination

---

4. Zapata appeared specially and moved to set aside service of process outside the country. Justice Karminski of the High Court of Justice denied the motion on the ground the contractual choice-of-forum provision conferred jurisdiction and would be enforced, absent a factual showing it would not be "fair and right" to do so. He did not believe Zapata had made such a showing, and held that it should be required to "stick to (its) bargain." The Court of Appeal dismissed an appeal on the ground that Justice Karminski had properly applied the English rule. Lord Justice Willmer stated that rule as follows:

"The law on the subject, I think, is not open to doubt. . . . It is always open to parties to stipulate . . . that a particular Court shall have jurisdiction over any dispute arising out of their contract. Here, the parties chose to stipulate that disputes were to be referred to the London Court, which I take as meaning the High Court in this country. Prima facie it is the policy of the Court to hold parties to the bargain into which they have entered. . . . But that is not an inflexible rule . . .

"I approach the matter, therefore, in this way, that the Court has a discretion, but it is a discretion which, in the ordinary way and in the absence of strong reason to the contrary, will be exercised in favour of holding parties to their bargain. The question is whether sufficient circumstances have been shown to exist in this case to make it desirable, on the grounds of balance of convenience, that proceedings should not take place in this country. . . ."

of the controversy in the High Court of Justice in London and granted Zapata's motion to restrain Unterweser from litigating further in the London court. The District Judge ruled that, having taken jurisdiction in the limitation proceeding, he had jurisdiction to determine all matters relating to the controversy. He ruled that Unterweser should be required to "do equity" by refraining from also litigating the controversy in the London court, not only for the reasons he had previously stated for denying Unterweser's first motion to stay Zapata's action, but also because Unterweser had invoked the United States court's jurisdiction to obtain the benefit of the Limitation Act.

On appeal, a divided panel of the Court of Appeals affirmed, and on rehearing en banc the panel opinion was adopted, with six of the 14 en banc judges dissenting. As had the District Court, the majority rested on the *Carbon Black* decision, concluding that "at the very least" that case stood for the proposition that a forum-selection clause "will not be enforced unless the selected state would provide a more convenient forum than the state in which suit is brought." From that premise the Court of Appeals proceeded to conclude that, apart from the forum-selection clause, the District Court did not abuse its discretion in refusing to decline jurisdiction on the basis of forum non conveniens. It noted that (1) the flotilla never "escaped the Fifth Circuit's mare nostrum, and the casualty occurred in close proximity to the district court;" (2) a considerable number of potential witnesses, including Zapata crewmen, resided in the Gulf Coast area; (3) preparation for the voyage and inspection and repair work had been performed in the Gulf area; (4) the testimony of the Bremen crew was available by way of deposition; (5) England had no interest in or contact with the controversy other than the forum-selection clause. The Court of Appeals majority further noted that Zapata was a United States citizen and "(t)he discretion of the district court to remand the case to a foreign forum was consequently limited"—especially since it appeared likely that the English courts would enforce the exculpatory clauses. In the Court of Appeals' view, enforcement of such clauses would be contrary to public policy in American courts. Therefore, "(t)he district court was entitled to consider that remanding Zapata to a foreign forum, with no practical contact with the controversy, could raise a bar to recovery by a United States citizen which its own convenient courts would not countenance."[9]

We hold, with the six dissenting members of the Court of Appeals, that far too little weight and effect were given to the forum clause in resolving this controversy. For at least two decades we have witnessed an expansion of overseas commercial activities by business enterprises based in the United States. The barrier of distance that once tended to confine a business concern to a modest territory no longer does so. Here we see an

---

9. The Court of Appeals also indicated in passing that even if it took the view that choice-of-forum clauses were enforceable unless "unreasonable" it was "doubtful" that enforcement would be proper here because the exculpatory clauses would deny Zapata relief to which it was "entitled" and because England was "seriously inconvenient" for trial of the action.

American company with special expertise contracting with a foreign company to tow a complex machine thousands of miles across seas and oceans. The expansion of American business and industry will hardly be encouraged if, notwithstanding solemn contracts, we insist on a parochial concept that all disputes must be resolved under our laws and in our courts. Absent a contract forum, the considerations relied on by the Court of Appeals would be persuasive reasons for holding an American forum convenient in the traditional sense, but in an era of expanding world trade and commerce, the absolute aspects of the doctrine of the *Carbon Black* case have little place and would be a heavy hand indeed on the future development of international commercial dealings by Americans. We cannot have trade and commerce in world markets and international waters exclusively on our terms, governed by our laws, and resolved in our courts.

Forum-selection clauses have historically not been favored by American courts. Many courts, federal and state, have declined to enforce such clauses on the ground that they were "contrary to public policy," or that their effect was to "oust the jurisdiction" of the court. Although this view apparently still has considerable acceptance, other courts are tending to adopt a more hospitable attitude toward forum-selection clauses. This view, advanced in the well-reasoned dissenting opinion in the instant case, is that such clauses are prima facie valid and should be enforced unless enforcement is shown by the resisting party to be "unreasonable" under the circumstances. We believe this is the correct doctrine to be followed by federal district courts sitting in admiralty. It is merely the other side of the proposition recognized by this Court in *National Equipment Rental, Ltd. v. Szukhent*, 375 U.S. 311 (1964), holding that in federal courts a party may validly consent to be sued in a jurisdiction where he cannot be found for service of process through contractual designation of an "agent" for receipt of process in that jurisdiction. In so holding, the Court stated: "(I)t is settled ... that parties to a contract may agree in advance to submit to the jurisdiction of a given court to permit notice to be served by the opposing party, or even to waive notice altogether."

This approach is substantially that followed in other common-law countries including England. It is the view advanced by noted scholars and that adopted by the *Restatement of the Conflict of Laws*. It accords with ancient concepts of freedom of contract and reflects an appreciation of the expanding horizons of American contractors who seek business in all parts of the world. Not surprisingly, foreign businessmen prefer, as do we, to have disputes resolved in their own courts, but if that choice is not available, then in a neutral forum with expertise in the subject matter. Plainly, the courts of England meet the standards of neutrality and long experience in admiralty litigation. The choice of that forum was made in an arm's-length negotiation by experienced and sophisticated businessmen, and absent some compelling and countervailing reason it should be honored by the parties and enforced by the courts.

The argument that such clauses are improper because they tend to "oust" a court of jurisdiction is hardly more than a vestigial legal fiction.

It appears to rest at core on historical judicial resistance to any attempt to reduce the power and business of a particular court and has little place in an era when all courts are overloaded and when businesses once essentially local now operate in world markets. It reflects something of a provincial attitude regarding the fairness of other tribunals. No one seriously contends in this case that the forum selection clause "ousted" the District Court of jurisdiction over Zapata's action. The threshold question is whether that court should have exercised its jurisdiction to do more than give effect to the legitimate expectations of the parties, manifested in their freely negotiated agreement, by specifically enforcing the forum clause.

There are compelling reasons why a freely negotiated private international agreement, unaffected by fraud, undue influence, or overweening bargaining power,[14] such as that involved here, should be given full effect. In this case, for example, we are concerned with a far from routine transaction between companies of two different nations contemplating the tow of a extremely costly piece of equipment from Louisiana across the Gulf of Mexico and the Atlantic Ocean, through the Mediterranean Sea to its final destination in the Adriatic Sea. In the course of its voyage, it was to traverse the waters of many jurisdictions. The Chaparral could have been damaged at any point along the route, and there were countless possible ports of refuge. That the accident occurred in the Gulf of Mexico and the barge was towed to Tampa in an emergency were mere fortuities. It cannot be doubted for a moment that the parties sought to provide for a neutral forum for the resolution of any disputes arising during the tow. Manifestly much uncertainty and possibly great inconvenience to both parties could arise if a suit could be maintained in any jurisdiction in which an accident might occur or if jurisdiction were left to any place where the Bremen or Unterweser might happen to be found.[15] The

---

14. The record here refutes any notion of overweening bargaining power. Judge Wisdom, dissenting, in the Court of Appeals noted:

Zapata has neither presented evidence of nor alleged fraud or undue bargaining power in the agreement. Unterweser was only one of several companies bidding on the project. No evidence contradicts its Managing Director's affidavit that it specified English courts "in an effort to meet Zapata Off–Shore Company half way." Zapata's Vice President has declared by affidavit that no specific negotiations concerning the forum clause took place. But this was not simply a form contract with boilerplate language that Zapata had no power to alter. The towing of an oil rig across the Atlantic was a new business. Zapata did make alterations to the contract submitted by Unterweser. The forum clause could hardly be ignored. It is the final sentence of the agreement, immediately preceding the date and the parties' signatures. . . .

15. At the very least, the clause was an effort to eliminate all uncertainty as to the nature, location, and outlook of the forum in which these companies of differing nationalities might find themselves. Moreover, while the contract here did not specifically provide that the substantive law of England should be applied, it is the general rule in English courts that the parties are assumed, absent contrary indication, to have designated the forum with the view that it should apply its own law. It is therefore reasonable to conclude that the forum clause was also an effort to obtain certainty as to the applicable substantive law.

The record contains an affidavit of a Managing Director of Unterweser stating that Unterweser considered the choice-of-forum provision to be of "overriding importance" to the transaction. He stated that Unterweser towage contracts ordinarily provide for exclusive German jurisdiction and application of German law, but that "(i)n this instance, in an effort to meet (Zapata) half way, (Unterweser) proposed the London Court of Justice. Had this provision not been accepted by (Zapata), (Unterweser) would not have entered into the towage contract. . . ." He also stated that the parties intended, by designating the London forum, that English law would be applied. A

elimination of all such uncertainties by agreeing in advance on a forum acceptable to both parties is an indispensable element in international trade, commerce, and contracting. There is strong evidence that the forum clause was a vital part of the agreement,[16] and it would be unrealistic to think that the parties did not conduct their negotiations, including fixing the monetary terms, with the consequences of the forum clause figuring prominently in their calculations. Under these circumstances, as Justice Karminski reasoned in sustaining jurisdiction over Zapata in the High Court of Justice, "(t)he force of an agreement for litigation in this country, freely entered into between two competent parties, seems to me to be very powerful."

Thus, in the light of present-day commercial realities and expanding international trade we conclude that the forum clause should control absent a strong showing that it should be set aside. Although their opinions are not altogether explicit, it seems reasonably clear that the District Court and the Court of Appeals placed the burden on Unterweser to show that London would be a more convenient forum than Tampa, although the contract expressly resolved that issue. The correct approach would have been to enforce the forum clause specifically unless Zapata could clearly show that enforcement would be unreasonable and unjust, or that the clause was invalid for such reasons as fraud or overreaching. Accordingly, the case must be remanded for reconsideration.

We note, however, that there is nothing in the record presently before us that would support a refusal to enforce the forum clause. The Court of Appeals suggested that enforcement would be contrary to the public policy of the forum because of the prospect that the English courts would enforce the clauses of the towage contract purporting to exculpate Unterweser from liability for damages to the Chaparral. A contractual choice-of-forum clause should be held unenforceable if enforcement would contravene a strong public policy of the forum in which suit is brought, whether declared by statute or by judicial decision. It is clear, however, that whatever the proper scope of the policy expressed in *Bisso*, it does not reach this case. *Bisso* rested on considerations with respect to the towage business strictly in American waters, and those considerations are not controlling in an international commercial agreement. Speaking for the dissenting judges in the Court of Appeals, Judge Wisdom pointed out:

> (W)e should be careful not to overemphasize the strength of the (*Bisso*) policy. . . . (T)wo concerns underlie the rejection of exculpatory agreements: that they may be produced by overweening bargaining

responsive affidavit by Hoyt Taylor, a vice president of Zapata, denied that there were any discussions between Zapata and Unterweser concerning the forum clause or the question of the applicable law.

16. Zapata has denied specifically discussing the forum clause with Unterweser, but, as Judge Wisdom pointed out, Zapata made numerous changes in the contract without altering the forum clause, which could hardly have escaped its attention. Zapata is clearly not unsophisticated in such matters. The contract of its wholly owned subsidiary with an Italian corporation covering the contemplated drilling operations in the Adriatic Sea provided that all disputes were to be settled by arbitration in London under English law, and contained broad exculpatory clauses.

power; and that they do not sufficiently discourage negligence.... Here the conduct in question is that of a foreign party occurring in international waters outside our jurisdiction. The evidence disputes any notion of overreaching in the contractual agreement. And for all we know, the uncertainties and dangers in the new field of trans-oceanic towage of oil rigs were so great that the tower was unwilling to take financial responsibility for the risks, and the parties thus allocated responsibility for the voyage to the tow. It is equally possible that the contract price took this factor into account. I conclude that we should not invalidate the forum selection clause here unless we are firmly convinced that we would thereby significantly encourage negligent conduct within the boundaries of the United States.

Courts have also suggested that a forum clause, even though it is freely bargained for and contravenes no important public policy of the forum, may nevertheless be "unreasonable" and unenforceable if the chosen forum is seriously inconvenient for the trial of the action. Of course, where it can be said with reasonable assurance that at the time they entered the contract, the parties to a freely negotiated private international commercial agreement contemplated the claimed inconvenience, it is difficult to see why any such claim of inconvenience should be heard to render the forum clause unenforceable. We are not here dealing with an agreement between two Americans to resolve their essentially local disputes in a remote alien forum. In such a case, the serious inconvenience of the contractual forum to one or both of the parties might carry greater weight in determining the reasonableness of the forum clause. The remoteness of the forum might suggest that the agreement was an adhesive one, or that the parties did not have the particular controversy in mind when they made their agreement; yet even there the party claiming should bear a heavy burden of proof. Similarly, selection of a remote forum to apply differing foreign law to an essentially American controversy might contravene an important public policy of the forum. For example, so long as *Bisso* governs American courts with respect to the towage business in American waters, it would quite arguably be improper to permit an American tower to avoid that policy by providing a foreign forum for resolution of his disputes with an American towee.

This case, however, involves a freely negotiated international commercial transaction between a German and an American corporation for towage of a vessel from the Gulf of Mexico to the Adriatic Sea. As noted, selection of a London forum was clearly a reasonable effort to bring vital certainty to this international transaction and to provide a neutral forum experienced and capable in the resolution of admiralty litigation. Whatever "inconvenience" Zapata would suffer by being forced to litigate in the contractual forum as it agreed to do was clearly foreseeable at the time of contracting. In such circumstances it should be incumbent on the party seeking to escape his contract to show that trial in the contractual forum will be so gravely difficult and inconvenient that he will for all practical purposes be deprived of his day in court. Absent that, there is no basis for concluding that it would be unfair, unjust, or unreasonable to hold that party to his bargain.

In the course of its ruling on Unterweser's second motion to stay the proceedings in Tampa, the District Court did make a conclusory finding that the balance of convenience was "strongly" in favor of litigation in Tampa. However, as previously noted, in making that finding the court erroneously placed the burden of proof on Unterweser to show that the balance of convenience was strongly in its favor.[19] Moreover, the finding falls far short of a conclusion that Zapata would be effectively deprived of its day in court should it be forced to litigate in London. Indeed, it cannot even be assumed that it would be placed to the expense of transporting its witnesses to London. It is not unusual for important issues in international admiralty cases to be dealt with by deposition. Both the District Court and the Court of Appeals majority appeared satisfied that Unterweser could receive a fair hearing in Tampa by using deposition testimony of its witnesses from distant places, and there is no reason to conclude that Zapata could not use deposition testimony to equal advantage if forced to litigate in London as it bound itself to do. Nevertheless, to allow Zapata opportunity to carry its heavy burden of showing not only that the balance of convenience is strongly in favor of trial in Tampa (that is, that it will be far more inconvenient for Zapata to litigate in London than it will be for Unterweser to litigate in Tampa), but also that a London trial will be so manifestly and gravely inconvenient to Zapata that it will be effectively deprived of a meaningful day in court, we remand for further proceedings.

Zapata's remaining contentions do not require extended treatment. It is clear that Unterweser's action in filing its limitation complaint in the District Court in Tampa was, so far as Zapata was concerned, solely a defensive measure made necessary as a response to Zapata's breach of the forum clause of the contract. When the six-month statutory period for filing an action to limit its liability had almost run without the District Court's having ruled on Unterweser's initial motion to dismiss or stay Zapata's action pursuant to the forum clause, Unterweser had no other prudent alternative but to protect itself by filing for limitation of its liability. Its action in so doing was a direct consequence of Zapata's failure to abide by the forum clause of the towage contract. There is no basis on

---

19. Applying the proper burden of proof, Justice Karminski in the High Court of Justice at London made the following findings, which appear to have substantial support in the record:

> (Zapata) pointed out that in this case the balance of convenience so far as witnesses were concerned pointed in the direction of having the case heard and tried in the United States District Court at Tampa in Florida because the probability is that most, but not necessarily all, of the witnesses will be American. The answer, as it seems to me, is that a substantial minority at least of witnesses are likely to be German. The tug was a German vessel and was, as far as I know, manned by a German crew ... Where they all are mow or are likely to be when this matter is litigated I do not know, because the experience of the Admiralty Court here strongly points out that maritime witnesses in the course of their duties move about freely. The homes of the German crew presumably are in Germany. There is probably a balance of numbers in favour of the Americans, but not, as I am inclined to think, a very heavy balance. It should also be noted that if the exculpatory clause is enforced in the English courts, many of Zapata's witnesses on the questions of negligence and damage may be completely unnecessary.

which to conclude that this purely necessary defensive action by Unter-weser should preclude it from relying on the forum clause it bargained for.

For the first time in this litigation, Zapata has suggested to this Court that the forum clause should not be construed to provide for an exclusive forum or to include *in rem* actions. However, the language of the clause is clearly mandatory and all-encompassing; the language of the clause in the Carbon Black case was far different.

The judgment of the Court of Appeals is vacated and the case is remanded for further proceedings consistent with this opinion.

Vacated and remanded.

MR. JUSTICE WHITE, concurring.

I concur in the opinion and judgment of the Court except insofar as the opinion comments on the issues which are remanded to the District Court. In my view these issues are best left for consideration by the District Court in the first instance.

MR. JUSTICE DOUGLAS, dissenting.

Petitioner Unterweser contracted with respondent to tow respon-dent's drilling barge from Louisiana to Italy. The towage contract con-tained a "forum selection clause" providing that any dispute must be litigated before the High Court of Justice in London, England. While the barge was being towed in the Gulf of Mexico a casualty was suffered. The tow made for Tampa Bay, the nearest port, where respondent brought suit for damages in the District Court. * * *

Chief Justice Taft, in discussing the Limitation of Liability Act said that "the great object of the statute was to encourage shipbuilding and to induce the investment of money in this branch of industry by limiting the venture of those who build the ship to the loss of the ship itself or her freight then pending, in cases of damage or wrong happening, without the privity or knowledge of the ship owner, and by the fault or neglect of the master or other persons on board; that the origin of this proceeding for limitation of liability is to be found in the general maritime law differing from the English maritime law; and that such a proceeding is entirely within the constitutional grant of power to Congress to establish courts of admiralty and maritime jurisdiction."

Chief Justice Taft went on to describe how the owner of a vessel who, in case the vessel is found at fault, may limit his liability to the value of the vessel and may bring all claimants "into concourse in the proceeding by monition" and they may be enjoined from suing the owner and the vessel on such claims in any other court.

Chief Justice Taft concluded: "(T)his Court has by its rules and decisions given the statute a very broad and equitable construction for the purpose of carrying out its purpose, and for facilitating a settlement of the whole controversy over such losses as are comprehended within it, and that all the ease with which rights can be adjusted in equity is intended to be given to the proceeding. It is the administration of equity in an admiralty court.... The proceeding partakes in a way of the features of a bill to enjoin a multiplicity of suits, a bill in the nature of an interpleader, and a creditor's bill. It looks to a complete and just disposition of a many cornered controversy, and is applicable to proceedings in rem against the ship, as well as to proceedings *in personam* against the owner; the limitation extending to the owner's property as well as to his person."

The Limitation Court is a court of equity and traditionally an equity court may enjoin litigation in another court where equitable considerations indicate that the other litigation might prejudice the proceedings in the Limitation Court. Petitioners' petition for limitation subjects them to the full equitable powers of the Limitation Court.

Respondent is a citizen of this country. Moreover, if it were remitted to the English court, its substantive rights would be adversely affected. Exculpatory provisions in the towage control provide (1) that petitioners, the masters and the crews "are not responsible for defaults and/or errors in the navigation of the tow" and (2) that "(d)amages suffered by the towed object are in any case for account of its Owners."

Under our decision in *Dixilyn Drilling Corp. v. Crescent Towing & Salvage Co.,* "a contract which exempts the tower from liability for its own negligence" is not enforceable, though there is evidence in the present record that it is enforceable in England. That policy was first announced in *Bisso v. Inland Waterways Corp.* Although the casualty occurred on the high seas, the *Bisso* doctrine is nonetheless applicable.

Moreover, the casualty occurred close to the District Court, a number of potential witnesses, including respondent's crewmen, reside in that area, and the inspection and repair work were done there. The testimony of the tower's crewmen, residing in Germany, is already available by way of depositions taken in the proceedings.

All in all, the District Court judge exercised his discretion wisely in enjoining petitioners from pursuing the litigation in England.*

---

* It is said that because these parties specifically agreed to litigate their disputes before the London Court of Justice, the District Court, absent "unreasonable" circumstances, should have honored that choice by declining to exercise its jurisdiction. The forum-selection clause, however, is part and parcel of the exculpatory provision in the towing agreement which, as mentioned in the text, is not enforceable in American courts. For only by avoiding litigation in the United States could petitioners hope to evade the *Bisso* doctrine.

Judges in this country have traditionally been hostile to attempts to circumvent the public policy against exculpatory agreements. For example, clauses specifying that the law of a foreign place (which favors such releases) should control have regularly been ignored. Thus, in *The Kensington,* the Court held void an exemption from liability despite the fact that the contract provided that it should be construed under Belgian law which was more tolerant.

The instant stratagem of specifying a foreign forum is essentially the same as invoking a foreign law of construction except that the present circumvention also requires the American party to travel across an ocean to seek relief. Unless we are prepared to overrule *Bisso* we should not countenance devices designed solely for the purpose of evading its prohibition.

It is argued, however, that one of the rationales of the *Bisso* doctrine, "to protect those in need of goods or services from being overreached by others who have power to drive hard bargains" does not apply here because these parties may have been of equal bargaining stature. Yet we have often adopted prophylactic rules rather than attempt to sort the core cases from the marginal

I would affirm the judgment below.

* * *

CARNIVAL CRUISE LINES, INC. v. SHUTE
499 U.S. 585 (1991)

Justice Blackmun delivered the opinion of the Court.

In this admiralty case we primarily consider whether the United States Court of Appeals for the Ninth Circuit correctly refused to enforce a forum-selection clause contained in tickets issued by petitioner Carnival Cruise Lines, Inc., to respondents Eulala and Russel Shute.

I

The Shutes, through an Arlington, Wash., travel agent, purchased passage for a 7–day cruise on petitioner's ship, the *Tropicale*. Respondents paid the fare to the agent who forwarded the payment to petitioner's headquarters in Miami, Fla. Petitioner then prepared the tickets and sent them to respondents in the State of Washington. The face of each ticket, at its left-hand lower corner, contained this admonition:

"SUBJECT TO CONDITIONS OF CONTRACT ON LAST PAGES—IMPORTANT! PLEASE READ CONTRACT— ON LAST PAGES 1, 2, 3"

The following appeared on "contract page 1" of each ticket:

TERMS AND CONDITIONS OF PASSAGE CONTRACT TICKET

"3. (a) The acceptance of this ticket by the person or persons named hereon as passengers shall be deemed to be an acceptance and agreement by each of them of all of the terms and conditions of this Passage Contract Ticket.

* * *

"8. It is agreed by and between the passenger and the Carrier that all disputes and matters whatsoever arising under, in connection with or incident to this Contract shall be litigated, if at all, in and before a Court located in the State of Florida, U.S.A., to the exclusion of the Courts of any other state or country."

The last quoted paragraph is the forum-selection clause at issue.

II

Respondents boarded the *Tropicale* in Los Angeles, Cal. The ship sailed to Puerto Vallarta, Mexico, and then returned to Los Angeles. While the ship was in international waters off the Mexican coast, respondent

---

ones. In any event, the other objective of the *Bisso* doctrine, to "discourage negligence by making wrongdoers pay damages" applies here and in every case regardless of the relative bargaining strengths of the parties.

Eulala Shute was injured when she slipped on a deck mat during a guided tour of the ship's galley. Respondents filed suit against petitioner in the United States District Court for the Western District of Washington, claiming that Mrs. Shute's injuries had been caused by the negligence of Carnival Cruise Lines and its employees.

Petitioner moved for summary judgment, contending that the forum clause in respondents' tickets required the Shutes to bring their suit against petitioner in a court in the State of Florida. Petitioner contended, alternatively, that the District Court lacked personal jurisdiction over petitioner because petitioner's contacts with the State of Washington were insubstantial. The District Court granted the motion, holding that petitioner's contacts with Washington were constitutionally insufficient to support the exercise of personal jurisdiction.

The Court of Appeals reversed. Reasoning that "but for" petitioner's solicitation of business in Washington, respondents would not have taken the cruise and Mrs. Shute would not have been injured, the court concluded that petitioner had sufficient contacts with Washington to justify the District Court's exercise of personal jurisdiction.*

Turning to the forum-selection clause, the Court of Appeals acknowledged that a court concerned with the enforceability of such a clause must begin its analysis with *The Bremen v. Zapata Off–Shore Co.,* where this Court held that forum-selection clauses, although not "historically . . . favored," are "prima facie valid." The appellate court concluded that the forum clause should not be enforced because it "was not freely bargained for." As an "independent justification" for refusing to enforce the clause, the Court of Appeals noted that there was evidence in the record to indicate that "the Shutes are physically and financially incapable of pursuing this litigation in Florida" and that the enforcement of the clause would operate to deprive them of their day in court and thereby contravene this Court's holding in *The Bremen.*

We granted certiorari to address the question whether the Court of Appeals was correct in holding that the District Court should hear respondents' tort claim against petitioner. Because we find the forum-selection clause to be dispositive of this question, we need not consider petitioner's constitutional argument as to personal jurisdiction.

III

We begin by noting the boundaries of our inquiry. First, this is a case in admiralty, and federal law governs the enforceability of the forum-

---

* The Court of Appeals had filed an earlier opinion also reversing the District Court and ruling that the District Court had personal jurisdiction over the cruise line and that the forum-selection clause in the tickets was unreasonable and was not to be enforced. That opinion, however, was withdrawn when the court certified to the Supreme Court of Washington the question whether the Washington long-arm statute conferred personal jurisdiction over Carnival Cruise Lines for the claim asserted by the Shutes. The Washington Supreme Court answered the certified question in the affirmative on the ground that the Shutes' claim "arose from" petitioner's advertisement in Washington and the promotion of its cruises there. The Court of Appeals then "refiled" its opinion "as modified herein."

selection clause we scrutinize. Second, we do not address the question whether respondents had sufficient notice of the forum clause before entering the contract for passage. Respondents essentially have conceded that they had notice of the forum-selection provision. ("The respondents do not contest the incorporation of the provisions nor [*sic*] that the forum selection clause was reasonably communicated to the respondents, as much as three pages of fine print can be communicated"). Additionally, the Court of Appeals evaluated the enforceability of the forum clause under the assumption, although "doubtful," that respondents could be deemed to have had knowledge of the clause.

Within this context, respondents urge that the forum clause should not be enforced because, contrary to this Court's teachings in *The Bremen*, the clause was not the product of negotiation, and enforcement effectively would deprive respondents of their day in court. Additionally, respondents contend that the clause violates the Limitation of Vessel Owner's Liability Act. We consider these arguments in turn.

IV

A

Both petitioner and respondents argue vigorously that the Court's opinion in *The Bremen* governs this case, and each side purports to find ample support for its position in that opinion's broad-ranging language. This seeming paradox derives in large part from key factual differences between this case and *The Bremen*, differences that preclude an automatic and simple application of *The Bremen*'s general principles to the facts here.

In *The Bremen*, this Court addressed the enforceability of a forum-selection clause in a contract between two business corporations. An American corporation, Zapata, made a contract with Unterweser, a German corporation, for the towage of Zapata's oceangoing drilling rig from Louisiana to a point in the Adriatic Sea off the coast of Italy. The agreement provided that any dispute arising under the contract was to be resolved in the London Court of Justice. After a storm in the Gulf of Mexico seriously damaged the rig, Zapata ordered Unterweser's ship to tow the rig to Tampa, Fla., the nearest point of refuge. Thereafter, Zapata sued Unterweser in admiralty in federal court at Tampa. Citing the forum clause, Unterweser moved to dismiss. The District Court denied Unterweser's motion, and the Court of Appeals for the Fifth Circuit, sitting en banc on rehearing, and by a sharply divided vote, affirmed.

This Court vacated and remanded, stating that, in general, "a freely negotiated private international agreement, unaffected by fraud, undue influence, or overweening bargaining power, such as that involved here, should be given full effect." The Court further generalized that "in the light of present-day commercial realities and expanding international trade we conclude that the forum clause should control absent a strong showing that it should be set aside." The Court did not define precisely the circumstances that would make it unreasonable for a court to enforce a forum clause. Instead, the Court discussed a number of factors that made it reasonable to enforce the clause at issue in *The Bremen* and that, presumably, would be pertinent in any determination whether to enforce a similar clause.

In this respect, the Court noted that there was "strong evidence that the forum clause was a vital part of the agreement, and [that] it would be unrealistic to think that the parties did not conduct their negotiations, including fixing the monetary terms, with the consequences of the forum clause figuring prominently in their calculations." Further, the Court observed that it was not "dealing with an agreement between two Americans to resolve their essentially local disputes in a remote alien forum," and that in such a case, "the serious inconvenience of the contractual forum to one or both of the parties might carry greater weight in determining the reasonableness of the forum clause." The Court stated that even where the forum clause establishes a remote forum for resolution of conflicts, "the party claiming [unfairness] should bear a heavy burden of proof."

In applying *The Bremen,* the Court of Appeals in the present litigation took note of the foregoing "reasonableness" factors and rather automatically decided that the forum-selection clause was unenforceable because, unlike the parties in *The Bremen,* respondents are not business persons and did not negotiate the terms of the clause with petitioner. Alternatively, the Court of Appeals ruled that the clause should not be enforced because enforcement effectively would deprive respondents of an opportunity to litigate their claim against petitioner.

The Bremen concerned a "far from routine transaction between companies of two different nations contemplating the tow of an extremely costly piece of equipment from Louisiana across the Gulf of Mexico and the Atlantic Ocean, through the Mediterranean Sea to its final destination in the Adriatic Sea." These facts suggest that, even apart from the evidence of negotiation regarding the forum clause, it was entirely reasonable for the Court in *The Bremen* to have expected Unterweser and Zapata to have negotiated with care in selecting a forum for the resolution of disputes arising from their special towing contract.

In contrast, respondents' passage contract was purely routine and doubtless nearly identical to every commercial passage contract issued by petitioner and most other cruise lines. In this context, it would be entirely unreasonable for us to assume that respondents—or any other cruise passenger—would negotiate with petitioner the terms of a forum-selection clause in an ordinary commercial cruise ticket. Common sense dictates that a ticket of this kind will be a form contract the terms of which are not subject to negotiation, and that an individual purchasing the ticket will not have bargaining parity with the cruise line. But by ignoring the crucial differences in the business contexts in which the respective contracts were executed, the Court of Appeals' analysis seems to us to have distorted somewhat this Court's holding in *The Bremen*.

In evaluating the reasonableness of the forum clause at issue in this case, we must refine the analysis of *The Bremen* to account for the realities of form passage contracts. As an initial matter, we do not adopt the Court of Appeals' determination that a non-negotiated forum-selection clause in a form ticket contract is never enforceable simply because it is not the subject of bargaining. Including a reasonable forum clause in a form contract of this kind well may be permissible for several reasons: First, a cruise line has a special interest in limiting the fora in which it potentially could be subject to suit. Because a cruise ship typically carries passengers from many locales, it is not unlikely that a mishap on a cruise could subject the cruise line to litigation in several different fora. Additionally, a clause establishing *ex ante* the forum for dispute resolution has the salutary effect of dispelling any confusion about where suits arising from the contract must be brought and defended, sparing litigants the time and expense of pretrial motions to determine the correct forum and conserving judicial resources that otherwise would be devoted to deciding those motions. Finally, it stands to reason that passengers who purchase tickets containing a forum clause like that at issue in this case benefit in the form of reduced fares reflecting the savings that the cruise line enjoys by limiting the fora in which it may be sued.

We also do not accept the Court of Appeals' "independent justification" for its conclusion that *The Bremen* dictates that the clause should not be enforced because "[t]here is evidence in the record to indicate that the Shutes are physically and financially incapable of pursuing this litigation in Florida." We do not defer to the Court of Appeals' findings of fact. In dismissing the case for lack of personal jurisdiction over petitioner, the District Court made no finding regarding the physical and financial impediments to the Shutes' pursuing their case in Florida. The Court of Appeals' conclusory reference to the record provides no basis for this Court to validate the finding of inconvenience. Furthermore, the Court of Appeals did not place in proper context this Court's statement in *The Bremen* that "the serious inconvenience of the contractual forum to one or both of the parties might carry greater weight in determining the reasonableness of the forum clause." The Court made this statement in evaluating a hypothetical "agreement between two Americans to resolve their essentially local disputes in a remote alien forum." In the present case, Florida is not a "remote alien forum," nor—given the fact that Mrs. Shute's accident occurred off the coast of Mexico—is this dispute an essentially local one inherently more suited to resolution in the State of Washington than in Florida. In light of these distinctions, and because respondents do not claim lack of notice of the forum clause, we conclude that they have not satisfied the "heavy burden of proof" required to set aside the clause on grounds of inconvenience.

It bears emphasis that forum-selection clauses contained in form passage contracts are subject to judicial scrutiny for fundamental fairness.

In this case, there is no indication that petitioner set Florida as the forum in which disputes were to be resolved as a means of discouraging cruise passengers from pursuing legitimate claims. Any suggestion of such a bad-faith motive is belied by two facts: Petitioner has its principal place of business in Florida, and many of its cruises depart from and return to Florida ports. Similarly, there is no evidence that petitioner obtained respondents' accession to the forum clause by fraud or overreaching. Finally, respondents have conceded that they were given notice of the forum provision and, therefore, presumably retained the option of rejecting the contract with impunity. In the case before us, therefore, we conclude that the Court of Appeals erred in refusing to enforce the forum-selection clause.

B

Respondents also contend that the forum-selection clause at issue violates 46 U.S.C. App. § 183c. That statute, enacted in 1936, provides:

> It shall be unlawful for the . . . owner of any vessel transporting passengers between ports of the United States or between any such port and a foreign port to insert in any rule, regulation, contract, or agreement any provision or limitation (1) purporting, in the event of loss of life or bodily injury arising from the negligence or fault of such owner or his servants, to relieve such owner . . . from liability, or from liability beyond any stipulated amount, for such loss or injury, or (2) purporting in such event to lessen, weaken, or avoid the right of any claimant to a trial by court of competent jurisdiction on the question of liability for such loss or injury, or the measure of damages therefor. All such provisions or limitations contained in any such rule, regulation, contract, or agreement are hereby declared to be against public policy and shall be null and void and of no effect.

By its plain language, the forum-selection clause before us does not take away respondents' right to "a trial by [a] court of competent jurisdiction" and thereby contravene the explicit proscription of § 183c. Instead, the clause states specifically that actions arising out of the passage contract shall be brought "if at all," in a court "located in the State of Florida," which, plainly, is a "court of competent jurisdiction" within the meaning of the statute.

Respondents appear to acknowledge this by asserting that although the forum clause does not directly prevent the determination of claims against the cruise line, it causes plaintiffs unreasonable hardship in asserting their rights and therefore violates Congress' intended goal in enacting § 183c. Significantly, however, respondents cite no authority for their contention that Congress' intent in enacting § 183c was to avoid having a plaintiff travel to a distant forum in order to litigate. The legislative history of § 183c suggests instead that this provision was enacted in response to passenger-ticket conditions purporting to limit the shipowner's liability for negligence or to remove the issue of liability from the scrutiny of any court by means of a clause providing that "the question of liability and the measure of damages shall be determined by arbitration." There was no prohibition of a forum-selection clause. Because the clause before us allows for judicial resolution of claims against petitioner and does not purport to limit petitioner's liability for negligence, it does not violate § 183c.

V

The judgment of the Court of Appeals is reversed.

It is so ordered.

JUSTICE STEVENS, with whom JUSTICE MARSHALL joins, dissenting.

The Court prefaces its legal analysis with a factual statement that implies that a purchaser of a Carnival Cruise Lines passenger ticket is fully and fairly notified about the existence of the choice of forum clause in the fine print on the back of the ticket. Even if this implication were accurate, I would disagree with the Court's analysis. But, given the Court's preface, I begin my dissent by noting that only the most meticulous passenger is likely to become aware of the forum-selection provision. I have therefore appended to this opinion a facsimile of the relevant text, using the type size that actually appears in the ticket itself. A careful reader will find the forum-selection clause in the 8th of the 25 numbered paragraphs.

Of course, many passengers, like the respondents in this case, will not have an opportunity to read paragraph 8 until they have actually purchased their tickets. By this point, the passengers will already have accepted the condition set forth in paragraph 16(a), which provides that "[t]he Carrier shall not be liable to make any refund to passengers in respect of ... tickets wholly or partly not used by a passenger." Not knowing whether or not that provision is legally enforceable, I assume that the average passenger would accept the risk of having to file suit in Florida in the event of an injury, rather than canceling-without a refund-a planned vacation at the last minute. The fact that the cruise line can reduce its litigation costs, and therefore its liability insurance premiums, by forcing this choice on its passengers does not, in my opinion, suffice to render the provision reasonable. Cf. *Steven v. Fidelity & Casualty Co. of New York* (refusing to enforce limitation on liability in insurance policy because insured "must purchase the policy before he even knows its provisions").

Even if passengers received prominent notice of the forum-selection clause before they committed the cost of the cruise, I would remain persuaded that the clause was unenforceable under traditional principles of federal admiralty law and is "null and void" under the terms of Limitation of Vessel Owners Liability Act which was enacted in 1936 to invalidate expressly stipulations limiting shipowners' liability for negligence.

Exculpatory clauses in passenger tickets have been around for a long time. These clauses are typically the product of disparate bargaining power between the carrier and the passenger, and they undermine the strong public interest in deterring negligent conduct. For these reasons, courts long before the turn of the century consistently held such clauses unenforceable under federal admiralty law. Thus, in a case involving a ticket provision purporting to limit the shipowner's liability for the negligent handling of baggage, this Court wrote:

> It is settled in the courts of the United States that exemptions limiting carriers from responsibility for the negligence of themselves or their servants are both unjust and unreasonable, and will be deemed as wanting in the element of voluntary assent; and, besides, that such conditions are in conflict with public policy. This doctrine was announced so long ago, and has been so frequently reiterated, that it is elementary.

Clauses limiting a carrier's liability or weakening the passenger's right to recover for the negligence of the carrier's employees come in a variety of forms. Complete exemptions from liability for negligence or limitations on the amount of the potential damage recovery, requirements that notice of claims be filed within an unreasonably short period of time, provisions mandating a choice of law that is favorable to the defendant in negligence cases, and forum-selection clauses are all similarly designed to put a thumb on the carrier's side of the scale of justice.[4]

Forum-selection clauses in passenger tickets involve the intersection of two strands of traditional contract law that qualify the general rule that courts will enforce the terms of a contract as written. Pursuant to the first strand, courts traditionally have reviewed with heightened scrutiny the terms of contracts of adhesion, form contracts offered on a take-or-leave basis by a party with stronger bargaining power to a party with weaker power. Some commentators have questioned whether contracts of adhesion can justifiably be enforced at all under traditional contract theory because the adhering party generally enters into them without manifesting knowing and voluntary consent to all their terms.

The common law, recognizing that standardized form contracts account for a significant portion of all commercial agreements, has taken a less extreme position and instead subjects terms in contracts of adhesion to scrutiny for reasonableness. Judge J. Skelly Wright set out the state of the law succinctly in *Williams v. Walker–Thomas Furniture Co.*:

> Ordinarily, one who signs an agreement without full knowledge of its terms might be held to assume the risk that he has entered a one-sided bargain. But when a party of little bargaining power, and hence little real choice, signs a commercially unreasonable contract with little or no knowledge of its terms, it is hardly likely that his consent, or even an objective manifestation of his consent, was ever

---

4. All these clauses will provide passengers who purchase tickets containing them with a "benefit in the form of reduced fares reflecting the savings that the cruise line enjoys by limiting [its exposure to liability]." Under the Court's reasoning, all these clauses, including a complete waiver of liability, would be enforceable, a result at odds with longstanding jurisprudence.

given to all of the terms. In such a case the usual rule that the terms of the agreement are not to be questioned should be abandoned and the court should consider whether the terms of the contract are so unfair that enforcement should be withheld.

The second doctrinal principle implicated by forum-selection clauses is the traditional rule that "contractual provisions, which seek to limit the place or court in which an action may ... be brought, are invalid as contrary to public policy." Although adherence to this general rule has declined in recent years, particularly following our decision in *The Bremen v. Zapata Off–Shore Co.,* the prevailing rule is still that forum-selection clauses are not enforceable if they were not freely bargained for, create additional expense for one party, or deny one party a remedy. A forum-selection clause in a standardized passenger ticket would clearly have been unenforceable under the common law before our decision in *The Bremen,* in my opinion, remains unenforceable under the prevailing rule today.

The Bremen, which the Court effectively treats as controlling this case, had nothing to say about stipulations printed on the back of passenger tickets. That case involved the enforceability of a forum-selection clause in a freely negotiated international agreement between two large corporations providing for the towage of a vessel from the Gulf of Mexico to the Adriatic Sea. The Court recognized that such towage agreements had generally been held unenforceable in American courts, but held that the doctrine of those cases did not extend to commercial arrangements between parties with equal bargaining power.

The federal statute that should control the disposition of the case before us today was enacted in 1936 when the general rule denying enforcement of forum-selection clauses was indisputably widely accepted. The principal subject of the statute concerned the limitation of ship-owner liability, but as the following excerpt from the House Report explains, the section that is relevant to this case was added as a direct response to ship-owners' ticketing practices.

> During the course of the hearings on the bill (H.R. 9969) there was also brought to the attention of the committee a practice of providing on the reverse side of steamship tickets that in the event of damage or injury caused by the negligence or fault of the owner or his servants, the liability of the owner shall be limited to a stipulated amount, in some cases $5,000, and in others substantially lower amounts, or that in such event the question of liability and the measure of damages *shall be determined by arbitration.* The amendment to chapter 6 of title 48 of the Revised Statutes proposed to be made by section 2 of the committee amendment is intended to, and in the opinion of the committee will, *put a stop to all such practices and practices of a like character.*

The intent to "put a stop to all such practices and practices of a like character" was effectuated in the second clause of the statute. It reads:

> It shall be unlawful for the manager, agent, master, or owner of any vessel transporting passengers between ports of the United States

or between any such port and a foreign port to insert in any rule, regulation, contract, or agreement any provision or limitation (1) purporting, in the event of loss of life or bodily injury arising from the negligence or fault of such owner or his servants, to relieve such owner, master, or agent from liability, or from liability beyond any stipulated amount, for such loss or injury, or (2) *purporting in such event to lessen, weaken, or avoid the right of any claimant to a trial by court of competent jurisdiction on the question of liability for such loss or injury, or the measure of damages therefor.* All such provisions or limitations contained in any such rule, regulation, contract, or agreement are declared to be against public policy and shall be null and void and of no effect.

The stipulation in the ticket that Carnival Cruise sold to respondents certainly lessens or weakens their ability to recover for the slip and fall incident that occurred off the west coast of Mexico during the cruise that originated and terminated in Los Angeles, California. It is safe to assume that the witnesses—whether other passengers or members of the crew— can be assembled with less expense and inconvenience at a west coast forum than in a Florida court several thousand miles from the scene of the accident.

A liberal reading of the 1936 statute is supported by both its remedial purpose and by the legislative history's general condemnation of "all such practices." Although the statute does not specifically mention forum-selection clauses, its language is broad enough to encompass them. The absence of a specific reference is adequately explained by the fact that such clauses were already unenforceable under common law and would not often have been used by carriers, which were relying on stipulations that purported to exonerate them from liability entirely.

The Courts of Appeals, construing an analogous provision of the Carriage of Goods by Sea Act, have unanimously held invalid as limitations on liability forum-selection clauses requiring suit in foreign jurisdictions. Commentators have also endorsed this view. The forum-selection clause here does not mandate suit in a foreign jurisdiction, and therefore arguably might have less of an impact on a plaintiff's ability to recover. However, the plaintiffs in this case are not large corporations but individuals, and the added burden on them of conducting a trial at the opposite end of the country is likely proportional to the additional cost to a large corporation of conducting a trial overseas.

Under these circumstances, the general prohibition against stipulations purporting "to lessen, weaken, or avoid" the passenger's right to a trial certainly should be construed to apply to the manifestly unreasonable stipulation in these passengers' tickets. Even without the benefit of the statute, I would continue to apply the general rule that prevailed prior to our decision in *The Bremen* to forum-selection clauses in passenger tickets.

I respectfully dissent.

* * *

V. CHOOSING THE FORUM (SUBJECT MATTER JURISDICTION)

A. DIVERSITY JURISDICTION AND SPECIAL DIVERSITY PROBLEMS

Diversity of Citizenship

28 U.S.C. § 1332

(a) The district courts shall have original jurisdiction of all civil actions where the matter in controversy exceeds the sum or value of $75,000, exclusive of interest and costs, and is between—

(1) citizens of different States;

(2) citizens of a State and citizens or subjects of a foreign state, except that the district courts shall not have original jurisdiction under this subsection of an action between citizens of a State and citizens or subjects of a foreign state who are lawfully admitted for permanent residence in the United States and are domiciled in the same state.

(3) citizens of different States and in which citizens or subjects of a foreign state are additional parties; and

(4) a foreign state, defined in section 1603(a) of this title, as plaintiff and citizens of a State or of different States.

For the purposes of this section, section 1335, and section 1441, an alien admitted to the United States for permanent residence shall be deemed a citizen of the State in which such alien is domiciled.

(b) Except when express provision therefore is otherwise made in a statute of the United States, where the plaintiff who files the case originally in the Federal courts is finally adjudged to be entitled to recover less than the sum or value of $75,000, computed without regard to any setoff or counterclaim to which the defendant may be adjudged to be entitled, and exclusive of interest and costs, the district court may deny costs to the plaintiff and, in addition, may impose costs on the plaintiff.

(c) For the purposes of this section and section 1441 of this title—

(1) a corporation shall be deemed to be a citizen of every State and foreign state by which it has been incorporated and of every State and foreign state where it has its principal place of business, except that in any direct action against the insurer of a policy or contract of liability insurance, whether incorporated or unincorporated, to which action the insured is not joined as a party-defendant, such insurer shall be deemed a citizen of—

(A) every State and foreign state of which the insured is a citizen;

(B) every State and foreign state by which the insurer has been incorporated; and

(C) the State or foreign state where the insurer has its principal place of business; and

(2) the legal representative of the estate of a decedent shall be deemed to be a citizen only of the same State as the decedent, and the legal representative of an infant or incompetent shall be deemed to be a citizen only of the same State as the infant or incompetent.

* * *

[28 U.S.C. § 1332(d), relating to diversity jurisdiction over class actions, is set forth in Chapter XIV.]

* * *

Federal Rule of Civil Procedure 12

Rule 12. Defenses and Objections: When and How Presented

* * *

(b) How to Present Defenses. Every defense to a claim for relief in any pleading must be asserted in the responsive pleading if one is required. But a party may assert the following defenses by motion:

(1) lack of subject-matter jurisdiction * * *

* * *

Federal Rule of Civil Procedure 17. Plaintiff and Defendant; Capacity; Public Officers

(a) Real Party in Interest.

(1) *Designation in General.* An action must be prosecuted in the name of the real party in interest. The following may sue in their own names without joining the person for whose benefit the action is brought:

(A) an executor;

(B) an administrator;

(C) a guardian;

(D) a bailee;

(E) a trustee of an express trust;

(F) a party with whom or in whose name a contract has been made for another's benefit; and

(G) a party authorized by statute.

(2) *Action in the Name of the United States for Another's Use or Benefit.* When a federal statute so provides, an action for another's use or benefit must be brought in the name of the United States.

(3) *Joinder of the Real Party in Interest.* The court may not dismiss an action for failure to prosecute in the name of the real

party in interest until, after an objection, a reasonable time has been allowed for the real party in interest to ratify, join, or be substituted into the action. After ratification, joinder, or substitution, the action proceeds as if it had been originally commenced by the real party in interest.

(b) Capacity to Sue or Be Sued. Capacity to sue or be sued is determined as follows:

(1) for an individual who is not acting in a representative capacity, by the law of the individual's domicile;

(2) for a corporation, by the law under which it was organized; and

(3) for all other parties, by the law of the state where the court is located, except that:

(A) a partnership or other unincorporated association with no such capacity under that state's law may sue or be sued in its common name to enforce a substantive right existing under the United States Constitution or laws; and

(B) 28 U.S.C. §§ 754 and 959(a) govern the capacity of a receiver appointed by a United States court to sue or be sued in a United States court.

(c) Minor or Incompetent Person.

(1) *With a Representative.* The following representatives may sue or defend on behalf of a minor or an incompetent person:

(A) a general guardian;

(B) a committee;

(C) a conservator; or

(D) a like fiduciary.

(2) *Without a Representative.* A minor or an incompetent person who does not have a duly appointed representative may sue by a next friend or by a guardian *ad litem.* The court must appoint a guardian *ad litem*—or issue another appropriate order—to protect a minor or incompetent person who is unrepresented in an action.

(d) Public Officer's Title and Name. A public officer who sues or is sued in an official capacity may be designated by official title rather than by name, but the court may order that the officer's name be added.

* * *

MAS v. PERRY

489 F.2d 1396 (5th Cir. 1974)

Before Wisdom, Ainsworth and Clark, Circuit Judges.

Ainsworth, Circuit Judge:

This case presents questions pertaining to federal diversity jurisdiction under 28 U.S.C. § 1332, which, pursuant to article III, section II of the Constitution, provides for original jurisdiction in federal district courts of all civil actions that are between, inter alia, citizens of different States or citizens of a State and citizens of foreign states and in which the amount in controversy is more than $10,000.

Appellees Jean Paul Mas, a citizen of France, and Judy Mas were married at her home in Jackson, Mississippi. Prior to their marriage, Mr. and Mrs. Mas were graduate assistants, pursuing coursework as well as performing teaching duties, for approximately nine months and one year, respectively, at Louisiana State University in Baton Rouge, Louisiana. Shortly after their marriage, they returned to Baton Rouge to resume their duties as graduate assistants at LSU. They remained in Baton Rouge for approximately two more years, after which they moved to Park Ridge, Illinois. At the time of the trial in this case, it was their intention to return to Baton Rouge while Mr. Mas finished his studies for the degree of Doctor of Philosophy. Mr. and Mrs. Mas were undecided as to where they would reside after that.

Upon their return to Baton Rouge after their marriage, appellees rented an apartment from appellant Oliver H. Perry, a citizen of Louisiana. This appeal arises from a final judgment entered on a jury verdict awarding $5,000 to Mr. Mas and $15,000 to Mrs. Mas for damages incurred by them as a result of the discovery that their bedroom and bathroom contained 'two-way' mirrors and that they had been watched through them by the appellant during three of the first four months of their marriage.

At the close of the appellees' case at trial, appellant made an oral motion to dismiss for lack of jurisdiction. The motion was denied by the district court. Before this Court, appellant challenges the final judgment below solely on jurisdictional grounds, contending that appellees failed to prove diversity of citizenship among the parties and that the requisite jurisdictional amount is lacking with respect to Mr. Mas. Finding no merit to these contentions, we affirm. Under section 1332(a)(2), the federal judicial power extends to the claim of Mr. Mas, a citizen of France, against the appellant, a citizen of Louisiana. Since we conclude that Mrs. Mas is a citizen of Mississippi for diversity purposes, the district court also properly had jurisdiction under section 1332(a)(1) of her claim.

It has long been the general rule that complete diversity of parties is required in order that diversity jurisdiction obtain; that is, no party on one side may be a citizen of the same State as any party on the other side. *Strawbridge v. Curtiss*, 7 U.S. (3 Cranch) 267, 2 L.Ed. 435 (1806). This determination of one's State Citizenship for diversity purposes is controlled by federal law, not by the law of any State. As is the case in other areas of federal jurisdiction, the diverse citizenship among adverse parties must be present at the time the complaint is filed. Jurisdiction is unaffected by subsequent changes in the citizenship of the parties. The burden of pleading the diverse citizenship is upon the party invoking federal jurisdiction; and if the diversity jurisdiction is properly challenged, that party also bears the burden of proof.

To be a citizen of a State within the meaning of section 1332, a natural person must be both a citizen of the United States, and a domiciliary of that State. For diversity purposes, citizenship means domicile; mere residence in the State is not sufficient.

A person's domicile is the place of "his true, fixed, and permanent home and principal establishment, and to which he has the intention of returning whenever he is absent therefrom. . . ." A change of domicile may be effected only by a combination of two elements: (a) taking up residence in a different domicile with (b) the intention to remain there.

It is clear that at the time of her marriage, Mrs. Mas was a domiciliary of the State of Mississippi. While it is generally the case that the domicile of the wife—and, consequently, her State citizenship for purposes of diversity jurisdiction—is deemed to be that of her husband, we find no precedent for extending this concept to the situation here, in which the husband is a citizen of a foreign state but resides in the United States. Indeed, such a fiction would work absurd results on the facts before us. If Mr. Mas were considered a domiciliary of France—as he would be since he had lived in Louisiana as a student-teaching assistant prior to filing this suit—then Mrs. Mas would also be deemed a domiciliary, and thus, fictionally at least, a citizen of France. She would not be a citizen of any State and could not sue in a federal court on that basis; nor could she invoke the alienage jurisdiction to bring her claim in federal court, since she is not an alien. On the other hand, if Mrs. Mas's domicile were Louisiana, she would become a Louisiana citizen for diversity purposes and could not bring suit with her husband against appellant, also a Louisiana citizen, on the basis of diversity jurisdiction. These are curious results under a rule arising from the theoretical identity of person and interest of the married couple.

An American woman is not deemed to have lost her United States citizenship solely by reason of her marriage to an alien. Similarly, we conclude that for diversity purposes a woman does not have her domicile or State Citizenship changed solely by reason of her marriage to an alien.

Mrs. Mas's Mississippi domicile was disturbed neither by her year in Louisiana prior to her marriage nor as a result of the time she and her husband spent at LSU after their marriage, since for both periods she was a graduate assistant at LSU. Though she testified that after her marriage she had no intention of returning to her parents' home in Mississippi, Mrs. Mas did not effect a change of domicile since she and Mr. Mas were in Louisiana only as students and lacked the requisite intention to remain there. Until she acquires a new domicile, she remains a domiciliary, and thus a citizen, of Mississippi.[2]

---

2. The original complaint in this case was filed within several days of Mr. and Mrs. Mas's realization that they had been watched through the mirrors, quite some time before they moved

Appellant also contends that Mr. Mas's claim should have been dismissed for failure to establish the requisite jurisdictional amount for diversity cases of more than $10,000. In their complaint Mr. and Mrs. Mas alleged that they had each been damaged in the amount of $100,000. As we have noted, Mr. Mas ultimately recovered $5,000.

It is well settled that the amount in controversy is determined by the amount claimed by the plaintiff in good faith. Federal jurisdiction is not lost because a judgment of less than the jurisdictional amount is awarded. That Mr. Mas recovered only $5,000 is, therefore, not compelling. As the Supreme Court stated in *St. Paul Mercury Indemnity Co. v. Red Cab Co.*, 303 U.S. 283:

> The sum claimed by the plaintiff controls if the claim is apparently made in good faith.

> It must appear to a legal certainty that the claim is really for less than the jurisdictional amount to justify dismissal. The inability of the plaintiff to recover an amount adequate to give the court jurisdiction does not show his bad faith or oust the jurisdiction. . . .

> . . . His good faith in choosing the federal forum is open to challenge not only by resort to the face of his complaint, but by the facts disclosed at trial, and if from either source it is clear that his claim never could have amounted to the sum necessary to give jurisdiction there is no injustice in dismissing the suit.

Having heard the evidence presented at the trial, the district court concluded that the appellees properly met the requirements of section 1332 with respect to jurisdictional amount. Upon examination of the record in this case, we are also satisfied that the requisite amount was in controversy.

Thus the power of the federal district court to entertain the claims of appellees in this case stands on two separate legs of diversity jurisdiction: a claim by an alien against a State citizen; and an action between citizens of different States. We also note, however, the propriety of having the federal district court entertain a spouse's action against a defendant, where the district court already has jurisdiction over a claim, arising from the same transaction, by the other spouse against the same defendant. In the case before us, such a result is particularly desirable. The claims of Mr. and Mrs. Mas arise from the same operative facts, and there was almost complete interdependence between their claims with respect to the proof required and the issues raised at trial. Thus, since the district court had jurisdiction of Mr. Mas's action, sound judicial administration militates strongly in favor of federal jurisdiction of Mrs. Mas's claim.

Affirmed.

---

to Park Ridge, Illinois. Because the district court's jurisdiction is not affected by actions of the parties subsequent to the commencement of the suit, the testimony concerning Mr. and Mrs. Mas's moves after that time is not determinative of the issue of diverse citizenship, though it is of interest insofar as it supports their lack of intent to remain permanently in Louisiana.

28 U.S.C. § 1441. REMOVAL OF CIVIL ACTIONS

(a) Generally.—Except as otherwise expressly provided by Act of Congress, any civil action brought in a State court of which the district courts of the United States have original jurisdiction, may be removed by the defendant or the defendants, to the district court of the United States for the district and division embracing the place where such action is pending.

(b) Removal based on diversity of citizenship.—

   (1) In determining whether a civil action is removable on the basis of the jurisdiction under section 1332(a) of this title, the citizenship of defendants sued under fictitious names shall be disregarded.

   (2) A civil action otherwise removable solely on the basis of the jurisdiction under section 1332(a) of this title may not be removed if any of the parties in interest properly joined and served as defendants is a citizen of the State in which such action is brought.

(c) Joinder of Federal law claims and State law claims.—

   (1) If a civil action includes

   (A) a claim arising under the Constitution, laws, or treaties of the United States (within the meaning of section 1331 of this title), and

   (B) a claim not within the original or supplemental jurisdiction of the district court or a claim that has been made nonremovable by statute, the entire action may be removed if the action would be removable without the inclusion of the claim described in subparagraph (B).

   (2) Upon removal of an action described in paragraph (1), the district court shall sever from the action all claims described in paragraph (1)(B) and shall remand the severed claims to the State court from which the action was removed. Only defendants against whom a claim described in paragraph (1)(A) has been asserted are required to join in or consent to the removal under paragraph (1).

* * *

THE HERTZ CORPORATION v. FRIEND

130 S.Ct. 1181 (2010)

JUSTICE BREYER delivered the opinion of the Court.

The federal diversity jurisdiction statute provides that "a corporation shall be deemed to be a citizen of any State by which it has been incorporated and of the State where it has its principal place of business." 28 U.S.C. § 1332(c)(1). We seek here to resolve different interpretations that the Circuits have given this phrase. In doing so, we place primary weight upon the need for judicial administration of a jurisdictional statute to remain as simple as possible. And we conclude that the phrase "principal place of business" refers to the place where the corporation's high level officers direct, control, and coordinate the corporation's activities. Lower federal courts have often metaphorically called that place the corporation's "nerve center." We believe that the "nerve center" will typically be found at a corporation's headquarters.

I

In September 2007, respondents Melinda Friend and John Nhieu, two California citizens, sued petitioner, the Hertz Corporation, in a California state court. They sought damages for what they claimed were violations of California's wage and hour laws. And they requested relief on behalf of a potential class composed of California citizens who had allegedly suffered similar harms.

Hertz filed a notice seeking removal to a federal court. 28 U.S.C. §§ 1332(d)(2), 1441(a). Hertz claimed that the plaintiffs and the defendant were citizens of different States. §§ 1332(a)(1), (c)(1). Hence, the federal court possessed diversity-of-citizenship jurisdiction. Friend and Nhieu, however, claimed that the Hertz Corporation was a California citizen, like themselves, and that, hence, diversity jurisdiction was lacking.

To support its position, Hertz submitted a declaration by an employee relations manager that sought to show that Hertz's "principal place of business" was in New Jersey, not in California. The declaration stated, among other things, that Hertz operated facilities in 44 States; and that California—which had about 12% of the Nation's population accounted for 273 of Hertz's 1,606 car rental locations; about 2,300 of its 11,230 fulltime employees; about $811 million of its $4.371 billion in annual revenue; and about 3.8 million of its approximately 21 million annual transactions, i.e., rentals. The declaration also stated that the "leadership of Hertz and its domestic subsidiaries" is located at Hertz's "corporate headquarters" in Park Ridge, New Jersey; that its "core executive and administrative functions ... are carried out" there and "to a lesser extent" in Oklahoma City, Oklahoma; and that its "major administrative operations ... are found" at those two locations.

The District Court of the Northern District of California accepted Hertz's statement of the facts as undisputed. But it concluded that, given those facts, Hertz was a citizen of California. In reaching this conclusion, the court applied Ninth Circuit precedent, which instructs courts to identify a corporation's "principal place of business" by first determining the amount of a corporation's business activity State by State. If the amount of activity is "significantly larger" or "substantially predominates" in one State, then that State is the corporation's "principal place of business." If there is no such State, then the "principal place of business" is the corporation's " 'nerve center,' " i.e., the place where " 'the majority of its executive and administrative functions are performed.' "

Applying this test, the District Court found that the "plurality of each of the relevant business activities" was in California, and that "the differential between the amount of those activities" in California and the amount in "the next closest state" was "significant." Hence, Hertz's "principal place of business" was California, and diversity jurisdiction was thus lacking. The District Court consequently remanded the case to the state courts.

Hertz appealed the District Court's remand order. The Ninth Circuit affirmed in a brief memorandum opinion. Hertz filed a petition for certiorari. And, in light of differences among the Circuits in the application of the test for corporate citizenship, we granted the writ.

II

[Discussion of jurisdictional objection omitted—*ed.*]

III

We begin our "principal place of business" discussion with a brief review of relevant history. The Constitution provides that the "judicial Power shall extend" to "Controversies ... between Citizens of different States." Art. III, § 2. This language, however, does not automatically confer diversity jurisdiction upon the federal courts. Rather, it authorizes Congress to do so and, in doing so, to determine the scope of the federal courts' jurisdiction within constitutional limits. Congress first authorized federal courts to exercise diversity jurisdiction in 1789 when, in the First Judiciary Act, Congress granted federal courts authority to hear suits "between a citizen of the State where the suit is brought, and a citizen of another State." The statute said nothing about corporations. In 1809, Chief Justice Marshall, writing for a unanimous Court, described a corporation as an "invisible, intangible, and artificial being" which was "certainly not a citizen." *Bank of United States v. Deveaux* (1809). But the Court held that a corporation could invoke the federal courts' diversity jurisdiction based on a pleading that the corporation's shareholders were all citizens of a different State from the defendants, as "the term citizen ought to be understood as it is used in the constitution, and as it is used in other laws. That is, to describe the real persons who come into court, in this case, under their corporate name." In *Louisville C. & C. R. Co. v. Letson* (1844), the Court modified this initial approach. It held that a corporation was to be deemed an artificial person of the State by which it had been created, and its citizenship for jurisdictional purposes determined accordingly. Ten years later, the Court in *Marshall v. Baltimore & Ohio R. Co.* (1854), held that the reason a corporation was a citizen of its State of incorporation was that, for the limited purpose of determining corporate citizenship, courts could conclusively (and artificially) presume that a corporation's shareholders were citizens of the State of incorporation. And it reaffirmed *Letson*. Whatever the rationale, the practical upshot was that, for diversity purposes, the federal courts considered a corporation to be a citizen of the State of its incorporation.

In 1928 this Court made clear that the "state of incorporation" rule was virtually absolute. It held that a corporation closely identified with State A could proceed in a federal court located in that State as long as the corporation had filed its incorporation papers in State B, perhaps a State where the corporation did no business at all. *See Black and White Taxicab & Transfer Co. v. Brown and Yellow Taxicab & Transfer Co.* (refusing to question corporation's reincorporation motives and finding diversity jurisdiction). Subsequently, many in Congress and those who testified before it pointed out that this interpretation was at odds with diversity jurisdiction's basic rationale, namely, opening the federal courts' doors to those who might otherwise suffer from local prejudice against out-of-state parties. Through its choice of the State of incorporation, a corporation could manipulate federal-court jurisdiction, for example, opening the federal courts' doors in a State where it conducted nearly all its business by filing incorporation papers elsewhere. ("Since the Supreme Court has decided that a corporation is a citizen ... it has become a common practice for corporations to be incorporated in one State while they do business in another. And there is no doubt but that it often occurs simply for the purpose of being able to have the advantage of choosing between two tribunals in case of litigation"). Although various legislative proposals to curtail the corporate use of diversity jurisdiction were made, none of these proposals were enacted into law.

At the same time as federal dockets increased in size, many judges began to believe those dockets contained too many diversity cases. A committee of the Judicial Conference of the United States studied the matter. And on March 12, 1951, that committee, the Committee on Jurisdiction and Venue, issued a report.

Among its observations, the committee found a general need "to prevent frauds and abuses" with respect to jurisdiction. The committee recommended against eliminating diversity cases altogether. Instead it recommended, along with other proposals, a statutory amendment that would make a corporation a citizen both of the State of its incorporation and any State from which it received more than half of its gross income (requiring corporation to show that "less than fifty per cent of its gross income was derived from business transacted within the state where the Federal court is held"). If, for example, a citizen of California sued (under state law in state court) a corporation that received half or more of its gross income from California, that corporation would not be able to remove the case to federal court, even if Delaware was its State of incorporation.

During the spring and summer of 1951 committee members circulated their report and attended circuit conferences at which federal judges discussed the report's recommendations. Reflecting those criticisms, the committee filed a new report in September, in which it revised its corporate citizenship recommendation. It now proposed that " 'a corporation shall be deemed a citizen of the state of its original creation ... [and] shall also be deemed citizen of a state where it has its principal place of business.' " The committee wrote that this new language would provide a "simpler and more practical formula" than the "gross income" test. It added that the language "ha[d] a precedent in the jurisdictional provisions of the Bankruptcy Act."

In mid–1957 the committee presented its reports to the House of Representatives Committee on the Judiciary. Judge Albert Maris, representing Judge John Parker (who had chaired the Judicial Conference Committee), discussed various proposals that the Judicial Conference had made to restrict the scope of diversity jurisdiction. In respect to the "principal place of business" proposal, he said that the relevant language "ha[d] been defined in the Bankruptcy Act." He added:

> "All of those problems have arisen in bankruptcy cases, and as I recall the cases—and I wouldn't want to be bound by this statement because I haven't them before me—I think the courts have generally taken the view that where a corporation's interests are rather widespread, the principal place of business is an actual rather than a theoretical or legal one. It is the actual place where its business operations are coordinated, directed, and carried out, which would ordinarily be the place where its officers carry on its day-to-day business, where its accounts are kept, where its payments are made, and not necessarily a State in which it may have a plant, if it is a big corporation, or something of that sort.

> "But that has been pretty well worked out in the bankruptcy cases, and that law would all be available, you see, to be applied here without having to go over it again from the beginning."

The House Committee reprinted the Judicial Conference Committee Reports along with other reports and relevant testimony and circulated it to the general public "for the purpose of inviting further suggestions and comments." Subsequently, in 1958, Congress both codified the courts' traditional place of incorporation test and also enacted into law a slightly modified version of the Conference Committee's proposed "principal place of business" language. A corporation was to "be deemed a citizen of any State by which it has been incorporated and of the State where it has its principal place of business."

IV

The phrase "principal place of business" has proved more difficult to apply than its originators likely expected. Decisions under the Bankruptcy Act did not provide the firm guidance for which Judge Maris had hoped because courts interpreting bankruptcy law did not agree about how to determine a corporation's "principal place of business." After Congress' amendment, courts were similarly uncertain as to where to look to determine a corporation's "principal place of business" for diversity purposes. If a corporation's headquarters and executive offices were in the same State in which it did most of its business, the test seemed straightforward. The "principal place of business" was located in that State. But suppose those corporate headquarters, including executive offices, are in one State, while the corporation's plants or other centers of business activity are located in other States? In 1959 a distinguished federal district judge, Edward Weinfeld, relied on the Second Circuit's interpretation of the Bankruptcy Act to answer this question in part: "Where a corporation is engaged in far-flung and varied activities which are carried on in different states, its principal place of business is the nerve center from which it radiates out to its constituent parts and from which its officers direct, control and coordinate all activities without regard to locale, in the furtherance of the corporate objective. The test applied by our Court of Appeals, is that place where the corporation has an 'office from which its business was directed and controlled'—the place where 'all of its business was under the supreme direction and control of its officers.' "

Numerous Circuits have since followed this rule, applying the "nerve center" test for corporations with "far-flung" business activities.

Scot's analysis, however, did not go far enough. For it did not answer what courts should do when the operations of the corporation are not "far-flung" but rather limited to only a few States. When faced with this question, various courts have focused more heavily on where a corporation's actual business activities are located.

Perhaps because corporations come in many different forms, involve many different kinds of business activities, and locate offices and plants for different reasons in different ways in different regions, a general "business activities" approach has proved unusually difficult to apply.

Courts must decide which factors are more important than others: for example, plant location, sales or servicing centers; transactions, payrolls, or revenue generation.

The number of factors grew as courts explicitly combined aspects of the "nerve center" and "business activity" tests to look to a corporation's "total activities," sometimes to try to determine what treatises have described as the corporation's "center of gravity." A major treatise confirms this growing complexity, listing Circuit by Circuit, cases that highlight different factors or emphasize similar factors differently, and reporting that the "federal courts of appeals have employed various tests"— tests which "tend to overlap" and which are sometimes described in "language" that "is imprecise." (describing, in 14 pages, major tests as looking to the "nerve center," "locus of operations," or "center of corporate activities"). Not surprisingly, different circuits (and sometimes different courts within a single circuit) have applied these highly general multifactor tests in different ways (noting that the First Circuit "has never explained a basis for choosing between 'the center of corporate activity' test and the 'locus of operations' test"; the Second Circuit uses a "two-part test" similar to that of the Fifth, Ninth, and Eleventh Circuits involving an initial determination as to whether "a corporation's activities are centralized or decentralized" followed by an application of either the "place of operations" or "nerve center" test; the Third Circuit applies the "center of corporate activities" test searching for the "headquarters of a corporation's day-to-day activity"; the Fourth Circuit has "endorsed neither [the 'nerve center' or 'place of operations'] test to the exclusion of the other"; the Tenth Circuit directs consideration of the "total activity of the company considered as a whole"). *See also* 13F Wright & Miller § 3625 (describing, in 73 pages, the "nerve center," "corporate activities," and "total activity" tests as part of an effort to locate the corporation's "center of gravity," while specifying different ways in which different circuits apply these or other factors).

This complexity may reflect an unmediated judicial effort to apply the statutory phrase "principal place of business" in light of the general purpose of diversity jurisdiction, i.e., an effort to find the State where a corporation is least likely to suffer out-of-state prejudice when it issued in a local court. But, if so, that task seems doomed to failure. After all, the relevant purposive concern—prejudice against an out-of-state party—will often depend upon factors that courts cannot easily measure, for example, a corporation's image, its history, and its advertising, while the factors that courts can more easily measure, for example, its office or plant location, its sales, its employment, or the nature of the goods or services it supplies, will sometimes bear no more than a distant relation to the likelihood of prejudice. At the same time, this approach is at war with administrative simplicity. And it has failed to achieve a nationally uniform interpretation of federal law, an unfortunate consequence in a federal legal system.

V

A

In an effort to find a single, more uniform interpretation of the statutory phrase, we have reviewed the Courts of Appeals' divergent and increasingly complexions. Having done so, we now return to, and expand, Judge Weinfeld's approach, as applied in the Seventh Circuit. We conclude that "principal place of business" is best read as referring to the place where a corporation's officers direct, control, and coordinate the corporation's activities. It is the place that Courts of Appeals have called the corporation's "nerve center." And in practice it should normally be the place where the corporation maintains its headquarters—provided that the headquarters is the actual center of direction, control, and coordination, i.e., the "nerve center," and not simply an office where the corporation holds its board meetings (for example, attended by directors and officers who have traveled there for the occasion).

Three sets of considerations, taken together, convince us that this approach, while imperfect, is superior to other possibilities. First, the statute's language supports the approach. The statute's text deems a corporation a citizen of the "State where it has its principal place of business." 28 U.S.C. § 1332(c)(1). The word "place" is in the singular, not the plural. The word "principal" requires us to pick out the "main, prominent" or "leading" place. 12 OXFORD ENGLISH DICTIONARY 495 (2d ed.

1989) (def. (A)(I)(2)). *Cf. Commissioner v. Soliman*, 506 U. S. 168, 174 (1993) (interpreting "principal place of business" for tax purposes to require an assessment of "whether any one business location is the 'most important, consequential, or influential' one"). And the fact that the word "place" follows the words "State where" means that the "place" is a place within a State. It is not the State itself.

A corporation's "nerve center," usually its main headquarters, is a single place. The public often (though not always) considers it the corporation's main place of business. And it is a place within a State. By contrast, the application of a more general business activities test hassled some courts, as in the present case, to look, not at a particular place within a State, but incorrectly at the State itself, measuring the total amount of business activities that the corporation conducts there and determining whether they are "significantly larger" than in the next ranking State.

This approach invites greater litigation and can lead to strange results, as the Ninth Circuit has since recognized. Namely, if a "corporation may be deemed a citizen of California on th[e] basis" of "activities [that] roughly reflect California's larger population . . . nearly every national retailer—no matter how far flung its operations—will be deemed a citizen of California for diversity purposes." But why award or decline diversity jurisdiction on the basis of a State's population, whether measured directly, indirectly (say proportionately), or with modifications?

Second, administrative simplicity is a major virtue in a jurisdictional statute. Complex jurisdictional tests complicate a case, eating up time and money as the parties litigate, not the merits of their claims, but which court is the right court to decide those claims. Complex tests produce appeals and reversals, encourage gamesmanship, and, again, diminish the likelihood that results and settlements will reflect a claim's legal and factual merits. Judicial resources too are at stake. Courts have an independent obligation to determine whether subject-matter jurisdiction exists, even when no party challenges it. So courts benefit from straightforward rules under which they can readily assure themselves of their power to hear a case.

Simple jurisdictional rules also promote greater predictability. Predictability is valuable to corporations making business and investment decisions. Predictability also benefits plaintiffs deciding whether to file suit in a state or federal court.

A "nerve center" approach, which ordinarily equates that "center" with a corporation's headquarters, is simple to apply comparatively speaking. The metaphor of a corporate "brain," while not precise, suggests a single location. By contrast, a corporation's general business activities more often lack a single principal place where they take place. That is to say, the corporation may have several plants, many sales locations, and employees located in many different places. If so, it will not be as easy to determine which of these different business locales is the "principal" or most important "place."

Third, the statute's legislative history, for those who accept it, offers a simplicity-related interpretive benchmark. The Judicial Conference provided an initial version of its proposal that suggested a numerical test. A corporation would be deemed a citizen of the State that accounted for more than half of its gross income. The Conference changed its mind in light of criticism that such a test would prove too complex and impractical to apply. That history suggests that the words "principal place of business" should be interpreted to be no more complex than the initial "half of gross income" test. A "nerve center" test offers such a possibility. A general business activities test does not.

B

We recognize that there may be no perfect test that satisfies all administrative and purposive criteria. We recognize as well that, under the "nerve center" test we adopt today, there will be hard cases. For example, in this era of telecommuting, some corporations may divide their command and coordinating functions among officers who work at several different locations, perhaps communicating over the Internet. That said, our test nonetheless points courts in a single direction, towards the center of overall direction, control, and coordination. Courts do not have to try to weigh corporate functions, assets, or revenues different in kind, one from the other. Our approach provides a sensible test that is relatively easier to apply, not a test that will, in all instances, automatically generate a result. We also recognize that the use of a "nerve center" test may in some cases produce results that seem to cut against the basic rationale for 28 U.S.C. § 1332. For example, if the bulk of a company's business activities visible to the public take place in New Jersey, while its top officers direct those activities just across the river in New York, the "principal place of business" is New York. One could argue that members of the public in New Jersey would be less likely to be prejudiced against the corporation than persons in New York—yet the corporation will still be entitled to remove a New Jersey state case to federal court. And note too that the same corporation would be unable to remove a New York state case to federal court, despite the New York public's presumed prejudice against the corporation. We understand that such seeming anomalies will arise.

However, in view of the necessity of having a clearer rule, we must accept them. Accepting occasionally counterintuitive results is the price the legal system must pay to avoid overly complex jurisdictional administration while producing the benefits that accompany a more uniform legal system.

The burden of persuasion for establishing diversity jurisdiction, of course, remains on the party asserting it. When challenged on allegations of jurisdictional facts, the parties must support their allegations by competent proof. And when faced with such a challenge, we reject suggestions such as, for example, the one made by petitioner that the mere filing of a form like the Securities and Exchange Commission's Form 10–K listing a corporation's "principal executive offices" would, without more, be sufficient proof to establish a corporation's "nerve center." Such possibilities would readily permit jurisdictional manipulation, thereby subverting a major reason for the insertion of the "principal place of business" language in the diversity statute. Indeed, if the record reveals attempts at manipulation—for example, that the alleged "nerve center" is nothing more than a mail drop box, a bare office with a computer, or the location of an annual executive retreat—the courts should instead take as the "nerve center" the place of actual direction, control, and coordination, in the absence of such manipulation.

VI

Petitioner's unchallenged declaration suggests that Hertz's center of direction, control, and coordination, its "nerve center," and its corporate headquarters are one and the same, and they are located in New Jersey, not in California. Because respondents should have a fair opportunity to litigate their case in light of our holding, however, we vacate the Ninth Circuit's judgment and remand the case for further proceedings consistent with this opinion.

It is so ordered.

B. SPECIAL PROBLEMS IN DIVERSITY JURISDICTION: COLLUSIVE JOINDER

28 U.S.C. § 1359. PARTIES COLLUSIVELY JOINED OR MADE

A district court shall not have jurisdiction of a civil action in which any party, by assignment or otherwise, has been improperly or collusively made or joined to invoke the jurisdiction of such court.

* * *

KRAMER v. CARIBBEAN MILLS, INC.

394 U.S. 823 (1969)

MR. JUSTICE HARLAN delivered the opinion of the Court.

The sole question presented by this case is whether the Federal District Court in which it was brought had jurisdiction over the cause, or whether that court was deprived of jurisdiction by 28 U.S.C. § 1359. That section provides:

> A district court shall not have jurisdiction of a civil action in which any party, by assignment or otherwise, has been improperly or collusively made or joined to invoke the jurisdiction of such court.

The facts were these. Respondent Caribbean Mills, Inc. (Caribbean) is a Haitian corporation. In May 1959 it entered into a contract with an individual named Kelly and the Panama and Venezuela Finance Company (Panama), a Panamanian Corporation. The agreement provided that Caribbean would purchase from Panama 125 shares of corporate stock, in return for payment of $85,000 down and an additional $165,000 in 12 annual installments.

No installment payments ever were made, despite requests for payment by Panama. In 1964, Panama assigned its entire interest in the 1959 contract to petitioner Kramer, an attorney in Wichita Falls, Texas. The stated consideration was $1. By a separate agreement dated the same day, Kramer promised to pay back to Panama 95% of any net recovery on the assigned cause of action,[1] "solely as a Bonus."

Kramer soon thereafter brought suit against Caribbean for $165,000 in the United States District Court for the Northern District of Texas, alleging diversity of citizenship between himself and Caribbean.[2] The District Court denied Caribbean's motion to dismiss for want of jurisdiction. The case proceeded to trial, and a jury returned a $165,000 verdict in favor of Kramer.

On appeal, the Court of Appeals for the Fifth Circuit reversed, holding that the assignment was "improperly or collusively made" within the meaning of 28 U.S.C. § 1359, and that in consequence the District Court lacked jurisdiction. We granted certiorari. For reasons which follow, we affirm the judgment of the Court of Appeals.

I

The issue before us is whether Kramer was "improperly or collusively made" a party "to invoke the jurisdiction" of the District Court, within the meaning of 28 U.S.C. § 1359. We look first to the legislative background.

Section 1359 has existed in its present form only since the 1948 revision of the Judicial Code. Prior to that time, the use of devices to create diversity was regulated by two federal statutes. The first, known as the "assignee clause" provided that, with certain exceptions not here relevant:

> No district court shall have cognizance of any suit * * * to recover upon any promissory note or other chose in action in favor of any assignee * * * unless such suit might have been prosecuted in such court * * * if no assignment had been made.

The second pre–1948 statute stated that a district court should dismiss an action whenever:

> it shall appear to the satisfaction of the * * * court * * * that such suit does not really and substantially involve a dispute or controversy properly within the jurisdiction of (the) court, or that the parties to

---

1. That is, Kramer would receive 5%, and Panama 95%, of the net proceeds remaining after payment of attorneys' fees and expenses of litigation.

2. Title 28 U.S.C. § 1332(a)(2) grants district courts original jurisdiction of civil actions in which the matter in controversy exceeds $10,000 and is between "citizens of a State, and foreign states or citizens or subjects thereof * * *." The District Court would have had no jurisdiction of a suit brought by Panama against Caribbean, since both were alien corporations.

said suit have been improperly or collusively made or joined * * * for the purpose of creating (federal jurisdiction).

As part of the 1948 revision, § 80 was amended to produce the present § 1359. The assignee clause was simultaneously repealed. The Reviser's Note describes the amended assignee clause as a "jumble of legislative jargon," and states that "(t)he revised section changes this clause by confining its application to cases wherein the assignment is improperly or collusively made * * *. Furthermore, * * * the original purpose of (the assignee) clause is better served by substantially following section 80." That purpose was said to be "to prevent the manufacture of Federal jurisdiction by the device of assignment."

II

Only a small number of cases decided under § 1359 have involved diversity jurisdiction based on assignments, and this Court has not considered the matter since the 1948 revision. Because the approach of the former assignee clause was to forbid the grounding of jurisdiction upon any assignment, regardless of its circumstances or purpose, decisions under that clause are of little assistance. However, decisions of this Court under the other predecessor statute, 28 U.S.C. § 80, seem squarely in point. These decisions, together with the evident purpose of § 1359, lead us to conclude that the Court of Appeals was correct in finding that the assignment in question was "improperly or collusively made."

The most compelling precedent is *Farmington Village Corp. v. Pillsbury*. There Maine holders of bonds issued by a Maine village desired to test the bonds' validity in the federal courts. In an effort to accomplish this, they cut the coupons from their bonds and transferred them to a citizen of Massachusetts, who gave in return a non-negotiable two-year note for $500 and a promise to pay back 50% of the net amount recovered above $500. The jurisdictional question was certified to this Court, which held that there was no federal jurisdiction because the plaintiff had been "improperly or collusively" made a party within the meaning of the predecessor statute to 28 U.S.C. § 80. The Court pointed out that the plaintiff could easily have been released from his non-negotiable note, and found that apart from the hoped-for creation of federal jurisdiction the only real consequence of the transfer was to enable the Massachusetts plaintiff to "retain one-half of what he collects for the use of his name and his trouble in collecting." The Court concluded that "the transfer of the coupons was a mere contrivance, a pretense, the result of a collusive arrangement to create" federal jurisdiction.

We find the case before us indistinguishable from *Farmington* and other decisions of like tenor. When the assignment to Kramer is considered together with his total lack of previous connection with the matter and his simultaneous reassignment of a 95% interest back to Panama, there can be little doubt that the assignment was for purposes of collection, with Kramer to retain 5% of the net proceeds "for the use of his name and his trouble in collecting."[9] If the suit had been unsuccessful, Kramer would have been out only $1, plus costs. Moreover, Kramer candidly admits that the "assignment was in substantial part motivated by a desire by (Panama's) counsel to make diversity jurisdiction available * * *."

The conclusion that this assignment was "improperly or collusively made" within the meaning of § 1359 is supported not only by precedent but also by consideration of the statute's purpose. If federal jurisdiction could be created by assignments of this kind, which are easy to arrange and involve few disadvantages for the assignor, then a vast quantity of ordinary contract and tort litigation could be channeled into the federal courts at the will of one of the parties. Such "manufacture of Federal jurisdiction" was the very thing which Congress intended to prevent when it enacted § 1359 and its predecessors.

III

Kramer nevertheless argues that the assignment to him was not "improperly or collusively made" within the meaning of § 1359, for two main reasons. First, he suggests that the undisputed legality of the assignment under Texas law necessarily rendered it valid for purposes of federal jurisdiction. We cannot accept this contention. The existence of federal jurisdiction is a matter of federal, not state law. Under the predecessor section, 28 U.S.C. § 80, this Court several times held that an assignment could be "improperly or collusively made" even though binding under state law, and nothing in the language or legislative history of § 1359 suggests that a different result should be reached under that statute. Moreover, to accept this argument would render § 1359 largely incapable of accomplishing its purpose; this very case demonstrates the ease with which a party may "manufacture" federal jurisdiction by an assignment which meets the requirements of state law.

Second, Kramer urges that this case is significantly distinguishable from earlier decisions because it involves diversity jurisdiction under 28 U.S.C. § 1332(a)(2), arising from the alienage of one of the parties, rather than the more common diversity jurisdiction based upon the parties' residence in different States. We can perceive no substance in this argument: by its terms, § 1359 applies equally to both types of diversity

---

9. Hence, we have no occasion to re-examine the cases in which this Court has held that where the transfer of a claim is absolute, with the transferor retaining no interest in the subject matter, then the transfer is not "improperly or collusively made," regardless of the transferor's motive.

Nor is it necessary to consider whether, in cases in which suit is required to be brought by an administrator or guardian, a motive to create diversity jurisdiction renders the appointment of an out-of-state representative "improper" or "collusive." Cases involving representatives vary in several respects from those in which jurisdiction is based on assignments: (1) in the former situation, some representative must be appointed before suit can be brought, while in the latter the assignor normally is himself capable of suing in state court; (2) under state law, different kinds of guardians and administrators may possess discrete sorts of powers; and (3) all such representatives owe their appointment to the decree of a state court, rather than solely to an action of the parties. It is not necessary to decide whether these distinctions amount to a difference for purposes of amount to a difference for purposes of § 1359.

jurisdiction, and there is no indication that Congress intended them to be treated differently.

IV

In short, we find that this assignment falls not only within the scope of § 1359 but within its very core. It follows that the District Court lacked jurisdiction to hear this action, and that petitioner must seek his remedy in the state courts. The judgment of the Court of Appeals is affirmed.

Affirmed.

MR. JUSTICE FORTAS took no part in the consideration or decision of this case.

ROSE v. GIAMATTI

721 F.Supp. 906 (S.D. Ohio 1989)

HOLSCHUH, DISTRICT JUDGE.

I. INTRODUCTION

This action by Peter Edward Rose against A. Bartlett Giamatti and others, initially filed in the Court of Common Pleas of Hamilton County, Ohio at Cincinnati, and removed to the United States District Court for the Southern District of Ohio on July 3, 1989.... In [a] transfer order, Judges Rubin and Weber stated:

> Plaintiff is not just another litigant. He is instead a baseball figure of national reputation closely identified with the Cincinnati Reds and the City of Cincinnati. Under such circumstances, it would appear advisable that [this case] be transferred to a city of the Southern District of Ohio other than Cincinnati.

Although in that same order Judges Rubin and Weber expressed doubt whether this action is removable to federal court, that doubt was expressed, of course, without the benefit of the extensive briefs, voluminous exhibits and oral argument presented to the undersigned judge subsequent to removal. Within the expedited time schedule set by the Court and the parties, I have resolved those issues based upon the record now before me.

The Court emphasizes that the issues decided by this Memorandum and Order are solely questions of law concerning the jurisdiction of a United States district court when a case is removed from a state court based upon diversity of citizenship of the parties to the controversy. The essential facts relative to these jurisdictional issues are not in dispute, and the merits of the controversy between plaintiff Rose and defendant Giamatti are not before the Court at this time.... The sole question raised by the notice of removal and the motion to remand is whether, under applicable law, the federal court has jurisdiction over the subject matter of this action. For the reasons stated hereafter, I conclude that the action was properly removed to this Court, and that this Court does have jurisdiction over the action which I have a duty to recognize and to enforce.

II. PROCEDURAL HISTORY

Plaintiff, Peter Edward Rose, is the Field Manager of the Cincinnati Reds baseball team. In February of this year, then Commissioner of Baseball Peter V. Ueberroth and then Commissioner of Baseball-elect A. Bartlett Giamatti initiated an investigation regarding allegations that Rose wagered on major league baseball games. On February 23, 1989 Giamatti retained John M. Dowd as Special Counsel for the purpose of conducting the investigation. On May 9, 1989 Dowd submitted a report to Giamatti summarizing the evidence obtained during the investigation. Commissioner Giamatti ultimately scheduled a hearing concerning the allegations for June 26, 1989.

In an effort to prevent Commissioner Giamatti from conducting the June 26 hearing, Rose filed an action in the Court of Common Pleas of Hamilton County, Ohio, on June 19, 1989, seeking a temporary restraining order and preliminary injunction against the pending disciplinary proceedings. Named as defendants in that action were A. Bartlett Giamatti, Major League Baseball, and the Cincinnati Reds. The crux of the complaint[1] is Rose's contention that he is being denied the right to a fair hearing on the gambling allegations by an unbiased decision-maker. The complaint requests permanent injunctive relief, which, if granted, would prevent Commissioner Giamatti from ever conducting a hearing to determine whether Rose has engaged in gambling activities in violation of the Rules of Major League Baseball. Rose asks that the Court of Common Pleas of Hamilton County, Ohio determine whether he has wagered on major league baseball games, including those of the Cincinnati Reds.

* * * On July 3, 1989, defendant Giamatti filed a notice of removal of the action from the state court to the United States District Court for the Southern District of Ohio, Western Division at Cincinnati, contending that the federal court has diversity jurisdiction over this action. Defendants Cincinnati Reds and Major League Baseball consented to the removal of the action.

On July 5, 1989, Rose filed a motion to remand this action to the Court of Common Pleas of Hamilton County, Ohio, asserting that there is a lack of complete diversity of citizenship between himself and the defendants. . . .

III. DIVERSITY JURISDICTION

The United States district courts are courts of limited jurisdiction, and the federal statute permitting removal of cases filed in state court restricts the types of cases which may be removed from state court to

---

1. The complaint alleges seven causes of action based upon state law claims of breach of contract, breach of an implied covenant of good faith and fair dealing, breach of fiduciary duty, promissory estoppel, tortious interference with contract, negligence, and the common law of "due process and natural justice."

federal court. The removal statute provides in pertinent part that "any civil action brought in a State court of which the district courts of the United States have original jurisdiction, may be removed by the defendant or the defendants to the district court of the United States for the district and division embracing the place where such action is pending." 28 U.S.C. § 1441(a). * * *

Defendant Giamatti contends in his notice of removal that the district court has original jurisdiction of this action by virtue of 28 U.S.C. § 1332(a), which grants original jurisdiction to the district courts in civil actions where the amount in controversy exceeds $50,000 and the action is between citizens of different states. This jurisdiction of federal courts is commonly known as "diversity" jurisdiction. The reason for granting diversity jurisdiction to federal courts was stated many years ago by Chief Justice Marshall:

> However true the fact may be, that the tribunals of the states will administer justice as impartially as those of the nation, to parties of every description, it is not less true that the Constitution itself either entertains apprehensions on this subject, or views with such indulgence the possible fears and apprehensions of suitors, that it has established national tribunals for the decision of controversies between aliens and a citizen, or between citizens of different States.

Bank of the United States v. Deveaux.[2] The diversity statute has historically been interpreted to require complete diversity of citizenship: " . . . diversity jurisdiction does not exist unless *each* defendant is a citizen of a different State from *each* plaintiff." If diversity of citizenship is found to exist among the parties to this action and none of the defendants in interest properly joined and served is a citizen of Ohio, then the action is properly removable from the state court. If the required diversity of citizenship does not exist, then the action is not properly removable and must be remanded to the state court.

With regard to the citizenship of the parties to this controversy, the complaint contains the following allegations concerning their identity and citizenship. Rose is alleged to be a resident of Hamilton County, Ohio. Commissioner Giamatti's residence is not stated in the complaint; in the notice of removal, however, he is alleged to be a citizen of the State of New York. Defendant Major League Baseball is alleged in the complaint to be an unincorporated association headquartered in New York and consisting of the two principal professional baseball leagues (National and American) and their twenty-six professional baseball clubs. The Cincinnati Reds, *dba* the Cincinnati Reds Baseball Club, is identified in the complaint

---

2. In oral argument, counsel for the Commissioner argued that this case should be heard by a "national tribunal":

In the State Court in Cincinnati, I need not describe Mr. Rose's standing. He is a local hero, perhaps the first citizen of Cincinnati. And Commissioner Giamatti is viewed suspiciously as a foreigner from New York, trapped in an ivory tower, accused of bias by Mr. Rose. Your Honor, this is a textbook example of why diversity jurisdiction was created in the Federal Courts and why it exists to this very day.

as an Ohio limited partnership (hereinafter referred to in the singular as the "Cincinnati Reds").

The Court will accept as true for purposes of ruling on the motion to remand that plaintiff Rose is a citizen of the State of Ohio, that defendant Giamatti is a citizen of the State of New York, that defendant Cincinnati Reds is a citizen of the State of Ohio,[3] and that defendant Major League Baseball, assuming it exists as a legal entity, is comprised of the two major professional baseball leagues and their constituent twenty-six major league baseball clubs, at least one of which, the Cincinnati Reds, is a citizen of the State of Ohio.

In the present case, it appears from the allegations of the complaint that defendant Cincinnati Reds and defendant Major League Baseball are citizens of the same state as plaintiff Rose. Recognizing that diversity jurisdiction is not demonstrated on the face of the complaint, defendant Giamatti includes in his notice of removal a number of allegations in support of his contention that this Court has diversity jurisdiction over this action such that it is properly removable. First, with respect to the defendant identified as Major League Baseball, the notice asserts that defendant Major League Baseball is not a "juridical entity," but is only a trade name utilized by the professional baseball clubs of the American and National Leagues and thus has no citizenship for diversity purposes. Second, the notice asserts that any citizenship ascribed to Major League Baseball should be disregarded for purposes of removal, "since Major League Baseball is not a proper party to this action and is at most a nominal party against which no claim or cause of action has been asserted." Finally, the notice asserts that Major League Baseball was "fraudulently joined" as a defendant for the purpose of attempting to defeat the removal jurisdiction of this Court. In a similar vein, the notice asserts that the defendant Cincinnati Reds is not a proper party to this action, is only a nominal party, and was fraudulently joined for the same purpose of defeating this Court's removal jurisdiction.

The issues framed by the notice of removal, the motion to remand, and the briefs of the parties are, accordingly, as follows:

> 1.   Is the named defendant, Major League Baseball, a legal entity which has a state of citizenship for diversity purposes?
>
> 2.   Can the citizenship of either Major League Baseball or the Cincinnati Reds be disregarded for diversity purposes?
>
> * * *

The Court will address each of these issues in turn.

---

3. For purposes of diversity, a limited partnership is considered to be a citizen of each state in which its partners are citizens. Although there is no indication in the record of the state or states of citizenship of the partners in the Cincinnati Reds, the parties agree that the Cincinnati Reds is an Ohio resident. Therefore, the Court will assume for purposes of this motion that at least one of those partners is a citizen of the State of Ohio.

A. *THE CITIZENSHIP OF DEFENDANT MAJOR LEAGUE BASEBALL*

Rose asserts that Major League Baseball is an unincorporated association created by virtue of the execution of the "Major League Agreement," an agreement entered into by and between the National League of Professional Baseball Clubs and each of its twelve constituent member clubs, and the American League of Professional Baseball Clubs and each of its fourteen constituent member clubs. Rose argues that the Major League Agreement creates an unincorporated association which operates under the name Major League Baseball. He contends that the association has officers, has previously described itself as an unincorporated association, and has acted in this case and in other cases as an unincorporated association capable of bringing suit and subject to being sued. Commissioner Giamatti contends that Major League Baseball is merely a trade name and registered service mark under which the twenty-six major league professional baseball clubs do business with respect to certain commercial activities.

Although the parties have debated the nature of the unique organization created by the Major League Agreement, Rose asserts that in the final analysis it is of no consequence whether Major League Baseball is an entity created by the Major League Agreement or simply a collective name for the twenty-six major league professional baseball clubs acting in concert. The Commissioner agrees that the critical issue to be resolved by this Court is not a determination of the nature of the association formed by the twenty-six major league professional baseball clubs, but rather whether those clubs are proper parties to this action for the purpose of determining the jurisdiction of this Court.

The Court agrees that, for the purpose of ruling on Rose's motion to remand, the central issue is not whether Major League Baseball is the formal name of an unincorporated association created by the Major League Agreement or a trade name and service mark used by the major league baseball clubs in certain commercial activities. The critical issue is whether the presence of the two major leagues and their twenty-six clubs, if before the Court as defendants in the form of an unincorporated association, would destroy the necessary diversity of citizenship. Inasmuch as under the Court's analysis which follows, the joinder as a defendant of the leagues and clubs as an unincorporated association doing business under the name Major League Baseball would not defeat the required diversity of citizenship, the Court, for purposes of this motion, will accept Rose's contention that the twenty-six major league professional baseball clubs joined together in the Major League Agreement to form an unincorporated association known as Major League Baseball, and that the unincorporated association known as Major League Baseball is before this Court as a properly served defendant in this case.

It is undisputed that, for purposes of determining the citizenship of an unincorporated association, an unincorporated association has no citizenship of its own, but is a citizen of every state in which each of its constituent members is a citizen. *United Steelworkers of America, AFL–CIO v. R.H. Bouligny, Inc. . . .*

The Cincinnati Reds Baseball Club, a citizen of Ohio, is one of the twenty-six major league baseball clubs which are members of the association doing business as Major League Baseball. Therefore, Major League Baseball is deemed to be a citizen of Ohio for diversity purposes. Because plaintiff Rose and the defendants Major League Baseball and the Cincinnati Reds are all citizens of Ohio, if either Major League Baseball or the Cincinnati Reds is a party properly joined in this action and whose citizenship, for diversity purposes, cannot be ignored, the lack of diversity of citizenship between plaintiff and all defendants would require the Court to conclude that the removal of the case to this Court was improper. Consequently, the Court must determine whether, as the Commissioner contends, the citizenship of these defendants should be ignored for the purpose of determining whether the removal of this case to this Court was proper.

B. *DETERMINATION OF PROPER PARTIES TO THIS ACTION FROM "THE PRINCIPAL PURPOSE OF THE SUIT"*

It is fundamental law that a plaintiff cannot confer jurisdiction upon the federal court, nor prevent a defendant from removing a case to the federal court on diversity grounds, by plaintiff's own determination as to who are proper plaintiffs and defendants to the action. As Justice Frankfurter said:

> Litigation is the pursuit of practical ends, not a game of chess. Whether the necessary "collision of interests," exists, is therefore not to be determined by mechanical rules. It must be ascertained from the "principal purpose of the suit," and the "primary and controlling matter in dispute."

In considering whether diversity of citizenship exists with respect to the "principal purpose of the suit," certain doctrines are well established. First, a plaintiff cannot defeat a defendant's right of removal on the basis of diversity of citizenship by the "fraudulent joinder" of a non-diverse defendant against whom the plaintiff has no real cause of action. * * * The joinder of a resident defendant against whom no cause of action is stated is a patent sham, and though a cause of action be stated, the joinder is similarly fraudulent if in fact no cause of action exists. . . . With respect to this doctrine, the Sixth Circuit has stated:

> In fraudulent joinder cases the underlying reason for removal is that there is no factual basis upon which it can be claimed that the resident defendant is jointly liable or where there is such liability there is no purpose to prosecute the action against the resident defendant in good faith. In such cases the assertion of the cause of action against the resident defendant is treated as a sham.

Other courts have held that the party opposing remand has the burden of establishing either that there is no possibility that the plaintiff can establish a valid cause of action under state law against the non-diverse defendant, or that there has been an outright fraud in the plaintiff's pleading of jurisdictional facts.

In many cases, removability may be determined from the original pleadings, and normally an allegation of a cause of action against the resident defendant will be sufficient to prevent removal. But when a defendant alleges that there has been fraudulent joinder, the court "may pierce the pleadings, consider the entire record, and determine the basis of joinder by any means available."

Used in this sense, the term "fraudulent joinder" is a term of art and is not intended to impugn the integrity of a plaintiff or plaintiff's counsel. Although the doctrine of fraudulent joinder applies to situations in which there has been actual fraud committed in the plaintiff's pleading of jurisdictional facts for the purpose of defeating federal court jurisdiction, the Court emphasizes that there is no allegation of any fraud and no evidence of any fraud on the part of plaintiff or plaintiff's counsel in this case. To the contrary, plaintiff's counsel are highly distinguished attorneys of great integrity who have sincerely and vigorously argued that both the Cincinnati Reds and Major League Baseball are properly joined as defendants and whose citizenship cannot be ignored under any applicable rule of law.

Second, it is also a long-established doctrine that a federal court, in its determination of whether there is diversity of citizenship between the parties, must disregard nominal or formal parties to the action and determine jurisdiction based only upon the citizenship of the real parties to the controversy.

Early in its history, [the Supreme Court] established that the "citizens' upon whose diversity a plaintiff grounds jurisdiction must be real and substantial parties to the controversy." Thus a federal court must disregard nominal or formal parties and rest jurisdiction only upon the citizenship of real parties to the controversy.

A real party in interest defendant is one who, by the substantive law, has the duty sought to be enforced or enjoined. In contrast to a "real party in interest," a formal or nominal party is one who, in a genuine legal sense, has no interest in the result of the suit, or no actual interest or control over the subject matter of the litigation.

While these related governing principles of federal court jurisdiction are clear and not in dispute, the parties strongly disagree as to their application in the present case. But, as Justice Frankfurter stated, . . . "As is true of many problems in the law, the answer is to be found not in legal learning but in the realities of the record." . . . The Court turns, then, to the realities of the record in this case to determine the real parties to this controversy.

1. *Defendant Giamatti*

It is apparent from the complaint that the actual controversy in this case is between Rose and Commissioner Giamatti. The complaint is replete with allegations of wrongdoing on the part of Giamatti. For example, Rose asserts that Giamatti and investigators hired by him attempted to bolster the credibility of witnesses against Rose, prejudged the truthfulness of certain testimony given as a part of the investigation, acted unreasonably in demanding information from Rose, improperly threatened him with refusing to cooperate in the investigation, requested that Rose step aside as the Reds' Field Manager without revealing to him the evidence which had been compiled concerning his alleged gambling activities, and otherwise acted improperly in violation of Giamatti's alleged duty to provide Rose with a fair and impartial hearing with respect to the allegations against him. The ultimate purpose of the action is to prevent Giamatti from conducting any hearing because of his alleged improper conduct and bias against Rose.

The critical question now before the Court is whether, in this controversy between Rose and Giamatti, there is "the necessary collision of interests" between Rose on the one hand and the Cincinnati Reds and Major League Baseball on the other hand so that the citizenship of these defendants may not be disregarded by the Court. If the necessary collision of interests exists, then the action was improvidently removed and must be remanded to the state court. If, however, the Cincinnati Reds and Major League Baseball were fraudulently joined as parties or are only nominal parties in the controversy, then diversity of citizenship is not defeated and Rose's motion to remand this case to the Court of Common Pleas of Hamilton County, Ohio must be denied.

2. *The Cincinnati Reds*

Just as it is clear that the crux of the present controversy is between Rose and Giamatti, it is equally clear that, in reality, there is no controversy between Rose and the Cincinnati Reds. The complaint explicitly asserts that Rose "alleges no wrongful conduct on the part of the Reds." Despite this explicit assertion, Rose contends that "all defendants herein owe Pete Rose the contractual duty to ensure that the Commissioner adheres to the Major League Agreement and discharges his duties in accordance with the Rules of Procedure. . . ." In essence, Rose asserts that the Commissioner's rules of procedure concerning fair disciplinary hearings are incorporated as a part of his employment contract with the Cincinnati Reds, and that any action by Commissioner Giamatti in violation of his own rules of procedure would constitute a breach of Rose's contract with the Cincinnati Reds. It is Rose's position that the Cincinnati Reds owes him a contractual duty to see that the procedural rules are not violated, and that if Giamatti violates these rules by holding an unfair hearing and, as a result, sanctions Rose, the Reds will have failed in its duty and will have breached his contract. Rose's claim against the Cincinnati Reds, involving no present wrongful conduct on the part of the Reds, is for "anticipatory breach" of his contract.

The Major League Agreement, which unquestionably is incorporated as a part of Rose's contract with the Cincinnati Reds, creates the office of Commissioner of Baseball and vests extraordinary power in the Commissioner. The Commissioner has unlimited authority to investigate any act, transaction or practice that is even suspected to be "not in the best interests" of baseball. * * * These rules of procedure are not rules adopted by the members of Major League Baseball; they are rules promulgated solely by the Commissioner of Baseball.

In contrast to the Commissioner's own rules of procedure, the members of Major League Baseball have formally adopted extensive rules governing relations between clubs and their employees, misconduct of players and other persons, and many other matters. These rules are known as the "Major League Rules." These detailed rules governing major league professional baseball have been accepted by the twenty-six major league professional baseball clubs and are recognized as binding upon them.

Considering the Major League Agreement, with its provisions vesting in the Commissioner the authority to promulgate his own procedural rules governing his investigation of matters not in the best interests of baseball, and its provisions for the adoption of Major League Rules binding upon every league, club, and player in major league professional baseball, it is apparent that "the Major League ... Rules" which are expressly incorporated into Rose's contract with the Cincinnati Reds are the extensive rules of conduct formally adopted by the members of Major League Baseball and not the procedural rules independently promulgated by the Commissioner which govern only his own proceedings. Furthermore, and of greater importance, there is nothing in the Major League Agreement, the Major League Rules, or in Rose's contract with the Cincinnati Reds which gives the Reds any right to prevent the Commissioner from holding a disciplinary hearing or to interfere with proceedings within the jurisdiction of the Commissioner. In fact, the parties are in agreement that the Cincinnati Reds has no such right.

Rose concedes that the Cincinnati Reds has done nothing that would be considered a breach of his contract at this time, nor does he allege that the Cincinnati Reds has taken any action that indicates an intention to refuse to perform its contract with him in the future so as to constitute an anticipatory breach of his contract under Ohio law. Rose's argument that any violation by Giamatti of the Commissioner's own procedural rules would somehow constitute an automatic breach of Rose's contract with the Cincinnati Reds is without legal basis.

It is undeniable that the Cincinnati Reds has, as a practical matter, an interest in the outcome of these proceedings, but not in the legal sense that requires its joinder as a defendant in this action. Rose's complaint specifically alleges that there has been no wrongdoing on the part of the

Cincinnati Reds, and the Reds specifically states that it will comply with the terms and conditions of its contract with Rose; there is no real controversy between these parties. The Court concludes that, for the purpose of determining diversity of citizenship, the defendant Cincinnati Reds was, in a legal sense, fraudulently joined as a defendant and that it is, at best, a nominal party in this action. Consequently, the citizenship of the Cincinnati Reds as a defendant may be disregarded for the purpose of determining whether there is complete diversity of citizenship among the parties to this action. In addition to being sued individually as a defendant, the Cincinnati Reds, for the purpose of this analysis of diversity of citizenship, is also a member of Major League Baseball, and the Court turns next to the consideration of that named defendant.

3. *Major League Baseball*

If Major League Baseball were a typical unincorporated association, its jurisdictional status would be more easily determined. The reality, however, is that Major League Baseball is a unique organization * * *

Given the background of the Major League Agreement and the unique manner in which the twenty-six major league baseball clubs have agreed to govern the conduct of players and others by a completely independent Commissioner, it is clear that Major League Baseball cannot be compared or equated with a typical unincorporated association engaged in any other business. * * *

The Commissioner's jurisdiction under the Major League Agreement to investigate violations of Major League Rules, or any activity he believes is "not in the best interests" of baseball, is exclusive. The major leagues and the twenty-six major league clubs have absolutely no control over such an investigation or the manner in which the Commissioner conducts it. Rose does not challenge any provision of the Major League Agreement or the Major League Rules, including the rule prohibiting wagering on major league baseball games, nor does he challenge the Commissioner's authority to promulgate his own rules of procedure dealing with investigations of suspected violations of the Major League Rules. What Rose challenges is Commissioner Giamatti's conduct of the investigation and disciplinary proceedings in his particular case. In short, Rose's controversy is not with Major League Baseball, but is with the office of the Commissioner of Baseball for the Commissioner's alleged failure to follow his own procedural rules in conducting the investigation of Rose's alleged gambling activities. Clearly, complete relief can be afforded with regard to the primary relief sought in the complaint—preventing Commissioner Giamatti from conducting a disciplinary hearing—without the need for any order against Major League Baseball or its constituent major league professional baseball clubs.

There is nothing in Rose's contract with the Cincinnati Reds or in the Major League Agreement which gives to the Cincinnati Reds or any other member of Major League Baseball any right, much less a duty, to prevent the Commissioner from conducting hearings concerning conduct "deemed by the Commissioner not to be in the best interests of Baseball." The Major League Agreement empowers the Commissioner to formulate his own rules of procedure which, as previously noted, are not a part of the Major League Agreement, the Major League Rules, or Rose's contract with the Cincinnati Reds. Accordingly, disregard of those procedural rules by the Commissioner, while it may be the basis for an action against the Commissioner, would not impose contractual liability on the Cincinnati Reds or the other members of Major League Baseball based on either the Major League Agreement or Rose's own contract.

Rose contends that Commissioner Giamatti, in conducting disciplinary proceedings, is acting as the agent for Major League Baseball, and that Major League Baseball is therefore liable for any violation of a duty owed by the Commissioner to Rose to follow his own procedural rules. If Major League Baseball were a typical business organization, Rose's contention might have merit. However, "baseball cannot be analogized to any other business.... Baseball's management through a commissioner is ... an exception, anomaly and aberration...." Whatever other activity the Commissioner may be authorized to perform as an agent on behalf of Major League Baseball, it is clear that with regard to disciplinary matters, the major league baseball clubs have made the Commissioner totally independent of their control. Under the Major League Agreement, the Commissioner's status with respect to disciplinary matters is analogous to that of an independent contractor, a person employed by Major League Baseball to act as an arbitrator and judge independent of any control by the members of Major League Baseball. Under Ohio law, it is clear that a party cannot be held liable for the conduct of such a person over whom the party has no control.

* * * While th[e] agreement to submit to the discipline of the Commissioner does not mean that the Commissioner may with impunity ignore his own procedural rules, it does mean that Rose's claims are against the Commissioner and not against Major League Baseball, which, under the Major League Agreement and Rose's own contract, has no control over the Commissioner in disciplinary proceedings.

Finally, Rose argues that, "[m]ost important to the present case is the fact that it is the members of [Major League Baseball] who must act if any action is to be taken against Pete Rose." However, it is only if the Commissioner is allowed to proceed with a hearing, finds Rose has violated the Major League Rules concerning wagering on major league baseball games, and places him on the ineligible list does any obligation to take any action arise on the part of the major league baseball clubs. In the meantime, the member clubs of Major League Baseball occupy a necessarily neutral role in the dispute between Rose and the Commissioner. As neutral bystanders to the battle between Rose and the Commissioner which is the subject of this action, the member clubs of Major League Baseball have no legal interest in the controversy, and at most would be considered to be nominal parties for the purpose of determining diversity of citizenship.

Rose cites a number of cases in which various sports associations have been named as defendants in support of his contention that the defendant Major League Baseball is a proper party in this action. None of those cases, however, names Major League Baseball as a defendant and all of the cases are clearly distinguishable from the present action. Most involve anti-trust actions. Others involve allegations of trademark infringement, employment discrimination, the validity of the association's own rules, or the enforcement of a membership agreement involving a member of the association.

* * * The Court has examined the above authorities cited by Rose, as well as others, and concludes that none supports Rose's claims against Major League Baseball in this case. The controversy here, as stated, is between Rose and Commissioner Giamatti and not between Rose and the Cincinnati Reds or between Rose and Major League Baseball. Major League Baseball is, at best, a nominal party in this action. Therefore, the citizenship of Major League Baseball may be disregarded for diversity purposes.

* * *

V. CONCLUSION

In light of the foregoing analysis, the Court holds that the controversy in this case is between plaintiff Rose and defendant Giamatti; that they are the real parties in interest in this case; that the Cincinnati Reds and Major League Baseball, are, at best, nominal parties in this controversy; and that, consequently, the citizenship of the Cincinnati Reds and Major League Baseball may be disregarded for diversity purposes. The Court determines that diversity of citizenship exists between Rose, a citizen of Ohio, and Commissioner Giamatti is a citizen of New York, and that the Court has diversity subject matter jurisdiction over this action. Defendant Giamatti is not a citizen of the State of Ohio and has not waived his right to remove this action, therefore, the action was properly removable from the Court of Common Pleas of Hamilton County, Ohio. Plaintiff Rose's motion to remand is denied.

It is so ordered.

C. FEDERAL QUESTION JURISDICTION— "ARISING UNDER" JURISDICTION

Art. III, Section 2, Clause 1. JURISDICTION OF COURTS

Section 2. The judicial Power shall extend to all Cases, in Law and Equity, arising under this Constitution, the Laws of the United States, and Treaties made, or which shall be made, under their Authority;—to all Cases affecting Ambassadors, other public Ministers and Consuls;—to all Cases of admiralty and maritime Jurisdiction;—to Controversies to which the United States shall be a Party;—to Controversies between two or more

States;—between a State and Citizens of another State;—between Citizens of different States;—between Citizens of the same State claiming Lands under Grants of different States, and between a State, or the Citizens thereof, and foreign States, Citizens or Subjects.

28 U.S.C. § 1331. FEDERAL QUESTION

The district courts shall have original jurisdiction of all civil actions arising under the Constitution, laws, or treaties of the United States.

28 U.S.C. § 1338. PATENTS, PLANT VARIETY PROTECTION, COPYRIGHTS, MASK WORKS, DESIGNS, TRADEMARKS, AND UNFAIR COMPETITION

(a) The district courts shall have original jurisdiction of any civil action arising under any Act of Congress relating to patents, plant variety protection, copyrights and trademarks. No State court shall have jurisdiction over any claim for relief arising under any Act of Congress relating to patents, plant variety protection, or copyrights. . . .

(b) The district courts shall have original jurisdiction of any civil action asserting a claim of unfair competition when joined with a substantial and related claim under the copyright, patent, plant variety protection or trademark laws.

AMERICAN NATIONAL RED CROSS v. S.G. AND A.E.

505 U.S. 247 (1992)

JUSTICE SOUTER delivered the opinion of the Court.

The Charter of the American National Red Cross authorizes the organization "to sue and be sued in courts of law and equity, State or Federal, within the jurisdiction of the United States." In this case we consider whether that "sue and be sued" provision confers original jurisdiction on federal courts over all cases to which the Red Cross is a party, with the consequence that the organization is thereby authorized to remove from state to federal court any state-law action it is defending. We hold that the clause does confer such jurisdiction.

I

In 1988 respondents filed a state-law tort action in a court of the State of New Hampshire, alleging that one of respondents had contracted AIDS from a transfusion of contaminated blood during surgery, and naming as defendants the surgeon and the manufacturer of a piece of medical equipment used during the procedure. After discovering that the Red Cross had supplied the tainted blood, respondents sued it, too, again in state court, and moved to consolidate the two actions. Before the state court decided that motion, the Red Cross invoked the federal removal statute, 28 U.S.C. § 1441, to remove the latter suit to the United States District Court for the District of New Hampshire. The Red Cross claimed federal jurisdiction based both on the diversity of the parties and on the "sue and be sued" provision of its charter, which it argued conferred original federal jurisdiction over suits involving the organization. The

District Court rejected respondents' motion to remand the case to state court, holding that the charter provision conferred original federal jurisdiction.

On interlocutory appeal, the United States Court of Appeals for the First Circuit reversed. The Court of Appeals compared the Red Cross Charter's "sue and be sued" provision with analogous provisions in federal corporate charters previously examined by this Court, and concluded that the relevant language in the Red Cross Charter was similar to its cognates in the charter of the first Bank of the United States, construed in *Bank of the United States v. Deveaux* (1809), and in that of the federally chartered railroad construed in *Bankers Trust Co. v. Texas & Pacific R. Co.* (1916), in neither of which cases did we find a grant of federal jurisdiction. The Court of Appeals distinguished *Osborn v. Bank of United States* (1824), where we reached the opposite result under the charter of the second Bank of the United States, the Court of Appeals finding it significant that the second Bank's authorization to sue and be sued spoke of a particular federal court and of state courts already possessed of jurisdiction. The Court of Appeals also discounted the Red Cross's reliance on our opinion in *D'Oench, Duhme & Co. v. Federal Deposit Ins. Corp.* (1942), concluding that in that case we had "not[ed] only incidentally" that federal jurisdiction was based on the "sue and be sued" clause in the FDIC's charter. The Court of Appeals found support for its conclusion in the location of the Red Cross Charter's "sue and be sued" provision in the section "denominat[ing] standard corporate powers," as well as in legislative history of the amendment to the Red Cross Charter adding the current "sue and be sued" language, and in the different form of analogous language in other federal corporate charters enacted contemporaneously with that amendment.

We granted certiorari to answer this difficult and recurring question.[1]

II

Since its founding in 1881 as part of an international effort to ameliorate soldiers' wartime suffering, the American Red Cross has expanded its activities to include, among others, the civilian blood-supply services here at issue. The organization was reincorporated in 1893, and in 1900 received its first federal charter, which was revised in 1905.

The 1905 charter empowered the Red Cross "to sue and be sued in courts of law and equity within the jurisdiction of the United States." At that time the provision would not have had the jurisdictional significance of its modern counterpart, since the law of the day held the involvement of a federally chartered corporation sufficient to render any case one "arising under" federal law for purposes of general statutory federal-question jurisdiction. In 1925, however, Congress restricted the reach of this jurisdictional theory to federally chartered corporations in which the

---

1. Although more than 40 District Court cases have considered this issue, no result clearly predominates. Reflecting this confusion, the only other Court of Appeals to consider this issue decided differently from the First Circuit.

United States owned more than one-half of the capital stock. Since the effect of the 1925 law on non-stock corporations like the Red Cross is unclear,[3] its enactment invested the charter's "sue and be sued" clause with a potential jurisdiction significance previously unknown to it.

Its text, nevertheless, was left undisturbed for more than 20 years further, until its current form, authorizing the Red Cross "to sue and be sued in courts of law and equity, State or Federal, within the jurisdiction of the United States," took shape with the addition of the term "State or Federal" to the 1905 language, as part of an overall revision of the organization's charter and bylaws. It is this language upon which the Red Cross relies, and which the Court of Appeals held to have conferred no federal jurisdiction.

III

A

As indicated earlier, we do not face a clean slate. Beginning with Chief Justice Marshall's opinion in 1809, we have had several occasions to consider whether the "sue and be sued" provision of a particular federal corporate charter conferred original federal jurisdiction over cases to which that corporation was a party, and our readings of those provisions not only represented our best efforts at divining congressional intent retrospectively, but have also placed Congress on prospective notice of the language necessary and sufficient to confer jurisdiction. Those cases therefore require visitation with care.

In *Deveaux,* we considered whether original federal jurisdiction over suits by or against the first Bank of the United States was conferred by its charter. The language in point authorized the Bank " 'to sue and be sued, plead and be impleaded, answer and be answered, defend and be defended, in courts of record, or any other place whatsoever' ". In the opinion written by Chief Justice Marshall, the Court held this language to confer no federal jurisdiction, reading it as a mere grant to the bank of the normal corporate capacity to sue. The Court contrasted the charter's "sue and be sued" provision with one authorizing the institution of certain suits against the bank's officers "in any court of record of the United States, or of [sic] either of them," a provision the Court described as "expressly authoriz[ing] the bringing of that action in the federal or state courts." The Chief Justice concluded that this latter provision "evince[d] the opinion of congress, that the right to sue does not imply a right to sue in the courts of the union, unless it be expressed."

The same issue came to us again 15 years later in *Osborn.* By this time Congress had established the second Bank of the United States, by a charter that authorized it "to sue and be sued, plead and be impleaded, answer and be answered, defend and be defended, in all state courts

---

3. We do not address this question, as we hold that the "sue and be sued" provision of the Red Cross's Charter suffices to confer federal jurisdiction independently of the organization's federal incorporation.

having competent jurisdiction, and in any circuit court of the United States." In its interpretation of this language, the Court, again speaking through Chief Justice Marshall, relied heavily on its *Deveaux* analysis, and especially on the contrast developed there between the first bank charter's "sue and be sued" provision and its provision authorizing suits against bank officers. Holding that the language of the second bank's charter "could not be plainer by explanation," in conferring federal jurisdiction, the *Osborn* Court distinguished *Deveaux* as holding that "a general capacity in the Bank to sue, without mentioning the courts of the Union, may not give a right to sue in those courts."

With the basic rule thus established, our next occasion to consider the issue did not arise until *Bankers Trust,* nearly a century later. The federal charter considered in that case authorized a railroad corporation "to sue and be sued, plead and be impleaded, defend and be defended, in all courts of law and equity within the United States." Testing this language against that construed in *Deveaux* and *Osborn,* we concluded that it "d[id] not literally follow" its analogues considered in either of the earlier cases, but held, nevertheless that it had "the same generality and natural import" as the clause contained in the first Bank charter. Thus, we followed *Deveaux* and found in the failure to authorize federal court litigation expressly no grant of federal jurisdiction.

Last came *D'Oench, Duhme,* where we held that the FDIC's charter granted original federal jurisdiction. That jurisdiction was not, we explained, "based on diversity of citizenship. Respondent, a federal corporation, brings this suit under an Act of Congress authorizing it to sue or be sued 'in any court of law or equity, State or Federal.' " It is perfectly true, as respondents stressed in argument, that in an accompanying footnote we quoted without comment another part of the same statute, providing that " '[a]ll suits of a civil nature at common law or in equity to which the Corporation shall be a party shall be deemed to arise under the laws of the United States: *Provided,* That any such suit to which the Corporation is a party in its capacity as receiver of a State bank and which involves only the rights or obligations of depositors, creditors, stockholders and such State bank under State law shall not be deemed to arise under the laws of the United States.' " The footnote did not, however, raise any doubt that the Court held federal jurisdiction to rest on the terms of the "sue and be sued" clause. Quite the contrary, the footnote's treatment naturally expressed the subordinate importance of the provision it quoted. While as a state bank's receiver the FDIC might lose the benefit of the deemer clause as a grant of federal jurisdiction, the "sue and be sued" clause would settle the jurisdictional question conclusively, in any case.

B

These cases support the rule that a congressional charter's "sue and be sued" provision may be read to confer federal court jurisdiction if, but only if, it specifically mentions the federal courts. In *Deveaux,* the Court found a "conclusive argument" against finding a jurisdictional grant in the "sue and be sued" clause in the fact that another provision of the same document authorized suits by and against bank officers "in any court of record of the United States, or of [*sic*] either of them...." In contrasting these two provisions the *Deveaux* Court plainly intended to indicate the degree of specificity required for a jurisdictional grant. That is certainly how the *Osborn* Court understood *Deveaux,* as it described the latter provision as an "express grant of jurisdiction," in contrast to the first Bank charter's "sue and be sued" provision, which, "without mentioning the courts of the Union," was held merely to give the Bank "a general capacity ... to sue [but not] a right to sue in those courts."[7] The *Osborn* Court thus found a jurisdictional grant sufficiently stated in the second Bank charter's "sue and be sued" provision, with its express federal reference, remarking that "[t]o infer from [*Deveaux*] that words expressly conferring a right to sue in those courts do not give the right, is surely a conclusion which the premises do not warrant."

Applying the rule thus established, in *Bankers Trust* we described the railroad charter's "sue and be sued" provision, with its want of any reference to federal courts, and, holding it up against its analogues in *Deveaux* and *Osborn,* we found it closer to the former.[9] Finally, in *D'Oench, Duhme* we based our finding of jurisdiction on the "sue and be sued" provision of the FDIC charter, which mentioned the federal courts in general, but not a particular federal court.

The rule established in these cases makes it clear that the Red Cross Charter's "sue and be sued" provision should be read to confer jurisdiction. In expressly authorizing the organization to sue and be sued in federal courts, using language resulting in a "sue and be sued" provision in all relevant respects identical to one on which we based a holding of federal jurisdiction just five years before, the provision extends beyond a mere grant of general corporate capacity to sue, and suffices to confer federal jurisdiction.

IV

Respondents offer several arguments against this conclusion, none of which we find availing.

---

7. The dissent accuses us of repeating what it announces as Chief Justice Marshall's misunderstanding, in *Osborn,* of his own previous opinion in *Deveaux.* We are honored.

9. The dissent is playful in manufacturing a conflict between our synthesis of the cases and the opinion in *Bankers Trust Co. v. Texas and Pacific R. Co.* The dissent first quotes the Court's construction in the *Bankers Trust* opinion, that the clause at issue there implied no jurisdictional grant, but simply rendered the corporation " 'capable of suing and being sued by its corporate name in any court of law or equity—Federal, state or territorial—whose jurisdiction as otherwise competently defined was adequate to the occasion.' " The dissent then concludes that "[t]hat paraphrasing of the railroad charter, in terms that would spell jurisdiction under the key the Court adopts today, belies any notion that *Bankers Trust* was using the same code-book." The dissent thus attempts to set up a conflict between our analysis and the result in *Bankers Trust,* by suggesting that that Court's interpretation of the provision (*i.e.,* to confer capacity to sue in courts including federal ones) should itself be subject to a second-order interpretation, which under our analysis might require a holding of jurisdiction, the conclusion rejected by the *Bankers Trust* Court. This "interpretation of an interpretation" methodology is simply illegitimate, originating not in our opinion but in the dissent's whimsy. Like our predecessors, we are construing a charter, not a paraphrase.

A

First, we can make short work of respondents' argument that the charter's conferral of federal jurisdiction is nevertheless subject to the requirements of the "well-pleaded complaint" rule (that the federal question must appear on the face of a well-pleaded complaint) limiting the removal of cases from state to federal court. Respondents erroneously invoke that rule outside the realm of statutory "arising under" jurisdiction, *i.e.,* jurisdiction based on 28 U.S.C. § 1331, to jurisdiction based on a separate and independent jurisdictional grant, in this case, the Red Cross Charter's "sue and be sued" provision. The "well-pleaded complaint" rule applies only to statutory "arising under" cases; it has no applicability here.

B

Respondents also claim that language used in congressional charters enacted closely in time to the 1947 amendment casts doubt on congressional intent thereby to confer federal jurisdiction over cases involving the Red Cross. Respondents argue that the 1948 amendment to the charter of the Commodity Credit Corporation (CCC), the 1947 amendment to the charter of the Federal Crop Insurance Corporation (FCIC), and the 1935 amendment to the FDIC's charter, each of which includes explicit grants of federal jurisdiction, together demonstrate "a practice of using clear and explicit language to confer federal jurisdiction over corporations [Congress] had created."

The argument does not hold up. The CCC amendment is irrelevant to this enquiry, as it conferred exclusive, rather than concurrent, federal jurisdiction. There is every reason to expect Congress to take great care in its use of explicit language when it wishes to confer exclusive jurisdiction, given our longstanding requirement to that effect. Its employment of explicitly jurisdictional language in the CCC's case thus raises no suggestion that its more laconic Red Cross amendment was not meant to confer concurrent federal jurisdiction.

Nor do the other two enactments support respondents' argument. The statutes were passed 12 years apart and employed verbally and doctrinally distinct formulations. These differences are not merely semantic: the jurisdictional effect of the FDIC's provision depends on the 28 U.S.C. § 1331 grant of general federal-question jurisdiction, while the FCIC's provision functions independently of § 1331. These differences of both form and substance belie respondents' claim of a coherent drafting pattern against which to judge the ostensible intent behind the Red Cross amendment.

If, indeed, respondents' argument could claim any plausibility, it would have to be at the cost of ignoring the 1942 *D'Oench, Duhme* opinion citing the FDIC charter's "sue and be sued" provision as the source of federal jurisdiction in that case. If the "sue and be sued" clause is sufficient for federal jurisdiction when it occurs in the same charter with the language respondents claim to be at odds with its jurisdictional significance, it is certainly sufficient standing alone. In any event, the fact that our opinion in *D'Oench, Duhme* was handed down before the 1947 amendment to the Red Cross Charter indicates that Congress may well have relied on that holding to infer that amendment of the Red Cross Charter's "sue and be sued" provision to make it identical to the FDIC's would suffice to confer federal jurisdiction. Congress was, in any event, entitled to draw the inference.

C

Respondents would have us look behind the statute to find quite a different purpose when they argue that the 1947 amendment may have been meant not to confer jurisdiction, but to clarify the Red Cross's capacity to sue in federal courts where an independent jurisdictional basis exists. The suggestion is that Congress may have thought such a clarification necessary after passage of the 1925 statute generally bringing an end to federal incorporation as a jurisdictional basis. But this suggestion misconstrues § 1349 as somehow affecting a federally chartered corporation's capacity to sue, when by its own terms it speaks only to jurisdiction. If, then, respondents are correct that the enactment of § 1349 motivated the 1947 amendment, that motivation cuts against them, given that § 1349 affected only jurisdiction.

The legislative history of the 1947 amendment cuts against them, as well, to the extent it points in any direction.[13] Congress's revision of the charter was prompted by, and followed, the recommendations of a private advisory committee of the Red Cross. The Advisory Report had recommended that "[t]he charter should make it clear that the Red Cross can sue and be sued in the Federal Courts," reasoning that "[t]he Red Cross has in several instances sued in the Federal Courts, and its powers in this respect have not been questioned. However, in view of the limited nature of the jurisdiction of the Federal Courts, it seems desirable that this right be clearly stated in the Charter."

The Advisory Report's explicit concern with the limited jurisdiction of the federal courts indicates that the recommended change, which prompted the amendment to the "sue and be sued" provision, spoke to jurisdiction rather than capacity to sue. Against this, respondents argue only that the Advisory Report's use of the words "can" and "power" indicate concern with the latter, not the former. This is fine phrasing, too fine to overcome the overall jurisdictional thrust of the Report's recommendation.

In a final look toward the text, respondents speculate that the 1947 amendment can be explained as an attempt to clarify the Red Cross's

---

13. The only debate on the 1947 amendment to the charter's "sue and be sued" provision occurred at a Senate Committee hearing. The only two relevant comments, both made by Senator George, appear to be mutually contradictory on the matter at issue here. At one point Senator George said: "I think the purpose of the bill is very clear, and that is to give the jurisdiction in State courts and Federal courts, and I think we had better leave it there." Later, however, he stated: "I think there might be some question about the right of a Federal corporation to be sued in a State court. I thought that was, and I still think it is, the purpose of this provision."

capacity to enter the federal courts under their diversity jurisdiction. The argument turns on the theory that federally chartered corporations are not citizens of any particular State, and thus may not avail themselves of diversity jurisdiction. Respondents completely fail, however, to explain how the addition of the words "State or Federal" to the "sue and be sued" provision might address this claimed jurisdictional problem. Indeed, the 1947 amendment, by specifying the particular courts open to the Red Cross, as opposed to the Red Cross's status as a party, seems particularly ill-suited to rectifying an asserted party-based jurisdictional deficiency.

Perhaps most obviously, respondents' argument violates the ordinary sense of the language used, as well as some basic canons of statutory construction. The 1905 charter, authorizing the Red Cross "to sue and be sued in courts of law and equity within the jurisdiction of the United States," simply cannot be read as failing to empower the Red Cross to sue in federal courts having jurisdiction. That fact, when combined with the Advisory Report's justification of the 1947 amendment by reference to federal courts' limited jurisdiction, leaves it extremely doubtful that capacity to sue *simpliciter* motivated that amendment. Indeed, the Red Cross's clear pre-amendment capacity to sue in federal courts calls into play the canon of statutory construction requiring a change in language to be read, if possible, to have some effect, a rule which here tugs hard toward a jurisdictional reading of the 1947 amendment.[15]

V

Our holding leaves the jurisdiction of the federal courts well within Article III's limits. As long ago as *Osborn*, this Court held that Article III's "arising under" jurisdiction is broad enough to authorize Congress to confer federal-court jurisdiction over actions involving federally chartered

---

15. The dissent adopts and refines respondents' argument that the 1947 amendment's parallel treatment of federal and state courts counsels against reading that amendment as conferring jurisdiction. The short answer is that *D'Oench, Duhme* forecloses the argument, since the charter language we held to confer federal jurisdiction in that case made exactly the same parallel mention of federal and state courts. But going beyond that, the reference to state as well as federal courts presumably was included lest a mention of federal courts alone (in order to grant jurisdiction to them) be taken as motivated by an intent to confer exclusive federal jurisdiction. Moreover, the Red Cross Charter's "sue and be sued" provision, like its counterparts construed in *Osborn* and *D'Oench, Duhme,* confers both capacity to sue and jurisdiction. While capacity to sue in both federal and state courts was already clearly established before the 1947 amendment, it may have been feared that the addition of the word "Federal" to confer federal jurisdiction would be misread to limit the Red Cross's capacity to sue in state courts, if it were not reaffirmed by explicit inclusion of the word "State."

It is the dissent's conclusion that the 1947 amendment was meant to "eliminat[e] the possibility that the language 'courts of law and equity within the jurisdiction of the United States' that was contained in the original charter . . . might be read to limit the grant of capacity to sue in federal court;" that is difficult to justify. Such a motivation is nowhere even hinted at in the Advisory Report, the document both Houses of Congress acknowledged as the source for the amendment; indeed, the relevant part of the Advisory Report does not even mention state courts. It is hardly a "reasonable construction" of the amendment to view it as granting something the Advisory Report never requested. While the dissent notes one of Senator George's comments supporting its hypothesis, it ignores the other, which explicitly notes a federal jurisdiction-conferring motivation behind the amendment. Neither party reads the 1947 amendment to clarify the Red Cross's capacity to sue in state courts, and, as there is no evidence of such an intent, we do not embrace that reading here.

corporations.[16] We have consistently reaffirmed the breadth of that holding. We would be loath to repudiate such a longstanding and settled rule, on which Congress has surely been entitled to rely, and this case gives us no reason to contemplate overruling it.

VI

The judgment of the Court of Appeals is reversed, and the case is remanded for proceedings consistent with this opinion.

It is so ordered.

JUSTICE SCALIA, with whom THE CHIEF JUSTICE, JUSTICE O'CONNOR, and JUSTICE KENNEDY join, dissenting.

The Court today concludes that whenever a statute granting a federally chartered corporation the "power to sue and be sued" specifically mentions the federal courts (as opposed to merely embracing them within general language), the law will be deemed not only to confer on the corporation the capacity to bring and suffer suit (which is all that the words say), but also to confer on federal district courts *jurisdiction* over any and all controversies to which that corporation is a party. This wonderland of linguistic confusion—in which words are sometimes read to mean only what they say and other times read also to mean what they do not say—is based on the erroneous premise that our cases in this area establish a "magic words" jurisprudence that departs from ordinary rules of English usage. In fact, our cases simply reflect the fact that the natural reading of *some* "sue and be sued" clauses is that they confer both capacity and jurisdiction. Since the natural reading of the Red Cross Charter is that it confers only capacity, I respectfully dissent.

I

Section 2 of the Red Cross Charter, 36 U.S.C. § 2, sets forth the various powers of the corporation, such as the power "to have and to hold ... real and personal estate"; "to adopt a seal"; "to ordain and establish bylaws and regulations"; and to "do all such acts and things as may be necessary to ... promote [its] purposes." The second item on this list is "the power to sue and be sued in courts of law and equity, State or Federal, within the jurisdiction of the United States." The presence of this language amidst a list of more or less ordinary corporate powers confirms what the words themselves suggest: It merely establishes that the Red Cross is a juridical person which may be party to a lawsuit in an American court, and that the Red Cross—despite its status as a federally chartered corporation—does not share the Government's general immunity from suit. Cf. Fed. Rule Civ. Proc. 17(b) ("The capacity of a corporation to sue or be sued shall be determined by the law under which it was organized").

---

16.   Again, it should be pointed out that statutory jurisdiction in this case is not based on the Red Cross's federal incorporation, but rather upon a specific statutory grant. In contrast, the constitutional question asks whether Article III's provision for federal jurisdiction over cases "arising under federal law" is sufficiently broad to allow that grant.

It is beyond question that nothing in the language of this provision suggests that it has anything to do with regulating the jurisdiction of the federal courts. The grant of corporate power to sue and be sued in no way implies a grant of federal-court jurisdiction; it merely places the corporation on the same footing as a natural person, who must look elsewhere to establish grounds for getting his case into court. Words conferring *authority* upon a *corporation* are a most illogical means of conferring *jurisdiction* upon a *court,* and would not normally be understood that way. Moreover, it would be extraordinary to confer a new subject-matter jurisdiction upon "federal courts" in general, rather than upon a particular federal court or courts.

The Court apparently believes that the language of § 2 is functionally equivalent to a specific reference to the district courts, since no other court could reasonably have been intended to be the recipient of the jurisdictional grant. Perhaps so, but applying that intuition requires such a random butchering of the text that it is much more reasonable to assume that *no* court was the intended recipient. The Red Cross is clearly granted the *capacity* to sue and be sued in *all* federal courts, so that it could appear, for example, as a party in a third-party action in the Court of International Trade and in an action before the United States Claims Court. There is simply no textual basis, and no legal basis except legal intuition, for saying that it must *in addition* establish an independent basis of jurisdiction to proceed in those courts, though it does *not* in the district courts.

In fact, the language of this provision not only does not distinguish among federal courts, it also does not treat federal courts differently from state courts; the Red Cross is granted the "power" to sue in both. This parallel treatment of state and federal courts even further undermines a jurisdictional reading of the statute, since the provision cannot reasonably be read as allowing the Red Cross to enter a state court without establishing the independent basis of jurisdiction appropriate under state law. Such a reading would present serious constitutional questions. Since the language of the Red Cross Charter cannot fairly be read to create federal jurisdiction but not state jurisdiction, we should not construe it as creating either.

I therefore conclude—indeed, I do not think it seriously contestable— that the natural reading of the "sue and be sued" clause of 36 U.S.C. § 2 confers upon the Red Cross only the *capacity* to "sue and be sued" in state and federal courts; it does not confer jurisdiction upon any court, state or federal.

II

I do not understand the Court to disagree with my analysis of the ordinary meaning of the statutory language. Its theory is that, regardless of ordinary meaning, our cases have created what might be termed a "phrase of art," whereby a "sue and be sued" clause confers federal jurisdiction "if, but only if, it specifically mentions the federal courts."

Thus, while the uninitiated would consider the phrase "sue and be sued in any court in the United States" to mean the same thing as "sue and be sued in any court, state or federal," the Court believes that our cases have established the latter (but not the former) as a shorthand for "sue and be sued in any court, state or federal, *and the federal district courts shall have jurisdiction over any such action.*" Congress is assumed to have used this cleverly crafted code in enacting the charter provision at issue here. In my view, our cases do not establish the cryptology the Court attributes to them. Rather, the four prior cases in which we have considered the jurisdictional implications of "sue and be sued" clauses are best understood as simply applications of conventional rules of statutory construction.

In *Bank of the United States v. Deveaux* (1809), we held that a provision of the Act establishing the first Bank of the United States which stated that the Bank was "made able and capable in law ... to sue and be sued ... in courts of record, or any other place whatsoever," did not confer jurisdiction on the federal courts to adjudicate suits brought by the Bank. Construing the statutory terms in accordance with their ordinary meaning, we concluded (as I conclude with respect to the Red Cross Charter) that the provision merely gave "a *capacity* to the corporation to appear, as a corporation, in any court which would, by law, have cognisance of the cause, if brought by individuals." We expressly noted (as I have in this case) that the Act's undifferentiated mention of all courts compelled the conclusion that the provision was not jurisdictional: "*If jurisdiction is given by this clause to the federal courts, it is equally given to all courts having original jurisdiction, and for all sums however small they may be.*" (emphasis added). That statement is immediately followed by contrasting this provision with another section of the Act which provided that certain actions against the directors of the Bank "may ... be brought ... in any court of record of the United States, or of either of them." *That* provision, we said, "expressly authorizes the bringing of that action in the federal or state courts," which "evinces the opinion of congress, that the right to sue does not imply a right to sue in the courts of the union, unless it be expressed." It is clear, I think, that the reason the Court thought the right to have been "expressed" under the directors-suit provision, but not "expressed" under the provision before it, was *not* that the former happened to mention courts "of the United States." For that would have provided no contrast to the argument against jurisdiction (italicized above) that the Court had just made. Reference to suits "in any court of record of the United States, or of either of them," is no less universal in its operative scope than reference to suits "in courts of record," and hence is subject to the *same* objection (to which the Court was presumably giving a contrasting example) that jurisdiction was indiscriminately conferred on all courts of original jurisdiction and for any and all amounts.

Deveaux establishes not, as the Court claims, the weird principle that mention of the federal courts *in a "sue and be sued" clause* confers jurisdiction; but rather, the quite different (and quite reasonable) proposition that mention of the federal courts in a provision *allowing a particular cause of action to be brought* does so. The contrast between the "sue and be sued" clause and the provision authorizing certain suits against the directors lay, not in the mere substitution of one broad phrase for another, but in the fact that the latter provision, by authorizing particular actions to be *brought* in federal court, could not reasonably be read *not* to confer jurisdiction. A provision merely conferring a general *capacity* to bring actions, however, cannot reasonably be read to *confer* jurisdiction.[2]

This reading of *Deveaux* is fully consistent with our subsequent decision in *Osborn v. Bank of United States,* which construed the "sue and be sued" clause of the second Bank's charter as conferring jurisdiction on federal circuit courts. The second charter provided that the Bank was "made able and capable, in law ... to sue and be sued ... in all state courts having competent jurisdiction, and in any circuit court of the United States". By granting the Bank power to sue, not in all courts generally (as in *Deveaux*), but in *particular* federal courts, this suggested a grant of jurisdiction rather than merely of capacity to sue. And that suggestion was strongly confirmed by the fact that the Bank was empowered to sue in state courts "having competent jurisdiction," but in federal circuit courts *simpliciter*. If the statute had jurisdiction in mind as to the one, it must as to the other as well. Our opinion in *Osborn* did not invoke the "magic words" approach adopted by the Court today, but concluded that the charter language "admit[ted] of but one interpretation" and could not "be made plainer by explanation."

In distinguishing *Deveaux, Osborn* noted, and apparently misunderstood as the Court today does, that case's contrast between the "express grant of jurisdiction to the federal courts" over suits against directors and the "general words" of the "sue and be sued" clause, "which [did] not mention those courts." All it concluded from that, however, was that *Deveaux* established that "a general capacity in the bank to sue, without mentioning the courts of the Union, may not give a right to sue in those courts." There does not logically follow from that the rule which the Court announces today: that *any* grant of a general capacity to sue *with* mention of federal courts will suffice to confer jurisdiction. The Court's reading of this language from *Osborn* as giving talismanic significance to any "mention" of federal courts is simply inconsistent with the fact that *Osborn* (like *Deveaux*) did not purport to confer on the words of the clause any meaning other than that suggested by their natural import.

This reading of *Deveaux* and *Osborn* is confirmed by our later decision in *Bankers Trust Co. v. Texas & Pacific R. Co.* There we held it to be "plain" that a railroad charter provision stating that the corporation

---

2. The Court believes that *Deveaux*'s statement that "the right to sue does not imply the right to sue in the courts of the union *unless it be expressed*" (emphasis added), is somehow inconsistent with my analysis. Quite the opposite is true: The Court's simple statement that the grant of jurisdiction must "be expressed" is obviously a call, not to reach for the cryptograph, but to discern the plain meaning of the statutory language.

"shall be able to sue and be sued . . . in all courts of law and equity within the United States," did not confer jurisdiction on any court. Had our earlier cases stood for the "magic words" rule adopted by the Court today, we could have reached that conclusion simply by noting that the clause at issue did not contain a specific reference to the federal courts. That is not, however, what we did. Indeed, the absence of such specific reference *was not even mentioned* in the opinion. Instead, as before, we sought to determine the sense of the provision by considering the ordinary meaning of its language in context. We concluded that "Congress would have expressed [a] purpose [to confer jurisdiction] in altogether different words" than these, which had "the same generality and *natural import* as did those in the earlier bank act [in *Deveaux*]" (emphasis added). Considered in their context of a listing of corporate powers, these words established that:

> "Congress was not then concerned with the jurisdiction of courts but with the faculties and powers of the corporation which it was creating; and evidently all that was intended was to render this corporation capable of suing and being sued by its corporate name *in any court of law or equity Federal, state, or territorial* whose jurisdiction as otherwise competently defined was adequate to the occasion." (emphasis added).

That paraphrasing of the railroad charter, in terms that would spell jurisdiction under the key the Court adopts today, belies any notion that *Bankers Trust* was using the same code book.

The fourth and final case relied upon by the Court is *D'Oench, Duhme & Co. v. FDIC* (1942). In that case, we granted certiorari to consider whether a federal court in a non-diversity action must apply the conflict-of-laws rules of the forum State. We ultimately did not address that question (because we concluded that the rule of decision was provided by federal, rather than state law), but in the course of setting forth the question presented, we noted that, as all parties had conceded, the jurisdiction of the federal district court did not rest on diversity:

> Respondent, a federal corporation, brings this suit under an Act of Congress authorizing it to sue or be sued 'in any court of law or equity, State or Federal.' That subdivision of the Act further provides: 'All suits of a civil nature at common law or in equity to which the Corporation shall be a party shall be deemed to arise under the laws of the United States. . . .'

The Court relies heavily on this case, which it views as holding that a statute granting a corporation the power "to sue or be sued in any court of law or equity, State or Federal" establishes jurisdiction in federal district courts. Even if the quoted language did say that, it would be remarkable to attribute such great significance to a passing comment on a conceded point. But in my view it does not say that anyway, since the footnote must be read together with the text as explaining the single basis of jurisdiction (rather than, as the Court would have it, explaining two separate bases of jurisdiction in a case where even the explanation of one is *obiter*). The language quoted in the footnote is not, as the Court says, from "another part of the same statute." And the complaint in *D'Oench, Duhme* expressly predicated jurisdiction on the fact that the action was one "aris[ing] under the laws of the United States." The language in this case is a thin reed upon which to rest abandonment of the rudimentary principle (followed even in other "sue and be sued" cases) that a statute should be given the meaning suggested by the "natural import" of its terms.

III

Finally, the Court argues that a jurisdictional reading of the Red Cross Charter is required by the canon of construction that an amendment to a statute ordinarily should not be read as having no effect. The original "sue and be sued" clause in the Red Cross Charter did not contain the phrase "State or Federal," and the Court argues that its reading—which gives decisive weight to that addition—is therefore strongly to be preferred. I do not agree. Even if it were the case that my reading of the clause rendered this phrase superfluous, I would consider that a small price to pay for adhering to the competing (and more important) canon that statutory language should be construed in accordance with its ordinary meaning. And it would seem particularly appropriate to run the risk of surplusage here, since the amendment in question was one of a number of technical changes in a comprehensive revision.

But in any event, a natural-meaning construction of the "sue and be sued" clause does not render the 1947 amendment superfluous. The addition of the words "State or Federal" eliminates the possibility that the language "courts of law and equity *within the jurisdiction* of the United States" that was contained in the original charter (emphasis added), might be read to limit the grant of capacity to sue in *federal court*. State courts are not within the "jurisdiction" of the United States unless "jurisdiction" is taken in the relatively rare sense of referring to territory rather than power. The addition of the words "State or Federal" removes this ambiguity.

The Court rejects this argument on the ground that there is "no evidence of such an intent." The best answer to that assertion is that it is irrelevant: To satisfy the canon the Court has invoked, it is enough that there be a reasonable construction of the old and amended statutes that would explain why the amendment is not superfluous. Another answer to the assertion is that it is wrong. As the Court notes elsewhere in its opinion, one of the only comments made by a Member of Congress on this amendment was Senator George's statement, during the hearings, that the purpose of the provision was to confirm the Red Cross' capacity to sue in *state* court.[4]

---

4. The Court points out that Senator George also stated, in response to a question whether foreign courts should be covered by the amendment, that the purpose of the bill was " 'to give the jurisdiction in State courts and Federal courts, and I think we had better leave it there.' " Rather

Because the Red Cross Charter contains no language suggesting a grant of jurisdiction, I conclude that it grants only the capacity to "sue or be sued" in a state or federal court of appropriate jurisdiction. In light of this conclusion, I find it unnecessary to reach the constitutional question addressed in Part V of the Court's opinion. I would affirm the judgment of the Court of Appeals.

T. B. HARMS COMPANY v. ELISCU

339 F.2d 823 (2d Cir. 1964)

FRIENDLY, CIRCUIT JUDGE:

A layman would doubtless be surprised to learn that an action wherein the purported sole owner of a copyright alleged that persons claiming partial ownership had recorded their claim in the Copyright Office and had warned his licensees against disregarding their interests was not one "arising under any Act of Congress relating to * * * copyrights" over which 28 U.S.C. § 1338 gives the federal courts exclusive jurisdiction. Yet precedents going back for more than a century teach that lesson and lead us to affirm Judge Weinfeld's dismissal of the complaint.

The litigation concerns four copyrighted songs; we shall state the nub of the matter as alleged in the complaint without going into details irrelevant to the jurisdictional issue. The music for the songs was composed by Vincent Youmans for use in a motion picture, "Flying Down to Rio," pursuant to a contract made in 1933 with RKO Studios, Inc. He agreed to assign to RKO the recordation and certain other rights relating to the picture during the existence of the copyrights and any renewals. RKO was to employ a writer of the lyrics and to procure the publishing rights in these for Youmans, who was "to pay said lyric writer the usual and customary royalties on sheet music and mechanical records." Subject to this, Youmans could assign the publication and small performing rights to the music and lyrics as he saw fit. In fact RKO employed two lyric writers, Gus Kahn and the defendant Edward Eliscu, who agreed to assign to RKO certain rights described in a contract dated as of May 25, 1933. Max Dreyfus, principal stockholder of the plaintiff Harms, which has succeeded to his rights, acquired Youmans' reserved rights to the music and was his designee for the assignment with respect to the lyrics. Allegedly—and his denial of this is a prime subject of dispute—Eliscu then entered into an agreement dated June 30, 1933, assigning his rights to the existing and renewal copyrights to Dreyfus in return for certain royalties.

When the copyrights were about to expire, proper renewal applications were made by the children of Youmans, by the widow and children of Kahn, and by Eliscu. The two former groups executed assignments of their rights in the renewal copyrights to Harms. But Eliscu, by an instrument dated February 19, 1962, recorded in the Copyright Office,

---

than concluding (as seems obvious) that Senator George was speaking with imprecision in using the phrase "give the jurisdiction," the Court draws the far less likely conclusion that Senator George was flatly contradicting himself in what he said only a few minutes later.

assigned his rights in the renewal copyrights to defendant Ross Jungnickel, Inc., subject to a judicial determination of his ownership. Thereafter Eliscu's lawyer advised ASCAP and one Harry Fox—respectively the agents for the small performing rights and the mechanical recording license fees—that Eliscu had become vested with a half interest in the renewal copyrights and that any future payments which failed to reflect his interest would be made at their own risk; at the same time he demanded an accounting from Harms. Finally, Eliscu brought an action in the New York Supreme Court for a declaration that he owned a one-third interest in the renewal copyrights and for an accounting.

Harms then began the instant action in the District Court for the Southern District of New York for equitable and declaratory relief against Eliscu and Jungnickel. Jurisdiction was predicated on 28 U.S.C. § 1338; plaintiff alleged its own New York incorporation and did not allege the citizenship of the defendants, which concededly is in New York. Defendants moved to dismiss the complaint for failure to state a claim on which relief can be granted and for lack of federal jurisdiction; voluminous affidavits were submitted. The district court dismissed the complaint for want of federal jurisdiction.

In line with what apparently were the arguments of the parties, Judge Weinfeld treated the jurisdictional issue as turning solely on whether the complaint alleged any act or threat of copyright infringement. He was right in concluding it did not. Infringement, as used in copyright law, does not include everything that may impair the value of the copyright; it is doing one or more of those things which § 1 of the Act, 17 U.S.C. § 1, reserves exclusively to the copyright owner. The case did not even raise what has been the problem presented when a defendant licensed to use a copyright or a patent on certain terms is alleged to have forfeited the grant; in such cases federal jurisdiction is held to exist if the plaintiff has directed his pleading against the offending use, referring to the license only by way of anticipatory replication, but not if he has sued to set the license aside, seeking recovery for unauthorized use only incidentally or not at all. Here neither Eliscu nor Jungnickel had used or threatened to use the copyrighted material; their various acts, as the district judge noted, sought to establish their ownership of the copyrights by judicial and administrative action, including notice to the parties concerned.

However, the jurisdictional statute does not speak in terms of infringement, and the undoubted truth that a claim for infringement "arises under" the Copyright Act does not establish that nothing else can. Simply as a matter of language, the statutory phrasing would not compel the conclusion that an action to determine who owns a copyright does not arise under the Copyright Act, which creates the federal copyright with an implied right to license and an explicit right to assign. But the gloss afforded by history and good sense leads to that conclusion as to the complaint in this case.

Although Chief Justice Marshall, construing the "arising under" language in the context of Article III of the Constitution, indicated in *Osborn v. Bank of the United States* (1824), that the grant extended to every case in which federal law furnished a necessary ingredient of the claim even though this was antecedent and uncontested, the Supreme Court has long given a narrower meaning to the "arising under" language in statutes defining the jurisdiction of the lower federal courts. If the ingredient theory of Article III had been carried over to the general grant of federal question jurisdiction now contained in 28 U.S.C. § 1331, there would have been no basis—to take a well-known example—why federal courts should not have jurisdiction as to all disputes over the many western land titles originating in a federal patent, even though the controverted questions normally are of fact or of local land law. Quite sensibly, such extensive jurisdiction has been denied.

The cases dealing with statutory jurisdiction over patents and copyrights have taken the same conservative line. The problem apparently first reached the Supreme Court in *Wilson v. Sanford* (1850), which allowed appeal to the Court, irrespective of the amount, in actions "arising under" the patent laws. The suit aimed to prevent use of a patented invention by a licensee who allegedly had failed to comply with the terms of the license and thus had forfeited its rights. Chief Justice Taney, dismissing the appeal, held the statute inapplicable to a dispute as to license or contract rights which "depended altogether upon the rules and principles of equity, and in no degree whatever upon any act of Congress concerning patent rights." The same principle was applied, and sometimes stated less cautiously, in decisions construing later legislation granting the federal courts exclusive jurisdiction of all suits 'arising under' the patent or copyright laws of the United States. To take one of many examples, the Court said in *New Marshall Engine Co. v. Marshall Engine Co.* (1912):

> The Federal courts have exclusive jurisdiction of all cases arising under the patent laws, but not of all questions in which a patent may be the subject-matter of the controversy. For courts of a state may try questions of title, and may construe and enforce contracts relating to patents.

Just as with western land titles, the federal grant of a patent or copyright has not been thought to infuse with any national interest a dispute as to ownership or contractual enforcement turning on the facts or on ordinary principles of contract law. Indeed, the case for an unexpansive reading of the provision conferring exclusive jurisdiction with respect to patents and copyrights has been especially strong since expansion would entail depriving the state courts of any jurisdiction over matters having so little federal significance.

In an endeavor to explain precisely what suits arose under the patent and copyright laws, Mr. Justice Holmes stated that '(a) suit arises under the law that creates the cause of action'; in the case *sub judice*, injury to a business involving slander of a patent, he said, "whether it is a wrong or not depends upon the law of the State where the act is done" so that the suit did not arise under the patent laws. *American Well Works Co. v. Layne & Bowler Co.* (1916). The Holmes "creation" test explains the taking of federal jurisdiction in a great many cases, notably copyright and patent infringement actions, both clearly authorized by the respective federal acts, and thus unquestionably within the scope of 28 U.S.C. § 1338; indeed, in the many infringement suits that depend only on some point of fact and require no construction of federal law, no other explanation may exist.

Harms' claim is not within Holmes' definition. The relevant statutes create no explicit right of action to enforce or rescind assignments of copyrights, nor does any copyright statute specify a cause of action to fix the locus of ownership. To be sure, not every federal cause of action springs from an express mandate of Congress; federal civil claims have been "inferred" from federal statutes making behavior criminal or otherwise regulating it. Such statutes invariably impose a federal duty and usually create some express remedy as well, while the relevant copyright provision merely authorizes an assignment by written instrument. It is true that although this difference carries the present case outside the classic doctrine of implied remedies, expansion may not be foreclosed where appropriate; we would not be understood, for example, as necessarily agreeing with the implication of *Republic Pictures Corp. v. Security–First National Bank*, that federal jurisdiction would not exist if a complaint alleged that a state declined to enforce assignments of copyright valid under federal law. But no such case is here presented.

It has come to be realized that Mr. Justice Holmes' formula is more useful for inclusion than for the exclusion for which it was intended. Even though the claim is created by state law, a case may "arise under" a law of the United States if the complaint discloses a need for determining the meaning or application of such a law. The path-breaking opinion to this effect was *Smith v. Kansas City Title & Trust Co.* (1921), pointedly rendered over a dissent by Mr. Justice Holmes. A recent application of this principle to 28 U.S.C. § 1338 is *De Sylva v. Ballentine*, where the Supreme Court decided on the merits a claim to partial ownership of copyright renewal terms. Since there was no diversity of citizenship and no infringement, the only, and a sufficient, explanation for the taking of jurisdiction was the existence of two major questions of construction of the Copyright Act.[1] But Harms likewise does not meet this test. The crucial issue is whether or not Eliscu executed the assignment to Dreyfus; possibly the interpretation of the initial May, 1933, contract is also relevant, but if any aspect of the suit requires an interpretation of the Copyright Act, the complaint does not reveal it.

* * *

---

1. Although the parties did not question federal jurisdiction and the Court did not mention it, the issue had been sharply raised by a dissent in the Court of Appeals, and can hardly have passed unnoticed.

Mindful of the hazards of formulation in this treacherous area, we think that an action "arises under" the Copyright Act if and only if the complaint is for a remedy expressly granted by the Act, *e.g.*, a suit for infringement or for the statutory royalties for record reproduction, or asserts a claim requiring construction of the Act, or, at the very least and perhaps more doubtfully, presents a case where a distinctive policy of the Act requires that federal principles control the disposition of the claim. The general interest that copyrights, like all other forms of property, should be enjoyed by their true owner is not enough to meet this last test.

* * *

Affirmed.

D. FEDERAL QUESTION JURISDICTION—THE WELL–PLEADED COMPLAINT RULE

LOUISVILLE & NASHVILLE RAILROAD COMPANY v. MOTTLEY

211 U.S. 149 (1908)

Statement by MR. JUSTICE MOODY:

The appellees (husband and wife), being residents and citizens of Kentucky, brought this suit in equity in the circuit court of the United States for the western district of Kentucky against the appellant, a railroad company and a citizen of the same state. The object of the suit was to compel the specific performance of the following contract:

Louisville, Ky., Oct. 2d, 1871.

The Louisville & Nashville Railroad Company, in consideration that E. L. Mottley and wife, Annie E. Mottley, have this day released company from all damages or claims for damages for injuries received by them on the 7th of September, 1871, in consequence of a collision of trains on the railroad of said company at Randolph's Station, Jefferson County, Kentucky, hereby agrees to issue free passes on said railroad and branches now existing or to exist, to said E. L. & Annie E. Mottley for the remainder of the present year, and thereafter to renew said passes annually during the lives of said Mottley and wife or either of them.

The bill alleged that in September, 1871, plaintiffs, while passengers upon the defendant railroad, were injured by the defendant's negligence, and released their respective claims for damages in consideration of the agreement for transportation during their lives, expressed in the contract. It is alleged that the contract was performed by the defendant up to January 1, 1907, when the defendant declined to renew the passes. The bill then alleges that the refusal to comply with the contract was based solely upon that part of the act of Congress of June 29, 1906, which forbids the giving of free passes or free transportation. The bill further alleges: First, that the act of Congress referred to does not prohibit the giving of passes under the circumstances of this case; and, second, that, if the law is to be construed as prohibiting such passes, it is in conflict with the 5th Amendment of the Constitution, because it deprives the plaintiffs of their property without due process of law. The defendant demurred to the bill. The judge of the circuit court overruled the demurrer, entered a decree for the relief prayed for, and the defendant appealed directly to this court.

MR. JUSTICE MOODY, after making the foregoing statement, delivered the opinion of the court:

Two questions of law were raised by the demurrer to the bill, were brought here by appeal, and have been argued before us. They are, first, whether that part of the act of Congress of June 29, 1906, which forbids the giving of free passes or the collection of any different compensation for transportation of passengers than that specified in the tariff filed, makes it unlawful to perform a contract for transportation of persons who, in good faith, before the passage of the act, had accepted such contract in satisfaction of a valid cause of action against the railroad; and, second, whether the statute, if it should be construed to render such a contract unlawful, is in violation of the 5th Amendment of the Constitution of the United States. We do not deem it necessary, however, to consider either of these questions, because, in our opinion, the court below was without jurisdiction of the cause. Neither party has questioned that jurisdiction, but it is the duty of this court to see to it that the jurisdiction of the circuit court, which is defined and limited by statute, is not exceeded. This duty we have frequently performed of our own motion.

There was no diversity of citizenship, and it is not and cannot be suggested that there was any ground of jurisdiction, except that the case was a "suit ... arising under the Constitution or laws of the United States." It is the settled interpretation of these words, as used in this statute, conferring jurisdiction, that a suit arises under the Constitution and laws of the United States only when the plaintiff's statement of his own cause of action shows that it is based upon those laws or that Constitution. It is not enough that the plaintiff alleges some anticipated defense to his cause of action, and asserts that the defense is invalidated by some provision of the Constitution of the United States. Although such allegations show that very likely, in the course of the litigation, a question under the Constitution would arise, they do not show that the suit, that is, the plaintiff's original cause of action, arises under the Constitution. In *Tennessee v. Union & Planters' Bank*, the plaintiff, the state of Tennessee, brought suit in the circuit court of the United States to recover from the defendant certain taxes alleged to be due under the laws of the state. The plaintiff alleged that the defendant claimed an immunity from the taxation by virtue of its charter, and that therefore the tax was void, because in violation of the provision of the Constitution of the United States, which forbids any state from passing a law impairing the obligation of contracts. The cause was held to be beyond the jurisdiction of the circuit court, the court saying, by Mr. Justice Gray: "A suggestion of one party, that the other will or may set up a claim under the Constitution or laws of the United States, does not make the suit one arising under that Constitution or those laws." Again, in *Boston & M. Consol. Copper & S. Min. Co. v. Montana Ore Purchasing Co.*, the plaintiff brought suit in the circuit court of the United States for the conversion of copper ore and for an injunction against its continuance. The plaintiff then alleged, for the purpose of showing jurisdiction, in substance, that the defendant would set up in defense certain laws of the United States. The cause was held to be beyond the jurisdiction of the circuit court, the court saying, by Mr. Justice Peckham:

> It would be wholly unnecessary and improper, in order to prove complainant's cause of action, to go into any matters of defense which the defendants might possibly set up, and then attempt to reply to such defense, and thus, if possible, to show that a Federal question might or probably would arise in the course of the trial of the case. To allege such defense and then make an answer to it before the defendant has the opportunity to itself plead or prove its own defense is inconsistent with any known rule of pleading, so far as we are aware, and is improper.

> The rule is a reasonable and just one that the complainant in the first instance shall be confined to a statement of its cause of action, leaving to the defendant to set up in his answer what his defense is, and, if anything more than a denial of complainant's cause of action, imposing upon the defendant the burden of proving such defense.

> Conforming itself to that rule, the complainant would not, in the assertion or proof of its cause of action, bring up a single Federal question. The presentation of its cause of action would not show that it was one arising under the Constitution or laws of the United States.

> The only way in which it might be claimed that a Federal question was presented would be in the complainant's statement of what the defense of defendants would be, and complainant's answer to such defense. Under these circumstances the case is brought within the rule laid down in *Tennessee v. Union & Planters' Bank*. That case has been cited and approved many times since.

* * * The application of this rule to the case at bar is decisive against the jurisdiction of the circuit court.

It is ordered that the judgment be reversed and the case remitted to the circuit court with instructions to dismiss the suit for want of jurisdiction.

VI. CHOOSING THE FORUM—SUBJECT MATTER JURISDICTION

A. FEDERAL QUESTION JURISDICTION— EXPRESS AND IMPLIED ACTIONS

MERRELL DOW PHARMACEUTICALS INC. v. THOMPSON

478 U.S. 804 (1986)

JUSTICE STEVENS delivered the opinion of the Court.

The question presented is whether the incorporation of a federal standard in a state-law private action, when Congress has intended that there not be a federal private action for violations of that federal standard, makes the action one "arising under the Constitution, laws, or treaties of the United States," 28 U.S.C. § 1331.

I

The Thompson respondents are residents of Canada and the MacTavishes reside in Scotland. They filed virtually identical complaints against petitioner, a corporation, that manufactures and distributes the drug Bendectin. The complaints were filed in the Court of Common Pleas in Hamilton County, Ohio. Each complaint alleged that a child was born with multiple deformities as a result of the mother's ingestion of Bendectin during pregnancy. In five of the six counts, the recovery of substantial damages was requested on common-law theories of negligence, breach of warranty, strict liability, fraud, and gross negligence. In Count IV, respondents alleged that the drug Bendectin was "misbranded" in violation of the Federal Food, Drug, and Cosmetic Act (FDCA), because its labeling did not provide adequate warning that its use was potentially dangerous. Paragraph 26 alleged that the violation of the FDCA "in the promotion" of Bendectin "constitutes a rebuttable presumption of negligence." Paragraph 27 alleged that the "violation of said federal statutes directly and proximately caused the injuries suffered" by the two infants.

Petitioner filed a timely petition for removal from the state court to the Federal District Court alleging that the action was "founded, in part, on an alleged claim arising under the laws of the United States."[1] After removal, the two cases were consolidated. Respondents filed a motion to remand to the state forum on the ground that the federal court lacked subject-matter jurisdiction. Relying on our decision in *Smith v. Kansas*

---

1. The petition also alleged that the action "is between citizens of a State and citizens or subjects of a foreign state." Because petitioner is a corporation with its principal place of business in Ohio, however, the removal was not proper unless the action was founded on a claim arising under federal law. Title 28 U.S.C. § 1441(b) provides:

(b) Any civil action of which the district courts have original jurisdiction founded on a claim or right arising under the Constitution, treaties or laws of the United States shall be removable without regard to the citizenship or residence of the parties. Any other such action shall be removable only if none of the parties in interest properly joined and served as defendants is a citizen of the State in which such action is brought.

City Title & Trust Co., 255 U.S. 180 (1921), the District Court held that Count IV of the complaint alleged a cause of action arising under federal law and denied the motion to remand. It then granted petitioner's motion to dismiss on *forum non conveniens* grounds.

The Court of Appeals for the Sixth Circuit reversed. After quoting one sentence from the concluding paragraph in our recent opinion in *Franchise Tax Board v. Construction Laborers Vacation Trust,* 463 U.S. 1 (1983),[2] and noting "that the FDCA does not create or imply a private right of action for individuals injured as a result of violations of the Act," it explained:

> Federal question jurisdiction would, thus, exist only if plaintiffs' right to relief *depended necessarily* on a substantial question of federal law. Plaintiffs' causes of action referred to the FDCA merely as one available criterion for determining whether Merrell Dow was negligent. Because the jury could find negligence on the part of Merrell Dow without finding a violation of the FDCA, the plaintiffs' causes of action did not depend necessarily upon a question of federal law. Consequently, the causes of action did not arise under federal law and, therefore, were improperly removed to federal court.

We granted certiorari and we now affirm.

II

Article III of the Constitution gives the federal courts power to hear cases "arising under" federal statutes. That grant of power, however, is not self-executing, and it was not until the Judiciary Act of 1875 that Congress gave the federal courts general federal-question jurisdiction. Although the constitutional meaning of "arising under" may extend to all cases in which a federal question is "an ingredient" of the action, *Osborn v. Bank of the United States,* we have long construed the statutory grant of federal-question jurisdiction as conferring a more limited power.

Under our longstanding interpretation of the current statutory scheme, the question whether a claim "arises under" federal law must be determined by reference to the "well-pleaded complaint." *Franchise Tax Board.* A defense that raises a federal question is inadequate to confer federal jurisdiction. *Louisville & Nashville R. Co. v. Mottley.* Since a defendant may remove a case only if the claim could have been brought in federal court, 28 U.S.C. § 1441(b), moreover, the question for removal jurisdiction must also be determined by reference to the "well-pleaded complaint."

As was true in *Franchise Tax Board,* the propriety of the removal in this case thus turns on whether the case falls within the original "federal question" jurisdiction of the federal courts. There is no "single, precise

---

2. " 'Under our interpretations, Congress has given the lower courts jurisdiction to hear, originally or by removal from a state court, only those cases in which a well-pleaded complaint establishes either that federal law creates the cause of action or that the plaintiff's right to relief necessarily depends on resolution of a substantial question of federal law.' "

definition" of that concept; rather, "the phrase 'arising under' masks a welter of issues regarding the interrelation of federal and state authority and the proper management of the federal judicial system."

This much, however, is clear. The "vast majority" of cases that come within this grant of jurisdiction are covered by Justice Holmes' statement that a " 'suit arises under the law that creates the cause of action,' " quoting *American Well Works Co. v. Layne & Bowler Co.* Thus, the vast majority of cases brought under the general federal-question jurisdiction of the federal courts are those in which federal law creates the cause of action.

We have, however, also noted that a case may arise under federal law "where the vindication of a right under state law necessarily turned on some construction of federal law." *Franchise Tax Board.*[5] Our actual holding in *Franchise Tax Board* demonstrates that this statement must be read with caution; the central issue presented in that case turned on the meaning of the Employee Retirement Income Security Act of 1974, but we nevertheless concluded that federal jurisdiction was lacking.

This case does not pose a federal question of the first kind; respondents do not allege that federal law creates any of the causes of action that they have asserted. This case thus poses what Justice Frankfurter called the "litigation-provoking problem," *Textile Workers v. Lincoln Mills*, 353 U.S. 448 (1957) (dissenting opinion)—the presence of a federal issue in a state-created cause of action.

In undertaking this inquiry into whether jurisdiction may lie for the presence of a federal issue in a nonfederal cause of action, it is, of course, appropriate to begin by referring to our understanding of the statute conferring federal-question jurisdiction. We have consistently emphasized that, in exploring the outer reaches of § 1331, determinations about federal jurisdiction require sensitive judgments about congressional intent, judicial power, and the federal system. "If the history of the interpretation of judiciary legislation teaches us anything, it teaches the duty to reject treating such statutes as a wooden set of self-sufficient words.... The Act of 1875 is broadly phrased, but it has been continuously construed and limited in the light of the history that produced it, the

---

5. The case most frequently cited for that proposition is *Smith v. Kansas City Title & Trust Co.*, 255 U.S. 180 (1921). In that case the Court upheld federal jurisdiction of a shareholder's bill to enjoin the corporation from purchasing bonds issued by the federal land banks under the authority of the Federal Farm Loan Act on the ground that the federal statute that authorized the issuance of the bonds was unconstitutional. The Court stated:

The general rule is that where it appears from the bill or statement of the plaintiff that the right to relief depends upon the construction or application of the Constitution or laws of the United States, and that such federal claim is not merely colorable, and rests upon a reasonable foundation, the District Court has jurisdiction under this provision.

The effect of this view, expressed over Justice Holmes' vigorous dissent, on his *American Well Works* formulation has been often noted. *See, e.g., Franchise Tax Board* ("[I]t is well settled that Justice Holmes' test is more useful for describing the vast majority of cases that come within the district courts' original jurisdiction than it is for describing which cases are beyond district court jurisdiction"); *T.B. Harms Co. v. Eliscu* (Friendly, J.) ("It has come to be realized that Mr. Justice Holmes' formula is more useful for inclusion than for the exclusion for which it was intended").

demands of reason and coherence, and the dictates of sound judicial policy which have emerged from the Act's function as a provision in the mosaic of federal judiciary legislation." In *Franchise Tax Board,* we forcefully reiterated this need for prudence and restraint in the jurisdictional inquiry: "We have always interpreted what *Skelly Oil* called 'the current of jurisdictional legislation since the Act of March 3, 1875' . . . with an eye to practicality and necessity."

In this case, both parties agree with the Court of Appeals' conclusion that there is no federal cause of action for FDCA violations. For purposes of our decision, we assume that this is a correct interpretation of the FDCA. Thus, as the case comes to us, it is appropriate to assume that, under the settled framework for evaluating whether a federal cause of action lies, some combination of the following factors is present: (1) the plaintiffs are not part of the class for whose special benefit the statute was passed; (2) the indicia of legislative intent reveal no congressional purpose to provide a private cause of action; (3) a federal cause of action would not further the underlying purposes of the legislative scheme; and (4) the respondents' cause of action is a subject traditionally relegated to state law. In short, Congress did not intend a private federal remedy for violations of the statute that it enacted.

This is the first case in which we have reviewed this type of jurisdictional claim in light of these factors. That this is so is not surprising. The development of our framework for determining whether a private cause of action exists has proceeded only in the last 11 years, and its inception represented a significant change in our approach to congressional silence on the provision of federal remedies.

The recent character of that development does not, however, diminish its importance. Indeed, the very reasons for the development of the modern implied remedy doctrine—the "increased complexity of federal legislation and the increased volume of federal litigation," as well as "the desirability of a more careful scrutiny of legislative intent,"—are precisely the kind of considerations that should inform the concern for "practicality and necessity" that *Franchise Tax Board* advised for the construction of § 1331 when jurisdiction is asserted because of the presence of a federal issue in a state cause of action.

The significance of the necessary assumption that there is no federal private cause of action thus cannot be overstated. For the ultimate import of such a conclusion, as we have repeatedly emphasized, is that it would flout congressional intent to provide a private federal remedy for the violation of the federal statute. We think it would similarly flout, or at least undermine, congressional intent to conclude that the federal courts might nevertheless exercise federal-question jurisdiction and provide remedies for violations of that federal statute solely because the violation of the federal statute is said to be a "rebuttable presumption" or a "proximate cause" under state law, rather than a federal action under federal law.

III

Petitioner advances three arguments to support its position that, even in the face of this congressional preclusion of a federal cause of action for a violation of the federal statute, federal-question jurisdiction may lie for the violation of the federal statute as an element of a state cause of action.

First, petitioner contends that the case represents a straightforward application of the statement in *Franchise Tax Board* that federal-question jurisdiction is appropriate when "it appears that some substantial, disputed question of federal law is a necessary element of one of the well-pleaded state claims." *Franchise Tax Board,* however, did not purport to disturb the long-settled understanding that the mere presence of a federal issue in a state cause of action does not automatically confer federal-question jurisdiction. Indeed, in determining that federal-question jurisdiction was not appropriate in the case before us, we stressed Justice Cardozo's emphasis on principled, pragmatic distinctions: " 'What is needed is something of that common-sense accommodation of judgment to kaleidoscopic situations which characterizes the law in its treatment of causation . . . a selective process which picks the substantial causes out of the web and lays the other ones aside.' "

Far from creating some kind of automatic test, *Franchise Tax Board* thus candidly recognized the need for careful judgments about the exercise of federal judicial power in an area of uncertain jurisdiction. Given the significance of the assumed congressional determination to preclude federal private remedies, the presence of the federal issue as an element of the state tort is not the kind of adjudication for which jurisdiction would serve congressional purposes and the federal system. This conclusion is fully consistent with the very sentence relied on so heavily by petitioner. We simply conclude that the congressional determination that there should be no federal remedy for the violation of this federal statute is tantamount to a congressional conclusion that the presence of a claimed violation of the statute as an element of a state cause of action is insufficiently "substantial" to confer federal-question jurisdiction.

Second, petitioner contends that there is a powerful federal interest in seeing that the federal statute is given uniform interpretations, and that federal review is the best way of insuring such uniformity. In addition to the significance of the congressional decision to preclude a federal remedy, we do not agree with petitioner's characterization of the federal interest and its implications for federal-question jurisdiction. To the extent that petitioner is arguing that state use and interpretation of the FDCA pose a threat to the order and stability of the FDCA regime, petitioner should be arguing, not that federal courts should be able to review and enforce state FDCA-based causes of action as an aspect of federal-question jurisdiction, but that the FDCA pre-empts state-court jurisdiction over the issue in dispute. Petitioner's concern about the uniformity of interpretation, moreover, is considerably mitigated by the fact that, even if there is no original district court jurisdiction for these kinds of action, this Court retains power to review the decision of a federal issue in a state cause of action.[14]

Finally, petitioner argues that, whatever the general rule, there are special circumstances that justify federal-question jurisdiction in this case. Petitioner emphasizes that it is unclear whether the FDCA applies to sales in Canada and Scotland; there is, therefore, a special reason for having a federal court answer the novel federal question relating to the extraterritorial meaning of the Act. We reject this argument. We do not believe the question whether a particular claim arises under federal law depends on the novelty of the federal issue. Although it is true that federal jurisdiction cannot be based on a frivolous or insubstantial federal question, "the interrelation of federal and state authority and the proper management of the federal judicial system," *Franchise Tax Board,* would be ill served by a rule that made the existence of federal-question jurisdiction depend on the district court's case-by-case appraisal of the novelty of the federal question asserted as an element of the state tort. The novelty of an FDCA issue is not sufficient to give it status as a federal cause of action; nor should it be sufficient to give a state-based FDCA claim status as a jurisdiction-triggering federal question.

IV

We conclude that a complaint alleging a violation of a federal statute as an element of a state cause of action, when Congress has determined that there should be no private, federal cause of action for the violation, does not state a claim "arising under the Constitution, laws, or treaties of the United States." 28 U.S.C. § 1331.

The judgment of the Court of Appeals is affirmed.

It is so ordered.

JUSTICE BRENNAN, with whom JUSTICE WHITE, JUSTICE MARSHALL, and JUSTICE BLACKMUN join, dissenting.

Article III, § 2, of the Constitution provides that the federal judicial power shall extend to "all Cases, in Law and Equity, arising under this Constitution, the Laws of the United States, and Treaties made, or which shall be made, under their Authority." We have long recognized the great breadth of this grant of jurisdiction, holding that there is federal jurisdiction whenever a federal question is an "ingredient" of the action, *Osborn v. Bank of the United States,* and suggesting that there may even be

---

14. See *Moore v. Chesapeake & Ohio R. Co.*("Questions arising in actions in state courts to recover for injuries sustained by employees in intrastate commerce and relating to the scope or construction of the Federal Safety Appliance Acts are, of course, federal questions which may appropriately be reviewed in this Court.... But it does not follow that a suit brought under the state statute which defines liability to employees who are injured while engaged in intrastate commerce, and brings within the purview of the statute a breach of the duty imposed by the federal statute, should be regarded as a suit arising under the laws of the United States and cognizable in the federal court in the absence of diversity of citizenship"). Cf. *Franchise Tax Board* ("[T]he absence of original jurisdiction does not mean that there is no federal forum in which a pre-emption defense may be heard. If the state courts reject a claim of federal pre-emption, that decision may ultimately be reviewed on appeal by this Court").

jurisdiction simply because a case involves "potential federal questions."
* * *

Title 28 U.S.C. § 1331 provides, in language that parrots the language of Article III, that the district courts shall have original jurisdiction "of all civil actions arising under the Constitution, laws, or treaties of the United States." Although this language suggests that Congress intended in § 1331 to confer upon federal courts the full breadth of permissible "federal question" jurisdiction. Nonetheless, given the language of the statute and its close relation to the constitutional grant of federal-question jurisdiction, limitations on federal-question jurisdiction under § 1331 must be justified by careful consideration of the reasons underlying the grant of jurisdiction and the need for federal review. I believe that the limitation on federal jurisdiction recognized by the Court today is inconsistent with the purposes of § 1331. Therefore, I respectfully dissent.

I

While the majority of cases covered by § 1331 may well be described by Justice Holmes' adage that "[a] suit arises under the law that creates the cause of action," *American Well Works Co. v. Layne & Bowler Co.* (1916), it is firmly settled that there may be federal-question jurisdiction even though both the right asserted and the remedy sought by the plaintiff are state created. The rule as to such cases was stated in what Judge Friendly described as "[t]he path-breaking opinion" in *Smith v. Kansas City Title & Trust Co.* In *Smith,* a shareholder of the defendant corporation brought suit in the federal court to enjoin the defendant from investing corporate funds in bonds issued under the authority of the Federal Farm Loan Act. The plaintiff alleged that Missouri law imposed a fiduciary duty on the corporation to invest only in bonds that were authorized by a valid law and argued that, because the Farm Loan Act was unconstitutional, the defendant could not purchase bonds issued under its authority. Although the cause of action was wholly state created, the Court held that there was original federal jurisdiction over the case:

> The general rule is that where it appears from the bill or statement of the plaintiff that the right to relief depends upon the construction or application of the Constitution or laws of the United States, and that such federal claim is not merely colorable, and rests upon a reasonable foundation, the District Court has jurisdiction under [the statute granting federal question jurisdiction].

The continuing vitality of *Smith* is beyond challenge. We have cited it approvingly on numerous occasions, and reaffirmed its holding several times—most recently just three Terms ago by a unanimous Court in *Franchise Tax Board.* * * * Moreover, in addition to Judge Friendly's authoritative opinion in *T.B. Harms Co. v. Eliscu, Smith* has been widely cited and followed in the lower federal courts. * * * Furthermore, the principle of the *Smith* case has been recognized and endorsed by most commentators as well.[1]

There is, to my mind, no question that there is federal jurisdiction over the respondents' fourth cause of action under the rule set forth in *Smith* and reaffirmed in *Franchise Tax Board*. Respondents pleaded that petitioner's labeling of the drug Bendectin constituted "misbranding" in violation of the Federal Food, Drug, and Cosmetic Act (FDCA), and that this violation "directly and proximately caused" their injuries. Respondents asserted in the complaint that this violation established petitioner's negligence *per se* and entitled them to recover damages without more. No other basis for finding petitioner negligent was asserted in connection with this claim. As pleaded, then, respondents' "right to relief depend[ed]

---

1. Some commentators have argued that the result in *Smith* conflicts with our decision in *Moore v. Chesapeake & Ohio R. Co.,* 291 U.S. 205 (1934). In *Moore,* the plaintiff brought an action under Kentucky's Employer Liability Act, which provided that a plaintiff could not be held responsible for contributory negligence or assumption of risk where his injury resulted from the violation of any state or federal statute enacted for the safety of employees. The plaintiff in *Moore* alleged that his injury was due to the defendant's failure to comply with the Federal Safety Appliance Act; therefore, an important issue in the adjudication of the state cause of action was whether the terms of the federal law had been violated. The Court could have dismissed the complaint on the ground that the federal issue would arise only in response to a defense of contributory negligence or assumption of risk, and that therefore there was no jurisdiction under the well-pleaded complaint rule. Instead, the Court held that "a suit brought under the state statute which defines liability to employees who are injured while engaged in intrastate commerce, and brings within the purview of the statute a breach of the duty imposed by the federal statute, should [not] be regarded as a suit arising under the laws of the United States and cognizable in the federal court in the absence of diversity of citizenship."

The Court suggests that *Smith* and *Moore* may be reconciled if one views the question whether there is jurisdiction under § 1331 as turning upon "an evaluation of the *nature* of the federal interest at stake." Thus, the Court explains, while in *Smith* the issue was the constitutionality of "an important federal statute," in *Moore* the federal interest was less significant in that "the violation of the federal standard as an element of state tort recovery did not fundamentally change the state tort nature of the action."

In one sense, the Court is correct in asserting that we can reconcile *Smith* and *Moore* on the ground that the "nature" of the federal interest was more significant in *Smith* than in *Moore*. Indeed, as the Court appears to believe, we could reconcile many of the seemingly inconsistent results that have been reached under § 1331 with such a test. But this is so only because a test based upon an ad hoc evaluation of the importance of the federal issue is infinitely malleable: at what point does a federal interest become strong enough to create jurisdiction? What principles guide the determination whether a statute is "important" or not? Why, for instance, was the statute in *Smith* so "important" that direct review of a state-court decision (under our mandatory appellate jurisdiction) would have been inadequate? Would the result in *Moore* have been different if the federal issue had been a more important element of the tort claim? The point is that if one makes the test sufficiently vague and general, virtually any set of results can be "reconciled." However, the inevitable—and undesirable—result of a test such as that suggested in the Court's footnote 12 is that federal jurisdiction turns in every case on an appraisal of the federal issue, its importance and its relation to state-law issues. Yet it is precisely because the Court believes that federal jurisdiction would be "ill served" by such a case-by-case appraisal that it rejects petitioner's claim that the difficulty and importance of the statutory issue presented by its claim suffices to confer jurisdiction under § 1331. The Court cannot have it both ways.

My own view is in accord with those commentators who view the results in *Smith* and *Moore* as irreconcilable. That fact does not trouble me greatly, however, for I view *Moore* as having been a "sport" at the time it was decided and having long been in a state of innocuous desuetude. Unlike the jurisdictional holding in *Smith,* the jurisdictional holding in *Moore* has never been relied upon or even cited by this Court. *Moore* has similarly borne little fruit in the lower courts, leading Professor Redish to conclude after comparing the vitality of *Smith* and *Moore* that "the principle enunciated in *Smith* is the one widely followed by modern lower federal courts." Finally, as noted in text, the commentators have also preferred *Smith*. *Moore* simply has not survived the test of time; it is presently moribund, and, to the extent that it is inconsistent with the well-established rule of the *Smith* case, it ought to be overruled.

upon the construction or application of the Constitution or laws of the United States." *Smith; see also Franchise Tax Board* (there is federal jurisdiction under § 1331 where the plaintiff's right to relief "necessarily depends" upon resolution of a federal question). Furthermore, although petitioner disputes its liability under the FDCA, it concedes that respondents' claim that petitioner violated the FDCA is "colorable, and rests upon a reasonable foundation." *Smith.* Of course, since petitioner must make this concession to prevail in this Court, it need not be accepted at face value. However, independent examination of respondents' claim substantiates the conclusion that it is neither frivolous nor meritless. As stated in the complaint, a drug is "misbranded" under the FDCA if "the labeling or advertising fails to reveal facts material ... with respect to consequences which may result from the use of the article to which the labeling or advertising relates ...". Obviously, the possibility that a mother's ingestion of Bendectin during pregnancy could produce malformed children is material. Petitioner's principal defense is that the Act does not govern the branding of drugs that are sold in foreign countries. It is certainly not immediately obvious whether this argument is correct. Thus, the statutory question is one which "discloses a need for determining the meaning or application of [the FDCA]," *T.B. Harms Co. v. Eliscu,* and the claim raised by the fourth cause of action is one "arising under" federal law within the meaning of § 1331.

II

The Court apparently does not disagree with any of this—except, of course, for the conclusion. According to the Court, if we assume that Congress did not intend that there be a private federal cause of action under a particular federal law (and, presumably, *a fortiori* if Congress' decision not to create a private remedy is express), we must also assume that Congress did not intend that there be federal jurisdiction over a state cause of action that is determined by that federal law. Therefore, assuming—only because the parties have made a similar assumption—that there is no private cause of action under the FDCA, the Court holds that there is no federal jurisdiction over the plaintiffs' claim:

> The significance of the necessary assumption that there is no federal private cause of action thus cannot be overstated. For the ultimate import of such a conclusion, as we have repeatedly emphasized, is that it would flout congressional intent to provide a private federal remedy for the violation of the federal statute. We think it would similarly flout, or at least undermine, congressional intent to conclude that the federal courts might nevertheless exercise federal-question jurisdiction and provide remedies for violations of that federal statute solely because the violation of the federal statute is said to be a 'rebuttable presumption' or a 'proximate cause' under state law, rather than a federal action under federal law.

The Court nowhere explains the basis for this conclusion. Yet it is hardly self-evident. Why should the fact that Congress chose not to create a private federal *remedy* mean that Congress would not want there to be federal *jurisdiction* to adjudicate a state claim that imposes liability for violating the federal law? Clearly, the decision not to provide a private federal remedy should not affect federal jurisdiction unless the reasons Congress withholds a federal remedy are also reasons for withholding federal jurisdiction. Thus, it is necessary to examine the reasons for Congress' decisions to grant or withhold both federal jurisdiction and private remedies, something the Court has not done.

A

In the early days of our Republic, Congress was content to leave the task of interpreting and applying federal laws in the first instance to the state courts; with one short-lived exception, Congress did not grant the inferior federal courts original jurisdiction over cases arising under federal law until 1875. The reasons Congress found it necessary to add this jurisdiction to the district courts are well known. First, Congress recognized "the importance, and even necessity of *uniformity* of decisions throughout the whole United States, upon all subjects within the purview of the constitution." *Martin v. Hunter's Lessee* (Story, J.) (emphasis in original). Concededly, because federal jurisdiction is not always exclusive and because federal courts may disagree with one another, absolute uniformity has not been obtained even under § 1331. However, while perfect uniformity may not have been achieved, experience indicates that the availability of a federal forum in federal-question cases has done much to advance that goal. This, in fact, was the conclusion of the American Law Institute's Study of the Division of Jurisdiction Between State and Federal Courts.

In addition, § 1331 has provided for adjudication in a forum that specializes in federal law and that is therefore more likely to apply that law correctly. Because federal-question cases constitute the basic grist for federal tribunals, "[t]he federal courts have acquired a considerable expertness in the interpretation and application of federal law." By contrast, "it is apparent that federal question cases must form a very small part of the business of [state] courts." As a result, the federal courts are comparatively more skilled at interpreting and applying federal law, and are much more likely correctly to divine Congress' intent in enacting legislation.[6]

---

6. Another reason Congress conferred original federal-question jurisdiction on the district courts was its belief that state courts are hostile to assertions of federal rights. Although this concern may be less compelling today than it once was, the American Law Institute reported as recently as 1969 that "it is difficult to avoid concluding that federal courts are more likely to apply federal law sympathetically and understandingly than are state courts." In any event, this rationale is, like the rationale based on the expertise of the federal courts, simply an expression of Congress' belief that federal courts are more likely to interpret federal law correctly.

One might argue that this Court's appellate jurisdiction over state-court judgments in cases arising under federal law can be depended upon to correct erroneous state-court decisions and to insure that federal law is interpreted and applied uniformly. However, as any experienced observer of this Court can attest, "Supreme Court review of state courts, limited by docket pressures, narrow review of the facts, the debilitating possibilities of delay, and the necessity of deferring to adequate state grounds of decision, cannot do the whole job." Indeed, having served

These reasons for having original federal-question jurisdiction explain why cases like this one and *Smith*—*i.e.,* cases where the cause of action is a creature of state law, but an essential element of the claim is federal— "arise under" federal law within the meaning of § 1331. Congress passes laws in order to shape behavior; a federal law expresses Congress' determination that there is a federal interest in having individuals or other entities conform their actions to a particular norm established by that law. Because all laws are imprecise to some degree, disputes inevitably arise over what specifically Congress intended to require or permit. It is the duty of courts to interpret these laws and apply them in such a way that the congressional purpose is realized. As noted above, Congress granted the district courts power to hear cases "arising under" federal law in order to enhance the likelihood that federal laws would be interpreted more correctly and applied more uniformly. In other words, Congress determined that the availability of a federal forum to adjudicate cases involving federal questions would make it more likely that federal laws would shape behavior in the way that Congress intended.

By making federal law an essential element of a state-law claim, the State places the federal law into a context where it will operate to shape behavior: the threat of liability will force individuals to conform their conduct to interpretations of the federal law made by courts adjudicating the state-law claim. It will not matter to an individual found liable whether the officer who arrives at his door to execute judgment is wearing a state or a federal uniform; all he cares about is the fact that a sanction is being imposed—and may be imposed again in the future—because he failed to comply with the federal law. Consequently, the possibility that the federal law will be incorrectly interpreted in the context of adjudicating the state-law claim implicates the concerns that led Congress to grant the district courts power to adjudicate cases involving federal questions in precisely the same way as if it was federal law that "created" the cause of action. It therefore follows that there is federal jurisdiction under § 1331.

B

The only remaining question is whether the assumption that Congress decided not to create a private cause of action alters this analysis in a way that makes it inappropriate to exercise original federal jurisdiction. According to the Court, "the very reasons for the development of the modern implied remedy doctrine" support the conclusion that, where the legislative history of a particular law shows (whether expressly or by inference) that Congress intended that there be no private federal remedy, it must also mean that Congress would not want federal courts to exercise jurisdiction over a state-law claim making violations of that federal law actionable. These reasons are " 'the increased complexity of federal legislation,' " " 'the increased volume of federal litigation,' " and " 'the desirability of a more careful scrutiny of legislative intent.' "

---

on this Court for 30 years, it is clear to me that, realistically, it cannot even come close to "doing the whole job" and that § 1331 is essential if federal rights are to be adequately protected.

These reasons simply do not justify the Court's holding. Given the relative expertise of the federal courts in interpreting federal law, the increased complexity of federal legislation argues rather strongly in *favor* of recognizing federal jurisdiction. And, while the increased volume of litigation may appropriately be considered in connection with reasoned arguments that justify limiting the reach of § 1331, I do not believe that the day has yet arrived when this Court may trim a statute solely because it thinks that Congress made it too broad.[7]

This leaves only the third reason: " 'the desirability of a more careful scrutiny of legislative intent.' " I certainly subscribe to the proposition that the Court should consider legislative intent in determining whether or not there is jurisdiction under § 1331. But the Court has not examined the purposes underlying either the FDCA or § 1331 in reaching its conclusion that Congress' presumed decision not to provide a private federal remedy under the FDCA must be taken to withdraw federal jurisdiction over a private state remedy that imposes liability for violating the FDCA. Moreover, such an examination demonstrates not only that it is consistent with legislative intent to find that there is federal jurisdiction over such a claim, but, indeed, that it is the Court's contrary conclusion that is inconsistent with congressional intent.

The enforcement scheme established by the FDCA is typical of other, similarly broad regulatory schemes. Primary responsibility for overseeing implementation of the Act has been conferred upon a specialized administrative agency, here the Food and Drug Administration (FDA). Congress has provided the FDA with a wide-ranging arsenal of weapons to combat violations of the FDCA, including authority to obtain an *ex parte* court order for the seizure of goods subject to the Act, authority to initiate proceedings in a federal district court to enjoin continuing violations of the FDCA, and authority to request a United States Attorney to bring criminal proceedings against violators. Significantly, the FDA has no independent enforcement authority; final enforcement must come from the federal courts, which have exclusive jurisdiction over actions under the FDCA. Thus, while the initial interpretive function has been delegated to an expert administrative body whose interpretations are entitled to considerable deference, final responsibility for interpreting the statute in order to carry out the legislative mandate belongs to the federal courts.

Given that Congress structured the FDCA so that all express remedies are provided by the federal courts, it seems rather strange to conclude that it either "flout[s]" or "undermine[s]" congressional intent for the federal courts to adjudicate a private state-law remedy that is based upon

---

7. Cf. *Cohens v. Virginia* (1821) (Marshall, C.J.) ("It is most true that this Court will not take jurisdiction if it should not; but it is equally true, that it must take jurisdiction if it should.... We have no more right to decline the exercise of jurisdiction which is given, than to usurp that which is not given"). The narrow exceptions we have recognized to Chief Justice Marshall's famous dictum have all been justified by compelling judicial concerns of comity and federalism. It would be wholly illegitimate, however, for this Court to determine that there was no jurisdiction over a class of cases simply because the Court thought that there were too many cases in the federal courts.

violating the FDCA. That is, assuming that a state cause of action based on the FDCA is not pre-empted, it is entirely consistent with the FDCA to find that it "arises under" federal law within the meaning of § 1331. Indeed, it is the Court's conclusion that such a state cause of action must be kept *out* of the federal courts that appears contrary to legislative intent inasmuch as the enforcement provisions of the FDCA quite clearly express a preference for having federal courts interpret the FDCA and provide remedies for its violation.

It may be that a decision by Congress not to create a private remedy is intended to preclude all private enforcement. If that is so, then a state cause of action that makes relief available to private individuals for violations of the FDCA is pre-empted. But if Congress' decision not to provide a private federal remedy does *not* pre-empt such a state remedy, then, in light of the FDCA's clear policy of relying on the federal courts for enforcement, it also should not foreclose federal jurisdiction over that state remedy. Both § 1331 and the enforcement provisions of the FDCA reflect Congress' strong desire to utilize the federal courts to interpret and enforce the FDCA, and it is therefore at odds with both these statutes to recognize a private state-law remedy for violating the FDCA but to hold that this remedy cannot be adjudicated in the federal courts.

The Court's contrary conclusion requires inferring from Congress' decision not to create a private federal remedy that, while some private enforcement is permissible in state courts, it is "bad" if that enforcement comes from the *federal* courts. But that is simply illogical. Congress' decision to withhold a private right of action and to rely instead on public enforcement reflects congressional concern with obtaining more accurate implementation and more coordinated enforcement of a regulatory scheme. These reasons are closely related to the Congress' reasons for giving federal courts original federal-question jurisdiction. Thus, if anything, Congress' decision not to create a private remedy *strengthens* the argument in favor of finding federal jurisdiction over a state remedy that is not pre-empted.

B.   STATUTORY BASES

GRABLE & SONS METAL PRODUCTS, INC. v. DARUE ENGINEERING

545 U.S. 308 (2005)

JUSTICE SOUTER delivered the opinion of the Court.

The question is whether want of a federal cause of action to try claims of title to land obtained at a federal tax sale precludes removal to federal court of a state action with non-diverse parties raising a disputed issue of federal title law. We answer no, and hold that the national interest in providing a federal forum for federal tax litigation is sufficiently substantial to support the exercise of federal-question jurisdiction over the disputed issue on removal, which would not distort any division of labor between the state and federal courts, provided or assumed by Congress.

I

In 1994, the Internal Revenue Service seized Michigan real property belonging to petitioner Grable & Sons Metal Products, Inc., to satisfy Grable's federal tax delinquency. Title 26 U.S.C. § 6335 required the IRS to give notice of the seizure, and there is no dispute that Grable received actual notice by certified mail before the IRS sold the property to respondent Darue Engineering & Manufacturing. Although Grable also received notice of the sale itself, it did not exercise its statutory right to redeem the property within 180 days of the sale, and after that period had passed, the Government gave Darue a quitclaim deed.

Five years later, Grable brought a quiet title action in state court, claiming that Darue's record title was invalid because the IRS had failed to notify Grable of its seizure of the property in the exact manner required by § 6335(a), which provides that written notice must be "given by the Secretary to the owner of the property [or] left at his usual place of abode or business." Grable said that the statute required personal service, not service by certified mail.

Darue removed the case to Federal District Court as presenting a federal question, because the claim of title depended on the interpretation of the notice statute in the federal tax law. The District Court declined to remand the case at Grable's behest after finding that the "claim does pose a 'significant question of federal law,'" and ruling that Grable's lack of a federal right of action to enforce its claim against Darue did not bar the exercise of federal jurisdiction. On the merits, the court granted summary judgment to Darue, holding that although § 6335 by its terms required personal service, substantial compliance with the statute was enough.

The Court of Appeals for the Sixth Circuit affirmed. On the jurisdictional question, the panel thought it sufficed that the title claim raised an issue of federal law that had to be resolved, and implicated a substantial federal interest (in construing federal tax law). The court went on to affirm the District Court's judgment on the merits. We granted certiorari on the jurisdictional question alone, to resolve a split within the Courts of Appeals on whether *Merrell Dow Pharmaceuticals Inc. v. Thompson*, always requires a federal cause of action as a condition for exercising federal-question jurisdiction. We now affirm.

II

Darue was entitled to remove the quiet title action if Grable could have brought it in federal district court originally, 28 U.S.C. § 1441(a), as a civil action "arising under the Constitution, laws, or treaties of the United States," § 1331. This provision for federal-question jurisdiction is invoked by and large by plaintiffs pleading a cause of action created by federal law (*e.g.*, claims under 42 U.S.C. § 1983). There is, however, another longstanding, if less frequently encountered, variety of federal "arising under" jurisdiction, this Court having recognized for nearly 100 years that in certain cases federal-question jurisdiction will lie over state-law claims that implicate significant federal issues. The doctrine captures the commonsense notion that a federal court ought to be able to hear claims recognized under state law that nonetheless turn on substantial questions of federal law, and thus justify resort to the experience, solicitude, and hope of uniformity that a federal forum offers on federal issues.

The classic example is *Smith v. Kansas City Title & Trust Co.*, a suit by a shareholder claiming that the defendant corporation could not lawfully buy certain bonds of the National Government because their issuance was unconstitutional. Although Missouri law provided the cause of action, the Court recognized federal-question jurisdiction because the principal issue in the case was the federal constitutionality of the bond issue. *Smith* thus held, in a somewhat generous statement of the scope of the doctrine, that a state-law claim could give rise to federal-question jurisdiction so long as it "appears from the [complaint] that the right to relief depends upon the construction or application of [federal law]."

The *Smith* statement has been subject to some trimming to fit earlier and later cases recognizing the vitality of the basic doctrine, but shying away from the expansive view that mere need to apply federal law in a state-law claim will suffice to open the "arising under" door. As early as 1912, this Court had confined federal-question jurisdiction over state-law claims to those that "really and substantially involv[e] a dispute or controversy respecting the validity, construction or effect of [federal] law." This limitation was the ancestor of Justice Cardozo's later explanation that a request to exercise federal-question jurisdiction over a state action calls for a "common-sense accommodation of judgment to [the] kaleidoscopic situations" that present a federal issue, in "a selective process which picks the substantial causes out of the web and lays the other ones aside." It has in fact become a constant refrain in such cases that federal jurisdiction demands not only a contested federal issue, but a substantial one, indicating a serious federal interest in claiming the advantages thought to be inherent in a federal forum. *E.g., Chicago v. International College of Surgeons*; *Merrell Dow*; *Franchise Tax Bd. of Cal.*

But even when the state action discloses a contested and substantial federal question, the exercise of federal jurisdiction is subject to a possible veto. For the federal issue will ultimately qualify for a federal forum only if federal jurisdiction is consistent with congressional judgment about the sound division of labor between state and federal courts governing the application of § 1331. Thus, *Franchise Tax Bd.* explained that the appropriateness of a federal forum to hear an embedded issue could be evaluated only after considering the "welter of issues regarding the interrelation of federal and state authority and the proper management of the federal judicial system." Because arising-under jurisdiction to hear a state-law claim always raises the possibility of upsetting the state-federal line drawn (or at least assumed) by Congress, the presence of a disputed federal issue and the ostensible importance of a federal forum are never necessarily dispositive; there must always be an assessment of any disruptive portent in exercising federal jurisdiction. See also *Merrell Dow*.

These considerations have kept us from stating a "single, precise, all-embracing" test for jurisdiction over federal issues embedded in state-law claims between non-diverse parties. We have not kept them out simply because they appeared in state raiment, as Justice Holmes would have done, *see Smith,* but neither have we treated "federal issue" as a pass-word opening federal courts to any state action embracing a point of federal law. Instead, the question is, does a state-law claim necessarily raise a stated federal issue, actually disputed and substantial, which a federal forum may entertain without disturbing any congressionally approved balance of federal and state judicial responsibilities.

III

A

This case warrants federal jurisdiction. Grable's state complaint must specify "the facts establishing the superiority of [its] claim," and Grable has premised its superior title claim on a failure by the IRS to give it adequate notice, as defined by federal law. Whether Grable was given notice within the meaning of the federal statute is thus an essential element of its quiet title claim, and the meaning of the federal statute is actually in dispute; it appears to be the only legal or factual issue contested in the case. The meaning of the federal tax provision is an important issue of federal law that sensibly belongs in a federal court. The Government has a strong interest in the "prompt and certain collection of delinquent taxes," and the ability of the IRS to satisfy its claims from the property of delinquents requires clear terms of notice to allow buyers like Darue to satisfy themselves that the Service has touched the bases necessary for good title. The Government thus has a direct interest in the availability of a federal forum to vindicate its own administrative action, and buyers (as well as tax delinquents) may find it valuable to come before judges used to federal tax matters. Finally, because it will be the rare state title case that raises a contested matter of federal law, federal jurisdiction to resolve genuine disagreement over federal tax title provisions will portend only a microscopic effect on the federal-state division of labor.

This conclusion puts us in venerable company, quiet title actions having been the subject of some of the earliest exercises of federal-question jurisdiction over state-law claims. In *Hopkins,* the question was federal jurisdiction over a quiet title action based on the plaintiffs' allegation that federal mining law gave them the superior claim. Just as in this case, "the facts showing the plaintiffs' title and the existence and invalidity of the instrument or record sought to be eliminated as a cloud upon the title are essential parts of the plaintiffs' cause of action." As in this case again, "it is plain that a controversy respecting the construction and effect of the [federal] laws is involved and is sufficiently real and substantial." This Court therefore upheld federal jurisdiction in *Hopkins,* as well as in the similar quiet title matters.... Consistent with those cases, the recognition of federal jurisdiction is in order here.

B

Merrell Dow Pharmaceuticals Inc. v. Thompson, on which Grable rests its position, is not to the contrary. *Merrell Dow* considered a state tort claim resting in part on the allegation that the defendant drug company had violated a federal misbranding prohibition, and was thus presumptively negligent under Ohio law. The Court assumed that federal law would have to be applied to resolve the claim, but after closely examining the strength of the federal interest at stake and the implications of opening the federal forum, held federal jurisdiction unavailable. Congress had not provided a private federal cause of action for violation of the federal branding requirement, and the Court found "it would ... flout, or at least undermine, congressional intent to conclude that federal courts might nevertheless exercise federal-question jurisdiction and provide remedies for violations of that federal statute solely because the violation ... is said to be a ... 'proximate cause' under state law."

Because federal law provides for no quiet title action that could be brought against Darue, Grable argues that there can be no federal jurisdiction here, stressing some broad language in *Merrell Dow* (including the passage just quoted) that on its face supports Grable's position. But an opinion is to be read as a whole, and *Merrell Dow* cannot be read whole as overturning decades of precedent, as it would have done by effectively adopting the Holmes dissent in *Smith,* and converting a federal cause of action from a sufficient condition for federal-question jurisdiction into a necessary one.

In the first place, *Merrell Dow* disclaimed the adoption of any bright-line rule, as when the Court reiterated that "in exploring the outer reaches of § 1331, determinations about federal jurisdiction require sensitive judgments about congressional intent, judicial power, and the federal system." The opinion included a lengthy footnote explaining that questions of jurisdiction over state-law claims require "careful judgments," about the "nature of the federal interest at stake." And as a final indication that it did not mean to make a federal right of action mandatory, it expressly approved the exercise of jurisdiction sustained in *Smith,* despite the want of any federal cause of action available to *Smith's* shareholder plaintiff. *Merrell Dow* then, did not toss out, but specifically retained, the contextual enquiry that had been *Smith's* hallmark for over 60 years. At the end of *Merrell Dow,* Justice Holmes was still dissenting.

Accordingly, *Merrell Dow* should be read in its entirety as treating the absence of a federal private right of action as evidence relevant to, but not dispositive of, the "sensitive judgments about congressional intent" that § 1331 requires. The absence of any federal cause of action affected *Merrell Dow's* result two ways. The Court saw the fact as worth some consideration in the assessment of substantiality. But its primary importance emerged when the Court treated the combination of no federal cause of action and no preemption of state remedies for misbranding as an important clue to Congress's conception of the scope of jurisdiction to be exercised under § 1331. The Court saw the missing cause of action not as a missing federal door key, always required, but as a missing welcome mat, required in the circumstances, when exercising federal jurisdiction over a state misbranding action would have attracted a horde of original filings and removal cases raising other state claims with embedded federal issues. For if the federal labeling standard without a federal cause of action could get a state claim into federal court, so could any other federal standard without a federal cause of action. And that would have meant a tremendous number of cases.

One only needed to consider the treatment of federal violations generally in garden variety state tort law. "The violation of federal statutes and regulations is commonly given negligence per se effect in state tort proceedings." A general rule of exercising federal jurisdiction over state claims resting on federal mislabeling and other statutory violations would thus have heralded a potentially enormous shift of traditionally state cases into federal courts. Expressing concern over the "increased volume of federal litigation," and noting the importance of adhering to "legislative intent," *Merrell Dow* thought it improbable that the Congress, having made no provision for a federal cause of action, would have meant to welcome any state-law tort case implicating federal law "solely because the violation of the federal statute is said to [create] a rebuttable presumption [of negligence] . . . under state law." In this situation, no welcome mat meant keep out. *Merrell Dow's* analysis thus fits within the framework of examining the importance of having a federal forum for the issue, and the consistency of such a forum with Congress's intended division of labor between state and federal courts.

As already indicated, however, a comparable analysis yields a different jurisdictional conclusion in this case. Although Congress also indicated ambivalence in this case by providing no private right of action to Grable, it is the rare state quiet title action that involves contested issues of federal law. Consequently, jurisdiction over actions like Grable's would not materially affect, or threaten to affect, the normal currents of litigation. Given the absence of threatening structural consequences and the clear interest the Government, its buyers, and its delinquents have in the availability of a federal forum, there is no good reason to shirk from federal jurisdiction over the dispositive and contested federal issue at the heart of the state-law title claim.[7]

IV

The judgment of the Court of Appeals, upholding federal jurisdiction over Grable's quiet title action, is affirmed.

---

7. At oral argument Grable's counsel espoused the position that after *Merrell Dow,* federal-question jurisdiction over state-law claims absent a federal right of action could be recognized only where a constitutional issue was at stake. There is, however, no reason in text or otherwise to draw such a rough line. As *Merrell Dow* itself suggested, constitutional questions may be the more likely ones to reach the level of substantiality that can justify federal jurisdiction. But a flat ban on statutory questions would mechanically exclude significant questions of federal law like the one this case presents.

It is so ordered.

JUSTICE THOMAS, concurring.

The Court faithfully applies our precedents interpreting 28 U.S.C. § 1331 to authorize federal-court jurisdiction over some cases in which state law creates the cause of action but requires determination of an issue of federal law, *e.g., Smith v. Kansas City Title & Trust Co.; Merrell Dow Pharmaceuticals Inc.* In this case, no one has asked us to overrule those precedents and adopt the rule Justice Holmes set forth in *American Well Works Co. v. Layne & Bowler Co.,* limiting § 1331 jurisdiction to cases in which federal law creates the cause of action pleaded on the face of the plaintiff's complaint. In an appropriate case, and perhaps with the benefit of better evidence as to the original meaning of § 1331's text, I would be willing to consider that course.*

Jurisdictional rules should be clear. Whatever the virtues of the *Smith* standard, it is anything but clear (the standard "calls for a 'common-sense accommodation of judgment to [the] kaleidoscopic situations' that present a federal issue, in 'a selective process which picks the substantial causes out of the web and lays the other ones aside' "); ("[T]he question is, does a state-law claim necessarily raise a stated federal issue, actually disputed and substantial, which a federal forum may entertain without disturbing any congressionally approved balance of federal and state judicial responsibilities"); (" '[D]eterminations about federal jurisdiction require sensitive judgments about congressional intent, judicial power, and the federal system' "); ("the absence of a federal private right of action [is] evidence relevant to, but not dispositive of, the 'sensitive judgments about congressional intent' that § 1331 requires" (quoting *Merrell Dow*)).

Whatever the vices of the *American Well Works* rule, it is clear. Moreover, it accounts for the " 'vast majority' " of cases that come within § 1331 under our current case law, *Merrell Dow,* (quoting *Franchise Tax Bd. of Cal.*)—further indication that trying to sort out which cases fall within the smaller *Smith* category may not be worth the effort it entails. Accordingly, I would be willing in appropriate circumstances to reconsider our interpretation of § 1331.

MIMS v. ARROW FINANCIAL SERVICES, LLC.

132 S.Ct. 740 (2012)

JUSTICE GINSBURG delivered the opinion of the Court.

This case concerns enforcement, through private suits, of the Telephone Consumer Protection Act of 1991 (TCPA or Act), 47 U.S.C. § 227.

---

* This Court has long construed the scope of the statutory grant of federal-question jurisdiction more narrowly than the scope of the constitutional grant of such jurisdiction. See *Merrell Dow Pharmaceuticals Inc.* I assume for present purposes that this distinction is proper-that is, that the language of 28 U.S.C. § 1331, "[t]he district courts shall have original jurisdiction of all *civil actions arising under* the Constitution, laws, or treaties of the United States" (emphasis added), is narrower than the language of Art. III, § 2, cl. 1, of the Constitution, "[t]he judicial Power shall extend to all *Cases,* in Law and Equity, *arising under* this Constitution, the Laws of the United States, and Treaties made, or which shall be made, under their Authority ..." (emphasis added).

Voluminous consumer complaints about abuses of telephone technology—for example, computerized calls dispatched to private homes—prompted Congress to pass the TCPA. Congress determined that federal legislation was needed because telemarketers, by operating interstate, were escaping state-law prohibitions on intrusive nuisance calls. The Act bans certain practices invasive of privacy and directs the Federal Communications Commission (FCC or Commission) to prescribe implementing regulations. It authorizes States to bring civil actions to enjoin prohibited practices and to recover damages on their residents' behalf. The Commission must be notified of such suits and may intervene in them. Jurisdiction over state-initiated TCPA suits, Congress provided, lies exclusively in the U.S. district courts. Congress also provided for civil actions by private parties seeking redress for violations of the TCPA or of the Commission's implementing regulations.

Petitioner Marcus D. Mims, complaining of multiple violations of the Act by respondent Arrow Financial Services, LLC (Arrow), a debt-collection agency, commenced an action for damages against Arrow in the U.S. District Court for the Southern District of Florida. Mims invoked the court's "federal question" jurisdiction, *i.e.*, its authority to adjudicate claims "arising under the ... laws ... of the United States," 28 U.S.C. § 1331. The District Court, affirmed by the U.S. Court of Appeals for the Eleventh Circuit, dismissed Mims's complaint for want of subject-matter jurisdiction. Both courts relied on Congress' specification, in the TCPA, that a private person may seek redress for violations of the Act (or of the Commission's regulations thereunder) "in an appropriate court of [a] State," "if [such an action is] otherwise permitted by the laws or rules of court of [that] State."

The question presented is whether Congress' provision for private actions to enforce the TCPA renders state courts the *exclusive* arbiters of such actions. We have long recognized that "[a] suit arises under the law that creates the cause of action." *American Well Works Co. v. Layne & Bowler Co.* (1916). Beyond doubt, the TCPA is a federal law that both creates the claim Mims has brought and supplies the substantive rules that will govern the case. We find no convincing reason to read into the TCPA's permissive grant of jurisdiction to state courts any barrier to the U.S. district courts' exercise of the general federal-question jurisdiction they have possessed since 1875. We hold, therefore, that federal and state courts have concurrent jurisdiction over private suits arising under the TCPA.

I

A

In enacting the TCPA, Congress made several findings relevant here. "Unrestricted telemarketing," Congress determined, "can be an intrusive invasion of privacy." In particular, Congress reported, "[m]any consumers are outraged over the proliferation of intrusive, nuisance [telemarketing] calls to their homes." "[A]utomated or prerecorded telephone calls" made to private residences, Congress found, were rightly regarded by recipients as "an invasion of privacy. *Ibid.* (internal quotation marks omitted). Although over half the States had enacted statutes restricting telemarketing, Congress believed that federal law was needed because "telemarketers [could] evade [state-law] prohibitions through interstate operations."

Subject to exceptions not pertinent here, the TCPA principally outlaws four practices. First, the Act makes it unlawful to use an automatic telephone dialing system or an artificial or prerecorded voice message, without the prior express consent of the called party, to call any emergency telephone line, hospital patient, pager, cellular telephone, or other service for which the receiver is charged for the call. Second, the TCPA forbids using artificial or prerecorded voice messages to call residential telephone lines without prior express consent. Third, the Act proscribes sending unsolicited advertisements to fax machines. Fourth, it bans using automatic telephone dialing systems to engage two or more of a business' telephone lines simultaneously.

The TCPA delegates authority to the FCC to ban artificial and prerecorded voice calls to businesses, and to exempt particular types of calls from the law's requirements). The Act also directs the FCC to prescribe regulations to protect the privacy of residential telephone subscribers, possibly through the creation of a national "do not call" system.

Congress provided complementary means of enforcing the Act. State Attorneys General may "bring a civil action on behalf of [State] residents," if the Attorney General "has reason to believe that any person has engaged ... in a pattern or practice" of violating the TCPA or FCC regulations thereunder. "The district courts of the United States ... have exclusive jurisdiction" over all TCPA actions brought by State Attorneys General. The Commission may intervene in such suits.

Title 47 U.S.C. § 227(b)(3), captioned "Private right of action," provides:

> A person or entity may, if otherwise permitted by the laws or rules of court of a State, bring in an appropriate court of that State—
>
>> (A) an action based on a violation of this subsection or the regulations prescribed under this subsection to enjoin such violation,
>>
>> (B) an action to recover for actual monetary loss from such a violation, or to receive $500 in damages for each such violation, whichever is greater, or
>>
>> (C) both such actions.
>
> If the court finds that the defendant willfully or knowingly violated this subsection or the regulations prescribed under this subsection, the court may, in its discretion, increase the amount of the award to

an amount equal to not more than 3 times the amount available under subparagraph (B) of this paragraph.

A similar provision authorizes a private right of action for a violation of the FCC's implementing regulations.

B

Mims, a Florida resident, alleged that Arrow, seeking to collect a debt, repeatedly used an automatic telephone dialing system or prerecorded or artificial voice to call Mims's cellular phone without his consent. Commencing suit in the U.S. District Court for the Southern District of Florida, Mims charged that Arrow "willfully or knowingly violated the TCPA." He sought declaratory relief, a permanent injunction, and damages.

The District Court held that it lacked subject-matter jurisdiction over Mims's TCPA claim. Under Eleventh Circuit precedent, the District Court explained, federal-question jurisdiction under 28 U.S.C. § 1331 was unavailable "because Congress vested jurisdiction over [private actions under] the TCPA exclusively in state courts."

We granted certiorari to resolve a split among the Circuits as to whether Congress granted state courts exclusive jurisdiction over private actions brought under the TCPA. We now hold that Congress did not deprive federal courts of federal-question jurisdiction over private TCPA suits.

II

Federal courts, though "courts of limited jurisdiction," in the main "have no more right to decline the exercise of jurisdiction which is given, then to usurp that which is not given." Congress granted federal courts general federal-question jurisdiction in 1875. As now codified, the law provides: "The district courts shall have original jurisdiction of all civil actions arising under the Constitution, laws, or treaties of the United States." 28 U.S.C. § 1331. The statute originally included an amount-in-controversy requirement, set at $500. Recognizing the responsibility of federal courts to decide claims, large or small, arising under federal law, Congress in 1980 eliminated the amount-in-controversy requirement in federal-question (but not diversity) cases. Apart from deletion of the amount-in-controversy requirement, the general federal-question provision has remained essentially unchanged since 1875.

Because federal law creates the right of action and provides the rules of decision, Mims's TCPA claim, in 28 U.S.C. § 1331's words, plainly "aris[es] under" the "laws ... of the United States." As already noted, "[a] suit arises under the law that creates the cause of action." *American Well Works*. Although courts have described this formulation as "more useful for inclusion than for ... exclusion," *Merrell Dow Pharmaceuticals Inc. v. Thompson,* (quoting *T.B. Harms Co. v. Eliscu,* there is no serious debate that a federally created claim for relief is generally a "sufficient condition for federal-question jurisdiction." *Grable & Sons Metal Products, Inc. v. Darue Engineering & Mfg.*[8]

Arrow agrees that this action arises under federal law, but urges that Congress vested exclusive adjudicatory authority over private TCPA actions in state courts. In cases "arising under" federal law, we note, there is a "deeply rooted presumption in favor of concurrent state court jurisdiction," rebuttable if "Congress affirmatively ousts the state courts of jurisdiction over a particular federal claim." *E.g.*, 28 U.S.C. § 1333 ("The district courts shall have original jurisdiction, exclusive of the courts of the States, of: (1) Any civil case of admiralty or maritime jurisdiction. . . . "). The presumption of concurrent state-court jurisdiction, we have recognized, can be overcome "by an explicit statutory directive, by unmistakable implication from legislative history, or by a clear incompatibility between state-court jurisdiction and federal interests."

Arrow readily acknowledges the presumption of concurrent state-court jurisdiction, but maintains that 28 U.S.C. § 1331 creates no converse presumption in favor of federal-court jurisdiction. Instead, Arrow urges, the TCPA, a later, more specific statute, displaces § 1331, an earlier, more general prescription.

Section 1331, our decisions indicate, is not swept away so easily. As stated earlier, when federal law creates a private right of action and furnishes the substantive rules of decision, the claim arises under federal law, and district courts possess federal-question jurisdiction under § 1331.[9] That principle endures unless Congress divests federal courts of their § 1331 adjudicatory authority.

"[D]ivestment of district court jurisdiction" should be found no more readily than "divestmen[t] of state court jurisdiction," given "the longstanding and explicit grant of federal question jurisdiction in 28 U.S.C. § 1331." Accordingly, the District Court retains § 1331 jurisdiction over Mims's complaint unless the TCPA, expressly or by fair implication, excludes federal-court adjudication.

III

Arrow's arguments do not persuade us that Congress has eliminated § 1331 jurisdiction over private actions under the TCPA.

The language of the TCPA—"A person or entity may, if otherwise permitted by the laws or rules of court of a State, bring [an action] in an appropriate court of that State," Arrow asserts, is uniquely state-court

---

8. For a rare exception to the rule that a federal cause of action suffices to ground federal-question jurisdiction, see *Shoshone Mining Co. v. Rutter*. In *Shoshone Mining*, we held that a suit for a federal mining patent did not arise under federal law for jurisdictional purposes because "the right of possession" in controversy could be determined by "local rules or customs, or state statutes," or "may present simply a question of fact." Here, by contrast, the TCPA not only creates the claim for relief and designates the remedy; critically, the Act and regulations thereunder supply the governing substantive law.

9. Even when a right of action is created by state law, if the claim requires resolution of significant issues of federal law, the case may arise under federal law for 28 U.S.C. § 1331 purposes. See *Grable & Sons Metal Products, Inc.*.

oriented. That may be, but "[i]t is a general rule that the grant of jurisdiction to one court does not, of itself, imply that the jurisdiction is to be exclusive."

Nothing in the permissive language of § 227(b)(3) makes state-court jurisdiction exclusive, or otherwise purports to oust federal courts of their 28 U.S.C. § 1331 jurisdiction over federal claims. Congress may indeed provide a track for a federal claim exclusive of § 1331. Congress has done nothing of that sort here, however.

Title 47 U.S.C. § 227(b)(3) does not state that a private plaintiff may bring an action under the TCPA "only" in state court, or "exclusively" in state court. The absence of such a statement contrasts with the Act's instruction on suits instituted by State Attorneys General. As earlier noted, 47 U.S.C.A. § 227(g)(2)) vests "exclusive jurisdiction over [such] actions" in "[t]he district courts of the United States." Section 227(g)(2)'s exclusivity prescription "reinforce[s] the conclusion that [47 U.S.C. § 227(b)(3)'s] silence ... leaves the jurisdictional grant of § 1331 untouched. For where otherwise applicable jurisdiction was meant to be excluded, it was excluded expressly." The most natural interpretation of Congress' failure to use similar language in [47 U.S.C. §]227(b)(3) is that Congress did not intend to grant exclusive jurisdiction in that section."); ("[47 U.S.C.A. § 227(g)(2) (Supp.2011)] is explicit about exclusivity, while [47 U.S.C.] § 227(b)(3) is not; the natural inference is that the state forum mentioned in § 227(b)(3) is optional rather than mandatory.").

Arrow urges that Congress would have had no reason to provide for a private action "in an appropriate [state] court," § 227(b)(3), if it did not mean to make the state forum exclusive. Had Congress said nothing at all about bringing private TCPA claims in state courts, Arrow observes, those courts would nevertheless have concurrent jurisdiction. True enough, but Congress had simultaneously provided for TCPA enforcement actions by state authorities, and had made federal district courts exclusively competent in such cases. Congress may simply have wanted to avoid any argument that in private actions, as in actions brought by State Attorneys General, "federal jurisdiction is exclusive." Moreover, by providing that private actions may be brought in state court "if otherwise permitted by the laws or rules of court of [the] State," Congress arguably gave States leeway they would otherwise lack to "decide for [themselves] whether to entertain claims under the [TCPA]."[12]

Making state-court jurisdiction over § 227(b)(3) claims exclusive, Arrow further asserts, "fits hand in glove with [Congress'] objective": enabling States to control telemarketers whose interstate operations evaded state law. Even so, we have observed, jurisdiction conferred by 28

---

12. The Supremacy Clause declares federal law the "supreme law of the land," and state courts must enforce it "in the absence of a valid excuse." *Howlett v. Rose.* "An excuse that is inconsistent with or violates federal law is not a valid excuse: The Supremacy Clause forbids state courts to dissociate themselves from federal law because of disagreement with its content or a refusal to recognize the superior authority of its source." Without the "if otherwise permitted" language, 47 U.S.C. § 227(b)(3), there is little doubt that state courts would be obliged to hear TCPA claims.

U.S.C. § 1331 should hold firm against "mere implication flowing from subsequent legislation."

We are not persuaded, moreover, that Congress sought only to fill a gap in the States' enforcement capabilities. Had Congress so limited its sights, it could have passed a statute providing that out-of-state telemarketing calls directed into a State would be subject to the laws of the receiving State. Congress did not enact such a law. Instead, it enacted detailed, uniform, federal substantive prescriptions and provided for a regulatory regime administered by a federal agency. TCPA liability thus depends on violation of a federal statutory requirement or an FCC regulation, not on a violation of any state substantive law.

The federal interest in regulating telemarketing to "protec[t] the privacy of individuals" while "permit[ting] legitimate [commercial] practices," is evident from the regulatory role Congress assigned to the FCC. Congress' design would be less well served if consumers had to rely on "the laws or rules of court of a State," or the accident of diversity jurisdiction, to gain redress for TCPA violations.

Arrow emphasizes a statement made on the Senate floor by Senator Hollings, the TCPA's sponsor:

> Computerized calls are the scourge of modern civilization. They wake us up in the morning; they interrupt our dinner at night; they force the sick and elderly out of bed; they hound us until we want to rip the telephone right out of the wall.

> The substitute bill contains a private right-of-action provision that will make it easier for consumers to recover damages from receiving these computerized calls. The provision would allow consumers to bring an action in State court against any entity that violates the bill. The bill does not, because of constitutional constraints, dictate to the States which court in each State shall be the proper venue for such an action, as this is a matter for State legislators to determine. Nevertheless, it is my hope that States will make it as easy as possible for consumers to bring such actions, preferably in small claims court....

> Small claims court or a similar court would allow the consumer to appear before the court without an attorney. The amount of damages in this legislation is set to be fair to both the consumer and the telemarketer. However, it would defeat the purposes of the bill if the attorneys' costs to consumers of bringing an action were greater than the potential damages. I thus expect that the States will act reasonably in permitting their citizens to go to court to enforce this bill.

This statement does not bear the weight Arrow would place on it.

First, the views of a single legislator, even a bill's sponsor, are not controlling. Second, Senator Hollings did not mention federal-court jurisdiction or otherwise suggest that 47 U.S.C. § 227(b)(3) is intended to divest federal courts of authority to hear TCPA claims. Hollings no doubt believed that mine-run TCPA claims would be pursued most expeditiously in state small-claims court.[14] But one cannot glean from his statement any expectation that those courts, or state courts generally, would have exclusive jurisdiction over private actions alleging violations of the Act or of the FCC's implementing regulations. Third, even if we agreed with Arrow that Senator Hollings expected private TCPA actions to proceed solely in state courts, and even if other supporters shared his view, that expectation would not control our judgment on 28 U.S.C. § 1331's compass.

Among its arguments for state-court exclusivity, Arrow raises a concern about the impact on federal courts were we to uphold § 1331 jurisdiction over private actions under the TCPA. "[G]iven the enormous volume of telecommunications presenting potential claims," Arrow projects, federal courts could be inundated by $500–per–violation TCPA claims. "Moreover, if plaintiffs are free to bring TCPA claims in federal court under § 1331, then defendants sued in state court would be equally free to remove those cases to federal court under 28 U.S.C. § 1441." Indeed, Arrow suggests, defendants could use removal as a mechanism to force small-claims-court plaintiffs to abandon suit rather than "figh[t] it out" in the "more expensive federal forum."

Arrow's floodgates argument assumes "a shocking degree of noncompliance" with the Act, Reply Brief 11, and seems to us more imaginary than real. The current federal district court civil filing fee is $350. How likely is it that a party would bring a $500 claim in, or remove a $500 claim to, federal court? Lexis and Westlaw searches turned up 65 TCPA claims removed to federal district courts in Illinois, Indiana, and Wisconsin since the Seventh Circuit held, in October 2005, that the Act does not confer exclusive jurisdiction on state courts. All 65 cases were class actions, not individual cases removed from small-claims court.[15] There were also 26 private TCPA claims brought initially in federal district courts; of those, 24 were class actions.

IV

Nothing in the text, structure, purpose, or legislative history of the TCPA calls for displacement of the federal-question jurisdiction U.S. district courts ordinarily have under 28 U.S.C. § 1331. In the absence of direction from Congress stronger than any Arrow has advanced, we apply the familiar default rule: Federal courts have § 1331 jurisdiction over claims that arise under federal law. Because federal law gives rise to the claim for relief Mims has stated and specifies the substantive rules of

---

14. The complaint in this very case, we note, could not have been brought in small-claims court. Mims alleged some 12 calls, and sought treble damages ($1,500) for each. The amount he sought to recover far exceeded the $5,000 ceiling on claims a Florida small-claims court can adjudicate.

15. When Congress wants to make federal claims instituted in state court non-removable, it says just that. See 28 U.S.C. § 1445(a) ("A civil action in any State court against a railroad or its receivers or trustees, [arising under §§ 51–60 of Title 45,] may not be removed to any district court of the United States.") and 15 U.S.C. § 77v(a) ("[N]o case arising under this subchapter and brought in any State court of competent jurisdiction shall be removed to any court of the United States.")).

decision, the Eleventh Circuit erred in dismissing Mims's case for lack of subject-matter jurisdiction.

For the reasons stated, the judgment of the United States Court of Appeals for the Eleventh Circuit is reversed, and the case is remanded for further proceedings consistent with this opinion.

It is so ordered.

C. SUPPLEMENTAL JURISDICTION— COMMON LAW PRINCIPLES

PENDENT CLAIM AND PENDENT PARTY JURISDICTION

FEDERAL RULE OF CIVIL PROCEDURE 2. ONE FORM OF ACTION

There is one form of action—the civil action.

FEDERAL RULE OF CIVIL PROCEDURE 42. CONSOLIDATION; SEPARATE TRIALS

(a) Consolidation. If actions before the court involve a common question of law or fact, the court may:

(1) join for hearing or trial any or all matters at issue in the actions;

(2) consolidate the actions; or

(3) issue any other orders to avoid unnecessary cost or delay.

(b) Separate Trials. For convenience, to avoid prejudice, or to expedite and economize, the court may order a separate trial of one or more separate issues, claims, crossclaims, counterclaims, or third-party claims. When ordering a separate trial, the court must preserve any federal right to a jury trial.

UNITED MINE WORKERS OF AMERICA v. GIBBS
383 U.S. 715 (1966)

MR. JUSTICE BRENNAN delivered the opinion of the Court.

Respondent Paul Gibbs was awarded compensatory and punitive damages in this action against petitioner United Mine Workers of America (NMW) for alleged violations of § 303 of the Labor Management Relations Act, 1947, and of the common law of Tennessee. The case grew out of the rivalry between the United Mine Workers and the Southern Labor Union over representation of workers in the southern Appalachian coal fields. Tennessee Consolidated Coal Company, not a party here, laid off 100 miners of the UMW's Local 5881 when it closed one of its mines in southern Tennessee during the spring of 1960. Late that summer, Grundy Company, a wholly owned subsidiary of Consolidated, hired respondent as mine superintendent to attempt to open a new mine on Consolidated's property at nearby Gray's Creek through use of members of the Southern Labor Union. As part of the arrangement, Grundy also gave respondent a contract to haul the mine's coal to the nearest railroad loading point.

On August 15 and 16, 1960, armed members of Local 5881 forcibly prevented the opening of the mine, threatening respondent and beating an organizer for the rival union. The members of the local believed Consolidated had promised them the jobs at the new mine; they insisted that if anyone would do the work, they would. At this time, no representative of the UMW, their international union, was present. George Gilbert, the UMW's field representative for the area including Local 5881, was away at Middlesboro, Kentucky, attending an Executive Board meeting when the members of the local discovered Grundy's plan; he did not return to the area until late in the day of August 16. There was uncontradicted testimony that he first learned of the violence while at the meeting, and returned with explicit instructions from his international union superiors to establish a limited picket line, to prevent any further violence, and to see to it that the strike did not spread to neighboring mines. There was no further violence at the mine site; a picket line was maintained there for nine months; and no further attempts were made to open the mine during that period.

Respondent lost his job as superintendent, and never entered into performance of his haulage contract. He testified that he soon began to lose other trucking contracts and mine leases he held in nearby areas. Claiming these effects to be the result of a concerted union plan against him, he sought recovery not against Local 5881 or its members, but only against petitioner, the international union. The suit was brought in the United States District Court for the Eastern District of Tennessee, see, and jurisdiction was premised on allegations of secondary boycotts under § 303. The state law claim, for which jurisdiction was based upon the doctrine of pendent jurisdiction, asserted "an unlawful conspiracy and an unlawful boycott aimed at him and (Grundy) to maliciously, wantonly and willfully interfere with his contract of employment and with his contract of haulage."

The trial judge refused to submit to the jury the claims of pressure intended to cause mining firms other than Grundy to cease doing business with Gibbs; he found those claims unsupported by the evidence. The jury's verdict was that the UMW had violated both § 303 and state law. Gibbs was awarded $60,000 as damages under the employment contract and $14,500 under the haulage contract; he was also awarded $100,000 punitive damages. On motion, the trial court set aside the award of damages with respect to the haulage contract on the ground that damage was unproved. It also held that union pressure on Grundy to discharge respondent as supervisor would constitute only a primary dispute with Grundy, as respondent's employer, and hence was not cognizable as a claim under § 303. Interference with the employment relationship was cognizable as a state claim, however, and a remitted award was sustained on the state law claim. The Court of Appeals for the Sixth Circuit affirmed. We granted certiorari. We reverse.

A threshold question is whether the District Court properly entertained jurisdiction of the claim based on Tennessee law. . . . [H]ere respondent's claim is based in part on proofs of violence and intimidation. "(W)e have allowed the States to grant compensation for the consequences, as defined by the traditional law of torts, of conduct marked by violence and imminent threats to the public order. * * * State jurisdiction has prevailed in these situations because the compelling state interest, in the scheme of our federalism, in the maintenance of domestic peace is not overridden in the absence of clearly expressed congressional direction."

The fact that state remedies were not entirely pre-empted does not, however, answer the question whether the state claim was properly adjudicated in the District Court absent diversity jurisdiction. The Court held in *Hurn v. Oursler*, that state law claims are appropriate for federal court determination if they form a separate but parallel ground for relief also sought in a substantial claim based on federal law. The Court distinguished permissible from non-permissible exercises of federal judicial power over state law claims by contrasting "a case where two distinct grounds in support of a single cause of action are alleged, one only of which presents a federal question, and a case where two separate and distinct causes of action are alleged, one only of which is federal in character. In the former, where the federal question averred is not plainly wanting in substance, the federal court, even though the federal ground be not established, may nevertheless retain and dispose of the case upon the nonfederal ground; in the latter it may not do so upon the nonfederal cause of action." The question is into which category the present action fell.

Hurn was decided in 1933, before the unification of law and equity by the Federal Rules of Civil Procedure. At the time, the meaning of "cause of action" was a subject of serious dispute; the phrase might "mean one thing for one purpose and something different for another." The Court in *Hurn* identified what it meant by the term by citation of *Baltimore S.S. Co. v. Phillips*, a case in which "cause of action" had been used to identify the operative scope of the doctrine of res judicata. In that case the Court had noted that "the whole tendency of our decisions is to require a plaintiff to try his whole cause of action and his whole case at one time," It stated its holding in the following language, quoted in part in the *Hurn* opinion:

> Upon principle, it is perfectly plain that the respondent (a seaman suing for an injury sustained while working aboard ship) suffered but one actionable wrong, and was entitled to but one recovery, whether his injury was due to one or the other of several distinct acts of alleged negligence, or to a combination of some or all of them. In either view, there would be but a single wrongful invasion of a single primary right of the plaintiff, namely, the right of bodily safety, whether the acts constituting such invasion were one or many, simple or complex.

A cause of action does not consist of facts, but of the unlawful violation of a right which the facts show. The number and variety of the facts alleged do not establish more than one cause of action so long as their result, whether they be considered severally or in combination, is the violation of but one right by a single legal wrong. The mere multiplication of grounds of negligence alleged as causing the same injury does not result in multiplying the causes of action. 'The facts are merely the means, and not the end. They do not constitute the cause of action, but they show its existence by making the wrong appear.'

Had the Court found a jurisdictional bar to reaching the state claim in *Hurn*, we assume that the doctrine of res judicata would not have been applicable in any subsequent state suit. But the citation of *Baltimore S.S. Co.* shows that the Court found that the weighty policies of judicial economy and fairness to parties reflected in res judicata doctrine were in themselves strong counsel for the adoption of a rule which would permit federal courts to dispose of the state as well as the federal claims.

With the adoption of the Federal Rules of Civil Procedure and the unified form of action, Fed. Rule Civ. Proc. 2, much of the controversy over "cause of action" abated. The phrase remained as the keystone of the *Hurn* test, however, and, as commentators have noted, has been the source of considerable confusion. Under the Rules, the impulse is toward entertaining the broadest possible scope of action consistent with fairness to the parties; joinder of claims, parties and remedies is strongly encouraged. Yet because the *Hurn* question involves issues of jurisdiction as well as convenience, there has been some tendency to limit its application to cases in which the state and federal claims are, as in *Hurn*, "little more than the equivalent of different epithets to characterize the same group of circumstances."

This limited approach is unnecessarily grudging. Pendent jurisdiction, in the sense of judicial power, exists whenever there is a claim "arising under (the) Constitution, the Laws of the United States, and Treaties made, or which shall be made, under their Authority * * *," U.S. Const., Art. III, § 2, and the relationship between that claim and the state claim permits the conclusion that the entire action before the court comprises but one constitutional "case." The federal claim must have substance sufficient to confer subject matter jurisdiction on the court. The state and federal claims must derive from a common nucleus of operative fact. But if, considered without regard to their federal or state character, a plaintiff's claims are such that he would ordinarily be expected to try them all in one judicial proceeding, then, assuming substantiality of the federal issues, there is power in federal courts to hear the whole.

That power need not be exercised in every case in which it is found to exist. It has consistently been recognized that pendent jurisdiction is a doctrine of discretion, not of plaintiff's right. Its justification lies in considerations of judicial economy, convenience and fairness to litigants; if these are not present a federal court should hesitate to exercise jurisdiction over state claims, even though bound to apply state law to them.

Needless decisions of state law should be avoided both as a matter of comity and to promote justice between the parties, by procuring for them a surer-footed reading of applicable law. Certainly, if the federal claims are dismissed before trial, even though not insubstantial in a jurisdictional sense, the state claims should be dismissed as well. Similarly, if it appears that the state issues substantially predominate, whether in terms of proof, of the scope of the issues raised, or of the comprehensiveness of the remedy sought, the state claims may be dismissed without prejudice and left for resolution to state tribunals. There may, on the other hand, be situations in which the state claim is so closely tied to questions of federal policy that the argument for exercise of pendent jurisdiction is particularly strong. In the present case, for example, the allowable scope of the state claim implicates the federal doctrine of pre-emption; while this interrelationship does not create statutory federal question jurisdiction, its existence is relevant to the exercise of discretion. Finally, there may be reasons independent of jurisdictional considerations, such as the likelihood of jury confusion in treating divergent legal theories of relief, that would justify separating state and federal claims for trial, Fed. Rule Civ. Proc. 42(b). If so, jurisdiction should ordinarily be refused.

The question of power will ordinarily be resolved on the pleadings. But the issue whether pendent jurisdiction has been properly assumed is one which remains open throughout the litigation. Pretrial procedures or even the trial itself may reveal a substantial hegemony of state law claims, or likelihood of jury confusion, which could not have been anticipated at the pleading stage. Although it will of course be appropriate to take account in this circumstance of the already completed course of the litigation, dismissal of the state claim might even then be merited. For example, it may appear that the plaintiff was well aware of the nature of his proofs and the relative importance of his claims; recognition of a federal court's wide latitude to decide ancillary questions of state law does not imply that it must tolerate a litigant's effort to impose upon it what is in effect only a state law case. Once it appears that a state claim constitutes the real body of a case, to which the federal claim is only an appendage, the state claim may fairly be dismissed.

We are not prepared to say that in the present case the District Court exceeded its discretion in proceeding to judgment on the state claim. We may assume for purposes of decision that the District Court was correct in its holding that the claim of pressure on Grundy to terminate the employment contract was outside the purview of § 303. Even so, the § 303 claims based on secondary pressures on Grundy relative to the haulage contract and on other coal operators generally were substantial. Although § 303 limited recovery to compensatory damages based on secondary pressures, and state law allowed both compensatory and punitive damages, and allowed such damages as to both secondary and primary activity, the state and federal claims arose from the same nucleus of operative fact and reflected alternative remedies. Indeed, the verdict sheet sent in to the jury authorized only one award of damages, so that recovery could not be given separately on the federal and state claims.

It is true that the § 303 claims ultimately failed and that the only recovery allowed respondent was on the state claim. We cannot confidently say, however, that the federal issues were so remote or played such a minor role at the trial that in effect the state claim only was tried. Although the District Court dismissed as unproved the § 303 claims that petitioner's secondary activities included attempts to induce coal operators other than Grundy to cease doing business with respondent, the court submitted the § 303 claims relating to Grundy to the jury. The jury returned verdicts against petitioner on those § 303 claims, and it was only on petitioner's motion for a directed verdict and a judgment n.o.v. that the verdicts on those claims were set aside. The District Judge considered the claim as to the haulage contract proved as to liability, and held it failed only for lack of proof of damages. Although there was some risk of confusing the jury in joining the state and federal claims—especially since, as will be developed, differing standards of proof of UMW involvement applied—the possibility of confusion could be lessened by employing a special verdict form, as the District Court did. Moreover, the question whether the permissible scope of the state claim was limited by the doctrine of pre-emption afforded a special reason for the exercise of pendent jurisdiction; the federal courts are particularly appropriate bodies for the application of pre-emption principles. We thus conclude that although it may be that the District Court might, in its sound discretion, have dismissed the state claim, the circumstances show no error in refusing to do so.

* * *

Reversed.

THE CHIEF JUSTICE took no part in the decision of this case. MR. JUSTICE HARLAN, whom MR. JUSTICE CLARK joins, concurring.

I agree with and join in Part I of the Court's opinion relating to pendent jurisdiction. * * *

FINLEY v. UNITED STATES

490 U.S. 545 (1989)

JUSTICE SCALIA delivered the opinion of the Court.

On the night of November 11, 1983, a twin-engine plane carrying petitioner's husband and two of her children struck electric transmission lines during its approach to a San Diego, California, airfield. No one survived the resulting crash. Petitioner brought a tort action in state court, claiming that San Diego Gas and Electric Company had negligently positioned and inadequately illuminated the transmission lines, and that the city of San Diego's negligent maintenance of the airport's runway lights had rendered them inoperative the night of the crash. When she later discovered that the Federal Aviation Administration (FAA) was in fact the party responsible for the runway lights, petitioner filed the present action against the United States in the United States District Court for the Southern District of California. The complaint based jurisdiction upon the Federal Tort Claims Act (FTCA), 28 U.S.C. § 1346(b), alleging negligence in the FAA's operation and maintenance of the runway lights and performance of air traffic control functions. Almost a year later, she moved to amend the federal complaint to include claims against the original state-court defendants, as to which no independent basis for federal jurisdiction existed. The District Court granted petitioner's motion and asserted "pendent" jurisdiction under *Mine Workers v. Gibbs,* finding it "clear" that "judicial economy and efficiency" favored trying the actions together, and concluding that they arose "from a common nucleus of operative facts." The District Court certified an interlocutory appeal to the Court of Appeals for the Ninth Circuit. That court summarily reversed on the basis of its earlier opinion in *Ayala v. United States,* which had categorically rejected pendent-party jurisdiction under the FTCA. We granted certiorari, to resolve a split among the Circuits on whether the FTCA permits an assertion of pendent jurisdiction over additional parties.

The FTCA provides that "the district courts ... shall have exclusive jurisdiction of civil actions on claims against the United States" for certain torts of federal employees acting within the scope of their employment. 28 U.S.C. § 1346(b). Petitioner seeks to append her claims against the city and the utility to her FTCA action against the United States, even though this would require the District Court to extend its authority to additional parties for whom an independent jurisdictional base—such as diversity of citizenship, 28 U.S.C. § 1332(a)(1)—is lacking.

In 1807 Chief Justice Marshall wrote for the Court that "courts which are created by written law, and whose jurisdiction is defined by written law, cannot transcend that jurisdiction. It is unnecessary to state the reasoning on which this opinion is founded, because it has been repeatedly given by this court; and with the decisions heretofore rendered on this point, no member of the bench has, even for an instant, been dissatisfied." It remains rudimentary law that "[a]s regards all courts of the United States inferior to this tribunal, two things are necessary to create jurisdiction, whether original or appellate. The Constitution must have given to the court the capacity to take it, *and an act of Congress must have supplied it....* To the extent that such action is not taken, the power lies dormant."

Despite this principle, in a line of cases by now no less well established we have held, without specific examination of jurisdictional statutes, that federal courts have "pendent" claim jurisdiction—that is, jurisdiction over nonfederal claims between parties litigating other matters properly before the court—to the full extent permitted by the Constitution. *Mine Workers v. Gibbs; Hurn v. Oursler. Gibbs,* which has come to stand for the principle in question, held that "[p]endent jurisdiction, in the sense of judicial *power,* exists whenever there is a claim 'arising under

[the] Constitution, the Laws of the United States, and Treaties made, or which shall be made, under their Authority ...,' U.S. Const., Art. III, § 2, and the relationship between that claim and the state claim permits the conclusion that the entire action before the court comprises but one constitutional 'case.' " The requisite relationship exists, *Gibbs* said, when the federal and nonfederal claims "derive from a common nucleus of operative fact" and are such that a plaintiff "would ordinarily be expected to try them in one judicial proceeding." Petitioner contends that the same criterion applies here, leading to the result that her state-law claims against San Diego Gas and Electric Company and the city of San Diego may be heard in conjunction with her FTCA action against the United States.

Analytically, petitioner's case is fundamentally different from *Gibbs* in that it brings into question what has become known as pendent-*party* jurisdiction, that is, jurisdiction over parties not named in any claim that is independently cognizable by the federal court. We may assume, without deciding, that the constitutional criterion for pendent-party jurisdiction is analogous to the constitutional criterion for pendent-claim jurisdiction, and that petitioner's state-law claims pass that test. Our cases show, however, that with respect to the addition of parties, as opposed to the addition of only claims, we will not assume that the full constitutional power has been congressionally authorized, and will not read jurisdictional statutes broadly. * * *

[In 1976, the] the non-transferability of *Gibbs* to pendent-party claims was made explicit. In *Aldinger v. Howard,* 427 U.S. 1 (1976), the plaintiff brought federal claims under 42 U.S.C. § 1983 against individual defendants, and sought to append to them a related state claim against Spokane County, Washington. We specifically disapproved application of the *Gibbs* mode of analysis, finding a "significant legal difference." "[T]he addition of a completely new party," we said, "would run counter to the well-established principle that federal courts ... are courts of limited jurisdiction marked out by Congress." "Resolution of a claim of pendent-party jurisdiction ... calls for careful attention to the relevant statutory language." We held in *Aldinger* that the jurisdictional statute under which suit was brought, 28 U.S.C. § 1343, which conferred district court jurisdiction over civil actions of certain types "authorized by law to be commenced," did not mean to include as "authorized by law" a state-law claim against a party that had been statutorily insulated from similar federal suit. The county had been "*excluded* from liability in § 1983, and therefore by reference in the grant of jurisdiction under § 1343(3)."

We reaffirmed and further refined our approach to pendent-party jurisdiction in *Owen Equipment & Erection Co. v. Kroger,* ... focusing on the requirement that the suit be "between ... citizens of different states," rather than the requirement that it "excee[d] the sum or value of $10,000." We held that the jurisdiction which § 1332(a)(1) confers over a "matter in controversy" between a plaintiff and defendant of diverse citizenship cannot be read to confer pendent jurisdiction over a different non-diverse defendant, even if the *claim* involving that other defendant meets the *Gibbs* test. *"Gibbs,"* we said, "does not end the inquiry into whether a federal court has power to hear the nonfederal claims along with the federal ones. Beyond this constitutional minimum, there must be an examination of the posture in which the nonfederal claim is asserted and of the specific statute that confers jurisdiction over the federal claim."

The most significant element of "posture" or of "context," in the present case is precisely that the added claims involve added parties over whom no independent basis of jurisdiction exists. While in a narrow class of cases a federal court may assert authority over such a claim "ancillary" to jurisdiction otherwise properly vested—for example, when an additional party has a claim upon contested assets within the court's exclusive control—we have never reached such a result solely on the basis that the *Gibbs* test has been met. And little more basis than that can be relied upon by petitioner here. As in *Kroger,* the relationship between petitioner's added claims and the original complaint is one of "mere factual similarity," which is of no consequence since "neither the convenience of the litigants nor considerations of judicial economy can suffice to justify extension of the doctrine of ancillary jurisdiction." It is true that here, unlike in *Kroger,* the party seeking to bring the added claims had little choice but to be in federal rather than state court, since the FTCA permits the Federal Government to be sued only there. But that alone is not enough, since we have held that suits against the United States under the Tucker Act cannot include private defendants.

The second factor invoked by *Kroger,* the text of the jurisdictional statute at issue, likewise fails to establish petitioner's case. The FTCA, § 1346(b), confers jurisdiction over "civil actions on claims against the United States." It does not say "civil actions on claims that include requested relief against the United States," nor "civil actions in which there is a claim against the United States"—formulations one might expect if the presence of a claim against the United States constituted merely a minimum jurisdictional requirement, rather than a definition of the permissible scope of FTCA actions. Just as the statutory provision "between . . . citizens of different States" has been held to mean citizens of different States and no one else, so also here we conclude that "against the United States" means against the United States and no one else.[5] "Due regard for the rightful independence of state governments . . . requires that [federal courts] scrupulously confine their own jurisdiction to the precise limits which the statute has defined." The statute here

---

5. Justice STEVENS would distinguish *Kroger* from the present case on the ground that, where Congress "has unequivocally indicated its intent that the federal right be litigated in a federal forum, there is reason to believe that Congress did not intend that the substance of the federal right be diminished by the increased costs in efficiency and convenience of litigation in two forums." It seems to us, however, that one could say precisely the same thing about the diversity jurisdiction involved in *Kroger:* When Congress has unequivocally indicated its intent that a plaintiff have a right to bring a diversity action in federal court, there is reason to believe that Congress did not intend that the substance of that right be diminished, etc. We simply do not agree with the inference, in either context.

defines jurisdiction in a manner that does not reach defendants other than the United States.

Petitioner contends, however, that an affirmative grant of pendent-party jurisdiction is suggested by changes made to the jurisdictional grant of the FTCA as part of the comprehensive 1948 revision of the Judicial Code. In its earlier form, the FTCA had conferred upon district courts "exclusive jurisdiction to hear, determine, and render judgment *on any claim* against the United States" for specified torts. In the 1948 revision, this provision was changed to "exclusive jurisdiction of *civil actions on claims* against the United States." Petitioner argues that this broadened the scope of the statute, permitting the assertion of jurisdiction over any "civil action," so long as that action *includes* a claim against the United States. We disagree.

Under established canons of statutory construction, "it will not be inferred that Congress, in revising and consolidating the laws, intended to change their effect unless such intention is clearly expressed." Concerning the 1948 re-codification of the Judicial Code in particular, we have stated that "no changes in law or policy are to be presumed from changes of language in the revision unless an intent to make such changes is clearly expressed." We have found no suggestion, much less a clear expression, that the minor rewording at issue here imported a substantive change.

The change from "claim against the United States" to "civil actions on claims against the United States" would be a strange way to express the substantive revision asserted by petitioner-but a perfectly understandable way to achieve another objective. The 1948 re-codification came relatively soon after the adoption of the Federal Rules of Civil Procedure, which provide that "[t]here shall be one form of action to be known as 'civil action.'" Fed. Rule Civ. Proc. 2. Consistent with this new terminology, the 1948 revision inserted the expression "civil action" throughout the provisions governing district-court jurisdiction.

Reliance upon the 1948 re-codification also ignores the fact that the concept of pendent-party jurisdiction was not considered remotely viable until *Gibbs* liberalized the concept of pendent-claim jurisdiction—nearly 20 years later. Indeed, in 1948 even a relatively limited substantive expansion of pendent-*claim* jurisdiction with respect to unfair competition actions provoked considerable discussion. That change, in the already accepted realm of pendent-*claim* jurisdiction, was accomplished by wording that could not be mistaken, referring to "any civil action asserting a claim of unfair competition when joined with a substantial and related claim under the copyright, patent, or trademark laws." It is inconceivable that the much more radical change of adopting pendent-party jurisdiction would have been effected by the minor and obscure change of wording at issue here—especially when that revision is more naturally understood as stylistic.

Because the FTCA permits the Government to be sued only in federal court, our holding that parties to related claims cannot necessarily be sued there means that the efficiency and convenience of a consolidated action will sometimes have to be forgone in favor of separate actions in state and federal courts. We acknowledged this potential consideration in *Aldinger,* but now conclude that the present statute permits no other result.

* * *

As we noted at the outset, our cases do not display an entirely consistent approach with respect to the necessity that jurisdiction be explicitly conferred. The *Gibbs* line of cases was a departure from prior practice, and a departure that we have no intent to limit or impair. But *Aldinger* indicated that the *Gibbs* approach would not be extended to the pendent-party field, and we decide today to retain that line. Whatever we say regarding the scope of jurisdiction conferred by a particular statute can of course be changed by Congress. What is of paramount importance is that Congress be able to legislate against a background of clear interpretive rules, so that it may know the effect of the language it adopts. All our cases—*Zahn, Aldinger,* and *Kroger*—have held that a grant of jurisdiction over claims involving particular parties does not itself confer jurisdiction over additional claims by or against different parties. Our decision today reaffirms that interpretive rule; the opposite would sow confusion.

For the foregoing reasons, the judgment of the Court of Appeals is

Affirmed.

JUSTICE BLACKMUN, dissenting.

If *Aldinger v. Howard,* required us to ask whether the Federal Tort Claims Act embraced "an affirmative grant of pendent-party jurisdiction," I would agree with the majority that no such specific grant of jurisdiction is present. But, in my view, that is not the appropriate question under *Aldinger.* I read the Court's opinion in that case, rather, as requiring us to consider whether Congress has demonstrated an intent to *exempt* "the party as to whom jurisdiction pendent to the principal claim" is asserted from being haled into federal court. And, as those of us in dissent in *Aldinger* observed, the *Aldinger* test would be rendered meaningless if the required intent could be found in the failure of the relevant jurisdictional statute to mention the type of party in question, "because all instances of asserted pendent-party jurisdiction will by definition involve a party as to whom Congress has impliedly 'addressed itself' by not expressly conferring subject-matter jurisdiction on the federal courts."

In *Aldinger,* the Court found the requisite intent to exclude municipalities from the relevant jurisdictional statute, because (the Court then thought) municipalities had been affirmatively excluded by Congress from the scope of 42 U.S.C. § 1983. In such a case, the Court barred the use of the pendent-party doctrine, for otherwise the doctrine would permit an end run around an express congressional limitation of federal power.

In the present case, I find no such substantive limitation. Nor, in my view, is there any other expression of congressional intent to exclude private defendants from federal tort claims litigation. *United States v.*

Sherwood is not to the contrary. There, this Court held that Congress did not intend under the Tucker Act to permit the district courts to adjudicate any cause of action that could not have been brought in the Court of Claims, an Article I court in which no private party could be a defendant. *Sherwood* did not turn solely on a canon of "conservatism which is appropriate in the case of a waiver of sovereign immunity." It turned also upon "the history of the Court of Claims' jurisdiction." There is no equivalent history of adjudication of tort claims against the United States in a tribunal without power to litigate the liability of private tortfeasors; thus, *Sherwood* does not require the result the Court reaches today.

In a case not controlled by any express intent to limit the scope of a constitutional "case," *Aldinger* suggests that the appropriateness of pendent-party jurisdiction might turn on the "alignmen[t] of parties and claims," and that one significant factor is whether "the grant of jurisdiction to [the] federal court is exclusive," as is the situation here. Where, as here, Congress' preference for a federal forum for a certain category of claims makes the federal forum the *only* possible one in which the constitutional case may be heard as a whole, the sensible result is to permit the exercise of pendent-party jurisdiction. *Aldinger* imposes no obstacle to that result, and I would not reach out to create one. I therefore dissent.

JUSTICE STEVENS, with whom JUSTICE BRENNAN and JUSTICE MARSHALL join, dissenting.

The Court's holding is not faithful to our precedents and casually dismisses the accumulated wisdom of our best judges. As we observed more than 16 years ago, "numerous decisions throughout the courts of appeals since [*Mine Workers v. Gibbs*] have recognized the existence of judicial power to hear pendent claims involving pendent parties where 'the entire action before the court comprises but one constitutional "case" ' as defined in *Gibbs*." I shall first explain why the position taken by the overwhelming consensus of federal judges is correct and then comment on major flaws in the opinion the Court announces today.

I

Article III of the Constitution identifies the categories of "Cases" and "Controversies" that federal courts may have jurisdiction to decide. If a case is not within one of the specified categories, neither Congress nor the parties may authorize a federal court to decide it. Objections to a federal court's jurisdiction over the subject matter of a case cannot be waived. Although Article III strictly confines the subject-matter jurisdiction of federal courts, it does not limit the extent of the courts' personal jurisdiction over individual parties or their power to decide individual claims in cases within any of the specified categories. A party beyond the reach of a federal court's process may voluntarily submit to its jurisdiction over his person, but he cannot create subject-matter jurisdiction-by waiver, estoppel, or the filing of a lawsuit-over a non-Article III case.[6]

The case before us today is one in which the United States is a party. Given the plain language of Article III, there is not even an arguable basis for questioning the federal court's constitutional power to decide it. Moreover, by enacting the Federal Tort Claims Act (FTCA) in 1946, 28 U.S.C. § 1346(b), Congress unquestionably authorized the District Court to accept jurisdiction of "civil actions on claims against the United States." Thus, it is perfectly clear that the District Court has both constitutional and statutory power to decide this case.

It is also undisputed that this power will not be defeated by the joinder of two private defendants. Rule 14(a) of the Federal Rules of Civil Procedure expressly authorizes the defendant to implead joint tortfeasors,[8] and this Rule is applicable to FTCA cases. Moreover, if the claim against nonfederal defendants had been properly brought in a federal court, those defendants could require the United States to defend their claim for contribution in that action. The dispute between all the parties derives from a common nucleus of operative fact. There is accordingly ample basis for regarding this entire three-cornered controversy as a single "case" and for allowing petitioner to assert additional claims against the nonfederal defendants as she is authorized to do by Rule 20(a) of the Federal Rules.[11]

Prior to the adoption of the Federal Rules of Civil Procedure in 1938, the federal courts routinely decided state-law claims in cases in which they

---

6. *Gibbs* concerned a state-law claim jurisdictionally pendent to one of federal law, but no reason appears why the identical principles should not equally apply to pendent state-law claims involving the joinder of additional parties. In either case the Art. III question concerns only the subject matter and not the *in personam* jurisdiction of the federal courts. In either case the question of Art. III power in the federal judiciary to exercise subject-matter jurisdiction concerns whether the claims asserted are such as "would ordinarily be expected to [be tried] in one judicial proceeding," and the question of discretion addresses "considerations of judicial economy, convenience and fairness to litigants."

"To recognize that the addition of parties under the pendent jurisdiction of the federal courts will sometimes alter the balance of 'judicial economy, convenience and fairness,' or sometimes threaten to embroil federal courts in the resolution of uncertain questions of state law, and thereby make the exercise of this discretionary jurisdiction inappropriate, is only to speak to the question of the proper exercise of judicial discretion in the circumstances and does not vitiate the *Gibbs* analysis or its application to the question of pendent-party jurisdiction." *Aldinger v. Howard* (Brennan, J., dissenting).

The Court has upheld the authority of a federal court to entertain counterclaims against a plaintiff, and a third-party defendant, notwithstanding that the claims do not have an independent jurisdictional basis. *See also Owen Equipment & Erection Co. v. Kroger* ("[T]he exercise of ancillary jurisdiction over nonfederal claims has often been upheld in situations involving impleader, cross-claims or counterclaims").

8. Rule 14(a) provides in part:

At any time after commencement of the action a defending party, as a third-party plaintiff, may cause a summons and complaint to be served upon a person not a party to the action who is or may be liable to the third-party plaintiff for all or part of the plaintiff's claim against the third-party plaintiff.

11. Rule 20(a) provides in part:

All persons ... may be joined in one action as defendants if there is asserted against them jointly, severally, or in the alternative, any right to relief in respect of or arising out of the same transaction, occurrence, or series of transactions or occurrences and if any question of law or fact common to all defendants will arise in the action.

had subject-matter jurisdiction, see, *e.g., Hurn*; and granted relief against non-diverse parties on state claims as to which there was no independent basis for federal jurisdiction. Although the contours of the federal cause of action—or "case"—were then more narrowly defined than they are today, *see, e.g., Hurn,* the doctrine of "pendent" or "ancillary" jurisdiction had long been firmly established. The relevant change that was effectuated by the adoption of the Rules in 1938 was, in essence, a statutory broadening of the dimensions of the cases that federal courts may entertain.

The Court's unanimous opinion in *Mine Workers v. Gibbs* highlights the modern conception of a "civil action" and a "constitutional case." At issue was the exercise of pendent jurisdiction over a state-law claim in an action brought under the Labor Management Relations Act, 1947. [excerpt from Court's opinion in *Gibbs* omitted—ed.][15]

Immediately after *Gibbs* was decided,[16] federal judges throughout the Nation recognized that its reasoning applied to cases in which it was necessary to add an additional party on a pendent, nonfederal claim in order to grant complete relief. For example, Judge Henry Friendly considered this precise question in three separate opinions.... [H]e is universally recognized not only as one of our wisest judges,[18] ... with special learning and expertise in matters of federal jurisdiction [discussion of Judge friendly's decisions omitted—ed.]

Before Judge Friendly addressed this issue for the third time, we decided *Aldinger v. Howard.* In that case, after declining to announce any general rule governing pendent-party jurisdiction, we held that such jurisdiction should not be exercised if Congress has "expressly or by implication negated its existence" in the statute granting subject-matter jurisdiction over the particular claim before the Court. Specifically, we concluded that the Civil Rights Acts, as then interpreted, precluded the joinder of a municipal corporation as a defendant to a claim asserted pursuant to 42 U.S.C. § 1983 or to a state-law claim pendent to such a federal claim. Although a reasonable argument can be made that the Court misconstrued the intent of Congress in that case, there surely can be no quarrel with the proposition that Congress may withdraw or deny pendent jurisdiction over particular claims or parties.

In his third "pendent-party" opinion, Judge Friendly correctly described the limited scope of our holding in *Aldinger.* He wrote:

---

15. The Court is correct to treat *Gibbs* as established law. Just last Term we stated: "*Gibbs* establishes that the pendent jurisdiction doctrine is designed to enable courts to handle cases involving state-law claims in the way that will best accommodate the values of economy, convenience, fairness, and comity, and *Gibbs* further establishes that the judicial branch is to shape and apply the doctrine in that light." *Carnegie-Mellon Univ. v. Cohill,* 484 U.S. 343 (1988). *See also Merrell Dow Pharmaceuticals Inc. v. Thompson* ...

16. Although the Court suggests that "the concept of pendent-party jurisdiction was not considered remotely viable until *Gibbs* liberalized the concept of pendent-claim jurisdiction," some courts exercised a form of pendent-party jurisdiction even prior to that decision.

18. In 1963, Justice Frankfurter regarded him "as the best judge now writing opinions on the American scene"; Erwin Griswold has described him as "the ablest lawyer of my generation," and Judge Posner called him "the greatest federal appellate judge of his time."

Although the *Aldinger* Court disapproved of the joinder of a pendent party defendant in the case before it, the Court explicitly limited its conclusion to "the issue of so-called 'pendent party' jurisdiction with respect to a claim brought under [28 U.S.C.] § 1343(3) and 42 U.S.C. § 1983," and noted that "[o]ther statutory grants and other alignments of parties and claims might call for a different result," and that "it would be as unwise as it would be unnecessary to lay down any sweeping pronouncement upon the existence or exercise of such jurisdiction."

The circumstances here are about as powerful for the exercise of pendent party jurisdiction as can be imagined. The exclusivity of federal jurisdiction over claims for violation of the Securities Exchange Act makes a federal court the only one where a complete disposition of federal and related state claims can be rendered.

In the *Weinberger* case the circumstances were "about as powerful for the exercise of pendent party jurisdiction as can be imagined" because Congress had vested the federal courts with exclusive jurisdiction over claims arising under the Securities Exchange Act. The Federal District Court was therefore the only forum in which the entire constitutional case could be tried at one time. That powerful circumstance is also present in cases arising under the FTCA. In fact, in dicta, the *Aldinger* Court suggested that pendent-party jurisdiction might be available under the FTCA for precisely this reason.

I would thus hold that the grant of jurisdiction to hear "civil actions on claims against the United States" authorizes the federal courts to hear state-law claims against a pendent party. As many other judges have recognized,[22] the fact that such claims are within the exclusive federal jurisdiction, together with the absence of any evidence of congressional disapproval of the exercise of pendent-party jurisdiction in FTCA cases, provides a fully sufficient justification for applying the holding in *Gibbs* to this case.

II

The Court's contrary conclusion rests on an insufficient major premise, a failure to distinguish between diversity and federal-question cases, and an implicit reliance on a narrow view of the waiver of sovereign immunity in the FTCA.

The Court treats the absence of an affirmative grant of jurisdiction by Congress as though it constituted the kind of implicit rejection of pendent jurisdiction that we found in *Aldinger v. Howard.* Its opinion laboriously demonstrates that the FTCA "defines jurisdiction in a manner that does not reach defendants other than the United States," and that the language of the statute cannot be construed as "adopting pendent-party

---

22. In *Moore,* in 1973, we noted that the Ninth Circuit rule denying pendent-party jurisdiction "stands virtually alone against this post-*Gibbs* trend in the courts of appeals." An overwhelming number of judges adhered to that view after *Aldinger* was decided.

jurisdiction." That, of course, is always the predicate for the question whether a federal court may rely on the doctrine of ancillary or pendent jurisdiction to fill a gap in the relevant jurisdictional statute. If the Court's demonstration were controlling, *Gibbs, Hurn,* and *Moore,* as well as a good many other cases, were incorrectly decided.

In *Aldinger,* we adopted a rule of construction that assumed the existence of pendent jurisdiction unless "Congress in the statutes conferring jurisdiction has ... expressly or by implication negated its existence." We rejected the assertion of pendent-party jurisdiction there because it arose "not in the context of congressional silence or tacit encouragement, but in quite the opposite context." Congress' exclusion of municipal corporations from the definition of persons under § 1983, we concluded, evinced an intent to preclude the exercise of federal-court jurisdiction over them. If congressional silence were sufficient to defeat pendent jurisdiction, the careful reasoning in our *Aldinger* opinion was wholly unnecessary, for obviously the civil rights statutes do not affirmatively authorize the joinder of any state-law claims.

* * * The Court today adopts a sharply different approach. Without even so much as acknowledging our statement in *Aldinger* that before a federal court may exercise pendent-party jurisdiction it must satisfy itself that Congress "has not expressly or by implication negated its existence," it now instructs that "a grant of jurisdiction over claims involving particular parties does not itself confer jurisdiction over additional claims by or against different parties." This rule, the Court asserts, is necessary to provide Congress "a background of clear interpretative rules" and to avoid sowing confusion. But as a method of statutory interpretation, the Court's approach is neither clear nor faithful to our judicial obligation to discern congressional intent. While with respect to the joinder of additional defendants on pendent state claims, the Court's mandate is now clear, its approach offers little guidance with respect to the many other claims that a court must address in the course of deciding a constitutional case. Because the Court provides no reason why the joinder of pendent defendants over whom there is no other basis of federal jurisdiction should differ from the joinder of pendent claims and other pendent parties, I fear that its approach will confuse more than it clarifies. How much more clear to assume—especially when the courts have long so held—that with respect to all of these situations Congress intended the Federal Rules to govern unless Congress has indicated otherwise.

The Court's focus on diversity cases may explain why it also loses sight of the purpose behind the principle of pendent jurisdiction. The doctrine of pendent jurisdiction rests in part on a recognition that forcing a federal plaintiff to litigate his or her case in both federal and state courts impairs the ability of the federal court to grant full relief, and "imparts a fundamental bias against utilization of the federal forum owing to the deterrent effect imposed by the needless requirement of duplicate litigation if the federal forum is chosen." *Aldinger.* "The courts, by recognizing pendent jurisdiction, are effectuating Congress' decision to provide the plaintiff with a federal forum for litigating a jurisdictionally sufficient claim." This is especially the case when, by virtue of the grant of exclusive federal jurisdiction, *"only* in a federal court may all of the claims be tried together." *Aldinger*. In such circumstances, in which Congress has unequivocally indicated its intent that the federal right be litigated in a federal forum, there is reason to believe that Congress did not intend that the substance of the federal right be diminished by the increased costs in efficiency and convenience of litigation in two forums. No such special federal interest is present when federal jurisdiction is invoked on the basis of the diverse citizenship of the parties and the state-law claims may be litigated in a state forum. To be sure "[w]hatever we say regarding the scope of jurisdiction conferred by a particular statute can ... be changed by Congress" but that does not relieve us of our responsibility to be faithful to the congressional design. The Court is quite incorrect to presume that because Congress did not sanction the exercise of pendent-party jurisdiction in the diversity context, it has not permitted its exercise with respect to claims within the exclusive federal jurisdiction.

* * *

Today we should be guided by the wisdom of Cardozo and Friendly rather than by the "unnecessarily grudging" approach that was unanimously rebuffed in *Gibbs*.

I respectfully dissent.

D.   SUPPLEMENTAL JURISDICTION— COMMON LAW PRINCIPLES

ANCILLARY JURISDICTION

FEDERAL RULE OF CIVIL PROCEDURE 14. THIRD–PARTY PRACTICE

(a)   When a Defending Party May Bring in a Third Party.

   (1)   *Timing of the Summons and Complaint.* A defending party may, as third-party plaintiff, serve a summons and complaint on a nonparty who is or may be liable to it for all or part of the claim against it. But the third-party plaintiff must, by motion, obtain the court's leave if it files the third-party complaint more than 14 days after serving its original answer.

   (2)   *Third-Party Defendant's Claims and Defenses.* The person served with the summons and third-party complaint—the "third-party defendant":

   (A) must assert any defense against the third-party plaintiff's claim under Rule 12;

   (B) must assert any counterclaim against the third-party plaintiff under Rule 13(a), and may assert any counterclaim against the third-party plaintiff under Rule 13(b) or any cross-claim against another third-party defendant under Rule 13(g);

(C) may assert against the plaintiff any defense that the third-party plaintiff has to the plaintiff's claim; and

(D) may also assert against the plaintiff any claim arising out of the transaction or occurrence that is the subject matter of the plaintiff's claim against the third-party plaintiff.

(3) *Plaintiff's Claims Against a Third–Party Defendant.* The plaintiff may assert against the third-party defendant any claim arising out of the transaction or occurrence that is the subject matter of the plaintiff's claim against the third-party plaintiff. The third-party defendant must then assert any defense under Rule 12 and any counterclaim under Rule 13(a), and may assert any counterclaim under Rule 13(b) or any cross-claim under Rule 13(g).

(4) *Motion to Strike, Sever, or Try Separately.* Any party may move to strike the third-party claim, to sever it, or to try it separately.

(5) *Third-Party Defendant's Claim Against a Nonparty.* A third-party defendant may proceed under this rule against a nonparty who is or may be liable to the third-party defendant for all or part of any claim against it.

* * *

OWEN EQUIPMENT AND ERECTION COMPANY v. KROGER

437 U.S. 365 (1978)

MR. JUSTICE STEWART delivered the opinion of the Court.

In an action in which federal jurisdiction is based on diversity of citizenship, may the plaintiff assert a claim against a third-party defendant when there is no independent basis for federal jurisdiction over that claim? The Court of Appeals for the Eighth Circuit held in this case that such a claim is within the ancillary jurisdiction of the federal courts. We granted certiorari, because this decision conflicts with several recent decisions of other Courts of Appeals.

I

On January 18, 1972, James Kroger was electrocuted when the boom of a steel crane next to which he was walking came too close to a high-tension electric power line. The respondent (his widow, who is the administratrix of his estate) filed a wrongful-death action in the United States District Court for the District of Nebraska against the Omaha Public Power District (OPPD). Her complaint alleged that OPPD's negligent construction, maintenance, and operation of the power line had caused

Kroger's death. Federal jurisdiction was based on diversity of citizenship, since the respondent was a citizen of Iowa and OPPD was a Nebraska corporation.

OPPD then filed a third-party complaint pursuant to Fed. Rule Civ. Proc. 14(a) against the petitioner, Owen Equipment and Erection Co. (Owen), alleging that the crane was owned and operated by Owen, and that Owen's negligence had been the proximate cause of Kroger's death.[3] OPPD later moved for summary judgment on the respondent's complaint against it. While this motion was pending, the respondent was granted leave to file an amended complaint naming Owen as an additional defendant. Thereafter, the District Court granted OPPD's motion for summary judgment in an unreported opinion. The case thus went to trial between the respondent and the petitioner alone.

The respondent's amended complaint alleged that Owen was "a Nebraska corporation with its principal place of business in Nebraska." Owen's answer admitted that it was "a corporation organized and existing under the laws of the State of Nebraska," and denied every other allegation of the complaint. On the third day of trial, however, it was disclosed that the petitioner's principal place of business was in Iowa, not Nebraska,[5] and that the petitioner and the respondent were thus both citizens of Iowa. The petitioner then moved to dismiss the complaint for lack of jurisdiction. The District Court reserved decision on the motion, and the jury thereafter returned a verdict in favor of the respondent. In an unreported opinion issued after the trial, the District Court denied the petitioner's motion to dismiss the complaint.

The judgment was affirmed on appeal. The Court of Appeals held that under this Court's decision in *Mine Workers v. Gibbs*, the District Court had jurisdictional power, in its discretion, to adjudicate the respondent's claim against the petitioner because that claim arose from the "core of 'operative facts' giving rise to both [respondent's] claim against OPPD and OPPD's claim against Owen." It further held that the District Court had properly exercised its discretion in proceeding to decide the case even after summary judgment had been granted to OPPD, because the petitioner had concealed its Iowa citizenship from the respondent. Rehearing en banc was denied by an equally divided court.

II

It is undisputed that there was no independent basis of federal jurisdiction over the respondent's state-law tort action against the peti-

---

3. Under Rule 14(a), a third-party defendant may not be impleaded merely because he may be liable to the *plaintiff*. While the third-party complaint in this case alleged merely that Owen's negligence caused Kroger's death, and the basis of Owen's alleged liability to OPPD is nowhere spelled out, OPPD evidently relied upon the state common-law right of contribution among joint tortfeasors. The petitioner has never challenged the propriety of the third-party complaint as such.

5. The problem apparently was one of geography. Although the Missouri River generally marks the boundary between Iowa and Nebraska, Carter Lake, Iowa, where the accident occurred and where Owen had its main office, lies west of the river, adjacent to Omaha, Neb. Apparently the river once avulsed at one of its bends, cutting Carter Lake off from the rest of Iowa.

tioner, since both are citizens of Iowa. And although Fed. Rule Civ. Proc. 14(a) permits a plaintiff to assert a claim against a third-party defendant, it does not purport to say whether or not such a claim requires an independent basis of federal jurisdiction. Indeed, it could not determine that question, since it is axiomatic that the Federal Rules of Civil Procedure do not create or withdraw federal jurisdiction.

In affirming the District Court's judgment, the Court of Appeals relied upon the doctrine of ancillary jurisdiction, whose contours it believed were defined by this Court's holding in *Mine Workers v. Gibbs*. The *Gibbs* case differed from this one in that it involved pendent jurisdiction, which concerns the resolution of a plaintiff's federal- and state-law claims against a single defendant in one action. By contrast, in this case there was no claim based upon substantive federal law, but rather state-law tort claims against two different defendants. Nonetheless, the Court of Appeals was correct in perceiving that *Gibbs* and this case are two species of the same generic problem: Under what circumstances may a federal court hear and decide a state-law claim arising between citizens of the same State? But we believe that the Court of Appeals failed to understand the scope of the doctrine of the *Gibbs* case.

The plaintiff in *Gibbs* alleged that the defendant union had violated the common law of Tennessee as well as the federal prohibition of secondary boycotts. This Court held that, although the parties were not of diverse citizenship, the District Court properly entertained the state-law claim as pendent to the federal claim. The crucial holding was stated as follows:

> "Pendent jurisdiction, in the sense of judicial *power*, exists whenever there is a claim 'arising under [the] Constitution, the Laws of the United States, and Treaties made, or which shall be made, under their Authority ...,' U.S. Const., Art. III, § 2, and the relationship between that claim and the state claim permits the conclusion that the entire action before the court comprises but one constitutional 'case.' ... The state and federal claims must derive from a common nucleus of operative fact. But if, considered without regard to their federal or state character, a plaintiff's claims are such that he would ordinarily be expected to try them all in one judicial proceeding, then, assuming substantiality of the federal issues, there is *power* in federal courts to hear the whole."

It is apparent that *Gibbs* delineated the constitutional limits of federal judicial power. But even if it be assumed that the District Court in the present case had constitutional power to decide the respondent's lawsuit against the petitioner, it does not follow that the decision of the Court of Appeals was correct. Constitutional power is merely the first hurdle that must be overcome in determining that a federal court has jurisdiction over a particular controversy. For the jurisdiction of the federal courts is limited not only by the provisions of Art. III of the Constitution, but also by Acts of Congress.

That statutory law as well as the Constitution may limit a federal court's jurisdiction over nonfederal claims[11] is well illustrated by two recent decisions of this Court, *Aldinger v. Howard*, and *Zahn v. International Paper Co.* In *Aldinger* the Court held that a Federal District Court lacked jurisdiction over a state-law claim against a county, even if that claim was alleged to be pendent to one against county officials under 42 U.S.C. § 1983. In *Zahn* the Court held that in a diversity class action under Fed. Rule Civ. Proc. 23(b)(3), the claim of each member of the plaintiff class must independently satisfy the minimum jurisdictional amount set by 28 U.S.C. § 1332(a), and rejected the argument that jurisdiction existed over those claims that involved $10,000 or less as ancillary to those that involved more. In each case, despite the fact that federal and nonfederal claims arose from a "common nucleus of operative fact," the Court held that the statute conferring jurisdiction over the federal claim did not allow the exercise of jurisdiction over the nonfederal claim.

The *Aldinger* and *Zahn* cases thus make clear that a finding that federal and nonfederal claims arise from a "common nucleus of operative fact," the test of *Gibbs*, does not end the inquiry into whether a federal court has power to hear the nonfederal claims along with the federal ones. Beyond this constitutional minimum, there must be an examination of the posture in which the nonfederal claim is asserted and of the specific statute that confers jurisdiction over the federal claim, in order to determine whether "Congress in [that statute] has ... expressly or by implication negated" the exercise of jurisdiction over the particular nonfederal claim. *Aldinger v. Howard.*

III

The relevant statute in this case, 28 U.S.C. § 1332(a)(1), confers upon federal courts jurisdiction over "civil actions where the matter in controversy exceeds the sum or value of $10,000 ... and is between ... citizens of different States." This statute and its predecessors have consistently been held to require complete diversity of citizenship. That is, diversity jurisdiction does not exist unless *each* defendant is a citizen of a different State from *each* plaintiff. Over the years Congress has repeatedly re-enacted or amended the statute conferring diversity jurisdiction, leaving intact this rule of complete diversity. Whatever may have been the original purposes of diversity-of-citizenship jurisdiction, this subsequent history clearly demonstrates a congressional mandate that diversity jurisdiction is not to be available when any plaintiff is a citizen of the same State as any defendant.

Thus it is clear that the respondent could not originally have brought suit in federal court naming Owen and OPPD as codefendants, since citizens of Iowa would have been on both sides of the litigation. Yet the

---

11. As used in this opinion, the term "nonfederal claim" means one as to which there is no independent basis for federal jurisdiction. Conversely, a "federal claim" means one as to which an independent basis for federal jurisdiction exists.

identical lawsuit resulted when she amended her complaint. Complete diversity was destroyed just as surely as if she had sued Owen initially. In either situation, in the plain language of the statute, the "matter in controversy" could not be "between ... citizens of different States."

It is a fundamental precept that federal courts are courts of limited jurisdiction. The limits upon federal jurisdiction, whether imposed by the Constitution or by Congress, must be neither disregarded nor evaded. Yet under the reasoning of the Court of Appeals in this case, a plaintiff could defeat the statutory requirement of complete diversity by the simple expedient of suing only those defendants who were of diverse citizenship and waiting for them to implead non-diverse defendants.[17] If, as the Court of Appeals thought, a "common nucleus of operative fact" were the only requirement for ancillary jurisdiction in a diversity case, there would be no principled reason why the respondent in this case could not have joined her cause of action against Owen in her original complaint as ancillary to her claim against OPPD. Congress' requirement of complete diversity would thus have been evaded completely.

It is true, as the Court of Appeals noted, that the exercise of ancillary jurisdiction over nonfederal claims has often been upheld in situations involving impleader, cross-claims or counterclaims. But in determining whether jurisdiction over a nonfederal claim exists, the context in which the nonfederal claim is asserted is crucial. *See Aldinger v. Howard.* And the claim here arises in a setting quite different from the kinds of nonfederal claims that have been viewed in other cases as falling within the ancillary jurisdiction of the federal courts.

First, the nonfederal claim in this case was simply not ancillary to the federal one in the same sense that, for example, the impleader by a defendant of a third-party defendant always is. A third-party complaint depends at least in part upon the resolution of the primary lawsuit. Its relation to the original complaint is thus not mere factual similarity but logical dependence. The respondent's claim against the petitioner, however, was entirely separate from her original claim against OPPD, since the petitioner's liability to her depended not at all upon whether or not OPPD was also liable. Far from being an ancillary and dependent claim, it was a new and independent one.

Second, the nonfederal claim here was asserted by the plaintiff, who voluntarily chose to bring suit upon a state-law claim in a federal court. By contrast, ancillary jurisdiction typically involves claims by a defending party haled into court against his will, or by another person whose rights might be irretrievably lost unless he could assert them in an ongoing

---

17. This is not an unlikely hypothesis, since a defendant in a tort suit such as this one would surely try to limit his liability by impleading any joint tortfeasors for indemnity or contribution. Some commentators have suggested that the possible abuse of third-party practice could be dealt with under 28 U.S.C. § 1359, which forbids collusive attempts to create federal jurisdiction. The dissenting opinion today also expresses this view. But there is nothing necessarily collusive about a plaintiff's selectively suing only those tortfeasors of diverse citizenship, or about the named defendants' desire to implead joint tortfeasors. Nonetheless, the requirement of complete diversity would be eviscerated by such a course of events.

action in a federal court. A plaintiff cannot complain if ancillary jurisdiction does not encompass all of his possible claims in a case such as this one, since it is he who has chosen the federal rather than the state forum and must thus accept its limitations. "[T]he efficiency plaintiff seeks so avidly is available without question in the state courts."[20]

It is not unreasonable to assume that, in generally requiring complete diversity, Congress did not intend to confine the jurisdiction of federal courts so inflexibly that they are unable to protect legal rights or effectively to resolve an entire, logically entwined lawsuit. Those practical needs are the basis of the doctrine of ancillary jurisdiction. But neither the convenience of litigants nor considerations of judicial economy can suffice to justify extension of the doctrine of ancillary jurisdiction to a plaintiff's cause of action against a citizen of the same State in a diversity case. Congress has established the basic rule that diversity jurisdiction exists under 28 U.S.C. § 1332 only when there is complete diversity of citizenship. "The policy of the statute calls for its strict construction." To allow the requirement of complete diversity to be circumvented as it was in this case would simply flout the congressional command.

Accordingly, the judgment of the Court of Appeals is reversed.

It is so ordered.

Mr. Justice White, with whom Mr. Justice Brennan joins, dissenting.

The Court today states that "[i]t is not unreasonable to assume that, in generally requiring complete diversity, Congress did not intend to confine the jurisdiction of federal courts so inflexibly that they are unable . . . effectively to resolve an entire, logically entwined lawsuit." In spite of this recognition, the majority goes on to hold that in diversity suits federal courts do not have the jurisdictional power to entertain a claim asserted by a plaintiff against a third-party defendant, no matter how entwined it is with the matter already before the court, unless there is an independent basis for jurisdiction over that claim. Because I find no support for such a requirement in either Art. III of the Constitution or in any statutory law, I dissent from the Court's "unnecessarily grudging" approach.

The plaintiff below, Mrs. Kroger, chose to bring her lawsuit against the Omaha Public Power District (OPPD) in Federal District Court. No one questions the power of the District Court to entertain this claim, for Mrs. Kroger at the time was a citizen of Iowa, OPPD was a citizen of Nebraska, and the amount in controversy was greater than $10,000; jurisdiction therefore existed under 28 U.S.C. § 1332(a). As permitted by Fed. Rule Civ. Proc. 14(a), OPPD impleaded petitioner Owen Equipment & Erection Co. (Owen). Although OPPD's claim against Owen did not raise a federal question and although it was alleged that Owen was a citizen of the same State as OPPD, the parties and the court apparently believed that the District Court's ancillary jurisdiction encompassed this claim. Subsequently, Mrs. Kroger asserted a claim against Owen, everyone

---

20. Whether Iowa's statute of limitations would now bar an action by the respondent in an Iowa court is, of course, entirely a matter of state law.

believing at the time that these two parties were citizens of different States. Because it later came to light that Mrs. Kroger and Owen were in fact both citizens of Iowa, the Court concludes that the District Court lacked jurisdiction over the claim.

In *Mine Workers v. Gibbs*, we held that once a claim has been stated that is of sufficient substance to confer subject-matter jurisdiction on the federal district court, the court has judicial power to consider a nonfederal claim if it and the federal claim are derived from "a common nucleus of operative fact." Although the specific facts of that case concerned a state claim that was said to be pendent to a federal-question claim, the Court's language and reasoning were broad enough to cover the instant factual situation: "[I]f, considered without regard to their federal or state character, a plaintiff's claims are such that he would ordinarily be expected to try them all in one judicial proceeding, then, assuming substantiality of the federal issues, there is *power* in federal courts to hear the whole." In the present case, Mrs. Kroger's claim against Owen and her claim against OPPD derived from a common nucleus of fact; this is necessarily so because in order for a plaintiff to assert a claim against a third-party defendant, Fed. Rule Civ. Proc. 14(a) requires that it "aris[e] out of the transaction or occurrence that is the subject matter of the plaintiff's claim against the third-party plaintiff...." Furthermore, the substantiality of the claim Mrs. Kroger asserted against OPPD is unquestioned. Accordingly, as far as Art. III of the Constitution is concerned, the District Court had power to entertain Mrs. Kroger's claim against Owen.

The majority correctly points out, however, that the analysis cannot stop here. As *Aldinger v. Howard* teaches, the jurisdictional power of the federal courts may be limited by Congress, as well as by the Constitution. In *Aldinger*, although the plaintiff's state claim against Spokane County was closely connected with her 42 U.S.C. § 1983 claim against the county treasurer, the Court held that the District Court did not have pendent jurisdiction over the state claim, for, under the Court's precedents at that time, it was thought that Congress had specifically determined not to confer on the federal courts jurisdiction over civil rights claims against cities and counties. That being so, the Court refused to allow "the federal courts to fashion a jurisdictional doctrine under the general language of Art. III enabling them to circumvent this exclusion...."[3]

In the present case, the only indication of congressional intent that the Court can find is that contained in the diversity jurisdictional statute, 28 U.S.C. § 1332(a), which states that "district courts shall have original jurisdiction of all civil actions where the matter in controversy exceeds the sum or value of $10,000 ... and is between ... citizens of different States...." Because this statute has been interpreted as requiring com-

---

3. We were careful in *Aldinger* to point out the limited nature of our holding:

There are, of course, many variations in the language which Congress has employed to confer jurisdiction upon the federal courts, and we decide here only the issue of so-called "pendent party" jurisdiction with respect to a claim brought under §§ 1343(3) and 1983. Other statutory grants and other alignments of parties and claims might call for a different result.

plete diversity of citizenship between each plaintiff and each defendant, *Strawbridge v. Curtiss,* the Court holds that the District Court did not have ancillary jurisdiction over Mrs. Kroger's claim against Owen. In so holding, the Court unnecessarily expands the scope of the complete-diversity requirement while substantially limiting the doctrine of ancillary jurisdiction.

The complete-diversity requirement, of course, could be viewed as meaning that in a diversity case, a federal district court may adjudicate only those claims that are between parties of different States. Thus, in order for a defendant to implead a third-party defendant, there would have to be diversity of citizenship; the same would also be true for cross-claims between defendants and for a third-party defendant's claim against a plaintiff. Even the majority, however, refuses to read the complete-diversity requirement so broadly; it recognizes with seeming approval the exercise of ancillary jurisdiction over nonfederal claims in situations involving impleader, cross-claims, and counterclaims. Given the Court's willingness to recognize ancillary jurisdiction in these contexts, despite the requirements of § 1332(a), I see no justification for the Court's refusal to approve the District Court's exercise of ancillary jurisdiction in the present case.

It is significant that a plaintiff who asserts a claim against a third-party defendant is not seeking to add a new party to the lawsuit. In the present case, for example, Owen had already been brought into the suit by OPPD, and, that having been done, Mrs. Kroger merely sought to assert against Owen a claim arising out of the same transaction that was already before the court. Thus the situation presented here is unlike that in *Aldinger,* wherein the Court noted:

> [I]t is one thing to authorize two parties, already present in federal court by virtue of a case over which the court has jurisdiction, to litigate in addition to their federal claim a state-law claim over which there is no independent basis of federal jurisdiction. But it is quite another thing to permit a plaintiff, who has asserted a claim against one defendant with respect to which there is federal jurisdiction, to join an entirely different defendant on the basis of a state-law claim over which there is no independent basis of federal jurisdiction, simply because his claim against the first defendant and his claim against the second defendant "derive from a common nucleus of operative fact." . . . True, the same considerations of judicial economy would be served insofar as plaintiff's claims "are such that he would ordinarily be expected to try them all in one judicial proceeding. . . ." [*Gibbs*]. But the addition of a completely new party would run counter to the well-established principle that federal courts, as opposed to state trial courts of general jurisdiction, are courts of limited jurisdiction marked out by Congress.

Because in the instant case Mrs. Kroger merely sought to assert a claim against someone already a party to the suit, considerations of judicial economy, convenience, and fairness to the litigants—the factors relied upon in *Gibbs*—support the recognition of ancillary jurisdiction here. Already before the court was the whole question of the cause of Mr. Kroger's death. Mrs. Kroger initially contended that OPPD was responsible; OPPD in turn contended that Owen's negligence had been the proximate cause of Mr. Kroger's death. In spite of the fact that the question of Owen's negligence was already before the District Court, the majority requires Mrs. Kroger to bring a separate action in state court in order to assert that very claim. Even if the Iowa statute of limitations will still permit such a suit, considerations of judicial economy are certainly not served by requiring such duplicative litigation.[4]

The majority, however, brushes aside such considerations of convenience, judicial economy, and fairness because it concludes that recognizing ancillary jurisdiction over a plaintiff's claim against a third-party defendant would permit the plaintiff to circumvent the complete-diversity requirement and thereby "flout the congressional command." Since the plaintiff in such a case does not bring the third-party defendant into the suit, however, there is no occasion for deliberate circumvention of the diversity requirement, absent collusion with the defendant. In the case of such collusion, of which there is absolutely no indication here,[5] the court can dismiss the action under the authority of 28 U.S.C. § 1359.[6] In the absence of such collusion, there is no reason to adopt an absolute rule prohibiting the plaintiff from asserting those claims that he may properly assert against the third-party defendant pursuant to Fed. Rule Civ. Proc. 14(a). The plaintiff in such a situation brings suit against the defendant only with absolutely no assurance that the defendant will decide or be able to implead a particular third-party defendant. Since the plaintiff has no control over the defendant's decision to implead a third party, the fact that he could not have originally sued that party in federal court should be irrelevant. Moreover, the fact that a plaintiff in some cases may be able to foresee the subsequent chain of events leading to the impleader does not seem to me to be a sufficient reason to declare that a district court does not have the *power* to exercise ancillary jurisdiction over the plaintiff's claims against the third-party defendant.[7]

---

4. It is true that prior to trial OPPD was dismissed as a party to the suit and that, as we indicated in *Gibbs*, the dismissal prior to trial of the federal claim will generally require the dismissal of the nonfederal claim as well. Given the unusual facts of the present case, however—in particular, the fact that the actual location of Owen's principal place of business was not revealed until the third day of trial—fairness to the parties would lead me to conclude that the District Court did not abuse its discretion in retaining jurisdiction over Mrs. Kroger's claim against Owen. Under the Court's disposition, of course, it would not matter whether or not the federal claim is tried, for in either situation the court would have no jurisdiction over the plaintiff's nonfederal claim against the third-party defendant.

5. When Mrs. Kroger brought suit, it was believed that Owen was a citizen of Nebraska, not Iowa. Therefore, had she desired at that time to make Owen a party to the suit, she would have done so directly by naming Owen as a defendant.

6. Section 1359 states: "A district court shall not have jurisdiction of a civil action in which any party, by assignment or otherwise, has been improperly or collusively made or joined to invoke the jurisdiction of such court."

7. Under the *Gibbs* analysis, recognition of the district court's power to hear a plaintiff's nonfederal claim against a third-party defendant in a diversity suit would not mean that the court

We have previously noted that "[s]ubsequent decisions of this Court indicate that *Strawbridge* is not to be given an expansive reading." In light of this teaching, it seems to me appropriate to view § 1332 as requiring complete diversity only between the plaintiff and those parties he actually brings into the suit. Beyond that, I would hold that in a diversity case the District Court has power, both constitutional and statutory, to entertain all claims among the parties arising from the same nucleus of operative fact as the plaintiff's original, jurisdiction-conferring claim against the defendant. Accordingly, I dissent from the Court's disposition of the present case.

---

would be required to entertain such claims in all cases. The district court would have the discretion to dismiss the nonfederal claim if it concluded that the interests of judicial economy, convenience, and fairness would not be served by the retention of the claim in the federal lawsuit. See *Gibbs*. Accordingly, the majority's concerns that lead it to conclude that ancillary jurisdiction should not be recognized in the present situation could be met on a case-by-case basis, rather than by the absolute rule it adopts.

VII. CHOOSING THE FORUM—SUPPLEMENTAL JURISDICTION, REMOVAL, VENUE

A. THE SUPPLEMENTAL JURISDICTION STATUTE

28 U.S.C. § 1367. SUPPLEMENTAL JURISDICTION

(a) Except as provided in subsections (b) and (c) or as expressly provided otherwise by Federal statute, in any civil action of which the district courts have original jurisdiction, the district courts shall have supplemental jurisdiction over all other claims that are so related to claims in the action within such original jurisdiction that they form part of the same case or controversy under Article III of the United States Constitution. Such supplemental jurisdiction shall include claims that involve the joinder or intervention of additional parties.

(b) In any civil action of which the district courts have original jurisdiction founded solely on section 1332 of this title, the district courts shall not have supplemental jurisdiction under subsection (a) over claims by plaintiffs against persons made parties under Rule 14, 19, 20, or 24 of the Federal Rules of Civil Procedure, or over claims by persons proposed to be joined as plaintiffs under Rule 19 of such rules, or seeking to intervene as plaintiffs under Rule 24 of such rules, when exercising supplemental jurisdiction over such claims would be inconsistent with the jurisdictional requirements of section 1332.

(c) The district courts may decline to exercise supplemental jurisdiction over a claim under subsection (a) if—

    (1) the claim raises a novel or complex issue of State law,

    (2) the claim substantially predominates over the claim or claims over which the district court has original jurisdiction,

    (3) the district court has dismissed all claims over which it has original jurisdiction, or

    (4) in exceptional circumstances, there are other compelling reasons for declining jurisdiction.

(d) The period of limitations for any claim asserted under subsection (a), and for any other claim in the same action that is voluntarily dismissed at the same time as or after the dismissal of the claim under subsection (a), shall be tolled while the claim is pending and for a period of 30 days after it is dismissed unless State law provides for a longer tolling period.

(e) As used in this section, the term "State" includes the District of Columbia, the Commonwealth of Puerto Rico, and any territory or possession of the United States.

EXXON MOBIL CORPORATION v. ALLAPATTAH SERVICES, INC.

545 U.S. 546 (2005)

JUSTICE KENNEDY delivered the opinion of the Court.

These consolidated cases present the question whether a federal court in a diversity action may exercise supplemental jurisdiction over additional plaintiffs whose claims do not satisfy the minimum amount-in-controversy requirement, provided the claims are part of the same case or controversy as the claims of plaintiffs who do allege a sufficient amount in controversy. Our decision turns on the correct interpretation of 28 U.S.C. § 1367. The question has divided the Courts of Appeals, and we granted certiorari to resolve the conflict.

We hold that, where the other elements of jurisdiction are present and at least one named plaintiff in the action satisfies the amount-in-controversy requirement, § 1367 does authorize supplemental jurisdiction over the claims of other plaintiffs in the same Article III case or controversy, even if those claims are for less than the jurisdictional amount specified in the statute setting forth the requirements for diversity jurisdiction. We affirm the judgment of the Court of Appeals for the Eleventh Circuit, and we reverse the judgment of the Court of Appeals for the First Circuit.

I

In 1991, about 10,000 Exxon dealers filed a class-action suit against the Exxon Corporation in the United States District Court for the Northern District of Florida. The dealers alleged an intentional and systematic scheme by Exxon under which they were overcharged for fuel purchased from Exxon. The plaintiffs invoked the District Court's § 1332(a) diversity jurisdiction. After a unanimous jury verdict in favor of the plaintiffs, the District Court certified the case for interlocutory review, asking whether it had properly exercised § 1367 supplemental jurisdiction over the claims of class members who did not meet the jurisdictional minimum amount in controversy.

The Court of Appeals for the Eleventh Circuit upheld the District Court's extension of supplemental jurisdiction to these class members. "[W]e find," the court held, "that § 1367 clearly and unambiguously provides district courts with the authority in diversity class actions to exercise supplemental jurisdiction over the claims of class members who do not meet the minimum amount in controversy as long as the district court has original jurisdiction over the claims of at least one of the class representatives." This decision accords with the views of the Courts of Appeals for the Fourth, Sixth, and Seventh Circuits. The Courts of Appeals for the Fifth and Ninth Circuits, adopting a similar analysis of the statute, have held that in a diversity class action the unnamed class members need not meet the amount-in-controversy requirement, provided the named class members do. These decisions, however, are unclear on whether all the named plaintiffs must satisfy this requirement.

In the other case now before us the Court of Appeals for the First Circuit took a different position on the meaning of § 1367(a). In that case, a 9-year-old girl sued Star–Kist in a diversity action in the United States District Court for the District of Puerto Rico, seeking damages for unusually severe injuries she received when she sliced her finger on a tuna can. Her family joined in the suit, seeking damages for emotional distress and certain medical expenses. The District Court granted summary judgment to Star–Kist, finding that none of the plaintiffs met the minimum amount-in-controversy requirement. The Court of Appeals for the First Circuit, however, ruled that the injured girl, but not her family members, had made allegations of damages in the requisite amount.

The Court of Appeals then addressed whether, in light of the fact that one plaintiff met the requirements for original jurisdiction, supplemental jurisdiction over the remaining plaintiffs' claims was proper under § 1367. The court held that § 1367 authorizes supplemental jurisdiction only when the district court has original jurisdiction over the action, and that in a diversity case original jurisdiction is lacking if one plaintiff fails to satisfy the amount-in-controversy requirement. Although the Court of Appeals claimed to "express no view" on whether the result would be the same in a class action, its analysis is inconsistent with that of the Court of Appeals for the Eleventh Circuit. The Court of Appeals for the First Circuit's view of § 1367 is, however, shared by the Courts of Appeals for the Third, Eighth, and Tenth Circuits, and the latter two Courts of Appeals have expressly applied this rule to class actions.

II

A

The district courts of the United States, as we have said many times, are "courts of limited jurisdiction. They possess only that power authorized by Constitution and statute." In order to provide a federal forum for plaintiffs who seek to vindicate federal rights, Congress has conferred on the district courts original jurisdiction in federal-question cases—civil actions that arise under the Constitution, laws, or treaties of the United States. 28 U.S.C. § 1331. In order to provide a neutral forum for what have come to be known as diversity cases, Congress also has granted district courts original jurisdiction in civil actions between citizens of different States, between U.S. citizens and foreign citizens, or by foreign states against U.S. citizens. § 1332. To ensure that diversity jurisdiction does not flood the federal courts with minor disputes, § 1332(a) requires that the matter in controversy in a diversity case exceed a specified amount, currently $75,000.

Although the district courts may not exercise jurisdiction absent a statutory basis, it is well established—in certain classes of cases—that, once a court has original jurisdiction over some claims in the action, it may exercise supplemental jurisdiction over additional claims that are part of the same case or controversy. The leading modern case for this principle is *Mine Workers v. Gibbs*. In *Gibbs,* the plaintiff alleged the defendant's conduct violated both federal and state law. The District Court, *Gibbs* held, had original jurisdiction over the action based on the federal claims. *Gibbs* confirmed that the District Court had the additional power (though not the obligation) to exercise supplemental jurisdiction over related state claims that arose from the same Article III case or controversy. ("The federal claim must have substance sufficient to confer subject matter jurisdiction on the court.... [A]ssuming substantiality of the federal issues, there is *power* in federal courts to hear the whole").

As we later noted, the decision allowing jurisdiction over pendent state claims in *Gibbs* did not mention, let alone come to grips with, the text of the jurisdictional statutes and the bedrock principle that federal courts have no jurisdiction without statutory authorization. *Finley v. United States*. In *Finley,* we nonetheless reaffirmed and rationalized *Gibbs* and its progeny by inferring from it the interpretive principle that, in cases involving supplemental jurisdiction over additional claims between parties properly in federal court, the jurisdictional statutes should be read broadly, on the assumption that in this context Congress intended to authorize courts to exercise their full Article III power to dispose of an " 'entire action before the court [which] comprises but one constitutional "case." ' "

We have not, however, applied *Gibbs'* expansive interpretive approach to other aspects of the jurisdictional statutes. For instance, we have consistently interpreted § 1332 as requiring complete diversity: In a case with multiple plaintiffs and multiple defendants, the presence in the action of a single plaintiff from the same State as a single defendant deprives the district court of original diversity jurisdiction over the entire action. *Strawbridge v. Curtiss*; *Owen Equipment & Erection Co. v. Kroger*. The complete diversity requirement is not mandated by the Constitution, or by the plain text of § 1332(a). The Court, nonetheless, has adhered to the complete diversity rule in light of the purpose of the diversity requirement, which is to provide a federal forum for important disputes where state courts might favor, or be perceived as favoring, home-state litigants. The presence of parties from the same State on both sides of a case dispels this concern, eliminating a principal reason for conferring § 1332 jurisdiction over any of the claims in the action. The specific purpose of the complete diversity rule explains both why we have not adopted *Gibbs'* expansive interpretive approach to this aspect of the jurisdictional statute and why *Gibbs* does not undermine the complete diversity rule. In order for a federal court to invoke supplemental jurisdiction under *Gibbs,* it must first have original jurisdiction over at least one claim in the action. Incomplete diversity destroys original jurisdiction with respect to all claims, so there is nothing to which supplemental jurisdiction can adhere.

In contrast to the diversity requirement, most of the other statutory prerequisites for federal jurisdiction, including the federal-question and amount-in-controversy requirements, can be analyzed claim by claim. True, it does not follow by necessity from this that a district court has authority to exercise supplemental jurisdiction over all claims provided there is original jurisdiction over just one. Before the enactment of § 1367, the Court declined in contexts other than the pendent-claim instance to follow *Gibbs'* expansive approach to interpretation of the jurisdictional statutes. The Court took a more restrictive view of the proper interpretation of these statutes in so-called pendent-party cases involving supplemental jurisdiction over claims involving additional parties-plaintiffs or defendants-where the district courts would lack original jurisdiction over claims by each of the parties standing alone.

Thus, with respect to plaintiff-specific jurisdictional requirements, the Court held in *Clark v. Paul Gray, Inc.* that every plaintiff must separately satisfy the amount-in-controversy requirement. Though *Clark* was a federal-question case, at that time federal-question jurisdiction had an amount-in-controversy requirement analogous to the amount-in-controversy requirement for diversity cases. "Proper practice," *Clark* held, "requires that where each of several plaintiffs is bound to establish the jurisdictional amount with respect to his own claim, the suit should be dismissed as to those who fail to show that the requisite amount is involved." The Court reaffirmed this rule, in the context of a class action brought invoking § 1332(a) diversity jurisdiction, in *Zahn v. International Paper Co.,* 414 U.S. 291 (1973). It follows "inescapably" from *Clark,* the Court held in *Zahn,* that "any plaintiff without the jurisdictional amount must be dismissed from the case, even though others allege jurisdictionally sufficient claims."

The Court took a similar approach with respect to supplemental jurisdiction over claims against additional defendants that fall outside the district courts' original jurisdiction. In *Aldinger v. Howard,* the plaintiff brought a 42 U.S.C. § 1983 action against county officials in District Court pursuant to the statutory grant of jurisdiction in 28 U.S.C. § 1343(3). The plaintiff further alleged the court had supplemental jurisdiction over her related state-law claims against the county, even though the county was not suable under § 1983 and so was not subject to § 1343(3)'s original jurisdiction. The Court held that supplemental jurisdiction could not be exercised because Congress, in enacting § 1343(3), had declined (albeit implicitly) to extend federal jurisdiction over any party who could not be sued under the federal civil rights statutes. "Before it can be concluded that [supplemental] jurisdiction [over additional parties] exists," *Aldinger* held, "a federal court must satisfy itself not only that Art[icle] III permits it, but that Congress in the statutes conferring jurisdiction has not expressly or by implication negated its existence."

In *Finley v. United States,* we confronted a similar issue in a different statutory context. * * * We held that the District Court lacked a sufficient statutory basis for exercising supplemental jurisdiction over these claims. Relying primarily on *Zahn, Aldinger,* and *Kroger,* we held in *Finley* that "a grant of jurisdiction over claims involving particular parties does not itself confer jurisdiction over additional claims by or against different parties." While *Finley* did not "limit or impair" *Gibbs'* liberal approach to interpreting the jurisdictional statutes in the context of supplemental jurisdiction over additional claims involving the same parties, *Finley* nevertheless declined to extend that interpretive assumption to claims involving additional parties. *Finley* held that in the context of parties, in contrast to claims, "we will not assume that the full constitutional power has been congressionally authorized, and will not read jurisdictional statutes broadly."

As the jurisdictional statutes existed in 1989, then, here is how matters stood: First, the diversity requirement in § 1332(a) required complete diversity; absent complete diversity, the district court lacked original jurisdiction over all of the claims in the action. *Strawbridge*; *Kroger*. Second, if the district court had original jurisdiction over at least one claim, the jurisdictional statutes implicitly authorized supplemental jurisdiction over all other claims between the same parties arising out of the same Article III case or controversy. *Gibbs*. Third, even when the district court had original jurisdiction over one or more claims between particular parties, the jurisdictional statutes did not authorize supplemental jurisdiction over additional claims involving other parties. *Clark*; *Zahn*; *Finley*.

B

In *Finley* we emphasized that "[w]hatever we say regarding the scope of jurisdiction conferred by a particular statute can of course be changed by Congress." In 1990, Congress accepted the invitation. It passed the Judicial Improvements Act, which enacted § 1367, the provision which controls these cases.

Section 1367 provides, in relevant part:

(a) Except as provided in subsections (b) and (c) or as expressly provided otherwise by Federal statute, in any civil action of which the district courts have original jurisdiction, the district courts shall have supplemental jurisdiction over all other claims that are so related to claims in the action within such original jurisdiction that they form part of the same case or controversy under Article III of the United States Constitution. Such supplemental jurisdiction shall include claims that involve the joinder or intervention of additional parties.

(b) In any civil action of which the district courts have original jurisdiction founded solely on section 1332 of this title, the district courts shall not have supplemental jurisdiction under subsection (a) over claims by plaintiffs against persons made parties under Rule 14, 19, 20, or 24 of the Federal Rules of Civil Procedure, or over claims by persons proposed to be joined as plaintiffs under Rule 19 of such rules, or seeking to intervene as plaintiffs under Rule 24 of such rules, when exercising supplemental jurisdiction over such claims would be inconsistent with the jurisdictional requirements of section 1332.

All parties to this litigation and all courts to consider the question agree that § 1367 overturned the result in *Finley*. There is no warrant, however, for assuming that § 1367 did no more than to overrule *Finley* and otherwise to codify the existing state of the law of supplemental jurisdiction. We must not give jurisdictional statutes a more expansive interpretation than their text warrants; but it is just as important not to adopt an artificial construction that is narrower than what the text provides. No sound canon of interpretation requires Congress to speak with extraordinary clarity in order to modify the rules of federal jurisdiction within appropriate constitutional bounds. Ordinary principles of statutory construction apply. In order to determine the scope of supplemental jurisdiction authorized by § 1367, then, we must examine the statute's text in light of context, structure, and related statutory provisions.

Section 1367(a) is a broad grant of supplemental jurisdiction over other claims within the same case or controversy, as long as the action is one in which the district courts would have original jurisdiction. The last sentence of § 1367(a) makes it clear that the grant of supplemental jurisdiction extends to claims involving joinder or intervention of additional parties. The single question before us, therefore, is whether a diversity case in which the claims of some plaintiffs satisfy the amount-in-controversy requirement, but the claims of other plaintiffs do not, presents a "civil action of which the district courts have original jurisdiction." If the answer is yes, § 1367(a) confers supplemental jurisdiction over all claims, including those that do not independently satisfy the amount-in-controversy requirement, if the claims are part of the same Article III case or controversy. If the answer is no, § 1367(a) is inapplicable and, in light of our holdings in *Clark* and *Zahn*, the district court has no statutory basis for exercising supplemental jurisdiction over the additional claims.

We now conclude the answer must be yes. When the well-pleaded complaint contains at least one claim that satisfies the amount-in-controversy requirement, and there are no other relevant jurisdictional defects, the district court, beyond all question, has original jurisdiction over that claim. The presence of other claims in the complaint, over which the district court may lack original jurisdiction, is of no moment. If the court has original jurisdiction over a single claim in the complaint, it has original jurisdiction over a "civil action" within the meaning of § 1367(a), even if the civil action over which it has jurisdiction comprises fewer claims than were included in the complaint. Once the court determines it has original jurisdiction over the civil action, it can turn to the question whether it has a constitutional and statutory basis for exercising supplemental jurisdiction over the other claims in the action.

Section 1367(a) commences with the direction that §§ 1367(b) and (c), or other relevant statutes, may provide specific exceptions, but otherwise § 1367(a) is a broad jurisdictional grant, with no distinction drawn between pendent-claim and pendent-party cases. In fact, the last sentence of § 1367(a) makes clear that the provision grants supplemental jurisdiction over claims involving joinder or intervention of additional parties. The terms of § 1367 do not acknowledge any distinction between pendent jurisdiction and the doctrine of so-called ancillary jurisdiction. Though the doctrines of pendent and ancillary jurisdiction developed separately as a historical matter, the Court has recognized that the doctrines are "two species of the same generic problem," *Kroger*. Nothing in § 1367 indicates a congressional intent to recognize, preserve, or create some meaningful, substantive distinction between the jurisdictional categories we have historically labeled pendent and ancillary.

If § 1367(a) were the sum total of the relevant statutory language, our holding would rest on that language alone. The statute, of course, instructs us to examine § 1367(b) to determine if any of its exceptions apply, so we proceed to that section. While § 1367(b) qualifies the broad rule of § 1367(a), it does not withdraw supplemental jurisdiction over the claims of the additional parties at issue here. The specific exceptions to § 1367(a) contained in § 1367(b), moreover, provide additional support for our conclusion that § 1367(a) confers supplemental jurisdiction over these claims. Section 1367(b), which applies only to diversity cases, withholds supplemental jurisdiction over the claims of plaintiffs proposed to be joined as indispensable parties under Federal Rule of Civil Procedure 19, or who seek to intervene pursuant to Rule 24. Nothing in the text of § 1367(b), however, withholds supplemental jurisdiction over the claims of plaintiffs permissively joined under Rule 20 or certified as class-action members pursuant to Rule 23. The natural, indeed the necessary, inference is that § 1367 confers supplemental jurisdiction over claims by Rule 20 and Rule 23 plaintiffs. This inference, at least with respect to Rule 20 plaintiffs, is strengthened by the fact that § 1367(b) explicitly excludes supplemental jurisdiction over claims against defendants joined under Rule 20.

We cannot accept the view, urged by some of the parties, commentators, and Courts of Appeals, that a district court lacks original jurisdiction over a civil action unless the court has original jurisdiction over every claim in the complaint. As we understand this position, it requires assuming either that all claims in the complaint must stand or fall as a single, indivisible "civil action" as a matter of definitional necessity—what we will refer to as the "indivisibility theory"—or else that the inclusion of a claim or party falling outside the district court's original jurisdiction somehow contaminates every other claim in the complaint, depriving the court of original jurisdiction over any of these claims—what we will refer to as the "contamination theory."

The indivisibility theory is easily dismissed, as it is inconsistent with the whole notion of supplemental jurisdiction. If a district court must have original jurisdiction over every claim in the complaint in order to have "original jurisdiction" over a "civil action," then in *Gibbs* there was no civil action of which the district court could assume original jurisdiction under § 1331, and so no basis for exercising supplemental jurisdiction over any of the claims. The indivisibility theory is further belied by our practice—in both federal-question and diversity cases—of allowing federal courts to cure jurisdictional defects by dismissing the offending parties rather than dismissing the entire action. *Clark,* for example, makes clear that claims that are jurisdictionally defective as to amount in controversy do not destroy original jurisdiction over other claims (dismissing parties who failed to meet the amount-in-controversy requirement but retaining jurisdiction over the remaining party). If the presence of jurisdictionally problematic claims in the complaint meant the district court was without original jurisdiction over the single, indivisible civil action before it, then the district court would have to dismiss the whole action rather than particular parties.

We also find it unconvincing to say that the definitional indivisibility theory applies in the context of diversity cases but not in the context of federal-question cases. The broad and general language of the statute does not permit this result. The contention is premised on the notion that the phrase "original jurisdiction of all civil actions" means different things in §§ 1331 and 1332. It is implausible, however, to say that the identical phrase means one thing (original jurisdiction in all actions where at least one claim in the complaint meets the following requirements) in § 1331 and something else (original jurisdiction in all actions where every claim in the complaint meets the following requirements) in § 1332.

The contamination theory, as we have noted, can make some sense in the special context of the complete diversity requirement because the presence of non-diverse parties on both sides of a lawsuit eliminates the justification for providing a federal forum. The theory, however, makes little sense with respect to the amount-in-controversy requirement, which is meant to ensure that a dispute is sufficiently important to warrant federal-court attention. The presence of a single nondiverse party may eliminate the fear of bias with respect to all claims, but the presence of a claim that falls short of the minimum amount in controversy does nothing to reduce the importance of the claims that do meet this requirement.

It is fallacious to suppose, simply from the proposition that § 1332 imposes both the diversity requirement and the amount-in-controversy requirement, that the contamination theory germane to the former is also relevant to the latter. There is no inherent logical connection between the amount-in-controversy requirement and § 1332 diversity jurisdiction. After all, federal-question jurisdiction once had an amount-in-controversy requirement as well. If such a requirement were revived under § 1331, it is clear beyond peradventure that § 1367(a) provides supplemental jurisdiction over federal-question cases where some, but not all, of the federal-law claims involve a sufficient amount in controversy. In other words, § 1367(a) unambiguously overrules the holding and the result in *Clark.* If that is so, however, it would be quite extraordinary to say that § 1367 did not also overrule *Zahn,* a case that was premised in substantial part on the holding in *Clark.* [discussion of related removal context omitted—ed.]

* * *

We also reject the argument . . . that while the presence of additional claims over which the district court lacks jurisdiction does not mean the civil action is outside the purview of § 1367(a), the presence of additional parties does. The basis for this distinction is not altogether clear, and it is in considerable tension with statutory text. Section 1367(a) applies by its terms to any civil action of which the district courts have original jurisdiction, and the last sentence of § 1367(a) expressly contemplates that the court may have supplemental jurisdiction over additional parties. So it cannot be the case that the presence of those parties destroys the court's original jurisdiction, within the meaning of § 1367(a), over a civil action otherwise properly before it. Also, § 1367(b) expressly withholds supplemental jurisdiction in diversity cases over claims by plaintiffs joined as indispensable parties under Rule 19. If joinder of such parties were sufficient to deprive the district court of original jurisdiction over the civil action within the meaning of § 1367(a), this specific limitation on supplemental jurisdiction in § 1367(b) would be superfluous. The argument that the presence of additional parties removes the civil action from the scope of § 1367(a) also would mean that § 1367 left the *Finley* result undisturbed. *Finley,* after all, involved a Federal Tort Claims Act suit against a federal defendant and state-law claims against additional defendants not otherwise subject to federal jurisdiction. Yet all concede that one purpose of § 1367 was to change the result reached in *Finley.*

Finally, it is suggested that our interpretation of § 1367(a) creates an anomaly regarding the exceptions listed in § 1367(b): It is not immediately obvious why Congress would withhold supplemental jurisdiction over plaintiffs joined as parties "needed for just adjudication" under Rule 19 but would allow supplemental jurisdiction over plaintiffs permissively joined under Rule 20. The omission of Rule 20 plaintiffs from the list of exceptions in § 1367(b) may have been an "unintentional drafting gap." If that is the case, it is up to Congress rather than the courts to fix it. The omission may seem odd, but it is not absurd. An alternative explanation for the different treatment of Rules 19 and 20 is that Congress was concerned that extending supplemental jurisdiction to Rule 19 plaintiffs would allow circumvention of the complete diversity rule: A non-diverse plaintiff might be omitted intentionally from the original action, but joined later under Rule 19 as a necessary party. The contamination theory described above, if applicable, means this ruse would fail, but Congress may have wanted to make assurance double sure. More generally, Congress may have concluded that federal jurisdiction is only appropriate if the district court would have original jurisdiction over the claims of all those plaintiffs who are so essential to the action that they could be joined under Rule 19.

To the extent that the omission of Rule 20 plaintiffs from the list of § 1367(b) exceptions is anomalous, moreover, it is no more anomalous than the inclusion of Rule 19 plaintiffs in that list would be if the alternative view of § 1367(a) were to prevail. If the district court lacks original jurisdiction over a civil diversity action where any plaintiff's claims fail to comply with all the requirements of § 1332, there is no need for a special § 1367(b) exception for Rule 19 plaintiffs who do not meet these requirements. Though the omission of Rule 20 plaintiffs from § 1367(b) presents something of a puzzle on our view of the statute, the inclusion of Rule 19 plaintiffs in this section is at least as difficult to explain under the alternative view.

And so we circle back to the original question. When the well-pleaded complaint in district court includes multiple claims, all part of the same case or controversy, and some, but not all, of the claims are within the court's original jurisdiction, does the court have before it "any civil action of which the district courts have original jurisdiction"? It does. Under § 1367, the court has original jurisdiction over the civil action comprising the claims for which there is no jurisdictional defect. No other reading of § 1367 is plausible in light of the text and structure of the jurisdictional statute. Though the special nature and purpose of the diversity require-ment mean that a single non-diverse party can contaminate every other claim in the lawsuit, the contamination does not occur with respect to jurisdictional defects that go only to the substantive importance of individ-ual claims.

It follows from this conclusion that the threshold requirement of § 1367(a) is satisfied in cases, like those now before us, where some, but not all, of the plaintiffs in a diversity action allege a sufficient amount in controversy. We hold that § 1367 by its plain text overruled *Clark* and *Zahn* and authorized supplemental jurisdiction over all claims by diverse parties arising out of the same Article III case or controversy, subject only to enumerated exceptions not applicable in the cases now before us.

C

The proponents of the alternative view of § 1367 insist that the statute is at least ambiguous and that we should look to other interpretive tools, including the legislative history of § 1367, which supposedly demon-strate Congress did not intend § 1367 to overrule *Zahn*. We can reject this argument at the very outset simply because § 1367 is not ambiguous. For the reasons elaborated above, interpreting § 1367 to foreclose supplemen-tal jurisdiction over plaintiffs in diversity cases who do not meet the minimum amount in controversy is inconsistent with the text, read in light of other statutory provisions and our established jurisprudence. Even if we were to stipulate, however, that the reading these proponents urge upon us is textually plausible, the legislative history cited to support it would not alter our view as to the best interpretation of § 1367.

Those who urge that the legislative history refutes our interpretation rely primarily on the House Judiciary Committee Report on the Judicial

Improvements Act. This Report explained that § 1367 would "authorize jurisdiction in a case like *Finley,* as well as essentially restore the pre-*Finley* understandings of the authorization for and limits on other forms of supplemental jurisdiction." The Report stated that § 1367(a) "generally authorizes the district court to exercise jurisdiction over a supplemental claim whenever it forms part of the same constitutional case or controversy as the claim or claims that provide the basis of the district court's original jurisdiction," and in so doing codifies *Gibbs* and fills the statutory gap recognized in *Finley.* The Report then remarked that § 1367(b) "is not intended to affect the jurisdictional requirements of [§ 1332] in diversity-only class actions, as those requirements were interpreted prior to *Finley.*" The Report noted that the "net effect" of § 1367(b) was to implement the "principal rationale" of *Kroger,* effecting only "one small change" in pre-*Finley* practice with respect to diversity actions: § 1367(b) would exclude "Rule 23(a) plaintiff-intervenors to the same extent as those sought to be joined as plaintiffs under Rule 19."

As we have repeatedly held, the authoritative statement is the statutory text, not the legislative history or any other extrinsic material. Extrinsic materials have a role in statutory interpretation only to the extent they shed a reliable light on the enacting Legislature's understanding of otherwise ambiguous terms. Not all extrinsic materials are reliable sources of insight into legislative understandings, however, and legislative history in particular is vulnerable to two serious criticisms. First, legislative history is itself often murky, ambiguous, and contradictory. Judicial investigation of legislative history has a tendency to become, to borrow Judge Leventhal's memorable phrase, an exercise in " 'looking over a crowd and picking out your friends.' " Second, judicial reliance on legislative materials like committee reports, which are not themselves subject to the requirements of Article I, may give unrepresentative committee members—or, worse yet, unelected staffers and lobbyists—both the power and the incentive to attempt strategic manipulations of legislative history to secure results they were unable to achieve through the statutory text. We need not comment here on whether these problems are sufficiently prevalent to render legislative history inherently unreliable in all circumstances, a point on which Members of this Court have disagreed. It is clear, however, that in this instance both criticisms are right on the mark.

First of all, the legislative history of § 1367 is far murkier than selective quotation from the House Report would suggest. The text of § 1367 is based substantially on a draft proposal contained in a Federal Court Study Committee working paper, which was drafted by a Subcommittee chaired by Judge Posner. While the Subcommittee explained, in language echoed by the House Report, that its proposal "basically restores the law as it existed prior to *Finley,*" it observed in a footnote that its proposal would overrule *Zahn* and that this would be a good idea. Although the Federal Courts Study Committee did not expressly adopt the Subcommittee's specific reference to *Zahn,* it neither explicitly disagreed with the Subcommittee's conclusion that this was the best reading of the proposed text nor substantially modified the proposal to avoid this result. Therefore, even if the House Report could fairly be read to reflect an understanding that the text of § 1367 did not overrule *Zahn,* the Subcommittee Working Paper on which § 1367 was based reflected the opposite understanding. The House Report is no more authoritative than the Subcommittee Working Paper. The utility of either can extend no further than the light it sheds on how the enacting Legislature understood the statutory text. Trying to figure out how to square the Subcommittee Working Paper's understanding with the House Report's understanding, or which is more reflective of the understanding of the enacting legislators, is a hopeless task.

Second, the worst fears of critics who argue legislative history will be used to circumvent the Article I process were realized in this case. The telltale evidence is the statement, by three law professors who participated in drafting § 1367, that § 1367 "on its face" permits "supplemental jurisdiction over claims of class members that do not satisfy section 1332's jurisdictional amount requirement, which would overrule *[Zahn]*. [There is] a disclaimer of intent to accomplish this result in the legislative history. . . . It would have been better had the statute dealt explicitly with this problem, and the legislative history was an attempt to correct the oversight." The professors were frank to concede that if one refuses to consider the legislative history, one has no choice but to "conclude that section 1367 has wiped *Zahn* off the books." So there exists an acknowledgment, by parties who have detailed, specific knowledge of the statute and the drafting process, both that the plain text of § 1367 overruled *Zahn* and that language to the contrary in the House Report was a *post hoc* attempt to alter that result. One need not subscribe to the wholesale condemnation of legislative history to refuse to give any effect to such a deliberate effort to amend a statute through a committee report.

In sum, even if we believed resort to legislative history were appropriate in these cases—a point we do not concede—we would not give significant weight to the House Report. The distinguished jurists who drafted the Subcommittee Working Paper, along with three of the participants in the drafting of § 1367, agree that this provision, on its face, overrules *Zahn.* This accords with the best reading of the statute's text, and nothing in the legislative history indicates directly and explicitly that Congress understood the phrase "civil action of which the district courts have original jurisdiction" to exclude cases in which some but not all of the diversity plaintiffs meet the amount-in-controversy requirement.

No credence, moreover, can be given to the claim that, if Congress understood § 1367 to overrule *Zahn,* the proposal would have been more controversial. We have little sense whether any Member of Congress would have been particularly upset by this result. This is not a case where one can plausibly say that concerned legislators might not have realized the possible effect of the text they were adopting. Certainly, any competent legislative aide who studied the matter would have flagged this issue if it were a matter of importance to his or her boss, especially in light of the Subcommittee Working Paper. There are any number of reasons why legislators did not spend more time arguing over § 1367, none of which are relevant to our interpretation of what the words of the statute mean.

D

Finally, we note that the Class Action Fairness Act (CAFA), enacted this year, has no bearing on our analysis of these cases. Subject to certain limitations, the CAFA confers federal diversity jurisdiction over class actions where the aggregate amount in controversy exceeds $5 million. It abrogates the rule against aggregating claims, a rule this Court recognized in *Ben-Hur* and reaffirmed in *Zahn*. The CAFA, however, is not retroactive and the views of the 2005 Congress are not relevant to our interpretation of a text enacted by Congress in 1990. The CAFA, moreover, does not moot the significance of our interpretation of § 1367, as many proposed exercises of supplemental jurisdiction, even in the class-action context, might not fall within the CAFA's ambit. The CAFA, then, has no impact, one way or the other, on our interpretation of § 1367.

* * *

The judgment of the Court of Appeals for the Eleventh Circuit is affirmed. The judgment of the Court of Appeals for the First Circuit is reversed, and the case is remanded for proceedings consistent with this opinion.

It is so ordered.

JUSTICE STEVENS, with whom JUSTICE BREYER joins, dissenting.

Justice Ginsburg's carefully reasoned (dissenting opinion), demonstrates the error in the Court's rather ambitious reading of this opaque jurisdictional statute. She also has demonstrated that "ambiguity" is a term that may have different meanings for different judges, for the Court has made the remarkable declaration that its reading of the statute is so obviously correct—and Justice Ginsburg's so obviously wrong—that the text does not even qualify as "ambiguous." Because ambiguity is apparently in the eye of the beholder, I remain convinced that it is unwise to treat the ambiguity *vel non* of a statute as determinative of whether legislative history is consulted. Indeed, I believe that we as judges are more, rather than less, constrained when we make ourselves accountable to *all* reliable evidence of legislative intent.

The legislative history of 28 U.S.C. § 1367 provides powerful confirmation of Justice Ginsburg's interpretation of that statute. It is helpful to consider in full the relevant portion of the House Report, which was also adopted by the Senate:

> This section would authorize jurisdiction in a case like *Finley*, as well as essentially restore the pre-*Finley* understandings of the authorization for and limits on other forms of supplemental jurisdiction. In federal question cases, it broadly authorizes the district courts to exercise supplemental jurisdiction over additional claims, including

claims involving the joinder of additional parties. In diversity cases, the district courts may exercise supplemental jurisdiction, except when doing so would be inconsistent with the jurisdictional requirements of the diversity statute.

* * *

Subsection 114(b) [§ 1367(b)] prohibits a district court in a case over which it has jurisdiction founded solely on the general diversity provision, 28 U.S.C. § 1332, from exercising supplemental jurisdiction in specified circumstances. [Footnote 16: 'The net effect of subsection (b) is to implement the principal rationale of *Owen Equipment*'.] In diversity-only actions the district courts may not hear plaintiffs' supplemental claims when exercising supplemental jurisdiction would encourage plaintiffs to evade the jurisdictional requirement of 28 U.S.C. § 1332 by the simple expedient of naming initially only those defendants whose joinder satisfies section 1332's requirements and later adding claims not within original federal jurisdiction against other defendants who have intervened or been joined on a supplemental basis. In accord with case law, the subsection also prohibits the joinder or intervention of persons or plaintiffs if adding them is inconsistent with section 1332's requirements. The section is not intended to affect the jurisdictional requirements of 28 U.S.C. § 1332 in diversity-only class actions, as those requirements were interpreted prior to *Finley*.

Subsection (b) makes one small change in pre-*Finley* practice. Anomalously, under current practice, the same party might intervene as of right under Federal Rule of Civil Procedure 23(a) and take advantage of supplemental jurisdiction, but not come within supplemental jurisdiction if parties already in the action sought to effect the joinder under Rule 19. Subsection (b) would eliminate this anomaly, excluding Rule 23(a) plaintiff-intervenors to the same extent as those sought to be joined as plaintiffs under Rule 19.

Not only does the House Report specifically say that § 1367 was not intended to upset *Zahn,* but its entire explanation of the statute demonstrates that Congress had in mind a very specific and relatively modest task-undoing this Court's 5-to-4 decision in *Finley*. In addition to overturning that unfortunate and much-criticized decision, the statute, according to the Report, codifies and preserves "the pre-*Finley* understandings of the authorization for and limits on other forms of supplemental jurisdiction," House Report, with the exception of making "one small change in pre-*Finley* practice," which is not relevant here.

The sweeping purpose that the Court's decision imputes to Congress bears no resemblance to the House Report's description of the statute. But this does not seem to trouble the Court, for its decision today treats statutory interpretation as a pedantic exercise, divorced from any serious attempt at ascertaining congressional intent. Of course, there are situations in which we do not honor Congress' apparent intent unless that intent is made "clear" in the text of a statute—in this way, we can be certain that Congress considered the issue and intended a disfavored outcome. But that principle provides no basis for discounting the House Report, given that our cases have never recognized a presumption in *favor* of expansive diversity jurisdiction.

The Court's reasons for ignoring this virtual billboard of congressional intent are unpersuasive. That a subcommittee of the Federal Courts Study Committee believed that an earlier, substantially similar version of the statute overruled *Zahn,* only highlights the fact that the statute is ambiguous. What is determinative is that the House Report explicitly rejected that broad reading of the statutory text. Such a report has special significance as an indicator of legislative intent. In Congress, committee reports are normally considered the authoritative explication of a statute's text and purposes, and busy legislators and their assistants rely on that explication in casting their votes.

The Court's second reason—its comment on the three law professors who participated in drafting § 1367—is similarly off the mark. In the law review article that the Court refers to, the professors were merely saying that the text of the statute was susceptible to an overly broad (and simplistic) reading, and that clarification in the House Report was therefore appropriate.[3] Significantly, the reference to *Zahn* in the House Report does not at all appear to be tacked on or out of place; indeed, it is wholly consistent with the Report's broader explanation of Congress' goal of overruling *Finley* and preserving pre-*Finley* law. To suggest that these professors participated in a "deliberate effort to amend a statute through a committee report," reveals an unrealistic view of the legislative process, not to mention disrespect for three law professors who acted in the role of public servants. To be sure, legislative history can be manipulated. But, in the situation before us, there is little reason to fear that an unholy conspiracy of "unrepresentative committee members," law professors, and "unelected staffers and lobbyists," endeavored to torpedo Congress' attempt to overrule (without discussion) two longstanding features of this Court's diversity jurisprudence.

After nearly 20 pages of complicated analysis, which explores subtle doctrinal nuances and coins various neologisms, the Court announces that § 1367 could not reasonably be read another way. That conclusion is difficult to accept. Given Justice Ginsburg's persuasive account of the statutory text and its jurisprudential backdrop, and given the uncommonly clear legislative history, I am confident that the majority's interpretation of § 1367 is mistaken. I respectfully dissent.

JUSTICE GINSBURG, with whom JUSTICE STEVENS, JUSTICE O'CONNOR, and JUSTICE BREYER join, dissenting.

---

3. The professors' account of the challenges they faced in drafting § 1367 gives some sense, I think, of why that statute has proved difficult to interpret: "More broadly, codifying a complex area like supplemental jurisdiction is itself complex business. A danger is that the result of the effort to deal with all the foreseeables will be a statute too prolix and baroque for everyday use and application by practitioners and judges. Section 1367 reflects an effort to provide sufficient detail without overdoing it. The statute is concededly not perfect. What it accomplishes, however, is to change the direction taken by the Supreme Court in *Finley,* to provide basic guidance, and then to trust the federal courts under the changed direction to interpret the statute sensibly...."

These cases present the question whether Congress, by enacting 28 U.S.C. § 1367, overruled this Court's decisions in *Clark* and *Zahn*. *Clark* held that, when federal-court jurisdiction is predicated on a specified amount in controversy, each plaintiff joined in the litigation must independently meet the jurisdictional amount requirement. *Zahn* confirmed that in class actions governed by Federal Rule of Civil Procedure 23(b)(3), "[e]ach [class member] . . . must satisfy the jurisdictional amount, and any [class member] who does not must be dismissed from the case."

Section 1367, all agree, was designed to overturn this Court's decision in *Finley*. *Finley* concerned not diversity-of-citizenship jurisdiction (28 U.S.C. § 1332), but original federal-court jurisdiction in cases arising under federal law (28 U.S.C. § 1331). * * * The plaintiff could not have brought her entire action in state court, because federal jurisdiction in FTCA actions is exclusive. Hence, absent federal jurisdiction embracing the state-law claims, she would be obliged to pursue two discrete actions, one in federal court, the other in state court. This Court held, nevertheless, that the District Court lacked jurisdiction over the "pendent-party" state-law claims. In so holding, the Court stressed that Congress held the control rein. Congress could reverse the result in *Finley,* and permit pendent jurisdiction over state-law claims against additional defendants, if it so chose.

What more § 1367 wrought is an issue on which courts of appeals have sharply divided. The Court today holds that § 1367, although prompted by *Finley,* a case in which original access to federal court was predicated on a federal question, notably enlarges federal diversity jurisdiction. The Court reads § 1367 to overrule *Clark* and *Zahn,* thereby allowing access to federal court by co-plaintiffs or class members who do not meet the now in excess of $75,000 amount-in-controversy requirement, so long as at least one co-plaintiff, or the named class representative, has a jurisdictionally sufficient claim.

The Court adopts a plausibly broad reading of § 1367, a measure that is hardly a model of the careful drafter's art. There is another plausible reading, however, one less disruptive of our jurisprudence regarding supplemental jurisdiction. If one reads § 1367(a) to instruct, as the statute's text suggests, that the district court must first have "original jurisdiction" over a "civil action" before supplemental jurisdiction can attach, then *Clark* and *Zahn* are preserved, and supplemental jurisdiction does not open the way for joinder of plaintiffs, or inclusion of class members, who do not independently meet the amount-in-controversy requirement. For the reasons that follow, I conclude that this narrower construction is the better reading of § 1367.

I

A

Section 1367, captioned "Supplemental jurisdiction," codifies court-recognized doctrines formerly labeled "pendent" and "ancillary" jurisdiction. Pendent jurisdiction involved the enlargement of federal-question litigation to include related state-law claims. Ancillary jurisdiction evolved primarily to protect defending parties, or others whose rights might be adversely affected if they could not air their claims in an ongoing federal-court action. Given jurisdiction over the principal action, federal courts entertained certain matters deemed ancillary regardless of the citizenship of the parties or the amount in controversy.

[In] *Mine Workers v. Gibbs,* . . . [t]his Court upheld the joinder of federal and state claims. "[T]here is *power* in federal courts to hear the whole," the Court said, when the state and federal claims "derive from a common nucleus of operative fact" and are so linked that the plaintiff "would ordinarily be expected to try them all in one judicial proceeding."

Gibbs involved the linkage of federal and state claims against the same defendant. In *Finley,* the Court contained *Gibbs.* Without congressional authorization, the Court admonished, the pendent jurisdiction umbrella could not be stretched to cover the joinder of additional parties. *Gibbs* had departed from earlier decisions recognizing that "jurisdiction [must] be explicitly conferred," the Court said. *Aldinger,* the Court observed, although resting "on a much narrower basis," had already signaled that "the *Gibbs* approach would not be extended to the pendent-party field," *Finley.* While the *Finley* Court did not "limit or impair" *Gibbs* itself, for further development of pendent jurisdiction, the Court made it plain, the initiative would lie in Congress' domain.[1]

Ancillary jurisdiction, which evolved as a more sprawling doctrine than pendent jurisdiction, was originally rooted in "the notion that [when] federal jurisdiction in [a] principal suit effectively controls the property or fund under dispute, other claimants thereto should be allowed to intervene in order to protect their interests, without regard to jurisdiction." *Aldinger.* In *Owen Equipment & Erection Co. v. Kroger,* the Court addressed the permissible scope of the doctrine in relation to the liberal provisions of the Federal Rules of Civil Procedure for joinder of parties and claims. [description of *Kroger* facts and holding omitted—ed.].

* * * In sum, in federal-question cases before § 1367's enactment, the Court recognized pendent-claim jurisdiction, *Gibbs,* but not pendent-party jurisdiction, *Finley.* As to ancillary jurisdiction, the Court adhered to the limitation that in diversity cases, throughout the litigation, all plaintiffs must remain diverse from all defendants. *See Kroger.*

Although pendent jurisdiction and ancillary jurisdiction evolved discretely, the Court has recognized that they are "two species of the same generic problem: Under what circumstances may a federal court hear and decide a state-law claim arising between citizens of the same State?"

B

Shortly before the Court decided *Finley,* Congress had established the Federal Courts Study Committee to take up issues relating to "the federal

---

1. "[B]oth the Finley result and its implications" sparked "considerable criticism."

courts' congestion, delay, expense, and expansion." Report of the Federal Courts Study Committee (hereinafter Committee Report). The Committee's charge was to conduct a study addressing the "crisis" in federal courts caused by the "rapidly growing" caseload.

Among recommendations, the Committee urged Congress to "authorize federal courts to assert pendent jurisdiction over parties without an independent federal jurisdictional base." If adopted, this recommendation would overrule *Finley.* Earlier, a Subcommittee had recommended that Congress overrule both *Finley* and *Zahn.* Report of the Subcommittee on the Role of the Federal Courts and Their Relationship to the States (hereinafter Subcommittee Report). In the Subcommittee's view, "[f]rom a policy standpoint," *Zahn* "ma[de] little sense." The full Committee, however, urged only the overruling of *Finley* and did not adopt the recommendation to overrule *Zahn.*

As a separate matter, a substantial majority of the Committee "strongly recommend[ed]" the elimination of diversity jurisdiction, save for "complex multi-state litigation, interpleader, and suits involving aliens." "[N]o other step," the Committee's Report maintained, "will do anywhere nearly as much to reduce federal caseload pressures and contain the growth of the federal judiciary."

Congress responded by adopting, as part of the Judicial Improvements Act of 1990, recommendations of the Federal Courts Study Committee ranked by the House Committee on the Judiciary as "modest" and "noncontroversial." Congress did not take up the Study Committee's immodest proposal to curtail diversity jurisdiction. It did, however, enact a supplemental jurisdiction statute, codified as 28 U.S.C. § 1367.

II

A

Section 1367, by its terms, operates only in civil actions "of which the district courts have original jurisdiction." The "original jurisdiction" relevant here is diversity-of-citizenship jurisdiction, conferred by § 1332. The character of that jurisdiction is the essential backdrop for comprehension of § 1367.

The Constitution broadly provides for federal-court jurisdiction in controversies "between Citizens of different States." Art. III, § 2, cl. 1. This Court has read that provision to demand no more than "minimal diversity," *i.e.,* so long as one party on the plaintiffs' side and one party on the defendants' side are of diverse citizenship, Congress may authorize federal courts to exercise diversity jurisdiction. Further, the Constitution includes no amount-in-controversy limitation on the exercise of federal jurisdiction. But from the start, Congress, as its measures have been construed by this Court, has limited federal-court exercise of diversity jurisdiction in two principal ways. First, unless Congress specifies otherwise, diversity must be "complete," *i.e.,* all parties on plaintiffs' side must be diverse from all parties on defendants' side. *Strawbridge v. Curtiss.*

Second, each plaintiff's stake must independently meet the amount-in-controversy specification: "When two or more plaintiffs, having separate and distinct demands, unite for convenience and economy in a single suit, it is essential that the demand of each be of the requisite jurisdictional amount."

The statute today governing federal-court exercise of diversity jurisdiction in the generality of cases, § 1332, like all its predecessors, incorporates both a diverse-citizenship requirement and an amount-in-controversy specification.[5] As to the latter, the statute reads: "The district courts shall have original jurisdiction [in diversity-of-citizenship cases] where the matter in controversy exceeds the sum ... of $75,000." § 1332(a). This Court has long held that, in determining whether the amount-in-controversy requirement has been satisfied, a single plaintiff may aggregate two or more claims against a single defendant, even if the claims are unrelated. But in multiparty cases, including class actions, we have unyieldingly adhered to the non-aggregation rule ... stated in *Troy Bank*.

This Court most recently addressed "[t]he meaning of [§ 1332's] 'matter in controversy' language" in *Zahn*. *Zahn* ... was a class action.... [I]n *Zahn*, the named plaintiffs had ... claims [large enough to satisfy the amount in controversy requirement]. Nevertheless, the Court declined to depart from its "longstanding construction of the 'matter in controversy' requirement of § 1332." The *Zahn* Court stated:

> *Snyder* invoked the well-established rule that each of several plaintiffs asserting separate and distinct claims must satisfy the jurisdictional-amount requirement if his claim is to survive a motion to dismiss. This rule plainly mandates not only that there may be no aggregation and that the entire case must be dismissed where none of the plaintiffs claims [meets the amount-in-controversy requirement] but also requires that any plaintiff without the jurisdictional amount must be dismissed from the case, even though others allege jurisdictionally sufficient claims.

The rule that each plaintiff must independently satisfy the amount-in-controversy requirement, unless Congress expressly orders otherwise, was thus the solidly established reading of § 1332 when Congress enacted the Judicial Improvements Act of 1990, which added § 1367 to Title 28.

B

These cases present the question whether Congress abrogated the non-aggregation rule long tied to § 1332 when it enacted § 1367. In

---

5. Endeavoring to preserve the "complete diversity" rule first stated in *Strawbridge*, the Court's opinion drives a wedge between the two components of 28 U.S.C. § 1332, treating the diversity-of-citizenship requirement as essential, the amount-in-controversy requirement as more readily disposable. Section 1332 itself, however, does not rank order the two requirements. What "[o]rdinary principl[e] of statutory construction" or "sound canon of interpretation," allows the Court to slice up § 1332 this way? In partial explanation, the Court asserts that amount in controversy can be analyzed claim by claim, but the diversity requirement cannot. It is not altogether clear why that should be so. The cure for improper joinder of a non-diverse party is the same as the cure for improper joinder of a plaintiff who does not satisfy the jurisdictional amount. In both cases, original jurisdiction can be preserved by dismissing the non-qualifying party.

answering that question, "context [should provide] a crucial guide." The Court should assume, as it ordinarily does, that Congress legislated against a background of law already in place and the historical development of that law. Here, that background is the statutory grant of diversity jurisdiction, the amount-in-controversy condition that Congress, from the start, has tied to the grant, and the non-aggregation rule this Court has long applied to the determination of the "matter in controversy."

* * * The Court is unanimous in reading § 1367(a) to permit pendent-party jurisdiction in federal-question cases, and thus, to overrule *Finley.* The basic jurisdictional grant, § 1331, provides that "[t]he district courts shall have original jurisdiction of all civil actions arising under the Constitution, laws, or treaties of the United States." Since 1980, § 1331 has contained no amount-in-controversy requirement. Once there is a civil action presenting a qualifying claim arising under federal law, § 1331's sole requirement is met. District courts, we have held, may then adjudicate, additionally, state-law claims "deriv[ing] from a common nucleus of operative fact." *Gibbs.* Section 1367(a) enlarges that category to include not only state-law claims against the defendant named in the federal claim, but also "[state-law] claims that involve the joinder or intervention of additional parties."

The Court divides, however, on the impact of § 1367(a) on diversity cases controlled by § 1332. Under the majority's reading, § 1367(a) permits the joinder of related claims cut loose from the non-aggregation rule that has long attended actions under § 1332. Only the claims specified in § 1367(b) would be excluded from § 1367(a)'s expansion of § 1332's grant of diversity jurisdiction. And because § 1367(b) contains no exception for joinder of plaintiffs under Rule 20 or class actions under Rule 23, the Court concludes, *Clark* and *Zahn* have been overruled.[8]

The Court's reading is surely plausible, especially if one detaches § 1367(a) from its context and attempts no reconciliation with prior interpretations of § 1332's amount-in-controversy requirement. But § 1367(a)'s text, as the First Circuit held, can be read another way, one that would involve no rejection of *Clark* and *Zahn.*

As explained by the First Circuit in *Ortega,* and applied to class actions by the Tenth Circuit, § 1367(a) addresses "civil action[s] of which the district courts have original jurisdiction," a formulation that, in diversity cases, is sensibly read to incorporate the rules on joinder and aggregation tightly tied to § 1332 at the time of § 1367's enactment. On this reading, a complaint must first meet that "original jurisdiction" measurement. If it does not, no supplemental jurisdiction is authorized. If it does, § 1367(a) authorizes "supplemental jurisdiction" over related claims. In other words, § 1367(a) would preserve undiminished, as part

---

8. Under the Court's construction of § 1367, Beatriz Ortega's family members can remain in the action because their joinder is merely permissive, *see* Fed. Rule Civ. Proc. 20. If, however, their presence was "needed for just adjudication," Rule 19, their dismissal would be required. The inclusion of those who may join, and exclusion of those who should or must join, defies rational explanation, and others adopting the interpretation the Court embraces have so acknowledged.

and parcel of § 1332 "original jurisdiction" determinations, both the "complete diversity" rule and the decisions restricting aggregation to arrive at the amount in controversy. Section 1367(b)'s office, then, would be "to prevent the erosion of the complete diversity [and amount-in-controversy] requirement[s] that might otherwise result from an expansive application of what was once termed the doctrine of ancillary jurisdiction." In contrast to the Court's construction of § 1367, which draws a sharp line between the diversity and amount-in-controversy components of § 1332, the interpretation presented here does not sever the two jurisdictional requirements.

The more restrained reading of § 1367 just outlined would yield affirmance of the First Circuit's judgment in *Ortega,* and reversal of the Eleventh Circuit's judgment in *Exxon.* It would not discard entirely, as the Court does, the judicially developed doctrines of pendent and ancillary jurisdiction as they existed when *Finley* was decided.[10] Instead, it would recognize § 1367 essentially as a codification of those doctrines, placing them under a single heading, but largely retaining their substance, with overriding *Finley* the only basic change: Supplemental jurisdiction, once the district court has original jurisdiction, would now include "claims that involve the joinder or intervention of additional parties." § 1367(a).

Pendent jurisdiction, as earlier explained, applied only in federal-question cases and allowed plaintiffs to attach nonfederal claims to their jurisdiction-qualifying claims. Ancillary jurisdiction applied primarily, although not exclusively, in diversity cases and "typically involve[d] claims *by a defending party* haled into court against his will." *Kroger.* As the First Circuit observed, neither doctrine permitted a plaintiff to circumvent the dual requirements of § 1332 (diversity of citizenship and amount in controversy) "simply by joining her [jurisdictionally inadequate] claim in an action brought by [a] jurisdictionally competent diversity plaintiff."

* * * The less disruptive view I take of § 1367 also accounts for the omission of Rule 20 plaintiffs and Rule 23 class actions in § 1367(b)'s text. If one reads § 1367(a) as a plenary grant of supplemental jurisdiction to federal courts sitting in diversity, one would indeed look for exceptions in § 1367(b). Finding none for permissive joinder of parties or class actions, one would conclude that Congress effectively, even if unintentionally, overruled *Clark* and *Zahn.* But if one recognizes that the non-aggregation rule delineated in *Clark* and *Zahn* forms part of the determination whether "original jurisdiction" exists in a diversity case, then plaintiffs who do not meet the amount-in-controversy requirement would fail at the § 1367(a) threshold. Congress would have no reason to resort to a § 1367(b) exception to turn such plaintiffs away from federal court, given that their claims, from the start, would fall outside the court's § 1332 jurisdiction.

---

10. The Court's opinion blends the two doctrines, according no significance to their discrete development.

* * * What is the utility of § 1367(b) under my reading of § 1367(a)? Section 1367(a) allows parties other than the plaintiff to assert *reactive* claims once entertained under the heading ancillary jurisdiction (... including compulsory counterclaims and impleader claims, over which federal courts routinely exercised ancillary jurisdiction). As earlier observed, § 1367(b) stops plaintiffs from circumventing § 1332's jurisdictional requirements by using another's claim as a hook to add a claim that the plaintiff could not have brought in the first instance. *Kroger* is the paradigm case. There, the Court held that ancillary jurisdiction did not extend to a plaintiff's claim against a non-diverse party who had been impleaded by the defendant under Rule 14. Section 1367(b), then, is corroborative of § 1367(a)'s coverage of claims formerly called ancillary, but provides exceptions to ensure that accommodation of added claims would not fundamentally alter "the jurisdictional requirements of section 1332."

While § 1367's enigmatic text defies flawless interpretation, the precedent-preservative reading, I am persuaded, better accords with the historical and legal context of Congress' enactment of the supplemental jurisdiction statute, and the established limits on pendent and ancillary jurisdiction. It does not attribute to Congress a jurisdictional enlargement broader than the one to which the legislators adverted, and it follows the sound counsel that "close questions of [statutory] construction should be resolved in favor of continuity and against change."[14]

* * *

For the reasons stated, I would hold that § 1367 does not overrule *Clark* and *Zahn*. I would therefore affirm the judgment of the Court of Appeals for the First Circuit and reverse the judgment of the Court of Appeals for the Eleventh Circuit.

B. REMOVAL JURISDICTION

* * *

28 U.S.C. § 1441. REMOVAL OF CIVIL ACTIONS

(a) Generally.—Except as otherwise expressly provided by Act of Congress, any civil action brought in a State court of which the district courts of the United States have original jurisdiction, may be removed by the defendant or the defendants, to the district court of the United States for the district and division embracing the place where such action is pending.

(b) Removal based on diversity of citizenship.—

  (1) In determining whether a civil action is removable on the basis of the jurisdiction under section 1332(a) of this title, the citizenship of defendants sued under fictitious names shall be disregarded.

---

14. While the interpretation of § 1367 described in this opinion does not rely on the measure's legislative history, that history, as Justice Stevens has shown, is corroborative of the statutory reading set out above.

(2) A civil action otherwise removable solely on the basis of the jurisdiction under section 1332(a) of this title may not be removed if any of the parties in interest properly joined and served as defendants is a citizen of the State in which such action is brought.

(c) Joinder of Federal law claims and State law claims.—

(1) If a civil action includes

(A) a claim arising under the Constitution, laws, or treaties of the United States (within the meaning of section 1331 of this title), and

(B) a claim not within the original or supplemental jurisdiction of the district court or a claim that has been made nonremovable by statute, the entire action may be removed if the action would be removable without the inclusion of the claim described in subparagraph (B).

(2) Upon removal of an action described in paragraph (1), the district court shall sever from the action all claims described in paragraph (1)(B) and shall remand the severed claims to the State court from which the action was removed. Only defendants against whom a claim described in paragraph (1)(A) has been asserted are required to join in or consent to the removal under paragraph (1).

(d) Actions against foreign States.—Any civil action brought in a State court against a foreign state as defined in section 1603(a) of this title may be removed by the foreign state to the district court of the United States for the district and division embracing the place where such action is pending. Upon removal the action shall be tried by the court without jury. Where removal is based upon this subsection, the time limitations of section 1446(b) of this chapter may be enlarged at any time for cause shown.

(e) Multiparty, multiforum jurisdiction.—

(1) Notwithstanding the provisions of subsection (b) of this section, a defendant in a civil action in a State court may remove the action to the district court of the United States for the district and division embracing the place where the action is pending if—

(A) the action could have been brought in a United States district court under section 1369 of this title; or

(B) the defendant is a party to an action which is or could have been brought, in whole or in part, under section 1369 in a United States district court and arises from the same accident as the action in State court, even if the action to be removed could not have been brought in a district court as an original matter.

The removal of an action under this subsection shall be made in accordance with section 1446 of this title, except that a notice of removal may also be filed before trial of the action in State court within 30 days after the date on which the defendant first becomes a party to an action under section 1369 in a United States district court that arises from the same accident as the action in State court, or at a later time with leave of the district court.

(2) Whenever an action is removed under this subsection and the district court to which it is removed or transferred under section 1407(j) has made a liability determination requiring further proceedings as to damages, the district court shall remand the action to the State court from which it had been removed for the determination of damages, unless the court finds that, for the convenience of parties and witnesses and in the interest of justice, the action should be retained for the determination of damages.

(3) Any remand under paragraph (2) shall not be effective until 60 days after the district court has issued an order determining liability and has certified its intention to remand the removed action for the determination of damages. An appeal with respect to the liability determination of the district court may be taken during that 60–day period to the court of appeals with appellate jurisdiction over the district court. In the event a party files such an appeal, the remand shall not be effective until the appeal has been finally disposed of. Once the remand has become effective, the liability determination shall not be subject to further review by appeal or otherwise.

(4) Any decision under this subsection concerning remand for the determination of damages shall not be reviewable by appeal or otherwise.

(5) An action removed under this subsection shall be deemed to be an action under section 1369 and an action in which jurisdiction is based on section 1369 of this title for purposes of this section and sections 1407, 1697, and 1785 of this title.

(6) Nothing in this subsection shall restrict the authority of the district court to transfer or dismiss an action on the ground of inconvenient forum.

(f) Derivative removal jurisdiction.—

The court to which a civil action is removed under this section is not precluded from hearing and determining any claim in such civil action because the State court from which such civil action is removed did not have jurisdiction over that claim.

28 U.S.C. § 1442. FEDERAL OFFICERS OR AGENCIES SUED OR PROSECUTED

(a) A civil action or criminal prosecution that is commenced in a State court and that is against or directed to any of the following may be removed by them to the district court of the United States for the district and division embracing the place wherein it is pending:

(1) The United States or any agency thereof or any officer (or any person acting under that officer) of the United States or of any agency thereof, in an official or individual capacity, for or relating to any act under color of such office or on account of any right, title or authority claimed under any Act of Congress for the apprehension or punishment of criminals or the collection of the revenue.

(2) A property holder whose title is derived from any such officer, where such action or prosecution affects the validity of any law of the United States.

(3) Any officer of the courts of the United States, for or relating to any act under color of office or in the performance of his duties;

(4) Any officer of either House of Congress, for or relating to any act in the discharge of his official duty under an order of such House.

(b) A personal action commenced in any State court by an alien against any citizen of a State who is, or at the time the alleged action accrued was, a civil officer of the United States and is a nonresident of such State, wherein jurisdiction is obtained by the State court by personal service of process, may be removed by the defendant to the district court of the United States for the district and division in which the defendant was served with process.

(c) As used in subsection (a), the terms "civil action" and "criminal prosecution" include any proceeding (whether or not ancillary to another proceeding) to the extent that in such proceeding a judicial order, including a subpoena for testimony or documents, is sought or issued. If removal is sought for a proceeding described in the previous sentence, and there is no other basis for removal, only that proceeding may be removed to the district court. As used in subsection (a), the terms "civil action" and "criminal prosecution" include any proceeding (whether or not ancillary to another proceeding) to the extent that in such proceeding a judicial order, including a subpoena for testimony or documents, is sought or issued. If removal is sought for a proceeding described in the previous sentence, and there is no other basis for removal, only that proceeding may be removed to the district court.

28 U.S.C. § 1443. Civil rights cases

Any of the following civil actions or criminal prosecutions, commenced in a State court may be removed by the defendant to the district court of the United States for the district and division embracing the place wherein it is pending:

(1) Against any person who is denied or cannot enforce in the courts of such State a right under any law providing for the equal civil rights of citizens of the United States, or of all persons within the jurisdiction thereof;

(2) For any act under color of authority derived from any law providing for equal rights, or for refusing to do any act on the ground that it would be inconsistent with such law.

28 U.S.C. § 1445. NONREMOVABLE ACTIONS

(a) A civil action in any State court against a railroad or its receivers or trustees, arising under sections 1–4 and 5–10 of the Act of April 22, 1908 . . . , may not be removed to any district court of the United States.

(b) A civil action in any State court against a carrier or its receivers or trustees to recover damages for delay, loss, or injury of shipments, . . . , may not be removed to any district court of the United States unless the matter in controversy exceeds $10,000, exclusive of interest and costs.

(c) A civil action in any State court arising under the workmen's compensation laws of such State may not be removed to any district court of the United States.

(d) A civil action in any State court arising under section 40302 of the Violence Against Women Act of 1994 may not be removed to any district court of the United States.

28 U.S.C. § 1446. PROCEDURE FOR REMOVAL OF CIVIL ACTIONS

(a) Generally.—A defendant or defendants desiring to remove any civil action from a State court shall file in the district court of the United States for the district and division within which such action is pending a notice of removal signed pursuant to Rule 11 of the Federal Rules of Civil Procedure and containing a short and plain statement of the grounds for removal, together with a copy of all process, pleadings, and orders served upon such defendant or defendants in such action.

(b) Requirements; generally.—

    (1) The notice of removal of a civil action or proceeding shall be filed within 30 days after the receipt by the defendant, through service or otherwise, of a copy of the initial pleading setting forth the claim for relief upon which such action or proceeding is based, or within 30 days after the service of summons upon the defendant if such initial pleading has then been filed in court and is not required to be served on the defendant, whichever period is shorter.

    (2)

        (A) When a civil action is removed solely under section 1441(a), all defendants who have been properly joined and served must join in or consent to the removal of the action.

        (B) Each defendant shall have 30 days after receipt by or service on that defendant of the initial pleading or summons described in paragraph (1) to file the notice of removal.

(C) If defendants are served at different times, and a later-served defendant files a notice of removal, any earlier-served defendant may consent to the removal even though that earlier-served defendant did not previously initiate or consent to removal.

(3) Except as provided in subsection (c), if the case stated by the initial pleading is not removable, a notice of removal may be filed within 30 days after receipt by the defendant, through service or otherwise, of a copy of an amended pleading, motion, order or other paper from which it may first be ascertained that the case is one which is or has become removable.

(c) Requirements; removal based on diversity of citizenship.—

(1) A case may not be removed under subsection (b)(3) on the basis of jurisdiction conferred by section 1332 more than 1 year after commencement of the action, unless the district court finds that the plaintiff has acted in bad faith in order to prevent a defendant from removing the action.

(2) If removal of a civil action is sought on the basis of the jurisdiction conferred by section 1332(a), the sum demanded in good faith in the initial pleading shall be deemed to be the amount in controversy, except that—

(A) the notice of removal may assert the amount in controversy if the initial pleading seeks—

(i) nonmonetary relief; or

(ii) a money judgment, but the State practice either does not permit demand for a specific sum or permits recovery of damages in excess of the amount demanded; and

(B) removal of the action is proper on the basis of an amount in controversy asserted under subparagraph (A) if the district court finds, by the preponderance of the evidence, that the amount in controversy exceeds the amount specified in section 1332(a).

(3)

(A) If the case stated by the initial pleading is not removable solely because the amount in controversy does not exceed the amount specified in section 1332(a), information relating to the amount in controversy in the record of the State proceeding, or in responses to discovery, shall be treated as an 'other paper' under subsection (b)(3).

(B) If the notice of removal is filed more than 1 year after commencement of the action and the district court finds that the plaintiff deliberately failed to disclose the actual amount in controversy to prevent removal, that finding shall be deemed bad faith under paragraph (1).

(d) Notice to adverse parties and State court.—Promptly after the filing of such notice of removal of a civil action the defendant or defendants shall give written notice thereof to all adverse parties and shall file a copy of the notice with the clerk of such State court, which shall effect the removal and the State court shall proceed no further unless and until the case is remanded.

(e) Counterclaim in 337 proceeding.—With respect to any counterclaim removed to a district court pursuant to section 337(c) of the Tariff Act of 1930, the district court shall resolve such counterclaim in the same manner as an original complaint under the Federal Rules of Civil Procedure, except that the payment of a filing fee shall not be required in such cases and the counterclaim shall relate back to the date of the original complaint in the proceeding before the International Trade Commission under section 337 of that Act.

[**(f)** Redesignated (e)]

(g) Where the civil action or criminal prosecution that is removable under section 1442(a) is a proceeding in which a judicial order for testimony or documents is sought or issued or sought to be enforced, the 30–day requirement of subsection (b) of this section and paragraph (1) of section 1455(b) is satisfied if the person or entity desiring to remove the proceeding files the notice of removal not later than 30 days after receiving, through service, notice of any such proceeding.

28 U.S.C. § 1447. PROCEDURE AFTER REMOVAL GENERALLY

(a) In any case removed from a State court, the district court may issue all necessary orders and process to bring before it all proper parties whether served by process issued by the State court or otherwise.

(b) It may require the removing party to file with its clerk copies of all records and proceedings in such State court or may cause the same to be brought before it by writ of certiorari issued to such State court.

(c) A motion to remand the case on the basis of any defect other than lack of subject matter jurisdiction must be made within 30 days after the filing of the notice of removal under section 1446(a). If at any time before final judgment it appears that the district court lacks subject matter jurisdiction, the case shall be remanded. An order remanding the case may require payment of just costs and any actual expenses, including attorney fees, incurred as a result of the removal. A certified copy of the order of remand shall be mailed by the clerk to the clerk of the State court. The State court may thereupon proceed with such case.

(d) An order remanding a case to the State court from which it was removed is not reviewable on appeal or otherwise, except that an order remanding a case to the State court from which it was removed pursuant to section 1442 or 1443 of this title shall be reviewable by appeal or otherwise.

(e) If after removal the plaintiff seeks to join additional defendants whose joinder would destroy subject matter jurisdiction, the court may deny joinder, or permit joinder and remand the action to the State court.

28 U.S.C. § 1448. PROCESS AFTER REMOVAL

In all cases removed from any State court to any district court of the United States in which any one or more of the defendants has not been served with process or in which the service has not been perfected prior to removal, or in which process served proves to be defective, such process or service may be completed or new process issued in the same manner as in cases originally filed in such district court.

This section shall not deprive any defendant upon whom process is served after removal of his right to move to remand the case.

CARLSBAD TECHNOLOGY, INC. v. HIF BIO, INC.

556 U.S. 635 (2009)

JUSTICE THOMAS delivered the opinion of the Court.

In this case, we decide whether a federal court of appeals has jurisdiction to review a district court's order that remands a case to state court after declining to exercise supplemental jurisdiction over state-law claims under 28 U.S.C. § 1367(c). The Court of Appeals for the Federal Circuit held that appellate review of such an order is barred by § 1447(d) because it viewed the remand order in this case as resting on the District Court's lack of subject-matter jurisdiction over the state-law claims. We disagree and reverse the judgment of the Court of Appeals.

I

In 2005, respondents filed a complaint against petitioner and others in California state court, alleging that petitioner had violated state and federal law in connection with a patent dispute. Petitioner removed the case to the United States District Court for the Central District of California pursuant to § 1441(c), which allows removal of an "entire case" when it includes at least one claim over which the federal district court has original jurisdiction. Petitioner then filed a motion to dismiss the only federal claim in the lawsuit, which arose under the Racketeer Influenced and Corrupt Organizations Act (RICO), 18 U.S.C. §§ 1961–1968, for failure to adequately allege a pattern of racketeering. The District Court agreed that respondents had failed to state a RICO claim upon which relief could be granted and dismissed the claim pursuant to Federal Rule of Civil Procedure 12(b)(6). The District Court also declined to exercise supplemental jurisdiction over the remaining state-law claims pursuant to 28 U.S.C. § 1367(c)(3), which provides that a district court "may decline to exercise supplemental jurisdiction over a claim" if "the district court has dismissed all claims over which it has original jurisdiction." The

District Court then remanded the case to state court as authorized by this Court's decision in *Carnegie-Mellon Univ. v. Cohill,* 484 U.S. 343 (1988).

Petitioner appealed to the United States Court of Appeals for the Federal Circuit, arguing that the District Court should have exercised supplemental jurisdiction over the state-law claims because they implicate federal patent-law rights. The Court of Appeals dismissed the appeal, finding that the remand order could "be colorably characterized as a remand based on lack of subject matter jurisdiction" and, therefore, could not be reviewed under §§ 1447(c) and (d), which provide in part that remands for "lack of subject matter jurisdiction" are "not reviewable on appeal or otherwise."

This Court has not yet decided whether a district court's order remanding a case to state court after declining to exercise supplemental jurisdiction is a remand for lack of subject-matter jurisdiction for which appellate review is barred by §§ 1447(c) and (d). We granted certiorari to resolve this question, and now hold that such remand orders are not based on a lack of subject-matter jurisdiction. Accordingly, we reverse the judgment of the Court of Appeals and remand for further proceedings.

II

Appellate review of remand orders is limited by 28 U.S.C. § 1447(d), which states:

> An order remanding a case to the State court from which it was removed is not reviewable on appeal or otherwise, except that an order remanding a case to the State court from which it was removed pursuant to section 1443 of this title shall be reviewable by appeal or otherwise.

This Court has consistently held that § 1447(d) must be read *in pari materia* with § 1447(c), thus limiting the remands barred from appellate review by § 1447(d) to those that are based on a ground specified in § 1447(c). *See Thermtron Products, Inc. v. Hermansdorfer,* 423 U.S. 336.*

One type of remand order governed by § 1447(c)—the type at issue in this case—is a remand order based on a lack of "subject matter jurisdiction." § 1447(c) (providing, in relevant part, that "[i]f at any time before final judgment it appears that the district court lacks subject matter jurisdiction, the case shall be remanded"). The question presented in this case is whether the District Court's remand order, which rested on its decision declining to exercise supplemental jurisdiction over respondents' state-law claims, is a remand based on a "lack of subject matter jurisdiction" for purposes of §§ 1447(c) and (d). It is not.

"Subject matter jurisdiction defines the court's authority to hear a given type of case;" it represents "the extent to which a court can rule on

---

* We do not revisit today whether *Thermtron* was correctly decided. Neither the brief for petitioner nor the brief for respondents explicitly asked the Court to do so here, and counsel for both parties clearly stated at oral argument that they were not asking for *Thermtron* to be overruled.

the conduct of persons or the status of things." This Court's precedent makes clear that whether a court has subject-matter jurisdiction over a claim is distinct from whether a court chooses to exercise that jurisdiction. *See, e.g., Quackenbush* (holding that an abstention-based remand is not a remand for "lack of subject matter jurisdiction" for purposes of §§ 1447(c) and (d)); *Ankenbrandt v. Richards,* 504 U.S. 689 (1992) (questioning whether, "even though subject matter jurisdiction might be proper, sufficient grounds exist to warrant abstention from the exercise of that jurisdiction") . . .

With respect to supplemental jurisdiction in particular, a federal court has subject-matter jurisdiction over specified state-law claims, which it may (or may not) choose to exercise. *See* §§ 1367(a), (c). A district court's decision whether to exercise that jurisdiction after dismissing every claim over which it had original jurisdiction is purely discretionary. *See* § 1367(c) ("The district courts *may* decline to exercise supplemental jurisdiction over a claim . . . if . . . the district court has dismissed all claims over which it has original jurisdiction"); ("Even if only state-law claims remained after resolution of the federal question, the District Court would have discretion, consistent with Article III, to retain jurisdiction"); ("[W]hen a court grants a motion to dismiss for failure to state a federal claim, the court generally retains discretion to exercise supplemental jurisdiction, pursuant to 28 U.S.C. § 1367, over pendent state-law claims"); *see also* FEDERAL PRACTICE AND PROCEDURE § 3567 (3d ed. 2008) ("Once it has dismissed the claims that invoked original bases of subject matter jurisdiction, all that remains before the federal court are state-law claims. . . . The district court retains discretion to exercise supplemental jurisdiction [over them]"). As a result, "the [district] court's exercise of its discretion under § 1367(c) is not a jurisdictional matter. Thus, the court's determination may be reviewed for abuse of discretion, but may not be raised at any time as a jurisdictional defect."

It is undisputed that when this case was removed to federal court, the District Court had original jurisdiction over the federal RICO claim pursuant to 28 U.S.C. § 1331 and supplemental jurisdiction over the state-law claims because they were "so related to claims in the action within such original jurisdiction that they form[ed] part of the same case or controversy under Article III of the United States Constitution." § 1367(a). Upon dismissal of the federal claim, the District Court retained its statutory supplemental jurisdiction over the state-law claims. Its decision declining to exercise that statutory authority was not based on a jurisdictional defect but on its discretionary choice not to hear the claims despite its subject-matter jurisdiction over them. *See Chicago v. International College of Surgeons,* 522 U.S. 156 (1997) ("Depending on a host of factors, then—including the circumstances of the particular case, the nature of the state law claims, the character of the governing state law, and the relationship between the state and federal claims—district courts may decline to exercise jurisdiction over supplemental state law claims"). The remand order, therefore, is not based on a "lack of subject matter jurisdiction" for purposes of the bar to appellate review created by §§ 1447(c) and (d).

The Court of Appeals held to the contrary based on its conclusion that "every § 1367(c) remand necessarily involves a predicate finding that the claims at issue lack an independent basis of subject matter jurisdiction." But, as explained above, §§ 1367(a) and (c) provide a basis for subject-matter jurisdiction over any properly removed state claim. We thus disagree with the Court of Appeals that the remand at issue here "can be colorably characterized as a lack of subject matter jurisdiction."

* * *

When a district court remands claims to a state court after declining to exercise supplemental jurisdiction, the remand order is not based on a lack of subject-matter jurisdiction for purposes of §§ 1447(c) and (d). The judgment of the Court of Appeals for the Federal Circuit is reversed, and the case is remanded for further proceedings consistent with this opinion.

It is so ordered.

JUSTICE STEVENS, concurring.

In his dissenting opinion in *Thermtron Products, Inc. v. Hermansdorfer,* then-Justice Rehnquist remarked that he could "perceive no justification for the Court's decision to ignore the express directive of Congress in favor of what it personally perceives to be 'justice' in this case." He began his dissent with a comment that is also applicable to the case before us today: "The Court of Appeals not unreasonably believed that 28 U.S.C. § 1447(d) means what it says. It says: 'An order remanding a case to the State court from which it was removed is not reviewable on appeal or otherwise....' "

Today, as in *Thermtron,* the Court holds that § 1447(d) does not mean what it says.

If we were writing on a clean slate, I would adhere to the statute's text. But *Thermtron*'s limiting construction applies equally to this case ... and *stare decisis* compels the conclusion that the District Court's remand order is reviewable notwithstanding § 1447(d)'s unambiguous contrary command. The Court's adherence to precedent in this case represents a welcome departure from its sometimes single-minded focus on literal text. Accordingly, I join the Court's opinion.

JUSTICE SCALIA, concurring.

The Court today does nothing more than accurately apply to the facts of this case our holding in *Thermtron Products, Inc.* As the Court notes, neither party has asked us to reconsider *Thermtron,* and we thus have no occasion to revisit that decision here.

I write separately, though, to note that our decision in *Thermtron* was questionable in its day and is ripe for reconsideration in the appropriate case. Title 28 U.S.C. § 1447(d) states that "[a]n order remanding a case to the State court from which it was removed is not reviewable on appeal or otherwise." The statute provides a single exception—not remotely implicated in this case—for certain civil rights cases removed under § 1443. *See* § 1447(d). As then-Justice Rehnquist understatingly observed in his *Thermtron* dissent, it would not be "unreasonabl[e][to] believ[e] that 28 U.S.C. § 1447(d) means what it says;" and what it says is no appellate review of remand orders. Since the District Court's order in this case "remand[ed] a case to the State court from which it was removed," it should be—in the words of § 1447(d)—"not reviewable on appeal or otherwise." Q.E.D.

Over the years, the Court has replaced the statute's clear bar on appellate review with a hodgepodge of jurisdictional rules that have no evident basis even in common sense. Under our decisions, there is no appellate jurisdiction to review remands for lack of subject-matter jurisdiction, though with exception; there is jurisdiction to review remands of supplemental state-law claims, and other remands based on abstention, though presumably no jurisdiction to review remands based on the "defects" referenced in § 1447(c). If this muddle represents a *welcome* departure from the literal text, *see* (Stevens, J., concurring), the world is mad.

This mess—entirely of our own making—does not in my view require expert reexamination of this area of the law, *see* (Breyer, J., concurring). It requires only the reconsideration of our decision in *Thermtron*—and a welcome *return* to the Court's focus on congressionally enacted text.

JUSTICE BREYER, with whom JUSTICE SOUTER joins, concurring.

I join the Court's opinion. I write separately to note an anomaly about the way 28 U.S.C. § 1447 works. In this case, we consider a District Court's decision not to retain on its docket a case that *once* contained federal law issues but *now* contains only state law issues. All agree that the law grants the District Court broad discretion to determine whether it should keep such cases on its docket, that a decision to do so (or not to do so) rarely involves major legal questions, and that (even if wrong) a district court decision of this kind will not often have major adverse consequences. We now hold that § 1447 *permits* appellate courts to review a district court decision of this kind, even if only for abuse of discretion.

Contrast today's decision with our decision two Terms ago in *Powerex Corp. v. Reliant Energy Services, Inc.,* 551 U.S. 224 (2007). In that case, we considered a District Court's decision to remand a case in which a Canadian province-owned power company had sought removal—a matter that the Foreign Sovereign Immunities Act of 1976 specifically authorizes federal judges (in certain instances) to decide. *See* §§ 1441(d); 1603(a). The case presented a difficult legal question involving the commercial activities of a foreign sovereign; and the District Court's decision (if wrong) had potentially serious adverse consequences, namely preventing a sovereign power from obtaining the *federal* trial to which the law (in its view) entitled it. We nonetheless held that § 1447 *forbids* appellate courts from reviewing a district court decision of this kind.

Thus, we have held that § 1447 *permits* review of a district court decision in an instance where that decision is unlikely to be wrong and where a wrong decision is unlikely to work serious harm. And we have held that § 1447 *forbids* review of a district court decision in an instance where that decision may well be wrong and where a wrong decision could work considerable harm. Unless the circumstances I describe are unusual, something is wrong. And the fact that we have read other exceptions in the statute's absolute-sounding language suggests that such circumstances are not all that unusual.

Consequently, while joining the majority, I suggest that experts in this area of the law reexamine the matter with an eye toward determining whether statutory revision is appropriate.

C. VENUE AND TRANSFER OF VENUE

28 U.S.C. § 1391. VENUE GENERALLY

(a) Applicability of section.—Except as otherwise provided by law—

(1) this section shall govern the venue of all civil actions brought in district courts of the United States; and

(2) the proper venue for a civil action shall be determined without regard to whether the action is local or transitory in nature.

(b) Venue in general.—A civil action may be brought in—

(1) a judicial district in which any defendant resides, if all defendants are residents of the State in which the district is located;

(2) a judicial district in which a substantial part of the events or omissions giving rise to the claim occurred, or a substantial part of property that is the subject of the action is situated; or

(3) if there is no district in which an action may otherwise be brought as provided in this section, any judicial district in which any defendant is subject to the court's personal jurisdiction with respect to such action.

(c) Residency.—For all venue purposes—

(1) a natural person, including an alien lawfully admitted for permanent residence in the United States, shall be deemed to reside in the judicial district in which that person is domiciled;

(2) an entity with the capacity to sue and be sued in its common name under applicable law, whether or not incorporated, shall be deemed to reside, if a defendant, in any judicial district in which such defendant is subject to the court's personal jurisdiction with respect to the civil action in question and, if a plaintiff, only in the judicial district in which it maintains its principal place of business; and

(3) a defendant not resident in the United States may be sued in any judicial district, and the joinder of such a defendant shall be disregarded in determining where the action may be brought with respect to other defendants.

(d) Residency of corporations in States with multiple districts.— For purposes of venue under this chapter, in a State which has more than one judicial district and in which a defendant that is a corporation is subject to personal jurisdiction at the time an action is commenced, such corporation shall be deemed to reside in any district in that State within which its contacts would be sufficient to subject it to personal jurisdiction if that district were a separate State, and, if there is no such district, the corporation shall be deemed to reside in the district within which it has the most significant contacts.

(e) Actions where defendant is officer or employee of the United States—

(1) In general.—A civil action in which a defendant is an officer or employee of the United States or any agency thereof acting in his official capacity or under color of legal authority, or an agency of the United States, or the United States, may, except as otherwise provided by law, be brought in any judicial district in which (A) a defendant in the action resides, (B) a substantial part of the events or omissions giving rise to the claim occurred, or a substantial part of property that is the subject of the action is situated, or (C) the plaintiff resides if no real property is involved in the action. Additional persons may be joined as parties to any such action in accordance with the Federal Rules of Civil Procedure and with such other venue requirements as would be applicable if the United States or one of its officers, employees, or agencies were not a party.

(2) Service.—The summons and complaint in such an action shall be served as provided by the Federal Rules of Civil Procedure except that the delivery of the summons and complaint to the officer or agency as required by the rules may be made by certified mail beyond the territorial limits of the district in which the action is brought.

(f) Civil actions against a foreign state—A civil action against a foreign state as defined in section 1603(a) of this title may be brought—

(1) in any judicial district in which a substantial part of the events or omissions giving rise to the claim occurred, or a substantial part of property that is the subject of the action is situated;

(2) in any judicial district in which the vessel or cargo of a foreign state is situated, if the claim is asserted under section 1605(b) of this title;

(3) in any judicial district in which the agency or instrumentality is licensed to do business or is doing business, if the action is brought against an agency or instrumentality of a foreign state as defined in section 1603(b) of this title; or

(4) in the United States District Court for the District of Columbia if the action is brought against a foreign state or political subdivision thereof.

(g) Multiparty, multiforum litigation—A civil action in which jurisdiction of the district court is based upon section 1369 of this title may be brought in any district in which any defendant resides or in which a substantial part of the accident giving rise to the action took place.

28 U.S.C. § 1404. CHANGE OF VENUE

(a) For the convenience of parties and witnesses, in the interest of justice, a district court may transfer any civil action to any other district or division where it might have been brought or to any district or division to which all parties have consented.

(b) Upon motion, consent or stipulation of all parties, any action, suit or proceeding of a civil nature or any motion or hearing thereof, may be transferred, in the discretion of the court, from the division in which pending to any other division in the same district. Transfer of proceedings in rem brought by or on behalf of the United States may be transferred under this section without the consent of the United States where all other parties request transfer.

(c) A district court may order any civil action to be tried at any place within the division in which it is pending.

(d) Transfers from a district court of the United States to the District Court of Guam, the District Court for the Northern Mariana Islands, or the District Court of the Virgin Islands shall not be permitted under this section. As otherwise used in this section, the term "district court" includes the District Court of Guam, the District Court for the Northern Mariana Islands, and the District Court of the Virgin Islands, and the term "district" includes the territorial jurisdiction of each such court.

28 U.S.C. § 1406. CURE OR WAIVER OF DEFECTS

(a) The district court of a district in which is filed a case laying venue in the wrong division or district shall dismiss, or if it be in the interest of justice, transfer such case to any district or division in which it could have been brought.

(b) Nothing in this chapter shall impair the jurisdiction of a district court of any matter involving a party who does not interpose timely and sufficient objection to the venue.

(c) As used in this section, the term "district court" includes the District Court of Guam, the District Court for the Northern Mariana Islands, and the District Court of the Virgin Islands, and the term "district" includes the territorial jurisdiction of each such court.

28 U.S.C. § 1407. MULTIDISTRICT LITIGATION

(a) When civil actions involving one or more common questions of fact are pending in different districts, such actions may be transferred to any district for coordinated or consolidated pretrial proceedings. Such transfers shall be made by the judicial panel on multidistrict litigation authorized by this section upon its determination that transfers for such proceedings will be for the convenience of parties and witnesses and will promote the just and efficient conduct of such actions. Each action so transferred shall be remanded by the panel at or before the conclusion of such pretrial proceedings to the district from which it was transferred unless it shall have been previously terminated: *Provided, however*, That the panel may separate any claim, cross-claim, counter-claim, or third-party claim and remand any of such claims before the remainder of the action is remanded.

(b) Such coordinated or consolidated pretrial proceedings shall be conducted by a judge or judges to whom such actions are assigned by the judicial panel on multidistrict litigation. For this purpose, upon request of the panel, a circuit judge or a district judge may be designated and assigned temporarily for service in the transferee district by the Chief Justice of the United States or the chief judge of the circuit, as may be required, in accordance with the provisions of chapter 13 of this title. With the consent of the transferee district court, such actions may be assigned by the panel to a judge or judges of such district. The judge or judges to whom such actions are assigned, the members of the judicial panel on multidistrict litigation, and other circuit and district judges designated when needed by the panel may exercise the powers of a district judge in any district for the purpose of conducting pretrial depositions in such coordinated or consolidated pretrial proceedings.

(c) Proceedings for the transfer of an action under this section may be initiated by—

(i) the judicial panel on multidistrict litigation upon its own initiative, or

(ii) motion filed with the panel by a party in any action in which transfer for coordinated or consolidated pretrial proceedings under this section may be appropriate. A copy of such motion shall be filed in the district court in which the moving party's action is pending.

The panel shall give notice to the parties in all actions in which transfers for coordinated or consolidated pretrial proceedings are contemplated, and such notice shall specify the time and place of any hearing to determine whether such transfer shall be made. Orders of the panel to set a hearing and other orders of the panel issued prior to the order either directing or denying transfer shall be filed in the office of the clerk of the district court in which a transfer hearing is to be or has been held. The panel's order of transfer shall be based upon a record of such hearing at which material evidence may be offered by any party to an action pending in any district that would be affected by the proceedings under this section, and shall be supported by findings of fact and conclusions of law based upon such record. Orders of transfer and such other orders as the panel may make thereafter shall be filed in the office of the clerk of the district court of the transferee district and shall be effective when thus filed. The clerk of the transferee district court shall forthwith transmit a certified copy of the panel's order to transfer to the clerk of the district court from which the action is being transferred. An order denying transfer shall be filed in each district wherein there is a case pending in which the motion for transfer has been made.

(d) The judicial panel on multidistrict litigation shall consist of seven circuit and district judges designated from time to time by the Chief Justice of the United States, no two of whom shall be from the same circuit. The concurrence of four members shall be necessary to any action by the panel.

(e) No proceedings for review of any order of the panel may be permitted except by extraordinary writ pursuant to the provisions of title 28, section 1651, United States Code. Petitions for an extraordinary writ to review an order of the panel to set a transfer hearing and other orders of the panel issued prior to the order either directing or denying transfer shall be filed only in the court of appeals having jurisdiction over the district in which a hearing is to be or has been held. Petitions for an extraordinary writ to review an order to transfer or orders subsequent to transfer shall be filed only in the court of appeals having jurisdiction over the transferee district. There shall be no appeal or review of an order of the panel denying a motion to transfer for consolidated or coordinated proceedings.

(f) The panel may prescribe rules for the conduct of its business not inconsistent with Acts of Congress and the Federal Rules of Civil Procedure.

(g) Nothing in this section shall apply to any action in which the United States is a complainant arising under the antitrust laws. "Antitrust laws" as used herein include those acts referred to in the Act of October 15, 1914, as amended (38 Stat. 730; 15 U.S.C. 12), and also include the Act of June 19, 1936 (49 Stat. 1526; 15 U.S.C. 13, 13a, and 13b) and the Act of September 26, 1914, as added March 21, 1938 (52 Stat. 116, 117; 15 U.S.C. 56); but shall not include section 4A of the Act of October 15, 1914, as added July 7, 1955 (69 Stat. 282; 15 U.S.C. 15a).

(h) Notwithstanding the provisions of section 1404 or subsection (f) of this section, the judicial panel on multidistrict litigation may consolidate and transfer with or without the consent of the parties, for both pretrial purposes and for trial, any action brought under section 4C of the Clayton Act.

* * *

BATES v. C & S ADJUSTERS, INC.

980 F.2d 865 (2d Cir. 1992)

JON O. NEWMAN, CIRCUIT JUDGE:

This appeal concerns venue in an action brought under the Fair Debt Collection Practices Act, 15 U.S.C. §§ 1692–1692o (1988). Specifically, the issue is whether venue exists in a district in which the debtor resides and to which a bill collector's demand for payment was forwarded. The issue arises on an appeal by Phillip E. Bates from the May 21, 1992, judgment of the District Court for the Western District of New York, dismissing his complaint because of improper venue. We conclude that venue was proper under 28 U.S.C.A. § 1391(b)(2) and therefore reverse and remand.

Background

Bates commenced this action in the Western District of New York upon receipt of a collection notice from C & S Adjusters, Inc. ("C & S"). Bates alleged violations of the Fair Debt Collection Practices Act, and demanded statutory damages, costs, and attorney's fees. The facts relevant to venue are not in dispute. Bates incurred the debt in question while he was a resident of the Western District of Pennsylvania. The creditor, a corporation with its principal place of business in that District, referred the account to C & S, a local collection agency which transacts no regular business in New York. Bates had meanwhile moved to the Western District of New York. When C & S mailed a collection notice to Bates at his Pennsylvania address, the Postal Service forwarded the notice to Bates' new address in New York.

In its answer, C & S asserted two affirmative defenses and also counterclaimed for costs, alleging that the action was instituted in bad faith and for purposes of harassment. C & S subsequently filed a motion to dismiss for improper venue, which the District Court granted.

Discussion

1. Venue and the 1990 amendments to 28 U.S.C. § 1391(b)

Bates concedes that the only plausible venue provision for this action is 28 U.S.C.A. § 1391(b)(2), which allows an action to be brought in "a judicial district in which a substantial part of the events or omissions giving rise to the claim occurred." Prior to 1990, section 1391 allowed for venue in "the judicial district ... in which the claim arose." 28 U.S.C. § 1391(b) (1988). This case represents our first opportunity to consider the significance of the 1990 amendments.

Prior to 1966, venue was proper in federal question cases, absent a special venue statute, only in the defendant's state of citizenship. If a plaintiff sought to sue multiple defendants who were citizens of different states, there might be no district where the entire action could be brought. Congress closed this "venue gap" by adding a provision allowing suit in the district "in which the claim arose." This phrase gave rise to a variety of conflicting interpretations. Some courts thought it meant that there could be only one such district; others believed there could be several. Different tests developed, with courts looking for "substantial contacts," the "weight of contacts," the place of injury or performance, or even to the boundaries of personal jurisdiction under state law. District courts within the Second Circuit used at least three of these approaches.

The Supreme Court gave detailed attention to section 1391(b) in *Leroy v. Great Western United Corp.*, 443 U.S. 173 (1979). The specific holding of *Leroy* was that Great Western, a Texas corporation, which had attempted to take over an Idaho corporation, could not bring suit in Texas against Idaho officials who sought to enforce a state anti-takeover law. Although the effect of the Idaho officials' action might be felt in Texas, the Court rejected this factor as a basis for venue, since it would allow the Idaho officials to be sued anywhere a shareholder of the target corporation could allege that he wanted to accept Great Western's tender offer. *Leroy*. The Court made several further observations: (1) the purpose of the 1966 statute was to close venue gaps and should not be read more broadly than necessary to close those gaps; (2) the general purpose of the venue statute was to protect defendants against an unfair or inconvenient trial location; (3) location of evidence and witnesses was a relevant factor; (4) familiarity of the Idaho federal judges with the Idaho anti-takeover statute was a relevant factor; (5) plaintiff's convenience was not a relevant factor; and (6) in only rare cases should there be more than one district in which a claim can be said to arise.

Subsequent to *Leroy* and prior to the 1990 amendment to section 1391(b), most courts have applied at least a form of the "weight of contacts" test. Courts continued to have difficulty in determining whether more than one district could be proper.

Against this background, we understand Congress' 1990 amendment to be at most a marginal expansion of the venue provision. The House Report indicates that the new language was first proposed by the American Law Institute in a 1969 Study, and observes:

> The great advantage of referring to the place where things happened ... is that it avoids the litigation breeding phrase "in which the claim arose." It also avoids the problem created by the frequent cases in which substantial parts of the underlying events have occurred in several districts.

Thus it seems clear that *Leroy's* strong admonition against recognizing multiple venues has been disapproved. Many of the factors in *Leroy*—for instance, the convenience of defendants and the location of evidence and witnesses—are most useful in distinguishing between two or more plausible venues. Since the new statute does not, as a general matter, require the District Court to determine the best venue, these factors will be of less significance. Apart from this point, however, *Leroy* and other precedents remain important sources of guidance.

2. Fair Debt Collection Practices Act

Under the version of the venue statute in force from 1966 to 1990, at least three District Courts held that venue was proper under the Fair Debt Collection Practices Act in the plaintiff's home district if a collection agency had mailed a collection notice to an address in that district or placed a phone call to a number in that district. None of these cases involved the unusual fact, present in this case, that the defendant did not deliberately direct a communication to the plaintiff's district.

We conclude, however, that this difference is inconsequential, at least under the current venue statute. The statutory standard for venue focuses not on whether a defendant has made a deliberate contact—a factor relevant in the analysis of personal jurisdiction[1]—but on the location where events occurred. Under the new version of section 1391(b)(2), we must determine only whether a "substantial part of the events . . . giving rise to the claim" occurred in the Western District of New York.

In adopting this statute, Congress was concerned about the harmful effect of abusive debt practices on consumers. *See* 15 U.S.C. § 1692(a) ("Abusive debt collection practices contribute to the number of personal bankruptcies, to marital instability, to the loss of jobs, and to invasions of individual privacy."). This harm does not occur until receipt of the collection notice. Indeed, if the notice were lost in the mail, it is unlikely that a violation of the Act would have occurred. Moreover, a debt collection agency sends its dunning letters so that they will be received. Forwarding such letters to the district to which a debtor has moved is an important step in the collection process. If the bill collector prefers not to be challenged for its collection practices outside the district of a debtor's original residence, the envelope can be marked "do not forward." We conclude that receipt of a collection notice is a substantial part of the events giving rise to a claim under the Fair Debt Collection Practices Act.

The relevant factors identified in *Leroy* add support to our conclusion. Although "bona fide error" can be a defense to liability under the Act, the alleged violations of the Act turn largely not on the collection agency's intent, but on the content of the collection notice. The most relevant evidence—the collection notice—is located in the Western District of New York. Because the collection agency appears not to have marked the notice with instructions not to forward, and has not objected to the assertion of personal jurisdiction, trial in the Western District of New York would not be unfair.

---

1. C & S has waived whatever claim it might have had that the District Court lacked personal jurisdiction over it. Waiver resulted from C & S's failure to allege lack of personal jurisdiction in its answer or motion to dismiss. *See* Fed.R.Civ.P. 12(b)(2), (h).

CONCLUSION

The judgment of the District Court is reversed, and the matter is remanded for further proceedings consistent with this decision.

HOFFMAN v. BLASKI

363 U.S. 335 (1960)

MR. JUSTICE WHITTAKER delivered the opinion of the Court.

To relieve against what was apparently thought to be the harshness of dismissal, under the doctrine of forum non conveniens, of an action brought in an inconvenient one of two or more legally available forums, *Gulf Oil Corp. v. Gilbert*, Congress, in 1948, enacted 28 U.S.C. § 1404(a), which provides:

> § 1404. Change of venue.
>
> (a) For the convenience of parties and witnesses, in the interest of justice, a district court may transfer any civil action to any other district or division where it might have been brought.

The instant cases present the question whether a District Court, in which a civil action has been properly brought, is empowered by § 1404(a) to transfer the action, on the motion of the defendant, to a district in which the plaintiff did not have a right to bring it.

Respondents, Blaski and others, residents of Illinois, brought this patent infringement action in the United States District Court for the Northern District of Texas against one Howell and a Texas corporation controlled by him, alleging that the defendants are residents of, and maintain their only place of business in, the City of Dallas, in the Northern District of Texas, where they are infringing respondents' patents. After being served with process and filing their answer, the defendants moved, under s 1404(a), to transfer the action to the United States District Court for the Northern District of Illinois.[2] Respondents objected to the transfer on the ground that, inasmuch as the defendants did not reside, maintain a place of business, or infringe the patents in, and could not have been served with process in, the Illinois district, the courts of that district lacked venue over the action and ability to command jurisdiction over the defendants; that therefore that district was not a forum in which the respondents had a right to bring the action, and, hence, the court was without power to transfer it to that district. Without mentioning that objection or the question it raised, the District Court found that "the motion should be granted for the convenience of the parties and

---

2. The asserted basis of the motion was that trial of the action in the Illinois District Court would be more convenient to the parties and witnesses and in the interest of justice because several actions involving the validity of these patents were then pending in that court, and that pretrial and discovery steps taken in those actions had developed a substantial amount of evidence that would be relevant and useful in this action.

Defendants also stated in the motion that, if and when the case be so transferred, they would waive all objections to the venue of the Illinois District Court over the action and would enter their appearance in the action in that court.

witnesses in the interest of justice," and ordered the case transferred to the Illinois district. Thereupon, respondents moved in the Fifth Circuit for leave to file a petition for a writ of mandamus directing the vacation of that order. That court, holding that "(t)he purposes for which § 1404(a) was enacted would be unduly circumscribed if a transfer could not be made 'in the interest of justice' to a district where the defendants not only waive venue but to which they seek the transfer," denied the motion.

Upon receipt of a certified copy of the pleadings and record, the Illinois District Court assigned the action to Judge Hoffman's calendar. Respondents promptly moved for an order remanding the action on the ground that the Texas District Court did not have power to make the transfer order and, hence, the Illinois District Court was not thereby vested with jurisdiction of the action. After expressing his view that the "weight of reason and logic" favored "retransfer of this case to Texas," Judge Hoffman, with misgivings, denied the motion. Respondents then filed in the Seventh Circuit a petition for a writ of mandamus directing Judge Hoffman to reverse his order. After hearing and rehearing, the Seventh Circuit, holding that "(w)hen Congress provided (in § 1404(a)) for transfer (of a civil action) to a district 'where it might have been brought,' it is hardly open to doubt but that it referred to a district where the plaintiff * * * had a right to bring the case," and that respondents did not have a right to bring this action in the Illinois district, granted the writ, one judge dissenting.

* * *

To settle the conflict that has arisen among the circuits respecting the proper interpretation and application of § 1404(a),we granted certiorari.

Without sacrifice or slight of any tenable position, the parties have in this Court commendably narrowed their contentions to the scope of the only relevant inquiry. The points of contention may be sharpened by first observing what is not in contest. Discretion of the district judges concerned is not involved. Propriety of the remedy of mandamus is not assailed. No claim is made here that the order of the Fifth Circuit denying the motion of respondents in the Blaski case for leave to file a petition for writ of mandamus, precluded Judge Hoffman or the Seventh Circuit from remanding that case.[9] Petitioners concede that these actions were properly brought in the respective transferor forums; that statutory venue did not exist over either of these actions in the respective transferee districts, and that the respective defendants were not within the reach of the process of the respective transferee courts. They concede, too, that § 1404(a), being "not unlimited," "may be utilized only to direct an action to any other district or division 'where it might have been brought,' " and that, like the superseded doctrine of forum non conveniens, *Gulf Oil Corp. v. Gilbert,*

---

9. That order did not purport to determine the jurisdiction of the transferee court and therefore did not preclude Judge Hoffman of power to determine his own jurisdiction, nor did it preclude the power of the Seventh Circuit to review his action.

the statute requires "an alternative forum in which plaintiff might proceed."

Petitioners' "thesis" and sole claim is that § 1404(a), being remedial, should be broadly construed, and, when so construed, the phrase "where it might have been brought" should be held to relate not only to the time of the bringing of the action, but also to the time of the transfer; and that "if at such time the transferee forum has the power to adjudicate the issues of the action, it is a forum in which the action might then have been brought." They argue that in the interim between the bringing of the action and the filing of a motion to transfer it, the defendants may move their residence to, or, if corporations, may begin the transaction of business in, some other district, and, if such is done, the phrase 'where it might have been brought' should be construed to empower the District Court to transfer the action, on motion of the defendants, to such other district; and that, similarly, if, as here, the defendants move to transfer the action to some other district and consent to submit to the jurisdiction of such other district, the latter district should be held one "in which the action might then have been brought."

We do not agree. We do not think the § 1404(a) phrase "where it might have been brought" can be interpreted to mean, as petitioners' theory would required, " 'where it may now be rebrought, with defendants' consent." This Court has said, in a different context, that § 1404(a) is "unambiguous, direct (and) clear," and that "the unequivocal words of § 1404(a) and the legislative history * * * (establish) that Congress indeed meant what it said." Like the Seventh Circuit, we think the dissenting opinion of Judges Hastie and McLaughlin in *Paramount Pictures, Inc. v. Rodney*, correctly answered this contention:

> But we do not see how the conduct of a defendant after suit has been instituted can add to the forums where 'it might have been brought.' In the normal meaning of words this language of Section 1404(a) directs the attention of the judge who is considering a transfer to the situation which existed when suit was instituted.

It is not to be doubted that the transferee courts, like every District Court, had jurisdiction to entertain actions of the character involved, but it is obvious that they did not acquire jurisdiction over these particular actions when they were brought in the transferor courts. The transferee courts could have acquired jurisdiction over these actions only if properly brought in those courts, or if validly transferred thereto under § 1404(a). Of course, venue, like jurisdiction over the person, may be waived. A defendant, properly served with process by a court having subject matter jurisdiction, waives venue by failing seasonably to assert it, or even simply by making default. But the power of a District Court under § 1404(a) to transfer an action to another district is made to depend not upon the wish or waiver of the defendant but, rather, upon whether the transferee district was one in which the action "might have been brought" by the plaintiff.

The thesis urged by petitioners would not only do violence to the plain words of § 1404(a), but would also inject gross discrimination. That thesis, if adopted, would empower a District Court, upon a finding of convenience, to transfer an action to any district desired by the defendants and in which they were willing to waive their statutory defenses as to venue and jurisdiction over their persons, regardless of the fact that such transferee district was not one in which the action "might have been brought" by the plaintiff. Conversely, that thesis would not permit the court, upon motion of the plaintiffs and a like showing of convenience, to transfer the action to the same district, without the consent and waiver of venue and personal jurisdiction defenses by the defendants. Nothing in § 1404(a), or in its legislative history, suggests such a unilateral objective and we should not, under the guise of interpretation, ascribe to Congress any such discriminatory purpose.

We agree with the Seventh Circuit that:

> If when a suit is commenced, plaintiff has a right to sue in that district, independently of the wishes of defendant, it is a district "where (the action) might have been brought." If he does not have that right, independently of the wishes of defendant, it is not a district "where it might have been brought," and it is immaterial that the defendant subsequently (makes himself subject, by consent, waiver of venue and personal jurisdiction defenses or otherwise, to the jurisdiction of some other forum).

Inasmuch as the respondents (plaintiffs) did not have a right to bring these actions in the respective transferee districts, it follows that the judgments of the Court of Appeals were correct and must be affirmed.

Affirmed.

D.   FORUM NON CONVENIENS

* * *

PIPER AIRCRAFT COMPANY v. REYNO

454 U.S. 235 (1981)

JUSTICE MARSHALL delivered the opinion of the Court.

These cases arise out of an air crash that took place in Scotland. Respondent, acting as representative of the estates of several Scottish citizens killed in the accident, brought wrongful-death actions against petitioners that were ultimately transferred to the United States District Court for the Middle District of Pennsylvania. Petitioners moved to dismiss on the ground of *forum non conveniens*. After noting that an alternative forum existed in Scotland, the District Court granted their motions. The United States Court of Appeals for the Third Circuit reversed. The Court of Appeals based its decision, at least in part, on the ground that dismissal is automatically barred where the law of the alternative forum is less favorable to the plaintiff than the law of the forum chosen by the plaintiff. Because we conclude that the possibility of an unfavorable change in law should not, by itself, bar dismissal, and because we conclude that the District Court did not otherwise abuse its discretion, we reverse.

I

A

In July 1976, a small commercial aircraft crashed in the Scottish highlands during the course of a charter flight from Blackpool to Perth. The pilot and five passengers were killed instantly. The decedents were all Scottish subjects and residents, as are their heirs and next of kin. There were no eyewitnesses to the accident. At the time of the crash the plane was subject to Scottish air traffic control.

The aircraft, a twin-engine Piper Aztec, was manufactured in Pennsylvania by petitioner Piper Aircraft Co. (Piper). The propellers were manufactured in Ohio by petitioner Hartzell Propeller, Inc. (Hartzell). At the time of the crash the aircraft was registered in Great Britain and was owned and maintained by Air Navigation and Trading Co., Ltd. (Air Navigation). It was operated by McDonald Aviation, Ltd. (McDonald), a Scottish air taxi service. Both Air Navigation and McDonald were organized in the United Kingdom. The wreckage of the plane is now in a hangar in Farnsborough, England.

The British Department of Trade investigated the accident shortly after it occurred. A preliminary report found that the plane crashed after developing a spin, and suggested that mechanical failure in the plane or the propeller was responsible. At Hartzell's request, this report was reviewed by a three-member Review Board, which held a 9–day adversary hearing attended by all interested parties. The Review Board found no evidence of defective equipment and indicated that pilot error may have contributed to the accident. The pilot, who had obtained his commercial pilot's license only three months earlier, was flying over high ground at an altitude considerably lower than the minimum height required by his company's operations manual.

In July 1977, a California probate court appointed respondent Gaynell Reyno administratrix of the estates of the five passengers. Reyno is not related to and does not know any of the decedents or their survivors; she was a legal secretary to the attorney who filed this lawsuit. Several days after her appointment, Reyno commenced separate wrongful-death actions against Piper and Hartzell in the Superior Court of California, claiming negligence and strict liability. Air Navigation, McDonald, and the estate of the pilot are not parties to this litigation. The survivors of the five passengers whose estates are represented by Reyno filed a separate action in the United Kingdom against Air Navigation, McDonald, and the pilot's estate. Reyno candidly admits that the action against Piper and Hartzell was filed in the United States because its laws regarding liability, capacity to sue, and damages are more favorable to her position than are those of Scotland. Scottish law does not recognize strict liability in tort. Moreover, it permits wrongful-death actions only when brought by a decedent's relatives. The relatives may sue only for "loss of support and society."

On petitioners' motion, the suit was removed to the United States District Court for the Central District of California. Piper then moved for transfer to the United States District Court for the Middle District of Pennsylvania, pursuant to 28 U.S.C. § 1404(a). Hartzell moved to dismiss for lack of personal jurisdiction, or in the alternative, to transfer. In December 1977, the District Court quashed service on Hartzell and transferred the case to the Middle District of Pennsylvania. Respondent then properly served process on Hartzell.

B

In May 1978, after the suit had been transferred, both Hartzell and Piper moved to dismiss the action on the ground of *forum non conveniens.* The District Court granted these motions in October 1979. It relied on the balancing test set forth by this Court in *Gulf Oil Corp. v. Gilbert,* 330 U.S. 501 (1947). In th[at] decision, the Court stated that a plaintiff's choice of forum should rarely be disturbed. However, when an alternative forum has jurisdiction to hear the case, and when trial in the chosen forum would "establish ... oppressiveness and vexation to a defendant ... out of all proportion to plaintiff's convenience," or when the "chosen forum [is] inappropriate because of considerations affecting the court's own administrative and legal problems," the court may, in the exercise of its sound discretion, dismiss the case. To guide trial court discretion, the Court provided a list of "private interest factors" affecting the convenience of the litigants, and a list of "public interest factors" affecting the convenience of the forum. *Gilbert.*[6]

After describing our decision[ ] in *Gilbert,* the District Court analyzed the facts of these cases. It began by observing that an alternative forum existed in Scotland; Piper and Hartzell had agreed to submit to the jurisdiction of the Scottish courts and to waive any statute of limitations defense that might be available. It then stated that plaintiff's choice of forum was entitled to little weight. The court recognized that a plaintiff's choice ordinarily deserves substantial deference. It noted, however, that Reyno "is a representative of foreign citizens and residents seeking a forum in the United States because of the more liberal rules concerning products liability law," and that "the courts have been less solicitous

---

6. The [*Gulf Oil v. Gilbert*] factors pertaining to the private interests of the litigants included the "relative ease of access to sources of proof; availability of compulsory process for attendance of unwilling, and the cost of obtaining attendance of willing, witnesses; possibility of view of premises, if view would be appropriate to the action; and all other practical problems that make trial of a case easy, expeditious and inexpensive." The public factors bearing on the question included the administrative difficulties flowing from court congestion; the "local interest in having localized controversies decided at home"; the interest in having the trial of a diversity case in a forum that is at home with the law that must govern the action; the avoidance of unnecessary problems in conflict of laws, or in the application of foreign law; and the unfairness of burdening citizens in an unrelated forum with jury duty.

when the plaintiff is not an American citizen or resident, and particularly when the foreign citizens seek to benefit from the more liberal tort rules provided for the protection of citizens and residents of the United States."

The District Court next examined several factors relating to the private interests of the litigants, and determined that these factors strongly pointed towards Scotland as the appropriate forum. Although evidence concerning the design, manufacture, and testing of the plane and propeller is located in the United States, the connections with Scotland are otherwise "overwhelming." The real parties in interest are citizens of Scotland, as were all the decedents. Witnesses who could testify regarding the maintenance of the aircraft, the training of the pilot, and the investigation of the accident—all essential to the defense—are in Great Britain. Moreover, all witnesses to damages are located in Scotland. Trial would be aided by familiarity with Scottish topography, and by easy access to the wreckage.

The District Court reasoned that because crucial witnesses and evidence were beyond the reach of compulsory process, and because the defendants would not be able to implead potential Scottish third-party defendants, it would be "unfair to make Piper and Hartzell proceed to trial in this forum." The survivors had brought separate actions in Scotland against the pilot, McDonald, and Air Navigation. "[I]t would be fairer to all parties and less costly if the entire case was presented to one jury with available testimony from all relevant witnesses." Although the court recognized that if trial were held in the United States, Piper and Hartzell could file indemnity or contribution actions against the Scottish defendants, it believed that there was a significant risk of inconsistent verdicts.[7]

The District Court concluded that the relevant public interests also pointed strongly towards dismissal. The court determined that Pennsylvania law would apply to Piper and Scottish law to Hartzell if the case were tried in the Middle District of Pennsylvania.[8] As a result, "trial in this forum would be hopelessly complex and confusing for a jury." In addition, the court noted that it was unfamiliar with Scottish law and thus would have to rely upon experts from that country. The court also found that the trial would be enormously costly and time-consuming; that it would be unfair to burden citizens with jury duty when the Middle District of

---

7. The District Court explained that inconsistent verdicts might result if petitioners were held liable on the basis of strict liability here, and then required to prove negligence in an indemnity action in Scotland. Moreover, even if the same standard of liability applied, there was a danger that different juries would find different facts and produce inconsistent results.

8. Under *Klaxon v. Stentor Electric Mfg. Co.*, 313 U.S. 487 (1941), a court ordinarily must apply the choice-of-law rules of the State in which it sits. However, where a case is transferred pursuant to 28 U.S.C. § 1404(a), it must apply the choice-of-law rules of the State from which the case was transferred. *Van Dusen v. Barrack*, 376 U.S. 612 (1964). Relying on these two cases, the District Court concluded that California choice-of-law rules would apply to Piper, and Pennsylvania choice-of-law rules would apply to Hartzell. It further concluded that California applied a "governmental interests" analysis in resolving choice-of-law problems, and that Pennsylvania employed a "significant contacts" analysis. The court used the "governmental interests" analysis to determine that Pennsylvania liability rules would apply to Piper, and the "significant contacts" analysis to determine that Scottish liability rules would apply to Hartzell.

Pennsylvania has little connection with the controversy; and that Scotland has a substantial interest in the outcome of the litigation.

In opposing the motions to dismiss, respondent contended that dismissal would be unfair because Scottish law was less favorable. The District Court explicitly rejected this claim. It reasoned that the possibility that dismissal might lead to an unfavorable change in the law did not deserve significant weight; any deficiency in the foreign law was a "matter to be dealt with in the foreign forum."

C

On appeal, the United States Court of Appeals for the Third Circuit reversed and remanded for trial. The decision to reverse appears to be based on two alternative grounds. First, the Court held that the District Court abused its discretion in conducting the *Gilbert* analysis. Second, the Court held that dismissal is never appropriate where the law of the alternative forum is less favorable to the plaintiff.

The Court of Appeals began its review of the District Court's *Gilbert* analysis by noting that the plaintiff's choice of forum deserved substantial weight, even though the real parties in interest are nonresidents. It then rejected the District Court's balancing of the private interests. It found that Piper and Hartzell had failed adequately to support their claim that key witnesses would be unavailable if trial were held in the United States: they had never specified the witnesses they would call and the testimony these witnesses would provide. The Court of Appeals gave little weight to the fact that Piper and Hartzell would not be able to implead potential Scottish third-party defendants, reasoning that this difficulty would be "burdensome" but not "unfair." Finally, the court stated that resolution of the suit would not be significantly aided by familiarity with Scottish topography, or by viewing the wreckage.

The Court of Appeals also rejected the District Court's analysis of the public interest factors. It found that the District Court gave undue emphasis to the application of Scottish law: " 'the mere fact that the court is called upon to determine and apply foreign law does not present a legal problem of the sort which would justify the dismissal of a case otherwise properly before the court.' " In any event, it believed that Scottish law need not be applied. After conducting its own choice-of-law analysis, the Court of Appeals determined that American law would govern the actions against both Piper and Hartzell. The same choice-of-law analysis apparently led it to conclude that Pennsylvania and Ohio, rather than Scotland, are the jurisdictions with the greatest policy interests in the dispute, and that all other public interest factors favored trial in the United States.[11]

---

11. The court's reasoning on this point is somewhat unclear. It states:

We have held that under the applicable choice of law rules Pennsylvania and Ohio are the jurisdictions with the greatest policy interest in this dispute. It follows that the other public interest factors that should be considered under the Supreme Court case[ ] of *Gilbert* favor[s] trial in this country rather than Scotland.

In any event, it appears that the Court of Appeals would have reversed even if the District Court had properly balanced the public and private interests. The court stated:

> [I]t is apparent that the dismissal would work a change in the applicable law so that the plaintiff's strict liability claim would be eliminated from the case. But ... a dismissal for forum non conveniens, like a statutory transfer, "should not, despite its convenience, result in a change in the applicable law." Only when American law is not applicable, or when the foreign jurisdiction would, as a matter of its own choice of law, give the plaintiff the benefit of the claim to which she is entitled here, would dismissal be justified.

In other words, the court decided that dismissal is automatically barred if it would lead to a change in the applicable law unfavorable to the plaintiff.

We granted certiorari ... to consider the questions they raise concerning the proper application of the doctrine of *forum non conveniens.*

II

The Court of Appeals erred in holding that plaintiffs may defeat a motion to dismiss on the ground of *forum non conveniens* merely by showing that the substantive law that would be applied in the alternative forum is less favorable to the plaintiffs than that of the present forum. The possibility of a change in substantive law should ordinarily not be given conclusive or even substantial weight in the *forum non conveniens* inquiry.

We expressly rejected the position adopted by the Court of Appeals in our decision in *Canada Malting Co. v. Paterson Steamships, Ltd.* That case arose out of a collision between two vessels in American waters. The Canadian owners of cargo lost in the accident sued the Canadian owners of one of the vessels in Federal District Court. The cargo owners chose an American court in large part because the relevant American liability rules were more favorable than the Canadian rules. The District Court dismissed on grounds of *forum non conveniens.* The plaintiffs argued that dismissal was inappropriate because Canadian laws were less favorable to them. This Court nonetheless affirmed:

> We have no occasion to enquire by what law the rights of the parties are governed, as we are of the opinion that, under any view of that question, it lay within the discretion of the District Court to decline to assume jurisdiction over the controversy.... "[T]he court will not take cognizance of the case if justice would be as well done by remitting the parties to their home forum."

The Court of Appeals concluded as part of its choice-of-law analysis that the United States had the greatest policy interest in the dispute. It apparently believed that this conclusion necessarily implied that the *forum non conveniens* public interest factors pointed toward trial in the United States.

The Court further stated that "[t]here was no basis for the contention that the District Court abused its discretion."

It is true that *Canada Malting* was decided before *Gilbert*, and that the doctrine of *forum non conveniens* was not fully crystallized until our decision in that case. However, *Gilbert* in no way affects the validity of *Canada Malting*. Indeed, by holding that the central focus of the *forum non conveniens* inquiry is convenience, *Gilbert* implicitly recognized that dismissal may not be barred solely because of the possibility of an unfavorable change in law. Under *Gilbert*, dismissal will ordinarily be appropriate where trial in the plaintiff's chosen forum imposes a heavy burden on the defendant or the court, and where the plaintiff is unable to offer any specific reasons of convenience supporting his choice.[15] If substantial weight were given to the possibility of an unfavorable change in law, however, dismissal might be barred even where trial in the chosen forum was plainly inconvenient.

The Court of Appeals' decision is inconsistent with this Court's earlier *forum non conveniens* decisions in another respect. Those decisions have repeatedly emphasized the need to retain flexibility. In *Gilbert*, the Court refused to identify specific circumstances "which will justify or require either grant or denial of remedy." Similarly, the Court rejected the contention that where a trial would involve inquiry into the internal affairs of a foreign corporation, dismissal was always appropriate. "That is one, but only one, factor which may show convenience." And ... we stated that we would not lay down a rigid rule to govern discretion, and that "[e]ach case turns on its facts." If central emphasis were placed on any one factor, the *forum non conveniens* doctrine would lose much of the very flexibility that makes it so valuable.

In fact, if conclusive or substantial weight were given to the possibility of a change in law, the *forum non conveniens* doctrine would become virtually useless. Jurisdiction and venue requirements are often easily satisfied. As a result, many plaintiffs are able to choose from among several forums. Ordinarily, these plaintiffs will select that forum whose choice-of-law rules are most advantageous. Thus, if the possibility of an unfavorable change in substantive law is given substantial weight in the *forum non conveniens* inquiry, dismissal would rarely be proper.

Except for the court below, every Federal Court of Appeals that has considered this question after *Gilbert* has held that dismissal on grounds of *forum non conveniens* may be granted even though the law applicable in the alternative forum is less favorable to the plaintiff's chance of recovery. Several courts have relied expressly on *Canada Malting* to hold that the possibility of an unfavorable change of law should not, by itself, bar dismissal.

---

15. In other words, *Gilbert* held that dismissal may be warranted where a plaintiff chooses a particular forum, not because it is convenient, but solely in order to harass the defendant or take advantage of favorable law. This is precisely the situation in which the Court of Appeals' rule would bar dismissal.

The Court of Appeals' approach is not only inconsistent with the purpose of the *forum non conveniens* doctrine, but also poses substantial practical problems. If the possibility of a change in law were given substantial weight, deciding motions to dismiss on the ground of *forum non conveniens* would become quite difficult. Choice-of-law analysis would become extremely important, and the courts would frequently be required to interpret the law of foreign jurisdictions. First, the trial court would have to determine what law would apply if the case were tried in the chosen forum, and what law would apply if the case were tried in the alternative forum. It would then have to compare the rights, remedies, and procedures available under the law that would be applied in each forum. Dismissal would be appropriate only if the court concluded that the law applied by the alternative forum is as favorable to the plaintiff as that of the chosen forum. The doctrine of *forum non conveniens*, however, is designed in part to help courts avoid conducting complex exercises in comparative law. As we stated in *Gilbert*, the public interest factors point towards dismissal where the court would be required to "untangle problems in conflict of laws, and in law foreign to itself."

Upholding the decision of the Court of Appeals would result in other practical problems. At least where the foreign plaintiff named an American manufacturer as defendant,[17] a court could not dismiss the case on grounds of *forum non conveniens* where dismissal might lead to an unfavorable change in law. The American courts, which are already extremely attractive to foreign plaintiffs, would become even more attractive. The flow of litigation into the United States would increase and further congest already crowded courts.[19]

The Court of Appeals based its decision, at least in part, on an analogy between dismissals on grounds of *forum non conveniens* and transfers between federal courts pursuant to § 1404(a). In *Van Dusen v. Barrack*, 376 U.S. 612 (1964), this Court ruled that a § 1404(a) transfer should not result in a change in the applicable law. Relying on dictum in an earlier Third Circuit opinion interpreting *Van Dusen*, the court below held that that principle is also applicable to a dismissal on *forum non*

---

17. In fact, the defendant might not even have to be American. A foreign plaintiff seeking damages for an accident that occurred abroad might be able to obtain service of process on a foreign defendant who does business in the United States. Under the Court of Appeals' holding, dismissal would be barred if the law in the alternative forum were less favorable to the plaintiff-even though none of the parties are American, and even though there is absolutely no nexus between the subject matter of the litigation and the United States.

19. In holding that the possibility of a change in law unfavorable to the plaintiff should not be given substantial weight, we also necessarily hold that the possibility of a change in law favorable to defendant should not be considered. Respondent suggests that Piper and Hartzell filed the motion to dismiss, not simply because trial in the United States would be inconvenient, but also because they believe the laws of Scotland are more favorable. She argues that this should be taken into account in the analysis of the private interests. We recognize, of course, that Piper and Hartzell may be engaged in reverse forum-shopping. However, this possibility ordinarily should not enter into a trial court's analysis of the private interests. If the defendant is able to overcome the presumption in favor of plaintiff by showing that trial in the chosen forum would be unnecessarily burdensome, dismissal is appropriate—regardless of the fact that defendant may also be motivated by a desire to obtain a more favorable forum.

conveniens grounds. However, § 1404(a) transfers are different than dismissals on the ground of *forum non conveniens.*

Congress enacted § 1404(a) to permit change of venue between federal courts. Although the statute was drafted in accordance with the doctrine of *forum non conveniens,* it was intended to be a revision rather than a codification of the common law. District courts were given more discretion to transfer under § 1404(a) than they had to dismiss on grounds of *forum non conveniens.*

The reasoning employed in *Van Dusen v. Barrack* is simply inapplicable to dismissals on grounds of *forum non conveniens.* That case did not discuss the common-law doctrine. Rather, it focused on "the construction and application" of § 1404(a). Emphasizing the remedial purpose of the statute, *Barrack* concluded that Congress could not have intended a transfer to be accompanied by a change in law. The statute was designed as a "federal housekeeping measure," allowing easy change of venue within a unified federal system. The Court feared that if a change in venue were accompanied by a change in law, forum-shopping parties would take unfair advantage of the relaxed standards for transfer. The rule was necessary to ensure the just and efficient operation of the statute.

We do not hold that the possibility of an unfavorable change in law should *never* be a relevant consideration in a *forum non conveniens* inquiry. Of course, if the remedy provided by the alternative forum is so clearly inadequate or unsatisfactory that it is no remedy at all, the unfavorable change in law may be given substantial weight; the district court may conclude that dismissal would not be in the interests of justice.[22] In these cases, however, the remedies that would be provided by the Scottish courts do not fall within this category. Although the relatives of the decedents may not be able to rely on a strict liability theory, and although their potential damages award may be smaller, there is no danger that they will be deprived of any remedy or treated unfairly.

III

The Court of Appeals also erred in rejecting the District Court's *Gilbert* analysis. The Court of Appeals stated that more weight should have been given to the plaintiff's choice of forum, and criticized the District Court's analysis of the private and public interests. However, the District Court's decision regarding the deference due plaintiff's choice of

---

22. At the outset of any *forum non conveniens* inquiry, the court must determine whether there exists an alternative forum. Ordinarily, this requirement will be satisfied when the defendant is "amenable to process" in the other jurisdiction. In rare circumstances, however, where the remedy offered by the other forum is clearly unsatisfactory, the other forum may not be an adequate alternative, and the initial requirement may not be satisfied. Thus, for example, dismissal would not be appropriate where the alternative forum does not permit litigation of the subject matter of the dispute. Cf. *Phoenix Canada Oil Co. Ltd. v. Texaco, Inc.* (Del.1978) (court refuses to dismiss, where alternative forum is Ecuador, it is unclear whether Ecuadorean tribunal will hear the case, and there is no generally codified Ecuadorean legal remedy for the unjust enrichment and tort claims asserted).

forum was appropriate. Furthermore, we do not believe that the District Court abused its discretion in weighing the private and public interests.

A

The District Court acknowledged that there is ordinarily a strong presumption in favor of the plaintiff's choice of forum, which may be overcome only when the private and public interest factors clearly point towards trial in the alternative forum. It held, however, that the presumption applies with less force when the plaintiff or real parties in interest are foreign.

The District Court's distinction between resident or citizen plaintiffs and foreign plaintiffs is fully justified. In *Koster*, the Court indicated that a plaintiff's choice of forum is entitled to greater deference when the plaintiff has chosen the home forum.[23] When the home forum has been chosen, it is reasonable to assume that this choice is convenient. When the plaintiff is foreign, however, this assumption is much less reasonable. Because the central purpose of any *forum non conveniens* inquiry is to ensure that the trial is convenient, a foreign plaintiff's choice deserves less deference.

B

The *forum non conveniens* determination is committed to the sound discretion of the trial court. It may be reversed only when there has been a clear abuse of discretion; where the court has considered all relevant public and private interest factors, and where its balancing of these factors is reasonable, its decision deserves substantial deference. *Gilbert*. Here, the Court of Appeals expressly acknowledged that the standard of review was one of abuse of discretion. In examining the District Court's analysis of the public and private interests, however, the Court of Appeals seems to have lost sight of this rule, and substituted its own judgment for that of the District Court.

(1)

In analyzing the private interest factors, the District Court stated that the connections with Scotland are "overwhelming." This characterization may be somewhat exaggerated. Particularly with respect to the question of relative ease of access to sources of proof, the private interests point in both directions. As respondent emphasizes, records concerning the design, manufacture, and testing of the propeller and plane are located

---

23. In *Koster*, we stated that "[i]n any balancing of conveniences, a real showing of convenience by a plaintiff who has sued in his home forum will normally outweigh the inconvenience the defendant may have shown." . . .

As the District Court correctly noted in its opinion, the lower federal courts have routinely given less weight to a foreign plaintiff's choice of forum.

A citizen's forum choice should not be given dispositive weight, however. Citizens or residents deserve somewhat more deference than foreign plaintiffs, but dismissal should not be automatically barred when a plaintiff has filed suit in his home forum. As always, if the balance of conveniences suggests that trial in the chosen forum would be unnecessarily burdensome for the defendant or the court, dismissal is proper.

in the United States. She would have greater access to sources of proof relevant to her strict liability and negligence theories if trial were held here. However, the District Court did not act unreasonably in concluding that fewer evidentiary problems would be posed if the trial were held in Scotland. A large proportion of the relevant evidence is located in Great Britain.

The Court of Appeals found that the problems of proof could not be given any weight because Piper and Hartzell failed to describe with specificity the evidence they would not be able to obtain if trial were held in the United States. It suggested that defendants seeking *forum non conveniens* dismissal must submit affidavits identifying the witnesses they would call and the testimony these witnesses would provide if the trial were held in the alternative forum. Such detail is not necessary. Piper and Hartzell have moved for dismissal precisely because many crucial witnesses are located beyond the reach of compulsory process, and thus are difficult to identify or interview. Requiring extensive investigation would defeat the purpose of their motion. Of course, defendants must provide enough information to enable the District Court to balance the parties' interests. Our examination of the record convinces us that sufficient information was provided here. Both Piper and Hartzell submitted affidavits describing the evidentiary problems they would face if the trial were held in the United States.

The District Court correctly concluded that the problems posed by the inability to implead potential third-party defendants clearly supported holding the trial in Scotland. Joinder of the pilot's estate, Air Navigation, and McDonald is crucial to the presentation of petitioners' defense. If Piper and Hartzell can show that the accident was caused not by a design defect, but rather by the negligence of the pilot, the plane's owners, or the charter company, they will be relieved of all liability. It is true, of course, that if Hartzell and Piper were found liable after a trial in the United States, they could institute an action for indemnity or contribution against these parties in Scotland. It would be far more convenient, however, to resolve all claims in one trial. The Court of Appeals rejected this argument. Forcing petitioners to rely on actions for indemnity or contributions would be "burdensome" but not "unfair." Finding that trial in the plaintiff's chosen forum would be burdensome, however, is sufficient to support dismissal on grounds of *forum non conveniens*.

The District Court's review of the factors relating to the public interest was also reasonable. On the basis of its choice-of-law analysis, it concluded that if the case were tried in the Middle District of Pennsylvania, Pennsylvania law would apply to Piper and Scottish law to Hartzell. It stated that a trial involving two sets of laws would be confusing to the jury. It also noted its own lack of familiarity with Scottish law. Consideration of these problems was clearly appropriate under *Gilbert*; in that case we explicitly held that the need to apply foreign law pointed towards dismissal.[29] The Court of Appeals found that the District Court's choice-of-law analysis was incorrect, and that American law would apply to both Hartzell and Piper. Thus, lack of familiarity with foreign law would not be a problem. Even if the Court of Appeals' conclusion is correct, however, all other public interest factors favored trial in Scotland.

Scotland has a very strong interest in this litigation. The accident occurred in its airspace. All of the decedents were Scottish. Apart from Piper and Hartzell, all potential plaintiffs and defendants are either Scottish or English. As we stated in *Gilbert*, there is "a local interest in having localized controversies decided at home." Respondent argues that American citizens have an interest in ensuring that American manufacturers are deterred from producing defective products, and that additional deterrence might be obtained if Piper and Hartzell were tried in the United States, where they could be sued on the basis of both negligence and strict liability. However, the incremental deterrence that would be gained if this trial were held in an American court is likely to be insignificant. The American interest in this accident is simply not sufficient to justify the enormous commitment of judicial time and resources that would inevitably be required if the case were to be tried here.

IV

The Court of Appeals erred in holding that the possibility of an unfavorable change in law bars dismissal on the ground of *forum non conveniens*. It also erred in rejecting the District Court's *Gilbert* analysis. The District Court properly decided that the presumption in favor of the respondent's forum choice applied with less than maximum force because the real parties in interest are foreign. It did not act unreasonably in deciding that the private interests pointed towards trial in Scotland. Nor did it act unreasonably in deciding that the public interests favored trial in Scotland. Thus, the judgment of the Court of Appeals is

Reversed.

JUSTICE POWELL took no part in the decision of these cases.

JUSTICE O'CONNOR took no part in the consideration or decision of these cases. JUSTICE WHITE, concurring in part and dissenting in part.

I join Parts I and II of the Court's opinion. However, like JUSTICE BRENNAN and JUSTICE STEVENS, I would not proceed to deal with the issues addressed in Part III. To that extent, I am in dissent.

JUSTICE STEVENS, with whom JUSTICE BRENNAN joins, dissenting.

[O]nly one question is presented for review to this Court:

Whether, in an action in federal district court brought by foreign plaintiffs against American defendants, the plaintiffs may defeat a motion to dismiss on the ground of *forum non conveniens* merely by

---

29. Many *forum non conveniens* decisions have held that the need to apply foreign law favors dismissal. Of course, this factor alone is not sufficient to warrant dismissal when a balancing of all relevant factors shows that the plaintiff's chosen forum is appropriate.

showing that the substantive law that would be applied if the case were litigated in the district court is more favorable to them than the law that would be applied by the courts of their own nation.

[In a companion appeal, T]he Court limited its grant of certiorari to the [same] question:

> Must a motion to dismiss on grounds of *forum non conveniens* be denied whenever the law of the alternate forum is less favorable to recovery than that which would be applied by the district court?

I agree that this question should be answered in the negative. Having decided that question, I would simply remand the case to the Court of Appeals for further consideration of the question whether the District Court correctly decided that Pennsylvania was not a convenient forum in which to litigate a claim against a Pennsylvania company that a plane was defectively designed and manufactured in Pennsylvania.

* * *

VIII. MODERN PLEADING

A. SELECTIONS FROM THE FIELD CODE (N.Y. LAWS 1848)

§ 62.   The distinction between actions at law and suits in equity, and the forms of all such actions and suits heretofore existing, are abolished; and, there shall be in this state, hereafter, but one form of action, for the enforcement or protection of private rights and the redress or prevention of private wrongs, which shall be denominated a civil action.

§ 118.   All the forms of pleading heretofore existing, are abolished; and hereafter, the forms of pleading in civil actions, and the rules by which the sufficiency of the pleadings is to be determined, shall be those which are prescribed by this act.

§ 119.   The first pleading on the part of the plaintiff, is the complaint.

§ 120.   The complaint shall contain:
1. The title of the cause, specifying the name of the court in which the action is brought, the name of the county in which the plaintiff desires the trial to be had, and the names of the parties to the action, plaintiff and defendant;
2. A statement of the facts constituting the cause of action, in ordinary and concise language, without repetition, and in such manner as to enable a person of common understanding to know what is intended;
3. A demand of the relief, to which the plaintiff supposes himself entitled. If the recovery of money be demanded, the amount thereof shall be stated.

§ 121.   The only pleading on the part of the defendant, is either a demurrer or an answer. It must be served within twenty days after service of the copy of the complaint.

§ 128.   The answer of the defendant shall contain:
1. In respect to each allegation of the complaint controverted by the defendant, a specific denial thereof, or any knowledge thereof sufficient to form a belief;
2. A statement of any new matter constituting a defence, in ordinary and concise language, without repetition, and in such a manner as to enable a person of common understanding to know what is intended.

§ 129.   The defendant may set forth in his answer, as many grounds of defence as he shall have. They shall be separately stated, and may refer to the causes of action which they are intended to answer, in any manner by which they may be intelligibly distinguished.

§ 131.   When the answer shall contain new matter, the plaintiff may within twenty days, reply to it, denying particularly each allegation controverted by him, or any knowledge thereof sufficient to form a belief; and he may allege, in ordinary and concise language, without repetition, and in such a manner as to enable a person of common and ordinary understanding to know what is intended, any new matter not inconsistent with the complaint, in avoidance of the answer.

§ 132.   No pleading shall be allowed, than the complaint, demurrer, answer and reply.

§ **136.** In the construction of a pleading, for the purpose of determining its effect, its allegations shall be liberally construed, with a view towards substantial justice between the parties.

§ **148.** Any pleading may be amended by the party of course, without costs, and without prejudice to the proceedings already had, at any time before the period for answering it shall expire. In such a case a copy of the amended pleading shall be served on the adverse party.

§ **151.** The court shall, in every stage of the action, disregard any error, or defect in the pleadings or proceedings, which shall not affect the substantial rights of the adverse party; and no judgment shall be reversed or affected by reason of such error or defect.

* * *

B. NOTICE PLEADING

FEDERAL RULE OF CIVIL PROCEDURE 1. SCOPE AND PURPOSE

These rules govern the procedure in all civil actions and proceedings in the United States district courts, except as stated in Rule 81. They should be construed and administered to secure the just, speedy, and inexpensive determination of every action and proceeding.

FEDERAL RULE OF CIVIL PROCEDURE 2. ONE FORM OF ACTION

There is one form of action—the civil action.

* * *

FEDERAL RULE OF CIVIL PROCEDURE 7. PLEADINGS ALLOWED; FORM OF MOTIONS AND OTHER PAPERS

(a) Pleadings. Only these pleadings are allowed:

 (1) a complaint;

 (2) an answer to a complaint;

 (3) an answer to a counterclaim designated as a counterclaim;

 (4) an answer to a cross-claim;

 (5) a third-party complaint;

 (6) an answer to a third-party complaint; and

 (7) if the court orders one, a reply to an answer.

(b) Motions and Other Papers.

 (1) *In General.* A request for a court order must be made by motion. The motion must:

  (A) be in writing unless made during a hearing or trial;

  (B) state with particularity the grounds for seeking the order; and

  (C) state the relief sought.

(2) *Form.* The rules governing captions and other matters of form in pleadings apply to motions and other papers.

* * *

FEDERAL RULE OF CIVIL PROCEDURE 7.1. DISCLOSURE STATEMENT

(a) **Who Must File; Contents.** A nongovernmental corporate party must file two copies of a disclosure statement that:

 (1) identifies any parent corporation and any publicly held corporation owning 10% or more of its stock; or

 (2) states that there is no such corporation.

(b) **Time to File; Supplemental Filing.** A party must:

 (1) file the disclosure statement with its first appearance, pleading, petition, motion, response, or other request addressed to the court; and

 (2) promptly file a supplemental statement if any required information changes.

* * *

FEDERAL RULE OF CIVIL PROCEDURE 8. GENERAL RULES OF PLEADING

(a) **Claim for Relief.** A pleading that states a claim for relief must contain:

 (1) a short and plain statement of the grounds for the court's jurisdiction, unless the court already has jurisdiction and the claim needs no new jurisdictional support;

 (2) a short and plain statement of the claim showing that the pleader is entitled to relief; and

 (3) a demand for the relief sought, which may include relief in the alternative or different types of relief.

* * *

(e) **Construing Pleadings.** Pleadings must be construed so as to do justice.

* * *

DIOGUARDI v. DURNING

139 F.2d 774 (2d Cir. 1944)

CLARK, CIRCUIT JUDGE.

In his complaint, obviously home drawn, plaintiff attempts to assert a series of grievances against the Collector of Customs at the Port of New York growing out of his endeavors to import merchandise from Italy "of great value, consisting of bottles of 'tonics.'" We may pass certain of his claims as either inadequate or inadequately stated and consider only these two: (1) that on the auction day, October 9, 1940, when defendant sold the merchandise at "public custom," "he sold my merchandise to another bidder with my price of $110, and not of his price of $120," and (2) "that three weeks before the sale, two cases, of 19 bottles each case, disappeared." Plaintiff does not make wholly clear how these goods came into the collector's hands, since he alleges compliance with the revenue laws; but he does say he made a claim for "refund of merchandise which was two-third paid in Milano, Italy," and that the collector denied the claim. These and other circumstances alleged indicate (what, indeed, plaintiff's brief asserts) that his original dispute was with his consignor as to whether anything more was due upon the merchandise, and that the collector, having held it for a year (presumably as unclaimed merchandise under 19 U.S.C.A. § 1491), then sold it, or such part of it as was left, at public auction. For his asserted injuries plaintiff claimed $5,000 damages, together with interest and costs, against the defendant individually and as collector. This complaint was dismissed by the District Court, with leave, however, to plaintiff to amend, on motion of the United States Attorney, appearing for the defendant, on the ground that it "fails to state facts sufficient to constitute a cause of action."

Thereupon plaintiff filed an amended complaint, wherein, with an obviously heightened conviction that he was being unjustly treated, he vigorously reiterates his claims, including those quoted above and how stated as that his "medicinal extracts" were given to the Springdale Distilling Company "with my betting (bidding?) price of $110: and not their price of $120," and "It isnt so easy to do away with two cases with 37 bottles of one quart. Being protected, they can take this chance." An earlier paragraph suggests that defendant had explained the loss of the two cases by "saying that they had leaked, which could never be true in the mauner they were bottled." On defendant's motion for dismissal on the same ground as before, the court made a final judgment dismissing the complaint, and plaintiff now comes to us with increased volubility, if not clarity.

It would seem, however, that he has stated enough to withstand a mere formal motion, directed only to the face of the complaint, and that here is another instance of judicial haste which in the long run makes waste. Under the new rules of civil procedure, there is no pleading requirement of stating "facts sufficient to constitute a cause of action," but only that there be "a short and plain statement of the claim showing that the pleader is entitled to relief," Federal Rules of Civil Procedure, rule 8(a); and the motion for dismissal under Rule 12(b) is for failure to state "a claim upon which relief can be granted." The District Court does not state why it concluded that the complaints showed no claim upon which relief could be granted; and the United States Attorney's brief before us does not help us, for it is limited to the prognostication— unfortunately ill founded so far as we are concerned—that "the most cursory examination" of them will show the correctness of the District Court's action.

We think that, however inartistically they may be stated, the plaintiff has disclosed his claims that the collector has converted or otherwise done away with two of his cases of medicinal tonics and has sold the rest in a manner incompatible with the public auction he had announced—and, indeed, required by 19 U.S.C.A. § 1491 and the Treasury Regulations promulgated under it. As to this latter claim, it may be that the collector's only error is a failure to collect an additional ten dollars from the Springdale Distilling Company; but giving the plaintiff the benefit of reasonable intendments in his allegations (as we must on this motion), the claim appears to be in effect that he was actually the first bidder at the price for which they were sold, and hence was entitled to the merchandise. Of course, defendant did not need to move on the complaint alone; he could have disclosed the facts from his point of view, in advance of a trial if he chose, by asking for a pre-trial hearing or by moving for a summary judgment with supporting affidavits. But, as it stands, we do not see how the plaintiff may properly be deprived of his day in court to show what he obviously so firmly believes and what for present purposes defendant must be taken as admitting. It appears to be well settled that the collector may be held personally for a default or for negligence in the performance of his duties.

On remand, the District Court may find substance in other claims asserted by plaintiff, which include a failure properly to catalogue the items (as the cited Regulations provide), or to allow plaintiff to buy at a discount from the catalogue price just before the auction sale (a claim whose basis is not apparent), and a violation of an agreement to deliver the merchandise to the plaintiff as soon as he paid for it, by stopping the payments. In view of plaintiff's limited ability to write and speak English, it will be difficult for the District Court to arrive at justice unless he consents to receive legal assistance in the presentation of his case. The record indicates that he refused further help from a lawyer suggested by the court, and his brief (which was a recital of facts, rather than an argument of law) shows distrust of a lawyer of standing at this bar. It is the plaintiff's privilege to decline all legal help; but we fear that he will be indeed ill advised to attempt to meet a motion for summary judgment or other similar presentation of the merits without competent advice and assistance.

Judgment is reversed and the action is remanded for further proceedings not inconsistent with this opinion.

* * *

FEDERAL RULE OF CIVIL PROCEDURE 84. FORMS

The forms in this Appendix suffice under the rules and illustrate the simplicity and brevity that these rules contemplate.

FORM 1. CAPTION

(Use on every summons, complaint, answer, motion, or other document.)

United States District Court
for the
_____ District of _____

A B, Plaintiff	)
	)
v.	)
	) Civil Action No. _____
C D, Defendant	)
	)
v.	)
	)
E F, Third–Party Defendant	)
(Use if needed.)	)

(Name of Document)

* * *

FORM 2. DATE, SIGNATURE, ADDRESS, E–MAIL ADDRESS, AND TELEPHONE NUMBER

(Use at the conclusion of pleadings and other papers that require a signature.)

Date _____

_____

(Signature of the attorney or
unrepresented party)

_____

(Printed name)

_____

(Address)

_____

(E-mail address)

_____

(Telephone number)

FORM 7. STATEMENT OF JURISDICTION

a. (For diversity-of-citizenship jurisdiction.) The plaintiff is [a citizen of Michigan] [a corporation incorporated under the laws of Michigan with its principal place of business in Michigan]. The defendant is [a citizen of New York] [a corporation incorporated under the laws of New York with its principal place of business in New York]. The amount in controversy, without interest and costs, exceeds the sum or value specified by 28 U.S.C. § 1332.

b.   (For federal-question jurisdiction.) This action arises under [the United States Constitution, specify the article or amendment and the section] [a United States treaty specify] [a federal statute, ___ U.S.C. § ___].

c.   (For a claim in the admiralty or maritime jurisdiction.) This is a case of admiralty or maritime jurisdiction. (To invoke admiralty status under Rule 9(h) use the following: This is an admiralty or maritime claim within the meaning of Rule 9(h).)

FORM 11. COMPLAINT FOR NEGLIGENCE

(Caption—See Form 1.)

1.   (Statement of Jurisdiction—See Form 7.)

2.   On date, at place, the defendant negligently drove a motor vehicle against the plaintiff.

3.   As a result, the plaintiff was physically injured, lost wages or income, suffered physical and mental pain, and incurred medical expenses of $_____.

Therefore, the plaintiff demands judgment against the defendant for $_____, plus costs.

(Date and sign—See Form 2).

FORM 16. THIRD-PARTY COMPLAINT

(Caption—See Form 1.)

1.   Plaintiff *name* has filed against defendant *name* a complaint, a copy of which is attached.

2.   (*State grounds entitling defendant's name to recover from third-party defendant's name for (all or an identified share) of any judgment for plaintiff's name against defendant's name.*)

Therefore, the defendant demands judgment against *third-party defendant's name* for *all or an identified share* of sums that may be adjudged against the defendant in the plaintiff's favor.

(Date and sign—See Form 2.)

CONLEY v. GIBSON

355 U.S. 41 (1957)

MR. JUSTICE BLACK delivered the opinion of the Court.

Once again Negro employees are here under the Railway Labor Act asking that their collective bargaining agent be compelled to represent them fairly. In a series of cases beginning with *Steele v. Louisville & Nashville R. Co.*, this Court has emphatically and repeatedly ruled that an exclusive bargaining agent under the Railway Labor Act is obligated to represent all employees in the bargaining unit fairly and without discrimination because of race and has held that the courts have power to protect employees against such invidious discrimination.

This class suit was brought in a Federal District Court in Texas by certain Negro members of the Brotherhood of Railway and Steamship Clerks, petitioners here, on behalf of themselves and other Negro employees similarly situated against the Brotherhood, its Local Union No. 28 and certain officers of both. In summary, the complaint made the following allegations relevant to our decision: Petitioners were employees of the Texas and New Orleans Railroad at its Houston Freight House. Local 28 of the Brotherhood was the designated bargaining agents under the Railway Labor Act for the bargaining unit to which petitioners belonged. A contract existed between the Union and the Railroad which gave the employees in the bargaining unit certain protection from discharge and loss of seniority. In May 1954, the Railroad purported to abolish 45 jobs held by petitioners or other Negroes all of whom were either discharged or demoted. In truth the 45 jobs were not abolished at all but instead filled by whites as the Negroes were ousted, except for a few instances where Negroes were rehired to fill their old jobs but with loss of seniority. Despite repeated pleas by petitioners, the Union, acting according to plan, did nothing to protect them against these discriminatory discharges and refused to give them protection comparable to that given white employees. The complaint then went on to allege that the Union had failed in general to represent Negro employees equally and in good faith. It charged that such discrimination constituted a violation of petitioners' right under the Railway Labor Act to fair representation from their bargaining agent. And it concluded by asking for relief in the nature of declaratory judgment, injunction and damages.

The respondents appeared and moved to dismiss the complaint on several grounds: (1) the National Railroad Adjustment Board had exclusive jurisdiction over the controversy; (2) the Texas and New Orleans Railroad, which had not been joined, was an indispensable party defendant; and (3) the complaint failed to state a claim upon which relief could be given. The District Court granted the motion to dismiss holding that Congress had given the Adjustment Board exclusive jurisdiction over the controversy. The Court of Appeals for the Fifth Circuit, apparently relying on the same ground, affirmed. Since the case raised an important question concerning the protection of employee rights under the Railway Labor Act we granted certiorari.

[The Court first addressed the jurisdictional argument, holding "it was error for the courts below to dismiss the complaint for lack of jurisdiction." The Court's analysis has been omitted. The Court's discussion whether the railroad company was an indispensable party, and whether the complaint failed to state a claim on which relief could be granted, also have been omitted—ed.]

* * *

Turning to respondents' final ground, we hold that under the general principles laid down in the *Steele*, *Graham*, and *Howard* cases the complaint adequately set forth a claim upon which relief could be granted. In appraising the sufficiency of the complaint we follow, of course, the accepted rule that a complaint should not be dismissed for failure to state a claim unless it appears beyond doubt that the plaintiff can prove no set of facts in support of his claim which would entitle him to relief. Here, the complaint alleged, in part, that petitioners were discharged wrongfully by the Railroad and that the Union, acting according to plan, refused to protect their jobs as it did those of white employees or to help them with their grievances all because they were Negroes. If these allegations are proven there has been a manifest breach of the Union's statutory duty to represent fairly and without hostile discrimination all of the employees in the bargaining unit.

This Court squarely held in *Steele* and subsequent cases that discrimination in representation because of race is prohibited by the Railway Labor Act. The bargaining representative's duty not to draw "irrelevant and invidious" distinctions among those it represents does not come to an abrupt end, as the respondents seem to contend, with the making of an agreement between union and employer. Collective bargaining is a continuing process. Among other things, it involves day-to-day adjustments in the contract and other working rules, resolution of new problems not covered by existing agreements, and the protection of employee rights already secured by contract. The bargaining representative can no more unfairly discriminate in carrying out these functions than it can in negotiating a collective agreement. A contract may be fair and impartial on its face yet administered in such a way, with the active or tacit consent of the union, as to be flagrantly discriminatory against some members of the bargaining unit.

The respondents also argue that the complaint failed to set forth specific facts to support its general allegations of discrimination and that its dismissal is therefore proper. The decisive answer to this is that the Federal Rules of Civil Procedure do not require a claimant to set out in detail the facts upon which he bases his claim. To the contrary, all the Rules require is "a short and plain statement of the claim"[8] that will give the defendant fair notice of what the plaintiff's claim is and the grounds upon which it rests. The illustrative forms appended to the Rules plainly demonstrate this. Such simplified "notice pleading" is made possible by the liberal opportunity for discovery and the other pretrial procedures established by the Rules to disclose more precisely the basis of both claim and defense and to define more narrowly the disputed facts and issues.[9] Following the simple guide of Rule 8(f) that "all pleadings shall be so

---

8. Rule 8(a)(2), 28 U.S.C.

9. *See, e.g.*, Rule 12(e) (motion for a more definite statement); Rule 12(f) (motion to strike portions of the pleading); Rule 12(c) (motion for judgment on the pleadings); Rule 16 (pre-trial procedure and formulation of issue); Rules 26–37 (depositions and discovery); Rule 56 (motion for summary judgment): Rule 15 (right to amend).

construed as to do substantial justice," we have no doubt that petitioners' complaint adequately set forth a claim and gave the respondents fair notice of its basis. The Federal Rules reject the approach that pleading is a game of skill in which one misstep by counsel may be decisive to the outcome and accept the principle that the purpose of pleading is to facilitate a proper decision on the merits.

The judgment is reversed and the cause is remanded to the District Court for further proceedings not inconsistent with this opinion.

It is so ordered.

Reversed and remanded with direction.

* * *

C. THE LIMITS OF NOTICE PLEADING

FEDERAL RULE OF CIVIL PROCEDURE 12(b)(6) (PLEASE REVIEW)

* * *

BELL ATLANTIC CORPORATION v. TWOMBLY

550 U.S. 544 (2007)

JUSTICE SOUTER delivered the opinion of the Court.

Liability under § 1 of the Sherman Act, 15 U.S.C. § 1, requires a "contract, combination . . ., or conspiracy, in restraint of trade or commerce." The question in this putative class action is whether a § 1 complaint can survive a motion to dismiss when it alleges that major telecommunications providers engaged in certain parallel conduct unfavorable to competition, absent some factual context suggesting agreement, as distinct from identical, independent action. We hold that such a complaint should be dismissed.

I

The upshot of the 1984 divestiture of the American Telephone & Telegraph Company's (AT & T) local telephone business was a system of regional service monopolies (variously called "Regional Bell Operating Companies," "Baby Bells," or "Incumbent Local Exchange Carriers" (ILECs)), and a separate, competitive market for long-distance service from which the ILECs were excluded. More than a decade later, Congress withdrew approval of the ILECs' monopolies by enacting the Telecommunications Act of 1996, which "fundamentally restructure[d] local telephone markets" and "subject[ed] [ILECs] to a host of duties intended to facilitate market entry." In recompense, the 1996 Act set conditions for authorizing ILECs to enter the long-distance market.

"Central to the [new] scheme [was each ILEC's] obligation . . . to share its network with competitors," which came to be known as "competitive local exchange carriers" (CLECs). A CLEC could make use of an

ILEC's network in any of three ways: by (1) "purchas[ing] local telephone services at wholesale rates for resale to end users," (2) "leas[ing] elements of the [ILEC's] network 'on an unbundled basis,'" or (3) "interconnect[ing] its own facilities with the [ILEC's] network." Owing to the "considerable expense and effort" required to make unbundled network elements available to rivals at wholesale prices, the ILECs vigorously litigated the scope of the sharing obligation imposed by the 1996 Act, with the result that the Federal Communications Commission (FCC) three times revised its regulations to narrow the range of network elements to be shared with the CLECs.

Respondents William Twombly and Lawrence Marcus (hereinafter plaintiffs) represent a putative class consisting of all "subscribers of local telephone and/or high speed internet services . . . from February 8, 1996 to present." In this action against petitioners, a group of ILECs, plaintiffs seek treble damages and declaratory and injunctive relief for claimed violations of § 1 of the Sherman Act, which prohibits "[e]very contract, combination in the form of trust or otherwise, or conspiracy, in restraint of trade or commerce among the several States, or with foreign nations."

The complaint alleges that the ILECs conspired to restrain trade in two ways, each supposedly inflating charges for local telephone and high-speed Internet services. Plaintiffs say, first, that the ILECs "engaged in parallel conduct" in their respective service areas to inhibit the growth of upstart CLECs. Their actions allegedly included making unfair agreements with the CLECs for access to ILEC networks, providing inferior connections to the networks, overcharging, and billing in ways designed to sabotage the CLECs' relations with their own customers. According to the complaint, the ILECs' "compelling common motivatio[n]" to thwart the CLECs' competitive efforts naturally led them to form a conspiracy; "[h]ad any one [ILEC] not sought to prevent CLECs . . . from competing effectively . . ., the resulting greater competitive inroads into that [ILEC's] territory would have revealed the degree to which competitive entry by CLECs would have been successful in the other territories in the absence of such conduct."

Second, the complaint charges agreements by the ILECs to refrain from competing against one another. These are to be inferred from the ILECs' common failure "meaningfully [to] pursu[e]" "attractive business opportunit[ies]" in contiguous markets where they possessed "substantial competitive advantages," and from a statement of Richard Notebaert, chief executive officer (CEO) of the ILEC Qwest, that competing in the territory of another ILEC " 'might be a good way to turn a quick dollar but that doesn't make it right.' "

The complaint couches its ultimate allegations this way:

> In the absence of any meaningful competition between the [ILECs] in one another's markets, and in light of the parallel course of conduct that each engaged in to prevent competition from CLECs within their respective local telephone and/or high speed internet

services markets and the other facts and market circumstances alleged above, Plaintiffs allege upon information and belief that [the ILECs] have entered into a contract, combination or conspiracy to prevent competitive entry in their respective local telephone and/or high speed internet services markets and have agreed not to compete with one another and otherwise allocated customers and markets to one another.

The United States District Court for the Southern District of New York dismissed the complaint for failure to state a claim upon which relief can be granted. The District Court acknowledged that "plaintiffs may allege a conspiracy by citing instances of parallel business behavior that suggest an agreement," but emphasized that "while '[c]ircumstantial evidence of consciously parallel behavior may have made heavy inroads into the traditional judicial attitude toward conspiracy[, . . .] "conscious parallelism" has not yet read conspiracy out of the Sherman Act entirely.'" Thus, the District Court understood that allegations of parallel business conduct, taken alone, do not state a claim under § 1; plaintiffs must allege additional facts that "ten[d] to exclude independent self-interested conduct as an explanation for defendants' parallel behavior." The District Court found plaintiffs' allegations of parallel ILEC actions to discourage competition inadequate because "the behavior of each ILEC in resisting the incursion of CLECs is fully explained by the ILEC's own interests in defending its individual territory." As to the ILECs' supposed agreement against competing with each other, the District Court found that the complaint does not "alleg[e] facts . . . suggesting that refraining from competing in other territories as CLECs was contrary to [the ILECs'] apparent economic interests, and consequently [does] not rais[e] an inference that [the ILECs'] actions were the result of a conspiracy."

The Court of Appeals for the Second Circuit reversed, holding that the District Court tested the complaint by the wrong standard. It held that "plus factors are not *required* to be pleaded to permit an antitrust claim based on parallel conduct to survive dismissal." Although the Court of Appeals took the view that plaintiffs must plead facts that "include conspiracy among the realm of 'plausible' possibilities in order to survive a motion to dismiss," it then said that "to rule that allegations of parallel anticompetitive conduct fail to support a plausible conspiracy claim, a court would have to conclude that there is no set of facts that would permit a plaintiff to demonstrate that the particular parallelism asserted was the product of collusion rather than coincidence."

We granted certiorari to address the proper standard for pleading an antitrust conspiracy through allegations of parallel conduct, and now reverse.

II

A

Because § 1 of the Sherman Act "does not prohibit [all] unreasonable restraints of trade . . . but only restraints effected by a contract, combination, or conspiracy," "[t]he crucial question" is whether the challenged anticompetitive conduct "stem[s] from independent decision or from an agreement, tacit or express." While a showing of parallel "business behavior is admissible circumstantial evidence from which the fact finder may infer agreement," it falls short of "conclusively establish[ing] agreement or . . . itself constitut[ing] a Sherman Act offense." Even "conscious parallelism," a common reaction of "firms in a concentrated market [that] recogniz[e] their shared economic interests and their interdependence with respect to price and output decisions" is "not in itself unlawful." ("The courts are nearly unanimous in saying that mere interdependent parallelism does not establish the contract, combination, or conspiracy required by Sherman Act § 1"); ("[M]ere interdependence of basic price decisions is not conspiracy").

The inadequacy of showing parallel conduct or interdependence, without more, mirrors the ambiguity of the behavior: consistent with conspiracy, but just as much in line with a wide swath of rational and competitive business strategy unilaterally prompted by common perceptions of the market. Accordingly, we have previously hedged against false inferences from identical behavior at a number of points in the trial sequence. An antitrust conspiracy plaintiff with evidence showing nothing beyond parallel conduct is not entitled to a directed verdict; proof of a § 1 conspiracy must include evidence tending to exclude the possibility of independent action; and at the summary judgment stage a § 1 plaintiff's offer of conspiracy evidence must tend to rule out the possibility that the defendants were acting independently.

B

This case presents the antecedent question of what a plaintiff must plead in order to state a claim under § 1 of the Sherman Act. Federal Rule of Civil Procedure 8(a)(2) requires only "a short and plain statement of the claim showing that the pleader is entitled to relief," in order to "give the defendant fair notice of what the . . . claim is and the grounds upon which it rests," *Conley v. Gibson*. While a complaint attacked by a Rule 12(b)(6) motion to dismiss does not need detailed factual allegations, a plaintiff's obligation to provide the "grounds" of his "entitle[ment] to relief" requires more than labels and conclusions, and a formulaic recitation of the elements of a cause of action will not do (on a motion to dismiss, courts "are not bound to accept as true a legal conclusion couched as a factual allegation"). Factual allegations must be enough to raise a right to relief above the speculative level.

In applying these general standards to a § 1 claim, we hold that stating such a claim requires a complaint with enough factual matter (taken as true) to suggest that an agreement was made. Asking for plausible grounds to infer an agreement does not impose a probability requirement at the pleading stage; it simply calls for enough fact to raise a reasonable expectation that discovery will reveal evidence of illegal agreement. And, of course, a well-pleaded complaint may proceed even if it strikes a savvy judge that actual proof of those facts is improbable, and "that a recovery is very remote and unlikely." In identifying facts that are suggestive enough to render a § 1 conspiracy plausible, we have the benefit of the prior rulings and considered views of leading commentators, already quoted, that lawful parallel conduct fails to bespeak unlawful agreement. It makes sense to say, therefore, that an allegation of parallel conduct and a bare assertion of conspiracy will not suffice. Without more, parallel conduct does not suggest conspiracy, and a conclusory allegation of agreement at some unidentified point does not supply facts adequate to show illegality. Hence, when allegations of parallel conduct are set out in order to make a § 1 claim, they must be placed in a context that raises a suggestion of a preceding agreement, not merely parallel conduct that could just as well be independent action.

The need at the pleading stage for allegations plausibly suggesting (not merely consistent with) agreement reflects the threshold requirement of Rule 8(a)(2) that the "plain statement" possess enough heft to "sho[w] that the pleader is entitled to relief." A statement of parallel conduct, even conduct consciously undertaken, needs some setting suggesting the agreement necessary to make out a § 1 claim; without that further circumstance pointing toward a meeting of the minds, an account of a defendant's commercial efforts stays in neutral territory. An allegation of parallel conduct is thus much like a naked assertion of conspiracy in a § 1 complaint: it gets the complaint close to stating a claim, but without some further factual enhancement it stops short of the line between possibility and plausibility of "entitle[ment] to relief." ("[T]erms like 'conspiracy,' or even 'agreement,' are border-line: they might well be sufficient in conjunction with a more specific allegation-for example, identifying a written agreement or even a basis for inferring a tacit agreement, . . . but a court is not required to accept such terms as a sufficient basis for a complaint").

We alluded to the practical significance of the Rule 8 entitlement requirement when we explained that something beyond the mere possibility of loss causation must be alleged, lest a plaintiff with " 'a largely groundless claim' " be allowed to " 'take up the time of a number of other people, with the right to do so representing an *in terrorem* increment of the settlement value.' " So, when the allegations in a complaint, however true, could not raise a claim of entitlement to relief, " 'this basic deficiency should . . . be exposed at the point of minimum expenditure of time and money by the parties and the court.' "

Thus, it is one thing to be cautious before dismissing an antitrust complaint in advance of discovery, but quite another to forget that proceeding to antitrust discovery can be expensive. As we indicated over 20 years "a district court must retain the power to insist upon some specificity in pleading before allowing a potentially massive factual controversy to proceed." That potential expense is obvious enough in the present case: plaintiffs represent a putative class of at least 90 percent of all subscribers to local telephone or high-speed Internet service in the continental United States, in an action against America's largest telecommunications firms (with many thousands of employees generating reams and gigabytes of business records) for unspecified (if any) instances of antitrust violations that allegedly occurred over a period of seven years.

It is no answer to say that a claim just shy of a plausible entitlement to relief can, if groundless, be weeded out early in the discovery process through "careful case management," given the common lament that the success of judicial supervision in checking discovery abuse has been on the modest side. And it is self-evident that the problem of discovery abuse cannot be solved by "careful scrutiny of evidence at the summary judgment stage," much less "lucid instructions to juries;" the threat of discovery expense will push cost-conscious defendants to settle even anemic cases before reaching those proceedings. Probably, then, it is only by taking care to require allegations that reach the level suggesting conspiracy that we can hope to avoid the potentially enormous expense of discovery in cases with no " 'reasonably founded hope that the [discovery] process will reveal relevant evidence' " to support a § 1 claim.[6]

Plaintiffs do not, of course, dispute the requirement of plausibility and the need for something more than merely parallel behavior, and their main argument against the plausibility standard at the pleading stage is its ostensible conflict with an early statement of ours construing Rule 8. Justice Black's opinion for the Court in *Conley v. Gibson* spoke not only of the need for fair notice of the grounds for entitlement to relief but of "the accepted rule that a complaint should not be dismissed for failure to state a claim unless it appears beyond doubt that the plaintiff can prove no set of facts in support of his claim which would entitle him to relief." This "no set of facts" language can be read in isolation as saying that any statement revealing the theory of the claim will suffice unless its factual impossibility may be shown from the face of the pleadings; and the Court of Appeals appears to have read *Conley* in some such way when formulat-

---

6. The dissent takes heart in the reassurances of plaintiffs' counsel that discovery would be "phased" and "limited to the existence of the alleged conspiracy and class certification." But determining whether some illegal agreement may have taken place between unspecified persons at different ILECs (each a multibillion dollar corporation with legions of management level employees) at some point over seven years is a sprawling, costly, and hugely time-consuming undertaking not easily susceptible to the kind of line drawing and case management that the dissent envisions. Perhaps the best answer to the dissent's optimism that antitrust discovery is open to effective judicial control is a more extensive quotation of the authority just cited, a judge with a background in antitrust law. Given the system that we have, the hope of effective judicial supervision is slim: "The timing is all wrong. The plaintiff files a sketchy complaint (the Rules of Civil Procedure discourage fulsome documents), and discovery is launched. A judicial officer does not know the details of the case the parties will present and in theory *cannot* know the details. Discovery is used to find the details. The judicial officer always knows less than the parties, and the parties themselves may not know very well where they are going or what they expect to find. A magistrate supervising discovery does not—cannot—know the expected productivity of a given request, because the nature of the requester's claim and the contents of the files (or head) of the adverse party are unknown. Judicial officers cannot measure the costs and benefits to the requester and so cannot isolate impositional requests. Requesters have no reason to disclose their own estimates because they gain from imposing costs on rivals (and may lose from an improvement in accuracy). The portions of the Rules of Civil Procedure calling on judges to trim back excessive demands, therefore, have been, and are doomed to be, hollow. We cannot prevent what we cannot detect; we cannot detect what we cannot define; we cannot define 'abusive' discovery except in theory, because in practice we lack essential information."

ing its understanding of the proper pleading standard (invoking *Conley's* "no set of facts" language in describing the standard for dismissal).

On such a focused and literal reading of *Conley's* "no set of facts," a wholly conclusory statement of claim would survive a motion to dismiss whenever the pleadings left open the possibility that a plaintiff might later establish some "set of [undisclosed] facts" to support recovery. So here, the Court of Appeals specifically found the prospect of unearthing direct evidence of conspiracy sufficient to preclude dismissal, even though the complaint does not set forth a single fact in a context that suggests an agreement. It seems fair to say that this approach to pleading would dispense with any showing of a " 'reasonably founded hope' " that a plaintiff would be able to make a case; Mr. Micawber's optimism would be enough.

Seeing this, a good many judges and commentators have balked at taking the literal terms of the *Conley* passage as a pleading standard. We could go on, but there is no need to pile up further citations to show that *Conley's* "no set of facts" language has been questioned, criticized, and explained away long enough. To be fair to the *Conley* Court, the passage should be understood in light of the opinion's preceding summary of the complaint's concrete allegations, which the Court quite reasonably understood as amply stating a claim for relief. But the passage so often quoted fails to mention this understanding on the part of the Court, and after puzzling the profession for 50 years, this famous observation has earned its retirement. The phrase is best forgotten as an incomplete, negative gloss on an accepted pleading standard: once a claim has been stated adequately, it may be supported by showing any set of facts consistent with the allegations in the complaint. *Conley,* then, described the breadth of opportunity to prove what an adequate complaint claims, not the minimum standard of adequate pleading to govern a complaint's survival.[8]

III

When we look for plausibility in this complaint, we agree with the District Court that plaintiffs' claim of conspiracy in restraint of trade comes up short. To begin with, the complaint leaves no doubt that plaintiffs rest their § 1 claim on descriptions of parallel conduct and not on any independent allegation of actual agreement among the ILECs. Although in form a few stray statements speak directly of agreement, on

---

8. Because *Conley's* " 'no set of facts' " language was one of our earliest statements about pleading under the Federal Rules, it is no surprise that it has since been "cited as authority" by this Court and others. Although we have not previously explained the circumstances and rejected the literal reading of the passage embraced by the Court of Appeals, our analysis comports with this Court's statements in the years since *Conley* . . . [citing cases].

The dissent finds relevance in Court of Appeals precedents from the 1940s, which allegedly gave rise to *Conley's* "no set of facts" language. Even indulging this line of analysis, these cases do not challenge the understanding that, before proceeding to discovery, a complaint must allege facts suggestive of illegal conduct.... Rather, these cases stand for the unobjectionable proposition that, when a complaint adequately states a claim, it may not be dismissed based on a district court's assessment that the plaintiff will fail to find evidentiary support for his allegations or prove his claim to the satisfaction of the fact-finder.

fair reading these are merely legal conclusions resting on the prior allegations. Thus, the complaint first takes account of the alleged "absence of any meaningful competition between [the ILECs] in one another's markets," "the parallel course of conduct that each [ILEC] engaged in to prevent competition from CLECs," "and the other facts and market circumstances alleged [earlier]"; "in light of" these, the complaint concludes "that [the ILECs] have entered into a contract, combination or conspiracy to prevent competitive entry into their . . . markets and have agreed not to compete with one another." The nub of the complaint, then, is the ILECs' parallel behavior, consisting of steps to keep the CLECs out and manifest disinterest in becoming CLECs themselves, and its sufficiency turns on the suggestions raised by this conduct when viewed in light of common economic experience.

We think that nothing contained in the complaint invests either the action or inaction alleged with a plausible suggestion of conspiracy. As to the ILECs' supposed agreement to disobey the 1996 Act and thwart the CLECs' attempts to compete, we agree with the District Court that nothing in the complaint intimates that the resistance to the upstarts was anything more than the natural, unilateral reaction of each ILEC intent on keeping its regional dominance. The 1996 Act did more than just subject the ILECs to competition; it obliged them to subsidize their competitors with their own equipment at wholesale rates. The economic incentive to resist was powerful, but resisting competition is routine market conduct, and even if the ILECs flouted the 1996 Act in all the ways the plaintiffs allege, there is no reason to infer that the companies had agreed among themselves to do what was only natural anyway; so natural, in fact, that if alleging parallel decisions to resist competition were enough to imply an antitrust conspiracy, pleading a § 1 violation against almost any group of competing businesses would be a sure thing.

The complaint makes its closest pass at a predicate for conspiracy with the claim that collusion was necessary because success by even one CLEC in an ILEC's territory "would have revealed the degree to which competitive entry by CLECs would have been successful in the other territories." But, its logic aside, this general premise still fails to answer the point that there was just no need for joint encouragement to resist the 1996 Act; as the District Court said, "each ILEC has reason to want to avoid dealing with CLECs" and "each ILEC would attempt to keep CLECs out, regardless of the actions of the other ILECs."[12]

Plaintiffs' second conspiracy theory rests on the competitive reticence among the ILECs themselves in the wake of the 1996 Act, which was supposedly passed in the " 'hop[e] that the large incumbent local monopo-

---

12. From the allegation that the ILECs belong to various trade associations, the dissent playfully suggests that they conspired to restrain trade, an inference said to be "buttressed by the common sense of Adam Smith." If Adam Smith is peering down today, he may be surprised to learn that his tongue-in-cheek remark would be authority to force his famous pinmaker to devote financial and human capital to hire lawyers, prepare for depositions, and otherwise fend off allegations of conspiracy; all this just because he belonged to the same trade guild as one of his competitors when their pins carried the same price tag.

ly companies ... might attack their neighbors' service areas, as they are the best situated to do so.' " Contrary to hope, the ILECs declined " 'to enter each other's service territories in any significant way,' " and the local telephone and high speed Internet market remains highly compartmentalized geographically, with minimal competition. Based on this state of affairs, and perceiving the ILECs to be blessed with "especially attractive business opportunities" in surrounding markets dominated by other ILECs, the plaintiffs assert that the ILECs' parallel conduct was "strongly suggestive of conspiracy."

But it was not suggestive of conspiracy, not if history teaches anything. In a traditionally unregulated industry with low barriers to entry, sparse competition among large firms dominating separate geographical segments of the market could very well signify illegal agreement, but here we have an obvious alternative explanation. In the decade preceding the 1996 Act and well before that, monopoly was the norm in telecommunications, not the exception. The ILECs were born in that world, doubtless liked the world the way it was, and surely knew the adage about him who lives by the sword. Hence, a natural explanation for the noncompetition alleged is that the former Government-sanctioned monopolists were sitting tight, expecting their neighbors to do the same thing.

In fact, the complaint itself gives reasons to believe that the ILECs would see their best interests in keeping to their old turf. Although the complaint says generally that the ILECs passed up "especially attractive business opportunit[ies]" by declining to compete as CLECs against other ILECs, it does not allege that competition as CLECs was potentially any more lucrative than other opportunities being pursued by the ILECs during the same period, and the complaint is replete with indications that any CLEC faced nearly insurmountable barriers to profitability owing to the ILECs' flagrant resistance to the network sharing requirements of the 1996 Act. Not only that, but even without a monopolistic tradition and the peculiar difficulty of mandating shared networks, "[f]irms do not expand without limit and none of them enters every market that an outside observer might regard as profitable, or even a small portion of such markets." The upshot is that Congress may have expected some ILECs to become CLECs in the legacy territories of other ILECs, but the disappointment does not make conspiracy plausible. We agree with the District Court's assessment that antitrust conspiracy was not suggested by the facts adduced under either theory of the complaint, which thus fails to state a valid § 1 claim.[14]

---

14. In reaching this conclusion, we do not apply any "heightened" pleading standard, nor do we seek to broaden the scope of Federal Rule of Civil Procedure 9, which can only be accomplished "by the process of amending the Federal Rules, and not by judicial interpretation." On certain subjects understood to raise a high risk of abusive litigation, a plaintiff must state factual allegations with greater particularity than Rule 8 requires. Fed. Rules Civ. Proc. 9(b)–(c). Here, our concern is not that the allegations in the complaint were insufficiently "particular[ized]"; rather, the complaint warranted dismissal because it failed *in toto* to render plaintiffs' entitlement to relief plausible.

* * * Here, in contrast, we do not require heightened fact pleading of specifics, but only enough facts to state a claim to relief that is plausible on its face. Because the plaintiffs here have not nudged their claims across the line from conceivable to plausible, their complaint must be dismissed.

* * *

The judgment of the Court of Appeals for the Second Circuit is reversed, and the cause is remanded for further proceedings consistent with this opinion.

It is so ordered.

JUSTICE STEVENS, with whom JUSTICE GINSBURG joins except as to Part IV, dissenting.

In the first paragraph of its 24–page opinion the Court states that the question to be decided is whether allegations that "major telecommunications providers engaged in certain parallel conduct unfavorable to competition" suffice to state a violation of § 1 of the Sherman Act. The answer to that question has been settled for more than 50 years. If that were indeed the issue, a summary reversal would adequately resolve this case. As [the Court] held, parallel conduct is circumstantial evidence admissible on the issue of conspiracy, but it is not itself illegal.

Thus, this is a case in which there is no dispute about the substantive law. If the defendants acted independently, their conduct was perfectly lawful. If, however, that conduct is the product of a horizontal agreement among potential competitors, it was unlawful. Plaintiffs have alleged such an agreement and, because the complaint was dismissed in advance of answer, the allegation has not even been denied. Why, then, does the case not proceed? Does a judicial opinion that the charge is not "plausible" provide a legally acceptable reason for dismissing the complaint? I think not.

Respondents' amended complaint describes a variety of circumstantial evidence and makes the straightforward allegation that petitioners "entered into a contract, combination or conspiracy to prevent competitive entry in their respective local telephone and/or high speed internet services markets and have agreed not to compete with one another and otherwise allocated customers and markets to one another."

The complaint explains that, contrary to Congress' expectation when it enacted the 1996 Telecommunications Act, and consistent with their own economic self-interests, petitioner Incumbent Local Exchange Carriers (ILECs) have assiduously avoided infringing upon each other's markets and have refused to permit non-incumbent competitors to access their networks. The complaint quotes Richard Notebaert, the former CEO of one such ILEC, as saying that competing in a neighboring ILEC's territory "might be a good way to turn a quick dollar but that doesn't make it right." Moreover, respondents allege that petitioners "communicate amongst themselves" through numerous industry associations. In sum, respondents allege that petitioners entered into an agreement that has long been recognized as a classic *per se* violation of the Sherman Act.

Under rules of procedure that have been well settled, a judge ruling on a defendant's motion to dismiss a complaint, "must accept as true all of the factual allegations contained in the complaint." But instead of requiring knowledgeable executives such as Notebaert to respond to these allegations by way of sworn depositions or other limited discovery—and indeed without so much as requiring petitioners to file an answer denying that they entered into any agreement—the majority permits immediate dismissal based on the assurances of company lawyers that nothing untoward was afoot. The Court embraces the argument of those lawyers that "there is no reason to infer that the companies had agreed among themselves to do what was only natural anyway;" that "there was just no need for joint encouragement to resist the 1996 Act;" and that the "natural explanation for the noncompetition alleged is that the former Government-sanctioned monopolists were sitting tight, expecting their neighbors to do the same thing."

The Court and petitioners' legal team are no doubt correct that the parallel conduct alleged is consistent with the absence of any contract, combination, or conspiracy. But that conduct is also entirely consistent with the *presence* of the illegal agreement alleged in the complaint. And the charge that petitioners "agreed not to compete with one another" is not just one of "a few stray statements;" it is an allegation describing unlawful conduct. As such, the Federal Rules of Civil Procedure, our longstanding precedent, and sound practice mandate that the District Court at least require some sort of response from petitioners before dismissing the case.

Two practical concerns presumably explain the Court's dramatic departure from settled procedural law. Private antitrust litigation can be enormously expensive, and there is a risk that jurors may mistakenly conclude that evidence of parallel conduct has proved that the parties acted pursuant to an agreement when they in fact merely made similar independent decisions. Those concerns merit careful case management, including strict control of discovery, careful scrutiny of evidence at the summary judgment stage, and lucid instructions to juries; they do not, however, justify the dismissal of an adequately pleaded complaint without even requiring the defendants to file answers denying a charge that they in fact engaged in collective decision-making. More importantly, they do not justify an interpretation of Federal Rule of Civil Procedure 12(b)(6) that seems to be driven by the majority's appraisal of the plausibility of the ultimate factual allegation rather than its legal sufficiency.

I

Rule 8(a)(2) of the Federal Rules requires that a complaint contain "a short and plain statement of the claim showing that the pleader is entitled to relief." The rule did not come about by happenstance and its language is not inadvertent. The English experience with Byzantine special pleading rules—illustrated by the hyper-technical Hilary rules of 1834—made obvious the appeal of a pleading standard that was easy for the common litigant to understand and sufficed to put the defendant on notice as to the nature of the claim against him and the relief sought. Stateside, David Dudley Field developed the highly influential New York Code of 1848, which required "[a] statement of the facts constituting the cause of action, in ordinary and concise language, without repetition, and in such a manner as to enable a person of common understanding to know what is intended." Substantially similar language appeared in the Federal Equity Rules adopted in 1912.

A difficulty arose, however, in that the Field Code and its progeny required a plaintiff to plead "facts" rather than "conclusions," a distinction that proved far easier to say than to apply. As commentators have noted,

> it is virtually impossible logically to distinguish among "ultimate facts," "evidence," and "conclusions." Essentially any allegation in a pleading must be an assertion that certain occurrences took place. The pleading spectrum, passing from evidence through ultimate facts to conclusions, is largely a continuum varying only in the degree of particularity with which the occurrences are described.

Rule 8 was directly responsive to this difficulty. Its drafters intentionally avoided any reference to "facts" or "evidence" or "conclusions." Under the relaxed pleading standards of the Federal Rules, the idea was not to keep litigants out of court but rather to keep them in. The merits of a claim would be sorted out during a flexible pretrial process and, as appropriate, through the crucible of trial.

II

It is in the context of this history that *Conley v. Gibson,* must be understood. * * *

Consistent with the design of the Federal Rules, *Conley's* "no set of facts" formulation permits outright dismissal only when proceeding to discovery or beyond would be futile. Once it is clear that a plaintiff has stated a claim that, if true, would entitle him to relief, matters of proof are appropriately relegated to other stages of the trial process. Today, however, in its explanation of a decision to dismiss a complaint that it regards as a fishing expedition, the Court scraps *Conley's* "no set of facts" language. Concluding that the phrase has been "questioned, criticized, and explained away long enough," the Court dismisses it as careless composition.

If *Conley's* "no set of facts" language is to be interred, let it not be without a eulogy. That exact language, which the majority says has "puzzl[ed] the profession for 50 years," has been cited as authority in a dozen opinions of this Court and four separate writings. In not one of those 16 opinions was the language "questioned," "criticized," or "explained away." Indeed, today's opinion is the first by any Member of this Court to express *any* doubt as to the adequacy of the *Conley* formulation.

Taking their cues from the federal courts, 26 States and the District of Columbia utilize as their standard for dismissal of a complaint the very language the majority repudiates: whether it appears "beyond doubt" that "no set of facts" in support of the claim would entitle the plaintiff to relief.

Petitioners have not requested that the *Conley* formulation be retired, nor have any of the six *amici* who filed briefs in support of petitioners. I would not rewrite the Nation's civil procedure textbooks and call into doubt the pleading rules of most of its States without far more informed deliberation as to the costs of doing so. Congress has established a process—a rulemaking process—for revisions of that order.

Today's majority calls *Conley's* "no set of facts" language "an incomplete, negative gloss on an accepted pleading standard: once a claim has been stated adequately, it may be supported by showing any set of facts consistent with the allegations in the complaint." This is not and cannot be what the *Conley* Court meant. First, as I have explained, and as the *Conley* Court well knew, the pleading standard the Federal Rules meant to codify does not require, or even invite, the pleading of facts. The "pleading standard" label the majority gives to what it reads into the *Conley* opinion—a statement of the permissible factual support for an adequately pleaded complaint—would not, therefore, have impressed the *Conley* Court itself. Rather, that Court would have understood the majority's remodeling of its language to express an *evidentiary* standard, which the *Conley* Court had neither need nor want to explicate. Second, it is pellucidly clear that the *Conley* Court was interested in what a complaint *must* contain, not what it *may* contain. In fact, the Court said without qualification that it was "appraising the *sufficiency* of the complaint." It was, to paraphrase today's majority, describing "the minimum standard of adequate pleading to govern a complaint's survival."

* * * We have consistently reaffirmed that basic understanding of the Federal Rules in the half century since *Conley*.

Everything today's majority says would therefore make perfect sense if it were ruling on a Rule 56 motion for summary judgment and the evidence included nothing more than the Court has described. But it should go without saying ... that a heightened production burden at the summary judgment stage does not translate into a heightened pleading burden at the complaint stage. The majority rejects the complaint in this case because—in light of the fact that the parallel conduct alleged is consistent with ordinary market behavior—the claimed conspiracy is "conceivable" but not "plausible." I have my doubts about the majority's assessment of the plausibility of this alleged conspiracy. But even if the majority's speculation is correct, its "plausibility" standard is irreconcilable with Rule 8 and with our governing precedents. As we made clear ... fear of the burdens of litigation does not justify factual conclusions supported only by lawyers' arguments rather than sworn denials or admissible evidence.

This case is a poor vehicle for the Court's new pleading rule, for we have observed that "in antitrust cases, where 'the proof is largely in the hands of the alleged conspirators,' ... dismissals prior to giving the plaintiff ample opportunity for discovery should be granted very sparingly."

III

Even if I were inclined to accept the Court's anachronistic dichotomy and ignore the complaint's actual allegations, I would dispute the Court's suggestion that any inference of agreement from petitioners' parallel conduct is "implausible." Many years ago a truly great economist perceptively observed that "[p]eople of the same trade seldom meet together, even for merriment and diversion, but the conversation ends in a conspiracy against the public, or in some contrivance to raise prices." I am not so cynical as to accept that sentiment at face value, but I need not do so here. Respondents' complaint points not only to petitioners' numerous opportunities to meet with each other, but also to Notebaert's curious statement that encroaching on a fellow incumbent's territory "might be a good way to turn a quick dollar but that doesn't make it right." What did he mean by that? One possible (indeed plausible) inference is that he meant that while it would be in his company's economic self-interest to compete with its brethren, he had agreed with his competitors not to do so. According to the complaint, that is how the Illinois Coalition for Competitive Telecom construed Notebaert's statement, and that is how Members of Congress construed his company's behavior.

Perhaps Notebaert meant instead that competition would be sensible in the short term but not in the long run. That's what his lawyers tell us anyway. But I would think that no one would know better what Notebaert meant than Notebaert himself. Instead of permitting respondents to ask Notebaert, however, the Court looks to other quotes from that and other articles and decides that what he meant was that entering new markets as a CLEC would not be a " 'sustainable economic model.' " Never mind that—as anyone ever interviewed knows—a newspaper article is hardly a verbatim transcript; the writer selects quotes to package his story, not to record a subject's views for posterity. But more importantly the District Court was required at this stage of the proceedings to construe Notebaert's ambiguous statement in the plaintiffs' favor. The inference the statement supports—that simultaneous decisions by ILECs not even to attempt to poach customers from one another once the law authorized them to do so were the product of an agreement—sits comfortably within the realm of possibility. That is all the Rules require.

To be clear, if I had been the trial judge in this case, I would not have permitted the plaintiffs to engage in massive discovery based solely on the allegations in this complaint. On the other hand, I surely would not have dismissed the complaint without requiring the defendants to answer the charge that they "have agreed not to compete with one another and otherwise allocated customers and markets to one another." Even a sworn denial of that charge would not justify a summary dismissal without giving the plaintiffs the opportunity to take depositions from Notebaert and at least one responsible executive representing each of the other defendants.

Respondents in this case proposed a plan of " 'phased discovery' " limited to the existence of the alleged conspiracy and class certification. Two petitioners rejected the plan. Whether or not respondents' proposed plan was sensible, it was an appropriate subject for negotiation.[13] Given the charge in the complaint—buttressed by the common sense of Adam Smith—I cannot say that the possibility that joint discussions and perhaps some agreements played a role in petitioners' decision-making process is so implausible that dismissing the complaint before any defendant has denied the charge is preferable to granting respondents even a minimal opportunity to prove their claims.

I fear that the unfortunate result of the majority's new pleading rule will be to invite lawyers' debates over economic theory to conclusively resolve antitrust suits in the absence of any evidence. It is no surprise that the antitrust defense bar—among whom "lament" as to inadequate judicial supervision of discovery is most "common"—should lobby for this state of affairs. But "we must recall that their primary responsibility is to win cases for their clients, not to improve law administration for the public." As we did in our prior decisions, we should have instructed them that their remedy was to seek to amend the Federal Rules—not our interpretation of them.

IV

Just a few weeks ago some of my colleagues explained that a strict interpretation of the literal text of statutory language is essential to avoid

---

13. The potential for "sprawling, costly, and hugely time-consuming" discovery, is no reason to throw the baby out with the bathwater. The Court vastly underestimates a district court's case-management arsenal. Before discovery even begins, the court may grant a defendant's Rule 12(e) motion; Rule 7(a) permits a trial court to order a plaintiff to reply to a defendant's answer, and Rule 23 requires "rigorous analysis" to ensure that class certification is appropriate. Rule 16 invests a trial judge with the power, backed by sanctions, to regulate pretrial proceedings via conferences and scheduling orders, at which the parties may discuss, *inter alia,* "the elimination of frivolous claims or defenses," Rule 16(c)(1); "the necessity or desirability of amendments to the pleadings," Rule 16(c)(2); "the control and scheduling of discovery," Rule 16(c)(6); and "the need for adopting special procedures for managing potentially difficult or protracted actions that may involve complex issues, multiple parties, difficult legal questions, or unusual proof problems," Rule 16(c)(12). Subsequently, Rule 26 confers broad discretion to control the combination of interrogatories, requests for admissions, production requests, and depositions permitted in a given case; the sequence in which such discovery devices may be deployed; and the limitations imposed upon them. Indeed, Rule 26(c) specifically permits a court to take actions "to protect a party or person from annoyance, embarrassment, oppression, or undue burden or expense" by, for example, disallowing a particular discovery request, setting appropriate terms and conditions, or limiting its scope.

In short, the Federal Rules contemplate that pretrial matters will be settled through a flexible process of give and take, of proffers, stipulations, and stonewalls, not by having trial judges screen allegations for their plausibility *vel non* without requiring an answer from the defendant. And should it become apparent over the course of litigation that a plaintiff's filings bespeak an *in terrorem* suit, the district court has at its call its own *in terrorem* device, in the form of a wide array of Rule 11 sanctions. *See* Rules 11(b), (c) (authorizing sanctions if a suit is presented "for any improper purpose, such as to harass or to cause unnecessary delay or needless increase in the cost of litigation").

judicial decisions that are not faithful to the intent of Congress. I happen to believe that there are cases in which other tools of construction are more reliable than text, but I agree of course that congressional intent should guide us in matters of statutory interpretation. This is a case in which the intentions of the drafters of three important sources of law—the Sherman Act, the Telecommunications Act of 1996, and the Federal Rules of Civil Procedure—all point unmistakably in the same direction, yet the Court marches resolutely the other way. Whether the Court's actions will benefit only defendants in antitrust treble-damages cases, or whether its test for the sufficiency of a complaint will inure to the benefit of all civil defendants, is a question that the future will answer. But that the Court has announced a significant new rule that does not even purport to respond to any congressional command is glaringly obvious.

The transparent policy concern that drives the decision is the interest in protecting antitrust defendants—who in this case are some of the wealthiest corporations in our economy—from the burdens of pretrial discovery. Even if it were not apparent that the legal fees petitioners have incurred in arguing the merits of their Rule 12(b) motion have far exceeded the cost of limited discovery, or that those discovery costs would burden respondents as well as petitioners, that concern would not provide an adequate justification for this law-changing decision. For in the final analysis it is only a lack of confidence in the ability of trial judges to control discovery, buttressed by appellate judges' independent appraisal of the plausibility of profoundly serious factual allegations, that could account for this stark break from precedent.

If the allegation of conspiracy happens to be true, today's decision obstructs the congressional policy favoring competition that undergirds both the Telecommunications Act of 1996 and the Sherman Act itself. More importantly, even if there is abundant evidence that the allegation is untrue, directing that the case be dismissed without even looking at any of that evidence marks a fundamental—and unjustified—change in the character of pretrial practice.

Accordingly, I respectfully dissent.

* * *

ASHCROFT v. IQBAL

556 U.S. 662 (2009)

JUSTICE KENNEDY delivered the opinion of the Court.

Respondent Javaid Iqbal is a citizen of Pakistan and a Muslim. In the wake of the September 11, 2001, terrorist attacks he was arrested in the United States on criminal charges and detained by federal officials. Respondent claims he was deprived of various constitutional protections while in federal custody. To redress the alleged deprivations, respondent filed a complaint against numerous federal officials, including John Ashcroft, the former Attorney General of the United States, and Robert Mueller, the Director of the Federal Bureau of Investigation (FBI). Ashcroft and Mueller are the petitioners in the case now before us. As to these two petitioners, the complaint alleges that they adopted an unconstitutional policy that subjected respondent to harsh conditions of confinement on account of his race, religion, or national origin.

In the District Court petitioners raised the defense of qualified immunity and moved to dismiss the suit, contending the complaint was not sufficient to state a claim against them. The District Court denied the motion to dismiss, concluding the complaint was sufficient to state a claim despite petitioners' official status at the times in question. Petitioners brought an interlocutory appeal in the Court of Appeals for the Second Circuit. The court, without discussion, assumed it had jurisdiction over the order denying the motion to dismiss; and it affirmed the District Court's decision.

Respondent's account of his prison ordeal could, if proved, demonstrate unconstitutional misconduct by some governmental actors. But the allegations and pleadings with respect to these actors are not before us here. This case instead turns on a narrower question: Did respondent, as the plaintiff in the District Court, plead factual matter that, if taken as true, states a claim that petitioners deprived him of his clearly established constitutional rights. We hold respondent's pleadings are insufficient.

I

Following the 2001 attacks, the FBI and other entities within the Department of Justice began an investigation of vast reach to identify the assailants and prevent them from attacking anew. The FBI dedicated more than 4,000 special agents and 3,000 support personnel to the endeavor. By September 18 "the FBI had received more than 96,000 tips or potential leads from the public."

In the ensuing months the FBI questioned more than 1,000 people with suspected links to the attacks in particular or to terrorism in general. Of those individuals, some 762 were held on immigration charges; and a 184–member subset of that group was deemed to be "of 'high interest'" to the investigation. The high-interest detainees were held under restrictive conditions designed to prevent them from communicating with the general prison population or the outside world.

Respondent was one of the detainees. According to his complaint, in November 2001 agents of the FBI and Immigration and Naturalization Service arrested him on charges of fraud in relation to identification documents and conspiracy to defraud the United States. Pending trial for those crimes, respondent was housed at the Metropolitan Detention Center (MDC) in Brooklyn, New York. Respondent was designated a person "of high interest" to the September 11 investigation and in January 2002 was placed in a section of the MDC known as the Administrative Maximum Special Housing Unit (ADMAX SHU). As the facility's name indicates, the ADMAX SHU incorporates the maximum security conditions allowable under Federal Bureau of Prison regulations. ADMAX SHU detainees were kept in lockdown 23 hours a day, spending the remaining hour outside their cells in handcuffs and leg irons accompanied by a four-officer escort.

Respondent pleaded guilty to the criminal charges, served a term of imprisonment, and was removed to his native Pakistan. He then filed a *Bivens* action in the United States District Court for the Eastern District of New York against 34 current and former federal officials and 19 "John Doe" federal corrections officers. The defendants range from the correctional officers who had day-to-day contact with respondent during the term of his confinement, to the wardens of the MDC facility, all the way to petitioners-officials who were at the highest level of the federal law enforcement hierarchy.

The 21–cause-of-action complaint does not challenge respondent's arrest or his confinement in the MDC's general prison population. Rather, it concentrates on his treatment while confined to the ADMAX SHU. The complaint sets forth various claims against defendants who are not before us. For instance, the complaint alleges that respondent's jailors "kicked him in the stomach, punched him in the face, and dragged him across" his cell without justification; subjected him to serial strip and body-cavity searches when he posed no safety risk to himself or others; and refused to let him and other Muslims pray because there would be "[n]o prayers for terrorists."

The allegations against petitioners are the only ones relevant here. The complaint contends that petitioners designated respondent a person of high interest on account of his race, religion, or national origin, in contravention of the First and Fifth Amendments to the Constitution. The complaint alleges that "the [FBI], under the direction of Defendant Mueller, arrested and detained thousands of Arab Muslim men . . . as part of its investigation of the events of September 11." It further alleges that "[t]he policy of holding post-September-11th detainees in highly restrictive conditions of confinement until they were 'cleared' by the FBI was approved by Defendants Ashcroft and Mueller in discussions in the weeks after September 11, 2001." Lastly, the complaint posits that petitioners "each knew of, condoned, and willfully and maliciously agreed to subject" respondent to harsh conditions of confinement "as a matter of policy, solely on account of [his] religion, race, and/or national origin and for no legitimate penological interest." The pleading names Ashcroft as the "principal architect" of the policy, and identifies Mueller as "instrumental in [its] adoption, promulgation, and implementation."

Petitioners moved to dismiss the complaint for failure to state sufficient allegations to show their own involvement in clearly established unconstitutional conduct. The District Court denied their motion. Accepting all of the allegations in respondent's complaint as true, the court held that "it cannot be said that there [is] no set of facts on which [respondent] would be entitled to relief as against" petitioners (relying on *Conley v. Gibson*). [P]etitioners filed an interlocutory appeal in the United States Court of Appeals for the Second Circuit. While that appeal was pending, this Court decided *Bell Atlantic Corp. v. Twombly,* which discussed the standard for evaluating whether a complaint is sufficient to survive a motion to dismiss.

The Court of Appeals considered *Twombly*'s applicability to this case. Acknowledging that *Twombly* retired the *Conley* no-set-of-facts test relied upon by the District Court, the Court of Appeals' opinion discussed at length how to apply this Court's "standard for assessing the adequacy of pleadings." It concluded that *Twombly* called for a "flexible 'plausibility standard,' which obliges a pleader to amplify a claim with some factual allegations in those contexts where such amplification is needed to render the claim *plausible*." The court found that petitioners' appeal did not present one of "those contexts" requiring amplification. As a consequence, it held respondent's pleading adequate to allege petitioners' personal involvement in discriminatory decisions which, if true, violated clearly established constitutional law.

Judge Cabranes concurred. He agreed that the majority's "discussion of the relevant pleading standards reflect[ed] the uneasy compromise ... between a qualified immunity privilege rooted in the need to preserve the effectiveness of government as contemplated by our constitutional structure and the pleading requirements of Rule 8(a) of the Federal Rules of Civil Procedure." Judge Cabranes nonetheless expressed concern at the prospect of subjecting high-ranking Government officials—entitled to assert the defense of qualified immunity and charged with responding to "a national and international security emergency unprecedented in the history of the American Republic"—to the burdens of discovery on the basis of a complaint as nonspecific as respondent's. Reluctant to vindicate that concern as a member of the Court of Appeals, Judge Cabranes urged this Court to address the appropriate pleading standard "at the earliest opportunity." We granted certiorari, and now reverse. * * *

III

In *Twombly,* the Court found it necessary first to discuss the antitrust principles implicated by the complaint. Here too we begin by taking note of the elements a plaintiff must plead to state a claim of unconstitutional discrimination against officials entitled to assert the defense of qualified immunity.

In *Bivens*—proceeding on the theory that a right suggests a remedy—this Court "recognized for the first time an implied private action for damages against federal officers alleged to have violated a citizen's constitutional rights." Because implied causes of action are disfavored, the Court has been reluctant to extend *Bivens* liability "to any new context or new category of defendants." That reluctance might well have disposed of respondent's First Amendment claim of religious discrimination. For while we have allowed a *Bivens* action to redress a violation of the equal protection component of the Due Process Clause of the Fifth Amendment, we have not found an implied damages remedy under the Free Exercise Clause. Indeed, we have declined to extend *Bivens* to a claim sounding in the First Amendment. Petitioners do not press this argument, however, so we assume, without deciding, that respondent's First Amendment claim is actionable under *Bivens*.

In the limited settings where *Bivens* does apply, the implied cause of action is the "federal analog to suits brought against state officials under 42 U.S.C. § 1983." Based on the rules our precedents establish, respondent correctly concedes that Government officials may not be held liable for the unconstitutional conduct of their subordinates under a theory of *respondeat superior*. Because vicarious liability is inapplicable to *Bivens* and § 1983 suits, a plaintiff must plead that each Government-official defendant, through the official's own individual actions, has violated the Constitution.

The factors necessary to establish a *Bivens* violation will vary with the constitutional provision at issue. Where the claim is invidious discrimination in contravention of the First and Fifth Amendments, our decisions make clear that the plaintiff must plead and prove that the defendant acted with discriminatory purpose. Under extant precedent purposeful discrimination requires more than "intent as volition or intent as awareness of consequences." It instead involves a decision-maker's undertaking a course of action " 'because of,' not merely 'in spite of,' [the action's] adverse effects upon an identifiable group." It follows that, to state a claim based on a violation of a clearly established right, respondent must plead sufficient factual matter to show that petitioners adopted and implemented the detention policies at issue not for a neutral, investigative reason but for the purpose of discriminating on account of race, religion, or national origin.

Respondent disagrees. He argues that, under a theory of "supervisory liability," petitioners can be liable for "knowledge and acquiescence in their subordinates' use of discriminatory criteria to make classification decisions among detainees." That is to say, respondent believes a supervisor's mere knowledge of his subordinate's discriminatory purpose amounts to the supervisor's violating the Constitution. We reject this argument. Respondent's conception of "supervisory liability" is inconsistent with his accurate stipulation that petitioners may not be held accountable for the misdeeds of their agents. In a § 1983 suit or a *Bivens* action—where masters do not answer for the torts of their servants—the term "supervisory liability" is a misnomer. Absent vicarious liability, each Government official, his or her title notwithstanding, is only liable for his or her own misconduct. In the context of determining whether there is a violation of clearly established right to overcome qualified immunity, purpose rather than knowledge is required to impose *Bivens* liability on the subordinate for unconstitutional discrimination; the same holds true for an official charged with violations arising from his or her superintendent responsibilities.

IV

A

We turn to respondent's complaint. Under Federal Rule of Civil Procedure 8(a)(2), a pleading must contain a "short and plain statement of the claim showing that the pleader is entitled to relief." As the Court held in *Twombly,* the pleading standard Rule 8 announces does not require "detailed factual allegations," but it demands more than an unadorned, the-defendant-unlawfully-harmed-me accusation. A pleading that offers "labels and conclusions" or "a formulaic recitation of the elements of a cause of action will not do." Nor does a complaint suffice if it tenders "naked assertion[s]" devoid of "further factual enhancement."

To survive a motion to dismiss, a complaint must contain sufficient factual matter, accepted as true, to "state a claim to relief that is plausible on its face." A claim has facial plausibility when the plaintiff pleads factual content that allows the court to draw the reasonable inference that the defendant is liable for the misconduct alleged. The plausibility standard is not akin to a "probability requirement," but it asks for more than a sheer possibility that a defendant has acted unlawfully. Where a complaint pleads facts that are "merely consistent with" a defendant's liability, it "stops short of the line between possibility and plausibility of 'entitlement to relief.' "

Two working principles underlie our decision in *Twombly.* First, the tenet that a court must accept as true all of the allegations contained in a complaint is inapplicable to legal conclusions. Threadbare recitals of the elements of a cause of action, supported by mere conclusory statements, do not suffice. (Although for the purposes of a motion to dismiss we must take all of the factual allegations in the complaint as true, we "are not bound to accept as true a legal conclusion couched as a factual allegation"). Rule 8 marks a notable and generous departure from the hyper-technical, code-pleading regime of a prior era, but it does not unlock the doors of discovery for a plaintiff armed with nothing more than conclusions. Second, only a complaint that states a plausible claim for relief survives a motion to dismiss. Determining whether a complaint states a plausible claim for relief will, as the Court of Appeals observed, be a context-specific task that requires the reviewing court to draw on its judicial experience and common sense. But where the well-pleaded facts do not permit the court to infer more than the mere possibility of misconduct, the complaint has alleged—but it has not "show[n]"—"that the pleader is entitled to relief." Fed. Rule Civ. Proc. 8(a)(2).

In keeping with these principles a court considering a motion to dismiss can choose to begin by identifying pleadings that, because they are no more than conclusions, are not entitled to the assumption of truth. While legal conclusions can provide the framework of a complaint, they must be supported by factual allegations. When there are well-pleaded factual allegations, a court should assume their veracity and then determine whether they plausibly give rise to an entitlement to relief.

Our decision in *Twombly* illustrates the two-pronged approach. There, we considered the sufficiency of a complaint alleging that incumbent telecommunications providers had entered an agreement not to compete and to forestall competitive entry, in violation of the Sherman Act, 15 U.S.C. § 1. Recognizing that § 1 enjoins only anticompetitive conduct "effected by a contract, combination, or conspiracy," the plaintiffs in *Twombly* flatly pleaded that the defendants "ha[d] entered into a contract, combination or conspiracy to prevent competitive entry ... and ha[d] agreed not to compete with one another." The complaint also alleged that the defendants' "parallel course of conduct ... to prevent competition" and inflate prices was indicative of the unlawful agreement alleged.

The Court held the plaintiffs' complaint deficient under Rule 8. In doing so it first noted that the plaintiffs' assertion of an unlawful agreement was a " 'legal conclusion' " and, as such, was not entitled to the assumption of truth. Had the Court simply credited the allegation of a conspiracy, the plaintiffs would have stated a claim for relief and been entitled to proceed perforce. The Court next addressed the "nub" of the plaintiffs' complaint—the well-pleaded, non-conclusory factual allegation of parallel behavior—to determine whether it gave rise to a "plausible suggestion of conspiracy." Acknowledging that parallel conduct was consistent with an unlawful agreement, the Court nevertheless concluded that it did not plausibly suggest an illicit accord because it was not only compatible with, but indeed was more likely explained by, lawful, unchoreographed free-market behavior. Because the well-pleaded fact of parallel conduct, accepted as true, did not plausibly suggest an unlawful agreement, the Court held the plaintiffs' complaint must be dismissed.

B

Under *Twombly*'s construction of Rule 8, we conclude that respondent's complaint has not "nudged [his] claims" of invidious discrimination "across the line from conceivable to plausible."

We begin our analysis by identifying the allegations in the complaint that are not entitled to the assumption of truth. Respondent pleads that petitioners "knew of, condoned, and willfully and maliciously agreed to subject [him]" to harsh conditions of confinement "as a matter of policy, solely on account of [his] religion, race, and/or national origin and for no legitimate penological interest." The complaint alleges that Ashcroft was the "principal architect" of this invidious policy, and that Mueller was "instrumental" in adopting and executing it. These bare assertions, much like the pleading of conspiracy in *Twombly*, amount to nothing more than a "formulaic recitation of the elements" of a constitutional discrimination claim, namely, that petitioners adopted a policy " 'because of,' not merely 'in spite of,' its adverse effects upon an identifiable group." As such, the allegations are conclusory and not entitled to be assumed true. *Twombly*. To be clear, we do not reject these bald allegations on the ground that they are unrealistic or nonsensical. We do not so characterize them any more than the Court in *Twombly* rejected the plaintiffs' express allegation of a " 'contract, combination or conspiracy to prevent competitive entry,' " because it thought that claim too chimerical to be maintained. It is the conclusory nature of respondent's allegations, rather than their extravagantly fanciful nature, that disentitles them to the presumption of truth.

We next consider the factual allegations in respondent's complaint to determine if they plausibly suggest an entitlement to relief. The complaint alleges that "the [FBI], under the direction of Defendant Mueller, arrested and detained thousands of Arab Muslim men . . . as part of its investigation of the events of September 11." It further claims that "[t]he policy of holding post-September-11th detainees in highly restrictive conditions of confinement until they were 'cleared' by the FBI was approved by Defendants Ashcroft and Mueller in discussions in the weeks after September 11, 2001." Taken as true, these allegations are consistent with petitioners' purposefully designating detainees "of high interest" because of their race, religion, or national origin. But given more likely explanations, they do not plausibly establish this purpose.

The September 11 attacks were perpetrated by 19 Arab Muslim hijackers who counted themselves members in good standing of al Qaeda, an Islamic fundamentalist group. Al Qaeda was headed by another Arab Muslim—Osama bin Laden—and composed in large part of his Arab Muslim disciples. It should come as no surprise that a legitimate policy directing law enforcement to arrest and detain individuals because of their suspected link to the attacks would produce a disparate, incidental impact on Arab Muslims, even though the purpose of the policy was to target neither Arabs nor Muslims. On the facts respondent alleges the arrests Mueller oversaw were likely lawful and justified by his nondiscriminatory intent to detain aliens who were illegally present in the United States and who had potential connections to those who committed terrorist acts. As between that "obvious alternative explanation" for the arrests, *Twombly*, and the purposeful, invidious discrimination respondent asks us to infer, discrimination is not a plausible conclusion.

But even if the complaint's well-pleaded facts give rise to a plausible inference that respondent's arrest was the result of unconstitutional discrimination, that inference alone would not entitle respondent to relief. It is important to recall that respondent's complaint challenges neither the constitutionality of his arrest nor his initial detention in the MDC. Respondent's constitutional claims against petitioners rest solely on their ostensible "policy of holding post-September-11th detainees" in the AD-MAX SHU once they were categorized as "of high interest." To prevail on that theory, the complaint must contain facts plausibly showing that petitioners purposefully adopted a policy of classifying post-September-11 detainees as "of high interest" because of their race, religion, or national origin.

This the complaint fails to do. Though respondent alleges that various other defendants, who are not before us, may have labeled him a person of "of high interest" for impermissible reasons, his only factual allegation against petitioners accuses them of adopting a policy approving "restrictive conditions of confinement" for post-September-11 detainees until they were " 'cleared' by the FBI." Accepting the truth of that allegation, the complaint does not show, or even intimate, that petitioners purposefully housed detainees in the ADMAX SHU due to their race, religion, or national origin. All it plausibly suggests is that the Nation's top law enforcement officers, in the aftermath of a devastating terrorist attack, sought to keep suspected terrorists in the most secure conditions available until the suspects could be cleared of terrorist activity. Respondent does not argue, nor can he, that such a motive would violate petitioners' constitutional obligations. He would need to allege more by way of factual content to "nudg[e]" his claim of purposeful discrimination "across the line from conceivable to plausible." *Twombly*.

To be sure, respondent can attempt to draw certain contrasts between the pleadings the Court considered in *Twombly* and the pleadings at issue here. In *Twombly*, the complaint alleged general wrongdoing that extended over a period of years, whereas here the complaint alleges discrete wrongs—for instance, beatings—by lower level Government actors. The allegations here, if true, and if condoned by petitioners, could be the basis for some inference of wrongful intent on petitioners' part. Despite these distinctions, respondent's pleadings do not suffice to state a claim. Unlike in *Twombly*, where the doctrine of *respondeat superior* could bind the corporate defendant, here, as we have noted, petitioners cannot be held liable unless they themselves acted on account of a constitutionally protected characteristic. Yet respondent's complaint does not contain any factual allegation sufficient to plausibly suggest petitioners' discriminatory state of mind. His pleadings thus do not meet the standard necessary to comply with Rule 8.

It is important to note, however, that we express no opinion concerning the sufficiency of respondent's complaint against the defendants who are not before us. Respondent's account of his prison ordeal alleges serious official misconduct that we need not address here. Our decision is limited to the determination that respondent's complaint does not entitle him to relief from petitioners.

C

Respondent offers three arguments that bear on our disposition of his case, but none is persuasive.

1

Respondent first says that our decision in *Twombly* should be limited to pleadings made in the context of an antitrust dispute. This argument is not supported by *Twombly* and is incompatible with the Federal Rules of Civil Procedure. Though *Twombly* determined the sufficiency of a complaint sounding in antitrust, the decision was based on our interpretation and application of Rule 8. That Rule in turn governs the pleading standard "in all civil actions and proceedings in the United States district courts." Fed. Rule Civ. P. 1. Our decision in *Twombly* expounded the pleading standard for "all civil actions," and it applies to antitrust and discrimination suits alike.

2

Respondent next implies that our construction of Rule 8 should be tempered where, as here, the Court of Appeals has "instructed the district court to cabin discovery in such a way as to preserve" petitioners' defense of qualified immunity "as much as possible in anticipation of a summary judgment motion." We have held, however, that the question presented by a motion to dismiss a complaint for insufficient pleadings does not turn on the controls placed upon the discovery process. *Twombly* ("It is no answer to say that a claim just shy of a plausible entitlement to relief can, if groundless, be weeded out early in the discovery process through careful case management given the common lament that the success of judicial supervision in checking discovery abuse has been on the modest side").

Our rejection of the careful-case-management approach is especially important in suits where Government-official defendants are entitled to assert the defense of qualified immunity. The basic thrust of the qualified-immunity doctrine is to free officials from the concerns of litigation, including "avoidance of disruptive discovery." There are serious and legitimate reasons for this. If a Government official is to devote time to his or her duties, and to the formulation of sound and responsible policies, it is counterproductive to require the substantial diversion that is attendant to participating in litigation and making informed decisions as to how it should proceed. Litigation, though necessary to ensure that officials comply with the law, exacts heavy costs in terms of efficiency and expenditure of valuable time and resources that might otherwise be directed to the proper execution of the work of the Government. The costs of diversion are only magnified when Government officials are charged with responding to, as Judge Cabranes aptly put it, "a national and international security emergency unprecedented in the history of the American Republic."

It is no answer to these concerns to say that discovery for petitioners can be deferred while pretrial proceedings continue for other defendants. It is quite likely that, when discovery as to the other parties proceeds, it would prove necessary for petitioners and their counsel to participate in the process to ensure the case does not develop in a misleading or slanted way that causes prejudice to their position. Even if petitioners are not yet themselves subject to discovery orders, then, they would not be free from the burdens of discovery.

We decline respondent's invitation to relax the pleading requirements on the ground that the Court of Appeals promises petitioners minimally intrusive discovery. That promise provides especially cold comfort in this pleading context, where we are impelled to give real content to the concept of qualified immunity for high-level officials who must be neither deterred nor detracted from the vigorous performance of their duties. Because respondent's complaint is deficient under Rule 8, he is not entitled to discovery, cabined or otherwise.

3

Respondent finally maintains that the Federal Rules expressly allow him to allege petitioners' discriminatory intent "generally," which he equates with a conclusory allegation. It follows, respondent says, that his complaint is sufficiently well pleaded because it claims that petitioners discriminated against him "on account of [his] religion, race, and/or national origin and for no legitimate penological interest." Were we required to accept this allegation as true, respondent's complaint would survive petitioners' motion to dismiss. But the Federal Rules do not require courts to credit a complaint's conclusory statements without reference to its factual context.

It is true that Rule 9(b) requires particularity when pleading "fraud or mistake," while allowing "[m]alice, intent, knowledge, and other conditions of a person's mind [to] be alleged generally." But "generally" is a relative term. In the context of Rule 9, it is to be compared to the particularity requirement applicable to fraud or mistake. Rule 9 merely excuses a party from pleading discriminatory intent under an elevated pleading standard. It does not give him license to evade the less rigid-though still operative-strictures of Rule 8. ("[A] rigid rule requiring the detailed pleading of a condition of mind would be undesirable because, absent overriding considerations pressing for a specificity requirement, as in the case of averments of fraud or mistake, the general 'short and plain statement of the claim' mandate in Rule 8(a) ... should control the second sentence of Rule 9(b)"). And Rule 8 does not empower respondent to plead the bare elements of his cause of action, affix the label "general allegation," and expect his complaint to survive a motion to dismiss.

V

We hold that respondent's complaint fails to plead sufficient facts to state a claim for purposeful and unlawful discrimination against petitioners. The Court of Appeals should decide in the first instance whether to remand to the District Court so that respondent can seek leave to amend his deficient complaint.

The judgment of the Court of Appeals is reversed, and the case is remanded for further proceedings consistent with this opinion.

It is so ordered.

JUSTICE SOUTER, with whom JUSTICE STEVENS, JUSTICE GINSBURG, and JUSTICE BREYER join, dissenting.

This case is here on the uncontested assumption that *Bivens v. Six Unknown Fed. Narcotics Agents,* allows personal liability based on a federal officer's violation of an individual's rights under the First and Fifth Amendments, and it comes to us with the explicit concession of petitioners Ashcroft and Mueller that an officer may be subject to *Bivens* liability as a supervisor on grounds other than *respondeat superior*. The Court apparently rejects this concession and, although it has no bearing on the majority's resolution of this case, does away with supervisory liability under *Bivens*. The majority then misapplies the pleading standard under *Bell Atlantic Corp. v. Twombly,* to conclude that the complaint fails to state a claim. I respectfully dissent from both the rejection of supervisory liability as a cognizable claim in the face of petitioners' concession, and from the holding that the complaint fails to satisfy Rule 8(a)(2) of the Federal Rules of Civil Procedure.

I

A

Respondent Iqbal was arrested in November 2001 on charges of conspiracy to defraud the United States and fraud in relation to identification documents, and was placed in pretrial detention at the Metropolitan Detention Center in Brooklyn, New York. He alleges that FBI officials carried out a discriminatory policy by designating him as a person " 'of high interest' " in the investigation of the September 11 attacks solely because of his race, religion, or national origin. Owing to this designation he was placed in the detention center's Administrative Maximum Special Housing Unit for over six months while awaiting the fraud trial. As I will mention more fully below, Iqbal contends that Ashcroft and Mueller were at the very least aware of the discriminatory detention policy and condoned it (and perhaps even took part in devising it), thereby violating his First and Fifth Amendment rights.

Iqbal claims that on the day he was transferred to the special unit, prison guards, without provocation, "picked him up and threw him against the wall, kicked him in the stomach, punched him in the face, and dragged him across the room." He says that after being attacked a second time he sought medical attention but was denied care for two weeks. According to Iqbal's complaint, prison staff in the special unit subjected him to unjustified strip and body cavity searches, verbally berated him as a "terrorist" and "Muslim killer," refused to give him adequate food, and intentionally turned on air conditioning during the winter and heating during the summer. He claims that prison staff interfered with his attempts to pray and engage in religious study, and with his access to counsel.

The District Court denied Ashcroft and Mueller's motion to dismiss Iqbal's discrimination claim, and the Court of Appeals affirmed.

* * *

II

Given petitioners' concession, the complaint satisfies Rule 8(a)(2). Ashcroft and Mueller admit they are liable for their subordinates' conduct if they "had actual knowledge of the assertedly discriminatory nature of the classification of suspects as being 'of high interest' and they were deliberately indifferent to that discrimination." Iqbal alleges that after the September 11 attacks the Federal Bureau of Investigation (FBI) "arrested and detained thousands of Arab Muslim men," that many of these men were designated by high-ranking FBI officials as being "of high interest," and that in many cases, including Iqbal's, this designation was made "because of the race, religion, and national origin of the detainees, and not because of any evidence of the detainees' involvement in supporting terrorist activity." The complaint further alleges that Ashcroft was the "principal architect of the policies and practices challenged," and that Mueller "was instrumental in the adoption, promulgation, and implementation of the policies and practices challenged." According to the complaint, Ashcroft and Mueller "knew of, condoned, and willfully and maliciously agreed to subject [Iqbal] to these conditions of confinement as a matter of policy, solely on account of [his] religion, race, and/or national origin and for no legitimate penological interest." The complaint thus alleges, at a bare minimum, that Ashcroft and Mueller knew of and condoned the discriminatory policy their subordinates carried out. Actually, the complaint goes further in alleging that Ashcroft and Muller affirmatively acted to create the discriminatory detention policy. If these factual allegations are true, Ashcroft and Mueller were, at the very least, aware of the discriminatory policy being implemented and deliberately indifferent to it.

Ashcroft and Mueller argue that these allegations fail to satisfy the "plausibility standard" of *Twombly*. They contend that Iqbal's claims are implausible because such high-ranking officials "tend not to be personally involved in the specific actions of lower-level officers down the bureaucratic chain of command." But this response bespeaks a fundamental misunderstanding of the enquiry that *Twombly* demands. *Twombly* does not require a court at the motion-to-dismiss stage to consider whether the factual allegations are probably true. We made it clear, on the contrary, that a court must take the allegations as true, no matter how skeptical the court may be. See *Twombly* (a court must proceed "on the assumption that all the allegations in the complaint are true (even if doubtful in fact)"); ("[A] well-pleaded complaint may proceed even if it strikes a savvy judge that actual proof of the facts alleged is improbable. The sole exception to this rule lies with allegations that are sufficiently fantastic to defy reality as we know it: claims about little green men, or the plaintiff's recent trip to Pluto, or experiences in time travel. That is not what we have here.").

Under *Twombly*, the relevant question is whether, assuming the factual allegations are true, the plaintiff has stated a ground for relief that is plausible. That is, in *Twombly*'s words, a plaintiff must "allege facts" that, taken as true, are "suggestive of illegal conduct." In *Twombly*, we were faced with allegations of a conspiracy to violate § 1 of the Sherman Act through parallel conduct. The difficulty was that the conduct alleged was "consistent with conspiracy, but just as much in line with a wide swath of rational and competitive business strategy unilaterally prompted by common perceptions of the market." We held that in that sort of circumstance, "[a]n allegation of parallel conduct is . . . much like a naked assertion of conspiracy in a § 1 complaint: it gets the complaint close to stating a claim, but without some further factual enhancement it stops short of the line between possibility and plausibility of 'entitlement to relief.'" Here, by contrast, the allegations in the complaint are neither confined to naked legal conclusions nor consistent with legal conduct. The complaint alleges that FBI officials discriminated against Iqbal solely on account of his race, religion, and national origin, and it alleges the knowledge and deliberate indifference that, by Ashcroft and Mueller's own admission, are sufficient to make them liable for the illegal action. Iqbal's complaint therefore contains "enough facts to state a claim to relief that is plausible on its face."

I do not understand the majority to disagree with this understanding of "plausibility" under *Twombly*. Rather, the majority discards the allegations discussed above with regard to Ashcroft and Mueller as conclusory, and is left considering only two statements in the complaint: that "the [FBI], under the direction of Defendant Mueller, arrested and detained thousands of Arab Muslim men . . . as part of its investigation of the events of September 11," and that "[t]he policy of holding post-September-11th detainees in highly restrictive conditions of confinement until they were 'cleared' by the FBI was approved by Defendants Ashcroft and Mueller in discussions in the weeks after September 11, 2001." I think the majority is right in saying that these allegations suggest only that Ashcroft and Mueller "sought to keep suspected terrorists in the most secure conditions available until the suspects could be cleared of terrorist activity," and that this produced "a disparate, incidental impact on Arab Muslims." And I agree that the two allegations selected by the majority, standing alone, do not state a plausible entitlement to relief for unconstitutional discrimination.

But these allegations do not stand alone as the only significant, nonconclusory statements in the complaint, for the complaint contains many allegations linking Ashcroft and Mueller to the discriminatory practices of their subordinates (Ashcroft was the "principal architect" of the discriminatory policy); (Mueller was "instrumental" in adopting and executing the discriminatory policy); (Ashcroft and Mueller "knew of, condoned, and willfully and maliciously agreed to subject" Iqbal to harsh conditions "as a matter of policy, solely on account of [his] religion, race, and/or national origin and for no legitimate penological interest").

The majority says that these are "bare assertions" that, "much like the pleading of conspiracy in *Twombly,* amount to nothing more than a 'formulaic recitation of the elements' of a constitutional discrimination claim" and therefore are "not entitled to be assumed true." The fallacy of the majority's position, however, lies in looking at the relevant assertions in isolation. The complaint contains specific allegations that, in the aftermath of the September 11 attacks, the Chief of the FBI's International Terrorism Operations Section and the Assistant Special Agent in

Charge for the FBI's New York Field Office implemented a policy that discriminated against Arab Muslim men, including Iqbal, solely on account of their race, religion, or national origin. Viewed in light of these subsidiary allegations, the allegations singled out by the majority as "conclusory" are no such thing. Iqbal's claim is not that Ashcroft and Mueller "knew of, condoned, and willfully and maliciously agreed to subject" him to a discriminatory practice that is left undefined; his allegation is that "they knew of, condoned, and willfully and maliciously agreed to subject" him to a particular, discrete, discriminatory policy detailed in the complaint. Iqbal does not say merely that Ashcroft was the architect of some amorphous discrimination, or that Mueller was instrumental in an ill-defined constitutional violation; he alleges that they helped to create the discriminatory policy he has described. Taking the complaint as a whole, it gives Ashcroft and Mueller " 'fair notice of what the ... claim is and the grounds upon which it rests.' " *Twombly* (quoting *Conley v. Gibson*).

That aside, the majority's holding that the statements it selects are conclusory cannot be squared with its treatment of certain other allegations in the complaint as non-conclusory. For example, the majority takes as true the statement that "[t]he policy of holding post-September-11th detainees in highly restrictive conditions of confinement until they were 'cleared' by the FBI was approved by Defendants Ashcroft and Mueller in discussions in the weeks after September 11, 2001." This statement makes two points: (1) after September 11, the FBI held certain detainees in highly restrictive conditions, and (2) Ashcroft and Mueller discussed and approved these conditions. If, as the majority says, these allegations are not conclusory, then I cannot see why the majority deems it merely conclusory when Iqbal alleges that (1) after September 11, the FBI designated Arab Muslim detainees as being of " 'high interest' " "because of the race, religion, and national origin of the detainees, and not because of any evidence of the detainees' involvement in supporting terrorist activity," and (2) Ashcroft and Mueller "knew of, condoned, and willfully and maliciously agreed" to that discrimination. By my lights, there is no principled basis for the majority's disregard of the allegations linking Ashcroft and Mueller to their subordinates' discrimination.

I respectfully dissent.

JUSTICE BREYER, dissenting.

I agree with Justice Souter and join his dissent. I write separately to point out that, like the Court, I believe it important to prevent unwarranted litigation from interfering with "the proper execution of the work of the Government." But I cannot find in that need adequate justification for the Court's interpretation of *Bell Atlantic Corp. v. Twombly,* and Federal Rule of Civil Procedure 8. The law, after all, provides trial courts with other legal weapons designed to prevent unwarranted interference. As the Second Circuit explained, where a Government defendant asserts a qualified immunity defense, a trial court, responsible for managing a case and "mindful of the need to vindicate the purpose of the qualified immunity defense," can structure discovery in ways that diminish the risk of imposing unwarranted burdens upon public officials. A district court, for example, can begin discovery with lower level government defendants before determining whether a case can be made to allow discovery related to higher level government officials. Neither the briefs nor the Court's opinion provides convincing grounds for finding these alternative case-management tools inadequate, either in general or in the case before us. For this reason, as well as for the independently sufficient reasons set forth in Justice Souter's opinion, I would affirm the Second Circuit.

* * *

D. FACT PLEADING REVITALIZED

FEDERAL RULE OF CIVIL PROCEDURE 9.   PLEADING SPECIAL MATTERS

(a) Capacity or Authority to Sue; Legal Existence.

> **(1)** *In General.* Except when required to show that the court has jurisdiction, a pleading need not allege:
>
> > **(A)** a party's capacity to sue or be sued;
> >
> > **(B)** a party's authority to sue or be sued in a representative capacity; or
> >
> > **(C)** the legal existence of an organized association of persons that is made a party.
>
> **(2)** *Raising Those Issues.* To raise any of those issues, a party must do so by a specific denial, which must state any supporting facts that are peculiarly within the party's knowledge.

(b) Fraud or Mistake; Conditions of Mind. In alleging fraud or mistake, a party must state with particularity the circumstances constituting fraud or mistake. Malice, intent, knowledge, and other conditions of a person's mind may be alleged generally.

(c) Conditions Precedent. In pleading conditions precedent, it suffices to allege generally that all conditions precedent have occurred or been performed. But when denying that a condition precedent has occurred or been performed, a party must do so with particularity.

(d) Official Document or Act. In pleading an official document or official act, it suffices to allege that the document was legally issued or the act legally done.

(e) Judgment. In pleading a judgment or decision of a domestic or foreign court, a judicial or quasi-judicial tribunal, or a board or officer, it suffices to plead the judgment or decision without showing jurisdiction to render it.

(f) Time and Place. An allegation of time or place is material when testing the sufficiency of a pleading.

(g) Special Damages. If an item of special damage is claimed, it must be specifically stated.

(h) Admiralty or Maritime Claim.

    (1) *How Designated.* If a claim for relief is within the admiralty or maritime jurisdiction and also within the court's subject-matter jurisdiction on some other ground, the pleading may designate the claim as an admiralty or maritime claim for purposes of Rules 14(c), 38(e), and 82 and the Supplemental Rules for Admiralty or Maritime Claims and Asset Forfeiture Actions. A claim cognizable only in the admiralty or maritime jurisdiction is an admiralty or maritime claim for those purposes, whether or not so designated.

* * *

TELLABS, INC. v. MAKOR ISSUES & RIGHTS, LTD.

551 U.S. 308 (2007)

JUSTICE GINSBURG delivered the opinion of the Court.

This Court has long recognized that meritorious private actions to enforce federal antifraud securities laws are an essential supplement to criminal prosecutions and civil enforcement actions brought, respectively, by the Department of Justice and the Securities and Exchange Commission (SEC). Private securities fraud actions, however, if not adequately contained, can be employed abusively to impose substantial costs on companies and individuals whose conduct conforms to the law. As a check against abusive litigation by private parties, Congress enacted the Private Securities Litigation Reform Act of 1995 (PSLRA).

Exacting pleading requirements are among the control measures Congress included in the PSLRA. The Act requires plaintiffs to state with particularity both the facts constituting the alleged violation, and the facts evidencing scienter, *i.e.,* the defendant's intention "to deceive, manipulate, or defraud." This case concerns the latter requirement. As set out in § 21D(b)(2) of the PSLRA, plaintiffs must "state with particularity facts giving rise to a strong inference that the defendant acted with the required state of mind."

Congress left the key term "strong inference" undefined, and Courts of Appeals have divided on its meaning. In the case before us, the Court of Appeals for the Seventh Circuit held that the "strong inference" standard would be met if the complaint "allege[d] facts from which, if true, a reasonable person could infer that the defendant acted with the required intent." That formulation, we conclude, does not capture the stricter demand Congress sought to convey in § 21D(b)(2). It does not suffice that a reasonable fact-finder plausibly could infer from the complaint's allegations the requisite state of mind. Rather, to determine whether a complaint's scienter allegations can survive threshold inspection for sufficiency, a court governed by § 21D(b)(2) must engage in a comparative evaluation; it must consider, not only inferences urged by the plaintiff, as the Seventh Circuit did, but also competing inferences rationally drawn from the facts alleged. An inference of fraudulent intent may be plausible, yet less cogent than other, non-culpable explanations for the defendant's conduct. To qualify as "strong" within the intendment of § 21D(b)(2), we hold, an inference of scienter must be more than merely plausible or reasonable—it must be cogent and at least as compelling as any opposing inference of non-fraudulent intent.

I

Petitioner Tellabs, Inc., manufactures specialized equipment used in fiber optic networks. During the time period relevant to this case, petitioner Richard Notebaert was Tellabs' chief executive officer and president. Respondents (Shareholders) are persons who purchased Tellabs stock between December 11, 2000, and June 19, 2001. They accuse Tellabs and Notebaert (as well as several other Tellabs executives) of engaging in a scheme to deceive the investing public about the true value of Tellabs' stock.

Beginning on December 11, 2000, the Shareholders allege, Notebaert (and by imputation Tellabs) "falsely reassured public investors, in a series of statements . . . that Tellabs was continuing to enjoy strong demand for its products and earning record revenues," when, in fact, Notebaert knew the opposite was true. From December 2000 until the spring of 2001, the Shareholders claim, Notebaert knowingly misled the public in four ways. First, he made statements indicating that demand for Tellabs' flagship networking device, the TITAN 5500, was continuing to grow, when in fact demand for that product was waning. Second, Notebaert made statements indicating that the TITAN 6500, Tellabs' next-generation networking device, was available for delivery, and that demand for that product was strong and growing, when in truth the product was not ready for delivery and demand was weak. Third, he falsely represented Tellabs' financial results for the fourth quarter of 2000 (and, in connection with those results, condoned the practice of "channel stuffing," under which Tellabs flooded its customers with unwanted products). Fourth, Notebaert made a series of overstated revenue projections, when demand for the TITAN 5500 was drying up and production of the TITAN 6500 was behind schedule. Based on Notebaert's sunny assessments, the Shareholders contend, market analysts recommended that investors buy Tellabs' stock.

The first public glimmer that business was not so healthy came in March 2001 when Tellabs modestly reduced its first quarter sales projections. In the next months, Tellabs made progressively more cautious statements about its projected sales. On June 19, 2001, the last day of the class period, Tellabs disclosed that demand for the TITAN 5500 had significantly dropped. Simultaneously, the company substantially lowered its revenue projections for the second quarter of 2001. The next day, the price of Tellabs stock, which had reached a high of $67 during the period, plunged to a low of $15.87.

On December 3, 2002, the Shareholders filed a class action in the District Court for the Northern District of Illinois. Their complaint stated that Tellabs and Notebaert had engaged in securities fraud in violation of § 10(b) of the Securities Exchange Act of 1934 and SEC Rule 10b–5, also that Notebaert was a "controlling person" under § 20(a) of the 1934 Act and therefore derivatively liable for the company's fraudulent acts. Tellabs moved to dismiss the complaint on the ground that the Shareholders had failed to plead their case with the particularity the PSLRA requires. The District Court agreed, and therefore dismissed the complaint without prejudice.

The Shareholders then amended their complaint, adding references to 27 confidential sources and making further, more specific, allegations concerning Notebaert's mental state. The District Court again dismissed, this time with prejudice. The Shareholders had sufficiently pleaded that Notebaert's statements were misleading, the court determined, but they had insufficiently alleged that he acted with scienter.

The Court of Appeals for the Seventh Circuit reversed in relevant part. Like the District Court, the Court of Appeals found that the Shareholders had pleaded the misleading character of Notebaert's statements with sufficient particularity. Unlike the District Court, however, the Seventh Circuit concluded that the Shareholders had sufficiently alleged that Notebaert acted with the requisite state of mind.

The Court of Appeals recognized that the PSLRA "unequivocally raise[d] the bar for pleading scienter" by requiring plaintiffs to "plea[d] sufficient facts to create a strong inference of scienter." In evaluating whether that pleading standard is met, the Seventh Circuit said, "courts [should] examine all of the allegations in the complaint and then ... decide whether collectively they establish such an inference." "[W]e will allow the complaint to survive," the court next and critically stated, "if it alleges facts from which, if true, a reasonable person could infer that the defendant acted with the required intent.... If a reasonable person could not draw such an inference from the alleged facts, the defendants are entitled to dismissal."

In adopting its standard for the survival of a complaint, the Seventh Circuit explicitly rejected a stiffer standard adopted by the Sixth Circuit, *i.e.,* that "plaintiffs are entitled only to the most plausible of competing inferences." The Sixth Circuit's standard, the court observed, because it involved an assessment of competing inferences, "could potentially infringe upon plaintiffs' Seventh Amendment rights." We granted certiorari to resolve the disagreement among the Circuits on whether, and to what extent, a court must consider competing inferences in determining whether a securities fraud complaint gives rise to a "strong inference" of scienter.

II

Section 10(b) of the Securities Exchange Act of 1934 forbids the "use or employ, in connection with the purchase or sale of any security ..., [of] any manipulative or deceptive device or contrivance in contravention of such rules and regulations as the [SEC] may prescribe as necessary or appropriate in the public interest or for the protection of investors." SEC Rule 10b–5 implements § 10(b) by declaring it unlawful:

(a) To employ any device, scheme, or artifice to defraud,

(b) To make any untrue statement of a material fact or to omit to state a material fact necessary in order to make the statements made . . . not misleading, or

(c) To engage in any act, practice, or course of business which operates or would operate as a fraud or deceit upon any person, in connection with the purchase or sale of any security.

Section 10(b), this Court has implied from the statute's text and purpose, affords a right of action to purchasers or sellers of securities injured by its violation. To establish liability under § 10(b) and Rule 10b–5, a private plaintiff must prove that the defendant acted with scienter, "a mental state embracing intent to deceive, manipulate, or defraud."

In an ordinary civil action, the Federal Rules of Civil Procedure require only "a short and plain statement of the claim showing that the pleader is entitled to relief." Fed. Rule Civ. Proc. 8(a)(2). Although the rule encourages brevity, the complaint must say enough to give the defendant "fair notice of what the plaintiff's claim is and the grounds upon which it rests." Prior to the enactment of the PSLRA, the sufficiency of a complaint for securities fraud was governed not by Rule 8, but by the heightened pleading standard set forth in Rule 9(b). Rule 9(b) applies to "all averments of fraud or mistake"; it requires that "the circumstances constituting fraud . . . be stated with particularity" but provides that "[m]alice, intent, knowledge, and other condition of mind of a person, may be averred generally."

Courts of Appeals diverged on the character of the Rule 9(b) inquiry in § 10(b) cases: Could securities fraud plaintiffs allege the requisite mental state "simply by stating that scienter existed," or were they required to allege with particularity facts giving rise to an inference of scienter? Circuits requiring plaintiffs to allege specific facts indicating scienter expressed that requirement variously. The Second Circuit's formulation was the most stringent. Securities fraud plaintiffs in that Circuit were required to "specifically plead those [facts] which they assert give rise to a *strong inference* that the defendants had" the requisite state of mind. The "strong inference" formulation was appropriate, the Second Circuit said, to ward off allegations of "fraud by hindsight."

Setting a uniform pleading standard for § 10(b) actions was among Congress' objectives when it enacted the PSLRA. Designed to curb perceived abuses of the § 10(b) private action—"nuisance filings, targeting of deep-pocket defendants, vexatious discovery requests and manipulation by class action lawyers,"—the PSLRA installed both substantive and procedural controls. Notably, Congress prescribed new procedures for the appointment of lead plaintiffs and lead counsel. This innovation aimed to increase the likelihood that institutional investors-parties more likely to balance the interests of the class with the long-term interests of the company-would serve as lead plaintiffs. Congress also "limit[ed] recoverable damages and attorney's fees, provide[d] a 'safe harbor' for forward-looking statements, ... mandate[d] imposition of sanctions for frivolous litigation, and authorize[d] a stay of discovery pending resolution of any motion to dismiss." And in § 21D(b) of the PSLRA, Congress "impose[d] heightened pleading requirements in actions brought pursuant to § 10(b) and Rule 10b–5."

Under the PSLRA's heightened pleading instructions, any private securities complaint alleging that the defendant made a false or misleading statement must: (1) "specify each statement alleged to have been misleading [and] the reason or reasons why the statement is misleading," and (2) "state with particularity facts giving rise to a strong inference that the defendant acted with the required state of mind." In the instant case, as earlier stated, the District Court and the Seventh Circuit agreed that the Shareholders met the first of the two requirements: The complaint sufficiently specified Notebaert's alleged misleading statements and the reasons why the statements were misleading. But those courts disagreed on whether the Shareholders, as required by § 21D(b)(2), "state[d] with particularity facts giving rise to a strong inference that [Notebaert] acted with [scienter]."

The "strong inference" standard "unequivocally raise[d] the bar for pleading scienter," and signaled Congress' purpose to promote greater uniformity among the Circuits. But "Congress did not ... throw much light on what facts ... suffice to create [a strong] inference," or on what "degree of imagination courts can use in divining whether" the requisite inference exists. While adopting the Second Circuit's "strong inference" standard, Congress did not codify that Circuit's case law interpreting the standard. With no clear guide from Congress other than its "inten[tion] to strengthen existing pleading requirements," Courts of Appeals have diverged again, this time in construing the term "strong inference." Among the uncertainties, should courts consider competing inferences in determining whether an inference of scienter is "strong"? Our task is to prescribe a workable construction of the "strong inference" standard, a reading geared to the PSLRA's twin goals: to curb frivolous, lawyer-driven litigation, while preserving investors' ability to recover on meritorious claims.

III

A

We establish the following prescriptions: *First,* faced with a Rule 12(b)(6) motion to dismiss a § 10(b) action, courts must, as with any motion to dismiss for failure to plead a claim on which relief can be granted, accept all factual allegations in the complaint as true. On this point, the parties agree.

Second, courts must consider the complaint in its entirety, as well as other sources courts ordinarily examine when ruling on Rule 12(b)(6) motions to dismiss, in particular, documents incorporated into the complaint by reference, and matters of which a court may take judicial notice. The inquiry, as several Courts of Appeals have recognized, is whether *all* of the facts alleged, taken collectively, give rise to a strong inference of scienter, not whether any individual allegation, scrutinized in isolation, meets that standard.

Third, in determining whether the pleaded facts give rise to a "strong" inference of scienter, the court must take into account plausible opposing inferences. The Seventh Circuit expressly declined to engage in such a comparative inquiry. A complaint could survive, that court said, as long as it "alleges facts from which, if true, a reasonable person could infer that the defendant acted with the required intent"; in other words, only "[i]f a reasonable person could not draw such an inference from the alleged facts" would the defendant prevail on a motion to dismiss. But in § 21D(b)(2), Congress did not merely require plaintiffs to "provide a factual basis for [their] scienter allegations," *i.e.,* to allege facts from which an inference of scienter rationally *could* be drawn. Instead, Congress required plaintiffs to plead with particularity facts that give rise to a "strong"—*i.e.,* a powerful or cogent-inference.

The strength of an inference cannot be decided in a vacuum. The inquiry is inherently comparative: How likely is it that one conclusion, as compared to others, follows from the underlying facts? To determine whether the plaintiff has alleged facts that give rise to the requisite "strong inference" of scienter, a court must consider plausible nonculpable explanations for the defendant's conduct, as well as inferences favoring the plaintiff. The inference that the defendant acted with scienter need not be irrefutable, *i.e.,* of the "smoking-gun" genre, or even the "most plausible of competing inferences." Recall in this regard that § 21D(b)'s pleading requirements are but one constraint among many the PSLRA installed to screen out frivolous suits, while allowing meritorious actions to move forward. Yet the inference of scienter must be more than merely "reasonable" or "permissible"—it must be cogent and compelling, thus strong in light of other explanations. A complaint will survive, we hold, only if a reasonable person would deem the inference of scienter cogent and at least as compelling as any opposing inference one could draw from the facts alleged.[5]

---

5. Justice Scalia objects to this standard on the ground that "[i]f a jade falcon were stolen from a room to which only A and B had access," it could not "*possibly* be said there was a 'strong inference' that B was the thief." I suspect, however, that law enforcement officials as well as the owner of the precious falcon would find the inference of guilt as to B quite strong—certainly strong enough to warrant further investigation. Indeed, an inference at least as likely as competing inferences can, in some cases, warrant recovery. *See Summers v. Tice* (plaintiff wounded by gunshot could recover from two defendants, even though the most he could prove was that each defendant was at least as likely to have injured him as the other); RESTATEMENT (THIRD) OF TORTS § 28(b), Comment *e,* p. 504 (Proposed Final Draft No. 1, Apr. 6, 2005) ("Since the publication of the Second Restatement in 1965, courts have generally accepted the alternative-liability principle of [*Summers v. Tice,* adopted in] § 433B(3), while fleshing out its limits.").

B

Tellabs contends that when competing inferences are considered, Notebaert's evident lack of pecuniary motive will be dispositive. The Shareholders, Tellabs stresses, did not allege that Notebaert sold any shares during the class period. While it is true that motive can be a relevant consideration, and personal financial gain may weigh heavily in favor of a scienter inference, we agree with the Seventh Circuit that the absence of a motive allegation is not fatal. As earlier stated, allegations must be considered collectively; the significance that can be ascribed to an allegation of motive, or lack thereof, depends on the entirety of the complaint.

Tellabs also maintains that several of the Shareholders' allegations are too vague or ambiguous to contribute to a strong inference of scienter. For example, the Shareholders alleged that Tellabs flooded its customers with unwanted products, a practice known as "channel stuffing." But they failed, Tellabs argues, to specify whether the channel stuffing allegedly known to Notebaert was the illegitimate kind (*e.g.,* writing orders for products customers had not requested) or the legitimate kind (*e.g.,* offering customers discounts as an incentive to buy). We agree that omissions and ambiguities count against inferring scienter, for plaintiffs must "state with particularity facts giving rise to a strong inference that the defendant acted with the required state of mind." We reiterate, however, that the court's job is not to scrutinize each allegation in isolation but to assess all the allegations holistically. In sum, the reviewing court must ask: When the allegations are accepted as true and taken collectively, would a reasonable person deem the inference of scienter at least as strong as any opposing inference?

IV

Accounting for its construction of § 21D(b)(2), the Seventh Circuit explained that the court "th[ought] it wis[e] to adopt an approach that [could not] be misunderstood as a usurpation of the jury's role." In our view, the Seventh Circuit's concern was undue.[7] A court's comparative assessment of plausible inferences, while constantly assuming the plaintiff's allegations to be true, we think it plain, does not impinge upon the

---

In any event, we disagree with Justice Scalia that the hardly stock term "strong inference" has only one invariably right ("natural" or "normal") reading—his.

   Justice Alito agrees with Justice Scalia, and would transpose to the pleading stage "the test that is used at the summary-judgment and judgment-as-a-matter-of-law stages." But the test at each stage is measured against a different backdrop. It is improbable that Congress, without so stating, intended courts to test pleadings, unaided by discovery, to determine whether there is "no genuine issue as to any material fact." *See* Fed. Rule Civ. Proc. 56(c). And judgment as a matter of law is a post-trial device, turning on the question whether a party has produced evidence "legally sufficient" to warrant a jury determination in that party's favor. *See* Rule 50(a)(1).

   7. The Seventh Circuit raised the possibility of a Seventh Amendment problem on its own initiative. The Shareholders did not contend below that dismissal of their complaint under § 21D(b)(2) would violate their right to trial by jury.

Seventh Amendment right to jury trial.[8]

Congress, as creator of federal statutory claims, has power to prescribe what must be pleaded to state the claim, just as it has power to determine what must be proved to prevail on the merits. It is the federal lawmaker's prerogative, therefore, to allow, disallow, or shape the contours of—including the pleading and proof requirements for—§ 10(b) private actions. No decision of this Court questions that authority in general, or suggests, in particular, that the Seventh Amendment inhibits Congress from establishing whatever pleading requirements it finds appropriate for federal statutory claims.[9]

* * * In the instant case, provided that the Shareholders have satisfied the congressionally "prescribe[d] ... means of making an issue," the case will fall within the jury's authority to assess the credibility of witnesses, resolve any genuine issues of fact, and make the ultimate determination whether Notebaert and, by imputation, Tellabs acted with scienter. We emphasize, as well, that under our construction of the "strong inference" standard, a plaintiff is not forced to plead more than she would be required to prove at trial. A plaintiff alleging fraud in a § 10(b) action, we hold today, must plead facts rendering an inference of scienter *at least as likely as* any plausible opposing inference. At trial, she must then prove her case by a "preponderance of the evidence." Stated otherwise, she must demonstrate that it is *more likely* than not that the defendant acted with scienter.

* * *

While we reject the Seventh Circuit's approach to § 21D(b)(2), we do not decide whether, under the standard we have described, the Shareholders' allegations warrant "a strong inference that [Notebaert and Tellabs] acted with the required state of mind." Neither the District Court nor the Court of Appeals had the opportunity to consider the matter in light of the prescriptions we announce today. We therefore vacate the Seventh Circuit's judgment so that the case may be reexamined in accord with our construction of § 21D(b)(2).

The judgment of the Court of Appeals is vacated, and the case is remanded for further proceedings consistent with this opinion.

It is so ordered.

JUSTICE SCALIA, concurring in the judgment.

I fail to see how an inference that is merely "at least as compelling as any opposing inference," can conceivably be called what the statute here at issue requires: a "strong inference." If a jade falcon were stolen from a

---

8. In numerous contexts, gate-keeping judicial determinations prevent submission of claims to a jury's judgment without violating the Seventh Amendment.

9. Any heightened pleading rule, including Fed. Rule Civ. Proc. 9(b), could have the effect of preventing a plaintiff from getting discovery on a claim that might have gone to a jury, had discovery occurred and yielded substantial evidence. In recognizing Congress' or the Federal Rule makers' authority to adopt special pleading rules, we have detected no Seventh Amendment impediment.

room to which only A and B had access, could it *possibly* be said there was a "strong inference" that B was the thief? I think not, and I therefore think that the Court's test must fail. In my view, the test should be whether the inference of scienter (if any) is *more plausible* than the inference of innocence.*

The Court's explicit rejection of this reading rests on two assertions. The first (doubtless true) is that the statute does not require that "[t]he inference that the defendant acted with scienter . . . be irrefutable, *i.e.,* of the 'smoking-gun' genre." It is up to Congress, however, and not to us, to determine what pleading standard would avoid those extremities while yet effectively deterring baseless actions. Congress has expressed its determination in the phrase "strong inference"; it is our job to give that phrase its normal meaning. And if we are to abandon text in favor of unexpressed purpose, as the Court does, it is inconceivable that Congress's enactment of stringent pleading requirements in the Private Securities Litigation Reform Act of 1995 somehow manifests the purpose of giving plaintiffs the edge in close cases.

The Court's second assertion (also true) is that "an inference at least as likely as competing inferences can, in some cases, warrant recovery." *Summers* is a famous case, however, because it sticks out of the ordinary body of tort law like a sore thumb. It represented "a relaxation" of "such proof as is ordinarily required" to succeed in a negligence action. There is no indication that the statute at issue here was meant to relax the ordinary rule under which a tie goes to the defendant. To the contrary, it explicitly strengthens that rule by extending it to the pleading stage of a case.

* * * The Court and the dissent criticize me for suggesting that there is only one reading of the text. They are both mistaken. I assert only that mine is the natural reading of the statute (*i.e.,* the normal reading), not that it is the only conceivable one. The Court has no standing to object to this approach, since it concludes that, in another respect, the statute admits of only one natural reading, namely, that competing inferences must be weighed because the strong-inference requirement "is inherently comparative." As for the dissent, it asserts that the statute cannot possibly have a natural and discernible meaning, since "Courts of Appeals" and "Members of this Court" "have divided" over the question. It was just weeks ago, however, that the author of the dissent, joined by the author of today's opinion for the Court, concluded that a statute's meaning was "plain," even though the Courts of Appeals and Members of this

---

* The Court suggests that "the owner of the precious falcon would find the inference of guilt as to B quite strong." If he should draw such an inference, it would only prove the wisdom of the ancient maxim *"aliquis non debet esse Judex in propria causa"*—no man ought to be a judge of his own cause. *Dr. Bonham's Case* (1610). For it is quite clear (from the dispassionate perspective of one who does not own a jade falcon) that a *possibility,* even a strong possibility, that B is responsible is not a strong *inference* that B is responsible. "Inference" connotes "belief" in what is inferred, and it would be impossible to form a strong belief that it was B and not A, or A and not B.

Court divided over the question. Was plain meaning then, as the dissent claims it is today, "in the eye of the beholder"?

It is unremarkable that various Justices in this case reach different conclusions about the correct interpretation of the statutory text. It is remarkable, however, that the dissent believes that Congress "implicitly delegated significant lawmaking authority to the Judiciary in determining how th[e] [strong-inference] standard should operate in practice." This is language usually employed to describe the discretion conferred upon administrative agencies, which need not adopt what courts would consider the interpretation most faithful to the text of the statute, but may choose some other interpretation, so long as it is within the bounds of the reasonable, and may later change to some *other* interpretation that is within the bounds of the reasonable. Courts, by contrast, *must* give the statute its single, most plausible, reading. To describe this as an exercise of "delegated lawmaking authority" seems to me peculiar—unless one believes in lawmakers who have no discretion. Courts must apply judgment, to be sure. But judgment is not discretion.

Even if I agreed with the Court's interpretation of "strong inference," I would not join the Court's opinion because of its frequent indulgence in the last remaining legal fiction of the West: that the report of a single committee of a single House expresses the will of Congress. The Court says, for example, that "Congress'[s] purpose" was "to promote greater uniformity among the Circuits," relying for that certitude upon the statement of managers accompanying a House Conference Committee Report whose text was never adopted by the House, much less by the Senate, and as far as we know was read by almost no one. The Court is sure that Congress " 'inten[ded] to strengthen existing pleading requirements,' " because—again—the statement of managers said so. I come to the same conclusion for the much safer reason that the law which Congress adopted (and which the Members of both Houses actually *voted* on) so indicates. And had the legislation not done so, the statement of managers assuredly could not have remedied the deficiency.

With the above exceptions, I am generally in agreement with the Court's analysis, and so concur in its judgment.

JUSTICE ALITO, concurring in the judgment.

I agree with the Court that the Seventh Circuit used an erroneously low standard for determining whether the plaintiffs in this case satisfied their burden of pleading "with particularity facts giving rise to a strong inference that the defendant acted with the required state of mind." I further agree that the case should be remanded to allow the lower courts to decide in the first instance whether the allegations survive under the correct standard. In two respects, however, I disagree with the opinion of the Court. First, the best interpretation of the statute is that only those facts that are alleged "with particularity" may properly be considered in determining whether the allegations of scienter are sufficient. Second, I agree with Justice Scalia that a "strong inference" of scienter, in the present context, means an inference that is more likely than not correct.

I

On the first point, the statutory language is quite clear. [The statute] states that "the complaint shall, with respect to each act or omission alleged to violate this chapter, state with particularity facts giving rise to a strong inference that the defendant acted with the required state of mind." Thus, "a strong inference" of scienter must arise from those facts that are stated "with particularity." It follows that facts not stated with the requisite particularity cannot be considered in determining whether the strong-inference test is met.

In dicta, however, the Court states that "omissions and ambiguities" merely "count against" inferring scienter, and that a court should consider all allegations of scienter, even non-particularized ones, when considering whether a complaint meets the "strong inference" requirement. Not only does this interpretation contradict the clear statutory language on this point, but it undermines the particularity requirement's purpose of preventing a plaintiff from using vague or general allegations in order to get by a motion to dismiss for failure to state a claim. Allowing a plaintiff to derive benefit from such allegations would permit him to circumvent this important provision.

Furthermore, the Court's interpretation of the particularity requirement in no way distinguishes it from normal pleading review, under which a court naturally gives less weight to allegations containing "omissions and ambiguities" and more weight to allegations stating particularized facts. The particularity requirement is thus stripped of all meaning.

Questions certainly may arise as to whether certain allegations meet the statutory particularity requirement, but where that requirement is violated, the offending allegations cannot be taken into account.

II

I would also hold that a "strong inference that the defendant acted with the required state of mind" is an inference that is stronger than the inference that the defendant lacked the required state of mind. Congress has provided very little guidance regarding the meaning of "strong inference," and the difference between the Court's interpretation (the inference of scienter must be at least as strong as the inference of no scienter) and Justice Scalia's (the inference of scienter must be at least marginally stronger than the inference of no scienter) is unlikely to make any practical difference. The two approaches are similar in that they both regard the critical question as posing a binary choice (either the facts give rise to a "strong inference" of scienter or they do not). But Justice Scalia's interpretation would align the pleading test under [the statute] with the test that is used at the summary-judgment and judgment-as-a-matter-of-law stages, whereas the Court's test would introduce a test previously unknown in civil litigation. It seems more likely that Congress meant to adopt a known quantity and thus to adopt Justice Scalia's approach.

JUSTICE STEVENS, dissenting.

As the Court explains, when Congress enacted a heightened pleading requirement for private actions to enforce the federal securities laws, it "left the key term 'strong inference' undefined." It thus implicitly delegated significant lawmaking authority to the Judiciary in determining how that standard should operate in practice. Today the majority crafts a perfectly workable definition of the term, but I am persuaded that a different interpretation would be both easier to apply and more consistent with the statute.

The basic purpose of the heightened pleading requirement in the context of securities fraud litigation is to protect defendants from the costs of discovery and trial in unmeritorious cases. Because of its intrusive nature, discovery may also invade the privacy interests of the defendants and their executives. Like citizens suspected of having engaged in criminal activity, those defendants should not be required to produce their private effects unless there is probable cause to believe them guilty of misconduct. Admittedly, the probable-cause standard is not capable of precise measurement, but it is a concept that is familiar to judges. As a matter of normal English usage, its meaning is roughly the same as "strong inference." Moreover, it is most unlikely that Congress intended us to adopt a standard that makes it more difficult to commence a civil case than a criminal case.

In addition to the benefit of its grounding in an already familiar legal concept, using a probable-cause standard would avoid the unnecessary conclusion that "in determining whether the pleaded facts give rise to a 'strong' inference of scienter, the court *must* take into account plausible opposing inferences." There are times when an inference can easily be deemed strong without any need to weigh competing inferences. For example, if a known drug dealer exits a building immediately after a confirmed drug transaction, carrying a suspicious looking package, a judge could draw a strong inference that the individual was involved in the aforementioned drug transaction without debating whether the suspect might have been leaving the building at that exact time for another unrelated reason.

If, using that same methodology, we assume the truth of the detailed factual allegations attributed to 27 different confidential informants described in the complaint, and view those allegations collectively, I think it clear that they establish probable cause to believe that Tellabs' chief executive officer "acted with the required intent," as the Seventh Circuit held.

Accordingly, I would affirm the judgment of the Court of Appeals.

IX. WEEK NINE: MODERN PLEADING

A. RESPONDING TO THE COMPLAINT

FEDERAL RULE OF CIVIL PROCEDURE 12 [PLEASE REVIEW RULE 12]

FEDERAL RULE OF CIVIL PROCEDURE 8(d)

(d) Pleading to Be Concise and Direct; Alternative Statements; Inconsistency.

    (1) *In General.* Each allegation must be simple, concise, and direct. No technical form is required.

    (2) *Alternative Statements of a Claim or Defense.* A party may set out two or more statements of a claim or defense alternatively or hypothetically, either in a single count or defense or in separate ones. If a party makes alternative statements, the pleading is sufficient if any one of them is sufficient.

    (3) *Inconsistent Claims or Defenses.* A party may state as many separate claims or defenses as it has, regardless of consistency.

(e) Construing Pleadings. Pleadings must be construed so as to do justice.

* * *

PAE GOVERNMENT SERVICES, INC. v. MPRI, INC.

514 F.3d 856 (9th Cir. 2007)

KOZINSKI, CHIEF JUDGE:

We consider whether a district court may strike allegations from an amended complaint because they contradict an earlier iteration of the same pleading.

Facts

PAE Government Services, Inc. and MPRI, Inc. sell services to government agencies. The companies agreed to work together to submit a bid for a government contract, and signed a "Teaming Agreement" that divided duties between them. MPRI submitted the bid as "prime contractor" and won. MPRI thereafter refused to subcontract to PAE all the work specified in the Teaming Agreement—or so PAE claimed in its original complaint.

The district court dismissed that complaint because, in its view, the Teaming Agreement is no more than an "agreement to agree." The agreement is governed by Virginia law, and the district court held that Virginia won't enforce agreements to agree. PAE thereupon amended its complaint to allege that, after MPRI won the government contract, it entered into a second agreement with PAE. According to the amended complaint, this second agreement was "confirmed" in "written communications" and by the parties' "course of conduct." The amended complaint also added a promissory estoppel claim against MPRI.

The district court found PAE's new allegations of a second agreement with MPRI to be "sham pleadings that contradict allegations made in the original Complaint." In particular, the allegation of a second agreement contradicted PAE's original claim that "[f]ollowing the award of the ... [government contract], MPRI failed and refused to enter into a subcontract with PAE." The district court therefore struck the new allegations from PAE's First Amended Complaint. After holding that Virginia law also barred PAE's promissory estoppel claim, the district court dismissed the complaint.

PAE amended its complaint yet again, adding more detail about its second agreement with MPRI. The district court remained unmoved; it deemed the Second Amended Complaint to be "merely a revision of the [First Amended Complaint] which alleges more specific facts evidencing the existence of a subsequent subcontract between the parties." The district court struck the additional allegations and dismissed the complaint—this time, with prejudice.

Analysis

1. By striking the allegations in PAE's amended complaint as a "sham," the district court effectively resolved those allegations on the merits. In other words, it determined that the allegations in the amended complaint were unfounded because they contradicted (in the district court's view) earlier allegations PAE made in its original complaint. But the Federal Rules of Civil Procedure do not authorize a district court to adjudicate claims on the merits at this early stage in the proceedings; the court may only review claims for legal sufficiency. *See* Fed. R. Civ. P. 12(b). Adjudication on the merits must await summary judgment or trial. Rule 12(f) does authorize the court to strike "any insufficient defense," which this is clearly not, and "any redundant, immaterial, impertinent, or scandalous matter." PAE's allegations of a second agreement are certainly not any of those things; they are normal contract claims that would not be in the least bit objectionable, but for the fact that they appeared, in the district court's view, to contradict allegations in an earlier version of the complaint.

Which brings us to the meat of the coconut: Does the fact that an amended complaint (or answer) contains an allegation that is apparently contrary to an earlier iteration of the same pleading render the later pleading a sham? The answer is: not necessarily. To begin with, allegations in the two versions of the complaint might not conflict at all. Here, for example, PAE explains that the allegations in the original complaint referred to MPRI's refusal to sign the specific subcontract contemplated in the Teaming Agreement; the amended complaint, by contrast, referred to an entirely different agreement reached over email. Only a careful comparison of the two documents, rather than a glance at isolated provisions, can determine whether PAE's account is plausible. We have not undertaken such a comparison, however, nor need we do so to resolve this case. Even assuming that the two pleadings were irreconcilably at odds with each other, this would not, by itself, establish that the later pleading is a sham.

At the time a complaint is filed, the parties are often uncertain about the facts and the law; and yet, prompt filing is encouraged and often required by a statute of limitations, laches, the need to preserve evidence and other such concerns. In recognition of these uncertainties, we do not require complaints to be verified, *see* Fed. R. Civ. P. 11(a), and we allow pleadings in the alternative—even if the alternatives are mutually exclusive. As the litigation progresses, and each party learns more about its case and that of its opponents, some allegations fall by the wayside as legally or factually unsupported. This rarely means that those allegations were brought in bad faith or that the pleading that contained them was a sham. Parties usually abandon claims because, over the passage of time and through diligent work, they have learned more about the available evidence and viable legal theories, and wish to shape their allegations to conform to these newly discovered realities. We do not call this process sham pleading; we call it litigation.[2]

This does not mean, of course, that allegations in a complaint can never be frivolous, or that a district court can never determine that a complaint or answer was filed in bad faith. But the mechanism for doing so is in Rule 11, which deals specifically with bad faith conduct. MPRI points to Rule 11 as a source of the district court's authority for the order it entered here. But Rule 11 can play no role in this case because the district court did not invoke the rule's procedural safeguards, nor did it employ the rule's substantive standard, which would have required a finding that PAE or its counsel acted in bad faith.[3] The district court has no free-standing authority to strike pleadings simply because it believes that a party has taken inconsistent positions in the litigation. Rather, the district court's powers are generally limited to those provided by the Federal Rules of Civil Procedure. Though the Federal Circuit reached a

---

2. PAE's earlier allegation may or may not have relevance to further proceedings in the case, including any under Rule 11. To the extent the superseded pleading is verified, it becomes something akin to a sworn declaration, and the party that presented it may suffer a loss of credibility before the trier of fact, which may be less inclined to believe a party that has sworn to inconsistent material statements. Also, a party's representations may judicially estop it from taking a contrary position in later proceedings. We mention this only as a theoretical possibility in the interest of completeness, not because we believe it could apply here. Indeed, the requirements for judicial estoppel are strict, and nothing we have seen in this record suggests those requirements are met here.

3. A prior version of Rule 11 did authorize a district court to "strike pleadings ... as sham and false," but this provision was eliminated in 1983. *See* Fed R. Civ. P. 11 advisory committee's note to 1983 amendment. The Advisory Committee notes to Rule 11 suggest that the 1983 amendment was designed to avoid precisely the type of error committed by the district court here: "confus[ing] the issue of attorney honesty with the merits of the action." Though false factual assertions may be evidence of bad faith, they are usually not; generally, they are the result of ignorance, misunderstanding or undue optimism. If bad faith is found, in accordance with the procedures outlined in Rule 11, the district court has wide latitude to impose sanctions, including the striking of the offending pleading. But absent a finding of bad faith, factual allegations in the complaint (or answer) must be tested through the normal mechanisms for adjudicating the merits.

contrary conclusion in *Bradley v. Chiron Corp.,* no other court of appeals has followed that decision, and we decline to do so.

The short of it is that there is nothing in the Federal Rules of Civil Procedure to prevent a party from filing successive pleadings that make inconsistent or even contradictory allegations. Unless there is a showing that the party acted in bad faith—a showing that can only be made after the party is given an opportunity to respond under the procedures of Rule 11—inconsistent allegations are simply not a basis for striking the pleading. The district court's order, which is based on the contrary conclusion, must be reversed.

2. Because MPRI made its alleged promises in connection with the Teaming Agreement, that agreement's choice-of-law clause governs PAE's promissory estoppel claim. The Teaming Agreement chooses Virginia law, which doesn't recognize promissory estoppel as a cause of action. We see no reason not to enforce the agreement's choice of law: Virginia has a substantial relationship to MPRI (which has its principal place of business there), and enforcing the clause won't violate a fundamental policy of California. The district court properly dismissed PAE's promissory estoppel claim.

* * *

Rule 12 provides no authority to dismiss "sham" pleadings. If a party believes that its opponent pled in bad faith, it can seek other means of redress, such as sanctions under Rule 11, 28 U.S.C. § 1927 or the court's inherent authority. *Chambers v. NASCO, Inc.,* 501 U.S. 32 (1991).

Reversed in part, affirmed in part and remanded. No costs.

* * *

FEDERAL RULE OF CIVIL PROCEDURE 12. DEFENSES AND OBJECTIONS: WHEN AND HOW PRESENTED; MOTION FOR JUDGMENT ON THE PLEADINGS; CONSOLIDATING MOTIONS; WAIVING DEFENSES; PRETRIAL HEARING

(a) Time to Serve a Responsive Pleading.

(1) *In General.* Unless another time is specified by this rule or a federal statute, the time for serving a responsive pleading is as follows:

(A) A defendant must serve an answer:

(i) within 21 days after being served with the summons and complaint; or

(ii) if it has timely waived service under Rule 4(d), within 60 days after the request for a waiver was sent, or within 90 days after it was sent to the defendant outside any judicial district of the United States.

(B) A party must serve an answer to a counterclaim or crossclaim within 21 days after being served with the pleading that states the counterclaim or crossclaim.

(**C**) A party must serve a reply to an answer within 21 days after being served with an order to reply, unless the order specifies a different time.

(**2**) *United States and Its Agencies, Officers, or Employees Sued in an Official Capacity.* The United States, a United States agency, or a United States officer or employee sued only in an official capacity must serve an answer to a complaint, counterclaim, or crossclaim within 60 days after service on the United States attorney.

(**3**) *United States Officers or Employees Sued in an Individual Capacity.* A United States officer or employee sued in an individual capacity for an act or omission occurring in connection with duties performed on the United States' behalf must serve an answer to a complaint, counterclaim, or crossclaim within 60 days after service on the officer or employee or service on the United States attorney, whichever is later.

(**4**) *Effect of a Motion.* Unless the court sets a different time, serving a motion under this rule alters these periods as follows:

(**A**) if the court denies the motion or postpones its disposition until trial, the responsive pleading must be served within 14 days after notice of the court's action; or

(**B**) if the court grants a motion for a more definite statement, the responsive pleading must be served within 14 days after the more definite statement is served.

(**b**) **How to Present Defenses.** Every defense to a claim for relief in any pleading must be asserted in the responsive pleading if one is required. But a party may assert the following defenses by motion:

(**1**) lack of subject-matter jurisdiction;

(**2**) lack of personal jurisdiction;

(**3**) improper venue;

(**4**) insufficient process;

(**5**) insufficient service of process;

(**6**) failure to state a claim upon which relief can be granted; and

(**7**) failure to join a party under Rule 19.

A motion asserting any of these defenses must be made before pleading if a responsive pleading is allowed. If a pleading sets out a claim for relief that does not require a responsive pleading, an opposing party may assert at trial any defense to that claim. No defense or objection is waived by joining it with one or more other defenses or objections in a responsive pleading or in a motion.

(**c**) **Motion for Judgment on the Pleadings.** After the pleadings are closed—but early enough not to delay trial—a party may move for judgment on the pleadings.

(d) Result of Presenting Matters Outside the Pleadings. If, on a motion under Rule 12(b)(6) or 12(c), matters outside the pleadings are presented to and not excluded by the court, the motion must be treated as one for summary judgment under Rule 56. All parties must be given a reasonable opportunity to present all the material that is pertinent to the motion.

(e) Motion for a More Definite Statement. A party may move for a more definite statement of a pleading to which a responsive pleading is allowed but which is so vague or ambiguous that the party cannot reasonably prepare a response. The motion must be made before filing a responsive pleading and must point out the defects complained of and the details desired. If the court orders a more definite statement and the order is not obeyed within 14 days after notice of the order or within the time the court sets, the court may strike the pleading or issue any other appropriate order.

(f) Motion to Strike. The court may strike from a pleading an insufficient defense or any redundant, immaterial, impertinent, or scandalous matter. The court may act:

    (1) on its own; or

    (2) on motion made by a party either before responding to the pleading or, if a response is not allowed, within 21 days after being served with the pleading.

(g) Joining Motions.

    (1) *Right to Join.* A motion under this rule may be joined with any other motion allowed by this rule.

    (2) *Limitation on Further Motions.* Except as provided in Rule 12(h)(2) or (3), a party that makes a motion under this rule must not make another motion under this rule raising a defense or objection that was available to the party but omitted from its earlier motion.

(h) Waiving and Preserving Certain Defenses.

    (1) *When Some Are Waived.* A party waives any defense listed in Rule 12(b)(2)-(5) by:

        (A) omitting it from a motion in the circumstances described in Rule 12(g)(2); or

        (B) failing to either:

            (i) make it by motion under this rule; or

            (ii) include it in a responsive pleading or in an amendment allowed by Rule 15(a)(1) as a matter of course.

        (2) *When to Raise Others.* Failure to state a claim upon which relief can be granted, to join a person required by Rule 19(b), or to state a legal defense to a claim may be raised:

    (A) in any pleading allowed or ordered under Rule 7(a);

    (B) by a motion under Rule 12(c); or

    (C) at trial.

    (3) *Lack of Subject–Matter Jurisdiction.* If the court determines at any time that it lacks subject-matter jurisdiction, the court must dismiss the action.

(i) Hearing Before Trial. If a party so moves, any defense listed in Rule 12(b)(1)-(7)—whether made in a pleading or by motion—and a motion under Rule 12(c) must be heard and decided before trial unless the court orders a deferral until trial.

GARCIA v. HILTON HOTELS INTERNATIONAL, INC.

97 F.Supp. 5 (D. Puerto Rico 1951)

ROBERTS, DISTRICT JUDGE.

The action here is for damages for defamation brought by plaintiff, a citizen and resident of Puerto Rico, against defendant, a Delaware corporation, in the District Court of Puerto Rico and removed to this Court by defendant corporation. The complaint sets forth two causes of action and the paragraphs considered herein are identical in each cause. Defendant has moved to dismiss the complaint for failure to state a claim upon which relief can be granted and, in the alternative, to strike Paragraphs 5, 6, 7 and 8 and for a more definite statement.

In support of its motion to dismiss, defendant contends that no publication of the alleged slanderous statement is alleged and that the complaint, therefore, fails to state a cause of action. This contention will be considered first with respect to Paragraph 4 of the complaint, which reads as follows: "4. On August 22, 1950, the plaintiff was violently discharged by the defendant, being falsely and slanderously accused of being engaged in bringing women from outside the Hotel and introducing them into the rooms thereof for the purpose of developing prostitution in the Hotel and that such women brought by him from outside the Hotel and introduced therein carried on acts of prostitution in said Hotel."

The motion to dismiss contemplated in Fed. Rules Civ. P. Rule 12(b)(6) is not concerned with failure of the pleader to state a cause of action, but only with failure to state a claim upon which relief can be granted. There is an obvious distinction between stating a cause of action and stating a claim upon which relief can be granted. It is clear from the terms of rule 8(a) that a pleader is required to set forth only "a short plain statement of the claim showing that the pleader is entitled to relief," and there is no pleading requirement that the pleader state a cause of action upon peril of having his complaint dismissed. "If a claim is stated which shows that the pleader is entitled to relief, it is enough to require the service of a responsive pleading; whether a cause of action can be and has been established is for the determination of the trial judge." In *Dioguardi* *v. Durning*, the Court of Appeals of the Second Circuit said: " * * * Under the new rules of civil procedure, there is no pleading requirement of stating facts sufficient to constitute a cause of action, but only that there be 'a short and plain statement of the claim showing that the pleader is entitled to relief,' Federal Rules of Civil Procedure, Rule 8(a), and the motion for dismissal under Rule 12(b) is for failure to state 'a claim upon which relief can be granted.' "

The controlling question here, with respect to the motion to dismiss, is whether the allegations of Paragraph 4 of the complaint, state a claim upon which relief can be granted. An examination of the authorities is persuasive that it does. It is settled, with respect to motions to dismiss for insufficiency of statement, that the complaint is to be construed in the light most favorable to the plaintiff with all doubts resolved in his favor and the allegations accepted as true. If, when a complaint is so considered, it reasonably may be anticipated that plaintiff, on the basis of what has been alleged, could make out a case at trial entitling him to some relief, the complaint should not be dismissed.

* * * Further, it has been a long recognized and generally accepted policy of the courts to look with disfavor upon the practice of terminating litigation, believed to be without merit, by dismissing the complaint for insufficiency of statement. [T]he District Court quoted with approval from . . . as follows: " * * * To warrant such dismissal, it should appear from the allegations that a cause of action does not exist, rather than that a cause of action has been defectively stated. * * * " "That rule of procedure should be followed which will be most likely to result in justice between the parties, and, generally speaking, that result is more likely to be attained by leaving the merits of the cause to be disposed of after answer and the submission of proof, than by attempting to deal with the merits on motion to dismiss the bill."

In the instant case, it is true that Paragraph 4, of the complaint, fails to state, in so many words, that there was a publication of the alleged slanderous utterance and, to that extent, the cause of action is defectively stated. However, it does not follow that the allegations do not state a claim upon which relief can be granted. It is alleged that plaintiff was "violently discharged" and was "falsely and slanderously accused" of procuring for prostitution. While in a technical sense, this language states a conclusion, it is clear that plaintiff used it intending to charge publication of the slanderous utterance and it would be unrealistic for defendant to claim that it does not so understand the allegations. Clearly, under such allegations it reasonably may be conceived that plaintiff, upon trial, could adduce evidence tending to prove a publication. If the provisions of Rule 8(a) are not to be negatived by recourse to Rule 12(b), the statement in Paragraph 4 of the complaint must be deemed sufficient.

In further support of its motion to dismiss, defendant contends that the alleged slanderous utterance was conditionally privileged. Conceding that to be so does not require that a difference conclusion be reached with respect to the motion to dismiss. Rule 12(b) requires that every defense in law or fact be asserted in a responsive pleading when one is required or permitted under the rules. The rule, however, enumerates certain defenses which may be asserted by motion to dismiss, all of which go to the jurisdiction except that of failure to state a claim upon which relief can be granted, Rule 12(b)(6). And this latter defense may be asserted successfully by a motion prior to responsive pleading only when it appears to a certainty that plaintiff would be entitled to no relief under any state of fact which could be proved in support of the claim asserted by him.

The conclusiveness of privilege as a defense depends upon whether the privilege involved is absolute or conditional. When the privilege involved is absolute, it constitutes a finally determinative or conclusive defense to an action based on the utterance. Consequently, when it appears from a complaint that absolute privilege exists, the defense of failure to state a claim properly may be asserted to accomplish a dismissal on motion under Rule 12(b). It is for the court to determine the existence of privilege and when absolute privilege is found, it constitutes an unassailable defense and, clearly, in such a case, the claim stated in one upon which relief cannot be granted.

But conditional privilege is not a conclusive defense to an action based on a slanderous utterance. It is but a qualified defense which may be lost to the defendant if plaintiff can prove abuse of the privilege or actual malice. "Qualified privilege is an affirmative defense and a defendant cannot get the benefit of this defense unless he sets it up in his answer as an affirmative defense." When from the allegations contained therein, a complaint indicates the availability of the defense of conditional privilege, it cannot be held therefrom as a matter of law, that there has been a failure to state a claim upon which relief can be granted, such as will warrant dismissal of the complaint on motion under Rule 12(b)(6), for the factual question remains whether defendant abused the privilege or made the communication maliciously.

As has been noted, on motion to dismiss for failure to state a claim, complaint must be construed in the light most favorable to plaintiff with all doubts resolved in his favor and the allegation taken as true. That being so, when allegations are sufficient to sustain the defense of conditional privilege they will be, generally, sufficient to permit the introduction of evidence tending to prove abuse of the privilege or actual malice. Save in some extraordinary situation, allegations which are adequate for the admission of evidence to prove the defense of qualified privilege are adequate for the admission of evidence to negative that defense. It appears from the complaint in the instant case that defendant is entitled to raise the defense of conditional privilege. But this defense may be lost to it if plaintiff proves abuse of the privilege or actual malice. And, clearly, plaintiff may introduce evidence under the allegations for the purpose of proving abuse of the privilege or actual malice. Therefore, it is concluded that defendant's motion to dismiss the complaint for failure to state a claim upon which relief can be granted should be denied.

The conclusion to deny defendant's motion to dismiss requires that consideration be given its alternative motion to strike Paragraphs 5, 6, 7 and 8 of the complaint. It is alleged in these paragraphs, in substance, that upon being discharged, plaintiff made claim with the Labor Department of Puerto Rico for severance pay and overtime as is provided for by law; that during a hearing on such claim held by the Labor Department, defendant, falsely and slanderously, repeated its charge that plaintiff had been engaged in procuring for prostitution; and, that, after said hearing defendant had compromised plaintiff's claim for severance pay and overtime. As respects defendant's motion to strike, the controlling allegations are contained in Paragraph 7 of this complaint.

Section 4 of "An Act Authorizing Civil Actions to Recover Damages for Libel and Slander," enacted by the Legislature of Puerto Rico and approved on February 19, 1902 provides in part as follows: "Section 4. A publication or communication shall not be held or deemed malicious when made in any legislative or judicial proceeding or in any other proceeding authorized by law. * * * "

The effect of the above quoted portions of the statute is to confer absolute privilege upon any communication made in any of the proceedings contemplated therein. If the hearing held by the Labor Department on plaintiff's claim for severance pay and overtime, referred to in Paragraph 7 of the complaint, is a proceeding within the meaning of the phrase "or any other proceeding authorized by law" as used in said Section 4 of the Act, the utterance was absolutely privileged and such privilege constitutes a conclusive defense in an action based on that utterance.

It appears that the hearing on plaintiff's claim by the Labor Department, referred to in Paragraph 7 of the complaint, is a proceeding "authorized by law" within the meaning of Section 4 of the Act. The Labor Department is authorized to hold such a hearing by Act No. 122 of the Legislature of Puerto Rico, which statute requires the Commissioner of Labor to enforce labor protecting laws. Act No. 122 reads in part as follows: "Section 5. It shall be the duty of the Commissioner to enforce the labor protecting laws. The Commissioner or any employee of the Department of Labor designated by him, shall investigate every complaint alleging the violation of any of the labor protecting laws now in force or hereafter enacted."

The statute further provides that the Commissioner shall have authority to "issue summonses for the appearance of witnesses and the production of any evidence, commissioner may compel obedience of such summonses through orders of the District Court demanding compliance on pain of contempt," and that "No natural or artificial person may refuse to obey a summons of the Commissioner of Labor or his duly authorized agents, or a judicial order so entered, on the allegation that the testimony or evidence required of him may tend to incriminate him or give cause for the imposition of a penalty upon him," and that any evidence given by such person pursuant to such summons may not be used in a criminal action against him.

It appears, upon examination, that this Statute has for its purpose the protection of the welfare of the workman and the furtherance of the public good, and that when hearings are held pursuant to its terms it is necessary, if those purposes are to be effectuated, that those called upon to give evidence therein must be protected against liability, civil or criminal, for communications given in evidence at such hearings. And this without regard for the motives of the witness or the truth or falsity of his statements. For otherwise, the giving of full, free and honest testimony, essential to the enforcement of such laws, will be discouraged. Therefore, communications made by witnesses in the course of such hearings, should be absolutely privileged in the same manner and to like extent as those made in the course of a judicial proceeding.

* * * The persuasive consideration is that the privilege attaches to the occasion of the utterance in the interest of public policy, that the public good requires that in such proceedings necessary information be freely and fully imparted and that this end justifies conferring absolute privilege on such occasions. Such considerations, standing alone, warrant holding communications made pursuant to the terms of Act No. 122 to be absolutely privileged. And this conviction is strengthened by the inescapable conclusion that the hearing held by the Labor Department referred to in Paragraph 7 of the complaint is a proceeding within the meaning of the words "or any other proceeding authorized by law" as used in Section 4 of the Act.

Clearly, then, the utterance of the defendant made during the Labor Department hearing referred to in Paragraph 7 of the complaint was absolutely privileged and that Paragraph 7 is, therefore, redundant in that it fails to state a claim upon which relief can be granted. It appears then, that defendant's motion to strike Paragraphs 5, 6, 7 and 8 should be granted.

The parties have agreed on hearing in open court that Paragraph 9 of the complaint should be stricken. And this Court being of the opinion that Paragraphs 5, 6, 7 and 8 should be stricken as redundant, defendant's motion for a more definite statement need be considered only with respect to the allegations of Paragraph 4 of the complaint.

As has been noted herein, conditional privilege is an affirmative defense which properly should be raised by its assertion in a responsive pleading. Consequently, when it appears from a complaint that the defense of conditional privilege may be available to a defendant, the allegations thereof should be reasonably adequate to permit the preparation of a responsive pleading asserting such defense. But when, in an action for slander, the complaint fails to set out substantially the utterance alleged to have been slanderously made or the facts relied upon to establish a publication of such utterance, such omission constitutes vagueness such as is a ground for granting a motion for more definite statement within the contemplation of Rule 12(e). Obviously, when such material allegations are insufficient, it would be unreasonable to require the defendant to prepare a responsive pleading without a more definite statement of the pertinent facts.

Considering the allegations of Paragraph 4 of the complaint, the defense of conditional privilege is indicated. However, the allegations suffer from vagueness with respect to the utterance alleged to have been slanderously made and the facts relied upon to establish a publication of the utterance. It is concluded that the defendant here is entitled to a more definite statement setting forth substantially the words alleged to have been slanderously uttered and the facts relied upon to establish a publication thereof.

Defendant's motion to dismiss the complaint for failure to state a claim upon which relief can be granted is denied. Defendant's motion to strike Paragraphs 5, 6, 7 and 8 of the complaint is granted. Defendant's motion for a more definite statement with respect to the matters prescribed in this opinion, is granted. Paragraph 9 of the complaint is ordered stricken. The decisions herein reached are hereby made applicable to the second cause of action set out in the complaint.

* * *

RUBERT–TORRES v. HOSPITAL SAN PABLO, INC.

205 F.3d 472 (1st Cir. 2000)

WALLACE, SENIOR CIRCUIT JUDGE.

Josefina Rubert–Torres appeals from the district court's summary judgment in favor of one defendant and from the judgment entered upon a jury verdict for the other defendant. The district court had jurisdiction pursuant to 28 U.S.C. § 1332, and we have jurisdiction over Rubert–Torres' timely appeal. We affirm in part, reverse in part, and remand for further proceedings.

I.

Rubert–Torres brought this medical malpractice action on behalf of her daughter Kimayra Cintrón-Rubert, a 21 year-old woman with cerebral palsy, against Dr. Néstor Rivera–Cotté, the doctor who delivered Kimayra, and Hospital San Pablo (Hospital), where Kimayra was born. Before trial, the district court entered summary judgment for the Hospital. At trial, Rubert–Torres's theory, supported by an obstetrical/gynecological (OB/GYN) expert and a neurological expert, was that physician error during her pregnancy and delivery of Kimayra caused Kimayra's disabilities. Dr. Rivera–Cotté's theory, supported by his own OB/GYN, neurological, and genetics experts, was that Kimayra's disabilities arose genetically. The jury returned a verdict for Dr. Rivera–Cotté.

II.

Rubert–Torres first contends that the district court erred in entering summary judgment *sua sponte* in favor of the Hospital. This argument is slightly mis-worded. The district court did not enter summary judgment *sua sponte*; rather, it converted the Hospital's motion for judgment on the pleadings, pursuant to Federal Rule of Civil Procedure 12(c), into a motion for summary judgment because Rubert–Torres attached an expert witness report to her opposition to the motion to dismiss. We review whether the district court properly converted a Rule 12 motion into a motion for summary judgment for abuse of discretion. Significantly, Rubert–Torres only makes this procedural argument against the entry of summary judgment; she does not contest the merits of the district court's decision.

We first recite the relevant facts. Rubert–Torres filed the complaint on July 14, 1996; the Hospital answered on October 7, 1996. Discovery started, and two scheduling conferences were held, with all parties represented, on November 26, 1996, and on April 30, 1997. At the second conference, the Hospital requested that Rubert–Torres support her allegations against it with specific facts, which she failed to do. At that point, discovery was apparently well underway: Rubert–Torres had received four expert witness reports and 20 years of medical records, interrogatories had been filed, and depositions taken.

When Rubert–Torres failed to support her allegations against the Hospital with specific facts, the Hospital filed a motion on May 7, 1997, for judgment on the pleadings, pursuant to Federal Rule of Civil Procedure 12(c). Rubert–Torres filed an opposition to the motion on May 14, 1997, including with it an expert witness report derived from discovery. On August 15, 1997, the district court, without previously providing notice, converted the motion for judgment on the pleadings into a motion for summary judgment, relied on the expert report, and entered an order for summary judgment in favor of the Hospital.

Rule 12(c) provides, in part:

> If, on a motion for judgment on the pleadings, matters outside the pleadings are presented to and not excluded by the court, the motion shall be treated as one for summary judgment and disposed of as provided in Rule 56, and all parties shall be given reasonable opportunity to present all material made pertinent to such a motion by Rule 56.

Fed. R. Civ. P. 12(c). In this regard, the rule is identical to Rule 12(b)(6), and relevant Rule 12(b)(6) case law on conversion assists this Rule 12(c) conversion case.

Conversion of a motion for judgment on the pleadings into one for summary judgment should only occur after the parties have been offered a "reasonable opportunity" to present pertinent summary judgment materials. Fed. R. Civ. P. 12(c). Whether the parties had an "opportunity to respond necessarily turns on the way in which the particular case under consideration has unfolded." Thus, we have disfavored conversion when (1) the motion comes quickly after the complaint was filed, (2) discovery is in its infancy and the nonmovant is limited in obtaining and submitting evidence to counter the motion, or (3) the nonmovant does not have reasonable notice that a conversion might occur.

In this case, however, these considerations are not present. The Rule 12(c) motion came 10 months after the complaint—and subsequent to the Hospital's request that Rubert–Torres support her allegations. There had been substantial discovery. Finally, Rubert–Torres was on constructive notice that conversion could occur. Explicit notice is not required. Rubert–Torres had constructive notice because *she* presented the district court with additional materials in her opposition memorandum. As we recently held, "a party receives constructive notice that the court has been afforded the option of conversion . . . when . . . the non-movant appends . . . materials [outside the pleadings] to [an] opposition and urges the court's consideration of them." When a plaintiff incorporates materials outside the pleadings into an opposition to a Rule 12(c) motion, the plaintiff "implicitly invite[s] conversion—and a party who invites conversion scarcely can be heard to complain when the trial court accepts the invitation."

Rubert–Torres argues that she did not invite the district court to convert the Rule 12(c) motion into a summary judgment motion because the attaching of the expert report was for the limited purpose of indicating "that further details regarding her claim against Hospital San Pablo had been provided in discovery." Her assertion is a stretch. In her response to the Hospital's Rule 12(c) motion, Rubert–Torres stated that the contentions in the motion were "more properly framed as a motion for a more definite statement under Federal Rule of Civil Procedure 12(e)," and that to "the extent that Hospital San Pablo's motion is in effect a 12(e) motion, it has been mooted by the provided report of plaintiff's obstetrical expert, Dr. Bernard Nathanson." However, Rubert–Torres not only relied upon Dr. Nathanson's report for the limited purpose of refuting the Hospital's motion, to the extent that it was a 12(e) motion, she also used it to argue the merits of the Rule 12(c) motion, stating: "The departures from the applicable standard of care identified by Dr. Nathanson show that Hospital San Pablo failed to comply with its legal duties under Puerto Rico law." This statement directly responded to the Hospital's contention that, pursuant to applicable law, it was not liable for Kimayra's condition, and implicitly invited the district court to consider the expert report for Rule 12(c) purposes.

It is true, as Rubert–Torres argues, that not every attachment to a Rule 12(c) motion or opposition thereto requires conversion into a motion for summary judgment. However, in this situation, Rubert–Torres invited the district court to consider Dr. Nathanson's report in its ruling on the merits of the Rule 12(c) motion, and thus invited the court to convert the

Rule 12(c) motion into one for summary judgment. The district court did not abuse its discretion when it accepted that invitation.

* * *

B. THE ANSWER; DENIALS AND AFFIRMATIVE DEFENSES

FEDERAL RULE OF CIVIL PROCEDURE 8(b)–(c)

(b) Defenses; Admissions and Denials.

   (1) *In General.* In responding to a pleading, a party must:

      (A) state in short and plain terms its defenses to each claim asserted against it; and

      (B) admit or deny the allegations asserted against it by an opposing party.

   (2) *Denials—Responding to the Substance.* A denial must fairly respond to the substance of the allegation.

   (3) *General and Specific Denials.* A party that intends in good faith to deny all the allegations of a pleading—including the jurisdictional grounds—may do so by a general denial. A party that does not intend to deny all the allegations must either specifically deny designated allegations or generally deny all except those specifically admitted.

   (4) *Denying Part of an Allegation.* A party that intends in good faith to deny only part of an allegation must admit the part that is true and deny the rest.

   (5) *Lacking Knowledge or Information.* A party that lacks knowledge or information sufficient to form a belief about the truth of an allegation must so state, and the statement has the effect of a denial.

   (6) *Effect of Failing to Deny.* An allegation—other than one relating to the amount of damages—is admitted if a responsive pleading is required and the allegation is not denied. If a responsive pleading is not required, an allegation is considered denied or avoided.

(c) Affirmative Defenses.

   (1) *In General.* In responding to a pleading, a party must affirmatively state any avoidance or affirmative defense, including:

      • accord and satisfaction;

      • arbitration and award;

      • assumption of risk;

      • contributory negligence;

      • duress;

- estoppel;
- failure of consideration;
- fraud;
- illegality;
- injury by fellow servant;
- laches;
- license;
- payment;
- release;
- res judicata;
- statute of frauds;
- statute of limitations; and
- waiver.

(2) *Mistaken Designation.* If a party mistakenly designates a defense as a counterclaim, or a counterclaim as a defense, the court must, if justice requires, treat the pleading as though it were correctly designated, and may impose terms for doing so.

* * *

ZIELINSKI v. PHILADELPHIA PIERS, INC.

139 F.Supp. 408 (E.D. Pa. 1956)

VAN DUSEN, DISTRICT JUDGE.

Plaintiff requests a ruling that, for the purposes of this case, the motor-driven fork lift operated by Sandy Johnson on February 9, 1953, was owned by defendant and that Sandy Johnson was its agent acting in the course of his employment on that date. The following facts are established by the pleadings, interrogatories, depositions and uncontradicted portions of affidavits:

1. Plaintiff filed his complaint on April 28, 1953, for personal injuries received on February 9, 1953, while working on Pier 96, Philadelphia, for J. A. McCarthy, as a result of a collision of two motor-driven forklifts.

2. Paragraph 5 of this complaint stated that "a motor-driven vehicle known as a fork lift or chisel, owned, operated and controlled by the defendant, its agents, servants and employees, was so negligently and carelessly managed * * * that the same * * * did come into contact with the plaintiff causing him to sustain the injuries more fully hereinafter set forth."

3. The "First Defense" of the Answer stated "Defendant * * * (c) denies the averments of paragraph 5 * * *."

4. The motor-driven vehicle known as a fork lift or chisel, which collided with the McCarthy fork lift on which plaintiff was riding, had on it the initials "P.P.I."

5. On February 10, 1953, Carload Contractors, Inc. made a report of this accident to its insurance company, whose policy No. CL 3964 insured Carload Contractors, Inc. against potential liability for the negligence of its employees contributing to a collision of the type described in paragraph 2 above.

6. By letter of April 29, 1953, the complaint served on defendant was forwarded to the above-mentioned insurance company. This letter read as follows:

> Gentlemen:
>
> As per telephone conversation today with your office, we attach hereto 'Complaint in Trespass' as brought against Philadelphia Piers, Inc. by one Frank Zielinski for supposed injuries sustained by him on February 9, 1953.
>
> We find that a fork lift truck operated by an employee of Carload Contractors, Inc. also insured by yourselves was involved in an accident with another chisel truck, which, was alleged, did cause injury to Frank Zielinski, and same was reported to you by Carload Contractors, Inc. at the time, and you assigned Claim Number OL 0153–94 to this claim.
>
> Should not this Complaint in Trespass be issued against Carload Contractors, Inc. and not Philadelphia Piers, Inc.?
>
> We forward for your handling.

7. Interrogatories 1 to 5 and the answers thereto,[1] which were sworn to by defendant's General Manager on June 12, 1953, and filed on June 22, 1953, read as follows:

> 1. State whether you have received any information of an injury sustained by the plaintiff on February 9, 1953, South Wharves. If so, state when and from whom you first received notice of such injury. A. We were first notified of this accident on or about February 9, 1953 by Thomas Wilson.
>
> 2. State whether you caused an investigation to be made of the circumstances of said injury and if so, state who made such investigation and when it was made. A. We made a very brief investigation on February 9, 1953 and turned the matter over to (our insurance company) for further investigation.
>
> 3. Give the names and addresses of all persons disclosed by such investigation to have been witnesses to the aforesaid occurrence. A. The witnesses whose names we have obtained so far are:

---

1. Plaintiff's argument that the answers to other interrogatories are misleading does not seem significant in view of the fact that plaintiff had the opportunity to frame these interrogatories (and could have filed requests for admissions) in a form that would have secured clearer answers and in view of the answer to Interrogatory 15. This order is being based on the inadequacy of the answer; and the inaccuracy of statements in the answers in the interrogatories, in view of the misleading effect of such inadequate answer and inaccurate statements under all the circumstances, including the inaccurate testimony of Sandy Johnson as described below.

Victor Marzo, 2005 E. Hart Lane, Philadelphia

Thomas Wilson, 6115 Reinhardt St., Philadelphia

Sandy Johnson, 1236 S. 16th Street, Philadelphia

4. State whether you have obtained any written statements from such witnesses and if so, identify such statements and state when and by whom they were taken. If in writing, attach copies of same hereto. A. We have obtained written statements from Victor Marzo, Thomas Wilson and Sandy Johnson and these statements are in the possession of our counsel * * *, who advises that copies need not be attached unless we are ordered by the court to do so.

5. Set forth the facts disclosed by such statements and investigation concerning the manner in which the accident happened. A. Sandy Johnson was moving boxes on Pier 96 and had stopped his towmotor when a towmotor operated by an employee of McCarthy Stevedoring Company with a person on the back, apparently the plaintiff, backed into the standing towmotor, injuring the plaintiff.

8. At a deposition taken August 18, 1953, Sandy Johnson testified that he was the employee of defendant on February 9, 1953, and had been their employee for approximately fifteen years.

9. At a pre-trial conference held on September 27, 1955, plaintiff first learned that over a year before February 9, 1953, the business of moving freight on piers in Philadelphia, formerly conducted by defendant, had been sold by it to Carload Contractors, Inc. and Sandy Johnson had been transferred to the payroll of this corporation without apparently realizing it, since the nature or location of his work had not changed.

10. As a result of the following answers to Supplementary Interrogatories 16 to 19, filed October 21, 1955, plaintiff learned the facts stated in paragraphs 5 and 6 above in the fall of 1955:

16. With reference to your answer to Interrogatory #1, state the name and address of the person employed by you who first received notice of this accident on or about February 9, 1953. A. Joseph Nolan, Office Manager.

17. With reference to your answer to Interrogatory #2, give the name and address of the person who conducted the investigation on February 9, 1953. A. Joseph Nolan, Office Manager.

18. With reference to your answer to Interrogatory #2, state the name and address of the person who turned the matter over to (your insurance company) and state whether the matter was turned over by telephone or by letter. If by letter, attach copy of same hereto. A. Joseph Nolan gave the information to James L. Maher, Office Manager, of Carload Contractors, Inc., as a result of which the attached accident report signed by Jonathan Wainwright, Treasurer of Carload Contractors, Inc. was forwarded to (the insurance company) on February 10, 1953.

19.   State whether or not any person on your behalf submitted a written report of the accident to (your insurance company). If so, give the name and address of such person, the date of said written report and attach copy of same hereto. A. Yes, the attached report dated April 29, 1953, was submitted to the insurance company after suit was started.

11.   Defendant now admits that on February 9, 1953, it owned the fork lift in the custody of Sandy Johnson and that this fork lift was leased to Carload Contractors, Inc. It is also admitted that the pier on which the accident occurred was leased by defendant.

12.   There is no indication of action by either party in bad faith and there is no proof of inaccurate statements being made with intent to deceive. Because defendant made a prompt investigation of the accident (see answers to Interrogatories 1, 2, 16 and 17), its insurance company has been representing the defendant since suit was brought, and this company insures Carload Contractors, Inc. also, requiring defendant to defend this suit, will not prejudice it.

Under these circumstances, and for the purposes of this action, it is ordered that the following shall be stated to the jury at the trial:

It is admitted that, on February 9, 1953, the towmotor or fork lift bearing the initials "P.P.I." was owned by defendant and that Sandy Johnson was a servant in the employ of defendant and doing its work on that date.

This ruling is based on the following principles:

1.   Under the circumstances of this case, the answer contains an ineffective denial of that part of paragraph 5 of the complaint which alleges that "a motor driven vehicle known as a fork lift or chisel (was) owned, operated and controlled by the defendant, its agents, servants and employees."

Fed. R. Civ. P. 8(b) provides:

A party shall state in short and plain terms his defenses to each claim asserted and shall admit or deny the averments upon which the adverse party relies. * * * Denials shall fairly meet the substance of the averments denied. When a pleader intends in good faith to deny only a part or a qualification of an averment, he shall specify so much of it as is true and material and shall deny only the remainder.

For example, it is quite clear that defendant does not deny the averment in paragraph 5 that the fork lift came into contact with plaintiff, since it admits, in the answers to interrogatories, that an investigation of an occurrence of the accident had been made and that a report dated February 10, 1953, was sent to its insurance company stating "While Frank Zielinski was riding on bumper of chisel and holding rope to secure cargo, the chisel truck collided with another chisel truck operated by Sandy Johnson causing injuries to Frank Zielinski's legs and hurt head of Sandy Johnson." Compliance with the above-mentioned rule required that defendant file a more specific answer than a general denial. A specific denial of parts of this paragraph and specific admission of other parts would have warned plaintiff that he had sued the wrong defendant.

In such a case, the defendant should make clear just what he is denying and what he is admitting. This answer to paragraph 5 does not make clear to plaintiff the defenses he must be prepared to meet.[8]

Under circumstances where an improper and ineffective answer has been filed, the Pennsylvania courts have consistently held that an allegation of agency in the complaint requires a statement to the jury that agency is admitted where an attempt to amend the answer is made after the expiration of the period of limitation.

Under the circumstances of this case, principles of equity require that defendant be estopped from denying agency because, otherwise, its inaccurate statements and statements in the record, which it knew (or had the means of knowing within its control) were inaccurate, will have deprived plaintiff of his right of action.

If Interrogatory 2 had been answered accurately[10] by saying that employees of Carload Contractors, Inc. had turned the matter over to the insurance company, it seems clear that plaintiff would have realized his mistake. The fact that if Sandy Johnson had testified accurately, the plaintiff could have brought its action against the proper party defendant within the statutory period of limitations is also a factor to be considered, since defendant was represented at the deposition and received knowledge of the inaccurate testimony.

At least one appellate court has stated that the doctrine of equitable estoppel will be applied to prevent a party from taking advantage of the statute of limitations where the plaintiff has been misled by conduct of such party.[12] In that case, the court said: "Of course, defendants were under no duty to advise complainants' attorney of his error, other than by appropriate pleadings, but neither did defendants have a right, knowing of the mistake, to foster it by its acts of omission."

---

8. [T]he existence of a poorly drawn complaint to which defendant has not objected under Fed. R. Civ. P. 12 is no ground excusing defendant from filing an answer in compliance with Fed. R. Civ. P. 8(b).

It should be noted that the Pennsylvania courts have consistently granted relief to a party to avoid a forfeiture of his rights resulting from neglect of his attorney.

Although plaintiff's counsel might have filed requests for admission or drawn his interrogatories more carefully, . . . a court should not permit a forfeiture of plaintiff's rights of action in a case such as this, particularly where the same insurance company, which insures both the defendant of record and the corporation which should have been made party defendant, received prompt notice of the suit.

10. At least one federal district court case has suggested that a contempt proceeding under 18 U.S.C. § 401 is the proper procedure to compensate the attorneys for one party who had been misled to their pecuniary damage by inaccurate answers to interrogatories. It suggested the imposition of a fine to be paid as civil liability to the attorneys for the complaining party.

12. When inaccurate statements are made under circumstances where there is foreseeable danger that another will rely on them to his prejudice, and he does in fact rely thereon, such statements are sufficient to invoke this doctrine even though fraud is not present.

This doctrine has been held to estop a party from taking advantage of a document of record where the misleading conduct occurred after the recording, so that application of this doctrine would not necessarily be precluded in a case such as this where the misleading answers to interrogatories and depositions were subsequent to the filing of the answer, even if the denial in the answer had been sufficient.

Closely related to this doctrine is the principle that a party may be estopped to deny agency or ratification.

Since this is a pre-trial order, it may be modified at the trial if the trial judge determines from the facts which then appear that justice so requires.

* * *

C. AMENDMENTS TO PLEADINGS

FEDERAL RULE OF CIVIL PROCEDURE 15.   AMENDED AND SUPPLEMENTAL PLEADINGS

(a) Amendments Before Trial.

(1) *Amending as a Matter of Course.* A party may amend its pleading once as a matter of course within:

    (A) 21 days after serving it, or

    (B) if the pleading is one to which a responsive pleading is required, 21 days after service of a responsive pleading or 21 days after service of a motion under Rule 12(b), (e), or (f), whichever is earlier.

(2) *Other Amendments.* In all other cases, a party may amend its pleading only with the opposing party's written consent or the court's leave. The court should freely give leave when justice so requires.

(3) *Time to Respond.* Unless the court orders otherwise, any required response to an amended pleading must be made within the time remaining to respond to the original pleading or within 14 days after service of the amended pleading, whichever is later.

(b) Amendments During and After Trial.

(1) *Based on an Objection at Trial.* If, at trial, a party objects that evidence is not within the issues raised in the pleadings, the court may permit the pleadings to be amended. The court should freely permit an amendment when doing so will aid in presenting the merits and the objecting party fails to satisfy the court that the evidence would prejudice that party's action or defense on the merits. The court may grant a continuance to enable the objecting party to meet the evidence.

(2) *For Issues Tried by Consent.* When an issue not raised by the pleadings is tried by the parties' express or implied consent, it must be treated in all respects as if raised in the pleadings. A party may move—at any time, even after judgment—to amend the pleadings to conform them to the evidence and to raise an unpleaded issue. But failure to amend does not affect the result of the trial of that issue.

(c) Relation Back of Amendments.

(1) *When an Amendment Relates Back.* An amendment to a pleading relates back to the date of the original pleading when:

(A) the law that provides the applicable statute of limitations allows relation back;

(B) the amendment asserts a claim or defense that arose out of the conduct, transaction, or occurrence set out—or attempted to be set out—in the original pleading; or

(C) the amendment changes the party or the naming of the party against whom a claim is asserted, if Rule 15(c)(1)(B) is satisfied and if, within the period provided by Rule 4(m) for serving the summons and complaint, the party to be brought in by amendment:

(i) received such notice of the action that it will not be prejudiced in defending on the merits; and

(ii) knew or should have known that the action would have been brought against it, but for a mistake concerning the proper party's identity.

(2) *Notice to the United States.* When the United States or a United States officer or agency is added as a defendant by amendment, the notice requirements of Rule 15(c)(1)(C)(i) and (ii) are satisfied if, during the stated period, process was delivered or mailed to the United States attorney or the United States attorney's designee, to the Attorney General of the United States, or to the officer or agency.

(d) Supplemental Pleadings. On motion and reasonable notice, the court may, on just terms, permit a party to serve a supplemental pleading setting out any transaction, occurrence, or event that happened after the date of the pleading to be supplemented. The court may permit supplementation even though the original pleading is defective in stating a claim or defense. The court may order that the opposing party plead to the supplemental pleading within a specified time.

* * *

KRUPSKI v. COSTA CROCIERE S. p. A.

130 S.Ct. 2485 (2010)

SOTOMAYOR, J., delivered the opinion of the Court, in which ROBERTS, C.J., and STEVENS, KENNEDY, THOMAS, GINSBURG, BREYER, AND ALITO, JJ., joined. SCALIA, J., filed an opinion concurring in part and concurring in the judgment.

JUSTICE SOTOMAYOR delivered the opinion of the Court.

Rule 15(c) of the Federal Rules of Civil Procedure governs when an amended pleading "relates back" to the date of a timely filed original pleading and is thus itself timely even though it was filed outside an applicable statute of limitations. Where an amended pleading changes a party or a party's name, the Rule requires, among other things, that "the party to be brought in by amendment ... knew or should have known that the action would have been brought against it, but for a mistake concerning the proper party's identity." Rule 15(c)(1)(C). In this case, the Court of Appeals held that Rule 15(c) was not satisfied because the plaintiff knew or should have known of the proper defendant before filing her original complaint. The court also held that relation back was not appropriate because the plaintiff had unduly delayed in seeking to amend. We hold that relation back under Rule 15(c)(1)(C) depends on what the party to be added knew or should have known, not on the amending party's knowledge or its timeliness in seeking to amend the pleading. Accordingly, we reverse the judgment of the Court of Appeals.

I

On February 21, 2007, petitioner, Wanda Krupski, tripped over a cable and fractured her femur while she was on board the cruise ship Costa Magica. Upon her return home, she acquired counsel and began the process of seeking compensation for her injuries. Krupski's passenger ticket-which explained that it was the sole contract between each passenger and the carrier, included a variety of requirements for obtaining damages for an injury suffered on board one of the carrier's ships. The ticket identified the carrier as

"Costa Crociere S. p. A., an Italian corporation, and all Vessels and other ships owned, chartered, operated, marketed or provided by Costa Crociere, S. p. A., and all officers, staff members, crew members, independent contractors, medical providers, concessionaires, pilots, suppliers, agents and assigns onboard said Vessels, and the manufacturers of said Vessels and all their component parts."

The ticket required an injured party to submit "written notice of the claim with full particulars ... to the carrier or its duly authorized agent within 185 days after the date of injury." The ticket further required any lawsuit to be "filed within one year after the date of injury" and to be "served upon the carrier within 120 days after filing." For cases arising from voyages departing from or returning to a United States port in which the amount in controversy exceeded $75,000, the ticket designated the United States District Court for the Southern District of Florida in Broward County, Florida, as the exclusive forum for a lawsuit. The ticket extended the "defenses, limitations and exceptions . . . that may be invoked by the CARRIER" to "all persons who may act on behalf of the CARRIER or on whose behalf the CARRIER may act," including "the CARRIER's parents, subsidiaries, affiliates, successors, assigns, representatives, agents, employees, servants, concessionaires and contractors" as well as "Costa Cruise Lines N. V.," identified as the "sales and marketing agent for the CARRIER and the issuer of this Passage Ticket Contract." The front of the ticket listed Costa Cruise Lines' address in Florida and stated that an entity called "Costa Cruises" was "the first cruise company in the world" to obtain a certain certification of quality.

On July 2, 2007, Krupski's counsel notified Costa Cruise Lines of Krupski's claims. On July 9, 2007, the claims administrator for Costa Cruise requested additional information from Krupski "[i]n order to facilitate our future attempts to achieve a pre-litigation settlement." The parties were unable to reach a settlement, however, and on February 1, 2008—three weeks before the 1–year limitations period expired—Krupski filed a negligence action against Costa Cruise, invoking the diversity jurisdiction of the Federal District Court for the Southern District of Florida. The complaint alleged that Costa Cruise "owned, operated, managed, supervised and controlled" the ship on which Krupski had injured herself; that Costa Cruise had extended to its passengers an invitation to enter onto the ship; and that Costa Cruise owed Krupski a duty of care, which it breached by failing to take steps that would have prevented her accident. The complaint further stated that venue was proper under the passenger ticket's forum selection clause and averred that, by the July 2007 notice of her claims, Krupski had complied with the ticket's presuit requirements. Krupski served Costa Cruise on February 4, 2008.

Over the next several months—after the limitations period had expired—Costa Cruise brought Costa Crociere's existence to Krupski's attention three times. First, on February 25, 2008, Costa Cruise filed its answer, asserting that it was not the proper defendant, as it was merely the North American sales and marketing agent for Costa Crociere, which was the actual carrier and vessel operator. Second, on March 20, 2008, Costa Cruise listed Costa Crociere as an interested party in its corporate disclosure statement. Finally, on May 6, 2008, Costa Cruise moved for summary judgment, again stating that Costa Crociere was the proper defendant.

On June 13, 2008, Krupski responded to Costa Cruise's motion for summary judgment, arguing for limited discovery to determine whether Costa Cruise should be dismissed. According to Krupski, the following sources of information led her to believe Costa Cruise was the responsible party: The travel documents prominently identified Costa Cruise and gave its Florida address; Costa Cruise's Web site listed Costa Cruise in Florida as the United States office for the Italian company Costa Crociere; and the Web site of the Florida Department of State listed Costa Cruise as the only "Costa" company registered to do business in that State. Krupski also observed that Costa Cruise's claims administrator had responded to her claims notification without indicating that Costa Cruise was not a responsible party. With her response, Krupski simultaneously moved to amend her complaint to add Costa Crociere as a defendant.

On July 2, 2008, after oral argument, the District Court denied Costa Cruise's motion for summary judgment without prejudice and granted Krupski leave to amend, ordering that Krupski effect proper service on Costa Crociere by September 16, 2008. Complying with the court's deadline, Krupski filed an amended complaint on July 11, 2008, and served Costa Crociere on August 21, 2008. On that same date, the District Court issued an order dismissing Costa Cruise from the case pursuant to the parties' joint stipulation, Krupski apparently having concluded that Costa Cruise was correct that it bore no responsibility for her injuries.

Shortly thereafter, Costa Crociere—represented by the same counsel who had represented Costa Cruise, at 100—moved to dismiss, contending that the amended complaint did not relate back under Rule 15(c) and was therefore untimely. The District Court agreed. Rule 15(c), the court explained, imposes three requirements before an amended complaint against a newly named defendant can relate back to the original complaint. First, the claim against the newly named defendant must have arisen "out of the conduct, transaction, or occurrence set out-or attempted to be set out-in the original pleading." Fed. Rules Civ. Proc. 15(c)(1)(B), (C). Second, "within the period provided by Rule 4(m) for serving the summons and complaint" (which is ordinarily 120 days from when the complaint is filed, see Rule 4(m)), the newly named defendant must have "received such notice of the action that it will not be prejudiced in defending on the merits." Rule 15(c)(1)(C)(i). Finally, the plaintiff must show that, within the Rule 4(m) period, the newly named defendant "knew or should have known that the action would have been brought against it, but for a mistake concerning the proper party's identity." Rule 15(c)(1)(C)(ii).

The first two conditions posed no problem, the court explained: The claim against Costa Crociere clearly involved the same occurrence as the original claim against Costa Cruise, and Costa Crociere had constructive notice of the action and had not shown that any unfair prejudice would result from relation back. But the court found the third condition fatal to Krupski's attempt to relate back, concluding that Krupski had not made a mistake concerning the identity of the proper party. Relying on Eleventh Circuit precedent, the court explained that the word "mistake" should not be construed to encompass a deliberate decision not to sue a party whose identity the plaintiff knew before the statute of limitations had run. Because Costa Cruise informed Krupski that Costa Crociere was the proper defendant in its answer, corporate disclosure statement, and motion for summary judgment, and yet Krupski delayed for months in moving to amend and then in filing an amended complaint, the court concluded that Krupski knew of the proper defendant and made no mistake.

The Eleventh Circuit affirmed in an unpublished *per curiam* opinion. Rather than relying on the information contained in Costa Cruise's filings, all of which were made after the statute of limitations had expired, as evidence that Krupski did not make a mistake, the Court of Appeals noted that the relevant information was located within Krupski's passenger ticket, which she had furnished to her counsel well before the end of the limitations period. Because the ticket clearly identified Costa Crociere as the carrier, the court stated, Krupski either knew or should have known of Costa Crociere's identity as a potential party. It was therefore appropriate to treat Krupski as having chosen to sue one potential party over another. Alternatively, even assuming that she first learned of Costa Crociere's identity as the correct party from Costa Cruise's answer, the Court of Appeals observed that Krupski waited 133 days from the time she filed her original complaint to seek leave to amend and did not file an amended complaint for another month after that. In light of this delay, the Court of Appeals concluded that the District Court did not abuse its discretion in denying relation back.

We granted certiorari to resolve tension among the Circuits over the breadth of Rule 15(c)(1)(C)(ii).

II

Under the Federal Rules of Civil Procedure, an amendment to a pleading relates back to the date of the original pleading when:

"(A) the law that provides the applicable statute of limitations allows relation back;

(B) the amendment asserts a claim or defense that arose out of the conduct, transaction, or occurrence set out—or attempted to be set out—in the original pleading; or

(C) the amendment changes the party or the naming of the party against whom a claim is asserted, if Rule 15(c)(1)(B) is satisfied and if, within the period provided by Rule 4(m) for serving the summons and complaint, the party to be brought in by amendment:

(i) received such notice of the action that it will not be prejudiced in defending on the merits; and

(ii) knew or should have known that the action would have been brought against it, but for a mistake concerning the proper party's identity." Rule 15(c)(1).

In our view, neither of the Court of Appeals' reasons for denying relation back under Rule 15(c)(1)(C)(ii) finds support in the text of the Rule. We consider each reason in turn.

A

The Court of Appeals first decided that Krupski either knew or should have known of the proper party's identity and thus determined that she had made a deliberate choice instead of a mistake in not naming Costa Crociere as a party in her original pleading. By focusing on Krupski's knowledge, the Court of Appeals chose the wrong starting point. The question under Rule 15(c)(1)(C)(ii) is not whether Krupski knew or should have known the identity of Costa Crociere as the proper defendant, but whether Costa Crociere knew or should have known that it would have been named as a defendant but for an error. Rule 15(c)(1)(C)(ii) asks what the prospective *defendant* knew or should have known during the Rule 4(m) period, not what the *plaintiff* knew or should have known at the time of filing her original complaint.

Information in the plaintiff's possession is relevant only if it bears on the defendant's understanding of whether the plaintiff made a mistake regarding the proper party's identity. For purposes of that inquiry, it would be error to conflate knowledge of a party's existence with the absence of mistake. A mistake is "[a]n error, misconception, or misunderstanding; an erroneous belief." Black's Law Dictionary 1092 (9th ed. 2009); *see also* Webster's THIRD NEW INTERNATIONAL DICTIONARY 1446 (2002) (defining "mistake" as "a misunderstanding of the meaning or implication of something"; "a wrong action or statement proceeding from faulty judgment, inadequate knowledge, or inattention"; "an erroneous belief"; or "a state of mind not in accordance with the facts"). That a plaintiff knows of a party's existence does not preclude her from making a mistake with respect to that party's identity. A plaintiff may know that a prospective defendant—call him party A—exists, while erroneously believing him to have the status of party B. Similarly, a plaintiff may know generally what party A does while misunderstanding the roles that party A and party B played in the "conduct, transaction, or occurrence" giving rise to her claim. If the plaintiff sues party B instead of party A under these circumstances, she has made a "mistake concerning the proper party's identity" notwithstanding her knowledge of the existence of both parties. The only question under Rule 15(c)(1)(C)(ii), then, is whether party A knew or should have known that, absent some mistake, the action would have been brought against him.

Respondent urges that the key issue under Rule 15(c)(1)(C)(ii) is whether the plaintiff made a deliberate choice to sue one party over another. We agree that making a deliberate choice to sue one party instead of another while fully understanding the factual and legal differences between the two parties is the antithesis of making a mistake concerning the proper party's identity. We disagree, however, with respondent's position that any time a plaintiff is aware of the existence of two parties and chooses to sue the wrong one, the proper defendant could reasonably believe that the plaintiff made no mistake. The reasonableness of the mistake is not itself at issue. As noted, a plaintiff might know that the prospective defendant exists but nonetheless harbor a misunderstanding about his status or role in the events giving rise to the claim at issue, and she may mistakenly choose to sue a different defendant based on that misimpression. That kind of deliberate but mistaken choice does not foreclose a finding that Rule 15(c)(1)(C)(ii) has been satisfied.

This reading is consistent with the purpose of relation back: to balance the interests of the defendant protected by the statute of limitations with the preference expressed in the Federal Rules of Civil Procedure in general, and Rule 15 in particular, for resolving disputes on their merits. A prospective defendant who legitimately believed that the limitations period had passed without any attempt to sue him has a strong interest in repose. But repose would be a windfall for a prospective defendant who understood, or who should have understood, that he escaped suit during the limitations period only because the plaintiff misunderstood a crucial fact about his identity. Because a plaintiff's knowledge of the existence of a party does not foreclose the possibility that she has made a mistake of identity about which that party should have been aware, such knowledge does not support that party's interest in repose.

Our reading is also consistent with the history of Rule 15(c)(1)(C). That provision was added in 1966 to respond to a recurring problem in suits against the Federal Government, particularly in the Social Security context. Individuals who had filed timely lawsuits challenging the administrative denial of benefits often failed to name the party identified in the statute as the proper defendant—the current Secretary of what was then the Department of Health, Education, and Welfare—and named instead the United States; the Department of Health, Education, and Welfare itself; the nonexistent "Federal Security Administration"; or a Secretary who had recently retired from office. By the time the plaintiffs discovered their mistakes, the statute of limitations in many cases had expired, and the district courts denied the plaintiffs leave to amend on the ground that the amended complaints would not relate back. Rule 15(c) was therefore "amplified to provide a general solution" to this problem. It is conceivable that the Social Security litigants knew or reasonably should have known the identity of the proper defendant either because of documents in their administrative cases or by dint of the statute setting forth the filing requirements. Nonetheless, the Advisory Committee clearly meant their filings to qualify as mistakes under the Rule.

Respondent suggests that our decision in *Nelson v. Adams USA, Inc.,* forecloses the reading of Rule 15(c)(1)(C)(ii) we adopt today. We disagree. In that case, *Adams USA, Inc.,* had obtained an award of attorney's fees against the corporation of which Donald Nelson was the president and sole shareholder. After Adams became concerned that the corporation did not have sufficient funds to pay the award, Adams sought to amend its pleading to add Nelson as a party and simultaneously moved to amend the judgment to hold Nelson responsible. The District Court granted both motions, and the Court of Appeals affirmed. We reversed, holding that the requirements of due process, as codified in Rules 12 and 15 of the Federal

Rules of Civil Procedure, demand that an added party have the opportunity to respond before judgment is entered against him. In a footnote explaining that relation back does not deny the added party an opportunity to respond to the amended pleading, we noted that the case did not arise under the "mistake clause" of Rule 15(c): "Respondent Adams made no such mistake. It knew of Nelson's role and existence and, until it moved to amend its pleading, chose to assert its claim for costs and fees only against [Nelson's company]."

Contrary to respondent's claim, *Nelson* does not suggest that Rule 15(c)(1)(C)(ii) cannot be satisfied if a plaintiff knew of the prospective defendant's existence at the time she filed her original complaint. In that case, there was nothing in the initial pleading suggesting that Nelson was an intended party, while there was evidence in the record (of which Nelson was aware) that Adams sought to add him only after learning that the company would not be able to satisfy the judgment. This evidence countered any implication that Adams had originally failed to name Nelson because of any "mistake concerning the proper party's identity," and instead suggested that Adams decided to name Nelson only after the fact in an attempt to ensure that the fee award would be paid. The footnote merely observes that Adams had originally been under no misimpression about the function Nelson played in the underlying dispute. We said, after all, that Adams knew of Nelson's "role" as well as his existence. Read in context, the footnote in *Nelson* is entirely consistent with our understanding of the Rule: When the original complaint and the plaintiff's conduct compel the conclusion that the failure to name the prospective defendant in the original complaint was the result of a fully informed decision as opposed to a mistake concerning the proper defendant's identity, the requirements of Rule 15(c)(1)(C)(ii) are not met. This conclusion is in keeping with our rejection today of the Court of Appeals' reliance on the plaintiff's knowledge to deny relation back.

B

The Court of Appeals offered a second reason why Krupski's amended complaint did not relate back: Krupski had unduly delayed in seeking to file, and in eventually filing, an amended complaint. The Court of Appeals offered no support for its view that a plaintiff's dilatory conduct can justify the denial of relation back under Rule 15(c)(1)(C), and we find none. The Rule plainly sets forth an exclusive list of requirements for relation back, and the amending party's diligence is not among them. Moreover, the Rule mandates relation back once the Rule's requirements are satisfied; it does not leave the decision whether to grant relation back to the district court's equitable discretion. *See* Rule 15(c)(1) ("An amendment ... *relates back* ... when" the three listed requirements are met (emphasis added)).

The mandatory nature of the inquiry for relation back under Rule 15(c) is particularly striking in contrast to the inquiry under Rule 15(a), which sets forth the circumstances in which a party may amend its pleading before trial. By its terms, Rule 15(a) gives discretion to the district court in deciding whether to grant a motion to amend a pleading to add a party or a claim. Following an initial period after filing a pleading during which a party may amend once "as a matter of course," "a party may amend its pleading only with the opposing party's written consent or the court's leave," which the court "should freely give . . . when justice so requires." Rules 15(a)(1)-(2). We have previously explained that a court may consider a movant's "undue delay" or "dilatory motive" in deciding whether to grant leave to amend under Rule 15(a). As the contrast between Rule 15(a) and Rule 15(c) makes clear, however, the speed with which a plaintiff moves to amend her complaint or files an amended complaint after obtaining leave to do so has no bearing on whether the amended complaint relates back.

Rule 15(c)(1)(C) does permit a court to examine a plaintiff's conduct during the Rule 4(m) period, but not in the way or for the purpose respondent or the Court of Appeals suggests. As we have explained, the question under Rule 15(c)(1)(C)(ii) is what the prospective defendant reasonably should have understood about the plaintiff's intent in filing the original complaint against the first defendant. To the extent the plaintiff's post-filing conduct informs the prospective defendant's understanding of whether the plaintiff initially made a "mistake concerning the proper party's identity," a court may consider the conduct. Cf. *Leonard v. Parry* ("[P]ost-filing events occasionally can shed light on the plaintiff's state of mind at an earlier time" and "can inform *a defendant's* reasonable beliefs concerning whether her omission from the original complaint represented a mistake (as opposed to a conscious choice)"). The plaintiff's post-filing conduct is otherwise immaterial to the question whether an amended complaint relates back.[5]

C

Applying these principles to the facts of this case, we think it clear that the courts below erred in denying relation back under Rule 15(c)(1)(C)(ii). The District Court held that Costa Crociere had "constructive notice" of Krupski's complaint within the Rule 4(m) period. Costa Crociere has not challenged this finding. Because the complaint made clear that Krupski meant to sue the company that "owned, operated, managed, supervised and controlled" the ship on which she was injured and also indicated (mistakenly) that Costa Cruise performed those roles, Costa Crociere should have known, within the Rule 4(m) period, that it was not named as a defendant in that complaint only because of Krupski's misunderstanding about which "Costa" entity was in charge of the ship— clearly a "mistake concerning the proper party's identity."

---

5. Similarly, we reject respondent's suggestion that Rule 15(c) requires a plaintiff to move to amend her complaint or to file and serve an amended complaint within the Rule 4(m) period. Rule 15(c)(1)(C)(i) simply requires that the prospective defendant has received sufficient "notice of the action" within the Rule 4(m) period that he will not be prejudiced in defending the case on the merits. The Advisory Committee Notes to the 1966 Amendment clarify that "the notice need not be formal."

Respondent contends that because the original complaint referred to the ticket's forum requirement and pre-suit claims notification procedure, Krupski was clearly aware of the contents of the ticket, and because the ticket identified Costa Crociere as the carrier and proper party for a lawsuit, respondent was entitled to think that she made a deliberate choice to sue Costa Cruise instead of Costa Crociere. As we have explained, however, that Krupski may have known the contents of the ticket does not foreclose the possibility that she nonetheless misunderstood crucial facts regarding the two companies' identities. Especially because the face of the complaint plainly indicated such a misunderstanding, respondent's contention is not persuasive. Moreover, respondent has articulated no strategy that it could reasonably have thought Krupski was pursuing in suing a defendant that was legally unable to provide relief.

Respondent also argues that Krupski's failure to move to amend her complaint during the Rule 4(m) period shows that she made no mistake in that period. But as discussed, any delay on Krupski's part is relevant only to the extent it may have informed Costa Crociere's understanding during the Rule 4(m) period of whether she made a mistake originally. Krupski's failure to add Costa Crociere during the Rule 4(m) period is not sufficient to make reasonable any belief that she had made a deliberate and informed decision not to sue Costa Crociere in the first instance.[6] Nothing in Krupski's conduct during the Rule 4(m) period suggests that she failed to name Costa Crociere because of anything other than a mistake.

It is also worth noting that Costa Cruise and Costa Crociere are related corporate entities with very similar names; "crociera" even means "cruise" in Italian. This interrelationship and similarity heighten the expectation that Costa Crociere should suspect a mistake has been made when Costa Cruise is named in a complaint that actually describes Costa Crociere's activities. Cf. *Morel v. DaimlerChrysler AG* (where complaint conveyed plaintiffs' attempt to sue automobile manufacturer and erroneously named the manufacturer as Daimler–Chrysler Corporation instead of the actual manufacturer, a legally distinct but related entity named DaimlerChrysler AG, the latter should have realized it had not been named because of plaintiffs' mistake); *Goodman v. Praxair, Inc.* (where complaint named parent company Praxair, Inc., but described status of subsidiary company Praxair Services, Inc., subsidiary company knew or should have known it had not been named because of plaintiff's mistake). In addition, Costa Crociere's own actions contributed to passenger confusion over "the proper party" for a lawsuit. The front of the ticket advertises that "Costa Cruises" has achieved a certification of quality, without clarifying whether "Costa Cruises" is Costa Cruise Lines, Costa Crociere, or some other related "Costa" company. Indeed, Costa Crociere

---

6. The Court of Appeals concluded that Krupski was not diligent merely because she did not seek leave to add Costa Crociere until 133 days after she filed her original complaint and did not actually file an amended complaint for another a month after that. It is not clear why Krupski should have been found dilatory for not accepting at face value the unproven allegations in Costa Cruise's answer and corporate disclosure form. In fact, Krupski moved to amend her complaint to add Costa Crociere within the time period prescribed by the District Court's scheduling order.

is evidently aware that the difference between Costa Cruise and Costa Crociere can be confusing for cruise ship passengers. *See, e.g., Suppa v. Costa Crociere, S.p.A.*(denying Costa Crociere's motion to dismiss the amended complaint where the original complaint had named Costa Cruise as a defendant after "find[ing] it simply inconceivable that Defendant Costa Crociere was not on notice . . . that . . . but for the mistake in the original Complaint, Costa Crociere was the appropriate party to be named in the action").

In light of these facts, Costa Crociere should have known that Krupski's failure to name it as a defendant in her original complaint was due to a mistake concerning the proper party's identity. We therefore reverse the judgment of the Court of Appeals for the Eleventh Circuit and remand the case for further proceedings consistent with this opinion.

It is so ordered.

Justice Scalia, concurring in part and concurring in the judgment.

I join the Court's opinion except for its reliance on the Notes of the Advisory Committee as establishing the meaning of Federal Rule of Civil Procedure 15(c)(1)(C). The Advisory Committee's insights into the proper interpretation of a Rule's text are useful to the same extent as any scholarly commentary. But the Committee's *intentions* have no effect on the Rule's meaning. Even assuming that we and the Congress that allowed the Rule to take effect read and agreed with those intentions, it is the text of the Rule that controls.

D. TRUTHFUL PLEADINGS AND SANCTIONS

Federal Rule of Civil Procedure 11. Signing Pleadings, Motions, and Other Papers; Representations to the Court; Sanctions

(a) **Signature.** Every pleading, written motion, and other paper must be signed by at least one attorney of record in the attorney's name—or by a party personally if the party is unrepresented. The paper must state the signer's address, e-mail address, and telephone number. Unless a rule or statute specifically states otherwise, a pleading need not be verified or accompanied by an affidavit. The court must strike an unsigned paper unless the omission is promptly corrected after being called to the attorney's or party's attention.

(b) **Representations to the Court.** By presenting to the court a pleading, written motion, or other paper—whether by signing, filing, submitting, or later advocating it—an attorney or unrepresented party certifies that to the best of the person's knowledge, information, and belief, formed after an inquiry reasonable under the circumstances:

   (1) it is not being presented for any improper purpose, such as to harass, cause unnecessary delay, or needlessly increase the cost of litigation;

(2) the claims, defenses, and other legal contentions are warranted by existing law or by a non-frivolous argument for extending, modifying, or reversing existing law or for establishing new law;

(3) the factual contentions have evidentiary support or, if specifically so identified, will likely have evidentiary support after a reasonable opportunity for further investigation or discovery; and

(4) the denials of factual contentions are warranted on the evidence or, if specifically so identified, are reasonably based on belief or a lack of information.

(c) Sanctions.

(1) *In General.* If, after notice and a reasonable opportunity to respond, the court determines that Rule 11(b) has been violated, the court may impose an appropriate sanction on any attorney, law firm, or party that violated the rule or is responsible for the violation. Absent exceptional circumstances, a law firm must be held jointly responsible for a violation committed by its partner, associate, or employee.

(2) *Motion for Sanctions.* A motion for sanctions must be made separately from any other motion and must describe the specific conduct that allegedly violates Rule 11(b). The motion must be served under Rule 5, but it must not be filed or be presented to the court if the challenged paper, claim, defense, contention, or denial is withdrawn or appropriately corrected within 21 days after service or within another time the court sets. If warranted, the court may award to the prevailing party the reasonable expenses, including attorney's fees, incurred for the motion.

(3) *On the Court's Initiative.* On its own, the court may order an attorney, law firm, or party to show cause why conduct specifically described in the order has not violated Rule 11(b).

(4) *Nature of a Sanction.* A sanction imposed under this rule must be limited to what suffices to deter repetition of the conduct or comparable conduct by others similarly situated. The sanction may include nonmonetary directives; an order to pay a penalty into court; or, if imposed on motion and warranted for effective deterrence, an order directing payment to the movant of part or all of the reasonable attorney's fees and other expenses directly resulting from the violation.

(5) *Limitations on Monetary Sanctions.* The court must not impose a monetary sanction:

(A) against a represented party for violating Rule 11(b)(2); or

(B) on its own, unless it issued the show-cause order under Rule 11(c)(3) before voluntary dismissal or settlement of the claims made by or against the party that is, or whose attorneys are, to be sanctioned.

(6) ***Requirements for an Order.*** An order imposing a sanction must describe the sanctioned conduct and explain the basis for the sanction.

(d) Inapplicability to Discovery. This rule does not apply to disclosures and discovery requests, responses, objections, and motions under Rules 26 through 37.

* * *

28 U.S.C. § 1927. COUNSEL'S LIABILITY FOR EXCESSIVE COSTS

Any attorney or other person admitted to conduct cases in any court of the United States or any Territory thereof who so multiplies the proceedings in any case unreasonably and vexatiously may be required by the court to satisfy personally the excess costs, expenses, and attorneys' fees reasonably incurred because of such conduct.

* * *

ROTH v. GREEN

466 F.3d 1179 (10th Cir. 2006)

BRISCOE, CIRCUIT JUDGE.

These appeals challenge a sanction award against counsel pursuant to Federal Rule of Civil Procedure 11 and 28 U.S.C. § 1927, as well as a fee award against two individual plaintiffs pursuant to 42 U.S.C. § 1988. Both appeals arise out of the same ill-fated § 1983 action.

Plaintiffs Stephen Roth and Ellen Gumeson, represented by attorney Robert Mulhern, filed suit under 42 U.S.C. § 1983 against various Colorado municipalities, counties, and local and state employees, arguing that the stop and search of their car, as well as their ensuing arrest, was unconstitutional. The district court granted defendants' motions to dismiss and/or for summary judgment. Plaintiffs appealed. While the appeal was pending the district court granted defendants' motions for sanctions and fees against attorney Mulhern. Thereafter, this court affirmed the district court's decision on the merits, granted a motion by one group of defendants for attorneys fees on appeal, and remanded the case to the district court for a determination of the proper amount of fees.

In Appeal No. 05–1129, attorney Mulhern appeals the district court's award of sanctions and fees against him and in favor of defendants. . . . In Appeal No. 05–1129, we reverse the district court's order granting Rule 11 sanctions against Mulhern and remand to the district court for a determination of the proper amount of fees to be assessed against Mulhern pursuant to 28 U.S.C. § 1927.

I.

Factual history

On June 15, 2000, officers associated with the Twenty–Second Judicial Drug Task Force in Colorado set up a narcotic "ruse" checkpoint on

Highway 145 just north of the town of Rico, in Dolores County, Colorado. As part of this "ruse" checkpoint, the officers placed a sign on the highway that stated a narcotics checkpoint was being conducted one mile ahead. A second sign was placed further down the highway stating that a drug dog was in use as part of the narcotics checkpoint. The statements made on the signs, however, were false. No narcotics checkpoint existed. Instead, officers were stationed in inconspicuous areas along the highway in the area of the signs watching for any illegal or suspicious activity. No stops were to be made unless officers observed or otherwise had reasonable suspicion of some type of illegal activity associated with a particular vehicle.

At approximately 4:30 p.m. on June 15, 2000, Deputy Hugh Richards of the Montezuma County Sheriff's Department was stationed between the two signs on Highway 145. Richards observed a female passenger in a blue Toyota throw an object out of the window. Based upon his observations, Richards radioed ahead and the blue Toyota was stopped for littering by task force member Dennis Spruell, a sergeant with the Cortez (Colorado) Police Department. After initially radioing Spruell, Richards retrieved the object, which turned out to be a wooden pipe with burnt residue and a screen. The pipe smelled of marijuana. Richards again radioed Spruell to advise him of what he had found. The driver of the vehicle, Stephen Roth, was advised that he had been stopped because his passenger had been observed throwing an object out the window. Roth stated that the object was a pop can. Roth was then asked if he would consent to a search of his vehicle. Roth declined to give consent. Spruell informed Roth and the passenger, Ellen Gumeson, that he suspected that marijuana contraband had been thrown from the vehicle, and thus he had reasonable suspicion that further evidence of contraband would be found in the vehicle. During the ensuing search, Spruell and Jeff Coleman, another member of the task force from the Durango (Colorado) Police Department, found a wooden marijuana pipe with burnt residue under the front driver's seat. Inside a cooler located in the back seat, officers found plastic baggies containing psilocybin mushrooms, a Schedule I controlled substance. Both Roth and Gumeson were arrested.

During the ensuing criminal proceedings in Dolores County, Roth unsuccessfully moved to suppress the evidence seized during the search of the vehicle. Gumeson subsequently pled guilty to littering. On December 11, 2001, Roth was found guilty at trial of possession of drug paraphernalia and fined $100.00. Roth appealed his conviction to the Colorado Court of Appeals (CCA), arguing that the evidence seized from his vehicle should have been suppressed because it was the fruit of an unconstitutional checkpoint employed by law enforcement officers, and because Deputy Richards could not reasonably have observed Gumeson throw anything out of the vehicle window and/or likely searched the incorrect area after observing Gumeson's actions. The CCA affirmed Roth's conviction on August 14, 2003. In doing so, the CCA held that the use of the fictitious drug checkpoint did not violate Roth's rights under the Fourth Amendment because the stop of his car was based on the officers' individualized suspicion of unlawful activity, and the officers had probable cause to believe the car contained evidence of a crime and thus were justified in searching the car and its contents. Although Roth filed petitions for writs of certiorari with the Colorado Supreme Court and the United States Supreme Court, those petitions were denied.

The original district court proceedings

On June 12, 2002, while Roth's state criminal appeal was still pending, Roth and Gumeson initiated this 42 U.S.C. § 1983 action by filing a complaint in federal district court against seventy-six defendants, including various state and county officials (e.g., the governor of the State of Colorado and the heads of at least three municipal police departments whose employees participated in the narcotics task force), several Colorado municipalities, and approximately fifty "unknown Doe defendants." In their complaint, Roth and Gumeson alleged that the defendants "created, established, and executed an unconstitutional drug checkpoint on ... June 15, 2000," that ultimately resulted in Roth and Gumeson being unlawfully stopped, detained, searched and arrested. The complaint, which alleged four separate causes of action under § 1983 arising out of the general allegations, sought general, special and punitive damages, attorneys' fees and costs, and declaratory relief.

Defendants moved to dismiss the complaint and/or for summary judgment. Rather than responding directly to those motions, Roth and Gumeson asked the district court to stay the case "until the appellate process, including any writs," in Roth's state criminal case was "completed." The district court denied the motion to stay and ordered Roth and Gumeson to respond to the defendants' pending motions. After responding to defendants' motions, Roth and Gumeson filed a motion asking the district court to stay all pretrial proceedings. That motion was granted by the magistrate judge on February 5, 2003.

On December 5, 2003, after allowing the parties to complete their briefing on the pending motions to dismiss and/or for summary judgment, the district court granted the motions and dismissed the action in its entirety. In doing so, the district court concluded: (1) it was precluded by the *Rooker-Feldman* doctrine from considering Roth's claims because the identical issues were decided against Roth in his state criminal proceedings; (2) Roth was precluded under the doctrine of collateral estoppel from challenging the constitutionality of the ruse checkpoint and his stop, detention and arrest; (3) both Roth and Gumeson were precluded from pursuing their § 1983 claims until such time, if ever, that they had successfully challenged their Colorado state convictions arising from the stop, search and arrest; (4) the claim of civil conspiracy asserted by Roth and Gumeson under § 1983 failed as a matter of law because they did not allege any "specific facts showing any agreement or collaboration between [the] Defendants to undertake an improper, illegal, or unconstitutional activity," and (5) in addition to these various bases for dismissal, defendants were entitled to summary judgment because the undisputed facts established that the "ruse checkpoint" was constitutional in light of [a Tenth Circuit decision], which the district court concluded involved "virtually identical facts and [wa]s dispositive." Judgment was entered in the case on December 11, 2003.

Roth and Gumeson filed a notice of appeal on January 5, 2004. On that same date, Roth and Gumeson filed a motion asking the district court for permission to proceed on appeal in forma pauperis. The district court denied that motion on February 2, 2004, concluding "th[e] appeal [wa]s not taken in good faith because plaintiffs ha[d] not shown the existence of a reasoned, nonfrivolous argument on the law and facts in support of the issues raised on appeal."

The motions for sanctions and/or fees and costs

In late December 2003 and in early January 2004, defendants filed motions for sanctions against Robert Mulhern, the attorney for Roth and Gumeson, and/or for attorney fees and costs pursuant to 28 U.S.C. § 1927. Mulhern filed a lengthy response to those motions on January 14, 2004. According to Mulhern, he filed the complaint on June 12, 2002, out of concern "that the Statute of Limitations was about to expire on June 15, 2002. . . ." Mulhern argued that the case was meritorious because: (1) the "case should have been stayed, not dismissed," until the conclusion of Roth's state criminal proceedings, (2) the holding in *Heck* was not applicable "to this search and seizure case," (3) he was not allowed to engage in discovery; (4) "all [defendants] were at least personally involved," (5) the case "should have been analyzed using checkpoint law, not individualized suspicion," and (6) "[t]he *Flynn* case [wa]s in conflict with decisions from not only the Supreme Court of the United States, but also a decision from the United States Court of Appeals for the Tenth Circuit, among other courts." In addition, Mulhern argued that the defendants failed to meet and confer with him prior to filing their motions, as required by the district court's local rules, and also failed to comply with the procedures outlined in Rule 11 by providing him with copies of their motions at least twenty-one days prior to filing those motions.

On February 13, 2004, Roth and Gumeson filed a motion for sanctions pursuant to Rule 11 and/or attorney fees and costs pursuant to 28 U.S.C. § 1927 against the defendants' attorneys. The only ground offered in support of the motion was that "the defendants' attorneys did not meet and confer with the plaintiffs, through their attorney of record, prior to filing the[ir] motions [for sanctions and/or fees and costs] and did not follow the required procedure for Rule 11 sanctions."

On June 15, 2004, the district court granted the defendants' motion for sanctions and/or fees and costs, and denied the plaintiffs' similar motion. In its order, the district court concluded that Rule 11 sanctions were appropriate because (1) the defendants' respective letters to Mulhern satisfied Rule 11's "safe harbor" requirement, (2) Mulhern's pursuit of the lawsuit, despite numerous Rule 11 "safe harbor" warnings from defendants, "created unnecessary delay and needlessly increased the cost of this litigation," (3) the plaintiffs' claims and legal contentions "were not warranted by existing law or by a non-frivolous argument for the extension, modification, or reversal of existing law or the establishment of new law," and (4) "the allegations and other factual contentions contained in Plaintiffs' claims lacked evidentiary support and would not have gained evidentiary support after further investigation or discovery." Although the district court stated it "ha[d] no information on Mulhern's ability to pay sanctions," or on his "history, experience, or ability," it "consider[ed] his offense severe in terms of wasted time and wasted money," and that "despite many opportunities to change his conduct—including a failed appeal in the Colorado Court of Appeals, and the Rule 11 safe-harbor letters here—Mulhern failed to do so." In short, the district court concluded that Mulhern "acted in bad faith," and thus "Rule 11 sanctions [we]re appropriate."

The district court also concluded that "charging fees and costs personally to ... Mulhern was appropriate" under 28 U.S.C. § 1927. "In suing twenty-six named Defendants and Does 1–50," the district court concluded, "Mulhern engaged in shotgun litigation, and ignored the realities of the Defendants' non-involvement in the circumstances applicable to his clients." In other words, the district court concluded, "Mulhern unreasonably and vexatiously multiplied the Defendants in this case, thereby recklessly increasing the amount of attorney and paralegal time spent on litigation, and the costs associated therewith." The district court also noted that "[d]efendants who clearly had no liability under the circumstances were forced to obtain counsel and defend against specious claims," and that "Mulhern refused to withdraw claims or dismiss various Defendants against whom claims could not be maintained."

In light of this vexatious conduct, "coupled with the need for Rule 11 sanctions," the district court "conclude[d] that Mulhern should be personally liable for the fees and costs associated with [the] ... Defendants' defense under § 1927." Together, these fees and costs totaled $92,044.77.

As for the plaintiffs' cross-motion for sanctions and/or fees and costs, the district court characterized it as "audacious," and concluded that by filing it "Plaintiffs ha[d] further increased the litigation costs of their fully unsubstantiated lawsuit." The district court also rejected the plaintiffs' arguments that defendants had failed to meet and confer as required by the local rules, or to provide plaintiffs with "safe-harbor" warnings under Rule 11.

This court's award of fees and costs to defendants

On February 3, 2005, this court issued an order and judgment affirming the district court's order dismissing the action on its merits, affirming the district court's order denying plaintiffs' motion for sanctions, and dismissing for lack of jurisdiction Mulhern's own appeal of the district court's order granting defendants' motions for sanctions and/or fees and costs against him.

On February 17, 2005, one group of defendants (Dennis Spruell, Danny Dufur, Roy Lane, and the City of Cortez, Colorado) filed a motion for an award of attorney fees and costs pursuant to Fed. R. App. P. 38 and 28 U.S.C. § 1912. In their motion, these defendants asked that the fees and costs be assessed against plaintiffs' attorney, Mulhern. Mulhern filed a response to the motion on behalf of himself, as well as on behalf of Roth and Gumeson. In his response, Mulhern argued that he had a reasonable basis for pursuing the appeal, sanctioning him would effectively result in the loss of his ability to practice law, and that "Roth and . . . Gumeson . . . ha[d] no money and c[ould] not pay costs." On March 28, 2005, this court granted the defendants' motion in part. Rather than relying on Fed. R. App. P. 38 or § 1912, however, this court awarded costs "in the amount of $363.20 pursuant to Fed. R. App. P. 39," and, "[p]ursuant to 42 U.S.C. § 1988," "award[ed] the defendants attorney's fees on appeal, in an amount to be determined by the district court on remand."

On remand, the defendants who prevailed on their motion for fees and costs filed a pleading and supporting documentation asking the district court to award them fees in the amount of $12,049.00. Roth and Gumeson responded, arguing in pertinent part that the requested fees were unreasonable and, as they had in their response filed with this court, that they were "paupers" who could not afford to pay any amount of fees. On May 12, 2005, the district court issued an order granting defendants' motion and directing Roth and Gumeson to pay fees in the requested amount ($12,049.00).

II.

In Appeal No. 05–1129, Mulhern challenges, on various grounds, the district court's decision to award sanctions against him and in favor of all the defendants pursuant to Rule 11 and 28 U.S.C. § 1927. We review for abuse of discretion the district court's decision to impose Rule 11 sanctions against Mulhern. Likewise, we review a district court's award of § 1927 sanctions for an abuse of discretion. Notably, this abuse of discretion standard does "not preclude [our] correction of a district court's legal errors. . . ." In other words, a district court will be deemed to have abused its discretion if its decision to impose sanctions under either Rule 11 or § 1927 "rest[ed] on an erroneous view of the law. . . ."

* * *

b) Did the § 1983 claims have merit?

Mulhern next contends that sanctions should not have been imposed against him because the § 1983 claims asserted in the complaint had merit. More specifically, Mulhern argues that (a) "the legal contentions [we]re warranted by existing law and by non-frivolous arguments for the reversal of existing law," including "the *Flynn* case," (b) "the allegations and other factual contentions ha[d] evidentiary support," and (c) "the claims [we]re not being presented to harass, cause unnecessary delay, or for the needless increase in the costs of the litigation in this case." In addition, Mulhern argues, the district court should have granted his request to stay the case pending the outcome of Roth's state criminal proceedings and, had the district court done so, "very little time, effort, and/or money would have been expended by the Court and/or [the defense] attorneys in this case."

The district court noted, and we agree, that there were a host of legal impediments to Roth and Gumeson prevailing on their claims. To begin with, the majority of the defendants named in the complaint had, at best, only tangential relationships to the "ruse" checkpoint, and thus were not properly named as defendants in the complaint. For example, defendant Bill Owens, the Governor of the State of Colorado, was not alleged to have had any direct connection with, or participation in, the "ruse" checkpoint.

Even with respect to the named defendants who directly participated in the "ruse" checkpoint, it is clear that their conduct was entirely legal. Although Mulhern continues to maintain that the claims asserted in the complaint were not controlled by our decision in *Flynn,* he is mistaken. In *Flynn,* the defendant (Mack Flynn), while driving on I–40 in Muskogee County, Oklahoma, encountered two road signs nearly identical to those encountered by plaintiffs Roth and Gumeson in this case (the first said "Drug Checkpoint 1/3 mile ahead" and the second said "Drug Dogs in Use"). The defendant, upon seeing the signs, "made an abrupt lane change and immediately took the [nearest] exit ramp" off of I–40. At the top of the exit ramp, the defendant briefly stopped his car while his passenger "opened the door and dropped a large sack from the car." Officers who were surveilling the highway examined the sack and determined it contained narcotics (it was later verified to be methamphetamine). The defendant was then stopped, placed under arrest, and charged with various federal offenses in connection with the incident. After the district court denied his motion to suppress, the defendant entered a conditional guilty plea to four drug-related offenses. On appeal, the defendant argued, in pertinent part, that his arrest was the result of "law enforcement's illegal conduct in operating a narcotics checkpoint." We rejected that argument, concluding that "[t]he posting of signs to create a ruse does not constitute illegal police activity," and that the defendant "never reached a drug checkpoint."

If there were any doubts about the legality of the ruse utilized by defendants in this case, those doubts should have ceased when we issued *Flynn.* Mulhern, in turn, upon receiving notice of the *Flynn* decision (and the record indicates he was repeatedly advised of the decision by the defendants in their respective letters to him), should have voluntarily dismissed the complaint. Stated differently, it was unreasonable, and a violation of his obligations as a licensed attorney, to continue to pursue the claims after the issuance of *Flynn.* Although Mulhern now argues that a reasonable basis exists for overruling the *Flynn* decision, he fails to offer any such basis.

Mulhern's assertion that he "had" to file the complaint to avoid the running of the statute of limitations, and that, in turn, the district court had an obligation to stay the case pending the outcome of Roth's state criminal proceedings, is simply wrong. "A plaintiff may not bring a civil rights suit if a favorable result in the suit would necessarily demonstrate the invalidity of an outstanding criminal judgment against the plaintiff." As correctly noted by the district court, that was precisely the situation here: by asserting that they were the victims of an unconstitutional drug checkpoint, Roth and Gumeson were effectively questioning the validity of their arrests and convictions. Thus, to recover damages based on their allegations, Roth and Gumeson were first obligated to " 'prove that the[ir] conviction[s] ... ha[d] been reversed on direct appeal, expunged by executive order, declared invalid by a state tribunal authorized to make such determination, or called into question by a federal court's issuance of a writ of habeas corpus.' " Not until they successfully did so would their § 1983 claims have arisen. In other words, " '[b]ecause the[ir] cause[s] of action d[id] not accrue until such time, the applicable statute of limitations d[id] not begin to run until the same time.' " Thus, Mulhern was in no way obligated to file suit against defendants, and indeed clearly should have waited until such time, if ever, as the Colorado state courts granted relief to Roth and Gumeson from their convictions.

In sum, the district court did not abuse its discretion in concluding that Mulhern violated the provisions of both Rule 11 and § 1927 in filing and pursuing the § 1983 claims on behalf of Roth and Gumeson.

c) *Did the defendants fail to meet and confer with Mulhern?*

Mulhern contends that sanctions were improperly imposed against him because the defendants failed to first "meet and confer" with him prior to filing their motions for sanctions, as required by Rule 7.1 of the district court's local rules. We review a district court's application of its local rules for abuse of discretion.

District of Colorado Local Rule 7.1 provides, in pertinent part, as follows:

> **A. Duty to Confer.** The court will not consider any motion, other than a motion under Fed. R. Civ. P. 12 or 56, unless counsel for the moving party or a pro se party, before filing the motion, has conferred or made reasonable, good-faith efforts to confer with opposing counsel or a pro se party to resolve the disputed matter. The moving party shall state in the motion, or in a certificate attached to the motion, the specific efforts to comply with this rule.

In its order granting defendants' motions for sanctions, the district court rejected Mulhern's assertion that defendants failed to comply with Local Rule 7.1. Specifically, the district court noted that each set of defendants sent Mulhern a "warning or 'safe-harbor' " letter outlining the deficiencies of each claim asserted in the complaint, asking that Mulhern voluntarily dismiss the complaint, and warning that Mulhern's failure to do so would result in the filing of motions for sanctions and fees. In the district court's view, these letters "substantially satisf[ied] ... the local rule."

Mulhern offers four reasons why the defendants' letters should not be deemed sufficient to satisfy Rule 7.1's "meet and confer" requirement. First, he argues that if defense counsel "did meet and confer [with him], they would have stated and were required to state in their sanctions motions and/or certify their specific efforts." Second, he argues that the letters "did not say anything about Rule 7.1A or that the letters were meet and confer letters." Third, he argues that the letters failed to address each of the grounds ultimately asserted by defendants in their respective motions to dismiss and/or for summary judgment. Fourth, he argues that the defendants' letters were sent to him "up to eleven (11) months prior to [defendants'] filing the motions for sanctions," and thus did not meet the spirit of Rule 7.1.

We reject Mulhern's arguments and conclude that the district court did not abuse its discretion in applying Rule 7.1. As noted, each letter advised Mulhern that, in the defendants' view, the claims asserted in the complaint were, for various reasons, meritless and should therefore be voluntarily dismissed. Further, each letter provided Mulhern with notice that, should he fail to voluntarily dismiss the complaint, defendants would move for sanctions against him. In short, each letter effectively complied with Local Rule 7.1 by attempting to seek a resolution of the issue (i.e., the frivolousness of the plaintiffs' claims) without first seeking resort to the district court's intervention. Although Mulhern complains that defendants failed to outline, in their motions, their efforts to meet and confer, he acknowledges that defendants attached to their motions copies of the letters they sent to him. In our view, the district court did not abuse its discretion in concluding that this "substantially satisfied" the requirements of Rule 7.1. Lastly, Rule 7.1 is silent with regard to precisely when the parties must meet and confer prior to the filing of a related motion. Thus, it was not a violation of Rule 7.1 for defendants to wait several months after sending their letters to Mulhern before filing their motions for sanctions (indeed, it arguably favored Mulhern by providing him with a considerable period of time in which to voluntarily dismiss the complaint).

d) Did defendants follow the procedures outlined in Rule 11?

Finally, Mulhern contends the district court should not have granted the defendants' motions for Rule 11 sanctions because defendants "did not serve [him] with their Rule 11 motions prior to filing the motions," and thus violated the so-called "safe harbor" provision of Rule 11. Mulhern also contends that "Rule 11 required that the motions for sanctions were to be served and filed before the conclusion of the civil rights case."

* * * The first question raised by Mulhern is whether defendants complied with the "safe harbor" provisions outlined in Rule 11(c)(1)(A). As noted, that subsection states that motions for sanctions "shall be

served ... but not filed with or presented to the court unless, within 21 days after service of the motion" the challenged pleadings or claims have not been "withdrawn or appropriately corrected." Although defendants all sent Mulhern warning letters well in advance of filing their motions for sanctions, it is uncontroverted that they did not, as required by subsection (c)(1)(A), serve him with copies of their actual motions for sanctions twenty-one days prior to filing those motions. Indeed, it appears from the record on appeal that the motions were served on Mulhern at the same time as, or after, the motions were actually filed.

As they did in the district court, however, defendants contend that the warning letters they sent to Mulhern months in advance of filing their motions for sanctions effectively satisfied the requirements of subsection (c)(1)(A) by providing Mulhern with notice of their intent to seek sanctions and an opportunity to withdraw the complaint prior to them filing their motions. Although the district court agreed with defendants, we conclude, for the reasons discussed below, that defendants' letters were not sufficient to satisfy the requirements of subsection (c)(1)(A), and thus the district court abused its discretion in granting defendants' motions for Rule 11 sanctions.

Contrary to defendants' arguments, nothing in subsection (c)(1)(A) suggests that a letter addressed to the alleged offending party will suffice to satisfy the safe harbor requirements. Rather, the plain language of subsection (c)(1)(A) requires a copy of the actual motion for sanctions to be served on the person(s) accused of sanctionable behavior at least twenty-one days prior to the filing of that motion. This conclusion is bolstered by the Advisory Committee's Notes to the 1993 amendment to Rule 11 (which added the safe harbor provision):

> The rule provides that requests for sanctions must be made as a separate motion, i.e., not simply included as an additional prayer for relief in another motion. *The motion for sanctions is not, however, to be filed until at least 21 days (or such other period as the court may set) after being served.* These provisions are intended to provide a type of "safe harbor" against motions under Rule 11 in that a party will not be subject to sanctions on the basis of another party's motion unless, *after receiving the motion,* it refuses to withdraw that position or to acknowledge candidly that it does not currently have evidence to support a specified allegation. * * *

> To stress the seriousness of a motion for sanctions and to define precisely the conduct claimed to violate the rule, the revision provides that the "safe harbor" period begins to run only upon service of the motion. In most cases, however, counsel should be expected to give informal notice to the other party, whether in person or by a telephone call or *letter,* of a potential violation *before proceeding to prepare and serve a Rule 11 motion.*

Fed. R. Civ. P. 11, advisory committee notes, 1993 Amendments (emphasis added). In other words, the Advisory Committee's Notes clearly suggest that warning letters, such as those sent by defendants to Mulhern, are supplemental to, and cannot be deemed an adequate substitute for, the service of the motion itself.

The reason for requiring a copy of the motion itself, rather than simply a warning letter, to be served on the allegedly offending party is clear. The safe harbor provisions were intended to "protect[ ] litigants from sanctions whenever possible in order to mitigate Rule 11's chilling effects, formaliz[e] procedural due process considerations such as notice for the protection of the party accused of sanctionable behavior, and encourag[e] the withdrawal of papers that violate the rule without involving the district court. . . ." Thus, "a failure to comply with them [should] result in the rejection of the motion for sanctions. . . ."

To be sure, the Seventh Circuit has, as noted by defendants, held that a letter sent to an offending party, rather than a copy of the actual motion, can constitute substantial compliance with Rule 11(c)(1)(A). We find this decision unpersuasive, however, because it contains no analysis of the language of Rule 11(c)(1)(A) or the Advisory Committee Notes, cites to no authority for its holding, and indeed is the only published circuit decision reaching such a conclusion.

Mulhern also contends that the motions for sanctions should have been denied because they were not filed until after the district court had dismissed the complaint. We agree. "The addition of the safe harbor provision in the 1993 amendment [to Rule 11] dramatically changed the effect that a final judgment or the dismissal of the claim has on the possibility of a Rule 11 proceeding." "[S]ervice of a sanctions motion after the district court has dismissed the claim or entered judgment prevents giving effect to the safe harbor provision or the policies and procedural protections it provides, and it will be rejected." *Id.; see Brickwood Contractors, Inc. v. Datanet Eng'g, Inc.* ("Because the rule requires that the party submitting the challenged pleading be given an opportunity to withdraw the pleading, sanctions cannot be sought after summary judgment has been granted."); *Tompkins v. Cyr* (affirming denial of motion for Rule 11 sanctions made after completion of trial); *Barber v. Miller* (holding that a party cannot wait until after summary judgment to move for sanctions, even if that party informally warned the offending party about the potential of Rule 11 sanctions); *Ridder v. City of Springfield* (holding that "a party cannot wait until after summary judgment to move for sanctions under Rule 11"); *see also AeroTech, Inc. v. Estes* (concluding that Rule 11 sanctions were unavailable to defendant who moved for sanctions after plaintiff moved to voluntarily dismiss its claims against defendant).

For these reasons, we conclude the district court abused its discretion in granting defendants' motions for sanctions under Rule 11. Because, however, the district court also awarded defendants fees under § 1927, we conclude the proper course is to reverse and remand to the district court to determine the proper amount of fees and costs to be assessed under

§ 1927 (i.e., "the excess costs ... and attorneys' fees reasonably incurred because of" his unreasonable and vexatious conduct).

* * *

In Appeal No. 05–1129, we reverse the district court's order granting Rule 11 sanctions against Mulhern and in favor of defendants, and remand to the district court for a determination of the proper amount of fees to be assessed against Mulhern pursuant to 28 U.S.C. § 1927.

* * *

X. WEEK TEN: JOINDER OF PARTIES AND CLAIMS

A. COUNTERCLAIMS

Federal Rule of Civil Procedure 13. Counterclaim and Cross-Claim

(a) Compulsory Counterclaim.

(1) In General. A pleading must state as a counterclaim any claim that—at the time of its service—the pleader has against an opposing party if the claim:

(A) arises out of the transaction or occurrence that is the subject matter of the opposing party's claim; and

(B) does not require adding another party over whom the court cannot acquire jurisdiction.

(2) Exceptions. The pleader need not state the claim if:

(A) when the action was commenced, the claim was the subject of another pending action; or

(B) the opposing party sued on its claim by attachment or other process that did not establish personal jurisdiction over the pleader on that claim, and the pleader does not assert any counterclaim under this rule.

(b) Permissive Counterclaim. A pleading may state as a counterclaim against an opposing party any claim that is not compulsory.

(c) Relief Sought in a Counterclaim. A counterclaim need not diminish or defeat the recovery sought by the opposing party. It may request relief that exceeds in amount or differs in kind from the relief sought by the opposing party.

(d) Counterclaim Against the United States. These rules do not expand the right to assert a counterclaim—or to claim a credit—against the United States or a United States officer or agency.

(e) Counterclaim Maturing or Acquired After Pleading. The court may permit a party to file a supplemental pleading asserting a counterclaim that matured or was acquired by the party after serving an earlier pleading.

(f) Abrogated.

(g) Crossclaim Against a Coparty. A pleading may state as a crossclaim any claim by one party against a coparty if the claim arises out of the transaction or occurrence that is the subject matter of the original action or of a counterclaim, or if the claim relates to any property that is the subject matter of the original action. The crossclaim may include a claim that the coparty is or may be liable to the crossclaimant for all or part of a claim asserted in the action against the crossclaimant.

(h) Joining Additional Parties. Rules 19 and 20 govern the addition of a person as a party to a counterclaim or crossclaim.

(i) Separate Trials; Separate Judgments. If the court orders separate trials under Rule 42(b), it may enter judgment on a counterclaim or cross-claim under Rule 54(b) when it has jurisdiction to do so, even if the opposing party's claims have been dismissed or otherwise resolved.

* * *

FEDERAL RULE OF CIVIL PROCEDURE 14.   THIRD–PARTY PRACTICE

(a) When a Defending Party May Bring in a Third Party.

(1) Timing of the Summons and Complaint. A defending party may, as third-party plaintiff, serve a summons and complaint on a nonparty who is or may be liable to it for all or part of the claim against it. But the third-party plaintiff must, by motion, obtain the court's leave if it files the third-party complaint more than 14 days after serving its original answer.

(2) Third–Party Defendant's Claims and Defenses. The person served with the summons and third-party complaint—the "third-party defendant"

(A) must assert any defense against the third-party plaintiff's claim under Rule 12;

(B) must assert any counterclaim against the third-party plaintiff under Rule 13(a), and may assert any counterclaim against the third-party plaintiff under Rule 13(b) or any crossclaim against another third-party defendant under Rule 13(g);

(C) may assert against the plaintiff any defense that the third-party plaintiff has to the plaintiff's claim; and

(D) may also assert against the plaintiff any claim arising out of the transaction or occurrence that is the subject matter of the plaintiff's claim against the third-party plaintiff.

(3) Plaintiff's Claims Against a Third–Party Defendant. The plaintiff may assert against the third-party defendant any claim arising out of the transaction or occurrence that is the subject matter of the plaintiff's claim against the third-party plaintiff. The third-party defendant must then assert any defense under Rule 12 and any counterclaim under Rule 13(a), and may assert any counterclaim under Rule 13(b) or any crossclaim under Rule 13(g).

(4) Motion to Strike, Sever, or Try Separately. Any party may move to strike the third-party claim, to sever it, or to try it separately.

(5) Third–Party Defendant's Claim Against a Nonparty. A third-party defendant may proceed under this rule against a nonparty who is or may be liable to the third-party defendant for all or part of any claim against it.

(6) Third–Party Complaint *In Rem*. If it is within the admiralty or maritime jurisdiction, a third-party complaint may be in rem. In that event, a reference in this rule to the "summons" includes the warrant of arrest, and a reference to the defendant or third-party plaintiff includes, when appropriate, a person who asserts a right under Supplemental Rule C(6)(a)(i) in the property arrested.

(b) When a Plaintiff May Bring in a Third Party. When a claim is asserted against a plaintiff, the plaintiff may bring in a third party if this rule would allow a defendant to do so.

(c) Admiralty or Maritime Claim.

(1) Scope of Impleader. If a plaintiff asserts an admiralty or maritime claim under Rule 9(h), the defendant or a person who asserts a right under Supplemental Rule C(6)(a)(i) may, as a third-party plaintiff, bring in a third-party defendant who may be wholly or partly liable—either to the plaintiff or to the third-party plaintiff—for remedy over, contribution, or otherwise on account of the same transaction, occurrence, or series of transactions or occurrences.

(2) Defending Against a Demand for Judgment for the Plaintiff. The third-party plaintiff may demand judgment in the plaintiff's favor against the third-party defendant. In that event, the third-party defendant must defend under Rule 12 against the plaintiff's claim as well as the third-party plaintiff's claim; and the action proceeds as if the plaintiff had sued both the third-party defendant and the third-party plaintiff.

* * *

JONES v. FORD MOTOR CREDIT COMPANY

358 F.3d 205 (2d Cir. 2004)

JON O. NEWMAN, CIRCUIT JUDGE.

This appeal concerns the availability of subject matter jurisdiction for permissive counterclaims. It also demonstrates the normal utility of early decision of a motion for class certification. Defendant–Appellant Ford Motor Credit Company ("Ford Credit") appeals from the June 14, 2002, judgment of the United States District Court for the Southern District of New York (Lawrence M. McKenna, District Judge) dismissing for lack of jurisdiction its permissive counterclaims against three of the four Plaintiffs–Appellees and its conditional counterclaims against members of the putative class that the Plaintiffs–Appellees seek to certify. We conclude that supplemental jurisdiction authorized by 28 U.S.C. § 1367 may be available for the permissive counterclaims, but that the District Court's discretion under subsection 1367(c) should not be exercised in this case until a ruling on the Plaintiffs' motion for class certification. We therefore vacate and remand.

Background

Plaintiffs–Appellees Joyce Jones, Martha L. Edwards, Lou Cooper, and Vincent E. Jackson ("Plaintiffs"), individually and as class representatives, sued Ford Credit alleging racial discrimination under the Equal Credit Opportunity Act ("ECOA"), 15 U.S.C. § 1691 et seq. (2003). They had purchased Ford vehicles under Ford Credit's financing plan. They alleged that the financing plan discriminated against African–Americans. Although the financing rate was primarily based on objective criteria, Ford Credit permitted its dealers to mark up the rate, using subjective criteria to assess non-risk charges. The Plaintiffs alleged that the mark-up policy penalized African–American customers with higher rates than those imposed on similarly situated Caucasian customers.

In its Answer, Ford Credit denied the charges of racial discrimination and also asserted state-law counterclaims against Jones, Edwards, and Cooper for the amounts of their unpaid car loans. Ford Credit alleged that Jones was in default on her obligations under her contract for the purchase of a 1995 Ford Windstar, and that Edwards and Cooper were in default on payments for their joint purchase of a 1995 Mercury Cougar. Additionally, in the event that a class was certified, Ford Credit asserted conditional counterclaims against any member of that class who was in default on a car loan from Ford Credit. The Plaintiffs moved to dismiss Ford Credit's counterclaims for lack of subject matter jurisdiction, Fed. R. Civ. P. 12(b)(1), lack of personal jurisdiction, Fed. R. Civ. P. 12(b)(2), improper venue, Fed. R. Civ. P. 12(b)(3), and failure to state a claim upon which relief could be granted, Fed. R. Civ. P. 12(b)(6).

The District Court granted the Plaintiffs' motion and dismissed Ford Credit's counterclaims, summarizing its reasons for doing so as follows: "[D]efendant's counterclaims do not meet the standard for compulsory counterclaims[, and] ... pursuant to § 1367(c)(4), ... there are compelling reasons to decline to exercise jurisdiction over the counterclaims."

In reaching these conclusions, Judge McKenna acknowledged some uncertainty. After determining that the counterclaims were permissive, he expressed doubt as to the jurisdictional consequence of that determination. On the one hand, he believed, as the Plaintiffs maintain, that permissive counterclaims must be dismissed if they lack an independent basis of federal jurisdiction. On the other hand, he acknowledged, that "there [was] some authority to suggest that ... the court should determine, based on the particular circumstances of the case, whether it ha[d] authority to exercise supplemental jurisdiction under § 1367(a)" over a counterclaim, regardless of whether it was compulsory or permissive.

To resolve his uncertainty, Judge McKenna initially ruled that the counterclaims, being permissive, "must be dismissed for lack of an independent basis of federal jurisdiction." He then ruled that, if he was wrong and if supplemental jurisdiction under section 1367 was available, he would still dismiss the counterclaims in the exercise of the discretion subsection 1367(c) gives district courts. Without explicitly stating on which of the four subdivisions of subsection 1367(c) he relied, Judge McKenna gave the following reasons for declining to exercise supplemental jurisdiction:

> [1] The claims and counterclaims arise out of the same occurrence only in the loosest terms.... There does not exist a logical relationship between the essential facts [to be proven] in the claim and those of the counterclaims.

> [2] [A]llowing defendant's counterclaims to proceed in this forum might undermine the ECOA enforcement scheme by discouraging plaintiffs from bringing ECOA claims due to the fear of counterclaims.

> [3] [T]he interests of judicial economy will not be served by joining the claim and counterclaims in one suit [because of] what would most likely be a tremendous number of separate collection actions, each based on facts specific to the individual plaintiffs involved.

Judge McKenna stated his belief that it would be "unfair and inexpedient" to require absent class members who resided outside of New York to litigate their debt collection actions in the Southern District of New York and that there was no good reason to litigate the debt collection actions in a federal court.

On March 27, 2003, the District Court entered judgment pursuant to Fed. R. Civ. P. 54(b) in favor of the Plaintiffs, dismissing Ford Credit's counterclaims without prejudice. Ford Credit appeals from this decision.

Discussion

I. Are Ford Credit's Counterclaims Permissive?

Fed. R. Civ. P. 13(a) defines a compulsory counterclaim as:

> any claim which at the time of serving the pleading the pleader has against any opposing party, if it arises out of the transaction or occurrence that is the subject matter of the opposing party's claim and does not require for its adjudication the presence of third parties of whom the court cannot obtain jurisdiction.

Such counterclaims are compulsory in the sense that if they are not raised, they are forfeited. Fed. R. Civ. P. 13(b) defines a permissive counterclaim as "any claim against an opposing party not arising out of the transaction or occurrence that is the subject matter of the opposing party's claim."

Whether a counterclaim is compulsory or permissive turns on whether the counterclaim "arises out of the transaction or occurrence that is the subject matter of the opposing party's claim," and this Circuit has long considered this standard met when there is a "logical relationship" between the counterclaim and the main claim.[1] Although the "logical relationship" test does not require "an absolute identity of factual backgrounds," the " 'essential facts of the claims [must be] so logically connected that considerations of judicial economy and fairness dictate that all the issues be resolved in one lawsuit.' "

We agree with the District Court that the debt collection counterclaims were permissive rather than compulsory. The Plaintiffs' ECOA claim centers on Ford Credit's mark-up policy, based on subjective factors, which allegedly resulted in higher finance charges on their purchase contracts than on those of similarly situated White customers. Ford Credit's debt collection counterclaims are related to those purchase contracts, but not to any particular clause or rate. Rather, the debt collection counterclaims concern the individual Plaintiffs' non-payment after the contract price was set. Thus, the relationship between the counterclaims and the ECOA claim is "logical" only in the sense that the sale, allegedly on discriminatory credit terms, was the "but for" cause of the non-payment. That is not the sort of relationship contemplated by our case law on compulsory counterclaims. The essential facts for proving the counterclaims and the ECOA claim are not so closely related that resolving both sets of issues in one lawsuit would yield judicial efficiency. Indeed, Ford Credit does not even challenge the ruling that its counterclaims are permissive.

II. Is There Jurisdiction over the Permissive Counterclaims?

For several decades federal courts have asserted that permissive counterclaims require an independent basis of jurisdiction, *i.e.,* that the counterclaim must be maintainable in a federal district court on some jurisdictional basis that would have sufficed had it been brought in a separate action. The origin of this proposition, the questioning of it before the statutory authorization of supplemental jurisdiction in section 1367, and the impact of that provision upon the proposition all merit careful consideration.

(A) *Origin of the independent basis doctrine.* The first suggestion of the requirement of an independent basis for permissive counterclaims is believed to have appeared in a case involving former Equity Rule 30. That rule distinguished in its two parts between what we would now call compulsory counterclaims "arising out of the transaction which is the subject matter of the suit" and what we would now call permissive counterclaims "which might be the subject of an independent suit in equity." In *Moore,* the Supreme Court ruled that the counterclaim in that case bore a sufficient relation to the underlying transaction under the first

---

1. The phrase "logical relationship," in the context of counterclaims, was first used by the Supreme Court in *Moore v. New York Cotton Exchange,* 270 U.S. 593 (1926). Referring to a counterclaim "arising out of the transaction which is the subject matter of the suit," as stated in former Equity Rule 30, the Court explained:

"Transaction" is a word of flexible meaning. It may comprehend a series of many occurrences, depending not so much upon the immediateness of their connection as upon their logical relationship.

part of the equity rule to be properly within federal jurisdiction and explicitly declined to "consider the point that, under the second branch [of the rule], federal jurisdiction independent of the original bill must appear."

By 1944, our Court somewhat tentatively observed that "[i]t seems to be accepted that a permissive counterclaim ... is not ancillary and requires independent grounds of jurisdiction." We stated the proposition more forcefully two years later, although our statement, like most of the language in the early cases concerning the proposition, was dictum.

Our first holding that independent jurisdiction is required for a permissive counterclaim occurred in 1968. Six years later, the Supreme Court stated, "*If* a counterclaim is compulsory, the federal court will have ancillary jurisdiction over it even though ordinarily it would be a matter for a state court," apparently implying that ancillary jurisdiction is not available for a permissive counterclaim.

Notably absent from this evolution of the case law is a reasoned explanation of why independent jurisdiction should be needed for permissive counterclaims. One early decision hinted at a reason by suggesting that the then restrictive rules concerning joinder of claims were applicable whether the claims were sought to be added by a plaintiff or a defendant. Likely also influencing the emergence of the doctrine was concern that, because under Rule 13 all counterclaims that are not compulsory are permissive, requiring independent jurisdiction was necessary to prevent federal court adjudication of every conceivable non-compulsory counterclaim that a defendant might happen to have against a plaintiff, some of which might be totally inappropriate for federal jurisdiction. A wife's federal law suit against her husband for a declaration of rights as a joint author, for example, ought not to be vehicle for his counterclaim seeking a divorce. Perhaps lurking beneath the surface of the casual statements about an independent jurisdiction requirement was apprehension that some counterclaims lacking such a basis would extend the lawsuit beyond Article III's limiting scope of "cases and controversies."

(B) *Questioning the doctrine prior to section 1367.* The first challenge to the independent jurisdiction requirement appeared in Professor Green's article in 1953. He mounted a powerful argument against the doctrine, demonstrating how it emerged from unreasoned dicta into unexplained holdings and why it was an unwarranted deviation from the general principle that "[t]wo court actions should not be encouraged where one will do." He particularly noted the incursion on the doctrine, well established even in 1953 when he wrote, that permitted some set-offs to be interposed against a plaintiff's claim in the absence of independent jurisdiction. Professor Green questioned why a defendant who can present evidence of a set-off that reduces a plaintiff's judgment to zero should not be able to obtain a counterclaim judgment to which his evidence would entitle him in a separate action.

In 1970, Judge Friendly, the acknowledged jurisdictional scholar of our Court, changed his mind about the independent jurisdiction doctrine and "reject[ed] the conventional learning." Judge Friendly noted Professor Green's persuasiveness: "The reasons why the conventional view is wrong are set out in detail in [Professor Green's article], and nothing would be gained by repetition."

In 1984, the Third Circuit, in a thoughtful opinion by Judge Becker, rejected the view that independent jurisdiction is required for all permissive counterclaims. Considering whether jurisdiction was available for a set-off, Judge Becker declined to uphold jurisdiction based on the previously recognized set-off exception to the independent jurisdiction requirement,[3] and instead argued broadly for ancillary jurisdiction, with some exceptions,[4] over set-offs and permissive counterclaims that satisfy the test of sharing a "common nucleus of operative fact," *United Mine Workers v. Gibbs,* with the plaintiff's underlying claim. "We conclude that the determination that a counterclaim is permissive within the meaning of Rule 13 is not dispositive of the constitutional question whether there is federal jurisdiction over the counterclaim."

(C) *The impact of section 1367.* The judge-made doctrine of ancillary jurisdiction, which had been invoked to provide a jurisdictional basis for compulsory counterclaims, was given statutory undergirding when Congress added section 1367 to Title 28 in 1990. The newly labeled "supplemental" jurisdiction explicitly extended federal courts' authority to "all other claims" in a civil action "so related to claims in the action within [the district court's] original jurisdiction that they form part of the same case or controversy under Article III of the United States Constitution." 28 U.S.C. § 1367(a).

The explicit extension to the limit of Article III of a federal court's jurisdiction over "all other claims" sought to be litigated with an underlying claim within federal jurisdiction recast the jurisdictional basis of permissive counterclaims into constitutional terms.[5] After section 1367, it

---

3. The set-off exception provides that "[w]here the permissive counterclaim is in the nature of a set-off interposed merely to defeat or reduce the opposing party's claim and does not seek affirmative relief, no independent jurisdictional grounds are required." As the court, the "defensive set-off exception does not fit squarely within the analytic framework set forth" in *United Mine Workers v. Gibbs,* because "under the exception, all defensive set-offs, whether or not they satisfy the *Gibbs* test, are within the ancillary jurisdiction of the court."

4. Anticipating considerations that would later be codified in 28 U.S.C. § 1367, Judge Becker suggested that a district court should decline to exercise ancillary jurisdiction over a defendant's claims where the exercise of jurisdiction would violate some federal policy limiting jurisdiction and be an inappropriate exercise of a district court's discretion, taking into account such factors as "fairness to the litigants, judicial economy, and the interests of federalism."

5. There is some doubt as to whether section 1367's expansion of supplemental jurisdiction to its constitutional limits renders the provision's scope broader than was contemplated in *Gibbs.* The text of subsection 1367(a) unambiguously extends jurisdiction to the limits of Article III, and the provision's legislative history indicates that Congress viewed the *Gibbs* "common nucleus" test as delineating those constitutional limits. Several commentators have suggested, however, that the extent of constitutional jurisdiction is broader than the *Gibbs* test, as Article III may not require a particular factual relationship between joined claims or counterclaims and federal claims that provide the basis for jurisdiction.

is no longer sufficient for courts to assert, without any reason other than dicta or even holdings from the era of judge-created ancillary jurisdiction, that permissive counterclaims require independent jurisdiction. Rising to the challenge, after enactment of section 1367, in a case strikingly similar to our pending case, the Seventh Circuit vacated the dismissal of a permissive counterclaim and remanded for exercise of the discretion contemplated by section 1367. As Judge Easterbrook stated, "Now that Congress has codified the supplemental jurisdiction in § 1367(a), courts should use the language of the statute to define the extent of their powers." He viewed section 1367's reach to the constitutional limits of Article III as requiring only "[a] loose factual connection between the claims," a standard that appears to be broader than the *Gibbs* test of "a common nucleus of operative facts," appropriate for permitting joinder of a plaintiff's non-federal claim. [H]e readily found the requisite "loose connection" to exist between the Consumer Leasing Act claim and the debt collection counterclaim.

We share the view that section 1367 has displaced, rather than codified, whatever validity inhered in the earlier view that a permissive counterclaim requires independent jurisdiction (in the sense of federal question or diversity jurisdiction). The issue in this case therefore becomes whether supplemental jurisdiction is available for Ford Credit's counterclaims.

III. Application of Section 1367's Standards for Supplemental Jurisdiction

Whether or not the *Gibbs* "common nucleus" standard provides the outer limit of an Article III "case,"[6] and is therefore a requirement for entertaining a permissive counterclaim that otherwise lacks a jurisdictional basis, the facts of Ford Credit's counterclaims and those of the Plaintiffs' ECOA claims satisfy that standard, even though the relationship is

---

In 1983, Professor Matasar, anticipating section 1367's authorization of supplemental jurisdiction for all claims within an Article III "case or controversy," advocated permitting joinder of all claims, whether those of the plaintiff or the defendant, to the full extent of "the system of rules lawfully adopted to govern procedure in the federal courts." He drew support from Chief Justice Marshall's statement that " '[the judicial] power is capable of acting only when the subject is submitted to [the judicial department], by a party who asserts his rights in the form prescribed by law.' " Professor Matasar would permit jurisdiction over any counterclaim authorized by federal rules, without requiring any factual relationship to the underlying claim.

More recently, Professor Fletcher (now Judge Fletcher) also advocated a broad view of the claims that could be joined in a "case or controversy" under section 1367. Like Professor Matasar, Professor Fletcher urged that the constitutional test of a "case" did not require a factual connection between joined claims, but would be satisfied under either the joinder standards applicable when the Constitution was adopted or modern joinder rules.

Congress's understanding of the extent of Article III is of course not binding as constitutional interpretation, and section 1367's legislative history cannot be read as an independent limit on subsection 1367(a)'s clear extension of jurisdiction to the limits of Article III. Thus, the correct reading of subsection 1367(a)'s reference to "the same case or controversy under Article III" remains unsettled.

6. If the *Gibbs* standard marks the outer limit of an Article III "case," congressional authorization to join counterclaims with a more tenuous connection to the underlying claim would be unconstitutional unless Congress has some authority to expand the constitutional scope of "case."

not such as would make the counterclaims compulsory.[7] The counter-claims and the underlying claim bear a sufficient factual relationship (if one is necessary) to constitute the same "case" within the meaning of Article III and hence of section 1367. Both the ECOA claim and the debt collection claims originate from the Plaintiffs' decisions to purchase Ford cars.

Satisfying the constitutional "case" standard of subsection 1367(a), however, does not end the inquiry a district court is obliged to make with respect to permissive counterclaims. A trial court must consider whether any of the four grounds set out in subsection 1367(c) are present to an extent that would warrant the exercise of discretion to decline assertion of supplemental jurisdiction.[8] Subsection 1367(c) provides:

> The district courts may decline to exercise supplemental jurisdiction over a claim under subsection (a) if—
>
> (1) the claim raises a novel or complex issue of State law,
>
> (2) the claim substantially predominates over the claim or claims over which the district court has original jurisdiction,
>
> (3) the district court has dismissed all claims over which it has original jurisdiction, or
>
> (4) in exceptional circumstances, there are other compelling reasons for declining jurisdiction.

We have indicated that, where at least one of the subsection 1367(c) factors is applicable, a district court should not decline to exercise supplemental jurisdiction unless it also determines that doing so would not promote the values articulated in *Gibbs*: economy, convenience, fairness, and comity.

Clearly the exception set forth in subsection 1367(c)(1) does not apply since Ford Credit's counterclaims do not raise a novel or complex issue of state law, but merely a standard contract question. Nor does subsection 1367(c)(3) apply since the District Court has not dismissed all claims over which it has original jurisdiction. That leaves subsections 1367(c)(2), permitting declination of supplemental jurisdiction where "the [counter-]claim substantially predominates over the claim or claims over which the district court has original jurisdiction," and 1367(c)(4), permitting declination "in exceptional circumstances, [where] there are other compelling reasons for declining jurisdiction." The District Court apparently based its

---

7. We note that the "common nucleus" test of *Gibbs*, expanding the prior test of *Hurn v. Oursler*, was developed to provide some limit upon the state law claims that a *plaintiff* could join with its federal law claims. That rationale does not necessarily apply to a defendant's counter-claims. A plaintiff might be tempted to file an insubstantial federal law claim as an excuse to tie to it one or more state law claims that do not belong in a federal court. There is no corresponding risk that a defendant will decline to file in state court an available state law claim, hoping to be lucky enough to be sued by his adversary on a federal claim so that he can assert a state law counterclaim.

8. Subsection 1367(b), precluding exercise of supplemental jurisdiction under some circum-stances where jurisdiction over the underlying claim is based solely on diversity of citizenship, does not apply here; the Plaintiffs' underlying claim is based on federal question jurisdiction.

decision on subsection 1367(c)(4), since it cited only that subsection in its opinion, but some of the concerns it discussed implicate the substantial predomination analysis of subsection 1367(c)(2) as well.

Judge Easterbrook canvassed the competing considerations bearing on whether the subsection (c)(2) and (c)(4) factors might permit declination of supplemental jurisdiction over collection counterclaims interposed against a claim under a consumer protection statute. Acknowledging a district court's discretion, the Seventh Circuit ultimately remanded because "[a]rguments under § 1367(c) are addressed to the district court's discretion." In *Channell,* however, the class had been certified, class members had been notified, and some had opted out. In our case, a ruling on the class motion has not yet been made.

Whether Ford Credit's counterclaims "predominate[ ]" over the Plaintiffs' claims and whether there are "exceptional circumstances" for declining jurisdiction cannot properly be determined until a decision has been made on the Plaintiffs' motion for class certification. Both the applicability of subsections 1367(c)(2) and (4), and the exercise of a district court's discretion in the event either or both are ruled applicable will be significantly influenced by the existence of a large class as sought by the Plaintiffs. The District Court's conclusions that it would be "unfair and inexpedient" to require out-of-state class members to litigate Ford's state law debt claims in New York, and that allowing the counterclaims might dissuade potential plaintiffs from joining the class, were therefore premature.

Class certification is to be decided "at an early practicable time" after the commencement of a suit. Fed. R. Civ. P. 23(c)(1). That course is especially important in this case. Accordingly, we remand this case with directions to rule on the class certification motion, and then, in light of that ruling, to proceed to determine whether to exercise or decline supplemental jurisdiction.

On remand, the District Court should exercise its discretion pursuant to subsection 1367(c), particularly the caution there expressed concerning use of subsection 1367(c)(4). In order to decline jurisdiction on this basis, the District Court should identify truly compelling circumstances that militate against exercising jurisdiction. Moreover, if the Court certifies the class action, its substantial predomination analysis under subsection 1367(c)(2) should take into account the methods by which the class action might be managed in order to prevent the state law counterclaims from predominating. By bifurcating the litigation, certifying a limited class (perhaps only in-state plaintiffs), or utilizing other management tools, the District Court might be able to structure the litigation in such a way as to prevent the state law claims from predominating over the federal basis of the action, while maintaining the advantages inherent in providing a forum in which all of the litigants' claims can be litigated.

Conclusion

The judgment dismissing Ford Credit's counterclaims is vacated, and the case is remanded for further proceedings consistent with this opinion. No costs.

* * *

B. CROSS–CLAIMS

FEDERAL RULE OF CIVIL PROCEDURE 13(g), (h), (i)

(g) Cross-claim Against a Co-party. A pleading may state as a cross-claim any claim by one party against a co-party if the claim arises out of the transaction or occurrence that is the subject matter of the original action or of a counterclaim, or if the claim relates to any property that is the subject matter of the original action. The cross-claim may include a claim that the co-party is or may be liable to the cross-claimant for all or part of a claim asserted in the action against the cross-claimant.

(h) Joining Additional Parties. Rules 19 and 20 govern the addition of a person as a party to a counterclaim or cross-claim.

(i) Separate Trials; Separate Judgments. If the court orders separate trials under Rule 42(b), it may enter judgment on a counterclaim or cross-claim under Rule 54(b) when it has jurisdiction to do so, even if the opposing party's claims have been dismissed or otherwise resolved.

* * *

FEDERAL RULE OF CIVIL PROCEDURE 18.   JOINDER OF CLAIMS

(a) In General. A party asserting a claim, counterclaim, cross-claim, or third-party claim may join, as independent or alternative claims, as many claims as it has against an opposing party.

(b) Joinder of Contingent Claims. A party may join two claims even though one of them is contingent on the disposition of the other; but the court may grant relief only in accordance with the parties' relative substantive rights. In particular, a plaintiff may state a claim for money and a claim to set aside a conveyance that is fraudulent as to that plaintiff, without first obtaining a judgment for the money.

* * *

FEDERAL RULE OF CIVIL PROCEDURE 20.   PERMISSIVE JOINDER OF PARTIES

(a) Persons Who May Join or Be Joined.

(1) **Plaintiffs.** Persons may join in one action as plaintiffs if:

(A) they assert any right to relief jointly, severally, or in the alternative with respect to or arising out of the same transaction, occurrence, or series of transactions or occurrences; and

(B) any question of law or fact common to all plaintiffs will arise in the action.

(2) Defendants. Persons—as well as a vessel, cargo, or other property subject to admiralty process *in rem*—may be joined in one action as defendants if:

(A) any right to relief is asserted against them jointly, severally, or in the alternative with respect to or arising out of the same transaction, occurrence, or series of transactions or occurrences; and

(B) any question of law or fact common to all defendants will arise in the action.

(3) Extent of Relief. Neither a plaintiff nor a defendant need be interested in obtaining or defending against all the relief demanded. The court may grant judgment to one or more plaintiffs according to their rights, and against one or more defendants according to their liabilities.

(b) Protective Measures. The court may issue orders—including an order for separate trials—to protect a party against embarrassment, delay, expense, or other prejudice that arises from including a person against whom the party asserts no claim and who asserts no claim against the party.

* * *

FEDERAL RULE OF CIVIL PROCEDURE 42.   CONSOLIDATION; SEPARATE TRIALS

(a) Consolidation. If actions before the court involve a common question of law or fact, the court may:

(1) join for hearing or trial any or all matters at issue in the actions;

(2) consolidate the actions; or

(3) issue any other orders to avoid unnecessary cost or delay.

(b) Separate Trials. For convenience, to avoid prejudice, or to expedite and economize, the court may order a separate trial of one or more separate issues, claims, cross-claims, counterclaims, or third-party claims. When ordering a separate trial, the court must preserve any federal right to a jury trial.

* * *

LASA PER L'INDUSTRIA DEL MARMO SOCIETA PER AZIONI OF LASA, ITALY v. ALEXANDER

414 F.2d 143 (6th Cir. 1969)

PHILLIPS, CIRCUIT JUDGE.

It has been said that the doctrine of ancillary jurisdiction providing for joinder of claims in the federal courts is "the child of necessity and the sire of confusion." The confusion in pleadings that can arise out of cross-claims, counterclaims and a third-party complaint, all involving the same construction project, is demonstrated by the present appeal.

The complicated procedural problems with which we are confronted arose out of the building of a new City Hall at Memphis, Tennessee.

The complaint was filed by an Italian corporation which had a contract with a subcontractor to furnish marble for the City Hall. Recovery is sought against the subcontractor, the prime contractor, its surety, and the City of Memphis for a balance alleged to be due for marble and labor.

Filed in the action were a series of counterclaims, cross-claims and a third-party.

Among the pleadings were a cross-claim filed by the defendant subcontractor, Alexander, against the prime contractor, its surety and the City of Memphis; a counterclaim filed by the prime contractor against Alexander; and a third-party complaint filed by Alexander against the architect. The third-party complaint was treated by the District Court as a cross-claim against the architect as was the counterclaim of the prime contractor against Alexander.

Construing Rules 13(g) and 13(h), Fed. R. Civ. P., the District Court dismissed the two cross-claims and the third-party complaint, holding that they do not arise out of the same transaction or occurrence that is the subject matter of the original action or of a counterclaim therein.

We reverse.

In the cross-claim of Alexander which was dismissed by the District Court, Alexander sues all cross-defendants for a balance of $158,061.75 alleged to be due under Alexander's subcontract with the prime contractor. In the second count of the same pleading Alexander sues the prime contractor for $250,000 in actual and punitive damages, averring that the prime contractor failed to prepare properly the concrete base upon which marble pieces were to be affixed and to install correct metal support angles in the concrete base; that the prime contractor required Alexander to work on marble installation in the most inclement cold and rainy weather, contrary to specifications; that the prime contractor terminated Alexander's subcontract without justification and brought in a new subcontractor at a highly inflated price, the cost of which was charged wrongfully to Alexander; and that the prime contractor damaged Alexander's business reputation and publicly blamed Alexander for many ills which were the fault of the prime contractor or the architect.

In its third-party complaint against the architect, treated by the District Court as a cross-claim under Rule 13(h), Alexander sued the architect for actual and punitive damages, alleging that the architect negligently provided improper specifications and insisted that they be followed; negligently failed to require the prime contractor to perform its work properly; wrongfully directed Alexander to install marble in inclement weather; willfully refused to approve Alexander's estimates for work done; influenced the prime contractor to terminate Alexander's subcontract and to bring in a new subcontractor at an inflated price and with preferred treatment through modified specifications; and wrongfully and maliciously injured Alexander's business reputation.

The prime contractor's cross-claim against Alexander, which also was dismissed by the District Court, seeks to hold Alexander liable for unliquidated damages for delays, faulty materials and workmanship and the failure of Alexander generally to conform to specifications. The count of the cross-claim of the prime contractor for indemnity against Alexander in the event of judgment for the plaintiff against the prime contractor was not dismissed.

After the dismissal of these claims there remain in the case now pending in the District Court the amended complaint, the answer and counterclaim of Alexander, the answer and counterclaim of the prime contractor, and the answer of the surety and the cross-claim by the prime contractor against Alexander for indemnity. Trial on these pleadings has been delayed pending disposition of the present appeal.

Under the Federal Rules of Civil Procedure the rights of all parties generally should be adjudicated in one action. Rules 13 and 14 are remedial and are construed liberally. Both Rules 13 and 14 are "intended to avoid circuity of action and to dispose of the entire subject matter arising from one set of facts in one action, thus administering complete and evenhanded justice expeditiously and economically." The aim of these rules "is facilitation not frustration of decisions on the merits."

A decision involving jurisdiction over cross-claims in litigation growing out of a construction project similar in some respects to the issues presented on this appeal, [a Ninth Circuit court] said:

> It is well settled that a grant of jurisdiction over particular subject matter includes the power to adjudicate all matters ancillary to the particular subject matter. * * * Therefore, if either a cross-claim under Rule 13 or a third-party claim under Rule 14 does arise out of the subject matter of the original action and involves the same persons and issues, the claim is ancillary to the original action. In such cases, if the court has jurisdiction to entertain the original action, no independent basis of jurisdiction for the cross-claim or third-party claim need be alleged or proved.

The District Court held that no part of Alexander's cross-claim against the prime contractor, his third-party complaint against the architect or of the prime contractor's cross-claim against Alexander for breach of contract arose out of the transaction or occurrence that is the subject matter of the original action or the two counterclaims. With deference to the well-written opinion of the District Judge, we disagree.

[T]he rule is stated as follows:

It is the theory of the rule that the defendant's right against the third party is merely the outgrowth of the same aggregate or core of facts which is determinative of the plaintiff's claim. In this view, the court which has jurisdiction over the aggregate of facts which constitutes the plaintiff's claim needs no additional ground of jurisdiction to determine the third-party claim which comprises the same core of facts. It is in this sense that the court is said to have ancillary jurisdiction over the third-party claim.

In *Moore v. N.Y. Cotton Exchange*, the Supreme Court construed the words "arising out of the transaction which is the subject matter of the suit" in Equity Rule 30, precursor of Rule 13. The Court said:

> "Transaction" is a word of flexible meaning. It may comprehend a series of many occurrences, depending not so much upon the immediateness of their connection as upon their logical relationship.

Our reading of the pleadings in this case convinces us that there is a "logical relationship" between the cross-claims (including the third party complaint against the architect) and the "transaction or occurrence" that is the subject matter of the complaint and the two pending counterclaims. Although different subcontracts are involved, along with the prime contract and specifications, all relate to the same project and to problems arising out of the marble used in the erection of the Memphis City Hall. The recurring question presented by the various pleadings is directed to the principal issue of who is responsible for the marble problems which arose on this job. Blame is sought to be placed upon plaintiff as furnisher of the marble, upon Alexander as subcontractor, upon the prime contractor and upon the architect. Many of the same or closely related factual and legal issues necessarily will be presented under the complaint, counterclaims and cross-claims in the resolution of these issues. It seems apparent that some of the same evidence will be required in the hearing on the cross-claims and in the hearing or hearings with respect to the complaint and the two pending counterclaims.

We understand it to be the purpose of Rule 13 and the related rules that all such matters may be tried and determined in one action and to make it possible for the parties to avoid multiplicity of litigation. The intent of the rules is that all issues be resolved in one action, with all parties before one court, complex though the action may be.

In support of the decision of the District Court it is argued that, since a jury trial has been demanded, the complications and confusions of the cross-claims are such that it would be impossible to try the numerous issues before the jury in an orderly manner. The short answer to this contention is that the District Judge is authorized by Rule 42(b) to order separate trials on any cross-claim, counterclaim, other claim or issues. If on the trial of this case the District Court concludes that separate trials on one or more of the counterclaims, cross-claims or issues would be conducive to expedition and economy, Rule 42(b) provides a practical solution to this problem.

Reversed and remanded for further proceedings not inconsistent with this opinion.

McAllister, Senior Circuit Judge (dissenting).

These cases, which hereafter will be generally referred to as a single case, involve a subcontractor's suit for a balance due on a contract against defendant subcontractor, as well as against the principal contractor, a surety for performance and payment of bills for labor and materials, and the City which had entered into the contract with the principal contractor. Counterclaims were filed against the plaintiff by the defendant subcontractor, as well as by the principal contractor, the surety, and the City. After filing its counterclaim against the plaintiff, the defendant subcontractor filed a cross-claim against the principal contractor, the surety, and the City. Defendant subcontractor also filed a third-party claim against the architect supervising the work done under the contract between the principal contractor and the City. The only issue in the case depends upon whether the defendant subcontractor was entitled to file a cross-claim against the principal contractor, the surety, and the City, and the third party claim against the architect, by virtue of Rule 13(g), (h), and Rule 20 of the Federal Rules of Civil Procedure.

The District Court held that the subcontractor was not entitled to file such cross-claim and third-party claim under the above-mentioned Rules, and, on motion, dismissed them. The court's order of dismissal of the defendant contractor's cross-claim against the principal contractor, and the third-party claim against the architect gives rise to this controversy.

From the foregoing recital, it is evident that this case involves solely a question of pleading. The facts in more comprehensive detail are as follows: The City of Memphis built a City Hall. Southern Builders, Inc. was the principal or prime contractor with the City for this project; and it furnished to the City a statutory bond for performance and payment of labor and materials. The surety in this bond was the Continental Casualty Company.

Southern Builders, Inc., the above-named contractor for the building of the City Hall, then entered into a contract with Alexander Marble and Tile Company, under which Alexander was to supply all marble and anchoring devices, and install the marble used in the building.

Alexander, the subcontractor, then entered into a contract with plaintiff-appellee, LASA Per L'Industria Del Marmo Societa Per Azioni of Lasa, Italy, in which LASA agreed to supply to Alexander all of the marble specified at a certain contract price.

LASA, alleging that the marble had been supplied as agreed, and that there was an unpaid balance of $127,240.80, filed a complaint against Alexander, with whom it had contracted to deliver the marble, Southern Builders, the principal contractor, Continental Casualty Company, the surety for the performance and payment of all labor and materials, and the City of Memphis.

To the original complaint of LASA, Alexander filed an answer and counterclaim in which it contended that LASA had failed to ship the marble as agreed; that it had threatened to cease shipments; and that, under duress, the price had been greatly increased; that much of the marble arrived late, was broken, or of the wrong type, and that LASA had failed to ship all of the marble it was obligated to furnish. Alexander, by this counterclaim, sued LASA for overpayment of the contract price and for damages in the amount of $350,000 for failure to ship the marble as agreed.

Furthermore, to the original complaint of LASA, the principal contractor, Southern Builders, and the surety for performance, Continental Casualty, filed answers and a counterclaim. They averred that Southern Builders was obligated to pay just and valid claims for labor and materials only, and that LASA had no such claims; that nothing was owed LASA for marble delivered and installed on the job. They denied that LASA had shipped the marble as agreed, and, by its counterclaim, Southern Builders sued LASA for its failure to ship the marble as agreed with the subcontractor, Alexander. Up to this point no question is raised with regard to the right of LASA to commence suit; with regard to the right of Alexander to file an answer and counterclaim against LASA; or with regard to the right of Southern Builders and Continental Casualty to file answers; and for Southern Builders to file its counterclaim against LASA for damages for failure to deliver the marble as it had agreed with Alexander.

Now comes the pleading that gives rise to the controversy in this suit. After Alexander had filed its answer and counterclaim against LASA, and Southern Builders and Continental Casualty had filed answers, and Southern Builders had filed its counterclaim against LASA, Alexander filed a cross-claim against Southern Builders, Continental Casualty, and the City of Memphis. Further, Alexander filed a cross-claim against A. L. Aydelott and Associates, and against Aydelott individually. Aydelott was the architect for the City Hall. Upon the filing of Alexander's cross-claim against Southern Builders, Continental Casualty, and the City of Memphis, and its cross-claim against Aydelott, Southern Builders and Aydelott filed motions to dismiss such cross-claims; and the District Court, as heretofore stated, after due consideration, dismissed them; and, from the order of dismissal, Alexander appeals.

In one count of its cross-claim against Southern Builders, Continental Casualty, and the City of Memphis, Alexander, claiming damages in the amount of $158,061.75, alleged that Southern Builders, upon the insistence of the architect, A. L. Aydelott, wrongfully hindered Alexander in the performance of the subcontract by failing properly to prepare the concrete base for the marble; by failing to install metal support angles; by insisting that Alexander work in inclement weather; by further insisting that Alexander install the marble in accordance with Aydelott's improper specifications; and by wrongfully refusing to pay over funds due to Alexander for work performed. Alexander further alleged, in a second count in his cross-claim, that Southern Builders, under the insistence of

Aydelott, and, necessarily cooperating with him, wrongfully terminated the subcontract, wrongfully forced Alexander off the job altogether; brought in another subcontractor who was allowed to finish the job not in accordance with the specifications and at an inflated price, all of which was wrongfully charged to the account of Alexander. In the same count in its cross-claim against Southern Builders, Alexander alleged that Southern Builders and Aydelott wrongfully injured the business reputation of Alexander by publicly blaming Alexander for many ills not its fault, and which were the fault of Southern Builders and Aydelott. In this count, Alexander asked for an additional amount of $250,000 for punitive damages, or a total, claimed in its cross-claim, of $408,061.75 with interest and costs.

Alexander further proceeded to file a third-party complaint-a cross-claim, as above mentioned, against the architect, A. L. Aydelott, claiming that Aydelott wrongfully and illegally induced Southern Builders to breach its contract with Alexander and, for such allegedly wrongful conduct, claimed from Aydelott treble damages in the amount of $750,000.

The issue in this case is whether the District Court was in error in dismissing Alexander's cross-claim against Southern Builders, and in dismissing its cross-claim against Aydelott.

The controlling law consists of the governing provisions of the Federal Rules of Civil Procedure as to joinder of parties, and the rules here applicable are: Rule 13(g) and (h).

As stated in MOORE'S FEDERAL PRACTICE:

> Hereafter, for the purpose of determining who must or may be joined as additional parties to a counterclaim or cross-claim, the party pleading the claim is to be regarded as plaintiff, and the additional parties as plaintiffs or defendants as the case may be, and amended Rules 19 and 20 are to be applied in the usual fashion.

With regard to Rule 20, it is to be emphasized that all persons may be joined in one action as defendants if there is asserted against them any right to relief arising out of the same transaction, "and if any question of law or fact common to all defendants will arise in the action." It is not enough then, in order to have the right to file cross-claims, that they arise out of the same transaction or occurrence, but there also must be a question of law or fact common to all defendants. [T]he court indicated that both requirements must be met—the common question and the requirements that the case arise out of the same transaction, occurrence, or series of transactions or occurrences. As the court stated:

> Rule 20, Fed. Rules Civil Procedure, permits joinder of plaintiffs or defendants whenever there is a common question of law or fact and the claims involved arise out of a single transaction, occurrence, or series of transactions or occurrences.

> Since joinder of parties is dependent on the concepts of "common question of law or fact" and "same transaction," these tests must

both be met in order for us to hold, as we do, that there is proper joinder of defendants in the case at bar.

The questions of fact or law involved in the original suit filed by LASA, and the counterclaim for overpayment filed by Alexander, are totally different from Alexander's claim against Southern Builders, claiming damages on the ground that Southern Builders wrongfully prevented and obstructed Alexander from performing its duties; wrongfully forced Alexander off the job; wrongfully brought in an outside subcontractor to complete the job at a highly inflated price, all of which was wrongfully and illegally charged to the account of Alexander—as well as Alexander's allegation in its same cross-claim against Southern Builders charging that Southern Builders and Aydelott entered upon a course of action wrongfully injuring the business reputation of Alexander for which it claimed $250,000 in punitive damages.

Alexander's cross-claim against Aydelott for treble damages in the amount of $750,000 for wrongfully and maliciously damaging Alexander's business reputation by abuse, harassment and public blame, and wrongfully and illegally inducing and procuring by inducement, persuasion or insistence, the breach and violation of Alexander's contract with Southern Builders, was an action in tort.

The suit brought by LASA was an action in contract to recover a balance due. The cross-claim of Alexander against Southern Builders constituted an action in tort.

Neither of these two cross-claims in tort, filed by Alexander, arises out of the transaction or occurrence that is the subject matter of the original action, or counterclaim thereto, as will hereafter more fully appear.

Alexander's cross-claim against Southern Builders does not arise out of the transaction or occurrence that is the subject matter of the original action-it does not arise out of the transaction or occurrence upon which LASA's suit is based, as is required by Rule 13(g); nor does it arise out of "a counterclaim therein"—that is, out of a counterclaim to LASA's suit. As the District Court properly held: "Rule 13(g) refers to counterclaims in the original action."

In like manner, Alexander's cross-claim against Aydelott does not arise out of the transaction or occurrence that is the subject matter of the original action—it does not arise out of the transaction or occurrence upon which LASA's suit is based. Nor does it arise out of "a counter-claim therein"—that is, out of a counterclaim in LASA's suit.

Where a surety company filed suit against a defendant on completion bonds, and defendant filed a counterclaim for damage to his reputation and credit allegedly resulting from malicious threats of public disgrace, financial ruin, and bankruptcy, and other similar allegations, the District Court held that the counterclaim was not based on the transaction or occurrence on which the principal suit was based, but upon subsequent events, and under Rule 13(a) and (b) dismissed the counterclaim, saying: "It is the opinion of the court that the counterclaim does not arise out of the transactions or occurrences upon which plaintiff's suit is based, but is bottomed entirely upon subsequent events and actions."

With regard to ancillary jurisdiction and joinder of claims, especially with respect to cross-claims, under Rule 13(g), the following test is applicable:

> A cross-claim which arises out of the transaction or occurrence that is the subject matter of the original action is within the ancillary jurisdiction of courts because it involves facts that are already subject to the jurisdiction of the court. * * *

> If the same issues of fact would determine both claims, they arise out of the same transaction or occurrence, but if the proof of one claim would have no connection with the proof of the other, the claims do not arise out of the same transaction or occurrence.

The foregoing test is accepted by Alexander which, in its brief filed in this court, submits:

> The question presented as to the court's jurisdiction of the cross-claims is "Do they arise out of the same transaction or occurrence which is the subject matter of the original claim, or of the counter-claims heretofore filed in this court." * * * Cross-claimants (Alexander) contend that their cross-claims clearly bear not only the requisite "logical relationship" with the original claim and counterclaims, but that they are intimately related, including absolute identity of the many factual and legal issues which must necessarily be presented at a hearing of these matters.

On the contrary, we are of the opinion that the cross-claims are not related to the original claim and the counterclaims, and that there is no identity of the many factual issues involved in the original claim and counterclaims, and in the cross-claims.

The proofs in LASA's suit and in Alexander's and Southern Builders' counterclaims against LASA would be entirely different from the proofs in Alexander's cross-claim against Southern Builders and its cross-claim against Aydelott.

The proofs in LASA's suit would consist of evidence showing a balance due on the contract to deliver marble. The proofs in Alexander's counterclaims and Southern Builders' counterclaims against LASA would consist of evidence showing a breach of LASA's contract to deliver the marble.

But the proof in Alexander's cross-claim against Southern Builders and Alexander's cross-claim against Aydelott would consist of entirely different evidence than that introduced in the original suit for recovery on the contract to deliver marble, and on the counterclaims for breach of that contract.

The proofs in Alexander's cross-claim against Southern Builders and Aydelott would consist of evidence of repeated, malicious, wrongful conduct in terminating Alexander's contract, and in forcing Alexander off the job and maliciously ruining its business reputation by abuse, harassment, and public blame.

The proofs in Alexander's cross-claim against Aydelott would consist only of evidence that Aydelott wrongfully and maliciously ruined Alexander's business reputation.

What is the controlling issue in the trial of LASA against Alexander and Southern Builders? Only whether Alexander or LASA breached the contract between them.

What is the question to be decided with regard to Alexander's cross-claims against Southern Builders and Aydelott? Only whether or not such cross-claims arise out of the same transaction or occurrence that is the subject matter of the original action or of the counterclaims filed therein.

The same issues of fact would not determine both the original action and Alexander's cross-claims. The cross-claims, therefore, do not arise out of the transaction or occurrence which is the subject matter of the original claim, or out of the counterclaims therein.

Considering appellant Alexander's claim that not only its cross-claim and its third-party claim include absolute identity of the many factual issues in the original claim of LASA and the counterclaims filed therein—a contention which we have hereinbefore found erroneous—we proceed to Alexander's argument that the cross-claim and the third-party claim against Southern Builders and Aydelott include absolute identity of the many legal issues in the original claim by LASA and the counterclaims filed therein.

The legal issue in the original claim filed by LASA is: Whether the contract is valid, and whether, under the contract, there is a balance due. The counterclaims of Alexander and Southern Builders are based on breach of contract by LASA. The only issue with regard to LASA's obligations under its agreement with Alexander and with regard to its breach of the agreement set forth in the counterclaims is determinable by the law of contract.

The only legal issue in Alexander's cross-claim against Southern Builders and its third-party claim against the architect, Aydelott, is whether Southern Builders and Aydelott are guilty of malicious, wrongful conduct which resulted in damages to Alexander. This issue is determinable by the law of torts.

There is, therefore, no identity of legal issues in the original claims of LASA and Alexander's and Southern Builders' counterclaims—all founded on contract and breach of contract—and Alexander's cross-claim against Southern Builders and its third-party claim against Aydelott—all founded in tort.

It seems clear then that, in this case, the proof of claim in tort would have no connection with the proof of claim in contract and that, consequently, the two different claims do not arise out of the same transaction or occurrence.

The only claims in this case that arise out of the transaction or occurrence that is the subject matter of the original action for balance due on a contract are the counterclaims filed against LASA by Alexander and Southern Builders, claiming breach of that contract-not Alexander's two cross-claims against Southern Builders and Aydelott for their claimed deliberately malicious, tortious, and damaging conduct, for which Alexander claimed damages of several hundred thousand dollars.

In accordance with the foregoing, in my opinion, the judgments of the District Court should be affirmed in accordance with the opinion of Chief Judge Bailey Brown.

* * *

C. PERSONS NEEDED FOR A JUST ADJUDICATION

REVIEW FEDERAL RULE OF CIVIL PROCEDURE 12(b)(7)

* * *

FEDERAL RULE OF CIVIL PROCEDURE 19. REQUIRED JOINDER OF PARTIES

(a) Persons Required to Be Joined if Feasible.

   (1) Required Party. A person who is subject to service of process and whose joinder will not deprive the court of subject-matter jurisdiction must be joined as a party if:

   (A) in that person's absence, the court cannot accord complete relief among existing parties; or

   (B) that person claims an interest relating to the subject of the action and is so situated that disposing of the action in the person's absence may:

   (i) as a practical matter impair or impede the person's ability to protect the interest; or

   (ii) leave an existing party subject to a substantial risk of incurring double, multiple, or otherwise inconsistent obligations because of the interest.

   (2) Joinder by Court Order. If a person has not been joined as required, the court must order that the person be made a party. A person who refuses to join as a plaintiff may be made either a defendant or, in a proper case, an involuntary plaintiff.

   (3) Venue. If a joined party objects to venue and the joinder would make venue improper, the court must dismiss that party.

(b) When Joinder Is Not Feasible. If a person who is required to be joined if feasible cannot be joined, the court must determine whether, in equity and good conscience, the action should proceed among the existing parties or should be dismissed. The factors for the court to consider include:

(1) the extent to which a judgment rendered in the person's absence might prejudice that person or the existing parties;

(2) the extent to which any prejudice could be lessened or avoided by:

(A) protective provisions in the judgment;

(B) shaping the relief; or

(C) other measures;

(3) whether a judgment rendered in the person's absence would be adequate; and

(4) whether the plaintiff would have an adequate remedy if the action were dismissed for nonjoinder.

(c) Pleading the Reasons for Nonjoinder. When asserting a claim for relief, a party must state:

(1) the name, if known, of any person who is required to be joined if feasible but is not joined; and

(2) the reasons for not joining that person.

(d) Exception for Class Actions. This rule is subject to Rule 23.

* * *

THE BANK OF CALIFORNIA v. THE SUPERIOR COURT OF SAN FRANCISCO

16 Cal.2d 516, 106 P.2d 879 (Cal. 1940)

GIBSON, C. J.

This is a petition for a writ of prohibition, to restrain the respondent superior court from proceeding with the trial of an action without bringing in certain parties alleged to be "necessary and indispensable".

Sara M. Boyd, the widow of Colin M. Boyd, died testate in June, 1937, leaving an estate valued at about $225,000. On July 8, 1937, in the superior court in San Francisco, her will was admitted to probate, and petitioner, Bank of California, was appointed executor. The will left individual legacies and bequests amounting to $60,000 to a large number of legatees, including charitable institutions and individuals, some residing in other states and in foreign countries. Petitioner, St. Luke's Hospital, was named residuary legatee and devisee, and thereby received the bulk of the estate.

On October 14, 1937, Bertha M. Smedley, a niece and legatee, brought an action to enforce the provisions of an alleged contract by which decedent agreed to leave her entire estate to the plaintiff. The complaint named as parties defendant the executor and all of the beneficiaries under the will, and prayed for a decree adjudging that plaintiff is, by virtue of the agreement, the owner of the entire estate of the decedent after payment of debts and expenses. It was further prayed that plaintiff's title to the property be quieted; that defendants be ordered to execute deeds to her, and that upon the failure of any defendant to do so the clerk should execute such an instrument.

Summons was served only upon petitioners, the executor and the residuary legatee. No other defendants were served, and none appeared. Petitioners filed separate answers. The action came to trial on November 15, 1939. Immediately upon its opening, petitioners made a motion under section 389 of the Code of Civil Procedure for an order to bring in the other defendants, and to have summons issued and served upon them. The motion was made on the ground that all the other defendants were "necessary and indispensable parties" to the action, and that the court could not proceed without them. The motion was denied by respondent court. Petitioners then applied for a writ of prohibition to restrain the trial until these other parties should be brought in.

In support of their application, petitioners point out that the complaint challenges the right of every legatee and devisee to share in the estate, and prays for an award of the entire property to plaintiff. It is contended that a trial and judgment without the absent defendants would adversely affect the rights of such parties, would result in a multiplicity of suits, and would subject the petitioning executor to inconvenience, expense and the burden of future litigation.

To test the theory of petitioners, it will be necessary to examine briefly the origin and nature of the rules on required or compulsory joinder of parties. We may eliminate, at the outset, the field of permissive joinder of "proper parties", for there is no doubt that the absent defendants are interested in the issues and subject of the action, and could properly be joined. For the same reason, these legatees, if they had not been named as defendants, could no doubt have intervened in the action. These propositions are conceded by all parties, and the precise issue is thus made clear, whether the absent defendants are not only proper parties but "indispensable parties" in the sense that service upon them or their appearance is essential to the jurisdiction of the court to proceed in the action. Prohibition, of course, cannot issue unless the procedural defect of parties is jurisdictional.

At common law, joinder of plaintiffs was compulsory where the parties, under the substantive law, were possessed of joint rights. Joint promisees under a contract, partners, and joint tenants were familiar examples. Equity courts developed another theory of compulsory joinder, to carry out the policy of avoiding piecemeal litigation and multiplicity of suits. Those persons necessary to a complete settlement of the controversy were usually required to be joined, in order that the entire matter might be concluded by a single suit. Obviously, this theory of joinder covered many situations where the substantive rights were not joint, and accordingly joinder would not have been required in an action at law. Generally speaking, the modern rule under the codes carries out the established equity doctrine. Thus, section 389 of the Code of Civil Procedure states: "The court may determine any controversy between parties before it, when it can be done without prejudice to the rights of others, or by saving their rights; but when a complete determination of the controversy cannot be had without the presence of other parties, the court must then order them to be brought in. ..." Such statutes have been interpreted as declaratory of the equity rule and practice.

But the equity doctrine as developed by the courts is loose and ambiguous in its expression and uncertain in its application. Sometimes it is stated as a mandatory rule, and at other times as a matter of discretion, designed to reach an equitable result if it is practicable to do so. And despite various attempts at reconciliation of conflicting expressions, a great deal of confusion still remains in the cases. Bearing in mind the fundamental purpose of the doctrine, we should, in dealing with "necessary" and "indispensable" parties, be careful to avoid converting a discretionary power or a rule of fairness in procedure into an arbitrary and burdensome requirement which may thwart rather than accomplish justice. These two terms have frequently been coupled together as if they have the same meaning; but there appears to be a sound distinction, both in theory and practice, between parties deemed "indispensable" and those considered merely "necessary". As Professor Clark has remarked: "It has been objected that the terms 'necessary' and 'indispensable' convey the same idea ... But a distinction has been drawn. While necessary parties are so interested in the controversy that they should normally be made parties in order to enable the court to do complete justice, yet if their interests are separable from the rest and particularly where their presence in the suit cannot be obtained, they are not indispensable parties. The latter are those without whom the court cannot proceed."

First, then, what parties are indispensable? There may be some persons whose interests, rights, or duties will inevitably be affected by any decree which can be rendered in the action. Typical are the situations where a number of persons have undetermined interests in the same property, or in a particular trust fund, and one of them seeks, in an action, to recover the whole, to fix his share, or to recover a portion claimed by him. The other persons with similar interests are indispensable parties. The reason is that a judgment in favor of one claimant for part of the property or fund would necessarily determine the amount or extent which remains available to the others. Hence, any judgment in the action would inevitably affect their rights. Thus, in an action by one creditor against assignees for the benefit of creditors, seeking an accounting and payment of his share of the assets, the other creditors were held indispensable; and in an action by plaintiff to enforce a trust, where he claimed the property in his own right, to the exclusion of another actual beneficiary, failure to join the latter was held fatal to the judgment. Where, also, the plaintiff seeks some other type of affirmative relief which, if granted, would injure or affect the interests of a third person not joined, that third person is an indispensable party. Thus, in an action by a lessor against a sublessee to forfeit a parent lease because of acts of the sublessee, the sublessors (original lessees) were indispensable parties, since a decree of forfeiture would deprive them of their lease. And in a suit to cancel illegal registration of voters, all voters whose registration was challenged were indispensable parties. Many other cases, illustrating the reasons for compulsory joinder, may be found.

All of these persons are, of course, "necessary" parties, but the decisions show that they come within a special classification of necessary parties, to which the term "indispensable" seems appropriate. An attempt to adjudicate their rights without joinder is futile. Many cases go so far as to say that the court would have no jurisdiction to proceed without them, and that its purported judgment would be void and subject to collateral attack. The objection being so fundamental, it need not be raised by the parties themselves; the court may, of its own motion, dismiss the proceedings, or refuse to proceed, until these indispensable parties are brought in. It follows that if the court does attempt to proceed, it is acting beyond its jurisdiction and may be restrained by prohibition.

The other classification includes persons who are interested in the sense that they might possibly be affected by the decision, or whose interests in the subject matter or transaction are such that it cannot be finally and completely settled without them; but nevertheless their interests are so separable that a decree may be rendered between the parties before the court without affecting those others. These latter may perhaps be "necessary" parties to a complete settlement of the entire controversy or transaction, but are not "indispensable" to any valid judgment in the particular case. They should normally be joined, and the court, following the equity rule, will usually require them to be joined, in order to carry out the policy of complete determination and avoidance of multiplicity of suits. But, since the rule itself is one of equity, it is limited and qualified by considerations of fairness, convenience, and practicability. Where, for example, it is impossible to find these other persons or impracticable to bring them in, the action may proceed as to those parties who are present.

* * * With the foregoing distinctions in mind, the present action may be examined to determine whether the absent defendants are indispensable or only necessary parties. The nature of such an action has been frequently discussed by the courts. The probate court cannot, of course, take cognizance of the contract, and an equity court cannot compel the making of a will. Hence, there is no specific performance of the contract in the strict sense. But equity gives relief which is the equivalent of specific performance. Though the estate may be probated and the property distributed accordingly, the court will, in an action by the promisee, impose a constructive trust upon any particular property in the hands of the individual distributee. This relief is sometimes called "*quasi* specific

performance", since it accomplishes the substantial result of enforcement of the contract.

The action in these cases is against the distributee personally, and not against the estate; and it is independent of the will and the probate proceeding. Each distributee is individually held as a constructive trustee solely of the property which came to him, and none is interested in the granting or denial of similar relief as to any other. Where there are a number of legatees and devisees, they would all appear to be "necessary" parties in the sense that the main issue, the validity of the testamentary disposition of the property of decedent, affects their property interests, and the entire matter, the disposition of all of the decedent's property, cannot be finally settled without a binding adjudication for or against every legatee or devisee. Hence, the court will usually order them served and brought in unless there is some good reason for not doing so. But the absent defendants in such a case are not indispensable parties. Unlike the situations discussed above, in which any judgment would necessarily affect the rights of the absent persons, the case here is one where plaintiff may litigate her claim against the appearing defendants alone and obtain a decree which binds them alone. The absent defendants, not being before the court, will not be bound by the judgment, whether favorable or unfavorable, and their property interests will not be affected.

* * * If, in this kind of action, the court has jurisdiction to try the case, and may render a valid judgment where the plaintiff sues or maintains the suit against less than all of the distributees, it must be clear that they are not indispensable parties. So, in the present case, the absent defendants are not indispensable parties, and the court has jurisdiction to proceed without them, to determine the rights of the parties actually before it.

Much stress is laid by petitioners upon the fact that plaintiff prays for judgment against all the defendants, and has not dismissed as to the absent parties. It is also pointed out that the prayer seeks a decree quieting title to the property. Petitioners argue that the court cannot have jurisdiction over the action in the form in which plaintiff seeks to maintain it, without bringing in the absent parties. The answer to this contention is that the court cannot lose jurisdiction of a proceeding merely because the prayer of the complaint seeks relief beyond that to which the plaintiff is entitled. The court may try the matters within its jurisdiction and render a valid judgment. It is not bound to follow plaintiff's theory and certainly it will not be presumed that it will follow an erroneous theory and act beyond its jurisdiction.

Only brief mention need be made of the contention that the prosecution of the action against less than all of the distributees will cause inconvenience and multiplicity of suits to the injury of the executor. These are all matters within the discretion of the court to consider in connection with its policy to settle the entire controversy in one proceeding, if possible. But the contention, as we have seen, does not go to the jurisdiction of the court.

We have refrained from discussing the question whether the lower court's denial of the motion to bring in the absent defendants was, under the circumstances, an abuse of discretion. If they were readily available and could have been brought in without serious difficulty, it may well be that the motion should have been granted. On the other hand, if, as is asserted by respondents, many reside outside the state or the country, great difficulty might be encountered in any attempt to bring them in, and the trial might be indefinitely delayed, to the detriment of the present parties. The fact that the interests of the absent defendants are trivial as compared with that of the residuary legatee, which received over seventy-five percent of the estate, is perhaps some indication of the reason why plaintiff chose to go to trial against the latter alone. All these considerations, however, were for the trial court in the first instance, and its determination, though reviewable in the proper manner, cannot be attacked on an application for writ of prohibition.

The alternative writ, heretofore issued is discharged, and the peremptory writ is denied.

* * *

PROVIDENT TRADESMENS BANK & TRUST CO. v. PATTERSON

390 U.S. 102 (1968)

Mr. Justice Harlan delivered the opinion of the Court.

This controversy, involving in its present posture the dismissal of a declaratory judgment action for non-joinder of an "indispensable" party, began nearly 10 years ago with a traffic accident. An automobile owned by Edward Dutcher, who was not present when the accident occurred, was being driven by Donald Cionci, to whom Dutcher had given the keys. John Lynch and John Harris were passengers. The automobile crossed the median strip of the highway and collided with a truck being driven by Thomas Smith. Cionci, Lynch, and Smith were killed and Harris was severely injured.

Three tort actions were brought. Provident Tradesmens Bank, the administrator of the estate of passenger Lynch and petitioner here, sued the estate of the driver, Cionci, in a diversity action. Smith's administratrix, and Harris in person, each brought a state-court action against the estate of Cionci, Dutcher, the owner, and the estate of Lynch. These Smith and Harris actions, for unknown reasons, have never gone to trial and are still pending. The Lynch action against Cionci's estate was settled for $50,000, which the estate of Cionci, being penniless, has never paid.

Dutcher, the owner of the automobile and a defendant in the as yet untried tort actions, had an automobile liability insurance policy with

Lumbermens Mutual Casualty Company, a respondent here. That policy had an upper limit of $100,000 for all claims arising out of a single accident. This fund was potentially subject to two different sorts of claims by the tort plaintiffs. First, Dutcher himself might be held vicariously liable as Cionci's "principal;" the likelihood of such a judgment against Dutcher is a matter of considerable doubt and dispute. Second, the policy by its terms covered the direct liability of any person driving Dutcher's car with Dutcher's "permission."

The insurance company had declined, after notice, to defend in the tort action brought by Lynch's estate against the estate of Cionci, believing that Cionci had not had permission and hence was not covered by the policy. The facts allegedly were that Dutcher had entrusted his car to Cionci, but that Cionci had made a detour from the errand for which Dutcher allowed his car to be taken. The estate of Lynch, armed with its $50,000 liquidated claim against the estate of Cionci, brought the present diversity action for a declaration that Cionci's use of the car had been "with permission" of Dutcher. The only named defendants were the company and the estate of Cionci. The other two tort plaintiffs were joined as plaintiffs. Dutcher, a resident of the State of Pennsylvania as were all the plaintiffs, was not joined either as plaintiff or defendant. The failure to join him was not adverted to at the trial level.

The major question of law contested at trial was a state-law question. The District Court had ruled that, as a matter of the applicable (Pennsylvania) law, the driver of an automobile is presumed to have the permission of the owner. Hence, unless contrary evidence could be introduced, the tort plaintiffs, now declaratory judgment plaintiffs, would be entitled to a directed verdict against the insurance company. The only possible contrary evidence was testimony by Dutcher as to restrictions he had imposed on Cionci's use of the automobile. The two estate plaintiffs claimed, however, that under the Pennsylvania "Dead Man Rule" Dutcher was incompetent to testify on this matter as against them. The District Court upheld this claim. It ruled that under Pennsylvania law Dutcher was incompetent to testify against an estate if he had an "adverse" interest to that of the estate. It found such adversity in Dutcher's potential need to call upon the insurance fund to pay judgments against himself, and his consequent interest in not having part or all of the fund used to pay judgments against Cionci. The District Court, therefore, directed verdicts in favor of the two estates. Dutcher was, however, allowed to testify as against the live plaintiff, Harris. The jury, nonetheless, found that Cionci had had permission, and hence awarded a verdict to Harris also.

Lumbermens appealed the judgment to the Court of Appeals for the Third Circuit, raising various state-law questions. The Court of Appeals did not reach any of these issues. Instead, after reargument *en banc*, it decided, 5–2, to reverse on two alternative grounds neither of which had been raised in the District Court or by the appellant.

The first of these grounds was that Dutcher was an indispensable party. The court held that the "adverse interests" that had rendered Dutcher incompetent to testify under the Pennsylvania Dead Man Rule also required him to be made a party. The court did not consider whether the fact that a verdict had already been rendered, without objection to the nonjoinder of Dutcher, affected the matter. Nor did it follow the provision of Rule 19 of the Federal Rules of Civil Procedure that findings of "indispensability" must be based on stated pragmatic considerations. It held, to the contrary, that the right of a person who "may be affected" by the judgment to be joined is a "substantive" right, unaffected by the federal rules; that a trial court "may not proceed" in the absence of such a person; and that since Dutcher could not be joined as a defendant without destroying diversity jurisdiction the action had to be dismissed.

Since this ruling presented a serious challenge to the scope of the newly amended Rule 19, we granted certiorari. Concluding that the inflexible approach adopted by the Court of Appeals in this case exemplifies the kind of reasoning that the Rule was designed to avoid, we reverse.

I.

[Court's recitation of Rule 19 omitted—ed.]

We may assume, at the outset, that Dutcher falls within the category of persons who, under s (a), should be "joined if feasible." The action was for an adjudication of the validity of certain claims against a fund. Dutcher, faced with the possibility of judgments against him, had an interest in having the fund preserved to cover that potential liability. Hence there existed, when this case went to trial, at least the possibility that a judgment might impede Dutcher's ability to protect his interest, or lead to later relitigation by him.

The optimum solution, an adjudication of the permission question that would be binding on all interested persons, was not "feasible," however, for Dutcher could not be made a defendant without destroying diversity. Hence the problem was the one to which Rule 19(b) appears to address itself: in the absence of a person who "should be joined if feasible," should the court dismiss the action or proceed without him? Since this problem emerged for the first time in the Court of Appeals, there were also two subsidiary questions. First, what was the effect, if any, of the failure of the defendants to raise the matter in the District Court? Second, what was the importance, if any, of the fact that a judgment, binding on the parties although not binding on Dutcher, had already been reached after extensive litigation? The three questions prove, on examination, to be interwoven.

We conclude, upon consideration of the record and applying the "equity and good conscience" test of Rule 19(b), that the Court of Appeals erred in not allowing the judgment to stand.

Rule 19(b) suggests four "interests" that must be examined in each case to determine whether, in equity and good conscience, the court should proceed without a party whose absence from the litigation is compelled. Each of these interests must, in this case, be viewed entirely from an appellate perspective since the matter of joinder was not considered in the trial court. First, the plaintiff has an interest in having a forum. Before the trial, the strength of this interest obviously depends upon whether a satisfactory alternative forum exists. On appeal, if the plaintiff has won, he has a strong additional interest in preserving his judgment. Second, the defendant may properly wish to avoid multiple litigation, or inconsistent relief, or sole responsibility for a liability he shares with another. After trial, however, if the defendant has failed to assert this interest, it is quite proper to consider it foreclosed.

Third, there is the interest of the outsider whom it would have been desirable to join. Of course, since the outsider is not before the court, he cannot be bound by the judgment rendered. This means, however, only that a judgment is not res judicata as to, or legally enforceable against, a nonparty. It obviously does not mean either (a) that a court may never issue a judgment that, in practice, affects a nonparty or (b) that (to the contrary) a court may always proceed without considering the potential effect on nonparties simply because they are not "bound" in the technical sense. Instead, as Rule 19(a) expresses it, the court must consider the extent to which the judgment may "as a practical matter impair or impede his ability to protect" his interest in the subject matter. When a case has reached the appeal stage the matter is more complex. The judgment appealed from may not in fact affect the interest of any outsider even though there existed, before trial, a possibility that a judgment affecting his interest would be rendered. When necessary, however, a court of appeals should, on its own initiative, take steps to protect the absent party, who of course had no opportunity to plead and prove his interest below.

Fourth, there remains the interest of the courts and the public in complete, consistent, and efficient settlement of controversies. We read the Rule's third criterion, whether the judgment issued in the absence of the non-joined person will be "adequate," to refer to this public stake in settling disputes by wholes, whenever possible, for clearly the plaintiff, who himself chose both the forum and the parties defendant, will not be heard to complain about the sufficiency of the relief obtainable against them. After trial, considerations of efficiency of course include the fact that the time and expense of a trial have already been spent.

Rule 19(b) also directs a district court to consider the possibility of shaping relief to accommodate these four interests. Commentators had argued that greater attention should be paid to this potential solution to a joinder stymie, and the Rule now makes it explicit that a court should consider modification of a judgment as an alternative to dismissal. Needless to say, a court of appeals may also properly require suitable modification as a condition of affirmance.

Had the Court of Appeals applied Rule 19's criteria to the facts of the present case, it could hardly have reached the conclusion it did. We begin with the plaintiff's viewpoint. It is difficult to decide at this stage whether they would have had an "adequate" remedy had the action been dismissed before trial for non-joinder: we cannot here determine whether the plaintiffs could have brought the same action, against the same parties plus Dutcher, in a state court. After trial, however, the "adequacy" of this hypothetical alternative, from the plaintiffs' point of view, was obviously greatly diminished. Their interest in preserving a fully litigated judgment should be overborne only by rather greater opposing considerations than would be required at an earlier stage when the plaintiffs' only concern was for a federal rather than a state forum.

Opposing considerations in this case are hard to find. The defendants had no stake, either asserted or real, in the joinder of Dutcher. They showed no interest in joinder until the Court of Appeals took the matter into its own hands. This properly forecloses any interest of theirs, but for purposes of clarity we note that the insurance company, whose liability was limited to $100,000, had or will have full opportunity to litigate each claim on that fund against the claimant involved. Its only concern with the absence of Dutcher was and is to obtain a windfall escape from its defeat at trial.

The interest of the outsider, Dutcher, is more difficult to reckon. The Court of Appeals, concluding that it should not follow Rule 19's command to determine whether, as a practical matter, the judgment impaired the nonparty's ability to protect his rights, simply quoted the District Court's reasoning on the Dead Man issue as proof that Dutcher had a "right" to be joined:

> The subject matter of this suit is the coverage of Lumbermens' policy issued to Dutcher. Depending upon the outcome of this trial, Dutcher may have the policy all to himself or he may have to share its coverage with the Cionci Estate, thereby extending the availability of the proceeds of the policy to satisfy verdicts and judgments in favor of the two Estate plaintiffs. Sharing the coverage of a policy of insurance with finite limits with another, and thereby making that policy available to claimants against that other person is immediately worth less than having the coverage of such policy available to Dutcher alone. By the outcome in the instant case, to the extent that the two Estate plaintiffs will have the proceeds of the policy available to them in their claims against Cionci's estate, Dutcher will lose a measure of protection. Conversely, to the extent that the proceeds of this policy are not available to the two Estate plaintiffs Dutcher will gain. * * * It is sufficient for the purpose of determining adversity (of interest) that it appears clearly that the measure of Dutcher's protection under this policy of insurance is dependent upon the outcome of this suit. That being so, Dutcher's interest in these proceedings is adverse to the interest of the two Estate plaintiffs, the parties who represent, on

this record, the interests of the deceased persons in the matter in controversy.

There is a logical error in the Court of Appeals' appropriation of this reasoning for its own quite different purposes: Dutcher had an "adverse" interest (sufficient to invoke the Dead Man Rule) because he would have been benefited by a ruling in favor of the insurance company; the question before the Court of Appeals, however, was whether Dutcher was harmed by the judgment against the insurance company.

The two questions are not the same. If the three plaintiffs had lost to the insurance company on the permission issue, that loss would have ended the matter favorably to Dutcher. If, as has happened, the three plaintiffs obtain a judgment against the insurance company on the permission issue, Dutcher may still claim that as a nonparty he is not estopped by that judgment from relitigating the issue. At that point it might be argued that Dutcher should be bound by the previous decision because, although technically a nonparty, he had purposely bypassed an adequate opportunity to intervene. We do not now decide whether such an argument would be correct under the circumstances of this case. If, however, Dutcher is properly foreclosed by his failure to intervene in the present litigation, then the joinder issue considered in the Court of Appeals vanishes, for any rights of Dutcher's have been lost by his own inaction.

If Dutcher is not foreclosed by his failure to intervene below, then he is not "bound" by the judgment in favor of the insurance company and, in theory, he has not been harmed. There remains, however, the practical question whether Dutcher is likely to have any need and if so will have any opportunity, to relitigate. The only possible threat to him is that if the fund is used to pay judgments against Cionci the money may in fact have disappeared before Dutcher has an opportunity to assert his interest. Upon examination, we find this supposed threat neither large nor unavoidable.

The state-court actions against Dutcher had lain dormant for years at the pleading stage by the time the Court of Appeals acted. Petitioner asserts here that under the applicable Pennsylvania vicarious liability law there is virtually no chance of recovery against Dutcher. We do not accept this assertion as fact, but the matter could have been explored below. Furthermore, even in the event of tort judgments against Dutcher, it is unlikely that he will be prejudiced by the outcome here. The potential claimants against Dutcher Himself are identical with the potential claimants against Cionci's estate. Should the claimants seek to collect from Dutcher personally, he may be able to raise the permission issue defensively, making it irrelevant that the actual monies paid from the fund may have disappeared: Dutcher can assert that Cionci did not have his permission and that therefore the payments made on Cionci's behalf out of Dutcher's insurance policy should properly be credited against Dutcher's own liability. Of course, when Dutcher raises this defense he may lose, either on the merits of the permission issue or on the ground that the issue is foreclosed by Dutcher's failure to intervene in the present case, but Dutcher will not have been prejudiced by the failure of the District Court here to order him joined.

If the Court of Appeals was unconvinced that the threat to Dutcher was trivial, it could nevertheless have avoided all difficulties by proper phrasing of the decree. The District Court, for unspecified reasons, had refused to order immediate payment on the Cionci judgment. Payment could have been withheld pending the suits against Dutcher and relitigation (if that became necessary) by him. In this Court, furthermore, counsel for petitioners represented orally that they, the tort plaintiffs, would accept a limitation of all claims to the amount of the insurance policy. Obviously such a compromise could have been reached below had the Court of Appeals been willing to abandon its rigid approach and seek ways to preserve what was, as to the parties, subject to the appellants' other contentions, a perfectly valid judgment.

The suggestion of potential relitigation of the question of "permission" raises the fourth "interest" at stake in joinder cases-efficiency. It might have been preferable, at the trial level, if there were a forum available in which both the company and Dutcher could have been made defendants, to dismiss the action and force the plaintiffs to go elsewhere. Even this preference would have been highly problematical, however, for the actual threat of relitigation by Dutcher depended on there being judgments against him and on the amount of the fund, which was not revealed to the District Court. By the time the case reached the Court of Appeals, however, the problematical preference on efficiency grounds had entirely disappeared: there was no reason then to throw away a valid judgment just because it did not theoretically settle the whole controversy.

II.

Application of Rule 19(b)'s "equity and good conscience" test for determining whether to proceed or dismiss would doubtless have led to a contrary result below. The Court of Appeals' reasons for disregarding the Rule remain to be examined. The majority of the court concluded that the Rule was inapplicable because "substantive" rights are involved, and substantive rights are not affected by the Federal Rules. Although the court did not articulate exactly what the substantive rights are, or what law determines them, we take it to have been making the following argument: (1) there is a category of persons called "indispensable parties;" (2) that category is defined by substantive law and the definition cannot be modified by rule; (3) the right of a person falling within that category to participate in the lawsuit in question is also a substantive matter, and is absolute.

With this we may contrast the position that is reflected in Rule 19. Whether a person is "indispensable," that is, whether a particular lawsuit must be dismissed in the absence of that person, can only be determined in the context of particular litigation. There is a large category, whose limits are not presently in question, of persons who, in the Rule's terminology, should be "joined if feasible," and who, in the older terminology, were called either necessary or indispensable parties. Assuming the existence of a person who should be joined if feasible, the only further question arises when joinder is not possible and the court must decide whether to dismiss or to proceed without him. To use the familiar but confusing terminology, the decision to proceed is a decision that the absent person is merely "necessary" while the decision to dismiss is a decision that he is "indispensable." decision whether to dismiss (i.e., the decision whether the person missing is "indispensable") must be based on factors varying with the different cases, some such factors being substantive, some procedural, some compelling by themselves, and some subject to balancing against opposing interests. Rule 19 does not prevent the assertion of compelling substantive interests; it merely commands the courts to examine each controversy to make certain that the interests really exist. To say that a court "must" dismiss in the absence of an indispensable party and that it "cannot proceed" without him puts the matter the wrong way around: a court does not know whether a particular person is "indispensable" until it had examined the situation to determine whether it can proceed without him.

* * *

We think it clear that the judgment below cannot stand. The judgment is vacated and the case is remanded to the Court of Appeals for consideration of those issues raised on appeal that have not been considered, and, should the Court of Appeals affirm the District Court as to those issues, for appropriate disposition preserving the judgment of the District Court and protecting the interests of non-joined persons.

It is so ordered.

Judgment vacated and case remanded to Court of Appeals.

* * *

D. INTERVENTION

FEDERAL RULE OF CIVIL PROCEDURE 24. INTERVENTION

(a) Intervention of Right. On timely motion, the court must permit anyone to intervene who:

> **(1)** is given an unconditional right to intervene by a federal statute; or

> **(2)** claims an interest relating to the property or transaction that is the subject of the action, and is so situated that disposing of the action may as a practical matter impair or impede the movant's ability to protect its interest, unless existing parties adequately represent that interest.

(b) Permissive Intervention.

   (1) In General. On timely motion, the court may permit anyone to intervene who:

      (A) is given a conditional right to intervene by a federal statute; or

      (B) has a claim or defense that shares with the main action a common question of law or fact.

   (2) By a Government Officer or Agency. On timely motion, the court may permit a federal or state governmental officer or agency to intervene if a party's claim or defense is based on:

      (A) a statute or executive order administered by the officer or agency; or

      (B) any regulation, order, requirement, or agreement issued or made under the statute or executive order.

   (3) Delay or Prejudice. In exercising its discretion, the court must consider whether the intervention will unduly delay or prejudice the adjudication of the original parties' rights.

(c) Notice and Pleading Required. A motion to intervene must be served on the parties as provided in Rule 5. The motion must state the grounds for intervention and be accompanied by a pleading that sets out the claim or defense for which intervention is sought.

* * *

GRUTTER v. BOLLINGER

188 F.3d 394 (6th Cir. 1999)

DAUGHTREY, CIRCUIT JUDGE.

Before us are two cases in which proposed defendant-intervenors were denied intervention under Federal Rule of Civil Procedure 24(a) and (b), in actions brought against the University of Michigan contesting the use of an applicant's race as a factor in determining admission. The appeals come from separate district courts but present similar, and in some instances the same, issues for our consideration. We have therefore consolidated the two cases for purposes of this opinion, and we find in both instances that the district courts erred in denying intervention under Rule 24(a).

Procedural and Factual Background

In each of the cases before the court, a group of students and one or more coalitions appeal the denial of their motion to intervene in a lawsuit brought to challenge a race-conscious admissions policy at the University of Michigan. The named plaintiffs in *Gratz v. Bollinger* are two white applicants who were denied admission to the College of Literature, Arts and Science. They allege that the College's admissions policy violates the Equal Protection Clause of the Fourteenth Amendment, 42 U.S.C. § 1981 and § 1983, and 42 U.S.C. §§ 2000d *et seq.* The plaintiffs seek compensatory and punitive damages, injunctive relief forbidding continuation of the alleged discriminatory admissions process, and admission to the College. The intervenors are 17 African–American and Latino/a individuals who have applied or intend to apply to the University, and the Citizens for Affirmative Action's Preservation (CAAP), a nonprofit organization whose stated mission is to preserve opportunities in higher education for African–American and Latino/a students in Michigan. The intervenors claim that the resolution of this case directly threatens the access of qualified African–American and Latino/a students to public higher education and that the University will not adequately represent their interest in educational opportunity. The district court denied their motion for intervention as of right, holding that the plaintiffs did not have a substantial interest in the litigation and that the University could adequately represent the proposed intervenors' interests. The district court also denied the proposed intervenors' alternative motion for permissive intervention.

The named plaintiff in *Grutter v. Bollinger* is a white woman challenging the admissions policy of the University of Michigan Law School. Like the plaintiffs in *Gratz*, she alleges that the race-conscious admissions policy utilized by the law school violates the Equal Protection Clause of the Fourteenth Amendment, 42 U.S.C. § 1981 and § 1983, and 42 U.S.C. §§ 2000d *et seq.* Grutter seeks compensatory and punitive damages, injunctive relief forbidding continuation of the alleged discriminatory admissions process, and admission to the law school. The proposed intervenors are 41 students and three pro-affirmative action coalitions. As described by the district court:

> [The] individual proposed intervenors include 21 undergraduate students of various races who currently attend [various undergraduate institutions], all of whom plan to apply to the law school for admission; five black students who currently attend [local high schools] and who also plan to apply to the law school for admission; 12 students of various races who currently attend the law school; a paralegal and a Latino graduate student at the University of Texas at Austin who intend to apply to the law school for admission; and a black graduate student at the University of Michigan who is a member of the Defend Affirmative Action Party.

The plaintiff opposed the motion to intervene, but the defendants, various officials of the Law School and the University, did not oppose the motion. The district court denied the motion to intervene as of right on the basis that the intervenors failed to show that their interests would not be adequately represented by the University. The district court also denied the proposed intervenors' alternative motion for permissive intervention.

Discussion

The proposed intervenors in each of these cases contend principally that the district court erred by denying their motion to intervene as of right. Fed. R. Civ. P. 24 provides in pertinent part:

Upon timely application anyone shall be permitted to intervene in an action ... (2) when the applicant claims an interest relating to the property or transaction which is the subject of the action and the applicant is so situated that the disposition of the action may as a practical matter impair or impede the applicant's ability to protect that interest, unless the applicant's interest is adequately represented by existing parties.

In this circuit, proposed intervenors must establish four elements in order to be entitled to intervene as a matter of right: (1) that the motion to intervene was timely; (2) that they have a substantial legal interest in the subject matter of the case; (3) that their ability to protect that interest may be impaired in the absence of intervention; and (4) that the parties already before the court may not adequately represent their interest. A district court's denial of intervention as of right is reviewed *de novo,* except for the timeliness element, which is reviewed for an abuse of discretion. The district court held in each of these cases that the motion for intervention was timely, and the plaintiffs do not contest this finding on appeal. We will therefore consider the motions timely and need address only the three remaining elements.

Substantial Legal Interest

The proposed intervenors must show that they have a substantial interest in the subject matter of this litigation. However, in this circuit we subscribe to a "rather expansive notion of the interest sufficient to invoke intervention of right." For example, an intervenor need not have the same standing necessary to initiate a lawsuit. We have also "cited with approval decisions of other courts 'reject[ing] the notion that Rule 24(a)(2) requires a specific legal or equitable interest.'" "The inquiry into the substantiality of the claimed interest is necessarily fact-specific."

The proposed intervenors argue that their interest in maintaining the use of race as a factor in the University's admissions program is a sufficient substantial legal interest to support intervention as of right. Specifically, they argue that they have a substantial legal interest in educational opportunity, which requires preserving access to the University for African–American and Latino/a students and preventing a decline in the enrollment of African–American and Latino/a students. The district court in *Grutter* "assumed without deciding" that the proposed intervenors do have a significant legal interest in this case and that their ability to protect that interest may be impaired by an adverse ruling in the underlying case. The district court in *Gratz,* however, determined that the proposed intervenors did *not* have a direct and substantial interest which is "legally protectable" and that they therefore failed to establish this required element. We conclude that Sixth Circuit precedent requires a finding to the contrary.

In *Jansen*, black applicants and employees of the city's fire department sought to intervene in a reverse discrimination lawsuit challenging the department's use of a quota system. We noted that the proposed intervenors were parties to an earlier consent decree setting goals for minority hiring and found that the proposed intervenors did have a significantly protectable interest in the affirmative action challenged in the lawsuit. The district court in *Gratz* distinguished *Jansen*, as well as *In re Birmingham Reverse Discrimination Employment Litig.*, aff'd. sub. nom., *Martin v. Wilks*, 490 U.S. 755 (1989), on which this court relied in *Jansen*, on the basis that the proposed intervenors in both *Jansen* and *In re Birmingham* had a legally protected interest only by virtue of their status as parties to a consent decree. As the proposed intervenors point out, however, neither *Jansen* nor *In re Birmingham* stands for the proposition that an interest must be protected by means of a consent decree or by any other particular means in order for the proposed intervenors to be able to establish that they have a substantial legal interest.

The *Gratz* district court's opinion relies heavily on the premise that the proposed intervenors do not have a significant legal interest unless they have a "legally enforceable right to have the existing admissions policy construed." We conclude that this interpretation results from a misreading of this circuit's approach to the issue. As noted earlier, we have repeatedly "cited with approval decisions of other courts 'reject[ing] the notion that Rule 24(a)(2) requires a specific legal or equitable interest.'" For example, in *Miller*, the Michigan Chamber of Commerce sought to intervene in a suit by labor unions challenging an amendment to Michigan's Campaign Finance Act, which extended the application of statutory restrictions on corporate political expenditures so that they applied to unions as well as to corporations. The majority found that the Chamber of Commerce did have a substantial legal interest by virtue of its role in the political process that resulted in the adoption of the contested amendments. The Chamber of Commerce was therefore allowed to intervene as of right, although the Chamber had no legal "right" to the enactment of the challenged legislation. We believe that the district court's attempt to distinguish *Miller*, as well as *Meek v. Metropolitan Dade County* (holding that voters and organizations were entitled to intervene in action by African–American and Latino citizens against the county for violation of Voting Rights Act) and *Citizens for Legislative Choice v. Miller* (holding that organization was entitled to intervene in action challenging constitutionality of term limits provision for which it had lobbied), on the sole basis that those cases involved challenges to legislation, was misguided. The case law of this circuit does not limit the finding of a substantial interest to cases involving the legislative context, any more than it limits such a finding to cases involving a consent decree. Neither a legislative context nor the existence of a consent decree is dispositive as to whether proposed intervenors have shown that they have a significant interest in the subject matter of the underlying case. We find that the interest implicated in the case now before us is even more direct, substantial, and compelling than the general interest of an organization in vindicating legislation that it had previously supported. This case is, if anything, a significantly stronger case for intervention than *Miller* and many of the cases on which *Miller* relied.

Even if it could be said that the question raised is a close one, "close cases should be resolved in favor of recognizing an interest under Rule 24(a)." The proposed intervenors have enunciated a specific interest in the subject matter of this case, namely their interest in gaining admission to the University, which is considerably more direct and substantial than the interest of the Chamber of Commerce in *Miller*—a much more general interest. We therefore hold that the district court erred in *Gratz* in failing to rule that the proposed intervenors have established that they have a substantial legal interest in the subject matter of this case.

Impairment

"To satisfy this element of the intervention test, a would-be intervenor must show only that impairment of its substantial legal interest is possible if intervention is denied. This burden is minimal." As noted above, the district court in *Grutter* "assumed without deciding" that the proposed intervenors met this element. The district court in *Gratz*, however, determined that because "the proposed intervenors [ ] failed to articulate the existence of a substantial legal interest in the subject matter of the instant litigation, it necessarily follows that the proposed intervenors cannot demonstrate an impairment of any interest." The proposed intervenors in *Gratz* continue to argue on appeal that a decision in favor of the plaintiff will adversely affect their interest in educational opportunity by diminishing their likelihood of obtaining admission to the University and by reducing the number of African–American and Latino/a students at the University.

As we have now decided, the district court erred in determining that the proposed intervenors did not have a substantial interest in the subject matter of this case. Consequently, we must likewise conclude that the district court erred in its analysis of the impairment element as well. There is little room for doubt that access to the University for African–American and Latino/a students will be impaired to some extent and that a substantial decline in the enrollment of these students may well result if the University is precluded from considering race as a factor in admissions. Recent experiences in California and Texas suggest such an outcome. The probability of similar effects in Michigan is more than sufficient to meet the minimal requirements of the impairment element.

Inadequate Representation

Finally, the prospective intervenors must show that the existing defendant, the University, may not adequately represent their interests. However, the proposed intervenors are "not required to show that the representation will in fact be inadequate." Indeed, "[i]t may be enough to show that the existing party who purports to seek the same outcome will not make all of the prospective intervenor's arguments."

As a preliminary matter, there is some dispute about the relevant standard for determining whether this element has been met when the existing defendant is a governmental entity. The district court in *Gratz* mentioned that the plaintiff relied on *Hopwood v. State of Texas* for the proposition that a stronger showing of inadequacy is required when a governmental agency is involved as the existing defendant. On reconsideration, however, the district court made clear that it had simply noted the plaintiff's argument in regard to the higher *Hopwood* standard but had not applied this higher standard. In *Grutter*, by contrast, the district court does appear to have applied the more demanding *Hopwood* standard. However, this circuit has declined to endorse a higher standard for inadequacy when a governmental entity in involved. For example, in *Miller*, where the defendants included the Secretary of State and the Attorney General, this court clearly stated that the proposed intervenors were required only to show that the representation *might* be inadequate. The district court in *Grutter* therefore erred in applying the higher standard articulated by the Fifth Circuit in *Hopwood*.

The proposed intervenors insist that there is indeed a possibility that the University will inadequately represent their interests, because the University is subject to internal and external institutional pressures that may prevent it from articulating some of the defenses of affirmative action that the proposed intervenors intend to present. They also argue that the University is at less risk of harm than the applicants if it loses this case and, thus, that the University may not defend the case as vigorously as will the proposed intervenors. The district court in *Gratz*, however, found that the proposed intervenors did not identify any specific separate or additional defenses that they will present that the University will not present. The district court in *Grutter* also found that the proposed intervenors failed to show that the University would not adequately represent their interests.

We conclude that the district court erred in each of these cases. The Supreme Court has held, and we have reiterated, that the proposed intervenors' burden in showing inadequacy is "minimal." *See Trbovich v. United Mine Workers*, 404 U.S. 528 (1972). The proposed intervenors need show only that there is a *potential* for inadequate representation. The proposed intervenors in these two cases have presented legitimate and reasonable concerns about whether the University will present particular defenses of the contested race-conscious admissions policies. We find persuasive their argument that the University is unlikely to present evidence of past discrimination by the University itself or of the disparate impact of some current admissions criteria, and that these may be important and relevant factors in determining the legality of a race-conscious admissions policy. We must therefore conclude that the proposed intervenors have articulated specific relevant defenses that the University may not present and, as a consequence, have established the possibility of inadequate representation.

Conclusion

For the reasons set out above, we find that the proposed intervenors have shown that they have a substantial legal interest in the subject matter of this matter, that this interest will be impaired by an adverse determination, and that the existing defendant, the University, may not adequately represent their interest. Hence, the proposed intervenors are entitled to intervene as of right and the district court's decision in each of these cases denying the motion for intervention as of right cannot be sustained. While this determination renders moot the question of permissive intervention under Rule 24(b), we do not believe that the denial of intervention on a permissive basis was erroneous.

The order of the district court in each case denying intervention is reversed and the cases are remanded for entry of an order permitting intervention by the proposed defendant-intervenors under Rule 24(a). The order previously entered in this court staying proceedings in the district courts is hereby vacated.

STAFFORD, DISTRICT JUDGE, dissenting.

I cannot agree that the proposed intervenors in these cases have established their right to intervene as of right. I do not believe, nor do I think *Michigan State AFL–CIO v. Miller* compels us to find, that the proposed intervenors' subjective fears are sufficient to satisfy their burden, however minimal, of showing that the University of Michigan will not adequately represent the proposed intervenors' interests in these two lawsuits. Unlike the State of Michigan in *Miller*, the University of Michigan here has in no way "demonstrated that it will not adequately represent and protect the interests held by the [proposed intervenors]." There is nothing in the record of either case to suggest that the University of Michigan will not zealously defend its voluntarily-adopted admissions policies, will not present all relevant evidence in support of its admissions policies, will not resist unspecified pressures that could temper its ability to defend its admissions policies, or will not raise all defenses or make all arguments that the prospective intervenors may raise or make. Because I do not think that we should substitute our judgment for the informed judgment of the two respective trial judges who determined that, based on the record before them, intervention was not merited, I must respectfully dissent.

* * *

XI. WEEK ELEVEN: DISCOVERY

A. SCOPE AND CONSTITUTIONALITY OF DISCOVERY

FEDERAL RULE OF CIVIL PROCEDURE 26. DUTY TO DISCLOSE; GENERAL PROVISIONS GOVERNING DISCOVERY

(a) Required Disclosures.

    (1) Initial Disclosure.

        (A) In General. Except as exempted by Rule 26(a)(1)(B) or as otherwise stipulated or ordered by the court, a party must, without awaiting a discovery request, provide to the other parties:

            (i) the name and, if known, the address and telephone number of each individual likely to have discoverable information—along with the subjects of that information—that the disclosing party may use to support its claims or defenses, unless the use would be solely for impeachment;

            (ii) a copy—or a description by category and location—of all documents, electronically stored information, and tangible things that the disclosing party has in its possession, custody, or control and may use to support its claims or defenses, unless the use would be solely for impeachment;

            (iii) a computation of each category of damages claimed by the disclosing party—who must also make available for inspection and copying as under Rule 34 the documents or other evidentiary material, unless privileged or protected from disclosure, on which each computation is based, including materials bearing on the nature and extent of injuries suffered; and

            (iv) for inspection and copying as under Rule 34, any insurance agreement under which an insurance business may be liable to satisfy all or part of a possible judgment in the action or to indemnify or reimburse for payments made to satisfy the judgment.

        (B) Proceedings Exempt from Initial Disclosure. The following proceedings are exempt from initial disclosure:

            (i) an action for review on an administrative record;

            (ii) a forfeiture action in rem arising from a federal statute;

            (iii) a petition for habeas corpus or any other proceeding to challenge a criminal conviction or sentence;

(iv) an action brought without an attorney by a person in the custody of the United States, a state, or a state subdivision;

(v) an action to enforce or quash an administrative summons or subpoena;

(vi) an action by the United States to recover benefit payments;

(vii) an action by the United States to collect on a student loan guaranteed by the United States;

(viii) a proceeding ancillary to a proceeding in another court; and

(ix) an action to enforce an arbitration award.

(C) **Time for Initial Disclosures—In General.** A party must make the initial disclosures at or within 14 days after the parties' Rule 26(f) conference unless a different time is set by stipulation or court order, or unless a party objects during the conference that initial disclosures are not appropriate in this action and states the objection in the proposed discovery plan. In ruling on the objection, the court must determine what disclosures, if any, are to be made and must set the time for disclosure.

(D) **Time for Initial Disclosures—For Parties Served or Joined Later.** A party that is first served or otherwise joined after the Rule 26(f) conference must make the initial disclosures within 30 days after being served or joined, unless a different time is set by stipulation or court order.

(E) **Basis for Initial Disclosure; Unacceptable Excuses.** A party must make its initial disclosures based on the information then reasonably available to it. A party is not excused from making its disclosures because it has not fully investigated the case or because it challenges the sufficiency of another party's disclosures or because another party has not made its disclosures.

(2) **Disclosure of Expert Testimony.**

(A) **In General.** In addition to the disclosures required by Rule 26(a)(1), a party must disclose to the other parties the identity of any witness it may use at trial to present evidence under Federal Rule of Evidence 702, 703, or 705.

(B) **Written Report.** Unless otherwise stipulated or ordered by the court, this disclosure must be accompanied by a written report—prepared and signed by the witness—if the witness is one retained or specially employed to provide expert testimony in the case or one whose duties as the party's employee regularly involve giving expert testimony. The report must contain:

    (i) a complete statement of all opinions the witness will express and the basis and reasons for them;

    (ii) the data or other information considered by the witness in forming them;

    (iii) any exhibits that will be used to summarize or support them;

    (iv) the witness's qualifications, including a list of all publications authored in the previous ten years;

    (v) a list of all other cases in which, during the previous four years, the witness testified as an expert at trial or by deposition; and

    (vi) a statement of the compensation to be paid for the study and testimony in the case.

(C) Witnesses Who Do Not Provide a Written Report. Unless otherwise stipulated or ordered by the court, if the witness is not required to provide a written report, this disclosure must state:

    (i) the subject matter on which the witness is expected to present evidence under Federal Rule of Evidence 702, 703, or 705; and

    (ii) a summary of the facts and opinions to which the witness is expected to testify.

(D) Time to Disclose Expert Testimony. A party must make these disclosures at the times and in the sequence that the court orders. Absent a stipulation or a court order, the disclosures must be made:

    (i) at least 90 days before the date set for trial or for the case to be ready for trial; or

    (ii) if the evidence is intended solely to contradict or rebut evidence on the same subject matter identified by another party under Rule 26(a)(2)(B) or (C), within 30 days after the other party's disclosure.

(E) Supplementing the Disclosure. The parties must supplement these disclosures when required under Rule 26(e).

(3) Pretrial Disclosures.

(A) In General. In addition to the disclosures required by Rule 26(a)(1) and (2), a party must provide to the other parties and promptly file the following information about the evidence that it may present at trial other than solely for impeachment:

(i) the name and, if not previously provided, the address and telephone number of each witness—separately identifying those the party expects to present and those it may call if the need arises;

(ii) the designation of those witnesses whose testimony the party expects to present by deposition and, if not taken stenographically, a transcript of the pertinent parts of the deposition; and

(iii) an identification of each document or other exhibit, including summaries of other evidence—separately identifying those items the party expects to offer and those it may offer if the need arises.

(B) **Time for Pretrial Disclosures; Objections.** Unless the court orders otherwise, these disclosures must be made at least 30 days before trial. Within 14 days after they are made, unless the court sets a different time, a party may serve and promptly file a list of the following objections: any objections to the use under Rule 32(a) of a deposition designated by another party under Rule 26(a)(3)(A)(ii); and any objection, together with the grounds for it, that may be made to the admissibility of materials identified under Rule 26(a)(3)(A)(iii). An objection not so made—except for one under Federal Rule of Evidence 402 or 403—is waived unless excused by the court for good cause.

(4) **Form of Disclosures.** Unless the court orders otherwise, all disclosures under Rule 26(a) must be in writing, signed, and served.

(b) **Discovery Scope and Limits.**

(1) **Scope in General.** Unless otherwise limited by court order, the scope of discovery is as follows: Parties may obtain discovery regarding any nonprivileged matter that is relevant to any party's claim or defense—including the existence, description, nature, custody, condition, and location of any documents or other tangible things and the identity and location of persons who know of any discoverable matter. For good cause, the court may order discovery of any matter relevant to the subject matter involved in the action. Relevant information need not be admissible at the trial if the discovery appears reasonably calculated to lead to the discovery of admissible evidence. All discovery is subject to the limitations imposed by Rule 26(b)(2)(C).

(2) **Limitations on Frequency and Extent.**

(A) **When Permitted.** By order, the court may alter the limits in these rules on the number of depositions and interrogatories or on the length of depositions under Rule 30. By order or local rule, the court may also limit the number of requests under Rule 36.

   (B) Specific Limitations on Electronically Stored Information. A party need not provide discovery of electronically stored information from sources that the party identifies as not reasonably accessible because of undue burden or cost. On motion to compel discovery or for a protective order, the party from whom discovery is sought must show that the information is not reasonably accessible because of undue burden or cost. If that showing is made, the court may nonetheless order discovery from such sources if the requesting party shows good cause, considering the limitations of Rule 26(b)(2)(C). The court may specify conditions for the discovery.

   (C) When Required. On motion or on its own, the court must limit the frequency or extent of discovery otherwise allowed by these rules or by local rule if it determines that:

      (i) the discovery sought is unreasonably cumulative or duplicative, or can be obtained from some other source that is more convenient, less burdensome, or less expensive;

      (ii) the party seeking discovery has had ample opportunity to obtain the information by discovery in the action; or

      (iii) the burden or expense of the proposed discovery outweighs its likely benefit, considering the needs of the case, the amount in controversy, the parties' resources, the importance of the issues at stake in the action, and the importance of the discovery in resolving the issues.

* * *

FEDERAL RULE OF CIVIL PROCEDURE 26(c) OMITTED; SEE BELOW

* * *

(d) Timing and Sequence of Discovery.

   (1) Timing. A party may not seek discovery from any source before the parties have conferred as required by Rule 26(f), except in a proceeding exempted from initial disclosure under Rule 26(a)(1)(B), or when authorized by these rules, by stipulation, or by court order.

   (2) Sequence. Unless, on motion, the court orders otherwise for the parties' and witnesses' convenience and in the interests of justice:

      (A) methods of discovery may be used in any sequence; and

      (B) discovery by one party does not require any other party to delay its discovery.

(e) Supplementing Disclosures and Responses.

(1) In General. A party who has made a disclosure under Rule 26(a)—or who has responded to an interrogatory, request for production, or request for admission—must supplement or correct its disclosure or response:

(A) in a timely manner if the party learns that in some material respect the disclosure or response is incomplete or incorrect, and if the additional or corrective information has not otherwise been made known to the other parties during the discovery process or in writing; or

(B) as ordered by the court.

(2) Expert Witness. For an expert whose report must be disclosed under Rule 26(a)(2)(B), the party's duty to supplement extends both to information included in the report and to information given during the expert's deposition. Any additions or changes to this information must be disclosed by the time the party's pretrial disclosures under Rule 26(a)(3) are due.

(f) Conference of the Parties; Planning for Discovery.

(1) Conference Timing. Except in a proceeding exempted from initial disclosure under Rule 26(a)(1)(B) or when the court orders otherwise, the parties must confer as soon as practicable—and in any event at least 21 days before a scheduling conference is to be held or a scheduling order is due under Rule 16(b).

(2) Conference Content; Parties' Responsibilities. In conferring, the parties must consider the nature and basis of their claims and defenses and the possibilities for promptly settling or resolving the case; make or arrange for the disclosures required by Rule 26(a)(1); discuss any issues about preserving discoverable information; and develop a proposed discovery plan. The attorneys of record and all unrepresented parties that have appeared in the case are jointly responsible for arranging the conference, for attempting in good faith to agree on the proposed discovery plan, and for submitting to the court within 14 days after the conference a written report outlining the plan. The court may order the parties or attorneys to attend the conference in person.

(3) Discovery Plan. A discovery plan must state the parties' views and proposals on:

(A) what changes should be made in the timing, form, or requirement for disclosures under Rule 26(a), including a statement of when initial disclosures were made or will be made;

(B) the subjects on which discovery may be needed, when discovery should be completed, and whether discovery should be conducted in phases or be limited to or focused on particular issues;

(C) any issues about disclosure or discovery of electronically stored information, including the form or forms in which it should be produced;

(D) any issues about claims of privilege or of protection as trial-preparation materials, including—if the parties agree on a procedure to assert these claims after production—whether to ask the court to include their agreement in an order;

(E) what changes should be made in the limitations on discovery imposed under these rules or by local rule, and what other limitations should be imposed; and

(F) any other orders that the court should issue under Rule 26(c) or under Rule 16(b) and (c).

(4) Expedited Schedule. If necessary to comply with its expedited schedule for Rule 16(b) conferences, a court may by local rule:

(A) require the parties' conference to occur less than 21 days before the scheduling conference is held or a scheduling order is due under Rule 16(b); and

(B) require the written report outlining the discovery plan to be filed less than 14 days after the parties' conference, or excuse the parties from submitting a written report and permit them to report orally on their discovery plan at the Rule 16(b) conference.

(g) Signing Disclosures and Discovery Requests, Responses, and Objections.

(1) Signature Required; Effect of Signature. Every disclosure under Rule 26(a)(1) or (a)(3) and every discovery request, response, or objection must be signed by at least one attorney of record in the attorney's own name—or by the party personally, if unrepresented—and must state the signer's address, e-mail address, and telephone number. By signing, an attorney or party certifies that to the best of the person's knowledge, information, and belief formed after a reasonable inquiry:

(A) with respect to a disclosure, it is complete and correct as of the time it is made; and

(B) with respect to a discovery request, response, or objection, it is:

(i) consistent with these rules and warranted by existing law or by a non-frivolous argument for extending, modifying, or reversing existing law, or for establishing new law;

(ii) not interposed for any improper purpose, such as to harass, cause unnecessary delay, or needlessly increase the cost of litigation; and

(iii) neither unreasonable nor unduly burdensome or expensive, considering the needs of the case, prior discovery in the case, the amount in controversy, and the importance of the issues at stake in the action.

(2) Failure to Sign. Other parties have no duty to act on an unsigned disclosure, request, response, or objection until it is signed, and the court must strike it unless a signature is promptly supplied after the omission is called to the attorney's or party's attention.

(3) Sanction for Improper Certification. If a certification violates this rule without substantial justification, the court, on motion or on its own, must impose an appropriate sanction on the signer, the party on whose behalf the signer was acting, or both. The sanction may include an order to pay the reasonable expenses, including attorney's fees, caused by the violation.

* * *

FEDERAL RULE OF CIVIL PROCEDURE 35. PHYSICAL AND MENTAL EXAMINATIONS

(a) Order for an Examination.

(1) In General. The court where the action is pending may order a party whose mental or physical condition—including blood group—is in controversy to submit to a physical or mental examination by a suitably licensed or certified examiner. The court has the same authority to order a party to produce for examination a person who is in its custody or under its legal control.

(2) Motion and Notice; Contents of the Order. The order:

(A) may be made only on motion for good cause and on notice to all parties and the person to be examined; and

(B) must specify the time, place, manner, conditions, and scope of the examination, as well as the person or persons who will perform it.

(b) Examiner's Report.

(1) Request by the Party or Person Examined. The party who moved for the examination must, on request, deliver to the requester a copy of the examiner's report, together with like reports of all earlier examinations of the same condition. The request may be made by the party against whom the examination order was issued or by the person examined.

(2) Contents. The examiner's report must be in writing and must set out in detail the examiner's findings, including diagnoses, conclusions, and the results of any tests.

(3) Request by the Moving Party. After delivering the reports, the party who moved for the examination may request—and is entitled to receive—from the party against whom the examination order was issued like reports of all earlier or later examinations of the same condition. But those reports need not be delivered by the party with custody or control of the person examined if the party shows that it could not obtain them.

(4) Waiver of Privilege. By requesting and obtaining the examiner's report, or by deposing the examiner, the party examined waives any privilege it may have—in that action or any other action involving the same controversy—concerning testimony about all examinations of the same condition.

(5) Failure to Deliver a Report. The court on motion may order— on just terms—that a party deliver the report of an examination. If the report is not provided, the court may exclude the examiner's testimony at trial.

(6) Scope. This subdivision (b) applies also to an examination made by the parties' agreement, unless the agreement states otherwise. This subdivision does not preclude obtaining an examiner's report or deposing an examiner under other rules.

* * *

SCHLAGENHAUF v. HOLDER

379 U.S. 104 (1964)

MR. JUSTICE GOLDBERG, delivered the opinion of the Court.

This case involves the validity and construction of Rule 35(a) of the Federal Rules of Civil Procedure as applied to the examination of a defendant in a negligence action. Rule 35(a) provides:

> Physical and Mental Examination of Persons. (a) Order for Examination. In an action in which the mental or physical condition of a party is in controversy, the court in which the action is pending may order him to submit to a physical or mental examination by a physician. The order may be made only on motion for good cause shown and upon notice to the party to be examined and to all other parties and shall specify the time, place, manner, conditions, and scope of the examination and the person or persons by whom it is to be made.

I.

An action based on diversity of citizenship was brought in the District Court seeking damages arising from personal injuries suffered by passengers of a bus which collided with the rear of a tractor-trailer. The named defendants were The Greyhound Corporation, owner of the bus; petitioner, Robert L. Schlagenhauf, the bus driver; Contract Carriers, Inc., owner of the tractor; Joseph L. McCorkhill, driver of the tractor; and National Lead Company, owner of the trailer. Answers were filed by each of the defendants denying negligence.

Greyhound then cross-claimed against Contract Carriers and National Lead for damage to Greyhound's bus, alleging that the collision was due solely to their negligence in that the tractor-trailer was driven at an unreasonably low speed, had not remained in its lane, and was not equipped with proper rear lights. Contract Carriers filed an answer to this cross-claim denying its negligence and asserting "(t)hat the negligence of the driver of the * * * bus (petitioner Schlagenhauf) proximately caused and contributed to * * * Greyhound's damages."

Pursuant to a pretrial order, Contract Carriers filed a letter—which the trial court treated as, and we consider to be, part of the answer—alleging that Schlagenhauf was "not mentally or physically capable" of driving a bus at the time of the accident.

Contract Carriers and National Lead then petitioned the District Court for an order directing petitioner Schlagenhauf to submit to both mental and physical examinations by one specialist in each of the following fields:

(1) Internal medicine;

(2) Ophthalmology;

(3) Neurology; and

(4) Psychiatry.

For the purpose of offering a choice to the District Court of one specialist in each field, the petition recommended two specialists in internal medicine, ophthalmology, and psychiatry, respectively, and three specialists in neurology—a total of nine physicians. The petition alleged that the mental and physical condition of Schlagenhauf was "in controversy" as it had been raised by Contract Carriers' answer to Greyhound's cross-claim. This was supported by a brief of legal authorities and an affidavit of Contract Carriers' attorney stating that Schlagenhauf had seen red lights 10 to 15 seconds before the accident, that another witness had seen the rear lights of the trailer from a distance of three-quarters to one-half mile, and that Schlagenhauf had been involved in a prior accident.

The certified record indicates that petitioner's attorneys filed in the District Court a brief in opposition to this petition asserting, among other things, that "the physical and mental condition of the defendant Robert L. Schlagenhauf is not 'in controversy' herein in the sense that these words are used in Rule 35 of the Federal Rules of Civil Procedure; (and) that good cause has not been shown for the multiple examinations prayed for by the cross-defendant * * *."

While disposition of this petition was pending, National Lead filed its answer to Greyhound's cross-claim and itself cross-claimed against Greyhound and Schlagenhauf for damage to its trailer. The answer asserted generally that Schlagenhauf's negligence proximately caused the accident. The cross-claim additionally alleged that Greyhound and Schlagenhauf were negligent "(b)y permitting said bus to be operated over and upon said public highway by the said defendant, Robert L. Schlagenhauf, when both the said Greyhound Corporation and said Robert L. Schlagenhauf knew that the eyes and vision of the said Robert L. Schlagenhauf was (sic) impaired and deficient."

The District Court, on the basis of the petition filed by Contract Carriers, and without any hearing, ordered Schlagenhauf to submit to nine examinations—one by each of the recommended specialists—despite the fact that the petition clearly requested a total of only four examinations.

Petitioner applied for a writ of mandamus in the Court of Appeals against the respondent, the District Court Judge, seeking to have set aside the order requiring his mental and physical examinations. The Court of Appeals denied mandamus, one judge dissenting. We granted certiorari to review undecided questions concerning the validity and construction of Rule 35.

* * *

II.

Rule 35 on its face applies to all "parties," which under any normal reading would include a defendant. Petitioner contends, however, that the application of the Rule to a defendant would be an unconstitutional invasion of his privacy, or, at the least, be a modification of substantive rights existing prior to the adoption of the Federal Rules of Civil Procedure and thus beyond the congressional mandate of the Rules Enabling Act.[9]

These same contentions were raised in *Sibbach v. Wilson & Co.*, by a plaintiff in a negligence action who asserted a physical injury as a basis for recovery. The Court, by a closely divided vote, sustained the Rule as there applied. Both the majority and dissenting opinions, however, agreed that Rule 35 could not be assailed on constitutional grounds. The division in the Court was on the issue of whether the Rule was procedural or a modification of substantive rights. The majority held that the Rule was a regulation of procedure and thus within the scope of the Enabling Act— the dissenters deemed it substantive. Petitioner does not challenge the holding in *Sibbach* as applied to plaintiffs. He contends, however, that it should not be extended to defendants. We can see no basis under the *Sibbach* holding for such a distinction. Discovery "is not a one-way proposition." *Hickman v. Taylor.* Issues cannot be resolved by a doctrine of favoring one class of litigants over another.

We recognize that, insofar as reported cases show, this type of discovery in federal courts has been applied solely to plaintiffs, and that some early state cases seem to have proceeded on a theory that a plaintiff who seeks redress for injuries in a court of law thereby "waives" his right to claim the inviolability of his person.

---

9. 28 U.S.C. § 2072, which provides that the Rules "shall not abridge, enlarge or modify any substantive right * * *."

However, it is clear that *Sibbach* was not decided on any "waiver" theory. As Mr. Justice Roberts, for the majority, stated, one of the rights of a person "is the right not to be injured in one's person by another's negligence, to redress infraction of which the present action was brought." For the dissenters, Mr. Justice Frankfurter pointed out that "(o)f course the Rule is compulsive in that the doors of the federal courts otherwise open may be shut to litigants who do not submit to such a physical examination."

These statements demonstrate the invalidity of any waiver theory. The chain of events leading to an ultimate determination on the merits begins with the injury of the plaintiff, an involuntary act on his part. Seeking court redress is just one step in this chain. If the plaintiff is prevented or deterred from this redress, the loss is thereby forced on him to the same extent as if the defendant were prevented or deterred from defending against the action.

Moreover, the rationalization of *Sibbach* on a waiver theory would mean that a plaintiff has waived a right by exercising his right of access to the federal courts. Such a result might create constitutional problems. Also, if a waiver theory is espoused, problems would arise as to a plaintiff who originally brought his action in a state court (where there was no equivalent of Rule 35) and then has the case removed by the defendant to federal court.

We hold that Rule 35, as applied to either plaintiffs or defendants to an action, is free of constitutional difficulty and is within the scope of the Enabling Act. We therefore agree with the Court of Appeals that the District Court had power to apply Rule 35 to a party defendant in an appropriate case.

IV.

There remains the issue of the construction of Rule 35. We enter upon determination of this construction with the basic premise "that the deposition-discovery rules are to be accorded a broad and liberal treatment," *Hickman v. Taylor*, to effectuate their purpose that "civil trials in the federal courts no longer need be carried on in the dark."

Petitioner contends that even if Rule 35 is to be applied to defendants, which we have determined it must, nevertheless it should not be applied to him as he was not a party in relation to Contract Carriers and National Lead—the movants for the mental and physical examinations—at the time the examinations were sought. The Court of Appeals agreed with petitioner's general legal proposition, holding that the person sought to be examined must be an opposing party vis-a-vis the movant (or at least one of them). While it is clear that the person to be examined must be a party to the case, we are of the view that the Court of Appeals gave an unduly restrictive interpretation to that term. Rule 35 only requires that the person to be examined be a party to the "action," not that he be an opposing party vis-a-vis the movant. There is no doubt that Schlagenhauf was a "party" to this "action" by virtue of the original complaint. Therefore, Rule 35 permitted examination of him (a party defendant) upon petition of Contract Carriers and National Lead (codefendants), provided, of course, that the other requirements of the Rule were met. Insistence that the movant have filed a pleading against the person to be examined would have the undesirable result of an unnecessary proliferation of cross-claims and counterclaims and would not be in keeping with the aims of a liberal, nontechnical application of the Federal Rules. *See Hickman v. Taylor.*

While the Court of Appeals held that petitioner was not a party vis-a-vis National Lead or Contract Carriers at the time the examinations were first sought, it went on to hold that he had become a party vis-a-vis National Lead by the time of a second order entered by the District Court and thus was a party within its rule. This second order, identical in all material respects with the first, was entered on the basis of supplementary petitions filed by National Lead and Contract Carriers. These petitions gave no new basis for the examinations, except for the allegation that petitioner's mental and physical condition had been additionally put in controversy by the National Lead answer and cross-claim, which had been filed subsequent to the first petition for examinations.

Petitioner next contends that his mental or physical condition was not "in controversy" and "good cause" was not shown for the examinations, both as required by the express terms of Rule 35.

The discovery devices sanctioned by the Federal Rules include the taking of oral and written depositions (Rules 26–32), interrogatories to parties (Rule 33), production of documents (Rule 34), and physical and mental examinations of parties (Rule 35). The scope of discovery in each instance is limited by Rule 26(b)'s provision that "the deponent may be examined regarding any matter, not privileged, which is relevant to the subject matter involved in the pending action," and by the provisions of Rule 30(b) permitting the district court, upon motion, to limit, terminate, or otherwise control the use of discovery devices so as to prevent either their use in bad faith or undue "annoyance, embarrassment, or oppression."

It is notable, however, that in none of the other discovery provisions is there a restriction that the matter be "in controversy," and only in Rule 34 is there Rule 35's requirement that the movant affirmatively demonstrate "good cause."

This additional requirement of "good cause" was reviewed by Chief Judge Sobeloff in the following words:

> Subject to * * * (the restrictions of Rules 26(b) and 30(b) and (d)), a party may take depositions and serve interrogatories without prior sanction of the court or even its knowledge of what the party is doing. Only if a deponent refuses to answer in the belief that the question is irrelevant, can the moving party request under Rule 37 a court order requiring an answer.

Significantly, this freedom of action, afforded a party who resorts to depositions and interrogatories, is not granted to one proceeding under Rules 34 and 35. Instead, the court must decide as an initial matter, and in every case, whether the motion requesting production of documents or the making of a physical or mental examination adequately demonstrates good cause. The specific requirement of good cause would be meaningless if good cause could be sufficiently established by merely showing that the desired materials are relevant, for the relevancy standard has already been imposed by Rule 26(b). Thus, by adding the words "good cause," the Rules indicate that there must be greater showing of need under Rules 34 and 35 than under the other discovery rules.

The courts of appeals in other cases have also recognized that Rule 34's good-cause requirement is not a mere formality, but is a plainly expressed limitation on the use of that Rule. This is obviously true as to the "in controversy" and "good cause" requirements of Rule 35. They are not met by mere conclusory allegations of the pleadings—nor by mere relevance to the case—but require an affirmative showing by the movant that each condition as to which the examination is sought is really and genuinely in controversy and that good cause exists for ordering each particular examination. Obviously, what may be good cause for one type of examination may not be so for another. The ability of the movant to obtain the desired information by other means is also relevant.

Rule 35, therefore, requires discriminating application by the trial judge, who must decide, as an initial matter in every case, whether the party requesting a mental or physical examination or examinations has adequately demonstrated the existence of the Rule's requirements of "in controversy" and "good cause," which requirements, as the Court of Appeals in this case itself recognized, are necessarily related. This does not, of course, mean that the movant must prove his case on the merits in order to meet the requirements for a mental or physical examination. Nor does it mean that an evidentiary hearing is required in all cases. This may be necessary in some cases, but in other cases the showing could be made by affidavits or other usual methods short of a hearing. It does mean, though, that the movant must produce sufficient information, by whatever means, so that the district judge can fulfill his function mandated by the Rule.

Of course, there are situations where the pleadings alone are sufficient to meet these requirements. A plaintiff in a negligence action who asserts mental or physical injury, places that mental or physical injury clearly in controversy and provides the defendant with good cause for an examination to determine the existence and extent of such asserted injury. This is not only true as to a plaintiff, but applies equally to a defendant who asserts his mental or physical condition as a defense to a claim, such as, for example, where insanity is asserted as a defense to a divorce action.

Here, however, Schlagenhauf did not assert his mental or physical condition either in support of or in defense of a claim. His condition was sought to be placed in issue by other parties. Thus, under the principles discussed above, Rule 35 required that these parties make an affirmative showing that petitioner's mental or physical condition was in controversy and that there was good cause for the examinations requested. This, the record plainly shows, they failed to do.

The only allegations in the pleadings relating to this subject were the general conclusory statement in Contract Carriers' answer to the cross-claim that "Schlagenhauf was not mentally or physically capable of operating" the bus at the time of the accident and the limited allegation in National Lead's cross-claim that, at the time of the accident, "the eyes and vision of * * * Schlagenhauf was (sic) impaired and deficient."

The attorney's affidavit attached to the petition for the examinations provided:

> That * * * Schlagenhauf, in his deposition * * * admitted that he saw red lights for 10 to 15 seconds prior to a collision with a semi-tractor trailer unit and yet drove his vehicle on without reducing speed and without altering the course thereof.

> The only eye-witness to this accident known to this affiant * * * testified that immediately prior to the impact between the bus and truck that he had also been approaching the truck from the rear and that he had clearly seen the lights of the truck for a distance of three-quarters to one-half mile to the rear thereof.

> * * * Schlagenhauf has admitted in his deposition * * * that he was involved in a (prior) similar type rear end collision. * * *

This record cannot support even the corrected order which required one examination in each of the four specialties of internal medicine, ophthalmology, neurology, and psychiatry. Nothing in the pleadings or affidavit would afford a basis for a belief that Schlagenhauf was suffering from a mental or neurological illness warranting wide-ranging psychiatric or neurological examinations. Nor is there anything stated justifying the broad internal medicine examination.[16]

The only specific allegation made in support of the four examinations ordered was that the "eyes and vision" of Schlagenhauf were impaired. Considering this in conjunction with the affidavit, we would be hesitant to set aside a visual examination if it had been the only one ordered. However, as the case must be remanded to the District Court because of the other examinations ordered, it would be appropriate for the District

---

16. Moreover, it seems clear that there was no compliance with Rule 35's requirement that the trial judge delineate the "conditions, and scope" of the examinations. Here the examinations were ordered in very broad, general areas. The internal medicine examination might for example, at the instance of the movant or its recommended physician extend to such things as blood tests, electrocardiograms, gastro-intestinal and other X-ray examinations. It is hard to conceive how some of these could be relevant under any possible theory of the case.

Judge to reconsider also this order in light of the guidelines set forth in this opinion.

The Federal Rules of Civil Procedure should be liberally construed, but they should not be expanded by disregarding plainly expressed limitations. The "good cause" and "in controversy" requirements of Rule 35 make it very apparent that sweeping examinations of a party who has not affirmatively put into issue his own mental or physical condition are not to be automatically ordered merely because the person has been involved in an accident—or, as in this case, two accidents—and a general charge of negligence is lodged. Mental and physical examinations are only to be ordered upon a discriminating application by the district judge of the limitations prescribed by the Rule. To hold otherwise would mean that such examinations could be ordered routinely in automobile accident cases. The plain language of Rule 35 precludes such an untoward result.

Accordingly, the judgment of the Court of Appeals is vacated and the case remanded to the District Court to reconsider the examination order in light of the guidelines herein formulated and for further proceedings in conformity with this opinion.

Vacated and remanded.

MR. JUSTICE BLACK, with whom MR. JUSTICE CLARK joins, concurring in part and dissenting in part.

I agree with the Court that under Rule 35(a): (1) a plaintiff and a defendant have precisely the same right to obtain a court order for physical or mental examination of the other party or parties to a lawsuit; (2) before obtaining such an order it must be shown that physical or mental health is "in controversy" as to a relevant and material issue in the case; and (3) such an order "may be made only on motion for good cause shown" after "notice to the party to be examined and to all other parties." Unlike the Court, however, I think this record plainly shows that there was a controversy as to Schlagenhauf's mental and physical health and that "good cause" was shown for a physical and mental examination of him, unless failure to deny the allegations amounted to an admission that they were true. While the papers filed in connection with this motion were informal, there can be no doubt that other parties in the lawsuit specifically and unequivocally charged that Schlagenhauf was not mentally or physically capable of operating a motor bus at the time of the collision, and that his negligent operation of the bus caused the resulting injuries and damage. The other parties filed an affidavit based on depositions of Schlagenhauf and a witness stating that Schlagenhauf, driving the bus along a four-lane highway in what apparently was good weather, had come upon a tractor-trailer down the road in front of him. The tractor-trailer was displaying red lights visible for at least half a mile, and Schlagenhauf admitted seeing them. Yet after coming in sight of the vehicle Schlagenhauf continued driving the bus in a straight line, without slowing down, for a full 10 or 15 seconds until the bus struck the tractor-trailer. Schlagenhauf admitted also that he had been involved in the very same kind of accident once before. Schlagenhauf has never at any time in the proceedings denied and he does not even now deny the charges that his mental and physical health and his eyes and vision were impaired and deficient.

In a collision case like this one, evidence concerning very bad eyesight or impaired mental or physical health which may affect the ability to drive is obviously of the highest relevance. It is equally obvious, I think, that when a vehicle continues down an open road and smashes into a truck in front of it although the truck is in plain sight and there is ample time and room to avoid collision, the chances are good that the driver has some physical, mental or moral defect. When such a thing happens twice, one is even more likely to ask, "What is the matter with that driver? Is he blind or crazy?" Plainly the allegations of the other parties were relevant and put the question of Schlagenhauf's health and vision "in controversy." The Court nevertheless holds that these charges were not a sufficient basis on which to rest a court-ordered examination of Schlagenhauf. It says with reference to the charges of impaired physical or mental health that the charges are "conclusory." I had not thought there was anything strange about pleadings being "conclusory"—that is their function, at least since modern rules of procedure have attempted to substitute simple pleadings for the complicated and redundant ones which long kept the common-law courts in disrepute. I therefore cannot agree that the charges about Schlagenhauf's health and vision were not sufficient upon which to base an order under Rule 35(a), particularly since he was a party who raised every technical objection to being required to subject himself to an examination but never once denied that his health and vision were bad. In these circumstances the allegations here should be more than enough to show probable cause to justify a court order requiring some kind of physical and mental examination.

While I dissent from the Court's holding that no examination at all was justified by this record, I agree that the order was broader than required. I do so in part because of the arguments made in the dissent in *Sibbach v. Wilson & Co.*, that physical examinations of people should be ordered by courts only when clearly and unequivocally required by law. By the same reasoning I think the courts should exercise great restraint in administering such a law once it has been enacted, as *Sibbach* held it had been when Rule 35 was approved. For this reason I agree to the Court's judgment remanding the case in order to give Schlagenhauf, if he now chooses, and the other parties an opportunity to produce any relevant facts to aid the District Judge in refashioning an order which will be neither too broad nor too narrow to give all the parties the rights which are theirs.

Mr. JUSTICE DOUGLAS, dissenting in part.

While I join the Court in reversing this judgment, I would, on the remand, deny all relief asked under Rule 35.

I do not suppose there is any licensed driver of a car or a truck who does not suffer from some ailment, whether it be ulcers, bad eyesight, abnormal blood pressure, deafness, liver malfunction, bursitis, rheumatism, or what not. If he or she is turned over to the plaintiff's doctors and psychoanalysts to discover the cause of the mishap, the door will be opened for grave miscarriages of justice. When the defendant's doctors examine plaintiff, they are normally interested only in answering a single question: did plaintiff in fact sustain the specific injuries claimed? But plaintiff's doctors will naturally be inclined to go on a fishing expedition in search of anything which will tend to prove that the defendant was unfit to perform the acts which resulted in the plaintiff's injury. And a doctor for a fee can easily discover something wrong with any patient—a condition that in prejudiced medical eyes might have caused the accident. Once defendants are turned over to medical or psychiatric clinics for an analysis of their physical well-being and the condition of their psyche, the effective trial will be held there and not before the jury. There are no lawyers in those clinics to stop the doctor from probing this organ or that one, to halt a further inquiry, to object to a line of questioning. And there is no judge to sit as arbiter. The doctor or the psychiatrist has a holiday in the privacy of his office. The defendant is at the doctor's (or psychiatrist's) mercy; and his report may either overawe or confuse the jury and prevent a fair trial.

The Court in *Sibbach v. Wilson & Co.* was divided when it came to submission of a plaintiff to a compulsory medical examination. The division was not over the constitutional power to require it but only as to whether Congress had authorized a rule to that effect. I accept that point as one governed by stare decisis. But no decision that when a plaintiff claims damages his "mental or physical condition" is "in controversy," within the meaning of Rule 35, governs the present case. The plaintiff by suing puts those issues "in controversy." A plaintiff, by coming into court and asserting that he has suffered an injury at the hands of the defendant, has thereby put his physical or mental condition "in controversy." Thus it may be only fair to provide that he may not be permitted to recover his judgment unless he permits an inquiry into the true nature of his condition.

A defendant's physical and mental condition is not, however, immediately and directly "in controversy" in a negligence suit. The issue is whether he was negligent. His physical or mental condition may of course be relevant to that issue; and he may be questioned concerning it and various methods of discovery can be used. But I balk at saying those issues are "in controversy" within the meaning of Rule 35 in every negligence suit or that they may be put "in controversy" by the addition of a few words in the complaint. As I have said, *Sibbach* proceeded on the basis that a plaintiff who seeks a decree of a federal court for his damages may not conceal or make difficult the proof of the claim he makes. The defendant, however, is dragged there; and to find "waiver" of the "inviolability of the person" is beyond reality.

Neither the Court nor Congress up to today has determined that any person whose physical or mental condition is brought into question during some lawsuit must surrender his right to keep his person inviolate. Congress did, according to *Sibbach*, require a plaintiff to choose between his privacy and his purse; but before today it has not been thought that any other "party" had lost this historic immunity. Congress and this Court can authorize such a rule. But a rule suited to purposes of discovery against defendants must be carefully drawn in light of the great potential of blackmail.

The Advisory Committee on Rules for Civil Procedure in its October 1955 Report of Proposed Amendments to the Rules of Civil Procedure for the United States District Courts proposed that Rule 35 be broadened to include situations where the mental or physical condition or "the blood relationship" of a party, or "of an agent or a person in the custody or under the legal control of a party," is "in controversy." We did not adopt that Rule in its broadened form. But concededly the issue with which we are now concerned was not exposed. It needs, in my opinion, full exposure so that if the Rule is to be applied to defendants as well as to plaintiffs, safeguards can be provided in the Rule itself against the awful risks of blackmail that exist in a Rule of that breadth.

This is a problem that we should refer to the Civil Rules Committee of the Judicial Conference so that if medical and psychiatric clinics are to be used in discovery against defendants—whether in negligence, libel, or contract cases—the standards and conditions will be discriminating and precise. If the bus driver in the instant case were not a defendant, could he be examined by doctors and psychiatrists? Lines must in time be drawn; and I think the new Civil Rules Committee is better equipped than we are to draw them initially.

MR. JUSTICE HARLAN, dissenting.

* * * The Court of Appeals having correctly concluded, as this Court now holds and as I agree, that the District Court had power to order the physical and mental examinations of this petitioner, and since I believe that there was no clear abuse of discretion in its so acting, I think the lower court was quite right in denying mandamus, and I would affirm its judgment on that basis.

* * *

B. PROTECTIVE ORDERS

FEDERAL RULE OF CIVIL PROCEDURE 26(c)

(c) Protective Orders.

> **(1) In General.** A party or any person from whom discovery is sought may move for a protective order in the court where the action is pending—or as an alternative on matters relating to a deposition, in the court for the district where the deposition will

be taken. The motion must include a certification that the movant has in good faith conferred or attempted to confer with other affected parties in an effort to resolve the dispute without court action. The court may, for good cause, issue an order to protect a party or person from annoyance, embarrassment, oppression, or undue burden or expense, including one or more of the following:

(A) forbidding the disclosure or discovery;

(B) specifying terms, including time and place, for the disclosure or discovery;

(C) prescribing a discovery method other than the one selected by the party seeking discovery;

(D) forbidding inquiry into certain matters, or limiting the scope of disclosure or discovery to certain matters;

(E) designating the persons who may be present while the discovery is conducted;

(F) requiring that a deposition be sealed and opened only on court order;

(G) requiring that a trade secret or other confidential research, development, or commercial information not be revealed or be revealed only in a specified way; and

(H) requiring that the parties simultaneously file specified documents or information in sealed envelopes, to be opened as the court directs.

(2) Ordering Discovery. If a motion for a protective order is wholly or partly denied, the court may, on just terms, order that any party or person provide or permit discovery.

(3) Awarding Expenses. Rule 37(a)(5) applies to the award of expenses.

* * *

Federal Rule of Civil Procedure 37. Failure to Make Disclosures or to Cooperate in Discovery; Sanctions

(a) Motion for an Order Compelling Disclosure or Discovery.

(1) In General. On notice to other parties and all affected persons, a party may move for an order compelling disclosure or discovery. The motion must include a certification that the movant has in good faith conferred or attempted to confer with the person or party failing to make disclosure or discovery in an effort to obtain it without court action.

(2) Appropriate Court. A motion for an order to a party must be made in the court where the action is pending. A motion for an order to a nonparty must be made in the court where the discovery is or will be taken.

(3) Specific Motions.

   (A) To Compel Disclosure. If a party fails to make a disclosure required by Rule 26(a), any other party may move to compel disclosure and for appropriate sanctions.

   (B) To Compel a Discovery Response. A party seeking discovery may move for an order compelling an answer, designation, production, or inspection. This motion may be made if:

     (i) a deponent fails to answer a question asked under Rule 30 or 31;

     (ii) a corporation or other entity fails to make a designation under Rule 30(b)(6) or 31(a)(4);

     (iii) a party fails to answer an interrogatory submitted under Rule 33; or

     (iv) a party fails to respond that inspection will be permitted—or fails to permit inspection—as requested under Rule 34.

   (C) Related to a Deposition. When taking an oral deposition, the party asking a question may complete or adjourn the examination before moving for an order.

(4) Evasive or Incomplete Disclosure, Answer, or Response. For purposes of this subdivision (a), an evasive or incomplete disclosure, answer, or response must be treated as a failure to disclose, answer, or respond.

(5) Payment of Expenses; Protective Orders.

   (A) If the Motion Is Granted (or Disclosure or Discovery Is Provided After Filing). If the motion is granted—or if the disclosure or requested discovery is provided after the motion was filed—the court must, after giving an opportunity to be heard, require the party or deponent whose conduct necessitated the motion, the party or attorney advising that conduct, or both to pay the movant's reasonable expenses incurred in making the motion, including attorney's fees. But the court must not order this payment if:

     (i) the movant filed the motion before attempting in good faith to obtain the disclosure or discovery without court action;

     (ii) the opposing party's nondisclosure, response, or objection was substantially justified; or

     (iii) other circumstances make an award of expenses unjust.

   (B) If the Motion Is Denied. If the motion is denied, the court may issue any protective order authorized under Rule 26(c) and must, after giving an opportunity to be heard, require the movant, the attorney filing the motion, or both to pay the party or deponent who opposed the motion its reasonable expenses incurred in opposing the motion, including attorney's fees. But the court must not order this payment if the motion was substantially justified or other circumstances make an award of expenses unjust.

(C) **If the Motion Is Granted in Part and Denied in Part.** If the motion is granted in part and denied in part, the court may issue any protective order authorized under Rule 26(c) and may, after giving an opportunity to be heard, apportion the reasonable expenses for the motion.

(b) **Failure to Comply with a Court Order.**

(1) **Sanctions in the District Where the Deposition Is Taken.** If the court where the discovery is taken orders a deponent to be sworn or to answer a question and the deponent fails to obey, the failure may be treated as contempt of court.

(2) **Sanctions in the District Where the Action Is Pending.**

(A) **For Not Obeying a Discovery Order.** If a party or a party's officer, director, or managing agent—or a witness designated under Rule 30(b)(6) or 31(a)(4)—fails to obey an order to provide or permit discovery, including an order under Rule 26(f), 35, or 37(a), the court where the action is pending may issue further just orders. They may include the following:

(i) directing that the matters embraced in the order or other designated facts be taken as established for purposes of the action, as the prevailing party claims;

(ii) prohibiting the disobedient party from supporting or opposing designated claims or defenses, or from introducing designated matters in evidence;

(iii) striking pleadings in whole or in part;

(iv) staying further proceedings until the order is obeyed;

(v) dismissing the action or proceeding in whole or in part;

(vi) rendering a default judgment against the disobedient party; or

(vii) treating as contempt of court the failure to obey any order except an order to submit to a physical or mental examination.

(B) **For Not Producing a Person for Examination.** If a party fails to comply with an order under Rule 35(a) requiring it to produce another person for examination, the court may issue any of the orders listed in Rule 37(b)(2)(A)(i) to (vi), unless the disobedient party shows that it cannot produce the other person.

(C) **Payment of Expenses.** Instead of or in addition to the orders above, the court must order the disobedient party, the attorney advising that party, or both to pay the reasonable expenses, including attorney's fees, caused by the failure, unless the failure was substantially justified or other circumstances make an award of expenses unjust.

(c) **Failure to Disclose, to Supplement an Earlier Response, or to Admit.**

(1) **Failure to Disclose or Supplement.** If a party fails to provide information or identify a witness as required by Rule 26(a) or (e), the party is not allowed to use that information or witness to supply evidence on a motion, at a hearing, or at a trial, unless the failure was substantially justified or is harmless. In addition to or instead of this sanction, the court, on motion and after giving an opportunity to be heard:

(A) may order payment of the reasonable expenses, including attorney's fees, caused by the failure;

(B) may inform the jury of the party's failure; and

(C) may impose other appropriate sanctions, including any of the orders listed in Rule 37(b)(2)(A)(i) to (vi).

(2) **Failure to Admit.** If a party fails to admit what is requested under Rule 36 and if the requesting party later proves a document to be genuine or the matter true, the requesting party may move that the party who failed to admit pay the reasonable expenses, including attorney's fees, incurred in making that proof. The court must so order unless:

(A) the request was held objectionable under Rule 36(a);

(B) the admission sought was of no substantial importance;

(C) the party failing to admit had a reasonable ground to believe that it might prevail on the matter; or

(D) there was other good reason for the failure to admit.

(d) **Party's Failure to Attend Its Own Deposition, Serve Answers to Interrogatories, or Respond to a Request for Inspection.**

(1) **In General.**

(A) **Motion; Grounds for Sanctions.** The court where the action is pending may, on motion, order sanctions if:

(i) a party or a party's officer, director, or managing agent— or a person designated under Rule 30(b)(6) or 31(a)(4)— fails, after being served with proper notice, to appear for that person's deposition; or

(ii) a party, after being properly served with interrogatories under Rule 33 or a request for inspection under Rule 34, fails to serve its answers, objections, or written response.

(B) Certification. A motion for sanctions for failing to answer or respond must include a certification that the movant has in good faith conferred or attempted to confer with the party failing to act in an effort to obtain the answer or response without court action.

(2) Unacceptable Excuse for Failing to Act. A failure described in Rule 37(d)(1)(A) is not excused on the ground that the discovery sought was objectionable, unless the party failing to act has a pending motion for a protective order under Rule 26(c).

(3) Types of Sanctions. Sanctions may include any of the orders listed in Rule 37(b)(2)(A)(i) to (vi). Instead of or in addition to these sanctions, the court must require the party failing to act, the attorney advising that party, or both to pay the reasonable expenses, including attorney's fees, caused by the failure, unless the failure was substantially justified or other circumstances make an award of expenses unjust.

(e) Failure to Provide Electronically Stored Information. Absent exceptional circumstances, a court may not impose sanctions under these rules on a party for failing to provide electronically stored information lost as a result of the routine, good-faith operation of an electronic information system.

(f) Failure to Participate in Framing a Discovery Plan. If a party or its attorney fails to participate in good faith in developing and submitting a proposed discovery plan as required by Rule 26(f), the court may, after giving an opportunity to be heard, require that party or attorney to pay to any other party the reasonable expenses, including attorney's fees, caused by the failure.

* * *

SEATTLE TIMES COMPANY v. RHINEHART

467 U.S. 20 (1984)

JUSTICE POWELL delivered the opinion of the Court.

This case presents the issue whether parties to civil litigation have a First Amendment right to disseminate, in advance of trial, information gained through the pretrial discovery process.

I

Respondent Rhinehart is the spiritual leader of a religious group, the Aquarian Foundation. The Foundation has fewer than 1,000 members, most of whom live in the State of Washington. Aquarian beliefs include life after death and the ability to communicate with the dead through a medium. Rhinehart is the primary Aquarian medium.

In recent years, the Seattle Times and the Walla Walla Union–Bulletin have published stories about Rhinehart and the Foundation.

Altogether 11 articles appeared in the newspapers during the years 1973, 1978, and 1979. The five articles that appeared in 1973 focused on Rhinehart and the manner in which he operated the Foundation. They described seances conducted by Rhinehart in which people paid him to put them in touch with deceased relatives and friends. The articles also stated that Rhinehart had sold magical "stones" that had been "expelled" from his body. One article referred to Rhinehart's conviction, later vacated, for sodomy. The four articles that appeared in 1978 concentrated on an "extravaganza" sponsored by Rhinehart at the Walla Walla State Penitentiary. The articles stated that he had treated 1,100 inmates to a 6-hour-long show, during which he gave away between $35,000 and $50,000 in cash and prizes. One article described a "chorus line of girls [who] shed their gowns and bikinis and sang. . . ." The two articles that appeared in 1979 referred to a purported connection between Rhinehart and Lou Ferrigno, star of the popular television program, "The Incredible Hulk."

II

Rhinehart brought this action in the Washington Superior Court on behalf of himself and the Foundation against the Seattle Times, the Walla Walla Union–Bulletin, the authors of the articles, and the spouses of the authors. Five female members of the Foundation who had participated in the presentation at the penitentiary joined the suit as plaintiffs.[1] The complaint alleges that the articles contained statements that were "fictional and untrue," and that the defendants—petitioners here—knew, or should have known, they were false. According to the complaint, the articles "did and were calculated to hold [Rhinehart] up to public scorn, hatred and ridicule, and to impeach his honesty, integrity, virtue, religious philosophy, reputation as a person and in his profession as a spiritual leader." With respect to the Foundation, the complaint also states: "[T]he articles have, or may have had, the effect of discouraging contributions by the membership and public and thereby diminished the financial ability of the Foundation to pursue its corporate purposes." The complaint alleges that the articles misrepresented the role of the Foundation's "choir" and falsely implied that female members of the Foundation had "stripped off all their clothes and wantonly danced naked. . . ." The complaint requests $14,100,000 in damages for the alleged defamation and invasions of privacy.[2]

Petitioners filed an answer, denying many of the allegations of the complaint and asserting affirmative defenses.[3] Petitioners promptly initi-

---

1. The record is unclear as to whether all five of the female plaintiffs participated in the "chorus line" described in the 1978 articles. The record also does not disclose whether any of the female plaintiffs were mentioned by name in the articles.

2. Although the complaint does not allege specifically that the articles caused a decline in membership of the Foundation, respondents' answers to petitioners' interrogatories raised this issue. In response to petitioners' request that respondents explain the damages they are seeking, respondents claimed that the Foundation had experienced a drop in membership in Hawaii and Washington "from about 300 people to about 150 people, and [a] concurrent drop in contributions."

3. Affirmative defenses included contentions that the articles were substantially true and accurate, that they were privileged under the First and Fourteenth Amendments, that the statute

ated extensive discovery. They deposed Rhinehart, requested production of documents pertaining to the financial affairs of Rhinehart and the Foundation, and served extensive interrogatories on Rhinehart and the other respondents. Respondents turned over a number of financial documents, including several of Rhinehart's income tax returns. Respondents refused, however, to disclose certain financial information,[4] the identity of the Foundation's donors during the preceding 10 years, and a list of its members during that period.

Petitioners filed a motion under the State's Civil Rule 37 requesting an order compelling discovery.[5] In their supporting memorandum, petitioners recognized that the principal issue as to discovery was respondents' "refusa[l] to permit any effective inquiry into their financial affairs, such as the source of their donations, their financial transactions, uses of their wealth and assets, and their financial condition in general." Respondents opposed the motion, arguing in particular that compelled production of the identities of the Foundation's donors and members would violate the First Amendment rights of members and donors to privacy, freedom of religion, and freedom of association. Respondents also moved for a protective order preventing petitioners from disseminating any information gained through discovery. Respondents noted that petitioners had stated their intention to continue publishing articles about respondents and this litigation, and their intent to use information gained through discovery in future articles.

In a lengthy ruling, the trial court initially granted the motion to compel and ordered respondents to identify all donors who made contributions during the five years preceding the date of the complaint, along with the amounts donated. The court also required respondents to divulge enough membership information to substantiate any claims of diminished membership. [T]he court refused to issue a protective order. It stated that the facts alleged by respondents in support of their motion for such an order were too conclusory to warrant a finding of "good cause" as required by Washington Superior Court Civil Rule 26(c).[7] The court

---

of limitations had run as to the 1973 articles, that the individual respondents had consented to any invasions of privacy, and that respondents had no reasonable expectation of privacy when performing before 1,100 prisoners.

4. Rhinehart also refused to reveal the current address of his residence. He submitted an affidavit stating that he had relocated out of fear for his safety and that disclosure of his current address would subject him to risks of bodily harm. Petitioners promptly moved for an order compelling Rhinehart to give his address and the trial court granted the motion.

5. Washington Superior Court Civil Rule 37 provides in relevant part: "A party, upon reasonable notice to other parties and all persons affected thereby, may apply to the court in the county where the deposition was taken, or in the county where the action is pending, for an order compelling discovery...."

7. Rule 26(c) provides:

Protective Orders. Upon motion by a party or by the person from whom discovery is sought, and for good cause shown, the court in which the action is pending or alternatively, on matters relating to a deposition, the court in the county where the deposition is to be taken may make any order which justice requires to protect a party or person from annoyance, embarrassment, oppression, or undue burden or expense, including one or more of the following: (1) that the discovery not be had; (2) that the discovery may be had only on specified terms and conditions,

stated, however, that the denial of respondents' motion was "without prejudice to [respondents'] right to move for a protective order in respect to specifically described discovery materials and a factual showing of good cause for restraining defendants in their use of those materials."

Respondents filed a motion for reconsideration in which they renewed their motion for a protective order. They submitted affidavits of several Foundation members to support their request. The affidavits detailed a series of letters and telephone calls defaming the Foundation, its members, and Rhinehart—including several that threatened physical harm to those associated with the Foundation. The affiants also described incidents at the Foundation's headquarters involving attacks, threats, and assaults directed at Foundation members by anonymous individuals and groups. In general, the affidavits averred that public release of the donor lists would adversely affect Foundation membership and income and would subject its members to additional harassment and reprisals.

Persuaded by these affidavits, the trial court issued a protective order covering all information obtained through the discovery process that pertained to "the financial affairs of the various plaintiffs, the names and addresses of Aquarian Foundation members, contributors, or clients, and the names and addresses of those who have been contributors, clients, or donors to any of the various plaintiffs." The order prohibited petitioners from publishing, disseminating, or using the information in any way except where necessary to prepare for and try the case. By its terms, the order did not apply to information gained by means other than the discovery process.[8] In an accompanying opinion, the trial court recognized that the protective order would restrict petitioners' right to publish information obtained by discovery, but the court reasoned that the restriction was necessary to avoid the "chilling effect" that dissemination would have on "a party's willingness to bring his case to court."

---

including a designation of the time or place; (3) that the discovery may be had only by a method of discovery other than that selected by the party seeking discovery; (4) that certain matters not be inquired into, or that the scope of the discovery be limited to certain matters; (5) that discovery be conducted with no one present except persons designated by the court; (6) that a deposition after being sealed be opened only by order of the court; (7) that a trade secret or other confidential research, development, or commercial information not be disclosed or be disclosed only in a designated way; (8) that the parties simultaneously file specified documents or information enclosed in sealed envelopes to be opened as directed by the court. . . .

Rule 26(c) is typical of the provisions adopted in many States.

8. The relevant portions of the protective order state:

2. Plaintiffs' motion for a protective order is granted with respect to information gained by the defendants through the use of all of the discovery processes regarding the financial affairs of the various plaintiffs, the names and addresses of Aquarian Foundation members, contributors, or clients, and the names and addresses of those who have been contributors, clients, or donors to any of the various plaintiffs.

3. The defendants and each of them shall make no use of and shall not disseminate the information defined in paragraph 2 which is gained through discovery, other than such use as is necessary in order for the discovering party to prepare and try the case. As a result, information gained by a defendant through the discovery process may not be published by any of the defendants or made available to any news media for publication or dissemination. This protective order has no application except to information gained by the defendants through the use of the discovery processes.

Respondents appealed from the trial court's production order, and petitioners appealed from the protective order. The Supreme Court of Washington affirmed both. With respect to the protective order, the court reasoned:

> Assuming then that a protective order may fall, ostensibly, at least, within the definition of a "prior restraint of free expression," we are convinced that the interest of the judiciary in the integrity of its discovery processes is sufficient to meet the "heavy burden" of justification. The need to preserve that integrity is adequate to sustain a rule like CR 26(c) which authorizes a trial court "to protect the confidentiality of information given for purposes of litigation."

The court noted that "[t]he information to be discovered concerned the financial affairs of the plaintiff Rhinehart and his organization, in which he and his associates had a recognizable privacy interest; and the giving of publicity to these matters would allegedly and understandably result in annoyance, embarrassment and even oppression." Therefore, the court concluded, the trial court had not abused its discretion in issuing the protective order.

The Supreme Court of Washington recognized that its holding conflicts with the holdings of the United States Court of Appeals for the District of Columbia Circuit and applies a different standard from that of the Court of Appeals for the First Circuit. We granted certiorari to resolve the conflict. We affirm.

III

Most States, including Washington, have adopted discovery provisions modeled on Rules 26 through 37 of the Federal Rules of Civil Procedure.[14] Rule 26(b)(1) provides that a party "may obtain discovery regarding any matter, not privileged, which is relevant to the subject matter involved in the pending action." It further provides that discovery is not limited to matters that will be admissible at trial so long as the information sought "appears reasonably calculated to lead to the discovery of admissible evidence."[15]

---

14. The Washington Supreme Court has stated that when the language of a Washington Rule and its federal counterpart are the same, courts should look to decisions interpreting the Federal Rule for guidance. The Washington Rule that provides for the scope of civil discovery and the issuance of protective orders is virtually identical to its counterpart in the Federal Rules of Civil Procedure.

15. Washington Superior Court Civil Rule 26(b)(1), identical to Federal Rule of Civil Procedure 26(b)(1) in effect at the time, provides in full:

> In General. Parties may obtain discovery regarding any matter, not privileged, which is relevant to the subject matter involved in the pending action, whether it relates to the claim or defense of the party seeking discovery or to the claim or defense of any other party, including the existence, description, nature, custody, condition and location of any books, documents, or other tangible things and the identity and location of persons having knowledge of any discoverable matter. It is not ground for objection that the information sought will be inadmissible at the trial if the information sought appears reasonably calculated to lead to the discovery of admissible evidence.

The Rules do not differentiate between information that is private or intimate and that to which no privacy interests attach. Under the Rules, the only express limitations are that the information sought is not privileged, and is relevant to the subject matter of the pending action. Thus, the Rules often allow extensive intrusion into the affairs of both litigants and third parties.[16] If a litigant fails to comply with a request for discovery, the court may issue an order directing compliance that is enforceable by the court's contempt powers.[17]

Petitioners argue that the First Amendment imposes strict limits on the availability of any judicial order that has the effect of restricting expression. They contend that civil discovery is not different from other sources of information, and that therefore the information is "protected speech" for First Amendment purposes. Petitioners assert the right in this case to disseminate any information gained through discovery. They do recognize that in limited circumstances, not thought to be present here, some information may be restrained. They submit, however:

> When a protective order seeks to limit expression, it may do so only if the proponent shows a compelling governmental interest. Mere speculation and conjecture are insufficient. Any restraining order, moreover, must be narrowly drawn and precise. Finally, before issuing such an order a court must determine that there are no alternatives which intrude less directly on expression.

We think the rule urged by petitioners would impose an unwarranted restriction on the duty and discretion of a trial court to oversee the discovery process.

IV

It is, of course, clear that information obtained through civil discovery authorized by modern rules of civil procedure would rarely, if ever, fall within the classes of unprotected speech identified by decisions of this Court. In this case, as petitioners argue, there certainly is a public interest in knowing more about respondents. This interest may well include most—and possibly all—of what has been discovered as a result of the court's order under Rule 26(b)(1). It does not necessarily follow, however, that a litigant has an unrestrained right to disseminate information that has been obtained through pretrial discovery. For even though the broad sweep of the First Amendment seems to prohibit all restraints on free

---

16. Under Rules 30 and 31, a litigant may depose a third party by oral or written examination. The litigant can compel the third party to be deposed and to produce tangible evidence at the deposition by serving the third party with a subpoena pursuant to Rule 45. Rule 45(b)(1) authorizes a trial court to quash or modify a subpoena of tangible evidence "if it is unreasonable and oppressive." Rule 45(f) provides: "Failure by any person without adequate excuse to obey a subpoena served upon him may be deemed a contempt of the court from which the subpoena issued."

17. In addition to its contempt power, Rule 37(b)(2) authorizes a trial court to enforce an order compelling discovery by other means including, for example, regarding designated facts as established for purposes of the action. *Cf.* Fed. Rule Civ. Proc. 37(b)(2)(A).

expression, this Court has observed that "[f]reedom of speech . . . does not comprehend the right to speak on any subject at any time."

The critical question that this case presents is whether a litigant's freedom comprehends the right to disseminate information that he has obtained pursuant to a court order that both granted him access to that information and placed restraints on the way in which the information might be used. In addressing that question it is necessary to consider whether the "practice in question [furthers] an important or substantial governmental interest unrelated to the suppression of expression" and whether "the limitation of First Amendment freedoms [is] no greater than is necessary or essential to the protection of the particular governmental interest involved."

A

At the outset, it is important to recognize the extent of the impairment of First Amendment rights that a protective order, such as the one at issue here, may cause. As in all civil litigation, petitioners gained the information they wish to disseminate only by virtue of the trial court's discovery processes. As the Rules authorizing discovery were adopted by the state legislature, the processes thereunder are a matter of legislative grace. A litigant has no First Amendment right of access to information made available only for purposes of trying his suit. ("The right to speak and publish does not carry with it the unrestrained right to gather information"). Thus, continued court control over the discovered information does not raise the same specter of government censorship that such control might suggest in other situations.

Moreover, pretrial depositions and interrogatories are not public components of a civil trial.[19] Such proceedings were not open to the public at common law, and, in general, they are conducted in private as a matter of modern practice. Much of the information that surfaces during pretrial discovery may be unrelated, or only tangentially related, to the underlying cause of action. Therefore, restraints placed on discovered, but not yet admitted, information are not a restriction on a traditionally public source of information.

Finally, it is significant to note that an order prohibiting dissemination of discovered information before trial is not the kind of classic prior restraint that requires exacting First Amendment scrutiny. As in this case, such a protective order prevents a party from disseminating only that information obtained through use of the discovery process. Thus, the

---

19. Discovery rarely takes place in public. Depositions are scheduled at times and places most convenient to those involved. Interrogatories are answered in private. Rules of Civil Procedure may require parties to file with the clerk of the court interrogatory answers, responses to requests for admissions, and deposition transcripts. *See* Fed. Rule Civ. Proc. 5(d). Jurisdictions that require filing of discovery materials customarily provide that trial courts may order that the materials not be filed or that they be filed under seal. Federal district courts may adopt local rules providing that the fruits of discovery are not to be filed except on order of the court. Thus, to the extent that courthouse records could serve as a source of public information, access to that source customarily is subject to the control of the trial court.

party may disseminate the identical information covered by the protective order as long as the information is gained through means independent of the court's processes. In sum, judicial limitations on a party's ability to disseminate information discovered in advance of trial implicates the First Amendment rights of the restricted party to a far lesser extent than would restraints on dissemination of information in a different context. Therefore, our consideration of the provision for protective orders contained in the Washington Civil Rules takes into account the unique position that such orders occupy in relation to the First Amendment.

B

Rule 26(c) furthers a substantial governmental interest unrelated to the suppression of expression. The Washington Civil Rules enable parties to litigation to obtain information "relevant to the subject matter involved" that they believe will be helpful in the preparation and trial of the case. Rule 26, however, must be viewed in its entirety. Liberal discovery is provided for the sole purpose of assisting in the preparation and trial, or the settlement, of litigated disputes. Because of the liberality of pretrial discovery permitted by Rule 26(b)(1), it is necessary for the trial court to have the authority to issue protective orders conferred by Rule 26(c). It is clear from experience that pretrial discovery by depositions and interrogatories has a significant potential for abuse.[20] This abuse is not limited to matters of delay and expense; discovery also may seriously implicate privacy interests of litigants and third parties.[21] The Rules do not distinguish between public and private information. Nor do they apply only to parties to the litigation, as relevant information in the hands of third parties may be subject to discovery.

There is an opportunity, therefore, for litigants to obtain—incidentally or purposefully—information that not only is irrelevant but if publicly released could be damaging to reputation and privacy. The government clearly has a substantial interest in preventing this sort of abuse of its processes. As stated by Judge Friendly "[w]hether or not the Rule itself authorizes [a particular protective order] ... we have no question as to the court's jurisdiction to do this under the inherent 'equitable powers of courts of law over their own process, to prevent abuses, oppression, and injustices'". The prevention of the abuse that can attend the coerced

---

20. *See* Comments of the Advisory Committee on the 1983 Amendments to Fed. Rule Civ. Proc. 26. In *Herbert v. Lando*, 441 U.S. 153 (1979), the Court observed: "There have been repeated expressions of concern about undue and uncontrolled discovery, and voices from this Court have joined the chorus. But until and unless there are major changes in the present Rules of Civil Procedure, reliance must be had on what in fact and in law are ample powers of the district judge to prevent abuse." But abuses of the Rules by litigants, and sometimes the inadequate oversight of discovery by trial courts, do not in any respect lessen the importance of discovery in civil litigation and the government's substantial interest in protecting the integrity of the discovery process.

21. Rule 26(c) includes among its express purposes the protection of a "party or person from annoyance, embarrassment, oppression or undue burden or expense." Although the Rule contains no specific reference to privacy or to other rights or interests that may be implicated, such matters are implicit in the broad purpose and language of the Rule.

production of information under a State's discovery rule is sufficient justification for the authorization of protective orders.[22]

C

We also find that the provision for protective orders in the Washington Rules requires, in itself, no heightened First Amendment scrutiny. To be sure, Rule 26(c) confers broad discretion on the trial court to decide when a protective order is appropriate and what degree of protection is required. The Legislature of the State of Washington, following the example of the Congress in its approval of the Federal Rules of Civil Procedure, has determined that such discretion is necessary, and we find no reason to disagree. The trial court is in the best position to weigh fairly the competing needs and interests of parties affected by discovery. The unique character of the discovery process requires that the trial court have substantial latitude to fashion protective orders.

V

The facts in this case illustrate the concerns that justifiably may prompt a court to issue a protective order. As we have noted, the trial court's order allowing discovery was extremely broad. It compelled respondents—among other things—to identify all persons who had made donations over a 5–year period to Rhinehart and the Aquarian Foundation, together with the amounts donated. In effect the order would compel disclosure of membership as well as sources of financial support. The Supreme Court of Washington found that dissemination of this information would "result in annoyance, embarrassment and even oppression." It is sufficient for purposes of our decision that the highest court in the State found no abuse of discretion in the trial court's decision to issue a protective order pursuant to a constitutional state law. We therefore hold that where, as in this case, a protective order is entered on a showing of good cause as required by Rule 26(c), is limited to the context of pretrial civil discovery, and does not restrict the dissemination of the information if gained from other sources, it does not offend the First Amendment.

The judgment accordingly is

Affirmed.

JUSTICE BRENNAN, with whom JUSTICE MARSHALL joins, concurring.

The Court today recognizes that pretrial protective orders, designed to limit the dissemination of information gained through the civil discovery process, are subject to scrutiny under the First Amendment. As the Court acknowledges, before approving such protective orders, "it is necessary to consider whether the 'practice in question [furthers] an important

---

22. The Supreme Court of Washington properly emphasized the importance of ensuring that potential litigants have unimpeded access to the courts: "[A]s the trial court rightly observed, rather than expose themselves to unwanted publicity, individuals may well forgo the pursuit of their just claims. The judicial system will thus have made the utilization of its remedies so onerous that the people will be reluctant or unwilling to use it, resulting in frustration of a right as valuable as that of speech itself."

or substantial governmental interest unrelated to the suppression of expression' and whether 'the limitation of First Amendment freedoms [is] no greater than is necessary or essential to the protection of the particular governmental interest involved.' "

In this case, the respondents opposed discovery, and in the alternative sought a protective order for discovered materials, because the "compelled production of the identities of the Foundation's donors and members would violate the First Amendment rights of members and donors to privacy, freedom of religion, and freedom of association." The Supreme Court of Washington found that these interests constituted the requisite "good cause" under the State's Rule 26(c) (upon "good cause shown," the court may make "any order which justice requires to protect a party or person from annoyance, embarrassment, oppression, or undue burden or expense"). Given this finding, the court approved a protective order limited to "information ... regarding the financial affairs of the various [respondents], the names and addresses of Aquarian Foundation members, contributors, or clients, and the names and addresses of those who have been contributors, clients, or donors to any of the various [respondents]." I agree that the respondents' interests in privacy and religious freedom are sufficient to justify this protective order and to overcome the protections afforded free expression by the First Amendment. I therefore join the Court's opinion.

* * *

C. WORK PRODUCT IMMUNITY

FEDERAL RULE OF CIVIL PROCEDURE 26(b)(3)

(3) Trial Preparation: Materials.

    (A) Documents and Tangible Things. Ordinarily, a party may not discover documents and tangible things that are prepared in anticipation of litigation or for trial by or for another party or its representative (including the other party's attorney, consultant, surety, indemnitor, insurer, or agent). But, subject to Rule 26(b)(4), those materials may be discovered if:

        (i) they are otherwise discoverable under Rule 26(b)(1); and

        (ii) the party shows that it has substantial need for the materials to prepare its case and cannot, without undue hardship, obtain their substantial equivalent by other means.

    (B) Protection Against Disclosure. If the court orders discovery of those materials, it must protect against disclosure of the mental impressions, conclusions, opinions, or legal theories of a party's attorney or other representative concerning the litigation.

    (C) Previous Statement. Any party or other person may, on request and without the required showing, obtain the person's own previous statement about the action or its subject matter. If the request is refused, the person may move for a court order, and Rule 37(a)(5) applies to the award of expenses. A previous statement is either:

    (i) a written statement that the person has signed or otherwise adopted or approved; or

    (ii) a contemporaneous stenographic, mechanical, electrical, or other recording—or a transcription of it—that recites substantially verbatim the person's oral statement.

* * *

(5) Claiming Privilege or Protecting Trial–Preparation Materials.

    (A) Information Withheld. When a party withholds information otherwise discoverable by claiming that the information is privileged or subject to protection as trial-preparation material, the party must:

        (i) expressly make the claim; and

        (ii) describe the nature of the documents, communications, or tangible things not produced or disclosed—and do so in a manner that, without revealing information itself privileged or protected, will enable other parties to assess the claim.

    (B) Information Produced. If information produced in discovery is subject to a claim of privilege or of protection as trial-preparation material, the party making the claim may notify any party that received the information of the claim and the basis for it. After being notified, a party must promptly return, sequester, or destroy the specified information and any copies it has; must not use or disclose the information until the claim is resolved; must take reasonable steps to retrieve the information if the party disclosed it before being notified; and may promptly present the information to the court under seal for a determination of the claim. The producing party must preserve the information until the claim is resolved.

* * *

FEDERAL RULE OF CIVIL PROCEDURE 30. DEPOSITIONS BY ORAL EXAMINATION

(a) When a Deposition May Be Taken.

    (1) Without Leave. A party may, by oral questions, depose any person, including a party, without leave of court except as provided in Rule 30(a)(2). The deponent's attendance may be compelled by subpoena under Rule 45.

    (2) With Leave. A party must obtain leave of court, and the court must grant leave to the extent consistent with Rule 26(b)(2):

        (A) if the parties have not stipulated to the deposition and:

(i) the deposition would result in more than 10 depositions being taken under this rule or Rule 31 by the plaintiffs, or by the defendants, or by the third-party defendants;

(ii) the deponent has already been deposed in the case; or

(iii) the party seeks to take the deposition before the time specified in Rule 26(d), unless the party certifies in the notice, with supporting facts, that the deponent is expected to leave the United States and be unavailable for examination in this country after that time; or

(B) if the deponent is confined in prison.

(b) Notice of the Deposition; Other Formal Requirements.

(1) Notice in General. A party who wants to depose a person by oral questions must give reasonable written notice to every other party. The notice must state the time and place of the deposition and, if known, the deponent's name and address. If the name is unknown, the notice must provide a general description sufficient to identify the person or the particular class or group to which the person belongs.

(2) Producing Documents. If a subpoena duces tecum is to be served on the deponent, the materials designated for production, as set out in the subpoena, must be listed in the notice or in an attachment. The notice to a party deponent may be accompanied by a request under Rule 34 to produce documents and tangible things at the deposition.

(3) Method of Recording.

(A) Method Stated in the Notice. The party who notices the deposition must state in the notice the method for recording the testimony. Unless the court orders otherwise, testimony may be recorded by audio, audiovisual, or stenographic means. The noticing party bears the recording costs. Any party may arrange to transcribe a deposition.

(B) Additional Method. With prior notice to the deponent and other parties, any party may designate another method for recording the testimony in addition to that specified in the original notice. That party bears the expense of the additional record or transcript unless the court orders otherwise.

(4) By Remote Means. The parties may stipulate—or the court may on motion order—that a deposition be taken by telephone or other remote means. For the purpose of this rule and Rules 28(a), 37(a)(2), and 37(b)(1), the deposition takes place where the deponent answers the questions.

(5) Officer's Duties.

(A) Before the Deposition. Unless the parties stipulate otherwise, a deposition must be conducted before an officer appointed or designated under Rule 28. The officer must begin the deposition with an on-the-record statement that includes:

(i) the officer's name and business address;

(ii) the date, time, and place of the deposition;

(iii) the deponent's name;

(iv) the officer's administration of the oath or affirmation to the deponent; and

(v) the identity of all persons present.

(B) Conducting the Deposition; Avoiding Distortion. If the deposition is recorded non-stenographically, the officer must repeat the items in Rule 30(b)(5)(A)(i) to (iii) at the beginning of each unit of the recording medium. The deponent's and attorneys' appearance or demeanor must not be distorted through recording techniques.

(C) After the Deposition. At the end of a deposition, the officer must state on the record that the deposition is complete and must set out any stipulations made by the attorneys about custody of the transcript or recording and of the exhibits, or about any other pertinent matters.

(6) Notice or Subpoena Directed to an Organization. In its notice or subpoena, a party may name as the deponent a public or private corporation, a partnership, an association, a governmental agency, or other entity and must describe with reasonable particularity the matters for examination. The named organization must then designate one or more officers, directors, or managing agents, or designate other persons who consent to testify on its behalf; and it may set out the matters on which each person designated will testify. A subpoena must advise a nonparty organization of its duty to make this designation. The persons designated must testify about information known or reasonably available to the organization. This paragraph (6) does not preclude a deposition by any other procedure allowed by these rules.

(c) Examination and Cross–Examination; Record of the Examination; Objections; Written Questions.

(1) Examination and Cross–Examination. The examination and cross-examination of a deponent proceed as they would at trial under the Federal Rules of Evidence, except Rules 103 and 615. After putting the deponent under oath or affirmation, the officer must record the testimony by the method designated under Rule 30(b)(3)(A). The testimony must be recorded by the officer personally or by a person acting in the presence and under the direction of the officer.

(2) Objections. An objection at the time of the examination—whether to evidence, to a party's conduct, to the officer's qualifications, to the manner of taking the deposition, or to any other aspect of the deposition—must be noted on the record, but the examination still proceeds; the testimony is taken subject to any objection. An objection must be stated concisely in a non-argumentative and non-suggestive manner. A person may instruct a deponent not to answer only when necessary to preserve a privilege, to enforce a limitation ordered by the court, or to present a motion under Rule 30(d)(3).

(3) **Participating Through Written Questions.** Instead of participating in the oral examination, a party may serve written questions in a sealed envelope on the party noticing the deposition, who must deliver them to the officer. The officer must ask the deponent those questions and record the answers verbatim.

(d) Duration; Sanction; Motion to Terminate or Limit.

(1) **Duration.** Unless otherwise stipulated or ordered by the court, a deposition is limited to 1 day of 7 hours. The court must allow additional time consistent with Rule 26(b)(2) if needed to fairly examine the deponent or if the deponent, another person, or any other circumstance impedes or delays the examination.

(2) **Sanction.** The court may impose an appropriate sanction—including the reasonable expenses and attorney's fees incurred by any party—on a person who impedes, delays, or frustrates the fair examination of the deponent.

(3) **Motion to Terminate or Limit.**

(A) **Grounds.** At any time during a deposition, the deponent or a party may move to terminate or limit it on the ground that it is being conducted in bad faith or in a manner that unreasonably annoys, embarrasses, or oppresses the deponent or party. The motion may be filed in the court where the action is pending or the deposition is being taken. If the objecting deponent or party so demands, the deposition must be suspended for the time necessary to obtain an order.

(B) **Order.** The court may order that the deposition be terminated or may limit its scope and manner as provided in Rule 26(c). If terminated, the deposition may be resumed only by order of the court where the action is pending.

(C) **Award of Expenses.** Rule 37(a)(5) applies to the award of expenses.

(e) Review by the Witness; Changes.

(1) **Review; Statement of Changes.** On request by the deponent or a party before the deposition is completed, the deponent must be allowed 30 days after being notified by the officer that the transcript or recording is available in which:

(A) to review the transcript or recording; and

    (B) if there are changes in form or substance, to sign a statement listing the changes and the reasons for making them.

  (2) Changes Indicated in the Officer's Certificate. The officer must note in the certificate prescribed by Rule 30(f)(1) whether a review was requested and, if so, must attach any changes the deponent makes during the 30–day period.

(f) Certification and Delivery; Exhibits; Copies of the Transcript or Recording; Filing.

  (1) Certification and Delivery. The officer must certify in writing that the witness was duly sworn and that the deposition accurately records the witness's testimony. The certificate must accompany the record of the deposition. Unless the court orders otherwise, the officer must seal the deposition in an envelope or package bearing the title of the action and marked "Deposition of [witness's name]" and must promptly send it to the attorney who arranged for the transcript or recording. The attorney must store it under conditions that will protect it against loss, destruction, tampering, or deterioration.

  (2) Documents and Tangible Things.

    (A) Originals and Copies. Documents and tangible things produced for inspection during a deposition must, on a party's request, be marked for identification and attached to the deposition. Any party may inspect and copy them. But if the person who produced them wants to keep the originals, the person may:

      (i) offer copies to be marked, attached to the deposition, and then used as originals—after giving all parties a fair opportunity to verify the copies by comparing them with the originals; or

      (ii) give all parties a fair opportunity to inspect and copy the originals after they are marked—in which event the originals may be used as if attached to the deposition.

    (B) Order Regarding the Originals. Any party may move for an order that the originals be attached to the deposition pending final disposition of the case.

  (3) Copies of the Transcript or Recording. Unless otherwise stipulated or ordered by the court, the officer must retain the stenographic notes of a deposition taken stenographically or a copy of the recording of a deposition taken by another method. When paid reasonable charges, the officer must furnish a copy of the transcript or recording to any party or the deponent.

  (4) Notice of Filing. A party who files the deposition must promptly notify all other parties of the filing.

(g) Failure to Attend a Deposition or Serve a Subpoena; Expenses. A party who, expecting a deposition to be taken, attends in person or by an attorney may recover reasonable expenses for attending, including attorney's fees, if the noticing party failed to:

    (1) attend and proceed with the deposition; or

    (2) serve a subpoena on a nonparty deponent, who consequently did not attend.

* * *

FEDERAL RULE OF CIVIL PROCEDURE 33.   INTERROGATORIES TO PARTIES

(a) In General.

    (1) Number. Unless otherwise stipulated or ordered by the court, a party may serve on any other party no more than 25 written interrogatories, including all discrete subparts. Leave to serve additional interrogatories may be granted to the extent consistent with Rule 26(b)(2).

    (2) Scope. An interrogatory may relate to any matter that may be inquired into under Rule 26(b). An interrogatory is not objectionable merely because it asks for an opinion or contention that relates to fact or the application of law to fact, but the court may order that the interrogatory need not be answered until designated discovery is complete, or until a pretrial conference or some other time.

(b) Answers and Objections.

    (1) Responding Party. The interrogatories must be answered:

       (A) by the party to whom they are directed; or

       (B) if that party is a public or private corporation, a partnership, an association, or a governmental agency, by any officer or agent, who must furnish the information available to the party.

    (2) Time to Respond. The responding party must serve its answers and any objections within 30 days after being served with the interrogatories. A shorter or longer time may be stipulated to under Rule 29 or be ordered by the court.

    (3) Answering Each Interrogatory. Each interrogatory must, to the extent it is not objected to, be answered separately and fully in writing under oath.

    (4) Objections. The grounds for objecting to an interrogatory must be stated with specificity. Any ground not stated in a timely objection is waived unless the court, for good cause, excuses the failure.

    (5) Signature. The person who makes the answers must sign them, and the attorney who objects must sign any objections.

(c) Use. An answer to an interrogatory may be used to the extent allowed by the Federal Rules of Evidence.

(d) Option to Produce Business Records. If the answer to an interrogatory may be determined by examining, auditing, compiling, abstracting, or summarizing a party's business records (including electronically stored information), and if the burden of deriving or ascertaining the answer will be substantially the same for either party, the responding party may answer by:

(1) specifying the records that must be reviewed, in sufficient detail to enable the interrogating party to locate and identify them as readily as the responding party could; and

(2) giving the interrogating party a reasonable opportunity to examine and audit the records and to make copies, compilations, abstracts, or summaries.

* * *

FEDERAL RULE OF CIVIL PROCEDURE 34. PRODUCING DOCUMENTS, ELECTRONICALLY STORED INFORMATION, AND TANGIBLE THINGS, OR ENTERING ONTO LAND, FOR INSPECTION AND OTHER PURPOSES

(a) In General. A party may serve on any other party a request within the scope of Rule 26(b):

(1) to produce and permit the requesting party or its representative to inspect, copy, test, or sample the following items in the responding party's possession, custody, or control:

(A) any designated documents or electronically stored information—including writings, drawings, graphs, charts, photographs, sound recordings, images, and other data or data compilations—stored in any medium from which information can be obtained either directly or, if necessary, after translation by the responding party into a reasonably usable form; or

(B) any designated tangible things; or

(2) to permit entry onto designated land or other property possessed or controlled by the responding party, so that the requesting party may inspect, measure, survey, photograph, test, or sample the property or any designated object or operation on it.

(b) Procedure.

(1) Contents of the Request. The request:

(A) must describe with reasonable particularity each item or category of items to be inspected;

(B) must specify a reasonable time, place, and manner for the inspection and for performing the related acts; and

(C) may specify the form or forms in which electronically stored information is to be produced.

(2) Responses and Objections.

    (A) Time to Respond. The party to whom the request is directed must respond in writing within 30 days after being served. A shorter or longer time may be stipulated to under Rule 29 or be ordered by the court.

    (B) Responding to Each Item. For each item or category, the response must either state that inspection and related activities will be permitted as requested or state an objection to the request, including the reasons.

    (C) Objections. An objection to part of a request must specify the part and permit inspection of the rest.

    (D) Responding to a Request for Production of Electronically Stored Information. The response may state an objection to a requested form for producing electronically stored information. If the responding party objects to a requested form—or if no form was specified in the request—the party must state the form or forms it intends to use.

    (E) Producing the Documents or Electronically Stored Information. Unless otherwise stipulated or ordered by the court, these procedures apply to producing documents or electronically stored information:

        (i) A party must produce documents as they are kept in the usual course of business or must organize and label them to correspond to the categories in the request;

        (ii) If a request does not specify a form for producing electronically stored information, a party must produce it in a form or forms in which it is ordinarily maintained or in a reasonably usable form or forms; and

        (iii) A party need not produce the same electronically stored information in more than one form.

(c) Nonparties. As provided in Rule 45, a nonparty may be compelled to produce documents and tangible things or to permit an inspection.

* * *

HICKMAN v. TAYLOR

329 U.S. 495 (1947)

MR. JUSTICE MURPHY delivered the opinion of the Court.

This case presents an important problem under the Federal Rules of Civil Procedure as to the extent to which a party may inquire into oral and written statements of witnesses, or other information, secured by an adverse party's counsel in the course of preparation for possible litigation after a claim has arisen. Examination into a person's files and records, including those resulting from the professional activities of an attorney, must be judged with care. It is not without reason that various safeguards have been established to preclude unwarranted excursions into the privacy of a man's work. At the same time, public policy supports reasonable and necessary inquiries. Properly to balance these competing interests is a delicate and difficult task.

On February 7, 1943, the tug "J. M. Taylor" sank while engaged in helping to tow a car float of the Baltimore & Ohio Railroad across the Delaware River at Philadelphia. The accident was apparently unusual in nature, the cause of it still being unknown. Five of the nine crew members were drowned. Three days later the tug owners and the underwriters employed a law firm, of which respondent Fortenbaugh is a member, to defend them against potential suits by representatives of the deceased crew members and to sue the railroad for damages to the tug.

A public hearing was held on March 4, 1943, before the United States Steamboat Inspectors, at which the four survivors were examined. This testimony was recorded and made available to all interested parties. Shortly thereafter, Fortenbaugh privately interviewed the survivors and took statements from them with an eye toward the anticipated litigation; the survivors signed these statements on March 29. Fortenbaugh also interviewed other persons believed to have some information relating to the accident and in some cases he made memoranda of what they told him. At the time when Fortenbaugh secured the statements of the survivors, representatives of two of the deceased crew members had been in communication with him. Ultimately claims were presented by representatives of all five of the deceased; four of the claims, however, were settled without litigation. The fifth claimant, petitioner herein, brought suit in a federal court under the Jones Act on November 26, 1943, naming as defendants the two tug owners, individually and as partners, and the railroad.

One year later, petitioner filed 39 interrogatories directed to the tug owners. The 38th interrogatory read: "State whether any statements of the members of the crews of the Tugs 'J. M. Taylor' and 'Philadelphia' or of any other vessel were taken in connection with the towing of the car float and the sinking of the Tug 'John M. Taylor'. Attach hereto exact copies of all such statements if in writing, and if oral, set forth in detail the exact provisions of any such oral statements or reports."

Supplemental interrogatories asked whether any oral or written statements, records, reports or other memoranda had been made concerning any matter relative to the towing operation, the sinking of the tug, the salvaging and repair of the tug, and the death of the deceased. If the answer was in the affirmative, the tug owners were then requested to set forth the nature of all such records, reports, statements or other memoranda.

The tug owners, through Fortenbaugh, answered all of the interrogatories except No. 38 and the supplemental ones just described. While admitting that statements of the survivors had been taken, they declined to summarize or set forth the contents. They did so on the ground that such requests called "for privileged matter obtained in preparation for litigation" and constituted "an attempt to obtain indirectly counsel's private files." It was claimed that answering these requests "would involve practically turning over not only the complete files, but also the telephone records and, almost, the thoughts of counsel."

In connection with the hearing on these objections, Fortenbaugh made a written statement and gave an informal oral deposition explaining the circumstances under which he had taken the statements. But he was not expressly asked in the deposition to produce the statements. The District Court for the Eastern District of Pennsylvania, sitting *en banc*, held that the requested matters were not privileged. The court then decreed that the tug owners and Fortenbaugh, as counsel and agent for the tug owners forthwith "Answer Plaintiff's 38th interrogatory and supplemental interrogatories; produce all written statements of witnesses obtained by Mr. Fortenbaugh, as counsel and agent for Defendants; state in substance any fact concerning this case which Defendants learned through oral statements made by witnesses to Mr. Fortenbaugh whether or not included in his private memoranda and produce Mr. Fortenbaugh's memoranda containing statements of fact by witnesses or to submit these memoranda to the Court for determination of those portions which should be revealed to Plaintiff." Upon their refusal, the court adjudged them in contempt and ordered them imprisoned until they complied.

The Third Circuit Court of Appeals, also sitting *en banc*, reversed the judgment of the District Court. It held that the information here sought was part of the "work product of the lawyer" and hence privileged from discovery under the Federal Rules of Civil Procedure. The importance of the problem, which has engendered a great divergence of views among district courts, led us to grant certiorari.

The pre-trial deposition-discovery mechanism established by Rules 26 to 37 is one of the most significant innovations of the Federal Rules of Civil Procedure. Under the prior federal practice, the pre-trial functions of notice-giving issue-formulation and fact-revelation were performed primarily and inadequately by the pleadings. Inquiry into the issues and the facts before trial was narrowly confined and was often cumbersome in method. The new rules, however, restrict the pleadings to the task of general notice-giving and invest the deposition-discovery process with a vital role in the preparation for trial. The various instruments of discovery now serve (1) as a device, along with the pre-trial hearing under Rule 16, to narrow and clarify the basic issues between the parties, and (2) as a device for ascertaining the facts, or information as to the existence or whereabouts of facts, relative to those issues. Thus civil trials in the federal courts no longer need be carried on in the dark. The way is now clear, consistent with recognized privileges, for the parties to obtain the fullest possible knowledge of the issues and facts before trial.

There is an initial question as to which of the deposition-discovery rules is involved in this case. Petitioner, in filing his interrogatories, thought that he was proceeding under Rule 33. That rule provides that a party may serve upon any adverse party written interrogatories to be answered by the party served. The District Court proceeded on the same assumption in its opinion, although its order to produce and its contempt order stated that both Rules 33 and 34 were involved. Rule 34 establishes a procedure whereby, upon motion of any party showing good cause therefor and upon notice to all other parties, the court may order any party to produce and permit the inspection and copying or photographing of any designated documents, etc., not privileged, which constitute or contain evidence material to any matter involved in the action and which are in his possession, custody or control.

The Circuit Court of Appeals, however, felt that Rule 26 was the crucial one. Petitioner, it said, was proceeding by interrogatories and, in connection with those interrogatories, wanted copies of memoranda and statements secured from witnesses. While the court believed that Rule 33 was involved, at least as to the defending tug owners, it stated that this rule could not be used as the basis for condemning Fortenbaugh's failure to disclose or produce the memoranda and statements, since the rule applies only to interrogatories addressed to adverse parties, not to their agents or counsel. And Rule 34 was said to be inapplicable since petitioner was not trying to see an original document and to copy or photograph it, within the scope of that rule. The court then concluded that Rule 26 must be the one really involved. That provides that the testimony of any person, whether a party or not, may be taken by any party by deposition upon oral examination or written interrogatories for the purpose of discovery or for use as evidence; and that the deponent may be examined regarding any matter, not privileged, which is relevant to the subject matter involved in the pending action, whether relating to the claim or defense of the examining party or of any other party, including the existence, description, nature, custody, condition and location of any books, documents or other tangible things.

The matter is not without difficulty in light of the events that transpired below. We believe, however, that petitioner was proceeding primarily under Rule 33. He addressed simple interrogatories solely to the individual tug owners, the adverse parties, as contemplated by that rule. He did not, and could not under Rule 33, address such interrogatories to their counsel, Fortenbaugh. Nor did he direct these interrogatories either to the tug owners or to Fortenbaugh by way of deposition; Rule 26 thus could not come into operation. And it does not appear from the record that petitioner filed a motion under Rule 34 for a court order directing the producetion of the documents in question. Indeed, such an order could not have been entered as to Fortenbaugh since Rule 34, like Rule 33, is limited to parties to the proceeding, thereby excluding their counsel or agents.

Thus to the extent that petitioner was seeking the production of the memoranda and statements gathered by Fortenbaugh in the course of his activities as counsel, petitioner misconceived his remedy. Rule 33 did not permit him to obtain such memoranda and statements as dejuncts to the interrogatories addressed to the individual tug owners. A party clearly cannot refuse to answer interrogatories on the ground that the information sought is solely within the knowledge of his attorney. But that is not this case. Here production was sought of documents prepared by a party's attorney after the claim has arisen. Rule 33 does not make provision for such production, even when sought in connection with permissible interrogatories. Moreover, since petitioner was also foreclosed from securing them through an order under Rule 34, his only recourse was to take Fortenbaugh's deposition under Rule 26 and to attempt to force Fortenbaugh to produce the materials by use of a subpoena duces tecum in accordance with Rule 45. But despite petitioner's faulty choice of action, the District Court entered an order, apparently under Rule 34, commanding the tug owners and Fortenbaugh, as their agent and counsel, to produce the materials in question. Their refusal led to the anomalous result of holding the tug owners in contempt for failure to produce that which was in the possession of their counsel and of holding Fortenbaugh in contempt for failure to produce that which he could not be compelled to produce under either Rule 33 or Rule 34.

But under the circumstances we deem it unnecessary and unwise to rest our decision upon this procedural irregularity, an irregularity which is not strongly urged upon us and which was disregarded in the two courts below. It matters little at this later stage whether Fortenbaugh fails to answer interrogatories filed under Rule 26 or under Rule 33 or whether he refuses to produce the memoranda and statements pursuant to a subpoena under Rule 45 or a court order under Rule 34. The deposition-discovery rules create integrated procedural devices. And the basic question at stake is whether any of those devices may be used to inquire into materials collected by an adverse party's counsel in the course of preparation for possible litigation. The fact that the petitioner may have used the wrong method does not destroy the main thrust of his attempt. Nor does it relieve us of the responsibility of dealing with the problem raised by that attempt. It would be inconsistent with the liberal atmosphere surrounding these rules to insist that petitioner now go through the empty formality of pursuing the right procedural device only to reestablish precisely the same basic problem now confronting us. We do not mean to say, however, that there may not be situations in which the failure to proceed in accordance with a specific rule would be important or decisive. But in the present circumstances, for the purposes of this decision, the procedural irregularity is not material. Having noted the proper procedure, we may accordingly turn our attention to the substance of the underlying problem.

In urging that he has a right to inquire into the materials secured and prepared by Fortenbaugh, petitioner emphasizes that the deposition-discovery portions of the Federal Rules of Civil Procedure are designed to enable the parties to discover the true facts and to compel their disclosure wherever they may be found. It is said that inquiry may be made under these rules, epitomized by Rule 26, as to any relevant matter which is not privileged; and since the discovery provisions are to be applied as broadly and liberally as possible, the privilege limitation must be restricted to its narrowest bounds. On the premise that the attorney-client privilege is the one involved in this case, petitioner argues that it must be strictly confined to confidential communications made by a client to his attorney. And since the materials here in issue were secured by Fortenbaugh from third persons rather than from his clients, the tug owners, the conclusion is reached that these materials are proper subjects for discovery under Rule 26.

As additional support for this result, petitioner claims that to prohibit discovery under these circumstances would give a corporate defendant a tremendous advantage in a suit by an individual plaintiff. Thus in a suit by an injured employee against a railroad or in a suit by an insured person against an insurance company the corporate defendant could pull a dark veil of secrecy over all the pertinent facts it can collect after the claim arises merely on the assertion that such facts were gathered by its large staff of attorneys and claim agents. At the same time, the individual plaintiff, who often has direct knowledge of the matter in issue and has no counsel until some time after his claim arises could be compelled to disclose all the intimate details of his case. By endowing with immunity from disclosure all that a lawyer discovers in the course of his duties, it is said, the rights of individual litigants in such cases are drained of vitality and the lawsuit becomes more of a battle of deception than a search for truth.

But framing the problem in terms of assisting individual plaintiffs in their suits against corporate defendants is unsatisfactory. Discovery concededly may work to the disadvantage as well as to the advantage of individual plaintiffs. Discovery, in other words, is not a one-way proposition. It is available in all types of cases at the behest of any party, individual or corporate, plaintiff or defendant. The problem thus far transcends the situation confronting this petitioner. And we must view that problem in light of the limitless situations where the particular kind of discovery sought by petitioner might be used.

We agree, of course, that the deposition-discovery rules are to be accorded a broad and liberal treatment. No longer can the time-honored cry of "fishing expedition" serve to preclude a party from inquiring into the facts underlying his opponent's case. Mutual knowledge of all the relevant facts gathered by both parties is essential to proper litigation. To that end, either party may compel the other to disgorge whatever facts he has in his possession. The deposition-discovery procedure simply advances the stage at which the disclosure can be compelled from the time of trial to the period preceding it, thus reducing the possibility of surprise. But discovery, like all matters of procedure, has ultimate and necessary boundaries. As indicated by Rules 30(b) and (d) and 31(d), limitations inevitably arise when it can be shown that the examination is being conducted in bad faith or in such a manner as to annoy, embarrass or oppress the person subject to the inquiry. And as Rule 26(b) provides, further limitations come into existence when the inquiry touches upon the irrelevant or encroaches upon the recognized domains of privilege.

We also agree that the memoranda, statements and mental impressions in issue in this case fall outside the scope of the attorney-client privilege and hence are not protected from discovery on that basis. It is unnecessary here to delineate the content and scope of that privilege as recognized in the federal courts. For present purposes, it suffices to note that the protective cloak of this privilege does not extend to information which an attorney secures from a witness while acting for his client in anticipation of litigation. Nor does this privilege concern the memoranda, briefs, communications and other writings prepared by counsel for his own use in prosecuting his client's case; and it is equally unrelated to writings which reflect an attorney's mental impressions, conclusions, opinions or legal theories.

But the impropriety of invoking that privilege does not provide an answer to the problem before us. Petitioner has made more than an ordinary request for relevant, non-privileged facts in the possession of his adversaries or their counsel. He has sought discovery as of right of oral and written statements of witnesses whose identity is well known and whose availability to petitioner appears unimpaired. He has sought production of these matters after making the most searching inquiries of his opponents as to the circumstances surrounding the fatal accident, which inquiries were sworn to have been answered to the best of their information and belief. Interrogatories were directed toward all the events prior to, during and subsequent to the sinking of the tug. Full and honest answers to such broad inquiries would necessarily have included all pertinent information gleaned by Fortenbaugh through his interviews with the witnesses. Petitioner makes no suggestion, and we cannot assume, that the tug owners or Fortenbaugh were incomplete or dishonest in the framing of their answers. In addition, petitioner was free to examine the public testimony of the witnesses taken before the United States Steamboat Inspectors. We are thus dealing with an attempt to secure the production of written statements and mental impressions contained in the files and the mind of the attorney Fortenbaugh without any showing of necessity or any indication or claim that denial of such production would unduly prejudice the preparation of petitioner's case or cause him any hardship or injustice. For aught that appears, the essence of what petitioner seeks either has been revealed to him already through the interrogatories or is readily available to him direct from the witnesses for the asking.

The District Court, after hearing objections to petitioner's request, commanded Fortenbaugh to produce all written statements of witnesses and to state in substance any facts learned through oral statements of witnesses to him. Fortenbaugh was to submit any memoranda he had made of the oral statements so that the court might determine what portions should be revealed to petitioner. All of this was ordered without any showing by petitioner, or any requirement that he make a proper showing, of the necessity for the production of any of this material or any demonstration that denial of production would cause hardship or injustice. The court simply ordered production on the theory that the facts sought were material and were not privileged as constituting attorney-client communications.

In our opinion, neither Rule 26 nor any other rule dealing with discovery contemplates production under such circumstances. That is not because the subject matter is privileged or irrelevant, as those concepts are used in these rules.[9] Here is simply an attempt, without purported necessity or justification, to secure written statements, private memoranda and personal recollections prepared or formed by an adverse party's counsel in the course of his legal duties. As such, it falls outside the arena of discovery and contravenes the public policy underlying the orderly prosecution and defense of legal claims. Not even the most liberal of discovery theories can justify unwarranted inquiries into the files and the mental impressions of an attorney.

Historically, a lawyer is an officer of the court and is bound to work for the advancement of justice while faithfully protecting the rightful interests of his clients. In performing his various duties, however, it is essential that a lawyer work with a certain degree of privacy, free from unnecessary intrusion by opposing parties and their counsel. Proper preparation of a client's case demands that he assemble information, sift what he considers to be the relevant from the irrelevant facts, prepare his legal theories and plan his strategy without undue and needless interference. That is the historical and the necessary way in which lawyers act within the framework of our system of jurisprudence to promote justice and to protect their clients' interests. This work is reflected, of course, in interviews, statements, memoranda, correspondence, briefs, mental impressions, personal beliefs, and countless other tangible and intangible ways-aptly though roughly termed by the Circuit Court of Appeals in this case as the "Work product of the lawyer." Were such materials open to opposing counsel on mere demand, much of what is now put down in writing would remain unwritten. An attorney's thoughts, heretofore inviolate, would not be his own. Inefficiency, unfairness and sharp practices would inevitably develop in the giving of legal advice and in the preparation of cases for trial. The effect on the legal profession would be

---

9. The English courts have developed the concept of privilege to include all documents prepared by or for counsel with a view to litigation. "All documents which are called into existence for the purpose—but not necessarily the sole purpose—of assisting the deponent or his legal advisers in any actual or anticipated litigation are privileged from production. * * * Thus all proofs, briefs, draft pleadings, etc., are privileged; but not counsel's indorsement on the outside of his brief * * *, nor any deposition or notes of evidence given publicly in open Court. * * * So are all papers prepared by any agent of the party bona fide for the use of his solicitor for the purposes of the action, whether in fact so used or not. * * * Reports by a company's servant, if made in the ordinary course of routine, are not privileged, even though it is desirable that the solicitor should have them and they are subsequently sent to him; but if the solicitor has requested that such documents shall always be prepared for his use and this was one of the reasons why they were prepared, they need not by disclosed."

demoralizing. And the interests of the clients and the cause of justice would be poorly served.

We do not mean to say that all written materials obtained or prepared by an adversary's counsel with an eye toward litigation are necessarily free from discovery in all cases. Where relevant and non-privileged facts remain hidden in an attorney's file and where production of those facts is essential to the preparation of one's case, discovery may properly be had. Such written statements and documents might, under certain circumstances, be admissible in evidence or give clues as to the existence or location of relevant facts. Or they might be useful for purposes of impeachment or corroboration. And production might be justified where the witnesses are no longer available or can be reached only with difficulty. Were production of written statements and documents to be precluded under such circumstances, the liberal ideals of the deposition-discovery portions of the Federal Rules of Civil Procedure would be stripped of much of their meaning. But the general policy against invading the privacy of an attorney's course of preparation is so well recognized and so essential to an orderly working of our system of legal procedure that a burden rests on the one who would invade that privacy to establish adequate reasons to justify production through a subpoena or court order. That burden, we believe, is necessarily implicit in the rules as now constituted.

Rule 30(b), as presently written, gives the trial judge the requisite discretion to make a judgment as to whether discovery should be allowed as to written statements secured from witnesses. But in the instant case there was no room for that discretion to operate in favor of the petitioner. No attempt was made to establish any reason why Fortenbaugh should be forced to produce the written statements. There was only a naked, general demand for these materials as of right and a finding by the District Court that no recognizable privilege was involved. That was insufficient to justify discovery under these circumstances and the court should have sustained the refusal of the tug owners and Fortenbaugh to produce.

But as to oral statements made by witnesses to Fortenbaugh, whether presently in the form of his mental impressions or memoranda, we do not believe that any showing of necessity can be made under the circumstances of this case so as to justify production. Under ordinary conditions, forcing an attorney to repeat or write out all that witnesses have told him and to deliver the account to his adversary gives rise to grave dangers of inaccuracy and untrustworthiness. No legitimate purpose is served by such production. The practice forces the attorney to testify as to what he remembers or what he saw fit to write down regarding witnesses' remarks. Such testimony could not qualify as evidence; and to use it for impeachment or corroborative purposes would make the attorney much less an officer of the court and much more an ordinary witness. The standards of the profession would thereby suffer.

Denial of production of this nature does not mean that any material, non-privileged facts can be hidden from the petitioner in this case. He need not be unduly hindered in the preparation of his case, in the discovery of facts or in his anticipation of his opponents' position. Searching interrogatories directed to Fortenbaugh and the tug owners, production of written documents and statements upon a proper showing and direct interviews with the witnesses themselves all serve to reveal the facts in Fortenbaugh's possession to the fullest possible extent consistent with public policy. Petitioner's counsel frankly admits that he wants the oral statements only to help prepare himself to examine witnesses and to make sure that he has overlooked nothing. That is insufficient under the circumstances to permit him an exception to the policy underlying the privacy of Fortenbaugh's professional activities. If there should be a rare situation justifying production of these matters, petitioner's case is not of that type.

We fully appreciate the wide-spread controversy among the members of the legal profession over the problem raised by this case. It is a problem that rests on what has been one of the most hazy frontiers of the discovery process. But until some rule or statute definitely prescribes otherwise, we are not justified in permitting discovery in a situation of this nature as a matter of unqualified right. When Rule 26 and the other discovery rules were adopted, this Court and the members of the bar in general certainly did not believe or contemplate that all the files and mental processes of lawyers were thereby opened to the free scrutiny of their adversaries. And we refuse to interpret the rules at this time so as to reach so harsh and unwarranted a result.

We therefore affirm the judgment of the Circuit Court of Appeals.

Affirmed.

MR. JUSTICE JACKSON, concurring.

The narrow question in this case concerns only one of thirty-nine interrogatories which defendants and their counsel refused to answer. As there was persistence in refusal after the court ordered them to answer it, counsel and clients were committed to jail by the district court until they should purge themselves of contempt.

The interrogatory asked whether statements were taken from the crews of the tugs involved in the accident, or of any other vessel, and demanded "Attach hereto exact copies of all such statements if in writing, and if oral, set forth in detail the exact provisions of any such oral statements or reports." The question is simply whether such a demand is authorized by the rules relating to various aspects of "discovery."

The primary effect of the practice advocated here would be on the legal profession itself. But it too often is overlooked that the lawyer and the law office are indispensable parts of our administration of justice. Law-abiding people can go nowhere else to learn the ever changing and constantly multiplying rules by which they must behave and to obtain redress for their wrongs. The welfare and tone of the legal profession is therefore of prime consequence to society, which would feel the consequences of such a practice as petitioner urges secondarily but certainly.

"Discovery" is one of the working tools of the legal profession. It traces back to the equity bill of discovery in English Chancery practice and seems to have had a forerunner in Continental practice. Since 1848 when the draftsmen of New York's Code of Procedure recognized the importance of a better system of discovery, the impetus to extend and expand discovery, as well as the opposition to it, has come from within the Bar itself. It happens in this case that it is the plaintiff's attorney who demands such unprecedented latitude of discovery and, strangely enough, amicus briefs in his support have been filed by several labor unions representing plaintiffs as a class. It is the history of the movement for broader discovery, however, that in actual experience the chief opposition to its extension has come from lawyers who specialize in representing plaintiffs because defendants have made liberal use of it to force plaintiffs to disclose their cases in advance. Discovery is a two-edged sword and we cannot decide this problem on any doctrine of extending help to one class of litigants.

It seems clear and long has been recognized that discovery should provide a party access to anything that is evidence in his case. It seems equally clear that discovery should not nullify the privilege of confidential communication between attorney and client. But those principles give us no real assistance here because what is being sought is neither evidence nor is it a privileged communication between attorney and client.

To consider first the most extreme aspect of the requirement in litigation here, we find it calls upon counsel, if he has had any conversations with any of the crews of the vessels in question or of any other, to "set forth in detail the exact provision of any such oral statements or reports." Thus the demand is not for the production of a transcript in existence but calls for the creation of a written statement not in being. But the statement by counsel of what a witness told him is not evidence when written plaintiff could not introduce it to prove his case. What, then, is the purpose sought to be served by demanding this of adverse counsel?

Counsel for the petitioner candidly said on argument that he wanted this information to help prepare himself to examine witnesses, to make sure he overlooked nothing. He bases his claim to it in his brief on the view that the Rules were to do away with the old situation where a law suit developed into "a battle of wits between counsel." But a common law trial is and always should be an adversary proceeding. Discovery was hardly intended to enable a learned profession to perform its functions either without wits or on wits borrowed from the adversary.

The real purpose and the probable effect of the practice ordered by the district court would be to put trials on a level even lower than a "battle of wits." I can conceive of no practice more demoralizing to the Bar than to require a lawyer to write out and deliver to his adversary an account of what witnesses have told him. Even if his recollection were perfect, the statement would be his language permeated with his inferences. Every one who has tried it knows that it is almost impossible so fairly to record the expressions and emphasis of a witness that when he testifies in the environment of the court and under the influence of the leading question there will not be departures in some respects. Whenever the testimony of the witness would differ from the "exact" statement the lawyer had delivered, the lawyer's statement would be whipped out to impeach the witness. Counsel producing his adversary's "inexact" statement could lose nothing by saying, "Here is a contradiction, gentlemen of the jury. I do not know whether it is my adversary or his witness who is not telling the truth, but one is not." Of course, if this practice were adopted, that scene would be repeated over and over again. The lawyer who delivers such statements often would find himself branded a deceiver afraid to take the stand to support his own version of the witness's conversation with him, or else he will have to go on the stand to defend his own credibility-perhaps against that of his chief witness, or possibly even his client.

Every lawyer dislikes to take the witness stand and will do so only for grave reasons. This is partly because it is not his role; he is almost invariably a poor witness. But he steps out of professional character to do it. He regrets it; the profession discourages it. But the practice advocated here is one which would force him to be a witness, not as to what he has seen or done but as to other witnesses' stories, and not because he wants to do so but in self-defense.

And what is the lawyer to do who has interviewed one whom he believes to be a biased, lying or hostile witness to get his unfavorable statements and know what to meet? He must record and deliver such statements even though he would not vouch for the credibility of the witness by calling him. Perhaps the other side would not want to call him either, but the attorney is open to the charge of suppressing evidence at the trial if he fails to call such a hostile witness even though he never regarded him as reliable or truthful.

Having been supplied the names of the witnesses, petitioner's lawyer gives no reason why he cannot interview them himself. If an employee-witness refuses to tell his story, he, too, may be examined under the Rules. He may be compelled on discovery as fully as on the trial to disclose his version of the facts. But that is his own disclosure—it can be used to impeach him if he contradicts it and such a deposition is not useful to promote an unseemly disagreement between the witness and the counsel in the case.

It is true that the literal language of the Rules would admit of an interpretation that would sustain the district court's order. So the literal language of the Act of Congress which makes "Any writing or record * * * made as a memorandum or record of any * * * occurrence, or event," admissible as evidence, would have allowed the railroad company to put its engineer's accident statements in evidence. But all such procedural measures have a background of custom and practice which was assumed by those who wrote and should be by those who apply them. We reviewed the background of the Act and the consequences on the trial of negligence cases of allowing railroads and others to put in their statements and thus to shield the crew from cross-examination. We said, "Such a major change which opens wide the door to avoidance of cross-examination should not be left to implication." We pointed out that there, as here, the "several hundred years of history behind the Act * * * indicate the nature of the reforms which it was designed to effect." We refused to apply it beyond that point. We should follow the same course of reasoning here. Certainly nothing in the tradition or practice of discovery up to the time of these Rules would have suggested that they would authorize such a practice as here proposed.

The question remains as to signed statements or those written by witnesses. Such statements are not evidence for the defendant. Nor should I think they ordinarily could be evidence for the plaintiff. But such a statement might be useful for impeachment of the witness who signed it, if he is called and if he departs from the statement. There might be circumstances, too, where impossibility or difficulty of access to the witness or his refusal to respond to requests for information or other facts would show that the interests of justice require that such statements be made available. Production of such statements are governed by Rule 34 and on "Showing good cause therefore" the court may order their inspection, copying or photographing. No such application has here been made; the demand is made on the basis of right, not on showing of cause.

I agree to the affirmance of the judgment of the Circuit Court of Appeals which reversed the district court.

* * *

D. ATTORNEY–CLIENT PRIVILEGE

UPJOHN COMPANY v. UNITED STATES

449 U.S. 383 (1981)

JUSTICE REHNQUIST delivered the opinion of the Court.

We granted certiorari in this case to address important questions concerning the scope of the attorney-client privilege in the corporate context and the applicability of the work-product doctrine in proceedings to enforce tax summonses. With respect to the privilege question the parties and various *amici* have described our task as one of choosing between two "tests" which have gained adherents in the courts of appeals. We are acutely aware, however, that we sit to decide concrete cases and not abstract propositions of law. We decline to lay down a broad rule or series of rules to govern all conceivable future questions in this area, even were we able to do so. We can and do, however, conclude that the attorney-client privilege protects the communications involved in this case from compelled disclosure and that the work-product doctrine does apply in tax summons enforcement proceedings.

I

Petitioner Upjohn Co. manufactures and sells pharmaceuticals here and abroad. In January 1976 independent accountants conducting an audit of one of Upjohn's foreign subsidiaries discovered that the subsidiary made payments to or for the benefit of foreign government officials in order to secure government business. The accountants, so informed petitioner, Mr. Gerard Thomas, Upjohn's Vice President, Secretary, and General Counsel. Thomas is a member of the Michigan and New York Bars, and has been Upjohn's General Counsel for 20 years. He consulted with outside counsel and R. T. Parfet, Jr., Upjohn's Chairman of the Board. It was decided that the company would conduct an internal investigation of what were termed "questionable payments." As part of this investigation the attorneys prepared a letter containing a questionnaire which was sent to "All Foreign General and Area Managers" over the Chairman's signature. The letter began by noting recent disclosures that several American companies made "possibly illegal" payments to foreign government officials and emphasized that the management needed full information concerning any such payments made by Upjohn. The letter indicated that the Chairman had asked Thomas, identified as "the company's General Counsel," "to conduct an investigation for the purpose of determining the nature and magnitude of any payments made by the Upjohn Company or any of its subsidiaries to any employee or official of a foreign government." The questionnaire sought detailed information concerning such payments. Managers were instructed to treat the investigation as "highly confidential" and not to discuss it with anyone other than Upjohn employees who might be helpful in providing the requested information. Responses were to be sent directly to Thomas. Thomas and outside counsel also interviewed the recipients of the questionnaire and some 33 other Upjohn officers or employees as part of the investigation.

On March 26, 1976, the company voluntarily submitted a preliminary report to the Securities and Exchange Commission on Form 8–K disclosing certain questionable payments. A copy of the report was simultaneously submitted to the Internal Revenue Service, which immediately began an investigation to determine the tax consequences of the payments. Special agents conducting the investigation were given lists by Upjohn of all those interviewed and all who had responded to the questionnaire. On November 23, 1976, the Service issued a summons demanding production of:

> All files relative to the investigation conducted under the supervision of Gerard Thomas to identify payments to employees of foreign governments and any political contributions made by the Upjohn Company or any of its affiliates since January 1, 1971 and to determine whether any funds of the Upjohn Company had been improperly accounted for on the corporate books during the same period.

The records should include but not be limited to written questionnaires sent to managers of the Upjohn Company's foreign affiliates, and memorandums or notes of the interviews conducted in the United States and abroad with officers and employees of the Upjohn Company and its subsidiaries.

The company declined to produce the documents specified in the second paragraph on the grounds that they were protected from disclosure by the attorney-client privilege and constituted the work product of attorneys prepared in anticipation of litigation. On August 31, 1977, the United States filed a petition seeking enforcement of the summons in the United States District Court for the Western District of Michigan. That court adopted the recommendation of a Magistrate who concluded that the summons should be enforced. Petitioners appealed to the Court of Appeals for the Sixth Circuit which rejected the Magistrate's finding of a waiver of the attorney-client privilege, but agreed that the privilege did not apply "[t]o the extent that the communications were made by officers and agents not responsible for directing Upjohn's actions in response to legal advice ... for the simple reason that the communications were not the 'client's.'" The court reasoned that accepting petitioners' claim for a broader application of the privilege would encourage upper-echelon management to ignore unpleasant facts and create too broad a "zone of silence." Noting that Upjohn's counsel had interviewed officials such as the Chairman and President, the Court of Appeals remanded to the District Court so that a determination of who was within the "control group" could be made. In a concluding footnote the court stated that the work-product doctrine "is not applicable to administrative summonses."

II

Federal Rule of Evidence 501 provides that "the privilege of a witness ... shall be governed by the principles of the common law as they may be interpreted by the courts of the United States in light of reason and experience." The attorney-client privilege is the oldest of the privileges for confidential communications known to the common law. Its purpose is to encourage full and frank communication between attorneys and their clients and thereby promote broader public interests in the observance of law and administration of justice. The privilege recognizes that sound legal advice or advocacy serves public ends and that such advice or advocacy depends upon the lawyer's being fully informed by the client. As we stated last Term: "The lawyer-client privilege rests on the need for the advocate and counselor to know all that relates to the client's reasons for seeking representation if the professional mission is to be carried out." And ... we recognized the purpose of the privilege to be "to encourage clients to make full disclosure to their attorneys." This rationale for the privilege has long been recognized by the Court (privilege "is founded upon the necessity, in the interest and administration of justice, of the aid of persons having knowledge of the law and skilled in its practice, which assistance can only be safely and readily availed of when free from the consequences or the apprehension of disclosure"). Admittedly complications in the application of the privilege arise when the client is a corporation, which in theory is an artificial creature of the law, and not an individual; but this Court has assumed that the privilege applies when the client is a corporation and the Government does not contest the general proposition.

The Court of Appeals, however, considered the application of the privilege in the corporate context to present a "different problem," since the client was an inanimate entity and "only the senior management, guiding and integrating the several operations, ... can be said to possess an identity analogous to the corporation as a whole." The first case to articulate the so-called "control group test" adopted by the court below, reflected a similar conceptual approach:

> Keeping in mind that the question is, Is it the corporation which is seeking the lawyer's advice when the asserted privileged communication is made?, the most satisfactory solution, I think, is that if the employee making the communication, of whatever rank he may be, is in a position to control or even to take a substantial part in a decision about any action which the corporation may take upon the advice of the attorney, ... then, in effect, *he is (or personifies) the corporation* when he makes his disclosure to the lawyer and the privilege would apply.

Such a view, we think, overlooks the fact that the privilege exists to protect not only the giving of professional advice to those who can act on it but also the giving of information to the lawyer to enable him to give sound and informed advice. The first step in the resolution of any legal problem is ascertaining the factual background and sifting through the facts with an eye to the legally relevant. *See* ABA Code of Professional Responsibility, Ethical Consideration 4–1:

> A lawyer should be fully informed of all the facts of the matter he is handling in order for his client to obtain the full advantage of our legal system. It is for the lawyer in the exercise of his independent professional judgment to separate the relevant and important from the irrelevant and unimportant. The observance of the ethical obligation of a lawyer to hold inviolate the confidences and secrets of his client not only facilitates the full development of facts essential to proper representation of the client but also encourages laymen to seek early legal assistance.

See also *Hickman v. Taylor.*

In the case of the individual client the provider of information and the person who acts on the lawyer's advice are one and the same. In the corporate context, however, it will frequently be employees beyond the control group as defined by the court below—"officers and agents ... responsible for directing [the company's] actions in response to legal advice"—who will possess the information needed by the corporation's lawyers. Middle-level- and indeed lower-level-employees can, by actions within the scope of their employment, embroil the corporation in serious legal difficulties, and it is only natural that these employees would have the relevant information needed by corporate counsel if he is adequately to advise the client with respect to such actual or potential difficulties. This fact was noted:

> In a corporation, it may be necessary to glean information relevant to a legal problem from middle management or non-management personnel as well as from top executives. The attorney dealing with a complex legal problem "is thus faced with a 'Hobson's choice'. If he interviews employees not having 'the very highest authority', their communications to him will not be privileged. If, on the other hand, he interviews *only* those employees with the 'very highest authority', he may find it extremely difficult, if not impossible, to determine what happened."

The control group test adopted by the court below thus frustrates the very purpose of the privilege by discouraging the communication of relevant information by employees of the client to attorneys seeking to render legal advice to the client corporation. The attorney's advice will also frequently be more significant to non-control group members than to those who officially sanction the advice, and the control group test makes it more difficult to convey full and frank legal advice to the employees who will put into effect the client corporation's policy. ("After the lawyer forms his or her opinion, it is of no immediate benefit to the Chairman of the Board or the President. It must be given to the corporate personnel who will apply it").

The narrow scope given the attorney-client privilege by the court below not only makes it difficult for corporate attorneys to formulate sound advice when their client is faced with a specific legal problem but also threatens to limit the valuable efforts of corporate counsel to ensure their client's compliance with the law. In light of the vast and complicated array of regulatory legislation confronting the modern corporation, corporations, unlike most individuals, "constantly go to lawyers to find out how to obey the law," particularly since compliance with the law in this area is hardly an instinctive matter ("the behavior proscribed by the [Sherman] Act is often difficult to distinguish from the gray zone of socially acceptable and economically justifiable business conduct").[2] The test adopted by the court below is difficult to apply in practice, though no abstractly formulated and unvarying "test" will necessarily enable courts to decide questions such as this with mathematical precision. But if the purpose of the attorney-client privilege is to be served, the attorney and client must be able to predict with some degree of certainty whether particular

---

2. The Government argues that the risk of civil or criminal liability suffices to ensure that corporations will seek legal advice in the absence of the protection of the privilege. This response ignores the fact that the depth and quality of any investigations, to ensure compliance with the law would suffer, even were they undertaken. The response also proves too much, since it applies to all communications covered by the privilege: an individual trying to comply with the law or faced with a legal problem also has strong incentive to disclose information to his lawyer, yet the common law has recognized the value of the privilege in further facilitating communications.

discussions will be protected. An uncertain privilege, or one which purports to be certain but results in widely varying applications by the courts, is little better than no privilege at all. The very terms of the test adopted by the court below suggest the unpredictability of its application. The test restricts the availability of the privilege to those officers who play a "substantial role" in deciding and directing a corporation's legal response. Disparate decisions in cases applying this test illustrate its unpredictability.

The communications at issue were made by Upjohn employees to counsel for Upjohn acting as such, at the direction of corporate superiors in order to secure legal advice from counsel. As the Magistrate found, "Mr. Thomas consulted with the Chairman of the Board and outside counsel and thereafter conducted a factual investigation to determine the nature and extent of the questionable payments *and to be in a position to give legal advice to the company with respect to the payments.*" Information, not available from upper-echelon management, was needed to supply a basis for legal advice concerning compliance with securities and tax laws, foreign laws, currency regulations, duties to shareholders, and potential litigation in each of these areas. The communications concerned matters within the scope of the employees' corporate duties, and the employees themselves were sufficiently aware that they were being questioned in order that the corporation could obtain legal advice. The questionnaire identified Thomas as "the company's General Counsel" and referred in its opening sentence to the possible illegality of payments such as the ones on which information was sought. A statement of policy accompanying the questionnaire clearly indicated the legal implications of the investigation. The policy statement was issued "in order that there be no uncertainty in the future as to the policy with respect to the practices which are the subject of this investigation." It began "Upjohn will comply with all laws and regulations," and stated that commissions or payments "will not be used as a subterfuge for bribes or illegal payments" and that all payments must be "proper and legal." Any future agreements with foreign distributors or agents were to be approved "by a company attorney" and any questions concerning the policy were to be referred "to the company's General Counsel." This statement was issued to Upjohn employees worldwide, so that even those interviewees not receiving a questionnaire were aware of the legal implications of the interviews. Pursuant to explicit instructions from the Chairman of the Board, the communications were considered "highly confidential" when made, and have been kept confidential by the company. Consistent with the underlying purposes of the attorney-client privilege, these communications must be protected against compelled disclosure.

The Court of Appeals declined to extend the attorney-client privilege beyond the limits of the control group test for fear that doing so would entail severe burdens on discovery and create a broad "zone of silence" over corporate affairs. Application of the attorney-client privilege to communications such as those involved here, however, puts the adversary in no worse position than if the communications had never taken place. The privilege only protects disclosure of communications; it does not protect disclosure of the underlying facts by those who communicated with the attorney:

> [T]he protection of the privilege extends only to *communications* and not to facts. A fact is one thing and a communication concerning that fact is an entirely different thing. The client cannot be compelled to answer the question, "What did you say or write to the attorney?" but may not refuse to disclose any relevant fact within his knowledge merely because he incorporated a statement of such fact into his communication to his attorney.

Here the Government was free to question the employees who communicated with Thomas and outside counsel. Upjohn has provided the IRS with a list of such employees, and the IRS has already interviewed some 25 of them. While it would probably be more convenient for the Government to secure the results of petitioner's internal investigation by simply subpoenaing the questionnaires and notes taken by petitioner's attorneys, such considerations of convenience do not overcome the policies served by the attorney-client privilege. As Justice Jackson noted in his concurring opinion in *Hickman v. Taylor*: "Discovery was hardly intended to enable a learned profession to perform its functions . . . on wits borrowed from the adversary."

Needless to say, we decide only the case before us, and do not undertake to draft a set of rules which should govern challenges to investigatory subpoenas. Any such approach would violate the spirit of Federal Rule of Evidence 501. While such a "case-by-case" basis may to some slight extent undermine desirable certainty in the boundaries of the attorney-client privilege, it obeys the spirit of the Rules. At the same time we conclude that the narrow "control group test" sanctioned by the Court of Appeals, in this case cannot, consistent with "the principles of the common law as . . . interpreted . . . in the light of reason and experience," Fed. Rule Evid. 501, govern the development of the law in this area.

III

Our decision that the communications by Upjohn employees to counsel are covered by the attorney-client privilege disposes of the case so far as the responses to the questionnaires and any notes reflecting responses to interview questions are concerned. The summons reaches further, however, and Thomas has testified that his notes and memoranda of interviews go beyond recording responses to his questions. To the extent that the material subject to the summons is not protected by the attorney-client privilege as disclosing communications between an employee and counsel, we must reach the ruling by the Court of Appeals that the work-product doctrine does not apply to IRS summonses.

The Government concedes, wisely, that the Court of Appeals erred and that the work-product doctrine does apply to IRS summonses. This doctrine was announced by the Court over 30 years ago in *Hickman v. Taylor*. In that case the Court rejected "an attempt, without purported necessity or justification, to secure written statements, private memoranda and personal recollections prepared or formed by an adverse party's counsel in the course of his legal duties." The Court noted that "it is essential that a lawyer work with a certain degree of privacy" and reasoned that if discovery of the material sought were permitted

> much of what is now put down in writing would remain unwritten. An attorney's thoughts, heretofore inviolate, would not be his own. Inefficiency, unfairness and sharp practices would inevitably develop in the giving of legal advice and in the preparation of cases for trial. The effect on the legal profession would be demoralizing. And the interests of the clients and the cause of justice would be poorly served.

The "strong public policy" underlying the work-product doctrine was reaffirmed recently and has been substantially incorporated in Federal Rule of Civil Procedure 26(b)(3).

As we stated last Term, the obligation imposed by a tax summons remains "subject to the traditional privileges and limitations." Nothing in the language of the IRS summons provisions or their legislative history suggests an intent on the part of Congress to preclude application of the work-product doctrine. Rule 26(b)(3) codifies the work-product doctrine, and the Federal Rules of Civil Procedure are made applicable to summons enforcement proceedings by Rule 81(a)(3). While conceding the applicability of the work-product doctrine, the Government asserts that it has made a sufficient showing of necessity to overcome its protections. The Magistrate apparently so found. The Government relies on the following language in *Hickman*:

> We do not mean to say that all written materials obtained or prepared by an adversary's counsel with an eye toward litigation are necessarily free from discovery in all cases. Where relevant and non-privileged facts remain hidden in an attorney's file and where production of those facts is essential to the preparation of one's case, discovery may properly be had.... And production might be justified where the witnesses are no longer available or can be reached only with difficulty.

The Government stresses that interviewees are scattered across the globe and that Upjohn has forbidden its employees to answer questions it considers irrelevant. The above-quoted language from *Hickman*, however, did not apply to "oral statements made by witnesses ... whether presently in the form of [the attorney's] mental impressions or memoranda." As to such material the Court did "not believe that any showing of necessity can be made under the circumstances of this case so as to justify production.... If there should be a rare situation justifying production of these matters petitioner's case is not of that type." Forcing an attorney to disclose notes and memoranda of witnesses' oral statements is particularly disfavored because it tends to reveal the attorney's mental processes ("what he saw fit to write down regarding witnesses' remarks"); ("the statement would be his [the attorney's] language, permeated with his inferences") (Jackson, J., concurring).[8]

Rule 26 accords special protection to work product revealing the attorney's mental processes. The Rule permits disclosure of documents and tangible things constituting attorney work product upon a showing of substantial need and inability to obtain the equivalent without undue hardship. This was the standard applied by the Magistrate. Rule 26 goes on, however, to state that "[i]n ordering discovery of such materials when the required showing has been made, the court shall protect against disclosure of the mental impressions, conclusions, opinions or legal theories of an attorney or other representative of a party concerning the litigation." Although this language does not specifically refer to memoranda based on oral statements of witnesses, the *Hickman* court stressed the danger that compelled disclosure of such memoranda would reveal the attorney's mental processes. It is clear that this is the sort of material the draftsmen of the Rule had in mind as deserving special protection. See Notes of Advisory Committee on 1970 Amendment to Rules ("The subdivision . . . goes on to protect against disclosure the mental impressions, conclusions, opinions, or legal theories . . . of an attorney or other representative of a party. The *Hickman* opinion drew special attention to the need for protecting an attorney against discovery of memoranda prepared from recollection of oral interviews. The courts have steadfastly safeguarded against disclosure of lawyers' mental impressions and legal theories . . .").

Based on the foregoing, some courts have concluded that *no* showing of necessity can overcome protection of work product which is based on oral statements from witnesses. Those courts declining to adopt an absolute rule have nonetheless recognized that such material is entitled to special protection. ("special considerations . . . must shape any ruling on the discoverability of interview memoranda . . .; such documents will be discoverable only in a 'rare situation' ").

We do not decide the issue at this time. It is clear that the Magistrate applied the wrong standard when he concluded that the Government had made a sufficient showing of necessity to overcome the protections of the work-product doctrine. The Magistrate applied the "substantial need" and "without undue hardship" standard articulated in the first part of Rule 26(b)(3). The notes and memoranda sought by the Government here, however, are work product based on oral statements. If they reveal communications, they are, in this case, protected by the attorney-client privilege. To the extent they do not reveal communications, they reveal the attorneys' mental processes in evaluating the communications. As

---

8. Thomas described his notes of the interviews as containing "what I considered to be the important questions, the substance of the responses to them, my beliefs as to the importance of these, my beliefs as to how they related to the inquiry, my thoughts as to how they related to other questions. In some instances they might even suggest other questions that I would have to ask or things that I needed to find elsewhere."

Rule 26 and *Hickman* make clear, such work product cannot be disclosed simply on a showing of substantial need and inability to obtain the equivalent without undue hardship.

While we are not prepared at this juncture to say that such material is always protected by the work-product rule, we think a far stronger showing of necessity and unavailability by other means than was made by the Government or applied by the Magistrate in this case would be necessary to compel disclosure. Since the Court of Appeals thought that the work-product protection was never applicable in an enforcement proceeding such as this, and since the Magistrate whose recommendations the District Court adopted applied too lenient a standard of protection, we think the best procedure with respect to this aspect of the case would be to reverse the judgment of the Court of Appeals for the Sixth Circuit and remand the case to it for such further proceedings in connection with the work-product claim as are consistent with this opinion.

Accordingly, the judgment of the Court of Appeals is reversed, and the case remanded for further proceedings.

It is so ordered.

CHIEF JUSTICE BURGER, concurring in part and concurring in the judgment.

I join in Parts I and III of the opinion of the Court and in the judgment. As to Part II, I agree fully with the Court's rejection of the so-called "control group" test, its reasons for doing so, and its ultimate holding that the communications at issue are privileged. As the Court states, however, "if the purpose of the attorney-client privilege is to be served, the attorney and client must be able to predict with some degree of certainty whether particular discussions will be protected." For this very reason, I believe that we should articulate a standard that will govern similar cases and afford guidance to corporations, counsel advising them, and federal courts.

The Court properly relies on a variety of factors in concluding that the communications now before us are privileged. Because of the great importance of the issue, in my view the Court should make clear now that, as a general rule, a communication is privileged at least when, as here, an employee or former employee speaks at the direction of the management with an attorney regarding conduct or proposed conduct within the scope of employment. The attorney must be one authorized by the management to inquire into the subject and must be seeking information to assist counsel in performing any of the following functions: (a) evaluating whether the employee's conduct has bound or would bind the corporation; (b) assessing the legal consequences, if any, of that conduct; or (c) formulating appropriate legal responses to actions that have been or may be taken by others with regard to that conduct. Other communications between employees and corporate counsel may indeed be privileged—as the petitioners and several *amici* have suggested in their proposed formulations—but the need for certainty does not compel us now to prescribe all the details of the privilege in this case.

Nevertheless, to say we should not reach all facets of the privilege does not mean that we should neglect our duty to provide guidance in a case that squarely presents the question in a traditional adversary context. Indeed, because Federal Rule of Evidence 501 provides that the law of privileges "shall be governed by the principles of the common law as they may be interpreted by the courts of the United States in the light of reason and experience," this Court has a special duty to clarify aspects of the law of privileges properly before us. Simply asserting that this failure "may to some slight extent undermine desirable certainty," neither minimizes the consequences of continuing uncertainty and confusion nor harmonizes the inherent dissonance of acknowledging that uncertainty while declining to clarify it within the frame of issues presented.

* * *

XII. SUMMARY JUDGMENT, TRIAL MOTIONS, AND POST–TRIAL MOTIONS

A. EVIDENTIARY BURDENS AND CREDIBILITY ISSUES

FEDERAL RULE OF CIVIL PROCEDURE 56. SUMMARY JUDGMENT

(a) Motion for Summary Judgment or Partial Summary Judgment. A party may move for summary judgment, identifying each claim or defense—or the part of each claim or defense—on which summary judgment is sought. The court shall grant summary judgment if the movant shows that there is no genuine dispute as to any material fact and the movant is entitled to judgment as a matter of law. The court should state on the record the reasons for granting or denying the motion.

(b) Time to File a Motion. Unless a different time is set by local rule or the court orders otherwise, a party may file a motion for summary judgment at any time until 30 days after the close of all discovery.

(c) Procedures.

    (1) Supporting Factual Positions. A party asserting that a fact cannot be or is genuinely disputed must support the assertion by:

        (A) citing to particular parts of materials in the record, including depositions, documents, electronically stored information, affidavits or declarations, stipulations (including those made for purposes of the motion only), admissions, interrogatory answers, or other materials; or

        (B) showing that the materials cited do not establish the absence or presence of a genuine dispute, or that an adverse party cannot produce admissible evidence to support the fact.

    (2) Objection That a Fact Is Not Supported by Admissible Evidence. A party may object that the material cited to support or dispute a fact cannot be presented in a form that would be admissible in evidence.

    (3) Materials Not Cited. The court need consider only the cited materials, but it may consider other materials in the record.

    (4) Affidavits or Declarations. An affidavit or declaration used to support or oppose a motion must be made on personal knowledge, set out facts that would be admissible in evidence, and show that the affiant or declarant is competent to testify on the matters stated.

(d) When Facts Are Unavailable to the Nonmovant. If a nonmovant shows by affidavit or declaration that, for specified reasons, it cannot present facts essential to justify its opposition, the court may:

    (1) defer considering the motion or deny it;

(2) allow time to obtain affidavits or declarations or to take discovery; or

(3) issue any other appropriate order.

(e) Failing to Properly Support or Address a Fact. If a party fails to properly support an assertion of fact or fails to properly address another party's assertion of fact as required by Rule 56(c), the court may:

(1) give an opportunity to properly support or address the fact;

(2) consider the fact undisputed for purposes of the motion;

(3) grant summary judgment if the motion and supporting materials—including the facts considered undisputed—show that the movant is entitled to it; or

(4) issue any other appropriate order.

(f) Judgment Independent of the Motion. After giving notice and a reasonable time to respond, the court may:

(1) grant summary judgment for a nonmovant;

(2) grant the motion on grounds not raised by a party; or

(3) consider summary judgment on its own after identifying for the parties material facts that may not be genuinely in dispute.

(g) Failing to Grant All the Requested Relief. If the court does not grant all the relief requested by the motion, it may enter an order stating any material fact—including an item of damages or other relief—that is not genuinely in dispute and treating the fact as established in the case.

(h) Affidavit or Declaration Submitted in Bad Faith. If satisfied that an affidavit or declaration under this rule is submitted in bad faith or solely for delay, the court—after notice and a reasonable time to respond—may order the submitting party to pay the other party the reasonable expenses, including attorney's fees, it incurred as a result. An offending party or attorney may also be held in contempt or subjected to other appropriate sanctions.

* * *

LUNDEEN v. CORDNER
354 F.2d 401 (8th Cir. 1966)

GIBSON, CIRCUIT JUDGE.

This is an appeal from the United States District Court for the District of Minnesota in a diversity action concerning the proceeds of a group life insurance policy and annuity contributions. The basic issue of the case is the determination of the rightful beneficiaries. The trial court awarded a summary judgment to intervenor and defendant, Northwestern National Bank of Minneapolis, (Northwestern) Trustee under the Last

Will and Testament of Joseph F. Cordner, the insured and prospective annuitant.

Appellant, plaintiff below, (hereinafter referred to as plaintiff) is a former wife of one Joseph Cordner, deceased. During their marriage two children were born, Maureen Joan Cordner and Michael Joseph Cordner. Prior to the time of his death Joseph Cordner was working in Libya. Mr. Cordner's employer Socony Mobil Oil Company, Inc. (Socony) carried a group life insurance contract with Metropolitan Life Insurance Company, (Metropolitan) under which Mr. Cordner as the insured had in 1956 designated his children, Maureen and Michael, as equal beneficiaries. In 1958 Joseph Cordner, having been divorced by plaintiff, married intervener, France Jeanne Cordner. In April 1960 a child was born of this second marriage. On October 3, 1962 Joseph Cordner died. During all periods above mentioned Mr. Cordner was in the employ of Socony stationed in Libya. The insurance policy and the annuity were in effect and due proof of loss was made. The contest for the proceeds arises between adverse claimants; the original designated beneficiaries, Maureen Joan and Michael Joseph Cordner; and France Jeanne Cordner, the second wife of assured, and Northwestern, as Trustee under the Last Will and Testament of Joseph F. Cordner, deceased.

On November 5, 1963, plaintiff as guardian and on behalf of her two children Maureen and Michael Cordner, the named beneficiaries, sued the insurer, Metropolitan, to recover the proceeds of the policy. Metropolitan answered that there were adverse claims to the policy benefits. Thereafter, Northwestern as the Trustee under the Last Will and Testament of the deceased, Joseph Cordner, was interpleaded as an additional defendant. Appellee, France J. Cordner, then intervened in the action. Both intervener and Northwestern allege that sometime in 1961 the decedent effected a change of beneficiaries. As a result of this alleged change, intervener states she is entitled to one-fourth of the insurance proceeds with the remaining three-fourths going to defendant, Northwestern in trust pursuant to Mr. Cordner's Will, which provided that income from the proceeds of the insurance policy would be paid to all three children of Joseph Cordner until they reach the age of 18, with the principal then going to intervenor.

It is clear that the first two children of decedent, Maureen and Michael, are the named beneficiaries. However, it is asserted that Joseph Cordner did everything within his power to effect a change of beneficiaries as alleged by intervener. Intervener presented affidavits and exhibits in support of her position and moved for summary judgment. The motion was granted and plaintiff contests this ruling on the ground that a summary judgment is not proper at this point in the litigation and that there remains a genuine issue on a material fact. It is now our task to determine if the summary judgment was properly granted.

The policy clearly allows the insured to change the beneficiaries at will.

The employer Socony was the admitted duly authorized representative of Metropolitan and kept all of the records relevant to the policy beneficiaries and any changes made in beneficiaries. In addition, as a matter of Socony policy all certificates (of insurance) held by employees working in foreign countries were held in Socony's New York office; therefore, any notice to Socony of a change in beneficiary would be operative to effectuate such a change; and it would be the ministerial function and duty of Socony to endorse the change requested on the retained certificate. Plaintiff accepts as controlling the general rule of law that an insured's attempt to change his beneficiary will be given effect if all that remains to be done is a ministerial duty on the part of the insurer.

Therefore, if deceased completed all the necessary steps required of him to change the beneficiary in his policy, intervener would be entitled to judgment. Furthermore, if intervenor can demonstrate this fact so clearly that there is no longer a genuine issue of fact, summary judgment may be properly granted under provisions of Rule 56(c) of the Fed. R. Civ. P.

We are of the opinion that the affidavits and exhibits introduced by intervener clearly and undeniably indicate that deceased made a change in his policy's beneficiaries. First, it appears that after deceased's marriage in 1958 to intervenor he amended his group hospitalization and employee savings plan to include intervener. Furthermore, certain correspondence conclusively indicates that a change in the life insurance was actually made.

Mr. Iten, an employee of Socony in Libya, whose duties included administration of company benefit plans, advising employees concerning the plans, referring questions about the plans to the New York office, issuing change of beneficiary forms on request, and offering necessary guidance on completion and execution of forms, (after consultation with the deceased in April 1961) prepared a letter to the New York office, dated April 19, 1961, stating that Joseph Cordner desired information as to who were his present beneficiaries under the company benefit plans and that Mr. Cordner had married for a second time and was not certain whether he had changed his beneficiary. This letter from the Libyan office was answered under date of May 3, 1961 informing him that his designated beneficiaries were Maureen Joan Cordner, 50 per cent, and Michael Joseph Cordner, 50 per cent; the letter further gratuitously asking whether he would prefer the entire benefit to be paid to any survivor in the event of the death of any of the named beneficiaries.

Mr. Iten was transferred from Libya shortly thereafter and his duties were assumed by Mr. Burks. Burks by affidavit stated that early in 1961 Mr. Cordner came to him with a request to change his beneficiaries; that Burks issued the necessary forms to Cordner and gave him instructions on how to complete the forms, at which time Cordner produced a copy of his Will made in North Dakota while vacationing from Libya in 1960. They discussed the form of beneficiary designation which might be appropriate under the terms of the Will. Mr. Cordner personally completed the forms, endorsed the beneficiary changes he wished to make on the back of each form, signed the forms in Burks' presence, (the latter acting as a witness to the signature) and then left the completed forms with Burks for transmittal. Since Burks was unfamiliar with the type of beneficiary changes endorsed on the forms he made a thermofax copy of Cordner's Will and sent this reproduction together with the completed change of beneficiary forms to the New York office in a letter dated May 11, 1961, which letter in part reads as follows:

> "Please review the enclosed employee change of beneficiary forms and advise us if this designation is acceptable under the plan."

The Home Office responded by stating in a letter dated June 1, 1961:

> "We are processing the Change of Beneficiary forms completed by the above employee (J. F. Cordner) and forwarded to us. * * * We see no reason why the designation will not be acceptable."

Mr. Burks in his earlier affidavit of March 30, 1963 states that to the best of his recollection the change of beneficiary requested by Cordner was as follows:

> "One-fourth of the proceeds to my wife France Jeanne Cordner and the balance to the Northwestern National Bank of Minneapolis, Minneapolis, Minnesota in trust for the uses and purposes set forth in my Last Will and Testament."

Burks in his second affidavit prepared for the purpose of the summary judgment proceeding confirmed the factual statements in his earlier affidavit and detailed the discussion and the procedures employed in the requested change of beneficiary by Cordner. He further stated that since the New York office had the Certificate for endorsement and since the Home Office stated in its letter of June 1, 1961 that they were processing the change of beneficiary forms he had no reason to believe that the processing of the changes had not proceeded to completion in the normal course. He was in the New York office at the time when a search of the files was made for the change of beneficiary forms, which, of course, they were unable to locate. When he returned to Tripoli, with instructions from the New York office to continue the search and to forward to New York all company papers having to do with Mr. Cordner's employment, he found a copy of a letter addressed to Cordner by his attorney suggesting the form of beneficiary designation required to effect the provisions of his Will. Burks then recalled that Mr. Cordner had referred to this same letter when discussing beneficiary changes in 1961 and that Cordner had used the suggested language in completing his change of beneficiary forms. After stating that he cannot restate from memory the text of the changes, he said that "I can and do reconfirm, upon my own direct knowledge and positive recollection that beneficiary changes so made by Joseph Franklin Cordner were in the form suggested by his attorney's letter and quoted verbatim from that letter in my prior affidavit."

Further correspondence indicates that the change of beneficiary forms were forwarded to the employer's Annuity and Insurance Department. A search of the department, however, never uncovered the form or the exact language used therein. It also appears by affidavit that all of the above related correspondence was properly identified and was prepared, mailed, received and kept as part of the business records of the company.

Plaintiff presents no counter evidence nor in any way indicates that intervenor's evidence is not worthy of belief. Therefore, we believe there is no genuine issue of fact on this point. It is clear that Joseph Cordner actually made a change in the beneficiaries of his life insurance policy.

However, to entitle intervenor to summary judgment, it must not only be clear that a change was made, but the wording of that change must be shown beyond any reasonable and genuine dispute. This point, too, was well covered in intervener's supporting papers.

While in the United States in July 1960, Joseph Cordner consulted a North Dakota attorney, one John Traynor, regarding a Last Will and Testament. By affidavit Mr. Traynor states that deceased informed him, "that he wished to make his wife beneficiary of 1/4 part of the proceeds (of the insurance policy) and to place the balance in trust for his children," and "that he prepared the Will in accordance with the plan." In order to place his client's expressed desire into operation Traynor drafted a Will that stated in part:

"That portion of my life insurance on my life payable to NORTH-WESTERN NATIONAL BANK OF MINNEAPOLIS, in Minneapolis, Minnesota, I give and bequeath to NORTHWESTERN NATIONAL BANK OF MINNEAPOLIS IN TRUST for the following uses and purposes, to wit: * * *

"The Trustee shall pay to my children, Maureen Joan Cordner, Michael Joseph Cordner, Geoffrey Philip Cordner and any other children that may hereafter be born of my present marriage, the entire income * * * in equal shares * * * until he or she reaches the age of eighteen (18) years." (at which time the entire principal of the Trust Estate shall be paid to France Jeanne Cordner.)

To further effectuate his client's wishes, Mr. Traynor advised Mr. Cordner how to change his insurance policy. He set forth this advice in a letter to Mr. Cordner reading in part as follows:

"In order to make the Trust arrangement in your Will effective, you should change the beneficiaries on your life insurance policy as follows:

" 'One-fourth of the proceeds to my wife, France Jeanne Cordner, and the balance to the Northwestern National Bank of Minneapolis, Minnesota, in Trust for the uses and purposes set forth in my Last Will and Testament.' "

From the affidavit of the attorney concerning the discussion of deceased's desires, from the letter written by the attorney explaining how the beneficiaries should be changed to effectuate these desires, and from the wording of the Last Will and Testament it is clear that Joseph Cordner intended to change the beneficiaries of his insurance policy by giving one-fourth to intervenor and the balance to Northwestern in trust. We can presume that this intent remained with Mr. Cordner during the intervening ten months between the Will's execution and the date of the beneficiary change. This presumption is supported by the presence of his unrevoked Will, which in itself indicates that he maintained this intent even until the time of his death, a year and a half after the change in beneficiary was sent to the company's home office. When we take this information along with the proof that some sort of beneficiary change was actually made by Mr. Cordner, and that the only change discovered was set out in Mr. Traynor's letter, we can presume that the change was made in accordance with this expressed intent. Otherwise, this unrevoked provision in Mr. Cordner's Will would have no force or effect.

However, in addition to this presumption we have the uncontested affidavits of a non-interested third party who was in a position to be aware of the actual wording of the change. The affiant, Mr. Harold Burks, was a fellow employee of Mr. Cordner in Libya, and supervised Mr. Cordner in filling out the required change of beneficiary forms. Mr. Burks is probably the only person that was in a position to be aware of the wording of the document. His affidavits are entitled to considerable weight in determining the merits of a summary judgment motion, especially where there is no indication of any counter-evidence. Moreover, Mr. Burks' assistance in processing the change in beneficiary was done in the regular course of business of Socony, and pursuant to his assigned duties. It has been held that the clear affidavits from the only persons in a position to be aware of a factual situation can well serve as the basis for a summary judgment.

Mr. Burks' first affidavit executed in Libya and forwarded to the company before any litigation had commenced said that Mr. Cordner made a change in beneficiaries and the change read as follows:

> "One-fourth of the proceeds to my wife France Jeanne Cordner and the balance to the Northwestern National Bank of Minneapolis, Minneapolis, Minnesota, in trust for the uses and purposes set forth in my Last Will and Testament."

The second affidavit of Mr. Burks executed by him in Singapore, Malaysia and made in anticipation of this litigation, confirmed the factual statements made in his first affidavit.

So, in support of intervenor's claim there is undisputed proof that Mr. Cordner had manifested an intent to give intervener one-fourth of his insurance proceeds with the balance going into the trust established by his Will. It is likewise clear beyond any shadow of doubt that Mr. Cordner subsequently made a change in his insurance beneficiaries. The logical conclusion is clear. He made the change in accordance with his prior expressed intent. This presumption is supported by the two affidavits of Mr. Burks which recite from direct and positive recollection that the beneficiary changes were copied from Mr. Cordner's letter from his attorney and were in form exactly as alleged by intervener.

In response to the overwhelming documentary evidence supported by affidavits all of which consistently showed that Cordner had requested a change of beneficiary in accordance with his lawyer's letter and his own Last Will and Testament, the plaintiff submitted her own counter-affidavit to the effect that Mr. Cordner was very much interested in the welfare of his first two children (the named beneficiaries) and was aware of the future financial difficulties they would face. No further information was offered. The Court, therefore, was not presented with a situation where it was asked to weigh conflicting affidavits. The problem was only, did the affidavits and exhibits of intervener sustain the necessary burden in order to allow a summary judgment? The trial court felt the burden was sustained, and from the above related facts we agree with the trial court's conclusion. The showing made by intervenor on the motion for summary judgment covers all of the material issues of fact in the case and as found by the trial judge, Cordner had "effectively changed the beneficiaries in his group policy and that he did all that he was required to do."[3]

We are of the opinion that if this information were presented at trial, intervenor would be entitled to a directed verdict in her favor, and it has been said that if the information presented entitles one to a directed verdict, a summary judgment is in order. Intervenor having made a sufficient showing, it then rests upon the plaintiff to specify at least some evidence which could be produced at trial. Plaintiff apparently is of the opinion that, since she makes a prima facie case by merely introducing the Certificate showing her children as designated beneficiaries, she is entitled to a trial on the issue of (1) whether any change of beneficiary was made, and (2) if so, what changes were actually made. This we do not feel is a correct view of the law.

The counter-affidavit of the plaintiff does not meet the issues raised and supported by the intervenor. This leaves no genuine issue as to any material fact, and presents a predicate for a summary judgment under Rule 56(c), Fed. R. Civ. P.

Rule 56(e) provides that "The court may permit affidavits to be supplemented or opposed by depositions, answers to interrogatories, or further affidavits." If there were any question about the affidavits made by Mr. Burks and Mr. Iten, the plaintiff should have raised an issue

---

3. A portion of Judge Nordbye's opinion reads as follows:

The Court is well aware that a summary judgment should not be granted except when it appears that the movant's position for such relief is made "with such clarity as to leave no room for controversy; with all reasonable doubts touching the existence of a genuine issue as to a material fact resolved against the movant; giving the benefit of all reasonable inferences that may reasonably be drawn from the evidence to the party moved against." But applying that rigid test, it would seem that only one possible conclusion could be reached on this showing, and that is that on or about May 11, 1961, Cordner caused to be transmitted to Socony Mobil Oil Company in New York the form submitted by Socony Mobil Oil Company in change of beneficiaries in this group policy in the language as noted in Mr. Traynor's letter to him under date of July 28, 1960.

thereto by affidavit or by requesting additional time to depose these affiants by deposition or by written interrogatories under Rule 28(b) or Rule 31 of Fed. R. Civ. P. This the plaintiff failed to do. The 1963 amendment to Rule 56(e) adds:

> When a motion for summary judgment is made and supported as provided in this rule, an adverse party may not rest upon the mere allegations or denials of his pleading, but his response, by affidavits or as otherwise provided in this rule, must set forth specific facts showing that there is a genuine issue for trial. If he does not so respond, summary judgment, if appropriate, shall be entered against him.

Having completely failed to respond in any meaningful way to intervenor's clear showing of the absence of a genuine issue, this amendment clearly authorizes the entry of a summary judgment. Plaintiff failing to place in issue any elements of intervener's documented case would translate a trial into a useless formality, thus making a summary judgment proper.

The real gravamen of plaintiff's objection is not that there is conflicting evidence but rather that the summary judgment rests upon the affidavits of Harold Burks. His testimony being so vital to intervener's cause, it is asserted that the case should proceed to trial in order that the demeanor of the witness could be observed and his testimony subjected to the test of cross-examination.

In passing on this contention it might be well to make four preliminary observations. First, affiant Burks appears to be an unbiased witness. He has no financial or personal interest in the outcome of this litigation. Second, there is no doubt but what his testimony is competent both in regard to his mental capacity and his being in a position to directly observe the facts related in his affidavits. Third, his participation in the change of beneficiaries was in the regular course of his duties with Socony. Finally, both affidavits are positive, internally consistent, unequivocal, and in full accord with the documentary exhibits. Therefore, even though cross-examination is a trial right which must be carefully protected, in this case, unlike many others there is no obvious advantage to be gained from a cross-examination. If there were, a summary judgment might arguably be improper. But where there is no indication that the affiant was biased, dishonest, mistaken, unaware or unsure of the facts, the cases declaring that cross-examination is necessary when one of the above is present, have no application here. There being no positive showing that this witness's testimony could be impeached or that he might have additional testimony valuable to plaintiff, summary judgment was properly granted. The opposing party cannot as a matter of course force a trial merely in order to cross-examine such an affiant, nor must the Court deny the motion for summary judgment on the basis of a vague supposition that something might turn up at the trial.

There is absolutely no showing that a trial would produce any different or additional evidence. It appears that Burks is now stationed in Singapore, far beyond the subpoena powers of the trial court. Neither party would be able to compel his attendance before the trial court. Since this witness is out of the jurisdiction, any of the parties, on the other hand, would be free to introduce Burks' testimony by use of a deposition. Therefore, in all likelihood Burks would never have to appear in open court. What would plaintiff have to gain by forcing a trial under these circumstances? We feel very little, if anything. A full trial would not give plaintiff an opportunity to cross-examine Burks in open court, nor would it unveil his demeanor to the trier of fact.

In the event of a trial plaintiff would only be free to obtain Burks' sworn testimony by deposition or upon written interrogatories ... Plaintiff, however, was free to take this action even prior to the present motion for summary judgment but chose not to do so. When the motion for summary judgment was presented, plaintiff, if she felt Burks had information valuable to her cause, was again free to move for a delay in judgment and secure Burks' deposition. Again plaintiff took no action. Apparently plaintiff felt she had nothing to gain by a deposition, yet under the circumstances of this case that is probably the most she could expect even if this case went to trial. Therefore, we do not feel that plaintiff is in a position at this time to force a trial. A trial would not secure Burks' presence, it would only force the taking of his deposition, a course previously open to plaintiff which she elected not to pursue.

* * * The position declaring that a party opposed to a summary judgment based upon affidavits must assume some initiative in showing that a factual issue actually exists is perfectly sound in the light of Rule 56, which specifically allows the use of affidavits in summary judgment proceedings. For if plaintiff's position is correct that an affiant's credibility is always an issue for the trial court, then the granting of a summary judgment would be virtually impossible when it is based in any way upon an affidavit. Rule 56 would be nullified by the prevailing party's use of one affidavit and the bald objection by the opposing party to the affiant's credibility. The reference in this rule to "affidavits" would therefore be of no effect.

This does not mean that an affiant's credibility cannot properly be put in issue by a litigant, but in doing so specific facts must be properly produced. At this point the 1963 amendment to Rule 56(e) comes into play requiring the opposing party to respond or suffer the fate of a summary judgment, if otherwise appropriate. Plaintiff failed to respond to the adequate and substantial showing of intervener, so the trial court properly granted the summary judgment. Keeping in mind that the purpose of the summary judgment is to avoid useless trials, from the circumstances of this case we believe a trial would indeed be a useless waste of time and expense to the parties as well as a needless inconvenience to the Court.

It also appears from the noncontroverted evidence in this case that any change of beneficiary requested by Cordner would be effective when placed in the hands of Mr. Burks, an employee of Socony specifically charged with the duty of processing beneficiary changes for Socony's employees under company benefit plans. Since Socony was the duly authorized agent for Metropolitan notice to an employee of Socony charged with the departmentalized duty of assisting, aiding and counseling in the making of such changes could be considered as effectuating a change of beneficiary at this point, the employee having done all that he could do to transmit to the company his intention of a change and the wording of the change. The Certificate had previously been surrendered to the company and was retained by the company for the benefit of the employee. Hence, Socony had the administrative and ministerial duty of endorsing any requested change on the Certificate.

As a matter of law, if Joseph Cordner did all that he could do to comply with the requirements, a requested change in beneficiary will be declared effective regardless of the fact that the insurance company or its duly authorized agent failed to complete the change. This fact was clearly demonstrated by the affidavits and exhibits of intervener to the point we believe that the trial court was justified in declaring that there no longer remained any genuine issue. Therefore, the summary judgment was properly granted.

Judgment affirmed.

* * *

CROSS v. UNITED STATES

336 F.2d 431 (2d Cir. 1964)

MOORE, CIRCUIT JUDGE:

In this income tax refund suit, plaintiffs-appellees claim that they were entitled to a deduction of $1,300 on their joint return for the year 1954 because of expenses incurred by Professor Ephraim Cross in connection with his summer travel to various Mediterranean and European countries. Upon appellees' motion for summary judgment, the district court, whose examination of the facts included the affidavits of several professors tending to indicate the desirability of foreign travel for a teacher of languages as well as the pre-trial deposition of Professor Cross, concluded that there was no genuine issue as to any material fact, and granted appellees' motion. The Government opposed the summary judgment procedure, claiming a right to cross-examine appellees as to the nature of their expenses and the educational benefits allegedly sought and also to cross-examine the affiant professors. On this appeal the only issue is whether there are triable issues of fact which render the award of summary judgment erroneous.

In 1954 Professor Cross was an Assistant Professor at City College in New York where he taught French, Spanish and romance linguistics (described by him as the study of the development of Latin into the romance languages, the study of the various dialects and the historic stages of those dialects). He, his wife and a pet dog sailed from New York on June 30, 1954 aboard a French freighter. The ship put in briefly in Portugal, Morocco, Tangiers, Oran, Algiers, Naples and Genoa and appellees spent a day or so in each place. When the freighter arrived at Marseilles, twenty-one days after leaving New York, appellees separated. Mrs. Cross joined a friend and continued touring while Professor Cross and their pet dog travelled to Paris. Although he did not pursue a formal course of study or engage in research, Professor Cross did visit schools, courts of law, churches, book publishers, theaters, motion pictures, restaurants, cafes and other places of amusement, read newspapers, listen to radio broadcasts, converse with students and teachers and attend political meetings. He rejoined his wife in this country on September 23, 1954 after his return aboard a French passenger liner.

Section 162(a), Int. Rev. Code of 1954 permits a deduction for "all the ordinary and necessary expenses paid or incurred * * * in carrying on any trade or business * * *." The Regulations promulgated under that section, Treas. Reg. 1.162–5, state:

> Expenses for education—(a) Expenditures made by a taxpayer for his education are deductible if they are for education (including research activities) undertaken primarily for the purpose of:
>
> (1) Maintaining or improving skills required by the taxpayer in his employment or trade or business, * * *
>
> Whether or not education is of the type referred to in subparagraph (1) of this paragraph shall be determined upon the basis of all the facts of each case. If it is customary for other established members of the taxpayer's trade or business to undertake such education, the taxpayer will ordinarily be considered to have undertaken this education for the purposes described in subparagraph (1) of this paragraph.
>
> * * *
>
> (c) In general, a taxpayer's expenditures for travel (including travel while on sabbatical leave) as a form of education shall be considered as primarily personal in nature and therefore not deductible.

Appellees claim, and the district court held, that all of Professor Cross's expenses are deductible. Professor Cross asserted in his deposition, which was taken for discovery purposes and did not include cross-examination,

> My purpose (in making the trip) was to maintain my contacts with my foreign languages for the purpose of maintaining and improving my skill as a linguist and teacher of languages, and to make my general teaching more effective, and to extend my contacts with foreign culture which I have to teach in connection with my teaching

of foreign languages per se, and this can be done effectively and properly only by going into a foreign language area.

The Government disputes this explanation. It contends that all or at least part of Professor Cross's travel was a vacation and thus a personal living expense for which a deduction is not allowed under Section 162. Moreover, the Government challenges the amount of the claimed deduction and questions whether any portion of that sum was expended on behalf of Mrs. Cross.

We believe that summary judgment was improvidently granted and that the Government is entitled to a trial at which all the circumstances may be developed for the consideration of the trier of fact. Rule 56(c) permits summary judgment only where "there is no genuine issue as to any material fact," a state of affairs not normally encountered where the problem is whether expenses are ordinary and necessary in carrying on a taxpayer's trade or business. Before travelling expenses can be allowed as deductible, there must be a factual determination of what parts, if any, are to be attributed to vacation travel or to educational advancement.

The essentially factual character of the issue is particularly apparent here, where the ultimate facts were warmly contested. While there was no dispute that Professor Cross was a teacher of languages and that he travelled abroad, many of the facts remain largely within his own knowledge and the Government should have the opportunity to test his credibility on cross-examination. Summary judgment is particularly inappropriate where "the inferences which the parties seek to have drawn deal with questions of motive, intent and subjective feelings and reactions." "A judge may not, on a motion for summary judgment, draw fact inferences. * * * Such inferences may be drawn only on a trial." While we have recently emphasized that ordinarily the bare allegations of the pleadings, unsupported by specific evidentiary data, will not alone defeat a motion for summary judgment, this principle does not justify summary relief where, as here, the disputed questions of fact turn exclusively on the credibility of movants' witnesses.

To the teacher of modern languages, particularly in a country far removed from the European continent, it is highly important that his linguistic ear be retuned as frequently as possible to the ways in which a foreign language is expressed. Moreover, a thorough familiarity with the current social, political and cultural climate of a country properly may be regarded as a prerequisite to effective classroom presentation of its language. The enlightened teaching of modern languages in our schools and colleges has assumed a position of unique importance in the world today. International understanding and its correlative, peaceful living by nations, is immeasurably aided by common language denominators. A recent Revenue Ruling has recognized these notions:

> If a teacher of French, while on sabbatical leave granted for the purpose of travel, journeys throughout France in order to improve his knowledge of the French language, the expenses of his travel (includ-

ing transportation and expenses necessarily incurred for meals and lodging) are deductible as education expenses if the taxpayer can show that his itinerary was chosen and the major portion of his activities during the trip was undertaken for the primary purpose of maintaining or improving his skills in the use and the teaching of the French language and that the places visited and his activities were of a nature calculated to result in actual or potential benefit to him in his position as a teacher of French. This is true even though his activities while travelling may consist largely of visiting French schools and families, attending motion pictures, plays or lectures in the French language, and the like.

On the other hand, a mere pleasure trip through various countries by a professor who has some fluency with the language of each country might well not fall within the deductible category. Thus, Revenue Ruling 64–176 goes on to state:

> Because travel of the type which teachers usually engage in for its educational value is generally of the same type as that on which other taxpayers embark for purely recreational and personal purposes, the expenses of a teacher for such travel will be deductible as ordinary and necessary business expenses only if and to the extent that the travel is directly related to the duties of the teacher in his teaching position, due consideration being given to the normal duties of that position.

Who can doubt that the alert American trial lawyer as a part of a summer vacation might not profit greatly by spending some time at the Old Bailey listening to British barristers exhibit their skills. The surgeon, too, might be benefitted in his profession by observing some delicate operation conducted by a European surgeon of renown. Yet it is questionable whether such tangible evidences of constant interest in one's profession entitle a taxpayer to deduct all his summer vacation expenses.

In addition to determining whether the trip was devoted in whole or in part to educational advancement, the trier of the facts will have to ascertain such amounts as are to be attributed to such purpose. Were the preliminary twenty-one days prior to the Marseilles landing all part of an educational program? What part, if any, was allocable to Mrs. Cross? What charges were incurred by the dog? Although probably de minimis, the Treasury frequently watches every penny and might not be generously inclined even though the dog were a French poodle.

The district court reasoned that summary judgment should be granted because the Government did not adduce facts to refute Professor Cross's claims as to the purpose of his trip, and that the Government had an opportunity to cross-examine when taking his deposition. The "right to use depositions for discovery * * * does not mean that they are to supplant the right to call and examine the adverse party * * * before the jury." * * * "We cannot very well overestimate the importance of having the witness examined and cross-examined in presence of the court and jury." By the same process, Professor Cross will have an opportunity to show with greater particularity that his more modern approach to the problem of linguistic improvement is far superior to the old-fashioned classroom lecture method.

Reversed and remanded for trial.

* * *

B. MODERN SUMMARY JUDGMENT STANDARDS

CELOTEX CORPORATION v. CATRETT
477 U.S. 317 (1986)

JUSTICE REHNQUIST delivered the opinion of the Court.

The United States District Court for the District of Columbia granted the motion of petitioner Celotex Corporation for summary judgment against respondent Catrett because the latter was unable to produce evidence in support of her allegation in her wrongful-death complaint that the decedent had been exposed to petitioner's asbestos products. A divided panel of the Court of Appeals for the District of Columbia Circuit reversed, however, holding that petitioner's failure to support its motion with evidence tending to *negate* such exposure precluded the entry of summary judgment in its favor. This view conflicted with that of the Third Circuit. We granted certiorari to resolve the conflict, and now reverse the decision of the District of Columbia Circuit.

Respondent commenced this lawsuit in September 1980, alleging that the death in 1979 of her husband, Louis H. Catrett, resulted from his exposure to products containing asbestos manufactured or distributed by 15 named corporations. Respondent's complaint sounded in negligence, breach of warranty, and strict liability. Two of the defendants filed motions challenging the District Court's *in personam* jurisdiction, and the remaining 13, including petitioner, filed motions for summary judgment. Petitioner's motion, which was first filed in September 1981, argued that summary judgment was proper because respondent had "failed to produce evidence that any [Celotex] product . . . was the proximate cause of the injuries alleged within the jurisdictional limits of [the District] Court." In particular, petitioner noted that respondent had failed to identify, in answering interrogatories specifically requesting such information, any witnesses who could testify about the decedent's exposure to petitioner's asbestos products. In response to petitioner's summary judgment motion, respondent then produced three documents which she claimed "demonstrate that there is a genuine material factual dispute" as to whether the decedent had ever been exposed to petitioner's asbestos products. The three documents included a transcript of a deposition of the decedent, a letter from an official of one of the decedent's former employers whom petitioner planned to call as a trial witness, and a letter from an insurance company to respondent's attorney, all tending to establish that the decedent had been exposed to petitioner's asbestos products in Chicago during 1970–1971. Petitioner, in turn, argued that the three documents were inadmissible hearsay and thus could not be considered in opposition to the summary judgment motion.

In July 1982, almost two years after the commencement of the lawsuit, the District Court granted all of the motions filed by the various defendants. The court explained that it was granting petitioner's summary judgment motion because "there [was] no showing that the plaintiff was exposed to the defendant Celotex's product in the District of Columbia or elsewhere within the statutory period." Respondent appealed only the grant of summary judgment in favor of petitioner, and a divided panel of the District of Columbia Circuit reversed. The majority of the Court of Appeals held that petitioner's summary judgment motion was rendered "fatally defective" by the fact that petitioner "made no effort to adduce *any* evidence, in the form of affidavits or otherwise, to support its motion." According to the majority, Rule 56(e) of the Federal Rules of Civil Procedure, and this Court's decision in *Adickes v. S.H. Kress & Co.,* 398 U.S. 144 (1970), establish that "the party opposing the motion for summary judgment bears the burden of responding *only after* the moving party has met its burden of coming forward with proof of the absence of any genuine issues of material fact." The majority therefore declined to consider petitioner's argument that none of the evidence produced by respondent in opposition to the motion for summary judgment would have been admissible at trial. The dissenting judge argued that "[t]he majority errs in supposing that a party seeking summary judgment must always make an affirmative evidentiary showing, even in cases where there is not a triable, factual dispute." According to the dissenting judge, the majority's decision "undermines the traditional authority of trial judges to grant summary judgment in meritless cases."

We think that the position taken by the majority of the Court of Appeals is inconsistent with the standard for summary judgment set forth in Rule 56(c) of the Federal Rules of Civil Procedure. Under Rule 56(c), summary judgment is proper "if the pleadings, depositions, answers to interrogatories, and admissions on file, together with the affidavits, if any, show that there is no genuine issue as to any material fact and that the moving party is entitled to a judgment as a matter of law." In our view, the plain language of Rule 56(c) mandates the entry of summary judgment, after adequate time for discovery and upon motion, against a party who fails to make a showing sufficient to establish the existence of an element essential to that party's case, and on which that party will bear the burden of proof at trial. In such a situation, there can be "no genuine issue as to any material fact," since a complete failure of proof concerning an essential element of the nonmoving party's case necessarily renders all other facts immaterial. The moving party is "entitled to a judgment as a matter of law" because the nonmoving party has failed to make a sufficient showing on an essential element of her case with respect to which she has the burden of proof. "[T]h[e] standard [for granting summary judgment] mirrors the standard for a directed verdict under Federal Rule of Civil Procedure 50(a)....." *Anderson v. Liberty Lobby, Inc.* (1986).

Of course, a party seeking summary judgment always bears the initial responsibility of informing the district court of the basis for its motion, and identifying those portions of "the pleadings, depositions, answers to interrogatories, and admissions on file, together with the affidavits, if any," which it believes demonstrate the absence of a genuine issue of material fact. But unlike the Court of Appeals, we find no express or implied requirement in Rule 56 that the moving party support its motion with affidavits or other similar materials *negating* the opponent's claim. On the contrary, Rule 56(c), which refers to "the affidavits, *if any*" (emphasis added), suggests the absence of such a requirement. And if there were any doubt about the meaning of Rule 56(c) in this regard, such doubt is clearly removed by Rules 56(a) and (b), which provide that claimants and defendants, respectively, may move for summary judgment *"with or without supporting affidavits"* (emphasis added). The import of these subsections is that, regardless of whether the moving party accompanies its summary judgment motion with affidavits, the motion may, and should, be granted so long as whatever is before the district court demonstrates that the standard for the entry of summary judgment, as set forth in Rule 56(c), is satisfied. One of the principal purposes of the summary judgment rule is to isolate and dispose of factually unsupported claims or defenses, and we think it should be interpreted in a way that allows it to accomplish this purpose.

Respondent argues, however, that Rule 56(e), by its terms, places on the nonmoving party the burden of coming forward with rebuttal affidavits, or other specified kinds of materials, only in response to a motion for summary judgment "made and supported as provided in this rule." According to respondent's argument, since petitioner did not "support" its motion with affidavits, summary judgment was improper in this case. But as we have already explained, a motion for summary judgment may be made pursuant to Rule 56 "with or without supporting affidavits." In cases like the instant one, where the nonmoving party will bear the burden of proof at trial on a dispositive issue, a summary judgment motion may properly be made in reliance solely on the "pleadings, depositions, answers to interrogatories, and admissions on file." Such a motion, whether or not accompanied by affidavits, will be "made and supported as provided in this rule," and Rule 56(e) therefore requires the nonmoving party to go beyond the pleadings and by her own affidavits, or by the "depositions, answers to interrogatories, and admissions on file," designate "specific facts showing that there is a genuine issue for trial."

We do not mean that the nonmoving party must produce evidence in a form that would be admissible at trial in order to avoid summary judgment. Obviously, Rule 56 does not require the nonmoving party to depose her own witnesses. Rule 56(e) permits a proper summary judgment motion to be opposed by any of the kinds of evidentiary materials listed in

Rule 56(c), except the mere pleadings themselves, and it is from this list that one would normally expect the nonmoving party to make the showing to which we have referred.

The Court of Appeals in this case felt itself constrained, however, by language in our decision in *Adickes v. S.H. Kress & Co.* There we held that summary judgment had been improperly entered in favor of the defendant restaurant in an action brought under 42 U.S.C. § 1983. In the course of its opinion, the *Adickes* Court said that "both the commentary on and the background of the 1963 amendment conclusively show that it was not intended to modify the burden of the moving party . . . to show initially the absence of a genuine issue concerning any material fact." We think that this statement is accurate in a literal sense, since we fully agree with the *Adickes* Court that the 1963 amendment to Rule 56(e) was not designed to modify the burden of making the showing generally required by Rule 56(c). It also appears to us that, on the basis of the showing before the Court in *Adickes,* the motion for summary judgment in that case should have been denied. But we do not think the *Adickes* language quoted above should be construed to mean that the burden is on the party moving for summary judgment to produce evidence showing the absence of a genuine issue of material fact, even with respect to an issue on which the nonmoving party bears the burden of proof. Instead, as we have explained, the burden on the moving party may be discharged by "showing"—that is, pointing out to the district court-that there is an absence of evidence to support the nonmoving party's case.

The last two sentences of Rule 56(e) were added, as this Court indicated in *Adickes,* to disapprove a line of cases allowing a party opposing summary judgment to resist a properly made motion by reference only to its pleadings. While the *Adickes* Court was undoubtedly correct in concluding that these two sentences were not intended to *reduce* the burden of the moving party, it is also obvious that they were not adopted to *add to* that burden. Yet that is exactly the result which the reasoning of the Court of Appeals would produce; in effect, an amendment to Rule 56(e) designed to *facilitate* the granting of motions for summary judgment would be interpreted to make it *more difficult* to grant such motions. Nothing in the two sentences themselves requires this result, for the reasons we have previously indicated, and we now put to rest any inference that they do so.

Our conclusion is bolstered by the fact that district courts are widely acknowledged to possess the power to enter summary judgments *sua sponte,* so long as the losing party was on notice that she had to come forward with all of her evidence. It would surely defy common sense to hold that the District Court could have entered summary judgment *sua sponte* in favor of petitioner in the instant case, but that petitioner's filing of a motion requesting such a disposition precluded the District Court from ordering it.

Respondent commenced this action in September 1980, and petitioner's motion was filed in September 1981. The parties had conducted discovery, and no serious claim can be made that respondent was in any sense "railroaded" by a premature motion for summary judgment. Any potential problem with such premature motions can be adequately dealt with under Rule 56(f), which allows a summary judgment motion to be denied, or the hearing on the motion to be continued, if the nonmoving party has not had an opportunity to make full discovery.

In this Court, respondent's brief and oral argument have been devoted as much to the proposition that an adequate showing of exposure to petitioner's asbestos products was made as to the proposition that no such showing should have been required. But the Court of Appeals declined to address either the adequacy of the showing made by respondent in opposition to petitioner's motion for summary judgment, or the question whether such a showing, if reduced to admissible evidence, would be sufficient to carry respondent's burden of proof at trial. We think the Court of Appeals with its superior knowledge of local law is better suited than we are to make these determinations in the first instance.

The Federal Rules of Civil Procedure have for almost 50 years authorized motions for summary judgment upon proper showings of the lack of a genuine, triable issue of material fact. Summary judgment procedure is properly regarded not as a disfavored procedural shortcut, but rather as an integral part of the Federal Rules as a whole, which are designed "to secure the just, speedy and inexpensive determination of every action." Fed. Rule Civ. Proc. 1. Before the shift to "notice pleading" accomplished by the Federal Rules, motions to dismiss a complaint or to strike a defense were the principal tools by which factually insufficient claims or defenses could be isolated and prevented from going to trial with the attendant unwarranted consumption of public and private resources. But with the advent of "notice pleading," the motion to dismiss seldom fulfills this function any more, and its place has been taken by the motion for summary judgment. Rule 56 must be construed with due regard not only for the rights of persons asserting claims and defenses that are adequately based in fact to have those claims and defenses tried to a jury, but also for the rights of persons opposing such claims and defenses to demonstrate in the manner provided by the Rule, prior to trial, that the claims and defenses have no factual basis.

The judgment of the Court of Appeals is accordingly reversed, and the case is remanded for further proceedings consistent with this opinion.

It is so ordered.

JUSTICE WHITE, concurring.

I agree that the Court of Appeals was wrong in holding that the moving defendant must always support his motion with evidence or affidavits showing the absence of a genuine dispute about a material fact. I also agree that the movant may rely on depositions, answers to interrogatories, and the like, to demonstrate that the plaintiff has no evidence to prove his case and hence that there can be no factual dispute. But the movant must discharge the burden the Rules place upon him: It is not enough to move for summary judgment without supporting the motion in any way or with a conclusory assertion that the plaintiff has no evidence to prove his case.

A plaintiff need not initiate any discovery or reveal his witnesses or evidence unless required to do so under the discovery Rules or by court order. Of course, he must respond if required to do so; but he need not also depose his witnesses or obtain their affidavits to defeat a summary judgment motion asserting only that he has failed to produce any support for his case. It is the defendant's task to negate, if he can, the claimed basis for the suit.

Petitioner Celotex does not dispute that if respondent has named a witness to support her claim, summary judgment should not be granted without Celotex somehow showing that the named witness' possible testimony raises no genuine issue of material fact. It asserts, however, that respondent has failed on request to produce any basis for her case. Respondent, on the other hand, does not contend that she was not obligated to reveal her witnesses and evidence but insists that she has revealed enough to defeat the motion for summary judgment. Because the Court of Appeals found it unnecessary to address this aspect of the case, I agree that the case should be remanded for further proceedings.

JUSTICE BRENNAN, with whom THE CHIEF JUSTICE and JUSTICE BLACKMUN join, dissenting.

This case requires the Court to determine whether Celotex satisfied its initial burden of production in moving for summary judgment on the ground that the plaintiff lacked evidence to establish an essential element of her case at trial. I do not disagree with the Court's legal analysis. The Court clearly rejects the ruling of the Court of Appeals that the defendant must provide affirmative evidence disproving the plaintiff's case. Beyond this, however, the Court has not clearly explained what is required of a moving party seeking summary judgment on the ground that the nonmoving party cannot prove its case.[1] This lack of clarity is unfortunate: district courts must routinely decide summary judgment motions, and the Court's opinion will very likely create confusion. For this reason, even if I agreed with the Court's result, I would have written separately to explain more clearly the law in this area. However, because I believe that Celotex did not meet its burden of production under Federal Rule of Civil Procedure 56, I respectfully dissent from the Court's judgment.

---

1. It is also unclear what the Court of Appeals is supposed to do in this case on remand. Justice White—who has provided the Court's fifth vote—plainly believes that the Court of Appeals should reevaluate whether the defendant met its initial burden of production. However, the decision to reverse rather than to vacate the judgment below implies that the Court of Appeals should assume that Celotex has met its initial burden of production and ask only whether the plaintiff responded adequately, and, if so, whether the defendant has met its ultimate burden of persuasion that no genuine issue exists for trial. Absent some clearer expression from the Court to the contrary, Justice White's understanding would seem to be controlling.

I

Summary judgment is appropriate where the Court is satisfied "that there is no genuine issue as to any material fact and that the moving party is entitled to a judgment as a matter of law." Fed. Rule Civ. Proc. 56(c). The burden of establishing the nonexistence of a "genuine issue" is on the party moving for summary judgment. This burden has two distinct components: an initial burden of production, which shifts to the nonmoving party if satisfied by the moving party; and an ultimate burden of persuasion, which always remains on the moving party. The court need not decide whether the moving party has satisfied its ultimate burden of persuasion[2] unless and until the Court finds that the moving party has discharged its initial burden of production.

The burden of production imposed by Rule 56 requires the moving party to make a prima facie showing that it is entitled to summary judgment. The manner in which this showing can be made depends upon which party will bear the burden of persuasion on the challenged claim at trial. If the *moving* party will bear the burden of persuasion at trial, that party must support its motion with credible evidence—using any of the materials specified in Rule 56(c)—that would entitle it to a directed verdict if not controverted at trial. Such an affirmative showing shifts the burden of production to the party opposing the motion and requires that party either to produce evidentiary materials that demonstrate the existence of a "genuine issue" for trial or to submit an affidavit requesting additional time for discovery. Fed. Rules Civ. Proc. 56(e), (f).

If the burden of persuasion at trial would be on the *non-moving* party, the party moving for summary judgment may satisfy Rule 56's burden of production in either of two ways. First, the moving party may submit affirmative evidence that negates an essential element of the nonmoving party's claim. Second, the moving party may demonstrate to the Court that the nonmoving party's evidence is insufficient to establish an essential element of the nonmoving party's claim. If the nonmoving party cannot muster sufficient evidence to make out its claim, a trial would be useless and the moving party is entitled to summary judgment as a matter of law.

Where the moving party adopts this second option and seeks summary judgment on the ground that the nonmoving party—who will bear the burden of persuasion at trial—has no evidence, the mechanics of discharging Rule 56's burden of production are somewhat trickier. Plainly, a conclusory assertion that the nonmoving party has no evidence is

---

2. The burden of persuasion imposed on a moving party by Rule 56 is a stringent one. Summary judgment should not be granted unless it is clear that a trial is unnecessary, and any doubt as to the existence of a genuine issue for trial should be resolved against the moving party. In determining whether a moving party has met its burden of persuasion, the court is obliged to take account of the entire setting of the case and must consider all papers of record as well as any materials prepared for the motion. As explained by the Court of Appeals for the Third Circuit "[i]f ... there is any evidence in the record from any source from which a reasonable inference in the [nonmoving party's] favor may be drawn, the moving party simply cannot obtain a summary judgment...."

insufficient. Such a "burden" of production is no burden at all and would simply permit summary judgment procedure to be converted into a tool for harassment. Rather, as the Court confirms, a party who moves for summary judgment on the ground that the nonmoving party has no evidence must affirmatively show the absence of evidence in the record. This may require the moving party to depose the nonmoving party's witnesses or to establish the inadequacy of documentary evidence. If there is literally no evidence in the record, the moving party may demonstrate this by reviewing for the court the admissions, interrogatories, and other exchanges between the parties that are in the record. Either way, however, the moving party must affirmatively demonstrate that there is no evidence in the record to support a judgment for the nonmoving party.

If the moving party has not fully discharged this initial burden of production, its motion for summary judgment must be denied, and the Court need not consider whether the moving party has met its ultimate burden of persuasion. Accordingly, the nonmoving party may defeat a motion for summary judgment that asserts that the nonmoving party has no evidence by calling the Court's attention to supporting evidence already in the record that was overlooked or ignored by the moving party. In that event, the moving party must respond by making an attempt to demonstrate the inadequacy of this evidence, for it is only by attacking all the record evidence allegedly supporting the nonmoving party that a party seeking summary judgment satisfies Rule 56's burden of production.[3] Thus, if the record disclosed that the moving party had overlooked a witness who would provide relevant testimony for the nonmoving party at trial, the Court could not find that the moving party had discharged its initial burden of production unless the moving party sought to demonstrate the inadequacy of this witness' testimony. Absent such a demonstration, summary judgment would have to be denied on the ground that the moving party had failed to meet its burden of production under Rule 56.

The result in *Adickes v. S.H. Kress & Co,* is fully consistent with these principles. In that case, petitioner was refused service in respondent's lunchroom and then was arrested for vagrancy by a local policeman as she left. Petitioner brought an action under 42 U.S.C. § 1983 claiming that the refusal of service and subsequent arrest were the product of a conspiracy between respondent and the police; as proof of this conspiracy, petitioner's complaint alleged that the arresting officer was in respondent's store at the time service was refused. Respondent subsequently moved for summary judgment on the ground that there was no actual

---

3. Once the moving party has attacked whatever record evidence—if any—the nonmoving party purports to rely upon, the burden of production shifts to the nonmoving party, who must either (1) rehabilitate the evidence attacked in the moving party's papers, (2) produce additional evidence showing the existence of a genuine issue for trial as provided in Rule 56(e), or (3) submit an affidavit explaining why further discovery is necessary as provided in Rule 56(f). Summary judgment should be granted if the nonmoving party fails to respond in one or more of these ways, or if, after the nonmoving party responds, the court determines that the moving party has met its ultimate burden of persuading the court that there is no genuine issue of material fact for trial.

evidence in the record from which a jury could draw an inference of conspiracy. In response, petitioner pointed to a statement from her own deposition and an unsworn statement by a Kress employee, both already in the record and both ignored by respondent, that the policeman who arrested petitioner was in the store at the time she was refused service. We agreed that "[i]f a policeman were present, ... it would be open to a jury, in light of the sequence that followed, to infer from the circumstances that the policeman and Kress employee had a 'meeting of the minds' and thus reached an understanding that petitioner should be refused service." Consequently, we held that it was error to grant summary judgment "on the basis of this record" because respondent had "failed to fulfill its initial burden" of demonstrating that there was no evidence that there was a policeman in the store.

The opinion in *Adickes* has sometimes been read to hold that summary judgment was inappropriate because the respondent had not submitted affirmative evidence to negate the possibility that there was a policeman in the store. The Court of Appeals apparently read *Adickes* this way and therefore required Celotex to submit evidence establishing that plaintiff's decedent had not been exposed to Celotex asbestos. I agree with the Court that this reading of *Adickes* was erroneous and that Celotex could seek summary judgment on the ground that plaintiff could not prove exposure to Celotex asbestos at trial. However, Celotex was still required to satisfy its initial burden of production.

II

I do not read the Court's opinion to say anything inconsistent with or different than the preceding discussion. My disagreement with the Court concerns the application of these principles to the facts of this case.

Defendant Celotex sought summary judgment on the ground that plaintiff had "failed to produce" any evidence that her decedent had ever been exposed to Celotex asbestos. Celotex supported this motion with a two-page "Statement of Material Facts as to Which There is No Genuine Issue" and a three-page "Memorandum of Points and Authorities" which asserted that the plaintiff had failed to identify any evidence in responding to two sets of interrogatories propounded by Celotex and that therefore the record was "totally devoid" of evidence to support plaintiff's claim.

Approximately three months earlier, Celotex had filed an essentially identical motion. Plaintiff responded to this earlier motion by producing three pieces of evidence which she claimed "[a]t the very least ... demonstrate that there is a genuine factual dispute for trial": (1) a letter from an insurance representative of another defendant describing asbestos products to which plaintiff's decedent had been exposed; (2) a letter from T.R. Hoff, a former supervisor of decedent, describing asbestos products to which decedent had been exposed; and (3) a copy of decedent's deposition from earlier workmen's compensation proceedings. Plaintiff also apparently indicated at that time that she intended to call Mr. Hoff as a witness at trial.

Celotex subsequently withdrew its first motion for summary judgment. However, as a result of this motion, when Celotex filed its second summary judgment motion, the record *did* contain evidence—including at least one witness—supporting plaintiff's claim. Indeed, counsel for Celotex admitted to this Court at oral argument that Celotex was aware of this evidence and of plaintiff's intention to call Mr. Hoff as a witness at trial when the second summary judgment motion was filed. Moreover, plaintiff's response to Celotex' second motion pointed to this evidence—noting that it had already been provided to counsel for Celotex in connection with the first motion—and argued that Celotex had failed to "meet its burden of proving that there is no genuine factual dispute for trial."

On these facts, there is simply no question that Celotex failed to discharge its initial burden of production. Having chosen to base its motion on the argument that there was no evidence in the record to support plaintiff's claim, Celotex was not free to ignore supporting evidence that the record clearly contained. Rather, Celotex was required, as an initial matter, to attack the adequacy of this evidence. Celotex' failure to fulfill this simple requirement constituted a failure to discharge its initial burden of production under Rule 56, and thereby rendered summary judgment improper.[6]

This case is indistinguishable from *Adickes*. Here, as there, the defendant moved for summary judgment on the ground that the record contained no evidence to support an essential element of the plaintiff's claim. Here, as there, the plaintiff responded by drawing the court's attention to evidence that was already in the record and that had been ignored by the moving party. Consequently, here, as there, summary judgment should be denied on the ground that the moving party failed to satisfy its initial burden of production.

JUSTICE STEVENS, dissenting.

As the Court points out, petitioner's motion for summary judgment was based on the proposition that respondent could not prevail unless she proved that her deceased husband had been exposed to petitioner's products "within the jurisdictional limits" of the District of Columbia. Respondent made an adequate showing—albeit possibly not in admissible form—that her husband had been exposed to petitioner's product in Illinois. Although the basis of the motion and the argument had been the lack of exposure *in the District of Columbia,* the District Court stated at the end of the argument: "The Court will grant the defendant Celotex's motion for summary judgment there being no showing that the plaintiff was exposed to the defendant Celotex's product in the District of Columbia *or elsewhere* within the statutory period." The District Court offered no additional

---

6. If the plaintiff had answered Celotex' second set of interrogatories with the evidence in her response to the first summary judgment motion, and Celotex had ignored those interrogatories and based its second summary judgment motion on the first set of interrogatories only, Celotex obviously could not claim to have discharged its Rule 56 burden of production. This result should not be different simply because the evidence plaintiff relied upon to support her claim was acquired by Celotex other than in plaintiff's answers to interrogatories.

explanation and no written opinion. The Court of Appeals reversed on the basis that Celotex had not met its burden; the court noted the incongruity of the District Court's opinion in the context of the motion and argument, but did not rest on that basis because of the "or elsewhere" language.

Taken in the context of the motion for summary judgment on the basis of no exposure in the District of Columbia, the District Court's decision to grant summary judgment was palpably erroneous. The court's bench reference to "or elsewhere" neither validated that decision nor raised the complex question addressed by this Court today. In light of the District Court's plain error, therefore, it is perfectly clear that, even after this Court's abstract exercise in Rule construction, we should nonetheless affirm the reversal of summary judgment on that narrow ground.

I respectfully dissent.

* * *

SCOTT v. HARRIS

550 U.S. 372 (2007)

JUSTICE SCALIA delivered the opinion of the Court.

We consider whether a law enforcement official can, consistent with the Fourth Amendment, attempt to stop a fleeing motorist from continuing his public-endangering flight by ramming the motorist's car from behind. Put another way: Can an officer take actions that place a fleeing motorist at risk of serious injury or death in order to stop the motorist's flight from endangering the lives of innocent bystanders?

I

In March 2001, a Georgia county deputy clocked respondent's vehicle traveling at 73 miles per hour on a road with a 55-mile-per-hour speed limit. The deputy activated his blue flashing lights indicating that respondent should pull over. Instead, respondent sped away, initiating a chase down what is in most portions a two-lane road, at speeds exceeding 85 miles per hour. The deputy radioed his dispatch to report that he was pursuing a fleeing vehicle, and broadcast its license plate number. Petitioner, Deputy Timothy Scott, heard the radio communication and joined the pursuit along with other officers. In the midst of the chase, respondent pulled into the parking lot of a shopping center and was nearly boxed in by the various police vehicles. Respondent evaded the trap by making a sharp turn, colliding with Scott's police car, exiting the parking lot, and speeding off once again down a two-lane highway.

Following respondent's shopping center maneuvering, which resulted in slight damage to Scott's police car, Scott took over as the lead pursuit vehicle. Six minutes and nearly 10 miles after the chase had begun, Scott decided to attempt to terminate the episode by employing a "Precision Intervention Technique ('PIT') maneuver, which causes the fleeing vehicle to spin to a stop." Having radioed his supervisor for permission, Scott was told to " '[g]o ahead and take him out.' " Instead, Scott applied his push bumper to the rear of respondent's vehicle. As a result, respondent lost control of his vehicle, which left the roadway, ran down an embankment, overturned, and crashed. Respondent was badly injured and was rendered a quadriplegic.

Respondent filed suit against Deputy Scott and others under 42 U.S.C. § 1983, alleging, a violation of his federal constitutional rights viz. use of excessive force resulting in an unreasonable seizure under the Fourth Amendment. In response, Scott filed a motion for summary judgment based on an assertion of qualified immunity. The District Court denied the motion, finding that "there are material issues of fact on which the issue of qualified immunity turns which present sufficient disagreement to require submission to a jury." On interlocutory appeal, the United States Court of Appeals for the Eleventh Circuit affirmed the District Court's decision to allow respondent's Fourth Amendment claim against Scott to proceed to trial. Taking respondent's view of the facts as given, the Court of Appeals concluded that Scott's actions could constitute "deadly force" and that the use of such force in this context "would violate [respondent's] constitutional right to be free from excessive force during a seizure. Accordingly, a reasonable jury could find that Scott violated [respondent's] Fourth Amendment rights." The Court of Appeals further concluded that "the law as it existed [at the time of the incident], was sufficiently clear to give reasonable law enforcement officers 'fair notice' that ramming a vehicle under these circumstances was unlawful." The Court of Appeals thus concluded that Scott was not entitled to qualified immunity. We granted certiorari and now reverse.

II

In resolving questions of qualified immunity, courts are required to resolve a "threshold question: Taken in the light most favorable to the party asserting the injury, do the facts alleged show the officer's conduct violated a constitutional right? This must be the initial inquiry." If, and only if, the court finds a violation of a constitutional right, "the next, sequential step is to ask whether the right was clearly established . . . in light of the specific context of the case." Although this ordering contradicts "[o]ur policy of avoiding unnecessary adjudication of constitutional issues," we have said that such a departure from practice is "necessary to set forth principles which will become the basis for a [future] holding that a right is clearly established." We therefore turn to the threshold inquiry: whether Deputy Scott's actions violated the Fourth Amendment.

III

A

The first step in assessing the constitutionality of Scott's actions is to determine the relevant facts. As this case was decided on summary judgment, there have not yet been factual findings by a judge or jury, and respondent's version of events (unsurprisingly) differs substantially from

Scott's version. When things are in such a posture, courts are required to view the facts and draw reasonable inferences "in the light most favorable to the party opposing the [summary judgment] motion." In qualified immunity cases, this usually means adopting (as the Court of Appeals did here) the plaintiff's version of the facts.

There is, however, an added wrinkle in this case: existence in the record of a videotape capturing the events in question. There are no allegations or indications that this videotape was doctored or altered in any way, nor any contention that what it depicts differs from what actually happened. The videotape quite clearly contradicts the version of the story told by respondent and adopted by the Court of Appeals.[5] For example, the Court of Appeals adopted respondent's assertions that, during the chase, "there was little, if any, actual threat to pedestrians or other motorists, as the roads were mostly empty and [respondent] remained in control of his vehicle." Indeed, reading the lower court's opinion, one gets the impression that respondent, rather than fleeing from police, was attempting to pass his driving test:

> [T]aking the facts from the non-movant's viewpoint, [respondent] remained in control of his vehicle, slowed for turns and intersections, and typically used his indicators for turns. He did not run any motorists off the road. Nor was he a threat to pedestrians in the shopping center parking lot, which was free from pedestrian and vehicular traffic as the center was closed. Significantly, by the time the parties were back on the highway and Scott rammed [respondent], the motorway had been cleared of motorists and pedestrians allegedly because of police blockades of the nearby intersections.

The videotape tells quite a different story. There we see respondent's vehicle racing down narrow, two-lane roads in the dead of night at speeds that are shockingly fast. We see it swerve around more than a dozen other cars, cross the double-yellow line, and force cars traveling in both directions to their respective shoulders to avoid being hit.[6] We see it run multiple red lights and travel for considerable periods of time in the occasional center left-turn-only lane, chased by numerous police cars forced to engage in the same hazardous maneuvers just to keep up. Far from being the cautious and controlled driver the lower court depicts,

---

5. Justice Stevens suggests that our reaction to the videotape is somehow idiosyncratic, and seems to believe we are misrepresenting its contents. ("In sum, the factual statements by the Court of Appeals quoted by the Court ... were entirely accurate"). We are happy to allow the videotape to speak for itself.

6. Justice Stevens hypothesizes that these cars "had already pulled to the side of the road or were driving along the shoulder because they heard the police sirens or saw the flashing lights," so that "[a] jury could certainly conclude that those motorists were exposed to no greater risk than persons who take the same action in response to a speeding ambulance." It is not our experience that ambulances and fire engines careen down two-lane roads at 85-plus miles per hour, with an unmarked scout car out in front of them. The risk they pose to the public is vastly less than what respondent created here. But even if that were not so, it would in no way lead to the conclusion that it was unreasonable to eliminate the threat to life that respondent posed. Society accepts the risk of speeding ambulances and fire engines in order to save life and property; it need not (and assuredly does not) accept a similar risk posed by a reckless motorist fleeing the police.

what we see on the video more closely resembles a Hollywood-style car chase of the most frightening sort, placing police officers and innocent bystanders alike at great risk of serious injury.[7]

At the summary judgment stage, facts must be viewed in the light most favorable to the nonmoving party only if there is a "genuine" dispute as to those facts. Fed. Rule Civ. Proc. 56(c). As we have emphasized, "[w]hen the moving party has carried its burden under Rule 56(c), its opponent must do more than simply show that there is some metaphysical doubt as to the material facts.... Where the record taken as a whole could not lead a rational trier of fact to find for the nonmoving party, there is no 'genuine issue for trial.'" "[T]he mere existence of *some* alleged factual dispute between the parties will not defeat an otherwise properly supported motion for summary judgment; the requirement is that there be no *genuine* issue of *material* fact." When opposing parties tell two different stories, one of which is blatantly contradicted by the record, so that no reasonable jury could believe it, a court should not adopt that version of the facts for purposes of ruling on a motion for summary judgment.

That was the case here with regard to the factual issue whether respondent was driving in such fashion as to endanger human life. Respondent's version of events is so utterly discredited by the record that no reasonable jury could have believed him. The Court of Appeals should not have relied on such visible fiction; it should have viewed the facts in the light depicted by the videotape.

B

Judging the matter on that basis, we think it is quite clear that Deputy Scott did not violate the Fourth Amendment. Scott does not contest that his decision to terminate the car chase by ramming his bumper into respondent's vehicle constituted a "seizure." "[A] Fourth Amendment seizure [occurs] ... when there is a governmental termination of freedom of movement through means intentionally applied." It is also conceded, by both sides, that a claim of "excessive force in the course of making [a] ... 'seizure' of [the] person ... [is] properly analyzed under the Fourth Amendment's 'objective reasonableness' standard." The question we need to answer is whether Scott's actions were objectively reasonable.[8]

* * *

---

7. This is not to say that each and every factual statement made by the Court of Appeals is inaccurate. For example, the videotape validates the court's statement that when Scott rammed respondent's vehicle it was not threatening any other vehicles or pedestrians. (Undoubtedly Scott *waited* for the road to be clear before executing his maneuver.)

8. Justice Stevens incorrectly declares this to be "a question of fact best reserved for a jury," and complains we are "usurp[ing]" the jury's fact-finding function." At the summary judgment stage, however, once we have determined the relevant set of facts and drawn all inferences in favor of the nonmoving party *to the extent supportable by the record,* the reasonableness of Scott's actions—or, in Justice Stevens' parlance, "[w]hether [respondent's] actions have risen to a level warranting deadly force," is a pure question of law.

* * * The car chase that respondent initiated in this case posed a substantial and immediate risk of serious physical injury to others; no reasonable jury could conclude otherwise. Scott's attempt to terminate the chase by forcing respondent off the road was reasonable, and Scott is entitled to summary judgment. The Court of Appeals' decision to the contrary is reversed.

It is so ordered.

JUSTICE GINSBURG, concurring.

I join the Court's opinion and would underscore two points. First, I do not read today's decision as articulating a mechanical, per se rule. Cf. (Breyer, J., concurring). The inquiry described by the Court is situation specific. Among relevant considerations: Were the lives and well-being of others (motorists, pedestrians, police officers) at risk? Was there a safer way, given the time, place, and circumstances, to stop the fleeing vehicle? "[A]dmirable" as "[an] attempt to craft an easy-to-apply legal test in the Fourth Amendment context [may be]," the Court explains, "in the end we must still slosh our way through the factbound morass of 'reasonableness.'"

Second, were this case suitable for resolution on qualified immunity grounds, without reaching the constitutional question, Justice Breyer's discussion would be engaging. In joining the Court's opinion, however, Justice Breyer apparently shares the view that, in the appeal before us, the constitutional question warrants an answer. The video footage of the car chase, he agrees, demonstrates that the officer's conduct did not transgress Fourth Amendment limitations. Confronting Saucier, therefore, is properly reserved for another day and case.

JUSTICE BREYER, concurring.

I join the Court's opinion with one suggestion and two qualifications. Because watching the video footage of the car chase made a difference to my own view of the case, I suggest that the interested reader take advantage of the link in the Court's opinion and watch it. Having done so, I do not believe a reasonable jury could, in this instance, find that Officer Timothy Scott (who joined the chase late in the day and did not know the specific reason why the respondent was being pursued) acted in violation of the Constitution.

Second, the video makes clear the highly fact-dependent nature of this constitutional determination. And that fact dependency supports the argument that we should overrule the requirement, announced in *Saucier v. Katz* (2001), that lower courts must first decide the "constitutional question" before they turn to the "qualified immunity question." ("[T]he first inquiry must be whether a constitutional right would have been violated on the facts alleged"). Instead, lower courts should be free to decide the two questions in whatever order makes sense in the context of a particular case. Although I do not object to our deciding the constitutional question in this particular case, I believe that in order to lift the burden from lower courts we can and should reconsider *Saucier's* requirement as well.

Sometimes (e.g., where a defendant is clearly entitled to qualified immunity) *Saucier's* fixed order-of-battle rule wastes judicial resources in that it may require courts to answer a difficult constitutional question unnecessarily. Sometimes (e.g., where the defendant loses the constitutional question but wins on qualified immunity) that order-of-battle rule may immunize an incorrect constitutional ruling from review. Sometimes, as here, the order-of-battle rule will spawn constitutional rulings in areas of law so fact dependent that the result will be confusion rather than clarity. And frequently the order-of-battle rule violates that older, wiser judicial counsel "not to pass on questions of constitutionality . . . unless such adjudication is unavoidable." ("The Court will not pass upon a constitutional question although properly presented by the record, if there is also present some other ground upon which the case may be disposed of"). In a sharp departure from this counsel, *Saucier* requires courts to embrace unnecessary constitutional questions not to avoid them.

It is not surprising that commentators, judges, and, in this case, 28 States in an amicus brief have invited us to reconsider *Saucier's* requirement . . . I would accept that invitation.

While this Court should generally be reluctant to overturn precedents, stare decisis concerns are at their weakest here. ("Considerations in favor of stare decisis" are at their weakest in cases "involving procedural and evidentiary rules"). The order-of-battle rule is relatively novel, it primarily affects judges, and there has been little reliance upon it.

Third, I disagree with the Court insofar as it articulates a per se rule. The majority states: "A police officer's attempt to terminate a dangerous high-speed car chase that threatens the lives of innocent bystanders does not violate the Fourth Amendment, even when it places the fleeing motorist at risk of serious injury or death." This statement is too absolute. As Justice Ginsburg points out, whether a high-speed chase violates the Fourth Amendment may well depend upon more circumstances than the majority's rule reflects. With these qualifications, I join the Court's opinion.

JUSTICE STEVENS, dissenting.

Today, the Court asks whether an officer may "take actions that place a fleeing motorist at risk of serious injury or death in order to stop the motorist's flight from endangering the lives of innocent bystanders." Depending on the circumstances, the answer may be an obvious "yes," an obvious "no," or sufficiently doubtful that the question of the reasonableness of the officer's actions should be decided by a jury, after a review of the degree of danger and the alternatives available to the officer. A high speed chase in a desert in Nevada is, after all, quite different from one that travels through the heart of Las Vegas.

Relying on a *de novo* review of a videotape of a portion of a nighttime chase on a lightly traveled road in Georgia where no pedestrians or other "bystanders" were present, buttressed by uninformed speculation about the possible consequences of discontinuing the chase, eight of the jurors on this Court reach a verdict that differs from the views of the judges on both the District Court and the Court of Appeals who are surely more familiar with the hazards of driving on Georgia roads than we are. The Court's justification for this unprecedented departure from our well-settled standard of review of factual determinations made by a district court and affirmed by a court of appeals is based on its mistaken view that the Court of Appeals' description of the facts was "blatantly contradicted by the record" and that respondent's version of the events was "so utterly discredited by the record that no reasonable jury could have believed him."

Rather than supporting the conclusion that what we see on the video "resembles a Hollywood-style car chase of the most frightening sort,"[1] the tape actually confirms, rather than contradicts, the lower courts' appraisal of the factual questions at issue. More important, it surely does not provide a principled basis for depriving the respondent of his right to have a jury evaluate the question whether the police officers' decision to use deadly force to bring the chase to an end was reasonable.

Omitted from the Court's description of the initial speeding violation is the fact that respondent was on a four-lane portion of Highway 34 when the officer clocked his speed at 73 miles per hour and initiated the chase.[2] More significant—and contrary to the Court's assumption that respondent's vehicle "force[d] cars traveling in both directions to their respective shoulders to avoid being hit"—a fact unmentioned in the text of the opinion explains why those cars pulled over prior to being passed by respondent. The sirens and flashing lights on the police cars following respondent gave the same warning that a speeding ambulance or fire engine would have provided.[3] The 13 cars that respondent passed on his side of the road before entering the shopping center, and both of the cars that he passed on the right after leaving the center, no doubt had already pulled to the side of the road or were driving along the shoulder because

---

1. I can only conclude that my colleagues were unduly frightened by two or three images on the tape that looked like bursts of lightning or explosions, but were in fact merely the headlights of vehicles zooming by in the opposite lane. Had they learned to drive when most high-speed driving took place on two-lane roads rather than on superhighways—when split-second judgments about the risk of passing a slow-poke in the face of oncoming traffic were routine—they might well have reacted to the videotape more dispassionately.

2. According to the District Court record, when respondent was clocked at 73 miles per hour, the deputy who recorded his speed was sitting in his patrol car on Highway 34 between Lora Smith Road and Sullivan Road in Coweta County, Georgia. At that point, as well as at the point at which Highway 34 intersects with Highway 154—where the deputy caught up with respondent and the videotape begins—Highway 34 is a four-lane road, consisting of two lanes in each direction with a wide grass divider separating the flow of traffic.

3. While still on the four-lane portion of Highway 34, the deputy who had clocked respondent's speed turned on his blue light and siren in an attempt to get respondent to pull over. It was when the deputy turned on his blue light that the dash-mounted video camera was activated and began to record the pursuit.

they heard the police sirens or saw the flashing lights before respondent or the police cruisers approached.[4] A jury could certainly conclude that those motorists were exposed to no greater risk than persons who take the same action in response to a speeding ambulance, and that their reactions were fully consistent with the evidence that respondent, though speeding, retained full control of his vehicle.

The police sirens also minimized any risk that may have arisen from running "multiple red lights." In fact, respondent and his pursuers went through only two intersections with stop lights and in both cases all other vehicles in sight were stationary, presumably because they had been warned of the approaching speeders. Incidentally, the videos do show that the lights were red when the police cars passed through them but, because the cameras were farther away when respondent did so and it is difficult to discern the color of the signal at that point, it is not entirely clear that he ran either or both of the red lights. In any event, the risk of harm to the stationary vehicles was minimized by the sirens, and there is no reason to believe that respondent would have disobeyed the signals if he were not being pursued.

My colleagues on the jury saw respondent "swerve around more than a dozen other cars," and "force cars traveling in both directions to their respective shoulders," but they apparently discounted the possibility that those cars were already out of the pursuit's path as a result of hearing the sirens. Even if that were not so, passing a slower vehicle on a two-lane road always involves some degree of swerving and is not especially dangerous if there are no cars coming from the opposite direction. At no point during the chase did respondent pull into the opposite lane other than to pass a car in front of him; he did the latter no more than five times and, on most of those occasions, used his turn signal. On none of these occasions was there a car traveling in the opposite direction. In fact, at one point, when respondent found himself behind a car in his own lane and there were cars traveling in the other direction, he slowed and waited for the cars traveling in the other direction to pass before overtaking the car in front of him while using his turn signal to do so. This is hardly the stuff of Hollywood. To the contrary, the video does not reveal any incidents that could even be remotely characterized as "close calls."

In sum, the factual statements by the Court of Appeals quoted by the Court, were entirely accurate. That court did not describe respondent as a "cautious" driver as my colleagues imply, but it did correctly conclude that there is no evidence that he ever lost control of his vehicle. That court also correctly pointed out that the incident in the shopping center parking lot did not create any risk to pedestrians or other vehicles because the chase occurred just before 11 p.m. on a weekday night and the center was closed. It is apparent from the record (including the videotape) that local police had blocked off intersections to keep respondent from entering

---

4. Although perhaps understandable, because their volume on the sound recording is low (possibly due to sound proofing in the officer's vehicle), the Court appears to minimize the significance of the sirens audible throughout the tape recording of the pursuit.

residential neighborhoods and possibly endangering other motorists. I would add that the videos also show that no pedestrians, parked cars, sidewalks, or residences were visible at any time during the chase. The only "innocent bystanders" who were placed "at great risk of serious injury," were the drivers who either pulled off the road in response to the sirens or passed respondent in the opposite direction when he was driving on his side of the road.

I recognize, of course, that even though respondent's original speeding violation on a four-lane highway was rather ordinary, his refusal to stop and subsequent flight was a serious offense that merited severe punishment. It was not, however, a capital offense, or even an offense that justified the use of deadly force rather than an abandonment of the chase. The Court's concern about the "imminent threat to the lives of any pedestrians who might have been present," while surely valid in an appropriate case, should be discounted in a case involving a nighttime chase in an area where no pedestrians were present.

What would have happened if the police had decided to abandon the chase? We now know that they could have apprehended respondent later because they had his license plate number. Even if that were not true, and even if he would have escaped any punishment at all, the use of deadly force in this case was no more appropriate than the use of a deadly weapon against a fleeing felon. In any event, any uncertainty about the result of abandoning the pursuit has not prevented the Court from basing its conclusions on its own factual assumptions.[5] The Court attempts to avoid the conclusion that deadly force was unnecessary by speculating that if the officers had let him go, respondent might have been "just as likely" to continue to drive recklessly as to slow down and wipe his brow. That speculation is unconvincing as a matter of common sense and improper as a matter of law. Our duty to view the evidence in the light most favorable to the nonmoving party would foreclose such speculation if the Court had not used its observation of the video as an excuse for replacing the rule of law with its ad hoc judgment. There is no evidentiary basis for an assumption that dangers caused by flight from a police pursuit will continue after the pursuit ends. Indeed, rules adopted by countless police departments throughout the country are based on a judgment that differs from the Court's. ("During a pursuit, the need to apprehend the suspect should always outweigh the level of danger created by the pursuit. When the immediate danger to the public created by the pursuit is greater than

---

5. In noting that Scott's action "was *certain* to eliminate the risk that respondent posed to the public" while "ceasing pursuit was not," the Court prioritizes total elimination of the risk of harm to the public over the risk that respondent may be seriously injured or even killed. The Court is only able to make such a statement by assuming, based on its interpretation of events on the videotape, that the risk of harm posed in this case, and the type of harm involved, rose to a level warranting deadly force. These are the same types of questions that, when disputed, are typically resolved by a jury; this is why both the District Court and the Court of Appeals saw fit to have them be so decided. Although the Court claims only to have drawn factual inferences in respondent's favor *"to the extent supportable by the record,"* its own view of the record has clearly precluded it from doing so to the same extent as the two courts through which this case has already traveled.

the immediate or potential danger to the public should the suspect remain at large, then the pursuit should be discontinued or terminated.... [P]ursuits should usually be discontinued when the violator's identity has been established to the point that later apprehension can be accomplished without danger to the public").

Although [prior precedent] may not, as the Court suggests, "establish a magical on/off switch that triggers rigid preconditions" for the use of deadly force, [the Court's precedents] did set a threshold under which the use of deadly force would be considered constitutionally unreasonable.

Whether a person's actions have risen to a level warranting deadly force is a question of fact best reserved for a jury.[6] Here, the Court has usurped the jury's fact-finding function and, in doing so, implicitly labeled the four other judges to review the case unreasonable. It chastises the Court of Appeals for failing to "vie[w] the facts in the light depicted by the videotape" and implies that no reasonable person could view the videotape and come to the conclusion that deadly force was unjustified. However, the three judges on the Court of Appeals panel apparently did view the videotapes entered into evidence and described a very different version of events:

> At the time of the ramming, apart from speeding and running two red lights, Harris was driving in a non-aggressive fashion (i.e., without trying to ram or run into the officers). Moreover, ... Scott's path on the open highway was largely clear. The videos introduced into evidence show little to no vehicular (or pedestrian) traffic, allegedly because of the late hour and the police blockade of the nearby intersections. Finally, Scott issued absolutely no warning (e.g., over the loudspeaker or otherwise) prior to using deadly force.

If two groups of judges can disagree so vehemently about the nature of the pursuit and the circumstances surrounding that pursuit, it seems eminently likely that a reasonable juror could disagree with this Court's characterization of events. Moreover, it is certainly possible that "a jury could conclude that Scott unreasonably used deadly force to seize Harris by ramming him off the road under the instant circumstances."

The Court today sets forth a *per se* rule that presumes its own version of the facts: "A police officer's attempt to terminate a dangerous high-speed car chase *that threatens the lives of innocent bystanders* does not violate the Fourth Amendment, even when it places the fleeing motorist at risk of serious injury or death." Not only does that rule fly in the face of the flexible and case-by-case "reasonableness" approach, but it is also arguably inapplicable to the case at hand, given that it is not clear that this chase threatened the life of any "innocent bystande[r]." In my view, the risks inherent in justifying unwarranted police conduct on the basis of

---

6. In its opinion, the Court of Appeals correctly noted: "We reject the defendants' argument that Harris' driving must, as a matter of law, be considered sufficiently reckless to give Scott probable cause to believe that he posed a substantial threat of imminent physical harm to motorists and pedestrians. This is a disputed issue to be resolved by a jury."

unfounded assumptions are unacceptable, particularly when less drastic measures—in this case, the use of stop sticks or a simple warning issued from a loudspeaker—could have avoided such a tragic result. In my judgment, jurors in Georgia should be allowed to evaluate the reasonableness of the decision to ram respondent's speeding vehicle in a manner that created an obvious risk of death and has in fact made him a quadriplegic at the age of 19.

I respectfully dissent.

* * *

C. JUDGMENT AS A MATTER OF LAW (DIRECTED VERDICT)

FEDERAL RULE OF CIVIL PROCEDURE 50. JUDGMENT AS A MATTER OF LAW IN A JURY TRIAL; RELATED MOTION FOR A NEW TRIAL; CONDITIONAL RULING

(a) Judgment as a Matter of Law.

(1) In General. If a party has been fully heard on an issue during a jury trial and the court finds that a reasonable jury would not have a legally sufficient evidentiary basis to find for the party on that issue, the court may:

(A) resolve the issue against the party; and

(B) grant a motion for judgment as a matter of law against the party on a claim or defense that, under the controlling law, can be maintained or defeated only with a favorable finding on that issue.

(2) Motion. A motion for judgment as a matter of law may be made at any time before the case is submitted to the jury. The motion must specify the judgment sought and the law and facts that entitle the movant to the judgment.

(b) Renewing the Motion After Trial; Alternative Motion for a New Trial. If the court does not grant a motion for judgment as a matter of law made under Rule 50(a), the court is considered to have submitted the action to the jury subject to the court's later deciding the legal questions raised by the motion. No later than 28 days after the entry of judgment—or if the motion addresses a jury issue not decided by a verdict, no later than 28 days after the jury was discharged—the movant may file a renewed motion for judgment as a matter of law and may include an alternative or joint request for a new trial under Rule 59. In ruling on the renewed motion, the court may:

(1) allow judgment on the verdict, if the jury returned a verdict;

(2) order a new trial; or

(3) direct the entry of judgment as a matter of law.

(c) Granting the Renewed Motion; Conditional Ruling on a Motion for a New Trial.

    (1) In General. If the court grants a renewed motion for judgment as a matter of law, it must also conditionally rule on any motion for a new trial by determining whether a new trial should be granted if the judgment is later vacated or reversed. The court must state the grounds for conditionally granting or denying the motion for a new trial.

    (2) Effect of a Conditional Ruling. Conditionally granting the motion for a new trial does not affect the judgment's finality; if the judgment is reversed, the new trial must proceed unless the appellate court orders otherwise. If the motion for a new trial is conditionally denied, the appellee may assert error in that denial; if the judgment is reversed, the case must proceed as the appellate court orders.

(d) Time for a Losing Party's New–Trial Motion. Any motion for a new trial under Rule 59 by a party against whom judgment as a matter of law is rendered must be filed no later than 28 days after the entry of the judgment.

(e) Denying the Motion for Judgment as a Matter of Law; Reversal on Appeal. If the court denies the motion for judgment as a matter of law, the prevailing party may, as appellee, assert grounds entitling it to a new trial should the appellate court conclude that the trial court erred in denying the motion. If the appellate court reverses the judgment, it may order a new trial, direct the trial court to determine whether a new trial should be granted, or direct the entry of judgment.

* * *

GALLOWAY v. UNITED STATES

319 U.S. 372 (1943)

Mr. Justice Rutledge delivered the opinion of the Court.

Petitioner seeks benefits for total and permanent disability by reason of insanity he claims existed May 31, 1919. On that day his policy of yearly renewable term insurance lapsed for nonpayment of premium.[1]

The suit was filed June 15, 1938. At the close of all the evidence the District Court granted the Government's motion for a directed verdict.

---

    1. The contract was issued pursuant to the War Risk Insurance Act and insured against death or total permanent disability. Pursuant to statutory authority, provided:

    Any impairment of mind or body which renders it impossible for the disabled person to follow continuously any substantially gainful occupation shall be deemed * * * to be total disability.

    Total disability shall be deemed to be permanent whenever it is founded upon conditions which render it reasonably certain that it will continue throughout the life of the person suffering from it.

Judgment was entered accordingly. The Circuit Court of Appeals affirmed. Both courts held the evidence legally insufficient to sustain a verdict for petitioner. He says this was erroneous and, in effect, deprived him of trial by jury, contrary to the Seventh Amendment.

The constitutional argument, as petitioner has made it, does not challenge generally the power of federal courts to withhold or withdraw from the jury cases in which the claimant puts forward insufficient evidence to support a verdict. The contention is merely that his case as made was substantial, the courts' decisions to the contrary were wrong, and therefore their effect has been to deprive him of a jury trial. Upon the record and the issues as the parties have made them, the only question is whether the evidence was sufficient to sustain a verdict for petitioner. On that basis, we think the judgments must be affirmed.

I.

Certain facts are undisputed. Petitioner worked as a longshoreman in Philadelphia and elsewhere prior to enlistment in the Army November 1, 1917.[3] He became a cook in a machine gun battalion. His unit arrived in France in April, 1918. He served actively until September 24. From then to the following January he was in a hospital with influenza. He then returned to active duty. He came back to the United States, and received honorable discharge April 29, 1919. He enlisted in the Navy January 15, 1920, and was discharged for bad conduct in July. The following December he again enlisted in the Army and served until May, 1922, when he deserted. Thereafter he was carried on the Army records as a deserter.

In 1930 began a series of medical examinations by Veterans' Bureau physicians. On May 19 that year his condition was diagnosed as "Moron, low grade; observation, dementia praecox, simple type." In November, 1931, further examination gave the diagnosis, "Psychosis with other diseases or conditions (organic disease of the central nervous system-type undetermined)." In July, 1934, still another examination was made, with diagnosis: "Psychosis manic and depressive insanity incompetent; hypertension, moderate; otitis media, chronic, left; varicose veins left, mild; abscessed teeth roots; myocarditis, mild."

Petitioner's wife, the nominal party in this suit, was appointed guardian of his person and estate in February, 1932. Claim for insurance benefits was made in June, 1934, and was finally denied by the Board of Veterans' Appeals in January, 1936. This suit followed two and a half years later.

Petitioner concededly is now totally and permanently disabled by reason of insanity and has been for some time prior to institution of this suit. It is conceded also that he was sound in mind and body until he arrived in France in April, 1918.

---

3. The record does not show whether this employment was steady and continuous or was spotty and erratic. But there is no contention petitioner's behavior was abnormal before he arrived in France in April, 1918.

The theory of his case is that the strain of active service abroad brought on an immediate change, which was the beginning of a mental breakdown that has grown worse continuously through all the later years. Essential in this is the view it had become a total and permanent disability not later than May 31, 1919.

The evidence to support this theory falls naturally into three periods, namely, that prior to 1923; the interval from then to 1930; and that following 1930. It consists in proof of incidents occurring in France to show the beginnings of change; testimony of changed appearance and behavior in the years immediately following petitioner's return to the United States as compared with those prior to his departure; the medical evidence of insanity accumulated in the years following 1930; and finally the evidence of a physician, given largely as medical opinion, which seeks to tie all the other evidence together as foundation for the conclusion, expressed as of 1941, that petitioner's disability was total and permanent as of a time not later than May of 1919.

Documentary exhibits included military, naval and Veterans' Bureau records. Testimony was given by deposition or at the trial chiefly by five witnesses. One, O'Neill, was a fellow worker and friend from boyhood; two, Wells and Tanikawa, served with petitioner overseas; Lt. Col. Albert K. Mathews, who was an Army chaplain, observed him or another person of the same name at an Army hospital in California during early 1920; and Dr. Wilder, a physician, examined him shortly before the trial and supplied the only expert testimony in his behalf. The petitioner also put into evidence the depositions of Commander Platt and Lt. Col. James E. Matthews, his superior officers in the Navy and the Army, respectively, during 1920–22.

What happened in France during 1918–19 is shown chiefly by Wells and Tanikawa. Wells testified to an incident at Aisonville, where the unit was billeted shortly after reaching France and before going into action. Late at night petitioner created a disturbance, "hollering, screeching, swearing. * * * The men poured out from the whole section." Wells did not see the incident, but heard petitioner swearing at his superior officers and saw "the result, a black eye for Lt. Warner." However, he did not see "who gave it to him." Wells personally observed no infraction of discipline except this incident, and did not know what brought it on. Petitioner's physical appearance was good, he "carried on his duties as a cook all right," and the witness did not see him after June 1, except for about three days in July when he observed petitioner several times at work feeding stragglers.

Tanikawa, Hawaiian-born citizen, served with petitioner from the latter's enlistment until September, 1918, when Galloway was hospitalized, although the witness thought they had fought together and petitioner was "acting queer" at the Battle of the Argonne in October. At Camp Greene, North Carolina, petitioner was "just a regular soldier, very normal, * * * pretty neat." After reaching France "he was getting nervous * * *, kind of irritable, always picking a fight with other soldier." This began at Aisonville. Tanikawa saw Galloway in jail, apparently before June. It is not clear whether these are references to the incident Wells described.

Tanikawa described another incident in June "when we were on the Marne," the Germans "were on the other side and we were on this side." It was a new front, without trenches. The witness and petitioner were on guard duty with others. Tanikawa understood the Germans were getting ready for a big drive. "One night he (petitioner) screamed. He said, 'The Germans are coming' and we all gagged him." There was no shooting, the Germans were not coming, and there was nothing to lead the witness to believe they were. Petitioner was court martialed for the matter, but Tanikawa did not know "what they did with him." He did not talk with Galloway that night, because "he was out of his mind" and appeared insane. Tanikawa did not know when petitioner left the battalion or what happened to him after (as the witness put it) the Argonne fight, but heard he went to the hospital, "just dressing station I guess." The witness next saw Galloway in 1936, at a disabled veterans' post meeting in Sacramento, California. Petitioner then "looked to me like he wasn't all there. Insane. About the same * * * as compared to the way he acted in France, particularly when they gagged him * * *."

O'Neill was "born and raised with" petitioner, worked with him as a longshoreman, and knew him "from when he come out of the army for seven years, * * * I would say five or six years." When petitioner returned in April or May, 1919, "he was a wreck compared to what he was when he went away. The fellow's mind was evidently unbalanced." Symptoms specified were withdrawing to himself; crying spells; alternate periods of normal behavior and nonsensical talk; expression of fears that good friends wanted "to beat him up"; spitting blood and remarking about it in vulgar terms. Once petitioner said, "G-d-it, I must be a Doctor Jekyll and Mr. Hyde."

O'Neill testified these symptoms and this condition continued practically the same for about five years. In his opinion petitioner was "competent at times and others was incompetent." The intervals might be "a couple of days, a couple of months." In his normal periods Galloway "would be his old self * * * absolutely O.K."

O'Neill was definite in recalling petitioner's condition and having seen him frequently in 1919, chiefly however, and briefly, on the street during lunch hour. He was not sure Galloway was working and was "surprised he got in the Navy, I think in the Navy or in the Government service."

O'Neill maintained he saw petitioner "right on from that (1920) at times." But his recollection of dates, number of opportunities for observation, and concrete events was wholly indefinite. He would fix no estimate for the number of times he had seen petitioner: "In 1920 I couldn't recall whether it was one or a thousand." For later years he would not say whether it was "five times or more or less." When he was pinned down by cross-examination, the effect of his testimony was that he recalled petitioner clearly in 1919 "because there was such a vast contrast in the man," but for later years he could give little or no definite information. The excerpt from the testimony set forth in the margin[5] shows this contrast. We also summarize below[6] other evidence which explains or illustrates the vagueness of the witness' recollection for events after 1919. O'Neill recalled one specific occasion after 1919 when petitioner returned to Philadelphia, "around 1920 or 1921, but I couldn't be sure," to testify in a criminal proceeding. He also said, "After he was away for five or six years, he came back to Philadelphia, but I wouldn't know nothing about dates on that. He was back in Philadelphia for five or six months or so, and he was still just evidently all right, and then he would be off."

Lt. Col. (Chaplain) Mathews said he observed a Private Joseph Galloway, who was a prisoner for desertion and a patient in the mental ward at Fort MacArthur Station Hospital, California, during a six weeks period early in 1920. The chaplain's testimony gives strong evidence the man he observed was insane. However, there is a fatal weakness in this

---

5. 'X Can you tell us approximately how many times you saw him in 1919?

'A. No; I seen him so often that it would be hard to give any estimate.

'X And the same goes for 1920?

'A. I wouldn't be sure about 1920. I remember him more when he first came home because there was such a vast contrast in the man. Otherwise, if nothing unusual happened, I wouldn't probably recall him at all, you know, that is, recall the particular time and all.

'X Well, do you recall him at all in 1920?

'A. I can't say.

'X And could you swear whether or not you ever saw him in 1921?

'A. I think I seen him both in 1921 and 1920 and 1921 and right on. I might not see him for a few weeks or months at a time, but I think I saw him a few times in all the years right up to, as I say, at least five years after.

'X Can you give us an estimate as to the number of times you saw him in 1920?

'A. No, I would not.

'X Was it more than five times or less?

'A. In 1920 I couldn't recall whether it was one or a thousand. The time I recall him well is when he first come home, but I know that I seen him right on from that at times.

'X And the same goes for 1921, 1922, 1923 and 1924?

'A. I would say for five years afterwards, but I don't know just when or how often I seen him except when he first come home for the first couple of months.

'X But for years after his return you couldn't say definitely whether you saw him five times or more or less, could you?

'A. No, because it was a thing that there was a vast contrast when he first come home and everybody noticed it and remarked about it and it was more liable to be remembered. You could ask me about some more friends I knew during those years and I wouldn't know except there was something unusual.'

6. Petitioner's own evidence shows without dispute he was on active duty in the Navy from January 15, 1920, to July of that year and in the Army from December, 1920, to May 6, 1922. As is noted in the text, O'Neill was not sure he was working and "was surprised he got in the Navy, I think in the Navy or in the Government service." He only "heard some talk" of petitioner's having reenlisted in the Army, but "if it was the fact, I would be surprised that he could do it owing to his mental condition." O'Neill was not certain that he saw Galloway in uniform after the first week of his return to Philadelphia from overseas, although he said he saw petitioner during "the periods of those reenlistments * * * but I can't recall about it."

evidence. In his direct testimony, which was taken by deposition, the chaplain said he was certain that the soldier was petitioner. When confronted with the undisputed fact that petitioner was on active duty in the Navy during the first half of 1920, the witness at first stated that he might have been mistaken as to the time of his observation. Subsequently he reasserted the accuracy of his original statement as to the time of observation, but admitted that he might have been mistaken in believing that the patient-prisoner was petitioner. In this connection he volunteered the statement, "Might I add, sir, that I could not now identify that soldier if I were to meet him face to face, and that is because of the long lapse of time." The patient whom the witness saw was confined to his bed. The record is barren of other evidence, whether by the hospital's or the Army's records or otherwise, to show that petitioner was either patient or prisoner at Fort MacArthur in 1920 or at any other time.

Commander Platt testified that petitioner caused considerable trouble by disobedience and leaving ship without permission during his naval service in the first half of 1920. After "repeated warnings and punishments, leading to court martials," he was sentenced to a bad conduct discharge.

Lt. Col. James E. Matthews (not the chaplain) testified by deposition which petitioner's attorney interrupted Dr. Wilder's testimony to read into evidence. The witness was Galloway's commanding officer from early 1921 to the summer of that year, when petitioner was transferred with other soldiers to another unit. At first Colonel Matthews considered making petitioner a corporal, but found him unreliable and had to discipline him. Petitioner "drank considerably," was "what we called a bolshevik," did not seem loyal, and "acted as if he was not getting a square deal." The officer concluded "he was a moral pervert and probably used narcotics," but could not secure proof of this. Galloway was court martialed for public drunkenness and disorderly conduct, served a month at hard labor, and returned to active duty. At times he "was one of the very best soldiers I had," at others undependable. He was physically sound, able to do his work, perform close order drill, etc., "very well." He had alternate periods of gaiety and depression, talked incoherently at times, gave the impression he would fight readily, but did not resent orders and seemed to get along well with other soldiers. The officer attributed petitioner's behavior to alcohol and narcotics and it occurred to him at no time to question his sanity.

Dr. Wilder was the key witness. He disclaimed specializing in mental disease, but qualified as having given it "special attention." He first saw petitioner shortly before the trial, examined him "several times." He concluded petitioner's ailment "is a schizophrenic branch or form of praecox." Dr. Wilder heard the testimony and read the depositions of the other witnesses, and examined the documentary evidence. Basing his judgment upon this material, with inferences drawn from it, he concluded petitioner was born with "an inherent instability," though he remained normal until he went to France; began there "to be subjected to the strain of military life, then he began to go to pieces." In May, 1919, petitioner "was still suffering from the acuteness of the breakdown * * *. He is going downhill still, but the thing began with the breakdown * * *." Petitioner was "definitely insane, yes, sir," in 1920 and "has been insane at all times, at least since July, 1918, the time of this episode on the Marne"; that is, "to the point that he was unable to adapt himself. I don't mean he has not had moments when he could not perform some routine tasks," but "from an occupational standpoint * * * he has been insane." He could follow "a mere matter of routine," but would have no incentive, would not keep a steady job, come to work on time, or do anything he didn't want to do. Dr. Wilder pointed to petitioner's work record before he entered the service and observed: "At no time after he went into the war do we find him able to hold any kind of a job. He broke right down." He explained petitioner's enlistment in the Navy and later in the Army by saying, "It would have been no trick at all for a man who was reasonably conforming to get into the Service."

However, the witness knew "nothing whatever except his getting married" about petitioner's activities between 1925 and 1930, and what he knew of them between 1922 and 1925 was based entirely on O'Neill's testimony and a paper not of record here. Dr. Wilder at first regarded knowledge concerning what petitioner was doing between 1925 and 1930 as not essential. "We have a continuing disease, quite obviously beginning during his military service, and quite obviously continuing in 1930, and the minor incidents don't seem to me ." Counsel for the government interrupted to inquire, "Well, if he was continuously employed for eight hours a day from 1925 to 1930 would that have any hearing?" The witness replied, "It would have a great deal." Upon further questioning, however, he reverted to his first position, stating it would not be necessary or helpful for him to know what petitioner was doing from 1925 to 1930: "I testified from the information I had."

II.

This, we think, is the crux of the case and distinguishes it from the cases on which petitioner has relied. His burden was to prove total and permanent disability as of a date not later than May 31, 1919. He has undertaken to do this by showing incipience of mental disability shortly before that time and its continuance and progression throughout the succeeding years. He has clearly established incidence of total and permanent disability as of some period prior to 1938, when he began this suit.[9] For our purposes this may be taken as medically established by the Veterans' Bureau examination and diagnosis of July, 1934.[10]

---

9. He has not established a fixed date at which contemporaneous medical examination, both physical and mental, establishes totality and permanence prior to Dr. Wilder's examinations in 1941.

Dr. Wilder testified that on the evidence concerning petitioner's behavior at the time of his discharge in 1919, and without reference to the testimony as to later conduct, including O'Neill's, he would reserve his opinion on whether petitioner was then "crazy"—"I wouldn't have enough".

10. The previous examinations of 1930 and 1931 show possibility of mental disease in the one case and existence of psychosis with other disease, organic in character but with type undeter-

But if the record is taken to show that some form of mental disability existed in 1930, which later became total and permanent, petitioner's problem remains to demonstrate by more than speculative inference that this condition itself began on or before May 31, 1919 and continuously existed or progressed through the intervening years to 1930.

To show origin before the crucial date, he gives evidence of two abnormal incidents occurring while he was in France, one creating the disturbance before he came near the fighting front, the other yelling that the Germans were coming when he was on guard duty at the Marne. There is no other evidence of abnormal behavior during his entire service of more than a year abroad.

That he was court martialed for these sporadic acts and bound and gagged for one does not prove he was insane or had then a general breakdown in "an already fragile mental constitution," which the vicissitudes of a longshoreman's life had not been able to crack.

To these two incidents petitioner adds the testimony of O'Neill that he looked and acted like a wreck, compared with his former self, when he returned from France about a month before the crucial date, and O'Neill's vague recollections that this condition continued through the next two, three, four or five years.

O'Neill's testimony apparently takes no account of petitioner's having spent 101 days in a hospital in France with influenza just before he came home. But, given the utmost credence, as is required, it does no more than show that petitioner was subject to alternating periods of gaiety and depression for some indefinite period after his return, extending perhaps as late as 1922. But because of its vagueness as to time, dates, frequency of opportunity for observation, and specific incident, O'Neill's testimony concerning the period from 1922 to 1925 is hardly more than speculative.

We have then the two incidents in France followed by O'Neill's testimony of petitioner's changed condition in 1919 and its continuance to 1922.[11] There is also the testimony of Commander Platt and Lt. Col.

---

mined, in the other. These two examinations without more do not prove existence of total and permanent disability; on the contrary, they go far toward showing it could not be established then medically.

The 1930 diagnosis shows only that the examiner regarded petitioner as a moron of low grade, and recommended he be observed for simple dementia praecox. Dr. Wilder found no evidence in 1941 that petitioner was a moron. The 1931 examination is even less conclusive in one respect, namely, that "psychosis" takes the place of moronic status. Dr. Wilder also disagreed with this diagnosis. However, this examination first indicates existence of organic nervous disease. Not until the 1934 diagnosis is there one which might be regarded as showing possible total and permanent disability by medical evidence contemporaneous with the fact.

11. Chaplain Mathews' testimony would be highly probative of insanity existing early in 1920, if petitioner were sufficiently identified as its subject. However, the bare inference of identity which might otherwise be drawn from the mere identity of names cannot be made reasonably in view of its overwhelming contradiction by other evidence presented by petitioner and the failure to produce records from Fort MacArthur Hospital or the Army or from persons who knew the fact that petitioner had been there at any time. The omission eloquently testifies in a manner which no inference could overcome that petitioner never was there. The chaplain's testimony therefore should have been stricken, had the case gone to the jury, and petitioner can derive no aid from it here.

James E. Matthews as to his service in the Navy and the Army, respectively, during 1920–1922. Neither thought petitioner was insane or that his conduct indicated insanity. Then follows a chasm of eight years. The only evidence we have concerning this period is the fact that petitioner married his present guardian at some time within it, an act from which in the legal sense no inference of insanity can be drawn.

This period was eight years of continuous insanity, according to the inference petitioner would be allowed to have drawn. If so, he should have no need of inference. Insanity so long and continuously sustained does not hide itself from the eyes and ears of witnesses.[13] The assiduity which produced the evidence of two "crazy" incidents during a year and a half in France should produce one during eight years or, for that matter, five years in the United States.

* * * Inference is capable of bridging many gaps. But not, in these circumstances, one so wide and deep as this. Knowledge of petitioner's activities and behavior from 1922 or 1925 to 1930 was peculiarly within his ken and that of his wife, who has litigated this cause in his and presumably, though indirectly, in her own behalf. His was the burden to show continuous disability. What he did in this time, or did not do, was vital to his case. Apart from the mere fact of his marriage, the record is blank for five years and almost blank for eight. For all that appears, he may have worked full time and continuously for five and perhaps for eight, with only a possible single interruption.

No favorable inference can be drawn from the omission. It was not one of oversight or inability to secure proof. That is shown by the thoroughness with which the record was prepared for all other periods, before and after this one, and by the fact petitioner's wife, though she married him during the period and was available, did not testify. The only reasonable conclusion is that petitioner, or those who acted for him, deliberately chose, for reasons no doubt considered sufficient (and which we do not criticize, since such matters including tactical ones, are for the judgment of counsel) to present no evidence or perhaps to withhold

---

Tanikawa, it may be recalled, did not profess to have seen petitioner between October, 1918, and 1936.

13. The only attempt to explain the absence of testimony concerning the period from 1922 to 1930 is made by counsel in the reply brief: "The insured, it will be observed, was never apprehended after his desertion from the Army in 1922. It is only reasonable that a person with the status of a deserter at large * * *, whose mind was in the condition of that of this insured, would absent himself from those with whom he would usually associate because of fear of apprehension and punishment. His mental condition * * * at the time of trial * * * clearly shows that he could not have testified. * * * A lack of testimony from 1922 to 1930 is thus explained, and the jury could well infer that only the then (1941?) admittedly insane insured was in a position to know where he was and what he was doing during those years; as he had lost his mental faculties, the reason for lack of proof during these years is apparent."

The "explanation" is obviously untenable. It ignores the one fact proved with relation to the period, that petitioner was married during it. His wife was nominally a party to the suit, and obviously available as a witness. It disregards the fact petitioner continued in the status of deserter after 1930, yet produced evidence relating to the period from that time on. It assumes he was insane during the eight years, yet succeeded during that long time in absenting himself from persons who could testify in his favor.

evidence readily available concerning this long interval, and to trust to the genius of expert medical inference and judicial laxity to bridge this canyon.

In the circumstances exhibited, the former is not equal to the feat, and the latter will not permit it. No case has been cited and none has been found in which inference, however expert, has been permitted to make so broad a leap and take the place of evidence which, according to all reason, must have been at hand. To allow this would permit the substitution of inference, tenuous at best, not merely for evidence absent because impossible or difficult to secure, but for evidence disclosed to be available and not produced. This would substitute speculation for proof. Furthermore, the inference would be more plausible perhaps if the evidence of insanity as of May, 1919, were stronger than it is, such for instance as Chaplain Mathews' testimony would have furnished if it could be taken as applying to petitioner. But, on this record, the evidence of insanity as of that time is thin at best, if it can be regarded as at all more than speculative.

Beyond this, there is nothing to show totality or permanence. These come only by what the Circuit Court of Appeals rightly characterized as "long-range retroactive diagnosis." That might suffice, notwithstanding this crucial inference was a matter of opinion, if there were factual evidence over which the medical eye could travel and find continuity through the intervening years. But eight years are too many to permit it to skip, when the bridgeheads (if the figure may be changed) at each end are no stronger than they are here, and when the seer first denies, then admits, then denies again, that what took place in this time would make "a great deal" of difference in what he saw. Expert medical inference rightly can do much. But we think the feat attempted here too large for its accomplishment.

The Circuit Court of Appeals thought petitioner's enlistments and service in the Navy and Army in 1920–1922 were in themselves "such physical facts as refute any reasonable inferences which may be drawn from the evidence here presented by him that he was totally and permanently disabled during the life of his policy." The opinion also summarizes and apparently takes account of the evidence presented on behalf of the Government. In view of the ground upon which we have placed the decision, we need not consider these matters.

III.

What has been said disposes of the case as the parties have made it. For that reason perhaps nothing more need be said. But objection has been advanced that, in some manner not wholly clear, the directed verdict practice offends the Seventh Amendment.

It may be noted, first, that the Amendment has no application of its own force to this case. The suit is one to enforce a monetary claim against the United States. It hardly can be maintained that under the common law in 1791 jury trial was a matter of right for persons asserting claims against the sovereign. Whatever force the Amendment has therefore is derived because Congress in the legislation cited, has made it applicable. Even so, the objection made on the score of its requirements is untenable.

If the intention is to claim generally that the Amendment deprives the federal courts of power to direct a verdict for insufficiency of evidence, the short answer is the contention has been foreclosed by repeated decisions made here consistently for nearly a century. More recently the practice has been approved explicitly in the promulgation of the Federal Rules of Civil Procedure. Cf. Rule 50. The objection therefore comes too late.

Furthermore, the argument from history is not convincing. It is not that "the rules of the common law" in 1791 deprived trial courts of power to withdraw cases from the jury, because not made out, or appellate courts of power to review such determinations. The jury was not absolute master of fact in 1791. Then as now courts excluded evidence for irrelevancy and relevant proof for other reasons. The argument concedes they weighed the evidence, not only piecemeal but in toto for submission to the jury, by at least two procedures, the demurrer to the evidence and the motion for a new trial. The objection is not therefore to the basic thing, which is the power of the court to withhold cases from the jury or set aside the verdict for insufficiency of the evidence. It is rather to incidental or collateral effects, namely, that the directed verdict as now administered differs from both those procedures because, on the one hand, allegedly higher standards of proof are required and, on the other, different consequences follow as to further maintenance of the litigation. Apart from the standards of proof, the argument appears to urge that in 1791, a litigant could challenge his opponent's evidence, either by the demurrer, which when determined ended the litigation, or by motion for a new trial which if successful, gave the adversary another chance to prove his case; and therefore the Amendment excluded any challenge to which one or the other of these consequences does not attach.

The Amendment did not bind the federal courts to the exact procedural incidents or details of jury trial according to the common law in 1791, any more than it tied them to the common-law system of pleading or the specific rules of evidence then prevailing. Nor were "the rules of the common law" then prevalent, including those relating to the procedure by which the judge regulated the jury's role on questions of fact, crystalized in a fixed and immutable system. On the contrary, they were constantly changing and developing during the late eighteenth and early nineteenth centuries. In 1791 this process already had resulted in widely divergent common-law rules on procedural matters among the states, and between them and England. And none of the contemporaneous rules regarding judicial control of the evidence going to juries or its sufficiency to support a verdict had reached any precise, much less final, form. In addition, the passage of time has obscured much of the procedure which then may have had more or less definite form, even for historical purposes.

This difficulty, no doubt, accounts for the amorphous character of the objection now advanced, which insists, not that any single one of the features criticized, but that the cumulative total or the alternative effect of all, was embodied in the Amendment. The more logical conclusion, we think, and the one which both history and the previous decisions here support, is that the Amendment was designed to preserve the basic institution of jury trial in only its most fundamental elements, not the great mass of procedural forms and details, varying even then so widely among common-law jurisdictions.

Apart from the uncertainty and the variety of conclusion which follows from an effort at purely historical accuracy, the consequences flowing from the view asserted are sufficient to refute it. It may be doubted that the Amendment requires challenge to an opponent's case to be made without reference to the merits of one's own and at the price of all opportunity to have it considered. On the other hand, there is equal room for disbelieving it compels endless repetition of litigation and unlimited chance, by education gained at the opposing party's expense, for perfecting a case at other trials. The essential inconsistency of these alternatives would seem sufficient to refute that either or both, to the exclusion of all others, received constitutional sanctity by the Amendment's force. The first alternative, drawn from the demurrer to the evidence, attributes to the Amendment the effect of forcing one admission because another and an entirely different one is made, and thereby compels conclusion of the litigation once and for all. The true effect of imposing such a risk would not be to guarantee the plaintiff a jury trial. It would be rather to deprive the defendant (or the plaintiff if he were the challenger) of that right; or, if not that, then of the right to challenge the legal sufficiency of the opposing case. The Amendment was not framed or adopted to deprive either party of either right. It is impartial in its guaranty of both. To posit assertion of one upon sacrifice of the other would dilute and distort the full protection intended. The admitted validity of the practice on the motion for a new trial goes far to demonstrate this. It negatives any idea that the challenge must be made at such a risk as the demurrer imposed. As for the other alternative, it is not urged that the Amendment guarantees another trial whenever challenge to the sufficiency of evidence is sustained. That argument, in turn, is precluded by the practice on demurrer to the evidence.

Each of the classical modes of challenge, therefore, disproves the notion that the characteristic feature of the other, for effect upon continuing the litigation, became a part of the Seventh Amendment's guaranty to the exclusion of all others. That guaranty did not incorporate conflicting constitutional policies, that challenge to an opposing case must be made with the effect of terminating the litigation finally and, at the same time, with the opposite effect of requiring another trial. Alternatives so contradictory give room, not for the inference that one or the other is required, but rather for the view that neither is essential.

Finally, the objection appears to be directed generally at the standards of proof judges have required for submission of evidence to the jury. But standards, contrary to the objection's assumption, cannot be framed wholesale for the great variety of situations in respect to which the question arises. Nor is the matter greatly aided by substituting one general formula for another. It hardly affords help to insist upon "substantial evidence" rather than "some evidence" or "any evidence," or vice versa. The matter is essentially one to be worked out in particular situations and for particular types of cases. Whatever may be the general formulation, the essential requirement is that mere speculation be not allowed to do duty for probative facts, after making due allowance for all reasonably possible inferences favoring the party whose case is attacked. The mere difference in labels used to describe this standard, whether it is applied under the demurrer to the evidence or on motion for a directed verdict, cannot amount to a departure from "the rules of the common law" which the Amendment requires to be followed. If there is abuse in this respect, the obvious remedy is by correction on appellate review.

Judged by this requirement, or by any standard other than sheer speculation, we are unable to conclude that one whose burden, by the nature of his claim, is to show continuing and total disability for nearly twenty years supplies the essential proof of continuity when he wholly omits to show his whereabouts, activities or condition for five years, although the record discloses evidence must have been available, and, further, throws no light upon three additional years, except for one vaguely described and dated visit to his former home. Nothing in the Seventh Amendment requires it should be allowed to join forces with the jury system to bring about such a result. That guaranty requires that the jury be allowed to make reasonable inferences from facts proven in evidence having a reasonable tendency to sustain them. It permits expert opinion to have the force of fact when based on facts which sustain it. But it does not require that experts or the jury be permitted to make inferences from the withholding of crucial facts, favorable in their effects to the party who has the evidence of them in his peculiar knowledge and possession, but elects to keep it so. The words "total and permanent" are the statute's, not our own. They mean something more than incipient or occasional disability. We hardly need add that we give full credence to all of the testimony. But that cannot cure its inherent vagueness or supply essential elements omitted or withheld.

Accordingly, the judgment is

Affirmed.

Mr. Justice Black, with whom Mr. Justice Douglas and Mr. Justice Murphy concur, dissenting.

The Seventh Amendment to the Constitution provides:

In suits at common law, where the value in controversy shall exceed twenty dollars, the right of trial by jury shall be preserved, and no fact tried by a jury shall be otherwise re-examined in any Court of the United States, than according to the rules of the common law.

The Court here re-examines testimony offered in a common law suit, weighs conflicting evidence, and holds that the litigant may never take this case to a jury. The founders of our government thought that trial of fact by juries rather than by judges was an essential bulwark of civil liberty. For this reason, among others, they adopted Article III, § 2 of the Constitution, and the Sixth and Seventh Amendments. Today's decision marks a continuation of the gradual process of judicial erosion which in one hundred fifty years has slowly worn away a major portion of the essential guarantee of the Seventh Amendment.

I.

Alexander Hamilton in *The Federalist* emphasized his loyalty to the jury system in civil cases and declared that jury verdicts should be re-examined, if at all, only "by a second jury, either by remanding the cause to the court below for a second trial of the fact, or by directing an issue immediately out of the Supreme Court." He divided the citizens of his time between those who thought that jury trial was a "valuable safeguard to liberty" and those who thought it was "the very palladium of free government." However, he felt it unnecessary to include in the Constitution a specific provision placing jury trial in civil cases in the same high position as jury trial in criminal cases.

Hamilton's view, that constitutional protection of jury trial in civil cases was undesirable, did not prevail. On the contrary, in response to widespread demands from the various State Constitutional Conventions, the first Congress adopted the Bill of Rights containing the Sixth and Seventh Amendments, intended to save trial in both criminal and common law cases from legislative or judicial abridgment. The first Congress expected the Seventh Amendment to meet the objections of men like Patrick Henry to the Constitution itself. Henry, speaking in the Virginia Constitutional Convention, had expressed the general conviction of the people of the Thirteen States when he said, "Trial by jury is the best appendage of freedom. * * * We are told that we are to part with that trial by jury with which our ancestors secured their lives and property. * * * I hope we shall never be induced, by such arguments, to part with that excellent mode of trial. No appeal can now be made as to fact in common law suits. The unanimous verdict of impartial men cannot be reversed." The first Congress, therefore provided for trial of common law cases by a jury, even when such trials were in the Supreme Court itself.

In 1789, juries occupied the principal place in the administration of justice. They were frequently in both criminal and civil cases the arbiters not only of fact but of law. Less than three years after the ratification of the Seventh Amendment, this Court called a jury in a civil case brought under our original jurisdiction. There was no disagreement as to the facts of the case. Chief Justice Jay, charging the jury for a unanimous Court, three of whose members had sat in the Constitutional Convention, said:

"For as, on the one hand, it is presumed, that juries are the best judges of facts; it is, on the other hand, presumable, that the court(s) are the best judges of law. But still, both objects are lawfully within your power of decision." Similar views were held by state courts in Connecticut, Massachusetts, Illinois, Louisiana and presumably elsewhere.

The principal method by which judges prevented cases from going to the jury in the Seventeenth and Eighteenth Centuries was by the demurrer to the evidence, under which the defendant at the end of the trial admitted all facts shown by the plaintiff as well as all inferences which might be drawn from the facts, and asked for a ruling of the Court on the "law of the case." This practice fell into disuse in England in 1793, and in the United States federal courts in 1826. The power of federal judges to comment to the jury on the evidence gave them additional influence. The right of involuntary non-suit of a plaintiff, which might have been used to expand judicial power at jury expense was at first denied federal courts.

As Hamilton had declared in *The Federalist*, the basic judicial control of the jury function was in the court's power to order a new trial. In 1830, this Court said: "The only modes known to the common law to re-examine such facts, are the granting of a new trial by the court where the issue was tried, or to which the record was properly returnable; or the award of a venire facias de novo, by an appellate court, for some error of law which intervened in the proceedings." That retrial by a new jury rather than factual reevaluation by a court is a constitutional right of genuine value was restated recently.

A long step toward the determination of fact by judges instead of by juries was the invention of the directed verdict. In 1850, what seems to have been the first directed verdict case considered by this Court, was presented for decision. The Court held that the directed verdict serves the same purpose as the demurrer to the evidence, and that since there was "no evidence whatever" on the critical issue in the case, the directed verdict was approved. The decision was an innovation, a departure from the traditional rule restated only fifteen years before in which this Court had said: "Where there is no evidence tending to prove a particular fact, the court(s) are bound so to instruct the jury, when requested; but they cannot legally give any instruction which shall take from the jury the right of weighing the evidence and determining what effect it shall have."

This new device contained potentialities for judicial control of the jury which had not existed in the demurrer to the evidence. In the first place, demurring to the evidence was risky business, for in so doing the party not only admitted the truth of all the testimony against him but also all reasonable inferences which might be drawn from it; and upon joinder in demurrer the case was withdrawn from the jury while the court proceeded to give final judgment either for or against the demurrant. Imposition of this risk was no mere technicality; for by making withdrawal of a case from the jury dangerous to the moving litigant's cause, the early law went far to assure that facts would never be examined except by a jury. Under the directed verdict practice the moving party takes no such chance, for if his motion is denied, instead of suffering a directed verdict against him, his case merely continues into the hands of the jury. The litigant not only takes no risk by a motion for a directed verdict, but in making such a motion gives himself two opportunities to avoid the jury's decision; for under the federal variant of judgment notwithstanding the verdict, the judge may reserve opinion on the motion for a directed verdict and then give judgment for the moving party after the jury was formally found against him. In the second place, under the directed verdict practice the courts soon abandoned the "admission of all facts and reasonable inferences" standard referred to, and created the so-called "substantial evidence" rule which permitted directed verdicts even though there was far more evidence in the case than a plaintiff would have needed to withstand a demurrer.

The substantial evidence rule did not spring into existence immediately upon the adoption of the directed verdict device. For a few more years federal judges held to the traditional rule that juries might pass finally on facts if there was "any evidence" to support a party's contention. The rule that a case must go to the jury unless there was "no evidence" was completely repudiated, upon which the Court today relies in part. There the Court declared that "some" evidence was not enough—there must be evidence sufficiently persuasive to the judge so that he thinks "a jury can properly proceed." The traditional rule was given an ugly name, "the scintilla rule", to hasten its demise. For a time traces of the old formula remained, but the new spirit prevailed. The same transition from jury supremacy to jury subordination through judicial decisions took place in State courts.

Later cases permitted the development of added judicial control. New and totally unwarranted formulas, which should surely be eradicated from the law at the first opportunity, were added as recently as 1929 which, by sheerest dictum, made new encroachments on the jury's constitutional functions. There it was announced that a judge might weigh the evidence to determine whether he, and not the jury, thought it was "overwhelming" for either party, and then direct a verdict. With it, and other tools, jury verdicts on disputed facts have been set aside or directed verdicts authorized so regularly as to make the practice commonplace while the motion for directed verdict itself has become routine.

* * * Today the Court comes dangerously close to weighing the credibility of a witness and rejecting his testimony because the majority do not believe it.

The story thus briefly told depicts the constriction of a constitutional civil right and should not be continued. Speaking of an aspect of this problem, a contemporary writer saw the heart of the issue: "Such a reversal of opinion (as that of a particular State court concerning the jury function), if it were isolated, might have little significance, but when many other courts throughout the country are found to be making the same shift and to be doing so despite the provisions of statutes and constitutions there is revealed one aspect of that basic conflict in the legal history of America-the conflict between the people's aspiration for democratic government, and the judiciary's desire for the orderly supervision of public affairs by judges."

The language of the Seventh Amendment cannot easily be improved by formulas. The statement of a district judge represents, in my opinion, the minimum meaning of the Seventh Amendment:

> The Seventh Amendment to the Constitution guarantees a jury trial in law cases, where there is substantial evidence to support the claim of the plaintiff in an action. If a single witness testifies to a fact sustaining the issue between the parties, or if reasoning minds might reach different conclusions from the testimony of a single witness, one of which would substantially support the issue of the contending party, the issue must be left to the jury. Trial by jury is a fundamental guaranty of the rights of the people, and judges should not search the evidence with meticulous care to deprive litigants of jury trials.

The call for the true application of the Seventh Amendment is not to words, but to the spirit of honest desire to see that Constitutional right preserved. Either the judge or the jury must decide facts and to the extent that we take this responsibility, we lessen the jury function. Our duty to preserve this one of the Bill of Rights may be peculiarly difficult, for here it is our own power which we must restrain. We should not fail to meet the expectation of James Madison, who, in advocating the adoption of the Bill of Rights, said: "Independent tribunals of justice will consider themselves in a peculiar manner the guardians of those rights; * * * they will be naturally led to resist every encroachment upon rights expressly stipulated for in the Constitution by the declaration of right." So few of these cases come to this Court that, as a matter of fact, the judges of the District Courts and the Circuit Courts of Appeal are the primary custodians of the Amendment. As for myself, I believe that a verdict should be directed, if at all, only when, without weighing the credibility of the witnesses, there is in the evidence no room whatever for honest difference of opinion over the factual issue in controversy. I shall continue to believe that in all other cases a judge should, in obedience to the command of the Seventh Amendment, not interfere with the jury's function. Since this is a matter of high constitutional importance, appellate courts should be alert to insure the preservation of this constitutional right even though each case necessarily turns on its peculiar circumstances.

II.

The factual issue for determination here is whether the petitioner incurred a total and permanent disability not later than May 31, 1919. It is undisputed that the petitioner's health was sound in 1918, and it is evidently conceded that he was disabled at least since 1930. When in the intervening period, did the disability take place?

A doctor who testified diagnosed the petitioner's case as a schizophrenic form of dementia praecox. He declared it to be sound medical theory that while a normal man can retain his sanity in the face of severe mental or physical shock, some persons are born with an inherent instability so that they are mentally unable to stand sudden and severe strain. The medical testimony was that this petitioner belongs to the latter class and that the shock of actual conflict on the battle front brought on the incurable affliction from which he now suffers. The medical witness testified that the dominant symptoms of the condition are extreme introversion and preoccupation with personal interests, a persecution complex, and an emotional instability which may be manifested by extreme exhilaration alternating with unusual depression or irrational outbursts. Persons suffering from this disease are therefore unable to engage in continuous employment.

The petitioner relies on the testimony of wartime and post war companions and superiors to show that his present mental condition existed on the crucial date. There is substantial testimony from which reasonable men might conclude that the petitioner was insane from the date claimed.

Two witnesses testify as to the petitioner's mental irresponsibility while he was in France. The most striking incident in this testimony is the account of his complete breakdown while on guard duty as a result of which he falsely alarmed his military unit by screaming that the Germans were coming when they were not and was silenced only by being forceably bound and gagged. There was also other evidence that Galloway became nervous, irritable, quarrelsome and turbulent after he got to France. The Court disposes of this testimony, which obviously indicates some degree of mental unbalance, by saying no more than that it "does not prove he was insane." No reason is given, nor can I imagine any, why a jury should not be entitled to consider this evidence and draw its own conclusions.

The testimony of another witness, O'Neill, was offered to show that the witness had known the petitioner both before and after the war, and that after the war the witness found the petitioner a changed man; that the petitioner imagined that he was being persecuted; and that the petitioner suffered from fits of melancholia, depression and weeping. If O'Neill's testimony is to be believed, the petitioner suffered the typical symptoms of a schizophreniac for some years after his return to this country; therefore if O'Neill's testimony is believed, there can be no reasonable doubt about the right of a jury to pass on this case. The Court analyzes O'Neill's testimony for internal consistency, criticizes his failure to remember the details of his association with the petitioner fifteen years before his appearance in this case, and concludes that O'Neill's evidence shows no more than that "petitioner was subject to alternating periods of gaiety and depression for some indefinite period." This extreme emotional instability is an accepted symptom of the disease from which the petitioner suffers. If he exhibited the same symptoms in 1922, it is, at the minimum, probable that the condition has been continuous since an origin during the war. O'Neill's testimony coupled with the petitioner's present condition presents precisely the type of question which a jury should resolve.

The petitioner was in the Navy for six months in 1920, until he was discharged for bad conduct, and later was in the Army during 1921 and a part of 1922 until he deserted. The testimony of his Commanding Officer while he was in the Army, Col. Matthews, is that the petitioner had "periods of gaiety and exhilaration" and was then "depressed as if he had had a hangover"; that petitioner tried to create disturbances and dissatisfy the men; that he suffered from a belief that he was being treated unfairly; and that generally his actions "were not those of a normal man". The Colonel was not a doctor and might well not have recognized insanity had he seen it; as it was, he concluded that the petitioner was an alcoholic and a narcotic addict. However, the officer was unable, upon repeated investigations, to discover any actual use of narcotics. A jury fitting this information into the general pattern of the testimony might well have been driven to the conclusion that the petitioner was insane at the time the Colonel had him under observation.

All of this evidence, if believed, showed a man healthy and normal before he went to the war suffering for several years after he came back from a disease which had the symptoms attributed to schizophrenia and who was insane from 1930 until his trial. Under these circumstances, I think that the physician's testimony of total and permanent disability by reason of continuous insanity from 1918 to 1938 was reasonable. The fact that there was no direct testimony for a period of five years, while it might be the basis of fair argument to the jury by the government, does not, as the Court seems to believe, create a presumption against the petitioner so strong that his case must be excluded from the jury entirely. Even if during these five years the petitioner was spasmodically employed, we could not conclude that he was not totally and permanently disabled. It is not doubted that schizophrenia is permanent even though there may be a momentary appearance of recovery.

The court below concluded that the petitioner's admission into the military service between 1920 and 1923 showed conclusively that he was not totally and permanently disabled. Any inference which may be created by the petitioner's admission into the Army and the Navy is more than met by his record of court martial, dishonorable discharge, and desertion, as well as by the explicit testimony of his Commanding Officer, Colonel Matthews.

This case graphically illustrates the injustice resulting from permitting judges to direct verdicts instead of requiring them to await a jury decision and then, if necessary, allow a new trial. The chief reason given for approving a directed verdict against this petitioner is that no evidence except expert medical testimony was offered for a five to eight year period. Perhaps, now that the petitioner knows he has insufficient evidence to satisfy a judge even though he may have enough to satisfy a jury, he would be able to fill this time gap to meet any judge's demand. If a court would point out on a motion for new trial that the evidence as to this particular period was too weak, the petitioner would be given an opportunity to buttress the physician's evidence. If, as the Court believes, insufficient evidence has been offered to sustain a jury verdict for the petitioner, we should at least authorize a new trial.

I believe that there is a reasonable difference of opinion as to whether the petitioner was totally and permanently disabled by reason of insanity on May 31, 1919, and that his case therefore should have been allowed to go to the jury. The testimony of fellow soldiers, friends, supervisors, and of a medical expert whose integrity and ability is not challenged cannot be rejected by any process available to me as a judge.

* * *

D. JUDGMENT AS A MATTER OF LAW (POST–TRIAL MOTIONS)

NEELY v. MARTIN K. EBY CONSTRUCTION CO., INC.

386 U.S. 317 (1967)

Mr. Justice White delivered the opinion of the Court.

Petitioner brought this diversity action in the United States District Court for the District of Colorado alleging that respondent's negligent construction, maintenance, and supervision of a scaffold platform used in the construction of a missile silo near Elizabeth, Colorado, had proximately caused her father's fatal plunge from the platform during the course of his employment as Night Silo Captain for Sverdrup & Parcel, an engineering firm engaged in the construction of a missile launcher system in the silo. At the close of the petitioner's evidence and again at the close of all the evidence, respondent moved for a directed verdict. The trial judge denied both motions and submitted the case to a jury, which returned a verdict for petitioner for $25,000.

Respondent then moved for judgment notwithstanding the jury's verdict or, in the alternative, for a new trial, in accordance with Rule 50(b), Federal Rules of Civil Procedure. The trial court denied the motions and entered judgment for petitioner on the jury's verdict. Respondent appealed, claiming that its motion for judgment n.o.v. should have been granted. Petitioner, as appellee, urged only that the jury's verdict should be upheld.

The Court of Appeals held that the evidence at trial was insufficient to establish either negligence by respondent or proximate cause and reversed the judgment of the District Court "with instructions to dismiss the action." Without filing a petition for rehearing in the Court of Appeals, petitioner then sought a writ of certiorari, presenting the question whether the Court of Appeals could, consistent with the 1963 amendments to Rule 50 of the Federal Rules and with the Seventh Amendment's guarantee of a right to jury trial, direct the trial court to dismiss the action. Our order allowing certiorari directed the parties' attention to whether Rule 50(d) permit[s] this disposition by a court of appeals despite Rule 50(c)(2), which gives a party whose jury verdict is set aside by a trial court 10 days in which to invoke the trial court's discretion to order a new trial. We affirm.

Under Rule 50(b), if a party moves for a directed verdict at the close of the evidence and if the trial judge elects to send the case to the jury, the judge is "deemed" to have reserved decision on the motion. If the jury returns a contrary verdict, the party may within 10 days move to have judgment entered in accordance with his motion for directed verdict. This procedure is consistent with decisions of this Court rendered prior to the adoption of the Federal Rules in 1938. And it is settled that Rule 50(b) does not violate the Seventh Amendment's guarantee of a jury trial.

The question here is whether the Court of Appeals, after reversing the denial of a defendant's Rule 50(b) motion for judgment notwithstanding the verdict, may itself order dismissal or direct entry of judgment for defendant. As far as the Seventh Amendment's right to jury trial is concerned, there is no greater restriction on the province of the jury when an appellate court enters judgment n.o.v. than when a trial court does; consequently, there is no constitutional bar to an appellate court granting judgment n.o.v. Likewise, the statutory grant of appellate jurisdiction to the courts of appeals is certainly broad enough to include the power to direct entry of judgment n.o.v. on appeal.

This brings us to Federal Rules 50(c) and 50(d), which were added to Rule 50 in 1963 to clarify the proper practice under this Rule. Though Rule 50(d) is more pertinent to the facts of this case, it is useful to examine these interrelated provisions together. Rule 50(c) governs the case where a trial court has granted a motion for judgment n.o.v. Rule 50(c)(1) explains that, if the verdict loser has joined a motion for new trial with his motion for judgment n.o.v., the trial judge should rule conditionally on the new trial motion when he grants judgment n.o.v. If he conditionally grants a new trial, and if the court of appeals reverses his grant of judgment n.o.v., Rule 50(c) (1) provides that "the new trial shall proceed unless the appellate court has otherwise ordered."On the other hand, if the trial judge conditionally denies the motion for new trial, and if his grant of judgment n.o.v. is reversed on appeal, "subsequent proceedings shall be in accordance with the order of the appellate court." As the Advisory Committee's Note to Rule 50(c) makes clear, Rule 50(c)(1) contemplates that the appellate court will review on appeal both the grant of judgment n.o.v. and, if necessary, the trial court's conditional disposition of the motion for new trial.[4] This review necessarily includes the power to grant or to deny a new trial in appropriate cases.

---

4. The Advisory Committee explains: "If the motion for new trial has been conditionally granted * * * (t)he party against whom the judgment n.o.v. was entered below may, as appellant, besides seeking to overthrow that judgment, also attack the conditional grant of the new trial.

Rule 50(d) is applicable to cases such as this one where the trial court has denied a motion for judgment n.o.v. Rule 50(d) expressly preserves to the party who prevailed in the district court the right to urge that the court of appeals grant a new trial should the jury's verdict be set aside on appeal. Rule 50(d) also emphasizes that "nothing in this rule precludes" the court of appeals "from determining that the appellee is entitled to a new trial, or from directing the trial court to determine whether a new trial shall be granted." Quite properly, this Rule recognizes that the appellate court may prefer that the trial judge pass first upon the appellee's new trial suggestion. Nevertheless, consideration of the new trial question "in the first instance" is lodged with the court of appeals. And Rule 50(d) is permissive in the nature of its direction to the court of appeals: as in Rule 50(c)(1), there is nothing in Rule 50(d) indicating that the court of appeals may not direct entry of judgment n.o.v. in appropriate cases.

Rule 50(c)(2), is on its face inapplicable to the situation presented here. That Rule regulates the verdict winner's opportunity to move for a new trial if the trial court has granted a Rule 50(b) motion for judgment n.o.v. In this case, the trial court denied judgment n.o.v. and respondent appealed. Jurisdiction over the case then passed to the Court of Appeals, and petitioner's right to seek a new trial in the trial court after her jury verdict was set aside became dependent upon the disposition by the Court of Appeals under Rule 50(d).

As the Advisory Committee explained, these 1963 amendments were not intended to "alter the effects of a jury verdict or the scope of appellate review," as articulated in the prior decisions of this Court.

The opinions in [these] cases make it clear that an appellate court may not order judgment n.o.v. where the verdict loser has failed strictly to comply with the procedural requirements of Rule 50(b), or where the record reveals a new trial issue which has not been resolved. Part of the Court's concern has been to protect the rights of the party whose jury verdict has been set aside on appeal and who may have valid grounds for a new trial, some or all of which should be passed upon by the district court, rather than the court of appeals, because of the trial judge's firsthand knowledge of witnesses, testimony, and issues—because of his "feel" for the overall case. These are very valid concerns to which the court of appeals should be constantly alert. Where a defendant moves for n.o.v. in the trial court, the plaintiff may present, in connection with the motion or with a separate motion after n.o.v. is granted, his grounds for a new trial or voluntary nonsuit. Clearly, where he retains his verdict in the trial court and the defendant appeals, plaintiff should have the opportunity which 50(d) affords him to press those same or different grounds in the court of appeals. And obviously judgment for defendant-appellant should

---

And the appellate court, if it reverses the judgment n.o.v., may in an appropriate case also reverse the conditional grant of the new trial and direct that judgment be entered on the verdict."

not be ordered where the plaintiff-appellee urges grounds for a nonsuit or new trial which should more appropriately be addressed to the trial court.

But these considerations do not justify an ironclad rule that the court of appeals should never order dismissal or judgment for defendant when the plaintiff's verdict has been set aside on appeal. Such a rule would not serve the purpose of Rule 50 to speed litigation and to avoid unnecessary retrials. Nor do any of our cases mandate such a rule. * * * In view of these cases, the language of Rule 50(d), and the statutory grant of broad appellate jurisdiction, we think a more discriminating approach is preferable to the inflexible rule for which the petitioner contends.

There are, on the one hand, situations where the defendant's grounds for setting aside the jury's verdict raise questions of subject matter jurisdiction or dispositive issues of law which, if resolved in defendant's favor, must necessarily terminate the litigation. * * *

On the other hand, where the court of appeals sets aside the jury's verdict because the evidence was insufficient to send the case to the jury, it is not so clear that the litigation should be terminated. Although many of the plaintiff-appellee's possible grounds for a new trial, such as inadequacy of the verdict, will not survive a decision that the case should not have gone to the jury in the first place, there remain important considerations which may entitle him to a new trial. The erroneous exclusion of evidence which would have strengthened his case is an important possibility. Another is that the trial court itself caused the insufficiency in plaintiff-appellee's case by erroneously placing too high a burden of proof on him at trial. But issues like these are issues of law with which the courts of appeals regularly and characteristically must deal. The district court in all likelihood has already ruled on these questions in the course of the trial and, in any event, has no special advantage or competence in dealing with them. They are precisely the kind of issues that the losing defendant below may bring to the court of appeals without ever moving for a new trial in the district court. Likewise, if the plaintiff's verdict is set aside by the trial court on defendant's motion for judgment n.o.v., plaintiff may bring these very grounds directly to the court of appeals without moving for a new trial in the district court.[6] Final action on these issues normally rests with the court of appeals.

A plaintiff whose jury verdict is set aside by the trial court on defendant's motion for judgment n.o.v. may ask the trial judge to grant a voluntary nonsuit to give plaintiff another chance to fill a gap in his proof. The plaintiff-appellee should have this same opportunity when his verdict is set aside on appeal. Undoubtedly, in many cases this question will call for an exercise of the trial court's discretion. However, there is no substantial reason why the appellee should not present the matter to the

---

6. The Advisory Committee's Note to Rule 50(c)(2) explains: "Even if the verdict winner makes no motion for a new trial, he is entitled upon his appeal from the judgment n.o.v. not only to urge that that judgment should be reversed and judgment entered upon the verdict, but that errors were committed during the trial which at the least entitle him to a new trial."

court of appeals, which can if necessary remand the case to permit initial consideration by the district court.

In these cases where the challenge of the defendant-appellant is to the sufficiency of the evidence, the record in the court of appeals will very likely be a full one. Thus, the appellee will not be required to designate and print additional parts of the record to substantiate his grounds for a nonsuit (or a new trial), and it should not be an undue burden in the course of arguing for his verdict to indicate in his brief why he is entitled to a new trial should his judgment be set aside. Moreover, the appellee can choose for his own convenience when to make his case for a new trial: he may bring his grounds for new trial to the trial judge's attention when defendant first makes an n.o.v. motion, he may argue this question in his brief to the court of appeals, or he may in suitable situations seek rehearing from the court of appeals after his judgment has been reversed.

In our view, therefore, Rule 50(d) makes express and adequate provision for the opportunity—which the plaintiff-appellee had without this rule—to present his grounds for a new trial in the event his verdict is set aside by the court of appeals. If he does so in his brief—or in a petition for rehearing if the court of appeals has directed entry of judgment for appellant—the court of appeals may make final disposition of the issues presented, except those which in its informed discretion should be reserved for the trial court. If appellee presents no new trial issues in his brief or in a petition for rehearing, the court of appeals may, in any event, order a new trial on its own motion or refer the question to the district court, based on factors encountered in its own review of the case.

In the case before us, petitioner won a verdict in the District Court which survived respondent's motion for judgment n.o.v. In the Court of Appeals the issue was the sufficiency of the evidence and that court set aside the verdict. Petitioner, as appellee, suggested no grounds for a new trial in the event her judgment was reversed, nor did she petition for rehearing in the Court of Appeals, even though that court had directed a dismissal of her case. Neither was it suggested that the record was insufficient to present any new trial issues or that any other reason required a remand to the District Court. Indeed, in her brief in the Court of Appeals, petitioner stated, "This law suit was fairly tried and the jury was properly instructed." It was, of course, incumbent on the Court of Appeals to consider the new trial question in the light of its own experience with the case. But we will not assume that the court ignored its duty in this respect, although it would have been better had its opinion expressly dealt with the new trial question.

In a short passage at the end of her brief to this Court, petitioner suggested that she has a valid ground for a new trial in the District Court's exclusion of opinion testimony by her witnesses concerning whether respondent's scaffold platform was adequate for the job it was intended to perform. This matter was not raised in the Court of Appeals or in the petition for a writ of certiorari, even though the relevant portions of the transcript were made a part of the record on appeal. Under these circumstances, we see no cause for deviating from our normal policy of not considering issues which have not been presented to the Court of Appeals and which are not properly presented for review here.

Petitioner's case in this Court is pitched on the total lack of power in the Court of Appeals to direct entry of judgment for respondent. We have rejected that argument and therefore affirm. It is so ordered.

Affirmed.

Mr. Justice Douglas and Mr. Justice Fortas, while agreeing with the Court's construction of Rule 50, would reverse the judgment because in their view the evidence of negligence and proximate case was sufficient to go to the jury.

Mr. Justice Black, dissenting.

I dissent from the Court's decision in this case for three reasons: First, I think the evidence in this case was clearly sufficient to go to the jury on the issues of both negligence and proximate cause. Second, I think that under our prior decisions and Rule 50, a court of appeals, in reversing a trial court's refusal to enter judgment n.o.v. on the ground of insufficiency of the evidence, is entirely powerless to order the trial court to dismiss the case, thus depriving the verdict winner of any opportunity to present a motion for new trial to the trial judge who is thoroughly familiar with the case. Third, even if a court of appeals has that power, I find it manifestly unfair to affirm the Court of Appeals, judgment have without giving this petitioner a chance to present her grounds for a new trial to the Court of Appeals as the Court today for the first time holds she must.

I.

Petitioner and respondent, both in their briefs on the merits and in their oral argument, have vigorously and extensively addressed themselves to the question of whether the lower court was correct in holding that petitioner's evidence of negligence and proximate cause was insufficient to go to the jury. The Court, however, conveniently avoids facing this issue— which if resolved in petitioner's favor, would completely dispose of this case—by a footnote statement that this issue was not presented in the petition for certiorari nor encompassed by our order granting certiorari. Besides the fact that this seems to me to be an overly meticulous reading of the petition for certiorari and our order granting it, I see no reason for the Court's refusal to deal with an issue which is undoubtedly present in this case even though not specifically emphasized in the petition for certiorari. Although usually this Court will not consider questions not presented in the petition for certiorari, our Rule 40(1)(d)(2) has long provided that "the court, at its option, may notice a plain error not presented," and the Court has frequently disposed of cases by deciding crucial issues which the parties themselves failed to present. If, as I believe, the Court of Appeals was wrong in concluding that the evidence was insufficient to go to the jury, then its reversal of the jury's verdict was a violation of the Seventh Amendment, and certainly this is the kind of plain constitutional error that this Court can and should correct.

That the evidence was more than ample to prove both negligence and proximate cause is, I think, inescapably clear from even a cursory review of the undisputed facts in this record. Petitioner's father was killed while working on the construction of a missile-launching silo in Colorado. Neely worked for an engineering firm and his job was to work on certain concrete blocks suspended 130 feet from the bottom of the silo. Respondent, a carpentry firm responsible for the construction, maintenance, and supervision of all scaffolding in the silo, constructed a wooden platform between two of the concrete blocks in order to allow workers such as Neely to go from one block to the other. The platform, however, did not cover the entire distance between the blocks nor was it level with them. Instead, it was two feet horizontally away from either block and was raised two feet vertically above the blocks. Also, a railing was constructed on one side of the platform between it and one of the blocks. No railing was placed on the other side of the platform. When Neely along with three fellow workers arrived at the silo, they were told by respondent's foreman that the platform was ready. The only way they could get from the platform to the blocks was by jumping the gap between the platform and blocks. However, because of the railing on one side of the platform, the workers could not jump directly across the two-foot gap to the block on that side, but had either to jump three feet diagonally to the block or to climb over the railing. One worker successfully leaped to the block, fastened his safety belt, and then looked back and saw Neely, who was to follow, falling head first through the hole between the platform and the block. Neely, failing to make the jump, fell to his death 130 feet below.

Petitioner's case consisted of the testimony of the day foreman, one of the carpenters who constructed the platform, and the worker who was closest to Neely when he fell. Quite understandably, in view of the strong evidence, petitioner did not call to testify the two other workers who witnessed Neely's fall or the other carpenters who worked on the platform. She did, however introduce several revealing photographs of the platform, blocks, and intervening gap taken immediately after the accident. On respondent's objection, the trial judge excluded several other photographs which showed nets which, after the accident, were placed under the platform for the safety of the investigators. There was testimony that neither the railing nor platform broke and that there was no grease on the platform. But when petitioner's counsel asked the day foreman whether he considered the platform safe and adequate, he replied in the negative, though this testimony, on respondent's objection, was then ordered stricken as opinion evidence on an ultimate issue. The trial court refused to allow the same question to be asked of the other witnesses. At one time, the carpenter did testify that a railing was put on only one side of the platform because lunch hour was nearing and the platform had to be completed before then.

On this evidence, which the trial judge characterized as presenting a "close case," the Court of Appeals held a verdict should have been directed for respondent. Although the court was willing to assume that there might be some negligence in the size of the platform or the placing of the railing along one side, and though it was willing to concede "that the platform might possibly have had something to do with his (Neely's) fall," the court purported to find no evidence, not even circumstantial evidence, that the construction of the platform was the proximate cause of the fall. I think this holding cries for reversal. If constructing a platform 130 feet in the air, at which height workmen use safety belts, with a three-foot diagonal gap over which workers must leap and with a railing which makes a direct jump impossible, does not itself show negligence and proximate cause, then it is difficult to conceive of any evidence that would. Besides the size of the platform and the presence of the railing, the photographs shown to the jury, and reproduced in this record, reveal other possible defects in its construction: a vertical kickboard extending beyond the railing into the gap through which Neely jumped; rough boards on the floor of the platform. The fact that Neely was coming headfirst by the time he passed the block two feet below might have made it reasonable for the jury to have concluded that he tripped on these impediments rather than merely stepped in the opening. In short, I believe it was a clear violation of the Seventh Amendment to deprive petitioner of a jury verdict rendered on this evidence.

II.

Since the adoption of Rule 50, our cases have consistently and emphatically preserved the right of a litigant whose judgment—whether it be a judgment entered on the verdict or judgment n.o.v.—is set aside to invoke the discretion of the trial court in ruling on a motion for new trial.

* * * The question here, however, is whether the Court of Appeals, after holding that the District Court erred in failing to direct a verdict against the plaintiff, can then order the District Court to dismiss the case and thereby deprive the verdict winner of any opportunity to ask the trial judge for a new trial in order to cure a defect in proof in the first trial.

* * * This issue of whether a new trial is justified after a verdict is set aside either by a trial or an appellate court is a new issue which it was not necessary to decide in the original trial. It is a factual issue and that the trial court is the more appropriate tribunal to determine it has been almost universally accepted by both federal and state courts throughout the years. There are many reasons for this. Appellate tribunals are not equipped to try factual issues as trial courts are. A trial judge who has heard the evidence in the original case has a vast store of information and knowledge about it that the appellate court cannot get from a cold, printed record. Thus, as we said in Cone, the trial judge can base the broad discretion granted him in determining factual issues of a new trial on his own knowledge of the evidence and the issues "in a perspective peculiarly available to him alone." The special suitability of having a trial judge

decide the issue of a new trial in cases like this is emphasized by a long and unbroken line of decisions of this Court holding that the exercise of discretion by trial judges in granting or refusing new trials on factual grounds is practically unreviewable by appellate courts.

Today's decision is out of harmony with all the cases referred to above. The Court's opinion attempts to justify its grant of power to appellate courts by pointing to instances in which those courts, and even assertedly this Court, have utilized this power in the past.

* * * The Court also attempts to justify its new grant of power to appellate judges by a strained process of reasoning.

* * * The Court further purports to derive this power from the provisions of Rule 50(c) and (d). The Court notes that under Rule 50(c)(1), where the trial judge grants a judgment n.o.v. and either grants or denies the conditional motion for new trial, an appellate court in reversing the judgment n.o.v. has "the power to grant or to deny a new trial in appropriate cases." But, as the Court fails to recognize, the crucial prerequisite to the exercise of this appellate power is a ruling in the first instance, by the trial court on the motion for new trial. Here that crucial prerequisite is missing.

The Court then proceeds to find Rule 50(c)(2) inapplicable on its face to a situation where the trial court denies a judgment n.o.v. but an appellate court orders that one be entered. In doing so, the Court ignores the purpose of Rule 50(c)(2). The Rules Committee explained this provision as follows: "Subdivision (c)(2) is a reminder that the verdict-winner is entitled, even after entry of judgment n.o.v. against him, to move for a new trial in the usual course."

The rule does not remotely indicate that the verdict winner loses this right to move for a new trial if the trial court's entry of judgment n.o.v. against him is on direction by the appellate court rather than on its own initiative. Sections (c) and (d) were added to Rule 50 in 1963, after all the cases discussed above had been decided. As the Notes of the Rules Committee indicate, these amendments were made to implement those decisions which had emphasized the importance of having trial judges initially determine the factual issue of whether a new trial is justified in cases where judgment n.o.v. has been entered against the verdict winner, either by the trial or appellate court. The Committee at no place hinted that the amendments were meant to change the practice established by those cases, and, to the contrary, it specifically stated that, "The amendments do not alter the effects of a jury verdict or the scope of appellate review."

Certainly this is true of Rule 50(d). This section provides that the verdict winner, who prevailed on the motion for judgment n.o.v., "may, as appellee, assert grounds entitling him to a new trial in the event the appellate court concludes that the trial court erred in denying the motion for judgment notwithstanding the verdict" and that "nothing in this rule precludes it (the appellate court) from determining that the appellee is entitled to a new trial, or from directing the trial court to determine whether a new trial shall be granted." Because the Court finds that the rule "is permissive in the nature of its direction to the court of appeals," it concludes "there is nothing in Rule 50(d) indicating that the court of appeals may not direct entry of judgment n.o.v. in appropriate cases." The Court entirely overlooks the fact that the rule is likewise permissive in the nature of its direction to the verdict winner as appellee: it provides that the verdict winner "may" ask the Court of Appeals for a new trial; it does not provide that he must do so in order to protect his right to a new trial. Contrary to the Court, I think the express failure of Rule 50(d) to give the appellate court power to order a case dismissed indicates a clear intention to deny it any such power. The practice now permitted by Rule 50(d) was first embodied in the Notes of the Rules Committee to the proposed, but unadopted, amendments of 1946. The Notes suggested that a verdict winner could, as appellee, assign grounds for a new trial in the event the appellate court set aside his verdict. In Cone, however, we expressly rejected the contention that the verdict winner's failure, as appellee, to assign grounds for a new trial in the appellate court gave that court the power to deny him a new trial. This rejection was extensively discussed by the commentators, most of whom concluded that under Cone the verdict winner should be allowed a chance to present his motion for new trial at the trial court level. Finally, when Rule 50(d) was adopted, there was not the slightest indication that it was intended to adopt the practice that we found objectionable. In fact, it was carefully worded to avoid giving the appellate court any power to deny a new trial. I do not believe this omission unintentional, for the language of Rule 50(c)(1), adopted at the same time, does purport to give the appellate court this power when it reverses a judgment n.o.v. and the trial court has already denied the verdict loser's conditional motion for new trial. It does so clearly by providing that "subsequent proceedings shall be in accordance with the order of the appellate court."

In short, today's decision flies in the teeth of Rule 50(c)(2), and our cases which that rule was intended to implement, by giving the Court of Appeals the power, clearly withheld by Rule 50(d), to substitute its judgment for the trial court's and then decide that justice requires no new trial.

III.

Even were I to agree with the Court that courts of appeals have the power to deny a verdict winner a new trial, I could not agree to the affirmance of such a denial here. Here, so far as appears from the record, the Court of Appeals never even gave a thought to the question of whether petitioner was entitled to a new trial, but simply required that the district judge dismiss the lawsuit as though it were an automatic necessity. And petitioner, in seeking to support her verdict without directing the Court of Appeals' attention to any grounds for a new trial, had every right to rely on our past cases which plainly told her that she was entitled to make her motion for a new trial to the trial judge who is far more able to determine whether justice requires a new trial. While in one breath the Court says that it "will not assume that the court (of appeals) ignored its duty" to "consider the new trial question," in another breath it notes that "(t)his matter was not raised in the Court of Appeals." And because petitioner failed to present grounds for a new trial to the Court of Appeals, the Court, while recognizing that she here presents grounds for a new trial which might require decision by the trial court, refuses to consider these grounds.

* * * The record here clearly reveals that there were gaps in petitioner's case which she might, if given a chance, fill upon a new trial. First, only one of the three eye-witnesses to Neely's fall and only one of the carpenters who worked on the platform were called as witnesses. Second, the trial court excluded testimony by all the witnesses as to their opinions of the adequacy of the platform. Third, several of petitioner's very relevant photographs of the platform were excluded by the trial judge. From such circumstances as these the trial judge might properly have concluded that petitioner was entitled to a new trial to fill the gaps in her case. It is particularly pertinent in this respect that the Court of Appeals itself said: "It may, of course, be conceded that the platform might possibly have had something to do with his fall, but there is nothing in the record to show what it was."

It surely cannot be dismissed as idle conjecture to think that petitioner could, if given a chance, introduce sufficient evidence to prove to the most exacting fact finder that the three-foot diagonal gap in the platform 130 feet above the ground had something to do with this fall and this death.

* * *

XIII. CHOICE OF APPLICABLE LAW (*ERIE* DOCTRINE)

A. HISTORICAL BASIS: THE RULES OF DECISION ACT

28 U.S.C. § 1652. STATE LAWS AS RULES OF DECISION

The laws of the several states, except where the Constitution or treaties of the United States or Acts of Congress otherwise require or provide, shall be regarded as rules of decision in civil actions in the courts of the United States, in cases where they apply.

* * *

ERIE R. CO. v. TOMPKINS

304 U.S. 64 (1938)

MR. JUSTICE BRANDEIS delivered the opinion of the Court.

The question for decision is whether the oft-challenged doctrine of *Swift v. Tyson* shall now be disapproved.

Tompkins, a citizen of Pennsylvania, was injured on a dark night by a passing freight train of the Erie Railroad Company while walking along its right of way at Hughestown in that state. He claimed that the accident occurred through negligence in the operation, or maintenance, of the train; that he was rightfully on the premises as licensee because on a commonly used beaten footpath which ran for a short distance alongside the tracks; and that he was struck by something which looked like a door projecting from one of the moving cars. To enforce that claim he brought an action in the federal court for Southern New York, which had jurisdiction because the company is a corporation of that state. It denied liability; and the case was tried by a jury.

The Erie insisted that its duty to Tompkins was no greater than that owed to a trespasser. It contended, among other things, that its duty to Tompkins, and hence its liability, should be determined in accordance with the Pennsylvania law; that under the law of Pennsylvania, as declared by its highest court, persons who use pathways along the railroad right of way—that is, a longitudinal pathway as distinguished from a crossing—are to be deemed trespassers; and that the railroad is not liable for injuries to undiscovered trespassers resulting from its negligence, unless it be wanton or willful. Tompkins denied that any such rule had been established by the decisions of the Pennsylvania courts; and contended that, since there was no statute of the state on the subject, the railroad's duty and liability is to be determined in federal courts as a matter of general law.

The trial judge refused to rule that the applicable law precluded recovery. The jury brought in a verdict of $30,000; and the judgment entered thereon was affirmed by the Circuit Court of Appeals, which held that it was unnecessary to consider whether the law of Pennsylvania was as contended, because the question was one not of local, but of general, law, and that "upon questions of general law the federal courts are free, in absence of a local statute, to exercise their independent judgment as to what the law is; and it is well settled that the question of the responsibility of a railroad for injuries caused by its servants is one of general law. * * * Where the public has made open and notorious use of a railroad right of way for a long period of time and without objection, the company owes to persons on such permissive pathway a duty of care in the operation of its trains. * * * It is likewise generally recognized law that a jury may find that negligence exists toward a pedestrian using a permissive path on the railroad right of way if he is hit by some object projecting from the side of the train."

The Erie had contended that application of the Pennsylvania rule was required, among other things, by section 34 of the Federal Judiciary Act of September 24, 1789 which provides: "The laws of the several States, except where the Constitution, treaties, or statutes of the United States otherwise require or provide, shall be regarded as rules of decision in trials at common law, in the courts of the United States, in cases where they apply."

Because of the importance of the question whether the federal court was free to disregard the alleged rule of the Pennsylvania common law, we granted certiorari.

First. Swift v. Tyson held that federal courts exercising jurisdiction on the ground of diversity of citizenship need not, in matters of general jurisprudence, apply the unwritten law of the state as declared by its highest court; that they are free to exercise an independent judgment as to what the common law of the state is—or should be; and that, as there stated by Mr. Justice Story, "the true interpretation of the 34th section limited its application to state laws, strictly local, that is to say, to the positive statutes of the state, and the construction thereof adopted by the local tribunals, and to rights and titles to things having a permanent locality, such as the rights and titles to real estate, and other matters immovable and intra-territorial in their nature and character. It never has been supposed by us, that the section did apply, or was designed to apply, to questions of a more general nature, not at all dependent upon local statutes or local usages of a fixed and permanent operation, as, for example, to the construction of ordinary contracts or other written instruments, and especially to questions of general commercial law, where the state tribunals are called upon to perform the like functions as ourselves, that is, to ascertain, upon general reasoning and legal analogies, what is the true exposition of the contract or instrument, or what is the just rule furnished by the principles of commercial law to govern the case."

The Court in applying the rule of section 34 to equity cases, said: "The statute, however, is merely declarative of the rule which would exist in the absence of the statute." The federal courts assumed, in the broad field of "general law," the power to declare rules of decision which Congress was confessedly without power to enact as statutes. Doubt was repeatedly expressed as to the correctness of the construction given section 34, and as to the soundness of the rule which it introduced. But it was the more recent research of a competent scholar, who examined the original document, which established that the construction given to it by the Court was erroneous; and that the purpose of the section was merely to make certain that, in all matters except those in which some federal law is controlling, the federal courts exercising jurisdiction in diversity of citizenship cases would apply as their rules of decision the law of the state, unwritten as well as written.

Criticism of the doctrine became widespread after the decision of *Black & White Taxicab & Transfer Co. v. Brown & Yellow Taxicab & Transfer Co.* There, Brown & Yellow, a Kentucky corporation owned by Kentuckians, and the Louisville & Nashville Railroad, also a Kentucky corporation, wished that the former should have the exclusive privilege of soliciting passenger and baggage transportation at the Bowling Green, Ky., Railroad station; and that the Black & White, a competing Kentucky corporation, should be prevented from interfering with that privilege. Knowing that such a contract would be void under the common law of Kentucky, it was arranged that the Brown & Yellow reincorporate under the law of Tennessee, and that the contract with the railroad should be executed there. The suit was then brought by the Tennessee corporation in the federal court for Western Kentucky to enjoin competition by the Black & White; an injunction issued by the District Court was sustained by the Court of Appeals; and this Court, citing many decisions in which the doctrine of *Swift & Tyson* had been applied, affirmed the decree.

Second. Experience in applying the doctrine of *Swift v. Tyson*, had revealed its defects, political and social; and the benefits expected to flow from the rule did not accrue. Persistence of state courts in their own opinions on questions of common law prevented uniformity; and the impossibility of discovering a satisfactory line of demarcation between the province of general law and that of local law developed a new well of uncertainties.[8]

On the other hand, the mischievous results of the doctrine had become apparent. Diversity of citizenship jurisdiction was conferred in order to prevent apprehended discrimination in state courts against those not citizens of the state. *Swift v. Tyson* introduced grave discrimination by noncitizens against citizens. It made rights enjoyed under the unwritten "general law" vary according to whether enforcement was sought in the state or in the federal court; and the privilege of selecting the court in which the right should be determined was conferred upon the noncitizen.

---

8. Compare 2 Warren, THE SUPREME COURT IN UNITED STATES HISTORY, Rev. Ed. 1935, 89: "Probably no decision of the Court has ever given rise to more uncertainty as to legal rights; and though doubtless intended to promote uniformity in the operation of business transactions, its chief effect has been to render it difficult for business men to know in advance to what particular topic the Court would apply the doctrine. * * * " The Federal Digest through the 1937 volume, lists nearly 1,000 decisions involving the distinction between questions of general and of local law.

Thus, the doctrine rendered impossible equal protection of the law. In attempting to promote uniformity of law throughout the United States, the doctrine had prevented uniformity in the administration of the law of the state.

The discrimination resulting became in practice far-reaching. This resulted in part from the broad province accorded to the so-called "general law" as to which federal courts exercised an independent judgment. In addition to questions of purely commercial law, "general law" was held to include the obligations under contracts entered into and to be performed within the state, the extent to which a carrier operating within a state may stipulate for exemption from liability for his own negligence or that of his employee; the liability for torts committed within the state upon persons resident or property located there, even where the question of liability depended upon the scope of a property right conferred by the state; and the right to exemplary or punitive damages. Furthermore, state decisions construing local deeds, mineral conveyances, and even devises of real estate, were disregarded.

In part the discrimination resulted from the wide range of persons held entitled to avail themselves of the federal rule by resort to the diversity of citizenship jurisdiction. Through this jurisdiction individual citizens willing to remove from their own state and become citizens of another might avail themselves of the federal rule. And, without even change of residence, a corporate citizen of the state could avail itself of the federal rule by reincorporating under the laws of another state, as was done in the Taxicab Case.

The injustice and confusion incident to the doctrine of *Swift v. Tyson* have been repeatedly urged as reasons for abolishing or limiting diversity of citizenship jurisdiction. Other legislative relief has been proposed. If only a question of statutory construction were involved, we should not be prepared to abandon a doctrine so widely applied throughout nearly a century. But the unconstitutionality of the course pursued has now been made clear, and compels us to do so.

Third. Except in matters governed by the Federal Constitution or by acts of Congress, the law to be applied in any case is the law of the state. And whether the law of the state shall be declared by its Legislature in a statute or by its highest court in a decision is not a matter of federal concern. There is no federal general common law. Congress has no power to declare substantive rules of common law applicable in a state whether they be local in their nature or "general," be they commercial law or a part of the law of torts. And no clause in the Constitution purports to confer such a power upon the federal courts. As stated by Mr. Justice Field when protesting against ignoring the Ohio common law of fellow-servant liability: "I am aware that what has been termed the general law of the country—which is often little less than what the judge advancing the doctrine thinks at the time should be the general law on a particular subject—has been often advanced in judicial opinions of this court to control a conflicting law of a state. I admit that learned judges have fallen into the habit of repeating this doctrine as a convenient mode of brushing aside the law of a state in conflict with their views. And I confess that, moved and governed by the authority of the great names of those judges, I have, myself, in many instances, unhesitatingly and confidently, but I think now erroneously, repeated the same doctrine. But, notwithstanding the great names which may be cited in favor of the doctrine, and notwithstanding the frequency with which the doctrine has been reiterated, there stands, as a perpetual protest against its repetition, the constitution of the United States, which recognizes and preserves the autonomy and independence of the states,—independence in their legislative and independence in their judicial departments. Supervision over either the legislative or the judicial action of the states is in no case permissible except as to matters by the constitution specifically authorized or delegated to the United States. Any interference with either, except as thus permitted, is an invasion of the authority of the state, and, to that extent, a denial of its independence."

The fallacy underlying the rule declared in *Swift v. Tyson* is made clear by Mr. Justice Holmes. The doctrine rests upon the assumption that there is "a transcendental body of law outside of any particular State but obligatory within it unless and until changed by statute," that federal courts have the power to use their judgment as to what the rules of common law are; and that in the federal courts "the parties are entitled to an independent judgment on matters of general law":

> But law in the sense in which courts speak of it today does not exist without some definite authority behind it. The common law so far as it is enforced in a State, whether called common law or not, is not the common law generally but the law of that State existing by the authority of that State without regard to what it may have been in England or anywhere else. * * *

> The authority and only authority is the State, and if that be so, the voice adopted by the State as its own (whether it be of its Legislature or of its Supreme Court) should utter the last word.

Thus the doctrine of *Swift v. Tyson* is, as Mr. Justice Holmes said, "an unconstitutional assumption of powers by the Courts of the United States which no lapse of time or respectable array of opinion should make us hesitate to correct." In disapproving that doctrine we do not hold unconstitutional section 34 of the Federal Judiciary Act of 1789 or any other act of Congress. We merely declare that in applying the doctrine this Court and the lower courts have invaded rights which in our opinion are reserved by the Constitution to the several states.

Fourth. The defendant contended that by the common law of Pennsylvania as declared by its highest court, the only duty owed to the plaintiff was to refrain from willful or wanton injury. The plaintiff denied that such is the Pennsylvania law. In support of their respective contentions the parties discussed and cited many decisions of the Supreme Court of the state. The Circuit Court of Appeals ruled that the question of liability is one of general law; and on that ground declined to decide the issue of state law. As we hold this was error, the judgment is reversed and the case remanded to it for further proceedings in conformity with our opinion.

Reversed.

MR. JUSTICE CARDOZO took no part in the consideration or decision of this case.

MR. JUSTICE BUTLER (dissenting).

The case presented by the evidence is a simple one. Plaintiff was severely injured in Pennsylvania. While walking on defendant's right of way along a much-used path at the end of the cross-ties of its main track, he came into collision with an open door swinging from the side of a car in a train going in the opposite direction. Having been warned by whistle and headlight, he saw the locomotive approaching and had time and space enough to step aside and so avoid danger. To justify his failure to get out of the way, he says that upon many other occasions he had safely walked there while trains passed.

Invoking jurisdiction on the ground of diversity of citizenship, plaintiff, a citizen and resident of Pennsylvania, brought this suit to recover damages against defendant, a New York corporation, in the federal court for the Southern District of that state. The issues were whether negligence of defendant was a proximate cause of his injuries, and whether negligence of plaintiff contributed. He claimed that, by hauling the car with the open door, defendant violated a duty to him. The defendant insisted that it violated no duty, and that plaintiff's injuries were caused by his own negligence. The jury gave him a verdict on which the trial court entered judgment; the Circuit Court of Appeals affirmed.

Defendant maintained, citing [a Pennsylvania case], that the only duty owed plaintiff was to refrain from willfully or wantonly injuring him; it argued that the courts of Pennsylvania had so ruled with respect to persons using a customary longitudinal path, as distinguished from one crossing the track. The plaintiff insisted that the Pennsylvania decisions did not establish the rule for which the defendant contended. Upon that issue the Circuit Court of Appeals said: "We need not go into this matter since the defendant concedes that the great weight of authority in other states is to the contrary. This concession is fatal to its contention, for upon questions of general law the federal courts are free, in absence of a local statute, to exercise their independent judgment as to what the law is; and it is well settled that the question of the responsibility of a railroad for injuries caused by its servants is one of general law." Upon that basis the court held the evidence sufficient to sustain a finding that plaintiff's injuries were caused by the negligence of defendant. It also held the question of contributory negligence one for the jury.

Defendant's petition for writ of certiorari presented two questions: Whether its duty toward plaintiff should have been determined in accordance with the law as found by the highest court of Pennsylvania, and whether the evidence conclusively showed plaintiff guilty of contributory negligence. Plaintiff contends that, as always heretofore held by this Court, the issues of negligence and contributory negligence are to be determined by general law against which local decisions may not be held conclusive; that defendant relies on a solitary Pennsylvania case of doubtful applicability, and that, even if the decisions of the courts of that state were deemed controlling, the same result would have to be reached.

No constitutional question was suggested or argued below or here. And as a general rule, this Court will not consider any question not raised below and presented by the petition. Here it does not decide either of the questions presented, but, changing the rule of decision in force since the foundation of the government, remands the case to be adjudged according to a standard never before deemed permissible.

The opinion just announced states that: "The question for decision is whether the oft-challenged doctrine of *Swift v. Tyson* shall now be disapproved."

That case involved the construction of the Judiciary Act of 1789, § 34, 28 U.S.C.A. § [1652]: "The laws of the several States, except where the Constitution, treaties, or statutes of the United States otherwise require or provide, shall be regarded as rules of decision in trials at common law, in the courts of the United States, in cases where they apply." Expressing the view of all the members of the Court, Mr. Justice Story said:

> In the ordinary use of language, it will hardly be contended, that the decisions of courts constitute laws. They are, at most, only evidence of what the laws are, and are not, of themselves, laws. They are often reexamined, reversed, and qualified by courts themselves, whenever they are found to be either defective, or ill-founded, or otherwise incorrect. The laws of a state are more usually understood to mean the rules and enactments promulgated by the legislative authority thereof, or long-established local customs having the force of laws. In all the various cases, which have hitherto come before us for decision, this court have uniformly supposed, that the true interpretation of the 34th section limited its application to state laws strictly local, that is to say, to the positive statutes of the state, and the construction thereof adopted by the local tribunals, and to rights and titles to things having a permanent locality, such as the rights and titles to real estate, and other matters immovable and intraterritorial in their nature and character. It never has been supposed by us, that the section did apply, or was designed to apply, to questions of a more general nature, not at all dependent upon local statutes or local usages of a fixed and permanent operation, as, for example, to the construction of ordinary contracts or other written instruments, and especially to questions of general commercial law, where the state tribunals are called upon to perform the like functions as ourselves, that is, to ascertain, upon general reasoning and

legal analogies, what is the true exposition of the contract or instrument, or what is the just rule furnished by the principles of commercial law to govern the case. And we have not now the slightest difficulty in holding, that this section, upon its true intendment and construction, is strictly limited to local statutes and local usages of the character before stated, and does not extend to contracts and other instruments of a commercial nature, the true interpretation and effect whereof are to be sought, not in the decisions of the local tribunals, but in the general principles and doctrines of commercial jurisprudence. Undoubtedly, the decisions of the local tribunals upon such subjects are entitled to, and will receive, the most deliberate attention and respect of this court; but they cannot furnish positive rules or conclusive authority, by which our own judgments are to be bound up and governed.

The doctrine of that case has been followed by this Court in an unbroken line of decisions. So far as appears, it was not questioned until more than 50 years later, and then by a single judge. In that case, Mr. Justice Brewer, speaking for the Court, truly said "Whatever differences of opinion may have been expressed have not been on the question whether a matter of general law should be settled by the independent judgment of this court, rather than through an adherence to the decisions of the state courts, but upon the other question, whether a given matter is one of local or of general law."

And since that decision, the division of opinion in this Court has been of the same character as it was before. In 1910, Mr. Justice Holmes, speaking for himself and two other Justices, dissented from the holding that a court of the United States was bound to exercise its own independent judgment in the construction of a conveyance made before the state courts had rendered an authoritative decision as to its meaning and effect. But that dissent accepted as "settled" the doctrine of *Swift v. Tyson*, and insisted merely that the case under consideration was by nature and necessity peculiarly local.

Thereafter, as before, the doctrine was constantly applied. In *Black & White Taxicab Co. v. Brown & Yellow Taxicab Co.*, three judges dissented. The writer of the dissent, Mr. Justice Holmes said, however: "I should leave *Swift v. Tyson* undisturbed, ... but I would not allow it to spread the assumed dominion into new fields."

* * * Whenever possible, consistently with standards sustained by reason and authority constituting the general law, this Court has followed applicable decisions of state courts. Unquestionably, the determination of the issues of negligence and contributory negligence upon which decision of this case depends are questions of general law.

While amendments to section 34 have from time to time been suggested, the section stands as originally enacted. Evidently Congress has intended throughout the years that the rule of decision as construed should continue to govern federal courts in trials at common law. The opinion just announced suggests that Mr. Warren's research has established that from the beginning this Court has erroneously construed section 34. But that author's "New Light on the History of the Federal Judiciary Act of 1789" does not purport to be authoritative, and was intended to be no more than suggestive. The weight to be given to his discovery has never been discussed at this bar. Nor does the opinion indicate the ground disclosed by the research. In his dissenting opinion in the Taxicab Case, Mr. Justice Holmes referred to Mr. Warren's work, but failed to persuade the Court that "laws" as used in section 34 included varying and possibly ill-considered rulings by the courts of a state on questions of common law. It well may be that, if the Court should now call for argument of counsel on the basis of Mr. Warren's research, it would adhere to the construction it has always put upon section 34. Indeed, the opinion in this case so indicates. For it declares: "If only a question of statutory construction were involved, we should not be prepared to abandon a doctrine so widely applied throughout nearly a century. But the unconstitutionality of the course pursued has now been made clear and compels us to do so." This means that, so far as concerns the rule of decision now condemned, the Judiciary Act of 1789, passed to establish judicial courts to exert the judicial power of the United States, and especially section 34 of that act as construed, is unconstitutional; that federal courts are now bound to follow decisions of the courts of the state in which the controversies arise; and that Congress is powerless otherwise to ordain. It is hard to foresee the consequences of the radical change so made. Our opinion in the *Taxicab Case* cites numerous decisions of this Court which serve in part to indicate the field from which it is now intended forever to bar the federal courts. It extends to all matters of contracts and torts not positively governed by state enactments. Counsel searching for precedent and reasoning to disclose common-law principles on which to guide clients and conduct litigation are by this decision told that as to all of these questions the decisions of this Court and other federal courts are no longer anywhere authoritative.

This Court has often emphasized its reluctance to consider constitutional questions and that legislation will not be held invalid as repugnant to the fundamental law if the case may be decided upon any other ground. In view of grave consequences liable to result from erroneous exertion of its power to set aside legislation, the Court should move cautiously, seek assistance of counsel, act only after ample deliberation, show that the question is before the Court, that its decision cannot be avoided by construction of the statute assailed or otherwise, indicate precisely the principle or provision of the Constitutional held to have been transgressed, and fully disclose the reasons and authorities found to warrant the conclusion of invalidity. These safeguards against the improvident use of the great power to invalidate legislation are so well-grounded and familiar that statement of reasons or citation of authority to support them is no longer necessary.

So far as appears, no litigant has ever challenged the power of Congress to establish the rule as construed. It has so long endured that its destruction now without appropriate deliberation cannot be justified. There is nothing in the opinion to suggest that consideration of any constitutional question is necessary to a decision of the case. By way of reasoning, it contains nothing that requires the conclusion reached. Admittedly, there is no authority to support that conclusion. Against the protest of those joining in this opinion, the Court declines to assign the case for reargument. It may not justly be assumed that the labor and argument of counsel for the parties would not disclose the right conclusion and aid the Court in the statement of reasons to support it. Indeed, it would have been appropriate to give Congress opportunity to be heard before devesting it of power to prescribe rules of decision to be followed in the courts of the United States.

The course pursued by the Court in this case is repugnant to the Act of Congress of August 24, 1937, 28 U.S.C.A. § 17. It declares that: "Whenever the constitutionality of any Act of Congress affecting the public interest is drawn in question in any court of the United States in any suit or proceeding to which the United States, or any agency thereof, or any officer or employee thereof, as such officer or employee, is not a party, the court having jurisdiction of the suit or proceeding shall certify such fact to the Attorney General. In any such case the court shall permit the United States to intervene and become a party for presentation of evidence (if evidence is otherwise receivable in such suit or proceeding) and argument upon the question of the constitutionality of such Act. In any such suit or proceeding the United States shall, subject to the applicable provisions of law, have all the rights of a party and the liabilities of a party as to court costs to the extent necessary for a proper presentation of the facts and law relating to the constitutionality of such Act." That provision extends to this Court. If defendant had applied for and obtained the writ of certiorari upon the claim that, as now held, Congress has no power to prescribe the rule of decision, section 34 as construed, it would have been the duty of this Court to issue the prescribed certificate to the Attorney General in order that the United States might intervene and be heard on the constitutional question. Within the purpose of the statute and its true intent and meaning, the constitutionality of that measure has been "drawn in question." Congress intended to give the United States the right to be heard in every case involving constitutionality of an act affecting the public interest. In view of the rule that, in the absence of challenge of constitutionality, statutes will not here be invalidated on that ground, the Act of August 24, 1937 extends to cases where constitutionality is first "drawn in question" by the Court. No extraordinary or unusual action by the Court after submission of the cause should be permitted to frustrate the wholesome purpose of that act. The duty it imposes ought here to be willingly assumed. If it were doubtful whether this case is within the scope of the act, the Court should give the United States opportunity to intervene and, if so advised, to present argument on the constitutional question, for undoubtedly it is one of great public importance. That would be to construe the act according to its meaning.

The Court's opinion in its first sentence defines the question to be whether the doctrine of *Swift v. Tyson* shall now be disapproved; it recites that Congress is without power to prescribe rules of decision that have been followed by federal courts as a result of the construction of section 34 in *Swift v. Tyson* and since; after discussion, it declares that "the unconstitutionality of the course pursued (meaning the rule of decision resulting from that construction) * * * compels" abandonment of the doctrine so long applied; and then near the end of the last page, the Court states that it does not hold section 34 unconstitutional, but merely that, in applying the doctrine of *Swift v. Tyson* construing it, this Court and the lower courts have invaded rights which are reserved by the Constitution to the several states. But, plainly through the form of words employed, the substance of the decision appears; it strikes down as unconstitutional section 34 as construed by our decisions; it divests the Congress of power to prescribe rules to be followed by federal courts when deciding questions of general law. In that broad field it compels this and the lower federal courts to follow decisions of the courts of a particular state.

I am of opinion that the constitutional validity of the rule need not be considered, because under the law, as found by the courts of Pennsylvania and generally throughout the country, it is plain that the evidence required a finding that plaintiff was guilty of negligence that contributed to cause his injuries, and that the judgment below should be reversed upon that ground.

MR. JUSTICE MCREYNOLDS, concurs in this opinion. MR. JUSTICE REED (concurring in part).

I concur in the conclusion reached in this case, in the disapproval of the doctrine of *Swift v. Tyson*, and in the reasoning of the majority opinion, except in so far as it relies upon the unconstitutionality of the "course pursued" by the federal courts.

The "doctrine of *Swift v. Tyson*," as I understand it, is that the words "the laws," as used in section 34 of the Federal Judiciary Act of September 24, 1789 do not included in their meaning "the decisions of the local tribunals." Mr. Justice Story, in deciding that point, said: "Undoubtedly, the decisions of the local tribunals upon such subjects are entitled to, and will receive, the most deliberate attention and respect of this court; but they cannot furnish positive rules, or conclusive authority, by which our own judgments are to be bound up and governed."

To decide the case now before us and to "disapprove" the doctrine of *Swift v. Tyson* requires only that we say that the words "the laws" include in their meaning the decisions of the local tribunals. As the majority opinion shows, by its reference to Mr. Warren's researches and the first quotation from Mr. Justice Holmes, that this Court is now of the view that "laws" includes "decisions," it is unnecessary to go further and declare that the "course pursued" was "unconstitutional," instead of merely erroneous.

The "unconstitutional" course referred to in the majority opinion is apparently the ruling in Swift v. Tyson that the supposed omission of Congress to legislate as to the effect of decisions leaves federal courts free to interpret general law for themselves. I am not at all sure whether, in the absence of federal statutory direction, federal courts would be compelled to follow state decisions. There was sufficient doubt about the matter in 1789 to induce the first Congress to legislate. No former opinions of this Court have passed upon it. Mr. Justice Holmes evidently saw nothing "unconstitutional" which required the overruling of *Swift v. Tyson*, for he said in the very opinion quoted by the majority, "I should leave *Swift v. Tyson* undisturbed, . . . but I would not allow it to spread the assumed dominion into new fields." If the opinion commits this Court to the position that the Congress is without power to declare what rules of substantive law shall govern the federal courts, that conclusion also seems questionable. The line between procedural and substantive law is hazy, but no one doubts federal power over procedure. The Judiciary Article, 3, and the "necessary and proper" clause of article 1, § 8, may fully authorize legislation, such as this section of the Judiciary Act.

In this Court, *stare decisis*, in statutory construction, is a useful rule, not an inexorable command. It seems preferable to overturn an established construction of an act of Congress, rather than, in the circumstances of this case, to interpret the Constitution.

There is no occasion to discuss further the range or soundness of these few phrases of the opinion. It is sufficient now to call attention to them and express my own non-acquiescence.

* * *

KLAXON CO. v. STENTOR ELECTRIC MFG. CO., INC.

313 U.S. 487 (1941)

Mr. Justice Reed delivered the opinion of the Court.

The principal question in this case is whether in diversity cases the federal courts must follow conflict of laws rules prevailing in the states in which they sit. We left this open . . . The frequent recurrence of the problem, as well as the conflict of approach to the problem between the Third Circuit's opinion here and that of the First Circuit, led us to grant certiorari.

In 1918 respondent, a New York corporation, transferred its entire business to petitioner, a Delaware corporation. Petitioner contracted to use its best efforts to further the manufacture and sale of certain patented devices covered by the agreement, and respondent was to have a share of petitioner's profits. The agreement was executed in New York, the assets were transferred there, and petitioner began performance there although later it moved its operations to other states. Respondent was voluntarily dissolved under New York law in 1919. Ten years later it instituted this action in the United States District Court for the District of Delaware, alleging that petitioner had failed to perform its agreement to use its best efforts. Jurisdiction rested on diversity of citizenship. In 1939 respondent recovered a jury verdict of $100,000, upon which judgment was entered. Respondent then moved to correct the judgment by adding interest at the rate of six percent from June 1, 1929, the date the action had been brought. The basis of the motion was the provision in section 480 of the New York Civil Practice Act directing that in contract actions interest be added to the principal sum "whether theretofore liquidated or unliquidated." The District Court granted the motion, taking the view that the rights of the parties were governed by New York law and that under New York law the addition of such interest was mandatory. The Circuit Court of Appeals affirmed and we granted certiorari, limited to the question whether section 480 of the New York Civil Practice Act is applicable to an action in the federal court in Delaware.

The Circuit Court of Appeals was of the view that under New York law the right to interest before verdict under section 480 went to the substance of the obligation, and that proper construction of the contract in suit fixed New York as the place of performance. It then concluded that section 480 was applicable to the case because "it is clear by what we think is undoubtedly the better view of the law that the rules for ascertaining the measure of damages are not a matter of procedure at all, but are matters of substance which should be settled by reference to the law of the appropriate state according to the type of case being tried in the forum. The measure of damages for breach of a contract is determined by the law of the place of performance; Restatement, Conflict of Laws § 413." The court referred also to section 418 of the Restatement, which makes interest part of the damages to be determined by the law of the place of performance. Application of the New York statute apparently followed from the court's independent determination of the "better view" without regard to Delaware law, for no Delaware decision or statute was cited or discussed.

We are of [the] opinion that the prohibition declared in *Erie Railroad v. Tompkins* against such independent determinations by the federal courts extends to the field of conflict of laws. The conflict of laws rules to be applied by the federal court in Delaware must conform to those prevailing in Delaware's state courts. Otherwise the accident of diversity of citizenship would constantly disturb equal administration of justice in coordinate state and federal courts sitting side by side. *See Erie Railroad v. Tompkins.* Any other ruling would do violence to the principle of uniformity within a state upon which the *Tompkins* decision is based. Whatever lack of uniformity this may produce between federal courts in different states is attributable to our federal system, which leaves to a state, within the limits permitted by the Constitution, the right to pursue local policies diverging from those of its neighbors. It is not for the federal courts to thwart such local policies by enforcing an independent "general law" of conflict of laws. Subject only to review by this Court on any federal question that may arise, Delaware is free to determine whether a given matter is to be governed by the law of the forum or some other law. This Court's views are not the decisive factor in determining the applicable conflicts rule. And the proper function of the Delaware federal court is to ascertain what the state law is, not what it ought to be.

* * * Looking then to the Delaware cases, petitioner relies on one group to support his contention that the Delaware state courts would refuse to apply section 480 of the New York Civil Practice Act, and respondent on another to prove the contrary. We make no analysis of these Delaware decisions, but leave this for the Circuit Court of Appeals when the case is remanded.

Respondent makes the further argument that the judgment must be affirmed because, under the full faith and credit clause of the Constitution, Art. 4, § 1, the state courts of Delaware would be obliged to give effect to the New York statute. The argument rests mainly on the decision of this Court in *John Hancock Mutual Life Insurance Company v. Yates*, where a New York statute was held such an integral part of a contract of insurance that Georgia was compelled to sustain the contract under the full faith and credit clause. Here, however, section 480 of the New York Civil Practice Act is in no way related to the validity of the contract in suit, but merely to an incidental item of damages, interest, with respect to which courts at the forum have commonly been free to apply their own or some other law as they see fit. Nothing in the Constitution ensures unlimited extraterritorial recognition of all statutes or of any statute under all circumstances. The full faith and credit clause does not go so far as to compel Delaware to apply section 480 if such application would interfere with its local policy.

Accordingly, the judgment is reversed and the case remanded to the Circuit Court of Appeals for decision in conformity with the law of Delaware.

Reversed and remanded.

* * *

B. THE OUTCOME DETERMINATION TEST

GUARANTY TRUST CO. OF NEW YORK v. YORK
326 U.S. 99 (1945)

MR. JUSTICE FRANKFURTER delivered the opinion of the Court.

In *Russell v. Todd*, we had "no occasion to consider the extent to which federal courts, in the exercise of the authority conferred upon them by Congress to administer equitable remedies, are bound to follow state statutes and decisions affecting those remedies." The question thus carefully left open ... is now before us. It arises under the following circumstances.

In May, 1930, Van Sweringen Corporation issued notes to the amount of $30,000,000. Under an indenture of the same date, petitioner, Guaranty Trust Co., was named trustee with power and obligations to enforce the rights of the noteholders in the assets of the Corporation and of the Van Sweringen brothers. In October, 1930, petitioner, with other banks, made large advances to companies affiliated with the Corporation and wholly controlled by the Van Sweringens. In October, 1931, when it was apparent that the Corporation could not meet its obligations, Guaranty co-operated in a plan for the purchase of the outstanding notes on the basis of cash for 50% of the face value of the notes and twenty shares of Van Sweringen Corporation's stock for each $1,000 note. This exchange offer remained open until December 15, 1931.

Respondent York received $6,000 of the notes as a gift in 1934, her donor not having accepted the offer of exchange. In April, 1940, three accepting noteholders began suit against petitioner, charging fraud and misrepresentation. Respondent's application to intervene in that suit was denied, and summary judgment in favor of Guaranty was affirmed. After her dismissal from the Hackner litigation, respondent, on January 22, 1942, began the present proceedings.

The suit, instituted as a class action on behalf of non-accepting noteholders and brought in a federal court solely because of diversity of citizenship, is based on an alleged breach of trust by Guaranty in that it failed to protect the interests of the noteholders in assenting to the exchange offer and failed to disclose its self-interest when sponsoring the offer. Petitioner moved for summary judgment, which was granted, upon the authority of the Hackner case. On appeal, the Circuit Court of Appeals, one Judge dissenting, found that the Hackner decision did not foreclose this suit, and held that in a suit brought on the equity side of a federal district court that court is not required to apply the State statute of limitations that would govern like suits in the courts of a State where the federal court is sitting even though the exclusive basis of federal jurisdiction is diversity of citizenship. The importance of the question for the disposition of litigation in the federal courts led us to bring the case here.

In view of the basis of the decision below, it is not for us to consider whether the New York statute would actually bar this suit were it brought in a State court. Our only concern is with the holding that the federal courts in a suit like this are not bound by local law.

We put to one side the considerations relevant in disposing of questions that arise when a federal court is adjudicating a claim based on a federal law. Our problem only touches transactions for which rights and obligations are created by one of the States, and for the assertion of which, in case of diversity of the citizenship of the parties, Congress has made a federal court another available forum.

Our starting point must be the policy of federal jurisdiction which *Erie R. Co. v. Tompkins*, embodies. In overruling *Swift v. Tyson*, *Erie R. Co. v. Tompkins* did not merely overrule a venerable case. It overruled a particular way of looking at law which dominated the judicial process long after its inadequacies had been laid bare. Law was conceived as a "brooding omnipresence" of Reason, of which decisions were merely evidence and not themselves the controlling formulations. Accordingly, federal courts deemed themselves free to ascertain what Reason, and therefore Law, required wholly independent of authoritatively declared State law, even in cases where a legal right as the basis for relief was created by State authority and could not be created by federal authority and the case got into a federal court merely because it was "between Citizens of different States" under Art. III of the Constitution of the United States.

This impulse to freedom from the rules that controlled State courts regarding State-created rights was so strongly rooted in the prevailing views concerning the nature of law, that the federal courts almost imperceptibly were led to mutilating construction even of the explicit command given to them by Congress to apply State law in cases purporting to enforce the law of a State. The matter was fairly summarized by the statement that "During the period when *Swift v. Tyson* (1842–1938) ruled the decisions of the federal courts, its theory of their freedom in matters of general law from the authority of state courts pervaded opinions of this Court involving even state statutes or local law."

In relation to the problem now here, the real significance of *Swift v. Tyson* lies in the fact that it did not enunciate novel doctrine. Nor was it restricted to its particular situation. It summed up prior attitudes and expressions in cases that had come before this Court and lower federal courts for at least thirty years, at law as well as in equity. The short of it is that the doctrine was congenial to the jurisprudential climate of the time. Once established, judicial momentum kept it going. Since it was conceived that there was "a transcendental body of law outside of any particular State but obligatory within it unless and until changed by statute", State court decisions were not "the law" but merely someone's opinion—to be sure an opinion to be respected—concerning the content of this all-pervading law. Not unnaturally, the federal courts assumed power to find for themselves the content of such a body of law. The notion was stimulated by the attractive vision of a uniform body of federal law. To such sentiments for uniformity of decision and freedom from diversity in State law the federal courts gave currency, particularly in cases where equitable remedies were sought, because equitable doctrines are so often cast in terms of universal applicability when close analysis of the source of legal enforceability is not demanded.

In exercising their jurisdiction on the ground of diversity of citizenship, the federal courts, in the long course of their history, have not differentiated in their regard for State law between actions at law and suits in equity. Although § 34 of the Judiciary Act of 1789 directed that the "laws of the several States * * * shall be regarded as rules of decision in trials of common law," this was deemed, consistently for over a hundred years, to be merely declaratory of what would in any event have governed the federal courts and therefore was equally applicable to equity suits. Indeed, it may fairly be said that the federal courts gave greater respect to State-created "substantive rights," in equity than they gave them on the law side, because rights at law were usually declared by State courts and as such increasingly flouted by extension of the doctrine of *Swift v. Tyson*, while rights in equity were frequently defined by legislative enactment and as such known and respected by the federal courts.

Partly because the States in the early days varied greatly in the manner in which equitable relief was afforded and in the extent to which it was available, Congress provided that "the forms and modes of proceeding in suits * * * of equity" would conform to the settled uses of courts of equity. But this enactment gave the federal courts no power that they would not have had in any event when courts were given "cognizance," by the first Judiciary Act, of equity. From the beginning there has been a good deal of talk in the cases that federal equity is a separate legal system. And so it is, properly understood. The suits in equity of which the federal courts have had "cognizance" ever since 1789 constituted the body of law which had been transplanted to this country from the English Court of Chancery. But this system of equity "derived its doctrines, as well as its powers, from its mode of giving relief." In giving federal courts "cognizance" of equity suits in cases of diversity jurisdiction, Congress never gave, nor did the federal courts ever claim, the power to deny substantive rights created by State law or to create substantive rights denied by State law.

This does not mean that whatever equitable remedy is available in a State court must be available in a diversity suit in a federal court, or conversely, that a federal court may not afford an equitable remedy not available in a State court. Equitable relief in a federal court is of course subject to restrictions: the suit must be within the traditional scope of equity as historically evolved in the English Court of Chancery; a plain, adequate and complete remedy at law must be wanting; explicit Congressional curtailment of equity powers must be respected; the constitutional right to trial by jury cannot be evaded. That a State may authorize its courts to give equitable relief unhampered by any or all such restrictions cannot remove these fetters from the federal courts. State law cannot define the remedies which a federal court must give simply because a federal court in diversity jurisdiction is available as an alternative tribunal to the State's courts. Contrariwise, a federal court may afford an equitable remedy for a substantive right recognized by a State even though a State court cannot give it. Whatever contradiction or confusion may be produced by a medley of judicial phrases severed from their environment, the body of adjudications concerning equitable relief in diversity cases leaves no doubt that the federal courts enforced State-created substantive rights if the mode of proceeding and remedy were consonant with the traditional body of equitable remedies, practice and procedure, and in so doing they were enforcing rights created by the States and not arising under any inherent or statutory federal law.

Inevitably, therefore, the principle of *Erie R. Co. v. Tompkins*, an action at law, was promptly applied to a suit in equity.

And so this case reduces itself to the narrow question whether, when no recovery could be had in a State court because the action is barred by the statute of limitations, a federal court in equity can take cognizance of the suit because there is diversity of citizenship between the parties. Is the outlawry, according to State law, of a claim created by the States a matter of "substantive rights" to be respected by a federal court of equity when that court's jurisdiction is dependent on the fact that there is a State-created right, or is such statute of "a mere remedial character," which a federal court may disregard?

Matters of "substance" and matters of "procedure" are much talked about in the books as though they defined a great divide cutting across the whole domain of law. But, of course, "substance" and "procedure" are the same key-words to very different problems. Neither "substance" nor "procedure" represents the same invariants. Each implies different variables depending upon the particular problem for which it is used. And the different problems are only distantly related at best, for the terms are in common use in connection with situations turning on such different considerations as those that are relevant to questions pertaining to ex post facto legislation, the impairment of the obligations of contract, the enforcement of federal rights in the State courts and the multitudinous phases of the conflict of laws.

Here we are dealing with a right to recover derived not from the United States but from one of the States. When, because the plaintiff happens to be a nonresident, such a right is enforceable in a federal as well as in a State court, the forms and mode of enforcing the right may at times, naturally enough, vary because the two judicial systems are not identic. But since a federal court adjudicating a state-created right solely because of the diversity of citizenship of the parties is for that purpose, in effect, only another court of the State, it cannot afford recovery if the right to recover is made unavailable by the State nor can it substantially affect the enforcement of the right as given by the State.

And so the question is not whether a statute of limitations is deemed a matter of "procedure" in some sense. The question is whether such a statute concerns merely the manner and the means by which a right to recover, as recognized by the State, is enforced, or whether such statutory limitation is a matter of substance in the aspect that alone is relevant to our problem, namely, does it significantly affect the result of a litigation for a federal court to disregard a law of a State that would be controlling in an action upon the same claim by the same parties in a State court?

It is therefore immaterial whether statutes of limitation are characterized either as "substantive" or "procedural" in State court opinions in any use of those terms unrelated to the specific issue before us. *Erie R. Co.*

v. Tompkins was not an endeavor to formulate scientific legal terminology. It expressed a policy that touches vitally the proper distribution of judicial power between State and federal courts. In essence, the intent of that decision was to insure that, in all cases where a federal court is exercising jurisdiction solely because of the diversity of citizenship of the parties, the outcome of the litigation in the federal court should be substantially the same, so far as legal rules determine the outcome of a litigation, as it would be if tried in a State court. The nub of the policy that underlies *Erie R. Co. v. Tompkins* is that for the same transaction the accident of a suit by a non-resident litigant in a federal court instead of in a State court a block away, should not lead to a substantially different result. And so, putting to one side abstractions regarding "substance" and "procedure," we have held that in diversity cases the federal courts must follow the law of the State as to burden of proof, as to conflict of laws, *Klaxon Co. v. Stentor Co.*, as to contributory negligence. *Erie R. Co. v. Tompkins* has been applied with an eye alert to essentials in avoiding disregard of State law in diversity cases in the federal courts. A policy so important to our federalism must be kept free from entanglements with analytical or terminological niceties.

Plainly enough, a statute that would completely bar recovery in a suit if brought in a State court bears on a State-created right vitally and not merely formally or negligibly. As to consequences that so intimately affect recovery or non-recovery a federal court in a diversity case should follow State law. The fact that under New York law a statute of limitations might be lengthened or shortened, that a security may be foreclosed though the debt be barred, that a barred debt may be used as a set-off, are all matters of local law properly to be respected by federal courts sitting in New York when their incidence comes into play there. Such particular rules of local law, however, do not in the slightest change the crucial consideration that if a plea of the statute of limitations would bar recovery in a State court, a federal court ought not to afford recovery.

Prior to *Erie R. Co. v. Tompkins* it was not necessary, as we have indicated, to make the critical analysis required by the doctrine of that case of the nature of jurisdiction of the federal courts in diversity cases. But even before *Erie R. Co. v. Tompkins*, federal courts relied on statutes of limitations of the States in which they sat. In suits at law State limitations statutes were held to be "rules of decision" within § 34 of the Judiciary Act of 1789 and as such applied in "trials at common law." While there was talk of freedom of equity from such State statutes of limitations, the cases generally refused recovery where suit was barred in a like situation in the State courts, even if only by way of analogy.

To make an exception to *Erie R. Co. v. Tompkins* on the equity side of a federal court is to reject the considerations of policy which, after long travail, led to that decision. Judge Augustus N. Hand thus summarized below the fatal objection to such inroad upon *Erie R. Co. v. Tompkins*: "In my opinion it would be a mischievous practice to disregard state statutes of limitation whenever federal courts think that the result of adopting them may be inequitable. Such procedure would promote the choice of United States rather than of state courts in order to gain the advantage of different laws. The main foundation for the criticism of *Swift v. Tyson* was that a litigant in cases where federal jurisdiction is based only on diverse citizenship may obtain a more favorable decision by suing in the United States courts."

Diversity jurisdiction is founded on assurance to non-resident litigants of courts free from susceptibility to potential local bias. The Framers of the Constitution, according to Marshall, entertained "apprehensions" lest distant suitors be subjected to local bias in State courts, or, at least, viewed with "indulgence the possible fears and apprehensions" of such suitors. And so Congress afforded out-of-State litigants another tribunal, not another body of law. The operation of a double system of conflicting laws in the same State is plainly hostile to the reign of law. Certainly, the fortuitous circumstance of residence out of a State of one of the parties to a litigation ought not to give rise to a discrimination against others equally concerned but locally resident. The source of substantive rights enforced by a federal court under diversity jurisdiction, it cannot be said too often, is the law of the States. Whenever that law is authoritatively declared by a State, whether its voice be the legislature or its highest court, such law ought to govern in litigation founded on that law, whether the forum of application is a State or a federal court and whether the remedies be sought at law or may be had in equity.

Dicta may be cited characterizing equity as an independent body of law. To the extent that we have indicated, it is. But insofar as these general observations go beyond that, they merely reflect notions that have been replaced by a sharper analysis of what federal courts do when they enforce rights that have no federal origin. And so, before the true source of law that is applied by the federal courts under diversity jurisdiction was fully explored, some things were said that would not now be said. But nothing that was decided, unless it be the Kirby case, needs to be rejected.

The judgment is reversed and the case is remanded for proceedings not inconsistent with this opinion.

So ordered.

Reversed.

MR. JUSTICE RUTLEDGE.

I dissent. If the policy of judicial conservatism were to be followed in this case, which forbids deciding constitutional and other important questions hypothetically or prematurely, I would favor remanding the cause to the Court of Appeals for determination of the narrow and comparatively minor question whether, under the applicable local law, the cause of action has been barred by lapse of time. That question has not been decided, may be determined in respondent's favor, and in that event the important question affecting federal judicial power now resolved, in a manner contrary to all prior decision here, will have been determined without substantial ultimate effect upon the litigation.

But the Court conceives itself confronted with the necessity for making that determination and in doing so overturns a rule of decision which has prevailed in the federal courts from almost the beginning. I am unable to assent to that decision, for reasons stated by the Court of Appeals and others to be mentioned only briefly. One may give full adherence to the rule of *Erie R. Co. v. Tompkins*, and its extension to cases in equity in so far as they affect clearly substantive rights, without conceding or assuming that the long tradition, both federal and state, which regards statutes of limitations as falling within the category of remedial rather than substantive law, necessarily must be ruled in the same way; and without conceding further that only a different jurisprudential climate or a kind of "brooding omnipresence in the sky" has dictated the hitherto unvaried policy of the federal courts in their general attitude toward the strict application of local statutes of limitations in equity causes.

If any characteristic of equity jurisprudence has descended unbrokenly from and within "the traditional scope of equity as historically evolved in the English Court of Chancery," it is that statutes of limitations, often in terms applying only to actions at law, have never been deemed to be rigidly applicable as absolute barriers to suits in equity as they are to actions at law. That tradition, it would seem, should be regarded as having been incorporated in the various Acts of Congress which have conferred equity jurisdiction upon the federal courts. So incorporated, it has been reaffirmed repeatedly by the decisions of this and other courts. It is now excised from those Acts. If there is to be excision, Congress, not this Court, should make it.

Moreover, the decision of today does not in so many words rule that Congress could not authorize the federal courts to administer equitable relief in accordance with the substantive rights of the parties, notwithstanding state courts had been forbidden by local statutes of limitations to do so. Nevertheless the implication to that effect seems strong, in view of the reliance upon *Erie R. Co. v. Tompkins*. In any event, the question looms more largely in the issues than the Court's opinion appears to make it. For if legislative acquiescence in long-established judicial construction can make it part of a statute, it has done so in this instance. More is at stake in the implications of the decision, if not in the words of the opinion, than simply bringing federal and local law into accord upon matters clearly and exclusively within the constitutional power of the state to determine. It is one thing to require that kind of an accord in diversity cases when the question is merely whether the federal court must follow the law of the state as to burden of proof; contributory negligence; or perhaps in application of the so-called parol evidence rule. These ordinarily involve matters of substantive law, though nominated in terms of procedure. But in some instances their application may lie along the border between procedure or remedy and substance, where the one may or may not be in fact but another name for the other. It is exactly in this borderland, where procedural or remedial rights may or may not have the effect of determining the substantive ones completely, that caution is required in extending the rule of the *Erie* case by the very rule itself.

The words "substantive" and "procedural" or "remedial" are not talismanic. Merely calling a legal question by one or the other does not resolve it otherwise than as a purely authoritarian performance. But they have come to designate in a broad way large and distinctive legal domains within the greater one of the law and to mark, though often indistinctly or with overlapping limits, many divides between such regions.

One of these historically has been the divide between the substantive law and the procedural or remedial law to be applied by the federal courts in diversity cases, a division sharpened but not wiped out by *Erie R. Co. v. Tompkins* and subsequent decisions extending the scope of its ruling. The large division between adjective law and substantive law still remains, to divide the power of Congress from that of the states and consequently to determine the power of the federal courts to apply federal law or state law in diversity matters.

This division, like others drawn by the broad allocation of adjective or remedial and substantive, has areas of admixture of these two aspects of the law. In these areas whether a particular situation or issue presents one aspect or the other depends upon how one looks at the matter. As form cannot always be separated from substance in a work of art, so adjective or remedial aspects cannot be parted entirely from substantive ones in these borderland regions.

Whenever this integration or admixture prevails in a substantial measure, so that a clean break cannot be made, there is danger either of nullifying the power of Congress to control not only how the federal courts may act, but what they may do by way of affording remedies, or of usurping that function, if the Erie doctrine is to be expended judicially to include such situations to the utmost extent.

It may be true that if the matter were wholly fresh the barring of rights in equity by statutes of limitation would seem to partake more of the substantive than of the remedial phase of law. But the matter is not fresh and it is not without room for debate. A long tradition, in the states and here, as well as in the common law which antedated both state and federal law, has emphasized the remedial character of statutes of limitations, more especially in application to equity causes, on many kinds of issues requiring differentiation of such matters from more clearly and exclusively substantive ones. We have recently reaffirmed the distinction in relation to the power of a state to change its laws with retroactive effect ... Similar, though of course not identical, arguments were advanced in that case to bring about departure from the long-established rule, but without success. The tradition now in question is equally long and unvaried. I cannot say the tradition is clearly wrong in this case more than in that. Nor can I say, as was said in the *Erie* case, that the matter is beyond the power of Congress to control. If that be conceded, I think Congress should make the change if it is to be made. The *Erie* decision was rendered in 1938. Seven years have passed without action by Congress to extend the rule to these matters. That is long enough to justify the conclusion that Congress also regards them as not governed by *Erie* and as wishing to make no change. This should be reason enough for leaving the matter at rest until it decides to act.

Finally, this case arises from what are in fact if not in law interstate transactions. It involves the rights of security holders in relation to securities which were distributed not in New York or Ohio alone but widely throughout the country. They are the kind of rights which Congress acted to safeguard when it adopted the Securities and Exchange legislation. Specific provisions of that legislation are not involved in this litigation. The broad policies underlying it may be involved or affected, namely, by the existence of adequate federal remedies, whether judicial or legislative, for the protection of security holders against the misconduct of issuers or against the breach of rights by trustees. Even though the basic rights may be controlled by state law, in such situations the question is often a difficult one whether the law of one state or another applies; and this is true not only of rights clearly substantive but also of those variously characterized as procedural or remedial and substantive which involve the application of statutes of limitations.

Applicable statutes of limitations in state tribunals are not always the ones which would apply if suit were instituted in the courts of the state which creates the substantive rights for which enforcement is sought. The state of the forum is free to apply its own period of limitations, regardless of whether the state originating the right has barred suit upon it. Whether or not the action will be held to be barred depends therefore not upon the law of the state which creates the substantive right, but upon the law of the state where suit may be brought. This in turn will depend upon where it may be possible to secure service of process, and thus jurisdiction of the person of the defendant. It may be therefore that because of the plaintiff's inability to find the defendant in the jurisdiction which creates his substantive right, he will be foreclosed of remedy by the sheer necessity of going to the haven of refuge within which the defendant confines its "presence" for jurisdictional purposes. The law of the latter may bar the suit even though suit still would be allowed under the law of the state creating the substantive right.

It is not clear whether today's decision puts it into the power of corporate trustees, by confining their jurisdictional "presence" to states which allow their courts to give equitable remedies only within short periods of time, to defeat the purpose and intent of the law of the state creating the substantive right. If so, the "right" remains alive, with full-fledged remedy, by the law of its origin, and because enforcement must be had in another state, which affords refuge against it, the remedy and with it the right are nullified. I doubt that the Constitution of the United States requires this or that the Judiciary Acts permit it. A good case can be made, indeed has been made, that the diversity jurisdiction was created to afford protection against exactly this sort of nullifying state legislation.

In my judgment this furnishes added reason for leaving any change, if one is to be made, to the judgment of Congress. The next step may well be to say that in applying the doctrine of laches a federal court must surrender its own judgment and attempt to find out what a state court sitting a block away would do with that notoriously amorphous doctrine.

* * *

C. CONSTITUTIONAL CONCERNS:
THE BYRD BALANCING TEST

BYRD v. BLUE RIDGE RURAL ELECTRIC
COOPERATIVE, INC.

356 U.S. 525 (1958)

MR. JUSTICE BRENNAN delivered the opinion of the Court.

This case was brought in the District Court for the Western District of South Carolina. Jurisdiction was based on diversity of citizenship. The petitioner, a resident of North Carolina, sued respondent, a South Carolina corporation, for damages for injuries allegedly caused by the respondent's negligence. He had judgment on a jury verdict. The Court of Appeals for the Fourth Circuit reversed and directed the entry of judgment for the respondent. We granted certiorari and subsequently ordered reargument.

The respondent is in the business of selling electric power to subscribers in rural sections of South Carolina. The petitioner was employed as a lineman in the construction crew of a construction contractor. The contractor, R. H. Bouligny, Inc., held a contract with the respondent in the amount of $334,300 for the building of some 24 miles of new power lines, the reconversion to higher capacities of about 88 miles of existing lines, and the construction of 2 new substations and a breaker station. The petitioner was injured while connecting power lines to one of the new substations.

One of respondent's affirmative defenses was that under the South Carolina Workmen's Compensation Act, § 72–111,[1] the petitioner—because the work contracted to be done by his employer was work of the kind also done by the respondent's own construction and maintenance crews—had the status of a statutory employee of the respondent and was therefore barred from suing the respondent at law because obliged to

---

1. § 72–111. Liability of owner to workmen of subcontractor:

When any person, in this section . . . referred to as "owner," undertakes to perform or execute any work which is a part of his trade, business or occupation and contracts with any other person . . . for the execution or performance by or under such subcontractor of the whole or any part of the work undertaken by such owner, the owner shall be liable to pay to any workman employed in the work any compensation under this Title which he would have been liable to pay if the workman had been immediately employed by him.

accept statutory compensation benefits as the exclusive remedy for his injuries. Two questions concerning this defense are before us: (1) whether the Court of Appeals erred in directing judgment for respondent without a remand to give petitioner an opportunity to introduce further evidence; and (2) whether petitioner, state practice notwithstanding, is entitled to a jury determination of the factual issues raised by this defense.

I.

The Supreme Court of South Carolina has held that there is no particular formula by which to determine whether an owner is a statutory employer.

* * * The Court of Appeals disagreed with the District Court's construction of the statute. Relying on the decisions of the Supreme Court of South Carolina, the Court of Appeals held that the statute granted respondent immunity from the action if the proofs established that the respondent's own crews had constructed lines and substations which, like the work contracted to the petitioner's employer, were necessary for the distribution of the electric power which the respondent was in the business of selling. We ordinarily accept the interpretation of local law by the Court of Appeals and do so readily here since neither party now disputes the interpretation.

However, instead of ordering a new trial at which the petitioner might offer his own proof pertinent to a determination according to the correct interpretation, the Court of Appeals made its own determination on the record and directed a judgment for the respondent. The court noted that the Rural Electric Cooperative Act of South Carolina authorized the respondent to construct, acquire, maintain, and operate electric generating plants, buildings, and equipment, and any and all kinds of property which might be necessary or convenient to accomplish the purposes for which the corporation was organized, and pointed out that the work contracted to the petitioner's employer was of the class which respondent was empowered by its charter to perform.

The court resolved the uncertainties in the manager's testimony in a manner largely favorable to the respondent: "The testimony with respect to the construction of the substations of Blue Ridge, stated most favorably to the (petitioner), discloses that originally Blue Ridge built three substations with its own facilities, but that all of the substations where were built after the war, including the six it was operating at the time of the accident, were constructed for it by independent contractors, and that at the time of the accident it had no one in its direct employ capable of handling the technical detail of substation construction."

The court found that the respondent financed the work contracted to the petitioner's employer with a loan from the United States, purchased the materials used in the work, and entered into an engineering service contract with an independent engineering company for the design and supervision of the work, concluding from these findings that "the main actor in the whole enterprise was the Cooperative itself."

Finally, the court held that its findings entitled the respondent to the direction of a judgment in its favor. " * * * (T)here can be no doubt that Blue Ridge was not only in the business of supplying electricity to rural communities, but also in the business of constructing the lines and substations necessary for the distribution of the product * * *."

* * * We believe that the Court of Appeals erred. We do not agree with the petitioner's argument in this Court that the respondent's evidence was insufficient to withstand the motion to strike the defense and that he is entitled to our judgment reinstating the judgment of the District Court. But the petitioner is entitled to have the question determined in the trial court. This would be necessary even if petitioner offered no proof of his own. Although the respondent's evidence was sufficient to withstand the motion under the meaning given the statute by the Court of Appeals, it presented a fact question, which, in the circumstances of this case to be discussed, is properly to be decided by a jury. This is clear not only because of the issue of the credibility of the manager's vital testimony, but also because, even should the jury resolve that issue as did the Court of Appeals, the jury on the entire record—consistent with the view of the South Carolina cases that this question is in each case largely one of degree and of fact—might reasonably reach an opposite conclusion from the Court of Appeals as to the ultimate fact whether the respondent was a statutory employer.

At all events, the petitioner is plainly entitled to have an opportunity to try the issue under the Court of Appeals' interpretation.

II.

A question is also presented as to whether on remand the factual issue is to be decided by the judge or by the jury. The respondent argues [based on South Carolina precedent] ... that the issue of immunity should be decided by the judge and not by the jury. That was a negligence action brought in the state trial court against a store owner by an employee of an independent contractor who operated the store's millinery department. The trial judge denied the store owner's motion for a directed verdict made upon the ground that [the statute] barred the plaintiff's action. The jury returned a verdict for the plaintiff. The South Carolina Supreme Court reversed, holding that it was for the judge and not the jury to decide on the evidence whether the owner was a statutory employer, and that the store owner had sustained his defense. The court rested its holding on decisions involving judicial review of the Industrial Commission and said:

> Thus the trial court should have in this case resolved the conflicts in the evidence and determined the fact of whether (the independent contractor) was performing a part of the "trade, business or occupation" of the department store-appellant and, therefore, whether (the

employee's) remedy is exclusively under the Workmen's Compensation Law.

The respondent argues that this state-court decision governs the present diversity case and "divests the jury of its normal function" to decide the disputed fact question of the respondent's immunity under[the state statute]. This is to contend that the federal court is bound under *Erie R. Co. v. Tompkins*, to follow the state court's holding to secure uniform enforcement of the immunity created by the State.

First. It was decided in *Erie R. Co. v. Tompkins* that the federal courts in diversity cases must respect the definition of state-created rights and obligations by the state courts. We must, therefore, first examine the rule in *Adams* to determine whether it is bound up with these rights and obligations in such a way that its application in the federal court is required.

The Workmen's Compensation Act is administered in South Carolina by its Industrial Commission. The South Carolina courts hold that, on judicial review of actions of the Commission under [the statute], the question whether the claim of an injured workman is within the Commission's jurisdiction is a matter of law for decision by the court, which makes its own findings of fact relating to that jurisdiction. The South Carolina Supreme Court states no reasons in *Adams* why, although the jury decides all other factual issues raised by the cause of action and defenses, the jury is displaced as to the factual issue raised by the affirmative defense under § 72–111. The decisions cited to support the holding are concerned solely with defining the scope and method of judicial review of the Industrial Commission. A State may, of course, distribute the functions of its judicial machinery as it sees fit. The decisions relied upon, however, furnish no reason for selecting the judge rather than the jury to decide this single affirmative defense in the negligence action. They simply reflect a policy, that administrative determination of "jurisdictional facts" should not be final but subject to judicial review. The conclusion is inescapable that the *Adams* holding is grounded in the practical consideration that the question had theretofore come before the South Carolina courts from the Industrial Commission and the courts had become accustomed to deciding the factual issue of immunity without the aid of juries. We find nothing to suggest that this rule was announced as an integral part of the special relationship created by the statute. Thus the requirement appears to be merely a form and mode of enforcing the immunity, *Guaranty Trust Co. of New York v. York*, and not a rule intended to be bound up with the definition of the rights and obligations of the parties. The situation is therefore not analogous to that in *Dice v. Akron, C. & Y.R. Co.*, where this Court held that the right to trial by jury is so substantial a part of the cause of action created by the Federal Employers' Liability Act, that the Ohio courts could not apply, in an action under that statute, the Ohio rule that the question of fraudulent release was for determination by a judge rather than by a jury.

Second. But cases following *Erie* have evinced a broader policy to the effect that the federal courts should conform as near as may be—in the absence of other considerations—to state rules even of form and mode where the state rules may bear substantially on the question whether the litigation would come out one way in the federal court and another way in the state court if the federal court failed to apply a particular local rule. *E.g., Guaranty Trust Co. of New York v. York.* Concededly the nature of the tribunal which tries issues may be important in the enforcement of the parcel of rights making up a cause of action or defense, and bear significantly upon achievement of uniform enforcement of the right. It may well be that in the instant personal-injury case the outcome would be substantially affected by whether the issue of immunity is decided by a judge or a jury. Therefore, were "outcome" the only consideration, a strong case might appear for saying that the federal court should follow the state practice.

But there are affirmative countervailing considerations at work here. The federal system is an independent system for administering justice to litigants who properly invoke its jurisdiction. An essential characteristic of that system is the manner in which, in civil common-law actions, it distributes trial functions between judge and jury and, under the influence—if not the command—of the Seventh Amendment, assigns the decisions of disputed questions of fact to the jury. The policy of uniform enforcement of state-created rights and obligations, *see, e.g., Guaranty Trust Co. of New York v. York,* cannot in every case exact compliance with a state rule—not bound up with rights and obligations—which disrupts the federal system of allocating functions between judge and jury. Thus the inquiry here is whether the federal policy favoring jury decisions of disputed fact questions should yield to the state rule in the interest of furthering the objective that the litigation should not come out one way in the federal court and another way in the state court.

We think that in the circumstances of this case the federal court should not follow the state rule. It cannot be gainsaid that there is a strong federal policy against allowing state rules to disrupt the judge-jury relationship in the federal courts. In *Herron v. Southern Pacific Co.,* the trial judge in a personal-injury negligence action brought in the District Court for Arizona on diversity grounds directed a verdict for the defendant when it appeared as a matter of law that the plaintiff was guilty of contributory negligence. The federal judge refused to be bound by a provision of the Arizona Constitution which made the jury the sole arbiter of the question of contributory negligence. This Court sustained the action of the trial judge, holding that "state laws cannot alter the essential character or function of a federal court" because that function "is not in any sense a local matter, and state statutes which would interfere with the appropriate performance of that function are not binding upon the federal court under either the Conformity Act or the 'Rules of Decision' Act." Perhaps even more clearly in light of the influence of the Seventh Amendment, the function assigned to the jury "is an essential factor in the process for which the Federal Constitution provides." Concededly the *Herron* case was decided before *Erie R. Co. v. Tompkins*, but even when *Swift v. Tyson*, was governing law and allowed federal courts sitting in diversity cases to disregard state decisional law, it was never thought that state statutes or constitutions were similarly to be disregarded. Yet *Herron* held that state statutes and constitutional provisions could not disrupt or alter the essential character or function of a federal court.

Third. We have discussed the problem upon the assumption that the outcome of the litigation may be substantially affected by whether the issue of immunity is decided by a judge or a jury. But clearly there is not present here the certainty that a different result would follow, *cf. Guaranty Trust Co. of New York v. York*. There are factors present here which might reduce that possibility. The trial judge in the federal system has powers denied the judges of many States to comment on the weight of evidence and credibility of witnesses, and discretion to grant a new trial if the verdict appears to him to be against the weight of the evidence. We do not think the likelihood of a different result is so strong as to require the federal practice of jury determination of disputed factual issues to yield to the state rule in the interest of uniformity of outcome.

The Court of Appeals did not consider other grounds of appeal raised by the respondent because the ground taken disposed of the case. We accordingly remand the case to the Court of Appeals for the decision of the other questions, with instructions that, if not made unnecessary by the decision of such questions, the Court of Appeals shall remand the case to the District Court for a new trial of such issues as the Court of Appeals may direct.

Reversed and remanded.

MR. JUSTICE WHITTAKER concurring in part and dissenting in part.

* * * This Court now vacates the judgment of the Court of Appeals and remands the case to it for decision of questions not reached in its prior opinion, with directions, if not made unnecessary by its decision of such questions, to remand the case to the District Court for a new trial upon such issues as the Court of Appeals may direct.

I agree with and join in that much of the Court's opinion. I do so because—although, as found by the Court of Appeals, respondent's evidence was ample, prima facie, to sustain its affirmative jurisdictional defense—petitioner had not waived his right to adduce evidence in rebuttal upon that issue, in other words had not "rested," at the time the district judge erroneously struck respondent's jurisdiction defense and supporting evidence from the record. In these circumstances, I believe that the judgment of the Court of Appeals, insofar as it directed the District Court to enter judgment for respondent, would deprive petitioner of his legal right, which he had not waived, to adduce evidence which he claims to have and desires to offer in rebuttal of respondent's prima facie established jurisdictional defense.

* * * But the Court's opinion proceeds to discuss and determine the question whether, upon remand to the District Court, if such becomes necessary, the jurisdictional issue is to be determined by the judge or by the jury—a question which, to my mind, is premature, not now properly before us, and is one we need not and should not now reach for or decide. The Court, although premising its conclusion "upon the assumption that the outcome of the litigation may be substantially affected by whether the issue of immunity is decided by a judge or a jury," holds that the issue is to be determined by a jury—not by the judge. I cannot agree to this conclusion for the following reasons.

* * * It thus seems to be settled under the South Carolina Workmen's Compensation Law, and the decisions of the highest court of that State construing it, that the question whether exclusive jurisdiction, in cases like this, is vested in its Industrial Commission or in its courts of general jurisdiction is one for decision by the court, not by a jury. The Federal District Court, in this diversity case, is bound to follow the substantive South Carolina law that would be applied if the trial were to be held in a South Carolina court, in which State the Federal District Court sits. *Erie R. Co. v. Tompkins.* A Federal District Court sitting in South Carolina may not legally reach a substantially different result than would have been reached upon a trial of the same case "in a State court a block away." *Guaranty Trust Co. of New York v. York.*

The Court's opinion states: "Concededly the nature of the tribunal which tries issues may be important in the enforcement of the parcel of rights making up a cause of action or defense, and bear significantly upon achievement of uniform enforcement of the right. It may well be that in the instant personal-injury case the outcome would be substantially affected by whether the issue of immunity is decided by a judge or a jury." And the Court premises its conclusion "upon the assumption that the outcome of the litigation may be substantially affected by whether the issue of immunity is decided by a judge or a jury." Upon that premise, the Court's conclusion, to my mind, is contrary to our cases. "Here (as in *Guaranty Trust Co. of New York v. York*) we are dealing with a right to recover derived not from the United States but from one of the States. When, because the plaintiff happens to be a non-resident, such a right is enforceable in a federal as well as in a State court, the forms and mode of enforcing the right may at times, naturally enough, vary because the two judicial systems are not identic. But since a federal court adjudicating a state-created right solely because of the diversity of citizenship of the parties is for that purpose, in effect, only another court of the State, it cannot afford recovery if the right to recover is made unavailable by the State nor can it substantially affect the enforcement of the right as given by the State." *Guaranty Trust Co. of New York v. York.*

The words "substantive" and "procedural" are mere conceptual labels and in no sense talismanic. To call a legal question by one or the other of those terms does not resolve the question otherwise than as a purely authoritarian performance. When a question though denominated "procedural" is nevertheless so "substantive" as materially to affect the result of a trial, federal courts, in enforcing state-created rights, are not free to disregard it, on the ground that it is "procedural," for such would be to allow, upon mere nomenclature, a different result in a state court from that allowable in a federal court though both are, in effect, courts of the State and "sitting side by side." *Klaxon Co. v. Stentor Electric Mfg. Co.* "The federal court enforces the state-created right by rules of procedure which it has acquired from the Federal Government and which therefore are not identical with those of the state courts." Yet, in spite of that difference in procedure, the federal court enforcing a state-created right in a diversity case is, as we said in *Guaranty Trust Co. of New York v. York*, in substance "only another court of the State." The federal court therefore may not "substantially affect the enforcement of the right as given by the State." "Where local law qualifies or abridges (the right), the federal court must follow suit. Otherwise there is a different measure of the cause of action in one court than in the other, and the principle of *Erie R. Co. v. Tompkins* is transgressed." "It is therefore immaterial whether (state-created rights) are characterized either as 'substantive' or 'procedural' in State court opinions in any use of those terms unrelated to the specific issue before us. *Erie R. Co. v. Tompkins* was not an endeavor to formulate scientific legal terminology. It expressed a policy that touches vitally the proper distribution of judicial power between State and federal courts. In essence, the intent of that decision was to insure that, in all cases where a federal court is exercising jurisdiction solely because of the diversity of citizenship of the parties, the outcome of the litigation in the federal court should be substantially the same, so far as legal rules determine the outcome of a litigation, as it would be if tried in a State court. The nub of the policy that underlies *Erie R. Co. v. Tompkins* is that for the same transaction the accident of a suit by a non-resident litigant in a federal court instead of in a State court a block away should not lead to a substantially different result. And so, putting to one side abstractions regarding 'substance' and 'procedure', we have held that in diversity cases the federal courts must follow the law of the State * * *." *Guaranty Trust Co. of New York v. York.*

Inasmuch as the law of South Carolina, as construed by its highest court, requires its courts—not juries—to determine whether jurisdiction over the subject matter of cases like this is vested in its Industrial Commission, and inasmuch as the Court's opinion concedes "that in the instant personal-injury case the outcome would be substantially affected by whether the issue of immunity is decided by a judge or a jury," it follows that in this diversity case the jurisdictional issue must be determined by the judge—not by the jury. Insofar as the Court holds that the question of jurisdiction should be determined by the jury, I think the Court departs from its past decisions. I therefore respectfully dissent from part II of the opinion of the Court.

* * *

D. THE RULES ENABLING ACT

28 U.S.C. § 2071. Rule-Making Power Generally

(a) The Supreme Court and all courts established by Act of Congress may from time to time prescribe rules for the conduct of their business. Such rules shall be consistent with Acts of Congress and rules of practice and procedure prescribed under section 2072 of this title.

(b) Any rule prescribed by a court, other than the Supreme Court, under subsection (a) shall be prescribed only after giving appropriate public notice and an opportunity for comment. Such rule shall take effect upon the date specified by the prescribing court and shall have such effect on pending proceedings as the prescribing court may order.

(c) **(1)** A rule of a district court prescribed under subsection (a) shall remain in effect unless modified or abrogated by the judicial council of the relevant circuit.

    (2) Any other rule prescribed by a court other than the Supreme Court under subsection (a) shall remain in effect unless modified or abrogated by the Judicial Conference.

(d) Copies of rules prescribed under subsection (a) by a district court shall be furnished to the judicial council, and copies of all rules prescribed by a court other than the Supreme Court under subsection (a) shall be furnished to the Director of the Administrative Office of the United States Courts and made available to the public.

(e) If the prescribing court determines that there is an immediate need for a rule, such court may proceed under this section without public notice and opportunity for comment, but such court shall promptly thereafter afford such notice and opportunity for comment.

(f) No rule may be prescribed by a district court other than under this section.

* * *

28 U.S.C. § 2072. Rules of Procedure and Evidence; Power to Prescribe

(a) The Supreme Court shall have the power to prescribe general rules of practice and procedure and rules of evidence for cases in the United States district courts (including proceedings before magistrate judges thereof) and courts of appeals.

(b) Such rules shall not abridge, enlarge or modify any substantive right. All laws in conflict with such rules shall be of no further force or effect after such rules have taken effect.

(c) Such rules may define when a ruling of a district court is final for the purposes of appeal under section 1291 of this title.

* * *

FEDERAL RULE OF CIVIL PROCEDURE 83. RULES BY DISTRICT COURTS; JUDGE'S DIRECTIVES

(a) Local Rules.

> **(1) In General.** After giving public notice and an opportunity for comment, a district court, acting by a majority of its district judges, may adopt and amend rules governing its practice. A local rule must be consistent with—but not duplicate—federal statutes and rules adopted under 28 U.S.C. §§ 2072 and 2075, and must conform to any uniform numbering system prescribed by the Judicial Conference of the United States. A local rule takes effect on the date specified by the district court and remains in effect unless amended by the court or abrogated by the judicial council of the circuit. Copies of rules and amendments must, on their adoption, be furnished to the judicial council and the Administrative Office of the United States Courts and be made available to the public.

> **(2) Requirement of Form.** A local rule imposing a requirement of form must not be enforced in a way that causes a party to lose any right because of a non-willful failure to comply.

(b) Procedure When There Is No Controlling Law. A judge may regulate practice in any manner consistent with federal law, rules adopted under 28 U.S.C. §§ 2072 and 2075, and the district's local rules. No sanction or other disadvantage may be imposed for noncompliance with any requirement not in federal law, federal rules, or the local rules unless the alleged violator has been furnished in the particular case with actual notice of the requirement.

* * *

HANNA v. PLUMER

380 U.S. 460 (1965)

MR. CHIEF JUSTICE WARREN delivered the opinion of the Court.

The question to be decided is whether, in a civil action where the jurisdiction of the United States district court is based upon diversity of citizenship between the parties, service of process shall be made in the manner prescribed by state law or that set forth in Rule 4(d)(1) of the Federal Rules of Civil Procedure.

On February 6, 1963, petitioner, a citizen of Ohio, filed her complaint in the District Court for the District of Massachusetts, claiming damages in excess of $10,000 for personal injuries resulting from an automobile accident in South Carolina, allegedly caused by the negligence of one Louise Plumer Osgood, a Massachusetts citizen deceased at the time of the filing of the complaint. Respondent, Mrs. Osgood's executor and also a Massachusetts citizen, was named as defendant. On February 8, service was made by leaving copies of the summons and the complaint with respondent's wife at his residence, concededly in compliance with Rule 4(d)(1), which provides:

> The summons and complaint shall be served together. The plaintiff shall furnish the person making service with such copies as are necessary. Service shall be made as follows:

> (1) Upon an individual other than an infant or an incompetent person, by delivering a copy of the summons and of the complaint to him personally or by leaving copies thereof at his dwelling house or usual place of abode with some person of suitable age and discretion then residing therein * * *.

Respondent filed his answer on February 26, alleging, *inter alia*, that the action could not be maintained because it had been brought "contrary to and in violation of the provisions of Massachusetts General Laws § 9." That section provides:

> Except as provided in this chapter, an executor or administrator shall not be held to answer to an action by a creditor of the deceased which is not commenced within one year from the time of his giving bond for the performance of his trust, or to such an action which is commenced within said year unless before the expiration thereof the writ in such action has been served by delivery in hand upon such executor or administrator or service thereof accepted by him or a notice stating the name of the estate, the name and address of the creditor, the amount of the claim and the court in which the action has been brought has been filed in the proper registry of probate. * * *.

On October 17, 1963, the District Court granted respondent's motion for summary judgment, citing *Guaranty Trust Co. of New York v. York* in support of its conclusion that the adequacy of the service was to be measured by § 9, with which, the court held, petitioner had not complied. On appeal, petitioner admitted noncompliance with § 9, but argued that Rule 4(d)(1) defines the method by which service of process is to be effected in diversity actions. The Court of Appeals for the First Circuit, finding that "(r)elatively recent amendments (to § 9) evince a clear legislative purpose to require personal notification within the year," concluded that the conflict of state and federal rules was over "a substantive rather than a procedural matter," and unanimously affirmed. 331 F.2d 157. Because of the threat to the goal of uniformity of federal procedure posed by the decision below, we granted certiorari.

We conclude that the adoption of Rule 4(d)(1), designed to control service of process in diversity actions,[3] neither exceeded the congressional mandate embodied in the Rules Enabling Act nor transgressed constitutional bounds, and that the Rule is therefore the standard against which

---

3. "These rules govern the procedure in the United States district courts in all suits of a civil nature whether cognizable as cases at law or in equity with the exceptions stated in Rule 81. * * * " Fed. Rules Civ. P. 1.

This case does not come within any of the exceptions noted in Rule 81.

the District Court should have measured the adequacy of the service. Accordingly, we reverse the decision of the Court of Appeals.

The Rules Enabling Act, 28 U.S.C. § 2072 (1958 ed.), provides, in pertinent part:

> The Supreme Court shall have the power to prescribe, by general rules, the forms of process, writs, pleadings, and motions, and the practice and procedure of the district courts of the United States in civil actions.

> Such rules shall not abridge, enlarge or modify any substantive right and shall preserve the right of trial by jury * * *.

Under the cases construing the scope of the Enabling Act, Rule 4(d)(1) clearly passes muster. Prescribing the manner in which a defendant is to be notified that a suit has been instituted against him, it relates to the "practice and procedure of the district courts."

"The test must be whether a rule really regulates procedure,—the judicial process for enforcing rights and duties recognized by substantive law and for justly administering remedy and redress for disregard or infraction of them." *Sibbach v. Wilson & Co.*

In *Mississippi Pub. Corp. v. Murphree*, this Court upheld Rule 4(f), which permits service of a summons anywhere within the State (and not merely the district) in which a district court sits:

> We think that Rule 4(f) is in harmony with the Enabling Act * * *. Undoubtedly most alterations of the rules of practice and procedure may and often do affect the rights of litigants. Congress' prohibition of any alteration of substantive rights of litigants was obviously not addressed to such incidental effects as necessarily attend the adoption of the prescribed new rules of procedure upon the rights of litigants who, agreeably to rules of practice and procedure, have been brought before a court authorized to determine their rights. *Sibbach v. Wilson & Co.* The fact that the application of Rule 4(f) will operate to subject petitioner's rights to adjudication by the district court for northern Mississippi will undoubtedly affect those rights. But it does not operate to abridge, enlarge or modify the rules of decision by which that court will adjudicate its rights.

Thus were there no conflicting state procedure, Rule 4(d)(1) would clearly control. However, respondent, focusing on the contrary Massachusetts rule, calls to the Court's attention another line of cases, a line which—like the Federal Rules—had its birth in 1938. *Erie R. Co. v. Tompkins*, overruling *Swift v. Tyson*, held that federal courts sitting in diversity cases, when deciding questions of "substantive" law, are bound by state court decisions as well as state statutes. The broad command of *Erie* was therefore identical to that of the Enabling Act: federal courts are to apply state substantive law and federal procedural law. However, as subsequent cases sharpened the distinction between substance and procedure, the line of cases following *Erie* diverged markedly from the line construing the Enabling Act. *Guaranty Trust Co. of New York v. York*, made it clear that *Erie*-type problems were not to be solved by reference to any traditional or common-sense substance-procedure distinction:

> And so the question is not whether a statute of limitations is deemed a matter of 'procedure' in some sense. The question is * * * does it significantly affect the result of a litigation for a federal court to disregard a law of a State that would be controlling in an action upon the same claim by the same parties in a State court?

Respondent, by placing primary reliance on *York* and *Ragan*, suggests that the *Erie* doctrine acts as a check on the Federal Rules of Civil Procedure, that despite the clear command of Rule 4(d)(1), *Erie* and its progeny demand the application of the Massachusetts rule. Reduced to essentials, the argument is: (1) *Erie*, as refined in *York*, demands that federal courts apply state law whenever application of federal law in its stead will alter the outcome of the case. (2) In this case, a determination that the Massachusetts service requirements obtain will result in immediate victory for respondent. If, on the other hand, it should be held that Rule 4(d)(1) is applicable, the litigation will continue, with possible victory for petitioner. (3) Therefore, *Erie* demands application of the Massachusetts rule. The syllogism possesses an appealing simplicity, but is for several reasons invalid.

In the first place, it is doubtful that, even if there were no Federal Rule making it clear that in-hand service is not required in diversity actions, the *Erie* rule would have obligated the District Court to follow the Massachusetts procedure. "Outcome-determination" analysis was never intended to serve as a talisman. *Byrd v. Blue Ridge Rural Elec. Cooperative.* Indeed, the message of York itself is that choices between state and federal law are to be made not by application of any automatic, "litmus paper" criterion, but rather by reference to the policies underlying the *Erie* rule. *Guaranty Trust Co. of New York v. York.*

The *Erie* rule is rooted in part in a realization that it would be unfair for the character of result of a litigation materially to differ because the suit had been brought in a federal court.

"Diversity of citizenship jurisdiction was conferred in order to prevent apprehended discrimination in state courts against those not citizens of the state. *Swift v. Tyson* introduced grave discrimination by noncitizens against citizens. It made rights enjoyed under the unwritten 'general law' vary according to whether enforcement was sought in the state or in the federal court; and the privilege of selecting the court in which the right should be determined was conferred upon the noncitizen. Thus, the doctrine rendered impossible equal protection of the law." *Erie R. Co. v. Tompkins.*

The decision was also in part a reaction to the practice of "forum-shopping" which had grown up in response to the rule of *Swift v. Tyson*. That the *York* test was an attempt to effectuate these policies is demonstrated by the fact that the opinion framed the inquiry in terms of "substantial" variations between state and federal litigation. Not only are non-substantial, or trivial, variations not likely to raise the sort of equal protection problems which troubled the Court in *Erie*; they are also unlikely to influence the choice of a forum. The "outcome-determination" test therefore cannot be read without reference to the twin aims of the *Erie* rule: discouragement of forum-shopping and avoidance of inequitable administration of the laws.

The difference between the conclusion that the Massachusetts rule is applicable, and the conclusion that it is not, is of course at this point "outcome-determinative" in the sense that if we hold the state rule to apply, respondent prevails, whereas if we hold that Rule 4(d)(1) governs, the litigation will continue. But in this sense every procedural variation is "outcome-determinative." For example, having brought suit in a federal court, a plaintiff cannot then insist on the right to file subsequent pleadings in accord with the time limits applicable in state courts, even though enforcement of the federal timetable will, if he continues to insist that he must meet only the state time limit, result in determination of the controversy against him. So it is here. Though choice of the federal or state rule will at this point have a marked effect upon the outcome of the litigation, the difference between the two rules would be of scant, if any, relevance to the choice of a forum. Petitioner, in choosing her forum, was not presented with a situation where application of the state rule would wholly bar recovery; rather, adherence to the state rule would have resulted only in altering the way in which process was served. Moreover, it is difficult to argue that permitting service of defendant's wife to take the place of in-hand service of defendant himself alters the mode of enforcement of state-created rights in a fashion sufficiently "substantial" to raise the sort of equal protection problems to which the *Erie* opinion alluded.

There is, however, a more fundamental flaw in respondent's syllogism: the incorrect assumption that the rule of *Erie R. Co. v. Tompkins* constitutes the appropriate test of the validity and therefore the applicability of a Federal Rule of Civil Procedure. The *Erie* rule has never been invoked to void a Federal Rule. It is true that there have been cases where this Court has held applicable a state rule in the face of an argument that the situation was governed by one of the Federal Rules. But the holding of each such case was not that *Erie* commanded displacement of a Federal Rule by an inconsistent state rule, but rather that the scope of the Federal Rule was not as broad as the losing party urged, and therefore, there being no Federal Rule which covered the point in dispute, *Erie* commanded the enforcement of state law.

"Respondent contends in the first place that the charge was correct because of the fact that Rule 8(c) of the Rules of Civil Procedure makes contributory negligence an affirmative defense. We do not agree. Rule 8(c) covers only the manner of pleading. The question of the burden of establishing contributory negligence is a question of local law which federal courts in diversity of citizenship cases must apply."

Here, of course, the clash is unavoidable; Rule 4(d)(1) says—implicitly, but with unmistakable clarity—that in-hand service is not required in federal courts. At the same time, in cases adjudicating the validity of Federal Rules, we have not applied the *York* rule or other refinements of *Erie*, but have to this day continued to decide questions concerning the scope of the Enabling Act and the constitutionality of specific Federal Rules in light of the distinction set forth in *Sibbach*.

Nor has the development of two separate lines of cases been inadvertent. The line between "substance" and "procedure" shifts as the legal context changes. "Each implies different variables depending upon the particular problem for which it is used." *Guaranty Trust Co. of New York v. York*. It is true that both the Enabling Act and the *Erie* rule say, roughly, that federal courts are to apply state "substantive" law and federal 'procedural' law, but from that it need not follow that the tests are identical. For they were designed to control very different sorts of decisions. When a situation is covered by one of the Federal Rules, the question facing the court is a far cry from the typical, relatively unguided *Erie* Choice: the court has been instructed to apply the Federal Rule, and can refuse to do so only if the Advisory Committee, this Court, and Congress erred in their prima facie judgment that the Rule in question transgresses neither the terms of the Enabling Act nor constitutional restrictions.

We are reminded by the *Erie* opinion that neither Congress nor the federal courts can, under the guise of formulating rules of decision for federal courts, fashion rules which are not supported by a grant of federal authority contained in Article I or some other section of the Constitution; in such areas state law must govern because there can be no other law. But the opinion in *Erie*, which involved no Federal Rule and dealt with a question which was "substantive" in every traditional sense (whether the railroad owed a duty of care to Tompkins as a trespasser or a licensee), surely neither said nor implied that measures like Rule 4(d)(1) are unconstitutional. For the constitutional provision for a federal court system (augmented by the Necessary and Proper Clause) carries with it congressional power to make rules governing the practice and pleading in those courts, which in turn includes a power to regulate matters which, though falling within the uncertain area between substance and procedure, are rationally capable of classification as either. Neither York nor the cases following it ever suggested that the rule there laid down for coping with situations where no Federal Rule applies is coextensive with the limitation on Congress to which *Erie* had adverted. Although this Court has never before been confronted with a case where the applicable Federal Rule is in direct collision with the law of the relevant State, courts of appeals faced with such clashes have rightly discerned the implications of our decisions.

"One of the shaping purposes of the Federal Rules is to bring about uniformity in the federal courts by getting away from local rules." This is especially true of matters which relate to the administration of legal proceedings, an area in which federal courts have traditionally exerted strong inherent power, completely aside from the powers Congress expressly conferred in the Rules. The purpose of the *Erie* doctrine, even as extended in *York* and *Ragan*, was never to bottle up federal courts with "outcome-determinative" and "integral-relations" stoppers—when there are "affirmative countervailing (federal) considerations and when there is a Congressional mandate (the Rules) supported by constitutional authority."

Erie and its offspring cast no doubt on the long-recognized power of Congress to prescribe housekeeping rules for federal courts even though some of those rules will inevitably differ from comparable state rules. "When, because the plaintiff happens to be a non-resident, such a right is enforceable in a federal as well as in a State court, the forms and mode of enforcing the right may at times, naturally enough, vary because the two judicial systems are not identical." *Guaranty Trust Co. of New York v. York.* Thus, though a court, in measuring a Federal Rule against the standards contained in the Enabling Act and the Constitution, need not wholly blind itself to the degree to which the Rule makes the character and result of the federal litigation stray from the course it would follow in state courts, *Sibbach v. Wilson & Co.*, it cannot be forgotten that the Erie rule, and the guidelines suggested in *York*, were created to serve another purpose altogether. To hold that a Federal Rule of Civil Procedure must cease to function whenever it alters the mode of enforcing state-created rights would be to disembowel either the Constitution's grant of power over federal procedure or Congress' attempt to exercise that power in the Enabling Act. Rule 4(d)(1) is valid and controls the instant case.

Reversed.

MR. JUSTICE BLACK concurs in the result. MR. JUSTICE HARLAN, concurring. It is unquestionably true that up to now *Erie* and the cases following it have not succeeded in articulating a workable doctrine governing choice of law in diversity actions. I respect the Court's effort to clarify the situation in today's opinion. However, in doing so I think it has misconceived the constitutional premises of *Erie* and has failed to deal adequately with those past decisions upon which the courts below relied.

Erie was something more than an opinion which worried about "forum-shopping and avoidance of inequitable administration of the laws," although to be sure these were important elements of the decision. I have always regarded that decision as one of the modern cornerstones of our federalism, expressing policies that profoundly touch the allocation of judicial power between the state and federal systems. *Erie* recognized that there should not be two conflicting systems of law controlling the primary activity of citizens, for such alternative governing authority must necessarily give rise to a debilitating uncertainty in the planning of everyday affairs. And it recognized that the scheme of our Constitution envisions an allocation of law-making functions between state and federal legislative processes which is undercut if the federal judiciary can make substantive law affecting state affairs beyond the bounds of congressional legislative powers in this regard. Thus, in diversity cases *Erie* commands that it be the state law governing primary private activity which prevails.

The shorthand formulations which have appeared in some past decisions are prone to carry untoward results that frequently arise from oversimplification. The Court is quite right in stating that the "outcome-determinative" test of *Guaranty Trust Co. of New York v. York*, if taken literally, proves too much, for any rule, no matter how clearly "procedural," can affect the outcome of litigation if it is not obeyed. In turning from the "outcome" test of *York* back to the unadorned forum-shopping rationale of *Erie*, however, the Court falls prey to like oversimplification, for a simple forum-shopping rule also proves too much; litigants often choose a federal forum merely to obtain what they consider the advantages of the Federal Rules of Civil Procedure or to try their cases before a supposedly more favorable judge. To my mind the proper line of approach in determining whether to apply a state or a federal rule, whether "substantive" or "procedural," is to stay close to basic principles by inquiring if the choice of rule would substantially affect those primary decisions respecting human conduct which our constitutional system leaves to state regulation. If so, *Erie* and the Constitution require that the state rule prevail, even in the face of a conflicting federal rule.

The Court weakens, if indeed it does not submerge, this basic principle by finding, in effect, a grant of substantive legislative power in the constitutional provision for a federal court system, and through it, setting up the Federal Rules as a body of law inviolate.

"(T)he constitutional provision for a federal court system * * * carries with it congressional power * * * to regulate matters which, though falling within the uncertain area between substance and procedure, are rationally capable of classification as either."

So long as a reasonable man could characterize any duly adopted federal rule as "procedural," the Court, unless I misapprehend what is said, would have it apply no matter how seriously it frustrated a State's substantive regulation of the primary conduct and affairs of its citizens. Since the members of the Advisory Committee, the Judicial Conference, and this Court who formulated the Federal Rules are presumably reasonable men, it follows that the integrity of the Federal Rules is absolute. Whereas the unadulterated outcome and forum-shopping tests may err too far toward honoring state rules, I submit that the Court's "arguably procedural, ergo constitutional" test moves too fast and far in the other direction.

The courts below relied upon this Court's decisions in *Ragan v. Merchants Transfer & Warehouse Co.*, and *Cohen v. Beneficial Indus. Loan Corp.* Those cases deserve more attention than this Court has given them, particularly *Ragan* which, if still good law, would in my opinion call for affirmance of the result reached by the Court of Appeals. Further, a discussion of these two cases will serve to illuminate the "diversity" thesis I am advocating.

In *Ragan* a Kansas statute of limitations provided that an action was deemed commenced when service was made on the defendant. Despite Federal Rule 3 which provides that an action commences with the filing of the complaint, the Court held that for purposes of the Kansas statute of limitations a diversity tort action commenced only when service was made upon the defendant. The effect of this holding was that although the plaintiff had filed his federal complaint within the state period of limitations, his action was barred because the federal marshal did not serve a summons on the defendant until after the limitations period had run. I think that the decision was wrong. At most, application of the Federal Rule would have meant that potential Kansas tort defendants would have to defer for a few days the satisfaction of knowing that they had not been sued within the limitations period. The choice of the Federal Rule would have had no effect on the primary stages of private activity from which torts arise, and only the most minimal effect on behavior following the commission of the tort. In such circumstances the interest of the federal system in proceeding under its own rules should have prevailed.

Cohen v. Beneficial Indus. Loan Corp. held that a federal diversity court must apply a state statute requiring a small stockholder in a stockholder derivative suit to post a bond securing payment of defense costs as a condition to prosecuting an action. Such a statute is not "outcome determinative;" the plaintiff can win with or without it. The Court now rationalizes the case on the ground that the statute might affect the plaintiff's choice of forum, but as has been pointed out, a simple forum-shopping test proves too much. The proper view of *Cohen* is in my opinion, that the statute was meant to inhibit small stockholders from instituting "strike suits," and thus it was designed and could be expected to have a substantial impact on private primary activity. Anyone who was at the trial bar during the period when *Cohen* arose can appreciate the strong state policy reflected in the statute. I think it wholly legitimate to view Federal Rule 23 as not purporting to deal with the problem. But even had the Federal Rules purported to do so, and in so doing provided a substantially less effective deterrent to strike suits, I think the state rule should still have prevailed. That is where I believe the Court's view differs from mine; for the Court attributes such overriding force to the Federal Rules that it is hard to think of a case where a conflicting state rule would be allowed to operate, even though the state rule reflected policy considerations which, under *Erie*, would lie within the realm of state legislative authority.

It remains to apply what has been said to the present case. The Massachusetts rule provides that an executor need not answer suits unless in-hand service was made upon him or notice of the action was filed in the proper registry of probate within one year of his giving bond. The evident intent of this statute is to permit an executor to distribute the estate which he is administering without fear that further liabilities may be outstanding for which he could be held personally liable. If the Federal District Court in Massachusetts applies Rule 4(d)(1) of the Federal Rules of Civil Procedure instead of the Massachusetts service rule, what effect would that have on the speed and assurance with which estates are distributed? As I see it, the effect would not be substantial. It would mean simply that an executor would have to check at his own house or the federal courthouse as well as the registry of probate before he could distribute the estate with impunity. As this does not seem enough to give rise to any real impingement on the vitality of the state policy which the Massachusetts rule is intended to serve, I concur in the judgment of the Court.

* * *

XIV. REPRESENTATIONAL CLASS ACTION LITIGATION

A. DUE PROCESS CONSIDERATIONS

HANSBERRY v. LEE

311 U.S. 32 (1940)

MR. JUSTICE STONE delivered the opinion of the Court.

The question is whether the Supreme Court of Illinois, by its adjudication that petitioners in this case are bound by a judgment rendered in an earlier litigation to which they were not parties, has deprived them of the due process of law guaranteed by the Fourteenth Amendment.

Respondents brought this suit in the Circuit Court of Cook County, Illinois, to enjoin the breach by petitioners of an agreement restricting the use of land within a described area of the City of Chicago, which was alleged to have been entered into by some five hundred of the land owners. The agreement stipulated that for a specified period no part of the land should be "sold, leased to or permitted to be occupied by any person of the colored race," and provided that it should not be effective unless signed by the "owners of 95 per centum of the frontage" within the described area. The bill of complaint set up that the owners of 95 per cent of the frontage had signed; that respondents are owners of land within the restricted area who have either signed the agreement or acquired their land from others who did sign and that petitioners Hansberry, who are Negroes, have, with the alleged aid of the other petitioners and with knowledge of the agreement, acquired and are occupying land in the restricted area formerly belonging to an owner who had signed the agreement.

To the defense that the agreement had never become effective because owners of 95 per cent of the frontage had not signed it, respondents pleaded that that issue was res judicata by the decree in an earlier suit. To this petitioners pleaded, by way of rejoinder, that they were not parties to that suit or bound by its decree, and that denial of their right to litigate, in the present suit, the issue of performance of the condition precedent to the validity of the agreement would be a denial of due process of law guaranteed by the Fourteenth Amendment. It does not appear, nor is it contended that any of petitioners is the successor in interest to or in privity with any of the parties in the earlier suit.

The circuit court, after a trial on the merits, found that owners of only about 54 per cent of the frontage had signed the agreement, and that the only support of the judgment in the *Burke* case was a false and fraudulent stipulation of the parties that 95 per cent had signed. But it ruled that the issue of performance of the condition precedent to the validity of the agreement was res judicata as alleged and entered a decree for respondents. The Supreme Court of Illinois affirmed. We granted certiorari to resolve the constitutional question.

The Supreme Court of Illinois, upon an examination of the record in *Burke v. Kleiman*, found that that suit, in the Superior Court of Cook County, was brought by a landowner in the restricted area to enforce the agreement which had been signed by her predecessor in title, in behalf of herself and other property owners in like situation, against four named individuals who had acquired or asserted an interest in a plot of land formerly owned by another signer of the agreement; that upon stipulation of the parties in that suit that the agreement had been signed by owners of 95 per cent of all the frontage, the court had adjudged that the agreement was in force, that it was a covenant running with the land and binding all the land within the described area in the hands of the parties to the agreement and those claiming under them including defendants, and had entered its decree restraining the breach of the agreement by the defendants and those claiming under them, and that the appellate court had affirmed the decree. It found that the stipulation was untrue but held, contrary to the trial court, that it was not fraudulent or collusive. It also appears from the record in *Burke v. Kleiman* that the case was tried on an agreed statement of facts which raised only a single issue, whether by reason of changes in the restricted area, the agreement had ceased to be enforcible in equity.

From this the Supreme Court of Illinois concluded in the present case that *Burke v. Kleiman* was a "class" or "representative" suit and that in such a suit "where the remedy is pursued by a plaintiff who has the right to represent the class to which he belongs, other members of the class are bound by the results in the case unless it is reversed or set aside on direct proceedings;" that petitioners in the present suit were members of the class represented by the plaintiffs in the earlier suit and consequently were bound by its decree which had rendered the issue of performance of the condition precedent to the restrictive agreement res judicata, so far as petitioners are concerned. The court thought that the circumstance that the stipulation in the earlier suit that owners of 95 per cent of the frontage had signed the agreement was contrary to the fact as found in the present suit did not militate against this conclusion since the court in the earlier suit had jurisdiction to determine the fact as between the parties before it and that its determination, because of the representative character of the suit, even though erroneous, was binding on petitioners until set aside by a direct attack on the first judgment.

State courts are free to attach such descriptive labels to litigations before them as they may choose and to attribute to them such consequences as they think appropriate under state constitutions and laws, subject only to the requirements of the Constitution of the United States. But when the judgment of a state court, ascribing to the judgment of another court the binding force and effect of res judicata, is challenged for want of due process it becomes the duty of this Court to examine the course of procedure in both litigations to ascertain whether the litigant whose rights have thus been adjudicated has been afforded such notice and opportunity to be heard as are requisite to the due process which the Constitution prescribes.

It is a principle of general application in Anglo–American jurisprudence that one is not bound by a judgment *in personam* in a litigation in which he is not designated as a party or to which he has not been made a party by service of process. *Pennoyer v. Neff.* A judgment rendered in such circumstances is not entitled to the full faith and credit which the Constitution and statute of the United States, *Pennoyer v. Neff,* and judicial action enforcing it against the person or property of the absent party is not that due process which the Fifth and Fourteenth Amendments requires.

To these general rules there is a recognized exception that, to an extent not precisely defined by judicial opinion, the judgment in a "class" or "representative" suit, to which some members of the class are parties, may bind members of the class or those represented who were not made parties to it.

The class suit was an invention of equity to enable it to proceed to a decree in suits where the number of those interested in the subject of the litigation is so great that their joinder as parties in conformity to the usual rules of procedure is impracticable. Courts are not infrequently called upon to proceed with causes in which the number of those interested in the litigation is so great as to make difficult or impossible the joinder of all because some are not within the jurisdiction or because their whereabouts is unknown or where if all were made parties to the suit its continued abatement by the death of some would prevent or unduly delay a decree. In such cases where the interests of those not joined are of the same class as the interests of those who are, and where it is considered that the latter fairly represent the former in the prosecution of the litigation of the issues in which all have a common interest, the court will proceed to a decree.

It is evident that the considerations which may induce a court thus to proceed, despite a technical defect of parties, may differ from those which must be taken into account in determining whether the absent parties are bound by the decree or, if it is adjudged that they are, in ascertaining whether such an adjudication satisfies the requirements of due process and of full faith and credit. Nevertheless there is scope within the framework of the Constitution for holding in appropriate cases that a judgment rendered in a class suit is res judicata as to members of the class who are not formal parties to the suit. Here, as elsewhere, the Fourteenth Amendment does not compel state courts or legislatures to adopt any particular rule for establishing the conclusiveness of judgments in class suits; nor does it compel the adoption of the particular rules thought by this court to be appropriate for the federal courts. With a proper regard for divergent local institutions and interests, this Court is justified in saying that there has been a failure of due process only in those cases where it cannot be said that the procedure adopted, fairly insures the protection of the interests of absent parties who are to be bound by it.

It is familiar doctrine of the federal courts that members of a class not present as parties to the litigation may be bound by the judgment where they are in fact adequately represented by parties who are present, or where they actually participate in the conduct of the litigation in which members of the class are present as parties, or where the interest of the members of the class, some of whom are present as parties, is joint, or where for any other reason the relationship between the parties present and those who are absent is such as legally to entitle the former to stand in judgment for the latter.

In all such cases, so far as it can be said that the members of the class who are present are, by generally recognized rules of law, entitled to stand in judgment for those who are not, we may assume for present purposes that such procedure affords a protection to the parties who are represented though absent, which would satisfy the requirements of due process and full faith and credit. Nor do we find it necessary for the decision of this case to say that, when the only circumstance defining the class is that the determination of the rights of its members turns upon a single issue of fact or law, a state could not constitutionally adopt a procedure whereby some of the members of the class could stand in judgment for all, provided that the procedure were so devised and applied as to insure that those present are of the same class as those absent and that the litigation is so conducted as to insure the full and fair consideration of the common issue. We decide only that the procedure and the course of litigation sustained here by the plea of res judicata do not satisfy these requirements.

The restrictive agreement did not purport to create a joint obligation or liability. It valid and effective its promises were the several obligations of the signers and those claiming under them. The promises ran severally to every other signer. It is plain that in such circumstances all those alleged to be bound by the agreement would not constitute a single class in any litigation brought to enforce it. Those who sought to secure its benefits by enforcing it could not be said to be in the same class with or represent those whose interest was in resisting performance, for the agreement by its terms imposes obligations and confers rights on the owner of each plot of land who signs it. If those who thus seek to secure the benefits of the agreement were rightly regarded by the state Supreme Court as constituting a class, it is evident that those signers or their successors who are interested in challenging the validity of the agreement and resisting its performance are not of the same class in the sense that their interests are identical so that any group who had elected to enforce rights conferred by the agreement could be said to be acting in the interest of any others who were free to deny its obligation.

Because of the dual and potentially conflicting interests of those who are putative parties to the agreement in compelling or resisting its performance, it is impossible to say, solely because they are parties to it, that any two of them are of the same class. Nor without more, and with the due regard for the protection of the rights of absent parties which due process exacts, can some be permitted to stand in judgment for all.

It is one thing to say that some members of a class may represent other members in a litigation where the sole and common interest of the class in the litigation, is either to assert a common right or to challenge an asserted obligation. It is quite another to hold that all those who are free alternatively either to assert rights or to challenge them are of a single class, so that any group merely because it is of the class so constituted, may be deemed adequately to represent any others of the class in litigating their interests in either alternative. Such a selection of representatives for purposes of litigation, whose substantial interests are not necessarily or even probably the same as those whom they are deemed to represent, does not afford that protection to absent parties which due process requires. The doctrine of representation of absent parties in a class suit has not hitherto been thought to go so far. Apart from the opportunities it would afford for the fraudulent and collusive sacrifice of the rights of absent parties, we think that the representation in this case no more satisfies the requirements of due process than a trial by a judicial officer who is in such situation that he may have an interest in the outcome of the litigation in conflict with that of the litigants.

The plaintiffs in the *Burke* case sought to compel performance of the agreement in behalf of themselves and all others similarly situated. They did not designate the defendants in the suit as a class or seek any injunction or other relief against others than the named defendants, and the decree which was entered did not purport to bind others. In seeking to enforce the agreement the plaintiffs in that suit were not representing the petitioners here whose substantial interest is in resisting performance. The defendants in the first suit were not treated by the pleadings or decree as representing others or as foreclosing by their defense the rights of others, and even though nominal defendants, it does not appear that their interest in defeating the contract outweighed their interest in establishing its validity. For a court in this situation to ascribe to either the plaintiffs or defendants the performance of such functions on behalf of petitioners here, is to attribute to them a power that it cannot be said that they had assumed to exercise, and a responsibility which, in view of their dual interests it does not appear that they could rightly discharge.

Reversed.

* * *

B. CLASS CERTIFICATION

FEDERAL RULE OF CIVIL PROCEDURE 23. CLASS ACTIONS

(a) **Prerequisites.** One or more members of a class may sue or be sued as representative parties on behalf of all members only if:

(1) the class is so numerous that joinder of all members is impracticable;

(2) there are questions of law or fact common to the class;

(3) the claims or defenses of the representative parties are typical of the claims or defenses of the class; and

(4) the representative parties will fairly and adequately protect the interests of the class.

(b) Types of Class Actions. A class action may be maintained if Rule 23(a) is satisfied and if:

(1) prosecuting separate actions by or against individual class members would create a risk of:

    (A) inconsistent or varying adjudications with respect to individual class members that would establish incompatible standards of conduct for the party opposing the class; or

    (B) adjudications with respect to individual class members that, as a practical matter, would be dispositive of the interests of the other members not parties to the individual adjudications or would substantially impair or impede their ability to protect their interests;

(2) the party opposing the class has acted or refused to act on grounds that apply generally to the class, so that final injunctive relief or corresponding declaratory relief is appropriate respecting the class as a whole; or

(3) the court finds that the questions of law or fact common to class members predominate over any questions affecting only individual members, and that a class action is superior to other available methods for fairly and efficiently adjudicating the controversy. The matters pertinent to these findings include:

    (A) the class members' interests in individually controlling the prosecution or defense of separate actions;

    (B) the extent and nature of any litigation concerning the controversy already begun by or against class members;

    (C) the desirability or undesirability of concentrating the litigation of the claims in the particular forum; and

    (D) the likely difficulties in managing a class action.

(c) Certification Order; Notice to Class Members; Judgment; Issues Classes; Subclasses.

(1) Certification Order.

    (A) Time to Issue. At an early practicable time after a person sues or is sued as a class representative, the court must determine by order whether to certify the action as a class action.

    (B) Defining the Class; Appointing Class Counsel. An order that certifies a class action must define the class and the class claims, issues, or defenses, and must appoint class counsel under Rule 23(g).

(C) **Altering or Amending the Order.** An order that grants or denies class certification may be altered or amended before final judgment.

(2) **Notice.**

(A) **For (b)(1) or (b)(2) Classes.** For any class certified under Rule 23(b) or (b)(2), the court may direct appropriate notice to the class.

(B) **For (b)(3) Classes.** For any class certified under Rule 23(b)(3), the court must direct to class members the best notice that is practicable under the circumstances, including individual notice to all members who can be identified through reasonable effort. The notice must clearly and concisely state in plain, easily understood language:

(i) the nature of the action;

(ii) the definition of the class certified;

(iii) the class claims, issues, or defenses;

(iv) that a class member may enter an appearance through an attorney if the member so desires;

(v) that the court will exclude from the class any member who requests exclusion;

(vi) the time and manner for requesting exclusion; and

(vii) the binding effect of a class judgment on members under Rule 23(c)(3).

(3) **Judgment.** Whether or not favorable to the class, the judgment in a class action must:

(A) for any class certified under Rule 23(b)(1) or (b)(2), include and describe those whom the court finds to be class members; and

(B) for any class certified under Rule 23(b)(3), include and specify or describe those to whom the Rule 23(c)(2) notice was directed, who have not requested exclusion, and whom the court finds to be class members.

(4) **Particular Issues.** When appropriate, an action may be brought or maintained as a class action with respect to particular issues.

(5) **Subclasses.** When appropriate, a class may be divided into subclasses that are each treated as a class under this rule.

(d) **Conducting the Action.**

(1) **In General.** In conducting an action under this rule, the court may issue orders that:

(A) determine the course of proceedings or prescribe measures to prevent undue repetition or complication in presenting evidence or argument;

(**B**) require—to protect class members and fairly conduct the action—giving appropriate notice to some or all class members of:

    (**i**) any step in the action;

    (**ii**) the proposed extent of the judgment; or

    (**iii**) the members' opportunity to signify whether they consider the representation fair and adequate, to intervene and present claims or defenses, or to otherwise come into the action;

(**C**) impose conditions on the representative parties or on intervenors;

(**D**) require that the pleadings be amended to eliminate allegations about representation of absent persons and that the action proceed accordingly; or

(**E**) deal with similar procedural matters.

(**2**) **Combining and Amending Orders.** An order under Rule 23(d)(1) may be altered or amended from time to time and may be combined with an order under Rule 16.

(**e**) **Settlement, Voluntary Dismissal, or Compromise.** The claims, issues, or defenses of a certified class may be settled, voluntarily dismissed, or compromised only with the court's approval. The following procedures apply to a proposed settlement, voluntary dismissal, or compromise:

(**1**) The court must direct notice in a reasonable manner to all class members who would be bound by the proposal.

(**2**) If the proposal would bind class members, the court may approve it only after a hearing and on finding that it is fair, reasonable, and adequate.

(**3**) The parties seeking approval must file a statement identifying any agreement made in connection with the proposal.

(**4**) If the class action was previously certified under Rule 23(b)(3), the court may refuse to approve a settlement unless it affords a new opportunity to request exclusion to individual class members who had an earlier opportunity to request exclusion but did not do so.

(**5**) Any class member may object to the proposal if it requires court approval under this subdivision (e); the objection may be withdrawn only with the court's approval.

(**f**) **Appeals.** A court of appeals may permit an appeal from an order granting or denying class-action certification under this rule if a petition for permission to appeal is filed with the circuit clerk within 14 days after the order is entered. An appeal does not stay proceedings in the district court unless the district judge or the court of appeals so orders.

(g) Class Counsel.

(1) Appointing Class Counsel. Unless a statute provides otherwise, a court that certifies a class must appoint class counsel. In appointing class counsel, the court:

(A) must consider:

(i) the work counsel has done in identifying or investigating potential claims in the action;

(ii) counsel's experience in handling class actions, other complex litigation, and the types of claims asserted in the action;

(iii) counsel's knowledge of the applicable law; and

(iv) the resources that counsel will commit to representing the class;

(B) may consider any other matter pertinent to counsel's ability to fairly and adequately represent the interests of the class;

(C) may order potential class counsel to provide information on any subject pertinent to the appointment and to propose terms for attorney's fees and nontaxable costs;

(D) may include in the appointing order provisions about the award of attorney's fees or nontaxable costs under Rule 23(h); and

(E) may make further orders in connection with the appointment.

(2) Standard for Appointing Class Counsel. When one applicant seeks appointment as class counsel, the court may appoint that applicant only if the applicant is adequate under Rule 23(g)(1) and (4). If more than one adequate applicant seeks appointment, the court must appoint the applicant best able to represent the interests of the class.

(3) Interim Counsel. The court may designate interim counsel to act on behalf of a putative class before determining whether to certify the action as a class action.

(4) Duty of Class Counsel. Class counsel must fairly and adequately represent the interests of the class.

(h) Attorney's Fees and Nontaxable Costs. In a certified class action, the court may award reasonable attorney's fees and nontaxable costs that are authorized by law or by the parties' agreement. The following procedures apply:

(1) A claim for an award must be made by motion under Rule 54(d)(2), subject to the provisions of this subdivision (h), at a time the court sets. Notice of the motion must be served on all parties and, for motions by class counsel, directed to class members in a reasonable manner.

(2) A class member, or a party from whom payment is sought, may object to the motion.

(3) The court may hold a hearing and must find the facts and state its legal conclusions under Rule 52(a).

(4) The court may refer issues related to the amount of the award to a special master or a magistrate judge, as provided in Rule 54(d)(2)(D).

* * *

IN THE MATTER OF RHONE–POULENC RORER INC.

51 F.3d 1293 (7th Cir. 1995)

POSNER, CHIEF JUDGE.

Drug companies that manufacture blood solids are the defendants in a nationwide class action brought on behalf of hemophiliacs infected by the AIDS virus as a consequence of using the defendants' products. The defendants have filed with us a petition for mandamus, asking us to direct the district judge to rescind his order certifying the case as a class action. We have no *appellate* jurisdiction over that order. * * *

The suit to which the petition for mandamus relates, arises out of the infection of a substantial fraction of the hemophiliac population of this country by the AIDS virus because the blood supply was contaminated by the virus before the nature of the disease was well understood or adequate methods of screening the blood supply existed. The AIDS virus (HIV-human immunodeficiency virus) is transmitted by the exchange of bodily fluids, primarily semen and blood. Hemophiliacs depend on blood solids that contain the clotting factors whose absence defines their disease. These blood solids are concentrated from blood obtained from many donors. If just one of the donors is infected with the AIDS virus the probability that the blood solids manufactured in part from his blood will be infected is very high unless the blood is treated with heat to kill the virus.

First identified in 1981, AIDS was diagnosed in hemophiliacs beginning in 1982, and by 1984 the medical community agreed that the virus was transmitted by blood as well as by semen. That year it was demonstrated that treatment with heat could kill the virus in the blood supply and in the following year a reliable test for the presence of the virus in blood was developed. By this time, however, a large number of hemophiliacs had become infected. Since 1984 physicians have been advised to place hemophiliacs on heat-treated blood solids, and since 1985 all blood donated for the manufacture of blood solids has been screened and supplies discovered to be HIV-positive have been discarded. Supplies that test negative still are heat-treated, because the test is not infallible and in particular may fail to detect the virus in persons who became infected within six months before taking the test.

The plaintiffs have presented evidence that 2,000 hemophiliacs have died of AIDS and that half or more of the remaining U.S. hemophiliac population of 20,000 may be HIV-positive. Unless there are dramatic breakthroughs in the treatment of HIV or AIDS, all infected persons will die from the disease. The reason so many are infected even though the supply of blood for the manufacture of blood solids (as for transfusions) has been safe since the mid–80s is that the disease has a very long incubation period; the median period for hemophiliacs may be as long as 11 years. Probably most of the hemophiliacs who are now HIV-positive, or have AIDS, or have died of AIDS were infected in the early 1980s, when the blood supply was contaminated.

Some 300 lawsuits, involving some 400 plaintiffs, have been filed, 60 percent of them in state courts, 40 percent in federal district courts under the diversity jurisdiction, seeking to impose tort liability on the defendants for the transmission of HIV to hemophiliacs in blood solids manufactured by the defendants. Obviously these 400 plaintiffs represent only a small fraction of the hemophiliacs (or their next of kin, in cases in which the hemophiliac has died) who are infected by HIV or have died of AIDS. One of the 300 cases is *Wadleigh,* filed in September 1993, the case that the district judge certified as a class action. Thirteen other cases have been tried already in various courts around the country, and the defendants have won twelve of them. All the cases brought in federal court (like *Wadleigh*)—cases brought under the diversity jurisdiction—have been consolidated for pretrial discovery in the Northern District of Illinois by the panel on multidistrict litigation.

The plaintiffs advance two principal theories of liability. The first is that before anyone had heard of AIDS or HIV, it was known that Hepatitis B, a lethal disease though less so than HIV–AIDS, could be transmitted either through blood transfusions or through injection of blood solids. The plaintiffs argue that due care with respect to the risk of infection with Hepatitis B required the defendants to take measures to purge that virus from their blood solids, whether by treating the blood they bought or by screening the donors—perhaps by refusing to deal with *paid* donors, known to be a class at high risk of being infected with Hepatitis B. The defendants' failure to take effective measures was, the plaintiffs claim, negligent. Had the defendants not been negligent, the plaintiffs further argue, hemophiliacs would have been protected not only against Hepatitis B but also, albeit fortuitously or as the plaintiffs put it "serendipitously," against HIV.

The plaintiffs' second theory of liability is more conventional. It is that the defendants, again negligently, dragged their heels in screening donors and taking other measures to prevent contamination of blood solids by HIV when they learned about the disease in the early 1980s. The plaintiffs have other theories of liability as well, including strict products liability, but it is not necessary for us to get into them.

The district judge did not think it feasible to certify *Wadleigh* as a class action for the adjudication of the entire controversy between the plaintiffs and the defendants. Fed. R. Civ. P. 23(b)(3). The differences in the date of infection alone of the thousands of potential class members would make such a procedure infeasible. Hemophiliacs infected before anyone knew about the contamination of blood solids by HIV could not rely on the second theory of liability, while hemophiliacs infected after the blood supply became safe (not perfectly safe, but nearly so) probably were not infected by any of the defendants' products. Instead the judge certified the suit "as a class action with respect to particular issues" only. Fed. R. Civ. P. 23(c)(4)(A). He explained this decision in an opinion which implied that he did not envisage the entry of a final judgment but rather the rendition by a jury of a special verdict that would answer a number of questions bearing, perhaps decisively, on whether the defendants are negligent under either of the theories sketched above. If the special verdict found no negligence under either theory, that presumably would be the end of all the cases unless other theories of liability proved viable. If the special verdict found negligence, individual members of the class would then file individual tort suits in state and federal district courts around the nation and would use the special verdict, in conjunction with the doctrine of collateral estoppel, to block relitigation of the issue of negligence.

With all due respect for the district judge's commendable desire to experiment with an innovative procedure for streamlining the adjudication of this "mass tort," we believe that his plan so far exceeds the permissible bounds of discretion in the management of federal litigation as to compel us to intervene and order decertification.

* * * Nevertheless we shall assume in accordance with the judge's letter that eventually there will be a final judgment to review. Only it will come too late to provide effective relief to the defendants; and this is an important consideration in relation to the first condition for mandamus, that the challenged ruling of the district court have inflicted irreparable harm, which is to say harm that cannot be rectified by an appeal from the final judgment in the lawsuit. The reason that an appeal will come too late to provide effective relief for these defendants is the sheer *magnitude* of the risk to which the class action, in contrast to the individual actions pending or likely, exposes them. Consider the situation that would obtain if the class had not been certified. The defendants would be facing 300 suits. More might be filed, but probably only a few more, because the statutes of limitations in the various states are rapidly expiring for potential plaintiffs. The blood supply has been safe since 1985. That is ten years ago. The risk to hemophiliacs of having become infected with HIV has been widely publicized; it is unlikely that many hemophiliacs are unaware of it. Under the usual discovery statute of limitations, they would have to have taken steps years ago to determine their infection status, and

having found out file suit within the limitations period running from the date of discovery, in order to preserve their rights.

Three hundred is not a trivial number of lawsuits. The potential damages in each one are great. But the defendants have won twelve of the first thirteen, and, if this is a representative sample, they are likely to win most of the remaining ones as well. Perhaps in the end, if class-action treatment is denied (it has been denied in all the other hemophiliac HIV suits in which class certification has been sought), they will be compelled to pay damages in only 25 cases, involving a potential liability of perhaps no more than $125 million altogether. These are guesses, of course, but they are at once conservative and usable for the limited purpose of comparing the situation that will face the defendants if the class certification stands. All of a sudden they will face thousands of plaintiffs. Many may already be barred by the statute of limitations, as we have suggested, though its further running was tolled by the filing of *Wadleigh* as a class action.

Suppose that 5,000 of the potential class members are not yet barred by the statute of limitations. And suppose the named plaintiffs in *Wadleigh* win the class portion of this case to the extent of establishing the defendants' liability under either of the two negligence theories. It is true that this would only be prima facie liability, that the defendants would have various defenses. But they could not be confident that the defenses would prevail. They might, therefore, easily be facing $25 billion in potential liability (conceivably more), and with it bankruptcy. They may not wish to roll these dice. That is putting it mildly. They will be under intense pressure to settle. If they settle, the class certification—the ruling that will have forced them to settle—will never be reviewed. Judge Friendly, who was not given to hyperbole, called settlements induced by a small probability of an immense judgment in a class action "blackmail settlements." Judicial concern about them is legitimate, not "sociological," as it was derisively termed in *In re Sugar Antitrust Litigation.*

The defendants did not mention their concern about settlement pressures until the oral argument of this appeal, so we should consider whether the argument is waived and we therefore cannot consider it. If a party fails to present a ground for reversal, the appeals court will not supply it; this is the doctrine of waiver. The doctrine is not that if the party fails to offer a particular reason for its position, the court cannot consider that reason. Were that the rule, the role of an appellate court would be confined to weighing the reasons, pro and con a particular ground, that the parties happened to proffer. Appellate consideration so truncated could not produce durable rules to guide decision in future cases; judicial opinions would be impoverished if all they did were call balls and strikes. The defendants here properly asserted as the basis for mandamus the two necessary conditions: irreparable harm and clear violation of right. For obvious reasons they did not point out in support of the first condition that if mandamus is denied they will be forced to settle—for such an acknowledgment would greatly weaken them in any settlement negotiations. We should be realistic about what is feasible to put in a public brief.

We do not want to be misunderstood as saying that class actions are bad because they place pressure on defendants to settle. That pressure is a reality, but it must be balanced against the undoubted benefits of the class action that have made it an authorized procedure for employment by federal courts. We have yet to consider the balance. All that our discussion to this point has shown is that the first condition for the grant of mandamus—that the challenged ruling not be effectively reviewable at the end of the case—is fulfilled. The ruling will inflict irreparable harm; the next question is whether the ruling can fairly be described as usurpative. We have formulated this second condition as narrowly, as stringently, as can be, but even so formulated we think it is fulfilled. We do not mean to suggest that the district judge is engaged in a deliberate power-grab. We have no reason to suppose that he *wants* to preside over an unwieldy class action. We believe that he was responding imaginatively and in the best of faith to the challenge that mass torts, graphically illustrated by the avalanche of asbestos litigation, pose for the federal courts. But the plan that he has devised for the HIV-hemophilia litigation exceeds the bounds of allowable judicial discretion. Three concerns, none of them necessarily sufficient in itself but cumulatively compelling, persuade us to this conclusion.

The first is a concern with forcing these defendants to stake their companies on the outcome of a single jury trial, or be forced by fear of the risk of bankruptcy to settle even if they have no legal liability, when it is entirely feasible to allow a final, authoritative determination of their liability for the colossal misfortune that has befallen the hemophiliac population to emerge from a decentralized process of multiple trials, involving different juries, and different standards of liability, in different jurisdictions; and when, in addition, the preliminary indications are that the defendants are not liable for the grievous harm that has befallen the members of the class. These qualifications are important. In most class actions-and those the ones in which the rationale for the procedure is most compelling-individual suits are infeasible because the claim of each class member is tiny relative to the expense of litigation. That plainly is not the situation here. A notable feature of this case, and one that has not been remarked upon or encountered, so far as we are aware, in previous cases, is the demonstrated great likelihood that the plaintiffs' claims, despite their human appeal, lack legal merit. This is the inference from the defendants' having won 92.3 percent (12/13) of the cases to have gone to judgment. Granted, thirteen is a small sample and further trials, if they are held, may alter the pattern that the sample reveals. But whether they do or not, the result will be robust if these further trials are permitted to go forward, because the pattern that results will reflect a consensus, or at least a pooling of judgment, of many different tribunals.

For this consensus or maturing of judgment the district judge proposes to substitute a single trial before a single jury instructed in accordance with no actual law of any jurisdiction—a jury that will receive a kind of Esperanto instruction, merging the negligence standards of the 50 states and the District of Columbia. One jury, consisting of six persons (the standard federal civil jury nowadays consists of six regular jurors and two alternates), will hold the fate of an industry in the palm of its hand. This jury, jury number fourteen, may disagree with twelve of the previous thirteen juries—and hurl the industry into bankruptcy. That kind of thing can happen in our system of civil justice (it is not likely to happen, because the industry is likely to settle—whether or not it really is liable) without violating anyone's legal rights. But it need not be tolerated when the alternative exists of submitting an issue to multiple juries constituting in the aggregate a much larger and more diverse sample of decision-makers. That would not be a feasible option if the stakes to each class member were too slight to repay the cost of suit, even though the aggregate stakes were very large and would repay the costs of a consolidated proceeding. But this is not the case with regard to the HIV-hemophilia litigation. Each plaintiff if successful is apt to receive a judgment in the millions. With the aggregate stakes in the tens or hundreds of millions of dollars, or even in the billions, it is not a waste of judicial resources to conduct more than one trial, before more than six jurors, to determine whether a major segment of the international pharmaceutical industry is to follow the asbestos manufacturers into Chapter 11.

We have hinted at the second reason for concern that the district judge exceeded the bounds of permissible judicial discretion. He proposes to have a jury determine the negligence of the defendants under a legal standard that does not actually exist anywhere in the world. One is put in mind of the concept of "general" common law that prevailed in the era of *Swift v. Tyson*. The assumption is that the common law of the 50 states and the District of Columbia, at least so far as bears on a claim of negligence against drug companies, is basically uniform and can be abstracted in a single instruction. It is no doubt true that at some level of generality the law of negligence is one, not only nationwide but worldwide. Negligence is a failure to take due care, and due care a function of the probability and magnitude of an accident and the costs of avoiding it. A jury can be asked whether the defendants took due care. And in many cases such differences as there are among the tort rules of the different states would not affect the outcome. The Second Circuit was willing to assume *dubitante* that this was true of the issues certified for class determination in the *Agent Orange* litigation.

We doubt that it is true in general, and we greatly doubt that it is true in a case such as this in which one of the theories pressed by the plaintiffs, the "serendipity" theory, is novel. If one instruction on negligence will serve to instruct the jury on the legal standard of every state of the United States applicable to a novel claim, implying that the claim despite its controversiality would be decided identically in all 50 states and the District of Columbia, one wonders what the Supreme Court thought it was doing in the *Erie* case when it held that it was *unconstitutional* for federal courts in diversity cases to apply general common law rather than the common law of the state whose law would apply if the case were being tried in state rather than federal court. *Erie R.R. v. Tompkins*. The law of negligence, including subsidiary concepts such as duty of care, foreseeability, and proximate cause, may as the plaintiffs have argued forcefully to us differ among the states only in nuance, though we think not, for a reason discussed later. But nuance can be important, and its significance is suggested by a comparison of differing state pattern instructions on negligence and differing judicial formulations of the meaning of negligence and the subordinate concepts. "The common law is not a brooding omnipresence in the sky, but the articulate voice of some sovereign or quasi sovereign that can be identified." The voices of the quasi-sovereigns that are the states of the United States sing negligence with a different pitch.

The "serendipity" theory advanced by the plaintiffs in *Wadleigh* is that if the defendants did not do enough to protect hemophiliacs from the risk of Hepatitis B, they are liable to hemophiliacs for any consequences—including infection by the more dangerous and at the time completely unknown AIDS virus—that proper measures against Hepatitis B would, all unexpectedly, have averted. This theory of liability, dispenses, rightly or wrongly from the standpoint of the Platonic Form of negligence, with proof of foreseeability, even though a number of states, in formulating their tests for negligence, incorporate the foreseeability of the risk into the test. These states follow Judge Cardozo's famous opinion in *Palsgraf v. Long Island R.R.*, under which the HIV plaintiffs might (we do not say would—we express no view on the substantive issues in this litigation) be barred from recovery on the ground that they were unforeseeable victims of the alleged failure of the defendants to take adequate precautions against infecting hemophiliacs with Hepatitis B and that therefore the drug companies had not violated any duty of care to them.

The plaintiffs' second theory focuses on the questions when the defendants should have learned about the danger of HIV in the blood supply and when, having learned about it, they should have taken steps to eliminate the danger or at least warn hemophiliacs or their physicians of it. These questions also may be sensitive to the precise way in which a state formulates its standard of negligence. If not, one begins to wonder why this country bothers with different state legal systems.

Both theories, incidentally, may be affected by differing state views on the role of industry practice or custom in determining the existence of negligence. In some states, the standard of care for a physician, hospital, or other provider of medical services, including blood banks, is a professional standard, that is, the standard fixed by the relevant profession. In others, it is the standard of ordinary care, which may, depending on judge or jury, exceed the professional standard. Which approach a state follows, and whether in those states that follow the professional-standard approach manufacturers of blood solids would be assimilated to blood banks as providers of medical services entitled to shelter under the professional standard, could make a big difference in the liability of these manufacturers. We note that persons infected by HIV through blood transfusions appear to have had little better luck suing blood banks than HIV-positive hemophiliacs have had suing the manufacturers of blood solids.

The diversity jurisdiction of the federal courts is, after *Erie,* designed merely to provide an alternative forum for the litigation of state-law claims, not an alternative system of substantive law for diversity cases. But under the district judge's plan the thousands of members of the plaintiff class will have their rights determined, and the four defendant manufacturers will have their duties determined, under a law that is merely an amalgam, an averaging, of the non-identical negligence laws of 51 jurisdictions. No one doubts that Congress could constitutionally prescribe a uniform standard of liability for manufacturers of blood solids. It might we suppose promulgate pertinent provisions of the *Restatement (Second) of Torts.* The point of *Erie* is that Article III of the Constitution does not empower the federal courts to create such a regime for diversity cases.

If in the course of individual litigations by HIV-positive hemophiliacs juries render special verdicts that contain findings which do not depend on the differing state standards of negligence-for example a finding concerning the date at which one or more of the defendants learned of the danger of HIV contamination of the blood supply—these findings may be given collateral estoppel effect in other lawsuits, at least in states that allow "offensive" use of collateral estoppel. In that way the essential purpose of the class action crafted by Judge Grady will be accomplished. If there are relevant differences in state law, findings in one suit will not be given collateral estoppel effect in others—and that is as it should be.

The plaintiffs argue that an equally important purpose of the class certification is to overcome the shyness or shame that many people feel at acknowledging that they have AIDS or are HIV-positive even when the source of infection is not a stigmatized act. That, the plaintiffs tell us, is why so few HIV-positive hemophiliacs have sued. We do not see how a class action limited to a handful of supposedly common issues can alleviate *that* problem. Any class member who wants a share in any judgment for damages or in any settlement will have to step forward at some point and identify himself as having AIDS or being HIV-positive. He will have to offer jury findings as collateral estoppel, overcome the defendants' defenses to liability (including possible efforts to show that the class member became infected with HIV through a source other than the defendants' product), and establish his damages. If the privacy of these class members in these follow-on proceedings to the class action is sought to be protected by denominating them "John Does," that is something that can equally well be done in individual lawsuits. The "John Doe" device—and with it the issue of privacy—is independent of class certification.

The third respect in which we believe that the district judge has exceeded his authority concerns the point at which his plan of action proposes to divide the trial of the issues that he has certified for class-action treatment from the other issues involved in the thousands of actual and potential claims of the representatives and members of the class. Bifurcation and even finer divisions of lawsuits into separate trials are authorized in federal district courts. Fed.R.Civ.P. 42(b). And a decision to employ the procedure is reviewed deferentially. However, as we have been at pains to stress recently, the district judge must carve at the joint. Of particular relevance here, the judge must not divide issues between separate trials in such a way that the same issue is reexamined by different juries. The problem is not inherent in bifurcation. It does not arise when the same jury is to try the successive phases of the litigation. But most of the separate "cases" that compose this class action will be tried, after the initial trial in the Northern District of Illinois, in different courts, scattered throughout the country. The right to a jury trial in federal civil cases, conferred by the Seventh Amendment, is a right to have juriable issues determined by the first jury impaneled to hear them (provided there are no errors warranting a new trial), and not reexamined by another finder of fact. This would be obvious if the second finder of fact were a judge. *Byrd v. Blue Ridge Rural Electric Cooperative, Inc.* But it is equally true if it is another jury. In this limited sense, a jury verdict can have collateral estoppel effect.

The plan of the district judge in this case is inconsistent with the principle that the findings of one jury are not to be reexamined by a second, or third, or nth jury. The first jury will not determine liability. It will determine merely whether one or more of the defendants was negligent under one of the two theories. The first jury may go on to decide the additional issues with regard to the named plaintiffs. But it will not decide them with regard to the other class members. Unless the defendants settle, a second (and third, and fourth, and hundredth, and conceivably thousandth) jury will have to decide, in individual follow-on litigation by class members not named as plaintiffs in the *Wadleigh* case, such issues as comparative negligence—did any class members knowingly continue to use unsafe blood solids after they learned or should have learned of the risk of contamination with HIV?—and proximate causation. Both issues overlap the issue of the defendants' negligence. Comparative negligence entails, as the name implies, a comparison of the degree of negligence of plaintiff and defendant. Proximate causation is found by determining whether the harm to the plaintiff followed in some sense naturally, uninterruptedly, and with reasonable probability from the negligent act of the defendant. It overlaps the issue of the defendants' negligence even when the state's law does not (as many states do) make the foreseeability of the risk to which the defendant subjected the plaintiff an explicit ingredient of negligence. A second or subsequent jury might find that the defendants' failure to take precautions against infection with Hepatitis B could not be thought the *proximate* cause of the plaintiffs' infection with HIV, a different and unknown blood-borne virus. How the resulting inconsistency between juries could be prevented escapes us.

The protection of the right conferred by the Seventh Amendment to trial by jury in federal civil cases is a traditional office of the writ of mandamus. *Beacon Theatres v. Westover*; *Dairy Queen, Inc. v. Wood*. When the writ is used for that purpose, strict compliance with the stringent conditions on the availability of the writ (including the requirement of proving irreparable harm) is excused. In *Beacon,* for example, if the judge had gone ahead and tried the equitable claims first and made his decision collateral estoppel in the subsequent jury trial, the losing party would have been entitled to a new trial, wiping out the judge's decision. There was no irreparable harm, yet mandamus was granted—which is one reason why we have said that the use of the writ cannot be reduced to formula. But the looming infringement of Seventh Amendment rights is only one of our grounds for believing this to be a case in which the issuance of a writ of mandamus is warranted. The others as we have said are the undue and unnecessary risk of a monumental industry-busting error in entrusting the determination of potential multi-billion dollar liabilities to a single jury when the results of the previous cases indicate that the defendants' liability is doubtful at best and the questionable constitutionality of trying a diversity case under a legal standard in force in no state. We need not consider whether any of these grounds standing by itself would warrant mandamus in this case. Together they make a compelling case.

We know that an approach similar to that proposed by Judge Grady has been approved for asbestos litigation. Most federal courts, however, refuse to permit the use of the class-action device in mass-tort cases, even asbestos cases. Those courts that have permitted it have been criticized, and alternatives have been suggested which recognize that a sample of trials makes more sense than entrusting the fate of an industry to a single jury. The number of asbestos cases was so great as to exert a well-nigh irresistible pressure to bend the normal rules. No comparable pressure is exerted by the HIV-hemophilia litigation. That litigation can be handled in the normal way without undue inconvenience to the parties or to the state or federal courts.

The defendants have pointed out other serious problems with the district judge's plan, but it is unnecessary to discuss them. The petition for a writ of mandamus is granted, and the district judge is directed to decertify the plaintiff class.

ILANA DIAMOND ROVNER, CIRCUIT JUDGE, dissenting.

The majority today takes the extraordinary step of granting defendants' petition for a writ of mandamus and directing the district court to rescind its order certifying the plaintiff class. Although certification orders like this one are not immediately appealable, the majority seizes upon our mandamus powers to effectively circumvent that rule. Because, in my view, our consideration of Judge Grady's decision to certify an issue class under Fed. R. Civ. P. 23(c)(4) should await an appeal from the final judgment in *Wadleigh,* I would deny the writ.

* * * Finally, although the availability of review on direct appeal after final judgment makes it unnecessary for me to discuss the merits of the certification order, the majority's arguments addressed to the propriety of forcing "defendants to stake their companies on the outcome of a single jury trial" or of allowing a single jury to "hold the fate of an industry in the palm of its hand" seem to me at odds with Fed. R. Civ. P. 23 itself. That rule expressly permits class treatment of such claims when its requirements are met, regardless of the magnitude of potential liability. And I see nothing in Rule 23, or in any of the relevant cases, that would make likelihood of success on the merits a prerequisite for class certification. The majority's preference for avoiding a class trial and for submitting the negligence issue "to multiple juries constituting in the aggregate a much larger and more diverse sample of decision-makers" is a rationale for amending the rule, not for avoiding its application in a specific case.

I must concede that I too have doubts about whether the class trial proposed by Judge Grady will succeed, and I sympathize with many of the apprehensions of my brothers. But in my view, the law requires that Judge Grady's plan be given the opportunity to succeed. Class certification orders are, after all, conditional orders subject to modification or revocation as the circumstances warrant. Fed. R. Civ. P. 23(c)(1). If the problems envisioned by the majority were to materialize at a class trial, Judge Grady could always modify his earlier ruling or even abandon it altogether, and his response in that regard would be reviewable by this court on direct appeal, once the actual ramifications of the certification order were evident.

I respectfully dissent.

* * *

C. JURISDICTION AND CHOICE OF LAW ISSUES

28 U.S.C. § 1332(d). CLASS ACTIONS; DIVERSITY OF CITIZENSHIP; AMOUNT IN CONTROVERSY

(d) (1) In this subsection—

> **(A)** the term "class" means all of the class members in a class action;

> **(B)** the term "class action" means any civil action filed under rule 23 of the Federal Rules of Civil Procedure or similar State statute or rule of judicial procedure authorizing an action to be brought by 1 or more representative persons as a class action;

> **(C)** the term "class certification order" means an order issued by a court approving the treatment of some or all aspects of a civil action as a class action; and

(D) the term "class members" means the persons (named or unnamed) who fall within the definition of the proposed or certified class in a class action.

(2) The district courts shall have original jurisdiction of any civil action in which the matter in controversy exceeds the sum or value of $5,000,000, exclusive of interest and costs, and is a class action in which—

(A) any member of a class of plaintiffs is a citizen of a State different from any defendant;

(B) any member of a class of plaintiffs is a foreign state or a citizen or subject of a foreign state and any defendant is a citizen of a State; or

(C) any member of a class of plaintiffs is a citizen of a State and any defendant is a foreign state or a citizen or subject of a foreign state.

(3) A district court may, in the interests of justice and looking at the totality of the circumstances, decline to exercise jurisdiction under paragraph (2) over a class action in which greater than one-third but less than two-thirds of the members of all proposed plaintiff classes in the aggregate and the primary defendants are citizens of the State in which the action was originally filed based on consideration of—

(A) whether the claims asserted involve matters of national or interstate interest;

(B) whether the claims asserted will be governed by laws of the State in which the action was originally filed or by the laws of other States;

(C) whether the class action has been pleaded in a manner that seeks to avoid Federal jurisdiction;

(D) whether the action was brought in a forum with a distinct nexus with the class members, the alleged harm, or the defendants;

(E) whether the number of citizens of the State in which the action was originally filed in all proposed plaintiff classes in the aggregate is substantially larger than the number of citizens from any other State, and the citizenship of the other members of the proposed class is dispersed among a substantial number of States; and

(F) whether, during the 3–year period preceding the filing of that class action, 1 or more other class actions asserting the same or similar claims on behalf of the same or other persons have been filed.

(4) A district court shall decline to exercise jurisdiction under paragraph (2)—

(A) **(i)** over a class action in which—

(I) greater than two-thirds of the members of all proposed plaintiff classes in the aggregate are citizens of the State in which the action was originally filed;

(II) at least 1 defendant is a defendant—

(aa) from whom significant relief is sought by members of the plaintiff class;

(bb) whose alleged conduct forms a significant basis for the claims asserted by the proposed plaintiff class; and

(cc) who is a citizen of the State in which the action was originally filed; and

(III) principal injuries resulting from the alleged conduct or any related conduct of each defendant were incurred in the State in which the action was originally filed; and

(ii) during the 3–year period preceding the filing of that class action, no other class action has been filed asserting the same or similar factual allegations against any of the defendants on behalf of the same or other persons; or

(B) two-thirds or more of the members of all proposed plaintiff classes in the aggregate, and the primary defendants, are citizens of the State in which the action was originally filed.

(5) Paragraphs (2) through (4) shall not apply to any class action in which—

(A) the primary defendants are States, State officials, or other governmental entities against whom the district court may be foreclosed from ordering relief; or

(B) The number of members of all proposed plaintiff classes in the aggregate is less than 100.

(6) In any class action, the claims of the individual class members shall be aggregated to determine whether the matter in controversy exceeds the sum or value of $5,000,000, exclusive of interest and costs.

(7) Citizenship of the members of the proposed plaintiff classes shall be determined for purposes of paragraphs (2) through (6) as of the date of filing of the complaint or amended complaint, or, if the case stated by the initial pleading is not subject to Federal jurisdiction, as of the date of service by plaintiffs of an amended pleading, motion, or other paper, indicating the existence of Federal jurisdiction.

(8) This subsection shall apply to any class action before or after the entry of a class certification order by the court with respect to that action.

(9) Paragraph (2) shall not apply to any class action that solely involves a claim—

     (A) concerning a covered security as defined under 16(f)(3) of the Securities Act of 1933 (15 U.S.C. 78p(f)(3)) and section 28(f)(5)(E) of the Securities Exchange Act of 1934 (15 U.S.C. 78bb(f)(5)(E));

     (B) that relates to the internal affairs or governance of a corporation or other form of business enterprise and that arises under or by virtue of the laws of the State in which such corporation or business enterprise is incorporated or organized; or

     (C) that relates to the rights, duties (including fiduciary duties), and obligations relating to or created by or pursuant to any security (as defined under section 2(a)(1) of the Securities Act of 1933 (15 U.S.C. 77b(a)(1)) and the regulations issued thereunder).

(10) For purposes of this subsection and section 1453, an unincorporated association shall be deemed to be a citizen of the State where it has its principal place of business and the State under whose laws it is organized.

(11) **(A)** For purposes of this subsection and section 1453, a mass action shall be deemed to be a class action removable under paragraphs (2) through (10) if it otherwise meets the provisions of those paragraphs.

     (B) **(i)** As used in subparagraph (A), the term "mass action" means any civil action (except a civil action within the scope of section 1711(2)) in which monetary relief claims of 100 or more persons are proposed to be tried jointly on the ground that the plaintiffs' claims involve common questions of law or fact, except that jurisdiction shall exist only over those plaintiffs whose claims in a mass action satisfy the jurisdictional amount requirements under subsection (a).

     (ii) As used in subparagraph (A), the term "mass action" shall not include any civil action in which—

         (I) all of the claims in the action arise from an event or occurrence in the State in which the action was filed, and that allegedly resulted in injuries in that State or in States contiguous to that State;

         (II) the claims are joined upon motion of a defendant;

         (III) all of the claims in the action are asserted on behalf of the general public (and not on behalf of individual claimants or members of a purported class) pursuant to a State statute specifically authorizing such action; or

(IV) the claims have been consolidated or coordinated solely for pretrial proceedings.

(C) **(i)** Any action(s) removed to Federal court pursuant to this subsection shall not thereafter be transferred to any other court pursuant to section 1407, or the rules promulgated thereunder, unless a majority of the plaintiffs in the action request transfer pursuant to section 1407.

(ii) This subparagraph will not apply—

(I) to cases certified pursuant to rule 23 of the Federal Rules of Civil Procedure; or

(II) if plaintiffs propose that the action proceed as a class action pursuant to rule 23 of the Federal Rules of Civil Procedure.

(D) The limitations periods on any claims asserted in a mass action that is removed to Federal court pursuant to this subsection shall be deemed tolled during the period that the action is pending in Federal court.

* * *

28 U.S.C. § 1453. REMOVAL OF CLASS ACTIONS

(a) Definitions. In this section, the terms "class", "class action", "class certification order", and "class member" shall have the meanings given such terms under section 1332(d)(1).

(b) In general. A class action may be removed to a district court of the United States in accordance with section 1446 (except that the 1-year limitation under section 1446(b) shall not apply), without regard to whether any defendant is a citizen of the State in which the action is brought, except that such action may be removed by any defendant without the consent of all defendants.

(c) Review of remand orders.—

(1) In general. Section 1447 shall apply to any removal of a case under this section, except that notwithstanding section 1447(d), a court of appeals may accept an appeal from an order of a district court granting or denying a motion to remand a class action to the State court from which it was removed if application is made to the court of appeals not less than 10 days after entry of the order.

(2) Time period for judgment. If the court of appeals accepts an appeal under paragraph (1), the court shall complete all action on such appeal, including rendering judgment, not later than 60 days after the date on which such appeal was filed, unless an extension is granted under paragraph (3).

(3) Extension of time period. The court of appeals may grant an extension of the 60–day period described in paragraph (2) if—

(A) all parties to the proceeding agree to such extension, for any period of time; or

(B) such extension is for good cause shown and in the interests of justice, for a period not to exceed 10 days.

(4) Denial of appeal. If a final judgment on the appeal under paragraph (1) is not issued before the end of the period described in paragraph (2), including any extension under paragraph (3), the appeal shall be denied.

(d) Exception. This section shall not apply to any class action that solely involves—

(1) a claim concerning a covered security as defined under section 16(f)(3) of the Securities Act of 1933 (15 U.S.C. 78p(f)(3)) and section 28(f)(5)(E) of the Securities Exchange Act of 1934 (15 U.S.C. 78bb(f)(5)(E));

(2) a claim that relates to the internal affairs or governance of a corporation or other form of business enterprise and arises under or by virtue of the laws of the State in which such corporation or business enterprise is incorporated or organized; or

(3) a claim that relates to the rights, duties (including fiduciary duties), and obligations relating to or created by or pursuant to any security (as defined under section 2(a)(1) of the Securities Act of 1933 (15 U.S.C. 77b(a)(1)) and the regulations issued thereunder).

* * *

PHILLIPS PETROLEUM COMPANY v. SHUTTS

472 U.S. 797 (1985)

JUSTICE REHNQUIST delivered the opinion of the Court.

Petitioner is a Delaware corporation which has its principal place of business in Oklahoma. During the 1970's it produced or purchased natural gas from leased land located in 11 different States, and sold most of the gas in interstate commerce. Respondents are some 28,000 of the royalty owners possessing rights to the leases from which petitioner produced the gas; they reside in all 50 States, the District of Columbia, and several foreign countries. Respondents brought a class action against petitioner in the Kansas state court, seeking to recover interest on royalty payments which had been delayed by petitioner. They recovered judgment in the trial court, and the Supreme Court of Kansas affirmed the judgment over petitioner's contentions that the Due Process Clause of the Fourteenth

Amendment prevented Kansas from adjudicating the claims of all the respondents, and that the Due Process Clause and the Full Faith and Credit Clause of Article IV of the Constitution prohibited the application of Kansas law to all of the transactions between petitioner and respondents. We granted certiorari to consider these claims. We reject petitioner's jurisdictional claim, but sustain its claim regarding the choice of law.

Because petitioner sold the gas to its customers in interstate commerce, it was required to secure approval for price increases from what was then the Federal Power Commission, and is now the Federal Energy Regulatory Commission. Under its regulations the Federal Power Commission permitted petitioner to propose and collect tentative higher gas prices, subject to final approval by the Commission. If the Commission eventually denied petitioner's proposed price increase or reduced the proposed increase, petitioner would have to refund to its customers the difference between the approved price and the higher price charged, plus interest at a rate set by statute.

Although petitioner received higher gas prices pending review by the Commission, petitioner suspended any increase in royalties paid to the royalty owners because the higher price could be subject to recoupment by petitioner's customers. Petitioner agreed to pay the higher royalty only if the royalty owners would provide petitioner with a bond or indemnity for the increase, plus interest, in case the price increase was not ultimately approved and a refund was due to the customers. Petitioner set the interest rate on the indemnity agreements at the same interest rate the Commission would have required petitioner to refund to its customers. A small percentage of the royalty owners provided this indemnity and received royalties immediately from the interim price increases; these royalty owners are unimportant to this case.

The remaining royalty owners received no royalty on the unapproved portion of the prices until the Federal Power Commission approval of those prices became final. Royalties on the unapproved portion of the gas price were suspended three times by petitioner, corresponding to its three proposed price increases in the mid–1970's. In three written opinions the Commission approved all of petitioner's tentative price increases, so petitioner paid to its royalty owners the suspended royalties of $3.7 million in 1976, $4.7 million in 1977, and $2.9 million in 1978. Petitioner paid no interest to the royalty owners although it had the use of the suspended royalty money for a number of years.

Respondents Irl Shutts, Robert Anderson, and Betty Anderson filed suit against petitioner in Kansas state court, seeking interest payments on their suspended royalties which petitioner had possessed pending the Commission's approval of the price increases. Shutts is a resident of Kansas, and the Andersons live in Oklahoma. Shutts and the Andersons own gas leases in Oklahoma and Texas. Over petitioner's objection the Kansas trial court granted respondents' motion to certify the suit as a class action under Kansas law. The class as certified was comprised of

33,000 royalty owners who had royalties suspended by petitioner. The average claim of each royalty owner for interest on the suspended royalties was $100.

After the class was certified respondents provided each class member with notice through first-class mail. The notice described the action and informed each class member that he could appear in person or by counsel; otherwise each member would be represented by Shutts and the Andersons, the named plaintiffs. The notices also stated that class members would be included in the class and bound by the judgment unless they "opted out" of the lawsuit by executing and returning a "request for exclusion" that was included with the notice. The final class as certified contained 28,100 members; 3,400 had "opted out" of the class by returning the request for exclusion, and notice could not be delivered to another 1,500 members, who were also excluded. Less than 1,000 of the class members resided in Kansas. Only a minuscule amount, approximately one quarter of one percent, of the gas leases involved in the lawsuit were on Kansas land.

After petitioner's mandamus petition to decertify the class was denied, the case was tried to the court. The court found petitioner liable under Kansas law for interest on the suspended royalties to all class members. The trial court relied heavily on an earlier, unrelated class action involving the same nominal plaintiff and the same defendant. The Kansas Supreme Court had held that a gas company owed interest to royalty owners for royalties suspended pending final Commission approval of a price increase. No federal statutes touched on the liability for suspended royalties, and the court in *Shutts, Executor* held as a matter of Kansas equity law that the applicable interest rates for computation of interest on suspended royalties were the interest rates at which the gas company would have had to reimburse its customers had its interim price increase been rejected by the Commission. The court viewed these as the fairest interest rates because they were also the rates that petitioner required the royalty owners to meet in their indemnity agreements in order to avoid suspended royalties.

The trial court in the present case applied the rule from *Shutts, Executor,* and held petitioner liable for prejudgment and post-judgment interest on the suspended royalties, computed at the Commission rates governing petitioner's three price increases. The applicable interest rates were: 7% for royalties retained until October 1974; 9% for royalties retained between October 1974 and September 1979; and thereafter at the average prime rate. The trial court did not determine whether any difference existed between the laws of Kansas and other States, or whether another State's laws should be applied to non-Kansas plaintiffs or to royalties from leases in States other than Kansas.

Petitioner raised two principal claims in its appeal to the Supreme Court of Kansas. It first asserted that the Kansas trial court did not possess personal jurisdiction over absent plaintiff class members as required by *International Shoe Co. v. Washington* and similar cases. Related to this first claim was petitioner's contention that the "opt-out" notice to absent class members, which forced them to return the request for exclusion in order to avoid the suit, was insufficient to bind class members who were not residents of Kansas or who did not possess "minimum contacts" with Kansas. Second, petitioner claimed that Kansas courts could not apply Kansas law to every claim in the dispute. The trial court should have looked to the laws of each State where the leases were located to determine, on the basis of conflict of laws principles, whether interest on the suspended royalties was recoverable, and at what rate.

The Supreme Court of Kansas held that the entire cause of action was maintainable under the Kansas class-action statute, and the court rejected both of petitioner's claims. First, it held that the absent class members were plaintiffs, not defendants, and thus the traditional minimum contacts test of *International Shoe* did not apply. The court held that nonresident class-action plaintiffs were only entitled to adequate notice, an opportunity to be heard, an opportunity to opt out of the case, and adequate representation by the named plaintiffs. If these procedural due process minima were met, according to the court, Kansas could assert jurisdiction over the plaintiff class and bind each class member with a judgment on his claim. The court surveyed the course of the litigation and concluded that all of these minima had been met.

The court also rejected petitioner's contention that Kansas law could not be applied to plaintiffs and royalty arrangements having no connection with Kansas. The court stated that generally the law of the forum controlled all claims unless "compelling reasons" existed to apply a different law. The court found no compelling reasons, and noted that "[t]he plaintiff class members have indicated their desire to have this action determined under the laws of Kansas." The court affirmed as a matter of Kansas equity law the award of interest on the suspended royalties, at the rates imposed by the trial court. The court set the postjudgment interest rate on all claims at the Kansas statutory rate of 15%.

I

As a threshold matter we must determine whether petitioner has standing to assert the claim that Kansas did not possess proper jurisdiction over the many plaintiffs in the class who were not Kansas residents and had no connection to Kansas. Respondents claim that a party generally may assert only his own rights, and that petitioner has no standing to assert the rights of its adversary, the plaintiff class, in order to defeat the judgment in favor of the class.

Standing to sue in any Article III court is, of course, a federal question which does not depend on the party's prior standing in state court. Generally stated, federal standing requires an allegation of a present or immediate injury in fact, where the party requesting standing has "alleged such a personal stake in the outcome of the controversy as to assure that concrete adverseness which sharpens the presentation of issues." There must be some causal connection between the asserted injury and the challenged action, and the injury must be of the type "likely to be redressed by a favorable decision."

Additional prudential limitations on standing may exist even though the Article III requirements are met because "the judiciary seeks to avoid deciding questions of broad social import where no individual rights would be vindicated and to limit access to the federal courts to those litigants best suited to assert a particular claim." One of these prudential limits on standing is that a litigant must normally assert his own legal interests rather than those of third parties.

Respondents claim that petitioner is barred by the rule requiring that a party assert only his own rights; they point out that respondents and petitioner are adversaries and do not have allied interests such that petitioner would be a good proponent of class members' interests. They further urge that petitioner's interference is unneeded because the class members have had opportunity to complain about Kansas' assertion of jurisdiction over their claim, but none have done so.

Respondents may be correct that petitioner does not possess standing *jus tertii,* but this is not the issue. Petitioner seeks to vindicate its own interests. As a class-action defendant petitioner is in a unique predicament. If Kansas does not possess jurisdiction over this plaintiff class, petitioner will be bound to 28,100 judgment holders scattered across the globe, but none of these will be bound by the Kansas decree. Petitioner could be subject to numerous later individual suits by these class members because a judgment issued without proper personal jurisdiction over an absent party is not entitled to full faith and credit elsewhere and thus has no res judicata effect as to that party. Whether it wins or loses on the merits, petitioner has a distinct and personal interest in seeing the entire plaintiff class bound by res judicata just as petitioner is bound. The only way a class action defendant like petitioner can assure itself of this binding effect of the judgment is to ascertain that the forum court has jurisdiction over every plaintiff whose claim it seeks to adjudicate, sufficient to support a defense of res judicata in a later suit for damages by class members.

While it is true that a court adjudicating a dispute may not be able to predetermine the res judicata effect of its own judgment, petitioner has alleged that it would be obviously and immediately injured if this class-action judgment against it became final without binding the plaintiff class. We think that such an injury is sufficient to give petitioner standing on its own right to raise the jurisdiction claim in this Court.

Petitioner's posture is somewhat similar to the trust settlor defendant in *Hanson v. Denckla,* who we found to have standing to challenge the forum's personal jurisdiction over an out-of-state trust company which was an indispensable party under the forum State's law. Because the court could not proceed with the action without jurisdiction over the trust company, we observed that "any defendant affected by the court's judgment ha[d] that 'direct and substantial personal interest in the outcome' that is necessary to challenge whether that jurisdiction was in fact acquired."

II

Reduced to its essentials, petitioner's argument is that unless out-of-state plaintiffs affirmatively consent, the Kansas courts may not exert jurisdiction over their claims. Petitioner claims that failure to execute and return the "request for exclusion" provided with the class notice cannot constitute consent of the out-of-state plaintiffs; thus Kansas courts may exercise jurisdiction over these plaintiffs only if the plaintiffs possess the sufficient "minimum contacts" with Kansas as that term is used in cases involving personal jurisdiction over out-of-state defendants. *E.g., International Shoe Co. v. Washington; Shaffer v. Heitner; World-Wide Volkswagen Corp. v. Woodson.* Since Kansas had no pre-litigation contact with many of the plaintiffs and leases involved, petitioner claims that Kansas has exceeded its jurisdictional reach and thereby violated the due process rights of the absent plaintiffs.

In *International Shoe* we were faced with an out-of-state corporation which sought to avoid the exercise of personal jurisdiction over it as a defendant by a Washington state court. We held that the extent of the defendant's due process protection would depend "upon the quality and nature of the activity in relation to the fair and orderly administration of the laws. . . ." with whom the State had no contacts, ties, or relations. If the defendant possessed certain minimum contacts with the State, so that it was "reasonable and just, according to our traditional conception of fair play and substantial justice" for a State to exercise personal jurisdiction, the State could force the defendant to defend himself in the forum, upon pain of default, and could bind him to a judgment.

The purpose of this test, of course, is to protect a defendant from the travail of defending in a distant forum, unless the defendant's contacts with the forum make it just to force him to defend there. As we explained in *Woodson,* the defendant's contacts should be such that "he should reasonably anticipate being haled" into the forum. In *Insurance Corp. of Ireland v. Compagnie des Bauxites de Guinee,* we explained that the requirement that a court have personal jurisdiction comes from the Due Process Clause's protection of the defendant's personal liberty interest, and said that the requirement "represents a restriction on judicial power not as a matter of sovereignty, but as a matter of individual liberty."

Although the cases like *Shaffer* and *Woodson* which petitioner relies on for a minimum contacts requirement all dealt with out-of-state defendants or parties in the procedural posture of a defendant, petitioner claims that the same analysis must apply to absent class-action plaintiffs. In this regard petitioner correctly points out that a chose in action is a constitutionally recognized property interest possessed by each of the plaintiffs. An adverse judgment by Kansas courts in this case may extinguish the chose in action forever through res judicata. Such an adverse judgment, petitioner claims, would be every bit as onerous to an absent plaintiff as an adverse judgment on the merits would be to a defendant. Thus, the same due process protections should apply to absent plaintiffs: Kansas should not be able to exert jurisdiction over the plaintiff's claims unless the plaintiffs have sufficient minimum contacts with Kansas.

We think petitioner's premise is in error. The burdens placed by a State upon an absent class-action plaintiff are not of the same order or magnitude as those it places upon an absent defendant. An out-of-state defendant summoned by a plaintiff is faced with the full powers of the forum State to render judgment *against* it. The defendant must generally hire counsel and travel to the forum to defend itself from the plaintiff's claim, or suffer a default judgment. The defendant may be forced to participate in extended and often costly discovery, and will be forced to respond in damages or to comply with some other form of remedy imposed by the court should it lose the suit. The defendant may also face liability for court costs and attorney's fees. These burdens are substantial, and the minimum contacts requirement of the Due Process Clause prevents the forum State from unfairly imposing them upon the defendant.

A class-action plaintiff, however, is in quite a different posture. The Court noted this difference in *Hansberry v. Lee,* which explained that a "class" or "representative" suit was an exception to the rule that one could not be bound by judgment *in personam* unless one was made fully a party in the traditional sense. *Ibid.,* citing *Pennoyer v. Neff.* As the Court pointed out in *Hansberry,* the class action was an invention of equity to enable it to proceed to a decree in suits where the number of those interested in the litigation was too great to permit joinder. The absent parties would be bound by the decree so long as the named parties adequately represented the absent class and the prosecution of the litigation was within the common interest.

Modern plaintiff class actions follow the same goals, permitting litigation of a suit involving common questions when there are too many plaintiffs for proper joinder. Class actions also may permit the plaintiffs to pool claims which would be uneconomical to litigate individually. For example, this lawsuit involves claims averaging about $100 per plaintiff; most of the plaintiffs would have no realistic day in court if a class action were not available.

In sharp contrast to the predicament of a defendant haled into an out-of-state forum, the plaintiffs in this suit were not haled anywhere to defend themselves upon pain of a default judgment. As commentators have noted, from the plaintiffs' point of view a class action resembles a "quasi-administrative proceeding, conducted by the judge."

A plaintiff class in Kansas and numerous other jurisdictions cannot first be certified unless the judge, with the aid of the named plaintiffs and defendant, conducts an inquiry into the common nature of the named plaintiffs' and the absent plaintiffs' claims, the adequacy of representation, the jurisdiction possessed over the class, and any other matters that will bear upon proper representation of the absent plaintiffs' interest. Unlike a defendant in a civil suit, a class-action plaintiff is not required to fend for himself. The court and named plaintiffs protect his interests. Indeed, the class-action defendant itself has a great interest in ensuring that the absent plaintiff's claims are properly before the forum. In this case, for example, the defendant sought to avoid class certification by alleging that the absent plaintiffs would not be adequately represented and were not amenable to jurisdiction.

The concern of the typical class-action rules for the absent plaintiffs is manifested in other ways. Most jurisdictions, including Kansas, require that a class action, once certified, may not be dismissed or compromised without the approval of the court. In many jurisdictions such as Kansas the court may amend the pleadings to ensure that all sections of the class are represented adequately.

Besides this continuing solicitude for their rights, absent plaintiff class members are not subject to other burdens imposed upon defendants. They need not hire counsel or appear. They are almost never subject to counterclaims or cross-claims, or liability for fees or costs.[2] Absent plaintiff class members are not subject to coercive or punitive remedies. Nor will an adverse judgment typically bind an absent plaintiff for any damages, although a valid adverse judgment may extinguish any of the plaintiff's claims which were litigated.

Unlike a defendant in a normal civil suit, an absent class-action plaintiff is not required to do anything. He may sit back and allow the litigation to run its course, content in knowing that there are safeguards provided for his protection. In most class actions an absent plaintiff is provided at least with an opportunity to "opt out" of the class, and if he takes advantage of that opportunity he is removed from the litigation entirely. This was true of the Kansas proceedings in this case. The Kansas procedure provided for the mailing of a notice to each class member by first-class mail. The notice, as we have previously indicated, described the action and informed the class member that he could appear in person or by counsel, in default of which he would be represented by the named plaintiffs and their attorneys. The notice further stated that class members would be included in the class and bound by the judgment unless they "opted out" by executing and returning a "request for exclusion" that was included in the notice.

Petitioner contends, however, that the "opt out" procedure provided by Kansas is not good enough, and that an "opt in" procedure is required to satisfy the Due Process Clause of the Fourteenth Amendment. Insofar as plaintiffs who have no minimum contacts with the forum State are

---

2. Petitioner places emphasis on the fact that absent class members might be subject to discovery, counterclaims, cross-claims, or court costs. Petitioner cites no cases involving any such imposition upon plaintiffs, however. We are convinced that such burdens are rarely imposed upon plaintiff class members, and that the disposition of these issues is best left to a case which presents them in a more concrete way.

concerned, an "opt in" provision would require that each class member affirmatively consent to his inclusion within the class.

Because States place fewer burdens upon absent class plaintiffs than they do upon absent defendants in non-class suits, the Due Process Clause need not and does not afford the former as much protection from state-court jurisdiction as it does the latter. The Fourteenth Amendment does protect "persons," not "defendants," however, so absent plaintiffs as well as absent defendants are entitled to some protection from the jurisdiction of a forum State which seeks to adjudicate their claims. In this case we hold that a forum State may exercise jurisdiction over the claim of an absent class-action plaintiff, even though that plaintiff may not possess the minimum contacts with the forum which would support personal jurisdiction over a defendant. If the forum State wishes to bind an absent plaintiff concerning a claim for money damages or similar relief at law,[3] it must provide minimal procedural due process protection. The plaintiff must receive notice plus an opportunity to be heard and participate in the litigation, whether in person or through counsel. The notice must be the best practicable, "reasonably calculated, under all the circumstances, to apprise interested parties of the pendency of the action and afford them an opportunity to present their objections." The notice should describe the action and the plaintiffs' rights in it. Additionally, we hold that due process requires at a minimum that an absent plaintiff be provided with an opportunity to remove himself from the class by executing and returning an "opt out" or "request for exclusion" form to the court. Finally, the Due Process Clause of course requires that the named plaintiff at all times adequately represent the interests of the absent class members. *Hansberry.*

We reject petitioner's contention that the Due Process Clause of the Fourteenth Amendment requires that absent plaintiffs affirmatively "opt in" to the class, rather than be deemed members of the class if they do not "opt out." We think that such a contention is supported by little, if any, precedent, and that it ignores the differences between class-action plaintiffs, on the one hand, and defendants in non-class civil suits on the other. Any plaintiff may consent to jurisdiction. *Keeton v. Hustler Magazine, Inc.* The essential question, then, is how stringent the requirement for a showing of consent will be.

We think that the procedure followed by Kansas, where a fully descriptive notice is sent first-class mail to each class member, with an explanation of the right to "opt out," satisfies due process. Requiring a plaintiff to affirmatively request inclusion would probably impede the prosecution of those class actions involving an aggregation of small individual claims, where a large number of claims are required to make it

---

3. Our holding today is limited to those class actions which seek to bind known plaintiffs concerning claims wholly or predominately for money judgments. We intimate no view concerning other types of class actions, such as those seeking equitable relief. Nor, of course, does our discussion of personal jurisdiction address class actions where the jurisdiction is asserted against a *defendant* class.

economical to bring suit. The plaintiff's claim may be so small, or the plaintiff so unfamiliar with the law, that he would not file suit individually, nor would he affirmatively request inclusion in the class if such a request were required by the Constitution.[4] If, on the other hand, the plaintiff's claim is sufficiently large or important that he wishes to litigate it on his own, he will likely have retained an attorney or have thought about filing suit, and should be fully capable of exercising his right to "opt out."

In this case over 3,400 members of the potential class did "opt out," which belies the contention that "opt out" procedures result in guaranteed jurisdiction by inertia. Another 1,500 were excluded because the notice and "opt out" form was undeliverable. We think that such results show that the "opt out" procedure provided by Kansas is by no means *pro forma,* and that the Constitution does not require more to protect what must be the somewhat rare species of class member who is unwilling to execute an "opt out" form, but whose claim is nonetheless so important that he cannot be presumed to consent to being a member of the class by his failure to do so. Petitioner's "opt in" requirement would require the invalidation of scores of state statutes and of the class-action provision of the Federal Rules of Civil Procedure, and for the reasons stated we do not think that the Constitution requires the State to sacrifice the obvious advantages in judicial efficiency resulting from the "opt out" approach for the protection of the *rara avis* portrayed by petitioner.

We therefore hold that the protection afforded the plaintiff class members by the Kansas statute satisfies the Due Process Clause. The interests of the absent plaintiffs are sufficiently protected by the forum State when those plaintiffs are provided with a request for exclusion that can be returned within a reasonable time to the court. Both the Kansas trial court and the Supreme Court of Kansas held that the class received adequate representation, and no party disputes that conclusion here. We conclude that the Kansas court properly asserted personal jurisdiction over the absent plaintiffs and their claims against petitioner.

III

The Kansas courts applied Kansas contract and Kansas equity law to every claim in this case, notwithstanding that over 99% of the gas leases and some 97% of the plaintiffs in the case had no apparent connection to the State of Kansas except for this lawsuit. Petitioner protested that the Kansas courts should apply the laws of the States where the leases were located, or at least apply Texas and Oklahoma law because so many of the leases came from those States. The Kansas courts disregarded this contention and found petitioner liable for interest on the suspended royalties as

---

4. In this regard the Reporter for the 1966 amendments to the Federal Rules of Civil Procedure stated:

[R]equiring the individuals affirmatively to request inclusion in the lawsuit would result in freezing out the claims of people—especially small claims held by small people—who for one reason or another, ignorance, timidity, unfamiliarity with business or legal matters, will simply not take the affirmative step.

a matter of Kansas law, and set the interest rates under Kansas equity principles.

Petitioner contends that total application of Kansas substantive law violated the constitutional limitations on choice of law mandated by the Due Process Clause of the Fourteenth Amendment and the Full Faith and Credit Clause of Article IV, § 1. We must first determine whether Kansas law conflicts in any material way with any other law which could apply. There can be no injury in applying Kansas law if it is not in conflict with that of any other jurisdiction connected to this suit.

Petitioner claims that Kansas law conflicts with that of a number of States connected to this litigation, especially Texas and Oklahoma. These putative conflicts range from the direct to the tangential, and may be addressed by the Supreme Court of Kansas on remand under the correct constitutional standard. For example, there is no recorded Oklahoma decision dealing with interest liability for suspended royalties: whether Oklahoma is likely to impose liability would require a survey of Oklahoma oil and gas law. Even if Oklahoma found such liability, petitioner shows that Oklahoma would most likely apply its constitutional and statutory 6% interest rate rather than the much higher Kansas rates applied in this litigation.

Additionally, petitioner points to an Oklahoma statute which excuses liability for interest if a creditor accepts payment of the full principal without a claim for interest. Petitioner contends that by ignoring this statute the Kansas courts created liability that does not exist in Oklahoma.

Petitioner also points out several conflicts between Kansas and Texas law. Although Texas recognizes interest liability for suspended royalties, Texas has never awarded any such interest at a rate greater than 6%, which corresponds with the Texas constitutional and statutory rate. Moreover, at least one court interpreting Texas law appears to have held that Texas excuses interest liability once the gas company offers to take an indemnity from the royalty owner and pay him the suspended royalty while the price increase is still tentative. Such a rule is contrary to Kansas law as applied below, but if applied to the Texas plaintiffs or leases in this case, would vastly reduce petitioner's liability.

The conflicts on the applicable interest rates, alone—which we do not think can be labeled "false conflicts" without a more thoroughgoing treatment than was accorded them by the Supreme Court of Kansas— certainly amounted to millions of dollars in liability. We think that the Supreme Court of Kansas erred in deciding on the basis that it did that the application of its laws to all claims would be constitutional.

Four Terms ago we addressed a similar situation in *Allstate Ins. Co. v. Hague.* In that case we were confronted with two conflicting rules of state insurance law. Minnesota permitted the "stacking" of separate uninsured motorist policies while Wisconsin did not. Although the decedent lived in Wisconsin, took out insurance policies and was killed there, he was employed in Minnesota, and after his death his widow moved to Minnesota for reasons unrelated to the litigation, and was appointed personal representative of his estate. She filed suit in Minnesota courts, which applied the Minnesota stacking rule.

The plurality in *Allstate* noted that a particular set of facts giving rise to litigation could justify, constitutionally, the application of more than one jurisdiction's laws. The plurality recognized, however, that the Due Process Clause and the Full Faith and Credit Clause provided modest restrictions on the application of forum law. These restrictions required "that for a State's substantive law to be selected in a constitutionally permissible manner, that State must have a significant contact or significant aggregation of contacts, creating state interests, such that choice of its law is neither arbitrary nor fundamentally unfair." The dissenting Justices were in substantial agreement with this principle. The dissent stressed that the Due Process Clause prohibited the application of law which was only casually or slightly related to the litigation, while the Full Faith and Credit Clause required the forum to respect the laws and judgments of other States, subject to the forum's own interests in furthering its public policy.

The plurality in *Allstate* affirmed the application of Minnesota law because of the forum's significant contacts to the litigation which supported the State's interest in applying its law. Kansas' contacts to this litigation, as explained by the Kansas Supreme Court, can be gleaned from the opinion below.

Petitioner owns property and conducts substantial business in the State, so Kansas certainly has an interest in regulating petitioner's conduct in Kansas. Moreover, oil and gas extraction is an important business to Kansas, and although only a few leases in issue are located in Kansas, hundreds of Kansas plaintiffs were affected by petitioner's suspension of royalties; thus the court held that the State has a real interest in protecting "the rights of these royalty owners both as individual residents of [Kansas] and as members of this particular class of plaintiffs." The Kansas Supreme Court pointed out that Kansas courts are quite familiar with this type of lawsuit, and "[t]he plaintiff class members have indicated their desire to have this action determined under the laws of Kansas." Finally, the Kansas court buttressed its use of Kansas law by stating that this lawsuit was analogous to a suit against a "common fund" located in Kansas.

We do not lightly discount this description of Kansas' contacts with this litigation and its interest in applying its law. There is, however, no "common fund" located in Kansas that would require or support the application of only Kansas law to all these claims. As the Kansas court noted, petitioner commingled the suspended royalties with its general corporate accounts. There is no specific identifiable res in Kansas, nor is there any limited amount which may be depleted before every plaintiff is compensated. Only by somehow aggregating all the separate claims in this case could a "common fund" in any sense be created, and the term becomes all but meaningless when used in such an expansive sense.

We also give little credence to the idea that Kansas law should apply to all claims because the plaintiffs, by failing to opt out, evinced their desire to be bound by Kansas law. Even if one could say that the plaintiffs "consented" to the application of Kansas law by not opting out, plaintiff's desire for forum law is rarely, if ever controlling. In most cases the plaintiff shows his obvious wish for forum law by filing there. "If a plaintiff could choose the substantive rules to be applied to an action ... the invitation to forum shopping would be irresistible." Even if a plaintiff evidences his desire for forum law by moving to the forum, we have generally accorded such a move little or no significance. In *Allstate* the plaintiff's move to the forum was only relevant because it was unrelated and prior to the litigation. Thus the plaintiffs' desire for Kansas law, manifested by their participation in this Kansas lawsuit, bears little relevance.

The Supreme Court of Kansas in its opinion in this case expressed the view that by reason of the fact that it was adjudicating a nationwide class action, it had much greater latitude in applying its own law to the transactions in question than might otherwise be the case:

> The general rule is that the law of the forum applies unless it is expressly shown that a different law governs, and in case of doubt, the law of the forum is preferred.... Where a state court determines it has jurisdiction over a nationwide class action and procedural due process guarantees of notice and adequate representation are present, we believe the law of the forum should be applied unless compelling reasons exist for applying a different law.... Compelling reasons do not exist to require this court to look to other state laws to determine the rights of the parties involved in this lawsuit.

We think that this is something of a "bootstrap" argument. The Kansas class-action statute, like those of most other jurisdictions, requires that there be "common issues of law or fact." But while a State may, for the reasons we have previously stated, assume jurisdiction over the claims of plaintiffs whose principal contacts are with other States, it may not use this assumption of jurisdiction as an added weight in the scale when considering the permissible constitutional limits on choice of substantive law. It may not take a transaction with little or no relationship to the forum and apply the law of the forum in order to satisfy the procedural requirement that there be a "common question of law." The issue of personal jurisdiction over plaintiffs in a class action is entirely distinct from the question of the constitutional limitations on choice of law; the latter calculus is not altered by the fact that it may be more difficult or more burdensome to comply with the constitutional limitations because of the large number of transactions which the State proposes to adjudicate and which have little connection with the forum.

Kansas must have a "significant contact or significant aggregation of contacts" to the claims asserted by each member of the plaintiff class, contacts "creating state interests," in order to ensure that the choice of Kansas law is not arbitrary or unfair. *Allstate.* Given Kansas' lack of "interest" in claims unrelated to that State, and the substantive conflict with jurisdictions such as Texas, we conclude that application of Kansas law to every claim in this case is sufficiently arbitrary and unfair as to exceed constitutional limits.

When considering fairness in this context, an important element is the expectation of the parties. There is no indication that when the leases involving land and royalty owners outside of Kansas were executed, the parties had any idea that Kansas law would control. Neither the Due Process Clause nor the Full Faith and Credit Clause requires Kansas "to substitute for its own [laws], applicable to persons and events within it, the conflicting statute of another state," but Kansas "may not abrogate the rights of parties beyond its borders having no relation to anything done or to be done within them."

Here the Supreme Court of Kansas took the view that in a nationwide class action where procedural due process guarantees of notice and adequate representation were met, "the law of the forum should be applied unless compelling reasons exist for applying a different law." Whatever practical reasons may have commended this rule to the Supreme Court of Kansas, for the reasons already stated we do not believe that it is consistent with the decisions of this Court. We make no effort to determine for ourselves which law must apply to the various transactions involved in this lawsuit, and we reaffirm our observation in *Allstate* that in many situations a state court may be free to apply one of several choices of law. But the constitutional limitations laid down in cases such as *Allstate* and *Home Ins. Co. v. Dick, supra,* must be respected even in a nationwide class action.

We therefore affirm the judgment of the Supreme Court of Kansas insofar as it upheld the jurisdiction of the Kansas courts over the plaintiff class members in this case, and reverse its judgment insofar as it held that Kansas law was applicable to all of the transactions which it sought to adjudicate. We remand the case to that court for further proceedings not inconsistent with this opinion.

It is so ordered.

JUSTICE POWELL took no part in the decision of this case. JUSTICE STEVENS, concurring in part and dissenting in part.

For the reasons stated in Parts I and II of the Court's opinion, I agree that the Kansas courts properly exercised jurisdiction over this class action. I also recognize that the use of the word "compelling" in a portion of the Kansas Supreme Court's opinion, when read out of context, may create an inaccurate impression of that court's choice-of-law holding. Our job, however, is to review judgments, not to edit opinions, and I am firmly convinced that there is no constitutional defect in the judgment under review.

As the Court recognizes, there "can be no [constitutional] injury in applying Kansas law if it is not in conflict with that of any other jurisdiction connected to this suit." A fair reading of the Kansas Supreme Court's opinion reveals that the Kansas court has examined the laws of connected jurisdictions and has correctly concluded that there is no "direct" or "substantive" conflict between the law applied by Kansas and the laws of those other States. Kansas has merely developed general common-law principles to accommodate the novel facts of this litigation—other state courts either agree with Kansas or have not yet addressed precisely similar claims. Consequently, I conclude that the Full Faith and Credit Clause of the Constitution did not require Kansas to apply the law of any other State, and the Fourteenth Amendment's Due Process Clause did not prevent Kansas from applying its own law in this case.

The Court errs today because it applies a loose definition of the sort of "conflict" of laws required to state a *constitutional* claim, allowing Phillips a tactical victory here merely on allegations of "putative" or "likely" conflicts. The Court's choice-of-law analysis also treats the two relevant constitutional provisions as though they imposed the same constraints on the forum court. In my view, however, the potential impact of the Kansas choice on the interests of other sovereign States and the fairness of its decision to the litigants should be separately considered. See *Allstate Insurance Co. v. Hague.*

* * *

In *Shutts II,* the case now under review, the Kansas Supreme Court adopted its earlier analysis in *Shutts I* without repeating it. "Although a larger class is involved than in *Shutts I,* the legal issues presented are substantially the same. While these issues are complex they were thoroughly reviewed in *Shutts I.*" Noting that "Phillips has not satisfactorily established why this court should not apply the rule enunciated in *Shutts I,*" the Kansas court went on to state that once jurisdiction over a "nationwide class action" is properly asserted, "the law of the forum should be applied unless compelling reasons exist for applying a different law."

II

This Court, of course, can have no concern with the substantive merits of common-law decisions reached by state courts faithfully applying their own law or the law of another State. When application of purely state law is at issue, "[t]he power delegated to us is for the restraint of unconstitutional [actions] by the States, and not for the correction of alleged errors committed by their judiciary." The Constitution does not expressly mandate particular or correct choices of law. Rather, a state court's choice of law can invoke constitutional protections, and hence our jurisdiction, only if it contravenes some explicit constitutional limitation.

Thus it has long been settled that "a mere misconstruction by the forum of the laws of a sister State is not a violation of the Full Faith and Credit Clause." That Clause requires only that States accord "full faith and credit" to other States' laws—that is, acknowledge the validity and finality of such laws and attempt in good faith to apply them when necessary as they would be applied by home state courts. But as Justice Holmes explained, when there is "nothing to suggest that [one State's court] was not candidly construing [another State's law] to the best of its ability, . . . even if it was wrong something more than an error of construction is necessary" to invoke the Constitution.

Merely to state these general principles is to refute any argument that Kansas' decision below violated the Full Faith and Credit Clause. As the opinion in *Shutts I* indicates, the Kansas court made a careful survey of the relevant laws of Oklahoma and Texas, the only other States whose law is proffered as relevant to this litigation. But, as the Court acknowledges, no other State's laws or judicial decisions were precisely on point, and, in the Kansas court's judgment, roughly analogous Texas and Oklahoma cases supported the results the Kansas court reached. The Kansas court expressly declared that, in a multistate action, a "court should also give careful consideration, as we have attempted to do, to any possible conflict of law problems." While a common-law judge might disagree with the substantive legal determinations made by the Kansas court (although nothing in its opinion seems erroneous to me), that court's approach to the possible choices of law evinces precisely the "full faith and credit" that the Constitution requires.

It is imaginable that even a good-faith review of another State's law might still "unjustifiably infring[e] upon the legitimate interests of another State" so as to violate the Full Faith and Credit Clause. If, for example, a Texas oil company or a Texas royalty owner with an interest in a Texas lease were treated directly contrary to a stated policy of the State of Texas by a Kansas court through some honest blunder, the Constitution might bar such "parochial entrenchment" on Texas' interests. But this case is so distant from such a situation that I need not pursue this theoretical possibility. Even Phillips does not contend that any stated policies of other States have been plainly contravened, and the Court's discussion is founded merely on an *absence* of reported decisions and the Court's speculation of what Oklahoma or Texas courts might "most likely" do in a case like this. There is simply no demonstration here that the Kansas Supreme Court's decision has impaired the legitimate interests of any other States or infringed on their sovereignty in the slightest.

III

It is nevertheless possible for a State's choice of law to violate the Constitution because it is so "totally arbitrary or . . . fundamentally unfair" to a litigant that it violates the Due Process Clause. If the forum court has no connection to the lawsuit other than its jurisdiction over the parties, a decision to apply the forum State's law might so "frustrat[e] the justifiable expectations of the parties" as to be unconstitutional.

Again, however, a constitutional claim of "unfair surprise" cannot be based merely upon an unexpected choice of a particular State's law—it must rest on a persuasive showing of an unexpected *result* arrived at by application of that law. Thus, absent any *conflict* of laws, in terms of the results they produce, the Due Process Clause simply has not been violated. This is because the underlying theory of a choice-of-law due process claim must be that parties plan their conduct and contractual relations based upon their legitimate expectations concerning the subsequent legal consequences of their actions. For example, they might base a decision on the belief that the law of a particular State will govern. But a change in that State's law in the interim between the execution and the performance of the contract would not violate the Due Process Clause. Nor would the Constitution be violated simply because a state court made an unanticipated ruling on a previously unanswered question of law—perhaps a choice-of-law question.

In this case it is perfectly clear that there has been no due process violation because this is a classic "false conflicts" case. Phillips has not demonstrated that any significant conflicts exist merely because Oklahoma and Texas state case law is *silent* concerning the equitable theories developed by the Kansas courts in this litigation, or even because the language of some Oklahoma and Texas statutes suggests that those States would "most likely" reach different results. The Court's heavy reliance on the characterization of the law provided by Phillips is not an adequate substitute for a neutral review. ("Petitioner claims," "petitioner shows," "petitioner points to," "Petitioner also points out . . ."). As is unmistakable from a review of *Shutts I,* the Kansas Supreme Court has examined the same laws cited by the Court today as indicative of "direct" conflicts, and construed them as supportive of the Kansas result. Our precedents, to say nothing of the Constitution and our statutory jurisdiction to review state-court judgments, do not permit the Court to second-guess these substantive judgments. Moreover, an independent examination demonstrates solid support for the Kansas court's conclusions.

* * * The crux of my disagreement with the Court is over the standard applied to evaluate the sufficiency of allegations of choice-of-law conflicts necessary to support a constitutional claim. Rather than potential, "putative," or even "likely" conflicts, I would require demonstration of an *unambiguous* conflict with the *established* law of another State as an essential element of a constitutional choice-of-law claim. Arguments that a state court has merely applied general common-law principles in a novel manner, or reconciled arguably conflicting laws erroneously in the face of unprecedented factual circumstances should not suffice to make out a constitutional issue.

In this case, the Kansas Supreme Court's application of general principles of equity, its interpretation of the agreements, its reliance on the Commission's regulations, and its construction of general statutory terms contravened no established legal principles of other States and consequently cannot be characterized as either arbitrary or fundamentally unfair to Phillips. I therefore can find no due process violation in the Kansas court's decision.

IV

In final analysis, the Court today may merely be expressing its disagreement with the Kansas Supreme Court's statement that in a "nationwide class action . . . the law of the forum should be applied unless compelling reasons exist for applying a different law." Considering this statement against the background of the Kansas Supreme Court's careful analysis in *Shutts I,* however, I am confident that court would agree that every state court has an obligation under the Full Faith and Credit Clause to "respect the legitimate interests of other States and avoid infringement upon their sovereignty."

It is also agreed that "the fact that a choice-of-law decision may be unsound . . . does not necessarily implicate the federal concerns embodied in the Full Faith and Credit Clause." When a suit involves claims connected to States other than the forum State, the Constitution requires only that the relevant laws of other States that are brought to the attention of the forum court be examined fairly prior to making a choice of law. Because this Court "reviews judgments, not opinions," criticism of a portion of the Kansas court's opinion taken out of context provides an insufficient basis for reversing its judgment. Unless the actual *choice* of Kansas law violated substantial constitutional rights of the parties, our power to review judgments of state law—including the state law of choice of law—does not extend to reversal based on disagreement with the law's application. A review of the record and the underlying litigation here convincingly demonstrates that, despite Phillips' protestations regarding Kansas' development of common-law principles, no disregard for the laws of other States nor unfair application of Kansas law to the litigants has occurred. Phillips has no constitutional right to avoid judgment in Kansas because it might have convinced a court in another State to develop its law differently.

I do not believe the Court should engage in detailed evaluations of various States' laws. To the contrary, I believe our limited jurisdiction to review state-court judgments should foreclose such review. Accordingly, I trust that today's decision is no more than a momentary aberration, and that the Court's opinion will not be read as a decision to constitutionalize novel state-court developments in the common law whenever a litigant can claim that another State connected to the litigation "most likely" would reach a different result. The Court long ago decided that state-court choices of law are unreviewable here absent demonstration of an unambiguous conflict in the established laws of connected States.. "To hold otherwise would render it possible to bring to this court every case wherein the defeated party claimed that the statute of another State had been construed to his detriment." Having ignored this admonition today, the Court may be forced to renew its turn-of-the-century efforts to convince the bar that state-court judgments based on fair evaluations of other States' laws are final.

Accordingly, while I join Parts I and II of the Court's opinion, I respectfully dissent from Part III and from the judgment.

* * *

D.   SETTLEMENT CLASSES

AMCHEM PRODUCTS, INC. v. WINDSOR

521 U.S. 591 (1997)

JUSTICE GINSBURG delivered the opinion of the Court.

This case concerns the legitimacy under Rule 23 of the Federal Rules of Civil Procedure of a class-action certification sought to achieve global settlement of current and future asbestos-related claims. The class proposed for certification potentially encompasses hundreds of thousands, perhaps millions, of individuals tied together by this commonality: Each was, or some day may be, adversely affected by past exposure to asbestos products manufactured by one or more of 20 companies. Those companies, defendants in the lower courts, are petitioners here.

The United States District Court for the Eastern District of Pennsylvania certified the class for settlement only, finding that the proposed settlement was fair and that representation and notice had been adequate. That court enjoined class members from separately pursuing asbestos-related personal-injury suits in any court, federal or state, pending the issuance of a final order. The Court of Appeals for the Third Circuit vacated the District Court's orders, holding that the class certification failed to satisfy Rule 23's requirements in several critical respects. We affirm the Court of Appeals' judgment.

I

A

The settlement-class certification we confront evolved in response to an asbestos-litigation crisis. A United States Judicial Conference Ad Hoc Committee on Asbestos Litigation, appointed by the Chief Justice in September 1990, described facets of the problem in a 1991 report:

> [This] is a tale of danger known in the 1930s, exposure inflicted upon millions of Americans in the 1940s and 1950s, injuries that began to take their toll in the 1960s, and a flood of lawsuits beginning in the 1970s. On the basis of past and current filing data, and because of a latency period that may last as long as 40 years for some asbestos related diseases, a continuing stream of claims can be expected. The final toll of asbestos related injuries is unknown. Predictions have

been made of 200,000 asbestos disease deaths before the year 2000 and as many as 265,000 by the year 2015.

The most objectionable aspects of asbestos litigation can be briefly summarized: dockets in both federal and state courts continue to grow; long delays are routine; trials are too long; the same issues are litigated over and over; transaction costs exceed the victims' recovery by nearly two to one; exhaustion of assets threatens and distorts the process; and future claimants may lose altogether.

Real reform, the report concluded, required federal legislation creating a national asbestos dispute-resolution scheme. As recommended by the Ad Hoc Committee, the Judicial Conference of the United States urged Congress to act. To this date, no congressional response has emerged.

In the face of legislative inaction, the federal courts—lacking authority to replace state tort systems with a national toxic tort compensation regime—endeavored to work with the procedural tools available to improve management of federal asbestos litigation. Eight federal judges, experienced in the superintendence of asbestos cases, urged the Judicial Panel on Multidistrict Litigation (MDL Panel), to consolidate in a single district all asbestos complaints then pending in federal courts. Accepting the recommendation, the MDL Panel transferred all asbestos cases then filed, but not yet on trial in federal courts to a single district, the United States District Court for the Eastern District of Pennsylvania; pursuant to the transfer order, the collected cases were consolidated for pretrial proceedings before Judge Weiner. The order aggregated pending cases only; no authority resides in the MDL Panel to license for consolidated proceedings claims not yet filed.

B

After the consolidation, attorneys for plaintiffs and defendants formed separate steering committees and began settlement negotiations. Ronald L. Motley and Gene Locks—later appointed, along with Motley's law partner Joseph F. Rice, to represent the plaintiff class in this action—cochaired the Plaintiffs' Steering Committee. Counsel for the Center for Claims Resolution (CCR), the consortium of 20 former asbestos manufacturers now before us as petitioners, participated in the Defendants' Steering Committee. Although the MDL Panel order collected, transferred, and consolidated only cases already commenced in federal courts, settlement negotiations included efforts to find a "means of resolving ... future cases." ("primary purpose of the settlement talks in the consolidated MDL litigation was to craft a national settlement that would provide an alternative resolution mechanism for asbestos claims," including claims that might be filed in the future).

In November 1991, the Defendants' Steering Committee made an offer designed to settle all pending and future asbestos cases by providing a fund for distribution by plaintiffs' counsel among asbestos-exposed individuals. The Plaintiffs' Steering Committee rejected this offer, and negotiations fell apart. CCR, however, continued to pursue "a workable administrative system for the handling of future claims."

To that end, CCR counsel approached the lawyers who had headed the Plaintiffs' Steering Committee in the unsuccessful negotiations, and a new round of negotiations began; that round yielded the mass settlement agreement now in controversy. At the time, the former heads of the Plaintiffs' Steering Committee represented thousands of plaintiffs with then-pending asbestos-related claims-claimants the parties to this suit call "inventory" plaintiffs. CCR indicated in these discussions that it would resist settlement of inventory cases absent "some kind of protection for the future." (CCR communicated to the inventory plaintiffs' attorneys that once the CCR defendants saw a rational way to deal with claims expected to be filed in the future, those defendants would be prepared to address the settlement of pending cases).

Settlement talks thus concentrated on devising an administrative scheme for disposition of asbestos claims not yet in litigation. In these negotiations, counsel for masses of inventory plaintiffs endeavored to represent the interests of the anticipated future claimants, although those lawyers then had no attorney-client relationship with such claimants.

Once negotiations seemed likely to produce an agreement purporting to bind potential plaintiffs, CCR agreed to settle, through separate agreements, the claims of plaintiffs who had already filed asbestos-related lawsuits. In one such agreement, CCR defendants promised to pay more than $200 million to gain release of the claims of numerous inventory plaintiffs. After settling the inventory claims, CCR, together with the plaintiffs' lawyers CCR had approached, launched this case, exclusively involving persons outside the MDL Panel's province-plaintiffs without already pending lawsuits.

C

The class action thus instituted was not intended to be litigated. Rather, within the space of a single day, January 15, 1993, the settling parties—CCR defendants and the representatives of the plaintiff class described below—presented to the District Court a complaint, an answer, a proposed settlement agreement, and a joint motion for conditional class certification.

The complaint identified nine lead plaintiffs, designating them and members of their families as representatives of a class comprising all persons who had not filed an asbestos-related lawsuit against a CCR defendant as of the date the class action commenced, but who (1) had been exposed—occupationally or through the occupational exposure of a spouse or household member—to asbestos or products containing asbestos attributable to a CCR defendant, or (2) whose spouse or family member had been so exposed. Untold numbers of individuals may fall within this description. All named plaintiffs alleged that they or a member of their family had been exposed to asbestos-containing products of CCR defendants. More than half of the named plaintiffs alleged that they or their family members had already suffered various physical injuries as a result of the exposure. The others alleged that they had not yet manifested any asbestos-related condition. The complaint delineated no subclasses; all named plaintiffs were designated as representatives of the class as a whole.

The complaint invoked the District Court's diversity jurisdiction and asserted various state-law claims for relief, including (1) negligent failure to warn, (2) strict liability, (3) breach of express and implied warranty, (4) negligent infliction of emotional distress, (5) enhanced risk of disease, (6) medical monitoring, and (7) civil conspiracy. Each plaintiff requested unspecified damages in excess of $100,000. CCR defendants' answer denied the principal allegations of the complaint and asserted 11 affirmative defenses.

A stipulation of settlement accompanied the pleadings; it proposed to settle, and to preclude nearly all class members from litigating against CCR companies, all claims not filed before January 15, 1993, involving compensation for present and future asbestos-related personal injury or death. An exhaustive document exceeding 100 pages, the stipulation presents in detail an administrative mechanism and a schedule of payments to compensate class members who meet defined asbestos-exposure and medical requirements. The stipulation describes four categories of compensable disease: mesothelioma; lung cancer; certain "other cancers" (colon-rectal, laryngeal, esophageal, and stomach cancer); and "non-malignant conditions" (asbestosis and bilateral pleural thickening). Persons with "exceptional" medical claims-claims that do not fall within the four described diagnostic categories-may in some instances qualify for compensation, but the settlement caps the number of "exceptional" claims CCR must cover.

For each qualifying disease category, the stipulation specifies the range of damages CCR will pay to qualifying claimants. Payments under the settlement are not adjustable for inflation. Mesothelioma claimants— the most highly compensated category—are scheduled to receive between $20,000 and $200,000. The stipulation provides that CCR is to propose the level of compensation within the prescribed ranges; it also establishes procedures to resolve disputes over medical diagnoses and levels of compensation.

Compensation above the fixed ranges may be obtained for "extraordinary" claims. But the settlement places both numerical caps and dollar limits on such claims. The settlement also imposes "case flow maximums," which cap the number of claims payable for each disease in a given year.

Class members are to receive no compensation for certain kinds of claims, even if otherwise applicable state law recognizes such claims. Claims that garner no compensation under the settlement include claims by family members of asbestos-exposed individuals for loss of consortium, and claims by so-called "exposure-only" plaintiffs for increased risk of cancer, fear of future asbestos-related injury, and medical monitoring. "Pleural" claims, which might be asserted by persons with asbestos-related plaques on their lungs but no accompanying physical impairment, are also excluded. Although not entitled to present compensation, exposure-only claimants and pleural claimants may qualify for benefits when and if they develop a compensable disease and meet the relevant exposure and medical criteria. Defendants forgo defenses to liability, including statute of limitations pleas.

Class members, in the main, are bound by the settlement in perpetuity, while CCR defendants may choose to withdraw from the settlement after ten years. A small number of class members—only a few per year—may reject the settlement and pursue their claims in court. Those permitted to exercise this option, however, may not assert any punitive damages claim or any claim for increased risk of cancer. Aspects of the administration of the settlement are to be monitored by the AFL–CIO and class counsel. Class counsel are to receive attorneys' fees in an amount to be approved by the District Court.

D

On January 29, 1993, as requested by the settling parties, the District Court conditionally certified, under Federal Rule of Civil Procedure 23(b)(3), an encompassing opt-out class. The certified class included persons occupationally exposed to defendants' asbestos products, and members of their families, who had not filed suit as of January 15. Judge Weiner appointed Locks, Motley, and Rice as class counsel, noting that "[t]he Court may in the future appoint additional counsel if it is deemed necessary and advisable." At no stage of the proceedings, however, were additional counsel in fact appointed. Nor was the class ever divided into subclasses. In a separate order, Judge Weiner assigned to Judge Reed, also of the Eastern District of Pennsylvania, "the task of conducting fairness proceedings and of determining whether the proposed settlement is fair to the class." Various class members raised objections to the settlement stipulation, and Judge Weiner granted the objectors full rights to participate in the subsequent proceedings.

In preliminary rulings, Judge Reed held that the District Court had subject-matter jurisdiction, and he approved the settling parties' elaborate plan for giving notice to the class. The court-approved notice informed recipients that they could exclude themselves from the class, if they so chose, within a three-month opt-out period.

Objectors raised numerous challenges to the settlement. They urged that the settlement unfairly disadvantaged those without currently compensable conditions in that it failed to adjust for inflation or to account for changes, over time, in medical understanding. They maintained that compensation levels were intolerably low in comparison to awards available in tort litigation or payments received by the inventory plaintiffs. And they objected to the absence of any compensation for certain claims, for example, medical monitoring, compensable under the tort law of several States. Rejecting these and all other objections, Judge Reed concluded that the settlement terms were fair and had been negotiated without collusion. He also found that adequate notice had been given to class members, and that final class certification under Rule 23(b)(3) was appropriate.

As to the specific prerequisites to certification, the District Court observed that the class satisfied Rule 23(a)(1)'s numerosity requirement, a matter no one debates. The Rule 23(a)(2) and (b)(3) requirements of commonality and preponderance were also satisfied, the District Court held, in that "[t]he members of the class have all been exposed to asbestos products supplied by the defendants and all share an interest in receiving prompt and fair compensation for their claims, while minimizing the risks and transaction costs inherent in the asbestos litigation process as it occurs presently in the tort system. Whether the proposed settlement satisfies this interest and is otherwise a fair, reasonable and adequate compromise of the claims of the class is a predominant issue for purposes of Rule 23(b)(3)."

The District Court held next that the claims of the class representatives were "typical" of the class as a whole, a requirement of Rule 23(a)(3), and that, as Rule 23(b)(3) demands, the class settlement was "superior" to other methods of adjudication.

Strenuous objections had been asserted regarding the adequacy of representation, a Rule 23(a)(4) requirement. Objectors maintained that class counsel and class representatives had disqualifying conflicts of interests. In particular, objectors urged, claimants whose injuries had become manifest and claimants without manifest injuries should not have common counsel and should not be aggregated in a single class. Furthermore, objectors argued, lawyers representing inventory plaintiffs should not represent the newly formed class.

Satisfied that class counsel had ably negotiated the settlement in the best interests of all concerned, and that the named parties served as adequate representatives, the District Court rejected these objections. Subclasses were unnecessary, the District Court held, bearing in mind the added cost and confusion they would entail and the ability of class members to exclude themselves from the class during the three-month opt-out period. Reasoning that the representative plaintiffs "have a strong interest that recovery for *all* of the medical categories be maximized because they may have claims in *any,* or several categories," the District Court found "no antagonism of interest between class members with various medical conditions, or between persons with and without currently manifest asbestos impairment." Declaring class certification appropriate and the settlement fair, the District Court preliminarily enjoined all class members from commencing any asbestos-related suit against the CCR defendants in any state or federal court.

The objectors appealed. The United States Court of Appeals for the Third Circuit vacated the certification, holding that the requirements of Rule 23 had not been satisfied.

E

The Court of Appeals, in a long, heavily detailed opinion by Judge Becker, first noted several challenges by objectors to justiciability, subject-matter jurisdiction, and adequacy of notice. These challenges, the court said, raised "serious concerns." However, the court observed, "the jurisdictional issues in this case would not exist but for the [class-action] certification." Turning to the class-certification issues and finding them dispositive, the Third Circuit declined to decide other questions.

On class-action prerequisites, the Court of Appeals referred to an earlier Third Circuit decision, *In re General Motors Corp. Pick–Up Truck Fuel Tank Products Liability Litigation,* which held that although a class action may be certified for settlement purposes only, Rule 23(a)'s requirements must be satisfied as if the case were going to be litigated. The same rule should apply, the Third Circuit said, to class certification under Rule 23(b)(3). While stating that the requirements of Rule 23(a) and (b)(3) must be met "without taking into account the settlement," the Court of Appeals in fact closely considered the terms of the settlement as it examined aspects of the case under Rule 23 criteria.

The Third Circuit recognized that Rule 23(a)(2)'s "commonality" requirement is subsumed under, or superseded by, the more stringent Rule 23(b)(3) requirement that questions common to the class "predominate over" other questions. The court therefore trained its attention on the "predominance" inquiry. The harmfulness of asbestos exposure was indeed a prime factor common to the class, the Third Circuit observed. But uncommon questions abounded.

In contrast to mass torts involving a single accident, class members in this case were exposed to different asbestos-containing products, in different ways, over different periods, and for different amounts of time; some suffered no physical injury, others suffered disabling or deadly diseases. "These factual differences," the Third Circuit explained, "translate[d] into significant legal differences." State law governed and varied widely on such critical issues as "viability of [exposure-only] claims [and] availability of causes of action for medical monitoring, increased risk of cancer, and fear of future injury." "[T]he number of uncommon issues in this humongous class action," the Third Circuit concluded, barred a determination, under existing tort law, that common questions predominated.

The Court of Appeals next found that "serious intra-class conflicts preclude[d] th[e] class from meeting the adequacy of representation requirement" of Rule 23(a)(4). Adverting to, but not resolving charges of attorney conflict of interests, the Third Circuit addressed the question whether the named plaintiffs could adequately advance the interests of all class members. The Court of Appeals acknowledged that the District

Court was certainly correct to this extent: " '[T]he members of the class are united in seeking the maximum possible recovery for their asbestos-related claims.' " "But the settlement does more than simply provide a general recovery fund," the Court of Appeals immediately added; "[r]ather, it makes important judgments on how recovery is to be *allocated* among different kinds of plaintiffs, decisions that necessarily favor some claimants over others."

In the Third Circuit's view, the "most salient" divergence of interests separated plaintiffs already afflicted with an asbestos-related disease from plaintiffs without manifest injury (exposure-only plaintiffs). The latter would rationally want protection against inflation for distant recoveries. See *ibid.* They would also seek sturdy back-end opt-out rights and "causation provisions that can keep pace with changing science and medicine, rather than freezing in place the science of 1993." Already injured parties, in contrast, would care little about such provisions and would rationally trade them for higher current payouts. These and other adverse interests, the Court of Appeals carefully explained, strongly suggested that an undivided set of representatives could not adequately protect the discrete interests of both currently afflicted and exposure-only claimants.

The Third Circuit next rejected the District Court's determination that the named plaintiffs were "typical" of the class, noting that this Rule 23(a)(3) inquiry overlaps the adequacy of representation question: "both look to the potential for conflicts in the class." Evident conflict problems, the court said, led it to hold that "no set of representatives can be 'typical' of this class."

The Court of Appeals similarly rejected the District Court's assessment of the superiority of the class action. The Third Circuit initially noted that a class action so large and complex "could not be tried." The court elaborated most particularly, however, on the unfairness of binding exposure-only plaintiffs who might be unaware of the class action or lack sufficient information about their exposure to make a reasoned decision whether to stay in or opt out. "A series of statewide or more narrowly defined adjudications, either through consolidation under Rule 42(a) or as class actions under Rule 23, would seem preferable," the Court of Appeals said.

The Third Circuit, after intensive review, ultimately ordered decertification of the class and vacation of the District Court's antisuit injunction. Judge Wellford concurred, "fully subscrib[ing] to the decision of Judge Becker that the plaintiffs in this case ha[d] not met the requirements of Rule 23." He added that in his view, named exposure-only plaintiffs had no standing to pursue the suit in federal court, for their depositions showed that "[t]hey claimed no damages and no present injury."

We granted certiorari and now affirm.

II

Objectors assert in this Court, as they did in the District Court and Court of Appeals, an array of jurisdictional barriers. Most fundamentally, they maintain that the settlement proceeding instituted by class counsel and CCR is not a justiciable case or controversy within the confines of Article III of the Federal Constitution. In the main, they say, the proceeding is a non-adversarial endeavor to impose on countless individuals without currently ripe claims an administrative compensation regime binding on those individuals if and when they manifest injuries.

Furthermore, objectors urge that exposure-only claimants lack standing to sue: Either they have not yet sustained any cognizable injury or, to the extent the complaint states claims and demands relief for emotional distress, enhanced risk of disease, and medical monitoring, the settlement provides no redress. Objectors also argue that exposure-only claimants did not meet the then-current amount-in-controversy requirement (in excess of $50,000) specified for federal-court jurisdiction based upon diversity of citizenship.

As earlier recounted, the Third Circuit declined to reach these issues because they "would not exist but for the [class-action] certification." We agree that "[t]he class certification issues are dispositive," because their resolution here is logically antecedent to the existence of any Article III issues, it is appropriate to reach them first. We therefore follow the path taken by the Court of Appeals, mindful that Rule 23's requirements must be interpreted in keeping with Article III constraints, and with the Rules Enabling Act, which instructs that rules of procedure "shall not abridge, enlarge or modify any substantive right," 28 U.S.C. § 2072(b). *See also* Fed. Rule Civ. Proc. 82 ("rules shall not be construed to extend . . . the [subject-matter] jurisdiction of the United States district courts").

III

To place this controversy in context, we briefly describe the characteristics of class actions for which the Federal Rules provide. Rule 23, governing federal-court class actions, stems from equity practice and gained its current shape in an innovative 1966 revision. Rule 23(a) states four threshold requirements applicable to all class actions: (1) numerosity (a "class [so large] that joinder of all members is impracticable"); (2) commonality ("questions of law or fact common to the class"); (3) typicality (named parties' claims or defenses "are typical . . . of the class"); and (4) adequacy of representation (representatives "will fairly and adequately protect the interests of the class").

In addition to satisfying Rule 23(a)'s prerequisites, parties seeking class certification must show that the action is maintainable under Rule 23(b)(1), (2), or (3). Rule 23(b)(1) covers cases in which separate actions by or against individual class members would risk establishing "incompatible standards of conduct for the party opposing the class," Fed. Rule Civ. Proc. 23(b)(1)(A), or would "as a practical matter be dispositive of the interests" of nonparty class members "or substantially impair or impede their ability to protect their interests," Rule 23(b)(1)(B). Rule 23(b)(1)(A) "takes in cases where the party is obliged by law to treat the members of the class alike (a utility acting toward customers; a government imposing a tax), or where the party must treat all alike as a matter of practical necessity (a riparian owner using water as against downriver owners)." Rule 23(b)(1)(B) includes, for example, "limited fund" cases, instances in which numerous persons make claims against a fund insufficient to satisfy all claims.

Rule 23(b)(2) permits class actions for declaratory or injunctive relief where "the party opposing the class has acted or refused to act on grounds generally applicable to the class." Civil rights cases against parties charged with unlawful, class-based discrimination are prime examples. (subdivision (b)(2) "build[s] on experience mainly, but not exclusively, in the civil rights field").

In the 1966 class-action amendments, Rule 23(b)(3), the category at issue here, was "the most adventuresome" innovation. Rule 23(b)(3) added to the complex-litigation arsenal class actions for damages designed to secure judgments binding all class members save those who affirmatively elected to be excluded. Rule 23(b)(3) "opt-out" class actions superseded the former "spurious" class action, so characterized because it generally functioned as a permissive joinder ("opt-in") device.

Framed for situations in which "class-action treatment is not as clearly called for" as it is in Rule 23(b)(1) and (b)(2) situations, Rule 23(b)(3) permits certification where class suit "may nevertheless be convenient and desirable." To qualify for certification under Rule 23(b)(3), a class must meet two requirements beyond the Rule 23(a) prerequisites: Common questions must "predominate over any questions affecting only individual members"; and class resolution must be "superior to other available methods for the fair and efficient adjudication of the controversy." In adding "predominance" and "superiority" to the qualification-for-certification list, the Advisory Committee sought to cover cases "in which a class action would achieve economies of time, effort, and expense, and promote ... uniformity of decision as to persons similarly situated, without sacrificing procedural fairness or bringing about other undesirable results." Sensitive to the competing tugs of individual autonomy for those who might prefer to go it alone or in a smaller unit, on the one hand, and systemic efficiency on the other, the Reporter for the 1966 amendments cautioned: "The new provision invites a close look at the case before it is accepted as a class action. . . ."

Rule 23(b)(3) includes a non-exhaustive list of factors pertinent to a court's "close look" at the predominance and superiority criteria:

(A) the interest of members of the class in individually controlling the prosecution or defense of separate actions; (B) the extent and nature of any litigation concerning the controversy already commenced by or against members of the class; (C) the desirability or undesirability of concentrating the litigation of the claims in the particular forum; (D) the difficulties likely to be encountered in the management of a class action.

In setting out these factors, the Advisory Committee for the 1966 reform anticipated that in each case, courts would "consider the interests of individual members of the class in controlling their own litigations and carrying them on as they see fit." They elaborated:

> The interests of individuals in conducting separate lawsuits may be so strong as to call for denial of a class action. On the other hand, these interests may be theoretic rather than practical; the class may have a high degree of cohesion and prosecution of the action through representatives would be quite unobjectionable, or the amounts at stake for individuals may be so small that separate suits would be impracticable.

As the Third Circuit observed in the instant case: "Each plaintiff [in an action involving claims for personal injury and death] has a significant interest in individually controlling the prosecution of [his case]"; each "ha[s] a substantial stake in making individual decisions on whether and when to settle."

While the text of Rule 23(b)(3) does not exclude from certification cases in which individual damages run high, the Advisory Committee had dominantly in mind vindication of "the rights of groups of people who individually would be without effective strength to bring their opponents into court at all." As concisely recalled in a recent Seventh Circuit opinion:

> The policy at the very core of the class action mechanism is to overcome the problem that small recoveries do not provide the incentive for any individual to bring a solo action prosecuting his or her rights. A class action solves this problem by aggregating the relatively paltry potential recoveries into something worth someone's (usually an attorney's) labor.

To alert class members to their right to "opt out" of a (b)(3) class, Rule 23 instructs the court to "direct to the members of the class the best notice practicable under the circumstances, including individual notice to all members who can be identified through reasonable effort." Fed. Rule Civ. Proc. 23(c)(2); see *Eisen v. Carlisle & Jacquelin,* 417 U.S. 156 (1974) (individual notice to class members identifiable through reasonable effort is mandatory in (b)(3) actions; requirement may not be relaxed based on high cost).

No class action may be "dismissed or compromised without [court] approval," preceded by notice to class members. Fed. Rule Civ. Proc. 23(e). The Advisory Committee's sole comment on this terse final provision of Rule 23 restates the Rule's instruction without elaboration: "Subdivision (e) requires approval of the court, after notice, for the dismissal or compromise of any class action."

In the decades since the 1966 revision of Rule 23, class-action practice has become ever more "adventuresome" as a means of coping with claims too numerous to secure their "just, speedy, and inexpensive determination" one by one. *See* Fed. Rule Civ. Proc. 1. The development reflects concerns about the efficient use of court resources and the conservation of funds to compensate claimants who do not line up early in a litigation queue.

Among current applications of Rule 23(b)(3), the "settlement only" class has become a stock device. Although all Federal Circuits recognize the utility of Rule 23(b)(3) settlement classes, courts have divided on the extent to which a proffered settlement affects court surveillance under Rule 23's certification criteria.

In *GM Trucks*, and in the instant case, the Third Circuit held that a class cannot be certified for settlement when certification for trial would be unwarranted. Other courts have held that settlement obviates or reduces the need to measure a proposed class against the enumerated Rule 23 requirements.

A proposed amendment to Rule 23 would expressly authorize settlement class certification, in conjunction with a motion by the settling parties for Rule 23(b)(3) certification, "even though the requirements of subdivision (b)(3) might not be met for purposes of trial." In response to the publication of this proposal, voluminous public comments—many of them opposed to, or skeptical of, the amendment—were received by the Judicial Conference Standing Committee on Rules of Practice and Procedure. The Committee has not yet acted on the matter. We consider the certification at issue under the Rule as it is currently framed.

IV

We granted review to decide the role settlement may play, under existing Rule 23, in determining the propriety of class certification. The Third Circuit's opinion stated that each of the requirements of Rule 23(a) and (b)(3) "must be satisfied without taking into account the settlement." That statement, petitioners urge, is incorrect.

We agree with petitioners to this limited extent: Settlement is relevant to a class certification. The Third Circuit's opinion bears modification in that respect. But, as we earlier observed, the Court of Appeals in fact did not ignore the settlement; instead, that court homed in on settlement terms in explaining why it found the absentees' interests inadequately represented. The Third Circuit's close inspection of the settlement in that regard was altogether proper.

Confronted with a request for settlement-only class certification, a district court need not inquire whether the case, if tried, would present intractable management problems, *see* Fed. Rule Civ. Proc. 23(b)(3)(D), for the proposal is that there be no trial. But other specifications of the Rule—those designed to protect absentees by blocking unwarranted or overbroad class definitions—demand undiluted, even heightened, attention in the settlement context. Such attention is of vital importance, for a court asked to certify a settlement class will lack the opportunity, present when a case is litigated, to adjust the class, informed by the proceedings as they unfold. *See* Rule 23(c), (d).

And, of overriding importance, courts must be mindful that the Rule as now composed sets the requirements they are bound to enforce. Federal Rules take effect after an extensive deliberative process involving many reviewers: a Rules Advisory Committee, public commenters, the Judicial Conference, this Court, the Congress. The text of a rule thus proposed and reviewed limits judicial inventiveness. Courts are not free to amend a rule outside the process Congress ordered, a process properly tuned to the instruction that rules of procedure "shall not abridge . . . any substantive right." § 2072(b).

Rule 23(e), on settlement of class actions, reads in its entirety: "A class action shall not be dismissed or compromised without the approval of the court, and notice of the proposed dismissal or compromise shall be given to all members of the class in such manner as the court directs." This prescription was designed to function as an additional requirement, not a superseding direction, for the "class action" to which Rule 23(e) refers is one qualified for certification under Rule 23(a) and (b). (adequate representation does not eliminate additional requirement to provide notice). Subdivisions (a) and (b) focus court attention on whether a proposed class has sufficient unity so that absent members can fairly be bound by decisions of class representatives. That dominant concern persists when settlement, rather than trial, is proposed.

The safeguards provided by the Rule 23(a) and (b) class—qualifying criteria, we emphasize, are not impractical impediments—checks shorn of utility—in the settlement-class context. First, the standards set for the protection of absent class members serve to inhibit appraisals of the chancellor's foot kind-class certifications dependent upon the court's gestalt judgment or overarching impression of the settlement's fairness.

Second, if a fairness inquiry under Rule 23(e) controlled certification, eclipsing Rule 23(a) and (b), and permitting class designation despite the impossibility of litigation, both class counsel and court would be disarmed. Class counsel confined to settlement negotiations could not use the threat of litigation to press for a better offer, and the court would face a bargain proffered for its approval without benefit of adversarial investigation.

Federal courts, in any case, lack authority to substitute for Rule 23's certification criteria a standard never adopted—that if a settlement is "fair," then certification is proper. Applying to this case criteria the rulemakers set, we conclude that the Third Circuit's appraisal is essentially correct. Although that court should have acknowledged that settlement is a factor in the calculus, a remand is not warranted on that account. The Court of Appeals' opinion amply demonstrates why—with or without a settlement on the table—the sprawling class the District Court certified does not satisfy Rule 23's requirements.

A

We address first the requirement of Rule 23(b)(3) that "[common] questions of law or fact ... predominate over any questions affecting only individual members." The District Court concluded that predominance was satisfied based on two factors: class members' shared experience of asbestos exposure and their common "interest in receiving prompt and fair compensation for their claims, while minimizing the risks and transaction costs inherent in the asbestos litigation process as it occurs presently in the tort system." The settling parties also contend that the settlement's fairness is a common question, predominating over disparate legal issues that might be pivotal in litigation but become irrelevant under the settlement.

The predominance requirement stated in Rule 23(b)(3), we hold, is not met by the factors on which the District Court relied. The benefits asbestos-exposed persons might gain from the establishment of a grand-scale compensation scheme is a matter fit for legislative consideration, but it is not pertinent to the predominance inquiry. That inquiry trains on the legal or factual questions that qualify each class member's case as a genuine controversy, questions that preexist any settlement.

The Rule 23(b)(3) predominance inquiry tests whether proposed classes are sufficiently cohesive to warrant adjudication by representation. The inquiry appropriate under Rule 23(e), on the other hand, protects unnamed class members "from unjust or unfair settlements affecting their rights when the representatives become fainthearted before the action is adjudicated or are able to secure satisfaction of their individual claims by a compromise." But it is not the mission of Rule 23(e) to assure the class cohesion that legitimizes representative action in the first place. If a common interest in a fair compromise could satisfy the predominance requirement of Rule 23(b)(3), that vital prescription would be stripped of any meaning in the settlement context.

The District Court also relied upon this commonality: "The members of the class have all been exposed to asbestos products supplied by the defendants...." Even if Rule 23(a)'s commonality requirement may be satisfied by that shared experience, the predominance criterion is far more demanding. Given the greater number of questions peculiar to the several categories of class members, and to individuals within each category, and the significance of those uncommon questions, any overarching dispute about the health consequences of asbestos exposure cannot satisfy the Rule 23(b)(3) predominance standard.

The Third Circuit highlighted the disparate questions undermining class cohesion in this case:

> Class members were exposed to different asbestos-containing products, for different amounts of time, in different ways, and over different periods. Some class members suffer no physical injury or have only asymptomatic pleural changes, while others suffer from lung cancer, disabling asbestosis, or from mesothelioma.... Each has

a different history of cigarette smoking, a factor that complicates the causation inquiry.

The [exposure-only] plaintiffs especially share little in common, either with each other or with the presently injured class members. It is unclear whether they will contract asbestos-related disease and, if so, what disease each will suffer. They will also incur different medical expenses because their monitoring and treatment will depend on singular circumstances and individual medical histories.

Differences in state law, the Court of Appeals observed, compound these disparities. (citing *Phillips Petroleum Co. v. Shutts*).

No settlement class called to our attention is as sprawling as this one. Predominance is a test readily met in certain cases alleging consumer or securities fraud or violations of the antitrust laws. Even mass tort cases arising from a common cause or disaster may, depending upon the circumstances, satisfy the predominance requirement. The Advisory Committee for the 1966 revision of Rule 23, it is true, noted that "mass accident" cases are likely to present "significant questions, not only of damages but of liability and defenses of liability, . . . affecting the individuals in different ways." And the Committee advised that such cases are "ordinarily not appropriate" for class treatment. But the text of the Rule does not categorically exclude mass tort cases from class certification, and District Courts, since the late 1970's, have been certifying such cases in increasing number. The Committee's warning, however, continues to call for caution when individual stakes are high and disparities among class members great. As the Third Circuit's opinion makes plain, the certification in this case does not follow the counsel of caution. That certification cannot be upheld, for it rests on a conception of Rule 23(b)(3)'s predominance requirement irreconcilable with the Rule's design.

B

Nor can the class approved by the District Court satisfy Rule 23(a)(4)'s requirement that the named parties "will fairly and adequately protect the interests of the class." The adequacy inquiry under Rule 23(a)(4) serves to uncover conflicts of interest between named parties and the class they seek to represent. "[A] class representative must be part of the class and 'possess the same interest and suffer the same injury' as the class members."

As the Third Circuit pointed out, named parties with diverse medical conditions sought to act on behalf of a single giant class rather than on behalf of discrete subclasses. In significant respects, the interests of those within the single class are not aligned. Most saliently, for the currently injured, the critical goal is generous immediate payments. That goal tugs against the interest of exposure-only plaintiffs in ensuring an ample, inflation-protected fund for the future.

The disparity between the currently injured and exposure-only categories of plaintiffs, and the diversity within each category are not made insignificant by the District Court's finding that petitioners' assets suffice to pay claims under the settlement. Although this is not a "limited fund" case certified under Rule 23(b)(1)(B), the terms of the settlement reflect essential allocation decisions designed to confine compensation and to limit defendants' liability. For example, as earlier described, the settlement includes no adjustment for inflation; only a few claimants per year can opt out at the back end; and loss-of-consortium claims are extinguished with no compensation.

The settling parties, in sum, achieved a global compromise with no structural assurance of fair and adequate representation for the diverse groups and individuals affected. Although the named parties alleged a range of complaints, each served generally as representative for the whole, not for a separate constituency. In another asbestos class action, the Second Circuit spoke precisely to this point:

> [W]here differences among members of a class are such that subclasses must be established, we know of no authority that permits a court to approve a settlement without creating subclasses on the basis of consents by members of a unitary class, some of whom happen to be members of the distinct subgroups. The class representatives may well have thought that the Settlement serves the aggregate interests of the entire class. But the adversity among subgroups requires that the members of each subgroup cannot be bound to a settlement except by consents given by those who understand that their role is to represent solely the members of their respective subgroups.

The Third Circuit found no assurance here—either in the terms of the settlement or in the structure of the negotiations—that the named plaintiffs operated under a proper understanding of their representational responsibilities. That assessment, we conclude, is on the mark.

C

Impediments to the provision of adequate notice, the Third Circuit emphasized, rendered highly problematic any endeavor to tie to a settlement class persons with no perceptible asbestos-related disease at the time of the settlement. Many persons in the exposure-only category, the Court of Appeals stressed, may not even know of their exposure, or realize the extent of the harm they may incur. Even if they fully appreciate the significance of class notice, those without current afflictions may not have the information or foresight needed to decide, intelligently, whether to stay in or opt out.

Family members of asbestos-exposed individuals may themselves fall prey to disease or may ultimately have ripe claims for loss of consortium. Yet large numbers of people in this category—future spouses and children of asbestos victims—could not be alerted to their class membership. And current spouses and children of the occupationally exposed may know nothing of that exposure.

Because we have concluded that the class in this case cannot satisfy the requirements of common issue predominance and adequacy of representation, we need not rule, definitively, on the notice given here. In accord with the Third Circuit, however, we recognize the gravity of the question whether class action notice sufficient under the Constitution and Rule 23 could ever be given to legions so unselfconscious and amorphous.

V

The argument is sensibly made that a nationwide administrative claims processing regime would provide the most secure, fair, and efficient means of compensating victims of asbestos exposure. Congress, however, has not adopted such a solution. And Rule 23, which must be interpreted with fidelity to the Rules Enabling Act and applied with the interests of absent class members in close view, cannot carry the large load CCR, class counsel, and the District Court heaped upon it. As this case exemplifies, the rulemakers' prescriptions for class actions may be endangered by "those who embrace [Rule 23] too enthusiastically just as [they are by] those who approach [the Rule] with distaste."

* * *

For the reasons stated, the judgment of the Court of Appeals for the Third Circuit is

Affirmed.

JUSTICE O'CONNOR took no part in the consideration or decision of this case. JUSTICE BREYER, with whom JUSTICE STEVENS joins, concurring in part and dissenting in part.

Although I agree with the Court's basic holding that "[s]ettlement is relevant to a class certification," I find several problems in its approach that lead me to a different conclusion. First, I believe that the need for settlement in this mass tort case, with hundreds of thousands of lawsuits, is greater than the Court's opinion suggests. Second, I would give more weight than would the majority to settlement-related issues for purposes of determining whether common issues predominate. Third, I am uncertain about the Court's determination of adequacy of representation, and do not believe it appropriate for this Court to second-guess the District Court on the matter without first having the Court of Appeals consider it. Fourth, I am uncertain about the tenor of an opinion that seems to suggest the settlement is unfair. And fifth, in the absence of further review by the Court of Appeals, I cannot accept the majority's suggestions that "notice" is inadequate.

These difficulties flow from the majority's review of what are highly fact-based, complex, and difficult matters, matters that are inappropriate for initial review before this Court. The law gives broad leeway to district courts in making class certification decisions, and their judgments are to be reviewed by the court of appeals only for abuse of discretion. Indeed, the District Court's certification decision rests upon more than 300 findings of fact reached after five weeks of comprehensive hearings. Accordingly, I do not believe that we should in effect set aside the findings of the District Court. That court is far more familiar with the issues and litigants than is a court of appeals or are we, and therefore has "broad power and discretion . . . with respect to matters involving the certification" of class actions.

I do not believe that we can rely upon the Court of Appeals' review of the District Court record, for that review, and its ultimate conclusions, are infected by a legal error. There is no evidence that the Court of Appeals at any point considered the settlement as something that would help the class meet Rule 23. I find, moreover, the fact-related issues presented here sufficiently close to warrant further detailed appellate court review under the correct legal standard. And I shall briefly explain why this is so.

I

First, I believe the majority understates the importance of settlement in this case. Between 13 and 21 million workers have been exposed to asbestos in the workplace—over the past 40 or 50 years—but the most severe instances of such exposure probably occurred three or four decades ago. This exposure has led to several hundred thousand lawsuits, about 15% of which involved claims for cancer and about 30% for asbestosis. About half of the suits have involved claims for pleural thickening and plaques—the harmfulness of which is apparently controversial. Some of those who suffer from the most serious injuries, however, have received little or no compensation. ("[U]p to one-half of asbestos claims are now being filed by people who have little or no physical impairment. Many of these claims produce substantial payments (and substantial costs) even though the individual litigants will never become impaired"). These lawsuits have taken up more than 6% of all federal civil filings in one recent year, and are subject to a delay that is twice that of other civil suits.

Delays, high costs, and a random pattern of non-compensation led the Judicial Conference Ad Hoc Committee on Asbestos Litigation to transfer all federal asbestos personal-injury cases to the Eastern District of Pennsylvania in an effort to bring about a fair and comprehensive settlement. * * *

Although the transfer of the federal asbestos cases did not produce a general settlement, it was intertwined with and led to a lengthy year-long negotiation between the co-chairs of the Plaintiff's Multi–District Litigation Steering Committee and the 20 asbestos defendants who are before us here. These "protracted and vigorous" negotiations led to the present partial settlement, which will pay an estimated $1.3 billion and compensate perhaps 100,000 class members in the first 10 years. "The negotiations included a substantial exchange of information" between class counsel and the 20 defendant companies, including "confidential data" showing the defendants' historical settlement averages, numbers of claims filed and settled, and insurance resources. "Virtually no provision" of the settlement "was not the subject of significant negotiation," and the settlement terms "changed substantially" during the negotiations. In the end, the negotiations produced a settlement that, the District Court determined based on its detailed review of the process, was "the result of arms-length adversarial negotiations by extraordinarily competent and experienced attorneys."

The District Court, when approving the settlement, concluded that it improved the plaintiffs' chances of compensation and reduced total legal fees and other transaction costs by a significant amount. Under the previous system, according to the court, "[t]he sickest of victims often go uncompensated for years while valuable funds go to others who remain unimpaired by their mild asbestos disease." The court believed the settlement would create a compensation system that would make more money available for plaintiffs who later develop serious illnesses.

I mention this matter because it suggests that the settlement before us is unusual in terms of its importance, both to many potential plaintiffs and to defendants, and with respect to the time, effort, and expenditure that it reflects. All of which leads me to be reluctant to set aside the District Court's findings without more assurance than I have that they are wrong. I cannot obtain that assurance through comprehensive review of the record because that is properly the job of the Court of Appeals and that court, understandably, but as we now hold, mistakenly, believed that settlement was not a relevant (and, as I would say, important) consideration.

Second, the majority, in reviewing the District Court's determination that common "issues of fact and law predominate," says that the predominance "inquiry trains on the legal or factual questions that qualify each class member's case as a genuine controversy, questions that preexist any settlement." I find it difficult to interpret this sentence in a way that could lead me to the majority's conclusion. If the majority means that these pre-settlement questions are what matters, then how does it reconcile its statement with its basic conclusion that "settlement is relevant" to class certification, or with the numerous lower court authority that says that settlement is not only relevant, but important?

Nor do I understand how one could decide whether common questions "predominate" in the abstract—without looking at what is likely to be at issue in the proceedings that will ensue, namely, the settlement. Every group of human beings, after all, has some features in common, and some that differ. How can a court make a contextual judgment of the sort that Rule 23 requires without looking to what proceedings will follow? Such guideposts help it decide whether, in light of common concerns and differences, certification will achieve Rule 23's basic objective—"economies of time, effort, and expense." As this Court has previously observed, "sometimes it may be necessary for the court to probe behind the pleadings before coming to rest on the certification question." I am not saying that the "settlement counts only one way." Rather, the settlement may simply "add a great deal of information to the court's inquiry and will often expose diverging interests or common issues that were not evident or clear from the complaint" and courts "can and should" look to it to enhance the "ability . . . to make informed certification decisions."

The majority may mean that the District Court gave too much weight to the settlement. But I am not certain how it can reach that conclusion. It cannot rely upon the Court of Appeals, for that court gave no positive weight at all to the settlement. Nor can it say that the District Court relied solely on "a common interest in a fair compromise," for the District Court did not do so. Rather, it found the settlement relevant because it explained the importance of the class plaintiffs' common features and common interests. The court found predominance in part because: "The members of the class have all been exposed to asbestos products supplied by the defendants and all share an interest in receiving prompt and fair compensation for their claims, while minimizing the risks and transaction costs inherent in the asbestos litigation process as it occurs presently in the tort system."

The settlement is relevant because it means that these common features and interests are likely to be important in the proceeding that would ensue—a proceeding that would focus primarily upon whether or not the proposed settlement fairly and properly satisfied the interests class members had in common. That is to say, the settlement underscored the importance of (a) the common fact of exposure, (b) the common interest in receiving *some* compensation for certain rather than running a strong risk of *no* compensation, and (c) the common interest in avoiding large legal fees, other transaction costs, and delays.

Of course, as the majority points out, there are also important differences among class members. Different plaintiffs were exposed to different products for different times; each has a distinct medical history and a different history of smoking; and many cases arise under the laws of different States. The relevant question, however, is *how much* these differences matter in respect to the legal proceedings that lie ahead. Many, if not all, toxic tort class actions involve plaintiffs with such differences. And the differences in state law are of diminished importance in respect to a proposed settlement in which the defendants have waived all defenses and agreed to compensate all those who were injured.

These differences might warrant subclasses, though subclasses can have problems of their own. "There can be a cost in creating more distinct subgroups, each with its own representation. . . . [T]he more subclasses created, the more severe conflicts bubble to the surface and inhibit settlement. . . . The resources of defendants and, ultimately, the community must not be exhausted by protracted litigation." Or these differences may be too serious to permit an effort at group settlement. This kind of determination, as I have said, is one that the law commits to the discretion of the district court—reviewable for abuse of discretion by a court of appeals. I believe that we are far too distant from the litigation itself to reweigh the fact-specific Rule 23 determinations and to find them erroneous without the benefit of the Court of Appeals first having re-studied the matter with today's legal standard in mind.

Third, the majority concludes that the "representative parties" will not "fairly and adequately protect the interests of the class." Rule 23(a)(4). It finds a serious conflict between plaintiffs who are now injured and those who may be injured in the future because "for the currently injured, the critical goal is generous immediate payments," a goal that "tugs against the interest of exposure-only plaintiffs in ensuring an ample, inflation-protected fund for the future."

I agree that there is a serious problem, but it is a problem that often exists in toxic tort cases. And it is a problem that potentially exists whenever a single defendant injures several plaintiffs, for a settling plaintiff leaves fewer assets available for the others. With class actions, at least, plaintiffs have the consolation that a district court, thoroughly familiar with the facts, is charged with the responsibility of ensuring that the interests of no class members are sacrificed.

But this Court cannot easily safeguard such interests through review of a cold record. "What constitutes adequate representation is a question of fact that depends on the circumstances of each case." That is particularly so when, as here, there is an unusual baseline, namely, the " 'real and present danger' " described by the Judicial Conference Report. The majority's use of the lack of an inflation adjustment as evidence of inadequacy of representation for future plaintiffs, is one example of this difficulty. An inflation adjustment might not be as valuable as the majority assumes if most plaintiffs are old and not worried about receiving compensation decades from now. There are, of course, strong arguments as to its value. But that disagreement is one that this Court is poorly situated to resolve.

Further, certain details of the settlement that are not discussed in the majority opinion suggest that the settlement may be of greater benefit to future plaintiffs than the majority suggests. The District Court concluded that future plaintiffs receive a "significant value" from the settlement due to a variety of its items that benefit future plaintiffs, such as: (1) tolling the statute of limitations so that class members "will no longer be forced to file premature lawsuits or risk their claims being time-barred"; (2) waiver of defenses to liability; (3) payment of claims, if and when members become sick, pursuant to the settlement's compensation standards, which avoids "the uncertainties, long delays and high transaction costs [including attorney's fees] of the tort system"; (4) "some assurance that there will be funds available if and when they get sick," based on the finding that each defendant "has shown an ability to fund the payment of all qualifying claims" under the settlement; and (5) the right to additional compensation if cancer develops (many settlements for plaintiffs with noncancerous conditions bar such additional claims). For these reasons, and others, the District Court found that the distinction between present and future plaintiffs was "illusory."

I do not know whether or not the benefits are more or less valuable than an inflation adjustment. But I can certainly recognize an argument that they are.... The difficulties inherent in both knowing and understanding the vast number of relevant individual fact-based determinations here counsel heavily in favor of deference to district court decision-making in Rule 23 decisions. Or, at the least, making certain that appellate court review has taken place with the correct standard in mind.

Fourth, I am more agnostic than is the majority about the basic fairness of the settlement. The District Court's conclusions rested upon complicated factual findings that are not easily cast aside. It is helpful to consider some of them, such as its determination that the settlement provided "fair compensation ... while reducing the delays and transaction costs endemic to the asbestos litigation process" and that "the proposed class action settlement is superior to other available methods for the fair and efficient resolution of the asbestos-related personal injury claims of class members." ... I do not intend to pass judgment upon the settlement's fairness, but I do believe that these matters would have to be explored in far greater depth before I could reach a conclusion about fairness. And that task, as I have said, is one for the Court of Appeals.

Finally, I believe it is up to the District Court, rather than this Court, to review the legal sufficiency of notice to members of the class. The District Court found that the plan to provide notice was implemented at a cost of millions of dollars and included hundreds of thousands of individual notices, a wide-ranging television and print campaign, and significant additional efforts by 35 international and national unions to notify their members. Every notice emphasized that an individual did not currently have to be sick to be a class member. And in the end, the District Court was "confident" that Rule 23 and due process requirements were satisfied because, as a result of this "extensive and expensive notice procedure," "over six million" individuals "received actual notice materials," and "millions more" were reached by the media campaign. Although the majority, in principle, is reviewing a Court of Appeals' conclusion, it seems to me that its opinion might call into question the fact-related determinations of the District Court. To the extent that it does so, I disagree, for such findings cannot be so quickly disregarded. And I do not think that our precedents permit this Court to do so.

II

The issues in this case are complicated and difficult. The District Court might have been correct. Or not. Subclasses might be appropriate. Or not. I cannot tell. And I do not believe that this Court should be in the business of trying to make these fact-based determinations. That is a job suited to the district courts in the first instance, and the courts of appeals on review. But there is no reason in this case to believe that the Court of Appeals conducted its prior review with an understanding that the settlement could have constituted a reasonably strong factor in favor of class certification. For this reason, I would provide the courts below with an opportunity to analyze the factual questions involved in certification by vacating the judgment, and remanding the case for further proceedings.

* * *

PART TWO

ALTERNATIVE WEEKS

I. PROCEDURAL DUE PROCESS

A. REASONABLE NOTICE

U.S. CONST. AMEND. V.

No person shall be held to answer for a capital, or otherwise infamous crime, unless on a presentment or indictment of a Grand Jury, except in cases arising in the land or naval forces, or in the Militia, when in actual service in time of War or public danger; nor shall any person be subject for the same offence to be twice put in jeopardy of life or limb; nor shall be compelled in any criminal case to be a witness against himself, nor be deprived of life, liberty, or property, without due process of law; nor shall private property be taken for public use, without just compensation.

* * *

U.S. CONST. AMEND. XIV.

Section 1. All persons born or naturalized in the United States, and subject to the jurisdiction thereof, are citizens of the United States and of the State wherein they reside. No State shall make or enforce any law which shall abridge the privileges or immunities of citizens of the United States; nor shall any State deprive any person of life, liberty, or property, without due process of law; nor deny to any person within its jurisdiction the equal protection of the laws.

* * *

MULLANE v. CENTRAL HANOVER BANK & TRUST CO.

339 U.S. 306 (1950)

MR. JUSTICE JACKSON delivered the opinion of the Court.

This controversy questions the constitutional sufficiency of notice to beneficiaries on judicial settlement of accounts by the trustee of a common trust fund established under the New York Banking Law. The New York Court of Appeals considered and overruled objections that the statutory notice contravenes requirements of the Fourteenth Amendment and that by allowance of the account beneficiaries were deprived of property without due process of law.

Common trust fund legislation is addressed to a problem appropriate for state action. Mounting overheads have made administration of small trusts undesirable to corporate trustees. In order that donors and testators of moderately sized trusts may not be denied the service of corporate fiduciaries, the District of Columbia and some thirty states other than New York have permitted pooling small trust estates into one fund for investment administration. The income, capital gains, losses and expenses of the collective trust are shared by the constituent trusts in proportion to their contribution. By this plan, diversification of risk and economy of management can be extended to those whose capital standing alone would not obtain such advantage.

Statutory authorization for the establishment of such common trust funds is provided in the New York Banking Law. Under this Act a trust company may, with approval of the State Banking Board, establish a common fund and, within prescribed limits, invest therein the assets of an unlimited number of estates, trusts or other funds of which it is trustee. Each participating trust shares ratably in the common fund, but exclusive management and control is in the trust company as trustee, and neither a fiduciary nor any beneficiary of a participating trust is deemed to have ownership in any particular asset or investment of this common fund. The trust company must keep fund assets separate from its own, and in its fiduciary capacity may not deal with itself or any affiliate. Provisions are made for accountings twelve to fifteen months after the establishment of a fund and triennially thereafter. The decree in each such judicial settlement of accounts is made binding and conclusive as to any matter set forth in the account upon everyone having any interest in the common fund or in any participating estate, trust or fund.

In January, 1946, Central Hanover Bank and Trust Company established a common trust fund in accordance with these provisions, and in March, 1947, it petitioned the Surrogate's Court for settlement of its first account as common trustee. During the accounting period a total of 113 trusts, approximately half *inter vivos* and half testamentary, participated in the common trust fund, the gross capital of which was nearly three million dollars. The record does not show the number or residence of the beneficiaries, but they were many and it is clear that some of them were not residents of the State of New York.

The only notice given beneficiaries of this specific application was by publication in a local newspaper in strict compliance with the minimum requirements of N.Y. Banking Law § 100–c(12): "After filing such petition (for judicial settlement of its account) the petitioner shall cause to be issued by the court in which the petition is filed and shall publish not less than once in each week for four successive weeks in a newspaper to be designated by the court a notice or citation addressed generally without naming them to all parties interested in such common trust fund and in such estates, trusts or funds mentioned in the petition, all of which may be described in the notice or citation only in the manner set forth in said petition and without setting forth the residence of any such decedent or donor of any such estate, trust or fund." Thus the only notice required, and the only one given, was by newspaper publication setting forth merely the name and address of the trust company, the name and the date of establishment of the common trust fund, and a list of all participating estates, trusts or funds.

At the time the first investment in the common fund was made on behalf of each participating estate, however, the trust company, pursuant to the requirements of § 100–c(9), had notified by mail each person of full age and sound mind whose name and address was then known to it and who was "entitled to share in the income therefrom * * * (or) * * * who would be entitled to share in the principal if the event upon which such estate, trust or fund will become distributable should have occurred at the time of sending such notice." Included in the notice was a copy of those provisions of the Act relating to the sending of the notice itself and to the judicial settlement of common trust fund accounts.

Upon the filing of the petition for the settlement of accounts, appellant was, by order of the court pursuant to § 100–c(12), appointed special guardian and attorney for all persons known or unknown not otherwise appearing who had or might thereafter have any interest in the income of the common trust fund; and appellee Vaughan was appointed to represent those similarly interested in the principal. There were no other appearances on behalf of anyone interested in either interest or principal.

Appellant appeared specially, objecting that notice and the statutory provisions for notice to beneficiaries were inadequate to afford due process under the Fourteenth Amendment, and therefore that the court was without jurisdiction to render a final and binding decree. Appellant's objections were entertained and overruled, the Surrogate holding that the notice required and given was sufficient. A final decree accepting the accounts has been entered, affirmed by the Appellate Division of the Supreme Court.

The effect of this decree, as held below, is to settle "all questions respecting the management of the common fund." We understand that every right which beneficiaries would otherwise have against the trust company, either as trustee of the common fund or as trustee of any individual trust, for improper management of the common trust fund during the period covered by the accounting is sealed and wholly terminated by the decree.

We are met at the outset with a challenge to the power of the State— the right of its courts to adjudicate at all as against those beneficiaries who reside without the State of New York. It is contended that the proceeding is one *in personam* in that the decree affects neither title to nor possession of any res, but adjudges only personal rights of the beneficiaries to surcharge their trustee for negligence or breach of trust. Accordingly, it is said, under the strict doctrine of *Pennoyer v. Neff*, the Surrogate is without jurisdiction as to nonresidents upon whom personal service of process was not made.

Distinctions between actions *in rem* and those *in personam* are ancient and originally expressed in procedural terms what seems really to have been a distinction in the substantive law of property under a system quite unlike our own. The legal recognition and rise in economic importance of incorporeal or intangible forms of property have upset the ancient simplicity of property law and the clarity of its distinctions, while new forms of proceedings have confused the old procedural classification. American courts have sometimes classed certain actions as *in rem* because personal service of process was not required, and at other times have held personal service of process not required because the action was *in rem*.

Judicial proceedings to settle fiduciary accounts have been sometimes termed in rem, or more indefinitely *quasi in rem*, or more vaguely still, "in the nature of a proceeding *in rem*." It is not readily apparent how the courts of New York did or would classify the present proceeding, which has some characteristics and is wanting in some features of proceedings both *in rem* and *in personam*. But in any event we think that the requirements of the Fourteenth Amendment to the Federal Constitution do not depend upon a classification for which the standards are so elusive and confused generally and which, being primarily for state courts to define, may and do vary from state to state. Without disparaging the usefulness of distinctions between actions *in rem* and those *in personam* in many branches of law, or on other issues, or the reasoning which underlies them, we do not rest the power of the State to resort to constructive service in this proceeding upon how its courts or this Court may regard this historic antithesis. It is sufficient to observe that, whatever the technical definition of its chosen procedure, the interest of each state in providing means to close trusts that exist by the grace of its laws and are administered under the supervision of its courts is so insistent and rooted in custom as to establish beyond doubt the right of its courts to determine the interests of all claimants, resident or nonresident, provided its procedure accords full opportunity to appear and be heard.

Quite different from the question of a state's power to discharge trustees is that of the opportunity it must give beneficiaries to contest. Many controversies have raged about the cryptic and abstract words of the Due Process Clause but there can be no doubt that at a minimum they require that deprivation of life, liberty or property by adjudication be preceded by notice and opportunity for hearing appropriate to the nature of the case.

In two ways this proceeding does or may deprive beneficiaries of property. It may cut off their rights to have the trustee answer for negligent or illegal impairments of their interests. Also, their interests are presumably subject to diminution in the proceeding by allowance of fees and expenses to one who, in their names but without their knowledge, may conduct a fruitless or uncompensatory contest. Certainly the proceeding is one in which they may be deprived of property rights and hence notice and hearing must measure up to the standards of due process.

Personal service of written notice within the jurisdiction is the classic form of notice always adequate in any type of proceeding. But the vital interest of the State in bringing any issues as to its fiduciaries to a final settlement can be served only if interests or claims of individuals who are outside of the State can somehow be determined. A construction of the Due Process Clause which would place impossible or impractical obstacles in the way could not be justified.

Against this interest of the State we must balance the individual interest sought to be protected by the Fourteenth Amendment. This is defined by our holding that "The fundamental requisite of due process of law is the opportunity to be heard." This right to be heard has little reality or worth unless one is informed that the matter is pending and can choose for himself whether to appear or default, acquiesce or contest.

The Court has not committed itself to any formula achieving a balance between these interests in a particular proceeding or determining when constructive notice may be utilized or what test it must meet. Personal service has not in all circumstances been regarded as indispensable to the process due to residents, and it has more often been held unnecessary as to nonresidents. We disturb none of the established rules on these subjects. No decision constitutes a controlling or even a very illuminating precedent for the case before us. But a few general principles stand out in the books.

An elementary and fundamental requirement of due process in any proceeding which is to be accorded finality is notice reasonably calculated, under all the circumstances, to apprise interested parties of the pendency of the action and afford them an opportunity to present their objections. *Milliken v. Meyer.* The notice must be of such nature as reasonably to convey the required information, and it must afford a reasonable time for those interested to make their appearance. But if with due regard for the practicalities and peculiarities of the case these conditions are reasonably met the constitutional requirements are satisfied. "The criterion is not the possibility of conceivable injury, but the just and reasonable character of the requirements, having reference to the subject with which the statute deals."

But when notice is a person's due, process which is a mere gesture is not due process. The means employed must be such as one desirous of actually informing the absentee might reasonably adopt to accomplish it. The reasonableness and hence the constitutional validity of any chosen method may be defended on the ground that it is in itself reasonably certain to inform those affected, where conditions do not reasonably permit such notice, that the form chosen is not substantially less likely to bring home notice than other of the feasible and customary substitutes.

It would be idle to pretend that publication alone as prescribed here, is a reliable means of acquainting interested parties of the fact that their rights are before the courts. It is not an accident that the greater number of cases reaching this Court on the question of adequacy of notice have been concerned with actions founded on process constructively served through local newspapers. Chance alone brings to the attention of even a local resident an advertisement in small type inserted in the back pages of a newspaper, and if he makes his home outside the area of the newspaper's normal circulation the odds that the information will never reach him are large indeed. The chance of actual notice is further reduced when as here the notice required does not even name those whose attention it is supposed to attract, and does not inform acquaintances who might call it to attention. In weighing its sufficiency on the basis of equivalence with actual notice we are unable to regard this as more than a feint.

Nor is publication here reinforced by steps likely to attract the parties' attention to the proceeding. It is true that publication traditionally has been acceptable as notification supplemental to other action which in itself may reasonably be expected to convey a warning. The ways or an owner with tangible property are such that he usually arranges means to learn of any direct attack upon his possessory or proprietary rights. Hence, libel of a ship, attachment of a chattel or entry upon real estate in the name of law may reasonably be expected to come promptly to the owner's attention. When the state within which the owner has located such property seizes it for some reason, publication or posting affords an additional measure of notification. A state may indulge the assumption that one who has left tangible property in the state either has abandoned it, in which case proceedings against it deprive him of nothing, or that he has left some caretaker under a duty to let him know that it is being jeopardized. As phrased long ago by Chief Justice Marshall "It is the part of common prudence for all those who have any interest in (a thing), to guard that interest by persons who are in a situation to protect it."

In the case before us there is, of course, no abandonment. On the other hand these beneficiaries do have a resident fiduciary as caretaker of their interest in this property. But it is their caretaker who in the accounting becomes their adversary. Their trustee is released from giving notice of jeopardy, and no one else is expected to do so. Not even the special guardian is required or apparently expected to communicate with his ward and client, and, of course, if such a duty were merely transferred from the trustee to the guardian, economy would not be served and more likely the cost would be increased.

This Court has not hesitated to approve of resort to publication as a customary substitute in another class of cases where it is not reasonably possible or practicable to give more adequate warning. Thus it has been recognized that, in the case of persons missing or unknown, employment of an indirect and even a probably futile means of notification is all that the situation permits and creates no constitutional bar to a final decree foreclosing their rights.

Those beneficiaries represented by appellant whose interests or whereabouts could not with due diligence be ascertained come clearly within this category. As to them the statutory notice is sufficient. However great the odds that publication will never reach the eyes of such unknown parties, it is not in the typical case much more likely to fail than any of the choices open to legislators endeavoring to prescribe the best notice practicable.

Nor do we consider it unreasonable for the State to dispense with more certain notice to those beneficiaries whose interests are either conjectural or future or, although they could be discovered upon investigation, do not in due course of business come to knowledge of the common trustee. Whatever searches might be required in another situation under ordinary standards of diligence, in view of the character of the proceedings and the nature of the interests here involved we think them unnecessary. We recognize the practical difficulties and costs that would be attendant on frequent investigations into the status of great numbers of beneficiaries, many of whose interests in the common fund are so remote as to be ephemeral; and we have no doubt that such impracticable and extended searches are not required in the name of due process. The expense of keeping informed from day to day of substitutions among even current income beneficiaries and presumptive remaindermen, to say nothing of the far greater number of contingent beneficiaries, would impose a severe burden on the plan, and would likely dissipate its advantages. These are practical matters in which we should be reluctant to disturb the judgment of the state authorities.

Accordingly we overrule appellant's constitutional objections to published notice insofar as they are urged on behalf of any beneficiaries whose interests or addresses are unknown to the trustee.

As to known present beneficiaries of known place of residence, however, notice by publication stands on a different footing. Exceptions in the name of necessity do not sweep away the rule that within the limits of practicability notice must be such as is reasonably calculated to reach interested parties. Where the names and post office addresses of those affected by a proceeding are at hand, the reasons disappear for resort to means less likely than the mails to apprise them of its pendency.

The trustee has on its books the names and addresses of the income beneficiaries represented by appellant, and we find no tenable ground for dispensing with a serious effort to inform them personally of the accounting, at least by ordinary mail to the record addresses. Certainly sending them a copy of the statute months and perhaps years in advance does not answer this purpose. The trustee periodically remits their income to them, and we think that they might reasonably expect that with or apart from their remittances word might come to them personally that steps were being taken affecting their interests.

We need not weigh contentions that a requirement of personal service of citation on even the large number of known resident or nonresident beneficiaries would, by reasons of delay if not of expense, seriously interfere with the proper administration of the fund. Of course personal service even without the jurisdiction of the issuing authority serves the end of actual and personal notice, whatever power of compulsion it might lack. However, no such service is required under the circumstances. This type of trust presupposes a large number of small interests. The individual interest does not stand alone but is identical with that of a class. The rights of each in the integrity of the fund and the fidelity of the trustee are shared by many other beneficiaries. Therefore notice reasonably certain to reach most of those interested in objecting is likely to safeguard the interests of all, since any objections sustained would inure to the benefit of all. We think that under such circumstances reasonable risks that notice might not actually reach every beneficiary are justifiable. "Now and then an extraordinary case may turn up, but constitutional law, like other mortal contrivances, has to take some chances, and in the great majority of instances, no doubt, justice will be done."

The statutory notice to known beneficiaries is inadequate, not because in fact it fails to reach everyone, but because under the circumstances it is not reasonably calculated to reach those who could easily be informed by other means at hand. However it may have been in former times, the mails today are recognized as an efficient and inexpensive means of communication. Moreover, the fact that the trust company has been able to give mailed notice to known beneficiaries at the time the common trust fund was established is persuasive that postal notification at the time of accounting would not seriously burden the plan.

In some situations the law requires greater precautions in its proceedings than the business world accepts for its own purposes. In few, if any, will it be satisfied with less. Certainly it is instructive, in determining the reasonableness of the impersonal broadcast notification here used, to ask whether it would satisfy a prudent man of business, counting his pennies but finding it in his interest to convey information to many persons whose names and addresses are in his files. We are not satisfied that it would. Publication may theoretically be available for all the world to see, but it is too much in our day to suppose that each or any individual beneficiary does or could examine all that is published to see if something may be tucked away in it that affects his property interests. We have before indicated in reference to notice by publication that, "Great caution should be used not to let fiction deny the fair play that can be secured only by a pretty close adhesion to fact."

We hold the notice of judicial settlement of accounts required by the New York Banking Law is incompatible with the requirements of the Fourteenth Amendment as a basis for adjudication depriving known persons whose whereabouts are also known of substantial property rights. Accordingly the judgment is reversed and the cause remanded for further proceedings not inconsistent with this opinion.

Reversed.

MR. JUSTICE BURTON, dissenting.

These common trusts are available only when the instruments creating the participating trusts permit participation in the common fund.

Whether or not further notice to beneficiaries should supplement the notice and representation here provided is properly within the discretion of the State. The Federal Constitution does not require it here.

* * *

B. SERVICE OF PROCESS

FEDERAL RULE OF CIVIL PROCEDURE 4. SUMMONS

(a) Contents; Amendments.

    (1) *Contents.* A summons must:

        (A) name the court and the parties;

        (B) be directed to the defendant;

        (C) state the name and address of the plaintiff's attorney or—if unrepresented—of the plaintiff;

        (D) state the time within which the defendant must appear and defend;

        (E) notify the defendant that a failure to appear and defend will result in a default judgment against the defendant for the relief demanded in the complaint;

        (F) be signed by the clerk; and

        (G) bear the court's seal.

    (2) *Amendments.* The court may permit a summons to be amended.

(b) Issuance. On or after filing the complaint, the plaintiff may present a summons to the clerk for signature and seal. If the summons is properly completed, the clerk must sign, seal, and issue it to the plaintiff for service on the defendant. A summons—or a copy of a summons that is addressed to multiple defendants—must be issued for each defendant to be served.

(c) Service.

    (1) *In General.* A summons must be served with a copy of the complaint. The plaintiff is responsible for having the summons and complaint served within the time allowed by Rule 4(m) and must furnish the necessary copies to the person who makes service.

    (2) *By Whom.* Any person who is at least 18 years old and not a party may serve a summons and complaint.

    (3) *By a Marshal or Someone Specially Appointed.* At the plaintiff's request, the court may order that service be made by a United States marshal or deputy marshal or by a person specially appointed by the court. The court must so order if the plaintiff is authorized to proceed in forma pauperis under 28 U.S.C. § 1915 or as a seaman under 28 U.S.C. § 1916.

(d) Waiving Service.

   (1) *Requesting a Waiver.* An individual, corporation, or association that is subject to service under Rule 4(e), (f), or (h) has a duty to avoid unnecessary expenses of serving the summons. The plaintiff may notify such a defendant that an action has been commenced and request that the defendant waive service of a summons. The notice and request must:

   (A) be in writing and be addressed:

      (i) to the individual defendant; or

      (ii) for a defendant subject to service under Rule 4(h), to an officer, a managing or general agent, or any other agent authorized by appointment or by law to receive service of process;

   (B) name the court where the complaint was filed;

   (C) be accompanied by a copy of the complaint, two copies of a waiver form, and a prepaid means for returning the form;

   (D) inform the defendant, using text prescribed in Form 5, of the consequences of waiving and not waiving service;

   (E) state the date when the request is sent;

   (F) give the defendant a reasonable time of at least 30 days after the request was sent—or at least 60 days if sent to the defendant outside any judicial district of the United States—to return the waiver; and

   (G) be sent by first-class mail or other reliable means.

   (2) *Failure to Waive.* If a defendant located within the United States fails, without good cause, to sign and return a waiver requested by a plaintiff located within the United States, the court must impose on the defendant:

   (A) the expenses later incurred in making service; and

   (B) the reasonable expenses, including attorney's fees, of any motion required to collect those service expenses.

   (3) *Time to Answer After a Waiver.* A defendant who, before being served with process, timely returns a waiver need not serve an answer to the complaint until 60 days after the request was sent—or until 90 days after it was sent to the defendant outside any judicial district of the United States.

   (4) *Results of Filing a Waiver.* When the plaintiff files a waiver, proof of service is not required and these rules apply as if a summons and complaint had been served at the time of filing the waiver.

   (5) *Jurisdiction and Venue Not Waived.* Waiving service of a summons does not waive any objection to personal jurisdiction or to venue.

(e) Serving an Individual Within a Judicial District of the United States. Unless federal law provides otherwise, an individual—other than a minor, an incompetent person, or a person whose waiver has been filed—may be served in a judicial district of the United States by:

    (1) following state law for serving a summons in an action brought in courts of general jurisdiction in the state where the district court is located or where service is made; or

    (2) doing any of the following:

        (A) delivering a copy of the summons and of the complaint to the individual personally;

        (B) leaving a copy of each at the individual's dwelling or usual place of abode with someone of suitable age and discretion who resides there; or

        (C) delivering a copy of each to an agent authorized by appointment or by law to receive service of process.

(f) Serving an Individual in a Foreign Country. Unless federal law provides otherwise, an individual—other than a minor, an incompetent person, or a person whose waiver has been filed—may be served at a place not within any judicial district of the United States:

    (1) by any internationally agreed means of service that is reasonably calculated to give notice, such as those authorized by the Hague Convention on the Service Abroad of Judicial and Extrajudicial Documents;

    (2) if there is no internationally agreed means, or if an international agreement allows but does not specify other means, by a method that is reasonably calculated to give notice:

        (A) as prescribed by the foreign country's law for service in that country in an action in its courts of general jurisdiction;

        (B) as the foreign authority directs in response to a letter rogatory or letter of request; or

        (C) unless prohibited by the foreign country's law, by:

            (i) delivering a copy of the summons and of the complaint to the individual personally; or

            (ii) using any form of mail that the clerk addresses and sends to the individual and that requires a signed receipt; or

    (3) by other means not prohibited by international agreement, as the court orders.

(g) Serving a Minor or an Incompetent Person. A minor or an incompetent person in a judicial district of the United States must be served by following state law for serving a summons or like process on such a defendant in an action brought in the courts of general jurisdiction of the state where service is made. A minor or an incompetent person who is not within any judicial district of the United States must be served in the manner prescribed by Rule 4(f)(2)(A), (f)(2)(B), or (f)(3).

(h) Serving a Corporation, Partnership, or Association. Unless federal law provides otherwise or the defendant's waiver has been filed, a domestic or foreign corporation, or a partnership or other unincorporated association that is subject to suit under a common name, must be served:

(1) in a judicial district of the United States:

   (A) in the manner prescribed by Rule 4(e)(1) for serving an individual; or

   (B) by delivering a copy of the summons and of the complaint to an officer, a managing or general agent, or any other agent authorized by appointment or by law to receive service of process and—if the agent is one authorized by statute and the statute so requires—by also mailing a copy of each to the defendant; or

(2) at a place not within any judicial district of the United States, in any manner prescribed by Rule 4(f) for serving an individual, except personal delivery under (f)(2)(C)(i).

(i) Serving the United States and Its Agencies, Corporations, Officers, or Employees.

(1) *United States.* To serve the United States, a party must:

   (A) (i) deliver a copy of the summons and of the complaint to the United States attorney for the district where the action is brought—or to an assistant United States attorney or clerical employee whom the United States attorney designates in a writing filed with the court clerk—or

   (ii) send a copy of each by registered or certified mail to the civil-process clerk at the United States attorney's office;

   (B) send a copy of each by registered or certified mail to the Attorney General of the United States at Washington, D.C.; and

   (C) if the action challenges an order of a nonparty agency or officer of the United States, send a copy of each by registered or certified mail to the agency or officer.

(2) *Agency; Corporation; Officer or Employee Sued in an Official Capacity.* To serve a United States agency or corporation, or a United States officer or employee sued only in an official capacity, a party must serve the United States and also send a copy of the summons and of the complaint by registered or certified mail to the agency, corporation, officer, or employee.

(3) *Officer or Employee Sued Individually.* To serve a United States officer or employee sued in an individual capacity for an act or omission occurring in connection with duties performed on the United States' behalf (whether or not the officer or employee is also sued in an official capacity), a party must serve the United States and also serve the officer or employee under Rule 4(e), (f), or (g).

(4) ***Extending Time.*** The court must allow a party a reasonable time to cure its failure to:

   (A) serve a person required to be served under Rule 4(i)(2), if the party has served either the United States attorney or the Attorney General of the United States; or

   (B) serve the United States under Rule 4(i)(3), if the party has served the United States officer or employee.

(j) Serving a Foreign, State, or Local Government.

(1) ***Foreign State.*** A foreign state or its political subdivision, agency, or instrumentality must be served in accordance with 28 U.S.C. § 1608.

(2) ***State or Local Government.*** A state, a municipal corporation, or any other state-created governmental organization that is subject to suit must be served by:

   (A) delivering a copy of the summons and of the complaint to its chief executive officer; or

   (B) serving a copy of each in the manner prescribed by that state's law for serving a summons or like process on such a defendant.

(k) Territorial Limits of Effective Service.

(1) ***In General.*** Serving a summons or filing a waiver of service establishes personal jurisdiction over a defendant:

   (A) who is subject to the jurisdiction of a court of general jurisdiction in the state where the district court is located;

   (B) who is a party joined under Rule 14 or 19 and is served within a judicial district of the United States and not more than 100 miles from where the summons was issued; or

   (C) when authorized by a federal statute.

(2) ***Federal Claim Outside State–Court Jurisdiction.*** For a claim that arises under federal law, serving a summons or filing a waiver of service establishes personal jurisdiction over a defendant if:

   (A) the defendant is not subject to jurisdiction in any state's courts of general jurisdiction; and

   (B) exercising jurisdiction is consistent with the United States Constitution and laws.

(l) Proving Service.

    (1) *Affidavit Required.* Unless service is waived, proof of service must be made to the court. Except for service by a United States marshal or deputy marshal, proof must be by the server's affidavit.

    (2) *Service Outside the United States.* Service not within any judicial district of the United States must be proved as follows:

        (A) if made under Rule 4(f)(1), as provided in the applicable treaty or convention; or

        (B) if made under Rule 4(f)(2) or (f)(3), by a receipt signed by the addressee, or by other evidence satisfying the court that the summons and complaint were delivered to the addressee.

    (3) *Validity of Service; Amending Proof.* Failure to prove service does not affect the validity of service. The court may permit proof of service to be amended.

(m) Time Limit for Service. If a defendant is not served within 120 days after the complaint is filed, the court—on motion or on its own after notice to the plaintiff—must dismiss the action without prejudice against that defendant or order that service be made within a specified time. But if the plaintiff shows good cause for the failure, the court must extend the time for service for an appropriate period. This subdivision (m) does not apply to service in a foreign country under Rule 4(f) or 4(j)(1).

(n) Asserting Jurisdiction over Property or Assets.

    (1) *Federal Law.* The court may assert jurisdiction over property if authorized by a federal statute. Notice to claimants of the property must be given as provided in the statute or by serving a summons under this rule.

    (2) *State Law.* On a showing that personal jurisdiction over a defendant cannot be obtained in the district where the action is brought by reasonable efforts to serve a summons under this rule, the court may assert jurisdiction over the defendant's assets found in the district. Jurisdiction is acquired by seizing the assets under the circumstances and in the manner provided by state law in that district.

* * *

NATIONAL EQUIPMENT RENTAL, LTD. v. SZUKHENT

375 U.S. 311 (1964)

MR. JUSTICE STEWART delivered the opinion of the Court.

The Federal Rules of Civil Procedure provide that service of process upon an individual may be made "by delivering a copy of the summons and of the complaint to an agent authorized by appointment * * * to receive service of process." The petitioner is a corporation with its principal place of business in New York. It sued the respondents, residents of Michigan, in a New York federal court, claiming that the respondents had defaulted under a farm equipment lease. The only question now before us is whether the person upon whom the summons and complaint were served was "an agent authorized by appointment" to receive the same, so as to subject the respondents to the jurisdiction of the federal court in New York.

The respondents obtained certain farm equipment from the petitioner under a lease executed in 1961. The lease was on a printed form less than a page and a half in length, and consisted of 18 numbered paragraphs. The last numbered paragraph, appearing just above the respondents' signatures and printed in the same type used in the remainder of the instrument, provided that "the Lessee hereby designates Florence Weinberg, 47–21 Forty-first Street, Long Island City, N.Y., as agent for the purpose of accepting service of any process within the State of New York." The respondents were not acquainted with Florence Weinberg.

In 1962 the petitioner commenced the present action by filing in the federal court in New York a complaint which alleged that the respondents had failed to make any of the periodic payments specified by the lease. The Marshal delivered two copies of the summons and complaint to Florence Weinberg. That same day she mailed the summons and complaint to the respondents, together with a letter stating that the documents had been served upon her as the respondents' agent for the purpose of accepting service of process in New York, in accordance with the agreement contained in the lease.[4] The petitioner itself also notified the respondents by certified mail of the service of process upon Florence Weinberg.

Upon motion of the respondents, the District Court quashed service of the summons and complaint, holding that, although Florence Weinberg had promptly notified the respondents of the service of process and mailed copies of the summons and complaint to them, the lease agreement itself had not explicitly required her to do so, and there was therefore a "failure of the agency arrangement to achieve intrinsic and continuing reality." The Court of Appeals affirmed, and we granted certiorari. For the reasons stated in this opinion, we have concluded that Florence Weinberg was "an agent authorized by appointment * * * to receive service of process," and accordingly we reverse the judgment before us.

We need not and do not in this case reach the situation where no personal notice has been given to the defendant. Since the respondents did

---

4. The complaint, summons, and covering letter were sent by certified mail, and the letter read as follows:

Gentlemen:

Please take notice that the enclosed Summons and Complaint was duly served upon me this day by the United States Marshal, as your agent for the purpose of accepting service of process within the State of New York, in accordance with your contract with National Equipment Rental, Ltd.

Very truly yours,

Florence Weinberg

in fact receive complete and timely notice of the lawsuit pending against them, no due process claim has been made. The case before us is therefore quite different from cases where there was no actual notice, such as *Mullane v. Central Hanover Bank & Trust Co.* Similarly, as the Court of Appeals recognized, this Court's decision in *Wuchter v. Pizzutti*, is inapposite here. In that case a state nonresident motorist statute which failed to provide explicitly for communication of notice was held unconstitutional, despite the fact that notice had been given to the defendant in that particular case. *Wuchter* dealt with the limitations imposed by the Fourteenth Amendment upon a statutory scheme by which a State attempts to subject nonresident individuals to the jurisdiction of its courts. The question presented here, on the other hand, is whether a party to a private contract may appoint an agent to receive service of process within the meaning of Federal Rule of Civil Procedure 4(d)(1), where the agent is not personally known to the party, and where the agent has not expressly undertaken to transmit notice to the party.

The purpose underlying the contractual provision here at issue seems clear. The clause was inserted by the petitioner and agreed to by the respondents in order to assure that any litigation under the lease should be conducted in the State of New York. The contract specifically provided that "This agreement shall be deemed to have been made in Nassau County, New York, regardless of the order in which the signatures of the parties shall be affixed hereto, and shall be interpreted, and the rights and liabilities of the parties here determined, in accordance with the laws of the State of New York." And it is settled, as the courts below recognized, that parties to a contract may agree in advance to submit to the jurisdiction of a given court, to permit notice to be served by the opposing party, or even to waive notice altogether.

Under well-settled general principles of the law of agency Florence Weinberg's prompt acceptance and transmittal to the respondents of the summons and complaint pursuant to the authorization was itself sufficient to validate the agency, even though there was no explicit previous promise on her part to do so. "The principal's authorization may neither expressly nor impliedly request any expression of assent by the agent as a condition of the authority, and in such a case any exercise of power by the agent within the scope of the authorization, during the term for which it was given, or within a reasonable time if no fixed term was mentioned, will bind the principal."

We deal here with a Federal Rule, applicable to federal courts in all 50 States. But even if we were to assume that this uniform federal standard should give way to contrary local policies, there is no relevant concept of state law which would invalidate the agency here at issue. In Michigan, where the respondents reside, the statute which validates service of process under the circumstances present in this case contains no provision requiring that the appointed agent expressly undertake to notify the principal of the service of process Similarly, New York law, which it was agreed should be applicable to the lease provisions, does not require any such express promise by the agent in order to create a valid agency for receipt of process. The New York statutory short form of general power of attorney, which specifically includes the power to accept service of process, is entirely silent as to any such requirement. Indeed, the identical contractual provision at issue here has been held by a New York court to create a valid agency for service of process under the law of that State.

It is argued, finally, that the agency sought to be created in this case was invalid because Florence Weinberg may have had a conflict of interest. This argument is based upon the fact that she was not personally known to the respondents at the time of her appointment and upon a suggestion in the record that she may be related to an officer of the petitioner corporation. But such a contention ignores the narrowly limited nature of the agency here involved. Florence Weinberg was appointed the respondents' agent for the single purpose of receiving service of process. An agent with authority so limited can in no meaningful sense be deemed to have had an interest antagonistic to the respondents, since both the petitioner and the respondents had an equal interest in assuring that, in the event of litigation, the latter be given that adequate and timely notice which is a prerequisite to a valid judgment.

A different case would be presented if Florence Weinberg had not given prompt notice to the respondents, for then the claim might well be made that her failure to do so had operated to invalidate the agency. We hold only that, prompt notice to the respondents having been given, Florence Weinberg was their "agent authorized by appointment" to receive process within the meaning of Federal Rule of Civil Procedure 4(d)(1).

The judgment of the Court of Appeals is reversed and the case is remanded for further proceedings consistent with this opinion. It is so ordered.

Judgment of Court of Appeals reversed and case remanded.

Mr. Justice Black, dissenting.

The petitioner, National Equipment Rental, Ltd., is a Delaware corporation with its principal place of business in greater New York City. From that location it does a nationwide equipment rental business. The respondents, Steve and Robert Szukhent, father and son farming in Michigan, leased from National two incubators for their farm, signing in Michigan a lease contract which was a standard printed form obviously prepared by the New York company's lawyers. Included in the 18 paragraphs of fine print was the following provision: " * * * the Lessee hereby designates Florence Weinberg, 47–21 Forty-first Street, Long Island City, N.Y., as agent for the purpose of accepting service of any process within the State of New York."

The New York company later brought this suit for breach of the lease in the United States District Court for the Eastern District of New York. Rule 4(d)(1) of the Federal Rules of Civil Procedure authorizes service of process for suits in federal courts to be made on an "agent authorized by appointment or by law to receive service of process." Process was served on Mrs. Weinberg as "agent" of the Michigan farmers. She mailed notice of this service to the Szukhents. A New York lawyer appeared especially for them and moved to quash the service on the ground that Mrs. Weinberg was not their agent but was in reality the agent of the New York company.

The record on the motion to quash shows that the Szukhents had never had any dealings with Mrs. Weinberg, their supposed agent. They had never met, seen, or heard of her. She did not sign the lease, was not a party to it, received no compensation from the Szukhents, and undertook no obligation to them. In fact, she was handpicked by the New York company to accept service of process in any suits that might thereafter be filed by the company. Only after this suit was brought was it reluctantly revealed that Mrs. Weinberg was in truth the wife of one of the company's officers. The district judge, applying New York law to these facts, held that there had been no effective appointment of Mrs. Weinberg as agent of the Szukhents, that the service on her as their "agent" was therefore invalid, and that the service should be quashed. The Court of Appeals, one judge dissenting, affirmed, agreeing that no valid agency had been created. This Court now reverses both courts below and holds that the contractual provision purporting to appoint Mrs. Weinberg as agent is valid and that service of process on her as agent was therefore valid and effective under Rule 4(d)(1) as on an "agent authorized by appointment * * * to receive service of process." I disagree with that holding, believing that (1) whether Mrs. Weinberg was a valid agent upon whom service could validly be effected under Rule 4(d)(1) should be determined under New York law and that we should accept the holdings of the federal district judge and the Court of Appeals sitting in New York that under that State's law the purported appointment of Mrs. Weinberg was invalid and ineffective; (2) if however, Rule 4(d)(1) is to be read as calling upon us to formulate a new federal definition of agency for purposes of service of process, I think our formulation should exclude Mrs. Weinberg from the category of an "agent authorized by appointment * * * to receive service of process;" and (3) upholding service of process in this case raises serious questions as to whether these Michigan farmers have been denied due process of law in violation of the Fifth and Fourteenth Amendments.

I.

No federal statute has undertaken to regulate the sort of agency transaction here involved. There is only Rule 4(d)(1), which says nothing more than that in federal courts personal jurisdiction may be obtained by service on an "agent." The Rule does not attempt to define who is an "agent." To me it is evident that the draftsmen of the Rules did not, by using the word "agent," show any intention of throwing out the traditional body of state law and creating a new and different federal doctrine in this branch of the law of agency. Therefore, it is to the law of New York—

the State where this action was brought in federal court, the place where the contract was deemed by the parties to have been made, and the State the law of which was specified as determining rights and liabilities under the contract[3]—that we should turn to test the validity of the appointment.

I agree with the district judge that this agency is invalid under the laws of New York. The highest state court that has passed on the question has held that, because of New York statutes, the designation by a nonresident of New York of an agent to receive service of process is ineffective; the court, in denying an order for interpleader, held that only residents of New York can make such an appointment, and even then only in compliance with the terms of the controlling statute. Even the dissenting judge in the Court of Appeals in the present case acknowledged that the purported appointment of Mrs. Weinberg "would not subject the defendants to the jurisdiction of the courts of the State of New York." The company cites three decisions of trial judges in two of New York's 62 counties which have upheld service upon purported agents in circumstances like these. In fact, two of those cases, both decided in Nassau County, where the company does business, upheld service on this same Mrs. Weinberg as "agent" in suits brought for breach of contract by this same company, one against a defendant living in the distant State of California. But these trial courts did not even mention the Rosenthal case, decided by a higher court, and in fact cited no higher court opinions at all which dealt with the question here raised. In seeking to apply New York's definition of "agent" we should follow the considered opinions of the highest appellate courts which have passed upon the question, not unexamined decisions of trial courts. In so doing, we see that under New York law this service of process is invalid. Also, we should accept the view of the question taken by the federal courts sitting in the State whose law is being applied unless we are shown "clearly and convincingly" that these courts erred. Here there is no showing that the Court of Appeals—where neither the majority nor the dissenter disputed the District Court's view of New York law—has erred.[7]

II.

If Rule 4(d)(1) is to be read as requiring this Court to formulate new federal standards of agency to be resolved in each case as a federal question, rather than as leaving the question to state law, I think the standards we formulate should clearly and unequivocally denounce as invalid any alleged service of process on nonresidents based on purported agency contracts having no more substance than that naming Mrs. Weinberg.

---

3. If New York would look in turn to the law of Michigan, the place where the contract was signed by the Szukhents and was to be performed, then we should do the same. *Cf. Klaxon Co. v. Stentor Electric Mfg. Co.*

7. Since New York would not hold Mrs. Weinberg a valid agent to receive service of process, service cannot be upheld as authorized by that part of Rule 4(d)(7) which validates service "in the manner prescribed by the law of the state."

A. In the first place, we should interpret the federal rule as contemplating a genuine agent, not a sham. Here the "agent," Mrs. Weinberg, was unknown to respondents. She was chosen by the New York company, was under its supervision, and, indeed, was the wife of one of its officers-facts no one ever told these farmers. State courts in general quite properly refuse to uphold service of process on an agent who, though otherwise competent, has interests antagonistic to those of the person he is meant to represent. In Michigan, the place where the contract here involved was signed and where the machinery was delivered, the State Supreme Court has said that to hold otherwise would open "wide the door for the perpetration of fraud and maladministration of justice." There is no reason for a federal rule to tolerate a less punctilious regard for fair dealing in a matter so very important to a person being sued. I cannot believe that Rule 4(d)(1), which may under some circumstances be used to subject people to jurisdiction thousands of miles from home, was ever meant to bring a defendant into court by allowing service on an "agent" whose true loyalty is not to the person being sued but to the one bringing suit. The Canons of Ethics forbid a lawyer to serve conflicting parties, at least without express consent given after full disclosure. If we are to create a federal standard, I would hold a 4(d) (1) agent to a like duty. Furthermore, as the courts below pointed out, there was no provision in the contract assuring the defendants of notice of any action brought against them in New York, and no undertaking by their purported agent or anyone else to notify them. It is true that actual notice was given. But there is a prophylactic value, especially where contracts of this kind can in future cases be used to impose on a nonresident defendant, in requiring that the contract provide for notice in the first place. We have, on due process grounds, required as much of state statutes which declare a statutory agent for substituted service on nonresidents.

B. But even if this contract had named a disinterested agent and required that notice of service be given to the Szukhents, I think that any federal standards we formulate under Rule 4(d)(1) should invalidate purported service of process in the circumstances of cases like this one. To give effect to the clause about service of process in this standardized form contract amounts to a holding that when the Szukhents leased these incubators they then and there, long in advance of any existing justiciable dispute or controversy, effectively waived all objection to the jurisdiction of a court in a distant State the process of which could not otherwise reach them. Both the nature of the right given up and the nature of the contractual relation here make such an application of the contract impossible to square with the context of American law in which Rule 4(d)(1) was written. The right to have a case tried locally and be spared the likely injustice of having to litigate in a distant or burdensome forum is as ancient as the Magna Charta. States generally have refused to enforce agreements in notes purporting to consent to foreign jurisdiction along with consent to confession of judgment, sometimes because such provisions are outlawed by statutes and sometimes because they are outlawed by courts in the absence of specific statutory prohibitions. In countless cases courts have refused to allow insurance companies to arrange that suits against them on their policies may be brought only at the home office of the company. And prior decisions of our own Court have gone to great lengths to avoid giving enforcement to such provisions.

C. Where one party, at its leisure and drawing upon expert legal advice, drafts a form contract, complete with waivers of rights and privileges by the other, it seems to me to defy common sense for this Court to formulate a federal rule designed to treat this as an agreement coolly negotiated and hammered out by equals.

It is hardly likely that these Michigan farmers, hiring farm equipment, were in any position to dicker over what terms went into the contract they signed. Yet holding this service effective inevitably will mean that the Szukhents must go nearly a thousand miles to a strange city, hire New York counsel, pay witnesses to travel there, pay their own and their witnesses' hotel bills, try to explain a dispute over a farm equipment lease to a New York judge or jury, and in other ways bear the burdens of litigation in a distant, and likely a strange, city. The company, of course, must have had this in mind when it put the clause in the contract. It doubtless hoped, by easing into its contract this innocent looking provision for service of process in New York, to succeed in making it as burdensome, disadvantageous, and expensive as possible for lessees to contest actions brought against them. This Court, in applying the doctrine of forum non conveniens, has suggested that "(a) plaintiff sometimes is under temptation to resort to a strategy of forcing the trial at a most inconvenient place for an adversary." *Gulf Oil Corp. v. Gilbert*. What was there deemed to be a very unjust result is greatly aggravated, I think, by today's holding that a man can, by a cleverly drafted form, be successfully inveigled into giving up in advance of any controversy his traditional right to be served with process and sued at home. Rule 4(d)(1), designed in part to preserve the right to have a case tried in a convenient tribunal, should not be used to formulate federal standards of agency that defeat this purpose.

It should be understood that the effect of the Court's holding is not simply to give courts sitting in New York jurisdiction over these Michigan farmers. It is also, as a practical matter, to guarantee that whenever the company wishes to sue someone who has contracted with it, it can, by force of this clause, confine all such suits to courts sitting in New York. This Court and others have frequently refused to hold valid a contract which, before any controversy has arisen, attempts to restrict jurisdiction to a single court or courts. Here this contract as effectively ousts the Michigan courts of jurisdiction as if it had said so. Today's holding disregards Michigan's interest in supervising the protection of rights of its citizens who never leave the State but are sued by foreign companies with which they have done business.

D. To formulate standards of agency under Rule 4(d)(1) which allow a plaintiff with a form contract to extend a District Court's service of process for suits on that contract anywhere in the country (or, presumably, the world) is to do something which Congress has never done. Years ago Mr. Justice Brandeis, speaking for the Court, emphasized that Congress had always been reluctant to grant power to Federal District Courts to serve process outside the territorial borders of the State in which a District Court sits.

This Court should reject any construction of Rule 4(d)(1) or formulation of federal standards under it to help powerful litigants to achieve by unbargained take-it-or-leave-it contracts what Congress has consistently refused to permit by legislation.

The end result of today's holding is not difficult to foresee. Clauses like the one used against the Szukhents—clauses which companies have not inserted, I suspect, because they never dreamed a court would uphold them—will soon find their way into the "boilerplate" of everything from an equipment lease to a conditional sales contract. Today's holding gives a green light to every large company in this country to contrive contracts which declare with force of law that when such a company wants to sue someone with whom it does business, that individual must go and try to defend himself in some place, no matter how distant, where big business enterprises are concentrated, like, for example, New York Connecticut, or, Illinois, or else suffer a default judgment. In this very case the Court holds that by this company's carefully prepared contractual clause the Szukhents must, to avoid a judgment rendered without a fair and full hearing, travel hundreds of miles across the continent, probably crippling their defense and certainly depleting what savings they may have, to try to defend themselves in a court sitting in New York City. I simply cannot believe that Congress, when by its silence it let Rule 4(d)(1) go into effect, meant for that rule to be used as a means to achieve such a far-reaching, burdensome, and unjust result. Heretofore judicial good common sense has, on one ground or another, disregarded contractual provisions like this one, not encouraged them. It is a long trip from San Francisco—or from Honolulu or Anchorage—to New York, Boston, or Wilmington. And the trip can be very expensive, often costing more than it would simply to pay what is demanded. The very threat of such a suit can be used to force payment of alleged claims, even though they be wholly without merit. This fact will not be news to companies exerting their economic power to wangle such contracts. No statute and no rule requires this Court to place its imprimatur upon them. I would not.

III.

The Court's holding that these Michigan residents are compelled to go to New York to defend themselves in a New York court brings sharply into focus constitutional questions as to whether they will thereby be denied due process of law in violation of the Fifth and Fourteenth Amendments. While implicit in much of the oral arguments and in the briefs, these questions have not been adequately discussed. The questions are serious and involve matters of both historical and practical importance. These things lead me to believe that this case should be set down for reargument on these constitutional questions. Moreover, this Court might, after such arguments, conclude that these constitutional questions are so substantial and weighty that the non-constitutional issues should be decided in favor of the Michigan defendants, thereby making a constitutional decision unnecessary. While I would prefer to await more informative constitutional discussions before deciding these due process questions, the Court rules against a re-argument. In this situation I am compelled now to reach, consider, and decide the constitutional questions. My view is that the Court's holding denies the Szukhents due process of law for the following, among other, reasons.

It has been established constitutional doctrine since *Pennoyer v. Neff* was decided in 1878, that a state court is without power to serve its process outside the State's boundaries so as to compel a resident of another State against his will to appear as a defendant in a case where a personal judgment is sought against him. This rule means that an individual has a constitutional right not to be sued on such claims in the courts of any State except his own without his consent. The prime value of this constitutional right has not diminished since *Pennoyer v. Neff* was decided. Our States have increased from 38 to 50. Although improved methods of travel have increased its speed and ameliorated its discomforts, it can hardly be said that these almost miraculous improvements would make more palatable or constitutional now than in 1878 a system of law that would compel a man or woman from Hawaii, Alaska, or even Michigan to travel to New York to defend against civil lawsuits claiming a few hundred or thousand dollars growing out of an ordinary commercial contract.

It can of course be argued with plausibility that the *Pennoyer* constitutional rule has no applicability here because the process served on the Szukhents ran from a federal, not a state, court. But this case was in federal court solely because of the District Court's diversity jurisdiction. And in the absence of any overriding constitutional or congressional requirements the rights of the parties were to be preserved there as they would have been preserved in state courts. Neither the Federal Constitution nor any federal statute requires that a person who could not constitutionally be compelled to submit himself to a state court's jurisdiction forfeits that constitutional right because he is sued in a Federal District Court acting for a state court solely by reason of the happenstance of diversity jurisdiction. The constant aim of federal courts, at least since *Erie R. Co. v. Tompkins*, has been, so far as possible, to protect all the substantial rights of litigants in both courts alike. And surely the right of a person not to be dragged into the courts of a distant State to defend himself against a civil lawsuit cannot be dismissed as insubstantial. Happily, in considering this question we are not confronted with any congressional enactment designed to bring non-state residents into a Federal District Court passed pursuant to congressional power to establish a judicial system to hear federal questions under Article III of the Constitution, or its power to regulate commerce under Art. I, § 8, or any of the other constitutionally granted congressional powers; we are dealing only with its power to let federal courts try lawsuits when the litigants reside in different States. Whatever power Congress might have in these other areas to extend a District Court's power to serve process across state lines, such power does not, I think, provide sound argument to justify reliance upon diversity jurisdiction to destroy a man's constitutional right to have his civil lawsuit tried in his own State. The protection of such a right in cases growing out of local state lawsuits is the reason for and the heart of the *Pennoyer* constitutional doctrine relevant here.

The Court relies on the printed provision of the contract as a consent of the Szukhents to be sued in New York, making the *Pennoyer* rule inapplicable. In effect the Court treats the provision as a waiver of the Szukhents' constitutional right not to be compelled to go to a New York court to defend themselves against the company's claims. This printed form provision buried in a multitude of words is too weak an imitation of a genuine agreement to be treated as a waiver of so important a constitutional safeguard as is the right to be sued at home. Waivers of constitutional rights to be effective, this Court has said, must be deliberately and understandingly made and can be established only by clear, unequivocal, and unambiguous language. It strains credulity to suggest that these Michigan farmers ever read this contractual provision about Mrs. Weinberg and about "accepting service of any process within the State of New York." And it exhausts credulity to think that they or any other laymen reading these legalistic words would have known or even suspected that they amounted to an agreement of the Szukhents to let the company sue them in New York should any controversy arise. This Court should not permit valuable constitutional rights to be destroyed by any such sharp contractual practices. The idea that there was a knowing consent of the Szukhents to be sued in the courts of New York is no more than a fiction—not even an amiable one at that.

I would affirm the judgment.

MR. JUSTICE BRENNAN, with whom THE CHIEF JUSTICE and MR. JUSTICE GOLDBERG join, dissenting.

I would affirm. In my view, federal standards and not state law must define who is "an agent authorized by appointment" within the meaning of Rule 4(d) (1). In formulating these standards I would, first, construe Rule 4(d)(1) to deny validity to the appointment of a purported agent whose interests conflict with those of his supposed principal. Second, I would require that the appointment include an explicit condition that the agent after service transmit the process forthwith to the principal. Although our decision in *Wuchter v. Pizzutti* dealt with the constitutionality of a state statute, the reasoning of that case is persuasive that, in fashioning a federal agency rule, we should engraft the same requirement upon Rule 4(d)(1). Third, since the corporate plaintiff prepared the printed form contract, I would not hold the individual purchaser bound by the appointment without proof, in addition to his mere signature on the form, that the individual understandingly consented to be sued in a State not that of his residence. We must bear in mind ... that we must strive not to be "that 'blind' Court, against which Mr. Chief Justice Taft admonished in a famous passage, * * * that does not see what '(a)ll others can see and understand.' " It offends common sense to treat a printed form which closes an installment sale as embodying terms to all of which the individual knowingly assented. The sales pitch aims solely at getting the signature on the form and wastes no time explaining or even mentioning the print. Before I would find that an individual purchaser has knowingly and intelligently consented to be sued in another State, I would require more proof of that fact than is provided by his mere signature on the form.

Since these standards were not satisfied in this case, the service of the summons and complaint was properly quashed.

* * *

C. OPPORTUNITY TO BE HEARD: PRIOR HEARING

FUENTES v. SHEVIN

407 U.S. 67 (1972)

MR. JUSTICE STEWART delivered the opinion of the Court.

We here review the decisions of two three-judge federal District Courts that upheld the constitutionality of Florida and Pennsylvania laws authorizing the summary seizure of goods or chattels in a person's possession under a writ of replevin. Both statutes provide for the issuance of writs ordering state agents to seize a person's possessions, simply upon the ex parte application of any other person who claims a right to them and posts a security bond. Neither statute provides for notice to be given to the possessor of the property, and neither statute gives the possessor an opportunity to challenge the seizure at any kind of prior hearing. The question is whether these statutory procedures violate the Fourteenth Amendment's guarantee that no State shall deprive any person of property without due process of law.

I

The appellant in No. 5039, Margarita Fuentes, is a resident of Florida. She purchased a gas stove and service policy from the Firestone Tire and Rubber Co. (Firestone) under a conditional sales contract calling for monthly payments over a period of time. A few months later, she purchased a stereophonic phonograph from the same company under the same sort of contract. The total cost of the stove and stereo was about $500, plus an additional financing charge of over $100. Under the contracts, Firestone retained title to the merchandise, but Mrs. Fuentes was entitled to possession unless and until she should default on her installment payments.

For more than a year, Mrs. Fuentes made her installment payments. But then, with only about $200 remaining to be paid, a dispute developed between her and Firestone over the servicing of the stove. Firestone instituted an action in a small-claims court for repossession of both the stove and the stereo, claiming that Mrs. Fuentes had refused to make her remaining payments. Simultaneously with the filing of that action and before Mrs. Fuentes had even received a summons to answer its complaint, Firestone obtained a writ of replevin ordering a sheriff to seize the disputed goods at once.

In conformance with Florida procedure, Firestone had only to fill in the blanks on the appropriate form documents and submit them to the clerk of the small-claims court. The clerk signed and stamped the documents and issued a writ of replevin. Later the same day, a local deputy sheriff and an agent of Firestone went to Mrs. Fuentes' home and seized the stove and stereo.

Shortly thereafter, Mrs. Fuentes instituted the present action in a federal district court, challenging the constitutionality of the Florida prejudgment replevin procedures under the Due Process Clause of the Fourteenth Amendment. She sought declaratory and injunctive relief against continued enforcement of the procedural provisions of the state statutes that authorize prejudgment replevin.

The appellants in No. 5138 filed a very similar action in a federal district court in Pennsylvania, challenging the constitutionality of that State's prejudgment replevin process. Like Mrs. Fuentes, they had had possessions seized under writs of replevin. Three of the appellants had purchased personal property—a bed, a table, and other household goods— under installment sales contracts like the one signed by Mrs. Fuentes; and the sellers of the property had obtained and executed summary writs of replevin, claiming that the appellants had fallen behind in their installment payments. The experience of the fourth appellant, Rosa Washington, had been more bizarre. She had been divorced from a local deputy sheriff and was engaged in a dispute with him over the custody of their son. Her former husband, being familiar with the routine forms used in the replevin process, had obtained a writ that ordered the seizure of the boy's clothes, furniture, and toys.[4]

In both No. 5039 and No. 5138, three-judge District Courts were convened to consider the appellants' challenges to the constitutional validity of the Florida and Pennsylvania statutes. The courts in both cases upheld the constitutionality of the statutes. We noted probable jurisdiction of both appeals.

II

Under the Florida statute challenged here "(a)ny person whose goods or chattels are wrongfully detained by any other person ... may have a

---

4. Unlike Mrs. Fuentes in No. 5039, none of the appellants in No. 5138 was ever sued in any court by the party who initiated seizure of the property.

writ of replevin to recover them...." Fla. Stat. Ann. § 78.01. There is no requirement that the applicant make a convincing showing before the seizure that the goods are, in fact, "wrongfully detained." Rather, Florida law automatically relies on the bare assertion of the party seeking the writ that he is entitled to one and allows a court clerk to issue the writ summarily. It requires only that the applicant file a complaint, initiating a court action for repossession and reciting in conclusory fashion that he is "lawfully entitled to the possession" of the property, and that he file a security bond "in at least double the value of the property to be replevied conditioned that plaintiff will prosecute his action to effect and without delay and that if defendant recovers judgment against him in the action, he will return the property, if return thereof is adjudged, and will pay defendant all sums of money recovered against plaintiff by defendant in the action."

On the sole basis of the complaint and bond, a writ is issued "command(ing) the officer to whom it may be directed to replevy the goods and chattels in possession of defendant ... and to summon the defendant to answer the complaint." If the goods are "in any dwelling house or other building or enclosure," the officer is required to demand their delivery; but if they are not delivered, "he shall cause such house, building or enclosure to be broken open and shall make replevin according to the writ...."

Thus, at the same moment that the defendant receives the complaint seeking repossession of property through court action, the property is seized from him. He is provided no prior notice and allowed no opportunity whatever to challenge the issuance of the writ. After the property has been seized, he will eventually have an opportunity for a hearing, as the defendant in the trial of the court action for repossession, which the plaintiff is required to pursue. And he is also not wholly without recourse in the meantime. For under the Florida statute, the officer who seizes the property must keep it for three days, and during that period the defendant may reclaim possession of the property by posting his own security bond in double its value. But if he does not post such a bond, the property is transferred to the party who sought the writ, pending a final judgment in the underlying action for repossession.

The Pennsylvania law differs, though not in its essential nature, from that of Florida. As in Florida, a private party may obtain a prejudgment writ of replevin through a summary process of ex part application to a prothonotary. As in Florida, the party seeking the writ may simply post with his application a bond in double the value of the property to be seized. Pa. Rule Civ. Proc. 1073(a). There is no opportunity for a prior hearing and no prior notice to the other party. On this basis, a sheriff is required to execute the writ by seizing the specified property. Unlike the Florida statute, however, the Pennsylvania law does not require that there ever be opportunity for a hearing on the merits of the conflicting claims to possession of the replevied property. The party seeking the writ is not obliged to initiate a court action for repossession. Indeed, he need not even formally allege that he is lawfully entitled to the property. The most that is required is that he file an "affidavit of the value of the property to be replevied." If the party who loses property through replevin seizure is to get even a post-seizure hearing, he must initiate a lawsuit himself. He may also, as under Florida law, post his own counterbond within three days after the seizure to regain possession.

III

* * * Prejudgment replevin statutes like those of Florida and Pennsylvania are derived from this ancient possessory action in that they authorize the seizure of property before a final judgment. But the similarity ends there. As in the present cases, such statutes are most commonly used by creditors to seize goods allegedly wrongfully detained—not wrongfully taken—by debtors. At common law, if a creditor wished to invoke state power to recover goods wrongfully detained, he had to proceed through the action of debt or detinue. These actions, however, did not provide for a return of property before final judgment. And, more importantly, on the occasions when the common law did allow prejudgment seizure by state power, it provided some kind of notice and opportunity to be heard to the party then in possession of the property, and a state official made at least a summary determination of the relative rights of the disputing parties before stepping into the dispute and taking goods from one of them.

IV

For more than a century the central meaning of procedural due process has been clear: "Parties whose rights are to be affected are entitled to be heard; and in order that they may enjoy that right they must first be notified." It is equally fundamental that the right to notice and an opportunity to be heard "must be granted at a meaningful time and in a meaningful manner."

The primary question in the present cases is whether these state statutes are constitutionally defective in failing to provide for hearings "at a meaningful time." The Florida replevin process guarantees an opportunity for a hearing after the seizure of goods, and the Pennsylvania process allows a post-seizure hearing if the aggrieved party shoulders the burden of initiating one. But neither the Florida nor the Pennsylvania statute provides for notice or an opportunity to be heard before the seizure. The issue is whether procedural due process in the context of these cases requires an opportunity for a hearing before the State authorizes its agents to seize property in the possession of a person upon the application of another.

The constitutional right to be heard is a basic aspect of the duty of government to follow a fair process of decision-making when it acts to deprive a person of his possessions. The purpose of this requirement is not only to ensure abstract fair play to the individual. Its purpose, more particularly, is to protect his use and possession of property from arbitrary encroachment-to minimize substantively unfair or mistaken deprivations of property, a danger that is especially great when the State seizes goods simply upon the application of and for the benefit of a private party. So viewed, the prohibition against the deprivation of property without due process of law reflects the high value, embedded in our constitutional and political history, that we place on a person's right to enjoy what is his, free of governmental interference.

The requirement of notice and an opportunity to be heard raises no impenetrable barrier to the taking of a person's possessions. But the fair process of decision making that it guarantees works, by itself, to protect against arbitrary deprivation of property. For when a person has an opportunity to speak up in his own defense, and when the State must listen to what he has to say, substantively unfair and simply mistaken deprivations of property interests can be prevented. It has long been recognized that "fairness can rarely be obtained by secret, one-sided determination of facts decisive of rights.... (And n)o better instrument has been devised for arriving at truth than to give a person in jeopardy of serious loss notice of the case against him and opportunity to meet it."

If the right to notice and a hearing is to serve its full purpose, then, it is clear that it must be granted at a time when the deprivation can still be prevented. At a later hearing, an individual's possessions can be returned to him if they were unfairly or mistakenly taken in the first place. Damages may even be awarded to him for the wrongful deprivation. But no later hearing and no damage award can undo the fact that the arbitrary taking that was subject to the right of procedural due process has already occurred. "This Court has not ... embraced the general proposition that a wrong may be done if it can be undone."

This is no new principle of constitutional law. The right to a prior hearing has long been recognized by this Court under the Fourteenth and Fifth Amendments. Although the Court has held that due process tolerates variances in the form of a hearing "appropriate to the nature of the case," *Mullane v. Central Hanover Tr. Co.*, and "depending upon the importance of the interests involved and the nature of the subsequent proceedings (if any)," the Court has traditionally insisted that, whatever its form, opportunity for that hearing must be provided before the deprivation at issue takes effect. "That the hearing required by due process is subject to waiver, and is not fixed in form does not affect its root requirement that an individual be given an opportunity for a hearing before he is deprived of any significant property interest, except for extraordinary situations where some valid governmental interest is at stake that justifies postponing the hearing until after the event."

The Florida and Pennsylvania prejudgment replevin statutes fly in the face of this principle. To be sure, the requirements that a party seeking a writ must first post a bond, allege conclusorily that he is entitled to specific goods, and open himself to possible liability in damages if he is wrong, serve to deter wholly unfounded applications for a writ. But those requirements are hardly a substitute for a prior hearing, for they test no more than the strength of the applicant's own belief in his rights.[13] Since his private gain is at stake, the danger is all too great that his confidence in his cause will be misplaced. Lawyers and judges are familiar with the phenomenon of a party mistakenly but firmly convinced that his view of the facts and law will prevail, and therefore quite willing to risk the costs of litigation. Because of the understandable, self-interested fallibility of litigants, a court does not decide a dispute until it has had an opportunity to hear both sides—and does not generally take even tentative action until it has itself examined the support for the plaintiff's position. The Florida and Pennsylvania statutes do not even require the official issuing a writ of replevin to do that much.

The minimal deterrent effect of a bond requirement is, in a practical sense, no substitute for an informed evaluation by a neutral official. More specifically, as a matter of constitutional principle, it is no replacement for the right to a prior hearing that is the only truly effective safeguard against arbitrary deprivation of property. While the existence of these other, less effective, safeguards may be among the considerations that affect the form of hearing demanded by due process, they are far from enough by themselves to obviate the right to a prior hearing of some kind.

V

The right to a prior hearing, of course, attaches only to the deprivation of an interest encompassed within the Fourteenth Amendment's protection. In the present cases, the Florida and Pennsylvania statutes were applied to replevy chattels in the appellants' possession. The replevin was not cast as a final judgment; most, if not all, of the appellants lacked full title to the chattels; and their claim even to continued possession was a matter in dispute. Moreover, the chattels at stake were nothing more than an assortment of household goods. Nonetheless, it is clear that the appellants were deprived of possessory interests in those chattels that were within the protection of the Fourteenth Amendment.

A

A deprivation of a person's possessions under a prejudgment writ of replevin, at least in theory, may be only temporary. The Florida and Pennsylvania statutes do not require a person to wait until a post-seizure hearing and final judgment to recover what has been replevied. Within three days after the seizure, the statutes allowing him to recover the goods if he, in return, surrenders other property—a payment necessary to secure a bond in double the value of the goods seized from him.[14] But it is now

---

13. They may not even test that much. For if an applicant for the writ knows that he is dealing with an uneducated, uniformed consumer with little access to legal help and little familiarity with legal procedures, there may be a substantial possibility that a summary seizure of property—however unwarranted—may go unchallenged, and the applicant may feel that he can act with impunity.

14. The appellants argue that this opportunity for quick recovery exists only in theory. They allege that very few people in their position are able to obtain a recovery bond, even if they know

well settled that a temporary, nonfinal deprivation of property is nonetheless a "deprivation" in the terms of the Fourteenth Amendment. *Sniadach v. Family Finance Corp.*; *Bell v. Burson*. Both *Sniadach* and *Bell* involved takings of property pending a final judgment in an underlying dispute. In both cases, the challenged statutes included recovery provisions, allowing the defendants to post security to quickly regain the property taken from them. Yet the Court firmly held that these were deprivations of property that had to be preceded by a fair hearing.

The present cases are no different. When officials of Florida or Pennsylvania seize one piece of property from a person's possession and then agree to return it if he surrenders another, they deprive him of property whether or not he has the funds, the knowledge, and the time needed to take advantage of the recovery provision. The Fourteenth Amendment draws no bright lines around three-day, 10–day or 50–day deprivations of property. Any significant taking of property by the State is within the purview of the Due Process Clause. While the length and consequent severity of a deprivation may be another factor to weigh in determining the appropriate form of hearing, it is not decisive of the basic right to a prior hearing of some kind.

B

The appellants who signed conditional sales contracts lacked full legal title to the replevied goods. The Fourteenth Amendment's protection of "property," however, has never been interpreted to safeguard only the rights of undisputed ownership. Rather, it has been read broadly to extend protection to "any significant property interest," including statutory entitlements.

The appellants were deprived of such an interest in the replevied goods—the interest in continued possession and use of the goods. They had acquired this interest under the conditional sales contracts that entitled them to possession and use of the chattels before transfer of title. In exchange for immediate possession, the appellants had agreed to pay a major financing charge beyond the basic price of the merchandise. Moreover, by the time the goods were summarily repossessed, they had made substantial installment payments. Clearly, their possessory interest in the goods, dearly bought and protected by contract, was sufficient to invoke the protection of the Due Process Clause.

Their ultimate right to continued possession was, of course, in dispute. If it were shown at a hearing that the appellants had defaulted on their contractual obligations, it might well be that the sellers of the goods would be entitled to repossession. But even assuming that the appellants had fallen behind in their installment payments, and that they had no

---

of the possibility. Appellant Fuentes says that in her case she was never told that she could recover the stove and stereo and that the deputy sheriff seizing them gave them at once to the Firestone agent, rather than holding them for three days. She further asserts that of 442 cases of prejudgment replevin in small-claims courts in Dade County, Florida, in 1969, there was not one case in which the defendant took advantage of the recovery provision.

other valid defenses, that is immaterial here. The right to be heard does not depend upon an advance showing that one will surely prevail at the hearing. "To one who protests against the taking of his property without due process of law, it is no answer to say that in his particular case due process of law would have led to the same result because he had no adequate defense upon the merit." It is enough to invoke the procedural safeguards of the Fourteenth Amendment that a significant property interest is at stake, whatever the ultimate outcome of a hearing on the contractual right to continued possession and use of the goods.

C

Nevertheless, the District Courts rejected the appellants' constitutional claim on the ground that the goods seized from them—a stove, a stereo, a table, a bed, and so forth—were not deserving of due process protection, since they were not absolute necessities of life. The courts based this holding on a very narrow reading of *Sniadach v. Family Finance Corp.* and *Goldberg v. Kelly*, in which this Court held that the Constitution requires a hearing before prejudgment wage garnishment and before the termination of certain welfare benefits. They reasoned that *Sniadach* and *Goldberg*, as a matter of constitutional principle, established no more than that a prior hearing is required with respect to the deprivation of such basically "necessary" items as wages and welfare benefits.

This reading of *Sniadach* and *Goldberg* reflects the premise that those cases marked a radical departure from established principles of procedural due process. They did not. Both decisions were in the mainstream of past cases, having little or nothing to do with the absolute "necessities" of life but establishing that due process requires an opportunity for a hearing before a deprivation of property takes effect. In none of those cases did the court hold that this most basic due process requirement is limited to the protection of only a few types of property interests. While *Sniadach* and *Goldberg* emphasized the special importance of wages and welfare benefits, they did not convert that emphasis into a new and more limited constitutional doctrine.

Nor did they carve out a rule of "necessity" for the sort of nonfinal deprivations of property that they involved. That was made clear in *Bell v. Burson*, holding that there must be an opportunity for a fair hearing before mere suspension of a driver's license. A driver's license clearly does not rise to the level of "necessity" exemplified by wages and welfare benefits. Rather, as the Court accurately stated, it is an "important interest," entitled to the protection of procedural due process of law.

The household goods, for which the appellants contracted and paid substantial sums, are deserving of similar protection. While a driver's license, for example, "may become (indirectly) essential in the pursuit of a livelihood," a stove or a bed may be equally essential to provide a minimally decent environment for human beings in their day-to-day lives. It is, after all, such consumer goods that people work and earn a livelihood in order to acquire.

No doubt, there may be many gradations in the "importance" or "necessity" of various consumer goods. Stoves could be compared to television sets, or beds could be compared to tables. But if the root principle of procedural due process is to be applied with objectivity, it cannot rest on such distinctions. The Fourteenth Amendment speaks of "property" generally. And, under our free-enterprise system, an individual's choices in the marketplace are respected, however unwise they may seem to someone else. It is not the business of a court adjudicating due process rights to make its own critical evaluation of those choices and protect only the ones that, by its own lights, are "necessary."

VI

There are "extraordinary situations" that justify postponing notice and opportunity for a hearing. These situations, however, must be truly unusual.[22] Only in a few limited situations has this Court allowed outright seizure without opportunity for a prior hearing. First, in each case, the seizure has been directly necessary to secure an important governmental or general public interest. Second, there has been a special need for very prompt action. Third, the State has kept strict control over its monopoly of legitimate force; the person initiating the seizure has been a government official responsible for determining, under the standards of a narrowly drawn statute, that it was necessary and justified in the particular instance. Thus, the Court has allowed summary seizure of property to collect the internal revenue of the United States, to meet the needs of a national war effort, to protect against the economic disaster of a bank failure, and to protect the public from misbranded drugs and contaminated food.

The Florida and Pennsylvania prejudgment replevin statutes serve no such important governmental or general public interest. They allow summary seizure of a person's possessions when no more than private gain is directly at stake.[29] The replevin of chattels, as in the present cases, may

---

22. A prior hearing always imposes some costs in time, effort, and expense, and it is often more efficient to dispense with the opportunity for such a hearing. But these rather ordinary costs cannot outweigh the constitutional right. Procedural due process is not intended to promote efficiency or accommodate all possible interests: it is intended to protect the particular interests of the person whose possessions are about to be taken.

"The establishment of prompt efficacious procedures to achieve legitimate state ends is a proper state interest worthy of cognizance in constitutional adjudication. But the Constitution recognizes higher values than speed and efficiency. Indeed, one might fairly say of the Bill of Rights in general, and the Due Process Clause in particular, that they were designed to protect the fragile values of a vulnerable citizenry from the overbearing concern for efficiency and efficacy that may characterize praiseworthy government officials no less, and perhaps more, than mediocre ones."

29. By allowing repossession without an opportunity for a prior hearing, the Florida and Pennsylvania statutes may be intended specifically to reduce the costs for the private party seeking to seize goods in another party's possession. Even if the private gain at stake in repossession actions were equal to the great public interests recognized in this Court's past decisions, the Court has made clear that the avoidance of the ordinary costs imposed by the opportunity for a hearing is not sufficient to override the constitutional right. The appellees argue that the cost of holding hearings may be especially onerous in the context of the creditor-debtor relationship. But the Court's holding in *Sniadach v. Family Finance Corp.*, indisputably demon-

satisfy a debt or settle a score. But state intervention in a private dispute hardly compares to state action furthering a war effort or protecting the public health.

Nor do the broadly drawn Florida and Pennsylvania statutes limit the summary seizure of goods to special situations demanding prompt action. There may be cases in which a creditor could make a showing of immediate danger that a debtor will destroy or conceal disputed goods. But the statutes before us are not "narrowly drawn to meet any such unusual condition." And no such unusual situation is presented by the facts of these cases.

The statutes, moreover, abdicate effective state control over state power. Private parties, serving their own private advantage, may unilaterally invoke state power to replevy goods from another. No state official participates in the decision to seek a writ; no state official reviews the basis for the claim to repossession; and no state official evaluates the need for immediate seizure. There is not even a requirement that the plaintiff provide any information to the court on these matters. The State acts largely in the dark.[30]

VII

Finally, we must consider the contention that the appellants who signed conditional sales contracts thereby waived their basic procedural due process rights. The contract signed by Mrs. Fuentes provided that "in the event of default of any payment or payments, Seller at its option may take back the merchandise. . . ." The contracts signed by the Pennsylvania appellants similarly provided that the seller "may retake" or "repossess" the merchandise in the event of a "default in any payment." These terms were parts of printed form contracts, appearing in relatively small type and unaccompanied by any explanations clarifying their meaning.

In *D. H. Overmyer Co. v. Frick Co.*, the Court recently outlined the considerations relevant to determination of a contractual waiver of due process rights. Applying the standards governing waiver of constitutional

---

strates that ordinary hearing costs are no more able to override due process rights in the creditor-debtor context than in other contexts.

In any event, the aggregate cost of an opportunity to be heard before repossession should not be exaggerated. For we deal here only with the right to an opportunity to be heard. Since the issues and facts decisive of rights in repossession suits may very often be quite simple, there is a likelihood that many defendants would forgo their opportunity, sensing the futility of the exercise in the particular case. And, of course, no hearing need be held unless the defendant, having received notice of his opportunity, takes advantage of it.

30. The seizure of possessions under a writ of replevin is entirely different from the seizure of possessions under a search warrant. First, a search warrant is generally issued to serve a highly important governmental need—e.g., the apprehension and conviction of criminals—rather than the mere private advantage of a private party in an economic transaction. Second, a search warrant is generally issued in situations demanding prompt action. The danger is all too obvious that a criminal will destroy or hide evidence or fruits of his crime if given any prior notice. Third, the Fourth Amendment guarantees that the State will not issue search warrants merely upon the conclusory application of a private party. It guarantees that the State will not abdicate control over the issuance of warrants and that no warrant will be issued without a prior showing of probable cause. Thus, our decision today in no way implies that there must be opportunity for an adversary hearing before a search warrant is issued.

rights in a criminal proceeding—although not holding that such standards must necessarily apply—the Court held that, on the particular facts of that case, the contractual waiver of due process rights was "voluntarily, intelligently, and knowingly" made. The contract in *Overmyer* was negotiated between two corporations; the waiver provision was specifically bargained for and drafted by their lawyers in the process of these negotiations. As the Court noted, it was "not a case of unequal bargaining power or overreaching. The *Overmyer-Frick* agreement, from the start, was not a contract of adhesion." Both parties were "aware of the significance" of the waiver provision.

The facts of the present cases are a far cry from those of *Overmyer*. There was no bargaining over contractual terms between the parties who, in any event, were far from equal in bargaining power. The purported waiver provision was a printed part of a form sales contract and a necessary condition of the sale. The appellees made no showing whatever that the appellants were actually aware or made aware of the significance of the fine print now relied upon as a waiver of constitutional rights.

The Court in *Overmyer* observed that "where the contract is one of adhesion, where there is great disparity in bargaining power, and where the debtor receives nothing for the (waiver) provision, other legal consequences may ensue." Yet, as in *Overmyer*, there is no need in the present cases to canvass those consequences fully. For a waiver of constitutional rights in any context must, at the very least, be clear. We need not concern ourselves with the involuntariness or unintelligence of a waiver when the contractual language relied upon does not, on its face, even amount to a waiver.

The conditional sales contracts here simply provided that upon a default the seller "may take back," "may retake" or "may repossess" merchandise. The contracts included nothing about the waiver of a prior hearing. They did not indicate how or through what process—a final judgment, self-help, prejudgment replevin with a prior hearing, or prejudgment replevin without a prior hearing—the seller could take back the goods. Rather, the purported waiver provisions here are no more than a statement of the seller's right to repossession upon occurrence of certain events. The appellees do not suggest that these provisions waived the appellants' right to a full post-seizure hearing to determine whether those events had, in fact, occurred and to consider any other available defenses. By the same token, the language of the purported waiver provisions did not waive the appellants' constitutional right to a pre-seizure hearing of some kind.

VIII

We hold that the Florida and Pennsylvania prejudgment replevin provisions work a deprivation of property without due process of law insofar as they deny the right to a prior opportunity to be heard before chattels are taken from their possessor. Our holding, however, is a narrow one. We do not question the power of a State to seize goods before a final judgment in order to protect the security interests of creditors so long as those creditors have tested their claim to the goods through the process of a fair prior hearing. The nature and form of such prior hearings, moreover, are legitimately open to many potential variations and are a subject, at this point, for legislation—not adjudication. Since the essential reason for the requirement of a prior hearing is to prevent unfair and mistaken deprivations of property, however, it is axiomatic that the hearing must provide a real test. "(D)ue process is afforded only by the kinds of 'notice' and 'hearing' that are aimed at establishing the validity, or at least the probable validity, of the underlying claim against the alleged debtor before he can be deprived of his property...."

For the foregoing reasons, the judgments of the District Courts are vacated and these cases are remanded for further proceedings consistent with this opinion.

It is so ordered.

Vacated and remanded.

MR. JUSTICE WHITE, with whom THE CHIEF JUSTICE and MR. JUSTICE BLACKMUN join, dissenting.

Because the Court's opinion and judgment improvidently, in my view, call into question important aspects of the statutes of almost all the States governing secured transactions and the procedure for repossessing personal property, I must dissent for the reasons that follow.

First: It is my view that when the federal actions were filed in these cases and the respective District Courts proceeded to judgment there were state court proceedings in progress. It seems apparent to me that the judgments should be vacated and the District Courts instructed to reconsider these cases ...

Second: It goes without saying that in the typical installment sale of personal property both seller and buyer have interests in the property until the purchase price is fully paid, the seller early in the transaction often having more at stake than the buyer. Nor is it disputed that the buyer's right to possession is conditioned upon his making the stipulated payments and that upon default the seller is entitled to possession. Finally, there is no question in these cases that if default is disputed by the buyer he has the opportunity for a full hearing, and that if he prevails he may have the property or its full value as damages.

The narrow issue, as the Court notes, is whether it comports with due process to permit the seller, pending final judgment, to take possession of the property through a writ of replevin served by the sheriff without affording the buyer opportunity to insist that the seller establish at a hearing that there is reasonable basis for his claim of default. The interests of the buyer and seller are obviously antagonistic during this interim period: the buyer wants the use of the property pending final judgment; the seller's interest is to prevent further use and deterioration of his security. By the Florida and Pennsylvania laws the property is to all intents and purposes placed in custody and immobilized during this time. The buyer loses use of the property temporarily but is protected against loss; the seller is protected against deterioration of the property but must undertake by bond to make the buyer whole in the event the latter prevails.

In considering whether this resolution of conflicting interests is unconstitutional, much depends on one's perceptions of the practical considerations involved. The Court holds it constitutionally essential to afford opportunity for a probable-cause hearing prior to repossession. Its stated purpose is "to prevent unfair and mistaken deprivations of property." But in these typical situations, the buyer-debtor has either defaulted or he has not. If there is a default, it would seem not only "fair," but essential, that the creditor be allowed to repossess; and I cannot say that the likelihood of a mistaken claim of default is sufficiently real or recurring to justify a broad constitutional requirement that a creditor do more than the typical state law requires and permits him to do. Sellers are normally in the business of selling and collecting the price for their merchandise. I could be quite wrong, but it would not seem in the creditor's interest for a default occasioning repossession to occur; as a practical matter it would much better serve his interests if the transaction goes forward and is completed as planned. Dollar-and-cents considerations weigh heavily against false claims of default as well as against precipitate action that would allow no opportunity for mistakes to surface and be corrected. Nor does it seem to me that creditors would lightly undertake the expense of instituting replevin actions and putting up bonds.

The Court relies on prior cases, particularly *Goldberg v. Kelly* [and] *Bell v. Burson*. But these cases provide no automatic test for determining whether and when due process of law requires adversary proceedings. Indeed, "(t)he very nature of due process negates any concept of inflexible procedures universally applicable to every imaginable situation...." "(W)hat procedures due process may require under any given set of circumstances must begin with a determination of the precise nature of the government function involved as well as of the private interest that has been affected by governmental action." Viewing the issue before us in this light, I would not construe the Due Process Clause to require the creditors to do more than they have done in these cases to secure possession pending final hearing. Certainly, I would not ignore, as the Court does, the creditor's interest in preventing further use and deterioration of the property in which he has substantial interest. Surely under the Court's own definition, the creditor has a "property" interest as deserving of protection as that of the debtor. At least the debtor, who is very likely uninterested in a speedy resolution that could terminate his use of the property, should be required to make those payments, into court or otherwise, upon which his right to possession is conditioned.

Third: The Court's rhetoric is seductive, but in end analysis, the result it reaches will have little impact and represents no more than ideological tinkering with state law. It would appear that creditors could withstand attack under today's opinion simply by making clear in the controlling credit instruments that they may retake possession without a hearing, or, for that matter, without resort to judicial process at all. Alternatively, they need only give a few days' notice of a hearing, take possession if hearing is waived or if there is default; and if hearing is necessary merely establish probable cause for asserting that default has occurred. It is very doubtful in my mind that such a hearing would in fact result in protections for the debtor substantially different from those the present laws provide. On the contrary, the availability of credit may well be diminished or, in any event, the expense of securing it increased.

None of this seems worth the candle to me. The procedure that the Court strikes down is not some barbaric hangover from bygone days. The respective rights of the parties in secured transactions have undergone the most intensive analysis in recent years. The Uniform Commercial Code, which now so pervasively governs the subject matter with which it deals, provides in Art. 9, § 9–503, that: "Unless otherwise agreed a secured party has on default the right to take possession of the collateral. In taking possession a secured party may proceed without judicial process if this can be done without breach of the peace or may proceed by action. . . ."

Recent studies have suggested no changes in Art. 9 in this respect. I am content to rest on the judgment of those who have wrestled with these problems so long and often and upon the judgment of the legislatures that have considered and so recently adopted provisions that contemplate precisely what has happened in these cases.

* * *

D. ATTACHMENT STATUTES

CONNECTICUT v. DOEHR

501 U.S. 1 (1991)

JUSTICE WHITE delivered an opinion, Parts I, II, and III of which are the opinion of the Court.*

This case requires us to determine whether a state statute that authorizes prejudgment attachment of real estate without prior notice or hearing, without a showing of extraordinary circumstances, and without a requirement that the person seeking the attachment post a bond, satisfies the Due Process Clause of the Fourteenth Amendment. We hold that, as applied to this case, it does not.

I

On March 15, 1988, petitioner John F. DiGiovanni submitted an application to the Connecticut Superior Court for an attachment in the

---

* The Chief Justice, Justice Blackmun, Justice Kennedy, and Justice Souter join Parts I, II, and III of this opinion, and Justice Scalia joins Parts I and III.

amount of $75,000 on respondent Brian K. Doehr's home in Meriden, Connecticut. DiGiovanni took this step in conjunction with a civil action for assault and battery that he was seeking to institute against Doehr in the same court. The suit did not involve Doehr's real estate, nor did DiGiovanni have any pre-existing interest either in Doehr's home or any of his other property.

Connecticut law authorizes prejudgment attachment of real estate without affording prior notice or the opportunity for a prior hearing to the individual whose property is subject to the attachment. The State's prejudgment remedy statute provides, in relevant part:

> The court or a judge of the court may allow the prejudgment remedy to be issued by an attorney without hearing as provided in sections 52–278c and 52–278d upon verification by oath of the plaintiff or of some competent affiant, that there is probable cause to sustain the validity of the plaintiff's claims and (1) that the prejudgment remedy requested is for an attachment of real property.... Conn.Gen.Stat. § 52–278e (1991).

The statute does not require the plaintiff to post a bond to insure the payment of damages that the defendant may suffer should the attachment prove wrongfully issued or the claim prove unsuccessful.

As required, DiGiovanni submitted an affidavit in support of his application. In five one-sentence paragraphs, DiGiovanni stated that the facts set forth in his previously submitted complaint were true; that "I was willfully, wantonly and maliciously assaulted by the defendant, Brian K. Doehr"; that "[s]aid assault and battery broke my left wrist and further caused an ecchymosis to my right eye, as well as other injuries"; and that "I have further expended sums of money for medical care and treatment." The affidavit concluded with the statement, "In my opinion, the foregoing facts are sufficient to show that there is probable cause that judgment will be rendered for the plaintiff."

On the strength of these submissions the Superior Court Judge, by an order dated March 17, found "probable cause to sustain the validity of the plaintiff's claim" and ordered the attachment on Doehr's home "to the value of $75,000." The sheriff attached the property four days later, on March 21. Only after this did Doehr receive notice of the attachment. He also had yet to be served with the complaint, which is ordinarily necessary for an action to commence in Connecticut. As the statute further required, the attachment notice informed Doehr that he had the right to a hearing: (1) to claim that no probable cause existed to sustain the claim; (2) to request that the attachment be vacated, modified, or dismissed or that a bond be substituted; or (3) to claim that some portion of the property was exempt from execution.

Rather than pursue these options, Doehr filed suit against DiGiovanni in Federal District Court, claiming that § 52–278e(a)(1) was unconstitutional under the Due Process Clause of the Fourteenth Amendment. The District Court upheld the statute and granted summary judgment in favor of DiGiovanni. On appeal, a divided panel of the United States Court of Appeals for the Second Circuit reversed. Judge Pratt, who wrote the opinion for the court, concluded that the Connecticut statute violated due process in permitting *ex parte* attachment absent a showing of extraordinary circumstances. "The rule to be derived from *Sniadach v. Family Finance Corp. of Bay View,* and its progeny, therefore, is not that post-attachment hearings are generally acceptable provided that plaintiff files a factual affidavit and that a judicial officer supervises the process, but that a prior hearing may be postponed where exceptional circumstances justify such a delay, *and where* sufficient additional safeguards are present." This conclusion was deemed to be consistent with our decision in *Mitchell v. W.T. Grant Co.,* 416 U.S. 600 (1974), because the absence of a pre-attachment hearing was approved in that case based on the presence of extraordinary circumstances.

A further reason to invalidate the statute, the court ruled, was the highly factual nature of the issues in this case. In *Mitchell,* there were "uncomplicated matters that len[t] themselves to documentary proof" and "[t]he nature of the issues at stake minimize[d] the risk that the writ [would] be wrongfully issued by a judge." Similarly, in *Mathews v. Eldridge,* 424 U.S. 319 (1976), where an evidentiary hearing was not required prior to the termination of disability benefits, the determination of disability was "sharply focused and easily documented." Judge Pratt observed that in contrast the present case involved the fact-specific event of a fist fight and the issue of assault. He doubted that the judge could reliably determine probable cause when presented with only the plaintiff's version of the altercation. "Because the risk of a wrongful attachment is considerable under these circumstances, we conclude that dispensing with notice and opportunity for a hearing until after the attachment, without a showing of extraordinary circumstances, violates the requirements of due process." Judge Pratt went on to conclude that in his view, the statute was also constitutionally infirm for its failure to require the plaintiff to post a bond for the protection of the defendant in the event the attachment was ultimately found to have been improvident.

Judge Mahoney was also of the opinion that the statutory provision for attaching real property in civil actions, without a prior hearing and in the absence of extraordinary circumstances, was unconstitutional. He disagreed with Judge Pratt's opinion that a bond was constitutionally required. Judge Newman dissented from the holding that a hearing prior to attachment was constitutionally required and, like Judge Mahoney, disagreed with Judge Pratt on the necessity for a bond.

The dissent's conclusion accorded with the views of the Connecticut Supreme Court, which had previously upheld § 52–278e(b). We granted certiorari to resolve the conflict of authority.

II

With this case we return to the question of what process must be afforded by a state statute enabling an individual to enlist the aid of the

State to deprive another of his or her property by means of the prejudgment attachment or similar procedure. Our cases reflect the numerous variations this type of remedy can entail. In *Sniadach v. Family Finance Corp. of Bay View,* the Court struck down a Wisconsin statute that permitted a creditor to effect prejudgment garnishment of wages without notice and prior hearing to the wage earner. In *Fuentes v. Shevin,* the Court likewise found a due process violation in state replevin provisions that permitted vendors to have goods seized through an *ex parte* application to a court clerk and the posting of a bond. Conversely, the Court upheld a Louisiana *ex parte* procedure allowing a lienholder to have disputed goods sequestered in *Mitchell v. W.T. Grant. Mitchell,* however, carefully noted that *Fuentes* was decided against "a factual and legal background sufficiently different . . . that it does not require the invalidation of the Louisiana sequestration statute." Those differences included Louisiana's provision of an immediate post-deprivation hearing along with the option of damages; the requirement that a judge rather than a clerk determine that there is a clear showing of entitlement to the writ; the necessity for a detailed affidavit; and an emphasis on the lienholder's interest in preventing waste or alienation of the encumbered property. In *North Georgia Finishing, Inc. v. Di–Chem, Inc.,* 419 U.S. 601 (1975), the Court again invalidated an *ex parte* garnishment statute that not only failed to provide for notice and prior hearing but also failed to require a bond, a detailed affidavit setting out the claim, the determination of a neutral magistrate, or a prompt post-deprivation hearing.

These cases "underscore the truism that '[d]ue process, unlike some legal rules, is not a technical conception with a fixed content unrelated to time, place and circumstances.'" *Mathews v. Eldridge.* In *Mathews,* we drew upon our prejudgment remedy decisions to determine what process is due when the government itself seeks to effect a deprivation on its own initiative. That analysis resulted in the now familiar threefold inquiry requiring consideration of "the private interest that will be affected by the official action"; "the risk of an erroneous deprivation of such interest through the procedures used, and the probable value, if any, of additional or substitute safeguards"; and lastly "the Government's interest, including the function involved and the fiscal and administrative burdens that the additional or substitute procedural requirement would entail."

Here the inquiry is similar, but the focus is different. Prejudgment remedy statutes ordinarily apply to disputes between private parties rather than between an individual and the government. Such enactments are designed to enable one of the parties to "make use of state procedures with the overt, significant assistance of state officials," and they undoubtedly involve state action "substantial enough to implicate the Due Process Clause." Nonetheless, any burden that increasing procedural safeguards entails primarily affects not the government, but the party seeking control of the other's property. See *Fuentes v. Shevin,* (White, J., dissenting). For this type of case, therefore, the relevant inquiry requires, as in *Mathews,* first, consideration of the private interest that will be affected by the prejudgment measure; second, an examination of the risk of erroneous deprivation through the procedures under attack and the probable value of additional or alternative safeguards; and third, in contrast to *Mathews,* principal attention to the interest of the party seeking the prejudgment remedy, with, nonetheless, due regard for any ancillary interest the government may have in providing the procedure or forgoing the added burden of providing greater protections.

We now consider the *Mathews* factors in determining the adequacy of the procedures before us, first with regard to the safeguards of notice and a prior hearing, and then in relation to the protection of a bond.

III

We agree with the Court of Appeals that the property interests that attachment affects are significant. For a property owner like Doehr, attachment ordinarily clouds title; impairs the ability to sell or otherwise alienate the property; taints any credit rating; reduces the chance of obtaining a home equity loan or additional mortgage; and can even place an existing mortgage in technical default where there is an insecurity clause. Nor does Connecticut deny that any of these consequences occurs.

Instead, the State correctly points out that these effects do not amount to a complete, physical, or permanent deprivation of real property; their impact is less than the perhaps temporary total deprivation of household goods or wages. *See Sniadach*; *Mitchell*. But the Court has never held that only such extreme deprivations trigger due process concern. To the contrary, our cases show that even the temporary or partial impairments to property rights that attachments, liens, and similar encumbrances entail are sufficient to merit due process protection. Without doubt, state procedures for creating and enforcing attachments, as with liens, "are subject to the strictures of due process."

We also agree with the Court of Appeals that the risk of erroneous deprivation that the State permits here is substantial. By definition, attachment statutes premise a deprivation of property on one ultimate factual contingency—the award of damages to the plaintiff which the defendant may not be able to satisfy. For attachments before judgment, Connecticut mandates that this determination be made by means of a procedural inquiry that asks whether "there is probable cause to sustain the validity of the plaintiff's claim." The statute elsewhere defines the validity of the claim in terms of the likelihood "that judgment will be rendered in the matter in favor of the plaintiff." What probable cause means in this context, however, remains obscure. The State initially took the position, as did the dissent below, that the statute requires a plaintiff to show the objective likelihood of the suit's success. Doehr, citing ambiguous state cases, reads the provision as requiring no more than that a plaintiff demonstrate a subjective good-faith belief that the suit will succeed. At oral argument, the State shifted its position to argue that the statute requires something akin to the plaintiff stating a claim with sufficient facts to survive a motion to dismiss.

We need not resolve this confusion since the statute presents too great a risk of erroneous deprivation under any of these interpretations. If the statute demands inquiry into the sufficiency of the complaint, or, still less, the plaintiff's good-faith belief that the complaint is sufficient, requirement of a complaint and a factual affidavit would permit a court to make these minimal determinations. But neither inquiry adequately reduces the risk of erroneous deprivation. Permitting a court to authorize attachment merely because the plaintiff believes the defendant is liable, or because the plaintiff can make out a facially valid complaint, would permit the deprivation of the defendant's property when the claim would fail to convince a jury, when it rested on factual allegations that were sufficient to state a cause of action but which the defendant would dispute, or in the case of a mere good-faith standard, even when the complaint failed to state a claim upon which relief could be granted. The potential for unwarranted attachment in these situations is self-evident and too great to satisfy the requirements of due process absent any countervailing consideration.

Even if the provision requires the plaintiff to demonstrate, and the judge to find, probable cause to believe that judgment will be rendered in favor of the plaintiff, the risk of error was substantial in this case. As the record shows, and as the State concedes, only a skeletal affidavit need be, and was, filed. The State urges that the reviewing judge normally reviews the complaint as well, but concedes that the complaint may also be conclusory. It is self-evident that the judge could make no realistic assessment concerning the likelihood of an action's success based upon these one-sided, self-serving, and conclusory submissions. And as the Court of Appeals said, in a case like this involving an alleged assault, even a detailed affidavit would give only the plaintiff's version of the confrontation. Unlike determining the existence of a debt or delinquent payments, the issue does not concern "ordinarily uncomplicated matters that lend themselves to documentary proof." The likelihood of error that results illustrates that "fairness can rarely be obtained by secret, one-sided determination of facts decisive of rights. . . . [And n]o better instrument has been devised for arriving at truth than to give a person in jeopardy of serious loss notice of the case against him and opportunity to meet it."

What safeguards the State does afford do not adequately reduce this risk. Connecticut points out that the statute also provides an "expeditiou[s]" postattachment adversary hearing; notice for such a hearing; judicial review of an adverse decision; and a double damages action if the original suit is commenced without probable cause. Similar considerations were present in *Mitchell,* where we upheld Louisiana's sequestration statute despite the lack of pre-deprivation notice and hearing. But in *Mitchell,* the plaintiff had a vendor's lien to protect, the risk of error was minimal because the likelihood of recovery involved uncomplicated matters that lent themselves to documentary proof, and the plaintiff was required to put up a bond. None of these factors diminishing the need for a pre-deprivation hearing is present in this case. It is true that a later hearing might negate the presence of probable cause, but this would not cure the temporary deprivation that an earlier hearing might have prevented. "The Fourteenth Amendment draws no bright lines around three-day, 10–day or 50–day deprivations of property. Any significant taking of property by the State is within the purview of the Due Process Clause." *Fuentes*.

Finally, we conclude that the interests in favor of an *ex parte* attachment, particularly the interests of the plaintiff, are too minimal to supply such a consideration here. The plaintiff had no existing interest in Doehr's real estate when he sought the attachment. His only interest in attaching the property was to ensure the availability of assets to satisfy his judgment if he prevailed on the merits of his action. Yet there was no allegation that Doehr was about to transfer or encumber his real estate or take any other action during the pendency of the action that would render his real estate unavailable to satisfy a judgment. Our cases have recognized such a properly supported claim would be an exigent circumstance permitting postponing any notice or hearing until after the attachment is effected. *See Mitchell*; *Fuentes*; *Sniadach*. Absent such allegations, however, the plaintiff's interest in attaching the property does not justify the burdening of Doehr's ownership rights without a hearing to determine the likelihood of recovery.

No interest the government may have affects the analysis. The State's substantive interest in protecting any rights of the plaintiff cannot be any more weighty than those rights themselves. Here the plaintiff's interest is *de minimis*. Moreover, the State cannot seriously plead additional financial or administrative burdens involving pre-deprivation hearings when it already claims to provide an immediate post-deprivation hearing.

Historical and contemporary practices support our analysis. Prejudgment attachment is a remedy unknown at common law. Instead, "it traces its origin to the Custom of London, under which a creditor might attach money or goods of the defendant either in the plaintiff's own hands or in the custody of a third person, by proceedings in the mayor's court or in the sheriff's court." Generally speaking, attachment measures in both England and this country had several limitations that reduced the risk of erroneous deprivation which Connecticut permits. Although attachments ordinarily did not require prior notice or a hearing, they were usually authorized only where the defendant had taken or threatened to take some action that would place the satisfaction of the plaintiff's potential award in jeopardy. Attachments, moreover, were generally confined to claims by creditors. As we and the Court of Appeals have noted, disputes between debtors and creditors more readily lend themselves to accurate *ex parte* assessments of the merits. Tort actions, like the assault and battery claim at issue here, do not. Finally, as we will discuss below, attachment statutes historically required that the plaintiff post a bond.

Connecticut's statute appears even more suspect in light of current practice. A survey of state attachment provisions reveals that nearly every

State requires either a pre-attachment hearing, a showing of some exigent circumstance, or both, before permitting an attachment to take place. See Appendix to this opinion. Twenty-seven States, as well as the District of Columbia, permit attachments only when some extraordinary circumstance is present. In such cases, pre-attachment hearings are not required but post-attachment hearings are provided. Ten States permit attachment without the presence of such factors but require pre-writ hearings unless one of those factors is shown. Six States limit attachments to extraordinary circumstance cases, but the writ will not issue prior to a hearing unless there is a showing of some even more compelling condition. Three States always require a pre-attachment hearing. Only Washington, Connecticut, and Rhode Island authorize attachments without a prior hearing in situations that do not involve any purportedly heightened threat to the plaintiff's interests. Even those States permit *ex parte* deprivations only in certain types of cases: Rhode Island does so only when the claim is equitable; Connecticut and Washington do so only when real estate is to be attached, and even Washington requires a bond. Conversely, the States for the most part no longer confine attachments to creditor claims. This development, however, only increases the importance of the other limitations.

We do not mean to imply that any given exigency requirement protects an attachment from constitutional attack. Nor do we suggest that the statutory measures we have surveyed are necessarily free of due process problems or other constitutional infirmities in general. We do believe, however, that the procedures of almost all the States confirm our view that the Connecticut provision before us, by failing to provide a pre-attachment hearing without at least requiring a showing of some exigent circumstance, clearly falls short of the demands of due process.

IV

A

Although a majority of the Court does not reach the issue, Justices Marshall, Stevens, O'Connor, and I deem it appropriate to consider whether due process also requires the plaintiff to post a bond or other security in addition to requiring a hearing or showing of some exigency.

As noted, the impairments to property rights that attachments effect merit due process protection. Several consequences can be severe, such as the default of a homeowner's mortgage. In the present context, it need only be added that we have repeatedly recognized the utility of a bond in protecting property rights affected by the mistaken award of prejudgment remedies.

Without a bond, at the time of attachment, the danger that these property rights may be wrongfully deprived remains unacceptably high even with such safeguards as a hearing or exigency requirement. The need for a bond is especially apparent where extraordinary circumstances justify an attachment with no more than the plaintiff's *ex parte* assertion of a claim. We have already discussed how due process tolerates, and the States generally permit, the otherwise impermissible chance of erroneously depriving the defendant in such situations in light of the heightened interest of the plaintiff. Until a post-attachment hearing, however, a defendant has no protection against damages sustained where no extraordinary circumstance in fact existed or the plaintiff's likelihood of recovery was nil. Such protection is what a bond can supply. Both the Court and its individual Members have repeatedly found the requirement of a bond to play an essential role in reducing what would have been too great a degree of risk in precisely this type of circumstance.

But the need for a bond does not end here. A defendant's property rights remain at undue risk even when there has been an adversarial hearing to determine the plaintiff's likelihood of recovery. At best, a court's initial assessment of each party's case cannot produce more than an educated prediction as to who will win. This is especially true when, as here, the nature of the claim makes any accurate prediction elusive. In consequence, even a full hearing under a proper probable-cause standard would not prevent many defendants from having title to their homes impaired during the pendency of suits that never result in the contingency that ultimately justifies such impairment, namely, an award to the plaintiff. Attachment measures currently on the books reflect this concern. All but a handful of States require a plaintiff's bond despite also affording a hearing either before, or (for the vast majority, only under extraordinary circumstances) soon after, an attachment takes place. Bonds have been a similarly common feature of other prejudgment remedy procedures that we have considered, whether or not these procedures also included a hearing.

The State stresses its double damages remedy for suits that are commenced without probable cause. This remedy, however, fails to make up for the lack of a bond. As an initial matter, the meaning of "probable cause" in this provision is no more clear here than it was in the attachment provision itself. Should the term mean the plaintiff's good faith or the facial adequacy of the complaint, the remedy is clearly insufficient. A defendant who was deprived where there was little or no likelihood that the plaintiff would obtain a judgment could nonetheless recover only by proving some type of fraud or malice or by showing that the plaintiff had failed to state a claim. Problems persist even if the plaintiff's ultimate failure permits recovery. At best a defendant must await a decision on the merits of the plaintiff's complaint, even assuming that a § 52–568(a)(1) action may be brought as a counterclaim. Settlement, under Connecticut law, precludes seeking the damages remedy, a fact that encourages the use of attachments as a tactical device to pressure an opponent to capitulate. An attorney's advice that there is probable cause to commence an action constitutes a complete defense, even if the advice was unsound or erroneous. Finally, there is no guarantee that the original plaintiff will have adequate assets to satisfy an award that the defendant may win.

Nor is there any appreciable interest against a bond requirement. Section 52–278e(a)(1) does not require a plaintiff to show exigent circumstances nor any pre-existing interest in the property facing attachment. A party must show more than the mere existence of a claim before subjecting an opponent to prejudgment proceedings that carry a significant risk of erroneous deprivation.

B

Our foregoing discussion compels the four of us to consider whether a bond excuses the need for a hearing or other safeguards altogether. If a bond is needed to augment the protections afforded by pre-attachment and post-attachment hearings, it arguably follows that a bond renders these safeguards unnecessary. That conclusion is unconvincing, however, for it ignores certain harms that bonds could not undo but that hearings would prevent. The law concerning attachments has rarely, if ever, required defendants to suffer an encumbered title until the case is concluded without any prior opportunity to show that the attachment was unwarranted. Our cases have repeatedly emphasized the importance of providing a prompt post-deprivation hearing at the very least. Every State but one, moreover, expressly requires a pre-attachment or post-attachment hearing to determine the propriety of an attachment.

The necessity for at least a prompt post-attachment hearing is self-evident because the right to be compensated at the end of the case, if the plaintiff loses, for all provable injuries caused by the attachment is inadequate to redress the harm inflicted, harm that could have been avoided had an early hearing been held. An individual with an immediate need or opportunity to sell a property can neither do so, nor otherwise satisfy that need or recreate the opportunity. The same applies to a parent in need of a home equity loan for a child's education, an entrepreneur seeking to start a business on the strength of an otherwise strong credit rating, or simply a homeowner who might face the disruption of having a mortgage placed in technical default. The extent of these harms, moreover, grows with the length of the suit. Here, oral argument indicated that civil suits in Connecticut commonly take up to four to seven years for completion .. Many state attachment statutes require that the amount of a bond be anywhere from the equivalent to twice the amount the plaintiff seeks. These amounts bear no relation to the harm the defendant might suffer even assuming that money damages can make up for the foregoing disruptions. It should be clear, however, that such an assumption is fundamentally flawed. Reliance on a bond does not sufficiently account for the harms that flow from an erroneous attachment to excuse a State from reducing that risk by means of a timely hearing.

If a bond cannot serve to dispense with a hearing immediately after attachment, neither is it sufficient basis for not providing a pre-attachment hearing in the absence of exigent circumstances even if in any event a hearing would be provided a few days later. The reasons are the same: a wrongful attachment can inflict injury that will not fully be redressed by recovery on the bond after a prompt post-attachment hearing determines that the attachment was invalid.

Once more, history and contemporary practices support our conclusion. Historically, attachments would not issue without a showing of extraordinary circumstances even though a plaintiff bond was almost invariably required in addition. Likewise, all but eight States currently require the posting of a bond. Out of this 42–State majority, all but one requires a pre-attachment hearing, a showing of some exigency, or both, and all but one expressly require a post-attachment hearing when an attachment has been issued *ex parte*. This testimony underscores the point that neither a hearing nor an extraordinary circumstance limitation eliminates the need for a bond, no more than a bond allows waiver of these other protections. To reconcile the interests of the defendant and the plaintiff accurately, due process generally requires all of the above.

V

Because Connecticut's prejudgment remedy provision violates the requirements of due process by authorizing prejudgment attachment without prior notice or a hearing, the judgment of the Court of Appeals is affirmed, and the case is remanded to that court for further proceedings consistent with this opinion.

It is so ordered.

CHIEF JUSTICE REHNQUIST, with whom JUSTICE BLACKMUN joins, concurring in part and concurring in the judgment.

I agree with the Court that the Connecticut attachment statute, "as applied to this case," fails to satisfy the Due Process Clause of the Fourteenth Amendment. I therefore join Parts I, II, and III of its opinion. Unfortunately, the remainder of the opinion does not confine itself to the facts of this case, but enters upon a lengthy disquisition as to what combination of safeguards are required to satisfy due process in hypothetical cases not before the Court. I therefore do not join Part IV.

As the Court's opinion points out, the Connecticut statute allows attachment not merely for a creditor's claim, but for a tort claim of assault and battery; it affords no opportunity for a pre-deprivation hearing; it contains no requirement that there be "exigent circumstances," such as an effort on the part of the defendant to conceal assets; no bond is required from the plaintiff; and the property attached is one in which the plaintiff has no pre-existing interest. The Court's opinion is, in my view, ultimately correct when it bases its holding of unconstitutionality of the Connecticut statute as applied here on our cases of *Sniadach*; *Fuentes*; *Mitchell*, and *North Georgia Finishing, Inc. v. Di–Chem, Inc.*, 419 U.S. 601 (1975). But I do not believe that the result follows so inexorably as the Court's opinion suggests. All of the cited cases dealt with personalty—bank deposits or chattels—and each involved the physical seizure of the property itself, so that the defendant was deprived of its use. These cases, which represented something of a revolution in the jurisprudence of procedural due process, placed substantial limits on the methods by which creditors could obtain a lien on the assets of a debtor prior to judgment. But in all of them the debtor was deprived of the use and possession of the property. In the present case, on the other hand, Connecticut's prejudgment attachment on real property statute, which secures an incipient lien for the plaintiff, does not deprive the defendant of the use or possession of the property.

The Court's opinion therefore breaks new ground, and I would point out, more emphatically than the Court does, the limits of today's holding. * * *

Today's holding is a significant development in the law; the only cases dealing with real property cited in the Court's opinion . . . arose out of lien foreclosure sales in which the question was whether the owner was entitled to proper notice. The change is dramatically reflected when we compare today's decision with the almost casual statement of Justice Holmes, writing for a unanimous Court: "[N]othing is more common than to allow parties alleging themselves to be creditors to establish in advance by attachment a lien dependent for its effect upon the result of the suit." The only protection accorded to the debtor in that case was the right to contest his liability in a post-deprivation proceeding.

It is both unwise and unnecessary, I believe, for the plurality to proceed, as it does in Part IV, from its decision of the case before it to discuss abstract and hypothetical situations not before it. This is especially so where we are dealing with the Due Process Clause which, as the Court recognizes, "unlike some legal rules, is not a technical conception with a fixed content unrelated to time, place and circumstances." And it is even more true in a case involving constitutional limits on the methods by which the States may transfer or create interests in real property; in other areas of the law, dicta may do little damage, but those who insure titles or write title opinions often do not enjoy the luxury of distinguishing between dicta and holding.

The two elements of due process with which the Court concerns itself in Part IV—the requirements of a bond and of "exigent circumstances"—prove to be upon analysis so vague that the discussion is not only unnecessary, but not particularly useful. Unless one knows what the terms and conditions of a bond are to be, the requirement of a "bond" in the abstract means little. The amount to be secured by the bond and the conditions of the bond are left unaddressed—is there to be liability on the part of a plaintiff if he is ultimately unsuccessful in the underlying lawsuit, or is it instead to be conditioned on some sort of good-faith test? The "exigent circumstances" referred to by the Court are admittedly equally vague; non-residency appears to be enough in some States, an attempt to conceal assets is required in others, an effort to flee the jurisdiction in still others. We should await concrete cases which present questions involving bonds and exigent circumstances before we attempt to decide when and if the Due Process Clause of the Fourteenth Amendment requires them as prerequisites for a lawful attachment.

JUSTICE SCALIA, concurring in part and concurring in the judgment.

Since the manner of attachment here was not a recognized procedure at common law, I agree that its validity under the Due Process Clause should be determined by applying the test we set forth in *Mathews v. Eldridge*; and I agree that it fails that test. I join Parts I and III of the Court's opinion, and concur in the judgment of the Court.

* * *

II. RIGHT TO TRIAL BY JURY

A. HISTORICAL BASES AND MODERN APPROACH

U.S. CONST. AMEND. VII. CIVIL TRIALS

In Suits at common law, where the value in controversy shall exceed twenty dollars, the right of trial by jury shall be preserved, and no fact tried by a jury, shall be otherwise reexamined in any Court of the United States, than according to the rules of the common law.

* * *

FEDERAL RULE OF CIVIL PROCEDURE 38. RIGHT TO A JURY TRIAL; DEMAND

(a) Right Preserved. The right of trial by jury as declared by the Seventh Amendment to the Constitution—or as provided by a federal statute—is preserved to the parties inviolate.

(b) Demand. On any issue triable of right by a jury, a party may demand a jury trial by:

    (1) serving the other parties with a written demand—which may be included in a pleading—no later than 14 days after the last pleading directed to the issue is served; and

    (2) filing the demand in accordance with Rule 5(d).

(c) Specifying Issues. In its demand, a party may specify the issues that it wishes to have tried by a jury; otherwise, it is considered to have demanded a jury trial on all the issues so triable. If the party has demanded a jury trial on only some issues, any other party may— within 14 days after being served with the demand or within a shorter time ordered by the court—serve a demand for a jury trial on any other or all factual issues triable by jury.

(d) Waiver; Withdrawal. A party waives a jury trial unless its demand is properly served and filed. A proper demand may be withdrawn only if the parties consent.

(e) Admiralty and Maritime Claims. These rules do not create a right to a jury trial on issues in a claim that is an admiralty or maritime claim under Rule 9(h).

* * *

FEDERAL RULE OF CIVIL PROCEDURE 39. TRIAL BY JURY OR BY THE COURT

(a) When a Demand Is Made. When a jury trial has been demanded under Rule 38, the action must be designated on the docket as a jury action. The trial on all issues so demanded must be by jury unless:

    (1) the parties or their attorneys file a stipulation to a nonjury trial or so stipulate on the record; or

(2) the court, on motion or on its own, finds that on some or all of those issues there is no federal right to a jury trial.

(b) When No Demand Is Made. Issues on which a jury trial is not properly demanded are to be tried by the court. But the court may, on motion, order a jury trial on any issue for which a jury might have been demanded.

(c) Advisory Jury; Jury Trial by Consent. In an action not triable of right by a jury, the court, on motion or on its own:

(1) may try any issue with an advisory jury; or

(2) may, with the parties' consent, try any issue by a jury whose verdict has the same effect as if a jury trial had been a matter of right, unless the action is against the United States and a federal statute provides for a nonjury trial.

* * *

FEDERAL RULE OF CIVIL PROCEDURE 57.   DECLARATORY JUDGMENT

These rules govern the procedure for obtaining a declaratory judgment under 28 U.S.C. § 2201. Rules 38 and 39 govern a demand for a jury trial. The existence of another adequate remedy does not preclude a declaratory judgment that is otherwise appropriate. The court may order a speedy hearing of a declaratory-judgment action.

* * *

28 U.S.C. § 2201.   CREATION OF REMEDY

(a) In a case of actual controversy within its jurisdiction, . . . as determined by the administering authority, any court of the United States, upon the filing of an appropriate pleading, may declare the rights and other legal relations of any interested party seeking such declaration, whether or not further relief is or could be sought. Any such declaration shall have the force and effect of a final judgment or decree and shall be reviewable as such.

28 U.S.C. § 2202.   FURTHER RELIEF

Further necessary or proper relief based on a declaratory judgment or decree may be granted, after reasonable notice and hearing, against any adverse party whose rights have been determined by such judgment.

* * *

BEACON THEATRES, INC. v. WESTOVER

359 U.S. 500 (1959)

MR. JUSTICE BLACK delivered the opinion of the Court.

Petitioner, Beacon Theatres, Inc., sought by mandamus to require a district judge in the Southern District of California to vacate certain orders alleged to deprive it of a jury trial of issues arising in a suit brought against it by Fox West Coast Theatres, Inc. The Court of Appeals for the Ninth Circuit refused the writ, holding that the trial judge had acted within his proper discretion in denying petitioner's request for a jury. We granted certiorari because "Maintenance of the jury as a fact-finding body is of such importance and occupies so firm a place in our history and jurisprudence that any seeming curtailment of the right to a jury trial should be scrutinized with the utmost care." *Dimick v. Schiedt.*

Fox had asked for declaratory relief against Beacon alleging a controversy arising under the Sherman Antitrust Act and under the Clayton Act, which authorizes suits for treble damages against Sherman Act violators. According to the complaint Fox operates a movie theatre in San Bernardino, California, and has long been exhibiting films under contracts with movie distributors. These contracts grant if the exclusive right to show "first run" pictures in the "San Bernardino competitive area" and provide for "clearance"—a period of time during which no other theatre can exhibit the same pictures. After building a drive-in theatre about 11 miles from San Bernardino, Beacon notified Fox that it considered contracts barring simultaneous exhibitions of first-run films in the two theatres to be overt acts in violation of the antitrust laws. Fox's complaint alleged that this notification, together with threats of treble damage suits against Fox and its distributors, gave rise to "duress and coercion" which deprived Fox of a valuable property right, the right to negotiate for exclusive first-run contracts. Unless Beacon was restrained, the complaint continued, irreparable harm would result. Accordingly, while its pleading was styled a "Complaint for Declaratory Relief," Fox prayed both for a declaration that a grant of clearance between the Fox and Beacon theatres is reasonable and not in violation of the antitrust laws, and for an injunction, pending final resolution of the litigation, to prevent Beacon from instituting any action under the antitrust laws against Fox and its distributors arising out of the controversy alleged in the complaint. Beacon filed an answer, a counterclaim against Fox, and a cross-claim against an exhibitor who had intervened. These denied the threats and asserted that there was no substantial competition between the two theatres, that the clearances granted were therefore unreasonable, and that a conspiracy existed between Fox and its distributors to manipulate contracts and clearances so as to restrain trade and monopolize first-run pictures in violation of the antitrust laws. Treble damages were asked.

Beacon demanded a jury trial of the factual issues in the case as provided by Federal Rule of Civil Procedure 38(b). The District Court, however, viewed the issues raised by the "Complaint for Declaratory Relief," including the question of competition between the two theatres, as essentially equitable. Acting under the purported authority of Rules 42(b) and 57, it directed that these issues be tried to the court before jury determination of the validity of the charges of antitrust violations made in the counterclaim and cross-claim.[3] A common issue of the "Complaint for

---

3. Fed. Rule Civ. P. 42(b) reads: "The court in furtherance of convenience or to avoid prejudice may order a separate trial of any claim, cross-claim, counter-claim, or third-party claim,

Declaratory Relief," the counterclaim, and the cross-claim was the reasonableness of the clearances granted to Fox, which depended, in part, on the existence of competition between the two theatres. Thus the effect of the action of the District Court could be, as the Court of Appeals believed, "to limit the petitioner's opportunity fully to try to a jury every issue which has a bearing upon its treble damage suit," for determination of the issue of clearances by the judge might "operate either by way of res judicata or collateral estoppel so as to conclude both parties with respect thereto at the subsequent trial of the treble damage claim."

The District Court's finding that the Complaint for Declaratory Relief presented basically equitable issues draws no support from the Declaratory Judgment Act, 28 U.S.C. §§ 2201, 2202. That statute, while allowing prospective defendants to sue to establish their non-liability, specifically preserves the right to jury trial for both parties. It follows that if Beacon would have been entitled to a jury trial in a treble damage suit against Fox it cannot be deprived of that right merely because Fox took advantage of the availability of declaratory relief to sue Beacon first. Since the right to trial by jury applies to treble damage suits under the antitrust laws, and is, in fact, an essential part of the congressional plan for making competition rather than monopoly the rule of trade, the Sherman and Clayton Act issues on which Fox sought a declaration were essentially jury questions.

Nevertheless the Court of Appeals refused to upset the order of the district judge. It held that the question of whether a right to jury trial existed was to be judged by Fox's complaint read as a whole. In addition to seeking a declaratory judgment, the court said, Fox's complaint can be read as making out a valid plea for injunctive relief, thus stating a claim traditionally cognizable in equity. A party who is entitled to maintain a suit in equity for an injunction, said the court, may have all the issues in his suit determined by the judge without a jury regardless of whether legal rights are involved. The court then rejected the argument that equitable relief, traditionally available only when legal remedies are inadequate, was rendered unnecessary in this case by the filing of the counterclaim and cross-claim which presented all the issues necessary to a determination of the right to injunctive relief. Relying on *American Life Ins. Co. v. Stewart*, decided before the enactment of the Federal Rules of Civil Procedure, it invoked the principle that a court sitting in equity could retain jurisdiction even though later a legal remedy became available. In such instances the equity court had discretion to enjoin the later lawsuit in order to allow the whole dispute to be determined in one case in one court. Reasoning by analogy, the Court of Appeals held it was not an abuse of discretion for the district judge, acting under Federal Rule of Civil Procedure 42(b), to try the equitable cause first even though this might, through collateral

---

or of any separate issue or of any number of claims, cross-claims, counterclaims, third-party claims, or issues." Rule 57 reads in part: "The court may order a speedy hearing of an action for a declaratory judgment and may advance it on the calendar."

estoppel, prevent a full jury trial of the counterclaim and cross-claim which were as effectively stopped as by an equity injunction.[6]

Beacon takes issue with the holding of the Court of Appeals that the complaint stated a claim upon which equitable relief could be granted. As initially filed the complaint alleged that threats of lawsuits by petitioner against Fox and its distributors were causing irreparable harm to Fox's business relationships. The prayer for relief, however, made no mention of the threats but asked only that pending litigation of the claim for declaratory judgment, Beacon be enjoined from beginning any lawsuits under the antitrust laws against Fox and its distributors arising out of the controversy alleged in the complaint. Evidently of the opinion that this prayer did not state a good claim for equitable relief, the Court of Appeals construed it to include a request for an injunction against threats of lawsuits. This liberal construction of a pleading is in line with Rule 8 of the Federal Rules of Civil Procedure. *See Conley v. Gibson.* But this fact does not solve our problem. Assuming that the pleadings can be construed to support such a request and assuming additionally that the complaint can be read as alleging the kind of harassment by a multiplicity of lawsuits which would traditionally have justified equity to take jurisdiction and settle the case in one suit, we are nevertheless of the opinion that, under the Declaratory Judgment Act and the Federal Rules of Civil Procedure, neither claim can justify denying Beacon a trial by jury of all the issues in the antitrust controversy.

The basis of injunctive relief in the federal courts has always been irreparable harm and inadequacy of legal remedies. At least as much is required to justify a trial court in using its discretion under the Federal Rules to allow claims of equitable origins to be tried ahead of legal ones, since this has the same effect as an equitable injunction of the legal claims. And it is immaterial, in judging if that discretion is properly employed, that before the Federal Rules and the Declaratory Judgment Act were passed, courts of equity, exercising a jurisdiction separate from courts of law, were, in some cases, allowed to enjoin subsequent legal actions between the same parties involving the same controversy. This was because the subsequent legal action, though providing an opportunity to try the case to a jury, might not protect the right of the equity plaintiff to a fair and orderly adjudication of the controversy. Under such circumstances the legal remedy could quite naturally be deemed inadequate. Inadequacy of remedy and irreparable harm are practical terms, however. As such their existence today must be determined, not by precedents decided under discarded procedures, but in the light of the remedies now made available by the Declaratory Judgment Act and the Federal Rules.

Viewed in this manner, the use of discretion by the trial court under Rule 42(b) to deprive Beacon of a full jury trial on its counterclaim and cross-claim, as well as on Fox's plea for declaratory relief, cannot be

---

6. In *Ettelson v. Metropolitan Life Ins. Co.*, this Court recognized that orders enabling equitable causes to be tried before legal ones had the same effect as injunctions.

justified. Under the Federal Rules the same court may try both legal and equitable causes in the same action. Fed. Rules Civ. P. 1, 2, 18. Thus any defenses, equitable or legal, Fox may have to charges of antitrust violations can be raised either in its suit for declaratory relief or in answer to Beacon's counterclaim. On proper showing, harassment by threats of other suits, or other suits actually brought, involving the issues being tried in this case, could be temporarily enjoined pending the outcome of this litigation. Whatever permanent injunctive relief Fox might be entitled to on the basis of the decision in this case could, of course, be given by the court after the jury renders its verdict. In this way the issues between these parties could be settled in one suit giving Beacon a full jury trial of every antitrust issue. By contrast, the holding of the court below while granting Fox no additional protection unless the avoidance of jury trial be considered as such, would compel Beacon to split his antitrust case, trying part to a judge and part to a jury.[10] Such a result, which involves the postponement and subordination of Fox's own legal claim for declaratory relief as well as of the counterclaim which Beacon was compelled by the Federal Rules to bring,[11] is not permissible.

Our decision is consistent with the plan of the Federal Rules and the Declaratory Judgment Act to effect substantial procedural reform while retaining a distinction between jury and nonjury issues and leaving substantive rights unchanged. Since in the federal courts equity has always acted only when legal remedies were inadequate, the expansion of adequate legal remedies provided by the Declaratory Judgment Act and the Federal Rules necessarily affects the scope of equity. Thus, the justification for equity's deciding legal issues once it obtains jurisdiction, and refusing to dismiss a case, merely because subsequently a legal remedy becomes available, must be re-evaluated in the light of the liberal joinder provisions of the Federal Rules which allow legal and equitable causes to be brought and resolved in one civil action. Similarly the need for, and therefore, the availability of such equitable remedies as Bills of Peace, Quia Timet and Injunction must be reconsidered in view of the existence of the Declaratory Judgment Act as well as the liberal joinder provision of the Rules. This is not only in accord with the spirit of the Rules and the Act but is required by the provision in the Rules that "(t)he right of trial by jury as declared by the Seventh Amendment to the Constitution or as given by a statute of the United States shall be preserved * * * inviolate."[16]

---

10. Since the issue of violation of the antitrust laws often turns on the reasonableness of a restraint on trade in the light of all the facts, it is particularly undesirable to have some of the relevant considerations tried by one fact-finder and some by another.

11. Fed. Rule Civ. P. 13(a).

16. Fed. Rule Civ. P. 38(a). In delegating to the Supreme Court responsibility for drawing up rules, Congress declared that: "Such rules shall not abridge, enlarge or modify any substantive right and shall preserve the right of trial by jury as at common law and as declared by the Seventh Amendment to the Constitution." 28 U.S.C. § 2072. The Seventh Amendment reads: "In Suits at common law, where the value in controversy shall exceed twenty dollars, the right of trial by jury shall be preserved, and no fact tried by a jury, shall be otherwise reexamined in any Court of the United States, than according to the rules of the common law."

If there should be cases where the availability of declaratory judgment or joinder in one suit of legal and equitable causes would not in all respects protect the plaintiff seeking equitable relief from irreparable harm while affording a jury trial in the legal cause, the trial court will necessarily have to use its discretion in deciding whether the legal or equitable cause should be tried first. Since the right to jury trial is a constitutional one, however, while no similar requirement protects trials by the court, that discretion is very narrowly limited and must, wherever possible, be exercised to preserve jury trial. As this Court said in *Scott v. Neely*: "In the Federal courts this (jury) right cannot be dispensed with, except by the assent of the parties entitled to it; nor can it be impaired by any blending with a claim, properly cognizable at law, of a demand for equitable relief in aid of the legal action, or during its pendency."[18] This long-standing principle of equity dictates that only under the most imperative circumstances, circumstances which in view of the flexible procedures of the Federal Rules we cannot now anticipate, can the right to a jury trial of legal issues be lost through prior determination of equitable claims. We as have shown, this is far from being such a case.

Respondent claims mandamus is not available under the All Writs Act, 28 U.S.C. § 1651. Whatever differences of opinion there may be in other types of cases, we think the right to grant mandamus to require jury trial where it has been improperly denied is settled.

The judgment of the Court of Appeals is reversed.

MR. JUSTICE STEWART, with whom MR. JUSTICE HARLAN and MR. JUSTICE WHITTAKER concur, dissenting.

There can be no doubt that a litigant is entitled to a writ of mandamus to protect a clear constitutional or statutory right to a jury trial. But there was no denial of such a right here. The district judge simply exercised his inherent discretion, now explicitly confirmed by the Federal Rules of Civil Procedure, to schedule the trial of an equitable claim in advance of an action at law. Even an abuse of such discretion could not, I think, be attacked by the extraordinary writ of mandamus. In any event no abuse of discretion is apparent in this case.

The complaint filed by Fox stated a claim traditionally cognizable in equity. That claim, in brief, was that Beacon had wrongfully interfered with the right of Fox to compete freely with Beacon and other distributors for the licensing of films for first-run exhibition in the San Bernardino area. The complaint alleged that the plaintiff was without an adequate remedy at law and would be irreparably harmed unless the defendant were restrained from continuing to interfere—by coercion and threats of litigation—with the plaintiff's lawful business relationships.

The Court of Appeals found that the complaint, although inartistically drawn, contained allegations entitling the petitioner to equitable relief. That finding is accepted in the prevailing opinion today. If the complaint

---

18. This Court has long emphasized the importance of the jury trial.

had been answered simply by a general denial, therefore, the issues would under traditional principles have been triable as a proceeding in equity. Instead of just putting in issue the allegations of the complaint, however, Beacon filed pleadings which affirmatively alleged the existence of a broad conspiracy among the plaintiff and other theatre owners to monopolize the first-run exhibition of films in the San Bernardino area to refrain from competing among themselves, and to discriminate against Beacon in granting film licenses. Based upon these allegations, Beacon asked damages in the amount of $300,000. Clearly these conspiracy allegations stated a cause of action triable as of right by a jury. What was demanded by Beacon, however, was a jury trial not only of this cause of action, but also of the issues presented by the original complaint.

Upon motion of Fox the trial judge ordered the original action for declaratory and equitable relief to be tried separately to the court and in advance of the trial of the defendant's counter-claim and cross-claim for damages. The court's order, which carefully preserved the right to trial by jury upon the conspiracy and damage issues raised by the counterclaim and cross-claim, was in conformity with the specific provisions of the Federal Rules of Civil Procedure.[3] Yet it is decided today that the Court of Appeals must compel the district judge to rescind it.

Assuming the existence of a factual issue common both to the plaintiff's original action and the defendant's counterclaim for damages, I cannot agree that the District Court must be compelled to try the counterclaim first.[4] It is, of course, a matter of no great moment in what order the issues between the parties in the present litigation are tried.

---

3. Rule 42(b) provides: "(b) Separate Trials. The court in furtherance of convenience or to avoid prejudice may order a separate trial of any claim, cross-claim, counterclaim, or third-party claim, or of any separate issue or of any number of claims, cross-claims, counterclaims, third-party claims, or issues."

The Note to Rule 39 of the Advisory Committee on Rules states that, "When certain of the issues are to be tried by jury and others by the court, the court may determine the sequence in which such issues shall be tried." This language was at one time contained in a draft of the Rules, but was deleted because "the power is adequately given by Rule 42(b) * * *."

See also Rule 57, which provides that "The court may order a speedy hearing of an action for a declaratory judgment and may advance it on the calendar."

4. It is not altogether clear at this stage of the proceedings whether the existence of substantial competition between Fox and Beacon is actually a material issue of fact common to both the equitable claim and the counterclaim for damages. The respondent ingeniously argues that determination in the equitable suit of the issue of competition between the theatres would be determinative of little or nothing in the counterclaim for damages. "The fact issue in the action for equitable and declaratory relief is whether the Fox West Coast California Theatre and the Petitioner's drive-in are substantially competitive with each other. The fact issue in the counterclaim is whether the cross-defendants and co-conspirators therein named conspired together in restraint of trade and to monopolize in the manner alleged in the counterclaim. Absent conspiracy, whether or not the distributors licensed a single first run picture to Petitioner's drive-in, be it in substantial competition or not in substantial competition with other first run theatres in the San Bernardino area, Petitioner will not have made out a case on its counterclaim. * * * If Petitioner on its counterclaim should fail to prove conspiracy the issue of competition between the theatres is meaningless. If petitioner on the other hand success in proving the allegations of its counterclaim, the conspiracy to monopolize first run and to discriminate against the new drive-in, the existence or non-existence of competition between the theatres would exculpate none of the alleged wrongdoers, although if there was an absence of competition between the drive-in and the other first run theatres, as Petitioner contended in its answer to the complaint, it might have some difficulty proving injury to its business."

What is disturbing is the process by which the Court arrives at its decision—a process which appears to disregard the historic relationship between equity and law.

I.

The Court suggests that "the expansion of adequate legal remedies provided by the Declaratory Judgment Act * * * necessarily affects the scope of equity." Does the Court mean to say that the mere availability of an action for a declaratory judgment operates to furnish "an adequate remedy at law" so as to deprive a court of equity of the power to act? That novel line of reasoning is at least implied in the Court's opinion. But the Declaratory Judgment Act did not "expand" the substantive law. That Act merely provided a new statutory remedy, neither legal nor equitable, but available in the areas of both equity and law. When declaratory relief is sought, the right to trial by jury depends upon the basic context in which the issues are presented. If the basic issues in an action for declaratory relief are of a kind traditionally cognizable in equity, *e.g.*, a suit for cancellation of a written instrument, the declaratory judgment is not a "remedy at law." If, on the other hand, the issues arise in a context traditionally cognizable at common law, the right to a jury trial of course remains unimpaired, even though the only relief demanded is a declaratory judgment.

Thus, if in this case the complaint had asked merely for a judgment declaring that the plaintiff's specified manner of business dealings with distributors and other exhibitors did not render it liable to Beacon under the antitrust laws, this would have been simply a "juxtaposition of parties" case in which Beacon could have demanded a jury trial. But the complaint in the present case, as the Court recognizes, presented issues of exclusively equitable cognizance, going well beyond a mere defense to any subsequent action at law. Fox sought from the court protection against Beacon's allegedly unlawful interference with its business relationships-protection which this Court seems to recognize might not have been afforded by a declaratory judgment, unsupplemented by equitable relief. The availability of a declaratory judgment did not, therefore, operate to confer upon Beacon the right to trial by jury with respect to the issues raised by the complaint.

II.

The Court's opinion does not, of course, hold or even suggest that a court of equity may never determine "legal rights." For indeed it is precisely such rights which the Chancellor, when his jurisdiction has been properly invoked, has often been called upon to decide. Issues of fact are rarely either "legal" or "equitable." All depends upon the context in which they arise. The examples cited by Chief Judge Pope in his thorough opinion in the Court of Appeals in this case are illustrative: " * * * (I)n a suit by one in possession of real property to quiet title, or to remove a cloud on title, the court of equity may determine the legal title. In a suit for specific performance of a contract, the court may determine the making, validity and the terms of the contract involved. In a suit for an injunction against trespass to real property the court may determine the legal right of the plaintiff to the possession of that property."

Though apparently not disputing these principles, the Court holds, quite apart from its reliance upon the Declaratory Judgment Act, that Beacon by filing its counterclaim and cross-claim acquired a right to trial by jury of issues which otherwise would have been properly triable to the court. Support for this position is found in the principle that, "in the federal courts equity has always acted only when legal remedies were inadequate. * * *" Yet that principle is not employed in its traditional sense as a limitation upon the exercise of power by a court of equity. This is apparent in the Court's recognition that the allegations of the complaint entitled Fox to equitable relief—relief to which Fox would not have been entitled if it had had an adequate remedy at law. Instead, the principle is employed today to mean that because it is possible under the counterclaim to have a jury trial of the factual issue of substantial competition, that issue must be tried by a jury, even though the issue was primarily presented in the original claim for equitable relief. This is a marked departure from long-settled principles.

It has been an established rule "that equitable jurisdiction existing at the filing of a bill is not destroyed because an adequate legal remedy may have become available thereafter." It has also been long settled that the District Court in its discretion may order the trial of a suit in equity in advance of an action at law between the same parties, even if there is a factual issue common to both. In the words of Mr. Justice Cardozo, writing for a unanimous Court in American Life Ins. Co. v. Stewart:

> A court has control over its own docket. * * * In the exercise of a sound discretion it may hold one lawsuit in abeyance to abide the outcome of another, especially where the parties and the issues are the same. * * * If request had been made by the respondents to suspend the suits in equity till the other causes were disposed of, the District Court could have considered whether justice would not be done by pursuing such a course, the remedy in equity being exceptional and the outcome of necessity. * * * There would be many circumstances to be weighed, as, for instance, the condition of the court calendar, whether the insurer had been precipitate or its adversaries dilatory, as well as other factors. In the end, benefit and hardship would have to be set off, the one against the other, and a balance ascertained.

III.

The Court today sweeps away these basic principles as "precedents decided under discarded procedures." It suggests that the Federal Rules of Civil Procedure have somehow worked an "expansion of adequate legal remedies" so as to oust the District Courts of equitable jurisdiction, as well as to deprive them of their traditional power to control their own dockets. But obviously the Federal Rules could not and did not "expand" the substantive law one whit.

Like the Declaratory Judgment Act, the Federal Rules preserve inviolate the right to trial by jury in actions historically cognizable at common law, as under the Constitution they must. They do not create a right of trial by jury where that right "does not exist under the Constitution or statutes of the United States." Rule 39(a). Since Beacon's counterclaim was compulsory under the Rules, *see* Rule 13(a), it is apparent that by filing it Beacon could not be held to have waived its jury rights. But neither can the counterclaim be held to have transformed Fox's original complaint into an action at law.

The Rules make possible the trial of legal and equitable claims in the same proceeding, but they expressly affirm the power of a trial judge to determine the order in which claims shall be heard. Rule 42(b). Certainly the Federal Rules were not intended to undermine the basic structure of equity jurisprudence, developed over the centuries and explicitly recognized in the United States Constitution.

For these reasons I think the petition for a writ of mandamus should have been dismissed.

* * *

B.   CHARACTERIZING THE ISSUE

DAIRY QUEEN, INC. v. WOOD

369 U.S. 469 (1962)

Mr. Justice Black delivered the opinion of the Court.

The United States District Court for the Eastern District of Pennsylvania granted a motion to strike petitioner's demand for a trial by jury in an action now pending before it on the alternative grounds that either the action was "purely equitable" or, if not purely equitable, whatever legal issues that were raised were "incidental" to equitable issues, and, in either case, no right to trial by jury existed. The petitioner then sought mandamus in the Court of Appeals for the Third Circuit to compel the district judge to vacate this order. When that court denied this request without opinion, we granted certiorari because the action of the Court of Appeals seemed inconsistent with protections already clearly recognized for the important constitutional right to trial by jury in our previous decisions.

At the outset, we may dispose of one of the grounds upon which the trial court acted in striking the demand for trial by jury—that based upon the view that the right to trial by jury may be lost as to legal issues where those issues are characterized as "incidental" to equitable issues—for our previous decisions make it plain that no such rule may be applied in the federal courts. In *Scott v. Neely*, decided in 1891, this Court held that a court of equity could not even take jurisdiction of a suit "in which a claim properly cognizable only at law is united in the same pleadings with a claim for equitable relief." That holding, which was based upon both the historical separation between law and equity and the duty of the Court to insure "that the right to a trial by a jury in the legal action may be preserved intact," created considerable inconvenience in that it necessitated two separate trials in the same case whenever that case contained both legal and equitable claims. Consequently, when the procedure in the federal courts was modernized by the adoption of the Federal Rules of Civil Procedure in 1938, it was deemed advisable to abandon that part of the holding of *Scott v. Neely* which rested upon the separation of law and equity and to permit the joinder of legal and equitable claims in a single action. Thus Rule 18(a) provides that a plaintiff "may join either as independent or as alternate claims as many claims either legal or equitable or both as he may have against an opposing party." And Rule 18(b) provides: "Whenever a claim is one heretofore cognizable only after another claim has been prosecuted to a conclusion, the two claims may be joined in a single action; but the court shall grant relief in that action only in accordance with the relative substantive rights of the parties. In particular, a plaintiff may state a claim for money and a claim to have set aside a conveyance fraudulent as to him, without first having obtained a judgment establishing the claim for money."

The Federal Rules did not, however, purport to change the basic holding of *Scott v. Neely* that the right to trial by jury of legal claims must be preserved.[5] Quite the contrary, Rule 38(a) expressly reaffirms that constitutional principle, declaring: "The right of trial by jury as declared by the Seventh Amendment to the Constitution or as given by a statute of the United States shall be preserved to the parties inviolate." Nonetheless, after the adoption of the Federal Rules, attempts were made indirectly to undercut that right by having federal courts in which cases involving both legal and equitable claims were filed decide the equitable claim first. The result of this procedure in those cases in which it was followed was that any issue common to both the legal and equitable claims was finally determined by the court and the party seeking trial by jury on the legal claim was deprived of that right as to these common issues. This procedure finally came before us in *Beacon Theatres, Inc. v. Westover*, a case which, like this one, arose from the denial of a petition for mandamus to compel a district judge to vacate his order striking a demand for trial by jury.

Our decision reversing that case not only emphasizes the responsibility of the Federal Courts of Appeals to grant mandamus where necessary to protect the constitutional right to trial by jury but also limits the issues open for determination here by defining the protection to which that right

---

5. "Subdivision (b) (of Rule 18) does not disturb the doctrine of those cases (*Scott v. Neely and Cates v. Allen*) but is expressly bottomed upon their principles. This is true because the Federal Rules abolish the distinction between law and equity, permit the joinder of legal and equitable claims, and safeguard the right to jury trial of legal issues."

is entitled in cases involving both legal and equitable claims. The holding in *Beacon Theatres* was that where both legal and equitable issues are presented in a single case, "only under the most imperative circumstances, circumstances which in view of the flexible procedures of the Federal Rules we cannot now anticipate, can the right to a jury trial of legal issues be lost through prior determination of equitable claims." That holding, of course, applies whether the trial judge chooses to characterize the legal issues presented as "incidental" to equitable issues or not.[8] Consequently, in a case such as this where there cannot even be a contention of such "imperative circumstances," *Beacon Theatres* requires that any legal issues for which a trial by jury is timely and properly demanded be submitted to a jury. There being no question of the timeliness or correctness of the demand involved here, the sole question which we must decide is whether the action now pending before the District Court contains legal issues.

The District Court proceeding arises out of a controversy between petitioner and the respondent owners of the trademark "Dairy Queen" with regard to a written licensing contract made by them in December 1949, under which petitioner agreed to pay some $150,000 for the exclusive right to use that trademark in certain portions of Pennsylvania. The terms of the contract provided for a small initial payment with the remaining payments to be made at the rate of 50% of all amounts received by petitioner on sales and franchises to deal with the trademark and, in order to make certain that the $150,000 payment would be completed within a specified period of time, further provided for minimum annual payments regardless of petitioner's receipts. In August 1960, the respondents wrote petitioner a letter in which they claimed that petitioner had committed "a material breach of that contract" by defaulting on the contract's payment provisions and notified petitioner of the termination of the contract and the cancellation of petitioner's right to use the trademark unless this claimed default was remedied immediately. When petitioner continued to deal with the trademark despite the notice of termination, the respondents brought an action based upon their view that a material breach of contract had occurred.

The complaint filed in the District Court alleged, among other things, that petitioner had "ceased paying * * * as required in the contract;" that the default "under the said contract * * * (was) in excess of $60,000.000;" that this default constituted a "material breach" of that contract; that petitioner had been notified by letter that its failure to pay as alleged made it guilty of a material breach of contract which if not "cured" would result in an immediate cancellation of the contract; that the breach had not been cured but that petitioner was contesting the cancellation and continuing to conduct business as an authorized dealer; that to continue

---

8. "It is therefore immaterial that the case at bar contains a stronger basis for equitable relief than was present in *Beacon Theatres*. It would make no difference if the equitable cause clearly outweighed the legal cause so that the basic issue of the case taken as a whole is equitable. As long as any legal cause is involved the jury rights it creates control. This is the teaching of *Beacon Theatres*, as we construe it."

such business after the cancellation of the contract constituted an infringement of the respondents' trademark; that petitioner's financial condition was unstable; and that because of the foregoing allegations, respondents were threatened with irreparable injury for which they had no adequate remedy at law. The complaint then prayed for both temporary and permanent relief, including: (1) temporary and permanent injunctions to restrain petitioner from any future use of or dealing in the franchise and the trademark; (2) an accounting to determine the exact amount of money owing by petitioner and a judgment for that amount; and (3) an injunction pending accounting to prevent petitioner from collecting any money from "Dairy Queen" stores in the territory.

In its answer to this complaint, petitioner raised a number of defenses, including: (1) a denial that there had been any breach of contract, apparently based chiefly upon its allegation that in January 1955 the parties had entered into an oral agreement modifying the original written contract by removing the provision requiring minimum annual payments regardless of petitioner's receipts thus leaving petitioner's only obligation that of turning over 50% of all its receipts; (2) laches and estoppel arising from respondents' failure to assert their claim promptly, thus permitting petitioner to expend large amounts of money in the development of its right to use the trademark; and (3) alleged violations of the antitrust laws by respondents in connection with their dealings with the trademark. Petitioner indorsed upon this answer a demand for trial by jury in accordance with Rule 38(b) of the Federal Rules of Civil Procedure.

Petitioner's contention, as set forth in its petition for mandamus to the Court of Appeals and reiterated in its briefs before this Court, is that insofar as the complaint requests a money judgment it presents a claim which is unquestionably legal. We agree with that contention. The most natural construction of the respondents' claim for a money judgment would seem to be that it is a claim that they are entitled to recover whatever was owed them under the contract as of the date of its purported termination plus damages for infringement of their trademark since that date. Alternatively, the complaint could be construed to set forth a full claim based upon both of these theories—that is, a claim that the respondents were entitled to recover both the debt due under the contract and damages for trademark infringement for the entire period of the alleged breach including that before the termination of the contract. Or it might possibly be construed to set forth a claim for recovery based completely on either one of these two theories—that is, a claim based solely upon the contract for the entire period both before and after the attempted termination on the theory that the termination, having been ignored, was of no consequence, or a claim based solely upon the charge of infringement on the theory that the contract, having been breached, could not be used as a defense to an infringement action even for the period prior to its termination. We find it unnecessary to resolve this ambiguity in the respondents' complaint because we think it plain that their claim for a money judgment is a claim wholly legal in its nature however the complaint is construed. As an action on a debt allegedly due under a contract, it would be difficult to conceive of an action of a more traditionally legal character. And as an action for damages based upon a charge of trademark infringement, it would be no less subject to cognizance by a court of law.

The respondents' contention that this money claim is "purely equitable" is based primarily upon the fact that their complaint is cast in terms of an "accounting," rather than in terms of an action for "debt" or "damages." But the constitutional right to trial by jury cannot be made to depend upon the choice of words used in the pleadings. The necessary prerequisite to the right to maintain a suit for an equitable accounting, like all other equitable remedies, is, as we pointed out in *Beacon Theatres*, the absence of an adequate remedy at law. Consequently, in order to maintain such a suit on a cause of action cognizable at law, as this one is, the plaintiff must be able to show that the "accounts between the parties" are of such a "complicated nature" that only a court of equity can satisfactorily unravel them. In view of the powers given to District Courts by Federal Rule of Civil Procedure 53(b) to appoint masters to assist the jury in those exceptional cases where the legal issues are too complicated for the jury adequately to handle alone, the burden of such a showing is considerably increased and it will indeed be a rare case in which it can be met. But be that as it may, this is certainly not such a case. A jury, under proper instructions from the court, could readily determine the recovery, if any, to be had here, whether the theory finally settled upon is that of breach of contract, that of trademark infringement, or any combination of the two. The legal remedy cannot be characterized as inadequate merely because the measure of damages may necessitate a look into petitioner's business records.

Nor is the legal claim here rendered "purely equitable" by the nature of the defenses interposed by petitioner. Petitioner's primary defense to the charge of breach of contract—that is, that the contract was modified by a subsequent oral agreement—presents a purely legal question having nothing whatever to do either with novation, as the district judge suggested, or reformation, as suggested by the respondents here. Such a defense goes to the question of just what, under the law, the contract between the respondents and petitioner is and, in an action to collect a debt for breach of a contract between these parties, petitioner has a right to have the jury determine not only whether the contract has been breached and the extent of the damages if any but also just what the contract is.

We conclude therefore that the district judge erred in refusing to grant petitioner's demand for a trial by jury on the factual issues related to the question of whether there has been a breach of contract. Since these issues are common with those upon which respondents' claim to equitable relief is based, the legal claims involved in the action must be determined prior to any final court determination of respondents' equitable claims. The Court of Appeals should have corrected the error of the district judge by granting the petition for mandamus. The judgment is therefore reversed and the cause remanded for further proceedings consistent with this opinion.

Reversed and remanded.

MR. JUSTICE WHITE took no part in the consideration or decision of this case. MR. JUSTICE HARLAN, whom MR. JUSTICE DOUGLAS joins, concurring.

I am disposed to accept the view, strongly pressed at the bar, that this complaint seeks an accounting for alleged trademark infringement, rather than contract damages. Even though this leaves the complaint as formally asking only for equitable relief,* this does not end the inquiry. The fact that an "accounting" is sought is not of itself dispositive of the jury trial issue. To render this aspect of the complaint truly "equitable" it must appear that the substantive claim is one cognizable only in equity or that the "accounts between the parties" are of such a "complicated nature" that they can be satisfactorily unraveled only by a court of equity. It is manifest from the face of the complaint that the "accounting" sought in this instance is not of either variety. A jury, under proper instructions from the court, could readily calculate the damages flowing from this alleged trademark infringement, just as courts of law often do in copyright and patent cases.

Consequently what is involved in this case is nothing more than a joinder in one complaint of prayers for both legal and equitable relief. In such circumstances, under principles long since established, *Scott v. Neely*, the petitioner cannot be deprived of his constitutional right to a jury trial on the "legal" claim contained in the complaint.

On this basis I concur in the judgment of the Court.

* * *

ROSS v. BERNHARD

396 U.S. 531 (1970)

MR. JUSTICE WHITE delivered the opinion of the Court.

The Seventh Amendment to the Constitution provides that in "(s)uits at common law, where the value in controversy shall exceed twenty dollars, the right of trial by jury shall be preserved." Whether the Amendment guarantees the right to a jury trial in stockholders' derivative actions is the issue now before us.

Petitioners brought this derivative suit in federal court against the directors of their closed-end investment company, the Lehman Corporation and the corporation's brokers, Lehman Brothers. They contended that Lehman Brothers controlled the corporation through an illegally large representation on the corporation's board of directors, in violation of the Investment Company Act of 1940, and used this control to extract

---

* Except as to the damage claim there is no dispute but that the complaint seeks only equitable relief.

excessive brokerage fees from the corporation. The directors of the corporation were accused of converting corporate assets and of "gross abuse of trust, gross misconduct, willful misfeasance, bad faith, (and) gross negligence." Both the individual defendants and Lehman Brothers were accused of breaches of fiduciary duty. It was alleged that the payments to Lehman Brothers constituted waste and spoliation, and that the contract between the corporation and Lehman Brothers had been violated. Petitioners requested that the defendants "account for and pay to the Corporation for their profits and gains and its losses." Petitioners also demanded a jury trial on the corporation's claims.

On motion to strike petitioners' jury trial demand, the District Court held that a shareholder's right to a jury on his corporation's cause of action was to be judged as if the corporation were itself the plaintiff. Only the shareholder's initial claim to speak for the corporation had to be tried to the judge. Convinced that "there are substantial grounds for difference of opinion as to this question and * * * an immediate appeal would materially advance the ultimate termination of this litigation," the District Court permitted an interlocutory appeal. The Court of Appeals reversed, holding that a derivative action was entirely equitable in nature, and no jury was available to try any part of it. Because of [a] conflict, we granted certiorari.

We reverse the holding of the Court of Appeals that in no event does the right to a jury trial preserved by the Seventh Amendment extend to derivative actions brought by the stockholders of a corporation. We hold that the right to jury trial attaches to those issues in derivative actions as to which the corporation, if it had been suing in its own right, would have been entitled to a jury.

The Seventh Amendment preserves to litigants the right to jury trial in suits at common law—"not merely suits, which the common law recognized among its old and settled proceedings, but suits in which legal rights were to be ascertained and determined, in contradistinction to those where equitable rights alone were recognized, and equitable remedies were administered. * * * In a jury sense, the amendment then may well be construed to embrace all suits, which are not of equity and admiralty jurisdiction, whatever may be the peculiar form which they may assume to settle legal rights."

However difficult it may have been to define with precision the line between actions at law dealing with legal rights and suits in equity dealing with equitable matters, some proceedings were unmistakably actions at law triable to a jury. The Seventh Amendment, for example, entitled the parties to a jury trial in actions for damages to a person or property, for libel and slander, for recovery of land, and for conversion of personal property. Just as clearly, a corporation, although an artificial being, was commonly entitled to sue and be sued in the usual forms of action, at least in its own State. Whether the corporation was viewed as an entity separate from its stockholders or as a device permitting its stockholders to carry on their business and to sue and be sued, a corporation's suit to enforce a legal right was an action at common law carrying the right to jury trial at the time the Seventh Amendment was adopted.

The common law refused, however, to permit stockholders to call corporate managers to account in actions at law. The possibilities for abuse, thus presented, were not ignored by corporate officers and directors. Early in the 19th century, equity provided relief both in this country and in England. Without detailing these developments, it suffices to say that the remedy in this country ... provided redress not only against faithless officers and directors but also against third parties who had damaged or threatened the corporate properties and whom the corporation through its managers refused to pursue. The remedy made available in equity was the derivative suit, viewed in this country as a suit to enforce a corporate cause of action against officers, directors, and third parties. As elaborated in the cases, one precondition for the suit was a valid claim on which the corporation could have sued; another was that the corporation itself had refused to proceed after suitable demand, unless excused by extraordinary conditions. Thus the dual nature of the stockholder's action: first, the plaintiff's right to sue on behalf of the corporation and, second, the merits of the corporation claim itself.

Derivative suits posed no Seventh Amendment problems where the action against the directors and third parties would have been by a bill in equity had the corporation brought the suit. Our concern is with cases based upon a legal claim of the corporation against directors or third parties. Does the trial of such claims at the suit of a stockholder and without a jury violate the Seventh Amendment?

The question arose in this Court in the context of a derivative suit for treble damages under the antitrust laws. Noting that the bill in equity set up a claim of the corporation alone, Mr. Justice Holmes observed that if the corporation were the plaintiff, "no one can doubt that its only remedy would be at law," and inquired "why the defendants' right to a jury trial should be taken away because the present plaintiff cannot persuade the only party having a cause of action to sue—how the liability which is the principal matter can be converted into an incident of the plaintiff's domestic difficulties with the company that has been wronged?" His answer was that the bill did not state a good cause of action in equity. Agreeing that there were "cases in which the nature of the right asserted for the company, or the failure of the defendants concerned to insist upon their rights, or a different state system, has led to the whole matter being disposed of in equity," he concluded that when the penalty of triple damages is sought, the antitrust statute plainly anticipated a jury trial and should not be read as "attempting to authorize liability to be enforced otherwise than through the verdict of a jury in a court of common law." Although the decision had obvious Seventh Amendment overtones, its ultimate rationale was grounded in the antitrust laws.

Where penal damages were not involved, however, there was no authoritative parallel in the federal system squarely passing on the applicability of the Seventh Amendment to the trial of a legal claim presented in a pre-merger derivative suit. What can be gleaned from this Court's opinions is not inconsistent with the general understanding, reflected by the state court decisions and secondary sources, that equity could properly resolve corporate claims of any kind without a jury when properly pleaded in derivative suits complying with the equity rules.

Such was the prevailing opinion when the Federal Rules of Civil Procedure were adopted in 1938. It continued until 1963 when the Court of Appeals for the Ninth Circuit, relying on the Federal Rules as construed and applied in *Beacon Theatres Inc. v. Westover*, and *Dairy Queen Inc. v. Wood*, required the legal issues in a derivative suit to be tried to a jury. It was this decision that the District Court followed in the case before us and that the Court of Appeals rejected.

Under those cases [*Beacon* and *Dairy Queen*], where equitable and legal claims are joined in the same action, there is a right to jury trial on the legal claims which must not be infringed either by trying the legal issues as incidental to the equitable ones or by a court trial of a common issue existing between the claims. The Seventh Amendment question depends on the nature of the issue to be tried rather than the character of the overall action.[10] The principle of these cases bears heavily on derivative actions.

We have noted that the derivative suit has dual aspects: first, the stockholder's right to sue on behalf of the corporation, historically an equitable matter; second, the claim of the corporation against directors or third parties on which, if the corporation had sued and the claim presented legal issues, the company could demand a jury trial. As implied by Mr. Justice Holmes, legal claims are not magically converted into equitable issues by their presentation to a court of equity in a derivative suit. The claim pressed by the stockholder against directors or third parties "is not his own but the corporation's." The corporation is a necessary party to the action; without it the case cannot proceed. Although named a defendant, it is the real party in interest, the stockholder being at best the nominal plaintiff. The proceeds of the action belong to the corporation and it is bound by the result of the suit. The heart of the action is the corporate claim. If it presents a legal issue, one entitling the corporation to a jury trial under the Seventh Amendment, the right to a jury is not forfeited merely because the stockholder's right to sue must first be adjudicated as an equitable issue triable to the court. *Beacon* and *Dairy Queen* require no less.

If under older procedures, now discarded, a court of equity could properly try the legal claims of the corporation presented in a derivative

---

10. As our cases indicate, the "legal" nature of an issue is determined by considering, first, the pre-merger custom with reference to such questions; second, the remedy sought; and, third, the practical abilities and limitations of juries. Of these factors, the first, requiring extensive and possibly abstruse historical inquiry, is obviously the most difficult to apply.

suit, it was because irreparable injury was threatened and no remedy at law existed as long as the stockholder was without standing to sue and the corporation itself refused to pursue its own remedies. Indeed, from 1789 until 1938, the judicial code expressly forbade courts of equity from entertaining any suit for which there was an adequate remedy at law. This provision served "to guard the right of trial by jury preserved by the Seventh Amendment and to that end it should be liberally construed." If, before 1938, the law and had borrowed from equity, as it borrowed other things, the idea that stockholders could litigate for their recalcitrant corporation, the corporate claim, if legal, would undoubtedly have been tried to a jury.

Of course, this did not occur, but the Federal Rules had a similar impact. Actions are no longer brought as actions at law or suits in equity. Under the Rules there is only one action—a "civil action"—in which all claims may be joined and all remedies are available. Purely procedural impediments to the presentation of any issue by any party, based on the difference between law and equity, was destroyed. In a civil action presenting a stockholder's derivative claim, the court after passing upon the plaintiff's right to sue on behalf of the corporation is now able to try the corporate claim for damages with the aid of a jury. Separable claims may be tried separately, Fed. Rule Civ. P. 42(b), or legal and equitable issues may be handled in the same trial. The historical rule preventing a court of law from entertaining a shareholder's suit on behalf of the corporation is obsolete; it is no longer tenable for a district court, administering both law and equity in the same action, to deny legal remedies to a corporation, merely because the corporation's spokesmen are its share-holders rather than its directors. Under the rules, law and equity are procedurally combined; nothing turns now upon the form of the action or the procedural devices by which the parties happen to come before the court. The "expansion of adequate legal remedies provided by * * * the Federal Rules necessarily affects the scope of equity." *Beacon Theatres, Inc.*

Thus, for example, before-merger class actions were largely a device of equity, and there was no right to a jury even on issues that might, under other circumstances, have been tried to a jury. Although at least one post-merger court held that the device was not available to try legal issues, it now seems settled in the lower federal courts that class action plaintiffs may obtain a jury trial on any legal issues they present.

Derivative suits have been described as one kind of "true" class action. We are inclined to agree with the description, at least to the extent it recognizes that the derivative suit and the class action were both ways of allowing parties to be heard in equity who could not speak at law. After adoption of the rules there is no longer any procedural obstacle to the assertion of legal rights before juries, however the party may have acquired standing to assert those rights. Given the availability in a derivative action of both legal and equitable remedies, we think the Seventh Amendment preserves to the parties in a stockholder's suit the same right to a jury trial that historically belonged to the corporation and to those against whom the corporation pressed its legal claims.

In the instant case we have no doubt that the corporation's claim is, at least in part, a legal one. The relief sought is money damages. There are allegations in the complaint of a breach of fiduciary duty, but there are also allegations of ordinary breach of contract and gross negligence. The corporation, had it sued on its own behalf, would have been entitled to a jury's determination, at a minimum, of its damages against its broker under the brokerage contract and of its rights against its own directors because of their negligence. Under these circumstances it is unnecessary to decide whether the corporation's other claims are also properly triable to a jury. *Dairy Queen, Inc.* The decision of the Court of Appeals is reversed.

It is so ordered.

Decision of Court of Appeals reversed.

MR. JUSTICE STEWART, with whom THE CHIEF JUSTICE and MR. JUSTICE HARLAN join, dissenting.

In holding as it does that the plaintiff in a shareholder's derivative suit is constitutionally entitled to a jury trial, the Court today seems to rely upon some sort of ill-defined combination of the Seventh Amendment and the Federal Rules of Civil Procedure. Somehow the Amendment and the Rules magically interact to do what each separately was expressly intended not to do, namely, to enlarge the right to a jury trial in civil actions brought in the courts of the United States.

The Seventh Amendment, by its terms, does not extend, but merely preserves the right to a jury trial "(i)n Suits at common law." All agree that this means the reach of the Amendment is limited to those actions that were tried to the jury in 1791 when the Amendment was adopted. Suits in equity, which were historically tried to the court, were therefore unaffected by it. Similarly, Rule 38 of the Federal Rules has no bearing on the right to a jury trial in suits in equity, for it simply preserves inviolate "(t)he right of trial by jury as declared by the Seventh Amendment." Thus this Rule, like the Amendment itself, neither restricts nor enlarges the right to jury trial. Indeed nothing in the Federal Rules can rightly be construed to enlarge the right of jury trial, for in the legislation authorizing the Rules, Congress expressly provided that they "shall neither abridge, enlarge, nor modify the substantive rights of any litigant." I take this plain, simple, and straight-forward language to mean that after the promulgation of the Federal Rules, as before, the constitutional right to a jury trial attaches only to suits at common law. So, apparently, has every federal court that has discussed the issue. Since, as the Court concedes, a shareholder's derivative suit could be brought only in equity, it would seem to me to follow by the most elementary logic that in such suits there is no constitutional right to a trial by jury.[4] Today the Court tosses aside

---

4. Virtually every state and federal court that has faced this issue has similarly reasoned to the same conclusion. The equitable nature of the derivative suit has been recognized in several

history, logic and over 100 years of firm precedent to hold that the plaintiff in a shareholder's derivative suit does indeed have a constitutional right to a trial by jury. This holding has a questionable basis in policy and no basis whatever in the Constitution.

The Court begins by assuming the "dual nature" of the shareholder's action. While the plaintiff's right to get into court at all is conceded to be equitable, once he is there the Court says his claim is to be viewed as though it were the claim of the corporation itself. If the corporation would have been entitled to a jury trial on such a claim, then, it is said, so would the shareholder. This conceptualization is without any historical basis. For the fact is that a shareholder's suit was not originally viewed in this country, or in England, as a suit to enforce a corporate cause of action. Rather, the shareholder's suit was initially permitted only against the managers of the corporation—not third parties—and it was conceived of as an equitable action to enforce the right of a beneficiary against his trustee. The shareholder was not, therefore, in court to enforce indirectly the corporate right of action, but to enforce directly his own equitable right of action against an unfaithful fiduciary. Later the rights of the shareholder were enlarged to encompass suits against third parties harming the corporation, but "the postulated 'corporate cause of action' has never been thought to describe an actual historical class of suit which was recognized by courts of law." Indeed the commentators, including those cited by the Court as postulating the analytic duality of the shareholder's derivative suit, recognize that historically the suit has in practice always been treated as a single cause tried exclusively in equity. They agree that there is therefore no constitutional right to a jury trial even where there might have been one had the corporation itself brought the suit.

This has been not simply the "general" or "prevailing" view in the federal courts as the Court says, but the unanimous view with the single exception of the Ninth Circuit's 1963 decision in *DePinto v. Provident Security Life Ins. Co.*, a decision that has since been followed by no court until the present case.

The Court would have us discount all those decisions rendered before 1938, when the Federal Rules of Civil Procedure were adopted, because it says that before the promulgation of the Rules, "(p)urely procedural impediments" somehow blocked the exercise of a constitutional right. In itself this would seem a rather shaky premise upon which to build an argument. But the Court's position is still further weakened by the fact that any "(p)urely procedural impediments" to a jury trial in a derivative suit were eliminated, not in 1938, but at least as early as 1912. For Rule 23 of the Equity Rules of that year provided that if a "matter ordinarily determinable at law" arose in an equity suit it should "be determined in

---

decisions of this Court. It was also reflected in the adoption of Equity Rule 94 in 1882, and Rule 27 of the Equity Rules of 1912 which established the preconditions to bringing shareholders' derivative suits in the federal courts. These rules are the forerunners of Rule 23(b) of Fed. Rule Civ. P. of 1938, and of Fed. Rule Civ. P. 23.1 (1966), which now controls the initiation of such suits.

that suit according to the principles applicable, without sending the case or question to the law side of the court." These applicable principles included the right of jury trial.

* * * [P]re–1938 cases, then, firmly establish the unitary, equitable basis of shareholders' derivative suits and in no way support the Court's holding here. But, the Court says, whatever the situation may have been before 1938, the Federal Rules of Civil Procedure of that year, at least as construed in our decisions more than 20 years later in *Beacon Theatres, Inc. v. Westover* and *Dairy Queen, Inc. v. Wood*, in any event require the conclusion reached today. I can find nothing in either of these cases that leads to that conclusion.

In *Beacon Theatres* the plaintiff sought both an injunction preventing the defendant from instituting an antitrust action and a declaratory judgment that certain moving picture distribution contracts did not violate the antitrust laws. The defendant answered and counterclaimed for treble damages under the antitrust laws. He demanded a jury trial on the factual issues relating to his counterclaim. The district court held that even though there were factual issues common to both the complaint and the counterclaim, it would first hear the plaintiff's suit for equitable relief before submitting the counterclaim to a jury. The Court of Appeals affirmed, and this Court reversed, upon the ground that if the equitable claim were tried first, there might be an estoppel which would defeat the defendant's right to a full jury trial on all the factual issues raised in his counterclaim. Similarly in *Dairy Queen* the Court simply held that a plaintiff could not avoid a jury trial by joining legal and equitable causes of action in one complaint.

It is true that in *Beacon Theatres* it was stated that the 1938 Rules did diminish the scope of federal equity jurisdiction in certain particulars. But the Court's effort to force the facts of this case into the mold of *Beacon Theatres* and *Dairy Queen* simply does not succeed. Those cases involved a combination of historically separable suits, one in law and one in equity. Their facts fit the pattern of cases where, before the Rules, the equity cases where, before the Rules, the equity court would have disposed of the equitable claim and would then have either retained jurisdiction over the suit, despite the availability of adequate legal remedies, or enjoined a subsequent legal action between the same parties involving the same controversy.

But the present case is not one involving traditionally equitable claims by one party, and traditionally legal claims by the other. Nor is it a suit in which the plaintiff is asserting a combination of legal and equitable claims. For, as we have seen, a derivative suit has always been conceived of as a single, unitary, equitable cause of action. It is for this reason, and not because of "procedural impediments," that the courts of equity did not transfer derivative suits to the law side. In short, the cause of action is wholly a creature of equity. And whatever else can be said of *Beacon*

Theatres and *Dairy Queen*, they did not cast aside altogether the historic division between equity and law.

If history is to be so cavalierly dismissed, the derivative suit can, of course, be artificially broken down into separable elements. But so then can any traditionally equitable cause of action, and the logic of the Court's position would lead to the virtual elimination of all equity jurisdiction. An equitable suit for an injunction, for instance, often involves issues of fact which, if damages had been sought, would have been triable to a jury. Does this mean that in a suit asking only for injunctive relief these factual issues must be tried to the jury, with the judge left to decide only whether, given the jury's findings, an injunction is the appropriate remedy? Certainly the Federal Rules make it possible to try a suit for an injunction in that way, but even more certainly they were not intended to have any such effect. Yet the Court's approach, it seems, would require that if any "legal issue" procedurally could be tried to a jury, it constitutionally must be tried to a jury.

The fact is, of course, that there are, for the most part, no such things as inherently "legal issues" or inherently "equitable issues." There are only factual issues, and, "like chameleons (they) take their color from surrounding circumstances." Thus the Court's "nature of the issue" approach is hardly meaningful.

As a final ground for its conclusion, the Court points to a supposed analogy to suits involving class actions. It says that before the Federal Rules such suits were considered equitable and not triable to a jury, but that since promulgation of the Rules the federal courts have found that "plaintiffs may obtain a jury trial on any legal issues they present." Of course the plaintiff may obtain such a trial even in a derivative suit. Nothing in the Constitution or the Rules precludes the judge from granting a jury trial as a matter of discretion. But even if the Court means that some federal courts have ruled that the class action plaintiff in some situations has a constitutional right to a jury trial, the analogy to derivative suits is wholly unpersuasive. For it is clear that the draftsmen of the Federal Rules intended that Rule 23 as it pertained to class actions should be applicable, like other rules governing joinder of claims and parties, "to all actions, whether formerly denominated legal or equitable." This does not mean that a formerly equitable action is triable to a jury simply because it is brought on behalf of a class, but only that a historically legal cause of action can be tried to a jury even if it is brought as a class action. Since a derivative suit is historically wholly a creation of equity, the class action "analogy" is in truth no analogy at all.

The Court's decision today can perhaps be explained as a reflection of an unarticulated but apparently overpowering bias in favor of jury trials in civil actions. It certainly cannot be explained in terms of either the Federal Rules or the Constitution.

* * *

C. ADMINISTRATIVE FORUM

ATLAS ROOFING CO., INC. v. OCCUPATIONAL SAFETY AND HEALTH REVIEW COMM.

430 U.S. 442 (1977)

MR. JUSTICE WHITE delivered the opinion of the Court.

The issue in these cases is whether, consistent with the Seventh Amendment, Congress may create a new cause of action in the Government for civil penalties enforceable in an administrative agency where there is no jury trial.

I

After extensive investigation, Congress concluded, in 1970, that work-related deaths and injuries had become a "drastic" national problem Finding the existing state statutory remedies as well as state common-law actions for negligence and wrongful death to be inadequate to protect the employee population from death and injury due to unsafe working conditions, Congress enacted the Occupational Safety and Health Act of 1970 (OSHA or Act). The Act created a new statutory duty to avoid maintaining unsafe or unhealthy working conditions, and empowers the Secretary of Labor to promulgate health and safety standards. Two new remedies were provided permitting the Federal Government, proceeding before an administrative agency, (1) to obtain abatement orders requiring employers to correct unsafe working conditions and (2) to impose civil penalties on any employer maintaining any unsafe working condition. Each remedy exists whether or not an employee is actually injured or killed as a result of the condition, and existing state statutory and common-law remedies for actual injury and death remain unaffected.

Under the Act, inspectors, representing the Secretary of Labor, are authorized to conduct reasonable safety and health inspections. If a violation is discovered, the inspector, on behalf of the Secretary, issues a citation to the employer fixing a reasonable time for its abatement and, in his discretion, proposing a civil penalty. Such proposed penalties may range from nothing for *de minimis* and non-serious violations, to not more than $1,000 for serious violations, to a maximum of $10,000 for willful or repeated violations.

If the employer wishes to contest the penalty or the abatement order, he may do so by notifying the Secretary of Labor within 15 days, in which event the abatement order is automatically stayed. An evidentiary hearing is then held before an administrative law judge of the Occupational Safety and Health Review Commission. The Commission consists of three members, appointed for six-year terms, each of whom is qualified "by reason of training, education or experience" to adjudicate contested citations and assess penalties. At this hearing the burden is on the Secretary to establish the elements of the alleged violation and the propriety of his proposed abatement order and proposed penalty; and the judge is empowered to affirm, modify, or vacate any or all of these items, giving due consideration in his penalty assessment to "the size of the business of the employer ..., the gravity of the violation, the good faith of the employer, and the history of previous violations." The judge's decision becomes the Commission's final and appealable order unless within 30 days a Commissioner directs that it be reviewed by the full Commission.

If review is granted, the Commission's subsequent order directing abatement and the payment of any assessed penalty becomes final unless the employer timely petitions for judicial review in the appropriate court of appeals. The Secretary similarly may seek review of Commission orders, but, in either case, "(t)he findings of the Commission with respect to questions of fact, if supported by substantial evidence on the record considered as a whole, shall be conclusive." If the employer fails to pay the assessed penalty, the Secretary may commence a collection action in a federal district court in which neither the fact of the violation nor the propriety of the penalty assessed may be retried. Thus, the penalty may be collected without the employer's ever being entitled to a jury determination of the facts constituting the violation.

II

Petitioners were separately cited by the Secretary and ordered immediately to abate pertinent hazards after inspections of their respective worksites conducted in 1972 revealed conditions that assertedly violated a mandatory occupational safety standard promulgated by the Secretary. In each case an employee's death had resulted. Petitioner Irey was cited for a willful violation of a safety standard promulgated by the Secretary under the Act requiring the sides of trenches in "unstable or soft material" to be "shored, ... sloped, or otherwise supported by means of sufficient strength to protect the employees working within them." The Secretary proposed a penalty of $7,500 for this violation and ordered the hazard abated immediately.

Petitioner Atlas was cited for a serious violation of [other provisions of OSHA] which require that roof opening covers be "so installed as to prevent accidental displacement." The Secretary proposed a penalty of $600 for this violation and ordered the hazard abated immediately.

Petitioners timely contested these citations and were afforded hearings before Administrative Law Judges of the Commission. The judges, and later the Commission, affirmed the findings of violations and accompanying abatement requirements and assessed petitioner Irey a reduced civil penalty of $5,000 and petitioner Atlas the civil penalty of $600 which the Secretary had proposed. Petitioners respectively thereupon sought judicial review in the Courts of Appeals for the Third and Fifth Circuits, challenging both the Commission's factual findings that violations had occurred and the constitutionality of the Act's enforcement procedures.

A panel of the Court of Appeals for the Third Circuit affirmed the Commission's orders in the Irey case over petitioner's and a dissenter's contention that the failure to afford the employer a jury trial on the question whether he had violated OSHA was in violation of the Seventh Amendment to the United States Constitution which provides for jury trial in most civil suits at common law. On rehearing *en banc*, the Court of Appeals for the Third Circuit, over four dissents, adhered to the original panel's decision. It concluded that this Court's rulings to date "leave no doubt that the Seventh Amendment is not applicable, at least in the context of a case such as this one, and that Congress is free to provide an administrative enforcement scheme without the intervention of a jury at any stage."

The Court of Appeals for the Fifth Circuit also affirmed the Commission's order in the Atlas case over a similar claim that the enforcement scheme violated the Seventh Amendment. It stated: "Where adjudicative responsibility rests only in the administering agency, 'jury trials would be incompatible with the whole concept of administrative adjudication and would substantially interfere with the (agency's) role in the statutory scheme.'"

We granted the petitions for writs of certiorari limited to the important question whether the Seventh Amendment prevents Congress from assigning to an administrative agency, under these circumstances the task of adjudicating violations of OSHA.

III

The Seventh Amendment provides that "(i)n Suits at common law, where the value in controversy shall exceed twenty dollars, the right of trial by jury shall be preserved ..." The phrase "Suits at common law" has been construed to refer to cases tried prior to the adoption of the Seventh Amendment in courts of law in which jury trial was customary as distinguished from courts of equity or admiralty in which jury trial was not. Petitioners claim that a suit in a federal court by the Government for civil penalties for violation of a statute is a suit for a money judgment which is classically a suit at common law; and that the defendant therefore has a Seventh Amendment right to a jury determination of all issues of fact in such a case. Petitioners then claim that to permit Congress to assign the function of adjudicating the Government's rights to civil penalties for violation of the statute to a different forum an administrative agency in which no jury is available would be to permit Congress to deprive a defendant of his Seventh Amendment jury right. We disagree. At least in cases in which "public rights" are being litigated *e. g.*, cases in which the Government sues in its sovereign capacity to enforce public rights created by statutes within the power of Congress to enact the Seventh Amendment does not prohibit Congress from assigning the fact-finding function and initial adjudication to an administrative forum with which the jury would be incompatible.

Congress has often created new statutory obligations, provided for civil penalties for their violation, and committed exclusively to an administrative agency the function of deciding whether a violation has in fact occurred. These statutory schemes have been sustained by this Court, albeit often without express reference to the Seventh Amendment. Thus taxes may constitutionally be assessed and collected together with penalties, with the relevant facts in some instances being adjudicated only by an administrative agency. Neither of these cases expressly discussed the question whether the taxation scheme violated the Seventh Amendment. However, in *Helvering v. Mitchell*, the Court said, in rejecting a claim under the Sixth Amendment that the assessment and adjudication of tax penalties could not be made without a jury, that "the determination of the facts upon which liability is based may be by an administrative agency instead of a jury." Similarly, Congress has entrusted to an administrative agency the task or adjudicating violations of the customs and immigration laws and assessing penalties based thereon. ("(D)ue process of law does not require that the courts, rather than administrative officers, be charged ... with determining the facts upon which the imposition of (fines) depends").

In Block v. Hirsh, the Court sustained Congress' power to pass a statute, applicable to the District of Columbia, temporarily suspending landlords' legal remedy of ejectment and relegating them to an administrative fact-finding forum charged with determining fair rents at which tenants could hold over despite the expiration of their leases. In that case the Court squarely rejected a challenge to the statute based on the Seventh Amendment, stating:

> The statute is objected to on the further ground that landlords and tenants are deprived by it of a trial by jury on the right to possession of the land. If the power of the Commission established by the statute to regulate the relation is established, as we think it is, by what we have said, this objection amounts to little. To regulate the relation and to decide the facts affecting it are hardly separable.

In *Crowell v. Benson*, apparently referring to the above-cited line of authority, the Court stated:

> (T)he distinction is at once apparent between cases of private right and those which arise between the Government and persons subject to its authority in connection with the performance of the constitutional functions of the executive or legislative departments.... (T)he Congress, in exercising the powers confided to it may establish "legislative" courts ... to serve as special tribunals "to examine and determine various matters, arising between the government and others, which from their nature do not require judicial determination and yet are susceptible of it." But "the mode of determining matters of this class is completely within congressional control. Congress may reserve to itself the power to decide, may delegate that power to executive officers, or may commit it to judicial tribunals." ... Famil-

iar illustrations of administrative of such matters are found in connection with the exercise of the congressional power as to interstate and foreign commerce, taxation, immigration, the public lands, public health, the facilities of the post office, pensions, and payments to veterans.

In *NLRB v. Jones & Laughlin Steel Corp.*, the Court squarely addressed the Seventh Amendment issue involved when Congress commits the fact-finding function under a new statute to an administrative tribunal. Under the National Labor Relations Act, Congress had committed to the National Labor Relations Board, in a proceeding brought by its litigating arm, the task of deciding whether an unfair labor practice had been committed and of ordering backpay where appropriate. The Court stated:

> The instant case is not a suit at common law or in the nature of such a suit. The proceeding is one unknown to the common law. It is a statutory proceeding. Reinstatement of the employee and payment for time lost are requirements (administratively) imposed for violation of the statute and are remedies appropriate to its enforcement. The contention under the Seventh Amendment is without merit.

This passage from *Jones & Laughlin* has recently been explained in *Curtis v. Loether*, in which the Court held the Seventh Amendment applicable to private damages suits in federal courts brought under the housing discrimination provisions of the Civil Rights Act of 1968. The Court rejected the argument that Jones & Laughlin held the Seventh Amendment inapplicable to any action based on a statutorily created right even if the action was brought before a tribunal which customarily utilizes a jury as its fact-finding arm. Instead, we concluded that Jones & Laughlin upheld "congressional power to entrust enforcement of statutory rights to an administrative process or specialized court of equity free from the strictures of the Seventh Amendment."

Finally, in *Pernell v. Southall Realty*, we stated:

> *Block v. Hirsh* merely stands for the principle that the Seventh Amendment is generally inapplicable in administrative proceedings, where jury trials would be incompatible with the whole concept of administrative adjudication.... We may assume that the Seventh Amendment would not be a bar to a congressional effort to entrust landlord-tenant disputes, including those over the right to possession, to an administrative agency. Congress has not seen fit to do so, however, but rather has provided that actions under s 16–1501 be brought as ordinary civil actions in the District of Columbia's court of general jurisdiction. Where it has done so, and where the action involves rights and remedies recognized at common law, it must preserve to parties their right to a jury trial.

In sum, the cases discussed above stand clearly for the proposition that when Congress creates new statutory "public rights," it may assign their adjudication to an administrative agency with which a jury trial would be incompatible, without violating the Seventh Amendment's injunction that jury trial is to be "preserved" in "suits at common law." Congress is not required by the Seventh Amendment to choke the already crowded federal courts with new types of litigation or prevented from committing some new types of litigation to administrative agencies with special competence in the relevant field. This is the case even if the Seventh Amendment would have required a jury where the adjudication of those rights is assigned instead to a federal court of law instead of an administrative agency. Petitioners would nevertheless have us disregard the interpretation of *Jones & Laughlin* which we recently espoused in *Curtis v. Loether* and *Pernell v. Southall Realty*, reading it instead as a holding solely that the entire proceeding before the NLRB was really equitable in nature; and they would have us entirely disregard *Block v. Hirsh*. They would have us disregard the dictum in *Crowell v. Benson*, that the adjudication of congressionally created public rights may be assigned to administrative agencies, as well as similar [holdings].

None of the grounds tendered for so reinterpreting the Seventh Amendment is convincing. It is suggested that in some of the cases, the Seventh Amendment was not expressly put in issue. But these cases are clear enough that in the context involved, there was no requirement that the courts be involved at all in the fact-finding process in the first instance. It is difficult to believe that these holdings or dicta did not subsume the proposition that a jury trial was not required. Furthermore, there are the remaining cases where the Court expressly held or observed that the Seventh Amendment did not bar administrative fact-findings.

Second, it is argued with some force that [some cited] cases all deal with the exercise of sovereign powers that are inherently in the exclusive domain of the Federal Government and critical to its very existence the power over immigration, the importation of goods, and taxation and that the theory of those cases is inapplicable where the Government exercises other powers that petitioners apparently regard as less fundamental, less exclusive, and less vital to the existence of the Nation, such as the power to regulate commerce among the several States, the latter being the power Congress sought to exercise in enacting the statute at issue here. The difficulty with this argument is that the Court in these cases, and in others, did not appear to confine its holdings in this manner.

* * * Third is the assertion that the right to jury trial was never intended to depend on the identity of the forum to which Congress has chosen to submit a dispute; otherwise, it is said, Congress could utterly destroy the right to a jury trial by always providing for administrative rather than judicial resolution of the vast range of cases that now arise in the courts. The argument is well put, but it overstates the holdings of our prior cases and is in any event unpersuasive. Our prior cases support administrative fact-finding in only those situations involving "public rights," e. g., where the Government is involved in its sovereign capacity under an otherwise valid statute creating enforceable public rights. Wholly

private tort, contract, and property cases, as well as a vast range of other cases as well are not at all implicated.

More the point, it is apparent from the history of jury trial in civil matters that fact-finding, which is the essential function of the jury in civil cases, was never the exclusive province of the jury under either the English or American legal systems at the time of the adoption of the Seventh Amendment; and the question whether a fact would be found by a jury turned to a considerable degree on the nature of the forum in which a litigant found himself. Critical fact-finding was performed without juries in suits in equity, and there were no juries in admiralty; nor were there juries in the military justice system. The jury was the fact-finding mode in most suits in the common-law courts, but it was not exclusively so: Condemnation was a suit at common law but constitutionally could be tried without a jury. "(M)any civil as well as criminal proceedings at common law were without a jury." The question whether a particular case was to be tried in a court of equity without a jury or a court of law with a jury did not depend on whether the suit involved fact-finding or on the nature of the facts to be found. Fact-finding could be a critical matter either at law or in equity. Rather, as a general rule, the decision turned on whether courts of law supplied a cause of action and an adequate remedy to the litigant. If it did, then the case would be tried in a court of law before a jury. Otherwise the case would be tried to a court of equity sitting without a jury. Thus, suits for damages for breach of contract, for example, were suits at common law with the issues of the making of the contract and its breach to be decided by a jury; but specific performance was a remedy unavailable in a court of law and where such relief was sought the case would be tried in a court of equity with the facts as to making and breach to be ascertained by the court.

The Seventh Amendment was declaratory of the existing law, for it required only that jury trial in suits at common law was to be "preserved." It thus did not purport to require a jury trial where none was required before. Moreover, it did not seek to change the fact-finding mode in equity or admiralty or to freeze equity jurisdiction as it existed in 1789, preventing it from developing new remedies where those available in courts of law were inadequate. *Ross v. Bernhard* is instructive in this respect. We there held that a jury trial is required in stockholder derivative suits where, if the corporation itself had sued, a jury trial would have been available to the corporation. It is apparent, however, that prior to the 1938 Federal Rules of Civil Procedure merging the law and equity functions of the federal courts, the very suit involved in Bernhard would have been in a court of equity sitting without a jury, not because the underlying issue was any different at all from the issue the corporation would have presented had it sued, but because the stockholder plaintiff who was denied standing in a court of law to sue on the issue was enabled in proper circumstances, starting in the early part of the 19th century, to sue in equity on behalf of the company.

The point is that the Seventh Amendment was never intended to establish the jury as the exclusive mechanism for fact-finding in civil cases. It took the existing legal order as it found it, and there is little or no basis for concluding that the Amendment should now be interpreted to provide an impenetrable barrier to administrative fact-finding under otherwise valid federal regulatory statutes. We cannot conclude that the Amendment rendered Congress powerless when it concluded that remedies available in courts of law were inadequate to cope with a problem within Congress' power to regulate to create new public rights and remedies by statute and commit their enforcement, if it chose, to a tribunal other than a court of law such as an administrative agency in which facts are not found by juries. Indeed, as the Oceanic opinion said, the "settled judicial construction" was to the contrary "from the beginning." That case indicated that the Government could commit the enforcement of statutes and the imposition and collection of fines to the judiciary, in which event jury trial would be required, but that the United States could also validly opt for administrative enforcement, without judicial trials.

Thus, history and our cases support the proposition that the right to a jury trial turns not solely on the nature of the issue to be resolved but also on the forum in which it is to be resolved. Congress found the common-law and other existing remedies for work injuries resulting from unsafe working conditions to be inadequate to protect the Nation's working men and women. It created a new cause of action, and remedies therefor, unknown to the common law, and placed their enforcement in a tribunal supplying speedy and expert resolutions of the issues involved. The Seventh Amendment is no bar to the creation of new rights or to their enforcement outside the regular courts of law.

The judgments below are affirmed.

It is so ordered.

* * *

D. STATUTORY CIVIL PENALTY ACTIONS

TULL v. UNITED STATES

481 U.S. 412 (1987)

JUSTICE BRENNAN delivered the opinion of the Court.

The question for decision is whether the Seventh Amendment guaranteed petitioner a right to a jury trial on both liability and amount of penalty in an action instituted by the Federal Government seeking civil penalties and injunctive relief under the Clean Water Act.

I

The Clean Water Act prohibits discharging, without a permit, dredged or fill material into "navigable waters," including the wetlands adjacent to the waters. "Wetlands" are "swamps, marshes, bogs and similar areas." The Government sued petitioner, a real estate developer, for dumping fill on wetlands on the island of Chincoteague, Virginia. The Government alleged in the original complaint that petitioner dumped fill on three sites: Ocean Breeze Mobile Homes Sites, Mire Pond Properties, and Eel Creek. The Government later amended the complaint to allege that petitioner also placed fill in a manmade waterway, named Fowling Gut Extended, on the Ocean Breeze property.

Section 1319 enumerates the remedies available under the Clean Water Act. Subsection (b) authorizes relief in the form of temporary or permanent injunctions. Subsection (d) provides that violators of certain sections of the Act "shall be subject to a civil penalty not to exceed $10,000 per day" during the period of the violation. The Government sought in this case both injunctive relief and civil penalties. When the complaint was filed, however, almost all of the property at issue had been sold by petitioner to third parties. Injunctive relief was therefore impractical except with regard to a small portion of the land. The Government's complaint demanded the imposition of the maximum civil penalty of $22,890,000 under subsection (d).

Petitioner's timely demand for a trial by jury was denied by the District Court. During the 15-day bench trial, petitioner did not dispute that he had placed fill at the locations alleged and did not deny his failure to obtain a permit. Petitioner contended, however, that the property in question did not constitute "wetlands." The Government concedes that triable issues of fact were presented by disputes between experts involving the composition and nature of the fillings.

The District Court concluded that petitioner had illegally filled in wetland areas on all properties in question, but drastically reduced the amount of civil penalties sought by the Government. With respect to the Ocean Breeze Mobile Homes Sites, the court imposed a civil fine of $35,000, noting that petitioner had sold seven lots at a profit of $5,000 per lot. The court fined petitioner another $35,000 for illegal fillings on the Mire Pond Properties, and $5,000 for filling that affected a single lot in Eel Creek, although petitioner had realized no profit from filling in these properties. In addition, the court imposed on petitioner a $250,000 fine to be suspended, however, "on the specific condition that he restore the extension of Fowling Gut to its former navigable condition. . . ." Although petitioner argued that such restoration required purchasing the land from third parties at a cost of over $700,000, thus leaving him no choice but to pay the fine, the court refused to alter this order. The court also granted separate injunctive relief: it ordered the restoration of wetlands on the portions of Mire Pond and Eel Creek still owned by petitioner, and further ordered the removal of fillings on five lots of the Ocean Breeze Mobile Home Sites unless petitioner were granted an "after-the-fact permit" validating the fillings.

The Court of Appeals affirmed over a dissent, rejecting petitioner's argument that, under the Seventh Amendment, he was entitled to a jury trial. The court expressly declined to follow the decision of the Court of Appeals for the Second Circuit in *United States v. J.B. Williams Co.,* which held that there was a Seventh Amendment " 'right of jury trial when the United States sues ... to collect a [statutory civil] penalty, even though the statute is silent on the right of jury trial.' " The Court of Appeals in this case also found unpersuasive the dictum in *Hepner v. United States* and in *United States v. Regan,* that the Seventh Amendment's guarantee applies to civil actions to collect a civil penalty. The court concluded that, while in *Hepner* and *Regan* the civil penalties were statutorily prescribed fixed amounts, the District Court in the present case exercised "statutorily conferred equitable power in determining the amount of the fine." The Court of Appeals also noted that the District Court fashioned a " 'package' of remedies" containing both equitable and legal relief with "one part of the package affecting assessment of the others."

In *Atlas Roofing Co. v. Occupational Safety and Health Review Comm'n,* we explicitly declined to decide whether the dictum of *Hepner* and *Regan* "correctly divines the intent of the Seventh Amendment." To resolve this question and the conflict between Circuits, we granted certiorari. We reverse.

II

The Seventh Amendment provides that, "[i]n Suits at common law, where the value in controversy shall exceed twenty dollars, the right of trial by jury shall be preserved...." The Court has construed this language to require a jury trial on the merits in those actions that are analogous to "Suits at common law." Prior to the Amendment's adoption, a jury trial was customary in suits brought in the English *law* courts. In contrast, those actions that are analogous to 18th-century cases tried in courts of equity or admiralty do not require a jury trial. This analysis applies not only to common-law forms of action, but also to causes of action created by congressional enactment. See *Curtis v. Loether.*

To determine whether a statutory action is more similar to cases that were tried in courts of law than to suits tried in courts of equity or admiralty, the Court must examine both the nature of the action and of the remedy sought. First, we compare the statutory action to 18th-century actions brought in the courts of England prior to the merger of the courts of law and equity. See, *e.g., Pernell v. Southall Realty; Dairy Queen, Inc. v. Wood.* Second, we examine the remedy sought and determine whether it is legal or equitable in nature. See, *e.g., Curtis v. Loether; Ross v. Bernhard.*[4]

---

4. The Court has also considered the practical limitations of a jury trial and its functional compatibility with proceedings outside of traditional courts of law in holding that the Seventh Amendment is not applicable to administrative proceedings. See, *e.g., Atlas Roofing Co. v. Occupational Safety and Health Review Comm'n; Pernell v. Southall Realty.* But the Court has not used these considerations as an independent basis for extending the right to a jury trial under the Seventh Amendment.

A

Petitioner analogizes this Government suit under § 1319(d) to an action in debt within the jurisdiction of English courts of law. Prior to the enactment of the Seventh Amendment, English courts had held that a civil penalty suit was a particular species of an action in debt that was within the jurisdiction of the courts of law.

After the adoption of the Seventh Amendment, federal courts followed this English common law in treating the civil penalty suit as a particular type of an action in debt, requiring a jury trial. ("[A]lthough the recovery of a penalty is a proceeding criminal in nature, yet in this class of cases it may be enforced in a civil action, and in the same manner that debts are recovered in the ordinary civil courts"). Actions by the Government to recover civil penalties under statutory provisions therefore historically have been viewed as one type of action in debt requiring trial by jury.

It was against this historical background that the Court in *Hepner v. United States* considered the propriety of a directed verdict by a District Court Judge in favor of the Government where there was undisputed evidence that a defendant had committed an offense under § 8 of the Alien Immigration Act of 1903, which provided for a $1,000 civil penalty. The Court held that a directed verdict was permissible and did not violate the defendant's right to a jury trial under the Seventh Amendment. The Court said:

> The objection made in behalf of the defendant, that an affirmative answer to the question certified could be used so as to destroy the constitutional right of trial by jury, is without merit and need not be discussed. *The defendant was, of course, entitled to have a jury summoned in this case,* but that right was subject to the condition, fundamental in the conduct of civil actions, that the court may withdraw a case from the jury and direct a verdict, according to the law if the evidence is uncontradicted and raises only a question of law.

In *United States v. Regan,* the Court assumed that a jury trial was required in civil penalty actions. In that case, the Court upheld the validity of a jury instruction in an action brought by the Government under the Alien Immigration Act of 1907. The Court stated that the instruction requiring proof beyond a reasonable doubt was incorrect because:

> While the defendant was entitled to have the issues tried before a jury, this right did not arise from Article III of the Constitution or from the Sixth Amendment, for both relate to prosecutions which are strictly criminal in their nature, but it derives out of the fact that in a civil action of debt involving more than twenty dollars a jury trial is demandable.

In the instant case, the Government sought penalties of over $22 million for violation of the Clean Water Act and obtained a judgment in the sum of $325,000. This action is clearly analogous to the 18th-century action in debt, and federal courts have rightly assumed that the Seventh Amendment required a jury trial.

The Government argues, however, that—rather than an action in debt—the closer historical analog is an action to abate a public nuisance. In 18th-century English law, a public nuisance was "an act or omission 'which obstructs or causes inconvenience or damage to the public in the exercise of rights common to all Her Majesty's subjects.' " The Government argues that the present suit is analogous to two species of public nuisances. One is the suit of the sovereign in the English courts of equity for a "purpresture" to enjoin or order the repair of an enclosure or obstruction of public waterways; the other is the suit of the sovereign to enjoin "offensive trades and manufactures" that polluted the environment.

It is true that the subject matter of this Clean Water Act suit—the placement of fill into navigable waters—resembles these two species of public nuisance. Whether, as the Government argues, a public nuisance action is a better analogy than an action in debt is debatable. But we need not decide the question. As *Pernell v. Southall Realty* cautioned, the fact that the subject matter of a modern statutory action and an 18th-century English action are close equivalents "is irrelevant for Seventh Amendment purposes," because "that Amendment requires trial by jury in actions unheard of at common law." It suffices that we conclude that both the public nuisance action and the action in debt are appropriate analogies to the instant statutory action.

The essential function of an action to abate a public nuisance was to provide a civil means to redress "a miscellaneous and diversified group of minor criminal offenses, based on some interference with the interests of the community, or the comfort or convenience of the general public." Similarly, the essential function of an action in debt was to recover money owed under a variety of statutes or under the common law. Both of these 18th-century actions, then, could be asserted by the sovereign to seek relief for an injury to the public in numerous contexts.

We need not rest our conclusion on what has been called an "abstruse historical" search for the nearest 18th-century analog. See *Ross v. Bernhard*. We reiterate our previously expressed view that characterizing the relief sought is "[m]ore important" than finding a precisely analogous common-law cause of action in determining whether the Seventh Amendment guarantees a jury trial. *Curtis v. Loether*.[6]

---

6. The Government contends that both the cause of action and the remedy must be legal in nature before the Seventh Amendment right to a jury trial attaches. It divides the Clean Water Act action for civil penalties into a cause of action and a remedy, and analyzes each component as if the other were irrelevant. Thus, the Government proposes that a public nuisance action is the better historical analog for the cause of action, and that an action for disgorgement is the proper analogy for the remedy. We reject this novel approach. Our search is for a single historical analog, taking into consideration the nature of the cause of action and the remedy as two important factors. *See Pernell v. Southall Realty; Curtis v. Loether.*

B

A civil penalty was a type of remedy at common law that could only be enforced in courts of law. Remedies intended to punish culpable individuals, as opposed to those intended simply to extract compensation or restore the status quo, were issued by courts of law, not courts of equity. See, *e.g., Curtis v. Loether* (punitive damages remedy is legal, not equitable, relief); *Ross v. Bernhard* (treble-damages remedy for securities violation is a penalty, which constitutes legal relief). The action authorized by § 1319(d) is of this character. Subsection (d) does not direct that the "civil penalty" imposed be calculated solely on the basis of equitable determinations, such as the profits gained from violations of the statute, but simply imposes a maximum penalty of $10,000 per day of violation. The legislative history of the Act reveals that Congress wanted the district court to consider the need for retribution and deterrence, in addition to restitution, when it imposed civil penalties. A court can require retribution for wrongful conduct based on the seriousness of the violations, the number of prior violations, and the lack of good-faith efforts to comply with the relevant requirements. It may also seek to deter future violations by basing the penalty on its economic impact. Subsection 1319(d)'s authorization of punishment to further retribution and deterrence clearly evidences that this subsection reflects more than a concern to provide equitable relief. In the present case, for instance, the District Court acknowledged that petitioner received no profits from filling in properties in Mire Pond and Eel Creek, but still imposed a $35,000 fine. Thus, the District Court intended not simply to disgorge profits but also to impose punishment. Because the nature of the relief authorized by § 1319(d) was traditionally available only in a court of law, petitioner in this present action is entitled to a jury trial on demand.

The punitive nature of the relief sought in this present case is made apparent by a comparison with the relief sought in an action to abate a public nuisance. A public nuisance action was a classic example of the kind of suit that relied on the injunctive relief provided by courts in equity. "Injunctive relief [for enjoining a public nuisance at the request of the Government] is traditionally given by equity upon a showing of [peril to health and safety]." The Government, in fact, concedes that public nuisance cases brought in equity sought injunctive relief, not monetary penalties. Indeed, courts in equity refused to enforce such penalties.

The Government contends, however, that a suit enforcing civil penalties under the Clean Water Act is similar to an action for disgorgement of improper profits, traditionally considered an equitable remedy. It bases this characterization upon evidence that the District Court determined the amount of the penalties by multiplying the number of lots sold by petitioner by the profit earned per lot. An action for disgorgement of improper profits is, however, a poor analogy. Such an action is a remedy only for restitution—a more limited form of penalty than a civil fine. Restitution is limited to "restoring the status quo and ordering the return of that which rightfully belongs to the purchaser or tenant." As the above discussion indicates, however, § 1319(d)'s concerns are by no means limited to restoration of the status quo.

The Government next contends that, even if the civil penalties under § 1319(d) are deemed legal in character, a jury trial is not required. A court in equity was empowered to provide monetary awards that were incidental to or intertwined with injunctive relief. The Government therefore argues that its claim under § 1319(b), which authorizes injunctive relief, provides jurisdiction for monetary relief in equity. This argument has at least three flaws. First, while a court in equity may award monetary restitution as an adjunct to injunctive relief, it may not enforce civil penalties. Second, the Government was aware when it filed suit that relief would be limited primarily to civil penalties, since petitioner had already sold most of the properties at issue. A potential penalty of $22 million hardly can be considered incidental to the modest equitable relief sought in this case.

Finally, the Government was free to seek an equitable remedy in addition to, or independent of, legal relief. Section 1319 does not intertwine equitable relief with the imposition of civil penalties. Instead each kind of relief is separably authorized in a separate and distinct statutory provision. Subsection (b), providing injunctive relief, is independent of subsection (d), which provides only for civil penalties. In such a situation, if a "legal claim is joined with an equitable claim, the right to jury trial on the legal claim, including all issues common to both claims, remains intact. The right cannot be abridged by characterizing the legal claim as 'incidental' to the equitable relief sought." *Curtis v. Loether*. Thus, petitioner has a constitutional right to a jury trial to determine his liability on the legal claims.

III

The remaining issue is whether petitioner additionally has a Seventh Amendment right to a jury assessment of the civil penalties. At the time this case was tried, § 1319(d) did not explicitly state whether juries or trial judges were to fix the civil penalties. The legislative history of the 1977 Amendments to the Clean Water Act shows, however, that Congress intended that trial judges perform the highly discretionary calculations necessary to award civil penalties after liability is found. ("[P]enalties assessed by judges should be sufficiently higher than penalties to which the Agency would have agreed in settlement to encourage violators to settle"). We must decide therefore whether Congress can, consistent with the Seventh Amendment, authorize judges to assess civil penalties.

The Seventh Amendment is silent on the question whether a jury must determine the remedy in a trial in which it must determine liability. The answer must depend on whether the jury must shoulder this responsibility as necessary to preserve the "substance of the common-law right of trial by jury." Is a jury role necessary for that purpose? We do not think so. " 'Only those incidents which are regarded as fundamental, as inherent in and of the essence of the system of trial by jury, are placed beyond the reach of the legislature.'" ("[T]he Amendment was designed to preserve the basic institution of jury trial in only its most fundamental elements"). The assessment of a civil penalty is not one of the "most fundamental elements." Congress' authority to fix the penalty by statute has not been questioned, and it was also the British practice. In the United States, the action to recover civil penalties usually seeks the amount fixed by Congress. The assessment of civil penalties thus cannot be said to involve the "substance of a common-law right to a trial by jury," nor a "fundamental element of a jury trial."

Congress' assignment of the determination of the amount of civil penalties to trial judges therefore does not infringe on the constitutional right to a jury trial. Since Congress itself may fix the civil penalties, it may delegate that determination to trial judges. In this case, highly discretionary calculations that take into account multiple factors are necessary in order to set civil penalties under the Clean Water Act. These are the kinds of calculations traditionally performed by judges. We therefore hold that a determination of a civil penalty is not an essential function of a jury trial, and that the Seventh Amendment does not require a jury trial for that purpose in a civil action.

IV

We conclude that the Seventh Amendment required that petitioner's demand for a jury trial be granted to determine his liability, but that the trial court and not the jury should determine the amount of penalty, if any. The judgment of the Court of Appeals is therefore reversed, and the case is remanded for further proceedings consistent with this opinion.

It is so ordered.

JUSTICE SCALIA, with whom JUSTICE STEVENS joins, concurring in part and dissenting in part.

I join the Court's disposition, and Parts I and II of its opinion. I do not join Part III because in my view the right to trial by jury on whether a civil penalty of unspecified amount is assessable also involves a right to trial by jury on what the amount should be. The fact that the Legislature could elect to fix the amount of penalty has nothing to do with whether, if it chooses not to do so, that element comes within the jury-trial guarantee. Congress could, I suppose, create a private cause of action by one individual against another for a fixed amount of damages, but it surely does not follow that if it creates such a cause of action *without* prescribing the amount of damages, that issue could be taken from the jury.

While purporting to base its determination (quite correctly) upon historical practice, the Court creates a form of civil adjudication I have never encountered. I can recall no precedent for judgment of civil liability by jury but assessment of amount by the court. Even punitive damages are assessed by the jury when liability is determined in that fashion. One is of course tempted to make an exception in a case like this, where the Government is imposing a non-compensatory remedy to enforce direct exercise of its regulatory authority, because there comes immediately to mind the role of the sentencing judge in a criminal proceeding. If criminal trials are to be the model, however, determination of liability by the jury should be on a standard of proof requiring guilt beyond a reasonable doubt. Having chosen to proceed in civil fashion, with the advantages which that mode entails, it seems to me the Government must take the bitter with the sweet. Since, as the Court correctly reasons, the proper analogue to a civil-fine action is the common-law action for debt, the Government need only prove liability by a preponderance of the evidence; but must, as in any action for debt, accept the amount of award determined not by its own officials but by 12 private citizens. If that tends to discourage the Government from proceeding in this fashion, I doubt that the Founding Fathers would be upset.

I would reverse and remand for jury determination of both issues.

* * *

III. INTERLOCUTORY APPEAL

A. THE FINAL JUDGMENT RULE

FEDERAL RULE OF CIVIL PROCEDURE 54.   JUDGMENT; COSTS

(a) Definition; Form. "Judgment" as used in these rules includes a decree and any order from which an appeal lies. A judgment should not include recitals of pleadings, a master's report, or a record of prior proceedings.

(b) Judgment on Multiple Claims or Involving Multiple Parties. When an action presents more than one claim for relief—whether as a claim, counterclaim, cross-claim, or third-party claim—or when multiple parties are involved, the court may direct entry of a final judgment as to one or more, but fewer than all, claims or parties only if the court expressly determines that there is no just reason for delay. Otherwise, any order or other decision, however designated, that adjudicates fewer than all the claims or the rights and liabilities of fewer than all the parties does not end the action as to any of the claims or parties and may be revised at any time before the entry of a judgment adjudicating all the claims and all the parties' rights and liabilities.

(c) Demand for Judgment; Relief to Be Granted. A default judgment must not differ in kind from, or exceed in amount, what is demanded in the pleadings. Every other final judgment should grant the relief to which each party is entitled, even if the party has not demanded that relief in its pleadings.

(d) Costs; Attorney's Fees.

  (1) *Costs Other Than Attorney's Fees.* Unless a federal statute, these rules, or a court order provides otherwise, costs—other than attorney's fees—should be allowed to the prevailing party. But costs against the United States, its officers, and its agencies may be imposed only to the extent allowed by law. The clerk may tax costs on 14 days' notice. On motion served within the next 7 days, the court may review the clerk's action.

  (2) *Attorney's Fees.*

   (A) *Claim to Be by Motion.* A claim for attorney's fees and related nontaxable expenses must be made by motion unless the substantive law requires those fees to be proved at trial as an element of damages.

   (B) *Timing and Contents of the Motion.* Unless a statute or a court order provides otherwise, the motion must:

    (i) be filed no later than 14 days after the entry of judgment;

    (ii) specify the judgment and the statute, rule, or other grounds entitling the movant to the award;

        (iii) state the amount sought or provide a fair estimate of it; and

        (iv) disclose, if the court so orders, the terms of any agreement about fees for the services for which the claim is made.

    (C) *Proceedings.* Subject to Rule 23(h), the court must, on a party's request, give an opportunity for adversary submissions on the motion in accordance with Rule 43(c) or 78. The court may decide issues of liability for fees before receiving submissions on the value of services. The court must find the facts and state its conclusions of law as provided in Rule 52(a).

    (D) *Special Procedures by Local Rule; Reference to a Master or a Magistrate Judge.* By local rule, the court may establish special procedures to resolve fee-related issues without extensive evidentiary hearings. Also, the court may refer issues concerning the value of services to a special master under Rule 53 without regard to the limitations of Rule 53(a)(1), and may refer a motion for attorney's fees to a magistrate judge under Rule 72(b) as if it were a dispositive pretrial matter.

    (E) *Exceptions.* Subparagraphs (A)–(D) do not apply to claims for fees and expenses as sanctions for violating these rules or as sanctions under 28 U.S.C. § 1927.

* * *

28 U.S.C. § 1291.   FINAL DECISIONS OF DISTRICT COURTS

The courts of appeals (other than the United States Court of Appeals for the Federal Circuit) shall have jurisdiction of appeals from all final decisions of the district courts of the United States, the United States District Court for the District of the Canal Zone, the District Court of Guam, and the District Court of the Virgin Islands, except where a direct review may be had in the Supreme Court. . . .

* * *

28 U.S.C. § 1292.   INTERLOCUTORY DECISIONS

(a) Except as provided in subsections (c) and (d) of this section, the courts of appeals shall have jurisdiction of appeals from:

    (1) Interlocutory orders of the district courts of the United States, the United States District Court for the District of the Canal Zone, the District Court of Guam, and the District Court of the Virgin Islands, or of the judges thereof, granting, continuing, modifying, refusing or dissolving injunctions, or refusing to dissolve or modify injunctions, except where a direct review may be had in the Supreme Court;

(2) Interlocutory orders appointing receivers, or refusing orders to wind up receiverships or to take steps to accomplish the purposes thereof, such as directing sales or other disposals of property;

(3) Interlocutory decrees of such district courts or the judges thereof determining the rights and liabilities of the parties to admiralty cases in which appeals from final decrees are allowed.

(b) When a district judge, in making in a civil action an order not otherwise appealable under this section, shall be of the opinion that such order involves a controlling question of law as to which there is substantial ground for difference of opinion and that an immediate appeal from the order may materially advance the ultimate termination of the litigation, he shall so state in writing in such order. The Court of Appeals which would have jurisdiction of an appeal of such action may thereupon, in its discretion, permit an appeal to be taken from such order, if application is made to it within ten days after the entry of the order: *Provided, however,* That application for an appeal hereunder shall not stay proceedings in the district court unless the district judge or the Court of Appeals or a judge thereof shall so order.

* * *

LIBERTY MUTUAL INSURANCE COMPANY v. WETZEL

424 U.S. 737 (1976)

MR. JUSTICE REHNQUIST delivered the opinion of the Court.

Respondents filed a complaint in the United States District Court for the Western District of Pennsylvania in which they asserted that petitioner's employee insurance benefits and maternity leave regulations discriminated against women in violation of Title VII of the Civil Rights Act of 1964 as amended by the Equal Employment Opportunity Act of 1972. The District Court ruled in favor of respondents on the issue of petitioner's liability under that Act, and petitioner appealed to the Court of Appeals for the Third Circuit. That court held that it had jurisdiction of petitioner's appeal under 28 U.S.C. § 1291, and proceeded to affirm on the merits the judgment of the District Court. We granted certiorari, and heard argument on the merits. Though neither party has questioned the jurisdiction of the Court of Appeals to entertain the appeal, we are obligated to do so on our own motion if a question thereto exists. Because we conclude that the District Court's order was not appealable to the Court of Appeals, we vacate the judgment of the Court of appeals with instructions to dismiss petitioner's appeal from the order of the District Court.

Respondents' complaint, after alleging jurisdiction and facts deemed pertinent to their claim, prayed for a judgment against petitioner embodying the following relief:

"(a) requiring that defendant establish non-discriminatory hiring, payment, opportunity, and promotional plans and programs;

"(b) enjoining the continuance by defendant of the illegal acts and practices alleged herein;

"(c) requiring that defendant pay over to plaintiffs and to the members of the class the damages sustained by plaintiffs and the members of the class by reason of defendant's illegal acts and practices, including adjusted backpay, with interest, and an additional equal amount as liquidated damages, and exemplary damages;

"(d) requiring that defendant pay to plaintiffs and to the members of the class the costs of this suit and a reasonable attorneys' fee, with interest; and

"(e) such other and further relief as the Court deems appropriate."

After extensive discovery, respondents moved for partial summary judgment only as to the issue of liability. Fed. Rule Civ. P. 56(c). The District Court on January 9, 1974, finding no issues of material fact in dispute, entered an order to the effect that petitioner's pregnancy-related policies violated Title VII of the Civil Rights Act of 1964. It also ruled that Liberty Mutual's hiring and promotion policies violated Title VII. Petitioner thereafter filed a motion for reconsideration which was denied by the District Court. Its order of February 20, 1974, denying the motion for reconsideration, contains the following concluding language:

In its Order the court stated it would enjoin the continuance of practices which the court found to be in violation of Title VII. The Plaintiffs were invited to submit the form of the injunction order and the Defendant has filed Notice of Appeal and asked for stay of any injunctive order. Under these circumstances the court will withhold the issuance of the injunctive order and amend the Order previously issued under the provisions of Fed. R. Civ. P. 54(b), as follows:

And now this 20th day of February, 1974, it is directed that final judgment be entered in favor of Plaintiffs that Defendant's policy of requiring female employees to return to work within three months of delivery of a child or be terminated is in violation of the provisions of Title VII of the Civil Rights Act of 1964; that Defendant's policy of denying disability income protection plan benefits to female employees for disabilities related to pregnancies or childbirth are (Sic) in violation of Title VII of the Civil Rights Act of 1964 and that it is expressly directed that Judgment be entered for the Plaintiffs upon these claims of Plaintiffs' Complaint; there being no just reason for delay.

It is obvious from the District Court's order that respondents, although having received a favorable ruling on the issue of petitioner's liability to them, received none of the relief which they expressly prayed for in the portion of their complaint set forth above. They requested an injunction, but did not get one; they requested damages, but were not awarded any; they requested attorneys' fees, but received none.

Counsel for respondents when questioned during oral argument in this Court suggested that at least the District Court's order of February 20 amounted to a declaratory judgment on the issue of liability pursuant to the provisions of 28 U.S.C. § 2201. Had respondents sought only a declaratory judgment, and no other form of relief, we would of course have a different case. But even if we accept respondents' contention that the District Court's order was a declaratory judgment on the issue of liability, it nonetheless left unresolved respondents' requests for an injunction, for compensatory and exemplary damages, and for attorneys' fees. It finally disposed of none of respondents' prayers for relief.

The District Court and the Court of Appeals apparently took the view that because the District Court made the recital required by Fed. Rule Civ. P. 54(b) that final judgment be entered on the issue of liability, and that there was no just reason for delay, the orders thereby became appealable as a final decision pursuant to 28 U.S.C. § 1291. We cannot agree with this application of the Rule and statute in question.

Rule 54(b) "does not apply to a single claim action.... It is limited expressly to multiple claims actions in which 'one or more but less than all' of the multiple claims have been finally decided and are found otherwise to be ready for appeal." *Sears, Roebuck & Co. v. Mackey.*[3] Here, however, respondents set forth but a single claim: that petitioner's employee insurance benefits and maternity leave regulations discriminated against its women employees in violation of Title VII of the Civil Rights Act of 1964. They prayed for several different types of relief in the event that they sustained the allegations of their complaint, *see* Fed. Rule Civ. P. 8(a)(3), but their complaint advanced a single legal theory which was applied to only one set of facts.[4] Thus, despite the fact that the District Court undoubtedly made the findings required under the Rule had it been applicable, those findings do not in a case such as this make the order appealable pursuant to 28 U.S.C. § 1291. See *Mackey.*

We turn to consider whether the District Court's order might have been appealed by petitioner to the Court of Appeals under any other theory. The order, viewed apart from its discussion of Rule 54(b), constitutes a grant of partial summary judgment limited to the issue of petitioner's liability. Such judgments are by their terms interlocutory, see Fed. Rule Civ. P. 56(c), and where assessment of damages or awarding of other relief remains to be resolved have never been considered to be "final" within the meaning of 28 U.S.C. § 1291. Thus the only possible authorization for an appeal from the District Court's order would be pursuant to the provisions of 28 U.S.C. § 1292.

---

3. Following *Mackey*, the Rule was amended to insure that orders finally disposing of some but not all of the parties could be appealed pursuant to its provisions. That provision is not implicated in this case, however, to which Mackey's exposition of the Rule remains fully accurate.

4. We need not here attempt any definitive resolution of the meaning of what constitutes a claim for relief within the meaning of the Rules. It is sufficient to recognize that a complaint asserting only one legal right, even if seeking multiple remedies for the alleged violation of that right, states a single claim for relief.

If the District Court had granted injunctive relief but had not ruled on respondents' other requests for relief, this interlocutory order would have been appealable under § 1292(a)(1). But, as noted above, the court did not issue an injunction. It might be argued that the order of the District Court, insofar as it failed to include the injunctive relief requested by respondents, is an interlocutory order refusing an injunction within the meaning of § 1292(a)(1). But even if this would have allowed *respondents* to then obtain review in the Court of Appeals, there was no denial of any injunction sought by Petitioner and it could not avail itself of that grant of jurisdiction.

Nor was this order appealable pursuant to 28 U.S.C. § 1292(b). Although the District Court's findings made with a view to satisfying Rule 54(b) might be viewed as substantial compliance with the certification requirement of that section, there is no showing in this record that petitioner made application to the Court of Appeals within the 10 days therein specified. And that court's holding that its jurisdiction was pursuant to § 1291 makes it clear that it thought itself obliged to consider on the merits petitioner's appeal. There can be no assurance that had the other requirements of § 1292(b) been complied with, the Court of Appeals would have exercised its discretion to entertain the interlocutory appeal.

Were we to sustain the procedure followed here, we would condone a practice whereby a district court in virtually any case before it might render an interlocutory decision on the question of liability of the defendant, and the defendant would thereupon be permitted to appeal to the court of appeals without satisfying any of the requirements that Congress carefully set forth. We believe that Congress, in enacting present §§ 1291 & 1292 of Title 28, has been well aware of the dangers of an overly rigid insistence upon a "final decision" for appeal in every case, and has in those sections made ample provision for appeal of orders which are not "final" so as to alleviate any possible hardship. We would twist the fabric of the statute more than it will bear if we were to agree that the District Court's order of February 20, 1974, was appealable to the Court of Appeals.

The judgment of the Court of Appeals is therefore vacated, and the case is remanded with instructions to dismiss the petitioner's appeal.

It is so ordered.

* * *

CURTISS–WRIGHT CORP. v. GENERAL ELECTRIC CO.

446 U.S. 1 (1980)

MR. CHIEF JUSTICE BURGER delivered the opinion of the Court.

Federal Rule of Civil Procedure 54(b) allows a district court dealing with multiple claims or multiple parties to direct the entry of final judgment as to fewer than all of the claims or parties; to do so, the court must make an express determination that there is no just reason for delay. We granted certiorari in order to examine the use of this procedural device.

I

From 1968 to 1972, respondent General Electric Co. entered into a series of 21 contracts with petitioner Curtiss–Wright Corp. for the manufacture of components designed for use in nuclear powered naval vessels. These contracts had a total value of $215 million.

In 1976, Curtiss–Wright brought a diversity action in the United States District Court for the District of New Jersey, seeking damages and reformation with regard to the 21 contracts. The complaint asserted claims based on alleged fraud, misrepresentation, and breach of contract by General Electric. It also sought $19 million from General Electric on the outstanding balance due on the contracts already performed.

General Electric counterclaimed for $1.9 million in costs allegedly incurred as the result of "extraordinary efforts" provided to Curtiss–Wright during performance of the contracts which enabled Curtiss–Wright to avoid a contract default. General Electric also sought, by way of counterclaim, to recover $52 million by which Curtiss–Wright was allegedly unjustly enriched as a result of these "extraordinary efforts."

The facts underlying most of these claims and counterclaims are in dispute. As to Curtiss–Wright's claims for the $19 million balance due, however, the sole dispute concerns the application of a release clause contained in each of the 21 agreements, which states that "Seller ... agree[s] as a condition precedent to final payment, that the Buyer and the Government ... are released from all liabilities, obligations and claims arising under or by virtue of this order." When Curtiss–Wright moved for summary judgment on the balance due, General Electric contended that so long as Curtiss–Wright's other claims remained pending, this provision constituted a bar to recovery of the undisputed balance.

The District Court rejected this contention and granted summary judgment for Curtiss–Wright on this otherwise undisputed claim. Applying New York law by which the parties had agreed to be bound, the District Court held that Curtiss–Wright was entitled to payment of the balance due notwithstanding the release clause. The court also ruled that Curtiss–Wright was entitled to prejudgment interest at the New York statutory rate of 6% per annum.

Curtiss–Wright then moved for a certification of the District Court's orders as final judgments under Federal Rule of Civil Procedure 54(b).

The court expressly directed entry of final judgment for Curtiss–Wright and made the determination that there was "no just reason for delay" pursuant to Rule 54(b).

The District Court also provided a written statement of reasons supporting its decision to certify the judgment as final. It acknowledged that Rule 54(b) certification was not to be granted as a matter of course, and that this remedy should be reserved for the infrequent harsh case because of the overload in appellate courts which would otherwise result from appeals of an interlocutory nature. The essential inquiry was stated to be "whether, after balancing the competing factors, finality of judgment should be ordered to advance the interests of sound judicial administration and justice to the litigants."

The District Court then went on to identify the relevant factors in the case before it. It found that certification would not result in unnecessary appellate review; that the claims finally adjudicated were separate, distinct, and independent of any of the other claims or counterclaims involved; that review of these adjudicated claims would not be mooted by any future developments in the case; and that the nature of the claims was such that no appellate court would have to decide the same issues more than once even if there were subsequent appeals.

Turning to considerations of justice to the litigants, the District Court found that Curtiss–Wright would suffer severe daily financial loss from nonpayment of the $19 million judgment because current interest rates were higher than the statutory prejudgment rate, a situation compounded by the large amount of money involved. The court observed that the complex nature of the remaining claims could, without certification, mean a delay that "would span many months, if not years."

The court found that solvency of the parties was not a significant factor, since each appeared to be financially sound. Although the presence of General Electric's counterclaims and the consequent possibility of a setoff recovery were factors which weighed against certification, the court, in balancing these factors, determined that they were outweighed by the other factors in the case. Accordingly, it granted Rule 54(b) certification. It also granted General Electric's motion for a stay without bond pending appeal.

A divided panel of the United States Court of Appeals for the Third Circuit held that the case was controlled by its decision in *Allis-Chalmers Corp. v. Philadelphia Electric Co.*, where the court had stated: "In the absence of unusual or harsh circumstances, we believe that the presence of a counterclaim, which could result in a set-off against any amounts due and owing to the plaintiff, weighs heavily against the grant of 54(b) certification."

In *Allis-Chalmers*, the court defined unusual or harsh circumstances as those factors "involving considerations of solvency, economic duress, etc."

In the Third Circuit's view, the question was which of the parties should have the benefit of the amount of the balance due pending final resolution of the litigation. The court held that *Allis-Chalmers* dictated "that the matter remain in status quo when non-frivolous counterclaims are pending, and in the absence of unusual or harsh circumstances." The Court of Appeals acknowledged that Curtiss–Wright's inability to have use of the money from the judgment might seem harsh, but noted that the same could be said for General Electric if it were forced to pay Curtiss–Wright now but later prevailed on its counterclaims.

The Court of Appeals concluded that the District Court had abused its discretion by granting Rule 54(b) certification in this situation and dismissed the case for want of an appealable order; it also directed the District Court to vacate its Rule 54(b) determination of finality. Curtiss–Wright's petition for rehearing and suggestion for rehearing en banc were denied. Four judges dissented from that denial, observing that the case was in conflict with [a Tenth Circuit decision]. We reverse.

II

Nearly a quarter of a century ago, in *Sears, Roebuck & Co. v. Mackey*, this Court outlined the steps to be followed in making determinations under Rule 54(b). A district court must first determine that it is dealing with a "final judgment." It must be a "judgment" in the sense that it is a decision upon a cognizable claim for relief, and it must be "final" in the sense that it is "an ultimate disposition of an individual claim entered in the course of a multiple claims action."

Once having found finality, the district court must go on to determine whether there is any just reason for delay. Not all final judgments on individual claims should be immediately appealable, even if they are in some sense separable from the remaining unresolved claims. The function of the district court under the Rule is to act as a "dispatcher." It is left to the sound judicial discretion of the district court to determine the "appropriate time" when each final decision in a multiple claims action is ready for appeal. This discretion is to be exercised "in the interest of sound judicial administration."

Thus, in deciding whether there are no just reasons to delay the appeal of individual final judgments in setting such as this, a district court must take into account judicial administrative interests as well as the equities involved. Consideration of the former is necessary to assure that application of the Rule effectively "preserves the historic federal policy against piecemeal appeals." It was therefore proper for the District Judge here to consider such factors as whether the claims under review were separable from the others remaining to be adjudicated and whether the nature of the claims already determined was such that no appellate court would have to decide the same issues more than once even if there were subsequent appeals.

Here the District Judge saw no sound reason to delay appellate resolution of the undisputed claims already adjudicated. The contrary conclusion of the Court of Appeals was strongly influenced by the existence of non-frivolous counterclaims. The mere presence of such claims, however, does not render a Rule 54(b) certification inappropriate. If it did, Rule 54(b) would lose much of its utility. In *Cold Metal Process Co. v. United Engineering & Foundry Co.*, this Court explained that counterclaims, whether compulsory or permissive, present no special problems for Rule 54(b) determinations; counterclaims are not to be evaluated differently from other claims. Like other claims, their significance for Rule 54(b) purposes turns on their interrelationship with the claims on which certification is sought. Here, the District Judge determined that General Electric's counterclaims were severable from the claims which had been determined in terms of both the factual and the legal issues involved. The Court of Appeals did not conclude otherwise.

What the Court of Appeals found objectionable about the District Judge's exercise of discretion was the assessment of the equities involved. The Court of Appeals concluded that the possibility of a setoff required that the status quo be maintained unless petitioner could show harsh or unusual circumstances; it held that such a showing had not been made in the District Court.

This holding reflects a misinterpretation of the standard of review for Rule 54(b) certifications and a misperception of the appellate function in such cases. The Court of Appeals relied on a statement of the Advisory Committee on the Rules of Civil Procedure, and its error derives from reading a description in the commentary as a standard of construction. When Rule 54(b) was amended in 1946, the Notes of the Advisory Committee which accompanied the suggested amendment indicated that the entire lawsuit was generally the appropriate unit for appellate review, "and that this rule needed only the exercise of a discretionary power to afford a remedy in the infrequent harsh case to provide a simple, definite, workable rule." However accurate it may be as a description of cases qualifying for Rule 54(b) treatment, the phrase "infrequent harsh case" in isolation is neither workable nor entirely reliable as a benchmark for appellate review. There is no indication it was ever intended by the drafters to function as such.

In *Sears*, the Court stated that the decision to certify was with good reason left to the sound judicial discretion of the district court. At the same time, the Court noted that "[w]ith equally good reason, any *abuse* of that discretion remains reviewable by the Court of Appeals." The Court indicated that the standard against which a district court's exercise of discretion is to be judged is the "interest of sound judicial administration." Admittedly this presents issues not always easily resolved, but the proper role of the court of appeals is not to reweigh the equities or reassess the facts but to make sure that the conclusions derived from those weighings and assessments are juridically sound and supported by the record.

There are thus two aspects to the proper function of a reviewing court in Rule 54(b) cases. The court of appeals must, of course, scrutinize the district court's evaluation of such factors as the interrelationship of the claims so as to prevent piecemeal appeals in cases which should be reviewed only as single units. But once such juridical concerns have been met, the discretionary judgment of the district court should be given substantial deference, for that court is "the one most likely to be familiar with the case and with any justifiable reasons for delay." *Sears.* The reviewing court should disturb the trial court's assessment of the equities only if it can say that the judge's conclusion was clearly unreasonable.

Plainly, sound judicial administration does not require that Rule 54(b) requests be granted routinely. That is implicit in commending them to the sound discretion of a district court. Because this discretion "is, with good reason, vested by the rule primarily" in the district courts, *Sears,* and because the number of possible situations is large, we are reluctant either to fix or sanction narrow guidelines for the district courts to follow. We are satisfied, however, that on the record here the District Court's assessment of the equities was reasonable.

One of the equities which the District Judge considered was the difference between the statutory and market rates of interest. Respondent correctly points out that adjustment of the statutory prejudgment interest rate is a matter within the province of the legislature, but that fact does not make the existing differential irrelevant for Rule 54(b) purposes. If the judgment is otherwise certifiable, the fact that a litigant who has successfully reduced his claim to judgment stands to lose money because of the difference in interest rates is surely not a "just reason for delay."

The difference between the prejudgment and market interest rates was not the only factor considered by the District Court. The court also noted that the debts in issue were liquidated and large, and that absent Rule 54(b) certification they would not be paid for "many months, if not years" because the rest of the litigation would be expected to continue for that period of time. The District Judge had noted earlier in his opinion on the merits of the release clause issue that respondent General Electric contested neither the amount of the debt nor the fact that it must eventually be paid. The only contest was over the effect of the release clause on the timing of the payment, an isolated and strictly legal issue on which summary judgment had been entered against respondent.

The question before the District Court thus came down to which of the parties should get the benefit of the difference between the prejudgment and market rates of interest on debts admittedly owing and adjudged to be due while unrelated claims were litigated. The central factor weighing in favor of General Electric was that its pending counterclaims created the possibility of a setoff against the amount it owed petitioner. This possibility was surely not an insignificant factor, especially since the counterclaims had survived a motion to dismiss for failure to state a claim. But the District Court took this into account when it determined that both litigants appeared to be in financially sound condition, and that Curtiss–Wright would be able to satisfy a judgment on the counterclaims should any be entered.

The Court of Appeals concluded that this was not enough, and suggested that the presence of such factors as economic duress and insolvency would be necessary to qualify the judgment for Rule 54(b) certification. But if Curtiss–Wright were under a threat of insolvency, that factor alone would weigh *against* qualifying; that very threat would cast doubt upon Curtiss–Wright's capacity to produce all or part of the $19 million should General Electric prevail on some of its counterclaims. Such a showing would thus in fact be self-defeating.

Nor is General Electric's solvency a dispositive factor; if its financial position were such that a delay in entry of judgment on Curtiss–Wright's claims would impair Curtiss–Wright's ability to collect on the judgment, that would weigh in favor of certification. But the fact that General Electric is capable of paying either now or later is not a "just reason for delay." At most, as the District Court found, the fact that neither party is or will become insolvent renders that factor neutral in a proper weighing of the equities involved.

The question in cases such as this is likely to be close, but the task of weighing and balancing the contending factors is peculiarly one for the trial judge, who can explore all the facets of a case. As we have noted, that assessment merits substantial deference on review. Here, the District Court's assessment of the equities between the parties was based on an intimate knowledge of the case and is a reasonable one. The District Court having found no other reason justifying delay, we conclude that it did not abuse its discretion in granting petitioner's motion for certification under Rule 54(b).

Accordingly, the judgment of the Court of Appeals is vacated, and the case is remanded for proceedings consistent with this opinion.

It is so ordered.

* * *

B. COLLATERAL ORDER DOCTRINE

COHEN v. BENEFICIAL INDUSTRIAL LOAN CORP.

337 U.S. 541 (1949)

MR. JUSTICE JACKSON delivered the opinion of the Court.

The ultimate question here is whether a federal court, having jurisdiction of a stockholder's derivative action only because the parties are of diverse citizenship, must apply a statute of the forum state which makes the plaintiff, if unsuccessful, liable for all expenses, including attorney's fees, of the defense and requires security for their payment as a condition of prosecuting the action.

Petitioners' decedent as plaintiff, brought in the United States District Court for New Jersey an action in the right of the Beneficial Industrial Loan Corporation, a Delaware corporation doing business in New Jersey. The defendants were the corporation and certain of its managers and directors. The complaint alleged generally that since 1929 the individual defendants engaged in a continuing and successful conspiracy to enrich themselves at the expense of the corporation. Specific charges of mismanagement and fraud extended over a period of eighteen years and the assets allegedly wasted or diverted thereby were said to exceed $100,000,000. The stockholder had demanded that the corporation institute proceedings for its recovery but, by their control of the corporation, the individual defendants prevented it from doing so. This stockholder, therefore, sought to assert the right of the corporation. One of 16,000 stockholders, he owned 100 of its more than two million shares, so that his holdings, together with 150 shares held by the intervenor, approximated 0.0125% of the outstanding stock and had a market value that had never exceeded $9,000.

The action was brought in 1943, and various proceedings had been taken therein when, in 1945, New Jersey enacted the statute which is here involved. Its general effect is to make a plaintiff having so small an interest liable for all expenses and attorney's fees of the defense if he fails to make good his complaint and to entitle the corporation to indemnity before the case can be prosecuted. These conditions are made applicable to pending actions. The corporate defendant therefore moved to require security, pointed to its by-laws by which it might be required to indemnify the individual defendants, and averred that a bond of $125,000 would be appropriate.

The District Court was of the opinion that the state enactment is not applicable to such an action when pending in a federal court. The Court of Appeals were of a contrary opinion and reversed and we granted certiorari.

Appealability

At the threshold we are met with the question whether the District Court's order refusing to apply the statute was an appealable one. Title 28 U.S.C. § 1291, provides, as did its predecessors, for appeal only "from all final decisions of the district courts," except when direct appeal to this Court is provided. Section 1292 allows appeals also from certain interlocutory orders, decrees and judgments, not material to this case except as they indicate the purpose to allow appeals from orders other than final judgments when they have a final and irreparable effect on the rights of the parties. It is obvious that, if Congress had allowed appeals only from those final judgments which terminate an action, this order would not be appealable.

The effect of the statute is to disallow appeal from any decision which is tentative, informal or incomplete. Appeal gives the upper court a power of review, not one of intervention. So long as the matter remains open, unfinished or inconclusive, there may be no intrusion by appeal. But the District Court's action upon this application was concluded and closed and its decision final in that sense before the appeal was taken.

Nor does the statute permit appeals, even from fully consummated decisions, where they are but steps towards final judgment in which they will merge. The purpose is to combine in one review all stages of the proceeding that effectively may be reviewed and corrected if and when final judgment results. But this order of the District Court did not make any step toward final disposition of the merits of the case and will not be merged in final judgment. When that time comes, it will be too late effectively to review the present order and the rights conferred by the statute, if it is applicable, will have been lost, probably irreparably. We conclude that the matters embraced in the decision appealed from are not of such an interlocutory nature as to affect, or to be affected by, decision of the merits of this case.

This decision appears to fall in that small class which finally determine claims of right separable from, and collateral to, rights asserted in the action, too important to be denied review and too independent of the cause itself to require that appellate consideration be deferred until the whole case is adjudicated. The Court has long given this provision of the statute this practical rather than a technical construction.

We hold this order appealable because it is a final disposition of a claimed right which is not an ingredient of the cause of action and does not require consideration with it. But we do not mean that every order fixing security is subject to appeal. Here it is the right to security that presents a serious and unsettled question. If the right were admitted or clear and the order involved only an exercise of discretion as to the amount of security, a matter the statute makes subject to reconsideration from time to time, appealability would present a different question.

Since this order may be reviewed on appeal, the petition in No. 512, whereby the corporation asserts the right to compel security by mandamus, is dismissed.

* * *

MOHAWK INDUSTRIES, INC. v. CARPENTER
130 S.Ct. 599 (2009)

JUSTICE SOTOMAYOR delivered the opinion of the Court.

Section 1291 of the Judicial Code confers on federal courts of appeals jurisdiction to review "final decisions of the district courts." 28 U.S.C. § 1291. Although "final decisions" typically are ones that trigger the entry of judgment, they also include a small set of prejudgment orders that are "collateral to" the merits of an action and "too important" to be denied immediate review. *Cohen v. Beneficial Industrial Loan Corp.* (1949). In this case, petitioner Mohawk Industries, Inc., attempted to bring a collateral order appeal after the District Court ordered it to disclose certain confidential materials on the ground that Mohawk had waived the attorney-client privilege. The Court of Appeals dismissed the appeal for want of jurisdiction.

The question before us is whether disclosure orders adverse to the attorney-client privilege qualify for immediate appeal under the collateral order doctrine. Agreeing with the Court of Appeals, we hold that they do not. Post-judgment appeals, together with other review mechanisms, suffice to protect the rights of litigants and preserve the vitality of the attorney-client privilege.

I

In 2007, respondent Norman Carpenter, a former shift supervisor at a Mohawk manufacturing facility, filed suit in the United States District Court for the Northern District of Georgia, alleging that Mohawk had terminated him in violation of 42 U.S.C. § 1985(2) and various Georgia laws. According to Carpenter's complaint, his termination came after he informed a member of Mohawk's human resources department in an e-mail that the company was employing undocumented immigrants. At the time, unbeknownst to Carpenter, Mohawk stood accused in a pending class-action lawsuit of conspiring to drive down the wages of its legal employees by knowingly hiring undocumented workers in violation of federal and state racketeering laws. Company officials directed Carpenter to meet with the company's retained counsel in the *Williams* case, and counsel allegedly pressured Carpenter to recant his statements. When he refused, Carpenter alleges, Mohawk fired him under false pretenses.

After learning of Carpenter's complaint, the plaintiffs in the *Williams* case sought an evidentiary hearing to explore Carpenter's allegations. In its response to their motion, Mohawk described Carpenter's accusations as "pure fantasy" and recounted the "true facts" of Carpenter's dismissal. According to Mohawk, Carpenter himself had "engaged in blatant and illegal misconduct" by attempting to have Mohawk hire an undocumented worker. The company "commenced an immediate investigation," during which retained counsel interviewed Carpenter. Because Carpenter's "efforts to cause Mohawk to circumvent federal immigration law" "blatantly violated Mohawk policy," the company terminated him.

As these events were unfolding in the *Williams* case, discovery was underway in Carpenter's case. Carpenter filed a motion to compel Mohawk to produce information concerning his meeting with retained counsel and the company's termination decision. Mohawk maintained that the requested information was protected by the attorney-client privilege.

The District Court agreed that the privilege applied to the requested information, but it granted Carpenter's motion to compel disclosure after concluding that Mohawk had implicitly waived the privilege through its representations in the *Williams* case. The court declined to certify its order for interlocutory appeal under 28 U.S.C. § 1292(b). But, recognizing "the seriousness of its [waiver] finding," it stayed its ruling to allow Mohawk to explore other potential "avenues to appeal ..., such as a petition for mandamus or appealing this Order under the collateral order doctrine."

Mohawk filed a notice of appeal and a petition for a writ of mandamus to the Eleventh Circuit. The Court of Appeals dismissed the appeal for lack of jurisdiction under 28 U.S.C. § 1291, holding that the District Court's ruling did not qualify as an immediately appealable collateral order within the meaning of *Cohen*. "Under *Cohen*," the Court of Appeals explained, "an order is appealable if it (1) conclusively determines the disputed question; (2) resolves an important issue completely separate from the merits of the action; and (3) is effectively unreviewable on appeal from a final judgment." According to the court, the District Court's waiver ruling satisfied the first two of these requirements but not the third, because "a discovery order that implicates the attorney-client privilege" can be adequately reviewed "on appeal from a final judgment." The Court of Appeals also rejected Mohawk's mandamus petition, finding no "clear usurpation of power or abuse of discretion" by the District Court. We granted certiorari, to resolve a conflict among the Circuits concerning the availability of collateral appeals in the attorney-client privilege context.[1]

II

A

By statute, Courts of Appeals "have jurisdiction of appeals from all final decisions of the district courts of the United States, ... except where a direct review may be had in the Supreme Court." 28 U.S.C. § 1291. A "final decisio[n]" is typically one "by which a district court disassociates itself from a case." This Court, however, "has long given" § 1291 a "practical rather than a technical construction." *Cohen*. As we held in *Cohen*, the statute encompasses not only judgments that "terminate an action," but also a "small class" of collateral rulings that, although they do not end the litigation, are appropriately deemed "final." "That small category includes only decisions that are conclusive, that resolve important questions separate from the merits, and that are effectively unreviewable on appeal from the final judgment in the underlying action."

In applying *Cohen*'s collateral order doctrine, we have stressed that it must "never be allowed to swallow the general rule that a party is entitled to a single appeal, to be deferred until final judgment has been entered." Our admonition reflects a healthy respect for the virtues of the final-judgment rule. Permitting piecemeal, prejudgment appeals, we have recognized, undermines "efficient judicial administration" and encroaches upon the prerogatives of district court judges, who play a "special role" in managing ongoing litigation ("[T]he district judge can better exercise [his or her] responsibility [to police the prejudgment tactics of litigants] if the appellate courts do not repeatedly intervene to second-guess prejudgment rulings").

The justification for immediate appeal must therefore be sufficiently strong to overcome the usual benefits of deferring appeal until litigation concludes. This requirement finds expression in two of the three traditional *Cohen* conditions. The second condition insists upon "*important* ques-

---

1. Three Circuits have permitted collateral order appeals of attorney-client privilege rulings. The remaining Circuits to consider the question have found such orders non-appealable.

tions separate from the merits." More significantly, "the third *Cohen* question, whether a right is 'adequately vindicable' or 'effectively reviewable,' simply cannot be answered without a judgment about the value of the interests that would be lost through rigorous application of a final judgment requirement." That a ruling "may burden litigants in ways that are only imperfectly reparable by appellate reversal of a final district court judgment ... has never sufficed." Instead, the decisive consideration is whether delaying review until the entry of final judgment "would imperil a substantial public interest" or "some particular value of a high order."

In making this determination, we do not engage in an "individualized jurisdictional inquiry." Rather, our focus is on "the entire category to which a claim belongs." As long as the class of claims, taken as a whole, can be adequately vindicated by other means, "the chance that the litigation at hand might be speeded, or a 'particular injustic[e]' averted," does not provide a basis for jurisdiction under § 1291.

B

In the present case, the Court of Appeals concluded that the District Court's privilege-waiver order satisfied the first two conditions of the collateral order doctrine—conclusiveness and separateness—but not the third—effective unreviewability. Because we agree with the Court of Appeals that collateral order appeals are not necessary to ensure effective review of orders adverse to the attorney-client privilege, we do not decide whether the other *Cohen* requirements are met.

Mohawk does not dispute that "we have generally denied review of pretrial discovery orders." Mohawk contends, however, that rulings implicating the attorney-client privilege differ in kind from run-of-the-mill discovery orders because of the important institutional interests at stake. According to Mohawk, the right to maintain attorney-client confidences— the *sine qua non* of a meaningful attorney-client relationship—is "irreparably destroyed absent immediate appeal" of adverse privilege rulings.

We readily acknowledge the importance of the attorney-client privilege, which "is one of the oldest recognized privileges for confidential communications." By assuring confidentiality, the privilege encourages clients to make "full and frank" disclosures to their attorneys, who are then better able to provide candid advice and effective representation. *Upjohn Co. v. United States*. This, in turn, serves "broader public interests in the observance of law and administration of justice."

The crucial question, however, is not whether an interest is important in the abstract; it is whether deferring review until final judgment so imperils the interest as to justify the cost of allowing immediate appeal of the entire class of relevant orders. We routinely require litigants to wait until after final judgment to vindicate valuable rights, including rights central to our adversarial system. See, *e.g., Richardson–Merrell* (holding an order disqualifying counsel in a civil case did not qualify for immediate appeal under the collateral order doctrine); *Flanagan v. United States*

(1984) (reaching the same result in a criminal case, notwithstanding the Sixth Amendment rights at stake). In *Digital Equipment,* we rejected an assertion that collateral order review was necessary to promote "the public policy favoring voluntary resolution of disputes." "It defies common sense," we explained, "to maintain that parties' readiness to settle will be significantly dampened (or the corresponding public interest impaired) by a rule that a district court's decision to let allegedly barred litigation go forward may be challenged as a matter of right only on appeal from a judgment for the plaintiff's favor."

We reach a similar conclusion here. In our estimation, post-judgment appeals generally suffice to protect the rights of litigants and assure the vitality of the attorney-client privilege. Appellate courts can remedy the improper disclosure of privileged material in the same way they remedy a host of other erroneous evidentiary rulings: by vacating an adverse judgment and remanding for a new trial in which the protected material and its fruits are excluded from evidence.

Dismissing such relief as inadequate, Mohawk emphasizes that the attorney-client privilege does not merely "prohibi[t] use of protected information at trial"; it provides a "right not to disclose the privileged information in the first place." Mohawk is undoubtedly correct that an order to disclose privileged information intrudes on the confidentiality of attorney-client communications. But deferring review until final judgment does not meaningfully reduce the *ex ante* incentives for full and frank consultations between clients and counsel.

One reason for the lack of a discernible chill is that, in deciding how freely to speak, clients and counsel are unlikely to focus on the remote prospect of an erroneous disclosure order, let alone on the timing of a possible appeal. Whether or not immediate collateral order appeals are available, clients and counsel must account for the possibility that they will later be required by law to disclose their communications for a variety of reasons—for example, because they misjudged the scope of the privilege, because they waived the privilege, or because their communications fell within the privilege's crime-fraud exception. Most district court rulings on these matters involve the routine application of settled legal principles. They are unlikely to be reversed on appeal, particularly when they rest on factual determinations for which appellate deference is the norm. The breadth of the privilege and the narrowness of its exceptions will thus tend to exert a much greater influence on the conduct of clients and counsel than the small risk that the law will be misapplied.

Moreover, were attorneys and clients to reflect upon their appellate options, they would find that litigants confronted with a particularly injurious or novel privilege ruling have several potential avenues of review apart from collateral order appeal. First, a party may ask the district court to certify, and the court of appeals to accept, an interlocutory appeal pursuant to 28 U.S.C. § 1292(b). The preconditions for § 1292(b) review— "a controlling question of law," the prompt resolution of which "may materially advance the ultimate termination of the litigation"—are most likely to be satisfied when a privilege ruling involves a new legal question or is of special consequence, and district courts should not hesitate to certify an interlocutory appeal in such cases. Second, in extraordinary circumstances—*i.e.,* when a disclosure order "amount[s] to a judicial usurpation of power or a clear abuse of discretion," or otherwise works a manifest injustice—a party may petition the court of appeals for a writ of mandamus. While these discretionary review mechanisms do not provide relief in every case, they serve as useful "safety valve[s]" for promptly correcting serious errors.

Another long-recognized option is for a party to defy a disclosure order and incur court-imposed sanctions. District courts have a range of sanctions from which to choose, including "directing that the matters embraced in the order or other designated facts be taken as established for purposes of the action," "prohibiting the disobedient party from supporting or opposing designated claims or defenses," or "striking pleadings in whole or in part." Fed. Rule Civ. Proc. 37(b)(2)(i)–(iii). Such sanctions allow a party to obtain post-judgment review without having to reveal its privileged information. Alternatively, when the circumstances warrant it, a district court may hold a non-complying party in contempt. The party can then appeal directly from that ruling, at least when the contempt citation can be characterized as a criminal punishment.

These established mechanisms for appellate review not only provide assurances to clients and counsel about the security of their confidential communications; they also go a long way toward addressing Mohawk's concern that, absent collateral order appeals of adverse attorney-client privilege rulings, some litigants may experience severe hardship. Mohawk is no doubt right that an order to disclose privileged material may, in some situations, have implications beyond the case at hand. But the same can be said about many categories of pretrial discovery orders for which collateral order appeals are unavailable. As with these other orders, rulings adverse to the privilege vary in their significance; some may be momentous, but others are more mundane. Section 1292(b) appeals, mandamus, and appeals from contempt citations facilitate immediate review of some of the more consequential attorney-client privilege rulings. Moreover, protective orders are available to limit the spillover effects of disclosing sensitive information. That a fraction of orders adverse to the attorney-client privilege may nevertheless harm individual litigants in ways that are "only imperfectly reparable" does not justify making all such orders immediately appealable as of right under § 1291.

In short, the limited benefits of applying "the blunt, categorical instrument of § 1291 collateral order appeal" to privilege-related disclosure orders simply cannot justify the likely institutional costs. Permitting parties to undertake successive, piecemeal appeals of all adverse attorney-client rulings would unduly delay the resolution of district court litigation and needlessly burden the Courts of Appeals. Attempting to downplay such concerns, Mohawk asserts that the three Circuits in which the collateral order doctrine currently applies to adverse privilege rulings have seen only a trickle of appeals. But this may be due to the fact that the practice in all three Circuits is relatively new and not yet widely known. Were this Court to approve collateral order appeals in the attorney-client privilege context, many more litigants would likely choose that route. They would also likely seek to extend such a ruling to disclosure orders implicating many other categories of sensitive information, raising an array of line-drawing difficulties.[4]

C

In concluding that sufficiently effective review of adverse attorney-client privilege rulings can be had without resort to the *Cohen* doctrine, we reiterate that the class of collaterally appealable orders must remain "narrow and selective in its membership." This admonition has acquired special force in recent years with the enactment of legislation designating rulemaking, "not expansion by court decision," as the preferred means for determining whether and when prejudgment orders should be immediately appealable. Specifically, Congress in 1990 amended the Rules Enabling Act, 28 U.S.C. § 2071 *et seq.*, to authorize this Court to adopt rules "defin[ing] when a ruling of a district court is final for the purposes of appeal under section 1291." § 2072(c). Shortly thereafter, and along similar lines, Congress empowered this Court to "prescribe rules, in accordance with [§ 2072], to provide for an appeal of an interlocutory decision to the courts of appeals that is not otherwise provided for under [§ 1292]." § 1292(e). These provisions, we have recognized, "warran[t] the Judiciary's full respect."

Indeed, the rulemaking process has important virtues. It draws on the collective experience of bench and bar, see 28 U.S.C. § 2073, and it facilitates the adoption of measured, practical solutions. We expect that the combination of standard post-judgment appeals, § 1292(b) appeals, mandamus, and contempt appeals will continue to provide adequate protection to litigants ordered to disclose materials purportedly subject to the attorney-client privilege. Any further avenue for immediate appeal of such rulings should be furnished, if at all, through rulemaking, with the opportunity for full airing it provides.

* * *

In sum, we conclude that the collateral order doctrine does not extend to disclosure orders adverse to the attorney-client privilege. Effective appellate review can be had by other means. Accordingly, we affirm the judgment of the Court of Appeals for the Eleventh Circuit.

It is so ordered.

---

4. Participating as *amicus curiae* in support of respondent Carpenter, the United States contends that collateral order appeals should be available for rulings involving certain governmental privileges "in light of their structural constitutional grounding under the separation of powers, relatively rare invocation, and unique importance to governmental functions." We express no view on that issue.

JUSTICE THOMAS, concurring in part and concurring in the judgment.

I concur in the judgment and in Part II–C of the Court's opinion because I wholeheartedly agree that "Congress's designation of the rule-making process as the way to define or refine when a district court ruling is 'final' and when an interlocutory order is appealable warrants the Judiciary's full respect." It is for that reason that I do not join the remainder of the Court's analysis.

The scope of federal appellate jurisdiction is a matter the Constitution expressly commits to Congress, see Art. I, § 8, cl. 9, and that Congress has addressed not only in 28 U.S.C. §§ 1291 and 1292, but also in the Rules Enabling Act amendments to which the Court refers. The Court recognizes that these amendments "designat[e] rulemaking, 'not expansion by court decision,' as the preferred means of determining whether and when prejudgment orders should be immediately appealable." Because that designation is entitled to our full respect, and because the privilege order here is not on all fours with orders we previously have held to be appealable under the collateral order doctrine, see *Cohen v. Beneficial Industrial Loan Corp.*, I would affirm the Eleventh Circuit's judgment on the ground that any "avenue for immediate appeal" beyond the three avenues addressed in the Court's opinion must be left to the "rulemaking process."

We need not, and in my view should not, further justify our holding by applying the *Cohen* doctrine, which prompted the rulemaking amendments in the first place. In taking this path, the Court needlessly perpetuates a judicial policy that we for many years have criticized and struggled to limit. The Court's choice of analysis is the more ironic because applying *Cohen* to the facts of this case requires the Court to reach conclusions on, and thus potentially prejudice, the very matters it says would benefit from "the collective experience of bench and bar" and the "opportunity for full airing" that rulemaking provides.

"Finality as a condition of review is an historic characteristic of federal appellate procedure" that was incorporated in the first Judiciary Act and that Congress itself has "departed from only when observance of it would practically defeat the right to any review at all." Until 1949, this Court's view of the appellate jurisdiction statute reflected this principle and the statute's text. *Cohen* changed all that when it announced that a "small class" of collateral orders that do not meet the statutory definition of finality nonetheless may be immediately appealable if they satisfy certain criteria that show they are "too important to be denied review."

Cohen and the early decisions applying it allowed § 1291 appeals of interlocutory orders concerning the posting of a bond, the attachment of a vessel in admiralty, and the imposition of notice costs in a class action. As the Court's opinion notes, later decisions sought to narrow *Cohen* lest its exception to § 1291 "'swallow' the final judgment rule." The Court has adhered to that narrowing approach, principally by raising the bar on what types of interests are "important enough" to justify collateral order appeals. See, *e.g.*, *Will* (explaining that an interlocutory order typically will be "important" enough to justify *Cohen* review only where "some particular value of a high order," such as "honoring the separation of powers, preserving the efficiency of government . . ., [or] respecting a State's dignitary interests," is "marshaled in support of the interest in avoiding trial" and the Court determines that denying review would "imperil" that interest); *Digital Equipment* (noting that appealability under *Cohen* turns on a "judgment about the value of the interests that would be lost through rigorous application of a final judgment requirement," and that an interest "qualifies as 'important' in *Cohen*'s sense" if it is "weightier than the societal interests advanced by the ordinary operation of final judgment principles"). As we recognized last Term, however, our attempts to contain the *Cohen* doctrine have not all been successful or persuasive. See *Ashcroft* ("[A]s a general matter, the collateral-order doctrine may have expanded beyond the limits dictated by its internal logic and the strict application of the criteria set out in *Cohen*"). In my view, this case presents an opportunity to improve our approach.

The privilege interest at issue here is undoubtedly important, both in its own right and when compared to some of the interests (*e.g.*, in bond and notice-cost rulings) we have held to be appealable under *Cohen*. Accordingly, the Court's *Cohen* analysis does not rest on the privilege order's relative unimportance, but instead on its effective reviewability after final judgment. Although I agree with the Court's ultimate conclusion, I see two difficulties with this approach. First, the Court emphasizes that the alternative avenues of review it discusses (which did not prove adequate in this case) would be adequate where the privilege ruling at issue is "particularly injurious or novel." If that is right, and it seems to me that it is, then the opinion raises the question why such avenues were not also adequate to address the orders whose unusual importance or particularly injurious nature we have held *justified* immediate appeal under *Cohen*. Second, the facts of this particular case seem in several respects to undercut the Court's conclusion that the benefits of collateral order review "cannot justify the likely institutional costs." The Court responds that these case-specific arguments miss the point because the focus of the *Cohen* analysis is whether the "entire category" or "class of claims" at issue merits appellate review under the collateral order doctrine. That is exactly right, and illustrates what increasingly has bothered me about making this kind of appealability determination via case-by-case adjudication. The exercise forces the reviewing court to subordinate the realities of each case before it to generalized conclusions about the "likely" costs and benefits of allowing an exception to the final judgment rule in an entire "class of cases." The Court concedes that Congress, which holds the constitutional reins in this area, has determined that such value judgments are better left to the "collective experience of bench and bar" and the "opportunity for full airing" that rulemaking provides. This determination is entitled to our full respect, indeed as well as in word. Accordingly, I would leave the value judgments the Court makes in its opinion to the rulemaking process, and in so doing take this opportunity to limit—effectively, predictably, and in a way we should have done long ago—the doctrine that, with a sweep of the Court's pen, subordinated what the appellate jurisdiction statute says to what the Court thinks is a good idea.

C. CERTIFIED ORDERS

YAMAHA MOTOR CORP., U.S.A. v. CALHOUN

516 U.S. 199 (1996)

JUSTICE GINSBURG delivered the opinion of the Court.

Twelve-year-old Natalie Calhoun was killed in a jet ski accident on July 6, 1989. At the time of her death, she was vacationing with family friends at a beach-front resort in Puerto Rico. Alleging that the jet ski was defectively designed or made, Natalie's parents sought to recover from the manufacturer pursuant to state survival and wrongful-death statutes. The manufacturer contended that state remedies could not be applied because Natalie died on navigable waters; federal, judge-declared maritime law, the manufacturer urged, controlled to the exclusion of state law.

Traditionally, state remedies have been applied in accident cases of this order—maritime wrongful-death cases in which no federal statute specifies the appropriate relief and the decedent was not a seaman, longshore worker, or person otherwise engaged in a maritime trade. We hold, in accord with the United States Court of Appeals for the Third Circuit, that state remedies remain applicable in such cases and have not been displaced by the federal maritime wrongful-death action.

I

Natalie Calhoun, the 12-year-old daughter of respondents Lucien and Robin Calhoun, died in a tragic accident on July 6, 1989. On vacation with family friends at a resort hotel in Puerto Rico, Natalie had rented a "WaveJammer" jet ski manufactured by Yamaha Motor Company, Ltd., and distributed by Yamaha Motor Corporation, U.S.A. (collectively, Yamaha), the petitioners in this case. While riding the WaveJammer, Natalie slammed into a vessel anchored in the waters off the hotel frontage, and was killed.

The Calhouns, individually and in their capacities as administrators of their daughter's estate, sued Yamaha in the United States District Court for the Eastern District of Pennsylvania. Invoking Pennsylvania's wrongful-death and survival statutes, the Calhouns asserted several bases for recovery (including negligence, strict liability, and breach of implied warranties), and sought damages for lost future earnings, loss of society, loss of support and services, and funeral expenses, as well as punitive damages. They grounded federal jurisdiction on both diversity of citizenship, 28 U.S.C. § 1332, and admiralty, 28 U.S.C. § 1333.

Yamaha moved for partial summary judgment, arguing that the federal maritime wrongful-death action this Court recognized in *Moragne v. States Marine Lines, Inc.,* provided the exclusive basis for recovery, displacing all remedies afforded by state law. Under *Moragne,* Yamaha contended, the Calhouns could recover as damages only Natalie's funeral expenses. The District Court agreed with Yamaha that *Moragne*'s maritime death action displaced state remedies; the court held, however, that loss of society and loss of support and services were compensable under *Moragne.*

Both sides asked the District Court to present questions for immediate interlocutory appeal pursuant to 28 U.S.C. § 1292(b). The District Court granted the parties' requests, and in its § 1292(b) certifying order stated:

> Natalie Calhoun, the minor child of plaintiffs Lucien B. Calhoun and Robin L. Calhoun, who are Pennsylvania residents, was killed in an accident not far off shore in Puerto Rico, in the territorial waters of the United States. Plaintiffs have brought a diversity suit against, *inter alia,* defendants Yamaha Motor Corporation, U.S.A. and Yamaha Motor Co., Ltd. The counts of the complaint directed against the Yamaha defendants allege that the accident was caused by a defect or defects in a Yamaha jet ski which Natalie Calhoun had rented and was using at the time of the fatal accident. Those counts sound in negligence, in strict liability, and in implied warranties of merchantability and fitness. The district court has concluded that admiralty jurisdiction attaches to these several counts and that they constitute a federal maritime cause of action. The questions of law certified to the Court of Appeals are whether, pursuant to such a maritime cause of action, plaintiffs may seek to recover (1) damages for the loss of the society of their deceased minor child, (2) damages for the loss of their child's future earnings, and (3) punitive damages.

Although the Court of Appeals granted the interlocutory review petition, the panel to which the appeal was assigned did not reach the questions presented in the certified order, for it determined that an anterior issue was pivotal. The District Court, as just recounted, had concluded that any damages the Calhouns might recover from Yamaha would be governed exclusively by federal maritime law. But the Third Circuit panel questioned that conclusion and inquired whether state wrongful-death and survival statutes supplied the remedial prescriptions for the Calhouns' complaint. The appellate panel asked whether the state remedies endured or were "displaced by a federal maritime rule of decision." Ultimately, the Court of Appeals ruled that state-law remedies apply in this case.

II

In our order granting certiorari, we asked the parties to brief a preliminary question: "Under 28 U.S.C. § 1292(b), can the courts of appeals exercise jurisdiction over any question that is included within the order that contains the controlling question of law identified by the district court?" The answer to that question, we are satisfied, is yes.

Section 1292(b) provides, in pertinent part:

> When a district judge, in making in a civil action an order not otherwise appealable under this section, shall be of the opinion that *such order* involves a controlling question of law as to which there is substantial ground for difference of opinion and that an immediate appeal *from the order* may materially advance the ultimate termination of the litigation, he shall so state in writing in such order. The Court of Appeals ... may thereupon, in its discretion, permit an appeal to be taken *from such order,* if application is made to it within ten days after the entry of the order. (Emphasis added.)

As the text of § 1292(b) indicates, appellate jurisdiction applies to the *order* certified to the court of appeals, and is not tied to the particular question formulated by the district court. The court of appeals may not reach beyond the certified order to address other orders made in the case. But the appellate court may address any issue fairly included within the certified order because "it is the *order* that is appealable, and not the controlling question identified by the district court." ("[T]he court of appeals may review the entire order, either to consider a question different than the one certified as controlling or to decide the case despite the lack of any identified controlling question.").

* * *

UNITED STATES v. PHILIP MORRIS USA INC.

396 F.3d 1190 (D.C. Cir. 2005)

SENTELLE, CIRCUIT JUDGE.

A group of cigarette manufacturers and related entities ("Appellants") appeal from a decision of the District Court denying summary judgment as to the Government's claim for disgorgement under the Racketeer Influenced and Corrupt Organizations Act ("RICO" or "the Act"). The relevant section of RICO, 18 U.S.C. § 1964(a), provides the District Courts jurisdiction only for forward-looking remedies that prevent and restrain violations of the Act. Because disgorgement, a remedy aimed at past violations, does not so prevent or restrain, we reverse the decision below and grant partial summary judgment for the Appellants.

I. Background

In 1999 the United States brought this claim against appellant cigarette manufacturers and research organizations, claiming that they engaged in a fraudulent pattern of covering up the dangers of tobacco use and marketing to minors. The Government sought damages under the Medical Care Recovery Act ("MCRA") and the Medicare Secondary Payer ("MSP") provisions of the Social Security Act to recover health-care related costs Appellants allegedly caused. The United States also claimed that Appellants engaged in a criminal enterprise to effect this cover-up, and sought equitable relief under RICO, including injunctive relief and disgorgement of proceeds from Appellants' allegedly unlawful activities. The Government sought this relief under 18 U.S.C. § 1964(a), which gives the District Court jurisdiction

> to prevent and restrain violations of [RICO] by issuing appropriate orders, including, but not limited to: ordering any person to divest himself of any interest, direct or indirect, in any enterprise; imposing reasonable restrictions on the future activities or investments of any person, including, but not limited to, prohibiting any person from engaging in the same type of endeavor as the enterprise engaged in, the activities of which affect interstate or foreign commerce; or ordering dissolution or reorganization of any enterprise. . . .

Appellants moved to dismiss the complaint in 2000. The District Court did dismiss the MCRA and MSP claims, but allowed the RICO claim to stand.

Section 1964(a) conferred jurisdiction on the District Court only to enter orders "to prevent and restrain violations of the statute." In considering whether disgorgement came within this jurisdictional grant, the court relied on a decision of the Second Circuit, the only circuit then to have considered "whether . . . disgorgements . . . are designed to 'prevent and restrain' *future* conduct rather than to punish *past* conduct." After noting that "RICO has a broad purpose [and] the legislative history of § 1964 indicates that the equitable relief available under RICO is intended to be 'broad enough to do all that is necessary,'" the *Carson* court went on to observe that it did not see how it could "serve[ ] any civil RICO purpose to order disgorgement of gains ill-gotten long ago. . . .". The portion of *Carson* relied upon by the District Court in the present controversy suggested that disgorgement *might* "serve the goal of 'preventing and restraining' future violations," but flatly held that the remedy would not do so "unless there is a finding that the gains are being used to fund or promote the illegal conduct, or constitute capital available for that purpose." The Second Circuit went on to caution that disgorgement would be better justified under this analysis where the "gains [were] ill-gotten relatively recently." The District Court accepted the Second Circuit's suggested holding that the appropriateness of disgorgement depends on whether the proceeds are available for the continuing of the criminal enterprise, but ruled that the question was premature, and denied the motion for dismissal on the RICO-disgorgement claim. Neither party sought leave to file an interlocutory appeal of that ruling.

The case proceeded, and the Government sought disgorgement of $280 billion that it traced to proceeds from Appellants' cigarette sales to the "youth addicted population" between 1971 and 2001. This population includes all smokers who became addicted before the age of 21, as measured by those who were smoking at least 5 cigarettes a day at that age.

After discovery, Appellants moved for summary judgment on the disgorgement claim arguing that (1) disgorgement is not an available remedy under § 1964(a), (2) even if disgorgement were available, the Government's model fails the *Carson* test for permissible disgorgement that will "prevent and restrain" future violations, and (3) even if disgorgement were available, the Government's proposed model is impermissible because it includes both legally and illegally obtained profits in violation of *SEC v. First City Financial Corp.* The District Court denied this motion in a memorandum order designated "#550." On motion of the defendants, the District Court certified Order #550 for interlocutory appeal pursuant to 28 U.S.C. § 1292(b). That section provides for interlocutory appeal where a district judge has certified that "an order not otherwise appealable ... involves a controlling question of law as to which there is substantial ground for difference of opinion and that an immediate appeal from the order may materially advance the ultimate termination of litigation...." Under § 1292(b), the Court of Appeals may then decide whether to permit the appeal to be taken from such order. In the present case, we allowed the appeal.

II. Analysis

A. Scope of Review

At the outset, the Government urges that our review should be limited to the narrow question of whether the disgorgement it seeks is consistent with the standards of *Carson,* not whether disgorgement *vel non* is an available remedy under civil RICO. The Government bases this argument on the theory that the order on appeal—that is the memorandum order denying "defendants' motion for partial summary judgment dismissing the Government's disgorgement claim"—was reiterating a prior order on the general question of availability of disgorgement Further, the Government argues, the order spoke anew only to the measure of disgorgement, assuming such disgorgement to be otherwise available. In support of its proposed limitation of our review, the Government relies upon *Yamaha Motor Corp., USA v. Calhoun.* In *Yamaha,* the Supreme Court dealt with the breadth of review properly conducted by a court of appeals under 28 U.S.C. § 1292(b). The Government selectively quotes from *Yamaha* the sentence that, "The court of appeals may not reach beyond the certified order to address others made in the case." Based on this sentence, the Government then argues that because the first order denying a motion to dismiss had dealt with the question of the availability of disgorgement, this certified interlocutory review of the subsequent summary judgment order is restricted to the new theory considered by the court on that occasion—that the disgorgement the Government pursued exceeded the standard available for such disgorgement as set by the Second Circuit in *Carson.*

Unfortunately for the Government's position, the *Yamaha* opinion did not end with the sentence upon which the Government relies. The Supreme Court went on to say in the same paragraph: "But the appellate court may address any issue fairly included within the certified order because 'it is the *order* that is appealable, and not the controlling question identified by the district court.' " Appellants' motion below was for "Summary Judgment Dismissing the Government's Disgorgement Claim," and granting this motion would have resulted in *complete dismissal* of the Government's claim for disgorgement with prejudice. Thus the District Court's denial was on the question of whether disgorgement would be allowed *at all,* and we may review it as such regardless of the grounds the District Court gave for its decision. In the memorandum accompanying its denial of this motion, evidencing an accurate understanding of the summary judgment standard provided by Rule 56 of the Federal Rules of Civil Procedure, the District Court noted that "summary judgment is appropriate if the pleadings, depositions, answers to interrogatories, and admissions on file, together with the affidavits, if any, show that there is no genuine issue as to any material fact and that the moving party is entitled to judgment as a matter of law." Significantly, the court further noted that "Defendants argue that any disgorgement which might be ordered upon a finding of liability must be limited by *both the text of Section 1964(a) itself and the holding in United States v. Carson ...* interpreting that section." Thus the court clearly implied the possibility that none might be ordered, and that statutory issues outside *Carson* were before the court.

Our dissenting colleague argues that the availability of the disgorgement claim *vel non* is not before us because Appellants did not fully restate their earlier arguments in their motion, but only expressed their reservation in a footnote referencing the District Court's prior rejection of their position. While it is true, as our colleague reminds us, that we have held that a "litigant does not properly raise an issue by addressing it in a 'cursory fashion,' with only 'bare-bones arguments,' " our prior holdings on that subject have been in very different contexts. In *Cement Kiln,* for example, and in *Wash. Legal Clinic for the Homeless v. Barry,* relied upon by the dissent, we were determining whether an issue was properly before us that had been raised in no other fashion. In the present case, we are reviewing a summary judgment decision, presumably according to the standards set forth by the Supreme Court in such decisions as *Yamaha,* and the issue in question was clearly decided by the District Court in the first rejection of the motion to dismiss. The issue was called to the attention of the court as a necessary antecedent in the second summary judgment order, now under direct review, and expressly pointed out in the footnote which our colleague disdains. Furthermore, the motion leading to the order presently before us sought summary judgment of dismissal of the disgorgement claim, not simply a limitation to such disgorgement as might have been supported by the *Carson* test or other factors. Given the Supreme Court's plain teaching in *Yamaha,* particularly its adoption from a learned treatise of the language "it is the order that is appealable, and not the controlling question identified by the district court," *Yamaha, Cement Kiln* and *Barry* have no applicability. *Yamaha* controls. We therefore proceed to review the denial of summary judgment, under the usually applicable standards, not simply the sole question to which the Appellees and the dissent would restrict us.

Our dissenting colleague suggests that we are limited by "our general policy of declining to consider arguments not made to the district court in the motion leading to the order under appeal." We know of no such "general policy" that the particular issue addressed has to have been raised in the particular motion. Rather, we understand our general policy to be following the instructions of the Supreme Court that we are to "address any issue fairly included within the certified order." *Yamaha.* Insofar as our colleague's differing understanding rests on *United States v. British Am. Tobacco (Invs.) Ltd.*, we do not read that case as supporting a general policy that limits consideration to those arguments raised in the particular motion leading to the certified order, as opposed to being "fairly included" within that order, or even to address the point. The court in *British American Tobacco* held only that an intervenor that had raised a privilege issue with respect to an entire collection of documents at one stage of the litigation, but that failed to participate at all in later proceedings focused on one of the documents, despite having notice, had not adequately preserved its objection as to that single document. It had nothing to do with the scope of review on an interlocutory appeal under § 1292(b). Neither it nor *Hylton* dealt in any fashion with the breadth of interlocutory review, nor was establishing any standard for the papers in which an argument must have been raised. Each rejected an attempt by an appellant to raise a new ground for the first time on appeal. Appellants before us raised and preserved their argument as set forth in the text above. We read nothing in *British American Tobacco* or *Hylton* to suggest a general policy barring our review under the *Yamaha* standard.

We find no history of such a general policy that would bar us from considering questions logically antecedent and essential to the order under review. Especially is this so given the Supreme Court's instructions in *Yamaha* that we are to "address any issue fairly included within the certified order." That must include at least issues that are logically interwoven with the explicitly identified issue and which were properly presented by the appellant. Even ignoring the apparent allusion to the broader issue of summary judgment preserved in the caption of the motion, the relief sought, and the footnote provided above, it is difficult to see how we could establish such a policy that would cause us to affirm a decision denying summary judgment when a ground compelling its grant is fairly encompassed within the order. Our colleague's interpretation of general policy would seem to compel us to return for trial a case before us for review of a denial of summary judgment, no matter how plain the absence of substantial question of material fact, on the grounds that the denial of summary judgment had been based on rejection of some other reasoning in a previous motion, even though the trial court had earlier erred in denying the first motion to dismiss—even when the appellant had called that denial to the court's attention in the caption of its motion, and a proposed order accompanying the second motion.

Our dissenting colleague finds in *Yamaha* support for the proposition that "the only issues 'fairly included' within a certified order are those decided in the district court's accompanying memorandum...." We understand the law to be, as suggested in *Yamaha,* that issues are not decided in memoranda at all, but rather in orders. Therefore, consistent with *Yamaha,* we review orders, not memoranda. Our colleague asserts that in *Yamaha* the Court "found 'fairly included' an issue that the district court had resolved in the same opinion in which it decided the issue identified as the controlling question of law." While this may well be the case, the Supreme Court not only did not stress that circumstance, it did not even mention it. Indeed, we note that our colleague had to repair to the unpublished opinion of the District Court to discover the truth of his proposition. We seriously doubt that the Supreme Court intended to establish a precedent that difficult to discover, let alone apply.

Nothing in *United States v. Stanley* is to the contrary. The passage relied upon by our dissenting colleague to the effect that courts considering interlocutory appeals under § 1292(b) should "not consider matters that were ruled upon in other orders," did not address a situation like the one before us. Here the order appealed from reiterated, and totally depended upon, an issue fairly encompassed within the motion before that court and the order now before us. In *Stanley,* the court of appeals undertook interlocutory review of an order dealing with one claim of a multi-claim complaint. In that order, the district court had refused to dismiss a claim asserted under the authority of *Bivens v. Six Unknown Fed. Narcotics Agents.* On appeal, the court of appeals not only affirmed the district court's conclusion as to the *Bivens* claim, but reached back in the record to order the district court to reinstate another claim for relief asserted under the Federal Tort Claims Act. In the present case, the disputed "prior order" had denied judgment of dismissal on the disgorgement claim. The order concededly before us denied judgment of dismissal on the same disgorgement claim. We see nothing in *Stanley* inconsistent with the later instruction in *Yamaha* recognizing our jurisdiction to "address any issue fairly included within the certified order." *Yamaha.* We therefore proceed, obedient to our understanding of *Yamaha,* to review the order before us denying summary judgment.* * *

TATEL, CIRCUIT JUDGE, dissenting.

I.

Under 28 U.S.C. § 1292(b), if a district court "shall be of the opinion that [an] order involves a controlling question of law as to which there is substantial ground for difference of opinion and that an immediate appeal from the order may materially advance the ultimate termination of the litigation," it may certify the order for interlocutory review, and the court of appeals "may thereupon, in its discretion, permit an appeal to be taken from such order." Section 1292(b) establishes a "two-tiered arrangement." Congress "chose to confer on district courts first line discretion to allow interlocutory appeals," *id.,* and "even if the district judge certifies the order under § 1292(b), the appellant still has the burden of persuading the court of appeals that exceptional circumstances justify a departure from the basic policy of postponing appellate review until after the entry of a final judgment," *Coopers & Lybrand v. Livesay.* In accepting this interlocutory appeal, this court not only (at the least) pushes the bounds of its jurisdiction, but also exercises its discretion on behalf of defendants whose litigating tactics leave much to be desired.

A.

In 2000, the tobacco companies—usually referred to in this opinion as "Philip Morris"—filed a motion to dismiss, arguing (among other things) that "disgorgement . . . is never available under a civil RICO count." Denying that motion, the district court held that disgorgement could be available under 18 U.S.C. § 1964(a), but did not address whether disgorgement would be available in this particular case. Philip Morris never sought certification of that order, though it could have done so at any time after the order's issuance. *See* Fed. R. App. P. 5(a)(3) (providing that the time for filing an appeal runs from when the district court amends the order to include certification, not from the issuance of the actual order); ("This latitude [in Rule 5(a)] makes it possible to employ § 1292(b) with some precision, deferring the question of appeal until it is clear that prompt appeal is apt to be useful.").

In 2004, Philip Morris sought summary judgment regarding the government's request for disgorgement in this case. Contrary to the court's statement, Philip Morris neither reargued the position it took in 2000 nor asked the district court to revisit its 2000 decision. Philip Morris's only reference to its prior position came in a one-sentence footnote: "As noted previously, Defendants respectfully disagree with the Court and maintain that disgorgement in any fashion is unavailable to the Government in a civil RICO action." Instead, Philip Morris urged the court to grant its motion for summary judgment for two primary reasons. First, relying on *United States v. Carson,* where the Second Circuit held that district courts may order disgorgement as a RICO remedy only where the gains "are being used to fund or promote the illegal conduct, or constitute capital available for that purpose," Philip Morris claimed that 18 U.S.C. § 1964(a) "limits disgorgement to the amount of ill-gotten gains that remain available to defendants to fund future RICO violations." Philip Morris further argued that "the Government deliberately has refused to develop the proof properly required under *Carson*" and this in turn "requires dismissal of the Government's disgorgement claim." Second, Philip Morris asserted that the government's disgorgement model fails as a matter of law to reasonably approximate the defendants' ill-gotten gains.

The district court rejected both arguments and denied summary judgment to Philip Morris. Interpreting section 1964(a) more broadly than had the Second Circuit, the court concluded that it could order disgorgement in situations besides those identified in *Carson*. Unsurprisingly, the district court did not revisit its 2000 decision, observing only (in a footnote) that this decision had held "that disgorgement is a permissible remedy under Section 1964(a)." The district court also rejected Philip Morris's contention regarding the government's disgorgement model.

Philip Morris then asked the district court to certify its 2004 order under section 1292(b). In its certification request, Philip Morris did not reassert its legal argument from 2000. Instead, it stated that "[w]hether the *Carson* standard applies to the Government's disgorgement claim is clearly a controlling question of law.... If the Government is wrong, and *Carson* applies, nothing is left of its claim in this case."

The district court agreed that a controlling question of law existed as to whether "the disgorgement allowed under 18 U.S.C. § 1964(a) is limited to those ill-gotten gains which are 'being used to fund or promote the illegal conduct or constitute capital available for that purpose.'" Although in its 2004 order the district court had rejected *Carson*'s interpretation of section 1964(a), it found substantial ground for difference of opinion on this issue, explaining that "it is obvious that the arguments to the contrary in *Carson* are neither insubstantial nor frivolous," and certified the 2004 order.

In its initial petition urging this court to accept the interlocutory appeal, Philip Morris never raised the broader question the district court had addressed in 2000, i.e., whether disgorgement is ever available under section 1964(a). Instead, Philip Morris focused on the narrower issue actually raised in its 2004 motion for summary judgment, arguing that the district court had erred in rejecting *Carson*'s interpretation of section 1964(a) and claiming that "[i]f this Court agrees with the Second Circuit in *Carson*, its decision on appeal would dispose of the Government's disgorgement claim." The government opposed Philip Morris's section 1292(b) petition, arguing that a host of factual issues would require resolution regardless of whether this court adopted *Carson*'s or the district court's interpretation of section 1964(a) and thus that "interlocutory appeal would not materially advance the termination of this litigation."

Responding to the government's opposition, Philip Morris suddenly changed tack and brought in play the issue decided in 2000. Philip Morris wrote:

> The district court rejected [the government's] argument [that an interlocutory appeal would not materially advance the litigation's termination] as a reason not to permit an appeal, and this Court should as well.
>
> First, and most obviously, if this Court reverses the district court's ruling that 'disgorgement is a permissible remedy under section 1964(a),' (Summary Judgment Order at 8 n.7), then the Government's $280 billion claim is precluded as a matter of law.

This entirely disingenuous statement conveyed the impression that the district court had *ruled* on this broader issue in the certified 2004 order rather than simply mentioning its 2000 decision. Moreover, by placing this statement under the heading "The District Court Properly Determined That an Appeal From Its Order Would Materially Advance This Litigation," Philip Morris insinuated that the district court had certified *this* issue to this court as opposed to the narrower question actually resolved in the 2004 order. The government, of course, had no opportunity to correct these misrepresentations, and a motions panel accepted Philip Morris's appeal, expressly leaving the merits panel free to reconsider and dismiss the appeal.

Philip Morris's opening brief on the merits reveals the scope of its bait and switch. The brief devotes forty pages to the issue decided in the 2000 order and only seven to the issues decided in the certified 2004 order. In response, the government urges us to dismiss the appeal entirely, suggesting that we lack jurisdiction over the issue decided in the 2000 order and observing that "Defendants' tactics subvert the mechanism for appeal established by section 1292(b)."

B.

As the foregoing discussion indicates, Philip Morris asks us—and the court now agrees—to decide an issue (1) not briefed in the motion leading up to the certified order, (2) not decided in the district court's opinion accompanying the certified order, (3) not raised by Philip Morris in its request for certification, (4) not discussed in the order granting certification, (5) not raised by Philip Morris in its section 1292(b) petition before this court, and (6) decided in an entirely different order which Philip Morris could at any time have asked the district court to certify. This presents serious questions on two separate fronts: our jurisdiction over this appeal under section 1292(b), and our general policy of declining to consider arguments not made to the district court in the motion leading to the order under appeal. Unlike the court, I cannot brush these concerns aside.

Regarding our jurisdiction under section 1292(b), the Supreme Court has made clear that an appellate court can review "any issue fairly included within the certified order" because "[a]s the text of § 1292(b) indicates, appellate jurisdiction applies to the *order* certified to the court of appeals, and is not tied to the particular question formulated by the district court." *Yamaha Motor Corp., USA v. Calhoun* (holding that where the district court decided two issues in the certified order but identified only the damages issue as the controlling question of law, the court of appeals could nonetheless address the other issue). But the "court of appeals may not reach beyond the certified order to address other orders made in the case." *Id.; see also United States v. Stanley* (holding that the court of appeals erred in addressing a claim not raised in the certified order though closely related to it). Both "[c]ommentators and courts have consistently observed that 'the scope of the issues open to the court of appeals is closely limited to the order appealed from [and][t]he court of appeals will not consider matters that were ruled upon in other orders.' "

This case falls near the intersection of these commands. For all intents and purposes, Philip Morris asks us to address the 2000 order. Today's decision overturns that order. This court has jurisdiction to do this under *Yamaha* only if the issue addressed in the 2000 order is "fairly included within the certified order." Taking a broad view of "fairly included," the court concludes that because the 2004 order denies dismissal of the government's disgorgement claim, we may review (at a minimum) any basis for summary judgment that is "logically interwoven with the explicitly identified issue." This approach not only gives us jurisdiction over the issue decided by the district court in the 2000 order, but also over the district court's 2002 determination, made in denying Philip Morris's motion for a jury trial, that disgorgement is an equitable remedy rather than a legal one. Indeed, although the concurrence apparently does not share this approach, the majority opinion suggests that any issue which would result in "*complete dismissal* of the Government's claim for disgorgement with prejudice" lies within our jurisdiction "regardless of the grounds the District Court gave for its decision." By this logic, we may also have interlocutory jurisdiction to review the district court's denial of the tobacco companies' 2000 motion to dismiss, where they claimed that the government has not "adequately alleged that Defendants' racketeering activity will continue into the future," and even the district court's denial of Liggett's 2000 motion to dismiss, where the company argued that (as to it) the government could not show two elements required for a RICO claim. Because victory for the tobacco companies on the first issue (and, for Liggett, victory on the second) could also trigger dismissal of the government's disgorgement claims, under the court's theory our interlocutory jurisdiction may extend to these issues as well.

The court's approach is problematic in several respects. Most significantly, it curtails the district court's section 1292(b) certification role. In this case, the district court had neither an opportunity to exercise "first line discretion to allow interlocutory appeal[ ]," on the broader issue resolved in its 2000 order nor notice that Philip Morris would raise this issue with us. In future cases, district courts will lose their flexibility to certify discrete issues for review, since the certification of one order may give this court jurisdiction over all sorts of prior orders. Today's situation illustrates this: under the court's theory, we have jurisdiction in this interlocutory appeal to review at a minimum two prior orders, neither of which Philip Morris sought to certify. Moreover, by reducing the opportunity for tailored review, the court's jurisdictional theory threatens this circuit with interlocutory overload. Parties who persuade us to accept an interlocutory appeal may feel encouraged to raise any or even all issues decided in prior orders that fall within our newfound jurisdiction especially since, according to the court, issues raised in prior orders are "preserved" for section 1292(b) purposes, and not simply for the purpose of appeal after final judgment.

By contrast, no harm of consequence would result from holding, as I would, that the only issues "fairly included" within a certified order are those decided in the district court's accompanying memorandum—exactly the situation with the issue reached by the Supreme Court in *Yamaha*. There, the Court found "fairly included" an issue that the district court had resolved in the same opinion in which it decided the issue identified as the controlling question of law. While the Court did not explicitly rely on this point, it is relevant to determining whether *Yamaha*'s "fairly included" language stands for the proposition that appellate courts have interlocutory jurisdiction over all possible bases for reversing a summary judgment denial (as my colleagues read it) or only over bases which the district court considered and resolved in this denial (as I read it).

My approach, moreover, respects the Court's instruction in *Stanley* that we should "not consider matters that were ruled upon in other orders." It is thus hardly surprising that the court today points to no case in which an appellate court has exercised interlocutory jurisdiction over an issue decided in a different order from the one under certification. True, under my approach a party seeking an interlocutory appeal on a matter split across two orders would need to seek certification of both orders to bring the matter fully to this court. But that seems a small burden. If the party fails to make this effort (as in this case) and we conclude that it would be inappropriate to address only the issues raised in the certified order (as I would here), then we have discretion under section 1292(b) to refuse to permit the interlocutory appeal altogether—a point this court overlooks.

In addition to resting on a dubious interpretation of section 1292(b), the court's decision to review the broader issue runs counter to this circuit's general rules regarding waiver. Parties may raise here only those arguments they presented to the district court in their papers seeking (and opposing) the order under review, since only in exceptional circumstances will we consider an argument not made to the district court. *See United States v. British Am. Tobacco (Invs.) Ltd.* (finding waiver based on a party's failure to appear and defend a privilege claim in the proceedings resulting in the interlocutory appeal, even though the party had asserted the privilege in a related proceeding in the same case). Here, as discussed earlier, Philip Morris never argued the broader issue in the relevant pleadings; a sentence-long footnote stating "respectful disagreement" is not an argument, particularly when offered in such a cursory fashion. Although it is true, as the court points out, that in the two just-cited cases the issues were apparently never raised at an earlier stage, here we are reviewing not the entire case but only the certified 2004 order, which sets the bounds of both our jurisdiction and waiver doctrine. Moreover, while we sometimes make exceptions to our waiver rules, I would not do so here given Philip Morris's questionable tactics. Even under my colleagues' jurisdictional theory, only by exercising our discretion to accept an argument not raised in the district court—and further exercising our discretion to accept the interlocutory appeal—does the broader issue stand before us.

In sum, whether viewed in terms of jurisdiction or waiver, only Philip Morris's narrower challenge is properly before us. True, this means we should dismiss the appeal altogether, as it makes little sense to decide the narrower question at this time when the broader question might be appealed later. But Philip Morris itself created this problem. It had several ways it could properly have brought the broader issue to our attention. In its 2004 motion for summary judgment, it could have reargued the broader question and asked the district court to reconsider its decision; the district court's denial of reconsideration would have brought the issue fairly into the challenged order. Even more appropriately, Philip Morris could have asked the district court to certify both the 2000 and 2004 orders and candidly explained that it wished this court to review the earlier order as well. Either way, the district court, having fair notice that Philip Morris wanted to raise both issues with us, could have performed its section 1292(b) gate-keeping function. Taking neither approach, Philip Morris instead not only jumped the fence at the district court level, but also circumvented our own screening process by waiting until after the government's opposition to raise the broader issue with the motions panel. This court should not be rewarding such tactics by exercising its discretion to hear this appeal.

I would therefore dismiss the interlocutory appeal. I reach this conclusion reluctantly because I certainly understand how hearing this interlocutory appeal could be helpful to Judge Kessler, who is presiding over a long and difficult trial. In my view, however, preserving section 1292(b)'s integrity and discouraging the kind of litigating tactics reflected in this record far outweigh the efficiency that hearing this interlocutory appeal might produce in this concededly complex case.

* * *

D. THE WRIT OF MANDAMUS

FEDERAL RULE OF CIVIL PROCEDURE 53. MASTERS

(a) Appointment.

 (1) *Scope.* Unless a statute provides otherwise, a court may appoint a master only to:

  (A) perform duties consented to by the parties;

  (B) hold trial proceedings and make or recommend findings of fact on issues to be decided without a jury if appointment is warranted by:

   (i) some exceptional condition; or

   (ii) the need to perform an accounting or resolve a difficult computation of damages; or

    (C) address pretrial and post-trial matters that cannot be effectively and timely addressed by an available district judge or magistrate judge of the district.

  (2) *Disqualification.* A master must not have a relationship to the parties, attorneys, action, or court that would require disqualification of a judge under 28 U.S.C. § 455, unless the parties, with the court's approval, consent to the appointment after the master discloses any potential grounds for disqualification.

  (3) *Possible Expense or Delay.* In appointing a master, the court must consider the fairness of imposing the likely expenses on the parties and must protect against unreasonable expense or delay.

(b) Order Appointing a Master.

  (1) *Notice.* Before appointing a master, the court must give the parties notice and an opportunity to be heard. Any party may suggest candidates for appointment.

  (2) *Contents.* The appointing order must direct the master to proceed with all reasonable diligence and must state:

    (A) the master's duties, including any investigation or enforcement duties, and any limits on the master's authority under Rule 53(c);

    (B) the circumstances, if any, in which the master may communicate ex parte with the court or a party;

    (C) the nature of the materials to be preserved and filed as the record of the master's activities;

    (D) the time limits, method of filing the record, other procedures, and standards for reviewing the master's orders, findings, and recommendations; and

    (E) the basis, terms, and procedure for fixing the master's compensation under Rule 53(g).

  (3) *Issuing.* The court may issue the order only after:

    (A) the master files an affidavit disclosing whether there is any ground for disqualification under 28 U.S.C. § 455; and

    (B) if a ground is disclosed, the parties, with the court's approval, waive the disqualification.

  (4) *Amending.* The order may be amended at any time after notice to the parties and an opportunity to be heard.

(c) Master's Authority.

  (1) *In General.* Unless the appointing order directs otherwise, a master may:

    (A) regulate all proceedings;

    (B) take all appropriate measures to perform the assigned duties fairly and efficiently; and

    (C) if conducting an evidentiary hearing, exercise the appointing court's power to compel, take, and record evidence.

  (2) *Sanctions.* The master may by order impose on a party any non-contempt sanction provided by Rule 37 or 45, and may recommend a contempt sanction against a party and sanctions against a nonparty.

(d) Master's Orders. A master who issues an order must file it and promptly serve a copy on each party. The clerk must enter the order on the docket.

(e) Master's Reports. A master must report to the court as required by the appointing order. The master must file the report and promptly serve a copy on each party, unless the court orders otherwise.

(f) Action on the Master's Order, Report, or Recommendations.

  (1) *Opportunity for a Hearing; Action in General.* In acting on a master's order, report, or recommendations, the court must give the parties notice and an opportunity to be heard; may receive evidence; and may adopt or affirm, modify, wholly or partly reject or reverse, or resubmit to the master with instructions.

  (2) *Time to Object or Move to Adopt or Modify.* A party may file objections to—or a motion to adopt or modify—the master's order, report, or recommendations no later than 20 days after a copy is served, unless the court sets a different time.

  (3) *Reviewing Factual Findings.* The court must decide de novo all objections to findings of fact made or recommended by a master, unless the parties, with the court's approval, stipulate that:

    (A) the findings will be reviewed for clear error; or

    (B) the findings of a master appointed under Rule 53(a)(1)(A) or (C) will be final.

  (4) *Reviewing Legal Conclusions.* The court must decide de novo all objections to conclusions of law made or recommended by a master.

  (5) *Reviewing Procedural Matters.* Unless the appointing order establishes a different standard of review, the court may set aside a master's ruling on a procedural matter only for an abuse of discretion.

(g) Compensation.

  (1) *Fixing Compensation.* Before or after judgment, the court must fix the master's compensation on the basis and terms stated in the appointing order, but the court may set a new basis and terms after giving notice and an opportunity to be heard.

  (2) *Payment.* The compensation must be paid either:

    (A) by a party or parties; or

(B) from a fund or subject matter of the action within the court's control.

(3) *Allocating Payment.* The court must allocate payment among the parties after considering the nature and amount of the controversy, the parties' means, and the extent to which any party is more responsible than other parties for the reference to a master. An interim allocation may be amended to reflect a decision on the merits.

(h) Appointing a Magistrate Judge. A magistrate judge is subject to this rule only when the order referring a matter to the magistrate judge states that the reference is made under this rule.

* * *

28 U.S.C. § 1651. WRITS

(a) The Supreme Court and all courts established by Act of Congress may issue all writs necessary or appropriate in aid of their respective jurisdictions and agreeable to the usages and principles of law.

* * *

LA BUY v. HOWES LEATHER COMPANY

352 U.S. 249 (1957)

MR. JUSTICE CLARK delivered the opinion of the Court.

These two consolidated cases present a question of the power of the Courts of Appeals to issue writs of mandamus to compel a District Judge to vacate his orders entered under Rule 53(b) of the Federal Rules of Civil Procedure, referring antitrust cases for trial before a master. The petitioner, a United States District Judge sitting in the Northern District of Illinois, contends that the Courts of Appeals have no such power and that, even if they did, these cases were not appropriate ones for its exercise. The Court of Appeals for the Seventh Circuit has decided unanimously that it has such power and, by a divided court, that the circumstances surrounding the references by the petitioner required it to issue the mandamus about which he complains. The importance of the question in the administration of the Federal Rules of Civil Procedure, together with the uncertainty existing on the issue among the Courts of Appeals, led to our grant of a writ of certiorari. We conclude that the Court of Appeals properly issued the writs of mandamus.

History of the Litigation.—These petitions for mandamus, filed in the Court of Appeals, arose from two antitrust actions instituted in the District Court in 1950. *Rohlfing* involves 87 plaintiffs, all operators of independent retail shoe repair shops. The claim of these plaintiffs against the six named defendants—manufacturers, wholesalers, and retail mail order houses and chain operators—is identical. The claim asserted in the complaint is a conspiracy between the defendants "to monopolize and to attempt to monopolize" and fix the price of shoe repair supplies sold in interstate commerce in the Chicago area, in violation of the Sherman Act. The allegations also include a price discrimination charge under the Robinson–Patman Act. Shaffer involves six plaintiffs, all wholesalers of shoe repair supplies, and six defendants, including manufacturers and wholesalers of such supplies and a retail shoe shop chain operator. The allegations here also include charges of monopoly and price fixing under the Sherman Act and price discrimination in violation of the Robinson–Patman Act. Both complaints pray for injunctive relief, treble damages, and an accounting with respect to the discriminatory price differentials charged.

The record indicates that the cases had been burdensome to the petitioner. In *Rohlfing* alone, 27 pages of the record are devoted to docket entries reflecting that petitioner had conducted many hearings on preliminary pleas and motions. The original complaint had been twice amended as a result of orders of the court in regard to misjoinders and severance; 14 defendants had been dismissed with prejudice; summary judgment hearings had resulted in a refusal to enter a judgment for some of the defendants on the pleadings; over 50 depositions had been taken; and hearings to compel testimony and require the production and inspection of records were held. It appears that several of the hearings were extended and included not only oral argument but submission of briefs, and resulted in the filing of opinions and memoranda by the petitioner. It is reasonable to conclude that much time would have been saved at the trial had petitioner heard the case because of his familiarity with the litigation.

The References to the Master.—The references to the master were made under the authority of Rule 53(b) of the Federal Rules of Civil Procedure. The cases were called on February 23, 1955, on a motion to reset them for trial. *Rohlfing* was "No. 1 below the black line" on the trial list, which gave it a preferred setting. All parties were anxious for an early trial, but plaintiffs wished an adjournment until May. The petitioner announced that "it has taken a long time to get this case at issue. I remember hearing more motions, I think, in this case than any case I have ever sat on in this court." The plaintiffs estimated that the trial would take six weeks, whereupon petitioner stated he did not know when he could try the case "if it is going to take this long." He asked if the parties could agree "to have a Master hear" it. The parties ignored this query and at a conference in chambers the next day petitioner entered the orders of reference *sua sponte*.[5] The orders declared that the court was "confronted with an extremely congested calendar" and that "exception (sic) condi-

---

5. The fact that the master is an active practitioner would make the comment of Chief Justice Vanderbilt with regard to the effect of references appropriate here. In his work, he states:

> There is one special cause of delay in getting cases on for trial that must be singled out for particular condemnation, the all-too-prevalent habit of sending matters to a reference. There is no more effective may of putting a case to sleep for an indefinite period than to permit it to go to a reference with a busy lawyer as referee. Only a drastic administrative rule, rigidly enforced, strictly limiting the matters in which a reference may be had and requiring weekly reports as to the progress of each reference will put to rout this inveterate enemy of dispatch in the trial of cases.

tions exist for this reason" requiring the references. The cases were referred to the master "to take evidence and to report the same to this Court, together with his findings of fact and conclusions of law." It was further ordered in each case that "the Master shall commence the trial of this cause" on a certain date and continue with diligence, and that the parties supply security for costs.

While the parties had deposited some $8,000 costs, the record discloses that all parties objected to the references and filed motions to vacate them. Upon petitioner's refusal to vacate the references, these mandamus actions were filed in the Court of Appeals seeking the issuance of writs ordering petitioner to do so. These applications were grounded on 28 U.S.C. § 1651 (the All Writs Act). In his answer to the show cause orders issued by the Court of Appeals, petitioner amplified the reasons for the references, stating "that the cases were very complicated and complex, that they would take considerable time to try," and that his "calendar was congested." Declaring that the references amounted to "a refusal on his (petitioner's) part, as a judge, to try the causes in due course," the Court of Appeals concluded that "in view of the extraordinary nature of these causes" the references must be vacated "if we find that the orders were beyond the court's power under the pertinent rule." And, it being so found, the writs issued under the authority of the All Writs Act. It is not disputed that the same principles and considerations as to the propriety of the issuance of the writs apply equally to the two cases.

The Power of the Courts of Appeals.—Petitioner contends that the power of the Courts of Appeals does not extend to the issuance of writs of mandamus to review interlocutory orders except in those cases where the review of the case on appeal after final judgment would be frustrated. Asserting that the orders of reference were in exercise of his jurisdiction under Rule 53(b), petitioner urges that such action can be reviewed only on appeal and not by writ of mandamus, since by congressional enactment appellate review of a District Court's orders may be had only after a final judgment. The question of naked power has long been settled by this Court. . . . Mr. Chief Justice Stone reviewed the decisions and, in considering the power of Courts of Appeals to issue writs of mandamus, the Court held that "the common-law writs, like equitable remedies, may be granted or withheld in the sound discretion of the court." The re-codification of the All Writs Act in 1948 did not affect the power of the Courts of Appeals to issue writs of mandamus in aid of jurisdiction. Since the Court of Appeals could at some stage of the antitrust proceedings entertain appeals in these cases, it has power in proper circumstances, as here, to issue writs of mandamus reaching them. This is not to say that the conclusion we reach on the facts of this case is intended, or can be used, to authorize the indiscriminate use of prerogative writs as a means of reviewing interlocutory orders. We pass on, then, to the only real question involved, i.e., whether the exercise of the power by the Court of Appeals was proper in the cases now before us.

The Discretionary Use of the Writs.—It appears from the docket entries to which we heretofore referred that the petitioner was well informed as to the nature of the antitrust litigation, the pleadings of the parties, and the gist of the plaintiffs' claims. He was well aware of the theory of the defense and much of the proof which necessarily was outlined in the various requests for discovery, admissions, interrogatories, and depositions. He heard arguments on motions to dismiss, to compel testimony on depositions, and for summary judgment. In fact, petitioner's knowledge of the cases at the time of the references, together with his long experience in the antitrust field, points to the conclusion that he could dispose of the litigation with greater dispatch and less effort than anyone else. Nevertheless, he referred both suits to a master on the general issue. Furthermore, neither the existence of the alleged conspiracy nor the question of liability *vel non* had been determined in either case. These issues, as well as the damages, if any, and the question concerning the issuance of an injunction, were likewise included in the references. Under all of the circumstances, we believe the Court of Appeals was justified in finding the orders of reference were an abuse of the petitioner's power under Rule 53(b). They amounted to little less than an abdication of the judicial function depriving the parties of a trial before the court on the basic issues involved in the litigation.

The use of masters is "to aid judges in the performance of specific judicial duties, as they may arise in the progress of a cause," and not to displace the court. The exceptional circumstances here warrant the use of the extraordinary remedy of mandamus. As this Court pointed out: " * * * (W)here the subject concerns the enforcement of the * * * (r)ules which by law it is the duty of this court to formulate and put in force, mandamus should issue to prevent such action thereunder so palpably improper as to place it beyond the scope of the rule invoked." As was said, were the Court " * * * to find that the rules have been practically nullified by a District Judge * * * it would not hesitate to restrain (him) * * *." . . .

* * * It is also contended that the Seventh Circuit has erroneously construed the All Writs Act as "conferring on it a 'roving commission' to supervise interlocutory orders of the District Courts in advance of final decision." Our examination of its opinions in this regard leads us to the conclusion that the Court of Appeals has exercised commendable self-restraint. It is true that mandamus should be resorted to only in extreme cases, since it places trial judges in the anomalous position of being litigants without counsel other than uncompensated volunteers. However, there is an end of patience and it clearly appears that the Court of Appeals has for years admonished the trial judges of the Seventh Circuit that the practice of making references "does not commend itself" and " * * * should seldom be made, and if at all only when unusual circumstances exist." Again, in 1942, it pointed out that the words "exception" and "exceptional" as used in the reference rule are not elastic terms with the trial court the sole judge of their elasticity. "Litigants are entitled to a

trial by the court, in every suit, save where exceptional circumstances are shown." Still the Court of Appeals did not disturb the reference practice by reversal or mandamus until this case was decided in October 1955. Again, Chief Judge ... called attention to the fact that the practice of referring cases to masters was " * * * all too common in the Northern District of Illinois * * *."

The record does not show to what extent references are made by the full bench of the District Court in the Northern District; however, it does reveal that petitioner has referred 11 cases to masters in the past 6 years. But even "a little cloud may bring a flood's downpour" if we approve the practice here indulged, particularly in the face of presently congested dockets, increased filings, and more extended trials. This is not to say that we are neither aware of nor fully appreciative of the unfortunate congestion of the court calendar in many of our District Courts. The use of procedural devices in the heavily congested districts has proven to be most helpful in reducing docket congestion. Illustrative of such techniques are provision for an assignment commissioner to handle the assignment of all cases; the assignment of judges to handle only motions, pleas, and pretrial proceedings; and separate calendars for civil and criminal trials in cases that have reached issue. We enumerate these merely as an example of the progress made in judicial administration through the use of enlightened procedural techniques. It goes without saying that they can be used effectively only where adaptable to the specific problems of a district.

But, be that as it may, congestion in itself is not such an exceptional circumstance as to warrant a reference to a master. If such were the test, present congestion would make references the rule rather than the exception. Petitioner realizes this, for in addition to calendar congestion he alleges that the cases referred had unusual complexity of issues of both fact and law. But most litigation in the antitrust field is complex. It does not follow that antitrust litigants are not entitled to a trial before a court. On the contrary, we believe that this is an impelling reason for trial before a regular, experienced trial judge rather than before a temporary substitute appointed on an ad hoc basis and ordinarily not experienced in judicial work. Nor does petitioner's claim of the great length of time these trials will require offer exceptional grounds. The final ground asserted by petitioner was with reference to the voluminous accounting which would be necessary in the event the plaintiffs prevailed. We agree that the detailed accounting required in order to determine the damages suffered by each plaintiff might be referred to a master after the court has determined the over-all liability of defendants, provided the circumstances indicate that the use of the court's time is not warranted in receiving the proof and making the tabulation.

We believe that supervisory control of the District Courts by the Courts of Appeals is necessary to proper judicial administration in the federal system. The All Writs Act confers on the Courts of Appeals the discretionary power to issue writs of mandamus in the exceptional circumstances existing here. Its judgment is therefore affirmed.

Affirmed.

Mr. Justice Brennan, with whom Mr. Justice Frankfurter, Mr. Justice Burton and Mr. Justice Harlan join, dissenting.

The issue here is not whether Judge La Buy's order was reviewable by the Court of Appeals. The sole question is whether review should have awaited final decision in the cause or whether the order was reviewable before final decision by way of a petition under the All Writs Act for the issuance of a writ of mandamus addressed to it. I do not agree that the writ directing Judge La Buy to vacate the order of reference was within the bounds of the discretionary power of the Court of Appeals to issue an extraordinary writ under the All Writs Act. Only last Term, in *Parr v. United States*, this Court restated those bounds:

> The power to issue them is discretionary and it is sparingly exercised. * * * This is not a case where a court has exceeded or refused to exercise its jurisdiction, nor one where appellate review will be defeated if a writ does not issue. Here the most that could be claimed is that the district courts have erred in ruling on matters within their jurisdiction. The extraordinary writs do not reach to such cases; they may not be used to thwart the congressional policy against piecemeal appeals.

The action of the Court of Appeals for the Seventh Circuit here under review is outside these limitations. The case before the Court of Appeals was "not a case where a court has exceeded or refused to exercise its jurisdiction * * *." Rule 53(b) of the Federal Rules of Civil Procedure vested Judge La Buy with discretionary power to make a reference if he found, and he did, that "some exceptional condition" required the reference. Here also "the most that could be claimed is that the district (court) * * * erred in ruling on matters within (its) jurisdiction." If Judge La Buy erred in finding that there was an "exceptional condition" requiring the reference or did not give proper weight to the caveat of the Rule that a "reference to a master shall be the exception and not the rule," that was mere error "in ruling on matters within (the District Court's) jurisdiction." Such mere error does not bring into play the power of the Court of Appeals to issue an extraordinary writ. Nor did Judge La Buy's order of reference present the Court of Appeals with a case "where appellate review will be defeated if a writ does not issue." The litigants may suffer added expense and possible delay in obtaining a decision as a consequence of the reference, but Roche settles that "that inconvenience is one which we must take if Congress contemplated in providing that only final judgments should be reviewable."

But, regrettable as is this Court's approval of what I consider to be a clear departure by the Court of Appeals from the settled principles governing the issuance of the extraordinary writs, what this Court says in reaching its result is reason for particularly grave concern. I think this Court has today seriously undermined the long-standing statutory policy against piecemeal appeals. My brethren say: "Since the Court of Appeals could at some stage of the antitrust proceedings entertain appeals in these cases, it has power in proper circumstances, as here, to issue writs of mandamus reaching them. * * * This is not to say that the conclusion we reach on the facts of this case is intended, or can be used, to authorize the indiscriminate use of prerogative writs as a means of reviewing interlocutory orders." I understand this to mean that proper circumstances are present for the issuance of a writ in this case because, if the litigants are not now heard, the Court of Appeals will not have an opportunity to relieve them of the burden of the added expense and delay of decision alleged to be the consequence of the reference. But that bridge was crossed by this Court in *Roche* and *Alkali*, where this very argument was rejected: "Here the inconvenience to the litigants results alone from the circumstance that Congress has provided for review of the district court's order only on review of the final judgment, and not from an abuse of judicial power, or refusal to exercise it, which it is the function of mandamus to correct."

What this Court is saying, therefore, is that the All Writs Act confers an independent appellate power in the Courts of Appeals to review interlocutory orders. I have always understood the law to be precisely to the contrary. The power granted to the Courts of Appeals by the All Writs Act is not an appellate power but merely an auxiliary power in aid of and to protect the appellate jurisdiction conferred by other provisions of law, e.g., the power to review final decisions granted by 28 U.S.C. § 1291 and to review specified exceptional classes of interlocutory orders granted by 28 U.S.C. § 1292. This holding that an independent appellate power is given by the All Writs Act not only discards the constraints upon the scope of the power to issue extraordinary writs restated in Parr, but, by the very fact of doing so, opens wide the crack in the door which, since the Judiciary Act of 1789, has shut out from intermediate appellate review all interlocutory actions of the District Courts not within the few exceptional classes now specified by the Congress in § 1292.

The power of the Courts of Appeals to issue extraordinary writs stems from § 14 of the Judiciary Act of 1789. Chief Judge Magruder provides us with an invaluable history of this power and of the judicial development of its scope. He demonstrates most persuasively that "(t)he all writs section does not confer an independent appellate power; the power is strictly of an auxiliary nature, in aid of a jurisdiction granted in some other provision of law . . . ."

The focal question posed for a Court of Appeals by a petition for the issuance of a writ is whether the action of the District Court tends to frustrate or impede the ultimate exercise by the Court of Appeals of its appellate jurisdiction granted in some other provision of the law. The answer is clearly in the affirmative where, for example, the order of the District Court transfers a cause to a District Court of another circuit for decision.

* * * The view now taken by this Court that the All Writs Act confers an independent appellate power, although not so broad as "to authorize the indiscriminate use of prerogative writs as a means of reviewing interlocutory orders," in effect engrafts upon federal appellate procedure a standard of interlocutory review never embraced by the Congress throughout our history, although it is written into the English Judicature Act and is followed in varying degrees in some of the States. That standard allows interlocutory appeals by leave of the appellate court. It is a compromise between conflicting viewpoints as to the extent that interlocutory appeals should be allowed. The federal policy of limited interlocutory review stresses the inconvenience and expense of piecemeal reviews and the strong public interest in favor of a single and complete trial with a single and complete review. The other view, of which the New York practice of allowing interlocutory review as of right from most orders is the extreme example, perceives danger of possible injustice in individual cases from the denial of any appellate review until after judgment at the trial.

The polestar of federal appellate procedure has always been "finality," meaning that appellate review of most interlocutory actions must await final determination of the cause at the trial level. "Finality as a condition of review is an historic characteristic of federal appellate procedure. It was written into the first Judiciary Act and has been departed from only when observance of it would practically defeat the right to any review at all." The Court's action today shatters that statutory policy. I protest, not only because we invade a domain reserved by the Constitution exclusively to the Congress, but as well because the encouragement to interlocutory appeals offered by this decision must necessarily aggravate further the already bad condition of calendar congestion in some of our District Courts and also add to the burden of work of some of our busiest Courts of Appeals. More petitions for interlocutory review, requiring the attention of the Courts of Appeals, add, of course, to the burden of work of those courts. Meanwhile final decision of the cases concerned is delayed while the District Courts mark time awaiting action upon the petitioners. Rarely does determination upon interlocutory review terminate the litigation. Moreover, the District Court calendars become longer with the addition of new cases before older ones are decided. This, then, interposes one more obstacle to the strong effort being made to better justice through improved judicial administration.

The power of the Court of Appeals to correct any error in Judge La Buy's reference is found exclusively in the power to review final decisions under § 1291. The Court of Appeals erred by assuming a nonexistent power under the All Writs Act to review this interlocutory order in advance of final decision. Insofar as the Court approves this error, I must respectfully dissent.

* * *

IV. RES JUDICATA AND PRECLUSION DOCTRINE

A. RES JUDICATA AND THE FINALITY OF JUDGMENTS

CROMWELL v. COUNTY OF SAC

94 U.S. 351 (1876)

MR. JUSTICE FIELD delivered the opinion of the court.

This was an action on four bonds of the county of Sac, in the State of Iowa, each for $1,000, and four coupons for interest, attached to them, each for $100. The bonds were issued in 1860, and were made payable to bearer, in the city of New York, in the years 1868, 1869, 1870, and 1871, respectively, with annual interest at the rate of ten per cent a year.

To defeat this action, the defendant relied upon the estoppel of a judgment rendered in favor of the county in a prior action brought by one Samuel C. Smith upon certain earlier maturing coupons on the same bonds, accompanied with proof that the plaintiff Cromwell was at the time the owner of the coupons in that action, and that the action was prosecuted for his sole use and benefit.

The questions presented for our determination relate to the operation of this judgment as an estoppel against the prosecution of the present action, and the admissibility of the evidence to connect the present plaintiff with the former action as a real party in interest.

In considering the operation of this judgment, it should be borne in mind, as stated by counsel, that there is a difference between the effect of a judgment as a bar or estoppel against the prosecution of a second action upon the same claim or demand, and its effect as an estoppel in another action between the same parties upon a different claim or cause of action. In the former case, the judgment, if rendered upon the merits, constitutes an absolute bar to a subsequent action. It is a finality as to the claim or demand in controversy, concluding parties and those in privity with them, not only as to every matter which was offered and received to sustain or defeat the claim or demand, but as to any other admissible matter which might have been offered for that purpose. Thus, for example, a judgment rendered upon a promissory note is conclusive as to the validity of the instrument and the amount due upon it, although it be subsequently alleged that perfect defences actually existed, of which no proof was offered, such as forgery, want of consideration, or payment. If such defences were not presented in the action, and established by competent evidence, the subsequent allegation of their existence is of no legal consequence. The judgment is as conclusive, so far as future proceedings at law are concerned, as though the defences never existed. The language, therefore, which is so often used, that a judgment estops not only as to every ground of recovery or defence actually presented in the action, but also as to every ground which might have been presented, is strictly accurate, when applied to the demand or claim in controversy. Such demand or claim, having passed into judgment, cannot again be brought into litigation between the parties in proceedings at law upon any ground whatever.

But where the second action between the same parties is upon a different claim or demand, the judgment in the prior action operates as an estoppel only as to those matters in issue or points controverted, upon the determination of which the finding or verdict was rendered. In all cases, therefore, where it is sought to apply the estoppel of a judgment rendered upon one cause of action to matters arising in a suit upon a different cause of action, the inquiry must always be as to the point or question actually litigated and determined in the original action, not what might have been thus litigated and determined. Only upon such matters is the judgment conclusive in another action.

The difference in the operation of a judgment in the two classes of cases mentioned is seen through all the leading adjudications upon the doctrine of estoppel. Thus, in the case of *Outram* v. *Morewood*, the defendants were held estopped from averring title to a mine, in an action of trespass for digging out coal from it, because, in a previous action for a similar trespass, they had set up the same title, and it had been determined against them. In commenting upon a decision cited in that case, Lord Ellenborough, in his elaborate opinion, said: "It is not the recovery, but the matter alleged by the party, and upon which the recovery proceeds, which creates the estoppel. The recovery of itself in an action of trespass is only a bar to the future recovery of damages for the same injury; but the estoppel precludes parties and privies from contending to the contrary of that point or matter of fact, which, having been once distinctly put in issue by them, or by those to whom they are privy in estate or law, has been, on such issue joined, solemnly found against them." And in the case of *Gardner* v. *Buckbee*, it was held by the Supreme Court of New York that a verdict and judgment in the Marine Court of the city of New York, upon one of two notes given upon a sale of a vessel, that the sale was fraudulent, the vessel being at the time unseaworthy, were conclusive upon the question of the character of the sale in an action upon the other note between the same parties in the Court of Common Pleas. The rule laid down in the celebrated opinion in the case of the *Duchess of Kingston* was cited, and followed: "That the judgment of a court of concurrent jurisdiction directly upon the point is as a plea a bar, or as evidence conclusive between the same parties upon the same matter directly in question in another court."

These cases, usually cited in support of the doctrine that the determination of a question directly involved in one action is conclusive as to that question in a second suit between the same parties upon a different cause of action, negative the proposition that the estoppel can extend beyond the point actually litigated and determined. The argument in these cases, that a particular point was necessarily involved in the finding in the original action, proceeded upon the theory that, if not thus involved, the judgment would be inoperative as an estoppel. In the case of *Miles* v. *Caldwell*, a judgment in ejectment in Missouri, where actions of that kind stand, with respect to the operation of a recovery therein, as a bar or estoppel, in the same position as other actions, was held by this court conclusive, in a subsequent suit in equity between the parties respecting the title, upon the question of the satisfaction of the mortgage under which the plaintiff claimed title to the premises in the ejectment, and the question as to the fraudulent character of the mortgage under which the defendant claimed, because these questions had been submitted to the jury in that action, and had been passed upon by them. The court held, after full consideration, that in cases of tort, equally as in those arising upon contract, where the form of the issue was so vague as not to show the questions of fact submitted to the jury, it was competent to prove by parol testimony what question or questions of fact were thus submitted and necessarily passed upon by them; and by inevitable implication also held that, in the absence of proof in such cases, the verdict and judgment were inconclusive, except as to the particular trespass alleged, whatever possible questions might have been raised and determined.

But it is not necessary to take this doctrine as a matter of inference from these cases. The precise point has been adjudged in numerous instances. It was so adjudged by this court in the case of *The Washington, Alexandria, & Georgetown Steam Packet Co.* v. *Sickles*. In that case, an action was brought upon a special parol contract for the use of Sickles's cut-off for saving fuel in the working of steam-engines, by which the plaintiffs, who had a patent for the cut-off, were to attach one of their machines to the engine of the defendants' boat, and were to receive for its use three-fourths of the saving of fuel thus produced, the payments to be made from time to time when demanded. To ascertain the saving of fuel an experiment was to be made in a specified manner, and the result taken as the rate of saving during the continuance of the contract. The plaintiffs in their declaration averred that the experiment had been made, at the rate of saving ascertained, and that the cut-off had been used on the boat until the commencement of the suit. In a prior action against the same defendant for an installment due, where the declaration set forth the same contract in two counts, the first of which was similar to the counts in the second action, and also the common counts, the plaintiffs had obtained verdict and judgment; and it was insisted that the defendant was estopped by the verdict and judgment produced from proving that there was no such contract as that declared upon, or that no saving of fuel had been obtained, or that the experiment was not made pursuant to the contract, or that the verdict was rendered upon all the issues, and not upon the first count specially. The Circuit Court assented to these views, and excluded the testimony offered by the defendants to prove those facts. But this court reversed the decision, and held that the defendants were not thus estopped.

"The record produced by the plaintiffs," said the court, "showed that the first suit was brought apparently upon the same contract as the second, and that the existence and validity of that contract might have been litigated. But the verdict might have been rendered upon the entire declaration, and without special reference to the first count. It was competent to the defendants to show the state of facts that existed at the trial, with a view to ascertain what was the matter decided upon by the verdict of the jury. It may have been that there was no contest in reference to the fairness of the experiment, or to its sufficiency to ascertain the premium to be paid for the use of the machine at the first trial, or it may have been that the plaintiffs abandoned their special counts and recovered their verdict upon the general counts. The judgment rendered in that suit, while it remains in force, and for the purpose of maintaining its validity, is conclusive of all the facts properly pleaded by the plaintiffs; but when it is presented as testimony in another suit, the inquiry is competent whether the same issue has been tried and settled by it.''

It is not believed that there are any cases going to the extent that because in the prior action a different question from that actually determined might have arisen and been litigated, therefore such possible question is to be considered as excluded from consideration in a second action between the same parties on a different demand, although loose remarks looking in that direction may be found in some opinions. On principle, a point not in litigation in one action cannot be received as conclusively settled in any subsequent action upon a different cause, because it might have been determined in the first action.

Various considerations, other than the actual merits, may govern a party in bringing forward grounds of recovery or defence in one action, which may not exist in another action upon a different demand, such as the smallness of the amount or the value of the property in controversy, the difficulty of obtaining the necessary evidence, the expense of the litigation, and his own situation at the time. A party acting upon considerations like these ought not to be precluded from contesting in a subsequent action other demands arising out of the same transaction. A judgment by default only admits for the purpose of the action the legality of the demand or claim in suit: it does not make the allegations of the declaration or complaint evidence in an action upon a different claim. The declaration may contain different statements of the cause of action in different counts. It could hardly be pretended that a judgment by default in such a case would make the several statements evidence in any other proceeding.

The case of *Howlett* v. *Tarte* supports this view. That was an action for rent, under a building agreement. The defendant pleaded a subsequent agreement, changing the tenancy into one from year to year, and its determination by notice to quit before the time for which the rent sued for was alleged to have accrued. The plaintiff replied that he had recovered a judgment in a former action against the defendant for rent under the same agreement, which had accrued after the alleged determination of the tenancy, in which action the defendant did not set up the defence pleaded in the second action. On demurrer, the replication, after full argument, was held bad. In deciding the case, Mr. Justice Willes said: "It is quite right that a defendant should be estopped from setting up in the same action a defence which he might have pleaded, but has chosen to let the proper time go by. But nobody ever heard of a defendant being precluded from setting up a defence in a second action because he did not avail himself of the opportunity of setting it up in the first action. . . . I think we should do wrong to favor the introduction of this new device into the law." Mr. Justice Byles said: "It is plain that there is no authority for saying that the defendant is precluded from setting up this defence." Mr. Justice Keating said: "This is an attempt on the part of the plaintiff to extend the doctrine of estoppel far beyond what any of the authorities warrant."

The language of the Vice–Chancellor, in the case of *Henderson* v. *Henderson* is sometimes cited as expressing a different opinion; but, upon examining the facts of that case, it will appear that the language used in no respect conflicts with the doctrine we have stated. In that case, a bill had been filed in the Supreme Court of Newfoundland, by the next of kin of an intestate, against A. and others, for an account of an estate and of certain partnership transactions. A decree was rendered against A., upon which the next of kin brought actions in England. A. then filed a bill there against the next of kin and personal representative of the intestate, stating that the intestate's estate was indebted to him, and alleging various errors and irregularities in the proceedings in the Supreme Court of the island, and praying that the estate of the intestate might be administered, the partnership accounts taken, and the amount of the debt due to him ascertained and paid. A demurrer to the bill was allowed for want of equity, on the ground that the whole of the matters were in question between the parties, and might properly have been the subject of adjudication in the suit before that court. It was with reference to the necessity of having the subject of particular litigation, as a whole, at once before the court, and not by piecemeal, that the Vice–Chancellor said:

> In trying this question, I believe I state the rule of court correctly, that when a given matter becomes the subject of litigation in and of adjudication by a court of competent jurisdiction, the court requires the parties to bring forward their whole case, and will not, except under special circumstances, permit the same parties to open the same subject of litigation in respect of matter which might have been brought forward as part of the subject in controversy, but which was not brought forward, only because they have, from negligence, inadvertence, or even accident, omitted part of the case. The plea of *res adjudicata* applies, except in special cases, not only to the points upon which the court was required by the parties to form an opinion, and pronounce a judgment, but to every point which properly belonged to the subject of litigation, and which the parties, exercising reasonable diligence, might have brought forward at the time.

There is nothing in this language, applied to the facts of the case, which gives support to the doctrine that, whenever in one action a party might have brought forward a particular ground of recovery or defence, and neglected to do so, he is, in a subsequent suit between the same parties upon a different cause of action, precluded from availing himself of such ground.

If, now, we consider the main question presented for our determination by the light of the views thus expressed and the authorities cited, its solution will not be difficult. It appears from the findings in the original action of Smith, that the county of Sac, by a vote of its people, authorized the issue of bonds to the amount of $10,000, for the erection of a courthouse; that bonds to that amount were issued by the county judge, and delivered to one Meserey, with whom he had made a contract for the erection of the court-house; that immediately upon receipt of the bonds the contractor gave one of them as a gratuity to the county judge; and that the court-house was never constructed by the contractor, or by any other person pursuant to the contract. It also appears that the plaintiff had become, before their maturity, the holder of twenty-five coupons, which had been attached to the bonds; but there was no finding that he had ever given any value for them. The court below held, upon these findings, that the bonds were void as against the county, and gave judgment accordingly. The case coming here on writ of error, this court held that the facts disclosed by the findings were sufficient evidence of fraud and illegality in the inception of the bonds to call upon the holder to show that he had given value for the coupons; and, not having done so, the judgment was affirmed. Reading the record of the lower court by the opinion and judgment of this court, it must be considered that the matters adjudged in that case were these: that the bonds were void as against the county in the hands of parties who did not acquire them before maturity and give value for them, and that the plaintiff, not having proved that he gave such value, was not entitled to recover upon the coupons. Whatever illegality or fraud there was in the issue and delivery to the contractor of the bonds affected equally the coupons for interest attached to them. The finding and judgment upon the invalidity of the bonds, as against the county, must be held to estop the plaintiff here from averring to the contrary. But as the bonds were negotiable instruments, and their issue was authorized by a vote of the county, and they recite on their face a compliance with the law providing for their issue, they would be held as valid obligations against the county in the hands of *a bona fide* holder taking them for value before maturity, according to repeated decisions of this court upon the character of such obligations. If, therefore, the plaintiff received the bond and coupons in suit before maturity for value, as he offered to prove, he should have been permitted to show that fact. There was nothing adjudged in the former action in the finding that the plaintiff had not made such proof in that case which can preclude the present plaintiff from making such proof here. The fact that a party may not have shown that he gave value for one bond or coupon is not even presumptive, much less conclusive, evidence that he may not have given value for another and different bond or coupon. The exclusion of the evidence offered by the plaintiff was erroneous, and for the ruling of the court in that respect the judgment must be reversed and a new trial had.

Judgment reversed, and cause remanded for a new trial.

MR. JUSTICE CLIFFORD dissenting.

* * * Suffice it to remark, in this connection, that these views were urged against the former judgment; but they did not prevail, and the judgment was rendered for the defendant, which is un-reversed and in full force. Suit is now brought upon the bonds to which those coupons were attached, and the sole question of any importance is whether the judgment in the former case is a bar to the present suit.

Nothing can be more certain in legal decision than the proposition that the title to the bonds and coupons are the same, as the coupons were annexed to the bonds when the bonds were executed and delivered to the original holder, in pursuance of the contract for building the court-house; and it is equally certain, that if it could be proved in defence that the consideration was illegal, or that the instruments were fraudulent in their inception, or that they had been lost or stolen before they were negotiated to the holder, the defence would apply to the bonds as well as the coupons.

Before proceeding to examine the legal question, it should be remarked that the former suit was prosecuted in the name of a different plaintiff; but the theory of the present defendants is that the present plaintiff was the real owner of the coupons in that action, and that the action was prosecuted for his sole use and benefit. Testimony to prove that theory was offered in the court below, and the majority of the court now hold that evidence to prove that proposition was properly admitted. Assume that to be so, and it follows that the parties, in legal contemplation, are the same; nor can it be denied that the cause of action, within the meaning of that requirement, as expounded and defined by decided cases of the highest authority, is the same as that in the former action, the rule being that the legal effect of the former judgment as a bar is not impaired, because the subject-matter of the second suit is different, provided the second suit involves the same title and depends upon the same question.

Holders of negotiable securities, as well as every other plaintiff litigant, are entitled to a full trial upon the merits of the cause of action; but if in such a trial judgment be rendered for the defendant, whether it be upon the verdict of a jury or upon a demurrer to a sufficient declaration, or to a material pleading involving the whole merits, the plaintiff can never after maintain against the same defendant or his privies any similar or concurrent action for the same cause, upon the same grounds as those disclosed in the first declaration, for the reason that the judgment, under such circumstances, determines the merits of the controversy, and a final judgment deciding the right must put an end to the dispute, else the litigation would be endless.

Allegations of an essential character may be omitted in the first declaration and be supplied in the second, in which event the judgment on demurrer in the first suit is not a bar to the second, for the reason that the merits of the cause as disclosed in the second declaration were not heard and decided in the first action.

Where the parties and the cause of action are the same, the *prima facie* presumption is that the questions presented for decision were the same, unless it appears that the merits of the controversy were not involved in the issue, the rule in such a case being that where every objection urged in the second suit was open to the party within the legitimate scope of the pleadings in the first suit, and that the whole defence might have been presented in that trial, the matter must be considered as having passed *in rem judicatam*, and the former judgment in such a case is conclusive between the parties.

Except in special cases, the plea of *res judicata* applies not only to points upon which the court was actually required to form an opinion and pronounce judgment, but to every point which properly belonged to the subject of the issue, and which the parties, exercising reasonable diligence, might have brought forward at the time.

Other text-writers of high authority substantially concur in that view; as, for example, Mr. Greenleaf says that "the rule should apply only to that which was directly in issue, and not to every thing which was incidentally brought into controversy during the trial;" and the reason given for that limitation is worthy of notice, which is, that the evidence must correspond with the allegations, and be confined to the point in issue; and he remarks that it is only to the material allegations of one party that the other can be called to answer, for to such alone can testimony be regularly adduced, and upon such an issue only is judgment to be rendered. Pursuant to those suggestions, he states his conclusion as follows: "A record, therefore, is not held conclusive as to the truth of any allegations which were not material nor traversable, but as to things material and traversable it is conclusive and final."

Unless the court, in rendering the former judgment, was called upon to determine the merits, the judgment is never a complete bar; and it is safe to add, that, if the trial went off on a technical defect, or because the debt was not yet due, or because the court had not jurisdiction, or because of a temporary disability of the plaintiff or the like, the judgment will be no bar to a future action.

[T]he general principle has always been conceded, that, when one is barred in any action, real or personal, by judgment or demurrer, confession or verdict, he is barred as to that or a similar action of the like nature for the same thing for ever. Demurrer for want of equity in such a case is allowed in chancery, because the whole matter in controversy is open in the first suit.

Contrary to that rule, a party brought a second bill of complaint, and the Vice–Chancellor, in disposing of the case, expressed himself as follows:—

Where a given matter becomes the subject of litigation in and of adjudication by a court of competent jurisdiction, the court requires the parties to bring forward their whole case, and will not, except under special circumstances, permit the same parties to open the same subject of litigation in respect of matter which might have been brought forward as part of the subject in contest, but which was not brought forward, only because the party has, from negligence, omitted part of his case.

And he added that the plea of *res judicata* applies, except in special cases, not only to points upon which the court was actually required by the parties to form an opinion and pronounce a judgment, but to every point which properly belonged to the subject of litigation, and which the parties, exercising reasonable diligence, might have brought forward at the time.

When a fact has been once determined in the course of a judicial proceeding, say the Supreme Court of Massachusetts, and final judgment has been rendered in accordance therewith, it cannot be again litigated between the same parties without virtually impeaching the correctness of the former decision, which, from motives of public policy, the law does not permit to be done; and they proceed to say that the estoppel is not confined to the judgment, but extends to all facts involved in it, as necessary steps, or the groundwork upon which it must have been founded.

Extended explanations upon the subject of estoppel by a prior judgment were made by this court nearly twenty years ago, by a judge very competent to perform that duty. Such a judgment, he said, in order that it may operate as an estoppel, must have been made by a court of competent jurisdiction upon the same subject matter between the same parties for the same purpose. He then proceeded to describe the cause of action in that case, which, as he stated, was a sum of money, being a part of the consideration or price for the use of a valuable machine for which the plaintiffs had a patent; that the sum demanded was the complement of a whole, of which the sum demanded in the declaration in the former suit is the other part. Both declarations contained similar special counts; and the court remarked, that a decision in the one suit on those counts in favor of the plaintiffs necessarily included and virtually determined the sufficiency of the declaration to sustain the title of the plaintiffs, and showed that the record was admissible in evidence.

Different views were entertained by the defendants, and they submitted the proposition that a judgment was not admissible in evidence as an estoppel, unless the record showed that the very point it is sought to estop was distinctly presented by an issue, and that it was expressly found by the jury; but the court remarked, that such a rule would be impracticable, as it would restrict the operation of *res judicata* within too narrow bounds, and the court decided that it was not necessary as between parties and privies that the record should show that matter of the estoppel was directly in issue, "but only that the said matter in controversy might have been litigated, and that extrinsic evidence would be admitted to prove that the particular question was material and was in fact contested, and that it was referred to the decision of the jury."

Attempt was made in that case to maintain the proposition that the judgment in the first suit could not be held to be an estoppel, unless it was shown by the record that the very point in controversy was distinctly presented by an issue, and that it was explicitly found by the jury; but the court held otherwise, and expressly overruled the proposition, although the defence of estoppel failed for other reasons.

Two notes, in another case, were given by the purchaser of a vessel to the vendor of the same, and payment of the first note being refused, the payee sued the maker; and the maker, at the trial, set up as a defence that the vessel was rotten and unseaworthy at the time of sale, and that those facts were known to the plaintiff. They went to trial, and the verdict and judgment were for the defendant. Subsequently the plaintiff sued the other note, and the defendant set up the judgment in the other case as a bar to the suit; and the Supreme Court of New York sustained the defence, holding that the former judgment, whether pleaded as an estoppel or given in evidence under the general issue, was conclusive that the sale was fraudulent, and that the plaintiff could not recover in the second action.

Certain sums of money, in a later case, were paid by a surety on two bonds given by an importer, in which the plaintiff and defendant were sureties. They were jointly liable; but the plaintiff paid the whole amount, and brought suit against the other surety for contribution. Service was made; and the defendant appeared and set up the defence that he had been released, with the consent of the plaintiff, before the payment was made; and the court sustained the defence upon demurrer, and gave judgment for the defendant.

Moneys were also paid by the same surety to discharge the liability under the second bond. Contribution being refused, the plaintiff brought a second suit, and the defendant set up the former judgment as a bar; and the court sustained the defence, it appearing that both bonds were given at the same time upon the same consideration, and as part of one and the same transaction.

Neither of the second suits in the two preceding cases were for the same cause of action as the first, but the defence was sustained because the suit was founded upon the same title.

Cases of that kind are quite numerous, and they show to a demonstration that a judgment may be a bar if the same title is involved, even though the cause of action may be founded on a different instrument, or for a different trespass upon the same premises.

In order to make a judgment conclusive, it is not necessary, said Mr. Justice Bigelow, that the cause of action should be the same in the first suit as that in which the judgment is pleaded or given in evidence, but it is essential that the issue should be the same. The judgment is then coextensive with the issue on which it is founded, and is conclusive only so far as the same fact or title is again in dispute.

Decided cases in that State to the same effect are numerous, the highest court of the State holding that it is well settled that a judgment in a former suit between the same parties is a bar to a subsequent action only when the point or question in issue is the same in both; that the judgment is conclusive in relation to all matters in the suit which were put in issue, but has no effect upon questions not involved in the issue, and which were neither open to inquiry nor the subjects of litigation.

Beyond question, the bar is not defeated because the subject matter of the second suit is different from the first, if it be founded on the same title; and the Supreme Court of Pennsylvania have held, in accordance with that view, that a judgment in trespass upon a traverse of *liberum tenementum* estops the party against whom it has been rendered, and his privies, from afterward controverting the title to the same freehold in a subsequent action of trespass.

Tested by these several considerations, it is clear that a former judgment is a bar in all cases where the matters put in issue in the first suit were the same as the matters in issue in the second suit. "It results from these authorities that an adjudication by a competent tribunal is conclusive, not only in the proceeding in which it is pronounced, but in every other where the right or title is the same, although the cause of action may be different."

Grant that, and still it is suggested that the plaintiff in the suit on the coupons did not introduce evidence to prove that he paid value for the bonds with the coupons; but the answer to that is, that he might have done so. He alleged in the declaration that he paid value, and consequently he might have given evidence to prove it, which shows that the question was directly involved in the issue between the parties.

Doubtless the plaintiff neglected to give evidence in that behalf, for the reason that he and his counsel were of the opinion that the evidence introduced by the defendants was not sufficient to repel the *prima facie* presumption, arising from his possession of the instruments, that he paid value for the transfer, and I am still of that opinion; but the remedy of the plaintiff, if surprised, was to except to the ruling, or to submit a motion for new trial.

Suggestions of that sort are now too late, nor are they sufficient to modify the effect of the judgment. When once finally rendered, the judgment must be considered conclusive, else litigation will be endless. Litigants sometimes prefer not to bring forward their whole case or defence, in order to enjoy the opportunity to bring up a reserve in case of defeat in the first contest; but a rule which would sanction that practice would be against public policy, as it would enable a party to protract the litigation as long as he could find means or credit to compel the attendance of witnesses and to secure the services of counsel.

* * *

RUSSELL v. PLACE

94 U.S. 606 (1876)

MR. JUSTICE FIELD delivered the opinion of the court.

This is a suit for an infringement of a patent to the complainant for an alleged new and useful improvement in the preparation of leather, and is similar in its general features to the suit of the complainant against Dodge. It is submitted upon substantially the same testimony, and presents, with one exception, the same questions for determination. That exception relates to the operation, as an estoppel against setting up the defences here made, of a judgment recovered by the complainant against the defendants in an action at law for the infringement of the patent.

The bill of complaint sets forth the invention claimed, the issue of a patent for the same, its surrender for alleged defective and insufficient description of the invention, its reissue with an amended specification, and the recovery of judgment against the defendants for damages in an action at law for a violation of the exclusive privileges secured by the patent.

The bill then alleges the subsequent manufacture, use, and sale by the defendants, without the license of the patentee, of the alleged invention and improvement, and prays that they may be decreed to account for the gains and profits thus acquired by them, and be enjoined from further infringement.

The answer admits the issue of the patent, its surrender and reissue, and, as a defence to this suit, sets up in substance the want of novelty in the invention, its use by the public for more than two years prior to the application for the patent, and that the reissue, so far as it differs from the original patent, is not for the same invention. The answer also admits the recovery by the complainant in the action at law of the judgment mentioned, but denies that the same issues were involved or tried in that action which are raised in this suit.

The action at law was brought in the Circuit Court of the United States for the Northern District of New York, in the ordinary form of such actions for infringement of the privileges secured by a patent. The defendants pleaded the general issue, and set up, by special notice under the act of Congress, the want of novelty in the invention, and its use by the public for more than two years prior to the application for a patent. The plaintiff obtained a verdict for damages, upon which the judgment mentioned was entered; and this judgment, it is now insisted, estops the defendants in this suit from insisting upon the want of novelty in the invention patented, and its prior use by the public, and also from insisting upon any ground going to the validity of the patent which might have been availed of as a defence in that action, and, of course, upon the want of identity in the invention covered by the reissue with that of the original patent.

It is undoubtedly settled law that a judgment of a court of competent jurisdiction, upon a question directly involved in one suit, is conclusive as to that question in another suit between the same parties. But to this operation of the judgment it must appear, either upon the face of the record or be shown by extrinsic evidence, that the precise question was raised and determined in the former suit. If there be any uncertainty on this head in the record—as, for example, if it appear that several distinct matters may have been litigated, upon one or more of which the judgment may have passed, without indicating which of them was thus litigated, and upon which the judgment was rendered—the whole subject-matter of the action will be at large, and open to a new contention, unless this uncertainty be removed by extrinsic evidence showing the precise point involved and determined. To apply the judgment, and give effect to the adjudication actually made, when the record leaves the matter in doubt, such evidence is admissible.

Thus, in the case of the *Washington, Alexandria, & Georgetown Steam–Packet Company* v. *Sickles*, a verdict and judgment for the plaintiff in a prior action against the same defendant on a declaration, containing a special count upon a contract, and the common counts, was held by this court not to be conclusive of the existence and validity of the contract set forth in the special count, because the verdict might have been rendered without reference to that count, and only upon the common counts. Extrinsic evidence showing the fact to have been otherwise was necessary to render the judgment an estoppel upon those points.

When the same case was before this court the second time, *Packet Company* v. *Sickles*, the general rule with respect to the conclusiveness of a verdict and judgment in a former suit between the same parties, when the judgment is used in pleading as an estoppel, or is relied upon as evidence, was stated to be substantially this: that, to render the judgment conclusive, it must appear by the record of the prior suit that the particular matter sought to be concluded was necessarily tried or determined—that is, that the verdict in the suit could not have been rendered without deciding that matter; or it must be shown by extrinsic evidence, consistent with the record, that the verdict and judgment necessarily involved the consideration and determination of the matter.

Tested by these views, the question presented by the plaintiff in this case, upon the effect as evidence of the verdict and judgment in the action at law, is of easy solution. The record of that action does not disclose the nature of the infringement for which damages were recovered. The declaration only avers that the plaintiff was the original and first inventor of a new and useful improvement in the preparation of leather, and that he obtained a patent for the same, and, on its surrender, a new patent, with an amended specification, without describing with other particularity the nature and operation of the invention; and alleges, as the infringement complained of, that the defendants have made and used the invention, and have caused others to make and use it. The patent contains two claims: one for the use of fat liquor generally in the treatment of leather, and the other for a process of treating barktanned lamb or sheep skin by means of a compound composed and applied in a particular manner. Whether the infringement for which the verdict and judgment passed consisted in the simple use of fat liquor in the treatment of leather, or in the use of the process specified, does not appear from the record. A recovery for an infringement of one claim of the patent is not of itself conclusive of an infringement of the other claim, and there was no extrinsic evidence offered to remove the uncertainty upon the record: it is left to conjecture what was in fact litigated and determined. The verdict may have been for an infringement of the first claim; it may have been for an infringement of the second; it may have been for an infringement of both. The validity of the patent was not necessarily involved, except with respect to the claim which was the basis of the recovery. A patent may be valid as to a single claim and not valid as to the others. The record wants, therefore, that certainty which is essential to its operation as an estoppel, and does not conclude the defendants from contesting the infringement or the validity of the patent in this suit.

The record is not unlike a record in an action for money had and received to the plaintiff's use. It would be impossible to affirm from such a record, with certainty, for what moneys thus received the action was brought, without extrinsic evidence showing the fact; and, of course, without such evidence the verdict and judgment would conclude nothing, except as to the amount of indebtedness established.

According to Coke, an estoppel must "be certain to every intent;" and if upon the face of a record any thing is left to conjecture as to what was necessarily involved and decided, there is no estoppel in it when pleaded, and nothing conclusive in it when offered as evidence.

Decree affirmed.

* * *

B. COLLATERAL ESTOPPEL: IDENTITY OF ISSUES

COMMISSIONER OF INTERNAL REVENUE v. SUNNEN
333 U.S. 591 (1948)

MR. JUSTICE MURPHY delivered the opinion of the Court.

The problem of the federal income tax consequences of intra-family assignments of income is brought into focus again by this case.

The stipulated facts concern the taxable years 1937 to 1941, inclusive, and may be summarized as follows:

The respondent taxpayer was an inventor-patentee and the president of the Sunnen Products Company, a corporation engaged in the manufacture and sale of patented grinding machines and other tools. He held 89% or 1,780 out of a total of 2,000 shares of the outstanding stock of the corporation. His wife held 200 shares, the vice-president held 18 shares and two others connected with the corporation held one share each. The corporation's board of directors consisted of five members, including the taxpayer and his wife. This board was elected annually by the stockholders. A vote of three directors was required to take binding action.

The taxpayer had entered into several non-exclusive agreements whereby the corporation was licensed to manufacture and sell various devices on which he had applied for patents. In return, the corporation agreed to pay to the taxpayer a royalty equal to 10% of the gross sales price of the devices. These agreements did not require the corporation to manufacture and sell any particular number of devices; nor did they specify a minimum amount of royalties. Each party had the right to cancel the licenses, without liability, by giving the other party written notice of either six months or a year. In the absence of cancellation, the agreements were to continue in force for ten years. The board of directors authorized the corporation to execute each of these contracts. No notices of cancellation were given. Two of the agreements were in effect throughout the taxable years 1937–1941, while the other two were in existence at all pertinent times after June 20, 1939.

The taxpayer at various times assigned to his wife all his right, title and interest in the various license contracts. She was given exclusive title and power over the royalties accruing under these contracts. All the assignments were without consideration and were made as gifts to the wife, those occurring after 1932 being reported by the taxpayer for gift tax purposes. The corporation was notified of each assignment.

In 1937 the corporation, pursuant to this arrangement, paid the wife royalties in the amount of $4,881.35 on the license contract made in 1928; no other royalties on that contract were paid during the taxable years in question. The wife received royalties from other contracts totaling $15,-518,68 in 1937, $17,318.80 in 1938, $25,243.77 in 1939, $50,492,50 in 1940, and $149,002.78 in 1941. She included all these payments in her income tax returns for those years, and the taxes she paid thereon have not been refunded.

Relying upon its own prior decision in *Estate of Dodson v. Commissioner*, the Tax Court held that, with one exception, all the royalties paid to the wife from 1937 to 1941 were part of the taxable income of the taxpayer. The one exception concerned the royalties of $4,881.35 paid in 1937 under the 1928 agreement. In an earlier proceeding in 1935, the Board of Tax Appeals dealt with the taxpayer's income tax liability for the years 1929–1931; it concluded that he was not taxable on the royalties paid to his wife during those years under the 1928 license agreement. This prior determination by the Board caused the Tax Court to apply the principle of res judicata to bar a different result as to the royalties paid pursuant to the same agreement during 1937.

The Tax Court's decision was affirmed in part and reversed in part by the Eighth Circuit Court of Appeals. Approval was given to the Tax Court's application of the res judicata doctrine to exclude from the taxpayer's income the $4,881.35 in royalties paid in 1937 under the 1928 agreement. But to the extent that the taxpayer had been held taxable on royalties paid to his wife during the taxable years of 1937–1941, the decision was reversed on the theory that such payments were not income to him. Because of that conclusion, the Circuit Court of Appeals found it unnecessary to decide the taxpayer's additional claim that the res judicata doctrine applied as well to the other royalties (those accruing apart from the 1928 agreement) paid in the taxable years. We then brought the case here on certiorari, the Commissioner alleging that the result below conflicts with prior decisions of this Court.

If the doctrine of res judicata is properly applicable so that all the royalty payments made during 1937–1941 are governed by the prior decision of the Board of Tax Appeals, the case may be disposed of without reaching the merits of the controversy. We accordingly cast our attention initially on that possibility, one that has been explored by the Tax Court and that has been fully argued by the parties before us.

It is first necessary to understand something of the recognized meaning and scope of res judicata, a doctrine judicial in origin. The general rule of res judicata applies to repetitious suits involving the same cause of action. It rests upon considerations of economy of judicial time and public policy favoring the establishment of certainty in legal relations. The rule provides that when a court of competent jurisdiction has entered a final judgment on the merits of a cause of action, the parties to the suit and their privies are thereafter bound "not only as to every matter which was offered and received to sustain or defeat the claim or demand, but as to any other admissible matter which might have been offered for that purpose." *Cromwell v. County of Sac.* The judgment puts an end to the cause of action, which cannot again be brought into litigation between the parties upon any ground whatever, absent fraud or some other factor invalidating the judgment.

But where the second action between the same parties is upon a different cause or demand, the principle of res judicata is applied much more narrowly. In this situation, the judgment in the prior action operates as an estoppel, not as to matters which might have been litigated and determined, but "only as to those matters in issue or points controverted, upon the determination of which the finding or verdict was rendered." *Cromwell v. County of Sac.* And see *Russell v. Place.* Since the cause of action involved in the second proceeding is not swallowed by the judgment in the prior suit, the parties are free to litigate points which were not at issue in the first proceeding, even though such points might have been tendered and decided at that time. But matters which were actually litigated and determined in the first proceeding cannot later be re-litigated. Once a party has fought out a matter in litigation with the other party, he cannot later renew that duel. In this sense, res judicata is usually and more accurately referred to as estoppel by judgment, or collateral estoppel.

These same concepts are applicable in the federal income tax field. Income taxes are levied on an annual basis. Each year is the origin of a new liability and of a separate cause of action. Thus if a claim of liability or non-liability relating to a particular tax year is litigated, a judgment on the merits is res judicata as to any subsequent proceeding involving the same claim and the same tax year. But if the later proceeding is concerned with a similar or unlike claim relating to a different tax year, the prior judgment acts as a collateral estoppel only as to those matters in the second proceeding which were actually presented and determined in the first suit. Collateral estoppel operates, in other words, to relieve the government and the taxpayer of "redundant litigation of the identical question of the statute's application to the taxpayer's status."

But collateral estoppel is a doctrine capable of being applied so as to avoid an undue disparity in the impact of income tax liability. A taxpayer may secure a judicial determination of a particular tax matter, a matter which may recur without substantial variation for some years thereafter. But a subsequent modification of the significant facts or a change or development in the controlling legal principles may make that determination obsolete or erroneous, at least for future purposes. If such a determination is then perpetuated each succeeding year as to the taxpayer involved in the original litigation, he is accorded a tax treatment different from that given to other taxpayers of the same class. As a result, there are inequalities in the administration of the revenue laws, discriminatory distinctions in tax liability, and a fertile basis for litigious confusion. Such consequences, however, are neither necessitated nor justified by the principle of collateral estoppel. That principle is designed to prevent repetitious lawsuits over matters which have once been decided and which have remained substantially static, factually and legally. It is not meant to create vested rights in decisions that have become obsolete or erroneous with time, thereby causing inequities among taxpayers.

And so where two cases involve income taxes in different taxable years, collateral estoppel must be used with its limitations carefully in mind so as to avoid injustice. It must be confined to situations where the matter raised in the second suit is identical in all respects with that decided in the first proceeding and where the controlling facts and applicable legal rules remain unchanged. If the legal matters determined in the earlier case differ from those raised in the second case, collateral estoppel has no bearing on the situation. And where the situation is vitally altered between the time of the first judgment and the second, the prior determination is not conclusive. As demonstrated by *Blair v. Commissioner*, a judicial declaration intervening between the two proceedings may so change the legal atmosphere as to render the rule of collateral estoppel inapplicable. But the intervening decision need not necessarily be that of a state court, as it was in the *Blair* case. While such a state court decision may be considered as having changed the facts for federal tax litigation purposes, a modification or growth in legal principles as enunciated in intervening decisions of this Court may also effect a significant change in the situation. Tax inequality can result as readily from neglecting legal modulations by this Court as from disregarding factual changes wrought by state courts. In either event, the supervening decision cannot justly be ignored by blind reliance upon the rule of collateral estoppel. It naturally follows that an interposed alternation in the pertinent statutory provisions or Treasury regulations can make the use of that rule unwarranted.

Of course, where a question of fact essential to the judgment is actually litigated and determined in the first tax proceeding, the parties are bound by that determination in a subsequent proceeding even though the cause of action is different. And if the very same facts and no others are involved in the second case, a case relating to a different tax year, the prior judgment will be conclusive as to the same legal issues which appear, assuming no intervening doctrinal change. But if the relevant facts in the two cases are separable, even though they be similar or identical, collateral estoppel does not govern the legal issues which recur in the second case. Thus the second proceeding may involve an instrument or transaction identical with, but in a form separable from, the one dealt with in the first proceeding. In that situation, a court is free in the second proceeding to make an independent examination of the legal matters at issue. It may then reach a different result or, if consistency in decision is considered just and desirable, reliance may be placed upon the ordinary rule of stare decisis. Before a party can invoke the collateral estoppel doctrine in these circumstances, the legal matter raised in the second proceeding must involve the same set of events or documents and the same bundle of legal principles that contributed to the rendering of the first judgment.

It is readily apparent in this case that the royalty payments growing out of the license contracts which were not involved in the earlier action before the Board of Tax Appeals and which concerned different tax years are free from the effects of the collateral estoppel doctrine. That is true even though those contracts are identical in all important respects with the 1928 contract, the only one that was before the Board, and even though the issue as to those contracts is the same as that raised by the 1928 contract. For income tax purposes, what is decided as to one contract is not conclusive as to any other contract which is not then in issue, however similar or identical it may be. In this respect, the instant case thus differs vitally from *Tait v. Western Md. R. Co.*, where the two proceedings involved the same instruments and the same surrounding facts.

A more difficult problem is posed as to the $4,881.35 in royalties paid to the taxpayer's wife in 1937 under the 1928 contract. Here there is complete identity of facts, issues and parties as between the earlier Board proceeding and the instant one. The Commissioner claims, however, that legal principles developed in various intervening decisions of this Court have made plain the error of the Board's conclusion in the earlier proceeding, thus creating a situation like that involved in *Blair v. Commissioner*, supra. This change in the legal picture is said to have been brought about by [various decisions]. These cases all imposed income tax liability on transferors who had assigned or transferred various forms of income to others within their family groups, although none specifically related to the assignment of patent license contracts between members of the same family. It must therefore be determined whether this *Clifford-Horst* line of cases represents an intervening legal development which is pertinent to the problem raised by the assignment of the 1928 agreement and which makes manifest the error of the result reached in 1935 by the Board. If that is the situation, the doctrine of collateral estoppel becomes inapplicable. A difference result is then permissible as to the royalties paid in 1937 under the agreement in question. But to determine whether the *Clifford-Horst* series of cases has such an effect on the instant proceeding necessarily requires inquiry into the merits of the controversy growing out of the various contract assignments from the taxpayer to his wife. To that controversy we now turn [discussion of case law omitted—*ed.*].

* * * The principles which have thus been recognized and developed by the *Clifford* and *Horst* cases, and those following them, are directly applicable to the transfer of patent license contracts between members of the same family. They are guideposts for those who seek to determine in a particular instance whether such an assignor retains sufficient control over the assigned contracts or over the receipt of income by the assignee to make it fair to impose income tax liability on him.

Moreover, the clarification and growth of these principles through the *Clifford-Horst* line of cases constitute, in our opinion, a sufficient change in the legal climate to render inapplicable in the instant proceeding, the doctrine of collateral estoppel relative to the assignment of the 1928 contract. True, these cases did not originate the concept that an assignor is taxable if he retains control over the assigned property or power to defeat the receipt of income by the assignee. But they gave much added emphasis and substance to that concept making it more suited to meet the "attenuated subtleties" created by taxpayers. So substantial was the amplification of this concept as to justify a reconsideration of earlier Tax Court decisions reached without the benefit of the expanded notions, decisions which are now sought to be perpetuated regardless of their present correctness. Thus in the earlier litigation in 1935, the Board of Tax Appeals was unable to bring to bear on the assignment of the 1928 contract the full breadth of the ideas enunciated in the *Clifford-Horst* series of cases. And, as we shall see, a proper application of the principles as there developed might well have produced a different result, such as was reached by the Tax Court in this case in regard to the assignments of the other contracts. Under those circumstances collateral estoppel should not have been used by the Tax Court in the instant proceeding to perpetuate the 1935 viewpoint of the assignment.

The initial determination of whether the assignment of the various contracts rendered the taxpayer immune from income tax liability was one to be made by the Tax Court. That is the agency designated by law to find and examine the facts and to draw conclusions as to whether a particular assignment left the assignor with substantial control over the assigned property or the income which accrues to the assignee. And it is well established that its decision is to be respected on appeal if firmly grounded in the evidence and if consistent with the law. That is the standard, therefore, for measuring the propriety of the Tax Court's decision on the merits of the controversy in this case.

The facts relative to the assignments of the contracts are undisputed. As to the legal foundation of the Tax Court's judgment on the tax consequences of the assignments, we are unable to say that its inferences and conclusions from those facts are unreasonable in the light of the pertinent statutory or administrative provisions or that they are inconsistent with any of the principles enunciated in the *Clifford-Horst* line of cases. Indeed, due regard for those principles leads one inescapably to the Tax Court's result. The taxpayer's purported assignment to his wife of the various license contracts may properly be said to have left him with something more than a memory. He retained very substantial interests in the contracts themselves, as well as power to control the payment of royalties to his wife, thereby satisfying the various criteria of taxability set forth in the *Clifford-Horst* group of cases.

* * * These factors make reasonable the Tax Court's conclusion that the assignments of the license contracts merely involved a transfer of the right to receive income rather than a complete disposition of all the taxpayer's interest in the contracts and the royalties. The existence of the taxpayer's power to terminate those contracts and to regulate the amount of the royalties rendered ineffective for tax purposes his attempt to dispose of the contracts and royalties. The transactions were simply a reallocation of income within the family group, a reallocation which did not shift the incidence of income tax liability.

The judgment below must therefore be reversed and the case remanded for such further proceedings as may be necessary in light of this opinion.

Reversed.

* * *

C. MUTUALITY OF ESTOPPEL

PARKLANE HOSIERY COMPANY, INC. v. SHORE
439 U.S. 322 (1979)

Mr. Justice Stewart delivered the opinion of the Court.

This case presents the question whether a party who has had issues of fact adjudicated adversely to it in an equitable action may be collaterally estopped from relitigating the same issues before a jury in a subsequent legal action brought against it by a new party.

The respondent brought this stockholder's class action against the petitioners in a Federal District Court. The complaint alleged that the petitioners, Parklane Hosiery Co., Inc. (Parklane), and 13 of its officers, directors, and stockholders, had issued a materially false and misleading proxy statement in connection with a merger. The proxy statement, according to the complaint, had violated §§ 14(a), 10(b), and 20(a) of the Securities Exchange Act of 1934, as well as various rules and regulations promulgated by the Securities and Exchange Commission (SEC). The complaint sought damages, rescission of the merger, and recovery of costs.

Before this action came to trial, the SEC filed suit against the same defendants in the Federal District Court, alleging that the proxy statement that had been issued by Parklane was materially false and misleading in essentially the same respects as those that had been alleged in the respondent's complaint. Injunctive relief was requested. After a 4-day trial, the District Court found that the proxy statement was materially false and misleading in the respects alleged, and entered a declaratory judgment to that effect. The Court of Appeals for the Second Circuit affirmed this judgment.

The respondent in the present case then moved for partial summary judgment against the petitioners, asserting that the petitioners were collaterally estopped from relitigating the issues that had been resolved against them in the action brought by the SEC. The District Court denied the motion on the ground that such an application of collateral estoppel would deny the petitioners their Seventh Amendment right to a jury trial. The Court of Appeals for the Second Circuit reversed, holding that a party who has had issues of fact determined against him after a full and fair opportunity to litigate in a nonjury trial is collaterally estopped from obtaining a subsequent jury trial of these same issues of fact. The appellate court concluded that "the Seventh Amendment preserves the right to jury trial only with respect to issues of fact, [and] once those issues have been fully and fairly adjudicated in a prior proceeding, nothing remains for trial, either with or without a jury." Because of an inter-circuit conflict, we granted certiorari.

I

The threshold question to be considered is whether, quite apart from the right to a jury trial under the Seventh Amendment, the petitioners can be precluded from relitigating facts resolved adversely to them in a prior equitable proceeding with another party under the general law of collateral estoppel. Specifically, we must determine whether a litigant who was not a party to a prior judgment may nevertheless use that judgment "offensively" to prevent a defendant from relitigating issues resolved in the earlier proceeding.[4]

---

4. In this context, offensive use of collateral estoppel occurs when the plaintiff seeks to foreclose the defendant from litigating an issue the defendant has previously litigated unsuccess-

A

Collateral estoppel, like the related doctrine of res judicata,[5] has the dual purpose of protecting litigants from the burden of relitigating an identical issue with the same party or his privy and of promoting judicial economy by preventing needless litigation. *Blonder-Tongue Laboratories, Inc. v. University of Illinois Foundation*. Until relatively recently, however, the scope of collateral estoppel was limited by the doctrine of mutuality of parties. Under this mutuality doctrine, neither party could use a prior judgment as an estoppel against the other unless both parties were bound by the judgment. Based on the premise that it is somehow unfair to allow a party to use a prior judgment when he himself would not be so bound,[7] the mutuality requirement provided a party who had litigated and lost in a previous action an opportunity to relitigate identical issues with new parties.

By failing to recognize the obvious difference in position between a party who has never litigated an issue and one who has fully litigated and lost, the mutuality requirement was criticized almost from its inception.[8] Recognizing the validity of this criticism, the Court in *Blonder-Tongue Laboratories, Inc. v. University of Illinois Foundation* abandoned the mutuality requirement, at least in cases where a patentee seeks to relitigate the validity of a patent after a federal court in a previous lawsuit has already declared it invalid. The "broader question" before the Court, however, was "whether it is any longer tenable to afford a litigant more than one full and fair opportunity for judicial resolution of the same issue." The Court strongly suggested a negative answer to that question:

> In any lawsuit where a defendant, because of the mutuality principle, is forced to present a complete defense on the merits to a claim which the plaintiff has fully litigated and lost in a prior action, there is an arguable misallocation of resources. To the extent the defendant in the second suit may not win by asserting, without contradiction, that the plaintiff had fully and fairly, but unsuccessfully, litigated the

fully in an action with another party. Defensive use occurs when a defendant seeks to prevent a plaintiff from asserting a claim the plaintiff has previously litigated and lost against another defendant.

5. Under the doctrine of res judicata, a judgment on the merits in a prior suit bars a second suit involving the same parties or their privies based on the same cause of action. Under the doctrine of collateral estoppel, on the other hand, the second action is upon a different cause of action and the judgment in the prior suit precludes relitigation of issues actually litigated and necessary to the outcome of the first action. *E. g., Commissioner of Internal Revenue v. Sunnen; Cromwell v. County of Sac.*

7. It is a violation of due process for a judgment to be binding on a litigant who was not a party or a privy and therefore has never had an opportunity to be heard. *Blonder-Tongue Laboratories, Inc. v. University of Illinois Foundation; Hansberry v. Lee.*

8. This criticism was summarized in the Court's opinion in *Blonder-Tongue Laboratories, Inc. v. University of Illinois Foundation*. The opinion of Justice Traynor for a unanimous California Supreme Court in *Bernhard v. Bank of America Nat. Trust & Savings Assn.*, made the point succinctly:

No satisfactory rationalization has been advanced for the requirement of mutuality. Just why a party who was not bound by a previous action should be precluded from asserting it as res judicata against a party who was bound by it is difficult to comprehend.

same claim in the prior suit, the defendant's time and money are diverted from alternative uses—productive or otherwise—to relitigation of a decided issue. And, still assuming that the issue was resolved correctly in the first suit, there is reason to be concerned about the plaintiff's allocation of resources. Permitting repeated litigation of the same issue as long as the supply of unrelated defendants holds out reflects either the aura of the gaming table or "a lack of discipline and of disinterestedness on the part of the lower courts, hardly a worthy or wise basis for fashioning rules of procedure." Although neither judges, the parties, nor the adversary system performs perfectly in all cases, the requirement of determining whether the party against whom an estoppel is asserted had a full and fair opportunity to litigate is a most significant safeguard.

B

The *Blonder-Tongue* case involved defensive use of collateral estoppel—a plaintiff was estopped from asserting a claim that the plaintiff had previously litigated and lost against another defendant. The present case, by contrast, involves offensive use of collateral estoppel—a plaintiff is seeking to estop a defendant from relitigating the issues which the defendant previously litigated and lost against another plaintiff. In both the offensive and defensive use situations, the party against whom estoppel is asserted has litigated and lost in an earlier action. Nevertheless, several reasons have been advanced why the two situations should be treated differently.

First, offensive use of collateral estoppel does not promote judicial economy in the same manner as defensive use does. Defensive use of collateral estoppel precludes a plaintiff from relitigating identical issues by merely "switching adversaries." *Bernhard v. Bank of America Nat. Trust & Savings Assn.*[12] Thus defensive collateral estoppel gives a plaintiff a strong incentive to join all potential defendants in the first action if possible. Offensive use of collateral estoppel, on the other hand, creates precisely the opposite incentive. Since a plaintiff will be able to rely on a previous judgment against a defendant but will not be bound by that judgment if the defendant wins, the plaintiff has every incentive to adopt a "wait and see" attitude, in the hope that the first action by another plaintiff will result in a favorable judgment. Thus offensive use of collateral estoppel will likely increase rather than decrease the total amount of litigation, since potential plaintiffs will have everything to gain and nothing to lose by not intervening in the first action.

A second argument against offensive use of collateral estoppel is that it may be unfair to a defendant. If a defendant in the first action is sued for small or nominal damages, he may have little incentive to defend vigorously, particularly if future suits are not foreseeable. Allowing offensive collateral estoppel may also be unfair to a defendant if the judgment

---

12. Under the mutuality requirement, a plaintiff could accomplish this result since he would not have been bound by the judgment had the original defendant won.

relied upon as a basis for the estoppel is itself inconsistent with one or more previous judgments in favor of the defendant.[14] Still another situation where it might be unfair to apply offensive estoppel is where the second action affords the defendant procedural opportunities unavailable in the first action that could readily cause a different result.[15]

C

We have concluded that the preferable approach for dealing with these problems in the federal courts is not to preclude the use of offensive collateral estoppel, but to grant trial courts broad discretion to determine when it should be applied. The general rule should be that in cases where a plaintiff could easily have joined in the earlier action or where, either for the reasons discussed above or for other reasons, the application of offensive estoppel would be unfair to a defendant, a trial judge should not allow the use of offensive collateral estoppel.

In the present case, however, none of the circumstances that might justify reluctance to allow the offensive use of collateral estoppel is present. The application of offensive collateral estoppel will not here reward a private plaintiff who could have joined in the previous action, since the respondent probably could not have joined in the injunctive action brought by the SEC even had he so desired. Similarly, there is no unfairness to the petitioners in applying offensive collateral estoppel in this case. First, in light of the serious allegations made in the SEC's complaint against the petitioners, as well as the foreseeability of subsequent private suits that typically follow a successful Government judgment, the petitioners had every incentive to litigate the SEC lawsuit fully and vigorously.[18] Second, the judgment in the SEC action was not inconsistent with any previous decision. Finally, there will in the respondent's action be no procedural opportunities available to the petitioners that were unavailable in the first action of a kind that might be likely to cause a different result.[19]

---

14. In Professor Currie's familiar example, a railroad collision injures 50 passengers all of whom bring separate actions against the railroad. After the railroad wins the first 25 suits, a plaintiff wins in suit 26. Professor Currie argues that offensive use of collateral estoppel should not be applied so as to allow plaintiffs 27 through 50 automatically to recover.

15. If, for example, the defendant in the first action was forced to defend in an inconvenient forum and therefore was unable to engage in full scale discovery or call witnesses, application of offensive collateral estoppel may be unwarranted. Indeed, differences in available procedures may sometimes justify not allowing a prior judgment to have estoppel effect in a subsequent action even between the same parties, or where defensive estoppel is asserted against a plaintiff who has litigated and lost. The problem of unfairness is particularly acute in cases of offensive estoppel, however, because the defendant against whom estoppel is asserted typically will not have chosen the forum in the first action.

18. After a 4–day trial in which the petitioners had every opportunity to present evidence and call witnesses, the District Court held for the SEC. The petitioners then appealed to the Court of Appeals for the Second Circuit, which affirmed the judgment against them. Moreover, the petitioners were already aware of the action brought by the respondent, since it had commenced before the filing of the SEC action.

19. It is true, of course, that the petitioners in the present action would be entitled to a jury trial of the issues bearing on whether the proxy statement was materially false and misleading had the SEC action never been brought—a matter to be discussed in Part II of this opinion. But

We conclude, therefore, that none of the considerations that would justify a refusal to allow the use of offensive collateral estoppel is present in this case. Since the petitioners received a "full and fair" opportunity to litigate their claims in the SEC action, the contemporary law of collateral estoppel leads inescapably to the conclusion that the petitioners are collaterally estopped from relitigating the question of whether the proxy statement was materially false and misleading.

II

The question that remains is whether, notwithstanding the law of collateral estoppel, the use of offensive collateral estoppel in this case would violate the petitioners' Seventh Amendment right to a jury trial.

A

"[T]he thrust of the [Seventh] Amendment was to preserve the right to jury trial as it existed in 1791." *Curtis v. Loether*. At common law, a litigant was not entitled to have a jury determine issues that had been previously adjudicated by a chancellor in equity.

Recognition that an equitable determination could have collateral-estoppel effect in a subsequent legal action was the major premise of this Court's decision in *Beacon Theatres, Inc. v. Westover*. In that case the plaintiff sought a declaratory judgment that certain arrangements between it and the defendant were not in violation of the antitrust laws, and asked for an injunction to prevent the defendant from instituting an antitrust action to challenge the arrangements. The defendant denied the allegations and counterclaimed for treble damages under the antitrust laws, requesting a trial by jury of the issues common to both the legal and equitable claims. The Court of Appeals upheld denial of the request, but this Court reversed, stating:

> [T]he effect of the action of the District Court could be, as the Court of Appeals believed, "to limit the petitioner's opportunity fully to try to a jury every issue which has a bearing upon its treble damage suit," for determination of the issue of clearances by the judge might "operate either by way of res judicata or collateral estoppel so as to conclude both parties with respect thereto at the subsequent trial of the treble damage claim."

It is thus clear that the Court in the *Beacon Theatres* case thought that if an issue common to both legal and equitable claims was first determined by a judge, relitigation of the issue before a jury might be foreclosed by res judicata or collateral estoppel. To avoid this result, the Court held that when legal and equitable claims are joined in the same action, the trial judge has only limited discretion in determining the sequence of trial and "that discretion ... must, wherever possible, be exercised to preserve jury trial."

---

the presence or absence of a jury as fact-finder is basically neutral, quite unlike, for example, the necessity of defending the first lawsuit in an inconvenient forum.

Both the premise of *Beacon Theatres*, and the fact that it enunciated no more than a general prudential rule were confirmed by this Court's decision in *Katchen v. Landy*. In that case the Court held that a bankruptcy court, sitting as a statutory court of equity, is empowered to adjudicate equitable claims prior to legal claims, even though the factual issues decided in the equity action would have been triable by a jury under the Seventh Amendment if the legal claims had been adjudicated first. The Court stated:

> Both *Beacon Theatres* and *Dairy Queen* recognize that there might be situations in which the Court could proceed to resolve the equitable claim first even though the results might be dispositive of the issues involved in the legal claim.

Thus the Court in *Katchen v. Landy* recognized that an equitable determination can have collateral-estoppel effect in a subsequent legal action and that this estoppel does not violate the Seventh Amendment.

B

Despite the strong support to be found both in history and in the recent decisional law of this Court for the proposition that an equitable determination can have collateral-estoppel effect in a subsequent legal action, the petitioners argue that application of collateral estoppel in this case would nevertheless violate their Seventh Amendment right to a jury trial. The petitioners contend that since the scope of the Amendment must be determined by reference to the common law as it existed in 1791, and since the common law permitted collateral estoppel only where there was mutuality of parties, collateral estoppel cannot constitutionally be applied when such mutuality is absent.

The petitioners have advanced no persuasive reason, however, why the meaning of the Seventh Amendment should depend on whether or not mutuality of parties is present. A litigant who has lost because of adverse factual findings in an equity action is equally deprived of a jury trial whether he is estopped from relitigating the factual issues against the same party or a new party. In either case, the party against whom estoppel is asserted has litigated questions of fact, and has had the facts determined against him in an earlier proceeding. In either case there is no further fact-finding function for the jury to perform, since the common factual issues have been resolved in the previous action.

The Seventh Amendment has never been interpreted in the rigid manner advocated by the petitioners. On the contrary, many procedural devices developed since 1791 that have diminished the civil jury's historic domain have been found not to be inconsistent with the Seventh Amendment. See *Galloway v. United States* (directed verdict does not violate the Seventh Amendment); *Gasoline Products Co. v. Champlin Refining Co.* (retrial limited to question of damages does not violate the Seventh Amendment even though there was no practice at common law for setting aside a verdict in part); *Fidelity & Deposit Co. v. United States* (summary judgment does not violate the Seventh Amendment).

The *Galloway* case is particularly instructive. There the party against whom a directed verdict had been entered argued that the procedure was unconstitutional under the Seventh Amendment. In rejecting this claim, the Court said:

> The Amendment did not bind the federal courts to the exact procedural incidents or details of jury trial according to the common law in 1791, any more than it tied them to the common-law system of pleading or the specific rules of evidence then prevailing. Nor were "the rules of the common law" then prevalent, including those relating to the procedure by which the judge regulated the jury's role on questions of fact, crystalized in a fixed and immutable system....

> The more logical conclusion, we think, and the one which both history and the previous decisions here support, is that the Amendment was designed to preserve the basic institution of jury trial in only its most fundamental elements, not the great mass of procedural forms and details, varying even then so widely among common-law jurisdictions.

The law of collateral estoppel, like the law in other procedural areas defining the scope of the jury's function, has evolved since 1791. Under the rationale of the *Galloway* case, these developments are not repugnant to the Seventh Amendment simply for the reason that they did not exist in 1791. Thus if, as we have held, the law of collateral estoppel forecloses the petitioners from relitigating the factual issues determined against them in the SEC action, nothing in the Seventh Amendment dictates a different result, even though because of lack of mutuality there would have been no collateral estoppel in 1791.

The judgment of the Court of Appeals is

Affirmed.

MR. JUSTICE REHNQUIST, dissenting.

It is admittedly difficult to be outraged about the treatment accorded by the federal judiciary to petitioners' demand for a jury trial in this lawsuit. Outrage is an emotion all but impossible to generate with respect to a corporate defendant in a securities fraud action, and this case is no exception. But the nagging sense of unfairness as to the way petitioners have been treated, engendered by the *imprimatur* placed by the Court of Appeals on respondent's "heads I win, tails you lose" theory of this litigation, is not dispelled by this Court's antiseptic analysis of the issues in the case. It may be that if this Nation were to adopt a new Constitution today, the Seventh Amendment guaranteeing the right of jury trial in civil cases in federal courts would not be included among its provisions. But any present sentiment to that effect cannot obscure or dilute our obligation to enforce the Seventh Amendment, which *was* included in the Bill of Rights in 1791 and which has not since been repealed in the only manner provided by the Constitution for repeal of its provisions.

The right of trial by jury in civil cases at common law is fundamental to our history and jurisprudence. Today, however, the Court reduces this valued right, which Blackstone praised as "the glory of the English law," to a mere "neutral" factor and in the name of procedural reform denies the right of jury trial to defendants in a vast number of cases in which defendants, heretofore, have enjoyed jury trials. Over 35 years ago, Mr. Justice Black lamented the "gradual process of judicial erosion which in one hundred fifty years has slowly worn away a major portion of the essential guarantee of the Seventh Amendment." *Galloway v. United States* (dissenting opinion). Regrettably, the erosive process continues apace with today's decision.

I

* * * The history of the Seventh Amendment has been amply documented by this Court and by legal scholars, and it would serve no useful purpose to attempt here to repeat all that has been written on the subject. Nonetheless, the decision of this case turns on the scope and effect of the Seventh Amendment, which, perhaps more than with any other provision of the Constitution, are determined by reference to the historical setting in which the Amendment was adopted. See It therefore is appropriate to pause to review, albeit briefly, the circumstances preceding and attending the adoption of the Seventh Amendment as a guide in ascertaining its application to the case at hand.

A

It is perhaps easy to forget, now more than 200 years removed from the events, that the right of trial by jury was held in such esteem by the colonists that its deprivation at the hands of the English was one of the important grievances leading to the break with England. The extensive use of vice-admiralty courts by colonial administrators to eliminate the colonists' right of jury trial was listed among the specific offensive English acts denounced in the Declaration of Independence. And after war had broken out, all of the 13 newly formed States restored the institution of civil jury trial to its prior prominence; 10 expressly guaranteed the right in their state constitutions and the 3 others recognized it by statute or by common practice. Indeed, "[t]he right to trial by jury was probably the only one universally secured by the first American state constitutions...."

One might justly wonder then why no mention of the right of jury trial in civil cases should have found its way into the Constitution that emerged from the Philadelphia Convention in 1787. Article III, § 2, cl. 3, merely provides that "The Trial of all Crimes, except in Cases of Impeachment, shall be by Jury." The omission of a clause protective of the civil jury right was not for lack of trying, however. Messrs. Pinckney and Gerry proposed to provide a clause securing the right of jury trial in civil cases, but their efforts failed. Several reasons have been advanced for this failure. The Federalists argued that the practice of civil juries among the several States varied so much that it was too difficult to draft constitutional language to accommodate the different state practices. Whatever the reason for the omission, however, it is clear that even before the delegates had left Philadelphia, plans were under way to attack the proposed Constitution on the ground that it failed to contain a guarantee of civil jury trial in the new federal courts.

The virtually complete absence of a bill of rights in the proposed Constitution was the principal focus of the Anti–Federalists' attack on the Constitution, and the lack of a provision for civil juries featured prominently in their arguments. Their pleas struck a responsive chord in the populace, and the price exacted in many States for approval of the Constitution was the appending of a list of recommended amendments, chief among them a clause securing the right of jury trial in civil cases. Responding to the pressures for a civil jury guarantee generated during the ratification debates, the first Congress under the new Constitution at its first session in 1789 proposed to amend the Constitution by adding the following language: "In suits at common law, between man and man, the trial by jury, as one of the best securities to the rights of the people, ought to remain inviolate." That provision, altered in language to what became the Seventh Amendment, was proposed by the Congress in 1789 to the legislatures of the several States and became effective with its ratification by Virginia on December 15, 1791.

The foregoing sketch is meant to suggest what many of those who oppose the use of juries in civil trials seem to ignore. The founders of our Nation considered the right of trial by jury in civil cases an important bulwark against tyranny and corruption, a safeguard too precious to be left to the whim of the sovereign, or, it might be added, to that of the judiciary. Those who passionately advocated the right to a civil jury trial did not do so because they considered the jury a familiar procedural device that should be continued; the concerns for the institution of jury trial that led to the passages of the Declaration of Independence and to the Seventh Amendment were not animated by a belief that use of juries would lead to more efficient judicial administration. Trial by a jury of laymen rather than by the sovereign's judges was important to the founders because juries represent the layman's common sense, the "passional elements in our nature," and thus keep the administration of law in accord with the wishes and feelings of the community. Those who favored juries believed that a jury would reach a result that a judge either could not or would not reach. It is with these values that underlie the Seventh Amendment in mind that the Court should, but obviously does not, approach the decision of this case.

B

The Seventh Amendment requires that the right of trial by jury be "preserved." Because the Seventh Amendment demands preservation of the jury trial right, our cases have uniformly held that the content of the right must be judged by historical standards. Thus, in *Baltimore &*

Carolina Line v. Redman, the Court stated that "[t]he right of trial by jury thus preserved is the right which existed under the English common law when the amendment was adopted." And in *Dimick v. Schiedt,* the Court held: "In order to ascertain the scope and meaning of the Seventh Amendment, resort must be had to the appropriate rules of the common law established at the time of the adoption of that constitutional provision in 1791." If a jury would have been impaneled in a particular kind of case in 1791, then the Seventh Amendment requires a jury trial today, if either party so desires.

To be sure, it is the substance of the right of jury trial that is preserved, not the incidental or collateral effects of common-law practice in 1791. "The aim of the amendment, as this Court has held, is to preserve the substance of the common-law right of trial by jury, as distinguished from mere matters of form or procedure, and particularly to retain the common-law distinction between the province of the court and that of the jury. . . ." "The Amendment did not bind the federal courts to the exact procedural incidents or details of jury trial according to the common law of 1791, any more than it tied them to the common-law system of pleading or the specific rules of evidence then prevailing." *Galloway v. United States.*

To say that the Seventh Amendment does not tie federal courts to the exact procedure of the common law in 1791 does not imply, however, that any nominally "procedural" change can be implemented, regardless of its impact on the functions of the jury. For to sanction creation of procedural devices which limit the province of the jury to a greater degree than permitted at common law in 1791 is in direct contravention of the Seventh Amendment. See *Neely v. Martin K. Eby Constr. Co.; Galloway v. United State; Dimick v. Schiedt.* And since we deal here not with the common law *qua* common law but with the Constitution, no amount of argument that the device provides for more efficiency or more accuracy or is fairer will save it if the degree of invasion of the jury's province is greater than allowed in 1791. To rule otherwise would effectively permit judicial repeal of the Seventh Amendment because nearly any change in the province of the jury, no matter how drastic the diminution of its functions, can always be denominated "procedural reform."

The guarantees of the Seventh Amendment will prove burdensome in some instances; the civil jury surely was a burden to the English governors who, in its stead, substituted the vice-admiralty court. But, as with other provisions of the Bill of Rights, the onerous nature of the protection is no license for contracting the rights secured by the Amendment. Because " '[m]aintenance of the jury as a fact-finding body is of such importance and occupies so firm a place in our history and jurisprudence . . . any seeming curtailment of the right to a jury trial should be scrutinized with the utmost care.' " *Dimick v. Schiedt,* quoted in *Beacon Theatres, Inc. v. Westover.*

C

Judged by the foregoing principles, I think it is clear that petitioners were denied their Seventh Amendment right to a jury trial in this case. Neither respondent nor the Court doubts that at common law as it existed in 1791, petitioners would have been entitled in the private action to have a jury determine whether the proxy statement was false and misleading in the respects alleged. The reason is that at common law in 1791, collateral estoppel was permitted only where the parties in the first action were identical to, or in privity with, the parties to the subsequent action. It was not until 1971 that the doctrine of mutuality was abrogated by this Court in certain limited circumstances. *Blonder-Tongue Laboratories, Inc. v. University of Illinois Foundation.* But developments in the judge-made doctrine of collateral estoppel, however salutary, cannot, consistent with the Seventh Amendment, contract in any material fashion the right to a jury trial that a defendant would have enjoyed in 1791. In the instant case, resort to the doctrine of collateral estoppel does more than merely contract the right to a jury trial: It eliminates the right entirely and therefore contravenes the Seventh Amendment.

The Court responds, however, that at common law "a litigant was not entitled to have a jury [in a subsequent action at law between the same parties] determine issues that had been previously adjudicated by a chancellor in equity," and that "petitioners have advanced no persuasive reason ... why the meaning of the Seventh Amendment should depend on whether or not mutuality of parties is present." But that is tantamount to saying that since a party would not be entitled to a jury trial if he brought an equitable action, there is no persuasive reason why he should receive a jury trial on virtually the same issues if instead he chooses to bring his lawsuit in the nature of a legal action. The persuasive reason is that the Seventh Amendment requires that a party's right to jury trial which existed at common law be "preserved" from incursions by the government or the judiciary. Whether this Court believes that use of a jury trial in a particular instance is necessary, or fair or repetitive is simply irrelevant. If that view is "rigid," it is the Constitution which commands that rigidity. To hold otherwise is to rewrite the Seventh Amendment so that a party is guaranteed a jury trial in civil cases unless this Court thinks that a jury trial would be inappropriate.

No doubt parallel "procedural reforms" could be instituted in the area of criminal jurisprudence, which would accomplish much the same sort of expedition of court calendars and conservation of judicial resources as would the extension of collateral estoppel in civil litigation. Government motions for summary judgment, or for a directed verdict in favor of the prosecution at the close of the evidence, would presumably save countless hours of judges' and jurors' time. It can scarcely be doubted, though, that such "procedural reforms" would not survive constitutional scrutiny under the jury trial guarantee of the Sixth Amendment. Just as the principle of separation of powers was not incorporated by the Framers into the Constitution in order to promote efficiency or dispatch in the business of government, the right to a jury trial was not guaranteed in order to facilitate prompt and accurate decision of lawsuits. The essence of that right lies in its insistence that a body of laymen not permanently attached to the sovereign participate along with the judge in the fact-finding necessitated by a lawsuit. And that essence is as much a part of the Seventh Amendment's guarantee in civil cases as it is of the Sixth Amendment's guarantee in criminal prosecutions.

Relying on *Galloway v. United States, Gasoline Products Co. v. Champlin Refining Co.*, and *Fidelity & Deposit Co. v. United States*, the Court seems to suggest that the offensive use of collateral estoppel in this case is permissible under the limited principle set forth above that a mere procedural change that does not invade the province of the jury and a defendant's right thereto to a greater extent than authorized by the common law is permissible. But the Court's actions today constitute a far greater infringement of the defendant's rights than it ever before has sanctioned. In *Galloway*, the Court upheld the modern form of directed verdict against a Seventh Amendment challenge, but it is clear that a similar form of directed verdict existed at common law in 1791. The modern form did not materially alter the function of the jury. Similarly, the modern device of summary judgment was found not to violate the Seventh Amendment because in 1791 a demurrer to the evidence, a procedural device substantially similar to summary judgment, was a common practice. The procedural devices of summary judgment and directed verdict are direct descendants of their common-law antecedents. They accomplish nothing more than could have been done at common law, albeit by a more cumbersome procedure. And while at common law there apparently was no practice of setting aside a verdict in part, the Court in *Gasoline Products* permitted a partial retrial of "distinct and separable" issues because the change in procedure would not impair the substance of the right to jury trial. The parties in *Gasoline Products* still enjoyed the right to have a jury determine all issues of fact.

By contrast, the development of non-mutual estoppel is a substantial departure from the common law and its use in this case completely deprives petitioners of their right to have a jury determine contested issues of fact. I am simply unwilling to accept the Court's presumption that the complete extinguishment of petitioners' right to trial by jury can be justified as a mere change in "procedural incident or detail." Over 40 years ago, Mr. Justice Sutherland observed in a not dissimilar case: "[T]his court in a very special sense is charged with the duty of construing and upholding the Constitution; and in the discharge of that important duty, it ever must be alert to see that a doubtful precedent be not extended by mere analogy to a different case if the result will be to weaken or subvert what it conceives to be a principle of the fundamental law of the land." *Dimick v. Schiedt.*

II

Even accepting, *arguendo*, the majority's position that there is no violation of the Seventh Amendment here, I nonetheless would not sanction the use of collateral estoppel in this case. The Court today holds: "The general rule should be that in cases where a plaintiff could easily have joined in the earlier action or where, either for the reasons discussed above or for other reasons, the application of offensive estoppel would be unfair to a defendant, a trial judge should not allow the use of offensive collateral estoppel."

In my view, it is "unfair" to apply offensive collateral estoppel where the party who is sought to be estopped has not had an opportunity to have the facts of his case determined by a jury. Since in this case petitioners were not entitled to a jury trial in the Securities and Exchange Commission (SEC) lawsuit. I would not estop them from relitigating the issues determined in the SEC suit before a jury in the private action. I believe that several factors militate in favor of this result.

First, the use of offensive collateral estoppel in this case runs counter to the strong federal policy favoring jury trials, even if it does not, as the majority holds, violate the Seventh Amendment. The Court's decision in *Beacon Threatres, Inc. v. Westover*, exemplifies that policy. In *Beacon Theatres* the Court held that where both equitable and legal claims or defenses are presented in a single case, "only under the most imperative circumstances, circumstances which in view of the flexible procedures of the Federal Rules we cannot now anticipate, can the right to a jury trial of legal issues be lost through prior determination of equitable claims." And in *Jacob v. New York*, the Court stated: "The right of jury trial in civil cases at common law is a basic and fundamental feature of our system of federal jurisprudence which is protected by the Seventh Amendment. A right so fundamental and sacred to the citizen, whether guaranteed by the Constitution or provided by statute, should be jealously guarded by the courts." Accord, *Byrd v. Blue Ridge Rural Electric Cooperative, Inc.* (strong federal policy in favor of juries requires jury trials in diversity cases, regardless of state practice). Today's decision will mean that in a large number of private cases defendants will no longer enjoy the right to jury trial.[20] Neither the Court nor respondent has adverted or cited to any unmanageable problems that have resulted from according defendants jury trials in such cases. I simply see no "imperative circumstances" requiring this wholesale abrogation of jury trials.[21]

Second, I believe that the opportunity for a jury trial in the second action could easily lead to a different result from that obtained in the first action before the court and therefore that it is unfair to estop petitioners from relitigating the issues before a jury. This is the position adopted in the *Restatement (Second) of Judgments*, which disapproves of the application of offensive collateral estoppel where the defendant has an opportuni-

---

20. The Court's decision today may well extend to other areas, such as antitrust, labor, employment discrimination, consumer protection, and the like, where a private plaintiff may sue for damages based on the same or similar violations that are the subject of government actions.

21. This is not to say that Congress cannot commit enforcement of statutorily created rights to an "administrative process or specialized court of equity." *Curtis v. Loether*; see *Atlas Roofing Co., Inc. v. Occupational Safety & Health Review Comm'n*; *Katchen v. Landy*; *NLRB v. Jones & Laughlin Steel Corp.*

ty for a jury trial in the second lawsuit that was not available in the first action. The Court accepts the proposition that it is unfair to apply offensive collateral estoppel "where the second action affords the defendant procedural opportunities unavailable in the first action that could readily cause a different result." Differences in discovery opportunities between the two actions are cited as examples of situations where it would be unfair to permit offensive collateral estoppel. But in the Court's view, the fact that petitioners would have been entitled to a jury trial in the present action is not such a "procedural opportunit[y]" because "the presence or absence of a jury as fact-finder is basically *neutral*, quite unlike, for example, the necessity of defending the first lawsuit in an inconvenient forum."

As is evident from the prior brief discussion of the development of the civil jury trial guarantee in this country, those who drafted the Declaration of Independence and debated so passionately the proposed Constitution during the ratification period, would indeed be astounded to learn that the presence or absence of a jury is merely "neutral," whereas the availability of discovery, a device unmentioned in the Constitution, may be controlling. It is precisely because the Framers believed that they might receive a different result at the hands of a jury of their peers than at the mercy of the sovereign's judges, that the Seventh Amendment was adopted. And I suspect that anyone who litigates cases before juries in the 1970's would be equally amazed to hear of the supposed lack of distinction between trial by court and trial by jury. The Court can cite no authority in support of this curious proposition. The merits of civil juries have been long debated, but I suspect that juries have never been accused of being merely "neutral" factors.

Contrary to the majority's supposition, juries can make a difference, and our cases have, before today at least, recognized this obvious fact. Thus, in *Colgrove v. Battin*, we stated that "the purpose of the jury trial in . . . civil cases [is] to assure a fair and equitable resolution of factual issues. . . ." And in *Byrd v. Blue Ridge Rural Electrical Cooperative*, the Court conceded that "the nature of the tribunal which tries issues may be important in the enforcement of the parcel of rights making up a cause of action or defense. . . . It may well be that in the instant personal-injury case the outcome would be substantially affected by whether the issue of immunity is decided by a judge or a jury." Jurors bring to a case their common sense and community values; their "very inexperience is an asset because it secures a fresh perception of each trial, avoiding the stereotypes said to infect the judicial eye."

The ultimate irony of today's decision is that its potential for significantly conserving the resources of either the litigants or the judiciary is doubtful at best. That being the case, I see absolutely no reason to frustrate so cavalierly the important federal policy favoring jury decisions of disputed fact questions. The instant case is an apt example of the minimal savings that will be accomplished by the Court's decision. As the Court admits, even if petitioners are collaterally estopped from relitigating whether the proxy was materially false and misleading, they are still entitled to have a jury determine whether respondent was injured by the alleged misstatements and the amount of damages, if any, sustained by respondent. Thus, a jury must be impaneled in this case in any event. The time saved by not trying the issue of whether the proxy was materially false and misleading before the jury is likely to be insubstantial. It is just as probable that today's decision will have the result of coercing defendants to agree to consent orders or settlements in agency enforcement actions in order to preserve their right to jury trial in the private actions. In that event, the Court, for no compelling reason, will have simply added a powerful club to the administrative agencies' arsenals that even Congress was unwilling to provide them.

* * *

D. FEDERALISM ISSUES

REVIEW U.S. CONST. ARTICLE IV § 1; 28 U.S.C. § 1738; FED. R. CIV. P. 8(c)(1)

DURFEE v. DUKE

375 U.S. 106 (1963)

MR. JUSTICE STEWART delivered the opinion of the Court.

The United States Constitution requires that "Full Faith and Credit shall be given in each State to the * * * judicial Proceedings of every other State." The case before us presents questions arising under this constitutional provision and under the federal statute enacted to implement it.

In 1956 the petitioners brought an action against the respondent in a Nebraska court to quiet title to certain bottom land situated on the Missouri River. The main channel of that river forms the boundary between the States of Nebraska and Missouri. The Nebraska court had jurisdiction over the subject matter of the controversy only if the land in question was in Nebraska. Whether the land was Nebraska land depended entirely upon a factual question-whether a shift in the river's course had been caused by avulsion or accretion. The respondent appeared in the Nebraska court and through counsel fully litigated the issues, explicitly contesting the court's jurisdiction over the subject matter of the controversy.[4] After a hearing the court found the issues in favor of the petitioners and ordered that title to the land be quieted in them. The respondent appealed, and the Supreme Court of Nebraska affirmed the judgment after a trial *de novo* on the record made in the lower court. The State Supreme Court specifically found that the rule of avulsion was applicable, that the land in question was in Nebraska, that the Nebraska courts therefore had

---

4. This is, therefore, not a case in which a party, although afforded an opportunity to contest subject-matter jurisdiction, did not litigate the issue.

jurisdiction of the subject matter of the litigation, and that title to the land was in the petitioners. The respondent did not petition this Court for a writ of certiorari to review that judgment.

Two months later the respondent filed a suit against the petitioners in a Missouri court to quiet title to the same land. Her complaint alleged that the land was in Missouri. The suit was removed to a Federal District Court by reason of diversity of citizenship. The District Court after hearing evidence expressed the view that the land was in Missouri, but held that all the issues had been adjudicated and determined in the Nebraska litigation, and that the judgment of the Nebraska Supreme Court was res judicata and "is now binding upon this court." The Court of Appeals reversed, holding that the District Court was not required to give full faith and credit to the Nebraska judgment, and that normal *res judicata* principles were not applicable because the controversy involved land and a court in Missouri was therefore free to retry the question of the Nebraska court's jurisdiction over the subject matter. We granted certiorari to consider a question important to the administration of justice in our federal system. For the reasons that follow, we reverse the judgment before us.

The constitutional command of full faith and credit, as implemented by Congress, requires that "judicial proceedings * * * shall have the same full faith and credit in every court within the United States * * * as they have by law or usage in the courts of such State * * * from which they are taken." Full faith and credit thus generally requires every State to give to a judgment at least the res judicata effect which the judgment would be accorded in the State which rendered it. "By the Constitutional provision for full faith and credit, the local doctrines of res judicata, speaking generally, become a part of national jurisprudence, and therefore federal questions cognizable here."

It is not questioned that the Nebraska courts would give full res judicata effect to the Nebraska judgment quieting title in the petitioners.[6] It is the respondent's position, however, that whatever effect the Nebraska courts might give to the Nebraska judgment, the federal court in Missouri was free independently to determine whether the Nebraska court in fact had jurisdiction over the subject matter, i.e., whether the land in question was actually in Nebraska.

In support of this position the respondent relies upon the many decisions of this Court which have held that a judgment of a court in one State is conclusive upon the merits in a court in another State only if the court in the first State had power to pass on the merits—had jurisdiction, that is, to render the judgment. As Mr. Justice Bradley stated: "we think

---

6. The Nebraska Supreme Court has clearly postulated the relevant law of the State: "This court adheres to the rule that if a court is one competent to decide whether or not the facts in any given proceeding confer jurisdiction, decides that it has jurisdiction, then its judgments entered within the scope of the subject matter over which its authority extends in proceedings following the lawful allegation of circumstances requiring the exercise of its jurisdiction, are not subject to collateral attack but conclusive against all the world unless reversed on appeal or avoided for error or fraud in a direct proceeding."

it clear that the jurisdiction of the court by which a judgment is rendered in any State may be questioned in a collateral proceeding in another State, notwithstanding the provision of the fourth article of the Constitution and the law of 1790, and notwithstanding the averments contained in the record of the judgment itself." The principle has been restated and applied in a variety of contexts.

However, while it is established that a court in one State, when asked to give effect to the judgment of a court in another State, may constitutionally inquire into the foreign court's jurisdiction to render that judgment, the modern decisions of this Court have carefully delineated the permissible scope of such an inquiry. From these decisions there emerges the general rule that a judgment is entitled to full faith and credit—even as to questions of jurisdiction—when the second court's inquiry discloses that those questions have been fully and fairly litigated and finally decided in the court which rendered the original judgment.

With respect to questions of jurisdiction over the person,[8] this principle was unambiguously established in *Baldwin v. Iowa State Traveling Men's Ass'n*. There it was held that a federal court in Iowa must give binding effect to the judgment of a federal court in Missouri despite the claim that the original court did not have jurisdiction over the defendant's person, once it was shown to the court in Iowa that that question had been fully litigated in the Missouri forum. "Public policy," said the Court, "dictates that there be an end of litigation; that those who have contested an issue shall be bound by the result of the contest; and that matters once tried shall be considered forever settled as between the parties. We see no reason why this doctrine should not apply in every case where one voluntarily appears, presents his case and is fully heard, and why he should not, in the absence of fraud, be thereafter concluded by the judgment of the tribunal to which he has submitted his cause."[9]

Following the *Baldwin* case, this Court soon made clear in a series of decisions that the general rule is no different when the claim is made that the original forum did not have jurisdiction over the subject matter. *Davis v. Davis*; *Stoll v. Gottlieb*; *Treinies v. Sunshine Mining Co.*; *Sherrer v. Sherrer*. In each of these cases the claim was made that a court, when asked to enforce the judgment of another forum, was free to retry the question of that forum's jurisdiction over the subject matter. In each case this Court held that since the question of subject-matter jurisdiction had been fully litigated in the original forum, the issue could not be retried in a subsequent action between the parties.

In the *Davis* case it was held that the courts of the District of Columbia were required to give full faith and credit to a decree of absolute

---

8. It is not disputed in the present case that the Nebraska courts had jurisdiction over the respondent's person. She entered a general appearance in the trial court, and initiated the appeal to the Nebraska Supreme Court.

9. This decision was adhered to the following year in *American Surety Co. v. Baldwin*. In his opinion for a unanimous Court in the case, Mr. Justice Brandeis said: "The principles of res judicata apply to questions of jurisdiction as well as to other issues."

divorce rendered in Virginia, despite the claim that the Virginia court had lacked jurisdiction because the plaintiff in the Virginia proceedings had not been domiciled in that State. In the course of the opinion the Court stated:

> As to petitioner's domicil for divorce and his standing to invoke jurisdiction of the Virginia court, its finding that he was a bona fide resident of that State for the required time is binding upon respondent in the courts of the District. She may not say that he was not entitled to sue for divorce in the state court, for she appeared there and by plea put in issue his allegation as to domicil, introduced evidence to show it false, took exceptions to the commissioner's report, and sought to have the court sustain them and uphold her plea. Plainly, the determination of the decree upon that point is effective for all purposes in this litigation.

This doctrine of jurisdictional finality was applied even more unequivocally in *Treinies*, involving title to personal property, and in *Sherrer*, involving, like *Davis*, recognition of a foreign divorce decree. In *Treinies*, the rule was succinctly stated: "One trial of an issue is enough. 'The principles of res judicata apply to questions of jurisdiction as well as to other issues,' as well to jurisdiction of the subject matter as of the parties."

The reasons for such a rule are apparent. In the words of the Court's opinion in *Stoll v. Gottlieb*, "We see no reason why a court in the absence of an allegation of fraud in obtaining the judgment, should examine again the question whether the court making the earlier determination on an actual contest over jurisdiction between the parties, did have jurisdiction of the subject matter of the litigation. * * * Courts to determine the rights of parties are an integral part of our system of government. It is just as important that there should be a place to end as that there should be a place to begin litigation. After a party has his day in court, with opportunity to present his evidence and his view of the law, a collateral attack upon the decision as to jurisdiction there rendered merely retries the issue previously determined. There is no reason to expect that the second decision will be more satisfactory than the first."

To be sure, the general rule of finality of jurisdictional determinations is not without exceptions. Doctrines of federal pre-emption or sovereign immunity may in some contexts be controlling. *Kalb v. Feuerstein*; United States v. United States Fidelity & Guaranty Co.[12] But no such overriding considerations are present here. While this Court has not before had occasion to consider the applicability of the rule of *Davis*, *Stoll*, *Treinies*, and *Sherrer* to a case involving real property, we can discern no reason why the rule should not be fully applicable.

It is argued that an exception to this rule of jurisdictional finality should be made with respect to cases involving real property because of

---

12. It is to be noted, however, that in neither of these cases had the jurisdictional issues actually been litigated in the first forum.

this Court's emphatic expressions of the doctrine that courts of one State are completely without jurisdiction directly to affect title to land in other States. This argument is wide of the mark. Courts of one State are equally without jurisdiction to dissolve the marriages of those domiciled in other States. But the location of land, like the domicile of a party to a divorce action, is a matter "to be resolved by judicial determination." The question remains whether, once the matter has been fully litigated and judicially determined, it can be retried in another State in litigation between the same parties. Upon the reason and authority of the cases we have discussed, it is clear that the answer must be in the negative.

It is to be emphasized that all that was ultimately determined in the Nebraska litigation was title to the land in question as between the parties to the litigation there. Nothing there decided, and nothing that could be decided in litigation between the same parties or their privies in Missouri, could bind either Missouri or Nebraska with respect to any controversy they might have, now or in the future, as to the location of the boundary between them, or as to their respective sovereignty over the land in question. Either State may at any time protect its interest by initiating independent judicial proceedings here.

For the reasons stated, we hold in this case that the federal court in Missouri had the power and, upon proper averments, the duty to inquire into the jurisdiction of the Nebraska courts to render the decree quieting title to the land in the petitioners. We further hold that when that inquiry disclosed, as it did, that the jurisdictional issues had been fully and fairly litigated by the parties and finally determined in the Nebraska courts, the federal court in Missouri was correct in ruling that further inquiry was precluded. Accordingly the judgment of the Court of Appeals is reversed, and that of the District Court is affirmed. It is so ordered.

Judgment of Court of Appeals reversed and judgment of District Court affirmed.

* * *

FEDERAL RULE OF CIVIL PROCEDURE 41. DISMISSAL OF ACTIONS

(a) Voluntary Dismissal.

    (1) *By the Plaintiff.*

        (A) *Without a Court Order.* Subject to Rules 23(e), 23.1(c), 23.2, and 66 and any applicable federal statute, the plaintiff may dismiss an action without a court order by filing:

            (i) a notice of dismissal before the opposing party serves either an answer or a motion for summary judgment; or

            (ii) a stipulation of dismissal signed by all parties who have appeared.

        (B) *Effect.* Unless the notice or stipulation states otherwise, the dismissal is without prejudice. But if the plaintiff previously dismissed any federal—or state—court action based on or including the same claim, a notice of dismissal operates as an adjudication on the merits.

(2) *By Court Order; Effect.* Except as provided in Rule 41(a)(1), an action may be dismissed at the plaintiff's request only by court order, on terms that the court considers proper. If a defendant has pleaded a counterclaim before being served with the plaintiff's motion to dismiss, the action may be dismissed over the defendant's objection only if the counterclaim can remain pending for independent adjudication. Unless the order states otherwise, a dismissal under this paragraph (2) is without prejudice.

(b) Involuntary Dismissal; Effect. If the plaintiff fails to prosecute or to comply with these rules or a court order, a defendant may move to dismiss the action or any claim against it. Unless the dismissal order states otherwise, a dismissal under this subdivision (b) and any dismissal not under this rule—except one for lack of jurisdiction, improper venue, or failure to join a party under Rule 19—operates as an adjudication on the merits.

(c) Dismissing a Counterclaim, Cross-claim, or Third–Party Claim. This rule applies to a dismissal of any counterclaim, cross-claim, or third-party claim. A claimant's voluntary dismissal under Rule 41(a)(1)(A)(i) must be made:

(1) before a responsive pleading is served; or

(2) if there is no responsive pleading, before evidence is introduced at a hearing or trial.

(d) Costs of a Previously Dismissed Action. If a plaintiff who previously dismissed an action in any court files an action based on or including the same claim against the same defendant, the court:

(1) may order the plaintiff to pay all or part of the costs of that previous action; and

(2) may stay the proceedings until the plaintiff has complied.

* * *

SEMTEK INT'L CORP. v. LOCKHEED MARTIN CORP.

531 U.S. 497 (2001)

JUSTICE SCALIA delivered the opinion of the Court.

This case presents the question whether the claim-preclusive effect of a federal judgment dismissing a diversity action on statute-of-limitations grounds is determined by the law of the State in which the federal court sits.

I

Petitioner filed a complaint against respondent in California state court, alleging inducement of breach of contract and various business torts. Respondent removed the case to the United States District Court for the Central District of California on the basis of diversity of citizenship, and successfully moved to dismiss petitioner's claims as barred by California's 2–year statute of limitations. In its order of dismissal, the District Court, adopting language suggested by respondent, dismissed petitioner's claims "in [their] entirety on the merits and with prejudice." Without contesting the District Court's designation of its dismissal as "on the merits," petitioner appealed to the Court of Appeals for the Ninth Circuit, which affirmed the District Court's order. Petitioner also brought suit against respondent in the State Circuit Court for Baltimore City, Maryland, alleging the same causes of action, which were not time barred under Maryland's 3–year statute of limitations. Respondent sought injunctive relief against this action from the California federal court under the All Writs Act, 28 U.S.C. § 1651, and removed the action to the United States District Court for the District of Maryland on federal-question grounds (diversity grounds were not available because Lockheed "is a Maryland citizen"). The California federal court denied the relief requested, and the Maryland federal court remanded the case to state court because the federal question arose only by way of defense. Following a hearing, the Maryland state court granted respondent's motion to dismiss on the ground of res judicata. Petitioner then returned to the California federal court and the Ninth Circuit, unsuccessfully moving both courts to amend the former's earlier order so as to indicate that the dismissal was not "on the merits." Petitioner also appealed the Maryland trial court's order of dismissal to the Maryland Court of Special Appeals. The Court of Special Appeals affirmed, holding that, regardless of whether California would have accorded claim-preclusive effect to a statute-of-limitations dismissal by one of its own courts, the dismissal by the California federal court barred the complaint filed in Maryland, since the res judicata effect of federal diversity judgments is prescribed by federal law, under which the earlier dismissal was on the merits and claim preclusive. After the Maryland Court of Appeals declined to review the case, we granted certiorari.

II

Petitioner contends that the outcome of this case is controlled by *Dupasseur v. Rochereau,* which held that the res judicata effect of a federal diversity judgment "is such as would belong to judgments of the State courts rendered under similar circumstances," and may not be accorded any "higher sanctity or effect." Since, petitioner argues, the dismissal of an action on statute-of-limitations grounds by a California state court would not be claim preclusive, it follows that the similar dismissal of this diversity action by the California federal court cannot be claim preclusive. While we agree that this would be the result demanded by *Dupasseur,* the case is not dispositive because it was decided under the Conformity Act of 1872, which required federal courts to apply the procedural law of the forum State in non-equity cases. That arguably affected the outcome of the case.

Respondent, for its part, contends that the outcome of this case is controlled by Federal Rule of Civil Procedure 41(b), which provides as follows:

> Involuntary Dismissal: Effect Thereof. For failure of the plaintiff to prosecute or to comply with these rules or any order of court, a defendant may move for dismissal of an action or of any claim against the defendant. Unless the court in its order for dismissal otherwise specifies, a dismissal under this subdivision and any dismissal not provided for in this rule, other than a dismissal for lack of jurisdiction, for improper venue, or for failure to join a party under Rule 19, operates as an adjudication upon the merits.

Since the dismissal here did not "otherwise specif[y]" (indeed, it specifically stated that it *was* "on the merits"), and did not pertain to the excepted subjects of jurisdiction, venue, or joinder, it follows, respondent contends, that the dismissal "is entitled to claim preclusive effect."

Implicit in this reasoning is the unstated minor premise that all judgments denominated "on the merits" are entitled to claim-preclusive effect. That premise is not necessarily valid. The original connotation of an "on the merits" adjudication is one that actually "pass[es] directly on the substance of [a particular] claim" before the court. That connotation remains common to every jurisdiction of which we are aware. ("The prototyp[ical] [judgment on the merits is] one in which the merits of [a party's] claim are in fact adjudicated [for or] against the [party] after trial of the substantive issues"). And it is, we think, the meaning intended in those many statements to the effect that a judgment "on the merits" triggers the doctrine of res judicata or claim preclusion. *See, e.g., Parklane Hosiery Co. v. Shore* ("Under the doctrine of res judicata, a judgment on the merits in a prior suit bars a second suit involving the same parties or their privies based on the same cause of action"); *Goddard v. Security Title Ins. & Guarantee Co.* ("[A] final judgment, rendered upon the merits by a court having jurisdiction of the cause ... is a complete bar to a new suit between [the parties or their privies] on the same cause of action" (internal quotation marks and citations omitted)).

But over the years the meaning of the term "judgment on the merits" "has gradually undergone change," and it has come to be applied to some judgments (such as the one involved here) that do *not* pass upon the substantive merits of a claim and hence do *not* (in many jurisdictions) entail claim-preclusive effect. That is why the Restatement of Judgments has abandoned the use of the term—"because of its possibly misleading connotations."

In short, it is no longer true that a judgment "on the merits" is necessarily a judgment entitled to claim-preclusive effect; and there are a number of reasons for believing that the phrase "adjudication upon the merits" does not bear that meaning in Rule 41(b). To begin with, Rule 41(b) sets forth nothing more than a default rule for determining the import of a dismissal (a dismissal is "upon the merits," with the three stated exceptions, unless the court "otherwise specifies"). This would be a highly peculiar context in which to announce a federally prescribed rule on the complex question of claim preclusion, saying in effect, "All federal dismissals (with three specified exceptions) preclude suit elsewhere, unless the court otherwise specifies."

And even apart from the purely default character of Rule 41(b), it would be peculiar to find a rule governing the effect that must be accorded federal judgments by other courts ensconced in rules governing the internal procedures of the rendering court itself. Indeed, such a rule would arguably violate the jurisdictional limitation of the Rules Enabling Act: that the Rules "shall not abridge, enlarge or modify any substantive right," 28 U.S.C. § 2072(b). In the present case, for example, if California law left petitioner free to sue on this claim in Maryland even after the California statute of limitations had expired, the federal court's extinguishment of that right (through Rule 41(b)'s mandated claim-preclusive effect of its judgment) would seem to violate this limitation.

Moreover, as so interpreted, the Rule would in many cases violate the federalism principle of *Erie R. Co. v. Tompkins,* by engendering " 'substantial' variations [in outcomes] between state and federal litigation" which would "[l]ikely ... influence the choice of a forum," *Hanna v. Plumer.* See also *Guaranty Trust Co. v. York.* With regard to the claim-preclusion issue involved in the present case, for example, the traditional rule is that expiration of the applicable statute of limitations merely bars the remedy and does not extinguish the substantive right, so that dismissal on that ground does not have claim-preclusive effect in other jurisdictions with longer, unexpired limitations periods. Out-of-state defendants sued on stale claims in California and in other States adhering to this traditional rule would systematically remove state-law suits brought against them to federal court—where, unless otherwise specified, a statute-of-limitations dismissal would bar suit everywhere.

Finally, if Rule 41(b) did mean what respondent suggests, we would surely have relied upon it in our cases recognizing the claim-preclusive effect of federal judgments in federal-question cases. Yet for over half a century since the promulgation of Rule 41(b), we have not once done so.

We think the key to a more reasonable interpretation of the meaning of "operates as an adjudication upon the merits" in Rule 41(b) is to be found in Rule 41(a), which, in discussing the effect of voluntary dismissal by the plaintiff, makes clear that an "adjudication upon the merits" is the opposite of a "dismissal without prejudice":

> Unless otherwise stated in the notice of dismissal or stipulation, the dismissal is without prejudice, except that a notice of dismissal operates as an adjudication upon the merits when filed by a plaintiff who has once dismissed in any court of the United States or of any state an action based on or including the same claim.

The primary meaning of "dismissal without prejudice," we think, is dismissal without barring the plaintiff from returning later, to the same court, with the same underlying claim. That will also ordinarily (though not always) have the consequence of not barring the claim from *other* courts, but its primary meaning relates to the dismissing court itself. Thus, Black's Law Dictionary defines "dismissed without prejudice" as "removed from the court's docket in such a way that the plaintiff may refile the same suit on the same claim," and defines "dismissal without prejudice" as "[a] dismissal that does not bar the plaintiff from refiling the lawsuit within the applicable limitations period."

We think, then, that the effect of the "adjudication upon the merits" default provision of Rule 41(b)—and, presumably, of the explicit order in the present case that used the language of that default provision—is simply that, unlike a dismissal "without prejudice," the dismissal in the present case barred refiling of the same claim in the United States District Court for the Central District of California. That is undoubtedly a necessary condition, but it is not a sufficient one, for claim-preclusive effect in other courts.

<h1 style="text-align:center">III</h1>

Having concluded that the claim-preclusive effect, in Maryland, of this California federal diversity judgment is dictated neither by *Dupasseur v. Rochereau,* as petitioner contends, nor by Rule 41(b), as respondent contends, we turn to consideration of what determines the issue. Neither the Full Faith and Credit Clause, U.S. Const., Art. IV, § 1, nor the full faith and credit statute, 28 U.S.C. § 1738, addresses the question. By their terms they govern the effects to be given only to state-court judgments (and, in the case of the statute, to judgments by courts of territories and possessions). And no other federal textual provision, neither of the Constitution nor of any statute, addresses the claim-preclusive effect of a judgment in a federal diversity action.

It is also true, however, that no federal textual provision addresses the claim-preclusive effect of a federal-court judgment in a federal-question case, yet we have long held that States cannot give those judgments merely whatever effect they would give their own judgments, but must accord them the effect that this Court prescribes. The reasoning of that line of cases suggests, moreover, that even when States are allowed to give federal judgments (notably, judgments in diversity cases) no more than the effect accorded to state judgments, that disposition is by direction of *this* Court, which has the last word on the claim-preclusive effect of *all* federal judgments:

> It is true that for some purposes and within certain limits it is only required that the judgments of the courts of the United States shall be given the same force and effect as are given the judgments of the courts of the States wherein they are rendered; but it is equally true that whether a Federal judgment has been given due force and effect in the state court is a Federal question reviewable by this court, which will determine for itself whether such judgment has been given due weight or otherwise. . . .

When is the state court obliged to give to Federal judgments only the force and effect it gives to state court judgments within its own jurisdiction? Such cases are distinctly pointed out in the opinion of Mr. Justice Bradley in *Dupasseur v. Rochereau* [which stated that the case was a diversity case, applying state law under state procedure].

In other words, in *Dupasseur* the State was allowed (indeed, required) to give a federal diversity judgment no more effect than it would accord one of its own judgments only because reference to state law was *the federal rule that this Court deemed appropriate*. In short, federal common law governs the claim-preclusive effect of a dismissal by a federal court sitting in diversity.

It is left to us, then, to determine the appropriate federal rule. And despite the sea change that has occurred in the background law since *Dupasseur* was decided—not only repeal of the Conformity Act but also the watershed decision of this Court in *Erie*—we think the result decreed by *Dupasseur* continues to be correct for diversity cases. Since state, rather than federal, substantive law is at issue there is no need for a uniform federal rule. And indeed, nationwide uniformity in the substance of the matter is better served by having the same claim-preclusive rule (the state rule) apply whether the dismissal has been ordered by a state or a federal court. This is, it seems to us, a classic case for adopting, as the federally prescribed rule of decision, the law that would be applied by state courts in the State in which the federal diversity court sits. As we have alluded to above, any other rule would produce the sort of "forum-shopping ... and ... inequitable administration of the laws" that *Erie* seeks to avoid, *Hanna,* since filing in, or removing to, federal court would be encouraged by the divergent effects that the litigants would anticipate from likely grounds of dismissal. See *Guaranty Trust Co. v. York.*

This federal reference to state law will not obtain, of course, in situations in which the state law is incompatible with federal interests. If, for example, state law did not accord claim-preclusive effect to dismissals for willful violation of discovery orders, federal courts' interest in the integrity of their own processes might justify a contrary federal rule. No such conflict with potential federal interests exists in the present case. Dismissal of this state cause of action was decreed by the California federal court only because the California statute of limitations so required; and there is no conceivable federal interest in giving that time bar more effect in other courts than the California courts themselves would impose.

* * *

Because the claim-preclusive effect of the California federal court's dismissal "upon the merits" of petitioner's action on statute-of-limitations grounds is governed by a federal rule that in turn incorporates California's law of claim preclusion (the content of which we do not pass upon today), the Maryland Court of Special Appeals erred in holding that the dismissal necessarily precluded the bringing of this action in the Maryland courts.

The judgment is reversed, and the case remanded for further proceedings not inconsistent with this opinion.

It is so ordered.

†